Contemporary
Literary Criticism

Guide to Gale Literary Criticism Series

For criticism on	Consult these Gale series
Authors now living or who died after December 31, 1959	*CONTEMPORARY LITERARY CRITICISM (CLC)*
Authors who died between 1900 and 1959	*TWENTIETH-CENTURY LITERARY CRITICISM (TCLC)*
Authors who died between 1800 and 1899	*NINETEENTH-CENTURY LITERATURE CRITICISM (NCLC)*
Authors who died between 1400 and 1799	*LITERATURE CRITICISM FROM 1400 TO 1800 (LC) SHAKESPEAREAN CRITICISM (SC)*
Authors who died before 1400	*CLASSICAL AND MEDIEVAL LITERATURE CRITICISM (CMLC)*
Black writers of the past two hundred years	*BLACK LITERATURE CRITICISM (BLC) AND BLACK LITERATURE CRITICISM SUPPLEMENT (BLCS)*
Authors of books for children and young adults	*CHILDREN'S LITERATURE REVIEW (CLR)*
Dramatists	*DRAMA CRITICISM (DC)*
Hispanic writers of the late nineteenth and twentieth centuries	*HISPANIC LITERATURE CRITICISM (HLC)*
Native North American writers and orators of the eighteenth, nineteenth, and twentieth centuries	*NATIVE NORTH AMERICAN LITERATURE (NNAL)*
Poets	*POETRY CRITICISM (PC)*
Short story writers	*SHORT STORY CRITICISM (SSC)*
Major authors from the Renaissance to the present	*WORLD LITERATURE CRITICISM, 1500 TO THE PRESENT (WLC)*
Major authors and works from the Bible to the present	*WORLD LITERATURE CRITICISM SUPPLEMENT (WLCS)*

ISSN 0091-3421

Volume 112

Contemporary Literary Criticism

Excerpts from Criticism of the Works
of Today's Novelists, Poets, Playwrights,
Short Story Writers, Scriptwriters, and
Other Creative Writers

Jeffrey W. Hunter
Deborah A. Schmitt
Timothy J. White
EDITORS

Tim Akers
Pamela S. Dear
Catherine V. Donaldson
Daniel Jones
John D. Jorgenson
Jerry Moore
Polly Vedder
Thomas Wiloch
Kathleen Wilson
ASSOCIATE EDITORS

GALE

DETROIT • LONDON

STAFF

Library of Congress Catalog Card Number 76-46132
ISBN 0-7876-2209-5
ISSN 0091-3421

Printed in the United States of America
10 9 8 7 6 5 4 3 2 1

Contents

Preface vii

Acknowledgments xi

Preface

A Comprehensive Information Source
on Contemporary Literature

Named "one of the twenty-five most distinguished reference titles published during the past twenty-five years" by *Reference Quarterly,* the *Contemporary Literary Criticism (CLC)* series provides readers with critical commentary and general information on more than 2,000 authors now living or who died after December 31, 1959. Previous to the publication of the first volume of *CLC* in 1973, there was no ongoing digest monitoring scholarly and popular sources of critical opinion and explication of modern literature. *CLC,* therefore, has fulfilled an essential need, particularly since the complexity and variety of contemporary literature makes the function of criticism especially important to today's reader.

Scope of the Series

CLC presents significant passages from published criticism of works by creative writers. Since many of the authors covered by *CLC* inspire continual critical commentary, writers are often represented in more than one volume. There is, of course, no duplication of reprinted criticism.

Authors are selected for inclusion for a variety of reasons, among them the publication or dramatic production of a critically acclaimed new work, the reception of a major literary award, revival of interest in past writings, or the adaptation of a literary work to film or television.

Attention is also given to several other groups of writers-authors of considerable public interest--about whose work criticism is often difficult to locate. These include mystery and science fiction writers, literary and social critics, foreign writers, and authors who represent particular ethnic groups within the United States.

Format of the Book

Each *CLC* volume contains about 500 individual excerpts taken from hundreds of book review periodicals, general magazines, scholarly journals, monographs, and books. Entries include critical evaluations spanning from the beginning of an author's career to the most current commentary. Interviews, feature articles, and other published writings that offer insight into the author's works are also presented. Students, teachers, librarians, and researchers will find that the generous excerpts and supplementary material in *CLC* provide them with vital information required to write a term paper, analyze a poem, or lead a book discussion group. In addition, complete bibliographical citations note the original source and all of the information necessary for a term paper footnote or bibliography.

Features

A *CLC* author entry consists of the following elements:

- The **Author Heading** cites the author's name in the form under which the author has most commonly published, followed by birth date, and death date when applicable. Uncertainty as to a birth or death date is indicated by a question mark.

- A **Portrait** of the author is included when available.

- A brief **Biographical and Critical Introduction** to the author and his or her work precedes the excerpted criticism. The first line of the introduction provides the author's full name, pseudonyms (if applicable), nationality, and a listing of genres in which the author has written. To provide users with easier access to information, the biographical and critical essay included in each author entry is divided into four categories: "Introduction," "Biographical Information," "Major Works," and "Critical Reception." The introductions to single-work entries--entries that focus on well known and frequently studied books, short stories, and poems--are similarly organized to quickly provide readers with information on the plot and major characters of the work being discussed, its major themes, and its critical reception. Previous volumes of *CLC* in which the author has been featured are also listed in the introduction.

- A list of **Principal Works** notes the most important writings by the author. When foreign-language works have been translated into English, the English-language version of the title follows in brackets.

- The **Excerpted Criticism** represents various kinds of critical writing, ranging in form from the brief review to the scholarly exegesis. Essays are selected by the editors to reflect the spectrum of opinion about a specific work or about an author's literary career in general. The excerpts are presented chronologically, adding a useful perspective to the entry. All titles by the author featured in the entry are printed in boldface type, which enables the reader to easily identify the works being discussed. Publication information (such as publisher names and book prices) and parenthetical numerical references (such as footnotes or page and line references to specific editions of a work) have been deleted at the editor's discretion to provide smoother reading of the text.

- Critical essays are prefaced by **Explanatory Notes** as an additional aid to readers. These notes may provide several types of valuable information, including: the reputation of the critic, the importance of the work of criticism, the commentator's approach to the author's work, the purpose of the criticism, and changes in critical trends regarding the author.

- A complete **Bibliographical Citation** designed to help the user find the original essay or book precedes each excerpt.

- Whenever possible, a recent, previously unpublished **Author Interview** accompanies each entry.

- A concise **Further Reading** section appears at the end of entries on authors for whom a significant amount of criticism exists in addition to the pieces reprinted in *CLC*. Each citation in this section is accompanied by a descriptive annotation describing the content of that article. Materials included in this section are grouped under various headings (e.g., Biography, Bibliography, Criticism, and Interviews) to aid users in their search for additional information. Cross-references to other useful sources published by Gale Research in which the author has appeared are also included: *Authors in the News, Black Writers, Children's Literature Review, Contemporary Authors, Dictionary of Literary Biography, DISCovering Authors, Drama Criticism, Hispanic Literature Criticism, Hispanic Writers, Native North American Literature, Poetry Criticism, Something about the Author, Short Story Criticism, Contemporary Authors Autobiography Series,* and *Something about the Author Autobiography Series.*

Other Features

CLC also includes the following features:

- An **Acknowledgments** section lists the copyright holders who have granted permission to reprint material in this volume of *CLC*. It does not, however, list every book or periodical reprinted or consulted during the preparation of the volume.

- Each new volume of *CLC* includes a **Cumulative Topic Index,** which lists all literary topics treated in *CLC, NCLC, TCLC,* and *LC 1400-1800.*

- A **Cumulative Author Index** lists all the authors who have appeared in the various literary criticism series published by Gale Research, with cross-references to Gale's biographical and autobiographical series. A full listing of the series referenced there appears on the first page of the indexes of this volume. Readers will welcome this cumulated author index as a useful tool for locating an author within the various series. The index, which lists birth and death dates when available, will be particularly valuable for those authors who are identified with a certain period but whose death dates cause them to be placed in another, or for those authors whose careers span two periods. For example, Ernest Hemingway is found in *CLC,* yet F. Scott Fitzgerald, a writer often associated with him, is found in *Twentieth-Century Literary Criticism.*

- A **Cumulative Nationality Index** alphabetically lists all authors featured in *CLC* by nationality, followed by numbers corresponding to the volumes in which the authors appear.

- An alphabetical **Title Index** accompanies each volume of *CLC.* Listings are followed by the author's name and the corresponding page numbers where the titles are discussed. English translations of foreign titles and variations of titles are cross-referenced to the title under which a work was originally published. Titles of novels, novellas, dramas, films, record albums, and poetry, short story, and essay collections are printed in italics, while all individual poems, short stories, essays, and songs are printed in roman type within quotation marks; when published separately (e.g., T. S. Eliot's poem *The Waste Land),* the titles of long poems are printed in italics.

- In response to numerous suggestions from librarians, Gale has also produced a **Special Paperbound Edition** of the *CLC* title index. This annual cumulation, which alphabetically lists all titles reviewed in the series, is available to all customers and is typically published with every fifth volume of *CLC.* Additional copies of the index are available upon request. Librarians and patrons will welcome this separate index: it saves shelf space, is easy to use, and is recyclable upon receipt of the next edition.

Citing *Contemporary Literary Criticism*

When writing papers, students who quote directly from any volume in the Literary Criticism Series may use the following general forms to footnote reprinted criticism. The first example pertains to material drawn from periodicals, the second to material reprinted in books:

[1]Alfred Cismaru, "Making the Best of It," *The New Republic,* 207, No. 24, (December 7, 1992), 30, 32; excerpted and reprinted in *Contemporary Literary Criticism,* Vol. 85, ed. Christopher Giroux (Detroit: Gale Research, 1995), pp. 73-4.

[2]Yvor Winters, *The Post-Symbolist Methods* (Allen Swallow, 1967); excerpted and reprinted in *Contemporary Literary Criticism,* Vol. 85, ed. Christopher Giroux (Detroit: Gale Research, 1995), pp. 223-26.

Suggestions Are Welcome

The editors hope that readers will find *CLC* a useful reference tool and welcome comments about the work. Send comments and suggestions to: Editors, *Contemporary Literary Criticism,* Gale Research, 27500 Drake Rd., Farmington Hills, MI 48333-3535.

Acknowledgments

The editors wish to thank the copyright holders of the excerpted criticism included in this volume and the permissions managers of many book and magazine publishing companies for assisting us in securing reproduction rights. We are also grateful to the staffs of the Detroit Public Library, the Library of Congress, the University of Detroit Mercy Library, Wayne State University Purdy/Kresge Library Complex, and the University of Michigan Libraries for making their resources available to us. Following is a list of the copyright holders who have granted us permission to reproduce material in this volume of CLC. Every effort has been made to trace copyright, but if omissions have been made, please let us know.

COPYRIGHTED EXCERPTS IN *CLC*, VOLUME 112, WERE REPRODUCED FROM THE FOLLOWING PERIODICALS:

The American Book Review, July-August, 1985. ©1985 by *The American Book Review.* Reproduced by permission.—*American Film,* v. 5, June, 1980 for "Carl Sagan's Guided Tour of the Universe" by Bruce Cook. Copyright 1980 by *American Film.* Reproduced by permission of the author.—*American Literature*, v. 63, March, 1991. Copyright © 1991 by Duke University Press, Durham, NC. Reproduced by permission.—*American Poetry,* v. 13, January-February, 1984. Reproduced by permission.—*Belles Lettres,* v. 8, Fall, 1992. Reproduced by permission.—*Book World--The Washington Post* August 13, 1989 for "Crackdown in Colombia" by Ross Thomas; May 5, 1996 for "Beneath a Jamaican Moon" by Liesl Schillinger; August 18, 1996 for "President Jack Ryan" by Michael R. Beschloss. © 1989, 1996 Washington Post Book World Service/Washington Post Writers Group. All reproduced by permission of the authors./September 14, 1969 for "A Warm Glow in a Cruel, Cold World" by Richard Freedman. © 1969 Washington Post Book World Service/Washington Post Writers Group. Reproduced by permission of the Literary Estate of Richard Freedman./December 3. 1978. © 1978 Washington Post Book World Service/Washington Post Writers Group. Reproduced by permission.—*Boundary 2,* v. 22, Spring, 1995. Copyright © 1995 by Duke University Press, Durham, NC. Reproduced by permission.—*Bulletin of the Atomic Scientists,* v. 47, March, 1991. Copyright © 1991 by the Educational Foundation for Nuclear Science, Chicago, IL 60637. Reproduced by permission of *Bulletin of the Atomic Scientists: A Magazine of Science and World Affairs.*—*Callaloo,* v. 18,Spring, 1995. Copyright © 1995 by Charles H. Rowell. Reproduced by permission of The Johns Hopkins University Press.—*Chicago Tribune---Books* May 6, 1990 for "Potok's Exiled Asher Lev Revisits His Hasidic Roots" by Andy Solomon; September 23, 1990 for "No Time for Any Barriers" by Charles R. Larson; May 17, 1992 for "Chaim Potok Traces a Korean War Orphan's Existentialist Journey" by Irving Abrahamson; May 31, 1992 for "No Time for Any Barriers" by Charles R. Larson; June 7, 1992 for "McInerney's Redemption" by Sven Birkerts. © copyrighted 1990, 1992 Chicago Tribune Company. All rights reserved. All reproduced by permission of the respective authors.—*The Christian Century,* May 16, 1984. Copyright 1984 Christian Century Foundation. Reproduced by permission from *The Christian Century.*—*The Christian Science Monitor,* July 20, 1967 for "Sight Becomes Insight" by Sandra Schmidt; January 9, 1969 for "Seeing the Classics as New" by Janet Overmyer; October 5, 1984 for "Having Fun in New York" by Ruth Doan MacDougall. © 1967, 1969, 1984 by the authors. All rights reserved. All reproduced by permission of the respective authors.—*Cineaste,* v. 19, Fall, 1992. Copyright © 1992 by Cineaste Publishers, Inc. Reproduced by permission.—*Commentary*, v. 49, May, 1970 for "Sequels" by Dorothy Rabinowitz; v. 94, September, 1992 for "High Life" by Evelyn Toynton. Copyright © 1970, 1992 American Jewish Committee. All rights reserved. Both reproduced by permission of the publisher and the resprctive authors.—*Comparative Literature Studies,* v. 32, Summer, 1995. Copyright © 1995 by The Pennsylvania State University. Reproduced by permission of The Pennsylvania State University Press.—*Contemporary Literature,* v. 37, Summer, 1996.© 1996 by the Board of Regents of the University of Wisconsin. Reproduced by permission of The University of Wisconsin Press.—*Critical Texts,* v. 5, 1988. Reproduced by permission.—*Critique: Studies in Contemporary Fiction,* v. 34, Fall, 1992. Reproduced with permission of the Helen Dwight Reid Educational Foundation, published by Heldref Publications, 119 18th Street, N. W., Washington, DC 20036-1802.—*Diplomatic History,* v. 17, Fall, 1993. Copyright 1993 by Blackwell Publishers. Reproduced by permission.—*ELH,* v. 57, Winter, 1990; v. 60, Spring, 1993. Copyright © 1990, 1993 by The Johns Hopkins University Press. All rights reserved. Both reproduced by permission.—*English Journal,* v. 85, April, 1996 for

1980; May 24, 1985. May 19, 1989; November 2, 1990; November 6, 1992; November 27, 1992; January 8, 1993, April 9, 1993; February 4, 1996; June 14, 1996. © The Times Supplements Limited 1967, 1971, 1980, 1985, 1989, 1990, 1992, 1993, 1996. All reproduced from *The Times Literary Supplement* by permission.—*Twentieth Century Literature,* v. 38, Winter, 1992. Copyright 1991 Hofstra University Press. Reproduced by permission.—*The Village Voice,* May 21, 1996. Copyright © V. V. Publishing Corporation. Reproduced by permission of the *The Village Voice.—Village Voice Literary Supplement,* May, 1990.Copyright © V. V. Publishing Corporation. Reproduced by permission of the *The Village Voice.—The Virginia Quarterly Review,* v. 69, Winter, 1993. Copyright, 1993, by *The Virginia Quarterly Review,* The University of Virginia. Reproduced by permission of the publisher.—*The Wall Street Journal,* May 15, 1967; April 29, 1985; September 16, 1988; August 16, 1989 ; May 18, 1992; June 12,1992; September 2, 1994; December 12, 1996. Copyright 1967, 1985, 1988, 1989, 1992, 1994, 1996 Dow Jones & Company, Inc. All rights reserved. All reproduced with permission of *The Wall Street Journal.—West Africa,* January 27, 1968. Copyright 1968. West Africa Publishing Co. Reproduced by permission.

COPYRIGHTED EXCERPTS IN *CLC,* VOLUME 112, WERE REPRODUCED FROM THE FOLLOWING BOOKS:

Abramson, Edward A. From *Chaim Potok.* Twayne Publishers, 1986. Copyright © 1986 by G. K. Hall & Co. All rights reserved. Reproduced by permission of Twayne Publishers, a division of Simon & Schuster, Inc.—Doane, Janice and Devon Hodges. From *Gender Studies: New Directions in Feminist Criticism.* Bowling Green State University Popular Press, 1986. Copyright © 1986 by Bowling Green State University Popular Press. Reproduced by permission.—Evans, Thomas. From "Kenneth Rexroth" in *American Poetry: The Modernist Ideal.* Edited by Clive Bloom and Brian Docherty. St. Martin's Press, 1995. © the Editorial Board, Lumiere (Co-operative Press) Ltd. 1995. All rights reserved. Reproduced by permission.—Faye, Jefferson. From"Cultural/Familial Estrangement: Self-Exile and Self-Destruction in Jay McInerney's Novels" in *The Literature of Emigration and Exile.* Edited by James Whitlark and Wendell Aycock. Texas Tech University Press, 1992. Copyright 1992 Texas Tech University Press. All rights reserved. Reproduced by permission.—Garson, Helen S. From *Tom Clancy A Critical Companion.* Greenwood Press, 1996. © 1996 by Greenwood Press. Reproduced by permission of Greenwood Publishing Group, Inc., Westport, CT.—Gibson, Morgan. From *Revolutionary Rexroth: Poet of East-West Wisdom.* Archon Books, 1986. © 1986 Morgan Gibson. All rights reserved. Reproduced by permission.—Hall, Donald. From "Kenneth Rexroth" in *American Writing Today.* Edited by Richard Kostelanetz. The Whitston Publishing Company, 1991. Copyright 1991 Richard Kostelanetz. Reproduced by permission.—Hendin, Josephine. From "Fictions of Acquisition" in *Culture in An Age of Money.* Edited by Nicolaus Mills. Ivan R. Dee, 1990. Copyright © 1990 by the Foundation for the Study of Independent Social Ideas. All rights reserved. Reproduced by permission.—Kremer, S. Lillian. From *Witness Throught the Imagination: Jewish American Holocaust Literature.* Wayne State University Press, 1989. Copyright © 1989 Wayne State University Press. All rights reserved. Reproduced by permission.—Prinz, Jessica. From "Spalding Gray's 'Swimming to Cambodia': A Performance Gesture" in *Staging the Impossible: The Fantastic Mode in Modern Drama.* Edited by Patrick D. Murphy. Greenwood Press, 1992. Copyright © 1992 by Patrick D. Murphy. All rights reserved. Reproduced by permission of Greenwood Publishing Group, Inc., Westport, CT.Reilly, Edward C. From *Understanding John Irving.* University of South Carolina Press, 1991. Copyright © 1991 University of South Carolina. Reproduced by permission.

PHOTOGRAPHS AND ILLUSTRATIONS APPEARING IN *CLC,* VOLUME 112, WERE RECEIVED FROM THE FOLLOWING SOURCES:

Clancy, Tom, photograph. AP/Wide World Photos. Reproduced by permission.
Gray, Spalding (holding up "Impossible Vacation"), photograph. AP/Wide World Photos. . Reproduced by permission.
Irving, John, photograph. AP/Wide World Photos. Reproduced by permission.
McInerey, Jay. Portrait of Jay McInerney.(c) Jerry Bauer. Reproduced by permission.
McMillan, Terry, photograph by Jerry Bauer. (c) Jerry Bauer. Reproduced by permission.
Potok, Chaim (arms crossed, wearing turtleneck), photograph by Jerry Bauer. (c) Jerry Bauer. Reproduced by

Aimé Césaire
1913-

(Full name Aimé Fernand Césaire) West Indian poet, dramatist, and essayist.

The following entry presents an overview of Césaire's career through 1995. For further information on his life and works, see *CLC,* Volumes 19 and 32.

INTRODUCTION

An acclaimed Caribbean poet, dramatist, and statesman, Césaire's fervent advocacy for black self-determination and heritage has won him international recognition. During the 1930s and 1940s, Césaire emerged as a founder and leading proponent of negritude, an artistic and political movement that sought to reclaim traditional black culture and racial identity in the wake of Western colonial ascendancy. The poetry of *Cahier d'un retour au pays natal* (1956; *Return to My Native Land*) is considered his masterpiece; also highly regarded are the three dramas *La Tragedie du roi Christophe* (1963; *The Tragedy of King Christophe*), *Une saison au Congo* (1966; *A Season in the Congo*), and *Une tempete* (1969; *A Tempest*). Much of his work reveals the influence of Surrealism, which Césaire adopted to liberate himself from European rationalism and literary convention. A revolutionary artist and lifelong political activist, Césaire's forceful opposition to imperialism, racism, and the assimilation of Western culture among non-Western people have exerted a profound influence on contemporary world literature.

Biographical Information

Césaire was born in Basse Pointe, Martinique, a French colony in the Caribbean where, during his childhood, he experienced the poverty and political oppression of the island's black citizens. An exceptional student, Césaire won a scholarship to travel to Paris in the early 1930s and studied literature and philosophy at the Ecole Normale Superieure. There he met Senegalese poet Leopold Sedar Senghor and founded, along with classmate Leon-Gontran Damas, *L'Etudiant noir,* the periodical in which the term negritude is believed to have originated. In 1939, the first version of Césaire's *Return to My Native Land* appeared in the magazine *Volontes;* a second version, with a preface by French Surrealist Andre Breton, was published in 1944, followed by the definitive edition in 1956. Upon the outbreak of the Second World War, Césaire returned to Martinique with his wife, Suzanne Roussy, whom he married in 1937. Both worked as teachers at Césaire's former school in Fort-de-France while Césaire became increasingly active in politics

and the Communist party. In 1945, Césaire was elected mayor of Fort-de-France and deputy for Martinique to the French National Assembly. He founded *Tropiques,* a literary journal significant for its advocacy of black culture and Surrealism, in 1941. Over the next decade, Césaire published several volumes of poetry, including *Les armes miraculeuses* (1944; *The Miracle Weapons*), which contains a versified version of the drama *Et les chiens se taisaient* (1956; *And the Dogs Were Silent*), *Soleil cou-coupe* (1948; *Beheaded Sun*), and *Corps perdu* (1949; *Disembodied*), as well as a series of essays condemning Fascism and European imperialism in *Discours sur le colonialisme* (1950; *Discourses on Colonialism*). Though Césaire renounced his affiliation with the Communist party in 1956, for reasons explained in the widely circulated pamphlet *Lettre a Maurice Thorez* (1956; *Letter to Maurice Thorez*), he maintained an active role in local Martinique politics. In 1957, Césaire founded the Martinique Progressive Party and was elected its president the next year. During the 1960s, he produced additional volumes of poetry, *Ferrements* (1960; *Shackles*) and *Cadastre* (1961), and his three major dramas—*The Tragedy of King Christophe, A Season in the Congo,* and *A Tempest.* Césaire's plays and verse were collected and published in *Oeuvres completes* (1976; *Complete Works*), with the exception of poetry from *Moi, laminaire* (1982). Césaire continued to serve as mayor of Fort-de-France until 1983 and deputy for Martinique until 1993.

Major Works

Césaire's preoccupation with the pernicious effects of decolonialization, cultural alienation, and the reconciliation of past and present pervades both his poetry and drama. *Return to My Native Land* is a long, surrealist poem in which Césaire relates his painful search for self-identity and meaning in the history and decayed culture of his people. The first part describes his early life on Martinique and the appalling poverty and social conditions that fostered apathy and self-loathing among its French-speaking black inhabitants. In the second part, Césaire expounds the principles of negritude as a remedy for such dejection, extolling the importance of racial self-awareness and reconnection with lost African heritage, which he celebrates in the final movement. Through the discovery of negritude, Césaire abandons passive disengagement to assume a powerful messianic voice that rallies the cause of all black people. As in much of his poetry, including that found in *The Miracle Weapons, Beheaded Sun,* and *Disembodied,* Césaire relies on the exotic imagery of African flora and fauna, rich vocabulary, discordant internal rhythms, and the combative tone of revolt to forge his idiosyncratic verse. In *Shackles,* whose title suggests the iron fetters of slavery, Césaire began to move away from hermetic, surrealist poetry in favor of a more accessible style through which he addressed political events in Africa, the Caribbean, and the United States during the 1950s. However, in the 1960s Césaire turned to theater to speak to his audiences more directly. His three major dramas are didactic, politicized presentations of important historical or literary figures that achieve archetypal symbolism. *The Tragedy of King Christophe* portrays the demise of nineteenth-century monarch Henri Christophe during the period of Haitian decolonialization. After mounting a successful revolution against French colonists, Christophe crowns himself king. However, his cruelty and despotic abuse of power eventually lead to rebellion and, finally, to his suicide. Through the failure of Christophe, an ambitious and well-meaning tyrant, Césaire satirizes aristocratic grandeur and the heroic pretensions of post-colonial dictators in Africa and other Third World countries. *A Season in the Congo* recounts the tragic death of Patrice Lumumba, the first prime minister of the Congo Republic and an African nationalist hero. The play follows Lumumba's efforts to free the Congolese from Belgian rule and the political struggles that eventually led to his assassination in 1961. Césaire depicts Lumumba as a sympathetic Christ figure whose conscious martyrdom reflects his self-sacrificing humanity and commitment to pan-Africanism. An adaptation of Shakespeare's *The Tempest,* Césaire's *A Tempest* examines Western colonialism and racial conflict through the relationship between Prospero and his slaves. Césaire's version portrays Prospero as a decadent imperialist, Ariel as a pacifistic mulatto slave, and Caliban as an unwilling black slave who openly rebels against Prospero and demands to be referred to as "X." After Caliban's attempted revolution fails, both he and Prospero declare their resolve to remain on the island and to resist each other with violence if necessary. As in his other works, Césaire contrasts the insidious machinations of neo-colonial subjugation with the liberating aspirations of negritude.

Critical Reception

Césaire is renowned as a leading voice of post-colonial emancipation and black self-affirmation. For his role in the definition of negritude, especially as found in *Return to My Native Land,* he is considered among the most important black writers of the postwar period. Andre Breton wrote that *Return to My Native Land* is "nothing less than the greatest lyrical monument of our time." John Paul Sartre also offered high praise in his seminal essay on negritude, "Black Orpheus." While disenfranchised people around the world found profound inspiration in Césaire's poetry, some critics note elements of obscurantism stemming from his affinity for Surrealism and dense vocabulary. Others cite apparent

contradictions in Césaire's reliance on European language and literary resources to exalt black self-sufficiency and racial integrity. Yet, the tension derived from such diverse formative influences is viewed as essential to the development of Césaire's unique personal aesthetic. As a playwright, Césaire has won widespread approval from critics and Third World audiences. His dramas have been compared to those of Bertolt Brecht, particularly *The Tragedy of King Christophe* and *A Season in the Congo,* for their instructive use of black comedy and satire. A visionary artist and legendary political leader in the West Indies, Césaire became an indispensable model for literary revolt and cultural reclamation among contemporary African and Caribbean writers.

PRINCIPAL WORKS

Les armes miraculeuses [*The Miracle Weapons*] (poetry) 1944

Soleil Cou-Coupe [*Beheaded Sun*] (poetry) 1948

Corps perdu [*Disembodied;* also translated as *Lost Body*] (poetry) 1949

Discours sur le colonialisme [*Discourses on Colonialism*] (essays) 1950

Cahier d'un retour au pays natal [*Return to My Native Land;* also translated as *Notebooks of a Return to My Native Land* and *Notebooks on Returning Home*] (poetry) 1956

Et les Chiens se Taisaient: Tragedie [*And the Dogs Were Silent: A Tragedy*] (drama) 1956

Lettre a Maurice Thorez [*Letter to Maurice Thorez*] (letter) 1956

Ferrements [*Shackles*] (poetry) 1960

Cadastre (poetry) 1961

Toussaint L'Ouverture: La revolution francaise et le probleme coloniale [*Toussaint L'Ouverture: The French Revolution and the Colonial Problem*] (historical study) 1960

La tragedie du roi Christophe [*The Tragedy of King Christophe*] (drama) 1963

Une saison au Congo [*A Season in the Congo*] (drama) 1966

Une tempete: d'apres "le tempete" de Shakespeare [*A Tempest*] (drama) 1969

Oeuvres completes [*Complete Works*] (poetry; three volumes) 1976

Moi, laminaire (poetry) 1982

The Collected Poetry of Aimé Césaire (poetry) 1983

CRITICISM

Abiola Irele (essay date 27 January 1968)

SOURCE: "Post-Colonial Negritude: The Political Plays of Aimé Césaire," in *West Africa,* January 27, 1968, pp. 100-01.

[*In the following essay, Irele discusses Césaire's preoccupation with post-colonial politics in* The Tragedy of King Christophe *and* A Season in the Congo.]

For some time Aimé Césaire's work has been devoted entirely to a cause; it represents in fact the most sustained effort so far to explore in literary terms the realities of the black man's experience in modern times as well as his intimate responses to his historical condition. The colonial situation has imposed a certain limitation upon Césaire's angle of vision upon the world, resulting in a simplification of his themes which obscured the less immediate but more profound significance of the issues with which he is concerned—the moral and spiritual implications of the Negro's collective experience, and their universal relevance.

The ending of the colonial era presently taking place has now permitted a certain broadening of Césaire's area of reference. The publication of his play, *La Tragédie du roi Christophe,* which has had a remarkable success on the stage in Europe and was a central attraction at the Dakar festival last year, marked this new trend in his work. Césaire has now followed up with another play, *Une Saison au Congo,* which confirms this evolution and indicates that if his attitude to the Negro condition in general and the African situation in particular remains unchanged, political changes and events in Africa have diverted his attention towards new concerns and dictated a new approach. For the common theme of these two plays is decolonisation, that is, the specific problems that beset newly freed men in their hopes and endeavours to create for themselves a new and acceptable collective life.

La Tragédie du Roi Christophe is set in the Haiti of the early nineteenth century, in the years immediately following Toussaint Louverture's revolution and the war of independence under Dessalines, who founded the state but died before he could consolidate it. His mantle fell upon General Christophe, a former slave and lieutenant successively of the two illustrious men. All the major characters depicted, as well as the principal events recalled in this play are strictly historical. Césaire reconstructs Christophe's subsequent career with all the fidelity that his personal research and the demands of his dramatic medium permit, the more firmly to underline his moral purpose in evoking this crucial phase of Negro history.

Christophe's conscious aspiration, upon assuming the direction of the new republic, is to be an effective leader and not the figurehead of the Haitian middle class, constituted mainly by the mulattoes, whose contribution to the struggle for freedom, though considerable, had been inspired more by their reaction against the aristocratic white settlers than by a feeling of a common destiny with the black slaves. To break the "hold on Haiti of the mulattoes" with whom the republican ideal is associated, Christophe sweeps aside the constitution which they had drawn up to limit his powers, and sets up a monarchy with himself as king whereupon the mulattoes, under their leader Pétion, withdrew to the southern part where they set up a rival republican state. Thus, in less than a decade after independence, there comes civil war.

> **For some time Aimé Césaire's work has been devoted entirely to a cause; it represents in fact the most sustained effort so far to explore in literary terms the realities of the black man's experience in modern times as well as his intimate responses to his historical condition.**
> —*Abiola Irele*

Christophe's intention in establishing a monarchy, however, is not so much to identify himself with the aspirations of his own people as to justify them, with the outer forms that contemporary "respectable" manners and opinions both offered and approved, in the eyes of the world, especially the former colonial master. In the same misguided spirit, he embarks upon an ambitious programme of national construction, symbolised by the erection of a citadel, to stand upon a promontory outside the capital as a monumental image of the national will. To vindicate his black subjects in their claim to their status as men, the new king chooses for them foreign models of action to channel their creative energies, models which bear no relation to their profound needs nor make a meaningful appeal to their real potential. Christophe's enterprise turns out to be a misdirection of his people's collective effort, not only because his objectives were grossly inappropriate and superficial, but also because these were inspired by an apologetic passion that previous domination and humiliation had bred in the Haitian leaders. His failure is thus significant in the way his slavish reference to foreign norms reveals both the real dilemmas that he faces in choosing a direction of purpose and his psychological handicaps.

The tragedy of Christophe unfolds itself at more than one level, running its course both in the deterioration that an impossible combination of objective factors create in his kingdom, and in the corruption of his noble purpose which is paralleled by his decline from a determined visionary to a sanguinary despot, a spiritual decline which bears close relation to the situation in which he is involved and is accentuated by his egocentric refusal to see Haiti as anything but a projection of himself. This finally dissociates him from his own people and leads to his fall.

The impact of Césaire's play derives mainly from the extraordinary scope of the central character, whose many facets are revealed and whose contradictions are plumbed at different levels. Christophe emerges not as a uniform character, and even less as some absurd villain—comparable for instance to Eugene O'Neill's "Emperor Jones" in the American's treatment of the same subject—but as a truly impressive figure whose hold on our imagination and on our emotions is made relentless by a poetic evocation of tremendous power. In language shorn of his former Surrealistic luxuriance to lay bare its stark, granite edge, Césaire has created an epic hero, at once warmly delineated and integrally realised:

> I would hold in hate my victory if it
>   held for you respite.
> For who then will call to life your
>   black rock,
> Ring clear your human note?
>
> Africa, my source of strength. . .
> The Kingfisher catching glint after
>   glint of oriflame
> Inventing itself a fresh morning of
>   drunken sunshine.

Indeed, the most striking thing about the whole play is its ambiguity, which reflects a more meditative consciousness on the part of Césaire of the complex nature of any human reality, and of the welter of impulses, rooted in men's minds, that determine human actions. This is what gives to his reconstruction of Christophe's career and of Haiti's early destiny, its quality of truth.

It is precisely this complexity which is missing in his evocation of Patrice Lumumba in *Une Saison au Congo*. Lumumba appears as a hero contemplated from the outside, but left unexplored, a mythical figure whose vital adhesion to his personal destiny is only summarily registered. He stands indeed for a passion, born out of a critical conjecture of events, but the driving force of this passion and its location in a human heart are not as much probed as rhetorically expressed. In other words, Césaire's Lumumba represents an ideal, but does not fully incarnate its reality. This is a pity, for the real situation in the Congo offered more than enough material for a fuller, more rounded treatment. The very title of the play, echoing as it does Rimbaud's *Saison en Enfer* (A Season in Hell), suggests in fact the nature of the highly dramatic situation that produced Lumumba—a Congo caught in a moment of stress, in which events, in their bewildering, tormenting pressure upon individuals, whipping up their minds to a turbulent pitch, shatter their wills in confused directions.

In Césaire's favour, however, it might be said that these events are too near us in time to permit a more detached and more profound appraisal: and even some of the major protagonists are still too much with us. Besides, Césaire is here making a statement that can only appear as supplementary to the essential message of the previous play. If the drama of the Congo loses some of its acuity in Césaire's representation, it is perhaps because his emphasis has, from one play to the other, shifted from a critical awareness of the problems he is tackling to an expression of the actual human tragedy played out in the Congo: the dreadful waste of lives sacrificed in futile conflicts, the intrigues of outside enemies sparking off or simply profiting from the ambitions of selfish politicians, and, in particular, the terrible helplessness of the masses, raised one moment to heights of hope, plunged the next to depths of suffering, of disillusionment and despair.

Further, the highly problematic situation which erupted into chaos in the Congo *did* produce characters who hardly seemed real men as much as stock types, and Lumumba himself ended up indeed as an archetype, whose fate stands as a symbol of the Congo's long season of distress and of the dreary prostration of the continent of which she is the heart.

In *Une Saison au Congo,* Césaire writes less as a committed observer than as a poet agonisingly aware that a drama of elemental intensity is here being enacted, the reversal of an old order prolonging itself in a disruption of the universal order, but out of which new life is created.
—*Abiola Irele*

In *Une Saison au Congo,* Césaire writes less as a committed observer than as a poet agonisingly aware that a drama of elemental intensity is here being enacted, the reversal of an old order prolonging itself in a disruption of the universal order, but out of which new life is created. Of this hope, Lumumba is the prophet:

> "As for Africa, I know that, for all her weakness
> and her divisions, she shall not fail us! For after
> all, here, of sift, sun and water—of their solemn
> mating—here man was born."

Thus is the parallel that Césaire overtly draws in *La Tragédie du roi Christophe* between the Haitian precedent some 150 years ago and the African situation today, driven home, as it were, in *Une Saison au Congo.* The identification between the Caribbean Negro and the African which is a prominent theme in Césaire's poetry, the bridge of feeling between them in his mind, today acquires a new edge.

These two plays represent then a capital turning point in Césaire's commitment to the Negro cause, but not in any sense a departure from the basic concerns he has demonstrated all along in his writings. Their topical relevance to the present situation in Africa give them an immediate significance that does not need to be emphasised, but they are far from indicating, as has been suggested, any change of attitude on his part. Rather, they cast a new light upon his work which now reveals itself more clearly as being not so much a finished statement upon the destiny of the black man, as an anxious interrogation of his historical experience, and ultimately, that of humanity.

Aimé Césaire does not renounce his négritude, he is quite simply pointing out its implications in the post-colonial era, exhorting us, at the same time, to brace ourselves up to meet their challenge.

Alfred Cismaru (essay date 1974)

SOURCE: "*Négritude* in Selected Works of Aimé Césaire," in *Renascence,* Vol. 26, 1974, pp. 105-11.

[*In the following essay, Cismaru offers an overview of Césaire's political concerns and literary accomplishments.*]

> White man, white because he was man, white as the day, white as truth, white as virtue, lit creation like a torch and unveiled the secret and white essence of things and beings. Today, the Black look at us, and we don't dare look back; now Black Torches light the world and our white heads are nothing but fragile street lights shaking in the wind . . . our whiteness is becoming a strange and pale varnish which prevents our skin from breathing, a white bathing trunk which no longer fits, and under which, if we could take it off, we would find the true human flesh, a flesh which has the color of black wine.

Sartre's lyricism notwithstanding, it is a fact that the Apostle of Existentialism saw almost a quarter of a century ago the inception of the advent of Black Literature in French letters. In fact, it was in the beginning of the 1920s that two friends who had met as students at the Sorbonne, the Senegalese Léopold Sédar Senghor and the Antillean Aimé Césaire, coined the word *négritude*. Because of subsequent political developments, however, the Africans and the Antilleans have somewhat different views concerning the meaning and the importance of the idea behind the word. In the 1950s and in the 1960s the French and Belgian colonial empires became dissipated; on the contrary, the French Caribbean islands have remained French Departments overseas. All French-speaking African countries obtained their independence between 1958 and 1960. Consequently, young African writers no longer saw in *négritude* a fundamental value. Not being any longer oppressed as Blacks, the Africans are more concerned with the economic disadvantages to which they are now submitted vis-à-vis the Western world. For the Antilleans, though, the word *négritude* still hides a purity and an innocence which they oppose to the dilapidated and decomposing European continent. The American theme of Black Power, for example, appears and reappears in the writings of many natives of Martinique and Guadeloupe; on the contrary, there is no mention of it in recent African literature. In fact, at the Festival of Black Art held at Dakar in 1966, and during the Pan African Cultural Festival held at Algiers in 1969, numerous were the instances of lack of solidarity between the black Africans and the black Antilleans. Literary magazines and newspapers all over the world gave, at the time, so much coverage to the different points of view advanced, and to the conflicting lists of priorities which emerged, that both groups felt the stigma of embarrassment for several months after each of the respective meetings. The rift might seem astonishing to those who recall that Blacks all over the world share in a common culture, which their dispersion throughout the planet did not manage to annihilate.

Nevertheless, soon after independence the African societies began to place a great deal more emphasis on immediate material problems than on loftier literary productions containing racial overtones. For the Antilleans, however, literature continued to provide a needed outlet for rebellion.

In France there is a small bibliography at the disposal of students of Black Literature; there is hardly anything in the United States, and there is nothing on Antillean poets who, perhaps better than their African brothers, and certainly earlier, had displayed a beautiful, strange and violent national lyricism heretofore encountered only in the best of Western writers. The purpose of the present essay will be, then, to fill this lacuna in Black Literary Studies by analyzing some of the work of Aimé Césaire, generally considered in Europe to be the best exponent of Black Caribbean culture in the twentieth century.

It will be recalled that Césaire was born in Martinique in 1913. As a young adult he went to France and was a student at the Ecole Normale Supérieure of Paris. Upon his return to Martinique he taught high school; later he was elected as the Island's representative at the National Assembly in Paris. His early adherence to the Communist Party was surely prompted more by the accidental fact that he was born in a French colony, than caused by deeply rooted political convictions. Temporarily he saw in Marxism a friendly point of view, perhaps even a solution. Later, he realized that his quarrel was not so much with a still colonizing Europe but with Whites as a whole. In 1956 he wrote to Maurice Thorez: "What I want is that Marxism and Communism be placed in the service of black people; I do not want the Black to be in the service of the Party." Specifically, he reproached the French Communist Party with the fact that it believed itself capable of solving the problems of colonized peoples. On the contrary, Césaire's idea of a black revolt and of black power implies an exclusively self-made solution. The poet's penchant for such an extreme position can be seen in *Cahier d'un retour au pays natal,* a poem dating back to 1935, (published however in 1947), when the author returned to Martinique after years of study in France. Notice the initial praise of a simple but innocent world, his, opposed to one encumbered by and weighed under its technical inventions:

> o friendly light
> o fresh source of life
> those who invented neither gunpowder, nor the compass
> those who never knew how to conquer steam nor electricity
> those who explored neither the seas nor the heavens
> but those without whom the earth would not be the earth . . .
> my blackness is not a stone . . .
> my blackness is not a spot of dead water on the dead cornea of the earth
> my blackness is neither a tower nor a cathedral
> it plunges however into the red flesh of the soil
> it plunges into the flaming flesh of the sky
> it is a perfect circle enclosing the world in a shut concordance

followed by a scornful attack on a morally and physically decaying Europe with which the Blacks can no longer deal, but to which they can still administer a final slap, that of commiseration:

> listen to the white world
> horribly tired of its immense effort
> listen to its predatory victories
> to its grandiose alibis
> have pity on our omniscient and naïve conquerors
> —*Cahier d'un retour au pays natal*

As soon as one begins to read Césaire, it becomes obvious that for him, unlike prose, poetry begins with extreme positions and espouses easily the most unexpected exaggerations. Giving himself entirely to the ancestral appeal of mother Africa, the poet often views *négritude* as virtue and whiteness as evil. His lyrical confrontation between white technology and black innocence has a quality of spontaneity about it, at once conquering and destructive. Moreover, his verbal incandescence appears to evoke a surrealistic lan-

guage saluted by André Breton himself, who saw in *Cahier d'un retour au pays natal* "the greatest lyrical monument of our time . . . transcending with every line the fear that the Black have for the Black who are imprisoned in a white society, identifying with this fear and becoming one with it, causing all poets to become one with it, all artists and all thinkers, by furnishing to them the bait of his verbal genius, and by making them all aware that the condition at the basis of this fear is as intolerable as it is changeable."

"Europe is indefensible," Césaire boasted once, at a time when he was closer to the tenets of the Communist Party. His quarrel with the old Continent stemmed, then, from the fact that he equated it with Christianity, which he considered at the source of the White's mania for colonization. "What is most responsible for the situation is Christian pedantry," he stated in his now famous *Discours sur le colonialisme:* for "it advanced the dishonest equations: Christianity = civilization; paganism = savagery." While admitting that exchanges between continents and rapports between different civilizations constitute the very oxygen of progress, Césaire denies that colonization did any good for the Black. Instead of human contact, what had happened, Césaire maintains, were simple liaisons of domination and of submission. To the White's statistics on roads, canals and railroads, he responds with lyrical pleas concerning the thousands of men sacrificed to the Congo-Océan and to the harbor of Abidjan dug by hand by generations of Blacks. But it is especially when he uses the device of causticity that his rebellion appears particularly effective. Such sentences as: "Neither Deterding, nor Royal Dutch, nor Standard Oil will ever console me for the loss of the Aztecs nor of the Incas," are effective precisely because they tend to distract the listener and the reader from content: how can it be proven that Royal Dutch or Standard Oil had anything to do with the disappearance of ancient civilizations?

But the *Discours sur le colonialisme* is not always dubious in content, nor sarcastic in style. When violent rebellion gives way to a more sedate approach, Césaire does manage to make some very good points. For example, in answer to some detractors, such as Roger Caillois, Emile Faguet and Jules Romains, he counters with a number of indisputable facts. To the often-made charge that "The black race has not yet yielded nor will ever give us an Einstein, nor a Stravinsky, nor a Gershwin," he lists a number of achievements attributable more or less directly to men of his heritage: "For example, the invention of arithmetic and of geometry by the Egyptians. For example, the discovery of astronomy by the Assyrians. For example, the appearance of Rationalism in the bosom of Islam at the time when western thought was furiously pre-logical."

Nevertheless, if in the past the Blacks constituted a proud and productive race, in more recent times it bent and submitted cowardly to foreign interventions and assimilation efforts. This is a theme which constantly lards the ***Discours sur le colonialisme*** and which reappears in a number of recent plays by Aimé Césaire. It should be noted immediately, however, that the poet's switch to the theatre did not really constitute an unusual metamorphosis. In writing for the stage he conserved intact the vigor of his poetry, his predilection for lyrical outbursts, and the use of Claudelian verset. Yet, in an unusual combination at which probably the Catholic poet would shiver, Claudel joins Brecht in Césaire's theatre. Let us mention for example ***La Tragédie du roi Christophe*** (1964), which takes place in Haiti at the beginning of the nineteenth century, and which seizes poignantly the aspirations of a Negro leader at first hailed by his people, then abandoned by them when it becomes obvious that freedom can only be secured at the cost of blood and tears. An even more striking example of the unusual fusion between Claudel's vocabulary and Brecht's propagandistic exhortations occurs in ***Une Saison au Congo,*** a play which follows closely the events which tore apart the Congo in 1960, and which lead to the assassination of its prime minister, Patrice Lumumba. The dominating figure of the African leader captures the imagination of spectators and readers to whom he is depicted as a misunderstood and solitary savior. Listen for example to Lumumba's lyrical hymn which evokes the birth of the Congo out of the ashes of an enslaved past:

> Congolese, today is a great day because for the first time in a long time we see daylight! It is the day when the world receives, among other nations, the Congo, our mother, and especially the Congo, our child. The child of our waiting, of our suffering, of our struggle. Comrades and fellow soldiers, may each of our wounds become a breast, may each of our thoughts, each of our hopes turn into a whip . . . I should like to be a *toucan,* the beautiful bird, in order to fly across the skies, and to announce, to races and languages, that our Congo has been born.
>   —*Une Saison au Congo*

And there are, of course, numerous other examples one could select in this and other plays by Césaire in which he combines successfully a majestic and violent lyricism which reassembles Claudelian tones, with those of the tam-tam African rhythms. Part of the attraction of this fusion, experienced even by those of different political persuasions, is in the fact that it recalls chant, mime, and dance, that is to say the traditional African culture which is essentially one based on oral and gesture communication. Moreover, this style is capable of expressing in a foreign language the divinations and the prophecies of the African temperament. The poet, synthesizing and synchronizing, manages to collect and to concretize a catching unity of great pulsations in which the *I* and the world are soldered into a mystical and quasi-erotic symbolism. In order to reach such an effect, Césaire's

genius finds a heretofore unexplored poetical expression, namely that of Claudel and Brecht mingled into a single voice: the most patented, partisan politics explicated in terms of motherhood ("the Congo, our mother . . . our child"); physical and spiritual injuries ("our wounds") evoking a most intimate part of the body ("breast") which is reminiscent of motherhood and nourishment; cogitation ("our thoughts") and expectations ("our hopes") metamorphosed into an offensive weapon ("a whip").

A Communist who could not stand the orthodoxy of the Communist Party, a Marxist who shook himself lose from Hegelian mechanisms, Aimé Césaire has always managed to hold on to his lyrical exuberance.
                                                        —*Alfred Cismaru*

A Communist who could not stand the orthodoxy of the Communist Party, a Marxist who shook himself lose from Hegelian mechanisms, Aimé Césaire has always managed to hold on to his lyrical exuberance. Moreover, his separation from Europe makes it possible for him to break with clarity and description, and to become intimate with the fundamental essence of things. Under his powerful, poetic eye, perception knows no limits and pierces appearances without pity. Words emerge and explode like firecrackers, catching the eye and the imagination of the reader. He makes use of the entire dictionary, of artificial and vulgar words, of elegant and forgotten ones, of technical and invented vocabulary, marrying it to Antillean and African syllables, and allowing it to play freely in a sort of flaming folly that is both a challenge and a tenacious attempt at mystification. Witness the following little poem, picked at random from among dozens which are available in his various collections of poetry;

> *Another Horizon*
> night devil-like stigma
> night telegraphic bushel planted in the ocean
> for the minute love of cetaceans
> night shut
> splendid atelier of maceration
> where with all of the strength of all its savage
>   colors flexes the violet muscle of the *aconitum*
>   *napallus* of another sun
>   —*Soleil cou coupé*

Its mysterious, cryptic tone notwithstanding, it is clear that the poet has communicated with Night, has identified with it, thus has managed to impart to us a most intimate and unusual experience clad in magic, powerful, and irrepressible vocabulary. Aimé Césaire's ability to convey is, therefore, not limited to topical themes, but it extends to very private and personal feelings enhanced by his genius and projected across the darkness of the world with the ease of a graceful manipulator of *chiaro-oscuros.* An exact accountant of his own suffering, Césaire is mysteriously aware of our own balance sheets on pain. He once stated in a collection already quoted:

> to go.
> just as there are hyena-men and cancer-men, I
> shall
>   be a Jew-man
> a Black of austral Africa
> a man-Hindu-from-Calcutta
> a man-from-Harlem-who-does-not-vote
> the hungry man, the insulted man, the tortured
> man
>   who can be seized at any moment and crushed
>   by blows and killed—killed entirely—without
>   anyone having to give an account to anybody
>   or to apologize to anybody
> a Jew-man
> a pogrom-man
> a young dog
> a beggar . . .
> I shall find the secret of great communications and
>   of great combustions. I shall tell the storm.
>   I shall tell the river. I shall tell the tornado.
> I shall tell the leaf. I shall tell the tree.
> I shall be drenched by all the rains, humectant
> with all the dews.
>
> *—Cahier d'un retour au pays natal*

Ambitious promises, of course, but Aimé Césaire has been able to deliver. He is a poet's poet when he stays clear of political questions, a tenacious and violent propagandist when the theme requires it. His place in contemporary French letters, already recognized by Sartre and other critics, is assured in spite of the fact that not many agree with his views on Whites in general, nor with his opinions on Europe, in particular. Some have seen a certain amount of naïveté in Césaire's choice of fighting intolerance with intolerance and hate with scorn. For example, speaking of him and of others who follow in his footsteps, Pierre de Boisdeffre remarked: "In acceding to the conquest of their national *I,* they continue to dream of a universal humanism of which Europe—whose grandeur they do not recognize because they have only seen its oppressive side—gave them the idea in the first place." The Everyman that he is, Césaire the Black, the Jew, the Colonized and the Freed, still uses, of course, a European language as his means of expression. That he is, at this point in history, incapable of admitting or seeing that his taste for freedom comes from the very people who have colonized and subjugated him, is of less importance than the fact that he is eminently able to become in-

carnated into a number of paradigms which shake the modern world and pain its conscience. Besides, unlike some Black Power advocates, Aimé Césaire sees, of course, the inadequacy of a return to what might be called the museum of African culture: the myriad languages of Africa would limit considerably the reading public of any poet, of any writer indeed. Césaire understood that African and Antillean vernaculars conserve simply an historic importance, and the only way not to have to pit one linguistic group against the other is to rely on French, which has been for so long the official administrative and scholarly language of millions of Blacks. That he does is of benefit to *aficionados* of literature everywhere.

Marjorie Perloff (review date January-February 1984)

SOURCE: "The French Connection," in *American Poetry Review,* Vol. 13, January-February, 1984, pp. 40-5.

[*In the following excerpt, Perloff offers praise for Césaire's poetry and its English translation upon publication of* The Collected Poetry of Aimé Césaire.]

I turn finally to what will surely be considered one of the most important translations from the French in 1983— Clayton Eshleman and Annette Smith's *Collected Poetry of Aimé Césaire.* A number of these translations had already appeared in Paul Auster's anthology, but it takes more than a handful of short poems to give the reader a sense of Césaire's astonishing poetic power, and the new California bilingual edition puts the entire lyric corpus before us for the first time.

The black poet Aimé Césaire was born in 1913 in Martinique. Creole is the first language of all black Martinicans, but Césaire's lower middle-class parents made strenuous efforts to secure their son the best French education possible: at eighteen, he won a scholarship to the famous Lycée Louis-le-Grand in Paris which, in turn, paved the way for his entrance to the Ecole Normale. In the Paris of the thirties, two influences converged to shape Césaire's future poetry: the Surrealism of André Breton and his circle, and the new interest in African ethnography, especially the work of Leo Frobenius. As Michel Leiris put it in his 1965 essay "Qui est Aimé Césaire?" (an English translation by A. James Arnold appeared in *Sulfur* 5 [1982]):

> Césaire found in surrealism a way of looking at the
> world that had to appeal to him. Wasn't surrealism
> in open revolt against the entire framework of west-
> ern rationalism, which the European intellectuals
> assembled around Breton rejected as an intolerable

tyranny, less tolerable still for a Black Antillean since that framework is, historically, the one the Whites *superimposed,* so to speak, on the slaves they imported from Africa and on their descendants?

Together with the African poet and statesman-to-be Léopold Senghor, Césaire developed the concept of *négritude,* which signifies not, as is often thought, "Blackness first," the belief in African superiority, but rather, as Leiris explains, the right to be what one is, the right to "remain *different*":

> For Césaire to be conscious of his negritude and to be conscious of it as Martinican requires that he pursue from the start two objectives: politically, to free his country of forms of economic exploitation that condemn the masses to pauperism; culturally, to bring the specifically Antillean element into proper relief, which implies that without underestimating the role of western civilization one must turn toward the African heritage that is so often forgotten or denied by colored Antilleans who want only to be first-class Frenchmen.

These are precisely the themes that find their way into Césaire's first great poem, the long *Cahier d'un retour au pays natal* (*Notebook of a Return to the Native Land*), published in its first version in 1939, when Césaire returned to Martinique. In the years that followed, Césaire became actively engaged in politics: first as editor of the radical journal *Tropiques,* then as a member of the fledgling Martinican Communist party which, at the end of World War II, elected him mayor of Fort-de-France and the same year as deputy to the Première Assemblée Nationale Constituante in Paris, where he participated in the formation of the new constitution of the Fourth Republic. In the decade that followed, Césaire wrote most of his lyric poetry; he also began to turn away from Communism and officially broke with the party in 1956 when the Soviets invaded Hungary. The precise nature of his Marxist philosophy is, as Smith and Eshleman point out, a complicated question: suffice it to say here that in 1958 he founded the independent socialist Martinican Progressive party (PPM) which has been returned to the French legislature in every subsequent election. A strong supporter of the Mitterand government, Césaire continues to write—in the last two decades chiefly drama and essays—and to engage in the cause of Martinican independence.

The appeal of Césaire's poetry depends, I think, on its particular blend of a native vitalism, a violent energy that celebrates the irrational, the strange, even the bestial, with a French sophistication, wit, and learning. If, as Eshleman and Smith note, the poetry is "a perpetual scene of dismemberment and mutilation," if it goes so far as to celebrate cannibalism as that which "symbolically eradicates the distinction

between the I and the Other, between human and nonhuman, between what is (anthropologically) edible and what is not, and, finally, between the subject and the object," it is also a self-consciously literary poetry, full of echoes of Rimbaud (especially the Rimbaud of the *Saison en enfer*), Lautréamont, Baudelaire, and Mallarmé. Again, if Césaire's rhythms are influenced by African dances and voodoo rituals, his syntax is so Latinate and his vocabulary so esoteric, that it brings to mind the reference shelf rather than the tribal dance. Sartre sums it up nicely in a comment cited on the book jacket of the Eshleman-Smith translation:

> In Aimé Césaire the great surrealist tradition draws to a close, achieves its definitive meaning and is destroyed: surrealism, a European movement in poetry is snatched from the Europeans by a black man who turns it against them and assigns a rigorously defined function to it . . . a Césaire poem explodes and whirls about itself like a rocket, suns burst forth whirling and exploding like new suns—it perpetually surpasses itself.

The rocket analogy is a good one: Césaire's is nothing if not an explosive poetry. *The Notebook of a Return to the Native Land,* for example, is a 1,055-line exorcism (part prose, part free verse) of the poet's "civilized" instincts, his lingering shame at belonging to a country and a race so abject, servile, petty and repressed as is his. A paratactic catalogue poem that piles up phrase upon phrase, image upon image, in a complex network of repetitions, its thrust is to define the threshold between sleep and waking—the sleep of oppression, the blind acceptance of the status quo, that gives way to rebirth, to a new awareness of what is and may be. Accordingly, it begins with the refrain line, repeated again and again in the first section of the poem, "Au bout du petit matin . . ." ("At the end of the little morning," a purposely childlike reference to dawn, which Eshleman and Smith awkwardly render as "At the end of the wee hours"), followed by a strophe that characterizes the poet's initial anguish, an anguish always laced with black humour:

> *Va-t'en, lui disais-je, gueule de flic, gueule de vache, va-t'en, je déteste les larbins de l'ordre et les hannetons de l'espérance. Va-t'en, mauvais gri-gri, punaise de moinillon. Puis je me tournais vers des paradis pour lui et les siens perdus, plus calme que la face d'une femme qui ment, et là, bercé par les effluves d'une pensée jamais lasse je nourrissais le vent, je délaçais les monstres et j'entendais monter de l'autre côté du désastre, un fleuve de tourterelles et de trèfles de la savane que je porte toujours dans mes profondeurs à hauteur inverse du vingtième étage des maisons les plus insolentes et par précaution contre la force putréfiante des*

ambiantes crépusculaires, arpentée nuit et jour d'un sacré soleil vénérien.

Beat it, I said to him, you cop, you lousy pig, beat it, I detest the flunkies of order and the cockchafers of hope. Beat it evil grigri, you bedbug of a petty monk. Then I turned toward paradises lost for him and his kin, calmer than the face of a woman telling lies, and there, rocked by the flux of a never exhausted thought I nourished the wind, I unlaced the monsters and heard rise, from the other side of disaster, a river of turtledoves and savanna clover which I carry forever in my depths height-deep as the twentieth floor of the most arrogant houses and as a guard against the putrefying force of crepuscular surroundings, surveyed night and day by a cursed veneral sun.

Here we have the hallmarks of Césaire's style: impassioned direct address ("Va-t'en"), name-calling ("gueule de flic," "gueule de vache"), parallel constructions that aren't quite parallel ("les larbins de l'ordre et les hannetons de l'espérance"), hyperbole ("la force putréfiante des ambiances crépusculaires"), oxymoron ("dans mes profondeurs à hauteur inverse du vingtième étage des maisons les plus insolents"), violent imagery ("sacré soleil vénérien"), and above all the chant-like rhythm created by the repetition of word and sound, as in "je nourrissais ... je délaçais ... j'entendais" or in "de l'autre côté du désastre, un fleuve de tourterelles et de trèfles."

The appeal of Césaire's poetry depends, I think, on its particular blend of a native vitalism, a violent energy that celebrates the irrational, the strange, even the bestial, with a French sophistication, wit, and learning.
—Marjorie Perloff

There is really nothing comparable to this mode in American poetry. In the long catalogue poems of Allen Ginsberg and Imamu Baraka, we find similarly impassioned repetition, parallelism, hyperbole; again, in a sequence like Galway Kinnell's *The Book of Nightmares*, we meet imagery of perhaps equal violence and stringency. But Césaire's poetry is quite different from Ginsberg's on the one hand or Kinnell's on the other in its curious conjunction of an intense realism (in the course of the *Notebook,* the topography of Martinique, its climate, architecture, and inhabitants are graphically described) with a surrealism that seems so inevitable it may almost escape our attention.

Who is it, for instance, that the poet meets "Au bout du petit matin"—a cop or a "bedbug of a petty monk"? Or both? If the former, then the paradise lost he cannot attain is one of a primitive society that had not learned the need for law-enforcement. If the latter, the enemy is primarily Christianity. These are, of course, part and parcel of the same complex for Césaire, but the point I am trying to make is that his is a language so violently charged with meaning that each word falls on the ear (or hits the eye) with resounding force. On "the other side of disaster," we read, there is "a river of turtledoves and savanna clover" which the poet carries so deep within himself that it surpasses the height of the most insolent twenty-floor house. But what is the disaster that has occurred? It will take the whole length of the poem to find out. And in the course of the poem, the town, "plate-étalée" ("sprawled-flat") like Van Gogh's little town in *The Starry Night,* must explode:

Elle rampe sur les mains sans jamais aucune envie de vriller le ciel d'une stature de protestation. Les dos des maisons ont peur du ciel truffé de feu, leurs pieds des noyades du sol, elles ont opté de se poser superficielles entre les surprises et les perfidies. Et pourtant elle avance la ville. Même qu'elle paît tous les jours outre sa marée de corridors carrelés, de persiennes pudibondes, de cours gluantes, de peintures qui dégoulinent. Et de petits scandales étouffés, de petites hontes tues, de petites haines immenses pétrissent en bosses et creux les rues étroites où le ruisseau grimace longitudinalement pari l'étron ...

It crawls on its hands without the slightest desire to drill the sky with a stature of protest. The backs of the houses are afraid of the sky truffled with fire, their feet of the drownings of the soil, they chose to perch shallowly between surprises and treacheries. And yet it advances, the town does. It even grazes every day further out into its tide of tiled corridors, prudish shutters, gluey courtyards, dripping paintwork. And petty hushed-up scandals, petty unvoiced guilts, petty immense hatreds knead the narrow streets into bumps and potholes where the waste-water grins longitudinally through turds ...

What strikes me as especially remarkable here and in Césaire's surrealist lyrics in **Les Armes Miraculeuses (The Miraculous Weapons)** of 1946 is the total absence of sentimentality or self-pity. He can see himself as:

—moi sur une route, enfant, mâchant une racine de canne à sucre
—traîné homme sur une route sanglante une corde au cou
—debout au milieu d'un cirque immense sur mon front noir une couronne de daturas

voum rooh

*—me on a road, a child chewing
sugar cane root
—a dragged man on a bloodspattered road
a rope around his neck
—standing in the center of a huge circus,
on my black forehead a crown of daturas
voum rooh*

without casting about for a scapegoat. For, as the "I" comes to realize in the course of the poem, "Nous vomissure de négrier" ("We the vomit of slave ships") must exorcise our own cowardice, fear, and hypocrisy before change can take place:

Et voici ceux qui ne se consolent point de n'être pas faits à la ressemblance de Dieu mais du diable, ceux qui considèrent que l'on est nègre comme commis de seconde classe: en attendant mieux et avec possibilité de monter plus haut; ceux qui battent la chamade devant soi-même . . . ceux qui disent à l'Europe: "Voyez, je sais comme vous faire des courbettes, comme vous présenter mes hommages, en somme, je ne suis pas différent de vous; ne faites pas attention à ma peau noire: c'est le soleil qui m'a brûlé."

And there are those who will never get over not being made in the likeness of God but of the devil, those who believe that being a nigger is like being a second-class clerk; waiting for a better deal and upward mobility; those who beat the drum of compromise in front of themselves, those who live in their own dungeon pit . . . those who say to Europe: "You see, I can bow and scrape, like you I pay my respects, in short, I am no different from you: pay no attention to my black skin: the sun did it."

Césaire, as the classical scholar Gregson Davis, himself a black Caribbean, argued in an essay of 1977, is notoriously difficult to translate. The use of arcane diction, technical vocabulary, Creole and African terms, homonyms, and neologisms, presents the translator with formidable problems, but, what is worse, Césaire's syntax seems to be, in Davis' words, "disordered and lubricous; and the lubricity, real or apparent, is partly a function of the total absence of punctuation." (This is less the case in *Notebook* than in the later work). It is often difficult to know whether a given adjectival modifier belongs to one noun or another; again, so Davis argues, Césaire's "specialized lyric vocabulary," especially his sequences of metaphors, cannot be tampered with without destroying the whole poetic structure. "Interpretation," he insists, "should take into account the total symbolic system of the lyric *oeuvre.*"

Eshleman and Smith, who refer to Davis' cautionary statements in their own "Translators' Notes," have clearly taken his lessons to heart. They affirm their desire to preserve Césaire's odd syntax as fully as possible and to reproduce his verbal patterns. Indeed, so careful are they to be literal, that they embed certain of the West Indian or technical terms in the English translation, for example:

Au bout du petit matin, le morne oublié, oublieux de sauter.

At the end of the wee hours, the morne forgotten, forgetful of leaping.

where *morne,* so the Notes tell us, "is a term used throughout the French West Indies to designate certain altitudes of volcanic origin" and hence "justly applied to the majority of Martinican hills." Or again, we read:

terre grande délire de la mentule de Dieu

earth great delirium of God's mentula

mentule being "probably a gallicization of the Latin 'mentula' (penis) based on an Indo-European stem designating a stick agitated to produce fire."

I find this practice of reproducing the foreign word irritating, for it destroys the continuity as well as the fiction of the text, reminding us that the English version is only, so to speak, a reproduction of the original. Even more irritating is the often dogged attempt to reproduce the exact syntax of the original as when, in the extract about the exploding town cited above. "Et pourtant elle avance la ville" is translated as "And yet it advances, the town does." In English, this sounds silly: "And yet the town advances" or "And yet the town moves forward" would have been quite sufficient.

Even at its best, this can hardly be called an elegant translation. "Pas un bout de ce monde qui ne porte mon empreinte digitale," which an earlier translator, Emile Snyder, rendered as "not a bit of this earth not smudged by my fingerprint," becomes "not an inch of this world devoid of my fingerprint," thus erasing the force of the "empreinte digitale" which Césaire wishes to convey. Again, it is hard to understand why "Ce qui est à moi / c'est un homme seul emprisonné de / blanc" is translated as "What is mine / a lonely man imprisoned in / whiteness," for an "homme seul" need not be lonely and Césaire's understatement is surely intentional.

"What is desperately needed in an enterprise so important and far-reaching as a translation of Césaire's lyric verse," says Gregson Davis, "is an interpreter who has a profound knowledge of Caribbean history and culture, on the one hand, and European literary history, ancient and modern, on the other." Davis is himself such an interpreter and I understand he will soon publish his own translation of Césaire. In the meantime, we have Clayton Eshleman and Annette Smith's brave attempt to come to terms with this difficult and brilliant poet. Smith's scholarship is impressive: the introduction, history of editions, translator's notes, and bibliography are very helpful. Eshleman, who won the National Book Award for his translation with José Rubia Barcia of César Vallejo (1978), seems less at ease with the surrealist complexities of Césaire than with the more direct emotive thrust of the Peruvian poet. But perhaps at this early stage of Césaire translation, it is ungrateful to ask for more than the California translators have given us. It is a genuine gift.

James A. Arnold (review date July 1985)

SOURCE: "Twentieth Century Stepchild," in *American Book Review,* Vol. 7, July, 1985, p. 3.

[*In the following review, Arnold praises the translation* The Collected Poems of Aimé Césaire *and discusses Césaire's perceived lack of national identity.*]

Aimé Césaire was heralded by the *Times Literary Supplement* in 1982 as one of the three most important poets of the twentieth century, alongside Artaud and Pasolini. This brilliant translation of his *Collected Poetry* (1939-1976) by Clayton Eshleman and Annette Smith, handsomely illustrated with line drawings by Césaire's friend, the Cuban artist Wifredo Lam, will allow readers to reach their own conclusions. At all events, an important new territory has been added to the poetic geography of our time by the availability in one volume of all but the most recent collection (*Moi, laminaire,* 1983) of the greatest living poet in the French language.

Césaire is a black Martinican who has been a Deputy in the French Chamber of Deputies since 1945. The fact that he is a Martinican, therefore a (neo-) colonial subject of France, has encouraged readers to assume that he is somehow outside the mainstream. The fact that he was the first major poet in the world to loudly proclaim that "it-is-beautiful-good-and-legitimate-to-be-a-nigger" (1939) has subjected Césaire to the vicissitudes of fashion regarding black writers. Insofar as he is recognized today, it is as a precursor of the Black Arts Movement in this country. When the revolutionary fervor and the rhetorical posturing of the sixties subsided, so did interest in Césaire. Our mistake was to tie him to a group of writers whose work was less permanent than Césaire's. Reading him as a Frantz Fanon in verse trivialized Césaire's poetry and reduced him to an epiphenomenon.

Gárcia Márquez, Vargas Llosa, in fiction, Neruda and Vallejo among Latin American poets, all write from within, even as they write against, recognizable national cultures. But the black writer from Martinique or Guadeloupe, having no national identity in the Caribbean, is the stepchild of the twentieth century. Saint-John Perse, born in Guadeloupe into the white planter class, rose to the top echelons of the French foreign service under his real name, Aléxis Saint-Léger Léger. He received the Nobel Prize for Literature in 1960. In the same year Aimé Césaire published *Ferraments,* probably his most accomplished collection of poems. His name has never appeared among the candidates for the Nobel.

The principal issue in reading, understanding and translating Césaire is his relationship to modernism and its antecedents. An only slightly less important issue is the potential of modernist poetics for awakening the political as well as the esthetic consciousness of its readers. Previous translators of Césaire stressed the political to the detriment of the esthetic. Clayton Eshleman and Annette Smith have struck a fine balance. They have given us strong poetry that features, sometimes alternately, sometimes in unexpected combinations, the asperity, the wit, the solemnity, and the sensual molding of sound that characterize the original. The fact that Annette Smith was born in colonial Algeria and has a feel for the French colonial milieu has contributed to keeping these translations very close to the tone and the affective sense of Césaire's writing.

The qualities of the *Notebook of a Return to the Native Land* (1939; standard edition, 1956) come through here for the first time in English. The reader can grasp the essence of this long poem (53 pages with the original French on the facing page) which became a source of moral and spiritual sustenance to readers involved in the decolonization of their countries in the late forties and fifties. Césaire's creation of an original form in this poem, where prophetic discourse of a distantly biblical flavor gives way to lyrical bursts and a prose that sometimes approaches narrative, has saved the *Notebook* from becoming a dated piece of anticolonialist poetry like so many others.

The Miraculous Weapons (1946) extends surrealism beyond the range it had acquired in Breton's practice, while retaining a muscular tension and a drive that seldom appear in Eluard's. *The Thoroughbreds,* one of the longer poems in the collection, evidences these characteristics in two successive passages: "But how how not bless / unlike anything dreamt by my logics / hard against the grain cracking their licy piles / and their saburra and more pathetic / than the fruit-bearing flower / the lucid chap of unreasons?" Then, in counterpoint: "And I hear the water mounting / the new the untouched the timeless water / toward the renewed air." The poem suggests the death and rebirth of a culture hero, the prelude to a new mythology freed from the dominating, raping will to power of the Western ethos. It culminates in a prophetic vision: "through knowing grasses time glides / the branches were pecking at a peace of green flames / and the earth breathed under the gauze of mists / and the earth stretched. There was a cracking / in its knotted shoulders. There was in its veins / a crackling of fire. . . ." In this mode Césaire frequently adopts an apocalyptic stance, positing ultimate renewal only after some telluric upheaval.

Lost Body, the title poem of a 1950 collection originally illustrated by Picasso, makes more explicit the impulse of the rootless to put down roots. Since the recent past of Afro-Americans (and, more generally, of the dispossessed) has been largely obliterated, those roots will probe an ancient substratum: "Things stand back make room among you / room for my repose carrying in waves / my frightening crest of anchor-like roots / looking for a place to take hold / Things I probe I probe / me the street-porter I am root-porter / and I bear down and I force and I arcane / I omphale / Ah who leads me back toward the harpoon / I am very weak / I hiss yes I hiss very ancient things. . . ."

In *Poetry and Knowledge* (1944) Césaire had expanded this notion in essay form. On the one hand, he claimed: "The poet's word is the primal word: rupestral design in the stuff of sound." No wonder then that the American poet to undertake the translation of Césaire's *oeuvre* should be Clayton Eshleman, whose recent collections *Hades in Manganese* (1981) and *Fracture* (1983) both concern themselves with the earliest human art and the dilemma of contemporary humanity. And it is characteristic of Eshleman's work in this translation that he makes his own another proposition in Césaire's *Poetry and Knowledge:* "the music of poetry . . . comes from a greater distance than sound. To seek to musicalize poetry is the crime against poetic music, which can only be the striking of the mental wave against the rock of the world." In *Hades in Manganese* Eshleman wrote that "words are energy deposits" (*The Shaft*) and *Winding Windows* suggests, in a style consonant with Césaire's poetic intention: "If there must be clarity, / let it be opaque, let the word be / as translucent as night stirred. . . ."

E. Anthony Hurley (essay date Spring 1992)

SOURCE: "Link and Lance: Aspects of Poetic Function in Césaire's *Cadastre*—An Analysis of Five Poems," in *L'Esprit Créateur,* Vol. XXXIII, No. 1, spring 1992, pp. 54-68.

[*In the following essay, Hurley discusses five of Césaire's poems taking into account peculiarities of his French Caribbean heritage and its lack of literary tradition.*]

It would be difficult to examine the notion of poetic function in relation to Aimé Césaire without taking into consideration the tension and ambivalence of Césaire's situation as a black intellectual and as a poet, functioning within a profoundly alienating white French sociocultural context. On the one hand, as a black man, and particularly as a black Martinican-Frenchman, Césaire is constantly confronted by identity issues, grounded in the unhealed and perhaps unhealable wound of slavery, of colonization, and of relatively forced assimilation into an alien culture, as well as in potential isolation and separation within the black/African diaspora. As a poet and black intellectual, Césaire serves as the voice of a leader for an audience and a people (fellow Blacks) on whom he depends and to whom he is inextricably linked for the integration of his identity. Césaire's situation therefore suggests the tension of a poetry that would tend to function simultaneously inwardly and outwardly, personally and politically, as both link and lance: as a link for exploring identity issues, a means of searching and solidifying, of facilitating and articulating identity; as a lance, a weapon of personal and political liberation, but also an instrument to open the festering wound of alienation and self-hatred in order to create hope and healing.

At the same time, Césaire is a citizen of France, albeit black and Martinican, writing poetry in the French language within an established French literary tradition with its own socio-symbolic order. While Césaire's awareness as an educated black man might tend to incline him towards consciously or unconsciously rejecting or subverting the French social order, he does not become "un-French," and both his use of the French language and his renown as a French (Caribbean) writer would tend to validate, and contribute to the survival of, the French social order to which he belongs.

> **A discussion of poetic function in relation to Césaire should . . . take into account the peculiarities of his French Caribbean situation and the ambivalence of his relationship to a metropolitan French literary tradition.**
> **—E. Anthony Hurley**

A discussion of poetic function in relation to Césaire should therefore take into account the peculiarities of his French Caribbean situation and the ambivalence of his relationship to a metropolitan French literary tradition. The term poetic function itself, however, though part of the rhetoric of the Western sociocultural tradition, tends to be somewhat elusive. Its meaning, for the purposes of this study, may be said to lie within the parameters of two modern critical and linguistic approaches, advanced by [Julia] Kristeva and [Roman] Jakobson. Kristeva's approach captures the irony of

Césaire's position vis-a-vis metropolitan French society. She posits a revolutionary and subversive function for poetry or poetic language within the context of a socio-symbolic order; poetry thus serves paradoxically both to transform the social order and to ensure its survival:

> Dans cet ordre socio-symbolique ainsi saturé sinon déjà clos, la poésie—disons plus exactement le langage poétique—rappelle ce qui fut depuis toujours sa fonction: introduire, à travers le symbolique, ce qui le travaille, le traverse et le menace. Ce que la théorie de l'inconscient cherche, le langage poétique le pratique à l'interieur et à l'encontre de l'ordre social: moyen ultime de sa mutation ou de sa subversion, condition de sa survie et de sa révolution. . . .

Kristeva's approach in relating poetry to the context of a social order shares linkages with Jakobson's analysis of linguistic communication. Jakobson identifies six constituent factors in linguistic processes: "destinateur," "destinataire," "message," "contexte," "code," and "contact." He relates poetic function to emphasis placed on the "message" itself: "l'accent mis sur le message pour son propre compte est ce qui caractérise la fonction poétique du langage. . . ." Césaire's poetry indeed necessarily emphasizes the "message," since it serves as a concrete manifestation of a communication link between poet and self and poet and people. In this study, therefore, poetic function will refer to the role of the poet and of the poem in relation to the sociopolitical context within which the poet writes.

The interpretation of Césaire's poetry as revolutionary, in relation to the nature and direction of the poet's communication, was suggested, long before the articulations of Jakobson and Kristeva, by Aristide Maugée, Césaire's close friend, fellow Martinican and co-contributor to the early 1940s Martinican journal, *Tropiques*. In a 1942 article, Maugée suggests aspects of the functions of Césaire's poetry that will become almost clichés in the years that follow: the poem as liberation, as verbal magic, as a means of exploring and discovering inner truths. He asserted:

> [Césaire] faconne da mots nouveaux, crée da images nouvelles pour exprimer la nuance exacte de sa perception, trouve des sonorités neuves pour libérer son chant interieur.
>
> Magie du son. Sortilège du Verbe.
>
> [. . .] par la désintégration du réel, le poéte recherche un monde nouveau: un monde de beauté et de vérité.
>
> Où le trouvera-t-il sinon dans la profondeur de sa conscience?

Moreover, Césaire himself, in his 1943 article in *Tropiques,* "Maintenir la poesie," had indicated that poetry as he conceived and practiced it had a deliberately subversive function, in relation to the existing social order:

> Se défendre du social par la création d'une zone d'incandescence, en deça de laquelle, à l'intérieur de laquelle fleurit dans une sécurité terrible la fleur inouïe du "Je"; [. . .] conquérir par la révolte la part franche où se susciter soi-même, intégral, telles sont quelques-unes des exigences qui [. . .] tendent à s'imposer à tout poète [. . .].
>
> Ici poésie égale insurrection [. . .]

Césaire's poetics have perhaps been most comprehensively articulated in **"Poésie et connaissance,"** in which he established an opposition between poetic and scientific processes of knowledge, affirming the superiority of the poetic process as a means of true cosmic knowledge. Césaire thus aligned himself with the revolutionary adventures of poets like Baudelaire, Rimbaud, Mallarmé, Lautréamont, Apollinaire and Breton. **"Poésie et connaissance"** ended with a summary of Césaire's poetics, expressed in seven propositions, the first of which asserts that "la poésie est cette démarche qui par le mot, l'image, le mythe, l'amour et l'humour m'installe au cccur vivant de moi-même et du monde".

Césaire's explicit alignment with these luminaries of modern French poetry has opened the door for Euro-centered critical approaches to his own poetry. Such approaches, however well meaning, however brilliantly executed, feed into the same dilemma from which Césaire as a French Caribbean writer has tried so courageously to escape: absorption into a socio-politico-cultural entity that has, through slavery, colonization, and assimilation, consistently denied a voice to him and his people. French Caribbean poets like Césaire are necessarily characterized by the problem of cultural identity, including the struggle of separation from France, and their textual voice is grounded in the geographical and sociocultural reality of the French Caribbean. Because of the peculiar situation of such poets, in terms of the dynamics of geography, language, history, and culture, it is inevitable that the signs of this situation will be literally inscribed in the texts produced. If these signs are unrecognized or ignored, much of the "significance" of the literary work will be missed.

Moreover, any approach to Césaire's poetry and indeed to the literature of the Caribbean that ignores the existence of an authentic and valid voice which compensates for an orality lost or repressed over the last few centuries will inevitably fall short of determining the profound significance of the literature.

No analysis of French Caribbean literature is ultimately meaningful if it does not directly engage the problematic of cultural identity with which every Caribbean writer is confronted. Approaches to Caribbean texts through the mediation of European theories tend to devalue and deny the pivotal thrust of French Caribbean literary production, which is ultimately to proclaim and assert its validity as an authentic cultural manifestation.

A problem arises, however, for, while it may be inappropriate to rely on Euro-centered critical approaches to explicate French Caribbean poetry, there is a lack of alternative approaches sensitive to this problematic. Since critical practice necessarily has political implications, there is a need for critical activity by scholars sensitive enough to the challenge posed by the special situation of French Caribbean letters not to adopt the easier task of imposing a traditional, metropolitan critical framework on French Caribbean texts, but to seek to develop approaches which will support the evolution of a French Caribbean literary canon on its own terms.

> **Césaire's poetry operates in two directions simultaneously: inwardly [and personally], the poetry serves as a vehicle for the poet to explore and resolve issues of personal identity and liberation, and as a means of personal salvation; outwardly [and politically], the poetry operates as a means of communicating with his people and with the supporters of the alienating social order, and as a means of affirmation, education, disalienation, and even of subversion.**
> —*E. Anthony Hurley*

The investigation which follows centers on the notion of poetic function in Césaire's *Cadastre,* with specific reference to five poems. *Cadastre,* published in 1961 by Seuil, is the re-edition of poems from two previously published collections, *Soleil cou-coupe* of 1948 and *Corps perdu* of 1950, with some of the original poems omitted and others revised. Césaire's poetic practice in this collection has been analyzed by A. James Arnold, who has sought to reconcile contrasting modernist and negritude approaches to Césaire. Arnold's assertion of a paradox in the negritude movement in that it "simultaneously cultivated a rhetoric of protest and an intensely subjective poetics", which colors his readings of Césaire's poems, suggests a practical and unreconciled separation between "lyrical" and "polemical" functions in Césaire's poetry not borne out by the texts themselves. Ronnie Scharfman, who has also produced penetrating analyses of many of Césaire's poems, seeks to address and supple-

ment "the absence of a problematic that could simultaneously articulate the difficulties of Césaire's poetic discourse and its political *engagement.*" Scharfman consequently reads each text "as an enactment of some conflict by or for the subject". While her analyses are consistently insightful, she has, by defining Césaire's genius as the "textualization of marginality", and by imposing European critical approaches on Césaire's poetic practice, perhaps underestimated the importance of the relationship existing between Césaire and his chosen "others."

As the title of this collection (*Cadastre*) suggests, the poet is concerned with making a survey—taking an inventory of his situation as a black man and as a poet. The poems suggest the tension implicit in the ambivalence of the relationship between the poet and the social order within which he functions, and serve to concretize the message of liberation. As mentioned earlier, Césaire's poetry operates in two directions simultaneously, inwardly and personally, and outwardly and politically: inwardly, the poetry serves as a vehicle for the poet to explore and resolve issues of personal identity and liberation, and as a means of personal salvation; outwardly, the poetry operates as a means of communicating with his people and with the supporters of the alienating social order, and as a means of affirmation, education, disalienation, and even of subversion.

Linking these two functions which represent the personal and political thrusts of Césaire's poetry is a connecting function which may be identified as creative, concerned with the poet's exploitation of the magical and prophetic potential of poetry. By a close textual reading that resists the temptation to assimilate the poetry into a predetermined European theoretical model, and that refrains from considering the poetry as other than what it is (French Caribbean poetry), I propose to illustrate the specific ways in which these functions operate. I shall attempt to answer the following questions: What voices speak within the poem? What are the roles and characteristics of the poetic voice? Whom does the poet address within the poem? How does the poem link poetic voice, addressee and context?

1. "Magique"

The title of this opening poem of the collection anticipates the magical metamorphosis which occurs at the end of the poem: the repositioning of "un dieu noir" (line 18). This metamorphosis takes place against a background of natural phenomena, an overcast sky in which only a thin slice of blue is visible ("une lèche de ciel"), and high winds ("vous bêtes qui sifflez"), which are characteristic of the destructive "tornade." The island, "ce quignon de terre," is represented as virtually dead, "cette morte," threatened by and at the mercy of the "bêtes" and the "fougères" that are shown to be already "libres." The metaphors signify a geopolitical context of conflict, between "vous bêtes" and "cette morte"; between "vous libres fougères" and "les roches assassines"; between "les conques," suggestive of the island, and "leur destin"; even between the implied light of "midi" and the darkness associated with "les étoiles." Césaire suggests here a conflict between forces of oppression and destruction and other forces with an impulse toward liberation. The struggle takes place on an island, but one that shares a situational bond of worthlessness with other islands, in that they are "englouties comme un sou," and "oubliées comme un sou."

Against this background, the poetic voice identifies itself through the plural "nous" of line 14 ("mol glissement des grains de l'été que nous fûmes"). This is significantly a communal identity, with an already realized potential for regeneration and metamorphosis. The poet also assumes the roles of "bouche," of "suffète des îles englouties," and of "prophetè des îles oubliées," attempting to communicate with an audience, designated as "vous bêtes" and "vous libres fougères." The context evoked, within which this communication takes place, is that of "l'île," "cette morte," featuring "roches assassines" and "conques trop vastes pour leur destin."

The voice of the poet in this situation attempts to transcend the limitations of the island: "la bouche aux parois du nid." The poet assumes the role of responsible leadership, that of "sufféte," but also that of "prophéte" announcing the future of his people. Through the vision and the prophecy of the poet, the dead island, "cette morte," is restored to life; through the poetic activity implicit in the poem a metamorphosis takes place, "ce mol glissement des grains d'été que nous fumes."

The hope of change is implicit throughout the poem. For, even in the midst of the atmosphere of menace and danger, signs of hope appear: the "lèche de ciel" bore within itself signs of good weather to come; the "étoiles" suggest not only darkness, but also light, with associations of good fortune, "trèfles au ciel," and vitality, "gouttes de lait chu." Hope is at the heart of the "message" of this poem: the restoration of the divinity of the black man ("réadjustent un dieu noir mal ne de son tonnerre").

The poem functions as a means of concretizing this hope, and of articulating the poet's prophetic voice, his sense of responsibility and leadership. It illustrates the identity dilemma confronting the French Caribbean poet. The poet as a linking voice magically emerges out of the silence historically imposed on Blacks in a neo-colonial situation. It is essentially through the poem that the "black" voice acquires validity.

2. "Couteaux midi"

In the first part of this poem, the subjective presence of the poet appears in the possessive and object pronouns of "ma foi," "mes paroles," "mes cris," "mes crocs de poivre," "mes lèvres," and "m'absente." The poet is evoked as a disembodied voice and mouth, involved in a dialogue, as the questions "Ils tirent à blanc?" and "Midi?" (posed five times) indicate. The poetic replies to the questions are always an affirmative "oui," which suggests the validity of the propositions advanced.

These propositions relate to the activities of blacks, and specifically to what the poet suggests occurs "quand les Nègres font la Révolution." He intimates, with evident irony, playing on common connotations of "blanc" and "noir," that "ils tirent à blanc," and supports the validity of the paradox by explaining that "le blanc est la juste force controversée du noir qu'ils portent dans le coeur. " The text suggests that the poet considers this an abortive, pseudo-revolution, doomed from the start by its own endemic contradictions, equivalent to a whitewashing process taking place under a pseudo midday sun, so pale in comparison to the tropical sun that it is to be greeted only with derisive laughter: "[. . .] les cornettes des soeurs de Saint Joseph de Cluny qu'elles lessivent sous les espèces de midi dans la jubilation solaire d'un savon tropical."

The poet, struck by the contrast between these two different noons, explores the significance which the tropical noon holds for him. He suggests that it provides a natural avenue of escape from the muzzling of his voice and limitations of a complacent and comfortable life: "Midi qui disperse dans le ciel la ouate trop complaisante qui capitonne mes paroles et où mes cris se prennent." The poetic voice shifts to a more assertive and affirmative mode, corresponding to the graphic shift from the common noun, "midi," disdain for which is suggested by "espèces de," to the proper "Midi." This contrasting "Midi" is invested with capacities which stand in opposition to the other "midi": the capacity for a presence affirmed even in darkness ("amande de la nuit"), and the capacity for speech ("langue"). This "Midi," too, is associated with the sensitivity that comes from emotional and social humiliations: "qui porte sur son dos de galeux." This "Midi" is suggestive of courageous patience and endurance and of the potential for creating movement: "met sur toutes les lignes de toutes les mains les trains." It is this "Midi" which, significantly, makes possible a break with the (white) world ("Midi somptueux qui de ce monde m'absente").

The attitude and activities of the poet change with the movement within the poem away from "ce monde." The poetic voice enters into full presence as the poem assumes a poetic "form" in the middle section of the poem. The poet becomes active and assumes the voice of revolt—a revolt so complete it embraces the extremes of "doux" and "dur":

Doux Seigneur!
durement je creche. Au visage des affameurs,
au visage des insulteurs, au visage des
paraschites it des éventreurs. Seigneur cur!
doux je siffle; je siffle doux. . .

The chiasma signals the parallelism of the roles of poet ("je")
and "Seigneur," as the poet moves from rebellion to acceptance. This new attitude is presented by the poet as indicative of his identity, characterized by wounds, but founded
on dignity and commitment: "Oh! je tiens mon pacte /
debout dans mes blessures où mon sang bat contre les fûts." The
poetic identity includes solidarity with others of his race and
the poetic voice sends a message of hope and humanitarianism, bringing into existence, at the end of this section, the
day of a new revolution that transcends hatred:

[. . .] c'est le jour,
un jour pour nos pieds fraternels
un jour pour nos mains sans rancunes
un jour pour nos souffles sans méfiance
un jour pour nos faces sans vergogne

The final short prose section, which continues the discussion of the opening section, links the role of the poet to that
of "les sorciers," suggesting the involvement of both poet
and sorcerer in harnessing powers of potential ferocity and
in creatively exploiting intimacy with the dark forces of nature: "l'intime férocité des étoiles."

The poet, in this poem, suggests a contrast, implicit in the
title, between violent physical pseudo-revolution
("couteaux") and the lucidity ("Midi") of true revolt. The
poet moves beyond embracing violence, to transform the
lance-"couteau" into a kind of magic wand, as he assumes
the role both of prophet predicting a future of hope, dignity
and love, and of sorcerer, using materials supplied by his
brother "Nègres" to participate in the creative activity of the
cosmos. Once again, the poem becomes the connecting link
between past and future, a hopeful echo of the "lost" black
voice in the present of the French Caribbean.

3. "Barbare"

The poetic voice makes itself heard from the first line of the
poem, in "C'est le mot qui me soutient," immediately suggesting the nature of the relationship between the poet and
"le mot," which functions as a source of needed support for
the poet. The poet is represented metonymically as "ma
carcasse," on whom "le mot," as voice, strikes to produce
sound and, by extension, life. In the second and third stanzas, the voice of the poet becomes identified and fused with
the voices of others, sharing with them "nos faces belles"
and "nos oreilles," within the context of the word that introduces and dominates even visually those two stanzas—

"Barbare." In the final stanza, the poet fully assumes the
identity of "barbare" and at the same time that of "le serpent cracheur," as he addresses a "vous," whose physical
presence is indicated in "la chair velue de vos poitrines."

Contrast and conflict between the barbarian group which includes the poet and the other hairy-chested group are clearly
indicated by the text. The poem thus sends a message of revolt, different from "les cris de révolte jamais entendus." The
revolt in the poem involves investing a word with pejorative and insulting resonances with an aura of primitive nobility and power. The resonance of the word "barbare" is a
reminder of psychological debasement, represented metaphorically in the text as the rusting effect of noon on the
poet's carcass, in which ironically only true barbarism, characterized by cowardice and dishonesty, is being destroyed:

C'est le mot qui me soutient
et frappe sur ma carcasse de cuivre jaune
où la lune dévore dans la soupente de la rouille
les os barbares
des lâches bêtes rôdeuses du mensonge.

In the second stanza, the poet suggests the magical power
of language to affirm the validity and beauty of "nos
faces"—an attitude of rejection which bears within itself the
power of creation. In the following stanza, the poet uses the
word "barbare" as a reminder of the past suffering and
present condition of people who have been characterized as
dead, but who are yet the life-blood of the earth, reminiscent of the situation of black South African miners: "des
morts qui circulent dans les veines de la terre." "Barbare"
is used also as a reminder of a spirit of revolt concealed behind a façade of dance and music: "et les cris de révolte
jamais entendus / qui tournent à mesure et à timbres de
musique."

The poet exploits the regenerative potential intrinsic in the
word "barbare," so that it is represented as the magical and
beautiful principle of life concealed in savage and reptilian
forms normally regarded as loathsome ("amphisbène," "serpent," "gekko"), and with which he completely identifies:
"Barbare moi." It is this vital principle that enables the poet
to metamorphose ("qui de mes putrifiantes chairs me
réveille") and adopt an attitude of direct and violent revolt
("me coller [. . .] aux lieux mêmes de la force").

Through the use of the explicit and implicit "barbare"-"moi"-
"poete" linkage, the poem itself functions as the theatre
where a subversive linguistic revolution takes place, and as
the means by which the word "barbare" achieves a truly healing significance. The poet, by appropriating and transforming the various implications of the word, validates the
cultural perspective of the French Caribbean.

4. "Mot"

The poet refers to himself directly only in the first two shorter sections of this poem. At the beginning of the poem, the poet's "moi" serves as the point of departure for the poem, as the context, as source or sender, and as receiver of this word: "Parmi moi / de moi-même / a moi-même / [. . .] en mes mains." At the beginning of the second section, the poet becomes a voice of hope: "j'aurai chance hors du labyrinthe." Soon afterwards, however, the poet becomes the object to be acted upon, at the mercy of, increasingly possessed by, the word ("me prendre," "me pendre," "que me clouent"). After this point, the poet virtually disappears from the poem as a self-referential voice. No further explicit references to a "moi" appear. The only direct indication of a subjective presence occurs in "savez-vous," while the vibration of the word "nègre" gathers momentum and dominates the remainder of the poem.

The word, unspecified at the opening of the poem, is lodged deep in the poet's psyche, inseparable from the poet's identity, and is evoked as a vital instinct, an automatic impulse of revolt: "le rare hoquet d'un ultime spasme délirant." The word becomes active and vibrates ("vibre") more and more throughout the poem. It is this vibration that gives the poet hope of escaping from the "labyrinthe" of his present situation. Hence, his willingness to submit to the emotional vibration, translated into a series of circular images that indicate the poet's delirium of magical possession, as he assumes the role, suggested by Arnold, of poet-priest and scapegoat at the center-stake of the voodoo temple: "au beau poteau-mitan des trés fraîches étoiles."

As the poem develops, the poet's "moi" is possessed by the word "nègre," which assumes an independent force of its own, evoking and conjuring, to the rhythm of a drum, images of humiliations, lynchings, horrible sufferings of mothers and children, and the burning of black bodies. The evocation of these horrors produces its own metamorphosis; the word "nègre," vibrating in the poet's unconscious, magically emerges as a symbol of resistance and revolt, of virility and dignity, successful beyond all expectation in obtaining liberty: "dru savez-vous / du tonnerre d'un été / que s'arrogent / des libertés incrédules."

The whole poem, therefore, concretely represents the transformation of the poetic "moi" into "le mot nègre," from the first to the second half of the poem, under the influence of a literal vibration within the poem itself. Hence, the poem functions as the arena within which this creative and liberating transformation takes place. The vibration of the word "nègre" within the poem has implications for the pivotal dilemma of French Caribbean writers. This poetic vibration counteracts the attempts at cultural silence and repression imposed on Blacks and becomes a manifestation of life, freedom, and creativity. The vibrant "mot" is the symbol of the authentic French Caribbean voice.

5. "Dit d'errance"

This poem, the poem with which **Cadastre** ends, illustrates the use of the poem as a means of both clarifying the poet's own identity and providing a catalyst, the poem itself, for other blacks, universally, to explore and validate their own identity as black people in a white-dominated society.

For the poet, there is a fusion between inner exploration and outward political commitment to his island and his people. At the beginning of the poem, he assumes the microcosmic mantle of all suffering humanity and of all alienation from self:

> Tout ce qui jamais fut déchiré
> en moi s'est déchiré
> tout ce qui jamais fut mutilé
> en moi s'est mutilé

This personal alienation is associated with an alienation in cosmic terms and necessitates a search for the other half of the identity: "au milieu de l'assiette de son souffle dénudé / le fruit coupé de la lune toujours en allee / vers le contour à inventer de l'autre moitié."

The reappraisal of the past that follows suggests only limited meaningful successes ("à peine peut-être certain sens") and even the possibility of having been led astray: "quand d'aucuns chantent Noël revenu / de songer aux astres / égarés." At this point, the poetic voice appears overwhelmed by a sense of failure, of lamentation: "tout est du tout déchu"; "j'ai bien en tête la saison si lacrimeuse." Indeed, the dominant characteristic of one part of the poet's fragmented identity, represented by his past experience of slavery, seems to be silence:

> Ciel éclaté courbe écorchée
> de dos d'esclaves fustigés
> peine trésorière des alizés
> grimoire fermè mob oubliés
> j'interroge mon passé muet

As the poet evokes the island which is part of his identity, "îls de sang," the island, like every island, is represented as sharing in the same condition of alienation and loss as the poet himself: "île maljointe île disjointe / toute île appelle / toute île est veuve." The loss for the island, as it is for the poet, is related to separation from the source of identity, Africa, represented by the civilizations of Bénin and Ifé, and his rhetorical question, in the name of all alienated Africans ("nous"), suggests his own doubt of ever being able to heal this breach: "tendrons-nous toujours les bras?"

The apostrophe that follows ("ô déchiré") may be read as an address to the poet's wounded and divided self, as he conjures up an image of triumphant reunification and healing, which leads him to a new state of consciousness, in which he assumes the priestly mantle of hope: "J'ai inventé un culte secret / mon soleil est celui que toujours on attend."

The poet adopts another role, that of lover ("corps féminin île retrouvée"), which becomes fused with his role as plaintive prophet ("moi sybille flébilant"). When he turns again to look back on his (shared) childhood past ("mes enfances"), the painful memories of communal failure with which he identifies ("j'ai vu un oiseau mâle sombrer") produce in him a sense of disillusionment: "je regarde le plus bas de l'année."

The poet's rather depressing impression of his past life, his doubts about his identity and his role, about whether he is indeed agent or victim, and about the validity of his concern with issues of black identity, are translated into lucid, self-reflexive ironic wit: "serais-je jouet de nigromance?" This question echoes the ambivalence of the title, "Dit d'errance," which suggests (in "errance") a lack of certainty on the part of the poet. As a result, however, of the process of rigorous self-examination and the awareness of identity linkages to Africa and his native island, the image of the "pierre" emerges to suggest both fixity and power, and the poem ends on a triumphant note, with the poet adopting the active, heroic role of lance:

> Or mieux qu'Antilia ni que Brazil
> pierre milliaire dans la distance
> épée d'une flamme qui me bourrelle
> j'abats les arbres du Paradis.

The foregoing analyses highlight certain aspects of poetic function in the poems: the relationship between the poet and a social order characterized by "vous"; the various roles assumed by the poet; the "messages" sent by the poem; and the general function of the poem itself. In *Cadastre* as a whole, the dominant roles adopted by the poet are those of leader and of voice: the leader and voice of revolt, the voice of prophecy and hope; the magician who protects the integrity and destiny of a people; even the scapegoat leader who endures and articulates the sufferings of his people in order to guarantee their survival and eventual triumph.

The poems presuppose a context of alienation from self, of loss of identity, dignity, nobility, beauty and power, of divisiveness and inhumanity. Within this context, which is in fact the social order in which the poem itself functions, the poetic act becomes an affirmation of contrary values. The constant "message" sent by the poems is one of hope: hope in the restoration of the dignity and divinity of the black man, hope in the triumph of humanitarianism, hope in the validity of true revolt.

Although references to an opposing "vous" occur, their relative rarity and indirectness, when compared to the references to a "moi" or a "nous," would tend to suggest that communication is directed not so much to the representatives of the oppressive and alienating social order but rather to the poet's self and to the group with whom the poet chooses to identify. This also tends to suggest that some of the implications of Scharfman's analysis, informed by Benveniste, are problematical. This factor, the direction of Césaire's communication, invests Césaire's poetry with a "revolutionary" function that is radically different from that discussed by Kristeva, who pointed to poetic language functioning paradoxically and unconsciously both to subvert and at the same time to maintain a social order, specifically the bourgeois technocratic structure of late nineteenth-century France. Césaire's poetry, in my view, deliberately transgresses such considerations. I see, furthermore, no separation in Césaire's poetic practice between the rhetoric of protest and subjective poetics, as Arnold suggests.

Indeed, the peculiarity of Césaire's situation, a poet with the problematical cultural identity of an educated Black, while at the same time a non-French Martinican Frenchman, gives a new significance to the term revolutionary. His poetic practice cannot be anything but revolutionary, as it operates harmoniously both inwardly and outwardly, linking and lancing, exploring, attacking, cutting, binding and healing all at once. This multifaceted revolutionary function of poetry, related to a need to affirm and protect the threatened integrity of identity, has remained a constant in Césaire's poetry. At the same time, Césaire has retained his conception of the poet as leader and prophet for a people. In a recent interview, discussing a poem entitled **"Dyâli,"** which he had written in honor of his longtime friend and colleague, Leopold Sedar Senghor, Césaire explains: "'**Dyâli**' autrement dit 'le diseur de parole', le 'poète' [. . .]. Le Dyâli c'est aussi celui qui montre le chemin [. . .]."

Césaire himself, by his continued literary and political activity, has also been showing the way. What he has shown, what his poetry shows by its very existence and by its function as a literary artifact, both within the context of and in opposition to the mainstream socioliterary order of metropolitan France, is that French Caribbean poetry exists. Césaire's poetry proclaims its own identity as an authentically distinct cultural manifestation which is essentially Caribbean.

Jonathan Ngaté (essay date Spring 1992)

SOURCE: "Aimé Césaire on Aimé Césaire: A Complementary Reading of 'Crevasses' (from *Moi, laminaire . . .*)," in *L'Esprit Créateur,* Vol. XXXII, No. 1, Spring 1992, pp. 41-53.

[*In the following essay, Ngaté examines Césaire's views as a literary critic, as expressed in Césaire's introductions and prefaces to other author's works.*]

The Césaire I am interested in here is not only the man who had very calmly but straightforwardly stated in 1956, in his *Lettre à Maurice Thorez,* that "aucune doctrine ne vaut que *repensée par nous, que repensée pour nous, que convertie à nous*" [emphasis added]; he is also, for this occasion again, Aimé Césaire in the role of informed and sensitive reader-and-critic of his own work and that of others. Much of great value has already been written about him as a committed and inspiring writer, a charismatic political figure and even (if less so) as a literary theorist, but not enough yet about him as a critic whose views have been expressed on numerous occasions in prefaces to other people's books or in the *Discours sur le colonialisme* (1954), that essay which, in its uplifting eloquence, is truly a monument to intellectual honesty and moral courage and also the passionate expression of a commitment to political action.

From a literary/critical point of view, the opinion I find the most illuminating in the *Discourse* for my purpose here is about the nineteenth-century French poet, Lautreamont, not only because it is concisely useful, but more importantly because of the way in which it succeeds so dearly in pointing to an unavoidable perspective on Césaire's own literary texts:

> the day will come when, with all the elements gathered together, all the sources analyzed, all the circumstances of the work elucidated, it will be possible to give the *Chants de Maldoror* a materialistic and historical interpretation which will bring to light an altogether unrecognized aspect of this frenzied epic, its implacable denunciation of a very particular form of society, as it could not escape the sharpest eyes around the year 1865.

No sharper eyes, it seems to me, have been looking into the Black worlds of Africa and the Americas (in their diversity) and into the overall world of the downtrodden since the 1930s than have Aimé Césaire's. And his uncanny ability to make pointed references to or to engage in a principled ransacking of the strongly similar colonial, and now neocolonial, experiences of people from those worlds should help make it clear that the "nous" (us) of the quotation from the *Lettre à Maurice Thorez* has very strong implications of racial and cultural as well as intellectual and ideological kinships. For a reader like myself, who has lived through the last decade or so of French colonial rule in Black Africa,

Césaire has been nothing if not he through whose eyes I have learned to see my *Umwelt,* with unsettling clarity, and he with whom I have been reasoning things out through the kind of dialogue made possible by the act of reading. The dialogue, a cross-generational one, has been based on my recognition of the fact that the driving force behind Césaire's writing has been a burning "désir d'attester une humanité contestée ou en danger et celui d'étre par et pour soi-même," as Eboussi Boulaga would say. That this view, which accounts for my attempt at providing a complementary reading of **"Crevasses,"** is not an idiosyncratic one will become evident from an overview of the ways in which some important writers and political activists of the post-World War Two generation have been responding to Césaire against the background of their own experiences with colonialism and neocolonialism.

I shall consider three of them, selected from different parts of Black Africa and the Caribbean: first, there is the late South African Steve Biko, founder of SASO (South African Students Organization) and the Black Consciousness movement, who highlighted the centrality of some of Aimé Césaire's pronouncements on race relations in his [Biko's] own analysis of the South African situation from the standpoint of Blacks as victims of apartheid by saying, in a 1972 article, that

> "No race possesses the monopoly of beauty, intelligence and force, and there is room for all of us at the rendezvous of victory." I do not think Aimé Césaire was thinking about South Africa when he said these words.

Given his concluding comment, Biko did not have to quote from Césaire's *Notebook of a Return to my Native Land* to make his point, but that he did so can arguably be read as the expression of the exasperation of a young man who had reached the conclusion that, fair and acceptable though it may be, Césaire's general observation in a long poem first published in 1939 was one that could still not be applied to the South Africa of the 1970s, one in which colonial-as-strictly-racist politics still meant that racial inequality remained the bedrock of a regime controlled by a racial minority. As he doubtless knew, Césaire had also observed in the *Discourse on Colonialism* (written at a time when France still had a colonial empire) that one did not colonize innocently. Thus there is, strictly speaking, nothing surprising about Biko's elaborating on the point he had already made in order to add, ominously, that

> so blatantly exploitative in terms of the mind and body is the practice of white racism that one wonders if the interests of blacks and whites in this country have not become so mutually exclusive as

to remove the possibility of there being "room for all of us at the rendezvous of victory."

The white rulers of his country proved him right in his assessment of the situation in South Africa by murdering him soon thereafter. Thus, his death and also the very disturbing circumstances under which it occurred (he was killed by elements of the security forces while still in detention) all point to Biko's justification in holding on to a healthy dose of skepticism in the 1970s about prospects for racial harmony in his native South Africa.

Second, I shall consider the Congolese Sony Labou Tansi, whose seemingly flippant remark, "je ne suis pas à développer mais à prendre ou à laisser," is nothing if not a strikingly appropriate updating of the defiant Césairian line from the *Cahier d'un retour au pays natal:* "Accommodez-vous de moi. Je ne m'accommode pas de vous."' Labou Tansi is a declared African admirer of Aimé Césaire who sees clearly how important a force the latter remains, both as a dramatist and a political thinker, in the context of the years of so-called independence on a continent that remains subjugated, with the bulk of its population still on bended knees, as it were:

> Le centre de ce lien [entre Césaire et l'Afrique] est le fait que l'Afrique est le plus recourbé des continents—or le drame césairien réside grosso modo dans un rapport douloureux avec la station verticale; il est celui de l'homme à la reconquête de la verticale.

Be it in *Et les chiens se taisaient, La Tragedie du roi Christophe, Une tempete* or *Une saison au Congo,* Césaire's theater is indeed insistently concerned with multiple forms of the struggles of the downtrodden, people bent to the breaking point under the full weight of their enslaving and/or neo-colonial masters. Labou Tansi's point here is therefore fairly clear: the people of Africa are engaged in a difficult struggle in order to be able to stand up by and for themselves and face the business of living as free human beings. Given this tragedy of the history of African peoples brought down to their collective knees by powerful and arrogant colonial masters and now, in many cases, by home-grown tyrants shamelessly manipulated by external forces in ways that give the very notion of political independence a new meaning, the point had to be made.

Finally, there is the Guadeloupean Danial Maximin whose literary filiation to Césaire in his very first novel *L'Isolé soleil* (1981) has been amply demonstrated by Clarisse Zimra. That she succeeds in making the intertextual link between Maximin and Césaire palpable is clear enough. But precisely because she does so, she is also able to make us aware that what is most striking about the novel is the fact

that at the very moment we are convinced that Césaire is being acknowledged as a literary *father,* the novel itself is, thematically, and quite literally, asking to be read against the background of its own main characters turning toward the *mother* for sustenance because they find it difficult to resist the temptation to get rid of both real and symbolic fathers who have left them only a legacy of death. If it is Adrien who blurts out that, "Parfois, je me demande s'il ne faut pas nous débarrasser d'urgence de tous ces péres qui ne nous ont laissé que leur mort comme souvenir éclatant," it is his friend Marie-Gabriel who sees the idea through to its radical conclusion. After admitting that, "Le sentiment croissant que l'histoire n'est qu'un mensonge des hommes m'arrête aussi. Mensonge par rapport à la manière dont les femmes vivent leur histoire," she chooses to act in a way that is succinctly described and insightfully interpreted in this gloss by Zimra:

> [. . .] on découvre, à la fin de *L'Isole soleil,* que la jeune fille a abandonné son projet de r/écriture du carnet paternel qui la forçait à écrire l'histoire des hommes, pour se tourner du côté du "Journal de Siméa."

> En effet, le cahier de cette mère morte en la mettant au monde va l'aider à accomplir une r/écriture des origines qui soit vraiment sienne; celle de sa propre naissance. La première ébauche, dédiée au père ("L'Aire de la mer"), est abandonnée au profit d'un nouveau récit qu'elle intitule "L'Air de la mere."

That Maximin should have succeeded in getting this message through in *L'Isole soleil* while foregrounding his literary father's identity is what I find significant. Césaire has indeed become the "fondement d'une littérature antillaise authentique," as the Maryse Condé epigraph has it. And if we think also of Steve Biko and Sony Labou Tansi then we will have to admit, again with Maryse Condé, that Césaire is without question a "référence essentielle pour les écrivains négro-africains," be they francophone or not. To that group one could add readers, who, like the writers just listed, do not blindly follow the Afro-Martinican writer and statesman but are well aware that they often cannot help but define themselves in relation to him.

No sharper eyes, it seems to me, have been looking into the Black worlds of Africa and the Americas (in their diversity) and into the overall world of the downtrodden since the 1930s than have Aimé Césaire's.
—Jonathan Ngaté

It is the sense of identification mentioned in the preceding paragraphs that enables me, as a reader coming out of French-speaking Black Africa, to feel fully justified in claiming the right to whisper along with Haitian poet Anthony Phelps, "Aimé Césaire/je vous viens de très prés," secure in the knowledge that the "pays natal" ("native land") that Césaire, as protagonist, longed for and "returned" to in his now famous poem, *Cahier d'un retour au pays natal,* is one that figuratively extends beyond the confines of the West Indies. The status of that "pays natal" was clear to yet another Haitian, Maximilien Laroche, when he evoked ". . . cette appartenance de tous les damnés de la terre à un même pays natal, terre de souffrance qui s'étend à tous les continents où se trouvent des exploités, des dominés et des colonisés."

In light of the above it should be possible to see why I am interested in the poem **"Crevasses,"** in which we find Césaire in the role of reader-as-critic, an informed and sensitive critic. What I would like to argue is that in this poem, from Césaire's latest published collection of poems, *Moi, laminaire . . .* (1982), the poet is involved in "reading" his whole *oeuvre* against the background of some responses to him and his work. But first, let us look at Bernadette Cailler's illuminating reading of this poem which she gave at the first international colloquium on Césaire's literary works in Paris in November 1985. I shall limit myself here to the major points she made and with which I generally agree. These will in turn, with some minor modifications, enable me to propose a complementary reading of the same poem.

It is Bernadette Cailler's contention that

> Dans le poème **"Crevasses,"** ainsi que dans d'autres textes du recueil [*Moi, laminaire. . .*], il semble qu'ait été privilégié le nadir du lieu de rêverie, point plus proche de la survie que de la résurrection, plus proche de l'instant fugitif que de l'éternité, point-merge, retrait lagunaire où se meut une constellation de vocables explorant l'efficacite du creux, de la blessure, de l'égratignure, de la dent.

The usefulness, or better still, the appositeness of the emphasis on the dream state involved here has to be recognized since it associates what is happening in this poem much more closely with survival (and the implied constant human struggle to ensure it) than with resurrection, which would point not only to an instantaneous result but also to the passivity of the humans involved and the necessary intervention of an external agent, a supernatural force. Instead, we are made to more fully appreciate the weight of the instant (or perhaps a succession of instants) in which, through words, the poetic subject explores and gives a reading of the implications of the metaphorical crevice he both is and inhabits: the things brought to the light of day as a result prove to be so many teethmarks of a history of continuous suffer-ing, a lived history, that has left a wound against which the power of metaphorical language is being tried.

And the speaker of the poem is described by Cailler as an "*on*narrateur-personnage (identité perdue?) le plus souvent rongeur, qui érode et use, ou insecte, qui rampe et s'insinue." Striking and of extreme importance here are not only the verbs of action used to describe the speaker but also their full implication: to erode and to wear out, to crawl, but only in order to insinuate the self into "la fissure" that the critic points to later. The speaker is indeed "à quatre pattes" but that is to be seen as part of a tactic of defense "contre la dangers la moins évidents, logés jusque dans la recoins les plus inattendus, y compris son propre trou de cloporte ou de poulpe."

Like the preceding thematic summary, the characterization of the poetic style of **"Crevasses"** is one I also find generally acceptable:

> Au plan poétique, au rêve d'une écriture épique, triomphante et jubilatoire, s'opposent ici de courts versets, à l'articulation peu élaborée, phrases à peine formées, déclarations quasi prosaïques, alliées à de courses exclamations ou questions; l'expression est ici réduite à des souffles-perceptions essentials: poétique de la clandestinité, de la survie. Il n'est ici ni cri brûlant de l'oiseau fabuleux, flamme sortie des cendres, ni parole incantatoire de sorcier, ni rythme haletant de danseur-musicien; il n'est ici ni narrateur ou personnage fabuleux héroïque, mythe producteur de mythes (Christophe, Toussaint . . .), ni texte fabuleux, poème tragique du Rebelle ou roman polyphonique d'une Histoire."

There is no denying the value of this description, even if, as we shall see, one is prepared to take issue with the view that what is involved here is merely a "poétique de la clandestinité." For as insightful as she is in her reading of the poem, Cailler seems to stumble toward the end of her analysis when she suggests that one could see in **"Crevasses"** the "articulation symbolique d'une politique de compromis, de la négociation, de la démarche prudente, pour ne pas dire craintive, stagnante, ou défaitiste." In context the last two adjectives prove to be too strong and, in the final analysis, unjustified.

If we start with Michael Dash's welcome reminder that *Moi, laminaire. . .* is a "guarded exercise in self-definition," we begin to understand the hesitancy in **"Crevasses"** to which Cailler is sensitive but whose importance she overstates. It should be understood that the persona of the poem is not so much a neutral *on* as it is the writer himself whose poetic self is being presented, or better still, dramatized as a metonym. Ronnie Scharfman's observations on the subject in Césaire's *Cahier* are helpful at this point:

> ... the subject is constantly finding itself and los-
> ing itself again, being decentered, writing itself,
> reading itself, and erasing itself. The text abounds
> in contradictory moments of selfhood for the sub-
> ject that must be appropriated as the diagnostic tools
> for a diacritical reading of the relationship between
> engagement and a language of the self."

Looking at the form of **"Crevasses,"** with its resort to question asking and the use of exclamations, and taking into account the tone of the poem (especially at the end), it is
possible to claim that, as an act of communication, the poem
dramatizes the persona's willingness both to explain and to
justify his own writing: the interlocutors, present only by
implication since they are never explicitly named, could fall
into two major groups. The first one would be comprised
of those people who have been taking to task both the writer
and his brand of Negritude, along with its translation into
political action. For Daniel Boukman, for instance, Césaire,
as "Orphée Volcan" is nothing but a tool of French colonial
forces on the island of Martinique. So necessary is Orphée
Volcan's presence that, when it is discovered that he has died,
no effort is spared to bring him back to life, for reasons that
the Banker of the play is made to give, rather melodramati-
cally:

> LE COMMERCANT—[. . .] Vous estimez donc in-
> dispensable de tout tenter pour le remettre sur pied?
>
> LE BANQUIER—Absolument! Il faut rallumer le
> phare pour qu'il recommence à fasciner les papil-
> lons qui tournoieront, tournoieront, et, phitt!
> disparus les problèmes et la réalite!
>
> LE COMMERCANT—Je ne comprends pas très
> bien. Qui tient le rôle du phare? Qui vent les papil-
> lons?
>
> LE BANQUIER—Le phare, c'est Orphée le poète;
> les papillons de nuit, ceux qui gobent ses poèsies;
> de petite fonctionnaires, la classe intellectuelle . . .
> le peuple, quoi, vous comprenez?

The second group of interlocutors would include people of
good will who might simply not be too sure they understand
the writer and his aims.

The net effect is that, whether they identify with one group
or the other, readers of this poem will find themselves fulfilling the function of a jury evaluating an answer to a question or a challenge that the very form of the poem itself is
acknowledging.

Published more than four decades after *Cahier, Moi,
laminaire. . .* could not help but draw attention to the fact
that its author is not just anybody but rather a "référence
essentielle" in Caribbean and francophone Black literature
in general, to quote Maryse Condé. To be a point of reference at this time in the history of the Black world is of course
to be in a position to generate controversy, even unwillingly.
And the preliminary notes to the whole of *Moi, laminaire. . .*
are clear on this point:

> Le non-temps impose au temps la tyrannic de sa
> spatialité: dans toute vie il y a un nord et un sud, et
> l'orient et l'occident. Au plus extrême, ou, pour le
> moins, au carrefour, c'est au fil des saisons
> survolées, l'inégale lutte de la vie et de la mort, de
> la fervour et de la lucidité, fût-ce celle du désespoir
> et de la retombée, la force aussi toujours de regarder
> demain. Ainsi va toute vie. Ainsi va ce livre, entre
> soleil et ombre, entre montagne et mangrove, entre
> chien et loup, claudiquant et binaire. Le temps aussi
> de régler leur compte à quelques fantasmes et à
> quelques fantômes.

Not surprisingly, Césaire-as-the-persona of **"Crevasses"**
gives every indication of being aware of the precariousness
of his position and that explains his determination to see to
it that he not be misunderstood. Consequently, the poet-as-
persona gradually turns into a close reader and a critic of
his own work and of some responses to it which, combined,
become the intertext for this poem.

The enunciating subject hides at first, as it were, behind the
"je" of the epigraph from Goethe's *Faust:* "Je grimpe depuis
trots cents ens/et ne puis atteindre le sommet." The tone here,
in this truncated passage, is not so much that of a complaint
as it is that of a statement of fact, with the emphasis on the
sustained effort to keep on climbing. Because the epigraph
comes from the "Walpurgis Night" scene in Part One of the
play, it could be read as a hint by the poet about his status
as one of the downtrodden and, in context, an outcast reduced to being a voice calling from below. But that is not
all: a quick look at *Faust* will reveal that not only did that
work set an impressive precedent for the variety of tones we
find in this poem but it also insistently returned to the very
theme Césaire draws attention to in his choice of verses for
the epigraph. Two examples should suffice: "For man must
strive, and striving he must err," we are told in Part One of
Faust, whereas Part Two chimes in with the no less revealing verses: "For he whose strivings never cease / is ours for
his redeeming." If the quotations represent a none too subtle
way of suggesting that the "I-subject" of this poem is Faust-
like, then it is only fair to point out that Goethe's Faust was
saved in the end, his "weaknesses" notwithstanding.

It is also worth noting that at another level, the 300 years of the epigraph are a clear enough echo of the title of an Edouard Glissant novel for example, *Le Quatrième siècle*, and thus it draws attention to a time frame that is of considerable importance to history-conscious Afro-Caribbeans. This in turn will remind us that the "je" of the epigraph is to be read as the promise of a "nous," a fact that is confirmed by the use of the French indefinite pronoun "on" in the text of the poem itself, an "on" that has the value of a "nous." Significant also is the use of "crevasses" (in the plural) in the title of the poem, whereas the persona concludes the poem by referring to himself as a "crevasse" (singular). As a "crevasse" among "crevasses" he is of course pointing to a continuity in Caribbean textual production that becomes his way of acknowledging the consciousness he has of his place in recent history.

The opening lines of the poem contain both a statement of general principle and an illustration of poetic practice, both of which draw attention to 1) the reliance on words to confront a world in which blackness still has to be asserted and, 2) the exploration made possible by the poet's habit of exploiting to the fullest extent possible the gap, that is to say also, the link, between sound and sense: "La sombre épellation établit sa loi: . . . Ure . . . Usure! Barbarie . . . Blessure!" The play of alliteration and assonance not only helps call attention to key words whose resonance for readers of Cesairian texts should be very obvious, it also helps keep the focus on the "blessure" (wound) that the persona has had to inhabit as a result of a history (represented by time with a capital T) he now seems to have taken a full measure of: "Le Temps, lui, connaît le blason et démasque à temps son mufle forban. Précisément." "Blessure" here is of course inseparable from verses such as the following from the *Cahier:*

> Que de sang dans ma mémoire! Dans ma memoire sont les / lagunes. Elles sont couvertes de têtes de morts. Elles / ne sont pas couvertes de nénuphars. Dans ma mémoire vent des lagunes. Sur leurs rives ne sont / pas étendus des pagnes de femmes.
> Ma mémoire est entourée de sang. Ma mémoire a sa ceinture / de cadavres!

If it is a full grasp of history that makes possible the identification of "je" (the I-subject) with "nous" (the we-subject), that identification is not an end in itself, nor does it offer sure protection against mistakes. Among them would be a possible fall into the trap of history itself which, in its multidimensionality, not to say its opacity, still has the potential for confounding: "On a toute licence: on avance, on pénètre dans le taillis, dans le fouillis. Tel est le piège." Only an awareness of the existence and the nature of that trap enables the collective self to adopt an outwardly humiliating posture, under the weight of history, without allowing it to prevent the self from moving along in time: "On marche à quatre pattes. On se dépêtre. Courbé toujours mais avancant." One cannot read such a passage without thinking indeed (as Cailler has noted) of the major characters of Césaire's plays: the Rebel, King Christophe, Lumumba, and Caliban. These are all characters who knew how to turn the weaknesses and the humiliation of their own people into fuel for action that would set them free and standing upright. In this light, Sony Labou Tansi's summary of what accounts for Césaire's power of attraction for African readers and theatergoers, cited earlier, is thoroughly convincing: ". . . or le drame césairien réside grosso modo dans un rapport douloureux avec la station verticale; il est celui de l'homme à la reconquête de la verticale." Success in that search for the opportunity to stand upright and to face (and in the process make) history is of course not something as inevitable as, say, a river flowing into another river or into the sea. Consequently, dogmatic assertions to the effect that there is one and only one ready-made answer to all the problems of the collective self is unacceptable:

> On tourne en rond. La naïvete est d'attendre qu'une voix, je dis bien qu'une vole vous disc: *par ici lo sortie!* N'existe que le noeud. Noeud sur noeud. Pas d'embouchure.

Reading such a passage now, we can better appreciate the care that had gone into the formulation of the definition of Negritude put forward by Césaire in the *Cahier;* long on what Negritude is not, it also emphasizes what it does without dogmatically pointing to very specific ways in which it ought to proceed:

> ma négritude n'est pas une pierre, sa surdité ruée contre / la clameur du jour
> ma négritude n'est pas une tale d'eau morte sur l'oeil mort de la terre
> ma négritude n'est ni une tour ni une cathédrale
> elle plonge dans la char rouge du sol
> elle plonge dans la char ardente du ciel
> elle troue l'accablement opaque de sa droite patience

The tone of this passage clearly runs counter to the openly heroic and confident one the self adopts later on in the same *Cahier:*

> je ne me dérobe point. Faites de ma tête une tête de proue et de moi-même, mon coeur, ne faites ni un père ni un frère ni un fils, mais le père, mais le frère, mais le fils ni un mari, mais l'amant de cet unique peuple.

Later on, in the play *Une saison au Congo,* Lumumba will be made to adopt a tone that is a successful mix of the aforementioned two, a tone that effectively prepares us for the language of **"Crevasses"**:

> C'est d'elle, d'elle-même, que l'Afrique a faim!
> C'est pourquoi je ne me veux ni messie ni mahdi.
> Je n'ai pour arme que ma parole, je parle, et
> j'éveille, je ne suis pas un redresseur de torts, pas
> un faiseur de miracles, je suds un redresseur de vie,
> je parle, et je rends l'Afrique à elle-même! Je parle,
> à je rends l'Afrique au monde! Je parle, et, attaquant
> à leur base, oppression et servitude, je rends pos-
> sible, pour la première fois possible, la fraternite!

Not surprisingly, this language of humility elicits a less than favorable response from the crowd that had been generally supportive of Lumumba up to that point in the play. It finds itself reacting with uncertainty, according to the stage direction.

I would like to suggest that it is a keen awareness of the fact of a similar reaction of uncertainty on the part of others (especially his own people) that makes the I-subject's language of humility sound so self-conscious and grounded in a present that is implicitly full of doubts, if not outright challenges in **"Crevasses."** If the self-consciousness accounts for the grammatical switch from "on" to the disjunctive pronoun "moi" and finally the subject pronoun "je," I am also prepared to argue that it is plainly an act of courage and intellectual honesty to admit what is being admitted at the end of the poem: "Moi qui rêvais autrefois d'une écriture belle de rage! Crevasse j'aurai tenté." In a very real sense, this acknowledgment by the I-subject could be read as a direct answer to Afro-Caribbean and especially Martinican texts such as Guy Cabort-Masson's *Lettre à Aimé Césaire* (1981), which is polemically modeled on Césaire's own polemical **Lettre à Maurice Thorez,** and generously quotes Césaire against himself in order to arrive at the conclusion that the "depute" and mayor of Fort-de-France no longer is the champion of his people. Understanding this, one would have to conclude that there is nothing clandestine going on here at all.

As the I-subject therefore, the Césaire we have in this poem is no longer the purveyor of, but rather a commentator on, a master-theme: the need to awaken and to give the "pays natal" (which at one level is Africa and its diaspora) back to itself. In the process of commenting on that master-theme, he also succeeds in justifying his *oeuvre,* which is nothing if not a master text, in the context of today's Black world as Maryse Condé makes clear. This major literary figure's challenge to his unnamed interlocutors in the poem, a challenge so deafening in the end precisely because it is not explicitly stated, is simply this: I have been doing my part for years. What are you really prepared to do?

Read this way, this poem is Césaire's invitation to a responsible "prise de parole" by his readers-as-his-people and, beyond that, a corollary commitment to meaningful action. And the focus at the end, once again, will have been shifted away from the I-subject to the we-subject and the need for an ongoing and fruitful dialogue, as opposed to mere name calling or posturing. This is really a poem about the responsibilities of "I and I," to use the language of the Rastafarians.

Clarisse Zimra (essay date Spring 1992)

SOURCE: "On Ancestral Ground: Heroic Figuring in Aimé Césaire," in *L'Esprit Créateur,* Vol. XXXII, No. 1, Spring 1992, pp. 16-29.

[*In the following essay, Zimra discusses Césaire's treatment of the recurring textual figure of the Ancestor.*]

It is hardly an exaggeration to say that contemporary Caribbean writers are obsessed with the past, an obsession made manifest by a recurring textual figure, that of the Ancestor. Both proponents and opponents of the tenets of Negritude, from Senghor to Soyinka, have tended to see the figure as heroic. In the Caribbean text, the ancestral trope plunges into an imaginary past predicated on collective history in order to gain access to a common future. Edouard Glissant calls it "a prophetic reading of the past" (preface to *Monsieur Toussaint).* But, as he also cautions in *Le Discours antillais,* this textual strategy may well elide an alienating present and prolong a self denying cultural stasis that renders political action impossible.

The sociological approach still predominates, whether among critics (I. F. Case's damning Césaire's inability to write about contemporary Martinique) or writers (Daniel Maximin condemning Glissant's unwillingness to do likewise as "evasiveness"). It would appear that the Caribbean corpus, a literature initially triggered by specific historical conditions, must always return to its ideological origins. This may account in no small part for the uneasy dance between myth and history in the Caribbean corpus, a feature particularly prominent in the Cesairean topos of the ancestral quest.

The question of the Ancestor remains a constant of Caribbean literature after Césaire as well. It took Maryse Condé a considerable African detour before she could trust herself to face her own "mangrove swamp." Her first novel stages this alienation with maximum impact when the child asks, "what were we before" and the Caribbean father refuses to entertain the notion that there may have been a past "before." Whether plaintive (in Condé's *Hérémakhônon),* wistful (in Léon Damas's *Hoquet:* "Désastre / parlez-moi du désastre / parlez-m'en"), or defiant (in Maximin's *L'Isolé soleil:* "Il nous faut drageonner nos pères"), the child's insistent question is the textual sign of a never-ending tug of war between the mythical and the historical dimension. From Derek Walcott's sobering words on selective amnesia in "The Muse of History,"' to Glissant's gradual evisceration of his once admirable "Negator," the question triggers an imaginery projection backward that must locate its object in an immemorial past before any move forward. **Cahier d'un retour au pays natal** is exemplary in this.

Admirable Question

In the wake of the **Cahier,** the poet had taken his stand. Fresh from the shock of his Haitian tour, Césaire delineated in the 1945 "Poesie et connaissance" his poetics of Caribbean authenticity as the weaving of the private, obsessional, self with the collective, ancestral, unconscious. But, as the whole *Tropiques* adventure made clear, it was a genetic unconscious nonetheless radically grounded in a specific moment:

> Ce qui émerge, c'est le fonds individuel. Les conflits intimes, les obsessions . . . Tou la chiffres du message personnel. . .

> Ce qui émerge aussi, c'est le vieux fonds ancestral. Images héreditaires, que seules peut remettre à jour, aux fins de déchiffrement, l'atmosphère poétique. . .

The poet starts with the retrieving of long forgotten selves buried deep within the collective memory. However, the very conditions of such a plunge are historically determined, as the **Cahier** finds time and again. At the time this was written, diving into the unconscious and recovering the African past seemed feasible, if not identical, projects. Thus, Suzanne Césaire in "Léo Frobénius et le problème des civilisations": ". . . l'Afrique ne signifie pas seulement pour nous un élargissement vers l'ailleurs, mais approfondissement de nous mêmes." The young rebels of Martinique, looking at Price-Mars's example on the next island, had every reason to be optimistic. The final movement of the **Cahier,** going downward and inward in order to expand outward and upward ("ailleurs"), attempts to answer the challenge it poses somewhat ironically for itself: "Qui et quels nous sommes? / Admirable question." Close to half-a-century later, in his 1982 preface to **moi, laminaire** Césaire would reconsider this poetic project and answer it otherwise, raising over his whole corpus the ghost of blind, self-deluded, limping Oedipus, torn between east and west, reason and imagination, past and present, myth and history: "Ainsi va toute vie. Ainsi va ce livre, entre soleil et ombre, entre montagne et mangrove, entre chien et loup, claudiquant et binaire."

My contention here is simple: it is against Césaire's definitions of the ancestral ground that much of subsequent Caribbean literature measures itself, whether deliberately or not.

To give but one example, Condé's paradigmatic "what were we before" destabilizes the solid ground of Césaire's earlier "who and what we are." To his glorious African depth sounding, she opposes a version of Walcott's radical amnesia, the surface of a blank Caribbean wall. Césaire's last work, **laminaire,** moves away from a unified, collective mythical dimension into a fragmented, tentative, historical consciousness, halfway between his glorious past soundings and Condé's radical negation. A clear understanding of the ancestral permutations in the Cesairean corpus, in turn, gives us a clearer sense of the writers who have followed in his footsteps.

> **My contention here is simple: it is against Césaire's definitions of the ancestral ground that much of subsequent Caribbean literature measures itself, whether deliberately or not.**
> **—Clarisse Zimra**

For the Negritude generation, Caribbean history consisted of a before and after, a reading often modeled after the paradigmatic metaphor of western intervention in the Caribbean, Shakespeare's *Tempest,* turned upside down. It was a frankly oppositional move, whose binary dance of difference was not always stable. Within this world, Césaire's Ancestor has remained a cipher of polarization both from within and from without, the trope of the Other's otherness. It represents the black self as non-white invading and engaging the white discourse; yet, it is also polarized within itself in a kind of mirroring effect oscillating between Caliban, the primal autonomous being, wild and free, and Toussaint, the all too willing victim of white cunning sacrificed on the altar of nationalism. In the Cesairean corpus, Caliban and Toussaint are sometimes figures of opposition and sometimes of complementarity, the Rebel borrowing from each. Toussaint, the ghost erased from white history books spitting up his lungs in Napoleon's dank cell, is a figure that the 1930s **Cahier** seeks simultaneously to reclaim for history, as the origin of black historical consciousness in the Caribbean, and turn into tragic myth, a dead hero greater than any one of his living descendants. As original presence on the primeval shore, Shakespeare's imaginary cannibal who at the end of **Une Tempête** sings his African freedom is a figure of myth too; for Césaire's 1969 play pointedly ends before the test of history begins. Or rather, with Prospero's final descent into lifeless impotence, colonial history has ended but post-colonial liberation has yet to begin. Conversely, from the 1946 oratorio to the 1956 play, the symbolic trajectory of **Et les chiens se taisaient** seems to move away from myth into more factual history. Yet, the successive versions of **Chiens,** down to the latest one in 1974, show clearly that neither dimension is relinquished. Trying to connect the corpus's fluctuations to the writer's own, critics have spent an inordinate amount of ink on the relationship between the poet and the politician. Given Césaire's highly oblique, deliberately opaque, style and the complexity of the issue itself, it is impossible to separate the strands neatly, even when the poet leaves the realm of openly creative writing for the more sobering arena of the political essay. In their biblical echoes, with their eternal present tense, the famous concluding words of *Toussaint Louverture:* "Au commencement est Toussaint Louverture," do indicate how hard it is for the Caribbean imagination to separate history from myth in excavating the ancestral ground.

In the Caribbean text, the absence of the Ancestor is everywhere. It represents simultaneously the inheritance and the eviscerating of a particularly obsessive sentimental reading of European Romanticism, from *Bug-Jargal* onward. The inversion of the false white father who refuses to acknowledge his mulatto progeny (from Sejour to Fanon, Capecia to Manicom), that of the defeated black father who could not protect his (from Thouret to Lacrosil, Condé to Schwarz-Bart), subtend Negritude's vision of an individual liberation that must precede the collective one at the risk of death—to follow Césaire's rough unfolding in the *Cahier.* What Ronnie Scharfman sees through Lacanian categories as the salient feature in the *Cahier,* "the binding of desire with violence," signals the inadequacy of the child-self to the intended father-Ancestor, perhaps because of the inadequacy of the model. The temptation—or the trap—is to posit a Negritude self as a phallic father indeed, but a better one. The famous, defiant passage on those who have invented nothing, a "how to" for black self-refashioning, briefly gives in to that urge, before transcending it in an epistemological shift. Among other things, the *Cahier* is also a warning on the simplistic danger of a binary oppositional vision.

In the justly famous and always moving shift, the shackled poetic self frees itself in a series of powerful kinetic images, starting with the simple standing *up* hand in hand with the beloved island; or rather hand in fist. For the child's tiny *open* hand, the gesture of trust, is engulfed by the giant knotted fist, a gesture of protection that triggers the total immersion downward into "la négraille," the nigger-scum, a plunge into a historically anchored collective self that prepares the illimited, unanchored self-hurtling upward of ritual rebirth. Reversing the initial roles, this now gigantic self leads, the tiny "mote-dust" of a country follows, each led ever upward by the ascending Dove: "monte, / Colombe / monte / monte / monte / Je te suis. . ."

The very intensity of this final prayer courts a realization ever deferred. Although it seeks to inscribe the autonomous black self in the text by establishing a clear line to an authentic Ancestor, the *Cahier* fails to maintain a stable ancestral figuring, as does Césaire's next dramatization of the

question, *Et les chiens se toisaient.* The Rebel attempting to sound his deeper African self must choose something or someone other than the false historical fathers, whose judgment he refuses by appealing to the African gods, primitive Greece dovetailing primeval Africa: "Pourquoi aurais-je peur du jugement de mes dieux? qui a dit que j'ai trahi?" As Suzanne Césaire had implied, the only way into the authentic self is through myth, a choice that signals a characteristic turning away from contemporary reality. The blood shed is called "communiel" and the emphasis kept firmly on the collective outcome. At the end of *Les Chiens,* the redoubling of motifs marks the fully mythical dimension: as the Ancestor of a new people, the Rebel becomes his own ancestor as well. But such outcome is still far in the future, as implied by the subjunctive mode, a vision rather than a fact: "que de mon sang oui, de mon sang / je fonde ce peuple."

The ideological gap between the two versions has usually been attributed to Césaire's own ideological fluctuations at the time. In this case, the autobiographical does not satisfactorily account for the fact that neither version chooses either mythical or historical dimension clearly. It might be more fruitful to look at the successive versions as modulating an ancestral question that has no fixed answer, given Césaire's habitually constant (rather than consistent) refiguring of symbols.

Ce qui est à moi

A precise scene connects the *Cahier* to *Les Chiens,* matrix whence all ancestral figuring flows. It is that of the blood baptism, the first step toward a Caribbean definition of self. In *Les Chiens,* the execution of the cockroach-eyed master, who, given the realities of plantation life, could well be the executioner's father, is claimed as the moment that ushers in the authentic self: "Que de sang au fond de ma mémoire (. . .) Je frappai, le sang gicla. C'est le seul baptême dont je me souvienne aujourd'hui." The execution that occurs out of the frame, off camera, before the beginning of *Les Chiens,* makes its symbolic significance possible. In *Le Cahier,* the phrase had appeared but had been undercut by a failure of nerve, the memory of rebellions eventually drowned in the master's liquor that made betrayal possible (as, we are told, Mackandal's was):

> Que de sang dans ma mémoire. Dans ma mémoire sont des lagunes, elles sont couvertes de têtes de morts . . .
>
> Ma mémoire est entourée de sang. Ma mémoire a sa ceinture de cadavres! et mitrailles de barils de rhum génialement arrosant nos révoltes ignobles . . .

Of course, the Rebel, too, has been betrayed by his own. However, *Le Cahier* reworks otherwise the theme of betrayal that is historically intertwined with the theme of constant uprisings, offering a historical ancestor that makes positive self-refiguring possible. To the dishonorable betrayal of Mackandal by his own people, his inebriated coconspirators, to the dishonorable betrayal of the Rebel by his own people, cowards afraid of white revenge, *Le Cahier* opposes an honorable counter-example, that of Toussaint kidnapped under the flag of truce by a dishonorable enemy:

> Ce qui est à moi
> c'est un homme seul emprisonné de
> blanc
> c'est un homme seul qui défie la cris
> blancs de la mort blanche
> (TOUSSAINT, TOUSSAINT LOUVERTURE)
>
> C'est un homme que fascine
> l'épervier blanc de la mort blanche . . .
> La splendeur de ce sang n'éclatera-t-elle point.

Retrieved from the silence of white history, the dying man is made to belong to black (rather than white) depth consciousness in a movement that answers violence with murder. "Ce qui est a mod" has been triggered by the gory sequence of the Middle Passage ("Et je me dis Bordeaux et Nantes et Liverpool et New York et San Francisco . . . / terres rouges, terres sanguines, terres consanguines," a sequence that is but the prelude to the Cesairean leitmotiv that connects several works ("que de sang dans ma mémoire"). This leitmotiv, in turn, introduces the sequence of the father-master's execution by the son-slave and signals the birthing of the true Caribbean now free, as in *Les Chiens*, to claim the Ancestor of his choice: himself. Thus, *Le Cahier* and *Les Chiens* present what looks like a joint version of positive self-birthing.

Critics have abundantly commented on the fact that, in the description of Toussaint's white death, Césaire operates an epistemological reversal. Deconstructing western values, the upending of color categories gives a heightened emotional impact to this scene of remembering that, in turn, makes the execution of the master possible. But it is, as well, a remembering of the contingency of defeat. In self-defeated Haiti, the fulgurant splendor of this sacrificial blood has yet to explode. Toussaint remains here trapped and his death in exile is further mocked by Christophe's own failure soon to come—as Césaire's next play was to explore, a political failure triggered by his people's failure of imagination (or, one might say more gently, their human frailties). By analogy, a pall is thrown over the true outcome of the Rebel's sacrifice (it, too, happens off camera and cannot be witnessed by us). Thus, the exaltation of the future tense, subtly undermined by the negative-interrogative form ("La splendeur de ce sang n'éclatera-t-elle point"), as in the final subjunctive wish of the Rebel ("que de mon sang . . . je fonde ce

peuple"), remains the sign of "a dream deferred." To wish it to happen is to acknowledge that it has not and, simultaneously, to fear that it may not.

Yet again myth seems to surge through the palimpsest of history, since the self-birthing voice who acknowledges Toussaint as Ancestor in a baptism of blood is, so nakedly, that of Caliban. The "ce qui est à moi" of *Le Cahier* is Caliban's response to Shakespearean Prospero's boast: "this thing of darkness is mine." The claim of common humanity makes Prospero unable or unwilling to relinquish moral responsibility for his acts, a position of liberal humanism that may hide the darker imperialist urge upon which Césaire's 1969 *Une Tempête* will eventually "signify" (to use Gates's fashionable term).

Une Tempête: Adaptation de 'La Tempête;' de Shakespeare pour un theatre noir may well hark back to a more ancient mode; that of *Les Chiens*. It is as if the limitations of history, as confronted in the intervening plays, *Christophe* and *Une Saison au Congo,* were to be replayed as myth, but a postlapsarian myth now put through the process of degradation by the recent "years of African independence." If we hear Caliban distinctly proclaiming "U'huru," at the beginning of the play, we can no longer see him at the end. The son of Sycorax sings himself in the Other's language ("la liberté, ohé, la liberté"), and we can barely make it out. Is it feebly heard because Caliban's own resolve—and, therefore, its exemplary quality—has weakened? Or is it feebly heard because we hear it through Prospero's own weakening physical and spiritual condition? Césaire leaves us with this ambivalence.

It is likewise with the white death, Toussaint's trope. Presented as the silenced collective history that must be reclaimed through the power of the imagination, it is immediately absorbed as a potentially mythical figuring of the past in *Le Cahier*—albeit one trailing historical contingencies in its turbulent wake. The famous "what is mine" sequence constructs an analogue between Haiti and Martinique, the past and the present, the humiliated nigger-scum and the emerging black self eager to inscribe otherwise the very past the white memory has appropriated. The binary temptation persists, a hint that the poetic self has a hard time moving out of the subject/object, myth/history trap when excavating the ancestral ground.

One can excavate this ancestral ground otherwise, and go back to the hortatory quotation cited above: "La splendeur de ce sang n'éclatera-t-elle point?" The future tense of spurted blood expressed the wish for the moment of explosive self-baptism, hallowed by another image of spurted blood, the Master's execution ("le sang gicla," a recurrent image in the Cesairean corpus), when the slave, by taking back his rightful name, that of Rebel, is giving birth to himself. This moment of fulgurant birthing connects us to that other constant of Césaire's poetic landscape, the volcano, cipher of physical as well as spiritual liberation, and anchors us back, squarely, on Caribbean soil.

With the natural imagery of the Caribbean landscape comes a fairly consistently polarized bestiary. To give but one instance, the positive thoroughbred ("pur sang," with its punning on racial purity as well as "bad blood," including that of the Rimbaldian variety), drawing on the boundless primeval freedom in the mythical time before time, is usually opposed to the negative mangy dog, steel jaws tearing the flesh of the runaway slave, drawing on the direct experience of a recent, historical past. As we observed before in Césaire, the outside polarization is often mirrored inside, within the same image cluster. For instance, **Les Chiens** is able to play on both registers, master's mastiffs and cynocephalic gods. Its signifying downward dive through Ancient religions (Egyptian or Greco-Roman) retrieves the positive god of a former consciousness: the psychopomp who presides over a different poetic passage, Anubis/Cerberus. Moreover, in the expanding doubling constitutive of myth, the dog-faced god is, often, also pictured as the monkey-faced god, willing mediator between the human and the divine. As the Yoruba trickster Eshu, his pranks emphasize the unpredictable nature of the human connection to the divine but never severs it. As the flying Anuman of India, he is the harbinger of the Word, who brings knowledge, culture and, above all, writing to the human species. He is, as well, the giant laughing Monkey-God carved into the stone of pre-Columbian temples all over the Mexican peninsula. A common symbol runs through all these avatars, one that, tapping the collective memory of the folktale, fuses myth and history without contradiction within the only syncretic ancestral trope that is uniquely Caribbean.

"Beau sang giclé" is an homage to the folktales rescued from oblivion in the pages of *Tropiques* by way of Lafcadio Hearn. Although the poem appears in **Ferrements** (1960), it clearly harks back, in its elusive imagery of a beheading, to the 1948 **Soleil cou coupé,** the collection that is usually considered Césaire's most "surrealistic," the critics' perplexed stamp of good housekeeping in the face of a violently fragmented subject. It is also connected to the earlier collection born of the war years, **Les Armes miraculeuses,** through two image clusters; first, the famous machete stab of the opening, a sort of beheading, and, second, the sacred bird: "Le grand coup de machète du plaisir rouge en plein front . . . quand mourir avait le goût du pain et la terre et la mer un goût d'ancêtre et cet oiseau qui me crie de ne pas me rendre. . ." The sacred bird of nonsurrender, often depicted with phoenix-like qualities, reappears throughout the corpus; to wit, the **Cahier**'s prayer ("pour que revienne le temps de promission/et l'oiseau qui savait mon nom"), or, in **Corps perdu,** "Dit d'errance" ("Par le soleil d'un nid

coiffé/où phénix meurt et renaît." By threading the fairly constant images of sacrificial dismemberment and/or beheading throughout Césaire's poetry, one may discern the patterns of sadistic torture that make up a universe where apocalyptic, yet primeval, beasts roam at will; a fusion of the before-time and the after-time characteristic of myth. It does not take great acumen to read the political referent in the myth, such descriptions also matching standard practices of slave torture. By connecting them to birds, one arrives at something more.

Vous connaissez le conte

"Beau sang giclé" is built on a famous folk subtext, but one probably undecipherable without some help for the non-Caribbean. The poem illustrates the story of Yé, who shot the sacred bird in order to feed his starving family: here, too, the political signifier keeps floating up to the surface on the mythical signified. *Tropiques* considered the AfroCaribbean folk tradition an integral element of political resistance and made little mystery of it, a fact which eventually led to its being banned:

> Un tambour. Le grand rire du Vaudou descend des mornes. Combien, au cours des siècles, de révoltes ainsi surgies! Que de victoires éphemères! Mais aussi, quelles défaites! Quelles répressions! Mains coupées, corps écartelés, gibets, voila ce qui peuple les allées de l'histoire coloniale. Et rien de tout cela n'aurait passé dans le folklore? Vous connaissez le conte de Colibri.

Césaire (and Menil) obligingly provide the folk connection between the story of Yé and "Conte Colibri." In a multiplicity of crisscrossing references, firmly connected by the central image of a beheading, the story of Yé spills into the tale of Colibri. The drum and the drum-bird stand for the primal Maroon, Caliban's last avatar. An obvious reference to the maroon's mode of communication, the drum functions both as an ontological metaphor (for instance, the vaudou ceremony in **Christophe** III, 7), and the poem as sample of the counter-poetics of "marronnage"; what Césaire wittily defined for Depestre in their famous friendly quarrel, "Réponse à Depestre, poète haïtien," as a symbolic system where nothing is what it seems.

Dismemberment connects the poem to **Les Chiens.** It also connects the tale of Colibri to that of Yé's sacred bird:

> Beau sang giclé
>
> tête trophée membres lacérés
> dard assassin beau sang giclé
> ramages perdus rivages ravis . . .

ô assassin attardé

l'oiseau aux plumes jadis plus belles que le passé
exige le compte de ses plumes dispersées.

On one level, the poem can be read as a riddle on the fact of colonization, predicting a successful revolt, if not revolution. The "standing nigger-scum" ("elle est debout la négraille") force the defeated colonizer, once triumphant trophy hunter, now defeated murderer, to acknowledge its dignity ("exige le compte de ses plumes dispersées"). On another level, Yé who would feed his children the body of the fallen god is replaying both those West African rituals of which Frazer and Freud made so much; and which, in their Mediterranean transformations, René Girard sees as the non-western foundations of our western beliefs—Christ's ritual sacrifice and "flesh-and-blood" communion embracing both. Willingly shedding his own "communial blood," the Rebel of *Les Chiens* is, among others, a (counter)version of Christ. On yet another level, the poem stages an allegorical replay of the Rebel's betrayal by his own people. If the ignorant trophy hunter may be compared to the ignorant betrayers of the oratorio, he has nonetheless committed a sacreligious crime for which he must atone; as, by inference, must they. The criticism of the betrayal is here muted, since Yé (metonym for the poorest "nigger-scum") was trying to feed his children (take charge of the people and so continue the Rebel's task). By forcing them to reconstitute its body, the sacred bird of Negritude is leading them to the selfawareness ("ever more beautiful than before") that precedes collective action. As usual with Césaire, any close-reading eventually proceeds in "expanding rings," to use Rilke's metaphor.

For it is the image of Afro-Caribbean consciousness that brings into the poem's semantic interplay its twin folktale, that of Colibri—not so coincidentally, the other Hearn selection reproduced by Césaire and Menil. "Conte colibri" is the story of the hummingbird who fights a succession of monsters sent by a jealous god to steal the bird's magic drum. When the last monster, Poisson-Armé, presents himself, a badly-wounded Colibri, "spurting blood," knows that he must die but gallantly accepts the challenge:

—Mon dernier combat, dit Colibri qui tomba mort.

Pouesson-Armé, en toute hate, ramassa un grand coutelas qui traînait par là, coupe la tête de Colibri, la mit sous la pierre de taille dans la cour de la maison. Alors, seulement, il prit le tambour l'emporta.

In "Beau sang giclé, the "trophy head" is the clue that Colibri and the sacred bird of the past are one. Like Osiris's and Orpheus's, Colibri's head must be severed after death to prevent reincarnation. But, as with Orpheus, the head buried in the house yard is immortal, drawing a perpetual potential reincarnation from Caribbean soil/self. The connection between the chtonic forces of the soil and the Rebel (who, sprawled on the ground, anoints his nape with crumbling earth), was made rather forcefully in the 1946 version of *Les Chiens*. Colibri may well be the Rebel's totem. We already know that it is Christophe's.

As Pestre d'Almeida has shown, parts of the pre-Columbian myth of the hummingbird correspond to aspects of the Ancient Phoenix as well as to the Aztec Hummingbird God; the latter represented the rising sun, the dawning of a new age—a particularly potent cluster in Césaire. In this overlapping of cultural traditions, Césaire has found the perfect syncretic Ancestor; and, as such, the model of the authentic Afro-Caribbean self: the eternal "bird of no surrender."

With its incredibly fast beating heart, the hummingbird is a living drum. And we remember that it is the sacred drum that Poisson-Armé stole from Colibri: in other words, along with his life, that which defined him, his self. Pushing the metaphor, one might also add, his music, his poetry, his language; or, in biblical terms, his Word. The tale of Colibri is that of an ontological murder. But it enfolds a possible rebirth. For, if Colibri did not, in the folktale, come back to life, Yé's magic bird did.

Colibri was a frame of reference in the Cesairean corpus every time the questions of ontological and historical authenticity were raised. With *moi, laminaire . . . ,* whose lower capped title is significant (all poems have lower capped titles as well), Césaire operates a bitter eviscerating:

rien de tout cela n'a la force d'aller bien loin
essoufflés
ce vent nos oiseaux tombant et retombant
alourdis par le surcroît de cendres da volcans

("éboulis")

The once fertile, revolution-nurturing landscape is now dry ashes. We can measure the depth of despair in this image of sterility and death for a man who once described himself as volcanic, "homme peleen," and praised the other pelean giant of Caribbean history, Louis Delgres who blew himself to bits on Matouba and who, like Césaire, was born on Basse-Terre. We have passed from the gigantic realm of an all embracing, all-creating, explosive imagination birthing an all-expanding consciousness (the sorcerer's incantations that create a new world and a new people) to a contracting, almost imploding universe. The poetic self, a figure of mythical resilience, once Phoenix-like in its stubborn Colibri-courage, is now confronting historical contingency, "limping," Oedipus-like, between self-knowledge and its reverse, self doubt: "Ainsi va toute vie. Ainsi va ce livre, entre soleil et ombre, entre montagne et mangrove, entre chien et loup, claudiquant et binaire." A shrunken giant wonders about his choice of ancestors: "j'ai tiré au sort mes ancétres" ("ibis-anubis"). The Ancient myths that so empowered him are now inoperative, reduced to arbitrary choices.

The heroic self has been reduced to a non-self, a modest life form that cannot stand separate from its marine environment for long, but sometimes manages self-consciousness, to "inhabit one of my wounds one minute at a time":

> j'habite de temps en temps une de mes plaies
> chaque minute je change d'appartement
> et toute paix m'effraie
> > ayant creché volcan mes entrailles d'eau
> > > vive
> > je reste avec mes pains de mots et mes
> > > minerais secrets
>
> j'habite donc une vaste pensée
> > **("calendrier lagunaire")**

The fragmented, tentative consciousness is all too aware of its vulnerability, yet tenaciously clinging to the hope of resurgence with a serenity born of experience at the end of a long life ("algues"):

> la relance
> > se fait
> > > algue laminaire

This is Colibri's last incarnation: limited and modest in its acts yet keeping the epic dream alive ("une vaste pensée"). In its last reincarnation, Césaire-Colibri acknowledges that his mission has not changed, and so finally answers the "admirable question," but this time without irony:

> il n'est pas question de livrer le monde aux
> assassins d'aube . . .
> une nouvelle bonte ne cesse de croître à l'horizon
> > **("nouvelle bonte")**

Somehow, this last incarnation is infinitely more touching, in its limitations, and stubborn hope, than the wildest of the Rebel's visions. Until we remember that, in Césaire's syncretic pantheon, Oedipus enfolds the smiling, limping figure of Legba-Eshu, cunning messenger of the gods, the liminal deity who never gave up. And so, infinitely refracted, the iconic figure of Colibri.

Hedy Kalikoff (essay date Spring 1995)

SOURCE: "Gender, Genre and Geography in Aimé Césaire's

Cahier d'un retour au pays natal," in *Callaloo*, Vol. 18, No. 2, Spring 1995, pp. 492-505.

[*In the following essay, Kalikoff examines epic qualities, gender-biased assumptions, and elements of female decolonization in Césaire's* Cahier d'un retour au pays natal.]

Aimé Césaire's **Cahier d'un retour au pays natal** is one of the acknowledged masterpieces of francophone Caribbean literature. A great work seems to require a great man, a hero who can act and speak for an entire people, and indeed the period **Cahier** inhabits in Caribbean literary history has been referred to as an era of "Heroic Negritude". There is scarcely any scholarship on the long poem which does not refer to it as "epic" and "heroic." What I would like to argue, however, is that these terms are inappropriate, for two reasons. First, they function to smooth out the disruptive quality of the poem by couching it in comfortably traditional categories of genre. And second, since the epic hero is always male and the trajectory of his journey has traditionally been gendered as masculine, these generic labels also serve to thwart discussion of the poem's figuration of gender by suppressing the role the feminine plays and reading the poem's figuration of masculinity as "natural." This ends up lending false coherence to the lyrical subject, suggesting an easily identifiable, active narrator moving through time and space, a notion **Cahier d'un retour** defies.

When one examines the way that the poem's complex imagery is gendered, one arrives at a point of reversal of terms, where what was once masculine (the sun) becomes feminine (the moon) and vice versa. This reversal is eventually overturned, yet a fundamental ambiguity remains and is never fully resolved. The poem's ending is both an attempt to rewrite the binary oppositions of masculine and feminine, vertical and horizontal, sun and moon, and a call to transcend a debilitating collective history. By unsettling this symbolic structure—what amounts to a "colonial Imaginary," in Althusserian terms—the poem unsettles the ideology which strove to justify the wrenching history of the African diaspora.

Once the poem undermines its own binary imagery and starts to sketch in a third term, one can see that what has been viewed as a sort of phallic negritude, where "negritude as phallus . . . revalorizes the black man", is nothing of the sort. The imposition of such Lacanian terms on the text leads to a reading of colonization and decolonization where the former is figured as emasculating and the latter as "rephallicizing." What I would like to do is to provide a reading which both illuminates the construction of gender in the poem, and shows how attempts to fit the poem into traditional generic concepts (hero and epic) and Lacanian structures (by way of Althusser and Fanon) unintentionally serve to preclude any possibility for female decolonization and to oversimplify the poem's obscurities. By drawing out the ambiguities of the poem's conclusion I hope to show just how ambitious the poem's decolonizing impulse is, and how difficult its project.

1. *Heroic Negritude*

A. James Arnold has called Aimé Césaire's **Cahier** "the epic of negritude," referring to Ezra Pound's definition of an epic as "a long poem with history in it". This definition is indeed a terse one, as Arnold writes, yet no matter how minimalist Pound's definition may be, it cannot denude the epic of its heroic proportions. This view is certainly not Arnold's alone. Aliko Songolo (in *Aimé Césaire: Une Poètique de la Découverte*) also calls the speaker of the poem "le poete-heros," not only upholding the notion of heroism but also eliding the distinction between the poet and the speaker of the poem. Indeed, this is one of the temptations **Cahier** poses. Césaire himself is such an extraordinary figure that his biography occasionally casts a shadow over interpretations of the poem. Yet this urge to read a hero into the work, in light of the textual evidence, is difficult to accept, particularly when one considers Ronnie Scharfman's convincing point that Césaire's poetry "is permeated not only with a sense of the arbitrariness of language but also with doubts as to the very possibility of mediating between the individual and the collective." Certainly the subject of the poem sometimes yearns to be the voice of the people, to be their leader, to singlehandedly decolonize them. However, this posture is not a constant one, and much of the poem strikes intensely personal, idiosyncratic notes which belie the stance of a public, heroic figure. As Eileen Julien has pointed out, the epic form is not one used by women writers, precisely because of its masculinist characteristics: "This hierarchic form is tied to nationalistic agendas and military might, which have been and continue to be, for the most part, provinces of patriarchy."

The world of the epic does not resemble that of *Cahier,* despite moments where heroism is invoked.
—*Hedy Kalikoff*

The world of the epic does not resemble that of **Cahier,** despite moments where heroism is invoked. As Mikhail Bakhtin has written,

> [t]he epic past is absolute and complete. It is as closed as a circle; inside it everything is finished, already over. There is no place in the epic world for any openendedness, indecision, indeterminacy.

However, indeterminacy, openendedness, and a constant interrogation of the past are important characteristics of Césaire's long poem. In a more recent example of scholarship on epic, and one perhaps more appropriate to literature of the African diaspora, Isidore Okpewho shows that "the hero is quite simply a comprehensive symbol of the ideals of human society and the dangers attendant upon such exaggerated expectations." The epic hero has a dual role: as champion of his community he is both a "man of the people" and a superior, noble creature endowed with supernatural powers. This comprehensive duality should not be mistaken for anything like the constant shifts and struggles of the poem's lyrical voice, for the epic hero's conflicts are the expression of a coherent identity, replete with biography and praise-singers. Nor should the mythic tone and historical references characteristic of Césaire's poem be read as evidence of epic qualities:

> History for the [traditional oral] artist is both what has actually happened and what is fabled to have happened. For him myth has considerable historical value; because it has been told all too often, it bears the stamp of truth.

What is so extraordinary and powerful about Césaire's poem is precisely that it is a story which had not previously been told. And in Césaire's case, this story is being told on the page; it is an extremely *written* text whose frequently esoteric vocabulary and imagery take it far from traditional oral art forms even while sometimes invoking them. If anything it is the notion of epic that Césaire interrogates in this poem, and this is perhaps a good example of the way that some colonial and postcolonial texts appropriate traditional genres in order to reinvent them.

When we turn from these theorists and critics to look at the poem's rhetoric, there is even more reason to avoid these generic labels, however casual their use may be. Perhaps one of the most frequently quoted lines from **Cahier** is one which places the poet in the position of lighting the way for his people, leading them to freedom:

> Je viendrais à ce pays mien et je lui dirais: / . . . / "Ma bouche sera la bouche des malheurs qui n'ont pas de bouche, ma voix, la liberté de celles qui s'affaissent au cachot du désespoir."

Only if this line is taken out of context could the subject of **Cahier** be seen as speaking continually and successfully as a representative for and of his people. The text itself resists this stance. Not only explicitly, as in "Mon héroïsme, quelle farce", but in the way that the passage above is phrased and presented. It is written in the conditional mood and, more importantly, it is placed within quotation marks. When the narrator says he would speak for "you" ("c'est pour vous que je parlerai"), it seems in retrospect to be a naive hope or intention, deflated upon actual arrival in the "pays natal." The triumphant cry, "Et voici que je suis venu!" is followed immediately by the vision of "cette vie clopinante devant moi, non pas cette vie, cette mort . . ." and the word "mort" will be repeated five times in this one stanza. This is a devastating rebuke of the fantasy that "ma bouche sera la bouche des malheurs qui n'ont pas de bouche." Scharfman points out the possibility that in this passage the subject is taking on a Christ-like voice and "by quoting it as if it were already poetry or gospel, the subject reveals itself as having been confined by a kind of textual grandiosity."

This moment of grandiose fantasy is quite different from what Okpewho has described as the typical immodesty of the epic hero: "[T]he hero has an exaggerated notion of his worth. He claims precedence above everyone else, his elders included, and expects others to recognize his greatness." The subject of **Cahier** only briefly imagines himself as a savior-figure before coming face to face with the morbid landscape of his island, "où la grandeur piteusement échoue." In traditional epic, there is no such bracing self-mockery.

Daniel Maximin's novel *L'Isole soleil* explicitly invokes **Cahier** as an important intertext, both responding to and reinterpreting Césaire's work, and for this reason I would like to use the novel as another way to comment on the poem. One of the characters in *L'Isole soleil* explains why a female reader might be frustrated with heroic epic: "Si on écoute nos poètes, nos révolutionnaires, nos romanciers et leurs historiens, la seule fonction des femmes noires serait d'enfanter nos heros." It is precisely this question as to the "fonction des femmes noires" in **Cahier** which will lead us into an examination of the way the poem manipulates gendered imagery.

2. *Male and Female Geography*

From the opening moments of **Cahier**, what is female appears in the text as a symbol of duplicity: "Puis je me tournais vers des paradis pour lui et les siens perdus, plus calme que la face d'une femme qui ment". A few lines later the phrase "menteusement souriante" will point the reader back to the first mention of "mensonge" and the lying, smiling female face will be established as a trope. This smile provokes the lyrical "je" of the poem into outrage: "on voit encore des madras aux reins des femmes des / anneaux a leurs oreilles des sourires à leurs bouches / des enfants à leurs mamelles et j'en passe: / ASSEZ DE CE SCANDALEI". It becomes clear that the poem's narrator is referring to the smiling face of the "doudou," the stereotypical *malâtresse* in her cheerful, French-loving mode about whom the song "Adieu fouiards, adieu madras" was written. The speaker's disdain and anger appear to be focused at the perpetuation of this stereotype. However, this may also

be an instance of scorn towards the women who, in the complicated colonial history of the French Caribbean, were able to raise their social status through sexual relations with white slaveowners. [This situation led to the differential treatment of free colored males and free colored females, enmiring mulatto women in sexual relations which exploited them while at the same time gave them access to white power.] This moment of hostility perhaps prefigures Frantz Fanon's (in)famous critique of Caribbean women who attempt to "lighten the race" by bedding white men.

The notion of duplicitousness, then, is linked to the image of degraded sexuality and the imagery which is gendered as female in the poem is inscribed along a horizontal line. The *mulâtresse* is the woman who represents lying down with the colonizer for survival. The city is marked as a degraded landscape, passive, horizontal, mute. "Cette ville plate-etalee" is associated with the powerless, faceless crowd which is in turn associated with "une femme". In a circular series of comparisons, the subject is as calm as the lying face of a smiling woman, and smiling, scandalous women are like the city which is laid out flat and passive as the body of a woman, and in this city there is a crowd which is silent and incomprehensible as a woman who would order a hypothetical rain not to fall. Occasionally what is horizontal is not passive and degraded but warm and fertile as the earth: "toi terre tendue terre / saoule / terre grand sexe leve vers le soleil / . . . la terre où tout est libre / et fraternal, ma terre".

The instability of the figuration is not limited to female symbols alone. The poem lurches and leaps back and forth from a dismal, colonized notion of "islandness" to moments of exalted joy in a pattern which has been described as having three large movements or three acts. Within these larger movements are smaller reversals, ascents and falls. The figuration changes according to the transformations of the subject's viewpoint. At its lowest point, the female is the city, the impoverished hybrid of urban modernism and colonialized squalor—flattened, sprawled, prostrated. In its antithesis, the female represents fertility. Both of these extremes are on a horizontal axis, whether positive or negative, whether they signify fertility or passivity.

Not surprisingly, then, what is vertical is usually gendered as male. I would like to focus on one primary and persistent figure of the masculine, "le soleil"—a conventional male symbol in traditional poetic imagery as well as in this poem.

The sun appears on the first page as cursed and venereal, a force on high, looking down on the colonized island. This is a gaze which inscribes an invisible vertical line, like a plumb line dropped from the sun to the island, surveying it authoritatively as a policeman would (". . . arpentée nuit et jour d'un sacré soleil venerien"). The metaphorics of verticality are immediately in play here, embodied by conflicting symbols, the most famous of which is the reference to "mes profondeurs a hauteur inverse du vingtieme etage," or as one of the translations puts it, "in my depths height-deep". There is a constant up-and-down movement, a vertical axis which is masculinized as one realizes that the speaker's voice is always a male voice. The sun, meanwhile, is infected by an illness, a malady of the colonizer, apparently the result of a contagious coupling, and the implication is that "la terre" or "la ville" has been infected by a diseased phallus.

In the second movement of the poem, with the introduction of the one-word sentence "Partir", the register changes. The sun is refigured. The earth, as we have seen, is the female sex raised towards the phallic sun, "la mentule de Dieu," and the sun now has the capacity not to infect but to fertilize, to turn golden that which is under its light. The sun will be represented as diseased once again in the poem—"Au bout du petit matin le soleil qui toussotte et crache ses poumons"—but this time the illness is tubercular. These shifts do not end here. Just before the beginning of the third movement, when the speaker calls to the sun with its curly hair like that of a black man ("Ange Soleil, Ange frisé du soleil"), he is asking it to help him affect a leap beyond the self-disgust which had permeated the preceding section. This is the pinnacle of the sun as symbol, the moment when it is personified and, most importantly, made into a black angel to help the subject ascend skyward, out of the depths of his colonized state. The vertical axis, at its most inspired, transcendent moments, stands for power, hope and independence. At its most negative it represents the diseased phallus, the colonial gaze, the surveillance and oppression of the colonizer, and the fall downward to despair.

3. *Trading Places*

Once the figural structure is established in the first half of the poem, the language and tone shift in a wave of ambiguous imagery. The gendered figures of sun and moon are reversed, changed back again, and then upset completely, plunging the poem into periods of instability and culminating in a profoundly obscure ending.

The major turning point comes at the famous, much-quoted section about the black man in the streetcar, "le nègre grand comme un pongo." This is the lowest moment for the "je" of the poem. He has just described the slave market under the guise of a horse market, rejected the notion that a glorious African past holds any hope, and evoked the despair in the hulls of slave ships. In a city streetcar, the speaker of the poem sees a hideous and pathetic black man and smiles along with the white women who sneer at him. Once he realizes his complicity with the disdain of the white gaze, he is as low as he can go, mired in self-hatred, "[c]omme cette ville dans la crasse et dans la boue couchée." He becomes completely prostrate, identifying for the first time in the

poem with the horizontal position which has up to now been gendered as female.

The poem's narrator remains flattened until the imagery of the poem starts to signal the advent of a new order: "je tremble maintenant du commun tremblement que / notre song docile change dans le madrépore." The madrépore is a particularly telling figure to use here. As Samuel Weber has pointed out, it is a term which has caused confusion: "Le madrépore, dont on a longtemps cru qu'il appartenait à la flore, est le site d'une erreur: son origine n'est pas végétale mais animale." The madrépore is a symbol of ambiguity and uncertainty, and it announces that the categories in the poem are shifting, the subject doubling and changing.

This is followed by several androgynous figures where masculine and feminine coexist side by side. When the word "silo" appears ("silo où se préserve et mûrit ce que la terre a de plus / terre"), we have a symbol whose shape is phallic and yet whose function is womblike, to house ripening grain until it is mature. In the passage, "ma negritude n'est pas une pierre . . .", the speaker seems to take on a masculine identity again:

> ma négritude n'est ni une tour ni une cathedrale /
> elle plonge dans la chair rouge du sol / elle plonge
> dans la chair ardente du ciel / elle troue
> l'accablement opaque de sa droite patience.

Yet, in this one passage, the text both denies an upright phallic shape ("ni une tour ni une cathedrale") and reaffirms it ("se droite patience") while reiterating a vertical movement from the earth to the sky, from a high tower to deep down in the soil. The earth here is red flesh being penetrated by "ma negritude," yet because "negritude" is feminine in French, the masculine movement of the speaker is expressed by a feminine pronoun: *"elle plonge* dans la chair rouge du sol."

The litany of flora and fauna which follows this places the narrator in the role of a Noah figure who "gathers lovingly all the beasts, birds, insects, saps, to shelter them from moral deluge". This is indeed the new beginning which the narrator had anticipated, both as the beginning of the end of the world and a rebirth of the self, a self-birthing.

At the end of this section the imagery becomes explicitly sexual:

> viennent les ovaires de l'eau où le futur agite ses
> petites têtes / viennent les loups qui paturent dans
> les orifices sauvages du corps à l'heure ou à
> l'auberge eliptique se / rencontrent *ma lune* et *ton
> soleil* (my emphasis)

Embedded in this passage is the startling reversal of symbols already referred to—at this moment the speaker no longer identifies himself with the masculine sun. He is the moon, and the "tu" of the poem is the sun. For the first time in the poem, masculine and feminine axes are realigned. This new identification continues through the next few stanzas. In the line, "Calme et berce ô ma parole l'enfant . . . ," the speaker appropriates a maternal posture. When he addresses himself to the light—"ô fraîche source de la lumiere"—he is speaking *to* the sun, the source of light whose supply will replenish him in his new identity as moon reflecting light.

On the next page, the symbols of the sun and the moon are explicitly restored to their conventional figuration and the sun becomes male once again: "le coeur mâle du soleil," "la fémininité de la lune au corps d'huile." In this stanza, there is a celebration of the notion of reconciliation. However, this realignment and "close concordance" are never so neat and unambiguous as they first seem.

4. *"Mon originale geographic"*

We have seen the gendered imagery suddenly reverse itself, going through a period of change heralded by a metaphorics of instability and androgyny. While the images seem to revert to their initial pattern, there is an element of ambiguity which never goes away. Masculinity is now insisted upon as the speaker of the poem seems to be trying to construct his own identity. This notion of renewal, restructuring and rethinking is underlined by the emphasis on geography. The "je" of the *Cahier* in redefining himself must also redraw the map of the world since his identity is so closely affiliated with the fragmented, volcanic islands, with the far-flung history of the diaspora, the middle passage, and the triangle inscribed by Africa, France and Martinique.

Now the speaker of the poem seems particularly muscular, sending up a "viril" prayer, asking for the faith of a sorcerer, for powerful hands, for the temper of a sword. He runs through the gamut of masculine roles, desiring to be "le frere . . . le fils . . . l'amant de cet unique peuple." The insistence and repetitiveness of the male imagery, the very foregrounding of the speaker's virility, signals that the constitution of the subject as masculine is in process, that he is trying singlehandedly to forge a new self, upright and masculine, capable of resisting oppression.

When the speaker of the poem intones an ironic and vituperative list of the outrages that he accepts, he includes his own geography, his own version of the world: "mon originale géographic aussi; la carte du / monde faite à mon usage . . . ." "Originale" here suggests a trajectory back to the beginning when earth, sun and moon were in their appropriate places. Yet original also signifies *new*, something never seen before. Not only is the narrator's version of the world new, it is also

eccentric and strange—the third meaning of the word "original" in French. The speaker of the poem is remaking the map of the world and of the universe as well. The very horizon is coming undone ("l'horizon se défait, recule et s'élargit"), the sun becomes a toy ball ("saute le soleil sur la raquette de mes mains") and this former symbol of masculine power is no longer adequate ("l'inegal soleil ne me suffit plus").

The speaker's explicit virility and sense of power intensify until they reach perhaps their most blatant image: "Et voici soudain que force et vie m'assaillent comme un taureau. . . ." With swords and sorcery at his command, embodied with the force of a bull, the speaker sounds just like a hero leading his people: "Et nous sommes debout maintenant, mon pays et moi. . . ." The poem rushes forward and upward towards its resolution, and with the constant vertical imagery and the insistence on standing and rising, "heroic negritude. does indeed seem implacably phallic.

5. *Phallic Negritude*

Standing upright is a metaphor for resistance and survival in the poem, which makes the vertical axis the more strongly privileged one in the figurative scheme. This has led some critics to read the poem's symbolic structure in Lacanian terms:

> The image of negritude as phallus serves several functions for the subject. As a corrective device, it revalorizes the black man, symbolically castrated throughout the text by the forces of oppression. It is the perfect metaphor for the desired union between the subject and primal forces in nature.

Lacan's notions about phallic power and castration in language are tempting ones to put to use here. But this is a temptation which should be resisted, for several reasons.

Lacan's conception of the phallus is a way of describing the subject's relation to language. The phallus is a signifier "c'est le signifiant destiné à désigner dans leur ensemble les effete de signifié, en tent que le signifiant les conditionne par sa presence de signifiant." The effects of the signified are that man's needs are alienated due to their expression in language. To be castrated in language is a condition of subjectivity; it implies that the speaking subject is incapable of expressing need in such a way that it can be satisfied.

The notion that language precedes the subject and that the subject is constructed through language but cannot master language has become a commonplace of poststructuralist theory. It is important to keep in mind that this alienation in language is as true for the colonizer as it is for the colonized. The alienation of those who are deprived of a political speaking voice under the conditions of colonization is quite different from the lack of mastery over language which is at the heart of subjectivity. To use a profoundly linguistic concept as a metaphor for a political one is, in this case, to risk attributing a kind of mastery to the colonial powers which would place colonial discourse at the mythic "center" of discourse; it would phallicize colonization by endowing it with complete control over language, with the absolute power to generate meaning as though colonial discourse stood somehow outside of language. Yet, "hegemony is a fragile and difficult process of containment," writes John Frow. "Further, there are historically quite distinct degrees of coherence of the 'dominant ideology'". If the colonizing subject were not castrated in language, the dominant ideology would then be perfectly coherent.

Fredric Jameson's long article on Lacan which serves as his attempt to reconcile psychoanalytic and Marxist schools of criticism does seem, as Scharfman notes, particularly helpful in the context of Césaire's **Cahier**. Jameson's intent in "Imaginary and Symbolic in Lacan" is to find a way of reading which would mediate "between social phenomena and what must be called private, rather than even merely individual, facts." He does this by relying on Althusser's definition of ideology as the "'representation' of the Imaginary's relationship of individuals to their Real conditions of existence." It is within representations of the Imaginary relationship of the colonized to the conditions of colonization that a historically grounded notion of alienation can be examined through the Symbolic order of language.

The real sticking point of Lacanian theory for feminist writers and theorists is the use of masculine terminology to represent ideas that are supposed to be gender-neutral. Lacan refers to the phallus as not being reducible to "l'organe, pénis ou clitoris, qu'il symbollse", suggesting that the phallus can refer to both male and female bodies. Yet this distinction between the phallus and the penis which Lacanians insist on is surely a tenuous one since it refuses to recognize the way these terms are inseparably associated by a larger culture within which individuals are powerless to dictate meaning. Merely willing it so will not strip the phallus of its male connotations. As Jane Gallop puts it, these Lacanian "attempts to remake language to one's own theoretical needs, as if language were merely a tool one could use, bespeaks a very un-Lacanian view of language." Gallop goes on to say that,

> as long as the attribute of power is a phallus which can only have meaning by referring to and being confused with a penis, this confusion will support a structure in which it seems reasonable that men have power and women do not.

If the purpose of figuring negritude as phallus is to revalorize the black man, one has to ask then where this schema leaves the question of female oppression, female resistance and decolonization and if this reading of negritude does not empower "the black man" in a way which seems "reasonable" while leaving female decolonization aside as a non-issue. But, does **Cahier d'un retour** really figure negritude as phallus? Do the rising tone and ecstatic imagery, the "arousal of ethnic consciousness" at the end of the poem, imply that the poem is, in fact, getting an erection?

If we look closely at the last pages of the poem, the powerful mounting rhythm is seen to be subtended by explosive imagery which insists on the mediatedness of this vertical movement. The axes which have structured the poem's imagery are erupting as the tension and tone intensify. The repeated images of verticality are interladen with an angry irony, palpable in the repetition of the heavy phrase "c'était un très bon nègre," and in the question, "Tenez, suis-je assez humble?" which both tend to weigh down the poem's final flight.

When the last lines of the poem finally appear, they are so idiosyncratic and inaccessible that the text ends on a note not of reconciliation but of obscurity, forcing a reconsideration of what came before. The last line of the text reads: "et le grand trou noir où je voulais me noyer l'autre lune / c'est la que je veux pêcher maintenant la langue maléfique de la nuit et son immobile verrition." In three different translations of the poem, the rendering of the last few words varies from "unmoving flick" to "motionless veerition" and "immutable truth." None of these makes the meaning of the last lines any clearer since Césaire ends the poem with a neologism:

> Césaire's great lyric about finding a voice, about returning to native ground, strands us, finally, with a made-up, Latinate, abstract-sounding question mark of a word. So much for expectations of direct, immediate linguistic "authenticity." With Césaire we are involved in a poetics of cultural *invention*. ([James] Clifford)

It is difficult, then, to agree that "dans le troisième acte, le poète reconcilié avec lui-même et avec son pays conduit son peuple vers la liberté desirée." At the end of the poem the sun is no longer adequate for the speaker, and he addresses himself to the wind. Bind me to the soil, he asks the wind, strangle me with your lasso of stars to the sky. Rise, dove, rise rise rise. Despite the exuberant upward movement, bounding and strangulation are perplexing images to use to express reconciliation and liberation.

The ending of the poem might be read instead not only as a "poetics of cultural invention" but as the attempt to constitute a decolonized subjectivity under a different imaginary scheme. To return to Althusser's very Lacanian conception of ideology, if the poem maps out an ideology which might be called negritude and in doing so decenters what I would conceptualize as a "colonial Imaginary," then what is its own Imaginary scheme?

To answer that question, I find it most useful to turn to the work of Luce Irigaray who has written lengthy critiques of Lacanian psychoanalytic theory and shown what a non-phallocentric Imaginary might look like, while still relying on Lacan's ideas. The most relevant aspect of Irigaray's work here is her insistence that Western philosophy is based on the "logic of sameness." Psychoanalysis, starting with Freud, has defined sexual difference according to phallic logic:

> Partie prenante d'une idéologie qu'il ne remet pas en cause, [Freud] affirme que le "masculin" est le modèle sexuel, que toute représentation de désir ne peut que s'y étalonner, s'y soumettre.

By this masculine standard, the clitoris is a smaller version of the penis, and the little girl is a "little man." This, of course, allows women to be viewed as the same as men, but inferior. Extending this logic to wider philosophical terms, "[c]ette domination du logos philosophique vient, pour une bonne part, de son pouvoir de *réduire tout autre dans l'économic du Même* (her emphasis). This economy of the same is the engine which powers colonial discourse and colonial self-justification. When the standard of measure is the white European male, the resulting philosophy holds that Africans, including Africans of the diaspora, fall far short of that standard, which, not coincidentally, makes them ripe for the "civilizing mission." From the insistent oppression of this colonial discourse stems what Fanon calls the "psychoexistential" inferiority complex of blacks, the internalization of racist ideology. Fanon's stated aim was to analyze the complex in order to destroy it.

Césaire, who was of course a great influence on Fanon, also has this destructive impulse as an aim; his text is linguistically disruptive in the same sense that Irigaray's is: "Irigaray attempts to disrupt symbolic discourse . . . by reimagining the female Imaginary." Césaire's poem with its eruptive, disruptive, denunciatory power aims to explode colonial discourse, the phallogocentric system on the other side of which lies a new map of the world, a different Imaginary. When the speaker of the poem associates himself with the masculine sun, he is filling in the role the colonizer had played. He is not upsetting the structure, but changing the players. In the historical context of the poem's production, this is an extraordinary move. However, as Irigaray puts it, "si [le] projet visait simplement à renverser l'ordre des choses—admettons même que cela soit possible . . . —l'histoire reviendrait finalement encore au *même*" (my emphasis). Césaire goes further than a reversal of terms: when the sun is removed from its privileged position, the rigid vertical-horizontal structure crumbles. The wind, which the speaker of the poem addresses throughout the last passage, serves

as a new metaphor, one which, in this poem, defies being categorized or even defined since it can be felt but not touched, heard but not seen, spoken to as if it were listening:

> . . . enroule-toi, vent, autour de ma nouvelle croissance / pose-toi sur mes doigts mesurés / je te livre ma conscience et son rythme de chair / . . . / je te livre mes paroles abruptes / dévore et enroule-toi / en t'enroulant embrasse-moi d'un plus vaste frisson / embrasse-moi jusqu'au nous furieux / embrasse, embrasse NOUS. . . .

Is the wind a voice which can be heard around the world? Is it a reference to oral culture and oral art? A non-material response to the aggressive sharpness of colonizing technology? A holy spirit? A form of resistance which does not imply phallic logic?

It is the "radical indeterminacy" of the poem's final stretch which the reader is left with at the end, yet the outlines of something new are sketched in. The poem's troublesome conclusion, with its complexity of image and language, introduces a third and perhaps mediating term, suggesting a new Imaginary which remains to be fully articulated. If we return to *L'Isolé soleil* for a moment, it is interesting to see the way that Maximin reiterates a Caribbean landscape of three elements and insists on the triangularization of meaning and desire: the sun, the volcano and the sea make up the three terms in Maximin's geography. Towards the end of the book "la voie lactée" joins "le soleil" and "la mer" in a more feminized version of the threesome. This figuring and refiguring of three terms includes the play of characters who often comprise two men and a woman, reinscribing the threesome who founded "Tropiques," Léon Damas, Aimé Césaire, and Suzanne Césaire. Maximin insists on the inclusion of a third term and of a female voice in what I would like to read as a novelistic continuation of Césaire's long poem. It is part of *L'Isolé soleil's* power that it recognizes the movement from two to three terms in **Cahier,** the triangularization of its imagery.

The poem's emphasis on vertical movement and insistence on masculinity should not, then, be read literally as the epic outpouring of a phallic leader, but rather as an attempt to subvert colonial discourse through reimagining the colonial Imaginary. The poem's blatant sexual images and gendered landscapes prove to be unstable and disruptive, suggesting a reading of the poem's masculinity that highlights its constructedness rather than its depiction of a natural process.

6. *Conclusion*

Negritude has long been subject to controversy. Heralded as a pan-Africanist response to colonialism by some, it has been derided as essentialist, globalizing and falsely idealist by others. Eventually, the topic lost some of its argumentative bite with the distance of time, negritude has been viewed in its historical specificity. As Clarisse Zimra has noted, "the quest which [negritude] expresses was defined primarily, according to the socio-political terms of the 1930s."

If negritude may be many things to many people, it has surely always been male from the nearly exclusive maleness of its participants to the supposedly phallic logic of its symbolic order. The question of whether there is a "negritude in the feminine mode," as Zimra puts it, has started to receive its share of scholarly attention. But the classics of negritude, including Césaire's **Cahier,** have remained strangely untouched.

While critics cannot ignore the explicit sexuality of Césaire's metaphors, the construction of both female and male in the text and the significance of gender for the work as a whole has itself been a fairly uncharted landscape.

The issues of female oppression and female decolonization tend to be silent spaces in the poem. Afterall, when the narrator allies himself with other oppressed people—"je serais un homme-juif / un homme-cafre / un homme-hindou-de Calcutta / un homme-de-Harlem-qui-ne-vote-pas"—the major omission on the list of sufferers is "un homme-femme." This is not to say that this absence undermines the text's extraordinary artistic power nor its force as a tool for "decolonizing the mind." However, this is something which stands to be remarked on, particularly if the text is to be taken as *the* epic of negritude, the blueprint for resistance and liberation.

If colonialism was an emasculating experience, how were the "always-already castrated" affected by it? Yet, colonialism was not of course literally emasculating; it has been figured as such, as the strongest mode of disempowerment some writers can imagine. Exactly what is missing from this schema is a different Imaginary. What the poem attempts to do in fact is to refigure the schema. The upsetting of the binary order and the introduction of the elements of a new one are crucial to the poem's revolutionary power.

It is easy to call **Cahier** an epic: it is a vast, complex and unwieldy text. To refer to it as a "long poem" seems somehow to slight its power. Yet, we need to foreground its unwieldness, since the poem's difficult form is one of the ways in which it bespeaks an unresolved historical struggle.

To try to disinvest **Cahier** of its heroic status is not to try to weaken the effect of the poem. As Trinh T. Minh-ha points out in another context, to posit a poet(-hero) lighting the way for his people is to suggest a liberation of the masses where "the masses are regarded as an aggregate of average persons condemned by their lack of personality or by their dim individualities to stay with the herd." One of Maximin's characters reiterates this point: "Quelle prétention chez tous ces écrivains mâles ou ces héros de romans. . . . Et tous ces moi-je toujours seuls face au peuple silencieux." The poem without its epic status and without a hero might not end in as clean and powerful a reconciliation as some of its readers might like, but it ends with the movement of struggle towards resolution. To deprive the poem of its final obscurity and struggle is to underestimate the difficulty of its project.

Laurence M. Porter (essay date Summer 1995)

SOURCE: "Aimé Césaire's Reworking of Shakespeare: Anticolonialist Discourse in *Une Tempête,*" in *Comparative Literature Studies,* Vol. 32, No. 3, Summer, 1995, pp. 360-81.

[*In the following essay, Porter provides comparative analysis of Césaire's adaptation of* The Tempest. *According to Porter, Césaire's parody of Shakespeare "constitutes a detailed condemnation of imperialism and racism, rivaled in Césaire's career only by his masterpiece, the* Cahier.*"*]

During most of the Vichy occupation of Martinique and the remaining years of World War II (April 1941 to September 1945), Aimé Césaire carried out the program announced two years earlier in his **Cahier d'un retour au pays natal,** opposing racism by inspiring pride in his people. His journal, *Tropiques,* published a series of articles intended to put the Martinicans in touch with their own land, history, and traditions. But his political resolve appears to have been crystallized in 1944 by his seven-month visit to Haiti, symbol and illustration of the possibility for black autonomy in the Caribbean. He soon was elected mayor of Martinique's principal city, Fort-de-France, and deputy to the French National Assembly in 1945. There he led the commission that drafted the bill of March 19, 1946, establishing the Départements d'Outre-Mer (D.O.M.). He has been severely criticized for missing the opportunity to make Martinique independent. But such criticism seems unjust: at that time, Martinique was too weak, economically, to stand alone, owing to the shortages caused by the Allied blockade, and was stifled politically by the highly centralized French administration. Only twelve years later was France to allow autonomy in her former colonies in Africa. In addition, Césaire respected the request voted on February 6, 1946, by the governing body of those he represented, the Conseil générale de la Martinique, which resolved: "Nous voulons l'assimilation, parce qu'elle est l'aboutissement de toute notre formation, trois fois séculaire." Within these limitations, Césaire had tried unsuccessfully to reserve special powers for the D.O.M.

His vocal support of anticolonialism, as a worldwide movement, was prepared by the independence movements in Madagascar and in Vietnam in the late 1940s, and provoked by Octave Mannoni's *Prospero and Caliban: The Psychology of Colonization.* Mannoni's psychoanalytical speculations attempted to negate the nationalistic implications of the 1947 uprising and its bloody suppression in the then French colony of Madagascar. Mannoni diagnosed the independence movement as the ambivalent symptom of the black person's "dependency complex," interacting with the white European colonizer's sublimated Oedipal desire for mastery, in rivalry with the symbolic father. That desire, Mannoni argued, led the European to quit country and family in quest of a freedom and autonomy that the Malagasy themselves—so Mannoni claimed—could neither imagine nor desire. To rule and dominate the latter was the Westerner's burden, as symbolic father, and by punishing the rebels, he would reassure them of the stability of his restraining power.

Césaire retorted promptly with his **Discours sur le colonialisme,** which reflects his emerging doubts about the efficacy of European Marxism for helping the Third World achieve eventual independence. At the same time that he refuted Mannoni's paternalistic views, he also rejected the Eurocentric left-wing views that would keep the Third World striving for autonomy, dependent on the guidance of Marxist thought. To redefine Caribbean experience in Caribbean terms, he founded his own socialist Progressive Party in 1958. From 1961 onward, he consistently advocated an autonomous federation of the D.O.M. in the Antilles and in Guyane. Throughout the 1960s, he attempted to prepare his constituents psychologically for self-rule and eventual nationhood through both political and cultural action.

As a form of cultural action, he wrote three plays that presented accessible, inspirational models of blacks' struggles for independence. The international context of the plays aimed to remind the Martinicans that morally, at least, they were not alone, and that their own striving for justice could in turn inspire others. Theater made Césaire's statements accessible to even the illiterate.

The last of these plays, **Une Tempête** (1969), parodies Shakespeare's original, satirizing the jarring contrast between the theory and practice of post-Shakespearean colonialism, between benevolent words and ready threats and uses of violence. It remains the only full-scale dramatic adaptation, and constitutes a detailed condemnation of imperialism and racism, rivaled in Césaire's career only by his masterpiece, the **Cahier.** Often studied, Césaire's parody deserves more attention than it has yet received, to explain the two added framing scenes, the landscape, and above all, the changes that transform Shakespeare's dreamlike drama into a vehicle for a satire of the Eurocentric, colonial imperialism articulated only after Shakespeare's time. Césaire's choice of a

prestigious model also suggests that no corner of white culture should be immune to skeptical scrutiny. Césaire's intent is not to attack Shakespeare as a racist. He is protesting the derogatory stereotypes of "natives" that *The Tempest*'s portrayal of a bestial Caliban clearly can be exploited to support—even though Caliban's mother herself came from Europe, so that he is only a second-generation settler. *The Tempest* itself implicitly evaluates the moral worth of each character according to the depth of his or her capacity to recognize Caliban as akin to the human.

> **For Césaire's purposes, that Shakespeare's original version locates the action on an exotic island makes it well suited for adaptation as a political allegory of the Antilles.**
> **—Laurence M. Porter**

The initial suggestion to adapt *The Tempest* came from Jean-Marie Serreau, the director of Césaire's two previously staged plays. In responding, Césaire insisted on a free hand and systematically transformed the original into a study of the master/slave relationship that generates "a critical reflection on the value system of western humanism." Here we must distinguish among three, not between only two viewpoints. Although Shakespeare clearly is influenced by Montaigne and aware of Indians, to whom he refers in his text, the initial shipwreck does occur in the Mediterranean, on a voyage from Tunis back to Europe. In his depiction of Caliban, Shakespeare himself primarily followed the medieval Wild Man topos, whose topographical reference, if any, would be Europe, not the Americas: *what if* the other *were not* civilized, if he lacked his own language (except, perhaps, in an incoherent, degenerate form) and literacy? The second viewpoint, against which Césaire contends, is the post-Shakespearean, racist, colonialist viewpoint, arguing that the other is *not* civilized. And the third viewpoint, Césaire's anticolonialist one, explains that it is the Europeans' greed or ignorance, or both, which prevent them from recognizing that the other *is in fact civilized,* although different.

For Césaire's purposes, that Shakespeare's original version locates the action on an exotic island makes it well suited for adaptation as a political allegory of the Antilles. The marooned Prospero, the chief racist from Césaire's point of view, must have recalled to him the thousands of French sailors stranded in the Antilles for many months after the Nazi invasion of France. The islanders had to host and support these foreigners—many were ignorant and crudely prejudiced—while frequently receiving little but hostility and contempt in return.

Shakespeare's essentialist views, not necessarily racist themselves, can readily be used by racists concerned with preserving the status quo. In *The Tempest* Caliban's revolt is only a secondary disturbance of the social nexus, destined to be set right as are all such disturbances in Shakespeare's plays. The cast of characters foretells the outcome: Prospero's evil brother is styled "the usurping Duke of Milan," and Prospero himself, "the right Duke of Milan." That the first words of the text are "The Scene, an uninhabited Island," underscores that Caliban and Ariel are not human to Shakespeare (Ariel himself acknowledges as much with his "were I human") and therefore possess no rights beyond those granted through the indulgence of Prospero. All of Shakespeare's story is told from Prospero's viewpoint—or more accurately, when other human characters' perceptions are directly presented, they are enchanted by love or magic, or deceived in the belief that they are the sole masters of their destiny.

Prospero assumes that because he has "created" Caliban as a civilized being, Caliban himself cannot be creative. Prospero's exclusive possession of "magic" (reaffirmed in Shakespeare, ultimately exposed as delusional in Césaire) betokens his (claim to a) monopoly on creativity. If Caliban defies him, it can only be as a fallen creature, a Galatea gone wrong.

To date, comparisons of Césaire and Shakespeare have limited themselves to content, neglecting the plays' overall form. By writing entirely in prose, Césaire removes the aestheticizing distraction of verse: he makes his text entirely businesslike, to function as a denunciation of colonialism. He thus also removes the hierarchical distinction, in Shakespeare, between those who speak in prose and those who speak in verse: the plebeian sailors, Stephano, and Trinculo, as opposed to the nobles. Erasing this invidious distinction, Césaire suggests that all have the same rights. In contrast, Shakespeare's and Césaire's Prosperos share the belief that Caliban is like an animal, has no language other than what Prospero taught him, and therefore, no valid viewpoint of his own. That Shakespeare's Ariel and Caliban often speak in verse, however, ennobles them linguistically and problematizes Prospero's elitist viewpoint.

The superficial significance of Césaire's leveling of language is that Prospero's claims to absolute superiority, in his confrontations with Caliban, are undercut by presenting the discourse of both on roughly the same level of elegance. The deeper implications, suggested by Caliban's occasional demonstrations of aesthetic and linguistic sensibilities in Shakespeare, are that, applied to drama, parody tends to flatten the text, whereas in lyric and narrative, it tends to enrich it. I mean that oppositional parody (German *Gegengesang* as distinguished from *Beigesang*) functions through a rhetoric that generates an intertextuality (as an awareness in the hearer or reader) calling into question the

self-sufficient, absolute status of an original, either by confronting it with another, external text, or by exposing its own inner contradictions. Thus parody complicates. But drama, a medley of conflicting voices, forms a sort of *Sängerkrieg* in which each voice seeks to impose itself. To make its point, parody simplifies drama; it reduces these voices to two, in sharp contrast: here, racist authoritarianism versus liberationist protest. Thus Césaire, for example, eliminates the serene, loving side of Prospero, and the inquisitive, role-playing, sexually aware Miranda. He passes over the moment when Miranda is less accepting of Caliban than is Prospero, when she expresses great reluctance even to see him: "Tis a villain, sir, / I do not love to look on," an exclamation that clearly prepares her "Abhorred slave" speech so often misattributed to Prospero, who at least wishes to tolerate Caliban's presence if only to exploit him. Césaire eliminates Miranda altogether from this confrontation with Caliban, so as to focus the racist voice in Prospero.

Both authors frame the play to emphasize its artificiality, but the respective effects are quite different. Shakespeare's frame glorifies Prospero: Césaire's diminishes him. The epilogue, a convention in Elizabethan plays though not in Shakespeare's, usually asks the indulgence and applause of the audience, in a deferred *captatio benevolentiae*. Shakespeare adopts it, for once, in this play, identifying himself with Prospero in a way that has been prepared throughout the final act. Thus he may be saying farewell to the magic of artistic creation and of the theater (after *The Tempest,* he was to write no more than, at most, *Henry VIII* and a few collaborations).

Césaire, in contrast, puts his framing scene at the beginning. In it an added character, "Le Meneur du Jeu," urges everyone to don a mask corresponding to his or her chosen role. Only half a page long, this scene is fraught with suggestions. Most obviously, it demystifies Prospero as the imperialist magician who stages most of the events at will. No longer is it he who is the chief master of illusion; no longer does the colonial usurper exercise an almost unquestioned authority close to that of the playwright himself. It is the "Meneur du jeu" who actually summons the tempest, implicitly identified as a Yoruba god, Shango, although Prospero later thinks he is summoning it. The failure of Césaire's Prospero in his attempts to function as "meneur du jeu" appears most blatantly at two later moments in the play. During the wedding and at the end, Prospero cannot orchestrate the spectacle of the assimilated savage (this oxymoronic phrase betrays the unconscious bad faith of the white man's condescension) becoming gratefully subject to the authority of his colonial master.

Moreover, after having overtly subtitled his play "Adaptation pour un théâtre nègre," Césaire simultaneously introduces the racial differences that reflect the Caribbean social hierarchy of the colonial era, by specifying that Caliban is black and Ariel mulatto, and denounces these differences as superficial by using masks. Likewise, Jean Genet, for example, had a few years earlier exposed the speciousness of sociopolitical hierarchies in his anticolonial play *Les Paravants.* Two generations ago, at the height of the *Négritude* movement, or one generation ago, at the height of the assertions of black pride, one might have seen in such a gesture the dangerous, self-deluding effort to deny the reality of race and to forswear one's heritage, in a manner attacked by Frantz Fanon in *Peau noire, masques blancs.* With the hindsight of a quarter century, however, Césaire's ostensible masking of his multiracial cast of characters seems surprisingly modern, reflecting as it does a position lucidly articulated by Henry Louis Gates, Jr.: "'race' is a metaphor for something else and not an essence or a thing in itself, apart from its creation by an act of language ... if we believe that races exist as things, as categories of being already 'there,' we cannot escape the danger of generalizing about observed differences between human beings as if these differences were consistent and determined, a priori ... It is the penchant to *generalize* based upon essences perceived as *biological* which defines 'racism.'"

At the same time, Césaire's casting and costuming scene also militates against emotional identification with individual actors by members of the audience. Through the calculated artificiality of the masking, the spectators are distanced from the ensuing action, as they are in the epic theater of Bertholt Brecht, so that they will think rather than feel. Césaire seeks not catharsis, as an end in itself, but provocation and incitement to action.

Césaire then increases Caliban's stature by greatly reducing the two competing plots. In Shakespeare, the revenge plot is primary; the secondary plot, the idyll between Miranda and Ferdinand, then provides the occasion for a reconciliation; and Caliban serves mainly to enhance an atmosphere of fantasy and to glorify Prospero's clemency, which extends even to monsters. In Césaire, in contrast, it is Caliban's slave revolt, rather than the love story, that provides the principal motivation for the reconciliation: Prospero makes common cause with the other whites as natural allies who will protect him against Caliban in a racial conflict.

In its own terms—whereby Caliban has an allegorical, rather than a literal, referent—Shakespeare's play seems to imply that Utopia is impossible, and that "the notion of an ideal state is corrupt in itself." But from the historical perspective of 1969, the play could seem the harbinger of a vast imperialist expansion, anticipated even in Shakespeare's time by the first settlements in North America, the founding of the East India Company, and the development of the British navy. Then the supernatural traits of Shakespeare's Ariel and Caliban could appear a mere ruse for robbing the "na-

tives" of humanity, so as to permit enslaving and torturing them with a clear conscience; and Prospero's magic could readily seem a metaphor for the mystifying rationalization of white superiority. For a traditional Shakespearean, Césaire's race-conscious reworking (his subtitle is "Adaptation pour un théâtre nègre") may well seem crudely reductive, if not wrong-headed: it exemplifies the bad manners and narrow focus of the protester. The offensive (in both senses of the word) mainspring of Césaire's parody is a metonymic reversal of cause and effect, whereby Shakespeare's diagnosis of political ills becomes their symptom.

> **Césaire's oppositional strategies include debunking the notion that the white colonizer is benevolent; exposing his hypocrisy through psychologizing; demystifying the myth of his superiority; and presenting the colonized person as an intellectual, social, and religious being with his own language, his own network of relationships, and his own beliefs and values.**
> **—*Laurence M. Porter***

Césaire's oppositional strategies include debunking the notion that the white colonizer is benevolent; exposing his hypocrisy through psychologizing; demystifying the myth of his superiority; and presenting the colonized person as an intellectual, social, and religious being with his own language, his own network of relationships, and his own beliefs and values. Regarding benevolence, among Césaire's whites, Gonzalo appears at first glance even more sympathetic than in Shakespeare. Césaire underlines the moral contrast, already prominent in the original, between the King's virtuous counselor and the other nobles. During the storm, in Césaire's version, Gonzalo remains calm while Antonio fears hell; Gonzalo advises seeking the eye of the hurricane to secure a brief respite to find harbor, while Antonio and Sebastian ignorantly deride him as a foolish old man. [Act 2, scene 2] gives him a much greater role than in Shakespeare. Césaire suggests he is superior to the other whites because he is more in touch with nature; yet even his attitude toward the isle, which he, like the other Europeans, sees as a potential colony, will be exposed as exploitative and self-centered. His interest in finding guano to use as fertilizer betrays the lowest common denominator of materialism. His reasoning, conforming to the fallacy "like causes, like effects" ("C'est clair: une terre merveilleuse ne peut porter que des êtres merveilleux"), unwittingly mocks both himself and Shakespeare. He does not seek conquest by force, but his very restraint is based on the condescending myth of the "noble savage," a form of admiration that attempts to relegate the other to an ornamental, peripheral role. He remarks:

"si l'île est habitée, comme je le pense, et que nous la colonisons [note the self-confident, indicative mood—where French would more often use the subjunctive—in the second of two successive if-clauses], comme je le souhaite, il faudra se garder comme de la peste d'y apporter nos défauts, oui, ce que nous appelons la civilisation. Qu'ils restent ce qu'ils sont: des sauvages, de bons sauvages, libres, sans complexes ni complications. Quelque chose comme un réservoir d'éternelle jouvence où nous viendrions périodiquement rafraîchir nos âmes vieillies et citadines."

Gonzalo's opening advice to seek the eye of the storm, added by Césaire, corresponds symbolically to his aspirations, suggested later in both plays, to find an outside to power while remaining within human society. He wishes to enjoy domination without guilt, to evade the violence stirred up by inequality while continuing to benefit from it as a member of a privileged class. Shakespeare had overtly denounced this delusion (Gonzalo: . . . no sovereignty. —Sebastian: Yet he would be king on't.). However benevolent, any appropriation of the Noble Savage effectively erases the other, even via the blandness of uncritical admiration, in the very act of treating him or her as a protected species. Césaire underscores this point by ascribing to Gonzalo a comical failure to exorcise Caliban, when, after his abortive revolt, he proves unrepentant: the native who fails to recognize the white man's divinely ordained dominion must be possessed by the devil.

As for Prospero, at the conclusion of the Shakespearean play, he has provided moral enlightenment for those who wronged him (excepting the unrepentant Antonio), and a moral test for the man who will wed his daughter. Thus *The Tempest* falls into the tradition of "teaching through fear" with the aid of allegorical pageants, rituals, and visions. Patricia Merivale has brilliantly traced this tradition from Mozart's *The Magic Flute* through Hesse's *Steppenwolf* to John Fowles's *The Magus* (itself, one should add, inspired by Shakespeare). Through the internal reduplication of a traditional masque to celebrate Miranda and Ferdinand's betrothal, through an assembly of the classical deities simulated by captive spirits, Prospero prepares to reintegrate his former oppressors into a now harmonious society that includes them all, but excludes Ariel and Caliban. Having achieved this end, he has no more reason to remain on his island. Aside from a final contemptuous order, the last word of Shakespeare's Prospero regarding Caliban is "this thing of darkness I / Acknowledge mine." This statement has been ingeniously interpreted in many ways; for instance, as Prospero's acknowledgement of his own dark side. In context, however, it is a flat assertion of jurisdiction. Three conspirators have robbed Prospero, attempted to take his life, and usurp his kingdom; of these, Stephano and Trinculo are Alonso's to discipline as he sees fit—by saying as much, Prospero renounces supreme authority in the island and prepares to leave; while the surveillance and punishment of Caliban remains Prospero's responsibility. Now doubly inferior, through his condition and through his crime, Caliban begs for forgiveness ("grace") and does his part in restoring order by returning to his proper role as an obedient servant. As Shakespeare sees it, he is so radically inferior that his only reasonable course is to submit to Prospero's guidance and domination.

Césaire's Caliban, in contrast, rejects the false image that Prospero has imposed on him:

> Un sous-développé, comme tu dis,
> un sous-capable,
> voilà comment tu m'as obligé à me voir,
> et cette image, je la hais! Et elle est fausse!

When asked what he wants, he offers the simplest of self-assertive answers: to be rid of Prospero and to regain his island and his freedom. Illustrating Césaire's parodic technique of questioning the motives of the master, Caliban knows that Prospero will choose to remain before Prospero knows it himself, and in advance, defies him.

To support a status quo favorable to him, the colonialist will consciously or unconsciously adopt the philosophical position of Platonic realism or essentialism. This involves the concept of "race" (dark skin as an outward and visible sign of a presumed absolute intellectual and moral inferiority, based on biology); and the myth of a transcendent origin and destiny for the ruler (the divine right of kings, the Apostolic succession, Manifest Destiny, and the like) that justifies governing without the consent of the governed. The other becomes an empty sign whose only value is the value added through the civilizing mission of the conqueror. First, the blacks and Indians had no culture, the imperialist argument runs; then they had European culture, and upon the extent of their assimilation depended the justification of their claims to be treated as human. The lucid slave is a happy and appropriately grateful slave who endorses his or her oppression. Any resemblance between a "native's" preexisting culture and that of Europe was seen as a depraved, revolting, and fallen parody.

The lie of the civilizing mission has deceived Césaire's Prospero himself. He has become intoxicated (Caliban's term) with the exercise of an arbitrary power that would have been impossible in Europe. Nor can Prospero leave the island, as Caliban has come to understand, without admitting to himself that his work of colonization has been pointless and ineffectual; he has not won Caliban's love; he has not converted Caliban to his values; and the isle itself could function perfectly without him. By remaining, he leaves open his relationship with Caliban, and can thus avoid confronting his moral defeat. More fundamentally (Césaire has the

Hegelian Master-Slave dialectic in mind, as we shall see), he has become enslaved to his slave, which is to say, dependent on him for his own sense of identity. This ultimate dependency emerges clearly in the final psychotic break in which his identity fuses with that of Caliban: "Toi et moi! Toi-Moi! Moi-Toi!" Caliban does not heed Prospero's desperate call.

In Césaire's play, the essence of Prospero's strategy for claiming cultural superiority is the rejection of reciprocity, a willful erasure of the other. He insists on always using his native language between them, while never bothering to learn a word of Caliban's tongue. He calls Caliban's use of his own language "impolite," and interprets his slave's articulate protests in Prospero's language as breakdowns of communication that justify brutality. (Even in Shakespeare, Prospero does not seem to notice that the unredeemable Caliban reforms as soon as he is no longer tortured and can envision the prospect of eventual freedom). For Prospero, only compliance counts as a proof of understanding: "Caliban, j'en ai assez! Attention! Si tu rouspètes, la trique! Et si tu lanternes, ou fais grève, ou sabotes, la trique! La trique, c'est le seul langage que tu comprennes; eh bien, tant pis pour toi, je te le parlerai haut et clair. Dépêche-toi!" In both Shakespeare's and Césaire's versions, Prospero insults and tortures his slave during their everyday interactions, not only to bolster his apparently shaky self-worth, but also to vent the excess rage that his conscience prevents him from venting on his European enemies. "The exchange of curses between Prospero and Caliban indicates that they have much in common. What Prospero hates and punishes in Caliban is the forbidden part of himself."

Against essentialist dogmas, Caliban, like other colonized persons, adopts the perspective of psychological relativism and represents the colonizer not as monolithic, but as split, at best, between benevolent protestations and tyrannical behavior. The colonized person considers this behavior in pragmatic terms. Whether the colonizer's protestations of benevolence are hypocritical or sincere, whether they depend on a conscious or unconscious bad faith, does not matter so long as they are exposed by the contrast between words and deeds, whenever "civilization," in practice, entails violence and murder. Similarly, the imposition of linguistic and cultural relativism on the conceptual map of the colonies, by oppositional discourse, means that the empty sign of the "native" is filled, thwarting the colonist's efforts to imagine a history starting with the present, and a "land without ghosts."

Regarding *The Tempest,* critics—and Shakespeareans in particular—could reject Caliban's psychologizing since it is both anachronistic and belated, as well as ignorant of the nature of fictional representation: it attributes an unconscious to Prospero as if he were a real person, thus reflecting an outmoded, nineteenth-century understanding of literary char-

acters. Powerful, regarding Shakespeare's world as such, this objection can nevertheless alert us to the essence of Césaire's revisionist strategy. In Shakespeare, Prospero feels justified in his ill treatment of Caliban because the latter, as he openly admits, had tried to rape Miranda: "Thou didst prevent me. I had peopled else / This isle with Calibans." Césaire's Caliban, in contrast, diagnoses in Prospero the phenomenon of psychic projection: "Violer! violer! Dis-donc, vieux bouc, tu me prêtes tes idées libidineuses. Sache-le: je n'ai que faire de ta fille." Césaire, to be sure, preserves ambiguity regarding Caliban's desires by having Miranda characterize him as "l'affreux Caliban, lequel me poursuit de ses assiduités et hurle mon nom dans ses rêves idiots!" But overall, Césaire's satire depends on questioning Prospero's motives. That these motives are represented as unconscious, refutes Ariel's argument that the colonizer can change for the better, and that *attentisme*—opposition rather than resistance—is therefore justifies.

Both Shakespeare's slaves will choose compliance, Ariel from the beginning. Faced with an insurmountable power differential, he only begs for justice and does not protest that justice deferred is justice denied. Césaire depicts him similarly, but with a message that becomes pointed when Ariel argues with Caliban. From the Martinican leader's viewpoint, Ariel's subservient attitude is explained by the preferential treatment he has received from Prospero, and from the lure of eventual emancipation that Prospero has dangled before him. In short, with reference to slavery in the United States, Caliban is the "field Negro" and Ariel is the "house Negro," the white-collar slave (so to speak) who, unlike Caliban, need not do heavy work with his hands; with reference to the Caribbean, Ariel is the collaborationist mulatto class, privileged owing to his lighter skin.

Shakespeare's Caliban moves from attempted resistance to compliance, seeking "grace" from his master. His initial intransigence causes a typically Shakespearean disturbance of the social nexus followed by a restoration of equilibrium, when the naturally inferior subject submits to his rightful lord. Césaire, in contrast, decenters Prospero by endowing Caliban with greater lucidity than his master. To dramatize it, he adds to Shakespeare's version (where Caliban may not even be aware of Ariel's—or, for that matter, Ferdinand's existence) a formal debate scene between the two slaves to reinforce his portrait of them as rational adults, not children whose weak impulse control makes them require constant surveillance and discipline. Moreover, "splitting the ambivalence" of the oppressed person's reactions between Ariel and Caliban allows the creation of a character (Césaire's Caliban) who is entirely and inspiringly resolute in his defiance:

CALIBAN

. . . a quoi t'ont servi ton obéissance, ta patience

d'oncle Tom, et toute cette lèche? Tu le vois bien, l'homme devient chaque jour plus exigeant et plus despotique . . .

ARIEL

. . . Ni violence, ni soumission. Comprends-moi bien. C'est Prospero qu'il faut changer. Troubler sa sérénité jusqu'à ce qu'il reconnaisse enfin l'existence de sa propre injustice et qu'il y mette un terme . . .

CALIBAN

. . . Que la conscience naisse à Prospero? Autant se mettre devant une pierre et attendre qu'il lui pousse des fleurs!

Césaire has inverted Shakespeare's terms so that it is the master, not the slave, who proves irredeemable (a condition underscored by Prospero's choosing to remain on Caliban's isle at the end). In the context of the 1960s, Caliban's temptation to violence recalls Frantz Fanon. Confronting Prospero, however, weapon in hand, Caliban will not strike unless his master defends himself, and Prospero taunts "Tu vois bien que tu n'es qu'un animal: tu ne sais pas tuer." As at the conclusion, Prospero equates civilization with murder. In contrast, Ariel's nonviolence recalls Martin Luther King. Together, these two figures reflect Césaire's ambivalence, determined by his own ambiguous, problematical role in founding the D.O.M. so as to preserve a French presence, like Prospero's at the end of the play. Césaire insisted that he saw himself in both Caliban and Ariel. Caliban himself eventually abjures violence in favor of separatism, which he—unlike Césaire, as a political leader—can achieve at once: Caliban's outcome may involve wish-fulfillment.

In Shakespeare, Caliban never appears on stage at the same time as either Ariel or Ferdinand (except when, in [act 3, scene 2], Ariel remains invisible and unrecognized). For Césaire to depict Caliban and Ariel's debate is to represent them as part of a social class, to deexoticize them, and to reinforce their added allegorical function as a symbol of oppressed peoples everywhere. Caliban's cries of "Uhuru!" ("Freedom!" in Swahili), "Freedom now!," and his allusion to Malcolm X, who dropped his white "slave name," ("Appelle-moi X. . . . Chaque fois que tu m'appeleras, ça me rappellera le fait fondamental, que tu m'as tout volé et jusqu'à mon identité! Uhuru!," in his first confrontation with Prospero, insert him into an international framework that, by implication, dignifies his revolt as a potential inspiration for others. The change of title from "*The Tempest*" to *A Tempest* similarly identifies Caliban's revolt as only one among many.

Shakespeare's play, like Césaire's, dramatizes all four possible courses of action for the slaves: collaboration, opposition, resistance, and separatism. But the added debate scene in Césaire makes these choices explicit, reversing Shakespeare's hierarchy of lucidity, in which Prospero alone possesses insight while the slaves have only instinct. It is Prospero's will to power, not the slaves' reactions, that Césaire wishes to characterize as unreasoning and instinctual.

From Caliban's viewpoint, Prospero's only superiority is technological; and his technology serves not to advance civilization but only to enable oppression. Faced with noncompliance, technology cannot negotiate or compromise, but only destroy. When Stephano and Trinculo complain of the mosquitoes, shortly after having joined Caliban in his assault on Prospero, Caliban explains: "C'est pas les moustiques. C'est un gaz qui vous pique le nez, la gorge, et donne des démangeaisons. Encore une invention de Prospero. Ça fait partie de son arsenal . . . anti-émeutes." The colonizer enjoys a purely material ascendancy; he lacks both moral authority and contact with nature, the ground of our existence. Nature is alien to him: in the psychotic break that concludes the play, Prospero fancies that the South American opossums gathering round his cave are leering at him, defying his civilizing mission. He reacts by firing his revolver wildly in all directions, killing all the inoffensive animals, with the cry "Je défendrai la civilisation!" Thus the naked brutality underlying colonialization is unmasked, and "civilization" imposed on others emerges again as only one more form of violence.

The Tempest, as far as we know, is one of only two plays whose plot was entirely invented by Shakespeare. When contrasted to the keen precision of the history plays, the fantasy setting of *The Tempest* can seem to imply that blacks have no history of their own because they have had no organized civilization, and that, therefore, they are not fully real. From there, it takes only a step to see a justification for benevolent despotism. Césaire, in a 1969 interview with L. Attoun, joins the opposing minority of those whom Berger called "the hard-nosed" as opposed to the "sentimental" interpreters of Prospero:

Je m'insurge lorsque l'on dit que c'est l'homme du pardon. Ce qui est essentiel chez lui, c'est la volonté de puissance. A mon avis, Prospero est l'homme de la raison froide, l'homme de la conquête, autrement dit, c'est un portrait de l'homme européen . . . campé en face du monde primitif colonisé.

Il ne faut dissimuler qu'en Europe, le monde de la raison conduit inévitablement à un totalitarisme.

En face, il y a Caliban, l'homme proche de la nature dont les communications avec elle ne sont pas encore interrompues, il participe à un monde merveilleux. Il est en même temps l'homme de la révolte, c'est un héros positif exactement comme chez Hegel: c'est l'esclave qui est le plus important, car c'est lui qui fait l'histoire.

In other words, the colonizer sees the slave as immanent, and himself, as transcendent. By invoking Hegel's Master-Slave dialectic, Césaire reverses these terms. It is not conquest but liberation that enables transcendence.

Shakespeare's Prospero, a superior person in Italy, whose only fault, perhaps, was a reluctance to exercise power there, returns home as soon as he is able. Césaire's Prospero, in contrast, is the white emigre who seeks in mastery over the colonized a compensation for his failure to compete successfully in his homeland. He can do to Caliban what Antonio had done to him. Therefore Prospero has no desire to return to Italy, even when the opportunity arises. As the only European in a "primitive" society, he can imagine himself as a culture hero orchestrating nature. With the supposed moral imperative of the white man's burden, Prospero's second major argument in defense of his "civilizing mission" is that there was nothing in the Third World before, that the "natives" are, culturally speaking, *tabulae rasae*. What the *Négritude* movement had tried to point out tactfully and indirectly, Césaire now affirms with vehemence, using Caliban as his spokesman: one person's "state of nature" is no more than another person's ignorance. Shakespeare had given Caliban no language until Mathilda taught him hers; you could even perversely claim that two signs of his superiority to many of the characters—his speaking in verse and his lyrical response to the magic of the isle—derive from his having had a lofty model, and that he himself deserves little credit for an independent linguistic sensibility. Césaire's Caliban, however, knows his mother's language, is fluent in French, and has at least shreds of English and Swahili.

Césaire's ending remains indeterminate, since Ariel has been freed but Caliban officially has not. Césaire thus implies that there may always be enslaved peoples somewhere in the world, but that they can preserve their dignity by continuing to fight for liberation. That Caliban can range untrammeled over the island at the conclusion, celebrating his autonomy, depends on Césaire's own magic. Unrealistically—in political terms—he eliminates from his version the acolytes through whom power is mediated (that is the mulattoes) throughout the colonial history of the Caribbean, and the commercial powers that presently keep the Third World in a state of economic dependency. Ariel and the Europeans (other than Prospero) simply depart. Then Césaire's Caliban has only to reject the myth of his inferiority for it to disappear. Thus he figures a mental liberation that, Césaire knows, must precede a political one.

Reflecting the awkward, embarrassing, and continuing presence of the French, Césaire's Prospero remains on the island, with his weapons and his "mission civilisatrice," and Caliban cannot drive him away. So Caliban remains involuntarily within the European orbit, but he is no longer of it. His master/slave symbiosis with Prospero now exists only in the latter's imagination. Indeed, Césaire suggests that French power will ultimately fade, when he has Prospero momentarily sense the vanity of power: "Tout cela passera un jour comme l'écume . . . Ma puissance a froid!" (one recalls that Caliban's major task in Shakespeare was to gather firewood). At the end of the play, Césaire's Caliban goes his own way, pursuing his own, unmediated projects, and the last words of the text are "La liberté!" The same words in the monster's comical, drunken, and deluded shout at the end of Shakespeare's [act 2, scene 2]—in the powerfully ironic context of absolute submission to a substitute, less worthy master—have been transformed by Césaire into the lucid affirmation of a newfound dignity.

How will this dignity be exercised, and how will it lead eventually to full independence? The one major character that Césaire added to the central play, the Yoruba trickster-god Eshu, suggests a gradualist approach in laying the groundwork for a new, black society, through the rediscovery of authentic, African cultural values. The white master, in Césaire's version, hopes to effect cultural genocide by erasing from the Brave New World of colonial empire all traces of the substrate of black civilization. Prospero has designed the betrothal ceremony for Miranda and Ferdinand to transmit his colonizer's values to the next generation, "leur *inculquer* [emphasis added] le spectacle de ce monde de demain: de raison, de beauté, d'harmonie, dont, à force de volonté, j'ai jeté le fondement." But as captive spirits enact Prospero's spectacle, they are interrupted by Eshu. Prospero's show has been ordered up, whereas Eshu's appearance is spontaneous. He bursts in, uninvited, with an obscene song that uncovers, beneath the ceremonial pomp, the realistic sexual dimension in marriage (one recalls how anxious Shakespeare's Prospero has been, before the wedding, to preserve Miranda's virginity) and more generally, the "democracy of the body," where all masters and slaves are equal. Eshu is a god who shows us that no humans are gods. He transforms a ritual affirming Prospero's power into a carnival that calls hierarchy into question.

From an autobiographical perspective, Prospero's show recalls the Eurocentric, classical education that Césaire received in Paris in the 30s. In contrast, Eshu represents an invigorating infusion of African and Caribbean cultural vitality from Jacques Roumain, Senghor, and others. Eshu is not just a clown: he represents the Yoruba religion from West Africa, which provided the major component of the syncretistic religions that, borrowing also from Catholicism, preserved black culture in the New World as voodoo (Haiti), santería (Cuba), and condomblé (Brazil). The irrepressible Eshu—like the Yoruba god of thunder, Shango, invoked by Caliban's hymns—implies that the slaves of the black diaspora retain an authentic cultural heritage far richer than that imagined by Shakespeare.

FURTHER READING

Criticism

Arnold, A. James. "Césaire's Negritude in Perspective." In his *Modernism and Negritude: The Poetry and Poetics of Aimé Césaire,* pp. 21-49. Cambridge, MA: Harvard University Press, 1981.

   Examines the influence of the Harlem Renaissance, Marxism, and various European, Caribbean, and African writers on the development of Césaire's political and artistic concerns.

Dayan, Joan. "Playing Caliban: Césaire's *Tempest.*" *Arizona Quarterly* 48, No. 2 (Winter 1992): 125-45.

   Discusses issues surrounding colonialism and historical representation in Césaire's *A Tempest.*

Hawkins, Hunt. "Aimé Césaire's Lesson about Decolonization in *La Tragédie du Roi Christophe.*" *CLA Journal* XXX, No. 2 (December 1986): 144-53.

   Examines Césaire's skepticism regarding decolonization and the actions of King Christophe as portrayed in *The Tragedy of King Christophe.*

Pallister, Janis L. "Return." In her *Aimé Césaire,* pp. 1-28. New York: Twayne Publishers, 1991.

   Provides extended analysis of *Return to My Native Land.*

Smith, Robert P. "Aimé Césaire Playwright Portrays Patrice Lumumba Man of Africa." *CLA Journal* XIV, No. 4 (June 1971): 371-9.

   Examines Césaire's portrayal of Patrice Lumumba in *A Season in the Congo.*

Smith, Robert P., and Robert J. Hudson. "Evoking Caliban: Césaire's Response to Shakespeare." *CLA Journal* 35, No. 4 (June 1992): 387-99.

   Examines the Caliban character in Césaire's adaptation of Shakespeare's *The Tempest.*

Wolitz, Seth L. "The Hero of Negritude in the Theater of Aimé Césaire." *Kentucky Romance Quarterly* 16 (1969): 195-208.

   Discusses the ideological rhetoric and didactic function of heroic protagonists in Césaire's dramatic works.

Interviews

Melsan, Annick Thebia. "The Liberating Power of Work." *UNESCO Courier* (May 1997): 4-7.

   Césaire comments on the affective power of poetry and the necessity for mutual recognition among differing cultures.

Additional coverage of Césaire's life and career is contained in the following sources published by Gale: *Black Literature Criticism; Black Writers,* **Vol. 2;** *Contemporary Authors,* **Vols. 65-68;** *Contemporary Authors New Revision Series,* **Vols. 24 and 43;** *DISCovering Authors Modules: Multicultural* **and** *Poets;* **and** *Major Twentieth-Century Writers.*

Tom Clancy
1947-

American novelist and nonfiction writer.

The following entry presents an overview of Clancy's career through 1996. For further information on his life and works, see *CLC,* Volume 45.

INTRODUCTION

Clancy is the best-selling author of popular thrillers featuring detailed military weaponry, high-tech espionage, and enthralling geopolitical crises. With the publication of his debut novel, *The Hunt for Red October* (1984), Clancy became a literary phenomenon, attracting a large and devoted audience that includes statesmen and high-ranking military officials. Several of his novels—*The Hunt for Red October, Patriot Games* (1987), and *Clear and Present Danger* (1989)—have been adapted into blockbuster Hollywood films. Considered an originator of the techno-thriller, a genre of contemporary fiction embodying combined characteristics of the thriller, spy fiction, and science fiction, Clancy's patriotic, strongly anti-Communist novels appeal to the atmosphere of national pride, military supremacy, and political conservatism at the end of the cold war.

Biographical Information

Born Thomas Lanier Clancy Jr. in Baltimore, Maryland, Clancy was raised in a middle-class home by his father, a mail carrier, and mother, a department store employee. An avid reader as a child, he soon developed a fascination with military machines and space technology. He attended local Roman Catholic schools, then enrolled at Loyola College in Baltimore, where he earned a bachelor's degree in English in 1969. While at Loyola, Clancy joined the U.S. Army Officers' Training Corp, but poor eyesight prevented him from serving during the Vietnam War. Clancy married Wanda Thomas the summer after his college graduation and immediately began work as an insurance agent in Baltimore; Hartford, Connecticut; and then Owings, Maryland, at a small insurance firm owned by his wife's grandfather. After purchasing the family company in 1980, Clancy found spare time to study military journals and revive his desire to write. Four years later he published *The Hunt for Red October* through the Naval Institute Press, a publisher of scholarly titles that had never printed an original work of fiction. Through enthusiastic word-of-mouth endorsements, including a fortuitous comment by President Ronald Reagan who praised the book as "a perfect yarn," *The Hunt for Red October* shot up best-seller lists to become an unexpected hit.

The incredible popularity of Clancy's first novel was duplicated by *Red Storm Rising* (1986), produced with the help of war game expert and friend Larry Bond, *Patriot Games, The Cardinal of the Kremlin* (1988), *Clear and Present Danger, The Sum of All Fears* (1991), *Without Remorse* (1994), *Debt of Honor* (1994), and *Executive Orders* (1996). With the enormous international sales of his novels, Clancy became one of the most popular and financially successful authors of the 1980s. Three of his novels have been adapted into films—*The Hunt for Red October* in 1990, starring Sean Connery and Alec Baldwin, *Patriot Games* in 1992, and *Clear and Present Danger* in 1994, both starring Harrison Ford. Clancy has also produced several nonfiction studies of military organizations and tactics, including *Submarine* (1993), *Marine* (1996), *Airborne* (1997), *Armored Cav* (1997), *Fighter Wing* (1997), and *Into the Storm* (1998). He currently resides at his estate overlooking the Chesapeake Bay in Huntingtown, Maryland.

Major Works

Clancy's techno-thriller novels revolve around description

of advanced military technology and intelligence operations employed by American government agents to subvert the nefarious machinations of international antagonists—mainly Soviets, Middle Eastern extremists, and terrorists. While the instruments of war and espionage figure prominently in his fiction, Clancy's novels also feature heroic male protagonists whose devotion to country and family underscore their superior moral authority and the triumphant destiny of the United States and its allies. In most of his books this central character is represented by Jack Ryan, a brilliant, though modest and happily married ex-Marine, CIA consultant, stockbroker, and scholar with a doctorate in economics and history. Ryan first appeared in *The Hunt for Red October,* a suspenseful thriller about the defection of a Soviet nuclear submarine under the command of Marko Ramius, a discontented Russian officer who seeks asylum in the United States. Pursued by both Soviet and American navies, Ramius survives a harrowing underwater chase, torpedo assaults, and a mutinous plot, and is guided to safety by Ryan and Bart Mancuso, captain of the American submarine *Dallas.* Clancy's second novel, *Red Storm Rising,* describes a future world war waged between the United States and Soviet Union with conventional weapons. The plot is set in motion when a key Siberian oil refinery is destroyed by Muslim fundamentalists, causing an energy shortage in the Soviet Union. The Russians respond by orchestrating a terrorist attack on their own people, used in turn as a pretext for invading Central Europe and Iceland while seizing Middle Eastern oil fields. Unlike other Clancy novels, Ryan is absent from the story and the protagonist role is shared by several American servicemen. Ryan reappears in *Patriot Games* to rescue members of the British royal family during a botched abduction scheme conducted by the Ulster Liberation Army, a fictional Maoist faction of the Irish Republican Army. Ryan is knighted by the British and befriended by the Prince of Wales, and returns to teaching at the U.S. Naval Academy in Annapolis, Maryland, where members of the ULA track him down to take revenge on him and the visiting royal family. In *The Cardinal of the Kremlin,* Ryan is embroiled in a complicated espionage scheme involving a jeopardized American spy in the Kremlin and the high stakes race between the United States and Soviet Union to deploy a "Star Wars" anti-ballistic missile defense system. *Clear and Present Danger* turns to the subject of powerful South American drug cartels and the American war on drugs. In this book, a U.S. president tacitly approves aggressive covert military operations against Colombian cocaine farmers and drug traffickers. When Ryan, now acting deputy of the CIA, discovers the unconstitutional American involvement, he intervenes to rescue betrayed U.S. soldiers cut off deep in the Colombian jungle to perish with their secrets. *The Sum of All Fears* follows the drastic efforts of an anti-Zionist faction to undermine a recently forged Vatican treaty, proposed by Ryan, to end hostilities among Israelis and Arabs. The terrorists, an amalgam of Arab extremists, European mer-

cenaries, and a Native American activist, detonate a pilfered nuclear weapon in Denver, Colorado, during an NFL Super Bowl game, bringing many casualties and nearly drawing the United States and Russia into war. *Without Remorse* features another major Clancy protagonist, John Kelly, a former Navy SEAL who returns to Vietnam with specially trained Marines to rescue American POWs. Set in the early 1970s, Kelly abducts a ruthless Soviet agent in Vietnam to force a diplomatic solution and, at home, secretly exterminates a Baltimore drug ring to avenge the brutal murder of his girlfriend. Due to his role in covert activities, John Kelly becomes John Clark with a new identity provided by the CIA. Jack Ryan reemerges in *Debt of Honor* as a national security advisor, then vice president of the United States, at the center of an international crisis stemming from strained economic relations between the United States and Japan. War breaks out when the Japanese government, newly installed with imperialist corporate tycoons, sabotages American financial markets, invades the Mariana Islands, sinks U.S. submarines, and threatens to use nuclear weapons. Ryan counterattacks with high-tech weapons and sophisticated espionage, involving the participation of John Clark from *Without Remorse.* In the end, however, a Japanese kamikaze pilot crashes into the U.S. Capitol, killing nearly everyone in government except Ryan, who thus becomes the next U.S. president. *Executive Orders* begins where *Debt of Honor* leaves off, placing Ryan at the helm of a crippled government while the newly formed United Islamic Republic, a merger of Iran and Iraq, conquers Kuwait and Saudi Arabia and plans to invade Afghanistan and Pakistan with the support of India and China. While struggling to reconstruct the leadership of the United States and the world, Ryan also contends with a deadly outbreak of the Ebola virus and a scheming Montana militia group. Clark returns in *Rainbow Six* (1998), now resigned from the CIA and leading an elite group of international counterterrorists based in England. Immediately successful in quelling three terrorist attacks in quick succession, the group draws unwanted attention from Soviet, Australian, and American factions.

Critical Reception

Clancy is a preeminent innovator of the techno-thriller genre. The huge commercial success and consistently intriguing plots of his action-packed novels distinguish his work from that of other contemporary mainstream authors. While most critics find little literary merit in his work, few deny his remarkable talent as a storyteller and impressive knowledge of state-of-the-art military and communications technology. His detractors are quick to cite many flaws in the quality of his writing, particularly uninspired prose, stereotypical characters, and verbosity. Many critics also object to pervasive examples of jingoism, racism, misogyny, and uncritical acceptance of authority and Judeo-Christian morality in his novels. A staunch conservative, Clancy is hailed by many

Republicans and right-leaning readers as a proponent of nationalism and a powerful American military spokesperson. Others view his glorification of advanced weaponry and American ascendancy as a backlash against anti-military sentiment following the Vietnam War and as propaganda for the military-industrial establishment. Despite such criticism concerning his literary skill and political ideals, Clancy has captivated legions of readers with his highly entertaining brand of escapist literature.

PRINCIPAL WORKS

The Hunt for Red October (novel) 1984
Red Storm Rising (novel) 1986
Patriot Games (novel) 1987
The Cardinal of the Kremlin (novel) 1988
Clear and Present Danger (novel) 1989
The Sum of All Fears (novel) 1991
Submarine (nonfiction) 1993
Without Remorse (novel) 1994
Debt of Honor (novel) 1994
Executive Orders (novel) 1996
Marine (nonfiction) 1996
Airborne (nonfiction) 1997
Armored Cav (nonfiction) 1997
Fighter Wing (nonfiction) 1997
Into the Storm (nonfiction) 1998
Rainbow Six (novel) 1998

CRITICISM

Walter Isaacson (review date 11 August 1986)

SOURCE: "Red Storm Rising," in *Time*, August 11, 1986, p. 64.

[*In the following review, Isaacson offers a generally favorable assessment of* Red Storm Rising.]

"What modern combat lacks in humanity, it more than makes up for in intensity," observes a reporter aboard an American frigate that has just repelled a Soviet missile attack. The same could be said of Tom Clancy's new military thriller, **Red Storm Rising**. In this version of blocs in conflict, the most compelling actors are the high-tech weapons that Clancy portrays with deadly accuracy.

The author, a Maryland insurance broker with a passion for military hardware, blipped onto the national radar screen with his 1984 novel, **The Hunt for Red October**, a tale of a defecting Soviet nuclear submarine and its conflicted crew.

Published by the Naval Institute Press, known primarily for academic and technical journals, the book was praised by Ronald Reagan as "the perfect yarn," became the sleeper of the year and stayed on the best-seller lists for seven months. With his new novel, Clancy has climbed out of the water. This time his subject is nothing less than World War III.

When Muslim fundamentalists disable a crucial Soviet oil refinery, Moscow works out a cold-blooded scheme to prevent the country's economy from collapsing: KGB agents blow up a group of Soviet schoolchildren visiting the Kremlin; the U.S.S.R. then blames the attack on West German terrorists, launches an invasion of Central Europe, captures Iceland and rushes the navy into action in an attempt to control the North Atlantic sea-lanes—all as a ruse for grabbing Persian Gulf oil facilities. The pretext serves Clancy better than it does the Soviets: it provides a fine backdrop for his account of strategies and shoot-outs.

Laymen tend to envision a future world war as instant Armageddon. Clancy knows better. Instead of staging yet another atomic holocaust, he imagines a scenario that accounts for much U.S. defense spending: a protracted showdown arising from a conventional Soviet attack on NATO. Although each side briefly contemplates "going nuclear," neither is willing to reach for the button; instead, the fighting involves a land war on the plains of Germany and games of hide-and-seek on the high seas.

For true military aficionados, the book offers an abundance of informed tidbits: an appearance by the secret radar-evading F-19 Stealth fighter plane, which the Pentagon has refused to admit exists even after one apparently crashed in California last month; descriptions of advances in antisubmarine weapons, among them passive sonars towed by computer-packed surveillance ships; and a stark examination of the critical role that Iceland plays in the naval strategy of the Western alliance.

Most of the material in the book was gathered from a number of unclassified sources and journals. The Navy provided unofficial support, allowing Clancy to visit nuclear submarines and spend a week aboard a frigate. To help simulate the look, sound and feel of combat, he worked with Larry Bond, an ex-naval officer who developed a war game called Harpoon. In it, players simulate naval engagements, using the newest and most sophisticated arms.

Throughout the war, missile and torpedo firings are described in harrowing (and sometimes reassuring) detail, and conversations among radar technicians are loaded with the requisite Pentagon jargon. Clancy convincingly shows the importance of electronic intelligence—gathered by satellites, ships, planes and submarines—to modern warfare. Yet it is an old-fashioned human component that proves to be a critical factor. One of the multitude of subplots involves four Americans wandering the barren terrain of occupied Iceland, reporting Soviet movements on a primitive two-way radio. At first, allied analysts are skeptical about the information, but it turns out to be crucial. Here Clancy goes off automatic pilot; there are even a few romantic interludes, as if to remind the reader that the most brilliantly designed war games must depend, sooner or later, on that unpredictable computer called the human brain.

For Homo sapiens fans, the Iceland episodes will be far too short—they are a mere fraction of the 43-chapter epic. The book has a variety of heroes and villains in its complex weave of plot strands, but the diffuse locales and the lack of an appealing main character make for a somewhat choppy narrative. Intrigues within the Politburo are interspersed with tense moments in the control rooms of submarines deep in the Atlantic, arguments among analysts in Scotland, daring assaults by fighter pilots on satellites, feats by covert commandos and battlefield maneuvers by intrepid tank commanders. The tightly focused **Hunt for Red October** allowed Clancy to develop the psychological and even religious motivations of the main characters. For too much of **Red Storm Rising,** the humans are obscured by the afterburn of their weapons systems.

Oddly enough, it is this very flaw that enhances the credibility of **Red Storm Rising.** World War III, by most postulates, is not likely to involve a grand Tolstoyan sweep of personal valor. Arsenals and tactics might indeed be set in motion by the frailties of flesh-and-blood players, but once launched the lethal machines would take on a life of their own—almost like characters in a novel. That possibility, vividly rendered, is what gives Clancy's book such a chilling ring of truth.

Anthony Hyde (review date 26 July 1987)

SOURCE: "Shadow of a Gunman," in *Book World—The Washington Post,* July 26, 1987, pp. 1-2.

[*In the following review, Hyde praises the entertainment value of* Patriot Games, *though concludes that the novel is "well below Clancy's previous efforts."*]

Tom Clancy's first two books were not so much novels as extended commentaries on war games—which I mean as a compliment, of course, not a complaint. In sitting down to play out Midway, I can't think of anyone else I'd rather have at my elbow, offering advice, except Admiral Spruance himself. But in both those early books, the deck was very much stacked in Clancy's favor. The map board was in place, the pieces arranged, the rules well established. Again, there's

nothing wrong with that, but it's interesting to see how Clancy has fared now that he's designed a game all on his own—for **Patriot Games** is about terrorism, where there are no rules, no uniforms and no set-piece battles at all.

Things begin well enough. Jack Ryan, Clancy's previous hero in **The Hunt for Red October,** is walking across St. James's Park in London when a splinter group of the IRA attempts to snatch Prince Charles, Princess Diana and Prince William. There's a lot of shooting and blood, but Jack is a good, decent man and an ex-Marine and so he plunges right in and saves the day, despite taking a bullet in the shoulder for his trouble.

A spirited opening. But immediately the book bogs down: we are forced to suffer, along with Jack, through 200 pages of his hospitalization and convalescence. Indeed, all that enlivens this section of the novel is the Royal Family. Of course, they have to be brought in—Jack, after all, has saved *two* princes of the realm. Graciously, Her Majesty knights him (leaving Maggie and Ron to sort out the legal technicalities) and then lays on a special tour of the Tower of London. This is ludicrous, of course, but it could be worse; you can more or less keep Prince Charles and Prince Philip separate in your mind as you read.

Clancy's difficulty here is that he attempts to assimilate the Royals to American values through the locker room—Charles is an all right guy because he flew Phantoms—and the sitcom: Elizabeth and Philip are old married hands straight out of *Father Knows Best,* while Di is happily preggers again. This is fine, as far as it goes, but it overlooks the crucial fact that these people are Brits. Clancy doesn't seem to understand that royal gratitude, in such circumstance, would be genuine enough, but certainly wouldn't extend to wanting Jack as a *friend.*

Still, he finally escapes them, and returns home to Annapolis. There, after a few cloying scenes of suburban bliss—Jack's wife is also expecting—the bracing American air finally gives the plot some get-up-and-go. The terrorists, it seems, are intent on revenge, and when Charles and Diana, on an American tour, drop by Jack's place for barbecue, they take their chance. Soon, we're back in a world of Redeye missiles, Browning automatics and police car chases. On this ground, few people can beat Clancy, and he gives us a bang-up climax with plenty of helicopters, dead bodies and a rousing sea chase—the prince, you'll be happy to know, acquits himself well.

There are two problems with this. The first is literary. In the end, Clancy is not quite sure which game he wants to play. Every once in a while, **Patriot Games** tries to be a spy story, but the intrigue is so feeble and artificial that Clancy quickly gives you the solution to his mysteries and reverts to the pyrotechnics of the adventure yarn. Here, he's more confident, but by dividing his attention he prevents the action from ever gaining momentum.

The second problem is even greater and yet, in a curious way, it saves the book. I can't remember when I last read a novel so politically naive. Clancy apparently subscribes to every single myth in which authority cloaks itself. They're all here: God, the home, the family; law and order; friendly British bobbies and stalwart NCOs—not to mention Her Majesty and Their Royal Highnesses. Of course, the values embodied in these myths are important enough, but surely Clancy doesn't need to take them so literally. The office of the presidency is no doubt worthy of respect, but I'd still be skeptical of Reagan's news conferences: and though I have the greatest appreciation for the extraordinarily fine, and delicate, tradition of authority represented by the monarchy, this doesn't require me to believe that the Princess of Wales has any more brains than Miss Universe.

Still, one should give Clancy his due. He has the virtue of his vice—enthusiasm. And though one can argue that this is the most dangerous virtue of all, it is the moving force in his book. I didn't believe a word of *Patriot Games,* but I certainly believed that Clancy believed, and that's enough to carry you through.

In short: *The Hardy Boys Meet the Royals*—well below Clancy's previous efforts, but some pop in the end. Beach bags should be bulging with it all through the summer.

Ross Thomas (review date 2 August 1987)

SOURCE: "White Knight, Green Villains," in *New York Times Book Review,* August 2, 1987, p. 11.

[*In the following review, Thomas offers a favorable review of* Patriot Games.]

Just after Jack Ryan, a 31-year-old American tourist and former Marine officer, joins his doctor wife and 4-year-old daughter in a park on the very first day of his first visit to London, he hears an explosion. Or "BOOM!" as Tom Clancy puts it. Two heavily armed men are attacking a just disabled Rolls-Royce. Ryan automatically classifies them as Irish Republican Army terrorists and instinctively, or at least without mulling it over much, blindsides, disarms and cripples one of them and kills the other, but not before being wounded himself in a shootout that takes place within hailing distance of Buckingham Palace.

Upon waking in a hospital, Ryan learns that the limousine's passengers were none other than the Prince of Wales; his wife, Princess Diana, and their 4-month-old infant. For his bravery, Ryan is knighted by an understandably grateful Queen Elizabeth; the British start calling him Sir John, and the reader, disbelief by now totally suspended, is still barely three dozen pages into Mr. Clancy's long and bloody novel about terrorism, revenge and how any number of complicated things really work.

Prince Charles, visiting Ryan in the hospital, confesses to being disturbed by press reports that question his own inaction during the attack. In a burst of robust camaraderie that might make some royalists wince, Ryan assures the Prince: "What do reporters know about anything? They don't do anything, for crying out loud. . . . You're not some dumb kid, sir. You're a trained pro. Start acting like one." Prince Charles, spine stiffened, thanks Ryan gravely and leaves with a presumably firmer step and steadier eye.

Back in Annapolis, where he teaches history at the Naval Academy while his wife performs eye surgery, Ryan slowly recovers from his wound and politely resists the blandishments of the C.I.A., which wants to recruit him for his brilliantly analytical mind.

Meanwhile, the terrorist band that calls itself the Ulster Liberation Army (U.L.A.), and is referred to as "a Maoist offshoot of the Provos," is dreaming up yet another terrorist operation that will wreak revenge on Jack Ryan in America and also discredit the rival Provos. It's an elegant but flawed scheme that drives Ryan straight into the willing arms of the C.I.A. There he uses the agency's enormous resources in an attempt to track down the terrorists who have nearly destroyed him and his family.

Sandwiched in between all this action are erudite and clear-as-day descriptions of such things as weapons large and small, satellite photography, eye surgery, the interstices of the Naval Academy and what may seem to some like the longest flight the Concorde ever made from Heathrow to Dulles International Airport.

Mr. Clancy's ability to describe mechanisms and how they work with absolute clarity carries over into his characterization. Not only does he make his protagonist, Jack Ryan, a white knight—both literally and figuratively—but he also makes his fellow heroes just as stalwart and nearly as stuffy.

Save for a lone American black, the villains in *Patriot Games* are all deeply dyed Irish ones, devoid of any compassion or hatred of social injustice or whatever it was, if anything, that turned them into terrorists in the first place.

Yet by sticking to the explicit and obvious, Mr. Clancy—well known as the author of the best sellers *The Hunt for*

Red October and *Red Storm Rising*—has written a novel that crackles more than it putters and should quite please those who, given the choice, will pick steadfast black and white over doubtful gray every time.

Robert Lekachman (review date 31 July 1988)

SOURCE: "Making the World Safe for Conventional War," in *New York Times Book Review,* July 31, 1988, p. 6.

[*In the following review, Lekachman offers praise for* The Cardinal of the Kremlin, *which he considers "by far the best of the Jack Ryan series."*]

Jack Ryan, the engaging, all-American hero of Tom Clancy's previous spy thrillers, *The Hunt for Red October* and *Patriot Games,* is entangled here in the high-stakes battle between America and the Soviet Union over the development of Star Wars. Mr. Clancy, a high-tech freak, permits no doubts about the feasibility of a space shield ultimately capable of rendering nuclear weapons obsolete. He is equally certain that, despite Soviet protestations to the contrary, our adversaries have committed more resources to Star Wars technology than we have.

Many technical obstacles impede the superpowers' progress toward a nuclear-free world in which wars will presumably be fought the old-fashioned way—via retail rather than wholesale slaughter. In order to achieve this balance of power, lasers, mirrors and computer software must operate in flawless coordination. After all, a leaky space shield may be worse than none at all if the enemy missiles that penetrate it provoke retaliatory strikes that are promptly followed by counterretaliation. It is needless to add that the country that masters space weaponry first will enormously enhance its bargaining position.

This is the logic that lies behind *The Cardinal of the Kremlin,* which is by far the best of the Jack Ryan series. In it, Mr. Clancy cuts back and forth from the United States to Moscow, from Pakistan to Afghanistan, touching down at various other locales in between. Nevertheless, it is always clear where we are, since the adventure on which Mr. Clancy sends us is of high quality. And while his prose is no better than workmanlike (the genre does not, after all, attract many budding Flauberts), the unmasking of the title's secret agent, the Cardinal, is as sophisticated an exercise in the craft of espionage as I have yet to encounter.

According to Mr. Clancy, the Russians and the Americans each lead and lag in some aspects of the exotic Star Wars technology. Both sides deploy their finest scientists and engineers in search of solutions to problems so intricate only

genius-class I.Q.'s can comprehend let alone solve them. The American ace is a certain Maj. Alan Gregory, a 29-year-old graduate of West Point who is the author of a doctoral dissertation on high-energy physics that is immediately classified Top Secret. Awed colleagues compare him to Stephen Hawking and Freeman Dyson. Like his Soviet opposite number, Col. Gennady Bondarenko, Gregory is devoted to achieving his country's technological primacy.

Research of the sort that Gregory and Bondarenko conduct is all very well, but theft can yield results a lot quicker. The American spy in the Kremlin, who is entrusted with this chore and who has been passing important information to the C.I.A. for three decades, is a highly decorated hero of World War II, the Great Patriotic War in Soviet parlance. His opposite number in America, who operates undercover for the Soviet Union at the laboratory where Gregory does his research, is a neurotic lesbian. Another of America's human assets turns out to be a man called simply the Archer, a heroic leader of the Afghan resistance who directs an assault on a Soviet research center that is temptingly close to the Afghan border.

Mr. Clancy keeps his readers well abreast of current politics and psychological theories as well as the latest technology. Part of the intrigue of the novel concerns the intricacies of power struggles within the Kremlin, where a character who resembles Mikhail Gorbachev does battle with an intractable ideologue modeled on Yegor Ligachev, the Soviet leader's second in command. A document very much like the Intermediate-Range Nuclear Forces treaty waits to be signed. An unreformed K.G.B. perfects the sensory-deprivation torture pioneered by Len Deighton in his 1963 novel, "The Ipcress File." And when American special forces are compelled to mount a "wet operation" in order to rescue Major Gregory from Russian agents, they fly in a psychiatrist to cope with the trauma that is induced by killing another human being. (Although this latter is a pleasant conceit, Mr. Clancy does not always come up with believable plot twists. In one of the less credible episodes, for example, his hero, Jack Ryan, lectures no less a personage than the Soviet General Secretary on the superiority of space shields over old-fashioned MAD—Mutually Assured Destruction.)

Mr. Clancy's publisher recently announced that he has signed a multi-book contract. I look forward to each one of the volumes yet to come, not least because their appearance will testify to Jack Ryan's continuing success in averting the next world war.

Ross Thomas (review date 13 August 1989)

SOURCE: "Crackdown in Colombia," in *Book World—The Washington Post,* August 13, 1989, pp. 1, 8.

[*In the following review, Thomas offers a favorable assessment of* Clear and Present Danger.]

In his search for a fictional clear and present danger that the nation might attack with its latest military hardware, Tom Clancy, novelist laureate of the military-industrial complex, has discovered the drug cartel that operates out of Medellin, Colombia, and that is getting enormously rich from America's apparently insatiable demand for cocaine.

And a rousing adventure it is, too, what with a fake military hanging aboard a Coast Guard cutter, plus several squads of U.S. Army infantrymen, all superbly trained killers, who are covertly infiltrated into Colombia only to be abandoned by a feckless national security adviser to the president.

There is also the reappearance of Clancy's favorite hero, Jack Ryan, U.S. Marine, stockbroker, history professor, knight of the British realm and now next in line to be the CIA's deputy director.

Not yet 40, Ryan reflects on his career with understandable satisfaction: "He's made his money in the brokerage business—and the money was still growing; he needed his CIA salary about as much as he needed a third shoe—gotten his doctor's degree, written his books, taught some history, made himself a new and interesting career, and worked his way to the top."

But before Ryan makes his presence known rather late in the novel, Clancy introduces us to the president, who's pretty much of a bubblehead, the slippery director of central intelligence and the first Jewish director of the FBI, who is assassinated while on a supposedly secret mission to Colombia.

Thus, the cat is set amongst the pigeons, and from there on the action intensifies. An American fighter pilot is ordered to shoot down unarmed planes suspected of drug smuggling. The U.S. infantrymen, Latinos all, are ordered to eliminate a number of coca leaf processing plants along with any number of Colombia peasants who, to me, immediately brought to mind visions of Juan Valdez.

But the novel's two most interesting antagonists are the pseudonymous Mr. Clark of the CIA and the equally pseudonymous Senor Gomez, a KGB-trained agent, now in the pay of the drug lords. Clark is a professional CIA killer, who admits he hasn't been given much work lately. Gomez, on the other hand, has only contempt for his rich employers, and is convinced that he himself could be a far more cost-effective lord of all drug lords.

Clancy displays his usual fascination and familiarity with the latest war toys, which he describes with gee-whiz enjoyment: "They're testing a new system called LPI—Low Probability of Intercept—radar . . . because of a combination of frequency agility, reduced side-lobes and relatively low power output, it's damned hard to detect the emissions from the set."

But what I appreciate even more about Clancy is his ability to crawl inside the heads of his characters and reveal their innermost thoughts because, I suspect, he is right on the mark. The low-wattage president, for example, is much given to musing aloud, either to himself or to the mirror, and his thought fragments are chilling. "'It's time those bastards were taught a lesson,' the President thought aloud." Some 250 pages later: "'Okay,' the President of the United States told the mirror. 'So you bastards want to play.'"

In yet another moment of introspection, the president thinks about how the world really works: "Terrorists, criminals, all manner of cowards . . . regularly hide behind or among the innocent, daring the mighty to act . . . but sometimes they had to be shown that it didn't work. And that was messy, wasn't it? Like some sort of international auto accident . . . But how the hell do I explain that to the American people?"

The might of the United States—Army, Navy, Coast Guard, Air Force, CIA and FBI—is employed to make that international auto accident happen. And to avoid having those Americans who do the killing perceived as mercenaries off on a bloody spree, Clancy gives virtually all of them a friend, lover or relative who has been devastated by drugs. This is known as taking out insurance.

Still, Clancy brings it off because he is a writer with the ability to make a convoluted tale as clear as the directions on a match folder. This is no small art, and if his asides and philosophical ramblings make your teeth hurt, you can always chuckle, sigh or ignore them and get on with a cracking good yarn. I know I did.

David Wise (review date 13 August 1989)

SOURCE: "Just Say Nuke 'Em," in *New York Times Book Review,* August 13, 1989, p. 9.

[*In the following review, Wise offers a tempered assessment of* Clear and Present Danger, *which he describes as "a ponderous thriller."*]

"It was odd, Cutter thought, how ideas grow. First the President had made an intemperate remark after learning that the cousin of a close friend had died of a drug overdose."

Next thing you know, Vice Adm. James Cutter, the President's national security adviser (and a certified baddie in Tom Clancy's new techno-thriller, *Clear and Present Danger*), has a chat with the C.I.A.'s senior spook. Before you can say Jack Armstrong, a team of Army commandos is assassinating workers at coca-processing sites in the jungles of Colombia and Navy smart bombs are blowing up the haciendas of the Medellin cocaine cartel, killing women and children as well as the evil drug lords. The body count is high.

Clearly, the new President has gone far beyond Nancy Reagan's "Just say no." A covert war has been launched against the drug cartel, and all the sophisticated weaponry, laser beams and enormous firepower so dear to Mr. Clancy's heart are unleashed.

At first, the reader might erroneously conclude that the author approves of these murderous and illegal activities—illegal because nobody bothered to tell Congress, and the President's complicity remains fuzzy. Echoes of Iran-contra are clear and present.

Ryan not only saves the American troops— or what is left of them—in the jungles of Colombia, he saves *Clear and Present Danger* from being just another beach thriller to enjoy among the sand fleas.
                                                    —*David Wise*

Aboard a Coast Guard cutter, where men are men, the legendary captain Red Wegener stages a mock execution to wring a confession from a suspected murderer and enforcer for the druggies. The suspect's arm is broken for good measure. Army commandos threaten to feed a drug-running pilot to a monster alligator, a method of eliciting information not contemplated by the Supreme Court in its Miranda decision. We are left with a sneaking suspicion that Mr. Clancy is not a staunch supporter of due process.

Wrong. Enter Jack Ryan, the C.I.A. good guy, who gradually uncovers the covert plot. Ryan not only saves the American troops—or what is left of them—in the jungles of Colombia, he saves *Clear and Present Danger* from being just another beach thriller to enjoy among the sand fleas.

The issues raised are real ones, and a jump ahead of the headlines. Does the drug traffic threaten America's national security? And if so, is the Government justified in murdering the suppliers? Jack Ryan is troubled by these questions (although not too much), and so he and the rest of us should be. It is not beyond belief, after all, that a President would encourage the C.I.A. to send covert teams against the

Medellin chiefs. Ryan concludes that this might be all right if Congress declared war on the drug cartels.

For Clancy fans, it probably won't make the least bit of difference that his dialogue has not improved one whit since *The Hunt for Red October.* One sample will suffice. A Cuban intelligence agent working for the drug lords beds down the vulnerable, widowed secretary to the Director of the F.B.I. Their pillow talk includes this exchange:

> "'It isn't just police work. They also do counterespionage. Chasing spies,' she added.

> "'That is CIA, no?'

> "'No. I can't talk about it, of course, but, no, that is a Bureau function.'"

And Mr. Clancy's readers won't be disappointed in the exhaustive list of gadgetry. He grooves on the Ground Laser Designator and the Varo Noctron-V night-sighting device, which help the C.I.A. drop the GBU-15 laser-guided bomb from a carrier-launched A-6E Intruder medium attack bomber. And so on, and on. Mr. Clancy lovingly describes the hardware of death; he is an indecent docent in a gallery of horrors. Heads roll (literally), body parts fly, blood flows.

It all takes a long, long time. The plot moves slowly, like a great, clanking clock, on the order of Big Ben. We see the gears turn and hear the machinery creaking and wonder if the big hand will ever get round. The patient reader is rewarded, however, the last hundred pages move with the speed of light.

But the excitement comes too late. Mr. Clancy has produced a contradiction in terms: a ponderous thriller. It won't bother his devotees, or the sand fleas.

Elliott Abrams (review date 16 August 1989)

SOURCE: "Operation Showboat: A Real War on Drugs," in *The Wall Street Journal,* August 16, 1989, p. A10.

[In the following review, Abrams offers a favorable assessment of Clear and Present Danger.*]*

Tom Clancy's *Clear and Present Danger* begins with a president sitting in his high-backed, bullet-resistant chair in the Oval Office, grumbling to his national security adviser. "I promised the American people that we'd do something about this problem and we haven't accomplished . . . ," he says, crossly buttering a croissant.

Mr. Clancy's new thriller revolves around the question: What do we do about drugs, when all the speeches are over? For Mr. Clancy's president, code name Wrangler, the answer is calling up the military in a covert operation after drug lords murder a high-ranking U.S. official. Soon, there's an undeclared war under way in Colombia, while the talk continues in Washington. Mr. Clancy revels in the proficiency, bravery and successes of the servicemen, but enough goes wrong with Operation Showboat to leave the reader wondering whether military action would ever work in the real world.

Which is about where the debate stands now in Washington: Civilians muse about hitting the traffickers hard, while the top brass at the Pentagon resists involvement as bitterly as it does a budget cut. The generals seem to fear taking on an ill-defined, and perhaps hopeless, task. They worry about the increased temptation for corruption. They view anti-drug activity as police work, if not indeed social work. And they point to the federal forces already mobilized and stepping on each other's toes: The Justice Department, the CIA, the U.S. Customs Service, the Coast Guard and the newly formed drug czardom.

One can certainly agree that as long as Americans demand more and more cocaine, and pay endless billions for it, no action on the supply side can possibly succeed. Demand reduction is the only long-term solution. Yet the generals, and others who counsel action only on the demand side, are wrong. In the short run, tough action to interdict supply routes, blow up laboratories and capture and extradite traffickers is critical. It will reduce the supply of drugs and, perhaps even more important, give the countries fighting on the front lines—Colombia, Peru and particularly Bolivia—the moral support and the resources they need to resist the immense power of the drug lords.

Since it is our citizens who, after all, create the cocaine market, do we have the right to urge those fragile Latin democracies to wage war on drugs if we plan to take a pacifist stance? Military action is no panacea, but it is an essential tool in this war as in any other.

Mr. Clancy grasps well the need to help, not blame, democracies fighting hard against drugs. Says his FBI director, later murdered by the drug mafia: "Colombia is trying damn hard to run a real democracy in a region where democracies are pretty rare . . . and you expect them to do—what? Trash what institutions they do have? . . . go fascist again to hunt down the druggies just because it suits us?" What helps to make *Clear and Present Danger* such compelling reading is a fairly sophisticated view of Latin politics combined with Mr. Clancy's patented, tautly shaped scenes, fleshed out with colorful technical data and tough talk.

Mr. Clancy's convincing portrait of Cuba under Castro comes through the comments of the novel's foulest character—a former Cuban intelligence officer who now works for the drug chieftains. Credit the author with a good nose for news about to happen. We read the ex-officer's musings and memories of the Cuba he left behind just as the headlines have reported Stalin-style show trials in Havana. Never mind Castro's most pious disclaimers, and the hanging of his close associates: Cuba is heavily involved with drug trafficking, and the new wave of repression is entirely consistent with the brutal, cynical communist system Mr. Clancy's villain recalls with great fondness.

The Cuban reflects happily that today "the yanquis had not yet discovered within themselves the courage to act in accordance with their power." It is clear that Mr. Clancy thinks this leaves the world a far less safe place.

Clear and Present Danger is another in Mr. Clancy's Jack Ryan series, focusing on the escapades of Ryan, his friends and family, and the assorted villains he meets. In *The Hunt For Red October, Red Storm Rising* and *The Cardinal of the Kremlin,* the bad guys were some type of communist: in *Patriot Games* they were terrorists. A few other familiar characters are also reintroduced, although Mr. Clancy minimizes character development and concentrates on his story—to put it politely.

Faithful fans of Mr. Clancy will not be disappointed with Ryan's new incarnation as "DDI," official lingo for deputy director of the CIA for intelligence analysis. Like Mr. Clancy, Ryan shows no signs of slowing down, much less losing his grip. It takes about five chapters to get all the characters straight, after which you won't stop until you hit the last pages, when Ryan and the president confront each other over the usefulness and legality of covert operations. With its allusions to events past and present, *Clear and Present Danger* makes absorbing reading.

Morton Kondracke (review date 28 July 1991)

SOURCE: "A Missile for Every Occasion," in *New York Times Book Review,* July 28, 1991, pp. 9-10.

[*In the following review, Kondracke offers a favorable assessment of* The Sum of All Fears. *According to Kondracke, "In its plotting, vividness and suspense, this is Mr. Clancy's best book since* The Hunt for Red October."]

One of Tom Clancy's many gifts as a writer of thrillers is that he constantly taps the current world situation for its imminent dangers and spins them into an engrossing tale. In 1984 and 1986, before United States-Soviet relations had begun to thaw, Mr. Clancy wrote *The Hunt for Red Octo-*

ber, in which the defection of a Soviet submarine captain nearly provokes World War III, and *Red Storm Rising,* in which a conventional World War III nearly leads to a nuclear war. In 1987, when Muammar el-Qaddafi seemed a greater menace than the Kremlin leadership, Mr. Clancy explored America's vulnerability to international terrorism in *Patriot Games.* In 1988, in *The Cardinal of the Kremlin,* he took the rivalry between Mikhail Gorbachev and his old-guard opposition, added some Afghan freedom fighters and a Star Wars arms race, and once again conjured up the specter of Armageddon. In 1989, with the cold war really ending, he mixed the then-trendy drug war with rogue White House operations a la the Iran-contra affair and cooked up a threat to constitutional liberty in *Clear and Present Danger.*

And now, after a two-year lull, *The Sum of All Fears* is exactly that: a treasure trove of geopolitical terrors. The cold war is over and the Gulf war has made a Middle East settlement possible. Ah, but what's peace for us good people is disaster and betrayal for the bad people, including Palestinian terrorists, European ultra-radicals and former East German secret police and military scientists. They get together, obtain a slightly damaged Israeli nuclear weapon and try to turn it into an H-bomb that, once exploded, will cause hardliners in the United States and the Soviet Union to seize control from panicked leaders and plunge the good guys into all-out war.

That's the main plot, based on the all too plausible present-day danger of nuclear proliferation. But it's another of Mr. Clancy's gifts that he can keep several sub-plots and sub-sub-plots in the air at the same time. In this book he's outdone himself. There is almost as much submarine action here as in *Red October.* There is as much intra-Soviet intrigue as in *Cardinal of the Kremlin,* more Washington intrigue than in *Clear and Present Danger* and all the terrorist and antiterrorist action of *Patriot Games.* There's also some conventional combat, as in *Red Storm Rising,* and even a touch of drug peddling.

In fact, Mr. Clancy does more than just keep all of these balls in the air. He makes his multiple sub-plots vivid by creating a set of characters to bring each one alive. The nuclear plot features a devout Palestinian guerrilla commander who's dying of cancer, a Red Army Faction survivor who's lost his wife and children to the cause of world revolution, one Arab and one German scientist who grow to respect each other even though their relationship is destined to end in murder, plus an American Indian militant who likes football.

The submarine plot is carried by an overambitious captain and his wise black executive officer, plus assorted admirals and enlisted men back from previous novels. In Moscow, there's a reformist president modeled on Mikhail Gorbachev, plus a dedicated democrat who's also a C.I.A. mole, and an

honest K.G.B. man. In Washington, there's an arrogant President, a scheming female national security adviser, a lazy C.I.A. director and dozens of F.B.I. men, C.I.A. men, Secret Service agents and military officers. Mr. Clancy's characters are drawn with enough individuality so that, even if they aren't forever memorable, one doesn't need a score card to keep them all straight.

Back again as our intrepid hero is Jack Ryan, who has risen from his roles as a C.I.A. analyst and Naval Academy instructor to be Deputy Director of Central Intelligence, Middle East peacemaker, the target of White House plotting and, ultimately, moral giant and savior of the world. Mr. Clancy has been criticized by some reviewers of his previous books for making Ryan an unbelievable paragon. This time out Mr. Clancy has given him flaws. Ryan smokes and drinks too much. He ignores his wife and children. He resents not getting credit for his achievements. He yells at people. He even suffers a bout of impotence. (Yes, for the first time, there's sex in a Tom Clancy novel.)

Mr. Clancy uses Ryan's flaws to carry his story along—his temper, for example, almost brings on the Apocalypse—but in the end they are just not credible. In moments of truth, we know Ryan is going to perform heroically, and he does. In his next novel (there are hints that it will be about a Japanese attempt to conquer the world economically), Mr. Clancy ought to keep Ryan a Superman in mufti.

As in all his previous novels, this one bulges with technological verisimilitude. In the earlier books, Mr. Clancy taught his readers more than any but experts could possibly absorb about submarine operations; air, land and sea war strategy; satellite photography; ballistic missiles and missile defense; small unit tactics, and the highest of high-tech communications. In this novel, he does the same with nuclear bomb fabrication, though he says in a postscript that he has altered some details so no one could use the novel to build a bomb.

I am not qualified to judge whether Mr. Clancy has got his technology right, but in a field I do know—Washington journalism—he is dismally inaccurate. The wicked national security adviser gives Washington's top investigative reporter and White House correspondent a false story accusing Ryan of sexual infidelity and professional ineptitude. The reporter, whom Mr. Clancy describes as a man of integrity and experience, writes the story as told to him without ever checking with Ryan or anyone else, even though he knows he is being manipulated. The story is leaked on "deep background," which normally means that no source is to be used; Mr. Clancy wrongly says the term means that an "administration official" can be cited.

When the falsehood of the story is made plain to him, the reporter then confidentially reveals the name of his source to a colleague of Ryan's, instead of blowing open the whole seamy (and also politically important) article in his newspaper. Mr. Clancy correctly understands that unsourced leaks are often used in bureaucratic warfare in Washington, and that some reporters will print anything. What he doesn't appreciate is that good journalists always check.

This is not a huge flaw, nor are such implausibilities as having all the Middle East's key disputes resolved in a matter of weeks and having the master terrorist carelessly drop fake identity cards with his picture on them in a waste basket near the body of a man whose throat he has just slashed, even if he does expect all the evidence to be incinerated in a nuclear blast. If there is anything significantly wrong with this book it is that it's just too long—and, at three pounds, almost too heavy for a beach bag.

In its plotting, vividness and suspense, this is Mr. Clancy's best book since *The Hunt for Red October.* To sustain interest, however, we simply do not have to watch each turn of the lathe and each shaving of plutonium that goes into making an H-bomb. This book remains a whiz-bang page-turner, but to be honest, not all the pages get read.

Bob Shacochis (review date 4 August 1991)

SOURCE: A review of *The Sum of All Fears*, in *Los Angeles Times Book Review,* August 4, 1991, pp. 3, 8.

[*In the following review, Shacochis offers praise for* The Sum of All Fears.]

OK, all of you despondent Desert Storm junkies, cheer up—the adventure continues (for a whopping 800 pages; none of this *Wham, Bam, Thank You, Saddam* stuff). *The Sum of All Fears* is the perfect panacea for anyone experiencing withdrawal symptoms from the Gulf War, unwilling to trust the White House to co-produce the sequel.

Whoever spends the bucks on Tom Clancy's sixth novel should be able to figure out how decent people become drug addicts, since Clancy is to storytelling what a voracious crack habit is to cocaine, firing narcotic blasts of 100% pure plot right down your pipes. And yet, if you're hankering for a little Escapist Lit from the guy, forget it; his MO is to animate the newspapers, enriching the radioactive wastes of international headlines with the intent of making himself the unequaled superpower of the best-selling universe.

To start with, our noblest aspirations, our prettiest dreams for the latest of our splendid little wars have come true. Is the would a safer place now? You bet. And it would be even safer, muses our hero, Jack Ryan, deputy director of Cen-

tral Intelligence, "if we could just do something about the Israeli side . . . It would be nice, he thought, to set the whole area to rest."

Nice, yeah. Count me in. Jack has a terrific idea, which he floats before the President's chief of staff and national security adviser. What if we turn Jerusalem into an International City of God, an ecumenical DMZ, administered by representatives of the three most trouble-making religions with dibs on the place, and persuade the Vatican to help us broker the deal, get the Swiss guard to police those holy mean streets, permanently station an armored U.S. Cavalry regiment on Israeli soil, give back the occupied territories, and that's that, and Earth can take a well-deserved vacation from the routine of 9-to-5 carnage?

Everybody agrees: nice. Yet, it's the same old pipe dream until the Arabs finally wise up, do the Martin Luther King thing, the Gandhi thing, organize a nonviolent sit-in, even singing "We shall overcome," to protest the plan of 10 fundamentalist rabbis to rebuild Solomon's Temple. While the CNN cameras roll, the Israeli police force fires rubber bullets into the demonstrators, who react, even as they are dying, with another chorus of the civil-rights anthem. A cross-wired Israeli captain goes berserk, murdering a young Palestinian leader in cold blood, close up and personal, for all the home viewers to see.

Oops, Israel's claim to moral superiority flies right out the geopolitical window. "A country whose police murder unarmed people has no legitimacy," pontificates the national security adviser. "We can no more support an Israel that does things like this than we could have supported Somoza, Marcos, or any other tin-pot dictator."

Not exactly words resonating with truth, but Jack Ryan's Vatican initiative—called Project PILGRIMAGE—jumps to the top of the list on Washington's dance card. The Russians come on board, natch. The Saudis, the Swiss. President Bob Fowler, a Quayle-like clone destined to become the Great Peacemaker (and later, in the clutch, the Crown Prince of Inadequacy), does some plain-talking: "We let Israel know that they either play ball or face the consequences, and that we're not kidding this time." Israel acquiesces. The deal is cut; the applause is euphoric.

But hold on, there's a 50-kiloton fly in the ointment. Not everybody, it seems, appreciates the New World Order; for instance, at least four terrorists nostalgic for the Cold War harbor a death wish for the Zionist Promised Land. Their agenda's fairly strict, and when they come into possession of a thermonuclear device—well, you knew it was going to happen some day—they detonate the sucker. In the ensuing confusion, Washington and Moscow prepare to nuke the daylights out of each other.

If Tom Clancy could only write as astutely as he narrates, if he found people as compelling as he finds facts and mechanisms and systems—weapons; cybernetics; intelligence-gathering systems—then perhaps Clancy would be our Tolstoy, rather than a Michener of the spook parade, the Stephen King of national-security affairs.

His characters are Front Page People, never penetrating their stereotypes, never shedding their prepackaged traits and images, and they can offer a reader no more emotional involvement than you might invest in a good Super Bowl team that's not your own. A lot of men are required to prove their manhood here, which I suppose explains why Clancy foreshadows his plot development with all the subtlety of a female dog in heat. And speaking of females, the author apparently doesn't like them much, especially the small-breasted variety.

Still, the scope is awesome, few writers have the muscle for it, and who wants to read Virgil at the beach anyway, when you can dig into Clancy's stash and blow your head right off with blockbusting excitement. What I'm saying is, whatever your gender, *The Sum of All Fears* will appeal to the most boy part of you.

Hey, Clancy: thumbs up, power weenie. You kicked ass.

Louis Menand (review date 16 September 1991)

SOURCE: "Very Popular Mechanics," in *The New Yorker,* September 16, 1991, pp. 91-2, 94-5.

[*In the following review, Menand provides analysis of* The Sum of All Fears *and Clancy's popularity.*]

I counted fifty-six references to coffee in Tom Clancy's new thriller, *The Sum of All Fears.* It's a long book, nearly eight hundred pages; still, that's a lot of coffee. Clancy's people need the caffeine, though, because freedom needs their vigilance. They are the intelligence analysts, fighter pilots, submariners, air-defense monitors, radar and sonar operators, secret-service agents, and other military, paramilitary, and civilian personnel on whose alertness the national security depends.

To describe Clancy's feeling for these people as respect is inadequate. He loves them; and his love includes an attentive sympathy for the special demands that a constant state of readiness, and the many cups of coffee needed to maintain it, can make. It is not unusual for one of his characters, in the midst of a sudden crisis that requires his complete concentration and on whose outcome the future of our way of life just might depend, to recall with a small but gratifying

sense of relief that he has recently made a trip to the bathroom.

There is something charming about a writer who, out of sheer infatuation with his subject, is capable of this sort of unaffected tactlessness, and it will be pretty clear to most readers of *The Sum of All Fears* that whatever it is Tom Clancy has, success has done nothing to spoil it. Clancy's own story is by now fairly well known. Less than ten years ago, he was a Maryland insurance agent; it was a steady job, but he wanted to be a paperback writer. He wrote in the time he could spare from his work and his obligations to his family, and his first effort was published, in 1984, by the Naval Institute Press, a noncommercial publisher in Annapolis which had never handled an original work of fiction before. The novel was *The Hunt for Red October,* a story about a Soviet nuclear submarine whose officers defect to the United States and bring their boat along with them. Soon after it came out, a Washington lobbyist (or so the story goes) sent a copy to the Reagans as a Christmas present. Nancy Reagan read it and passed it along to the President, who pronounced it "the perfect yarn." This well-placed endorsement (from a man who, whatever his shortcomings, does know something about yarns) helped make the book a national best-seller. Clancy quickly produced four more thrillers featuring the protagonist of *Red October*—an intelligence expert named Jack Ryan. They became best-sellers, too; the last of them, *Clear and Present Danger,* which appeared in 1989, is reported to have sold more copies than any other novel published in the nineteen-eighties, and Clancy now probably earns more for his books than any other writer in the world. But his work retains its homemade character; he is still, in his relation to the world he has imagined, a slightly awestruck amateur.

The clearest sign of this is his abiding admiration for professionalism. His heroes are daring and manly enough, but they are not cowboys. They are organization men, highly trained, disciplined, clean-cut, and honest, men who know how to push the edge of the envelope without tearing it. They are impatient with weak authority, but disrespectful of it only when a point of personal honor is at stake—just as they are blunt and sometimes vulgar but never (by their own lights, at any rate) tasteless or cruel.

Their professionalism makes them decent. It also makes them, in spite of their wholesomeness, a little bit cynical: because they know how hard it is to live up to principles, they know how easy it is to cheat on them, and this knowledge makes them at times acutely aware that the world is probably not entirely worthy of their dedication to its survival, and that there is something faintly absurd about their insistence on maintaining such high standards of conduct.

Clancy sees—and the perception is, I think, the one genuine imaginative accomplishment of his writing—that this cynicism must be a part of the kind of characters he creates. But he cannot share it. He cannot allow virtue to be its own reward; he must allot the virtuous every earthly reward, too. And he cannot allow crimes against virtue—even the most pitiful and craven ones—to escape retribution. He wants the world to be worthy of his heroes' exertions. He knows that he is writing fairy tales, but cannot keep from begging us, like Peter Pan, to clap our hands and make it so.

[Clancy's] heroes are daring and manly enough, but they are not cowboys. They are organization men, highly trained, disciplined, clean-cut, and honest, men who know how to push the edge of the envelope without tearing it.
—Louis Menand

The idea in *The Sum of All Fears* is that the bad fairies have got hold of a nuclear bomb and it's up to the good fairies to keep them from starting the Third World War. The bad fairies here are a sorry group; after all, the world's supply of bad fairies has fallen off rather sharply since 1984. In *The Hunt for Red October* Clancy was able, without departing much from official attitudes, to portray the leaders of the Soviet Union as unwashed thugs, people who routinely concluded policy disputes by having the losers shot. In *The Sum of All Fears,* though, the Cold War is over, and the Soviets have become friendly and well intentioned. The Soviet military, in particular, is praised for its competence and integrity, and the Soviet President, a Gorbachev-alike called Narmonov, behaves much more nobly in the book's climatic episode than his American counterpart, a vain, ineffectual fellow (he's a liberal) called Bob Fowler.

The book begins by tidying up the one nagging trouble spot left in the new world order. It has Jack, now the deputy director of the C.I.A., whip up a peace plan for the Middle East. Jack's brainstorm is pretty simple—but then that's always the way with the really big ideas, isn't it? His plan is to evacuate the Jewish settlements on the West Bank and hand it over to the Palestinians; make Jerusalem a dominion of the Vatican governed by an interfaith troika of clerics and policed by the Swiss Guard; and guarantee Israel's security by stationing American troops there permanently. The Israelis (in an extremely feeble concession to reality) are made to have a few reservations about this plan. But the rest of the world is enthusiastic, the Israelis come to realize that it's in their interest to cooperate, and the treaty is signed by the major powers, under the vague auspices of the Pope, in a ceremony at the Vatican.

Although some people—President Fowler, for instance—are ready to beat their swords into plowshares on the spot, Jack knows better. As he observes during a diplomatic chat with a Saudi prince (over coffee that is described as "thick, bitter, and hideously strong"): "Sir, the only constant factor in human existence is change."

Two teams of spoilers quickly (well, fairly quickly) emerge. The first is made up of President Fowler and his national-security adviser, a former political-science professor from Bennington called Liz Elliot, with whom the President happens to be sleeping. (They're both single; it's not that kind of book.) They are weak, ambitious people who resent Jack's brilliance and professionalism; they refuse to give him the credit he deserves for his peace plan, and plot to drive him out of the Administration.

The other bad fairies are a multicultural coalition of terrorists led by the notorious Qati, a fanatical anti-Zionist. His principal cohorts are Günther, a former member of a defunct German terrorist outfit, and Marvin, a Native American activist. Not a very impressive array of villains, you say. But suppose these folks were to come into possession of an atomic bomb that had been lost by the Israelis in the Golan Heights during the 1973 war; and suppose they were to buy the services of a former East German nuclear engineer, and he were to use materials from that bomb to manufacture a much more powerful hydrogen bomb; and suppose they were to take this hydrogen bomb to Denver and try to detonate it at the Super Bowl in the hope of triggering a nuclear war between the United States and the Soviet Union—not because that would solve the Palestinian problem or restore the rights of Native Americans but just because they are nasty, resentful people who, thanks in part to a series of personal disappointments, are filled with general misanthropy. Suppose these things (and throw in a couple of submarines), and you have supposed *The Sum of All Fears.*

For this is the most doggedly straightforward of stories. There are no puzzles to be solved and no secrets to be uncovered. We can't completely anticipate everything that is going to happen, of course, but as soon as something does happen we are almost always told everything we need to know about it. This directness pushes events forward without distraction and serves the book well when the climatic scenes are finally reached. But it is a very long way to the climax, and for the greater part of the book the sense of slowly unravelling mystery which one associates with most spy stories and other kinds of thrillers is almost entirely absent.

This is so, I think, because Clancy appears to have, as a writer, no technical resources for producing mystery. His chief device is to report a conversation and leave out the most important part. Here, for example, is Jack Ryan coming up with his peace plan during a meeting with members of the President's staff (they're drinking Coke, by the way, which, in addition to the caffeine, provides a quick energy boost):

> "You thinking about something, Jack?" Alden asked.
>
> "You know, we're all 'people of the book,' aren't we?" Ryan asked, seeing the outline of a new thought in the fog.
>
> "So?"
>
> "And the Vatican is a real country, with real diplomatic status, but no armed forces . . . they're Swiss . . . and Switzerland is neutral, not even a member of the UN. The Arabs do their banking and carousing there . . . gee, I wonder if he'd go for it . . .?" Ryan's face went blank again, and van Damm saw Jack's eyes center as the light bulb flashed on. It was always exciting to watch an idea being born, but less so when you didn't know what it was.
>
> "Go for what? *Who* go for *what?*" the Chief of Staff asked with some annoyance. Alden just waited.
>
> Ryan told them.

He doesn't tell *us,* though. It doesn't matter, since the plan is explained several chapters later and its details have no bearing on anything that happens in the interim. But it's Clancy's idea of suspense.

Jack himself, though he's a kind of superagent, is essentially an upright guy who's supposed to save the day without breaking the rules, and this means that he's never a particularly vivid character. One gets, for instance, almost no sense of what he looks like. It doesn't help much to learn, in one of the love scenes he's given (with his wife, and expressly for the purpose of making babies), that his hands are "strong but gentle." He is several times compared, by his nemesis Liz Elliot, to James Bond, and it's clear that we are supposed to regard the comparison as inaccurate, and an insult to Jack.

What is true of Jack is true of the rest of Clancy's people: they're cut out carefully along the dotted lines. If the story requires a professor, he will be absent-minded; if it requires a young cop, he will be gung ho and a little undisciplined. Politicians are fickle and self-serving, and reporters are jaded scandal-hounds. Asian-Americans have faith in education; Israelis are abrasive; Jesuit seminarians are more worldly-wise than they let on and don't mind sneaking a small glass of sherry before lunch.

That Clancy's world is mostly male is probably for the best, because when he creates a female character he cannot, for reasons that are not obvious to me, resist humiliating her. A female television reporter refuses to wear a bulletproof vest when she goes to interview a terrorist being staked out by the F.B.I., and when the terrorist is shot in the face and killed in front of her, his blood soaks her blouse. She is made to vomit from the shock and to rip off her shirt, "forgetting that there was nothing under it." Another woman, a convicted murderer, hangs herself in her cell after removing her dress and bra. A third, a housewife, is stripped and assassinated, and her body is sliced into pieces with a chain saw. The major female character, Liz Elliot, is grasping, contemptible, and a sexual predator. Her plots, needless to say, explode in her face, and at the end of the book her reaction to the global crisis she is supposed to help the President deal with is so hysterical that she has to be sedated.

This is all standard action-adventure stuff, no doubt, and it wouldn't be worth mentioning if it were not so unlike Clancy's treatment of his male characters. Plenty of his men die violently, and their deaths are recounted in detail that is certainly pointless enough ("The bullet entered the back of Fromm's skull, soon thereafter exiting through his forehead"), but Clancy has a kind of boyish respect for them all. Even his terrorists are accorded a certain dignity; they are, after all, by virtue of their bravery and dedication, psychotic mirror images of his heroes. But the women are punished. And not only the bad ones. Jack's wife, Cathy, though she's a crackerjack eye surgeon and supermom, is the subject of what must be one of the strangest lines ever written to conclude a love scene: "And then it was over, and he lay at her side. Cathy pulled him against her, his face to her regrettably flat chest."

Clancy's reputation is based not on his mastery of any of the standard storytelling techniques but on his enthusiasm for hardware: he is the inventor of the "techno-thriller." Before Clancy, technology in spy thrillers usually took the form of doomsday machines and fantastic gadgets to whose mechanics (except for guns) the hero was indifferent. ("*Try* to pay attention, 007.") What Clancy discovered when he wrote **The Hunt for Red October** was that instead of writing "The submarine started to submerge" you could write

> The reactor coolant pumps went to fast speed. An increased amount of hot, pressurized water entered the exchanger, where its heat was transferred to the steam on the outside loop. When the coolant returned to the reactor it was cooler than it had been and therefore denser. Being denser, it trapped more neutrons in the reactor pile, increasing the ferocity of the fission reaction and giving off yet more power. Farther aft, saturated steam in the "outside" or nonradioactive loop of the heat exchange system

emerged through clusters of control valves to strike the blades of the high-pressure turbine—

and people would line up to buy it.

The featured technological attraction in *The Sum of All Fears* is the nuclear bomb, of course. Many pages are devoted to its construction—there is a great deal of talk about tungsten-rhenium, beryllium, gallium-stabilized plutonium, and laser interferometry—and we are treated to a slow-motion account of what happens when such a bomb goes off:

> The plasma from the immolated straws pounded inward toward the second reservoir of lithium compounds. The dense uranium 238 fins just outside the Secondary pit also flashed to dense plasma, driving inward through the vacuum, then striking and compressing the tubular containment of more 238 U around the central container which held the largest quantity of lithium-deuteride/tritium. The forces were immense, and the structure was pounded with a degree of pressure greater than that of a healthy stellar core.

And so on. That we are to take all this seriously is made clear by an afterword in which the author explains that "certain technical details have been altered" in order to prevent readers from trying to build nuclear bombs in their basements.

It is certainly possible that my ignorance of how submarines run and why bombs explode is even more woeful than I suspect it is; but "The plasma from the immolated straws pounded inward toward the second reservoir of lithium compounds" is actually slightly less meaningful to me than "All mimsy were the borogoves." That Clancy's sentences about nuclear technology are grammatical is one positive indication that he actually understands what he is talking about, and is not simply paraphrasing some physics textbook; but it is the only indication I feel confident about. Millions of readers obviously feel differently, and either find these descriptions illuminating or don't care that they don't.

Whether fiction helps shape the world or only reflects it is a question that is usually answered according to one's taste for the particular fiction involved. But it is interesting that among Clancy's earliest admirers in the Reagan White House were Robert McFarlane, when he was the national-security adviser, and John Poindexter, who succeeded McFarlane at the National Security Council in 1985. For *The Hunt for Red October* reads today (subject matter aside) as obviously the novel of Iran-Contra. It is fairly radiant with the conviction, so central to the belief system that made the Iran-Contra affair possible, that the national security is much too important a matter to be left to those candy-colored clowns we

call the Congress; and it makes the same adolescent identification between great heroism and great secrecy which is manifest in the symbol of Iran-Contra, Oliver North.

The recent war in the Persian Gulf is referred to several times in *The Sum of All Fears;* and that war, as it played on American television, was unmistakably a Tom Clancy war. The wizardly technology that turned battle into a game of reflexes, like Ping-Pong, and the astonishingly detailed intelligence, gathered by electronic-surveillance devices that seemed able to tell us everything there was to know about the enemy until our bombs struck, but had nothing to report about the aftermath—it was all a spectacle after Clancy's own imagination. And then, interviewed as they walked to and from their amazing airplanes, there were the warriors themselves—clean-cut, professional, apparently indestructible, and, ever so slightly, cynical.

William F. Ryan (essay date Winter 1993)

SOURCE: "The Genesis of the Techno-Thriller," in *Virginia Quarterly Review,* Vol. 69, No. 1, Winter, 1993, pp. 24-40.

[*In the following excerpt, Ryan explores the origins and defining characteristics of the techno-thriller genre as popularized by Clancy's best-selling novels. Though Clancy is widely regarded as "the wizard inventor of the* techno-thriller," *Ryan cites literary precedents in the work of Jules Verne.*]

When Thomas Leo Clancy was a boy in Baltimore, he wanted to be a soldier. His heart beat for the stars and stripes. On good days he could catch the scent of sea spray from Chesapeake Bay. In his student years at Loyola College he carried no signs and made no audible protest. His mind was elsewhere, weighted stem to stern with the lore of the sea and warships. What he really wanted was to fight for his country in Vietnam. This didn't happen. His eyesight was, and is, too weak for combat. He was never a U.S. Marine. Too bad. Clancy was no doubt cut out for this, in spirit and sensibility. His intellect is keen and disciplined. And utterly military.

Instead, Tom Clancy became a writer of big books. Hefty novels for summer beaches or those long airline flights to spots where Clancy never goes. His first, *The Hunt for Red October,* arrived for sale in late 1984. Clancy's stars were clearly in place for Christmas. The publisher was the U.S. Naval Institute Press. Clancy's first book was the Institute's first gambit at publishing original fiction. It caught good attention in official Washington, D.C. Here at last was a fresh new thriller for career professionals in the Defense Department. Some important people in the State Depart-ment's diplomatic corps read the book and passed it around. The novel was mentioned at parties. A copy was placed under the White House Christmas tree. Not long after New Year's 1985, President Ronald Reagan told a *Time* interviewer that **Red October** is "the perfect yarn."

Only a few have questioned that praise. The book has no doubt carved a niche in cultural history as a phenomenon of the 1980's. It proved to be a pace setter for Clancy's further authorship and an impressive model to all Clancy disciples and imitators. This was the new way into big bucks from books. Surely this was a business after all . . . Or was it?

William S. Burroughs once asserted to me that every novelist writes as well as he or she can. He means that all writers produce at the peak of their skills or forms no matter what they say to seminars or interviewers. In the end, the collective aim of Melville, Faulkner, Kerouac, Mickey Spillane, and Iceberg Slim has been to earn two or three squares a day by one's pen. So if it's a business, it has some integrity.

The phenomenology of Clancy and devotees in his train occurs in literary circles. What spurred this discussion was the quick-draw jargon or newspeak of those three-minute oracles who review books for the mass media. I remain unwilling to call those persons critics. But their mission is to pinpoint trends, fads, shifts in the psychotic American breeze. By the late 1980's, one or more of them were calling Tom Clancy the wizard inventor of the *techno-thriller.*

To accept this blurb as literary history is to admit that Clancy created a new genre fiction. When his **Red October** and **Red Storm Rising** (1986) were published, no one else seemed to be writing or even talking about his kind of novel. Then came Stephen Coonts with *Flight of the Intruder* (U.S. Naval Institute Press, 1986) and Harold Coyle with *Team Yankee: A Novel of World War III* (1987). In short order a battalion of mimickers brought up the rear. Their colors are brazen and evident. Meanwhile, Clancy's sixth novel, **The Sum of All Fears,** was published by Putnam's in August 1991.

The techno-thrillers stand tall and thick in bookstores. The paperback renderings shimmer with glossy inks (good for reading in foxholes and duck blinds) and comic book graphics. The stories ring with patriotic fervor and a Manichean discernment of good versus evil. You always know your enemies. You quickly spot the good guys. You know from the outset which side will win because destiny commands it. These books are the proving grounds and playing fields of a warrior class. Heroes abound in the stories, most of them soldiers, seamen, fighter pilots, military officers, spies, or other mavens of espionage. The novels are just long enough

to become variously exciting, laborious, and silly. The plots and crucial sequences always rely on advanced technology for waging war. This quality of the techno-thriller links it to science fiction. Remember that or underline it. What annoys many readers is that such SF purists as Isaac Asimov and James E. Gunn sacrifice character development for scientific explication in their stories. The techno-thriller makes a similar sacrifice much of the time and mounts a paradox. Heroes and other soldiers are game pieces, mannequins, cardboard stand-ups in a showroom window. They have all the human complexity and élan of the Blackhawks or Batman and Robin of the World War II comic books. In inverse proportion, the Soviet enemies, terrorists, and other villains are sculpted to deliver character traits and singular menace. This is the case in all of Clancy's published novels to date.

> If there is a new genre, Clancy denies any connection with it. He insists that he writes novels, and they are thrillers. To make much more of it is to test his anger.
> —*William F. Ryan*

My initial supposition about the audience for these books was that only the techno-freaks attached to research and development firms, or troops in "Ollie's Army," would ever buy them. Those are in fact the true zealots. But much of the English-reading world has ingested works of this genre. C. S. Forester's "Hornblower" series and George MacDonald Fraser's "Flashman" frolics have now been outclassed—for now, at least—by Clancy's chronicles of Jack Ryan. I was bound to be curious sooner or later. With a lot of bothersome questions, I first approached Tom Clancy, and later, his friend Stephen Coonts.

If there is a new genre, Clancy denies any connection with it. He insists that he writes novels, and they are thrillers. To make much more of it is to test his anger. He referred to Michael Crichton's big seller, *The Andromeda Strain* (1969). "If anybody invented the techno-thriller, what about Crichton when I was in college? All you're doing is describing tools used by your characters. Technology is another word for tools."

The matter of Clancy's characters and how they function is a short subject made long by engaging the author in debate. He believes that he's done an exemplary job. His reinforcement comes from "people in the business" who read his books right on time and comment that what he does well is "capture the personalities." But what business is he talking about? The genre fiction that used to be just for newsstand pulps? What people in what business?

Not long after reading Clancy's **The Cardinal of the Kremlin** (1988), I got hold of a short story he had published in a high school literary magazine. Its title is **"The Wait."** Printed in 1965, it indexes the personality of a teenager who's patriotic and fine-tuned to world affairs. His concerns then are his concerns now. Clancy loathes revolutionaries and guerrillas, most likely because they flout the law. He emulates the tough, faceless soldier who puts his life on the line against Communism. **"The Wait"** is precisely the same schmaltz on a sub roll that he's been packaging for "thrillers" ever since. If Clancy refuses to own up to the techno-thriller, he might grant instead that he has given us five or six national security Westerns. The cowpokes wear black shoes and know how to fight showdowns with computers. Those are Clancy's people. Their business may not be for our eyes and ears. But trust Clancy.

He told me of a conversation from 1987, when he and his family visited England a second time. "A friend of mine was the skipper of H.M.S. *Boxer,* a frigate," he said. "We were having lunch in his stateroom aboard. He looked at me and he said, 'Tom, the technology in your books is not terribly impressive, but I think the characters are bloody accurate.' I wanted to grab him by the throat and say, 'Why don't you tell the God-damned critics?' But the people in the business tell me that the technology is no big deal, because any fool can do that. What I do well is capture the personalities."

What I've heard and read is just the reverse. Clancy has prodigious facility with high technology but his characters are tilting scarecrows. His third novel, *Patriot Games* (1987), deals less with war technology than with law enforcement and shooting it out with urban guerrillas. When we spoke, he said he regards this novel as his finest. Most reviews faulted this book more than his others, and on the same grounds. Only he and those "people in the business" have kind words for his characters. But the book sold extremely well as usual. Clancy need not defend himself.

In conversation with him I pushed the issue of his characters, perhaps a bit too far. I asked, for example, whether Prince Charles had shown any reaction to Clancy's portrayal of him in *Patriot Games.*

"No more than President Reagan had a reaction to the fact that there's a president in *Red October, Red Storm* and *Cardinal,*" he said. "He was a generic character. He was never intended to be Charles, Prince of Wales. He's just a character. If in any American political thriller novel you have a president, you don't necessarily mean President Reagan or President Ford or President Carter. You just mean a person who has the job. I simply treated the Prince of Wales as the same sort of literary invention. If you pay close attention there are enough clues to tell you that it's not Charles."

Again, please take note. The techno-thriller is bound to be inhabited by *generic* characters. Once the reader has ex-

pended those brain cells in processing data on machineries of devastation, he is perhaps amenable to drastic suspensions of disbelief. The existence of parallel worlds, for example. The one on which we walk, eat meals, read books, watch television, and gratefully go to sleep. The other is for Clancy's callow Prince, his renderings of nameless U.S. presidents who attain to dullness and stupidity, a martinet national security advisor named Jeffrey Pelt, a CIA director known as Judge Moore. Men with jobs. With each big book we get a cigar box full of tin men with guns. In the usual course of things, Clancy's women are as wan and insipid as tea left standing for three days. Clancy's recurring hero is Jack Ryan, very square and very opaque. With every book Jack's ties to the CIA are tighter. He advances upward, gets richer. The nation relies on him more and more. He could run for Congress if we ever knew anything meaningful about him.

Clancy insisted more than once that he writes about a "generic category of *hero.*" The idea by itself is specious outside the comic books. All the same, the legions of devotees who read his novels have not diminished. He tells a good story, spins an exciting yarn. The characters don't accomplish a thing in the techno-thriller. They generate no electricity. They are understood only by what they do. Their definition is the purpose of their mission.

Readers of this genre fiction are apt to find escapist fun but little or no artistry. Clancy told me that he thinks of himself as an entertainer with no pretense to literary matters or concerns. In my own fashion I looked for a durable message in the works of Tom Clancy. He often denies that he ever intends any such thing. But I asked anyway. In all those Cold War potboilers, isn't Clancy saying that there are ways to wage *peace* through a new balance of power in the world?

"You may be right," he answered. "As Claudius Appius the Blind said, '*Si vis pacem parate pro bellum.* . . . If you desire peace, prepare for war.' The other thing I say in there is that people we have wearing uniforms and carrying badges are important members of our society and entitled to respect. They don't have halos. You may not always want your daughter to go out and date one. But we should treat them decently because they're out there for us. The Pentagon Navy is not the same as the fleet Navy. I know that. And that may find its way into my next book."

II

Following the success of his *Team Yankee,* Harold Coyle wrote *Sword Point* (1988) and *Bright Star* (1990), both techno-thrillers from Simon & Schuster. Coyle is a friend to Tom Clancy, as is Stephen Coonts. After his *Flight of the Intruder,* Coonts encored with *Final Flight* (1988), then *The Minotaur* (1989) and *Under Siege* (1990). Standing in

Clancy's long shadow is no encumbrance for the other two. They are where they are because Clancy was the pathfinder. . . .

Some years ago, metacritics and a few popular novelists wrote and lectured on *moral fiction*. Where are those debates today? The techno-thriller and its practitioners may be standing athwart. Tom Clancy, for one, made it clear to me that he has no interest in contemporary literature as *Literature*. He perennially scorns any salon environs. He spoke of the legendary Algonquin Round Table in pejoratives. Never studied the modern novel as a course, never took creative writing in a school setting. He has warmth and praise for Frederick Forsyth as a wordsmith but would much prefer to talk about how his friend Freddy so spellbinds a reader with elegant language that he or she *becomes* a character such as Jackal. Forsyth is plainly Clancy's ideal. That is, for Tom Clancy he is a contemporary paragon. Underline *contemporary*.

For Coonts the works of Eric Ambler were sublime, especially two thrillers from 1943: *A Coffin for Dimitrios* and *Journey into Fear*. Today he admires John le Carre. *The Little Drummer Girl* he calls a masterpiece. But he finds the novels about George Smiley "too cerebral." Even in thriller genres there are lines rarely crossed. John le Carre may prove to be more daring than his younger *frères* in the business. But don't look for Smiley in a techno-thriller.

As with Clancy, the techno-thriller does not exist as a distinct genre for Stephen Coonts. Or so he says, when you first ask.

Coonts and Clancy are now fast friends. On many scores their opinions are alike. They no doubt swap war stories and gripes about book reviewers in the mass media. On the techno-thriller, Coonts remarked, "There's nothing new about it. I know that Tom sat down consciously to write a modern submarine tale that he hoped would be as good as *Run Silent, Run Deep*, by Edward L. Beach [1955], and told in the same style. In that novel you have all the elements of what is now called a techno-thriller. The military guys are the heroes. The tale is told in carefully crafted, solid, accurate technical details, all part of the story. You're told what it is the crew is doing and why they're doing it. That sets up the scene and the conflict, so it's part of the story. And it's an action-adventure story. Those are the elements of the so-called 'techno-thriller.'"

He said he didn't read **The Hunt for Red October** until his own first novel was accepted for publication by the U.S. Naval Institute Press. Coonts told me he intended a flying story modeled after Ernest K. Gann's *Fate Is the Hunter* (1961). That impressive book is a work of nonfiction. Coonts chose to write a novel because he believed the form would allow him generous space to interweave his own Vietnam experiences with those of other pilots.

"Gann puts you in the cockpit in an unobtrusive way," Coonts indicated. "He explains to you what the hell it is they're doing in there. You can't understand the story he's telling unless you realize what the pilots are doing. That's the essence of what *Flight of the Intruder* tries to do. You don't understand the problems Jake and Morgan and Tiger Cole have unless you understand what they're up against. How the airplane works, how the system works. You can't understand what it feels like to fly at 400 feet at night over North Vietnam dodging the flak, until you get a feel for what the crew is doing. And how Jake flies the airplane, and what he's looking at. The story can't be told without those details."

He credits Tom Clancy with rescuing the story of the hero in uniform and making it shine. After a long lapse the publishers could sell those swagger-and-salvo books in high volume. It isn't corn and camp any longer. So says Stephen Coonts. He looks back at 20 years of American fiction and sees the military image scarred by Vietnam recoil. The man in uniform was often painted as psychopathic, perverted, and criminal. But didn't the splendid novels of James Webb accomplish this revision years before the techno-thriller? Not as Coonts reads the flow chart. Jim Webb writes best sellers but they don't reap the rewards of the mammoth Clancy sagas. To Coonts this profit margin is ultimately a line of demarcation. On one side are war novelists the likes of Webb, James Jones, and Tim O'Brien. Their priorities have to do with realism and art. On the other are the new breed of genre writers who are mass-producing techno-thrillers. The difference for Coonts is between what he calls "realistic, thoughtful novels" and "popular commercial fiction" which "makes absolutely no pretenses of being literature."

Publishers have been contracting writers by the score to pound out techno-thrillers. The result has been a glut of this kind of book in the nation's drug stores, airline terminals, newsstands, supermarkets and—oh yes!—book shops. The mass-market paperbacks are frequently emblazoned with glossy allusions to Clancy and Coonts in their cover copy. This no doubt hastens the heartbeat of millions and does honor and justice to the genre. It also proves to the publicists in New York that you can always sell chicanery with its own gimcracks.

"I think that ultimately it's a fad," Coonts remarked. "A lot of the books are mediocre at best. I see a lot of shoot-'em-ups out there with high-tech stuff thrown in but not essential to the story. It's terrific that the guys who write them are breaking into publishing. Halleluia! But I think it'll pass. How many times can you do the next Korean War or the war in the Mideast? There's a limit on this stuff, and I think it's fast being reached. Tom Clancy can write anything he wants because he's a good-enough storyteller. He will always be able to sell his books. I'm a whole notch down from the public acceptance Tom Clancy's got. I'll have to grow and change to survive. But I guarantee you, I'm not about to do a book about the next Korean War or the war in the Mideast. I don't think the publishers are going to keep buying this stuff."

Recently I took a look at what is available around Washington, D.C., where five-dollar paperbacks are sold. Richard Herman, Jr.'s *Force* (1991) . . . about war in the Mideast. Patrick F. Rogers' *War God* (1990) . . . about facing the Soviets with SDI. *Hostage One,* by David E. Fisher and Col. Ralph Albertazzle (1990) . . . about the abduction of the U.S. President by a high-tech loony. Herbert Crowder's *Ambush at Osirak* (1989) . . . about war in the Mideast.

One of the problems confronting writers in this genre is collaring a plausible villain. Cessation of the Cold War has all but eliminated the Red Army, the KGB, and other Russian golems. The Gulf War didn't last long enough to suit the television networks, let alone the quick-book publishers. "The terrorists are the only plausible villains around right now who are obvious," Coonts said. Tom Clancy rounded up terrorists, gangsters, and corrupt public officials foreign and domestic when he wrote his big one for 1989, *Clear and Present Danger.* What we get is a pretty nifty book about the international drug war. Jack Ryan reappears as a three-star hero: CIA deputy director, concerned parent, and law-abiding citizen.

Jack Ryan would epitomize the "generic hero" if, as a character, he didn't raise such aggravating questions about himself. Annoying, because answers are never forthcoming. Reviewers and other readers often guess that he's the Walter Mitty projection of Tom Clancy.

Stephen Coonts presents another troublesome "generic" in the invention of Jake Grafton. Why should he warrant our attention? "Jake believes in himself," Coonts told me. "He is Everyman, with common sense and ability to do a good job. Jake Grafton is not wise, witty, or handsome. He is average. Jake is not a believer in high tech. Far from it. Jake has been in combat. He knows that, in real combat, anything more complex than a pocket watch won't work. Gadgets don't thrill Jake and don't thrill *me!* Jake is a timeless hero. I think that's Jake's appeal. He appeals to something basic in all of us."

But again, the hero of a brace of techno-thrillers has dimension because he has a job that he must do. This goes for all the techno-thrillers. The genre is about war, real, imagined, or inevitable. The job is warfare, the heroes are warriors. A case can be made that the authors in this genre are opting

for a warrior class. Clancy denies that he's glorifying any such class but defers to the multivolume "Brotherhood of War" series. Those popular thrillers are the work of Coonts' friend Bill Butterworth, using the nom de plume W.E.B. Griffin.

III

When he was a third-grade pupil, Tom Clancy began reading the fabulous novels of Jules Verne (1892-1905), the French author justly celebrated as the father of science fiction. Always an avid reader, Clancy has remained close to science fiction, for the pleasure of it and doubtless the inspiration in its other-worldly possibilities. While an English major at Baltimore's Loyola College, he completed an independent study program in science fiction. His reading list included Jules Verne, H. G. Wells, John Wyndham, Philip Wylie, and Isaac Asimov. He reached back to a literary genre that had captured his boyhood. It was clearly his intent to write science fiction stories. This he did, in some quantity, but was never fortunate to sell a single one to any publisher. Clancy told me that he never throws anything out. So, it's a safe bet that his SF manuscripts exist. Intuition tells me that they're probably well above average for contemporary SF tales. They would be the proving grounds for the techno-thriller.

Stephen Coonts insisted to me that he writes about people and "not hardware." High technology doesn't impress or inspire him. Long ago he was turned off by science fiction. Instead he is immersed in the idea of *change* within a story. How an author deals with changes in points of view, especially from a cockpit and through a bomb sight. Clancy refers back to the eternal "What if . . .?" of the science fiction visionaries. He applies their search for possibilities to modern warfare and foreign policy concerns. Among those classic prophetic writers, Jules Verne stands clearly apart as Tom Clancy's avatar.

In *The Hunt for Red October,* Clancy introduces Captain Marko Ramius, intrepid commander of the Soviet submarine *Red October.* Ramius is a man of parts. In early chapters the reader discovers his substance and ideals. Ramius proves to be more interesting than any other character in the story. His resemblance to an earlier seafaring warrior is unmistakable. *Twenty Thousand Leagues under the Sea* (1870) is considered by many to be Jules Verne's finest work. Its central figure is Captain Nemo, master of the mysterious submarine *Nautilus.* When Verne wrote his novel, submarines only broke the waves in the minds of dreamers. What Clancy wrote about was a submarine so ingenious that the most sophisticated sonar devices could scarcely trace its undersea whisper.

Verne's portrayal of Nemo remained cryptic. The indomitable submariner reappeared, a dying man aboard his *Nautilus,* in *The Mysterious Island* (1875). For all the readers knew, Captain Nemo was the sullen, embittered enemy of all oppressors. An undersea Robin Hood who settled scores and took out his personal vengeance on the world's maritime traffic. A close look shows no sure enemy to Nemo. In the last analysis he was a renegade avenger, an outlaw genius. Aside from his obvious rage and high-handed intimidation, he displayed noble traits. Near the close of *The Mysterious Island,* we learn that Nemo was an Indian prince whose family was slaughtered during the English colonial wars. His life mission had been revenge.

Jean Jules Verne, grandson of the great storyteller, relates how the author held vehement political convictions. He was incensed at the Russian oppression of the Polish people and others in Eastern Europe. Much of this acrimony found its way into an early draft of *Twenty Thousand Leagues Under the Sea.* Verne was prevailed upon by his business-wise publisher, Jules Hetzel, to purge any political material for the sake of high-volume international sales. Details of this restraint on the author are revealed in his grandson's *Jules Verne: A Biography.*

> The authorship of Tom Clancy resembles Jules Verne's in an important way. Both men are telling prophetic stories dealing with quirks or innovations in scientific technology.
> —*William F. Ryan*

Nemo the obsessive-compulsive maverick is reincarnated as Ramius in *The Hunt for Red October.* He reappears as the Soviet defector in *The Cardinal of the Kremlin,* but only the mincing, incoherent shade of the pirate who stole away with the *Red October.* Tom Clancy summoned perhaps his only realized fictional character and set him adrift.

The authorship of Tom Clancy resembles Jules Verne's in an important way. Both men are telling prophetic stories dealing with quirks or innovations in scientific technology. In all important cases, knowledge of what is going on—or what is anticipated—is known to only a select cabal of men (and no women). Only in rare instances do any of these men ever impress us as well-conceived or realized personalities. This is all right with Clancy because his men are "generic." Jules Verne was criticized when the details of Nemo's *Nautilus* nearly put the character Nemo in total eclipse. Nonetheless, Verne taught Clancy, and Clancy taught "generics" to all the rest.

Those cells of privileged information aren't very interesting in Tom Clancy's books. Nearly always they are cadres of

intelligence and secret weapons specialists who read Clausewitz in day school. Just drop a name like "Angleton" and you'll get a round of precise talk on the difference between *strategic* and *tactical.* Here are the Hollow Men. Heroes all.

Clancy told me that his favorite of his own novels is *Patriot Games,* the one he said was most "savaged" by reviewers. The story is outrageous and the characters are mostly clods. Technology is at a minimum. Instead we get bombs and an assortment of firearms, and the Clancy method of repelling international terrorists. The cabal is a bestiary of Irish nationalist guerrillas led by Sean Miller, a convicted bomber. In another place I have argued that Tom Clancy has such esteem for this work because it offered him an opportunity to pare his personality three ways. Accept Jack Ryan as Clancy's idealized self, no matter how loudly he denies it. His "generic" Prince of Wales appears callow, open-faced, a clean slate for the sage lessons of Jack Ryan. This Prince is an innocent with the power potential to be a warrior king. Perhaps another Clancy ideal. Sean Miller represents a special menace. When Jack Ryan testifies at the Old Bailey, he is chilled by Miller's cold stare. Clancy needed to create a duel, a shoot-out at Baltimore's Dundalk Marine Terminal, to do away with this ogre. I remain convinced that Sean Miller is Clancy's dark familiar, his *Doppelgänger,* the armed and dangerous one. Sean Miller is all that Clancy is not. Disorderly, unmilitary, reckless, anarchic. Clancy told me that he began to write *Patriot Games* well before he wrote *The Hunt for Red October.* By the luck of the Irish, the reading public came to know Tom Clancy far ahead of his prideful *Patriot Games.*

Curtis Church wrote a perceptive "Foreword" to the omnibus volume, *Works of Jules Verne* (1983). Therein, Church indicates Verne's schizoid outlook on modern science and its potentials. As much as he enjoyed science study and marveled at scientific advances, he dreaded the consequences of technology in mischievous or diabolical hands. Church further points to Verne's projection of his own personality in Captain Nemo and in Phileas Fogg, hero of *Around the World in Eighty Days* (1873; British, 1874). Thus the cabals, the secret enterprises of men who take dares and risk lives—their own or others. Jules Verne was a precise and thorough researcher. In his time he could never be faulted for inaccuracy. His personal insistence was on the plausible. The same is true of Tom Clancy today. He insisted to me that he has always relied on open, unclassified, or declassified source material, even though some of his novels have stunned and confounded people in Defense, as much of Verne was prophecy a century and more ago.

Verne's cabals are clusters of well-meaning eccentrics with mighty purpose. Like Clancy's heroes, they're going to have their day no matter what. In *A Journey to the Center of the*

Earth (1864; British, 1872), the sojourners underground are members of the Literary Society and Mechanics' Institute, which publishes educational books. Its roster includes "many foreign scholars of eminence" who are "honorary members." The gathering place is Hamburg. In *From the Earth to the Moon* (1865; British, 1873) and its sequel, *Round the Moon* (1870), Impey Barbicane and his fellow space travelers are officers of the Baltimore Gun Club, comprised of "artillerists" and sundry other militarists chiefly obsessed with warfare. In *Around the World in Eighty Days,* Phileas Fogg belongs to London's renowned Reform Club. Verne paints the club and its doings in lavish tones of opulent idleness. The all-male membership indulges in high-stakes gambling. Such a wager sends Fogg and his plucky valet, Passepartout, on a trip around the globe. In *The Mysterious Island,* five balloonists are stranded on what turns out to be Captain Nemo's secret island hideout. The men are an engineer, a journalist, a seaman, a black man who had been a slave, and a child. Jean Jules Verne has interpreted this configuration allegorically as the five who "represent the successive stages in the evolution of mankind." The novel begins at the close of the American Civil War. When Nemo is discovered, he is given ample room for philosophy.

Jules Verne loved the United States. He visited this country in the early spring of 1867 and traversed New York State, from Manhattan Island to Buffalo and the Canadian side of Niagara Falls. His letters and diaries from this vacation were ultimately the grist of one of his last novels, *Master of the World* (1904; not in English till 1914). This relatively short work is a true techno-thriller as the genre has been described. It brings back an earlier Verne villain, *Robur the Conqueror* (1886). The character Robur is a rogue scientist. His aim in the second tale about him is world domination. He pilots an infernal machine that can zoom across land, sail the seas and fly through the clouds. He commands a skeletal crew of loyal henchmen. Only this cabal knows about Robur's machine, called "the Terror," and its hiding places in the Appalachians and the Great Lakes region. The man sent in pursuit of "the Terror" is John Strock, "head inspector in the federal police department at Washington." He tracks Robur to Niagara Falls and then the Gulf of Mexico. At the close, the reader can only presume about Robur's destruction.

Old and sick at the turn of the 19th century, Jules Verne was wealthy, respected, admired—and jaded. When he died, March 24, 1905, he had excited more than four generations of young readers. He had made an adventure of science, geography, and certain ideas about geopolitics. In the long run he trusted less in the future of science. His life had spanned too many wars, too many imperialist land grabs accomplished by advanced war technology. He could read a newspaper and conjure the visage of a Robur or a Nemo, just across the Rhine or floating in the Strait of Dover. If the planet would make room for new sciences, systems, and ma-

chinery, would there be new ethics and morals also? Verne wouldn't live to know.

I don't know whether Tom Clancy's editors or publishers have tried to restrain him from expressing any ideas. His patriotism is evident in all he has written. His Russophobia was conspicuous in three of his first four novels. Uniforms, badges of authority, military decorations, Army tanks, Navy battleships and pep talks on the Strategic Defense Initiative can all make life worth living for him. When asked by others about the end of the Cold War, he said that he would almost surely continue to write *political thrillers.*

What does all this say about the techno-thriller genre? Is it for fun and escape, or is it a bill of goods? Maybe it is both. Jules Verne couldn't be reached for comment. But I don't think he ever conceived a novel about science and propaganda.

G. Gordon Liddy (review date 22 August 1993)

SOURCE: "The Smell of Napalm in the Morning," in *New York Times Book Review,* August 22, 1993, pp. 13-14.

[*In the following review, Liddy offers tempered criticism of* Without Remorse, *though concedes that "of the millions bound to read it, few will not enjoy it thoroughly."*]

It may seem a bit early, but why not revisit the cold war? After all, successful authors have been dining out on World War II for half a century and, if memory serves, they didn't wait long to start. The trick is to use the hottest part, Vietnam, and throw in a parallel story of revenge in the dirty world of drugs and prostitution that metastasized in our cities' streets as our involvement in Indochina progressed. In terms of the internal architecture of **Without Remorse,** the weaving of the two plots around the central actor in both, one John Kelly, the Navy Cross-winning former Seal introduced in earlier Tom Clancy novels, the author performs the trick well. His plotting is symmetrical and the satisfying resolution a setup for yet another sequel. If Mr. Clancy can cure Kelly's addiction to introspection (completely out of character for a Seal) Kelly will be a lot more popular than Jack Ryan, the hero of **Patriot Games** and other books.

The year is 1970, and the United States Government sends Kelly (nom de guerre John Clark) on a special mission to Vietnam just when he is fighting a self-declared war at home employing the same skills. The bad guys on the domestic front have anticipated the plot of a "Miami Vice" episode by more than a decade with the method they have devised of smuggling heroin into the United States, and have earned Kelly's lethal enmity by killing a close friend. Both plots are advanced by the plan-disrupting effects of leaks. No one in this book can keep his mouth shut, and that includes Kelly, who should know better.

Mr. Clancy's latest action thriller is certain to join his unbroken string of best sellers. Of the millions bound to read it, few will not enjoy it thoroughly.

Those few who won't will belong to either or both of two small, ever diminishing groups: those familiar with the operation and correct use of small arms (as we spend less and less on recruitment and training of the armed forces) and those familiar with the correct use of the English language (as we spend more and more on our public school systems). Both, unable to put down such a good story, will become increasingly exasperated at errors that could have been avoided easily.

To give Mr. Clancy the benefit of the doubt, perhaps the reason his description of how to make a suppressor to muffle the report of a firearm would leave a graduate of the mechanical shop class at Benedict Arnold Junior High laughing is that it's an attempt at social responsibility (we can't have all those grammar school kids carrying handguns with suppressors). But I doubt it. Mr. Clancy is one of the good guys. He correctly fingers the American left for supplying intelligence to the enemy during the Vietnam War, and his idea of proper behavior during that era would not serve as an outline for a biography of President Clinton.

Now there's nothing wrong with not knowing how to accomplish something so unusual as the manufacture of a suppressor, but if you don't know, why attempt it? It is gratuitous in any event, like naming the brand of the hero's suntan lotion (Coppertone). Just say he did it and move on. If not, find out how from someone who knows and who will, presumably, understand that it is necessary to provide a means to attach the device to the barrel of the pistol.

Even more irritating is Mr. Clancy's interchangeable use of the terms "magazine" and "clip." They are not the same. The M-1 Garand rifle, for example, uses a clip. The handgun of choice of John Kelly, the formidable 45-caliber ACP Colt model 1911 A-1 semiautomatic military service pistol, uses a spring-loaded magazine, not a clip. It gets worse. Kelly, like all Seals a small-arms expert, is described as disassembling his chosen handgun in a manner that is mechanically impossible. (No, I'm not going to tell you how to do it properly. This is, after all, supposed to be a book review, not a field manual. The problem is that as I read the book, from time to time I got the impression that it was a field manual, albeit one issued during the Carter Administration.)

Then there is the battle scene in Vietnam, earlier in the war,

wherein Kelly, supposedly a superbly trained and disciplined member of the psychologically and physiologically toughest special warfare-special operations organization in the world, is inserted alone in country on a mission to capture and bring back alive a specific enemy officer. Because Kelly witnesses that man doing some particularly nasty things before the rest of the team arrives, he mounts a one-man attack on 11 enemy soldiers and deliberately kills the officer he was sent to retrieve. Moreover, another of the enemy is "hosed down" with a fully automatic carbine by Kelly "emptying his magazine" (all remaining 22 rounds!) "into the running figure." That's no way to expend ammunition when you start out with only 180 rounds, surrounded by the enemy and deep in country.

We come now to that most lost of causes, the English language. Again, to be fair to Mr. Clancy, what follows is undoubtedly attributable to the appallingly under-reported nationwide editors' strike.

It is one thing to have a character ignorantly or carelessly confound the forms of the intransitive verb "lie" with those of the transitive verb "lay"; indeed, it may be required for verisimilitude (although not, one would hope, in the speech of Miss Sandy O'Toole, a nurse practitioner and the possessor of a master's degree, who nevertheless orders her patient to "lay down"). The striking editors could have been counted upon to point out, among other things, that "free" does not take "for"—one may get something "for nothing" but, if so, it is free; that there's a difference between "nauseous" and "nauseated," et cetera, ad nauseam.

Then there is my favorite passage in the book: "Food, nourishment, strength. He reached into a pocket, moving his hand slowly and withdrawing a pair of food bars. Nothing he'd eat by choice in any other place, but it was vital now. He tore off the plastic wrappers with his teeth and chewed them up slowly. The strength they imparted to his body was probably as much psychological as real, but both factors had their uses, as his body had to deal with both fatigue and stress." To say nothing of indigestion. Those plastic wrappers are hard on the stomach, even when chewed up slowly the way your mother always told you.

Enough. Eons ago, tribesmen sat around the campfires as the tellers of tales engaged their imaginations. A few years from now, Mr. Clancy will have a hearty last laugh on the few of us who care about these things as his visage fills the television screen, enabling him to deploy his narrative gifts to the delight of millions of graduates of "outcome based education," their illiterate little minds brimming with self-esteem, held in thrall by a master storyteller.

Walter L. Hixson (essay date Fall 1993)

SOURCE: "*Red Storm Rising*: Tom Clancy Novels and the Cult of National Security," in *Diplomatic History,* Vol. 17, No. 4, Fall, 1993, pp. 599-613.

[*In the following essay, Hixson examines the cultural significance of American jingoism and the glorification of advanced weaponry in* The Hunt for Red October, Red Storm Rising, *and* The Cardinal of the Kremlin. *According to Hixson, Clancy's novels "can be interpreted as popular representations of Reagan-era Cold War values."*]

> They're not just novels. They're read as the real thing.
> —Former Vice President Dan Quayle on Tom Clancy's novels

Prominent midcentury American social critics Dwight MacDonald and Clement Greenberg, inspired in part by Frankfurt school intellectuals, decried the growing influence of the mass media and popular culture on postindustrial society. They asserted that *kitsch,* ersatz culture for the masses, as represented in radio, television, popular music, cartoons, advertising, paperback novels, and the movies, would overwhelm the avant-garde and undermine elite, or high, culture. For many years, historians, who were among the last social scientists to take popular culture seriously, followed the lead of these intellectual critics in their disdain for the tastes of the masses. With the advent of the new social history, which focused on nonelites, and the recognition of the significance of the expansion of leisure time in postindustrial society, however, studies of popular culture have gained legitimacy. In recent years, for example, analyses of the popular culture of the Cold War have made significant contributions to our understanding of how Americans coped with atomic age anxieties and how they internalized the anti-Communist consensus.

Serious analysis of popular culture may be particularly relevant to understanding the 1980s, an era in which a Hollywood actor became one of the most popular chief executives in the nation's history, partly on the basis of his skill at invoking themes drawn directly from popular culture. To cite a few examples, Ronald Reagan once threatened a veto by assuming the role of Clint Eastwood's Dirty Harry ("go ahead, make my day"). On another occasion he promised to take the country "back to the future" and, recalling his own most famous role as the dying Notre Dame football player, he urged George Bush to "win one for the Gipper" in the 1988 presidential campaign.

Reagan's allusions to well-known movies suggest the extent to which popular culture leaves an imprint on mass consciousness. Because popular culture often conveys symbols and ideas that are familiar rather than original and is usually less developed aesthetically than elite representations, it has traditionally been condemned by intellectuals. But, as the "great communicator" himself clearly understood, lack of artistic merit does not render a book or film irrelevant to the public consciousness. Quite the contrary, as the French philosopher Jean-Paul Sartre once lamented with respect to literature, there are two kinds of books in the modern world: those that are unreadable, but are actually read by a great many people, and truly accomplished works, which are read by relatively few.

Students of popular culture have noted that its most successful practitioners are those who express what the audience yearns to hear and see. The "traditional function of popular culture," they argue, is to "articulate an existing idea, attitude or concern and, in the process, to reinforce people's convictions." Or, put another way, "The most important single function of popular culture [is] the dissemination of common values, symbols and attitudes in such a manner as to create sociocultural consensus."

Accordingly, research in mass culture should be useful to diplomatic historians, whose proper purview includes analysis of consensus making in foreign policy, especially in a democratic society. By exploring the relationship between popular culture and actual national security policy, foreign relations historians can better analyze the process through which society absorbs and perpetuates predominant themes of national security discourse. Use of popular culture allows the diplomatic historian to exploit a wider range of sources and include in the analysis the "bottom up" masses, whose exclusion has been the source of no little debate. Finally, such research lends itself to modernist methodologies, such as the "new cultural history," further enhancing the ability of diplomatic historians to interface with their colleagues in other fields.

In recent years, revealing studies have appeared on the popular culture of the Cold War, although most have focused on Hollywood representations. Relatively less attention has been paid to popular fiction. Studiously ignored by diplomatic historians has been the paperback spy thriller, even though it has been a highly popular genre and one with obvious Cold War resonances. Further research in this area might well illuminate popular perceptions of American foreign policy at a given point in time and might even represent the past more fully than traditional studies based solely on presidential decrees, State Department documents, and other official records.

The best-selling novels of Tom Clancy, the most popular writer of *any* type of fiction in the 1980s, with sales of more than thirty million books in the United States alone, show how fruitful research into this genre can be. Three of Clancy's novels—***The Hunt for Red October, Red Storm Rising,*** and ***The Cardinal of the Kremlin***—can be interpreted as popular representations of Reagan-era Cold War values. They reflect both popular perceptions of Soviet behavior and the predominant national security values of the Reagan era. They also perpetuate myths about the American past and reinforce the symbols, images, and historical lessons that have dominated Cold War discourse.

Clancy's novels are best understood in the context of the evolution of the thriller genre and the Cold War itself. Although espionage is sometimes described as the world's second oldest profession, it was not until the twentieth century that the spy thriller emerged as a distinct genre. The celebrated Dreyfus case in *fin de siécle* France and the bitter international rivalries that characterized the twentieth century created the conditions in which the new genre flourished. As one scholar has observed, "Thriller literature is crisis literature and has arisen in the same century as crisis theology and an existential philosophy, as a response to the crisis of our civilization."

Erskine Childers's *The Riddle of the Sands* (1903), Joseph Conrad's *The Secret Agent* (1907), and, most outstandingly, John Buchan's *The Thirty-Nine Steps* (1915) laid the foundation for the modern thriller. Buchan pioneered the formula of the heroic epic in which the gentleman amateur (Sir Richard Hannay in the Buchan novels) survives harrowing chases and direct encounters with evil and exotic villains in order to save Great Britain from intricate plots formulated by (usually German) spies. The highly moralistic heroic spy story formula dominated the genre until the 1950s, when the public, "tired of a devastating war and fearful of a nuclear future, clearly wanted escape, adventure, heroism, and romance, but remained suspicious of the pieties, the ascetic moralism, and the high-toned patriotism of the Buchan tradition."

It was in this climate that the morally ambiguous novels of Eric Ambler, Graham Greene, and John le Carré emerged. These authors wrote not merely spy tales but literature, and, in marked contrast to Buchan's heroic epics, their stories explored the excesses of superpatriotism, conflicting loyalties, and the complexities of the "the human factor," as Greene entitled one of his novels. There was little trace of the moral certainty characteristic of the heroic epic formula in Greene's *Quiet American,* in which CIA agent Alden Pyle kills innocent civilians in a reckless attempt to spread American values in Vietnam. Even more unsettling was le Carré's *The Spy Who Came in From the Cold,* published in 1962 and still considered the masterwork of spy fiction. In that novel Alec Leamas, the protagonist, finds himself trapped between the two in some respects indistinguishable Cold War antagonists. Betrayed by his own side and left alone out "in the cold," Leamas and his lover can only "come in" through their deaths at the Berlin Wall in the book's climactic scene. Le Carré's fiction reflected the daily uncertainties of real life

spying, which the CIA's legendary counterintelligence specialist James Angleton, himself once accused of being a "mole" for the KGB, lamented had become a complex "wilderness of mirrors" in which it was difficult to separate the patriots from the traitors, good from evil.

While the fiction of Ambler, Greene, and le Carré took the Cold War and its moral ambiguities seriously, Ian Fleming's James Bond could not resist the temptation of parody. Agent 007—the special designation gave him "a license to kill"—inhabited a world that shared characteristics with both Buchan's and le Carré's formulas. Like Buchan's Hannay, Bond lived in a manichean and melodramatic world in which the forces of evil—usually in the form of racially indeterminate characters such as Goldfinger and Dr. No—ultimately failed in their attempts to subvert world order. Unlike Hannay, but like the characters of Ambler, Greene, and le Carré, Bond operated in the context of a national security organization, which by this time had become a permanent fixture of Cold War fiction. After all, not even 007 could have been expected to tackle such postwar leviathans as SMERSH or SPECTRE without benefit of institutional support.

Although he stopped well short of outright satire, Fleming did not ask the readers of his fourteen Bond novels to take them too seriously. In any case, readers (including John F. Kennedy) were more entranced by the exotic locations, fast cars, casino gambling, and furious sexual liaisons with the likes of Honeychile Rider and Pussy Galore than in any serious reflections on the complexities of the Cold War. As John Cawelti has noted, "Fleming changed the spy story from a set of images heavily loaded with moral content into stories suffused with an amoral hedonism." By the time Albert R. Broccoli began to produce the Bond films, especially those starring Roger Moore, the parody that had lain just beneath the surface of the Fleming novels had become the centerpiece of films that attracted a cult following. Fleming's Bond was the most popular suspense hero since Sherlock Holmes and may yet enjoy an equally long literary and celluloid life.

Americans were heavy consumers of such spy stories, all of which were crafted by British authors, but the novels of Mickey Spillane were the first authentically American bestsellers to incorporate Cold War themes. While Spillane's Mike Hammer properly belongs to the genre of the hard-boiled detective, he could hardly avoid contact with domestic Communists, the "reds" who had infiltrated America's homes, schools, churches, cinemas, and, of course, the State Department in the early postwar years. From 1947 to 1952, Spillane's novels sold millions of copies even as the United States committed itself to global containment and the extirpation of domestic communism. Spillane's popular fiction reinforced the predominant national security values of the early Cold War much as Clancy's would do in the renascent Cold War of the Reagan years.

There was nothing subtle or morally ambiguous about Mike Hammer or Tiger Mann, an espionage agent who appeared in some of Spillane's later novels. They confronted evil villains, often either Communists, women, or both—and killed them. In Spillane's first novel, *I, the Jury* (1947), Hammer names himself judge, jury, and executioner of the woman who had been his lover but also, he discovered, had killed his partner. The book, which sold over eight million copies, was followed by equally lurid and misogynist releases such as *Vengeance Is Mine!* (1950), *My Gun Is Quick* (1950), *The Big Kill* (1951), and *Kiss Me, Deadly* (1952). While real American soldiers were fighting communism in Korea, Spillane published *One Lonely Night* (1951), in which Hammer exalted in killing more people in one night "than I have fingers on my hands. I shot them in cold blood and enjoyed every minute of it. . . . They were Commies . . . red sons of bitches who should have died long ago."

The series of rapid fire confrontations with evil seems to have exhausted even Spillane, who became a Jehovah's Witness and retired in 1952, only to reemerge in 1961, in the midst of the Kennedy Cold War crises, with a popular new series of novels. In *Bloody Sunrise* (1965), Tiger Mann, formerly of the wartime Office of Strategic Services but now an operative in a civilian anti-Communist agency, expresses the frustrations of unrepentant Cold Warriors embittered over the failure to defeat communism, even in "our own backyard." "This country wasn't founded on a goddam octopus government that lets mice like Castro and Kremlin bums pick us apart," Tiger Mann declares. "When something gets screwed up and the striped-pants boys can't handle it and the politicos are scared to death to touch it for fear of stepping on somebody's toes and maybe not getting reelected, then we do something about it."

From the mid-sixties to the late seventies, with the morally ambiguous spy formula pioneered by Ambler, Greene and le Carré dominating the genre, it was evident that Spillane's manichean imagery had been displaced. The Vietnam War, Watergate, revelations of CIA misconduct, détente, and the arms race all served to reinforce the ambiguities of espionage and international relations. It had never been more difficult to discern the good guys from the bad. Some of the most successful thrillers of this period led the reader to identify with evil doers. In Frederick Forsyth's *The Day of the Jackal* (1971), readers find themselves admiring the professionalism of the assassin whose mission is the elimination of Charles de Gaulle. In Jack Higgins's *The Eagle Has Landed* (1976), the reader is drawn to the actions of Nazi airborne commandos who aim to kill Winston Churchill, rather than to a heroic protagonist on the "right" side in World War II. In Len Deighton's *Spy Story* (1975), the evil

doers are prominent Englishmen. Thomas Grady's *Six Days of the Condor* (1974), later made into a popular movie starring Robert Redford, had the CIA cynically liquidating its own people because they had learned too much. The popular novels by Robert Ludlum did feature a traditional hero overcoming long odds in high-stakes confrontations with evil, but Ludlum employed a variety of villains, including even the FBI, and thus did little to eliminate moral ambiguity.

> **By the late 1970s, however, the malaise of the Carter years and frustration over the sense of impotence fostered by the "Vietnam syndrome" created conditions conducive to both the revitalization of the Cold War and the reemergence of the heroic epic formula with Tom Clancy as its champion.**
> —*Walter L. Hixson*

By the late 1970s, however, the malaise of the Carter years and frustration over the sense of impotence fostered by the "Vietnam syndrome" created conditions conducive to both the revitalization of the Cold War and the reemergence of the heroic epic formula with Tom Clancy as its champion. Jimmy Carter had begun his presidency by calling on the country to rise above its "inordinate fear of communism," but by the end of his term he had lost public support for his handling of foreign affairs. The Iran hostage crisis, the Soviet invasion of Afghanistan, the rejection of the SALT II treaty, and fears of Communist advances from Central America to the horn of Africa all combined to create a sense of crisis that Reagan exploited in his 1980 landslide election victory. The new president, drawing on the same Hollywood images of the cowboy that he had once romanticized on the "General Electric Theater" and "Death Valley Days," pledged that the nation would once again "stand tall" in world affairs. Vowing to contain communism across the globe, Reagan ordered a massive strategic buildup and employed military power in Lebanon, Grenada, and Libya. When the USSR shot down a South Korean civilian airliner (Flight 007, no less) that had penetrated deep into Soviet airspace on 1 September 1983, Reagan promptly declared, without evidence, that the Kremlin knew it was a commercial airliner but committed the "crime against humanity" all the same. Reagan responded to an outpouring of concern over the threat of nuclear war by abandoning a ten-year-old moratorium on defensive systems in order to promote the space-based Strategic Defense Initiative (SDI), which he asserted would one day render nuclear weapons "impotent and obsolete."

Just as Mickey Spillane reinforced the Truman administration's national security values, which found expression in NATO, Korea, and the global confrontation with communism propounded in NSC-68, Tom Clancy's work was the fictional incarnation of the Reagan administration's Cold War policy. Clancy's novels challenged the morally ambiguous Ambler-Greene-le Carré paradigm by reviving the heroic epic formula first popularized by John Buchan. Clancy's plots hinged on manichean struggles that invariably climaxed in the unambiguous triumph of good over evil. His protagonist, Jack Ryan, was in many respects a modern Sir Richard Hannay: clean-cut, patriotic, ingenious, and triumphant. Unlike Hannay, who was a product of pre-World War I innocence, however, Jack Ryan could not hope to win the epic struggles of the late twentieth century without the backing of a dedicated national security establishment and the ready availability of the most sophisticated military technology. And unlike James Bond, Ryan would never gamble and had little time for anything more than perfunctory sex, sometimes explicitly for procreation, and only with his wife. By "just saying 'no'" to vice, Ryan embodied the Reagan administration's "family values" as well as its national security policy.

Clancy's novels hinge on what might be called the cult of national security, a set of assumptions and policy formulations to which the Reagan administration adhered. Reviving orthodox perceptions of the early Cold War, Reagan administration national security planners embraced worst-case scenarios of Soviet behavior based on the assumption of the existence of a totalitarian regime bent on global expansion and, ultimately, "world domination." They perceived the USSR as beyond reform and utterly cynical with respect to the means it might employ to achieve its aggressive design. The cult of national security arrogated to Washington the primary responsibility to contain and deter the Soviet Union, thus invoking a language that reinforced the Cold War preoccupation with the adversary's capabilities rather than its intentions. National security policy also sanctioned intervention on behalf of authoritarian regimes, using, once again, the words containment and deterrence—defensive terms that implied that Washington actually sought to promote self-determination. The cult of national security mandated strict control over foreign policy by the executive branch of government and sought to manage or subvert, sometimes through covert, illegal, or constitutionally questionable means, congressional and public opposition. Adherents of the cult of national security equated negotiation with Communist adversaries with Munich-style appeasement and sought to discredit domestic proponents of détente.

Clancy's texts, like the Reagan administration itself, not only reflected the cult of national security but apotheosized the American dream as well. Indeed, Clancy's own rise from Maryland insurance salesman to best-selling author and

newsweekly cover star rivals any Horatio Alger tale. His six (through 1992) espionage and national security novels all topped the best-seller list for months and were translated into several languages, making him arguably the most widely read author in the Western world. Hollywood converted both *The Hunt for Red October* and *Patriot Games* into commercially successful films.

What accounts for the mass appeal of Clancy's novels? Even some of his most avid readers admit that the books do not thrive on literary merit. Clancy may be a more accomplished stylist than Spillane, but just barely. Critics have called attention to his "undistinguished prose"; "wooden dialogue"; "plastic characters . . . on a Victorian boy's book level"; and "rubber-band plot[s] that stretch credibility to the breaking point." Although Clancy sometimes succeeds in building suspense toward a page-turning climax—the elementary requirement of the genre—even in this respect he is no Frederick Forsyth. "If you don't share Clancy's reverence for the spectacle of a gigantic national-security apparatus mobilizing to repel foreign evildoers," noted critic Terrence Rafferty, "[Clancy's] stories are just a bore—you settle back in the bulletproof limo, close your eyes, and try to shut out the driver's jabbering."

Rather than thriving on their literary merit, it seems likely that Clancy's novels sell at least in part for the same reasons that Ronald Reagan was an immensely popular president. Much as Reagan did, Clancy rewards the public by invoking powerful themes that are embedded in the American cultural tradition. Perhaps the most potent theme invoked by both Reagan and Clancy is the enduring mythology of American exceptionalism—moral, political, and technological. In all three novels analyzed below, the American heroes—invariably patriotic white males employed by the nation's military or intelligence services—are virtuous products of a materially successful pluralist democracy. As yet another critic has noted, "What Clancy has to offer—and it makes his books emblematic of the Reagan administration's self-image—is an old-fashioned sense of certitude, righteousness and derring-do." Clancy's patriotic heroes are highly skilled, disciplined, honest, thoroughly professional, and only lose their cool when incompetent politicians or bureaucrats get in their way. Their unambiguous triumphs over evil provide symbolic relief from the legacy of the Vietnam War, the country's most recent actual conflict, in which military victory proved illusive and distinctions between good and evil proved illusory. There are numerous parallels between Reagan and Clancy. Clancy buries the legacy of Vietnam, just as Reagan attempted to do. Like Reagan, Clancy evokes nostalgic memories of American innocence and military victory in World War II, the "good war" in which the United States (the critical role played by its allies, especially the Soviet Union, having been minimized in U.S. cultural discourse) defeated Hitler as well as the "Japs" and enjoyed unparalleled security through its monopoly on atomic weapons. Clancy's texts thus complement the "Dr. Feel-good" Reagan era in that they succeed in reinvesting American culture with nostalgic images of military victory over external demons, and they resist accommodation to a new status of "relative decline" in world affairs.

Clancy's novels reinforce American exceptionalism by demonizing both foreign enemies and domestic political foes, much as the Reagan administration did also. As political scientist Michael Paul Rogin has argued, "political demonology" has been "a continuing feature of American politics." "The inflation, stigmatization, and dehumanization of political foes" reflect "a countersubversive tradition that exists at the core of American politics, not at its periphery." The monsters that have stalked American cultural history include "the Indian cannibal, the black rapist, the papal whore of Babylon, the monster-hydra United States Bank, the demon rum, the bomb-throwing anarchist, the many tentacled Communist conspiracy, [and] the agents of international terrorism." The Clancy novels employ Stalinist imagery, for the same reason Reagan did, to demonize the Soviet "evil empire" while promoting the mythology of American exceptionalism and the cult of national security. Clancy's demonization of the USSR and manichean imagery reflect a pattern of countersubversive behavior that has been embedded in American culture since colonial literature reduced the frontier to a struggle between the Indian savage and the hunter hero.

The Clancy novels demonize not only the external enemy but the internal one as well. Because the stories reflect and promote one conception of national security, they vilify American liberals, academics, homosexuals, the news media, and other putative challengers of the Cold War ethos. Like past proponents of red scare hysteria over internal security, Clancy's novels suggest that the United States could be undermined from within by spies and dupes of the international Communist conspiracy.

The triumph of American virtue only partially accounts for the appeal of Clancy's novels; equally important is *how* the heroes of his fiction triumph. Clancy's novels attach great importance to salvation through technology. Buchan's hero used only his own ingenuity to overcome evil doers. Although James Bond did employ deadly gadgets to get himself out of tight spots, he disdained being briefed about them ("*Try* to pay attention, 007!") and never used them to achieve the ultimate conquest of his adversary. Clancy, on the other hand, a self-confessed "technology freak" with a sure grasp of military hardware, has made his mark as "king of the technothriller." Virtually without exception American weapons—from nuclear submarines to the Stealth fighter to SDI—work unerringly and are decisive in the final resolution of his plots. Consistent with Reagan's promotion of such

programs as the MX "Peacekeeper" missile and SDI, Clancy's texts encourage the view that bolstering strategic arsenals, far from posing a threat to human existence, will enable the nation to deter and if necessary defeat aggressors as it fulfills its role as the exceptional guarantor of world order.

Clancy's first and perhaps best-crafted novel, **The Hunt for Red October** (1984) contains all these elements—an emphasis on American exceptionalism, demonized enemies, and an array of high-tech weaponry. The enduring appeal of the book stems in part from its success as a classic thriller. It is, one reviewer noted, "the most satisfactory novel of a sea chase since C. S. Forester perfected the form." The plot centers on the defection of a Soviet captain (Marko Ramius) to the United States in his nation's most advanced nuclear submarine while the Soviet navy gives chase and American officials try to clear his path. Despite the privileges that accrue to the Soviet navy's top submarine pilot, Ramius chooses to defect because he had begun to question Communist orthodoxies, and indeed had become "an individual in his thinking, and so unknowingly committed the gravest sin in the Communist pantheon [*sic*]."

Thus, the first forty pages of the novel establish the demonic nature of the USSR as the reader begins to identify with a Soviet protagonist who is exceptional because he acts as an individual in a regimented society founded on terror. (According to Clancy, the Soviet Union of the mid-1980s was still a state in which the KGB could "order the execution or imprisonment of a hundred men without blinking." In contrast to the redoubtable Ramius, most Soviet characters in **Red October** are dull-witted true believers in Marxism-Leninism. Clancy's American characters refer to the average Russian as "Ivan," evoking a more "terrible" image than does the noble-sounding Ramius, who is a Baltic European.

While the Soviet characters bumble their way toward strategic defeat, Jack Ryan and his colleagues skillfully guide **Red October** to U.S. shores, pulling off the whole enterprise so that neither the Soviets nor the American public are even aware of it. The novel highlights a U.S. intelligence operation that is both covert and successful, thus reassuring readers that their intelligence services may be accomplishing great things without their knowledge. U.S. intelligence services, the story suggests, should be amply funded and given license to conduct their business without the burden of external oversight. During the Iran-contra imbroglio, the Reagan administration showed that it shared the same view.

Through the character of Peter Henderson, Clancy underscores the dangers of democratic oversight while demonizing opponents of the national security cult. After progressing from Harvard, where he was an editor on the *Crimson* as well as an activist against the Vietnam War, Henderson became an aide to a U.S. senator and a KGB spy. The Henderson character alerts the reader to the dangers of congressional oversight by suggesting that congressmen may unwittingly pass information through disloyal aides into the hands of the tireless agents of international communism. Moreover, Henderson's character suggests that those who were involved in the antiwar movement and those with "liberal East Coast" and "liberal media" connections are potential traitors.

Despite the Henderson-Hiss-Lattimore attempts to stab America in the back, the mission succeeds, Ramius gains freedom, and Jack Ryan trumpets U.S. exceptionalism and material abundance. He informs a group of incredulous Russians that the United States is a land of unparalleled material wealth and equal opportunity. "Anything you want. . . . Beef, pork, lamb, turkey, chicken. . . . The United States feeds itself and has plenty left over. . . . Everyone has a car. Most people own their own homes. . . . The fact of the matter is that in our country if you have some brains . . . and you are willing to work . . . you will live a comfortable life even without any help." Moments later, Mannion, a black U.S. sailor, informs Ramius that all the Soviet propaganda he has heard about racism and the white bourgeois ruling class in America is just that—propaganda. Much like the Reagan administration itself, Clancy's characters dealt with poverty and racial inequality by acting as if they did not exist.

While demonization of the Soviet Union is an important element of *The Hunt for Red October,* it plays an even greater role in Clancy's second work, *Red Storm Rising* (1986). As the title image suggests, the novel emphasizes naked Soviet military aggression against the West. More than any other Clancy novel, *Red Storm Rising* promotes the worst-case scenarios of Soviet military behavior upon which the cult of national security depended. The book begins with dark-skinned, Koran-toting, Allah-quoting Soviet Muslim fanatics sabotaging a huge Siberian oil refining complex, thus depriving the USSR of 34 percent of its crude oil production and risking an internal rebellion on the part of "the faceless collection of men and women who toiled every day . . . in factories and on collective farms, their thoughts hidden behind unsmiling masks." The Soviet defense minister declares at an emergency Politburo meeting that "we must obtain more oil. It is as simple as that." Because not enough can be purchased, he concludes that "we must take it." The plot of *Red Storm Rising* thus reinforces the nightmarish image of an unstable totalitarian state that might at any moment resort to foreign "adventurism" to solve problems that flow from domestic instability. Like the Soviet bear, a large and powerful beast with a primitive mentality, Soviet leaders are violent and unpredictable. "In the Politburo, as in the jungle," the narrator avers, "the only rule was survival."

While the West is lulled to sleep by the détente line promoted by the new Communist party general secretary, the real decisions are being made in the Defense Ministry, which opts for total war to secure Soviet dominance of Europe and the Persian Gulf. Thus, the Politburo votes overwhelmingly (in the midst of a failed campaign in neighboring Afghanistan) to risk nuclear war by seizing the Persian Gulf after first launching an all-out invasion of NATO-occupied Western Europe. The Hitlerian nightmare unfolds with a reprise of Munich, as the Kremlin leadership trumpets détente before the world community and even proposes a 50 percent reduction, with verification, of superpower nuclear arsenals.

After encouraging appeasement in the West, the Soviets initiate hostilities in the most cynical fashion—by killing innocent *Soviet* children in a Kremlin explosion and blaming it on West Germany, which they then invade. After neutralizing Europe, the Red Army extends its *blitzkrieg* by invading Iceland in order to seize control of the Atlantic. Soviet storm troopers smash the tiny, nonviolent country, which is defended only by a national police force.

During the Icelandic invasion, Soviet soldiers kill the mother, father, and dog of a young—and of course pregnant—Icelandic woman, who is herself subjected to a gang rape. The rape and the subsequent rescue scene revive a narrative formula first popularized by James Fenimore Cooper's Leatherstocking tales and cemented in American cultural discourse ever since. The Cooperian mythology revolves around scenes of captivity, savagery, and violent regeneration through the heroism of the solitary hunter. In this case the solitary hunter is Mike Edwards, an air force lieutenant stationed at a NATO outpost on the western coast of Iceland. Like the self-made men who "tamed the frontier" before him, Edwards is not by nature a violent man, but even the mild-mannered air force meteorologist is compelled to adopt the savage frontier ethos. Sickened by the brutal rape and murders, Edwards and his fellow GIs cannot restrain themselves from summarily executing the Soviet prisoners who committed the atrocities. (The Icelandic woman falls in love with Edwards two days after being gang-raped.) The Russian soldiers thus merge with Spillane's "red sons of bitches" and with the savage Indians, Filipino "goo-goos," "Huns," "Japs," Nazis, and Vietnamese "gooks" as barbaric enemies who must be exterminated.

The Stealth fighter and bomber aircraft represent the theme of salvation through strategic technology in *Red Storm Rising.* "We nearly defeated you," the defeated Soviet General Alekseyev explains. "If those damned invisible bombers of yours hadn't hit our bridges on the first day, or if we had managed to smash three or four of your convoys, you would be offering me terms."

After drawing sharper criticism from reviewers of his third

novel, *Patriot Games,* a tale about IRA terrorist attempts to seize the British royal family, Clancy returned to the Soviet enemy in *The Cardinal of the Kremlin* (1988). Like *Red Storm Rising, Cardinal* opens with a reprise of an Allah-quoting, Koran-toting Afghani Muslim fanatic (with "dark pitiless eyes") gunning down Soviet soldiers in the mountains of Azerbaijan, where the Kremlin's operation Bright Star, an SDI-type system, is under construction. As Americans and Soviets seek to learn about and sabotage each other's SDI programs, a top CIA asset high in the Soviet defense ministry, Mikhail S. Filitov—the Cardinal of the Kremlin—is exposed and jailed and the top U.S. SDI scientist is kidnapped. The heroic Jack Ryan, aided by the *mujahideen* in Afghanistan (depicted as "freedom fighters" rather than Koran-toting fanatics), allows the United States to rescue its kidnapped scientist and free the Cardinal himself.

The Cardinal of the Kremlin promotes SDI as the means to salvation through technological advance. "Defense systems could not be stopped now," Filitov observes. "One might as easily try to stop the tide." The Soviet character Yazov obligingly confirms the Reagan administration line when he acknowledges that his country is not only deeply involved in research on strategic defensive systems but is also "further along in testing." Soviet negotiating offers, especially with respect to arms control, are dismissed as disingenuous ploys that mask malevolent intent. Only dupes in Congress and liberal peaceniks could think otherwise.

Like the rape and rescue scenes in *Red Storm Rising,* a demonization scene in *Cardinal* features Soviet savagery, this time directed at a beautiful Soviet woman who is an American spy. (Beautiful Soviet women are American spies; most Soviet women are depicted in Cold War popular culture as overweight matrons, like the uniformed comrade in the popular Wendy's television commercial that appeared in the late 1980s.) Following her capture, the blonde woman makes a drug-induced confession as the Nazi-like doctor caresses her naked body. Mind-altering drugs make her forget everything. The Nazi-Soviet doctor later explains: "Surely you have read *1984.* It might have been a dream when Orwell wrote it, but with modern technology we can do it." Invoking the most clichéed totalitarian imagery, the narrator describes the brainwashed woman's once animated face as "blank. What had been lively was now as emotionless as any face on a Moscow street." Big Brother no longer even needed to watch her. The imagery of totalitarian robotization is reinforced in other passages, where readers learn that Russians are "so grim all the time" (in part because their smiles "stop at their lips"); they don't "know how to have a good time"; and they themselves even admit that they "should have more Americans around."

This brief summary of the three Clancy novels shows the extent to which his popular fiction embodies the predomi-

nant national security values of the Reagan administration. Clancy's evocation of American exceptionalism, demonization of the Soviet Union, and his promotion of the national security *mentalité* indicate how deeply the United States invested in the language and symbols of the Cold War during the Reagan years. In the wake of defeat in Vietnam, the Watergate scandal, revelations of CIA misconduct, and the crises of the Carter years, Americans yearned to replace the morally ambiguous legacies of the Cold War with the unambiguous triumph of good over evil. Both Reagan's presidency and Clancy's novels were means to that end.

While the symbiosis between Clancy's texts and Reagan-era Cold War values seems clear, it is more difficult to assess the extent to which the books actually reinforced and promoted those values. It is not unreasonable to assume that the stress upon American exceptionalism, the demonization of the USSR, and the depiction of salvation through military technology reinforced the cult of national security in the minds of millions of Clancy readers. Clancy's novels, like those of Mickey Spillane, became best sellers in the same period that East-West tensions reached a new peak. It seems likely, therefore, that Clancy's fiction, like the Spillane novels of the early 1950s, helped bolster the Cold War ethos through the medium of popular culture.

> **The efforts of national security elites to promote Clancy's books, movies, and the author himself offer the best evidence that his popular fiction played a meaningful role in shaping opinion in the real world.**
> —*Walter L. Hixson*

The efforts of national security elites to promote Clancy's books, movies, and the author himself offer the best evidence that his popular fiction played a meaningful role in shaping opinion in the real world. The military establishment at first expressed some concern over Clancy's sure grasp of "secret" military technology, but it quickly concluded that such concerns were trivial when measured against the "great service" that Clancy's books performed by promoting the interests of the armed services and the military-industrial complex. Accordingly, the military establishment "adopted me," as Clancy himself once put it, by providing the popular author with privileged access to restricted facilities, job offers, and promotion of his books and films. "Everybody's willing to talk to Clancy," observed a Pentagon spokesman. "He's neat. He's one of the good guys." A Ford Foundation critic complained that leaks to Clancy were "the authorized winked-at way to leak information that will help the military procurement budget." Republican national strategist Edward Rollins and representative Newt Gingrich of Georgia found Clancy such an effective spokesman for the cult of national security that they urged him to challenge Maryland representative Roy Dyson, a prominent Democrat on the House Armed Services Committee, in 1992. Clancy declined.

The military establishment also gave the producers of the film version of **The Hunt for Red October** advice and technical assistance, as it often did when it approved of films. When producers of the film *Platoon,* which reflected critically on some U.S. military actions in Vietnam, requested similar assistance, however, the Pentagon refused. Additional efforts to exploit Clancy's fiction accompanied the opening of the film version of **The Hunt for Red October.** In theaters across the country the navy set up information tables, complete with model submarines, in the lobbies and hallways. Naval recruiters promoted the film as "the submariner's *Top Gun,*" a reference to the top grossing movie and video of the 1980s, which romanticized military service and prompted a 300-percent increase in naval aviation officer training enlistments.

The official embrace of **The Hunt for Red October** extended to the White House, where Clancy dined with the Reagans. Indeed, **The Hunt for Red October** became a publishing phenomenon only after Reagan called it "the perfect yarn" and recommended it to the nation. Senators, including Dan Quayle, who was then a senator from Indiana, praised Clancy, not as a novelist but as an authority on national security. During a debate on funding of anti-satellite weapons (ASAT) technology, Quayle held Clancy's **Red Storm Rising** aloft on the Senate floor and asked, "Have you read this book? ASAT technology is what wins the war!"

The reception accorded Clancy's novels in these circles makes it clear that national security elites exploited his popular fiction to promote the cult of national security. Millions of readers have absorbed Clancy's exaltation of American exceptionalism, demonization of foreign and domestic political enemies, and promotion of military technology and new weapons systems. One cannot conclusively prove that Clancy's novels reinforced or changed the way those readers thought about the Cold War or U.S. foreign policy any more than one can "prove" that the Truman Doctrine or John F. Kennedy's inaugural address shaped public perceptions about the Cold War. What can be demonstrated, in this case, is that Clancy's novels promoted ideologically constructed perceptions of foreign policy discourse—perceptions that were absorbed by millions of Americans and were actively promoted by a national security establishment whose interests they served.

John Calvin Batchelor (review date 21 August 1994)

SOURCE: "Tom Clancy's Damn-the-Literary-Torpedoes Style Dances at the Edge of the Daily News," in *Los Angeles Times Book Review,* August 21, 1994, pp. 1, 9.

[*In the following review, Batchelor offers praise for* Debt of Honor.]

Tom Clancy is America's most wish-fulfilling policy-maker, and in his eighth spectacular and scary novel, **Debt of Honor,** he plunges America into a foreign policy that is at once unthinkable and very thrilling—a campaign that the present State and Defense departments can only wish they had the talent to fight.

Real war with Japan. Real Japanese sneak attack against America's Pacific fleet, real paralyzing nuclear gamesmanship with rebuilt Soviet missiles, real state terrorism, real American territory taken by foreign troops, real dead Americans in the thousands, and all this in the immediate future.

The moment when the President learns of the war is the chilling instant of the book.

"You look like hell," President Durling remarks to Clancy's franchise player, super hero Jack Ryan.

They're in Air Force One, heading home from new ally Russia, alert to several spontaneous Third World crises that might be linked.

"What's the problem?" the President asks.

Ryan, now national security adviser, searches for the right emphasis on the mind-boggling news flashes: stock market crashing, two carriers out of action, two nuclear subs missing, terrorism in the Indian Ocean, chauvinist elections in Japan.

"Mr. President, based on information received over the last few hours, I believe that the United States of America is at war with Japan."

In one tight scene Tom Clancy has done the work of all the king's horses and men—he has put before you, as if you were the President, the possibility of a battle that is implicit in every economic headline this summer about the U.S. trade gap with Japan, the yen versus the dollar, and the fragility of the U.S. government bond market and the Nikkei stock market. War with Japan! Of course! So that's what's going on.

Clancy has spun this exact spider's web brilliantly before—brought together "what-if" scenarios with media agitprop with the dazzling hardware and tireless muscle of America's armed forces. In seven previous novels, Clancy has defended

America from the massive air-land-sea attacks of the Soviets (*Red Storm Rising*), the demonic sabotage of the Mideast fundamentalists (*Patriot Games, The Sum of All Fears*), the twisted minds of Vietnamese tyrants (*Without Remorse*), the hate-filled drug lords (*Clear and Present Danger*) and even the chicanery of allies and traitors (*Cardinal of the Kremlin, Hunt for Red October*).

For more than a decade Clancy has projected American power and ideals around the globe. If our foes want to know what we would do if attacked or tricked, they only need to look at Clancy to learn that they don't want to fool with Uncle Sam. (Clancy's two nonfiction works, *Submarine* and *Armored Cav,* for cavalry, are one boot stride into the twilight zone of what the Pentagon charmingly calls "warfighting.")

In his greatest achievement to date, *Red Storm Rising,* Clancy, with tech support from the skillful Larry Bond, played out the Soviet sneak attack on NATO and showed not only why the Soviet empire was evil but also that it was doomed to lose any scenario of conflict with the American military machine. The death of the Soviet Union followed Clancy's story like an afterthought, and in the history of Cold War fiction Clancy will always be remembered as the man who delivered the *coup de grâce.*

Debt of Honor raises the stakes for Clancy. Here he has us at war not with the infamous evil empire of the Cold War, not with the agreed-upon enemies of terrorists and druggies, but with the folk who own two Hollywood studios and Rockefeller Center: the Japanese.

In sum, war with the wrong foe. For the United States of America is not at present in a position either to defend itself from nor to counterattack a Japanese military strike.

"Jesus, the cupboard's that bare?" a stunned naval officer comments at the frail American order of battle in the Pacific at the war's opening.

Clancy responds to this question with his militant point: "The mighty United States Pacific Fleet, as recently as five years ago the most powerful naval force in the history of civilization, was now a frigate navy."

To convince the reader that war with the people who brought you the Nissan Pathfinder is credible, Clancy works diligently to build a 350-page case answering the why, who, where and how of a Japanese war.

This grinding detail is Clancy's gift. He atomizes the chain of events that leads from a mistaken manufacture of a Japanese automobile gas tank to the American political outrage

and turmoil to the mercantilist counterblow in the Congress to the textbook subterfuge of Japanese industrialists who are most threatened by a pending American embargo of all Japanese cars. It's all as logical as Kissinger's mind, domino by domino, and we watch the world move toward cataclysm with precision. When the Japanese take out the supercarriers Enterprise and John Stennis with a trick Mark-50 torpedo fusillade at their screw-propellers, it's clear that America is on the brink of Pearl Harbor II. And this time we won't have a chance to rearm because we've given the weapons locker away.

Fortunately the Irish ruthlessness of Jack Ryan is available to save his President and country once more from disaster. Harrison Ford has twice played Ryan perfectly—in the movie versions of *Patriot Games* and the new *Clear and Present Danger*—and it's impossible not to see Ford hunched over the desk in the Oval Office and biting off data-packed information for the President.

"There are ten birds here," Ryan says of the hidden Japanese nuclear missiles. "They're dug in deep, and the site seems to have been selected for relative immunity from attack. The next question is making sure we can hit them all."

At the same time, the sensationally savage CIA field officer, John Clark (hero of *Without Remorse*), has a critical role in countering the Japanese. Indeed Clancy brings all of his huge continuing cast of characters into play—the CIA families, the Secret Service and FBI agents, the sailors and aviators—and reading Clancy now is like attending a reunion. Everyone has a critical job, everyone performs admirably.

At the heart of the tale are the submarines, of course, for Clancy's love remains with his first success, *The Hunt for Red October.* The action language is always grand, but for me the dialogue in an attack submarine is pure science fiction pleasure:

"Bearing is constant. Not a wiggle. They heading straight for us or close to it. They pounding hard."

The last 200 pages of *Debt of Honor* are breathtaking. Only the elect who can read real-time satellite photos can get more excited than a Clancy reader at the climax of a war story. The White House situation room, Langley's communications links, COMCINCPAC operations, the flight deck of a B-2, the conn of a 688, the Ranger unit behind enemy lines—all this specificity jumping around from paragraph to paragraph without mercy for the uneducated. Clancy's passion is overwhelming. His sense of cliffhanging is state of the art. The close of this book is a five-run homer.

The lit crowd has long smirked at Clancy, and it will trip over its metaphors bad-mouthing this yarn as racism and paranoia and (zounds!) melodrama. Worth considering, however, is that Clancy is now embarked on a patriotic journey into the post Cold War future, where nightmares such as Haiti and Bosnia and North Korea await like wounded lions. What's going to happen will look much closer to Clancy's gunsight vision than to the Stone-Morrison-Smiley-Eco set of infinite feelings or meanings. Next time someone takes a cheap shot at your dogeared Clancy set, just bark back, "Bombs away!"

John Lehman (review date 2 September 1994)

SOURCE: "Jack Ryan's New Gizmos Save Another Day," in *The Wall Street Journal,* September 2, 1994, p. A7.

[*In the following review, Lehman offers a favorable assessment of* Debt of Honor.]

After **The Hunt for Red October** established Tom Clancy as the Pentagon's Boswell, he found himself accorded the honors and access of a field marshal. A former Marine and lifelong military buff, Mr. Clancy used this access to soak up even more of the technical detail and the cultural attitudes of the politico-military world. Thusly armed, he produced a new class of literature—techno-thriller.

So what if his prose reads like a government manual. What, I often wonder, do his critics think bureaucrats talk like? Billy Crystal? The very woodenness of the dialogue highlights the real stars, who are not the two-dimensional people but the three-dimensional weapons. Mr. Clancy's gift is in crafting a plausible story, full of thrills, that puts all the neat gadgets and elite forces through their paces. Anyone wishing to understand how nuclear reactors on a warship generate power by boiling water will please to turn to page 329. For readers new to Mr. Clancy, *Debt of Honor* is certainly a good starter. It has dueling submarines, terrorist hits, venal politicians, smarmy lobbyists and a familiar hero, Jack Ryan, recently embodied by Harrison Ford on the big screen. It also has way too many pages.

The scene opens with an administration confused by the post Cold War's new world order. Lest we think this is the Clinton administration, it is established right off that it is the vice president who is the womanizing lecher. The secretary of state is a feckless wimp and the secretary of defense and chairman of the Joint Chiefs of Staff are political hacks determined to dismantle the armed forces built by Ronald Reagan. America's Navy is half of what it was 10 years before. Trade policies have severely eroded relations with Japan, whose military has been busy building secret nuclear missiles. The ensuing economic chaos in Japan brings in a new government controlled by thuggish industrial tycoons.

These thorough baddies begin at once to execute a carefully planned destruction of the U.S. and its economy. They sabotage our financial systems by deploying a computer virus that erases an entire day's trading on Wall Street, and by shoving the president of the New York branch of the Federal Reserve in front of a taxi "with newly refurbished brakes"—this detail will be unconvincing to seasoned riders. They also disable the Seventh Fleet in the Pacific and occupy the Mariana Islands. Fortunately for the fate of the nation, Ryan has been persuaded to leave the world of investment banking and has joined the White House as national-security adviser. Before long Jack Ryan will be closer than ever to the Oval Office, but in the meanwhile he renews contact with some old pals in the KGB and figures out what the Japanese really want, namely Siberia.

Jack's counterattack is fiendishly clever, employing double agents, assassination, press manipulation and the use of every high-tech weapon not yet beaten into a ploughshare. Given current congressional attempts to kill several controversial weapons, it is amusing to see that Mr. Clancy has built them all and that they perform flawlessly. He activates the Air Force F-22 fighter, which currently exists only in prototype and will be capable of operating in "supercruise"—flying at supersonic speed without consuming a costly 120,000 pounds of fuel per hour, and he brings on a stealth Commanche helicopter for an attack on Japan.

Mr. Clancy's trademark obsession with detailed technical descriptions keeps the kettle boiling. He tells us how the orbits of CIA spy satellites can be redirected for real-time surveillance, for example, and how important copper mesh is to stealth. The material, placed as a lining, absorbs incoming radar (I guess this information is no longer classified).

But if all of this sounds too much like Boy Scouts run amok for your sensibilities, Mr. Clancy will soothe you with his sensitive, newly acquired political correctness. Now half of his fighter jocks are ladies, most of the good guys are black, Hispanic or acceptably ethnic; the wives and daughters are surgeons and lawyers; charges of sexual harassment bring down the vice president (thereby creating a vacancy for the upwardly mobile Jack); and just about everyone from the president to the sonarman agonizes deeply over the very caring Japanese in subs who are about to be pulverized into fish food.

The last chapter alone is worth the price of the book, at least for those of us who cannot look at the Capitol without thinking of term limits. Mr. Clancy carries out a fantasy I have dreamed about for years, one that involves a very large plane and a kamikaze pilot: "The entire east face of the building's southern half was smashed to gravel which shot westward—but the real damage took a second or two longer, barely time for the roof to start falling in on the nine hundred people in the chamber."

Christopher Buckley (review date 2 October 1994)

SOURCE: "Megabashing Japan," in *New York Times Book Review,* October 2, 1994, pp. 28-9.

[*Below, Buckley offers an unfavorable review of* Debt of Honor.]

Somewhere, if memory serves, Mark Twain said of one of Henry James's books, "Once you put it down, you can't pick it up." **Debt of Honor,** the eighth novel in Tom Clancy's *oeuvre,* is, at 766 pages, a herniating experience. Things don't really start to happen until about halfway through this book, by which time most authors, including even some turgid Russian novelists, are finished with theirs. But Tom Clancy must be understood in a broader context, not as a mere writer of gizmo-thrillers, destroyer of forests, but as an economic phenomenon. What are his editors—assuming they even exist; his books feel as if they go by modem from Mr. Clancy's computer directly to the printers—supposed to do? Tell him to cut? "You tell him it's too long." "No, *you* tell him."

Someone, on the other hand—friend, relative, spiritual adviser, I don't know—really ought to have taken him aside and said, "Uh, Tom, isn't this book kind of racist?" I bow to no one in my disapproval of certain Japanese trade practices, and I worked for a man who once conspicuously barfed into the lap of the Japanese Prime Minister, but this book is as subtle as a World War II anti-Japanese poster showing a mustachioed Tojo bayoneting Caucasian babies. If you thought Michael Crichton was a bit paranoid, "Rising Sun"-wise, well then, to quote Mr. Clancy's favorite President and original literary booster, Ronald Reagan, "You ain't seen nothing yet." His Japanese aren't one-dimensional, they're half-dimensional. They spend most of their time grunting in bathhouses. And yet, to echo "Dr. Strangelove"'s Group Captain Lionel Mandrake, "the strange thing is, they make such bloody good cameras."

The plot: Japan craftily sabotages the United States financial markets, occupies the Mariana Islands, sinks two American submarines, killing 250 sailors, and threatens us with nuclear weapons. Why, you ask, don't we just throw up on their laps and give them a countdown to a few toasty reruns of Hiroshima and Nagasaki? Because, fools that we are, we have got rid of all our nukes in a mad disarmament pact with the Russkies. (Plausible? Never mind.)

For a while it looks like sayonara for Western civ, until Jack Ryan, now White House national security adviser, masterminds such a brilliant response to the crisis that he ends up Vice President. To make way, the current V.P. must resign because of charges of—sexual harassment. I won't be ruining it for you by saying that Ryan's ascendancy does not stop there; the President and the entire Congress must be eliminated in an inadvertently comic deus ex machina piloted by a sullen Japanese airman who miraculously does not grunt "Banzai!" as he plows his Boeing 747 into the Capitol. Former Secretary of the Navy John Lehman has recently had the arguable taste to remark, apropos this episode in **Debt of Honor,** that this particular fantasy has long been his own. I don't like Congress either, but Abraham Lincoln, Lehman's fellow Republican and mine, did go to some pains to keep the Capitol's construction going during the Civil War as a symbol of the Union's continuity. Oh, well.

To be sure, the war enacted here is not the fruit of national Japanese will, but rather a manipulation of events by a *zaibatsu* businessman whose mother, father and siblings had jumped off a cliff in Saipan back in 1944 rather than be captured by evil American marines, and by a corrupt, America-hating politician. But that hardly lets Mr. Clancy off the hook, for the nasty characteristics ascribed to Yamata (the former) and Goto (the latter) are straightforwardly racial. To heat our blood further, Goto keeps a lovely American blonde as his geisha and does unspeakable naughties to her. When she threatens to become a political hot tomato, Yamata has the poor thing killed. It all plays into the crudest kind of cultural paranoia, namely, that what these beastly yellow inscrutables are really after is—*our women.* (A similar crime, recall, was at the heart of Mr. Crichton's novel "Rising Sun." Well, archetypes do do the job.) Her name, for these purposes, is perfect: Kimberly Norton. "Yamata had seen breasts before, even large Caucasian breasts." To judge from the number of mentions of them, it is fair to conclude that Caucasian breasts are at the very heart of Gotosan's *Weltanschauung.* Farther down that same page, he expresses his carnal delight to Yamata "coarsely" (naturally) in—shall we say—cavorting with American girls. Jack Ryan is therefore striking a blow for more than the American way of life: he is knight-defender of nothing less than American bimbohood.

It must be said that the hapless Kimberly Norton is a glaring exception among Clancy women: so much so that you wonder if he's been reading Susan Faludi under the covers at night. With this book, Mr. Clancy stakes his claim to being the most politically correct popular author in America, which is somewhat remarkable in such an outspoken, if not fire-breathing, right winger as himself. Practically everyone is either black, Hispanic, a woman or, at a minimum, ethnic. The Vice President is hauled off on charges of sexual harassment; the Japanese Prime Minister is a rapist; the deputy director of operations at the C.I.A. is a woman; there is Comdr. Roberta Peach (Peach? honestly) of the Navy; Ryan's wife receives a Lasker Award for her breakthroughs in ophthalmic surgery; one of the C.I.A. assassins is informed, practically in the middle of dispatching slanty-eyed despoilers of American women, that his own daughter has made dean's list and will probably get into medical school; secretaries, we are told again and again, are the real heroes, etc., etc.

All this would be more convincing were it not for the superseding macho that permeates each page like dried sweat. Ryan's Secret Service code name is, I kid you not, "Swordsman." And there's something a bit gamey about this description of the C.I.A.'s deputy director of operations: "Mary Pat entered the room, looking about normal for an American female on a Sunday morning." His feminism, if it can be called that, is pretty smarmy, like a big guy getting a woman in a choke hold and giving her a knuckly noogie on the top of her head by way of showing her she's "O.K." (Preferable, I admit, to the entertainments offered by the officers and gentlemen of the Tailhook Association.) And there is this hilarious description of Ryan's saintly wife saving someone's sight with laser surgery. "She lined up the crosshairs as carefully as a man taking down a Rocky Mountain sheep from half a mile, and thumbed the control." You've got to admire a man who can find the sheep-hunting metaphor in retinal surgery.

Tom Clancy is the James Fenimore Cooper of his day, which is to say, the most successful bad writer of his generation. This is no mean feat, for there are many, many more rich bad writers today than there were in Cooper's time. If Twain were alive now, he would surely be writing an essay entitled, "The Literary Crimes of Clancy." He would have loved **Debt of Honor,** the culmination, thus far, of Mr. Clancy's almost endearing Hardy Boys-"Jane's Fighting Ships" prose style:

> "The Indians were indeed getting frisky."

> "More surprisingly, people made way for him, especially women, and children positively shrank from his presence as though Godzilla had returned to crush their city."

> "'I will not become Prime Minister of my country,' Hiroshi Goto announced in a manner worthy of a stage actor, 'in order to become executor of its economic ruin.'"

> "The captain, Commander Tamaki Ugaki, was known as a stickler for readiness, and though he drilled his men hard, his was a happy ship because she was always a smart ship."

> "'This is better than the Concorde!' Cathy gushed at the Air Force corporal who served dinner."

> "Damn, how much crazier would this world get?"

> "But what kind of evil synergy was this?"

> "Night at sea is supposed to be a beautiful thing, but it was not so this time."

> "*But I'm not a symbol,* Jack wanted to tell him. *I'm a man, with doubts.*"
> "The dawn came up like thunder in this part of the world, or so the poem went."

> "'I knew Goto was a fool, but I didn't think him a madman.'"

> "'Gentlemen: this *will* work. It's just so damned outrageous, but maybe that works in our favor.'"

> "'Bloody clever,' the head of the Bank of England observed to his German counterpart. '*Jawohl,*' was the whispered reply."

And finally, this: "The man knew how to think on his feet, and though often a guy at the bottom of the food chain, he tended to see the big picture very clearly from down there."

Michael R. Beschloss (review date 18 August 1996)

SOURCE: "President Jack Ryan," in *Book World—The Washington Post,* August 18, 1996, pp. 1, 14.

[*In the following review, Beschloss offers a favorable assessment of* Executive Orders.]

As **Executive Orders** opens, Tom Clancy's hero, Jack Ryan, has just been confirmed as vice president after his predecessor, Edward Kealty, is caught in a sex scandal. After an abortive war between the United States and Japan, terrorists fly a Japan Airlines 747 into the Capitol, killing the president, hundreds of representatives and senators, the joint chiefs of staff, most of the cabinet and all nine justices of the Supreme Court. Ryan cries, "You're telling me I'm the whole government right now?" He must not only recompose the government and fend off hostile foreign powers but resolve a domestic crisis touched off when the venomous Kealty insists that he never actually resigned: "I've known Jack Ryan for ten years . . . He is, unfortunately, not the man to lead our country."

Clancy's publisher has announced a first printing of 2 million copies for this latest gripping example of his highly popular thrillers. By the time the hardcover, paperback, film and other incarnations of **Executive Orders** are out, conceivably a fifth of all Americans could wind up absorbed in the story related in this 874-page book. For the historian, mass entertainment reveals much about the passions and curiosities of a people at a particular moment. Subjects and plots that appear plausible and fascinating in the literature of one period can look bizarre or dated in another. What will the main narrative lines of *Executive Orders* tell scholars working in, say, 2096 about the Americans of our time?

Published in the wake of the World Trade Center and Oklahoma City bombings and during the same summer as the White House is blown up in "Independence Day," Clancy's new book shows that the current-day American is alert as never before to the possibility that no American landmark is safe from catastrophe. For most of our history, we have comforted ourselves with the exceptionalist notion that terrorism was a phenomenon generally practiced elsewhere. Had the Capitol or White House been exploded in a novel or motion picture of 50 years ago, the plot would probably have been dismissed as far-fetched, the author denounced as demented or un-American. Clancy anticipates the headlines of the past month by enlisting Ryan and Kealty in a conflict over anti-terrorism legislation that threatens encroachment upon Americans' civil liberties.

Especially considering that its author brandishes his 1980s-style sense of patriotism (the book is dedicated to the 40th president as "The Man Who Won the War," an odd locution for an author normally so aware of the contributions ordinary soldiers made to the defeat of the Soviet Union), Clancy's novel reflects surprising cynicism about our domestic political system. The author plays to Americans' current suspicions about their leaders' motives in his tale of the power grab by the elected vice president. Earlier in our history, a reader would have had a hard time accepting that, at a moment of unprecedented trauma, one of our leaders would shake the country further by selfishly challenging the presumed president's right to rule. In 1939, many Americans boycotted Frank Capra's "Mr. Smith Goes to Washington" to protest the portrayal of Jimmy Stewart's Senate colleagues as corrupt. Nowadays we do not blink at the notion that one of our leaders might turn a national tragedy into a great career move.

Executive Orders also opens a window on the American post-Cold War psyche. Dwight Eisenhower (another Clancy hero, who, as the author says in his narrative, "exercised power so skillfully that hardly anyone had noticed his doing anything at all") believed that when the confrontation with a Soviet empire ended, Americans would resume their essential benign composure; while retaining our world leadership, we would concentrate on education, farming, medicine and otherwise improving our society. Unlike his old colleague Gen. George Patton, Ike scoffed at the idea that

there was something in the American psychology that required an enemy.

Clancy is of the Patton school. He has an old Russian friend tell Ryan, "What a superb enemy you were." Had this book been written during the Cold War, Clancy almost certainly would have used his Capitol bombing to usher is some kind of conflagration with Moscow. But like the screenwriters of this decade's James Bond films, Clancy has to find his foe somewhere else. Looking to the Middle East, he invents a war-making "United Islamic Republic" of Iran and Iraq.

Germ warfare fought by Ebola virus is another large element of Clancy's book that is very much of this place and time. For most of the Cold War, the weapon of mass destruction that most Americans thought about was nuclear. Life-threatening epidemics such as tuberculosis and polio seemed under control. Now we live in an age of AIDS and flirtation by Iraqis and others with chemical and biological weapons, raising the specter of sudden new war-plagues of biblical proportions.

Perhaps the deepest wellspring of Clancy's appeal when he published *The Hunt for Red October* in the early 1980s was his ability to expose the details of military and intelligence technology. This was not surprising. The Cold War was threatening to grow dangerous. No issue was more timely. Thinking of the 1920s, when a shriveling American peacetime army and an inward-looking society made military thrillers poor performers in American publishing, one looks for signs that Clancy is trying to change his act. But although domestic political crisis and domestic terrorism loom large in *Executive Orders,* the author has wisely chosen not to abandon what he does so well (although, in its publicity materials, the publisher plays up the domestic drama and soft-pedals the foreign).

The book derives much of its action and suspense from the author's talent in exposing the inner workings of endless unseen chambers of our own and other governments—for example, the presidential briefcase containing nuclear attack plans called "the football": "The first section, Jack saw, was labeled MAJOR ATTACK OPTION. It showed a map of Japan, many of whose cities were marked with multicolored dots meant in terms of delivered megatonnage; probably another page would quantify the predicted deaths. Ryan opened the binder rings and removed the whole section. 'I want these pages burned. I want this MAO eliminated immediately.' That merely meant that it would be filed away in some drawer in Pentagon War Plans, and also in Omaha. Things like this never died."

There is little evidence that Clancy has grown more interested than in previous volumes in exploring the depths and complexities of human personality. The thinking and motivations of his characters are not remotely as interesting as the dramatic situations in which he places them. The historian of 2096 would find little in this book to demonstrate the fascination that Americans of the 1990s have with deconstructing personal character and understanding the psychohistory of our leaders.

As compelling entertainment, *Executive Orders* shows that, despite the end of the Cold War and the temptation to coast that conventional success may bring, Clancy has lost none of his verve. As cultural artifact, the book suggests a domestic America that is perilous and grim.

Paul Dean (review date 25 August 1996)

SOURCE: "Harrison Ford, Call Your Agent," in *Los Angeles Times Book Review,* August 25, 1996, p. 5.

[*In the following review, Dean offers tempered praise for* Executive Orders.]

In this, his longest and lumpiest collage of fundamental values and techno-babble, Tom Clancy resolves our Clinton-Dole-Perot-Nader uncertainties by suggesting the least of five evils: Jack Ryan for president.

Ryan—the indestructible, tighter-zippered superhero tied to Clancy and the CIA as closely as martini-weenie James Bond was to Ian Fleming and M15—certainly speaks what the electorate knows in its heart is right. "Please, do not send me politicians. I need people who do real things in the real world. I need people who do not want to live in Washington. I need people who will not try to work the system. . . ."

He knows what's been klutzing up the system: "What ever happened to the truth? . . . It's all a game and the object of the game isn't to do the right thing, the object of the game is to *stay* here."

And, for God's sake, don't tread on Jack Ryan: "Those guilty of . . . attack will face our justice. We will not send notes of protest. We will not call a special meeting of the U.N. Security Council. We will make war with all the power and rage this country and her citizens can muster."

Yes, Mr. President. Tell 'em to kiss ours. Or we'll kick theirs. Because we're No. 1.

So, Clancy fanatics, relax in this familiar and wildly right mood of *Executive Orders,* the logical, even plausible—lest we forget the World Trade Center or Lockerbie—sequel to *Debt of Honor.*

In that masterpiece of action mayhem, you'll remember, America's trade war with Japan escalates to a Pearl Harbor II sneak attack on Pacific Fleet carriers. Ryan—seemingly risen on derring-do alone from college professor to deputy director of the CIA to national security advisor in five easy novels—saves our turkey bacon and the Detroit auto industry.

And in yet another eerie echo of real headlines, Ivory-pure Ryan gets the vice president canned for some Bob Packwood moves on the ladies. Now, most national saviors would have settled for a Presidential Medal of Freedom and a condo in Maryland. Ryan stepped into the vice president's job until the next election. Then, in the book's multi-megaton conclusion, a Japanese airline skipper dusts off his roots and proves that old kamikaze pilots never die. They simply fade into sore losers and stuff a Boeing 747 into the Capitol building.

Ergo, the final chapter of *Debt of Honor* becomes the first page of *Executive Orders,* with Ryan up to his Irish eyebrows in rubble and gore. The president died when the Japan Airlines jumbo delivered its vote of no confidence. Also the Joint Chiefs of Staff and every Supreme Court Justice, most of the Senate, dozens of congressmen, and all but two Cabinet members.

So John Patrick Ryan is elected president by act of terrorism. His first thoughts don't exactly reflect the grit that carried his previous days against the Irish Republican Army, Colombian drug dealers, the Soviet Navy and Sean Connery. Ryan's musings, in fact, are more Dan Quayle than Abe Lincoln: "I don't know what to do. Where's the manual, the training course for this job? Whom do I ask? Where do I go?" (At least his grammar is correct.)

President Ryan, of course, does get his kit together and start saying and doing stuff fit for Harrison Ford or Alec Baldwin. All the time, courtesy of CNN, world leaders are watching Ryan in a global power vacuum. Some are former enemies stropping old scores or opportunists monitoring the teetering of American influence. Others are vultures seeing profit in our resources that may be up for grabs.

The bad guys—you win no lifetime subscription to National Review for guessing it's an ayatollah and those Iranians again—activate their death squads, cripple the military dictatorship of Iraq and forge a United Islamic Republic. Conquest of Kuwait and the Saudi kingdom and control of their oil supplies will be next. Then the baby UIR wants to crawl across Afghanistan and Pakistan and create a new, rich, powerful nation stretching from the Red Sea to China. With India and China its likely allies; with the United States and Russia its sworn enemies.

Executive Orders is a colossal read, which is praise for Clancy's ability to grind out exquisite details yet criticism of his inability to write an essentially simple geopolitical thriller in less than 874 pages. Quite worthy of note here is that the Cambridge text of the complete works of William Shakespeare ran only 125 pages longer; Raymond Chandler kissed off "The Big Sleep" in 155.

But if you can stay with him, if you can forgive Clancy some stereotyping here, some visible chauvinism there, there's no doubting the wizardry of his craft. His writing is too simplistic to place him among today's literati. But he is the honest-to-God creator of an exciting genre and a consistent producer of books that thunder, absorb and entertain.

Executive Orders proves both the shine and sludge of Clancy. There is gratuitous sexual equality that equates to sexism by afterthought ("angry men—and women") and bald racism ("How d'ya say 'tough' in rag-head?").

Blessedly, he seems to have diluted and unwound much of the Jane's All the World's GI-Speak that made earlier works required reading at Annapolis, West Point and the Air Force Academy. Still, old military habits are tough to nuke and the last 100 pages still read more like Desert Storm transcripts.

The biggest problem with Clancy novels is that they are sometimes raw, even clumsy. He uses an impressive word—say, *schadenfreude*—twice as though to tell readers he knows what it means and we don't. Or a character will ask a question. "Will they move?" The response comes 500 words later. "Yes, Mr. President. They will move."

Clancy is not one of the world's great romantics. At one point, after an 18-hour day touring a capital in bloody ruins, Ryan goes home to his wife. Hi, he says. She asks if it is all true. He nods. He asks about the kids. She says they are in bed. "And now?" she asks.

"I have to sleep," he says.

Hey, what about a hug or some tears? Or a "poor darling"? Or getting hammered on Bombay gin martinis?

Executive Orders is 874 pages in search of an executive order to find Clancy a good editor before he overwrites again. One is left with the impression that his one-ton manuscripts are delivered by fork-lift to Putnam and published unread, as is, because the author is Tom Clancy, builder of blockbusters and maker of millions for all.

Accepting that authors rarely write what they don't believe in, this volume is a hard look at where Clancy stands on just about everything: on gun control and tax reform; on com-

position of the Supreme Court, religion, abortion and the death penalty. Sounds very much like a party platform.

Could it be? Nah. Not Tom Clancy for president.

Christopher Hitchens (review date 14 November 1996)

SOURCE: "Something for the Boys," in *New York Review of Books*, November 14, 1996, pp. 34-6.

[*In the following review, Hitchens provides critical analysis of* Debt of Honor *and* Marine.]

The dedication page of this Behemoth carries a lapidary, capitalized inscription, "To Ronald Wilson Reagan, Fortieth President of the United States: The Man Who Won The War." And this is only fair. In 1984, the Naval Institute Press paid Tom Clancy an advance of $5,000 for **The Hunt for Red October.** It was the first fiction that the Naval Institute had knowingly or admittedly published. There matters might have rested, except that someone handed a copy to the Fortieth President, who (then at the zenith of his great parabola) gave it an unoriginal but unequivocal blurb. "The perfect yarn," he said, and the Baltimore insurance agent was on his way to blockbuster authorship. Putnam this past August issued a first printing of 2,211,101 copies of his newest novel, **Executive Orders,** and, on the Internet site devoted to Clancy, mayhem broke out as enthusiasts posted news of pre-publication copies available at Wal-Mart. Clancy's nine thrillers, as well as exemplifying an almost Reaganesque dream of American success, have catapulted him into that section of the cultural supermarket which is always designated by the hieroglyph #1. And this, too, is apt. Remember when America itself was #1? Are we not #1 today? Must we not be #1 tomorrow?

There are other superficial resemblances between the Reagan phenomenon and the Clancy one. Tom Clancy, the true-grit chronicler of air combat, has an aversion to flying and will not get on a plane unless he absolutely has to. Ronald Reagan became phobic about flying in 1937 and did not board another aircraft for almost thirty years. (While grounded, he played heroic airmen in *Secret Service of the Air, Murder in the Air, International Squadron,* and *Desperate Journey.*) When he wrote **Red October,** Clancy had never been on a submarine unless it was tethered to the dockside. Ronald Reagan, who never got further than the Hal Loach Training Studio on a Los Angeles backlot, told Yitzhak Shamir and Simon Wiesenthal that he had been present in person at the liberation of the Nazi camps, and often referred fondly to the wartime years he had spent "in uniform." Tom Clancy talks like a leatherneck when interviewed by the press, and keeps a large green M4A1 tank parked on the main lawn of his 4,000-acre estate on Chesapeake Bay. (There is a shooting range in the basement of the main house.) So the nation's two leading fans of vicarious combat make a good pairing. We cannot therefore be sure which "war," in the dedication. Reagan is supposed to have "won." It may be one of the wars that took place only in his head. I think that the millions of Clancy-consuming vicarious-war fans are supposed to assume, however, that it was that "cold" war, in which Tom Clancy was proposed by Vice-President Dan Quayle as a member of the National Space Council.

Clancy's fictional projection of his rather rotund and unadventurous self is Jack Ryan, who has now been animated on screen by Harrison Ford and Alec Baldwin. A child of the national security apparat. Ryan has captured a Soviet nuclear submarine (*The Hunt for Red October*), done battle with IRA gunmen (*Patriot Games*), outpointed the KGB (*The Cardinal of the Kremlin*), taken the war to the foe in the matter of the Colombian cartels (*Clear and Present Danger*), foiled a world-domination plot by the Indian Navy and a Japanese business consortium (*Debt of Honor*). On the cusp between *Debt of Honor* and *Executive Orders* he becomes Vice-President and President of the United States, all on the same day. Since Ryan has always been represented as an uncomplicated patriot with a distaste for politics and politicians, this transition might seem to offer a difficulty. But Clancy resolves it with a tremendous plot device, whereby a Japanese airliner crashes into a joint session of Congress, killing the Chief Executive, most of the members of the House and the Senate, most of the Cabinet, the Joint Chiefs, and all the Justices of the Supreme Court. Ryan has been appointed as a stopgap, can-do, pinch-hitting Veep, in the wake of the resignation of a scoundrelly incumbent. By nothing short of a miracle, he escapes the hecatomb of the Joint Session and finds not only that he is Leader of the Free World, but that he has a huge number of vacant appointments in his gift.

It rapidly becomes clear that Tom Clancy's political *beau ideal* is not really Ronald Reagan so much as it is Ross Perot. Ryan decides to hire a new Treasury Secretary and goes straight to a friend on Wall Street. He tells him:

> Buy a mop. I want your department cleaned up, streamlined and run like you want it to make a profit someday. How you do that is your problem. For Defense, I want the same thing. The biggest problem over there is administrative. I need somebody who can run a business and make a profit to cull the bureaucracy out. That's the biggest problem of all, for all the agencies.

There's a great deal more in this style of what I call "gruff stuff": husky admonitions and *semper fi* shoulder-punches

and injunctions not to stand on ceremony or go by the book. Is this, for one thing, a great country or is it not? As one young aide reflects, squeezing his eyes shut in a manly fashion:

> Only in America could a working-class kid who'd scratched into Harvard on a scholarship get befriended by the great son of a great family.

Read with any care, this assertion is only true to the extent that Harvard is in America. But care is just what Clancy doesn't exercise. As he once told an interviewer about an earlier volume in his oeuvre:

> I was never thinking about whether this was a good book or a bad book. I was thinking of the mission. You have to focus on the mission, and the mission is finishing the book, and everything else is a sideshow to the mission.

Here is the authentic voice of a man who must sometimes wish that he had not been excused from the draft on the grounds of his myopia. How he loves the argot, of "doing what you have to do to get the job done." Regrettably, in *Executive Orders* he sets himself too many missions and succumbs very early to what might be called imperial overstretch.

The outside world is, as is now notorious, a dangerous place. President Ryan is not to be allowed his honeymoon. In far-off Iran, a scheming ayatollah sees his chance. In distant, throbbing Zaire, a young Iranian physician starts to culture the Ebola virus. The glacial Stalinist mandarins of Beijing decide to test "this Ryan"—a very Fleming-like locution, incidentally, often employed to characterize the speech of a devious and fanatical foreigner. Even the nasty female who heads the government of India is in on the convoluted Sino-Iranian conspiracy, though it turns out to be a conspiracy with no objective beyond itself. The humiliation of the naive unsuspecting Americans is the general idea. They are so—heh, heh, heh—*enfeebled* by their attachment to democracy . . .

Nor are things at home all that propitious. Some bucolic fascists in Montana decide that their hour has struck. There may be a mole in the President's security detail. And of course, political and journalistic enemies never sleep. This salad of subplots, plucked alternately from the marquees of the Cineplex and the filler copy at *US News and World Report*, is narrated by means of intercutting, but will present serious problems of continuity for the studio which options it.

For a while, it seems Jack Ryan doesn't have a friend in the world. But he does, he does. There is Prince Charles, who of course we remember from Ryan's heroic rescue of the royals in *Patriot Games*. And there is the Israeli Mossad, without which no writer in this genre since the days of Frederick Forsyth has dared move a step. At the memorial for those massacred on Capitol Hill:

> "Mr. President." said the man in the Royal Navy mess jacket. His ambassador had positioned things nicely. On the whole, London rather liked the new arrangement. The "special relationship" would become more special, as President Ryan was an (honorary) Knight Commander of the Victorian Order.
>
> "Your highness." Jack paused, and allowed himself a smile as he shook the offered hand. "Long time since that day in London, pal."
>
> "Indeed."

I'm citing this not as a sample of Clancy's abysmal dialogue, because in point of fact it's much better crafted and more economical than most of the exchanges that he types, but because it illustrates two recurring Clancy tropes, which are his matey populism and his deference and snobbery. The two are as indissolubly linked, in this as in all Clancy narratives, as his taste for sadistic ruthlessness and his sentimentality.

These qualities are summarized, for me, in the way in which Clancy names his characters. "Jack Ryan" is a nothing name to start with, and the character is just an attitudinal cipher, with a tendency to long and sanctimonious monologues, who is naturally devoted to the children he never sees and who gets in bed with his wife only in order to go to sleep. We are informed at one point that he is "a student of human behavior," as who indeed is not? His associates and subordinates are called Pat Martin and Dave James and Bob Fowler. There's a John Clark and a Robert Jackson. And think of the ingenuity tax that must have been levied when Clancy had to come up with some tough but tender FBI veterans to be Ryan's only friends in the world (apart of course from the Windsors and the Israelis) and named them Patrick O'Day and Tony Caruso. It's like watching one of those macho "unit" movies from the Second World War, where there is a Kowalski and an O'Rourke and a Gambino in every platoon.

The geopolitics are evoked with the same skill. The Middle East, that renowned cauldron, is described as "a part of the world known for its interlocking non-sequiturs." I will say that I enjoyed that effortful oxymoron more than the immediately following revelation: "Like most Russians. Golovko had a deep respect for history." There is, then, inevitably, some talk about wolves and steppes and the uncomfortable conclusion that "Lying on the ground, the horizon could be surprisingly close." I dare say it could, if one were dangling.

We meet a handsome pro-American Saudi prince called Prince Ali Bin Sheik—a name as absurd in Arabic as it is in English. At one point, the saturnine Iranian doctor in the outback of Zaire makes a decision, lifts the phone, and calls the Iranian embassy in Kinshasa. Mr. Clancy's travels obviously haven't taken him to Zaire. The telephones there are down. You can't call the Iranian embassy—even if there is one—if you are already *in* Kinshasa.

Having commissioned the assassination of Saddam Hussein, the Iranian leadership is able to unite Iraq and Iran, on the basis of Shi'a solidarity, in a matter of days. The newly fused army is ready to reinvade Kuwait at once. Switzerland, on the other hand, hasn't changed since it was visited by Paul Erdman and Robert Ludlum. It is still, you will be reassured to hear, "a cold country in terms of both climate and culture, but a safe one, and for those with money to invest, an anonymous one." Books like *Executive Orders* depend on a species of paradox: vast changes in the natural order which leave the landscape of conventional wisdom unchanged. This is why Clancy, in a yarn of 874 pages, invents a few shocks but cannot bring off a nanosecond of real tension.

There comes a point when, chopping one's way through the hopeless tangle of Clancy's thoughts and Clancy's prose, one is compelled to ask who, if anybody, edits this stuff? Is it assumed that the customers will simply buy anything that bears the TC #1 franchise label? Even if so, both they and he are ill-served. That sinister Iranian physician "walked out of the room . . . removing his protective garb as he went, and dumping the articles in the proper container." A few pages later, "He left the room, stripping off his protective garb as he did so, depositing it in the proper containers." Sometimes the inattention creates miniature hilarities. "For the first time in a very long time, Clark went pale as a ghost." "Barry, I've never committed public suicide before." Sometimes, though, it results in a syntactical pileup from which there is no extrication:

> At every stop, the information was handed over raw, sometimes with the local assessment, but more often without, or if it were, placed at the bottom so that the national intelligence officers in charge of the various watches could make their own assessments, and duplicate the work of others. Mostly this made sense, but in fast-breaking situations it very often did not. The problem was that one couldn't tell the difference in a crisis.

Apparently not.

I believe that I can guess exactly the point at which Mr. Clancy gave up on his "mission" but kept going blindly on. Having been at some pains to show us the Ebola virus being bottled with diabolical care in vials of blood, he allows this blood to spill and permits the ultra-vigilant physician to notice that *something* sticky and liquid has escaped, only to dismiss the thought. The next person to encounter the spillage finds that "his seat was wet, with what he didn't know, but it was sticky and . . . red? Tomato juice or something, probably." The man making this suggestive blunder is an Iraqi Ba'athist secret policeman, who might be expected to know the difference between blood and Bloody Mary.

Clancy is forgiven much by his fans because he can deliver the high-octane military-industrial prose that is his hallmark.
—*Christopher Hitchens*

Clancy is forgiven much by his fans because he can deliver the high-octane military-industrial prose that is his hallmark. Writing of this caliber is essentially non-fictional, as is shown by Clancy's latest boy's-own guidebook, *Marine,* a breathless history and description of the real-life past and present of America's #1 military corps d'elite. But even *Marine* has a closing section in which fantasy is given its head and we are asked to accompany our boys on a future mission against those described as "rag-heads" in *Executive Orders:*

> Two minutes behind the B-2s came eight B-1B Lancers from the 7th Wing at Dyess AFB, Texas, also launched from Anderson AFB and refuelled from KC-10As at Diego Garcia. Their targets were two battalions of troops in barracks adjacent to Bushehr airport. Each unloaded twelve AGM-154 Joint Standoff Weapons (JSOWs) from their weapons bays, well outside Iranian airspace. Following a two-minute gliding flight, the ninety-six JSOWs, guided by onboard GPS receivers, unloaded their payloads of BLU-97/B Combined Effects Munitions (CEMs). They blanketed over a hundred acres of troop billeting and vehicle-parking areas with thousands of CEMs, and the effects were horrific. The two minutes since the bombs from the B-2 strike had given the troops time to thrown on their boots, grab weapons, and rush outside to be shredded into hamburger by exploding cluster munitions.

Here is another pileup, this time acronymic, culminating in a moment of sub-Mickey Spillane. It is the on-page equivalent of the "smart" videos from the Gulf War. (With this difference. After the Gulf War, staff officers who had viewed the non-virtual effects of cluster and fragmentation weapons decided not to put these triumphs on the air. The videos are still classified by the Department of Defense, whether out of squeamishness or not. But Clancy the gloating civilian is subject to no such inhibition.)

Descriptions like this bear the broken-backed weight of *Executive Orders,* too, and carry the badly injured plot toward its final foxhole. It's interesting to notice the amount of product endorsement that Clancy throws in to enhance the industrial side of his uncomplex military-industrial writing. Tributes to the excellence of Merck chemicals, Gulfstream aircraft, and Merrill Lynch brokers are plentiful, as are fulminations by Jack Ryan against the capital gains tax. The acknowledgments to *Marine* include the good people at Bell Textron, Boeing, Sikorsky, Texas Instruments, General Dynamics, and Hughes Aircraft. Are we entering the age of sponsorship in airport fiction?

Jack Ryan manages to battle successfully against the multiple and simultaneous subplots that conspire against him, but he succeeds chiefly because most of them just peter out. The Montana militiamen's scheme is discarded (by Clancy, not by the conspirators) and the Indians and Chinese seem just to change their minds. The ever-menacing Japanese are left out altogether on this occasion, while entire Ebola outbreaks, including one in Chicago and a nasty one in the Sudan, just vanish from the story. Having found a couple of tycoons to serve at Treasury and Defense, Ryan never does get around to any Supreme Court appointments. He even forgets to have a vice-president, which is a requirement of the very Constitution that he repeatedly tells us he is sworn to defend. Actually, Clancy only comes to life at all on those occasions when he can describe either a president trashing the Constitution or a field officer exceeding orders and kicking ass.

> Ryan's problem was that he really didn't *have* a political philosophy per se. He believed in things that worked, that produced the promised results and fixed whatever was broken. Whether these things adhered to one political slant or another was less important than the effects they had.

Will you adhere to my slant? But when it's a question of proclaiming martial law to combat Ebola, or of violating the prohibition on the assassination of foreign leaders, Ryan's pragmatism reveals itself for what it is—an authoritarian populism set out with more energy than grammar by its fictional author. The same goes for cutting out red tape on military expeditions:

> "How many can we kill before they make us stop, sir?"
>
> "If it's a tank, kill it. If it's BMP, kill it. If it's a truck, kill it. If it's south of the berm and it's holding a weapon, kill it. But the rules are serious about killing unresisting people. We don't break those rules. That's important."

"Fair 'nuff. Colonel."

"Don't take any unnecessary chances with prisoners, either."

"No, sir," the track commander promised. "I won't."

The implication of the passage is quite subtle by Clancy standards, but it shares in the same down-and-dirty, tough-guy pornography of which this is the soft version.

The usual throaty justification for such nastiness is, of course, the existence of women and children. As far as I can see. Clancy has fitted out Ryan with a spouse and some offspring simply so that he can experience paroxysms of justified male wrath when physical attacks are made on them. ("Why my kids, Jeff? I'm the one—here. If people get mad, it's supposed to be at me. Why do people like this go after children, tell me that . . .?") Strong, drivelling men like this are also traditionally very fond of committing minor infractions and then asking their subordinates not to tell the lady of the house or she'll have his guts for garters. Clancy does not spare us this convention. I lost count of the number of times that Ryan bummed a cigarette and then, likeably and democratically, cautioned the underling not to let "Cathy" know. This makes the mighty appear so much more . . . human, really.

Even though Clancy often seems bored by his own devices, there is one other subject—apart from political and military bullying—that gets him excited. Like many people who know absolutely nothing about Washington, and who reveal the fact by talking portentously of "this town," he believes that the press is out to "get" the man in charge. If a Jack Ryan had actually become President in the manner described here, and had then had to face a challenge from a newly united Iran-Iraq federation, he would have had the mass media at his disposal from early morn to dewy eve. "Bipartisanship" would not have been the half of it.

Instead, Clancy shows us a president who meekly submits to atrocious rudeness at press conferences, who is harried by reporters wherever he goes, who does five unrehearsed network interviews one after the other (on the same topic, in his private quarters), and who is subjected to a last-minute "set-up" grilling by a crafty presenter. Moreover, the Pentagon flies hostile correspondents directly to the scene of combat, while reporters call and get the National Security Advisor on the telephone at all times. A clue to Clancy's resentful caricature of the Fourth Estate is probably to be found in one such scene, where "a very liberated lady" reporter asks an impertinent question about *Roe v. Wade.* But I never want to read again that, say what you will about Clancy's losing armwrestle with the English language, he is at least good on the details.

Details can be suggestive, however, and some absorbing ones are to be found in *Marine.* We find that Clancy praises his favorite corps for capturing John Brown at Harper's Ferry (under the command of Virginia Army officers Robert E. Lee and J.E.B. Stuart); for subverting Mexico at Vera Cruz in 1847; for putting down Filipino rebels in 1899 and invading Nicaragua in 1913; for intervening in Haiti between 1915 and 1934; and for "pacifying the Panama Canal Zone" between 1901 and 1914, to say nothing of enforcing the Platt Amendment in Cuba. For Clancy, these are not disfigurements of a record that after all includes Iwo Jima, but glorious pages in and of themselves. As the novel began to recede in my memory, it was deposed and replaced by the image of Oliver North, a disgraced Marine officer for whom Clancy used to "do" fundraisers. There are obviously many "guys" out there, some of them perhaps living near bases threatened with closure, dwelling in the lost world of "choke points" and "arcs of crisis" and "daggers pointed at the heart of." For them, Clancy is a novelist and North is a hero. With no official enemy on the radar screen (and even the foul Iranians better-armed thanks to North and Reagan), Clancy has become the junk supplier of surrogate testosterone. His books bear the same relationship to reality as Oliver North's lachrymose and bragging speeches do to patriotism, and his writing is to prose what military music is to music.

Helen S. Garson (essay date 1996)

SOURCE: "In the Popular Tradition," in *Tom Clancy: A Critical Companion,* Greenwood Press, 1996, pp. 25-39.

[*In the following essay, Garson examines the combined elements of the conventional thriller, science fiction, detective fiction, and the techno-thriller in Clancy's novels.*]

For a long time Tom Clancy insisted he writes political thrillers, totally rejecting the term "technothriller" that numerous critics have bestowed on his work. But perhaps in recognition of the inevitable, he has finally given in. When Larry King on his 22 August 1994 television show introduced him as a writer of technothrillers, Clancy made no protest. As for labeling his work, a case could be made for both the large designation—thriller—and its subheading—technothriller, and also for spy/espionage fiction. Properties of all these types are easily found in Clancy's writing. Additionally, some book sellers, such as the Book-of-the-Month Club, list his novels under a more expansive and general category: Mystery/Suspense Fiction. This broad, all-encompassing term may be useful for libraries. However, it does little to help the reader distinguish the real differences between Clancy's work and the detective stories of Agatha Christie or the uncanny fiction of Stephen King, which are often placed alongside Clancy's in such indeterminate classifications.

When his first published book, **The Hunt for Red October,** appeared, reviewers found the technical aspects of the novel so impressive and unusual that it seemed that a word had to be coined to describe the type. Although nobody seems to be able to pinpoint the origin of the term "technothriller," Patrick Anderson of the *New York Times* gave that label to Clancy's work in 1988. In Anderson's review, Clancy became the "king" of such fiction. In that same year, Evan Thomas of *Newsweek* described Clancy as the "inventor" of the technothriller, although Clancy himself has said that Michael Crichton's *The Andromeda Strain* is the first technothriller. Nonetheless, Clancy is considered both inventor and king of the genre by many of the reviewers and critics who have interviewed him or written about his novels. The "king" has gained much more territory since the title was first bestowed on him by Anderson. Numerous technothriller books have been written by other novelists, often imitating him, but Clancy does not feel at all threatened by disciples. Within the decade following publication of **The Hunt for Red October,** similar novels became part of literary history. Publishers are eager to print technothrillers for a readership which has a large appetite for the type of fiction that Clancy has made popular. Still, among the crowds of technical writers, Clancy, from 1984 to 1995 the author of eight novels, continues to hold clear title to the crown.

Science Fiction

A few critics have suggested that Clancy is a science fiction (SF) writer, comparing his work to that of the legendary French novelist Jules Verne. Verne is the parent of technological fiction, although today his fiction is classified as SF. However, it is the technological aspect that has led to the comparison of his novels with Clancy's. Clancy, however, flatly rejects the idea that anything he has done is in the SF mode.

H. G. Wells, perhaps the most significant figure in SF writing, scornfully labeled Verne "a short-term technological popularizer." Because of Wells's description, there is some ambiguity about the use of the terms "technological" and "SF." Verne and those who followed his example used advanced technology but also worked with elements we associate with SF, for example, projection into the future. Even though Wells seems disdainful of Verne, he and other innovative and seminal science fiction writers did very much what Verne had with advanced technology, enhancing plots which would be unsuccessful without such technology.

The beginnings of SF go as far back as Plato and continue throughout the centuries with the work of Thomas More, Swift, William Blake, Verne, Wells, Asimov, and many other writers. Science fiction appeared as "fortunate island" stories, utopian and anti-utopian fiction, marvelous voyages, planetary novels, and political works. Although SF has changed throughout the centuries, certain key aspects hold. Science fiction is different from mimetic—imitative and observed forms—of literature in time, place, and character. It has any possible time—present, past, or future. There may be forms of religion and mythic situations, political philosophy and social structures, but they are outside the norm or the known. Although SF is a form of fantasy, within the limits set by the author the story is not ultimately impossible of fulfillment. It is "a realistic irreality, with humanized nonhumans" and "this-worldly Other Worlds." However, supernatural elements of horror, that is, the gothic, are not part of SF.

Science fiction writers reject the ordinary world of reality, creating instead new and strange worlds. Such writers (and many scientists) assume that there are other worlds inhabited by other forms of life. Within the conventions of SF there is no requirement that the writer be positive or negative toward the characters or their worlds, no preconceived notion of success, failure, or achievement. The search is for the unknown and for knowledge that goes beyond learning about character, about who we are or the world we live in. Science fiction characters and their surroundings are imaginary; yet the writer treats them factually and writes of them scientifically, perhaps bringing everything about science into play. Thus, SF is concerned with scientific philosophy, its politics, its psychology, and its anthropology. There is scientific logic in SF, so that it cannot go beyond nature. Although the material may be unrecognizable and unfamiliar to the reader, it is never so estranged as to be impossible to comprehend.

Clancy and Science Fiction

Because other worlds do not enter into Clancy's novels, he sees no fantasy in his work. What he creates is "real" to him, and he insists on his obligation to readers to write about reality, possibility, and probability. No matter that much science fiction has elements of possibility and sometimes probability; Clancy repudiates any resemblance to his work. Yet, examples abound. Clancy writes of some submarine equipment and experimental aircraft as if they were real; yet they do not exist. Further, he suggests that the Russians have developed a system to eliminate U.S. reconnaissance satellites (SDI in *Cardinal*). He treats these as operational actualities, though most experts would quarrel with his interpretation.

In **Red Storm Rising,** the reader accepts as possible, perhaps "real" in an SF sense, the projection of time into a future when a third world war is under way. The novel is both futuristic and scientific. Without the use of every type of technological information superior to that of the enemy, the forces of democracy could not defeat those of totalitarianism, the Soviets. The fact that the enemy is the USSR makes the plot plausible and also acceptably realistic (in a non-SF sense), given the state of the cold war in 1987, when the novel was published. The combination of elements lends itself to at least a partial classification of SF.

> **From early on, reviewers have spoken of Clancy as prophetic, as one might of a SF writer. Clancy's novels, like SF and some technothrillers, appear prophetic about current and future possibilities of scientific technology.**
> *—Helen S. Garson*

From early on, reviewers have spoken of Clancy as prophetic, as one might of a SF writer. Clancy's novels, like SF and some technothrillers, appear prophetic about current and future possibilities of scientific technology. In addition, SF books often involve politics, as do Clancy's, which have a political agenda along with scientific technology and prophetic characteristics. What seems unlikely today in a Clancy book, a science fiction novel, a work of political intrigue, or a technothriller is the reality of tomorrow. What if, as in Verne, a vessel could survive underwater? What if, as in Clancy, satellites and an SDI system could affect future wars and even determine outcomes? There is, however, one major difference between Clancy and SF writers. In science fiction "destiny" is not on anyone's side, although it looms large in technological fiction such as Clancy's, and that is an important distinction between his work and true science fiction.

The Thriller

Critics, reviewers, writers, and teachers have difficulty pinning down the word "thriller." Often we use it interchangeably with the terms spy/espionage story because of the many overlapping characteristics. Just as the technothriller may be subsumed by that more general term "thriller," so too may the spy story. However, not all thrillers are either spy or technological novels. They may be both or neither. They are also murder, suspense, or psychological stories. Terminology sometimes can be slippery, and labels often indistinct.

Ralph Harper calls the thriller "crisis literature," claiming that the crises always are about war. Other scholars, though, see additional subjects, often personal and with a variety of landscapes. The landscape may even be limited to the mind of a character. Thriller subjects may range from global situations (suspense thrillers, political thrillers) to individual disturbances (psychological thrillers), from an attack on a vast region to the murder of a person. Nevertheless, according to Harper, the basic issue in the thriller is "death and responsibility." Hostile acts are planned and executed, bringing vio-

lence and death as the story is played out. Resolution follows, though not invariably in the form of retribution or punishment.

Scholars disagree about the function of language and the importance of characters in thrillers. Some criticize the simplicity of language and form and the lack of character development typical of most thrillers. As a result, they believe too much attention is given to plot and not enough to character. Yet, another scholarly view holds "that in a thriller 'too much character clutters up the plot.'" Because of the differences it is useful to separate thrillers into categories of "entertainments" (popular fiction) and "high art." For thrillers by such writers as Graham Greene and John Le Carré, the classification "high art" applies because their interest is more in character than in plot, and in style more than suspense. Technothrillers by their very nature are popular fiction. Although at times the two types—popular fiction and high art—merge, generally they are separable.

Few thrillers are high art. Rather, most are popular entertainment and should be evaluated as such, with different measurements applied. Style is as changeable in the two types of thrillers as in unlike genres. Usually the most successful popular thriller style is simple and unsubtle. For the reader to be drawn into the story immediately there must be sufficient familiarity with language and form. Then too, thrillers have particular language patterns. The violent emotion, which is a vital characteristic, requires a flatness of tone with a dual function. It "underlines the violence" as well as serving to contain it. In the most exciting thrillers, the sentences are short, the structures imitative of news reports, frequently with a brevity suggestive of news bites.

Characters in popular art are familiar to readers, and because of their lack of individuality they border on stereotypes. To make them interesting and provocative, yet still generic, the author must create memorable and attention-getting figures, with qualities that attract readers and hold their attention. For that reason thrillers usually have heroes (heroines less often) who are exceptional, even fantastic people with whom most readers want to identify. Brave, dedicated heroes (heroines) represent the reader against deceitful and vicious enemies. Like us, heroes are vulnerable, but, unlike us, they overcome all odds. Heroes have developed over a long period of time and have changed little in basic ways from classical mythical figures to medieval knights to nineteenth-century adventurers. In nineteenth- and early twentieth-century popular fiction the heroes of adventure/suspense/mystery fiction were not professional detectives, policemen, or spies. They were amateurs, perhaps dilettantes, caught up in a situation they previously knew nothing about. Few of them had training to engage in the activities that became their lot. However, the hero was always someone with multiple skills learned perhaps in wartime or in some branch of service.

Until shortly before and after the time of World War II, professional agents or investigative figures were rarely depicted in fiction, but the growth of police departments and defense and undercover agencies throughout the century helped create a somewhat different type of hero. Modern warfare also played a part in making the hero an informed and knowledgeable professional. Nevertheless, the contemporary thriller hero still carries the marks of the traditional figure.

Thriller heroes rarely take on their tasks for money, even though they are paid for their activities. Some become involved for excitement, some to protect people, some to fulfill their sense of duty or social responsibility. But the major function of the thriller hero usually is the righting or prevention of wrongs, whether his country, a group, or an individual has been attacked or injured. The hero's role may change from novel to novel and even within the same novel. He may be either the hunter or the hunted. (Clancy's heroes fill both roles.) Whatever task he has, he is expected to perform honorably and loyally, even if he has to commit acts he may not approve of, be forced to play a deceptive game, or get involved in the deaths of innocent people. In one way or another, the hero is a vulnerable man. Guilt, as well as danger, is something he may always have to live with. No matter how he attempts to avoid danger, he is never free. Not only can he not escape his own fate, he may bring danger, pain, and suffering to those he loves.

Clancy and the Thriller

In a number of ways, Clancy's novels make a perfect fit as thriller, even though "technothriller" is a more exact term. Most of his novels have the large landscape of war that Harper considers a requirement for thrillers. His wars may not invariably be shooting wars, but wars they are. There is the cold war of *The Hunt for Red October.* The wars of terrorists are central to *Patriot Games* and *The Sum of All Fears.* Drug wars propel the action of *Clear and Present Danger,* and both drug wars and a shooting war are at the heart of *Without Remorse.* Economic war is related to actual warfare in *Debt of Honor.* Furthermore, Clancy's pages are brimming over with death and responsibility, elements that Harper considers essential. In all Clancy's work, violence in some form brings on death to large or small groups of people. Responsibility for hostile acts is always clear, so that the reader knows from the start where the blame lies, and it is never with "us"—the "good guys."

Clancy's novels, like most popular thrillers, have certainty in them. A single-minded philosophy puts the United States, its military, and preselected individuals in the good category and the opposition in the bad. No shades of gray are sketched in. Although Clancy's world is technologically complex, his "friendly forces" characters, as well as the private and public world they live in, are not. They are "our" people, know-

able and dependable. We can count on them to bring about justice as we understand it.

The heroes of Clancy's fiction risk their lives in the manner of medieval knights, even though at first nothing signals their special qualities. They may prefer to stay at home in a safe environment, doing familiar, enjoyable work, but when duty requires something else, they do it bravely. Toland in *Red Storm Rising* is an example. Ryan, the major Clancy hero, may be terrified of flying, but he does it anyway, just as he automatically risks his life again and again in dangerous situations. Ryan behaves that way from the moment he is introduced in *Red October* and on through each successive novel. There are also examples of ordinary, decent men who do not seem at first to have any of the makings of a hero. Yet, when events test them, they become leaders of men and saviors of women. Edwards, the meteorologist in *Red Storm Rising,* is that type of man. He would rather die than be a James Bond who secretly thrills to the idea of "the tang of rape" (*Casino Royale*). Clancy's heroes do not have such thoughts. They are men set apart from others, superior to those around them. Nevertheless, almost always they work within the establishment.

Jack Ryan, though individualized in memorable ways, comes through the traditional line of thriller novels and is an amalgam of traits of prior figures. Like sleuths and agents of early suspense fiction, Ryan has not chosen as his vocation any form of secret or investigative work, but it finds him. Although he differs from the low-key hero of some of the 1920s-30s Golden Age English detective, he does have a number of resemblances. (It is not surprising that we think of English figures, for both author and his hero show great affection for all things English.) The famed English writer Dorothy Sayers's Lord Peter Wimsey, for example, is rich, intelligent, well educated, a university graduate. He served and was injured in World War I, is an amateur sleuth but plays a role in government intelligence. Jack Ryan is also rich, well educated, successful even when he least expects it, a failure at nothing, a former marine, and involved in intelligence. In yet another bow to the English heroes, Clancy has the queen reward an exploit of Ryan's by dubbing him Sir Ryan.

When introduced in Clancy's first thriller, Ryan thinks of himself as an average citizen, a teacher/scholar. Of course the experienced thriller reader knows and expects him to be anything but average. With each book Ryan becomes more like the superstars of other thriller novels. He soon gives up his enjoyable teaching position to work for the CIA, and his exploits begin to rival those of any thriller hero. Not only does he place himself in harm's way but unwittingly does the same with his family. Family attachments also put him in greater danger. In *Patriot Games* when wife Caroline (Cathy) and daughter Sally are seriously injured by terrorists seeking vengeance on Ryan himself, he takes actions that he would not have followed had they not been attacked. Like other thriller heroes he refuses to let the law do all the work, and he throws himself into the center of action. He wins out, but there is a price, and over time, that is, over a ten-year series of novels, he changes. The quiet, cool-headed man of the first book becomes secretive, extremely active, and even explosive as he ages. With each novel we also see a more cynical Ryan, the result of his exposure to evil men and philosophy.

The Spy Novel

Another applicable description of Clancy's work is "spy novel." Lest someone protest that Clancy is not a spy writer, we have only to consider LeRoy Panek's judgment that a work is a spy novel if there is a single spy in it. Furthermore, that view is bolstered by Marc Cerasini's essay in *The Tom Clancy Companion*. In writing about "the birth of a genre," Cerasini describes Clancy's fusion of "military fiction with near-future apocalyptic science fiction, touches of espionage fiction, and a large dose of social realism." Those "touches of espionage fiction" in Clancy's work require consideration of the features of spy stories if we are to place it completely.

Critics assign different dates to the "first" or most important British spy novel, which is the true ancestor of American espionage fiction, even though occasionally someone will name the American James Fenimore Cooper's *The Spy* (1821) as the earliest example of the genre. Historians have said spying came about as early as the Middle Ages. Nevertheless, actual spies did not have the romantic aura that fiction conferred on them with the development of the spy novel in the nineteenth century. Scholars agree that spy stories are linked to the Industrial Revolution, which occurred in Great Britain and parts of Europe before the United States. As Britain became highly industrialized, its weaponry, naval power, and eventually its airplanes were seen as a threat, as well as a source of envy to foreign powers. Spying took on an important role in reality and in fiction.

Modern thriller/espionage writers (as well as detective story writers) are indebted to a number of nineteenth- and early twentieth-century authors who created the form. According to some scholars, the prolific novelist William LeQueux is said to have provided the major guidelines of the spy novel, in spite of the unreadability of most of his work. LeQueux's importance to the development of espionage fiction also comes through what Panek calls his "pseudo-histories." These resemble war prophecy novels and argue "for military preparedness." Although LeQueux was writing at the turn of the nineteenth century, his indirect effect may be seen in later writers who in turn influenced Clancy. LeQueux's work also suffers from what Panek calls "the worst brand

of Victorian sentiment." Sentiment, however, is not unique to LeQueux. Inasmuch as he is hardly the only author whose novels become mired in embarrassing mawkishness, we can't trace that tendency in Clancy back to LeQueux alone.

Also among the forerunners of the modern spy novel is the work of E. Phillips Oppenheimer, which provided one particular type of motif we find in Clancy. That is Oppenheimer's variation on the war prophecy novel, "prediction of an averted war instead of an actual one." Oppenheimer's spy fiction takes on issues common to both the war prophecy novel and the averted war novel, issues that Clancy makes use of also. Both novelists show concern about the sufficiency of defense, the strength and weaknesses of military preparedness, and secret weapons.

Most scholars agree that the first "good" spy fiction is a war prophecy novel, *The Riddle of the Sands,* written by Erskine Childers in 1903. Critic/novelist Julian Symons states it is that novel which established a double standard for spying. Enemy spies have evil motives, whereas "we" have only worthy intentions. (Depending on who the novelist is, the "we" may differ. In *Riddle of the Sands* it is the British, and in most spy fiction by English or American writers, their compatriots are the worthy "we.") Symons claims that the duality of the moral problem—we are good, they are bad—existed only through the first few decades of the twentieth century, coming to an end with the work of Eric Ambler. His position is belied not only by a reading of Clancy's novels but also by an examination of the varieties of fiction of the years following World War II.

The most important writer for our consideration of the "development of the spy novel or the detective novel" (and for examination of Clancy's relationship to them) is John Buchan. "The modern novel of espionage simply would not have developed along the same lines without him." Even today his novels continue to exert their influence on mystery—spy/thriller/adventure novels, and "in its best manifestations the spy novel returns to him." Even novelist John Le Carré tips his hat to the great earlier writer by using a Buchan title in one of his own books.

Like thrillers, all spy fiction is not the same. Several literary historians have called attention to two clear divisions in the spy fiction genre. One is in the heroic, conservative, traditional camp. The other is realistic and ironic, in the mode of modern fiction. The first, as defined by Symons, supports "authority," asserting "that agents are fighting to protect something valuable." He describes the other type as "radical, critical of authority," with claims "that agents perpetuate, and even create, false barriers between 'us' and 'them.'" Other critics note that the traditional archetypal form has more violence, as well as more vitality and hope than the later one. The earlier type generally has a happy and conclusive ending, much like the novels of the Victorian Age. All loose ends are tied, all issues settled, if only temporarily. The realistic spy novel with its antiheroes, its darkness, and sense of despair is much closer in tone to modern and postmodern thought. Not surprisingly, the spy novel that utilizes traditional motifs (even with updated variations) is the one that is most successful commercially even though it is the other type that literary pundits find more meaningful.

Clancy and the Spy Novel

By the 1980s the time was right for Clancy's unique blending of modes, the uniquely modern and the traditional. In traditional ways his work bears multiple resemblances to Buchan's. Both Buchan's novels and Clancy's are realistic in their use of actual historical events, but both mix them with fabricated incidents. Buchan's chief character Richard Hannay is, like the later Jack Ryan, a series figure. The two, who look and sound like the typical English or American reader, are a meld of romantic and ordinary figure. Buchan's fiction is a form of "Victorian" schoolboy literature, that is, it focuses on adventure, morality, heroism, and friendship. These same characteristics, though updated, are central to Clancy's work. Also notable in Buchan's novels is "the absence of believable, complete women characters." Though hardly a remarkable characteristic in any spy novels, it is another resemblance between Buchan and Clancy's fiction. Finally, one small link that seems appropriate to Buchan but somewhat entertaining in Clancy: Buchan's characters have memories of grouse shooting. Sir Jack Ryan also has such memories.

The Technothriller

Critics combined the words technology and thriller into "technothriller" to give a more precise definition to another variation in genre. The term "thriller" by itself does not suggest the differences in technological fiction. Although there is much overlapping of characteristics, the technological novel has some distinctive traits of its own.

Technothrillers are not completely the product of the modern age but have become significant additions to popular literature with the phenomenal advance of technology in the second half of the twentieth century. Contemporary writers have made use of technology unknown before the Second World War. These technothriller novelists build their work around technology that is both current and projected or futuristic. Every manner of complex machines, usually real but sometimes imagined, is fodder for the work. The technothriller may focus on any area from ocean to outer space. It may concern all forms of nuclear weaponry, missiles, submarines, aircraft. Perhaps it foregrounds computers that reach beyond human ability to solve problems. Laboratories with scientists—biologists, chemists, physicists, archaeolo-

gists—study unknown and as yet unsolved questions of existence, DNA, germs, viruses, extinct species.

In addition to the resemblances of technothriller to thriller fiction, there is sometimes the reminder of SF, and not only in the futuristic element. Still, some important distinctions exist. Unlike SF, the technothriller world is earthbound although its machines go out into space. It is the world the reader knows, even if its complexities are baffling. It is not the estranged world of SF. Scholars point out that characters in technothrillers are usually less interesting than the technology. However, people in technothrillers are recognizable humans, different from the fantasized, imaginary, or robotics figures of SF.

Although people are necessary to put things into motion (the thriller aspect), the plot in a technothriller depends more on advanced technology than on human character. Technothrillers are often a form of military fiction, with players who are soldiers, sailors, pilots. The novel serves as a subordinate backdrop to display advancements and projections of weaponry and war. Actual war, possible war, or averted war is fought on the pages of the technothriller. However, war is not limited to mass destruction of a martial nature. There may be other kinds of war, perhaps a financial war, dependent on modern technology, which could destroy the world economy. The crises and solutions in most technothrillers are mechanical. People may make mistakes, but the focus of the plot is on the machinery not on human limitations. The "good" characters in technothrillers are clearly delineated, are on the "right" side and, in the military fiction, are superpatriots. Invariably, the cast of characters is large. Although there may be a single traditional hero, the wide scope of the playing field requires a great many people, so many in fact that often they seem as faceless as their machines.

Clancy and the Technothriller

No matter how much technology dominates his books, Clancy's basic formula comes from the thriller. The fact that he sees himself as a writer of political thrillers further emphasizes the point that the thriller model is the primary one he has followed. Yet, his fiction has some SF connections and is especially close to espionage novels in its inclusion of spies, and, as critic William Ryan calls them, "other mavens of espionage." However, Clancy's enjoyment of gadgets, his early reading of SF stories, including those filled with gadgetry, his monitoring of scientific developments, his fascination with computers, his admiration for all things military, and his very strong sense of patriotism connect him to the technothriller.

Marc Cerasini provides some background for Clancy's work, by describing the fiction and films that preceded his novels. He tells of the changing attitudes of the second half of this century: "Traditional war novels, tales of personal heroism and self-sacrifice that reinforced higher values of social responsibility, the type of fiction characteristic of the years following the Second World War, were replaced with a fiction of cynicism and defeat." Antiwar novels and movies became popular for a time, one result of the unpopularity of the Vietnam War. But, even during the war, SF writers were creating promilitary novels and cleverly disguised war films. Cerasini writes that "Star Wars" is really a "reincarnation" of "unabashedly patriotic films of the 1940s." Filmmaker George Lucas, claims Cerasini, made "the villains clear-cut fascists, the good guys honest and noble." Similar films proved popular, and novels moved in the direction of technology and politics.

By the 1980s the time was ripe for the fiction of Clancy. All his novels employ technology, even *Patriot Games,* which the novelist considers a love story. Like the work of other technothriller writers, almost everything in Clancy's plots and their central episodes depends on advanced technology. For Clancy, like many other contemporary technothriller writers, that technology involves military matters. Because of that identification he has been described as "the novelist laureate of the military industrial complex."

His multiple characters are often flat and subordinate to the technology. Aside from his alter-ego character, Jack Ryan, and his other favorite, John Kelly (Clark), Clancy's people are types rather than individuals. Some reviewers also classify Ryan and Kelly that way, comments that anger the author greatly. He is exasperated by critics who describe his machines as more interesting, complex, and lifelike than his characterizations. He angrily defends his portrayal of characters. Even if he scoffs at the word "literature," and at critics, he wants to be known as a writer who understands everything about his creations. In his determination to make his people real, he provides family background, wives, children, a few friends. However, the same flatness of characterization pervasive in most technothriller writing holds for these. Rarely do the families come alive. The wives and children are too perfect, friends too understanding, invariably good-humored and supportive. But the humanizing element in his characters (and a quality that adds to suspense) is that they can occasionally make mistakes. They misread, or overlook, or make a poor judgment that leads to serious consequences. Still, the effect of such action is seen to propel plot, not to alter or develop character. The military and government agents in the author's drama do not change with success or failure.

Conclusion

All the many facets of Clancy's work may explain the esteem in which it is held by readers, and also the less praiseful attitudes of most literary critics. While Clancy is an inno-

vative and exciting writer in modern technological ways, paradoxically he is at the same time a traditional one. It is not pejorative to call his work formula writing. The entertainment technothriller, thriller, spy story always adheres to formula in language, plot, images and symbols. We readers like the assurance of that familiarity, while at the same time we want something new added in character or situation or "filler." (The filler is sometimes called "unbound motifs," that is, absorbing and interesting information but unnecessary to the progression of the story.) The pleasure readers gain from formula writing is the repetition of something we have experienced and enjoyed before, but with the excitement of newness. It might be the new plot or setting, or more about the serial hero, of whom we know much, yet never enough. We want to be told what he eats, drinks, drives, wears, what he feels about the world in which he functions. And, with all that, in such entertainments there is the promise of a complex world made comprehensible.

> **While Clancy is an innovative and exciting writer in modern technological ways, paradoxically he is at the same time a traditional one. It is not pejorative to call his work formula writing.**
> *—Helen S. Garson*

In Clancy's novels political views are central and powerful. He stirs old and new fears of the Russian bear, the Red menace, creeping communism, Asians and Latins, all these personified through evil characters. The enemy is known wherever or whenever he or she appears. The reader's apprehensions and the writer's become one. They are voiced by Fleming Meeks, who tells us Clancy plays on our "deep-seated geopolitical fears" as he "spins scary scenarios of world chaos." Works become popular when the reader shares or sympathizes with the point of view and feels a kinship to all or most of the values. Clancy brings about most of these responses in readers, who cannot wait for each new book to appear.

Then why the attacks of some reviewers on such popular material? To answer that, we might consider a comment made by Kingsley Amis about hostility to the James Bond novels of Ian Fleming. They, the critics, are angered, says Amis, by the "attraction of something one disapproves of." But few readers disapprove. For most, the use of formula brings the reassurance of safety even as the real or fictional world explodes. Our various repressed needs and longings are served. Many of us have an unconscious desire for danger and excitement, perhaps even violence, though in reality most of us do everything to avoid involvement. Through thrillers/spy novels we can cross the boundaries of actual life into the world of the forbidden or unattainable. In our escape into the fantasized world we find wish fulfillment. We can confront our foes, knowing someone else will act for us and win. Our hero—ourself—will live to fight another day. Then, as the poet A. E. Housman tells us, we'll "see the world as the world's not" and ourselves as "sterling lad[s]" ("Terence, This Is Stupid Stuff").

The experience is cathartic. Whether we can finally decide that there is a single label for Clancy's work doesn't matter. Rather it is our understanding of the ways the pieces of the puzzle fit together to make up the world of Clancy's fiction.

FURTHER READING

Criticism

Flick, Arend. "Traitors and Heroes." *Los Angeles Times Book Review* (26 July 1987): 1, 10.
    Offers tempered evaluation of *Patriot Games.*

Gibson, J. William. "Redeeming Vietnam: Techno-Thriller Novels of the 1980s." *Cultural Critique* 19 (Fall 1991): 179-202.
    Explores the sociocultural context and function of the techno-thriller, including Clancy's *The Hunt for Red October* and *Red Storm Rising.*

Lernoux, Penny. "Just Say Colombia." *Los Angeles Times Book Review* (10 September 1989): 4.
    A generally favorable review of *Clear and Present Danger.*

Miles, Jack. "An SDI 'Hamlet' without the Prince." *Los Angeles Times Book Review* (14 August 1988): 6.
    Offers tempered assessment of *The Cardinal of the Kremlin.*

Shiflett, Dave. "The Clancy Solution to Drug Dealing." *The Wall Street Journal* (13 August 1993): A5.
    Offers qualified praise for *Without Remorse.*

Stone, Oliver. "Who's That in the Oval Office?" *New York Times Book Review* (22 September 1996): 16-7.
    A tempered review of *Executive Orders.*

Additional coverage of Clancy's life and career is contained in the following sources published by Gale: *Authors and Artists for Young Adults,* **Vol. 9;** *Bestsellers,* **89:1 and 90:1;** *Contemporary Authors,* **Vols. 125 and 131;** *DISCovering Authors Modules: Novelists* **and** *Popular Fiction and Genre Authors;* **and** *Major Twentieth-Century Writers,* **second edition.**

Spalding Gray
1941-

American dramatist, novelist, actor, and short story writer.

The following entry presents an overview of Gray's career through 1996. For further information on his life and works, see *CLC*, Volume 49.

INTRODUCTION

Gray is numbered among the leading innovators of contemporary performance art. Through avant-garde experimentation with mainstream theater and media, Gray's improvised autobiographical monologues seek universal meaning in the absurd and often humorous particularities of white, middle-class American experience—especially his own. The stage performance of *Swimming to Cambodia* (1985), his best-known work, won critical praise, as did its film adaptation by director Jonathan Demme in 1987. While Gray's candid, self-deprecating public confessions dwell on the idiosyncracies of his own thought and personal crises, through such cathartic disclosures he attempts to bring about psychological healing and to raise social consciousness for both himself and his audience. An engaging storyteller and charismatic performer, Gray's insightful examination of the alternately mundane, personally embarrassing, and politically relevant illustrates the inseparable relationship between art and everyday life.

Biographical Information

Born in Barrington, Rhode Island, Gray and his two siblings grew up in a middle-class home. His father was a factory worker and his mother a homemaker who became a devout Christian Scientist after a series of nervous breakdowns. Upon graduating from Fryeburg Academy, a private secondary school in Maine, Gray attended Emerson College, where he studied acting and earned a bachelor's degree in 1965. For the next two years Gray worked as an actor in Cape Cod, Massachusetts, and Saratoga, New York, appearing in summer stock plays such as Eugene O'Neill's *Long Day's Journey into Night*. In 1967, he travelled to Texas and Mexico, but returned several months later upon news of his mother's suicide, a family trauma that plunged Gray into a long depression leading to a nervous breakdown nine years later. In 1967, Gray joined Richard Schechner's Performance Group, an experimental New York theater company with which he was associated until 1979. Gray produced *Sakonnet Point* (1975), *Rumstick Road* (1977), and *Nyatt School* (1978) with Elizabeth LeCompte, with whom he co-founded the Wooster Group in 1977. The three works were later performed as the trilogy *Three Places in Rhode Island* (1979), to which Gray added the epilogue *Point Judith* (1979). After teaching a summer workshop at the Santa Cruz campus of the University of California in 1978, Gray performed his first monologue, *Sex and Death to the Age 14* (1979), followed by *Booze, Cars, and College* (1979) and *India (And After)* (1979). He was awarded a grant from the National Endowment for the Arts in 1978 and a Rockefeller Foundation fellowship in 1979. During the early 1980s, Gray produced additional experimental monologues with *Interviewing the Audience* (1981), in which he solicits audience participation, and *In Search of Monkey Girl* (1981), a collaborative project with photographer Randal Levenson based on his experiences with carnival freaks at the Tennessee State Fair. In 1983, Gray appeared in the part of an American ambassador's aide in *The Killing Fields*, Roland Joffe's feature film about the Khmer Rouge reign of terror in Cambodia after the Vietnam War. Two years later, Gray produced the stage version of *Swimming to Cambodia*, a monologue about his experiences during filming in Thailand, for which he won a Guggenheim fellowship. Next was *Terrors of Pleasure* (1986), a monologue about his purchase of a dilapidated house in upstate New York, and *Rivkala's Ring* (1986), an adaptation of Anton Chekhov's short story "Orchards." Since his film debut in *The Killing Fields,* Gray has appeared in a Broadway revival of Thornton Wilder's *Our Town* and additional motion pictures including *True Stories, Clara's Heart* and *Beaches.*

Major Works

The origin of Gray's trademark stage persona and dramatic technique may be traced to the trilogy of autobiographical works produced with LeCompte and later performed together as *Three Places in Rhode Island.* The first two works, *Sakonnet Point* and *Rumstick Road,* deal with mental illness and Gray's efforts to come to terms with his mother's suicide. In *Sakonnet Point,* named after the Rhode Island resort town where Gray vacationed as a child, Gray employs non-verbal, dance-like actions to illustrate pre-verbal childhood consciousness. This work also reveals the influence of experimental European dramatists Antonin Artaud and Jerzy Grotowski. *Rumstick Road,* a more discontinuous and frantic work, probes Gray's childhood memories with audio recordings of actual family members and the psychiatrist who treated Gray's mother before her death. The third, *Nyatt School,* is a parody of T. S. Eliot's verse drama *The Cocktail Party* in which Gray deconstructs Eliot's text through the lecturing of a pedantic academic. Gray's role as the subject and leading actor in these early works prefigured his first monologue, *Sex and Death to the Age 14,* in which he discusses humorous anecdotes about his sexual awakening and Christian Science upbringing against the historical background of the Second World War, the dropping of the atomic bomb on Hiroshima, and the polio epidemic. *Booze, Cars, and College* chronicles his early adulthood and college misadventures up to the Cuban Missile Crisis, while *India (And After)* recounts events culminating in his nervous breakdown in 1976 after touring India with the Wooster Group. Gray similarly fused personal memory with contemporary American history in *Swimming to Cambodia,* a monologue based on his experiences during the production of *The Killing Fields,* a film about the brutal decimation of Cambodian civilians by Communist Khmer Rouge guerrillas during the mid-1970s. Accompanied on the stage by only a desk, two maps of Southeast Asia, and a glass of water as props, Gray discusses a myriad of topics. His focus includes: life on the set of a major motion picture; Thai culture and prostitutes; American foreign policy in Vietnam and Cambodia; Khmer Rouge atrocities; and his own quest for spiritual epiphany, or a "perfect moment," which he experiences while floating in the Indian Ocean. With impressive sensitivity, irony, and wit, Gray's observations reveal him as a troubled individual, a professional actor, an American, and a human being outraged at the horrifying cost of war. In *Monster in a Box* (1990) Gray speaks as a writer struggling to complete an unwieldy novel about his picaresque adventures. Invoking

his mother's suicide as a point of departure, Gray extemporizes about his travels to Nicaragua, Moscow, and both coasts of the United States. The "monster" is a massive manuscript that he is struggling to complete for his publisher. Gray adapted this monologue into his autobiographical novel *Impossible Vacation* (1992), changing the protagonist's name to Brewster North. Gray's alter ego reminisces about his dysfunctional family and perpetual search for enlightenment in theater, Zen, drugs, sex, and far-flung travels to Europe and India, promising himself a vacation to Bali once his life story has been recorded. Gray's recent monologues continue the chronicle of his personal life and neuroses. *Gray's Anatomy* (1993) deals with mortality and the artist's fear of going blind and *Its a Slippery Slope* (1996) relates Gray's compromising relationship with two women: his wife, Renee Shafransky, and a lover with whom he accidentally has a son.

Critical Reception

Gray is highly regarded as a brilliant performer and unflinching commentator on middle-class American self-consciousness. By openly dissecting his own shortcomings and existential despair with appealing humor, earnest bewilderment, and humility, Gray speaks to his audiences as a living example of the angst-ridden, self-obsessed modern person. Viewed as a mixture of avant-garde artist, "poetic journalist," and stand-up comedian, Gray has been compared to Samuel Beckett for the minimalist elements of his theater and Woody Allen for his neurotic self-absorption. While some critics find Gray's confessional monologues narcissistic and superficial, most praise his inimitable stage presence and great ability as a storyteller. *Swimming to Cambodia* is widely considered his masterpiece and received enthusiastic critical approval. Though faulted by some for elements of historical arrogance and misogyny, both the stage and film versions of this work are generally praised as an example of Gray's perceptive observations and remarkable talent for weaving personal experience and memory into the tapestry of world-historical consciousness. While stage performances of Gray's subsequent monologues received favorable critical attention, film adaptations of *Terrors of Pleasure, Monster in a Box, Gray's Anatomy,* and his autobiographical novel *Impossible Vacation* were greeted with mixed assessment. Admired for reviving the ancient art of epic oral history in his stylized chronicling of late twentieth-century self and society, Gray is recognized as an important creative force in contemporary American theater and performance art.

PRINCIPAL WORKS

Sakonnet Point [with Elizabeth LeCompte] (drama) 1975
Rumstick Road [with Elizabeth LeCompte] (drama) 1977
Nyatt School [with Elizabeth LeCompte] (drama) 1978

Three Places in Rhode Island [with Elizabeth LeCompte] (drama) 1979
Point Judith (drama) 1979
Sex and Death to the Age 14 (drama) 1979
Booze, Cars, and College Girls (drama) 1979
India (And After) (drama) 1979
A Personal History of the American Theatre (drama) 1980
In Search of Monkey Girl [with Randal Levenson] (drama) 1981
Interviewing the Audience (drama) 1981
Seven Scenes from a Family Album (short stories) 1981
Swimming to Cambodia (drama) 1985
Rivkala's Ring (drama) 1986
Terrors of Pleasure (drama) 1986
Travels through New England (drama) 1986
Swimming to Cambodia: The Collected Works of Spalding Gray (drama) 1987
Monster in a Box (drama) 1990
Impossible Vacation (novel) 1992
Gray's Anatomy (drama) 1993
It's a Slippery Slope (drama) 1996

CRITICISM

Cathleen McGuigan (essay date 28 July 1986)

SOURCE: "Gray's Eminence," in *Newsweek,* July 28, 1986, p. 69.

[*In the following essay, McGuigan discusses Gray's artistic concerns and Gray's performance in* Swimming to Cambodia.]

Spalding Gray walks onstage carrying a spiral notebook with a cartoon cover and wearing the kind of plaid cotton shirt that a nerd would button up to his Adam's apple. He sits at a table with a pull-down map behind him, as though he's about to give a class report. And he begins to talk, the words spilling out of him with the speed and candor of a precocious child. But there's nothing juvenile about his intricately crafted monologue, *Swimming to Cambodia.* A funny, moving soliloquy that Gray has been performing at Lincoln Center in New York, along with another monologue called *Terrors of Pleasure,* it manages in 100 minutes to sketch the history of Cambodian genocide, recount the filming of *The Killing Fields* (in which he had a part) and evoke a technicolor travelogue of paradise. It also provides a hilarious guided tour of Gray's neuroses (can't make a decision), fears (big ocean waves) and superstitions (turn off the radio only on a *positive* word). Don't worry, he's had professional help. His therapist, he notes, "was like a drinking buddy, but we never went drinking and I paid for all the drinks."

Gray is not, he insists, a performance artist, but an actor who comes to the theater each night and repeats certain actions and gestures. Whatever he is, he has reinvented the oral tradition. Unlike such solo performers as Lily Tomlin or Eric Bogosian, who present a gallery of personae, Gray plumbs just one character, himself. His material, all autobiographical, shows a great eye for detail, and he has a narrative gift for digressing and snaking neatly back to where he started.

In *Cambodia,* he threads in anecdotes about a nasty Manhattan neighbor or about sibling warfare at the Gray family dinner table, decades back in Barrington, R.I. He'll describe a man whose ears are so tiny they're like "pasta shells," or the T shirts the *The Killing Fields* crew wore one day that said, "Skip the Dialogue, Let's Blow Something Up." He'd rather not memorize the material; he checks his spiral notebook for an outline and cues, and every night he tries to spin the story as if for the first time.

> **Gray is not, he insists, a performance artist, but an actor who comes to the theater each night and repeats certain actions and gestures. Whatever he is, he has reinvented the oral tradition.**
> *—Cathleen McGuigan*

One day last week Gray, 45, sat in the Performing Garage in SoHo, his artistic home since 1970, and talked about his route from nonnarrative group-theater experiments to his solo work today. Trained as an actor, he worked with Richard Schechner's Performance Group, and it helped him overcome a fear of direct contact with an audience. "There were no seats," he recalls. "The audience would be perched on the edge of the set, like at a golf match." Later, with the Wooster Group, he developed a trilogy of autobiographical pieces; the most powerful, *Rumstick Road,* was about his mother's suicide.

With his first monologue in 1979, *Sex and Death to the Age of 14,* he was on his way to becoming the WASP Woody Allen. "It was a form of associative self-analysis," he says. Like the conceptual artist who lived in a storefront window in public view and called it a work of art, Gray's esthetic was based on extreme personal exposure—but his was artfully crafted and full of humor.

Decisions, Decisions

Although his work will remain personal, Gray is interested in monologues about "something larger than my own neuroses." He's much too busy for therapy, anyway. He's starring in David Byrne's movie *True Stories,* which comes out in October; director Jonathan Demme will film *Swimming to Cambodia* in November for theatrical release. Vintage Books has published a collection of his monologues and he's booked on the David Letterman show. But he keeps facing *decisions:* should he take his show to Broadway or go to the Mark Taper Forum for an intriguing project to search for natural storytellers on the streets of Los Angeles? Whatever he ends up doing, he's sure to be taking notes. "I'll never run out of material as long as I live," he says. "The only disappointment is that I probably won't be able to come back after I die and tell that experience."

Mervyn Rothstein (essay date 4 December 1988)

SOURCE: "A New Face in Grover's Corners," in *The New York Times,* December 4, 1988, pp. 1, 10.

[*In the following essay, Rothstein discusses Gray's artistic motivations and involvement in the Lincoln Center Theater revival of Thornton Wilder's* Our Town.]

Thornton Wilder, in his 1957 preface to "Three Plays":

> "*Our Town* is not offered as a picture of life in a New Hampshire village; or as a speculation about the conditions of life after death (that element I merely took from Dante's *Purgatory*). It is an attempt to find a value above all price for the smallest events in our daily life. I have made the claim as preposterous as possible, for I have set the village against the largest dimensions of time and place. The recurrent words in this play (few have noticed it) are 'hundreds,' 'thousands,' and 'millions.' Emily's joys and griefs, her algebra lessons and her birthday presents—what are they when we consider all the billions of girls who have lived, who are living, and who will live? Each individual's assertion to an absolute reality can be only inner, very inner."

The doorbell in the street is usually anonymous, but this morning a 47-year-old resident of the SoHo section of Manhattan has scribbled something to its right to provide a guide for a visitor.

"S. Gray," says the scrawl on the wall. The visitor rings the doorbell and waits as S. Gray races down four flights of stairs to open the door to the loft building where he lives. It is just down the street from the Performing Garage, where, first with the Performance Group and then with the Wooster Group, Spalding Gray performed and began creating the monologues for which he is best known.

Now the author of *Sex and Death to the Age 14, Terrors*

of Pleasure and *Swimming to Cambodia* has taken on a new role—that of the Stage Manager in Lincoln Center Theater's revival of Thornton Wilder's *Our Town.* The 1938 Pulitzer Prize-winning play about the residents of Grover's Corners, N. H. . . . is directed by Gregory Mosher and has a cast of 27, including Penelope Ann Miller, Eric Stoltz, James Rebhorn and Frances Conroy. It is, Mr. Gray says, his first major role in a play since he was Hoss in Sam Shepard's *Tooth of Crime* at the Performing Garage in 1974.

"When I was mulling over whether to do it, my girlfriend, Renée Shafransky, was playing devil's advocate," Mr. Gray recalls. "So she says to me, 'How are they going to do *Our Town* in Calcutta?' She was referring to New York City as Calcutta, because that's how we've been experiencing it."

He is seated at a bare wooden table next to a rear window in his apartment. It is a table not unlike the ones he has used in his monologues, and from time to time he will lean forward, elbows on the table, just as he does on stage. "At first I said no to Greg," Mr. Gray says.

> And he said, "Think it over for the day and call me back tonight." And I had said "No" because of the book I'm working on. It's a hardcover, autobiographic novel, and I was very anxious about it. So I went off for a walk to think it over. I always walk up to Barnes & Noble, on 18th Street—I have to have a point of reference to go to. And then I look at all the books on sale. I like to look at all the books on sale.

> And there was this guy outside. I always carry change with me and give it out, and this guy had such a sad story. He had had his head bashed in in San Francisco, and had been in a veterans' hospital, and he left prematurely, and he had no place to stay. And I thought, "No, I can't do *Our Town.* This is the answer. I must work with the homeless."

> And I went back all inspired. I thought I was going to go up to the Cathedral of St. John the Divine. And then I thought, "No, no, my talent is around the theater." And I know that doing this piece is in some way going to be important. In some way, this will create a dramatic dynamic between what is going on outside and what is going on on the stage; between the order of the theater and the absolute chaos of the streets.

His visitor asks for an example. "I don't think it's clear to me yet," he says.

> It's evolving. But when I came to work the first day, there were people dealing crack in the stage en-

trance, because no one had used the theater for such a long time. They had a suitcase open and they had bags the size of a hardcover book filled with what looked like rock candy. And I said, "Excuse me," and I stepped over the suitcase. I said, "I'm going to work now." They're not there anymore, because people are coming and the whole thing's alive. But they were there then.

Sex and Discipline to the Age 21

Mr. Mosher, the play's director and the director of Lincoln Center Theater, has brought to this production his personal view of the work. It is a view that closely relates the play to the vision of Samuel Beckett, and especially to one line from *Waiting for Godot:* ". . . they are born astride the grave."

"Somehow, in the 50's and 60's, the play was turned into a Hallmark card," Mr. Mosher recalled earlier this fall, on the day he announced that Mr. Gray had joined the cast. "It was reduced, not necessarily by anyone doing anything, but by a consensus that it was a superficial, nostalgic, flag-waving poem to a lost America.

"On the contrary," he said, "I think it's a very particular vision of what life in this century has been. The first act begins in 1901 and projects out into the future about the deepest sort of spiritual concerns that people have. It's a magnificent play to be doing side by side with *Godot.*

"They were written 10 years apart," he said—*Godot* was completed in 1948—"and while Beckett's vision is certainly a darker one, there's a searching in Thornton Wilder's play that simply can't exist when it's performed in a high school theater, as it often is. The students don't know about death, about dying in childbirth. There's that most famous line in *Godot* about being born astride the grave. And here in *Our Town* there's the most beautiful girl in the world giving birth and dying in childbirth."

Mr. Gray acknowledges the Beckett influence on the production. But he says that he has his own, very different, connections to the play. "Certainly that Beckett imagery is there," he says.

> But I don't relate to it as much as Gregory does. Beckett is not a favorite writer of mine, and *Godot* is not a favorite play.

> I would say that the kind of existential angst that Beckett has is mildly there. But there's something else—a kind of spirituality. There are hints of New England metaphysical Hinduism and Buddhism, as in Thoreau and Emerson. My first take on the play, and I still hold it, is that it's a New England grave-

yard meditation. It's a very heartfelt, dark piece, and, in this production, it's combined with a nice mix of lightness and humor.

Gertrude Stein is kind of my muse for the play. . . . I can hear her "Making of the Americans" in it, the way in which she repeats simple details about living. But Wilder is more condensed. And almost certainly there's the way Hemingway was influenced by her. They were trying to write the most uncomplicated sentences that would deliver the most information. It reminds me of dense Zen haikus, where they go on and on and on, but it's always nondelving nonpsychological, nonpsychoanalytic. It's clean surface statements that what you're seeing is what exists and all that exists beyond that is in your imagination, and mine.

Mr. Gray's connections to the play are related to his childhood, he says—to his birth in Barrington, R.I., and to his memories of growing up in New England, a New England 40 years after the time of *Our Town.*

"I refer to *Our Town* as the tip of the iceberg," he says.

> My book, my autobiographic novel, is the bottom. The book is like a parallel to *Peyton Place,* because it shows the more seamy, sordid side of New England, of why I left, of why I was driven out of it, and all the repressive aspects of it.

> When I see some of the scenes in the play, . . . I think about going to the Christian Science Sunday school, which you had to go to until you were 21, if you made it that far. These are associations I have while watching the play, and I watch it every night from the wings. I don't ever leave the presence of the play. I don't go to my dressing room, because I always want to know what I'm coming into when I come in as the Stage Manager—the energy field.

> I can remember my Sunday school teacher seeing me playing with my hands while I was listening, maybe nervously, and then him slapping my hands and saying, "We don't need that kind of distraction here." And I put my hands down, and then somewhere in the middle of the class, the same class, he got up and went over to the clock on the wall, an old pendulum clock, and he stopped it. And he said, "We don't need this kind of distraction either."

> And the other thing that I remember is when my mother found all my pinups behind my door— Marilyn Monroe included, that naked shot of her on red satin. I had put them on the back of my door so

that she'd never see them, but she went to dust behind the door, and she took them and put them all out on the coffee table down in the sun room. And she gave me a long lecture about how these would give me disturbing thoughts, bad thoughts.

So I think of that, . . . for instance, in the scene between Emily and her mother. When her mother says, Emily, "you're pretty enough for all normal purposes," I see this enormous New England repression around the idea of glorification of beauty. It's a wonderful line. It just brings home all of that puritanical stuff. It's the darker side, the one I always wanted to bust out of. It was meant to keep you in your place. The Australians call it the "tall poppy theory"—if you get too uppity, if you stand out too much, they cut you down.

But it had its good side too, he adds—"in the sense that it was always concerned with the enjoyment of very simple details, the Shaker aspect, the simple life.

"Wilder was writing it at the Macdowell Colony," he says, "and I was up there in March, so when I say the speech about the White Mountains I'm really seeing them, and it helps the connection. And I had climbed in the White Mountains—I climbed Mount Washington when I was 15 years old. It was the first mountain I climbed. So these connections mean much more to me than the Beckett one."

The Terrors of Performing

The play has in it something that he had not been in touch with for a while, Mr. Gray says.

It's a simple sense of heartfeltness. Taken over the edge, it would be sentiment, but we're not playing it that way. I don't think the play is a sentimental play, and I think the Stage Manager's role is to step in and cut the sentiment when it's right on the edge. I think of the Stage Manager as a kind of go-between between the audience and the piece. He interrupts all the scenes just before they can go into another realm—he brings it back to the point where he is saying, "This is a play we're doing." What I love about *Our Town* is I'm always saying that this is a play, and this convention feels good to me, because it's in a way working behind the scenes, which is the way I've always worked—telling the story under the story. When I'm trying to focus on "A," I think of "K."

But amid the love, there is a problem. "It's been a real project not to comment on what's going on around the pro-

duction," he says—"which is the construction of a very large building right next door," at Broadway and 45th Street.

"We've canceled Wednesday matinees now," he says, "because of that. But last Wednesday was a very interesting and memorable experience.

The workers were supposed to stop at 3 o'clock—that was the agreement they had with the Shubert Organization. Well, at 3 o'clock, it got worse. So in the middle of these incredible scenes there were these wonderful juxtapositions. It reminded me of when I first came to New York City, in 1967, and I went to see Merce Cunningham at the Brooklyn Academy of Music. Before the dance began, they said that they had no soundtrack, that the soundtrack was what's going on outside the Academy—the street sounds. As soon as they directed our attention there, of course, we accepted it and paid attention to it—it was a wonderful kind of John Cagean concept.

So here's this scene going on between Eric Stoltz—George Gibbs—and Jim Rebhorn, who plays his father, Doc Gibbs. They're talking about how the mother was cutting wood, how Doc Gibbs heard her cutting wood that morning, and how George should help his mother. And all you could hear was these buzz-saws cutting wood right next door—a big, big, ZZZZZZZEW, ZZZZZZZEW. And I thought, I hope it's quiet by the time we get to the cemetery and Emily's last speech.

Because I remembered that one night—there are no buildings next to the Lyceum now, so you can hear the sirens—and one night Emily was doing that "Oh, earth, you're too wonderful for anybody to realize you" speech, and there was full gridlock: sirens, police, ambulances.

Could all this be grist for a future monologue?

"Every monologue I've ever done was serendipitous," he says, "and came out of what I call a kind of leftover energy—things that weren't resolved, things that stood out, things that needed to be talked out to be understood. And they were always whatever I entered in my journal. And then I'll start to put together a fabric. I think that the next monologue is going to be very broad, and cover a lot of territory. It will be catching-up-with-what-has-happened-since-I've-last-spoken-to-you. Though Eric Stoltz is totally on guard about everything he says, because we share this dressing room."

He pauses and thinks for a moment. "I often think of the Lyceum Theater, when we're in it—and we've been in it a lot," he says, "as this huge, old cruise ship, going nowhere, in which the entire crew is condemned to perform *Our Town* every night. It's a strange experience, being with all these people and doing this piece, and I can't think that there won't be stories coming out of it."

The Killing Fields

"I'm thinking about Washington," Mr. Gray says. "I think that I'm going to move down there in the spring and begin to try to figure out what is going on there politically, because it's a foreign land to me. And I dislike it."

He pauses briefly. Onstage, he would probably take a sip of water. But there is no water on the table. "And this is why I want to go to Washington," he says.

> Because I feel that if there's any juxtaposition between this play and the world outside, it's how far we've come from the original ideals, the ideals of our forefathers.
>
> When I look at America now, I see a series of feudal states, feudal cities. You have your entertainment capital, in Los Angeles, your house of illusions; you have your drug city, in Miami; you have your bureaucratic law, lingo, policy-destroying-making city, Washington; you have the city of intellect and finance; you have the conservative breadbasket. You're so blown away now, and so dependent on media and press, which is the one unifier. And it makes me want to flee to *Our Town*.
>
> And so my bone-chilling line in the play, as someone called it, is when I say: "Over there are some Civil War veterans. Iron flags on their graves . . . New Hampshire boys . . . had a notion that the Union ought to be kept together, though they'd never seen more than 50 miles of it themselves. All they knew was the name, friends—the United States of America. The United States of America. And they went and died about it."

"And every night that has a different reading for me," he says. "And a different meaning. I just let it hang there, as a meditation, on what is the United States of America. And the juxtaposition is between what we were, or what we thought we were, as Americans, and what we are—and between what we might have been and what we are."

Peggy Phelan (essay date 1988)

SOURCE: "Spalding Gray's *Swimming to Cambodia:* The Article," in *Critical Texts,* Vol. 5, No. 1, 1988, pp. 27-30.

[*In the following essay, Phelan provides critical analysis of the stage, film, and text versions of* Swimming to Cambodia. *Phelan is critical of Gray's egocentrism and "opportunistic" discussion of Cambodian genocide as a foil for his own spiritual awakening.*]

The most remarkable thing about Spalding Gray's **Swimming to Cambodia** is its Zelig-like ability to change its form. First "an experience," then a memory of an experience, then an improvisational performance of a memory of an experience, then a performance script, then a book, then a film, **Swimming to Cambodia** is perhaps the ultimate postmodern text—ubiquitous, slippery, and apparently immune to the law of genre. But as Zelig soon discovered, such a Protean existence has its price. **Swimming to Cambodia**'s easy mutation suggests that its ontology lies less in its ability to be taken as a "vessel for great themes expressed through mighty events," as James Leverett intones in his Introduction to The Book, and more in its hollowness—its extremely malleable *surface* appeal.

Swimming to Cambodia is a dramatic monologue about Gray's experience playing the U.S. ambassador's aide during the making of Roland Joffe's *The Killing Fields* (1983). In the three live performances which were combined in Jonathan Demme's superbly edited film, Gray expertly employs four props—a notebook, a glass of water, a map, and a pointer—to expound the history of U.S. intervention in Cambodia, the ascendancy of the Khmer Rouge in 1975, and the subsequent deaths of about two million Cambodian people. Along the way, Gray also tells the story of noise squabbles with Soho neighbors, stand-offs with Renée Shafransky (his lover and the producer of the film), and his indefatigable pursuit of "Perfect Moments." This pursuit leads him deep into the waves of the Indian Ocean, into a severe economic lust which sends him to a Hollywood agent, and eventually to the performance/film itself. When he experiences his first Perfect Moment it is in the Indian Ocean; for Gray Perfect Moments are timeless perceptions distinguished by a nostalgic transcendental "oneness" with his surroundings:

> Suddenly there was no time and there was no fear and there was no body to bite. There were no longer any outlines. I was just one big ocean. My body had blended with the ocean. And there was just this round, smiling-ear-to-ear pumpkin-head perceiver on top bobbing up and down.

Gray wants to turn this perceiver into the performer and the "poetic reporter." He defines a poetic reporter in his "Author's Note" as:

> . . . more like an impressionist painter than a photographer. Most reporters get the facts out as quickly

as possible—fresh news is the best news. I do just the opposite. I give the facts a chance to settle down and at last they blend, bubble and mix in the swamp of dream, memory, and reflection.

Gray's theatrical minimalism and simple sentences fit well with his persona as poetic reporter in *Swimming*. Sitting behind a desk in a plaid flannel shirt and speaking for about an hour and a half, Gray seems more like a casual and slightly bemused academic than an actor with Hollywood aspirations. Gray's persona in *Swimming,* however, does not work as well with this material as it has in the past. Irony, his most congenial affect, is not a sufficiently complex attitude to treat the "gruesome period from 1966 to the present" which constitutes present-day Cambodia. In this monologue, Gray's ambition is greater than his skill.

In 1979 Gray explained that his move from acting in other people's plays to performing his own solo pieces was precipitated by the conviction that what he was doing on stage was akin to freestyle body-surfing: "The text was like a wave I was riding, and the way I rode that wave was up to me." As a member of Richard Schechner's Performing Garage and Elizabeth Le Compte's Wooster Group, Gray has had a long and distinguished career in avant-garde theater. In 1981, after playing Hoss in the Performing Garage's production of Sam Shepherd's *Tooth of Crime,* he remarked:

> After I do the long monologue about the fighter Richard [Schechner—the director] said to just finish that, stand in front of the audience and allow myself to come to a neutral place so I'm no longer the character, and just look at the audience's eyes. That time I could feel the charge that had been building up peel away like an onion and I came to this extremely neutral state. Everything disappeared and the audience and I were one, and from there I went on to the next scene playing the old man, and that was such a wonderful transition.

For Gray, performative Perfect Moments consist of these experiences of "oneness" between himself and the audience. In *Swimming to Cambodia,* however, we hear so much *about* other Perfect Moments that there is little time or energy for creating a new one there in the theater/film.

In his exuberant "Author's Note" to *Swimming,* Gray outlines his aesthetic theory: "all human culture is art. It is all a conscious contrivance for the purpose of survival. All I have to do is look around me." In practice, unfortunately, the liberating claim that all of human culture is potentially "performable" (able to be represented "on stage") becomes in Gray's text only another opportunity to see himself. This visual/psychological claustrophobia does not seem to trouble him; in fact, he celebrates his endless self-seeking: "You

never know when they're [Perfect Moments] coming. It's sort of like falling in love . . . with yourself." It seems never to have occurred to Gray that falling in love with someone else might be less than a Perfect Moment but more like a Textured History; nor does he consider that a psychological Textured History might be more suitable as a parallel narrative to the story of the tragedy of Cambodia. And perhaps most inexplicable of all is Gray's apparently unconscious exploitation of the history of Cambodia, which he uses essentially as a structure to frame his "poetic reports."

Pauline Kael's remarks in *The New Yorker* have succinctly outlined all the reasons why Gray's boyish irony about performing in a movie about Cambodia, finding an agent, struggling over weighty decisions about spending two weeks in Krummville, New York, or mainland Thailand, while also expressing outrage at the Khmer Rouge's decimation of the Cambodians, could be construed as opportunistic:

> The high point of his monologue comes when he hears for the first time about our secret bombing of Cambodia, and what the Khmer Rouge did to the Cambodian people in 1975, driving them out of the cities and to their deaths. Mostly, his tone has been gentle mockery of himself and everyone else, but now he's upset, indignant. He's incredulous and horrified as he describes the exodus; he's an actor who has just discovered strong material and he builds the tension. . . . Is he effective? To judge from reactions to his stage performances and to the new concert-film version, definitely. Yet I can't be alone in feeling that he's a total opportunist, and so unconsciously that it never even occurs to him that there's anything wrong about using a modern genocidal atrocity story to work up an audience.

Although this unconsciousness has been apparent in Gray's previous performance work, it comes acutely to the forefront in *Swimming to Cambodia* because the monologue purports to be at least in part "a portrait of an artist" coming to political consciousness. But the structure of Gray's monologue inevitably leads one to measure the death of two million Cambodian refugees against his epiphany in the Indian Ocean. Such inappropriate measuring is more than aesthetically unfortunate; it also is historically arrogant.

Gray's task as a performer is to use himself as a kind of epistemological gauge; all experience and all representations of that experience must be filtered through him. Diametrically opposed to the Stanislavskian approach in which the actor emptied himself in order to let the character live, Gray's performances attempt to use the performance situation itself to fill himself with becoming/expressing/being Spalding Gray. The logical outcome of this impulse is manifest in his performance called *Interviewing the Audience,* in which he does just that.

In theory, Gray's project is important and interesting. Performance Art's most radical and innovative work often involves a thrillingly difficult investigation of autobiography. By rejuvenating the possible ways of presenting and representing the self, Performance Art has changed the notion of theatrical presence and widened the methods by and through which the self can be narrated, parodied, held in contempt, and/or made to be the source of revelatory vision and thought. The divergent work of Linda Montano, Karen Finley, Stuart Sherman, Chris Burden, John Malpede, and Lily Tomlin, to name only some of the best-known artists (as distinct from the most interesting) involved in this project, gives some sense of the scope and range of this re-investigation. Gray's work, perhaps more than anyone else's, has been able to bridge the gap between avant-garde and pop culture. Gray has made no secret of his eagerness to be "a star" and he seems to have less hesitation than one might expect about "crossing over":

> I always wanted to be a star in the finest sense—to be there, to be brilliant. . . . [T]he only way to be a star in our culture is to enter into the media at large. You have to be a household word. I wanted to be in performance and also be a star.

The obvious risk in Gray's work is that this performed self will be inadequate, boring, superficial. In order to minimize that risk, Gray affects a blanket irony. But unlike most of the other performance artists engaged in rethinking autobiographical "texts," Gray's work consistently returns to one theme: his most consistently expressed emotion is one of loss. "I have had this feeling [of loss] for as long as I can remember. It is the feeling that the 'I' I call 'me' is only a visitor here. No, not even a visitor because a visitor goes elsewhere after he visits." The visits recorded in *Swimming to Cambodia,* paradoxically, are visits recorded by one who does not leave the tight moorings of the "I"; Gray never really swims off the shore that is Gray-in-Performance.

> **Gray is obviously an attractive and charismatic performer, but increasingly he is a "safe" one. His attempt to use himself as his own material is no longer unusual or raw; he himself has polished it and other performers' more radical self-explorations have inured us to the shock such an approach originally had.**
> —*Peggy Phelan*

In *Swimming,* this paradox is heightened because the narrative chronicles Gray's increasingly desperate attempts to lose himself (and his money) while swimming in the Indian Ocean; the increasing desperation comes from the painful realization that performing in a movie about "a modern genocidal atrocity" keeps the performer successfully insulated from the effects/affects of that atrocity. Gray repeatedly marvels at the fake blood, the fake fire, and the expensive composition of the fake "historical record" everywhere operative and visible in making *The Killing Fields.* But while Gray finds all this artifice perversely marvelous and absurdly appropriate, he also recognizes that it does not quite provide him with the material he needs to become "a poetic reporter" of anything but "absence." Hence, he begins to concentrate his will on experiencing a Perfect Moment—a performative "oneness" that he can embroider, embellish, and repeat in the performance. So eager is he to lose himself that he manufactures losses where there are none: he jumps to the conclusion that he has lost his swimming partner Ivan, when Ivan is himself safely bobbing beyond a wave Gray cannot ride. Gray's ubiquitous sense of loss is so great, his performances suggest, that as a spectator I can admire his strength for speaking about them, but I had better not ask him to let them go. In *Swimming,* Gray's "speaking" is not in any way an authentic exposure, nor is it a sincere attempt to "share" his selfhood: Gray's cathartic exercises are self-enclosed. More troubling, however, is that Gray's work manipulates the spectator into feeling either empathic sympathy or profound impassiveness. These are the only choices. And neither of them advance or invigorate theatrical performance.

Gray is obviously an attractive and charismatic performer, but increasingly he is a "safe" one. His attempt to use himself as his own material is no longer unusual or raw; he himself has polished it and other performers' more radical self-explorations have inured us to the shock such an approach originally had. Increasingly, Gray's work seems quite far from his purported project of using art "as a conscious contrivance for the purpose of survival." I don't begrudge Gray economic or popular success, but I am disappointed that he has not faced the truly radical innovative edge in his project. To face this edge in *Swimming* would require that Gray abandon his boyish unconsciousness and explore his own misogyny, racism, colonialism, and economic imperialism, which run like sludge throughout his text. Such an exploration would not abandon irony, but it would add to it a more challenging intelligence. I don't care one bit that Gray has all of these embarrassing attitudes toward other people and other cultures, most of us do; but what I find disappointing is his assumption that this can be glossed over without comment in favor of some boyish charm or political naiveté. He makes it clear early on that being apolitical is a bonus in Joffe's eyes. After hearing Joffe's plot summary of *Killing Fields,* Gray tells him: "'I know nothing about what you've told me. I'm not very political—in fact, I've never voted in my life.' And Roland said, 'Perfect! We're looking for the American ambassador's aide.'" This kind of joke is funny at first. But the humor never gets any smarter or any deeper, despite Gray's assertion in the "Author's Note" to The Book that he "still understand[s] and love[s] America, precisely for its sense of humor. . . . Humor. The bottom line." Gray seems unable or unwilling to consider the politics of most of the humor in *Swimming to Cambodia*. This quick-take approach gives *Swimming* an appealingly polished surface and a completely unthreatening substance. It also is responsible for the easy and multiple transformations to which the text has lent itself.

The most successful of these transformations is the filmic one, and a large part of that success comes from Jonathan Demme's ability to critique Gray's unconsciousness. Relying only on a few slides, some remarkable lighting effects, several well chosen clips from Joffe's film, a zippy musical score composed by Laurie Anderson, and Gray's commanding physical presence, Demme is able to enhance Gray's "epiphanies," transforming them into visual/psychological wonders. Perhaps the best moment in the film occurs when Gray is narrating his Perfect Moment in the middle of the Indian Ocean. Demme's camera starts to rock back and forth as if it too were in the ocean. Gray's narrative is so thrilling, Demme seems to suggest, that the camera itself is carried deep into the waves just to find out "what happens next." Moreover, as Gray describes his little perceptor/performer bobbing up and down on the ocean the camera seems to position itself in a logically impossible but visually compelling space: we seem to see both what Gray is seeing and we continue to see Gray seeing—Demme seems to locate the spectator *behind and in front of* Gray's eyes. (Perhaps the most celebrated example of this dualistic camera vision is in Hitchcock's *Vertigo,* when Jimmy Stewart is losing his mind and we see him fall through mental space; but that sequence relies on animation while Demme's is "naturalistic.") As Gray recites his narrative denouement—

> And up the perceiver would go with the waves, then down it would go, and the waves would come up around the perceiver, and it could have been in the middle of the Indian Ocean, because it could see no land. And then waves would take the perceiver up to where it could look down this great wall of water . . . far below, and then "Whoop!" the perceiver would go down again—

the camera rocks back and forth. Gray, still sitting in the Chair behind the desk, practices yoga head rolls while the camera "bobs" along with his modulating voice. Demme manages to find the perfect cinematic device to express Gray's Perfect Moment. Moreover, Demme underlines the failure of Gray's own vision. By virtue of appearing to be both inside and outside Gray's eyes, the camera effectively underlines Gray's inability to see anything other than him-

self. While the camera can, as it were, forget its own ontology and see as if it were Gray, Gray himself lacks precisely this visionary grasp.

William W. Demastes (essay date March 1989)

SOURCE: "Spalding Gray's *Swimming to Cambodia* and the Evolution of an Ironic Presence," in *Theatre Journal,* Vol. 41, No. 1, March, 1989, pp. 75-94.

[*In the following essay, Demastes examines the development and significance of Gray's innovative performance strategies for contemporary American drama. According to Demastes, "Gray has singularly succeeded in bringing to life on stage a political agenda similar to that demanded by experimentalists of an earlier epoch—the 1960s and 1970s—but in a manner that assures a 1980s reception."*]

Spalding Gray's career in the theatre has encompassed a variety of theories and practices. He was educated in traditional forms, then moved to Richard Schechner's Performance Group, and later worked with the Wooster Group. Gray's current involvement in auto-performance shows a tremendous debt to these earlier affiliations, yet many critics seem to have dismissed Gray's current work as indulgent, dilettantish, and no longer part of the serious avant-garde experimentalist's concern. He has, after all, been co-opted into mainstream American culture, as his critics are quick to note. This easy dismissal of Gray, however, seems premature. In fact, many of the reasons Gray is dismissed are exactly the reasons Gray should be reconsidered.

This essay is an effort to place Gray's work more clearly into a performance genre context by first outlining the general critical assessment that avant-garde theatre in the 1980s is dying, then considering Gray's debt to Richard Schechner and the Performance Group, evaluating Gray's affiliation with Wooster Group members, and then demonstrating how this rich background is evident in Gray's current auto-performance pieces. In these works Gray creates a sophisticated theatrical persona, who himself reenacts an awakening onstage designed to sensitize the audience to its own awareness. The awakening comes over the persona onstage, and the enactment undermines comforting surfaces, forcing the audience to face realities—political and others—that it perhaps would prefer to ignore. In *Swimming to Cambodia* in particular, Gray has singularly succeeded in bringing to life on the stage a political agenda similar to that demanded by experimentalists of an earlier epoch—the 1960s and 1970s—but in a manner that assures a 1980s reception.

Critical Concern for the Loss of a Political Avant-Garde Agenda

Richard Schechner's 1982 work, *The End of Humanism,* echoes the pain many practitioners and theorists have felt about the recent work of avant-garde American theatre, a theatre whose early vitality promised much but unfortunately soon dissipated. Schechner notes that this vitality centered around a political agenda, one particularly focused on the Peace Movement of the 1960s and opposition to the Vietnam War. But, as Schechner argues,

> Once the war ended and the recession of the mid-seventies hit, artists fell into a formalist deep freeze. Great work was done, but it was cut off: it did not manifest significant content. Instead a certain kind of "high art obscurity" took over.

Moving away from efforts to produce a politically conscious, culturally uniting forum, avant-garde theatre turned isolationist and narcissistic.

In *The Eye of Prey,* Herbert Blau similarly notes the turn toward isolationist undertakings. Reflecting on his own work in the theatre, Blau describes this transformation from the 1960s to current practices

> as a deviation from Brecht through Beckett into a highly allusive, refractory, intensely self-reflexive, ideographically charged process in which we were trying to understand, *to think through,* at the very quick of thought—words, words, unspeakably in the body—the metabolism of perception in the (de)materialization of the text.

Though Blau's style is (intentionally) oblique, he seems to be arguing that earlier efforts to fathom broader issues of community have been replaced by the pursuit of understanding individual means of perception. Blau adds, "As with the Conceptual Art of the late sixties—particularly that strain of it which jeopardized the body in the self-reflexive activity of thought—the subject of our work, and the danger of its becoming, was *solipsism.*"

But where Schechner saw vitality and "community" in the 1960s, Blau goes so far as to argue that the activist work of that decade itself was solipsistic in that its dream of paradise was naive and little more than an enfeebled attempt at political and idealistic awakening. The theatrical "recession" of the 1970s and 1980s merely brought greater attention to the fundamental flaws of the ideologies of the previous decade. Whatever their assessments of the 1960s, however, the two critics would agree on one matter. As Blau notes, "What seemed to be left in the recession, along with the new conservatism, was the dispossessed *subject* of the postmodern, reviewing the disenchantments, as if through the solipsistic orifice of a needle's eye." For both Schechner and Blau the unfortunate result of this "high art obscurity" with its attendant "dispossessed *subject*" was that avant-garde theatre lost its cultural base.

The results have become manifest in what Blau observed in *Blooded Thought* as a sort of "advocacy of confession in acting," of which "[t]here is also the offshoot of explicit autobiography, more or less disciplined, more or less confessed." Interestingly, at this point, Blau notes that the best of the genre are Gray's Rhode Island trilogy (formally entitled **Three Places in Rhode Island**) and Lee Breuer's *Animations,* but he adds, "Originally, the impulse had something devout about it, a kind of penance, as in the monastic period of Grotowski. . . ." Though he acknowledged that self-exposure is essential to powerful theatre, Blau insists that "[i]t is not mere authenticity we're talking about . . . , the self-indulgent spillover of existential sincerity"; rather it must be "a *critical* act as well, *exegetical,* an urgency in the mode of performance . . . , part of its *meaning,* that the Text be *understood,* though the meaning be ever deferred." Blau complains that too much of such work has thus far failed to go beyond documenting "authenticity." Exegesis of such events, or of the *presentations* of the events, has yet to be pursued to Blau's satisfaction.

The disenchantment that Schechner and Blau feel, however, is not shared by C. W. E. Bigsby. Bigsby does agree that the American avant-garde "became an expression of intensely private experience, moving from the gnomic tableau of Robert Wilson and Richard Foreman to the heavily autobiographical pieces of the Wooster Group (the Rhode Island trilogy) and the monologues of Spalding Gray." Bigsby agrees that the work of the isolated subject often "concern[s] itself with the nature of perception and consciousness," which on the surface may do little to establish community and more to increase isolation. But though the works may turn inwardly rather than reach outwardly, Bigsby points out that

> it may well be that in requiring audiences to offer their own completions, in provoking a degree of aesthetic complicity and imaginative collaboration, such theatre practitioners may be reminding them [audiences] of their capacity to act and to imagine a world beyond the banality of appearance.

Such art subtly requires an audience involvement, an "imaginative collaboration," that may ultimately establish a bond more true than any tangible "hand-holding" could strive for. Overt physical involvement has been replaced by a more subtle imaginative involvement, and the substitution, says Bigsby, may in fact be for the better. That such a *possibility* for bonding even exists under these circumstances is something Schechner clearly ignores and Blau seems skeptical that he has ever witnessed—at least he has not seen it in the efforts of performers like Gray and Breuer. For Bigsby, however, not only does the possibility exist, but in rare moments, so does the reality.

Gray's Wooster Agenda: The Rhode Island Trilogy

What Schechner particularly confronts in his *End of Humanism* assault on the "lost" theatre is the work of the auto-performers, which has dominated theatre recently. Schechner argues that the work is "brilliant, but not enough; personalistic rather than concerned with the *polis*, the life of the City, the life of the people." He concludes: "With this personalism comes a passivity, an acceptance of the City, the outer world, the world of social relations, economics, and politics, as it is." In his book, Schechner focuses on the evolution of his own splintered Performance Group, now called the Wooster Group, and the further splintering of that group by the individual efforts of Spalding Gray. Ironically, it was Schechner's own liberating teachings that caused the split and led Gray eventually to work on his own.

Gray explains the process of overturning his dependency on written texts and directorial leadership, a dependency he had grown accustomed to in his earlier, more traditional training:

> Richard Schechner reversed this process for me. He emphasized the performer, making him more than, or as important as, the text . . . [H]e was a liberator from assembly line acting techniques. The way that I interpreted Schechner's theories was that I was free to do what I wanted, be who I was, and trust that the text would give this freedom a structure.

Gray agrees with Blau's assessment, noted earlier, that his early effort after he separated from Schechner, the Rhode Island trilogy, was narcissistically confessional, noting, "I am by nature extremely narcissistic and reflective. For as long as I can remember, I have always been self-conscious and aware of my everyday actions." Gray adds, "I began my own work out of a desire to be both active and reflective at the same time before an audience." This process, however, extended beyond self-conscious presentation of his private life, becoming, in addition, a therapeutic endeavor. For example, Gray describes one of the trilogy pieces, **Sakonnet Point,** as a

> series of simple actions . . . that created a series of images like personal, living Rorschachs. These images were not unlike the blank, white wall in Zen meditations, nor were they unlike the mirror reflection of a good therapist.

Given this personal bent and its therapeutic design, such work could very easily be construed as isolationist. As Bigsby notes, "[F]or Richard Schechner this work [Gray's]

and that of others implied a regrettable shift not merely from a public to a private art but from a concern with subject to a concern with subjectivity." In fact, Bigsby notes the obvious conclusion to such thoughts when he observes of Schechner, "As the title of his book, *The End of Humanism,* seems to imply, he [Schechner] saw this as in some sense a betrayal." Gray, however, disagrees that any betrayal occurred, arguing in his own defense: "Often, what the audience saw was the reflection of their own minds, their own projections." In other words, the private art reached the public, though in subtler ways than Schechner might have advocated. Instead of direct surface confrontation, undercurrents began to play a central role.

One of the central reasons Schechner fails to see—or acknowledge—this approach as promoting audience involvement is that Gray and the Wooster Group abandoned Schechner's more overt practice of environmental participation between audience and performer and returned to a clear distinction between performance space and audience space. Bigsby reports the shift that Schechner bemoans:

> Where in the 1960s and early 1970s Off and Off-Off Broadway avant-garde theatre has seen itself as essentially a public art inviting the full physical participation of the audience, either as a gesture of solidarity with its political objectives or as evidence of a refusal of all restraints (including the special framing of the theatrical event), . . . the audience found itself excluded from the stage onto which it had once been invited and increasingly denied access to meaning.

The overall result, claims Schechner, is that "[w]ithout meaning to be, such productions became elitist: not necessarily for the economic elite . . . but for the artistically 'in.'" For Schechner, both the subject and the presentational methods have reduced the audience to coterie size instead of expanding it to build a larger sense of community.

That Gray's work is intensely personal is, of course, a given. But that it is more than just personal therapy is often overlooked, as is the fact that it does strive to embrace more than a coterie following. First of all, the techniques Gray used in the Rhode Island trilogy incorporate elements learned from Schechner, and they helped Gray overcome some of his intensely personal focus. Says Gray:

> Through being part of this [earlier] process, I developed an integrated understanding of how a group could collaborate in the creation of a mise-en-scène. This led directly to being able to work with some Group members and some people outside The Group on my own work. The source of the work was myself, but the final product was a result of the

collective conceptual actions of all involved. Thus, in the end, it is a group autobiography.

The "work was myself" idea escaped extreme solipsism since the work was reflected off of other "selves," such as Elizabeth LeCompte, Gray's confidante and directorial advisor. In that regard, at least, there was a nominal sense of community.

But the product was more than merely a blend and modification of selves isolated in a small group, as some would see it. It clearly entered the more universal realm of art in that it confronted aesthetic issues as traditional art did, though in a much more "open-nerved" manner. Says Gray:

> [I]t became not the art of pretending I was someone else but an art that began to approach the idea that I was someone else. I wanted to give up the names, to close the gaps. It was no longer to be the "Stanley Kowalski self" or the "Hamlet self," but now it was a play of moods, energies, aspects of self. It became the many-in-the-one that had its source in the archetype of the performer, not in the text.

The connection between performance in life and in art became a central concern, but it extended beyond Gray's own isolated self. Again, this aspect of Gray's style is one he learned from Schechner. It allowed him to discover "self," but in this presentation and discovery of self, he discovered "other" as well.

> By chance, I might suddenly find myself performing an action that was an aspect of me, and, upon reflection see it as an action belonging to Orpheus. Then, for that moment, I would be both Spalding and Orpheus. I was never one or the other and could be someone or something completely different for each audience member because they also live with their "names" and associations. It is their story as well as mine.

If the trilogy succeeds as intended, the piece should build foundations for community in the manner Bigsby describes, with results Schechner and Blau probably would finally approve. In requiring audiences to exact their own completions, as Bigsby describes it, Gray enables the audience to make contact with "self" and to communicate with "other" as well.

There is yet another aspect of Gray's trilogy work that could lead to charges of solipsism. Gray notes that "[a]ll of *Sakonnet Point* was built from free associations within the performing space. There were no 'ideas' about how it should be, nor was there any attempt to tell a meaningful story." James Bierman notes that the piece "is more evocative in style than expositional," and Arnold Aronson concludes that the play's "value lay not in any informational structure but in their capacity for evoking further images and moods. The creators did not intend to provoke thought but rather an inward contemplation." The result could very well be solipsistic.

The actors, of course, develop this inward contemplation, but communication transferral occurs when the audience feels the urge toward a similar development. According to Gray, "Often, what the audience saw was the reflection of their own minds, their own projections." But the process clearly requires an active desire on the part of the audience. Gray is aware of the need for active desire, having "desired" it himself while he viewed the works of other artists who strove to achieve the same subtle end. In fact, Gray identifies with a growing avant-garde tradition concerned with such involvement:

> I think *Sakonnet Point* was like the work of Robert Wilson and Meredith Monk. I had found that while watching their work my mind was left free to associate and my eye was grounded in watching the execution of their chosen actions. It was this grounding of my eye that gave my mind a quality of freedom I'd not experienced in theatre before. For me, the work of Wilson and Monk was dealing with the use of, and investigation into the nature of, mind projections. This seemed to be getting to the roots of what theatre and life are about. It is a kind of therapeutic lesson about how we create our own world through our projections.

Gray concludes his observations with a performer's perspective by noting that *Sakonnet Point* "was very involving and seemed therapeutic for the audience as well as the performer." In this regard, Schechner's advocacy of physical involvement of the audience has been replaced by a perceptual, conceptual, emotional, and mental involvement of the audience.

Another part of the trilogy, *Rumstick Road,* focused on Gray's mother's suicide, but as Gray notes, "Although the basis of the piece was the voices and pictures of my family, the other performers were free to take off from this material and develop their own scores." He admits that the piece was "confessional," but asserts "[i]t was also an act of distancing." Through distancing, Gray became, to use Blau's term, exegetical. Gray observes,

> Finally, if it is therapeutic, it is not so much so in the fact that it is confessional but in the fact that it is ART. The historic event of my mother's suicide is only a part of the fabric of that ART. Finally, the piece is not about suicide; it is about making ART.

Perhaps the clearest expression of analysis and exegesis in the trilogy's final piece, **Nyatt School,** which concentrates on the effects of being introduced to Freudian psychology. Gray argues that despite its distorted perspective on the world in general and language in particular, Freudian psychology is quite "real" nonetheless. Says Gray, "I felt and believed this at the time and wanted to make a theatre piece that was not only a reflection of that strange world, but the world itself."

Considering the trilogy as a unit, Gray states that he has moved beyond therapy and mere presentation of personal events to a realm of philosophical analysis of a more universal condition. His trilogy, he says,

> reflect[s] upon themes of loss. They are not just about the loss of my mother but about the feeling of loss itself. I have had this feeling for as long as I can remember. It is the feeling that the "I" that I call "me" is only a visitor here. No, not even a visitor because a visitor goes elsewhere after he visits. I have no word for it, and the work is the attempt at giving expression to that absent word.

If Gray begins with personal experience, he moves with that experience to a plane that reflects more than just his own condition. Gray admits, "I fantasize that if I am true to art it will be the graceful vehicle which will return me to life." But in this process something more than personal therapy occurs, for "[t]he very act of communication takes it into a 'larger vein' and brings it back to community."

Gray's transition from Group assisted work to performing monologues recounting his life stemmed from a double realization, one part taken from the Group, that "[s]omewhere along the line, every action became for me a piece of theatre" and the other a new one that saw "employing the old oral tradition [as] a fresh breath in these high tech times . . . with all its human energy and vividness." Gray's work has simply developed from an age-old observation that life is performance coupled with a new realization that life's tools, therefore, are performer's tools as well and are complete in themselves.

Gray notes, in a pattern similar to Richard Schechner's, that "Theatre is about presence = Life = Death" and asserts that reviving an oral tradition is his new "hope for passing it all down." With this new realization about performance/presence came a new outlook on theatre: "The personal confessional, stripped of its grand theatrical metaphors, is what matters to me now." Past avant-garde efforts to create a new theatrical "language"—his own efforts or others'—have consumed energy that otherwise could have been utilized for more substantial ends. Perhaps using current tools will be sufficient, and perhaps even returning to simple monologue

will be the most effective means of all. In one regard, at least, the return is fortunate. Being unable to establish a way to pass down the lessons and experiences of avant-garde theatre was one of Schechner's incidental concerns in *The End of Humanism.* Gray notes that an answer as simple as "oral tradition" was "one that Richard didn't mention." Since Gray's discovery of the potential of the oral tradition, it has been the avenue he has pursued.

The Wooster's L.S.D. Agenda

Returning to this traditional means of communication in avant-garde art, however, can hinder efforts to challenge the status quo. In particular, problems arise when an art form empowers a lone presence and when it empowers a tool—language—that has acquired a social or political tyranny over any liberating potential in that art. In this regard, Philip Auslander joins Blau and Schechner, expressing general concern that recent avant-garde theatre has turned apolitical or, even worse, reactionary. The concept of presence, and therefore of authority, according to Auslander, "is the specific problematic theatre theorists and practitioners must confront in reexamining our assumptions about political theatre and its function." He argues that "the theatre is precisely a locus at which critical/aesthetic and social practices intersect." The aesthetic of presence is necessarily entwined with the social, and therefore political, reality of presence, according to Auslander.

In addressing these issues, Auslander examines the work of the Wooster Group (without Gray) and in particular the piece *L.S.D. (. . . Just the High Points . . .),* arguing that the Group's efforts epitomize the as yet incomplete political efforts of the recent avant-garde to challenge authority as a socially/culturally entrenched power tool. The strategy the Group utilizes involves irony, in a manner that another critic, Elinor Fuchs, has described: "In the past, the Wooster Group's undercutting of one text by another, of one reading by another, and of both by the incisive use of segments of film, resulted in an almost wholly ironic dramaturgy." In the case of *L.S.D.,* the text of Miller's *The Crucible* is undermined. Although Fuchs concludes of this recent work that Wooster's "irony now seems unclear," Auslander asserts that the Group's efforts are moving in the right direction. He notes with approval the fact that Wooster entangled itself in the well-documented debate over its own right to manipulate Miller's text versus Miller's right to control performance of his work: "LeCompte [the Group's director] correctly describes the conflict with Miller as 'an inevitable outcome of our working process' and as a part of the Group's 'necessary relationship to authority.'"

But Auslander adds that LeCompte has failed to realize fully that "confrontation with authority is a *result* but not the *object* of the Group's process," noting that "[t]he Group seems blithely, perhaps utopianly, to proceed as if the poststructur-alist critical/theoretical concept of text as 'a tissue of quo-tations' belonging more to a culture than an individual were already in place as part of the social hegemony." The Group confronts the text as a product of a social/cultural power structure rather than the product of an individual "author," but before Wooster can attack the text as a social/cultural manifestation, it must first rigorously confront the authority of the individual—Miller—in its art rather than incidentally through outside litigation. So, rather irregularly,

> The effect of the Group's action is not so much to question Miller's rights over his text as to show what would be possible in the realm of cultural pro-duction if those rights were not in force, thus em-phasizing the importance of the connection between the cultural and the social/political.

According to Auslander, this assumption that as a text *The Crucible* asserts a social/cultural authority is accurate, but it needs further development, given the Group's naively uto-pian perspective on the issue.

As the Group undermines "authority" as a social/cultural manifestation, so must it strive to undermine "presence" it-self—in this case presence of the author—since suspicion has been cast upon presence. According to Auslander, the suspicion "derives from the apparent collusion between po-litical structures of authority and the pervasive power of pres-ence." The Wooster Group needs to continue its "transgressive" behavior in order to overcome the

> obvious inappropriateness of the political art strat-egies left over from the historical avant-garde of the early 20th century and from the 1960s, and by a widespread critical inability to conceive of aesthetic/political *praxis* in terms other than these inherited ones.

Continuing to refine means of undermining both authority and presence should remain part of the essential political avant-garde agenda.

A major problem arises, however, in the effort to realize that objective, and that has to do with the tool that conveys au-thority and confirms presence—language. Ideally, a new "language" needs to be constructed in order to free society from an old language rife with empowering prejudices. In response to Auslander's article, Schechner makes the follow-ing important concession: "Once I considered the Wooster Group nihilistic, and apolitical, but I was wrong." Though Schechner does not specify why he has changed his opin-ion, it can be assumed that he accepts Auslander's perspec-tive on the Wooster Group, that the politics of *L.S.D.* pulls Wooster out of the depths of nihilism and empty aesthetics.

However, Schechner calls attention to a central problem in-herent in Auslander's progressive goal of undermining pres-ence and authority in the theatre. Moving away from theatre in particular and seeing what he calls "several kinds of 'pro-gressive' thinking going on simultaneously" in the world at large, Schechner identifies "the problem's nub: translation is impossible; meaning is not separate from or prior to ex-pression."

By translation, Schechner means transferring meaning from one cultural (or professional) idiom to another. He concludes that "[t]he problem today is that ways of speaking are mu-tually untranslatable." Idioms themselves have become iso-lated in their very efforts to undermine the old and create new systems. In this regard Schechner notes that even a pos-sible dialogue between a "progressive" artist (LeCompte), theorist (Auslander), and politician (he uses Jesse Jackson) would be difficult, if not impossible, because their languages are so self-confined and so untranslatable into the others' idioms. The solipsistic dilemma arises again, this time out of a progressive agenda that strives to challenge power it-self, which entails challenging the language that enforces that power. For even those who have actually tried to challenge the power (LeCompte, Auslander, Jackson) have difficulty uniting under one flag, given the particular sources of power (and language) they are working to challenge. So, if in un-dermining current language and current cultural power in general these groups cannot unite and make significant con-tact *during* the struggle, what is the hope for more general cultural unity if such a progressive "revolution" succeeds?

Simply put, since language *is* a source of cultural/social power, any direct efforts at substantively changing the culture's/society's power structure entails reevaluating and "re-creating" language itself. The efforts that Auslander and other similar thinkers espouse seem fated to lead to an im-possible cultural/social order, since without communication there can be no community and since the lines of communi-cation have already been severed in the very attempt to com-municate this challenge of power. And in regard to art, such efforts can lead only to an impossible theatre. Finally, ef-forts such as those espoused by Auslander at creating a new cohesion lead to greater solipsism. Schechner seems quite rightly to concede that his earlier "environmental" efforts could be replaced by more subtle means of presentation, but he also quite accurately observes that the idealistic goals of this new generation of theorists/practitioners may ultimately be unattainable. Spalding Gray, however, provides an alter-native.

Gray's Auto-Performance Agenda

Gray left Schechner's Performance Group at about the same time Schechner himself left, and the Performance Group re-formed as the Wooster Group. Gray then separately collaborated with Elizabeth LeCompte, the current director of Wooster. The Rhode Island trilogy bears many marks of both groups' ensemble styles and can be considered one of many predecessors of the Wooster Group's later works, which culminated in *L.S.D.* (. . . *Just the High Points* . . .) But on a superficial level, at least, Gray's unscripted monologues bear little if any resemblance to the Group's work, since he relies almost completely on a single "presence" seated at a table *verbally* communicating to an audience, instead of opting for a more nondiscursive style that relied less heavily on an empowered language. As Don Shewey notes, "Unlike his colleagues in the Wooster Group and Mabou Mines, whose experimentation took them further into high-tech performance, Gray reclaimed the ancient art of storytelling, simply sitting at a desk and addressing an attentive audience in the intimacy of the Performance Garage." In fact, Vincent Canby notes that Gray's reliance on language has eliminated virtually any other form of communication, noting that "it would be a coup de theatre if he [Gray] just stood up." Ostensibly, Gray has given up on any idea of creating an alternative form of language for the theatre—technology assisted or otherwise—turning as he does to oral tradition as his means of communication.

This difference between Gray and his former colleagues, however, is more apparent than real. Though Gray is literally "telling" his story, there are indications that he is carrying on the Wooster tradition, utilizing a different approach to achieve virtually the same end. Reviews regularly have made note of Gray's WASP background, and Gray himself openly acknowledges in his monologues his comfortable middle-class, New England heritage. Given his privileged upbringing, it would seem that Gray had two options in pursuing an avant-garde, political agenda. He could reject his personal history and join the ranks of those out of power in an effort to enact change from without, and thus come to the theatre as less than a historically genuine spokesperson—a "have" joining in with the "have-nots." Or he could accept his personal history of privilege and work from within, accepting, at least for rhetorical purposes, his position of authority—"to the manor born"—complete with the empowering tools of that system, language certainly included. This second option, at first glance hardly a position for an avant-garde performer, is the option Gray has chosen. Choosing that option, it seems, was the cause for his split with his former colleagues.

If nothing else, Gray's separation from the Wooster Group and acceptance of his position of privilege circumvents one criticism Auslander advances concerning members of the Group who have been lured, however temporarily, away from the political/aesthetic theatre of the Group and into various commercial media. Such shifting, according to Auslander, "was not considered a worthy objective by the sixties generation," and now that it has occurred, "it could be seen as implying an alarming lack of integrity on the part of young experimental artists." Lack of integrity is, of course, a serious charge. Given Gray's decision to remain in the realm of the empowered, however, he *can* move from one format to another, and this mobility is the basis of his dramatic method.

In this method, several Spalding Grays are at work. First, the "observer-of-events," Spalding Gray the private citizen, works in a nearly reportorial fashion to uncover the system's shortcomings as he lives the life of a privileged middle-class male. The results of this espionage, in turn, are handed over to Gray the artist to create a work offering a critical perspective on the system. The piece is presented by Gray the *naive* performer, who appears fully incorporated into the system and is unaware of the ironies introduced into his presentation by the artist Gray, who shaped the material reported by the observer Gray. Who is the actual Spalding Gray? As far as his Wooster-rooted agenda is concerned, such a question is irrelevant. Gray's onstage work finally presents material, *seemingly* without comment, in an ironic manner that confronts the same power structure exposed by Wooster's *L.S.D.* Thus while Gray's work may *appear* supportive of the status quo, it presents a persona who ironically utilizes an empowered naivety to undermine itself and the authority it seems to uphold.

Gray's ironic approach apparently owes something to his association with Wooster. In fact, as Wooster's irony attempts to do, Gray's ironic posturing confronts both authority and presence, as Auslander hoped the avant-garde in general would do. But given the potential power of "presence" in performance in general and in Gray's work in particular, it would seem that auto-performance—especially monologues—would strengthen the hold of presence rather than weaken it. However, Fuchs has observed a kind of "revenge of writing," as she calls it, in many recent works of the avant-garde, a revenge whose aim, it seems, "is the undermining of theatrical Presence." Though she does not discuss Gray, Gray's performance "text" seeks just that end—the undermining of the performer's presence. Then what of Gray the behind-the-scenes author? The authority of Gray the author would be expected to assert itself. One must look back at the actual performance to understand how the text in turn undermines Gray the author's authority. One must realize that the performer has "misread" the text as he presents it, thereby undermining any of its discursive "meaning" in favor of a meaning that works to undermine textuality itself. For the audience, there may be—and usually is—a "pleasure in the text," but there is little real didactic substance that ultimately demands attention, and so there is even less attention paid to the authority of the text. Reaching beyond both written authority and physical presence is the design of Gray's works. Each consumes the other, leaving a void that forces the audience to doubt the power of either and search within itself for a replacement, empowering the audience, then, in the process.

In one regard, Gray's work can be seen, superficially, as an unconventional affirmation of the "conventional" itself. But going beneath surfaces, it becomes evident that the work is an attack on empowering convention in general, effected by high-lighting the ultimate empowering convention—language. The possibility for confusion is fortunate, for it has allowed Gray to enter the mainstream of popular culture, since his "hidden" agenda has been misread by the mass of socially/politically empowered literalists who have been unable to penetrate beneath Gray's surfaces. As a result Gray has been able to influence the order's very consciousness.

In *Rivkala's Ring,* his adaptation of a Chekhov story for the collection of short dramatic works entitled *Orchards,* Gray offers advice to others on how to perform the piece, advice that sums up his view of his own persona on stage:

> I see the character [in *Rivkala's Ring*] as a manic-y paranoid person who's spinning off these kind of paranoid delusions, trying to make order out of a very frightening and chaotic existence. So I see it fashioned after my character, the character of Spalding Gray that I do in the monologues.

The passage both acknowledges Gray's awareness of at least two Spalding Grays and outlines the personality of the stage persona Gray. Frank Rich sees the same split and notes,

> What makes Spalding Gray so theatrical in his seemingly nontheatrical way is not only his talent as a storyteller and social observer but also his ability to deepen the mystery of the demarcation line between performer and role.

Thus, although it may at times be difficult to distinguish Gray the private citizen from Gray the performer, Gray himself insists on drawing the distinction.

The "manic-y paranoia" is a deliberately manufactured characteristic. It renders the persona harmless and disarming, enabling him to draw the audience into the monologue, overcoming the defenses with which it would resist a political manifesto on the stage. As Novick notes, "Although he [Gray] was artistically nurtured by that company of screaming meemies, the Wooster Group, his art as a monologuist is the art of understatement." Gussow adds, speaking of the difference between the Rhode Island trilogy in general and a monologue like Gray's *47 Beds* in particular, that "[w]hile the performance pieces often sacrifice intelligibility in the interest of visual and aural stimulation, the solo work is as entertaining as it is eccentric."

The strategy is subtle yet effective in evoking the audience involvement Gray desired in his more frenetic Rhode Island trilogy but attained in a different manner. The audience is drawn in with entertaining twists, and the pleasure and attendant complacency are undermined through the same entertainingly palatable means. The man/presence who has charmed the audience onstage often is also drawn into the process of realization that the audience eventually experiences. It must be emphasized, however, that the language itself undermines, not any empowered presence. As Maslin notes, Gray the performer is "never inclined to talk with ironic detachment, no matter how absurd or strange or painful the circumstances he describes." Gray the performer is immersed; it is the behind-the-scenes artist Gray who is ironically detached and subtly confrontational. But that is not clearly seen in the performing area. Rather, since the persona onstage is guileless, it is left to the audience to deduce the ironies. Signals from either an empowered physical presence or from an unseen authority are virtually nonexistent.

The above analysis applies best to *Swimming to Cambodia,* but to a lesser degree it applies to most of Gray's monologues. David Guy notes that the collection of early auto-performance pieces (polished transcriptions of his stage work) entitled *Sex and Death to the Age 14* reveals a "belief on Mr. Gray's part . . . that there is more substance in the simple telling of stories than in more self-conscious art forms." Guy adds, "There is also a belief that the real truth in life lies in its most banal and embarrassing moments, that to pretty things up is to falsify them." The pieces go beyond mere documentation. Such works as *Interviewing the Audience,* for example, reveal an underlying motive even in Gray's most purely and simply confessional pieces of the period. Namely, they work, as Shewey notes, at "drawing others into his philosophical obsessions (is there a heaven? does true love exist?) and imparting to unbelievers the rewards of the examined life." As with Gray's trilogy agenda, "self-examination" is the essential point Gray tries to put across in these performance pieces. But here he has shifted approaches, presenting an insubstantial substance that works as bait to draw in his audience. Says Gray,

> There are two audiences for my work . . . There are people who live in the kind of life I have. They're very unrooted, they do a lot of different things, and they experience the world as fragmented. The other extreme is the householder who is my age now . . . who's right in the midst of raising two or three children, who's keeping down a job, and who's able to enjoy the stories vicariously, the same way he would Kerouac's *On the Road.*

Gray's work appeals to middle America, but for those who can see more than vicarious experience in the works, the pieces take on an ironic significance, revealing fragmentation and unrootedness that is a first step to a political awakening.

Having truly made the leap into mainstream American culture with his *Swimming to Cambodia*—first for the stage and recently as a screenplay—Gray has contributed to the postmodern blurring of high art and popular culture that Auslander discusses. But that is only an incidental result of his work. What is central is that the piece clearly moves toward a political agenda in a manner more obvious, it seems, than his earlier work. In this piece Gray clearly observes that he has moved beyond simple narcissism, if even he were merely narcissistic. With *Swimming to Cambodia*, Gray reports he found an objective situation that freed him from any narcissistic spell: "People writing reviews have called me a narcissist, and I would certainly admit to that. . . . But with *Swimming to Cambodia* I found a larger issue outside of my personal neuroses." Concerning this move to a "larger issue," Fuchs remarks, "*Swimming to Cambodia,* especially Part I, represents an artistic culmination for Gray as well as an impressive political breakthrough." Gray's method of presentation has finally found matter that allows him to exhibit his form's ironic agenda fully.

The work, in fact, succeeds in a way that led Fuchs to make the following comment: "Throughout, Gray's story proceeds by daring 'leaps and circles' . . . as if his perceptions of reality now imitated his earlier Cage-ean experiments." For Fuchs, Gray's presentation of multiple levels in the work clearly demonstrates the fruits of his "Cage-ean" Rhode Island, Wooster, and Performance Group exercises. It acknowledges processes that go beyond chronological construction and reflect psychological emphases expressed in apparently chaotic ramblings. In truth, however, the apparent rambling reflects a unity: A surface—and narcissistic—goal of finding a "perfect moment" is pursued—while a deeper underlying "moment of understanding" is exposed, and the critical instincts of the audience are required to discern the revelation beneath the naive presentation of Gray the stage persona. It is what Fuchs calls a "projection of Gray's WASP *persona* . . . onto the world scene" in an ironic manner that not only contributes to the piece's humor but also allows it to present historic and political verities without smelling of didacticism.

Looking for a "perfect moment" is one of the central pursuits in *Swimming to Cambodia.* In the tale Gray recounts, he refuses to leave Thailand because, as he says, "I hadn't had a Perfect Moment yet, and I always like to have one before I leave an exotic place." Amidst all the revelations of suffering and death Gray experiences while in Thailand, looking for a perfect moment remains his central obsession. This self-indulgent (or perhaps "therapeutic") end prevents the performer from becoming a reliable political spokesman; in fact, it positions Gray in the role of mindless American

oppressor, a part of the problem rather than part of a cure. Gray can even happily report in performance, "I'm not very political," which obviously undermines his authority. But one sees even more than Gray's undermining of himself when he turns into an American "Everyman" in the story by Roland Joffe, director of *The Killing Fields,* who hires Gray for the movie *because* of this comment: "Perfect! We're looking for the American ambassador's aide."

The event that triggered *Swimming to Cambodia* was the filming of *The Killing Fields,* in which Gray had a small part. The film, shot in Thailand, documents the holocaust in Cambodia under Pol Pot. Gray's participation in the film provided the opportunity for Gray the artist/reporter to present Gray the performer in circumstances that allow that persona unwittingly to present material transcending both his personal narcissism and the narcissism of the filming group, all egocentric artists and craftsmen whose work is undermined by Gray's artistic response. Even though he is a minor figure in the movie, Gray is pampered and coddled during production, given the impression that he is important, while he lacks any sense of awareness whatsoever.

But some of Gray the reporter/author infuses itself. For example, Gray the performer reports about when he learned of American involvement in Cambodia, first observing, "leave it to a Brit [Roland Joffe] to tell you your own history," and then tellingly adding, "as Roland reminded me, we're not living in a democracy." Messages from Gray the author slip through, but ever so subtly, and never supported by the authority of Gray the performer. The comment seems offered as little more than a curious bit of information for the audience to react to. As another example, when discussing the possibility of nuclear holocaust, Gray drops a line reminiscent of something Schechner himself would say: "Mother Earth needs a long, long rest." But the point is not developed any further; it is merely tossed out for the audience to consider.

Gray even directly addresses the issue of language and power that so concerns Auslander, through an anecdote set in New York in which he cannot communicate with his disorderly neighbors, observing: "I don't know the language. I knew the language when I was with my people in Boston in 1962, in whitebread homogeneous Boston, brick-wall Boston." He lifts this personal dilemma to a larger question when he concludes:

> I wonder how do we begin to approach the so-called Cold War (or Now-Heating-Up War) between Russia and America if I can't even begin to resolve the Hot War down on Northmoor and Greenwich in Lower Manhattan?

To a point Gray the performer seems to grow up, becoming

more aware of the world around him. But the moments when he "pronounces" judgment on the world are relatively rare, and even those are regularly undermined by his continual return to the narcissistic search for the "perfect moment." So too is any possible authority undermined, since the moments of awakening are little more than subplot *behind* the obsession about the "perfect moment." And Gray the performer loves that search for the "perfect moment," hungers for it.

Fuchs notes that "the actual story of the making of the film becomes a hallucinogenic recapitulation not only of the tragedy in Cambodia but of the universal torment by those who wield power over those who don't." Maslin notes, "What elevates this [monologue] above the realm of small talk is Mr. Gray's round-about—and peculiarly suspenseful—way of dramatizing the episode's [filming's] moral and political repercussions." These go beyond demonstrating the political power of some abstract government force over the oppressed in general to include the "innocent" abuses of the power-wielding camera crews, directors, and actors who manipulate the local inhabitants of the various film sites.

This control is illustrated by an innocent observation by Gray the performer. Recalling an ascent in a helicopter, he states, "I saw, my God, how much area the film covered!" In fact, the film controlled *more* than the physical territory Gray observed from above; there was economic and from that psychological and ethical control as well. As Gussow notes, among other things, *Swimming to Cambodia* "is a close-up, on-location analysis of the monumental absurdities of moviemaking." In making this point, Gray the artist has moved from a narcissistic and subjective perspective. He reveals the outside, well-intentioned efforts to portray the monumental destruction of war and revolution upon a culture as an invasion of that same oppressed culture. The effort to document the cruelties of oppression also is oppression.

Though the Gray persona's narcissistic shell hides overt commentary, Gray the artist clearly has abandoned narcissism. The piece makes the point that oppression is endemic to American culture, whether or not it is intentional. It is multi-layered, even in the performance, for *Swimming to Cambodia* challenges the oppression of *The Killing Fields* even as *The Killing Fields* documents the oppression of Pol Pot. Dika comments on this effect in *Swimming to Cambodia*: "What in *The Killing Fields* had seemed a complete, integrated rendition of reality is now disrupted. Gray's words serve to break the seamless flow of images, cracking them open like eggshells." The authority of *The Killing Fields* itself is undermined, very much the same way Wooster's *L.S.D.* worked to undermine *The Crucible*. The result is what Lisa Zeidner calls "a hall of mirrors because nothing is quite real." Determining the route through this hall of mirrors, ultimately, is left up to the audience.

Finally, at the end of the shorter version recorded as the movie, Gray makes a cryptic observation about the dangerous indulgences he has been part of when he pronounces, without further explanation: "And just as I was dozing off in the Pleasure Prison [what he calls the cast's hotel], I had a flash. An inkling. I suddenly thought I knew what it was that killed Marilyn Monroe." Gray the performer momentarily cracks here to reveal Gray the reporter (or maybe Gray the reintegrated self). The insider's view that Gray the artist has experienced has revealed exactly how destructive/oppressive the indulgences of the power elite can be, even/especially within their ranks.

An even more compelling tale concludes the transcription of the longer stage version. It is of a dream Gray has in which he witnesses a straw boy consumed by flame. The dream takes place in Hollywood, where Gray wanders the streets trying to tell the event to anyone who will listen, including several members of the Wooster Group. Gray concludes both the dream anecdote and the entire piece, with:

> And I knew all the time I was telling this story that
> it was a cover for the real story, the Straw Boy Story,
> which, for some reason, I found impossible to tell.

The text, finally, avoids the central issue, never even announces the issue, and thus the validity of the performer's presence is undermined, as is the entire text itself. Finally, *Swimming to Cambodia* strives to ground itself in some "other" that it cannot present because it *cannot* be presented. To fill the void, Gray has presented exactly what is *not* to be valued, which impacts on the audience all the more, since it *has* been valued, to some degree, throughout the performance. It is now all shown to be the very thing that destroys. In some ways what really needs to be told is too horrible to tell except by indirection, even if there were a language to tell it.

Gray has undermined a great many of the cultural icons that Wooster and many other more confrontational groups strive to undermine, but Gray clearly avoids doing so with any alienating revolutionary contempt; rather he employs a disarming process that works its way into establishment sensibilities with an alarming allure that charms as it undermines. But Gray goes even farther, having his own stage presence mesmerized as it mesmerizes the audience. The effect is that audiences are left not with a sense of betrayal, but with a sense that they have developed even as the onstage presence has developed; something of a community has been achieved.

The fact that Gray's work is *art* prevents it from exhibiting no authorial or presence power whatsoever. However, *Swimming to Cambodia* succeeds in minimizing that power in performance while, more importantly, it points out exactly how dangerously engulfing that power is. It critiques *The Killing Fields* and simultaneously undermines the perceived power of its own presence, whose spell has temporarily controlled the audience. Gray observes that we've all been consumed; in fact, he *demonstrates* it by "leading" with his own presence. Though Auslander's wish to see a movement toward no "power" at all seems fated never to occur, minimizing "power," undermining it, and demonstrating its danger seem to be the next best set of options, real options substituting for unreachable idealities.

The directly confrontational political agenda that many have looked for—and perhaps found elsewhere—does not exist in Gray. It is an agenda that owes a debt to the efforts of the 1960s and early 1970s but has indeed moved beyond those efforts. It is indebted to Schechner and the Performance Group, to Elizabeth LeCompte and the Wooster Group, and, though execution and performance does redirect itself, Gray's agenda follows directly, if sometimes obliquely, from the efforts of his predecessors.

Lee Lescaze (review date 18 May 1992)

SOURCE: "A Storyteller's Attempt at a Novel," in *The Wall Street Journal,* May 18, 1992, p. A8.

[*In the following review, Lescaze offers a tempered assessment of* Impossible Vacation.]

Spalding Gray is a comic storyteller in the rich tradition of American naifs to whom amazing things happen. He is a spinner of tales for the angst-bitten and the confused, for whom a part of life's basic joke is that they understand what's happening, they just don't know how to cope with it.

He became known first on stage and then on screen with his witty theatrical monologues, notably *Swimming to Cambodia,* relating his adventures as a bit player in the powerful Roland Joffe movie *The Killing Fields.*

Now, Mr. Gray has written his first novel, *Impossible Vacation.* The book has much in common with his works for the theater, and at its best it is sharply observed and amusing.

Impossible Vacation begins as though it were to be Mr. Gray's version of the coming-of-age novel. But it soon abandons structure in favor of the rambling—often charming—technique Mr. Gray has used with such success in the theater.

Funny things happen. Brewster North, the protagonist, joins an experimental theater group that takes its show on the road to the St. Louis suburbs. For its trouble, the group is judged

obscene and banned from Missouri for life. There were too many rips in the impoverished cast members' leotards and too much physical contact for the Show Me State's taste.

Brewster's retreat to a Zen center in the Poconos goes no better. During daily sessions of staring at a white wall, Brewster sees it come alive with pornographic images. When he finally achieves a moment of the sought-for "big mind," it quickly vanishes, leaving him back with the "small mind" of porn.

A Fourth of July barbecue with Brewster's father, stepmother and girlfriend is a nightmare out of Cheever by way of Bunuel. Dad and stepmother sniff the air expectantly as cocktail hour arrives. A barbecue turns into a blood ceremony.

"The more I chewed, the more I wanted. The more I ate, the less satisfied I felt. It was chew, chew, chew, angry chew, and then big gulps, swallow, wash down with more and more Lite beer . . . Dad drank the steak blood from a serving spoon. Babs killed flies."

In Mr. Gray's hands, the barbecue would make a great theater piece. So would Brewster's first LSD trip or his efforts to save drowning bugs from a swimming pool, or his venture into acting in X-rated films.

Sex, death and travel are Mr. Gray's major preoccupations. His tone, as in his monologues, is friendly, almost puppyish. The typical Gray protagonist avoids making accusations, never gets angry. He is a mostly good boy who sometimes does bad things in order to experience the sweetness of being forgiven. (This is often not a swell deal for his female companions.)

Mr. Gray has a gift for comic detail. When Brewster lands a job supervising a bunch of moving men, he finds they ignore his instructions until he takes to smoking cigars. When an Ohio woman tells her life story, it turns out the critical moment came when her husband learned about free love. How? By reading an article in that swingers' bible, *Time* magazine.

Perhaps none of Brewster's experiences would play better in a Spalding Gray monologue than the moment he and loyal companion Meg arrive at Agra to see the Taj Mahal, only to have Meg collapse, suffering the worst pain of her life. Does Brewster run for a doctor? Call the police? Seek out the nearest U.S. Consulate?

Hey, he's come a long way to see the Taj. He dashes off to sneak a look, leaving Meg moaning on the ground. "Of course I couldn't enjoy it. With the thought of Meg lying out there in a sick heap on the lawn, I could hardly see it."

By the time Brewster gets back, an Indian holy man is trying to force-feed Meg a dirty glass of vile liquid.

The good boy has been truly bad. But he is very charming about it—mostly to us, his readers, less to Meg. Meg sticks by him and we chuckle and smile.

Still, writing novels is very different from writing monologues. A novel needs characters and character development. A novel requires complexities. But make a theater piece too complex and the audience loses contact. Once in a while, a monologuist is well advised to throw his audience an obvious bit of summation just to make sure it is keeping up. On the page, such lines seem awkward and unnecessary.

A talented actor like Mr. Gray might be able to send an audience home with a smile after a resolution no greater than he gives his novel. After all, what structure *Swimming to Cambodia* has comes from Mr. Gray's claim to be searching for a "perfect moment." Mr. Gray has a fondness for water-based therapeutic moments, not so much a return to the womb as a return to the Leboyer birthing tub. In *Impossible Vacation,* he would have you believe that after 35 or so years of manic-depressive and immature behavior Brewster is cured by a soak in the chilly stream at the bottom of the Grand Canyon. Not only cured, but filled with a new determination to take hold of his life and become a writer.

If you find that easy to believe, you'll trust that Thelma and Louise's 1966 T-bird convertible is still floating over the Grand Canyon just as you saw it last.

Stanley Kaufmann (review date 6 July 1992)

SOURCE: A review of *Monster in a Box* and *Impossible Vacation,* in *New Republic,* July 6, 1992, pp. 26-8.

[*In the following review, Kaufmann offers a mixed assessment of* Monster in a Box *and* Impossible Vacation.]

Most of the comment about Spalding Gray, admiring though it rightly is, seems to me slightly skewed. He is praised for his heterodox, adventurous films, but that adventure of his begins in the theater. Why is *Monster in a Box* any more adventurous on film than it was on stage? (Likewise his previous film, *Swimming to Cambodia.*) It's assumed that Gray is more daring when he transfers his monologues to the screen because film demands greater visual variety than the theater and because film is inimical to language. Both of these assumptions are dubious (as plentiful examples show). To put it crassly, Gray runs just as much of a risk of tedium in the theater as he does on screen. The risks alter somewhat from one medium to another, but the success in the first venture emboldens the second.

Other one-person shows have been effectively transferred to film, Richard Pryor's and Lily Tomlin's, for prime instances; but Pryor deals in a series of riffs and Tomlin does a series of sketches. In thematically continuous, comic seriousness, I can think of only one forebear of Gray's work, Wallace Shawn's *My Dinner with Andre,* which, too, was done first in the theater by Shawn and Andre Gregory, then filmed under Louis Malle's direction. And this is a farfetched choice, of course, because next to Gray, Shawn's cast of two seems immense. But Gray, like Shawn, is earnestly funny and, above all else, articulate.

Gray sits before us at a desk—most of the time, anyway—as a companion, rather than a performer, not really old though with fluffy white hair, and recounts his adventures. He chooses where to begin, then (seemingly) free-associates for eighty-eight minutes. His previous monologue, *Cambodia,* was built around his engagement for a small role in *The Killing Fields.* This one is built around his signing with Knopf to write a novel. He has the monster 1,900-page manuscript on the desk, together with the box in which he carried the growing pile around, as he moved through New York, to Houston, to Hollywood, to the Soviet Union, to Nicaragua.

In all those places, Gray reveals himself as the sort of person to whom odd things happen; but then we see that the real difference between him and others is not really the oddity of the events but that he perceived them oddly and relishes them retrospectively. True, not many of us have been sent to Nicaragua by Columbia Pictures or have been engaged to play the Stage Manager in a Broadway production of *Our Town,* but he makes us feel that even if we had done those things, we wouldn't have picked the fruits of those experiences as he has done.

He begins by telling us blandly that, when his mother committed suicide in 1967, he was off vacationing in Mexico. That opening sets the key: a grim fact put in a bland context. A performer who was out only for boffos wouldn't have mentioned the suicide, and the way he mentions it relies on our understanding of why he gives those two facts almost equal weight. Further, the suicide, which comes up again later, serves as backdrop to this chronicle of a hip Candide.

The strongest elements in the piece is also the subtlest. If we ask what the purpose of the monologue is, what it really accomplishes, the answer is before us the whole time. What we are hearing about are some of the events that helped to create the person who is telling us this story.

Swimming to Cambodia was directed by Jonathan Demme,

who did as little as possible, relying on Gray—writer and performer—to hold us. Demme's directing (as I recall) conceded very little to the specific difficulties posed for film by Gray's form. Nick Bromfield, however, who directed **Monster,** starts with an inferiority complex toward the theater and a constant need to prove that film can deal with the piece. Every time there's a chance for a sound effect—traffic, earthquake rumbles, whatever—Bromfield lays it on. Every time there's the slightest excuse for a lighting change, sometimes even when there isn't an excuse, Bromfield pounces. And with the editor, Graham Hutchings, he does a lot of that arbitrary cutting from one side to another that TV frets about, in order to avoid the "talking head" charge. When a head can talk as well as Gray's, why not leave it alone as much as you can? Why inflict on it the strictures derived from lesser heads?

Only one quibble about Gray. He performs his piece on a stage in front of an audience (though we see them only at the beginning), thus he talks to them throughout. But from time to time, he looks at the camera, which is especially noticeable when it's directly to his left or right where the audience could not be. These looks are small fractures of the theater effect. If they are supposed to make the film more cinematic, they have the opposite effect. They reveal a worry that Gray should have been above.

Note on the **Monster.** Gray's novel, the ostinato of his piece, is called **Impossible Vacation,** has been condensed to 228 pages, and has just been published. It's a peculiar experience. After seeing Gray on stage and screen, it was difficult merely to read the book: I kept hearing it. Like his monologues, it's a first-person narrative and is couched in his customary "voice." For some reason, he has changed the narrator's name to Brewster North, but there is every intent to have us think the book autobiographical, especially since a few episodes—including his mother's suicide—are much the same as in **Monster in a Box.**

From time to time, markedly in the boyhood sections, the writing is lovely. ("I remember being there in bed thinking, or imagining—because back then there was no difference between thinking and imagining . . .") Very often through the book, the tone is pure Gray—quiet joy at having discovered how to savor life's smaller opportunities as well as the larger ones.

Example: he is in a Zen retreat where the diet is only vegetables with brown rice. "I'd never had such a pure and intense taste sensation before. Original sin, I began to think, was not Adam eating the apple but Adam not eating it slowly enough really to enjoy it."

But the colors in the novel are quite different from the monologue. It's as if, when he was preparing **Monster** (and even

Cambodia), Gray had winnowed out all the dark, troubled, frantic elements and saved them for this book: a lot of heavy drugging; a lot of wandering around the world in search of self, as far as Tibet; a jail term in Las Vegas; gay baths in Amsterdam; performing in a porno film in New York. (North/Gray was born in 1941, and some of these episodes are pure '60s.)

The book's interest—which it certainly has—depends on the novelty and variety of the episodes, as related by the narrator in the wide-eyed yet serene tone of an intelligent man discovering what it's possible to get into just through the accident of living. But inevitably it lacks what the monologues have throughout: the physical presence of Gray himself.

Benedict Nightingale (review date 12 July 1992)

SOURCE: "He Is a Few of His Favorite Things," in *The New York Times Book Review,* July 12, 1992, pp. 9-10.

[*In the following review, Nightingale offers a generally favorable assessment of* Monster in a Box *and* Impossible Vacation.]

According to **Monster in a Box,** the author and performance artist Spalding Gray's mother lowered her *Christian Science Monitor* one morning and looked him in the eyes more clearly, steadily and uncrazily than she had for a long time. "How shall I do it, dear?" she asked. "How shall I do it? Shall I do it in the garage with the car?"

It is almost exactly the same question the fictional Brewster North's fictional mother directs at him in **Impossible Vacation,** and it turns out to be no less ominous. Spalding Gray's mother gassed herself with exhaust fumes while he was on holiday in Mexico. Brewster is in the same place when an identical suicide occurs. Each young man returns home to Rhode Island to find his mother's ashes in a cardboard box beside his father's bed. Clearly the relationship between Gray and North, book and book, is in some ways as close as that between two Siamese twins whose nervous systems have become symbiotically enmeshed.

Spalding Gray's admirers have been aware of **Impossible Vacation** since 1990, when he opened **Monster in a Box,** the 13th of his autobiographical pieces, at Lincoln Center (it was recently released as a film). As always, the reminiscences and ruminations drifted this way and that; but the monologue mainly concerned "a man who can't write a book about a man who can't take a vacation." By way of emphasizing the hopelessness of this enterprise, a mass of paper crammed into a large, corrugated carton remained on the table as Mr. Gray sat and confided his secrets in his wry, mournful way. It was the book-to-be in unfinished and seemingly unfinishable form, an organism whose pages would go on chaotically multiplying until they filled first the stage and then the theater, a proliferating monster from the outer spaces of Mr. Gray's mind.

Well, at long last the manuscript has been not merely finished but edited into a novel that may be more than usually quirky but is only averagely long. The "monster in a box" has become *Impossible Vacation,* a 228-page exercise in what might be called neurotic picaresque. It would be impudent, and possibly libelous, to assume that it is wholly autobiographical. Suffice it to say that its protagonist's sometimes anguished adventures have the rambling, confessional feel of the memoirs Mr. Gray has so often presented onstage.

"To my mother, the Creator and Destroyer," reads the novel's dedication; but the destruction is more evident than the creation. Brewster's conventionally happy New England childhood is ruined by the "mad bird" in his mother's mind; his first halting attempts to achieve an adult identity are ended by her suicide; and he is left to roam America and the globe in search of his self and sexuality. The novel variously finds him appearing in a pornographic movie being filmed on East 86th Street, getting flung into jail in Las Vegas, ecstatically joining a group orgy in India, having a brusque encounter with a German man in a bathhouse in Amsterdam, shouting crazily to himself as he walks up Broadway, and everywhere sharing his internal mayhem with his long-suffering mistress, who has the same name as his mother and looks rather like her, too.

To accuse Brewster's narrative of being self-absorbed is as helpful as accusing glue of being sticky. Yet his attempts to unravel his Oedipal fixations can become a bit wearisome, and at times perhaps specious as well. How seriously can we take his claim, on befriending a wild, beautiful young woman and her wild, handsome son in California, that "I wanted to be the mother of this child, and for a moment I was"? The hurried and highly personal style means that characters other than the protagonist and, to a lesser extent, his mad mother seem shadowy and elusive. The emotional inadequacy of Brewster's father, a doggedly unimaginative rationalist, is not very vividly shown, and the old man's "almost fascistic craving . . . for order and control at all costs" is not shown at all. Nevertheless, several episodes are quintessential Gray, unique in their rueful blend of curiosity, self-mockery and panic.

You can hear Mr. Gray's singsong New England voice as Brewster describes painstakingly rescuing drowning bugs from his father's swimming pool, only to watch his stepmother slaughtering them with an antique fly gun; or desperately toiling with a woman named Janice and a man

named Gray to insure that the pornographers do not have to wait all afternoon to film the scene they want; or being run out of St. Louis by a school principal shocked by the improvised tale of the Tower of Babel he and some equally earnest performers have brought from New York. Like Mr. Gray, Brewster is an aspiring actor and, like him, he first finds success by doing monologues in which, as someone says, his "subconscious is so close to the surface I can see its periscope."

Actually, the genesis of that remark is a psychiatrist to whom Mr. Gray introduces us in *Monster in a Box,* itself just published in book form and as hilariously glum as any of his previous monologues. He accompanies an American fact-finding team to Nicaragua and tries to get hold of that increasingly rare commodity, vodka, in the old Soviet Union; he interviews a woman who claims to have been kidnapped by spacemen, begins to brood that he might somehow have contracted AIDS, and is attacked by the New York critics when he plays the Stage Manager in Thornton Wilder's *Our Town.* In the interstices of all this he struggles with *Impossible Vacation,* at one point deciding to throw the whole "solipsistic, narcissistic, self-indulgent pile of poop" off the Brooklyn Bridge.

The adjectives may be merited, but the nouns are not. This is the continuing paradox of Spalding Gray; the reason audiences, and now readers, should value him.

Spalding Gray with Dan Georgakas and Richard Porton (interview date Fall 1992)

SOURCE: "The Art of Autobiography: An Interview with Spalding Gray," in *Cineaste,* Vol. 19, No. 4, Fall, 1992, pp. 34-7.

[*In the following interview, Gray discusses the production of his stage and film performances, the evolution of his monologues, and his literary influences.*]

In many respects, the success of the film adaptations of two of Spalding Gray's more crowd-pleasing monologues, Jonathan Demme's *Swimming to Cambodia* (1987) and Nick Broomfield's *Monster in a Box* (1992), represents the ongoing 'mainstreaming' of portions of the downtown New York avant-garde, a trend which could also be observed in the solo film debuts of performers such as Laurie Anderson and Eric Bogosian. Yet, unlike Anderson or Bogosian, autobiography is Gray's chosen genre, and this choice has been both the source of Gray's appeal and the source of confusion. Autobiography can be naively understood as pure self-revelation, or more cannily recognized as cleverly wrought subterfuge. Gray's unabashedly autobiographical monologues seem like uncensored emotional outpourings, but are actually the result of carefully calculated artifice. The monologues' sudden shifts in tone from uproarious comedy to unmitigated anguish have stymied critics who, rather clumsily, compared Gray to such unlikely precursors as Mark Twain and Frank Harris. While realizing the risk of attempting similarly farfetched analogies, it might be said that Gray tempers the down-to-earth irony of humorists such as Jean Shepherd and Garrison Keillor with a manic-depressive lyricism that resembles the confessional zeal of his fellow New Englander, Robert Lowell.

Both *Swimming to Cambodia* and *Monster in a Box* integrate what would otherwise be a somewhat random series of ruminations into a decidedly comic picaresque structure. In the following interview, Gray acknowledges his debt to Jack Kerouac's version of the roman a clef, although in the monologues, unlike *On the Road,* there is no attempt to invent fictitious names for recurring characters such as film director Roland Joffe, Gray's wife Renee Shafransky (once a programmer at the late, lamented Collective for Living Cinema in New York), and, of course, 'Spalding' himself. The reference to Kerouac is a reminder of the fact that Gray has distinctly countercultural roots that become glaringly obvious when his past affiliation with Richard Schechner's Performance Group and Elizabeth LeCompte's Wooster Group is considered. The Performance Group shared the overtly Dionysian orientation of avant-garde theater during the late Sixties and early Seventies. The Wooster Group, a theatrical collective that promoted a somewhat more introspective esthetic, fueled their self-anointed "deconstructions" of hallowed theatrical texts such as *The Cocktail Party* with an anarchic spirit that was indebted at least as much to Lenny Bruce as to Artaud and Grotowski. Gray and LeCompte's trilogy, *Three Places in Rhode Island,* was the launching pad for many of Gray's subsequent autobiographical musings, although the somber tone of a performance piece such as *Rumstick Road* (the suicide of Gray's mother was the piece's departure point) contrasts sharply with the comic buoyancy of the later monologues, a cycle initiated at New York's Performing Garage with *Sex and Death to the Age 14.*

Spalding Gray has become something of a cottage industry, since his staged monologues have spawned published transcripts and compact discs as well as films. The 'monster' of *Monster in a Box* is, of course, a novel (*Impossible Vacation,* 1992) that borrows heavily from recollections previously featured in numerous monologues. Gray likes to emphasize that he is primarily an actor, although he has not always warmed to the roles doled out to him in lackluster Hollywood films such as *Stars and Bars* and *Beaches.* When *Cineaste* talked to Gray last fall, he seemed considerably more excited about his work in two soon-to-be-released features—Paul Mazursky's *The Pickle* and Steven Soderbergh's *King of the Hill.*

[*Cineaste:*] *Moving a piece conceived for the stage to film often involves opening up the material in some way. Neither* **Swimming to Cambodia** *nor* **Monster in a Box** *adopts that strategy, yet they are more than just filmed performances.*

[Spalding Gray:] What I did in both cases, with Jonathan Demme and Nick Broomfield, was to give over to their knowledge of film and the way they wanted to put it together. It was never my idea to put them on film. I always knew they worked best live. But I also knew and absolutely discovered after *Swimming* the value of putting them on film. It's less expensive to see, so you get an audience that cannot afford a theater ticket. Second, you get an audience that would never go to the theater at all, but which does go to the movies. The surprising thing that happened in retrospect is that because the film is so minimal, because there are no cutaways, the audience is required to make their own film. That's not to say that doesn't happen in the theater, but it happens differently in the movie theater. I think you come to film with certain expectations and conditioning. You have seen so many movies before that offer a kind of literal representation of reality. When it's not there, there is the motivation for the audience to make self-cinema.

Nick seems more or less to have followed Jonathan's formulas. The film is made from three performances and some pickup shots at a fourth session. It was a simple setup. We had three 35mm cameras. The idea was to have the cameras going at all times so I wouldn't have to interrupt the performance and break the flow. That was very important to me. I couldn't see breaking the flow. That's one of my objections to film acting, particularly when you have a running theme. So the film magazines were being changed all the time by runners. The pickup shots were things we couldn't get during the performances. We had one afternoon of that for *Monster.* Before that we had three whole performances shot with a live audience.

The idea of having a live audience was essential for me. I learned this doing *Swimming.* The first two nights of filming I was looking past the camera to find the audience, because I felt so guilty. Jonathan's only comment was "be generous to the camera" and I came to realize that the camera was the audience. So when we shot *Monster,* I informed the audience beforehand. I went out and thanked them for coming and told them that they would be looking at me looking at a camera and I hoped that would be interesting for them.

I like working with cameras but I prefer having an audience present. The best commercial example of that was recently when I did a small role with Dolly Parton in *Straight Talk.* We had to do it in front of a small studio audience in Chicago. When I was talking with Dolly I was supposed to be a guest on a live TV show. I could just feel the difference in the way Dolly responded and was energized.

Do you now have the sense that, with the piece on film, you need never perform it again?

Well, I can't do it for quite some time. That's in the contract. I'm thankful for that. In both cases I needed to have someone put their hand over my mouth because I didn't want to go on doing it, yet I could book it again and again. You go crazy at the idea of turning down a lucrative offer and you just do it. So the films saved me. The recent film shut me up and now I'm open again which is terrifying but productive. Before the films I always had the notion that people would stop me in the street and say I'd lost it. I'd be able to let it go at that point. It would be like dying. There would be no problem.

But in regard to your question about the form of the films, I think they are radical in the sense that they demonstrate that a talking head can be interesting. When I first started doing monologues, a guy at PBS who had a grant to do a film on storytellers asked me, "What are you going to do with your head?" What kind of cutaways did I suggest? I said, "Just keep the story going." He said, "We can't do that. That's a no-no." When I was doing *Swimming* in Los Angeles, I had film people calling me all the time to get it on tape. No contracts were offered. They just wanted to preserve it. So Renee thought, "Why don't we keep it in the family? I'll produce and you can choose a director." I got Jonathan, but it took two years to get the $400,000 needed to do it. The whole thing started with the film culture of L.A.

Your third monologue-like film, **Terrors of Pleasure,** *had cutaways rather than just the talking head.*

I would call that a comic interlude. It came between *Swimming* and *Monster.* It was done for HBO. I was annoyed with them because they cut out a whole half hour, but I didn't fight for it. I was excited that they were doing it at all and paying me so well. The director wanted to do something different than what Jonathan had done with *Swimming.* I allowed him to do cutaways, but I don't think it works. I think the cutaways distract the audience and make them ask, "Why not a movie?" They seem random to me. Of course, some of them are very funny. I would have liked to have done that as a genuine film with all the real people playing themselves.

The essence of your monologues is that they are constantly changing. Putting them on film seems to be a way of having your cake and eating it, too.

That's right. *Monster* was in the can for a year before it was released. The amount of changes that occurred through natural evolution was so enormous that, when I saw the film, I thought that if I were teaching a class I would use the film and then show a tape of a recent performance and just look at the differences. I'd see how it had changed its colors, its subtleties, its details, its rhythms. My monologues are not prewritten. They are developed with audiences. The new one has been done four times. It's still struggling to get information across in logical order. When you begin to know the information, you can play with it and comment on it and reflect on it and then you can turn it into music and begin to play all the rhythms. The last stage is getting the phrasing, like, "The banana being shot across the room almost hit me in the eye." ". . . almost hit an Australian housewife in the eye." ". . . almost hit me in the head." ". . . shot across the wall." ". . . stuck." ". . . slid down the wall." ". . . stopped and was instantly devoured by an army of giant cockroaches." You play phrases like a jazz musician might. It would never be there the first night. There would just be the struggle of telling a story.

Along the same lines I've noted the huge discrepancy between the novel *Impossible Vacation* and *Monster in a Box.* The novel only went through eight rewrites. That's all I could deal with. But the monologue has been rewritten a hundred times because every performance is a rewrite. The audience doesn't know that. It knows what it sees, and what it sees is not a rewrite, it's what the monologue is at that point. My process is to tape for the first three performances and then listen and listen and, after that, it begins to swing.

To make a monologue is a long process. That's why I'm resisting moving into this new one. I just don't want to get rolling in it too fast. One of my problems with it is that it's about my eye operation. I've now gotten adjusted to the way my eye is. So I have to go back and remember how I was feeling at the time and then act. When I'm working with existing reality or dealing with insecurity or chaos, that's an ongoing thing with me, it's nothing I have to do a lot of emotional recall about. The eye operation and the conditions leading up to it are over, so that's different intellectual and emotional process.

You've had a lot of negative things to say about most of your acting in films.

Well, I'm very pleased with one that I've just been involved with, so I can speak about that. I've just finished shooting *King of the Hill* with Steven Soderbergh. This is a big breakthrough for me, because Steven is the first person who has not cast me as a professional WASP or as a doctor. I think I have a problem in Hollywood because in the monologues I said the only reason to do a Hollywood film is for the health insurance. So the producers said, "Fuck him. We'll make him a doctor for the rest of his life." In Paul Mazursky's *The Pickle*, I am a doctor who goes into the Ritz Hotel to help Danny Aiello. Now, Paul has a great sense of humor and gave me a small doctor's card that reads, "Edward Spalding, M.D." What a beautiful in-joke! I get to rush in, open the door, and say, "Hello, I'm Doctor Spalding. Where's the patient?" My fans will roar and the rest of the audience won't get it.

But this new role in *King of the Hill* is different. I'm a real character named Mr. Mungo. The film deals with a thirteen-year-old boy growing up in the Great Depression. He lives in a hotel and has all these kinky neighbors, of which I am one. I've been successful at one point but I've declined. I wear linen suits with suspenders and hang out with the local prostitute. I'm always looking for cigar bands for the kid and I also get him to do whiskey runs for me. Eventually I kill myself by slitting my wrists in the sink. Blood and water run out under the door. Soderbergh pretty much shot in sequence and works very fast. The other good thing for me was that he wasn't giving me a lot of notes. He let me figure it out myself. I was ten days in St. Louis in the middle of August in a Hyatt Hotel located in a mall. When you opened the windows, you saw the mall. That was the air you were breathing. Believe me, by the time my scenes were shot, I was very disturbed.

Then I feared I had overacted. After the last setup, I rushed to go to the airport, but then I got so worried I told the taxi driver to take me back. I had to see the dailies. I was pleased to see that I had made a real character. It was me, but it was a soulful, sad part of myself that was coming through, the suicidal side, all the stuff that Steven allowed to surface by choosing me. And I was his first choice which I'd never had happen before. I asked him why he chose me. He said, "Mungo is ruled by regret." I asked how he knew that about me. He replied, "Your novel." So I got cast through my book.

I'm definitely ready to act again. I've been given the script of *And the Band Played On*. They were so vague with me that they said, "Tell us what role you want to play." Well, there are a hundred gay men and a hundred doctors, so what choice have I got? I'm going to be a doctor again.

How would you compare yourself with other performance artists who have gone into film? Eric Bogosian comes to mind, but Lily Tomlin and Whoopi Goldberg might be other examples.

First of all, I don't think of myself as a performance artist. Artist I am not. I am a humorist. I don't think many artists have a good sense of humor. I do first person narratives. There are very few people doing that. Wally Shawn is one and Josh Mostel is directing a guy from San Francisco doing *Red Diaper Baby*, and those are fairly true stories. Lily and Whoopi don't do monologues. They do cabaret acts as characters. I like that kind of work. I like Bogosian's work, but he does not get up and say, "I'm Eric Bogosian and this is what I'm going through in my life." There are very few critics who make these distinctions. They call everything a one-person show.

The other thing to remember is that I was trained as an actor. Bob Dylan used to say, "I may look like Robert Frost, but I feel like Jesse James." I say I may look like the American Ambassador's aide, a pediatrician, or a gynecologist, but I feel just like Woody Allen. I have all this stuff inside which isn't what my face is. Hollywood is always seeing the WASP. They cast from image. But I've been in fifty plays. Paul Mazursky told me he thought I was a very good actor but what I ought to do was the John Cheever Story. I said, "Sure. You direct and we'll raise the money on my name. We'll sell the story to the American public as the bisexual, alcoholic writer by the Hudson." I was being very facetious. But that's America. Hardly any films, just movies.

You could be a great CIA man.

Odd you should say that. I was just in Iowa with my agent and he kept telling me what a great CIA man I could play. I said, "That is just what I do not want to do. I want something with heart in it. I don't want to play a cold, straight CIA man." He said it would be a CIA man who sees the light, but those films don't come very often and, when they do, they hire someone from the club, someone like William Hurt.

But this can be a silly business. Two years ago my agent got word that Woody Allen wanted to audition me. I was told not to bring lunch as I'd probably be in there for thirty seconds. Renee said that, "Whatever you do, act cool, he'll want you if you're a cold, withholding WASP." But I don't want that. I don't want to be Sam Waterston. Anyway, I got there and Woody comes over looking like a pale mole. He said, "I saw your picture and I just wanted to see you in person. I'm doing a new film." He won't tell you more than that. I thought he had seen a photograph of me, but he was using the old term for movies. I said, "But did you see *Swimming to Cambodia?*" He said, "Yeah, I saw your picture and I wanted to see you." Withhold, withhold, withhold. So I turned in a circle and said, "Well, now I've seen your picture and I've seen you," and I left. I went outside to sit in the lobby to see how long other people were going to be in there. A minute was about the average. I came home and Renee asked what I had done. I said, "I just turned around." She said that most people did that. They turned around. Rotated.

How much of the Spalding Gray of the monologues and the 'pictures' is the real Spalding Gray?

Up until recently I'd have compared myself to Woody Allen. I have an enormous sense of humor in a public space and I can make people laugh. I help people laugh. But I don't laugh a lot myself. I'm rather morbid and have a somewhat depressive nature. I read heavy books to get to sleep. So there is a kind of taciturn, not really open person, a rigid New Englander who wishes he had been on Ken Kesey's bus but knows he would have been kicked out. I'm a Gemini. Split. The name Spalding in Old English means a meadow cleft by a spring.

I'm one thing on stage and some people think I'm like that all the time. A short time ago, I was honored at a party in Southampton. About seventeen people came. I don't know if I was supposed to be the Belle of the Ball, but I barely spoke. People are usually surprised by that. But that's how I am unless I have a lot to drink. Then I can get very loquacious. There is the extroverted side, the me of the performances, and then the me who retreats and listens and tries to get in touch with what is going on. I have to take things in. I'm not like Robin Williams. As soon as he perceives, he responds. He's right in the groove, just like that. I've been around him enough to have seen that. That's a big difference between us.

How did the Spalding Gray of the performances come into being?

The first confessional monologue was in 1971 with the Performance Group. Each of us was asked to go to a member of the audience and tell them a personal story about death. The immediate reference was the My Lai massacre which the director was trying to personalize. I whispered the story of my mother's suicide in Mexico in 1967 when I came home and found my mother's ashes and a note in a box on my father's bed. That's now in the novel and in **Monster** and it was the germ of my first active address.

The breakthrough came in 1977 when I was in the Wooster Group. I was able to get up and say, "My name is Spalding Gray. Spalding 'Spud' Gray. This is what happened to me and this is my house in Barrington, Rhode Island." Then the slide came up. A year later I had to get away from the Group. I rode a Greyhound bus across America. You could go coast to coast for $69 and get on and off as often as you liked. I was in Boulder at a cafe where people were all doing their version of Jack Kerouac's prose poetry. I knew I had to get up. I just had to. I had no idea what I would say. I got up and talked about everything that had happened to me since I left New York on the Greyhound and arrived in Boulder. Then I just got out of there. That was the first monologue outside of the Performance Group.

The confessional voice in American literature is often traced

to writers like Walt Whitman and Henry Miller. Did they have any impact on you?

Whitman is a bit too romantic for me. I prefer Robert Lowell. He's more existential. The tortured, alcoholic, overbred Irish Setter. I felt threatened by Miller. I've had to read him again, but I was left thinking he was boasting too much. He wouldn't show his vulnerability the way Kerouac would. He was not an anti-hero but a braggart. Miller's writing is like Paul Theroux's *My Secret History* which I hated because Paul refused any doubt about his sexuality.

You've referred to Kerouac often. Were there other influences from that time? It was a period when we relearned that poetry was something to be spoken, not just silently read.

I am a fan of the spoken word. When I listen to authors on tape I can visualize better than when I'm just reading the words. In college I didn't read Shakespeare, I listened to the plays on records. I listened to Dylan Thomas every night. I let it wash over me. Ginsberg was a great influence, but *Kaddish,* not *Howl.* I had a photograph of Kerouac on my wall and a friend of mine took a photograph of me reading *Howl.* I liked listening to cantors. There was also a jazz influence. I collect jazz. *On the Road* was one of the first books I ever sat down to read. What I liked was that he was alive. He had voice. All of that became clear to me when I was working on my novel at the McDowell Colony. I found that I was working from memory and I'm not that kind of writer. I'm not one of those guys who's read the complete works. I've read one or two things of authors I like.

What I came to understand in the late Seventies was that I wanted to control the whole thing—to be director, author, performer. I first formally tried that in 1979 after returning from the West. I speak rather than write. My words on a page are like everyone else's, but when you give it voice, it's different. The Spalding Gray of the monologues is a combination of Huckleberry Finn and Candide.

Jessica Prinz (essay date 1992)

SOURCE: "Spalding Gray's *Swimming to Cambodia:* A Performance Gesture," in *Staging the Impossible: The Fantastic Mode in Modern Drama,* Greenwood Press, 1992, pp. 156-68.

[*In the following essay, Prinz examines Gray's attempt to communicate and understand "the fantastic and seemingly impossible facts of history" in* Swimming to Cambodia.]

Laughter today—and this helps to explain why it often has a hollow sound and why so much contemporary humor takes the form of parody and self-parody—comes from people who are all too well aware of the bad news but have nevertheless made a determined effort to keep smiling.

—Christopher Lasch

Spalding Gray walks onstage at the Performing Garage in Soho. He sits down at a simple wooden table, takes a small sip of water, and begins to talk. He talks about his role in the making of *The Killing Fields;* he talks about Thailand, Cambodia, New York, and mostly he talks about Spalding Gray. Richard Schechner defines Gray as a pioneer in the new experimental theater of the 1980s, with its tendency toward the personal, the private, the monological, and the narcissistic. "By the 1980's," Schechner says, "the definitive mark of experimental theatre was one person alone in a small space." Neither classic theater, film, or literature, *Swimming to Cambodia* is nevertheless available to us in all of these forms—as drama, film, and text. Certainly we can read the book *Swimming to Cambodia,* but we would miss the essence of Gray's performance: his presence, his intonations, his facial expressions, vocal inflections, dialects, and gestures. These are indispensible elements of the new performance mode that Gray is helping to generate.

In *Swimming to Cambodia* Gray explores what it means to confront the fantastic but nevertheless true and tragic history of Cambodia. Within the performance, the simple set and staging, the minimal props, and quotidian talk are all, I will argue, a reaction to or defense mechanism against the fantastic and seemingly impossible facts of history. Tzvetan Todorov's definition of the fantastic is the most pertinent here: the fantastic causes the spectator to hesitate between supernatural and natural explanations of an event. "The fantastic," he says, "confronts us with a dilemma: to believe or not to believe." If in the "uncanny," supernatural events are explained as natural, in the "marvelous," supernatural events are accepted as such. But the fantastic hesitates between these two poles. While *Swimming to Cambodia* does not treat the supernatural, per se, it does describe and produce an epistemological hesitation of this kind. Gray is uncertain about where to locate "reality." The real history of Cambodia is impossible to understand and "much too far to swim to." The discussion of these issues will begin with an analysis of that quintessentially dramatic element: gesture.

As a concept addressed by psychologists, anthropologists, semioticians, and theoreticians of the theater, gesture is an interdisciplinary concept especially suited for an analysis of Gray's intermedial art. Interestingly enough, theorists in all of these disciplines strive in varied ways to separate gesture from language. Motivated by objectives defined by their own fields, they nevertheless almost univocally and universally dissociate the verbal from the gestural.

Antonin Artaud, Bertolt Brecht, and Jerzy Grotowsky, despite their differences, all celebrate a drama that is primarily gestural and only secondarily linguistic. Artaud, for instance, is opposed to the dominance, indeed tyranny, of speech in the theater and argues that theater is poetry in space, not in language. Brecht's A-Effect, or alienation effect, calls for a heightened self-consciousness to gesture, as in Chinese acting, where the actor is seen to observe his own gestures, or through purposeful contradiction between gestures and speech. Thus in his study of Brecht, Benjamin repeats: "Epic theatre is gestural. . . . The gesture is its raw material." For Grotowski, too, theatrical gesture is not subordinate to a language that it illustrates. Gesturality is supposed to free itself from discourse and form an autonomous semiotics for itself. According to Grotowski, it is only the "hypersensitive professor" who expects the theater to be a realization of a text.

Ray L. Birdwhistell is an anthropologist who has founded the science of gesture, *kinesics.* Although his work continuously draws analogies between gestures and language, Birdwhistell emphasizes repeatedly that gesture is an extralexical activity. In a 1968 essay on gesture, Julia Kristeva even more emphatically argues for a nonlinguistic model of gesture. For her it is important to see gesture as nonrepresentational; it is, she says, indicative but not signifying. This nonlinguistic and nonrepresentational concept of gesture allows her to create a semiotics that does not privilege language.

Finally, if we turn to the analysis of gesture by psychiatrists and psychologists, the conclusions are surprisingly similar. John P. Spiegel and Pavel Machotka begin their book *Messages of the Body* with this assertion: "To say that the communication system of the body is not like a linguistic system is not to deny that it is a set of coded messages; but its code and the program of encoding and decoding its messages probably bears a closer resemblance to music, drama, and the plastic arts than to words and language."

What these various theories do is help to foreground the surprisingly linguistic quality of Gray's acting in *Swimming to Cambodia.* In this performance piece, Gray's gestures mirror and reinforce the spoken text. Using the ordinary language of everyday talk, including its slang and sometimes profanity, Gray's facial expressions and gestures almost always translate the verbal into a visual and gestural code. This code switching merely produces a semantic redundancy.

There is a consistent reciprocity of gesture and text in Gray's work. Why, we might ask, does such a contemporary, even avant-garde artist, use gesture in such a traditional way? Why is gesture here an accessory to speech?

In her essay "Redundancy and the 'Readable' Text," Susan

Rubin Suleiman reminds us that, despite the negative connotation redundancy has in ordinary speech, linguists and information theorists view redundancy as a positive term, for without some redundancy communication is impossible. Clearly, Gray is determined to communicate with his audience, and as many theorists have noted, the postmodern audience is a wide one. Unlike the modern avant-garde, which was determined to antagonize, provoke, and even cancel its relation to the audience, along with other contemporary performance artists, Gray is determined to engage and communicate with it. Scholars as different as Harold Rosenberg, Fredric Jameson, Andreas Huyssen, and Umberto Eco have all noted this shift in postmodernism—the merging of high art and popular culture, fine art and mass media techniques, a shift in the relation to the audience so that the purpose is, as Eco says, to "reach . . . a vast audience."

The intermedial redundancy of *Swimming to Cambodia* ensures coherence and disambiguation, effecting greater communication between the performer and his audience. Yet the performance itself outlines numerous parables of failed communication. What does it mean to live in Manhattan, where people do not have a common language? The implications, for Gray, are finally political.

> But I say . . . how . . . how does a country like America, or rather how does America because certainly there is no country like it, begin to find the language to negotiate or talk with a country like Russia . . . if I can't even *begin* to get it with my people on the corner of Broadway and John Street?
> (*Swimming,* film version)

Acutely aware of the problematics of communication, Gray devises a performance mode that will establish communication with his own audience as effectively as possible.

The gestures within *Swimming to Cambodia,* like all gestures in the theater, help to extend Gray himself as an actor. In an excellent analysis of gesture, Patrice Pavis writes:

> The essential function of gesture is its capacity to designate the situation of the utterance, its being deictic, [or] a sign which refers to the presence of the stage and the actor. . . . Gesture is not dissociable from the actor who produces it . . . the actor is always anchored on the stage of innumerable corporal deictics, beginning with attitude, glance and mere physical presence.

Hence a primary function of gesture in *Swimming to Cambodia* is deictic, pointing to Gray's central presence in the action. In keeping with the narcissism built into the monological and autoperformative mode, many of Gray's gestures are self-directed. The focus of the performance is Gray himself as performer, character, and actor. Not only is he at the center of the narrative but symmetrical gestures often locate him at the center of a visual field.

Paradoxically, despite all this signaling of the self, Gray is presented in a way that also calls presence into question. Both Richard Schechner and Philip Auslander have noted that Gray enacts various Gray personae, creating a scene for his multiple selves. James Leverett writes, "It has gradually become Gray's chosen lot simultaneously to live his life and to play the role of Spalding Gray living his life, *and* to observe said Gray living his life in order to report on it in the next monologue." This self-diffraction is most pointedly expressed when Gray describes his excitement at the beach at Phuket, where he goes swimming with his friend Ivan: "I'd run down the beach and look back to try to see us there in the surf and each time I'd miss myself and then run back to try to be in it all again. Then down the beach and back and down the beach and back. . . ." (*Swimming,* film version)

Gray's performance is self-reflexive at a variety of levels and in many ways concerns its own involution. The narrative offers a metaphor for its own self-reflexiveness, as Gray describes a teak table he saw at the Vietnamese embassy:

> This table was exquisite. . . . On the surface there was a hand-carved, three-dimensional relief of elephants tearing down teak trees with their trunks in order to make the table—so you see, it was a reflective table—it told a story about itself. In fact, it was doubly reflective, even reflexive, because it had a piece of glass over it and every so often I would catch a reflection of myself in the glass.

Like the teak table, Gray's narrative is about itself, and it is also about his trying to catch glimpses of himself within it.

Swimming to Cambodia is a film about a film, a performance about performing, and a dramatic event that analyzes and describes acting. The Stanislavski "method" is satirized throughout the monologue, especially in Gray's description of Ira Wheeler trying to do an emotional memory and being on the verge of tears and in a deep funk all day, while the car in which they sit systematically falls to pieces. When Gray starts talking to the driver, Wheeler gets outraged and yells, "Will you stop talking. . . . I'm trying to have an emotional memory." Gray responds, "This man is about to get killed by an elephant. Try *that* one." "You would be amazed at what some people went through to get into character for this film," says Gray. The spoofs on Stanislavski accomplish at least two things in the narrative.

First, they emphasize how nonnaturalistic Gray's own acting style is. We never for a moment forget that his gestures in *Swimming to Cambodia* are the artificial products of a staged body. While his gestures are surprisingly *linguistic,* they are not therefore naturalistic or realistic (in the Stanislavsky mode). Rather the impetus of Gray's acting style is to undercut and resist realism in the way that many theorists of the theater advocate (Artaud, Brecht, Meyerhold, Witkeiwicz). In the performance piece *The Terrors of Pleasure,* Gray talks about the desire to find a piece of property with streams and rivers and describes how he became obsessed with water; then he pauses and takes a sip of water from a glass. The heightened literalism does not serve realism but undercuts it.

Second, and more important, the Stanislavsky method does not work in a situation, like that described by Gray, in which the boundaries between the illusory and the real have disintegrated:

> You don't have to Method-act. When those helicopter blades are whirring overhead, you shout to be heard. You don't have to Method-act when you look down and see a Thai peasant covered with chicken giblets and fake blood in 110-degree weather for fifteen hours a day for five dollars a day. (If they're real amputees they get seven-fifty.) It's just like the real event!

Where does acting leave off and reality begin? For Gray, life is an arena in which everyone acts for others. The Thai prostitutes deserve Academy Awards for their performances—they are so *apparently* happy. When Athol Fugard advises Gray to go home (saying there's no difference between Thailand and Krumville), Gray wonders with whom Fugard has been studying acting. "I wanted to say goodbye like a man," says Gray, "and if I couldn't be one, I was going to *act* like one. . . . And I went around to each person and acted as though I'd made up my mind." People don't have to act naturalistically, Gray seems to be implying, because they always are acting naturally already.

But the confusion of illusion and reality is even more pervasive and profound than this in *Swimming to Cambodia,* and it is this confusion that produces the "fantastic" within it. Here the distinction between the real and the simulated has dangerously dissolved. Gray gets into a helicopter and says, "I felt like I was in a movie, like I was in *Apocalypse Now,* and then I realized that I *was* in a movie!" The beautiful beach at Phuket is like "one big piece of calendar art" and Gray goes swimming on "a perfect Kodachrome day." Walking into a bar with Pat Pong is like stepping into a scene in *The Deer Hunter.* The producers of *The Killing Fields* build a real swimming pool and tennis court at a hotel in Wahen in order to better simulate the Hotel Phnom Phen. Spalding Gray points to a map of Cambodia, duplicating an image from *The Killing Fields;* it appears when Sidney Shanberg watches a video that shows Richard Nixon on tele-

vision pointing to a map of Cambodia. "Are those burning villages or burning tires set out by the special effects crew?" asks Leverett; "Is this history or just another take?" (*Swimming,* film version). Certainly we are in the realm of Jean Baudrillard's "Precession of Simulacra," where the mass media neutralize reality and the hyper-real and simulation supplant it.

Postmodern works like *Swimming to Cambodia* enact and describe the simulation process that Baudrillard describes. Throughout *Swimming to Cambodia* Gray struggles with the relation between reality and its replica, more specifically between the real history of Cambodia and its simulation in *The Killing Fields.* One might say that his monologue is an effort to kill the field of simulation produced by *The Killing Fields* in order to apprehend the "reality" behind it. In this sense it is an effort to "real"ize the fantastic, to make it real, to achieve a sense of reality. But that reality threatens to slip from Gray's grasp—and ours—intertwined as it is with the media and mediated images.

In his fascinating account of contemporary culture entitled *The Minimal Self,* Christopher Lasch maintains that the confusion of illusion and reality in contemporary media culture contributes to the narcissism of the 1980s. Epitomizing this wide cultural phenomenon, *Swimming to Cambodia* is narcissistic in both its form and content. Gray tells us that John Swain was the most narcissistic of the reporters, because he had come to watch himself being played in *The Killing Fields.* Then how much more narcissistic is Gray himself who creates a two-hour monologue concerning his own bit part in the film? The first scene in *Swimming to Cambodia* describes a hotel that Gray calls "the pleasure prison," where the crew is indulging in what the Thais call *sanug,* or pleasure. Gray's search for a perfect moment is a narcissistic urge to merge with the environment. At one point he says it is "like falling in love . . . with yourself." One form of self-indulgence is replaced by another, but pervading all is irony and self-parody: "What am I doing lying on the beach like an old hippie at forty-two years old, trying to have Perfect Moments in Thailand? What am I doing searching for Cosmic Consciousness? . . . Go directly to Hollywood and get an agent! Go! Get an agent!" Exhausted from this "epiphany," Gray falls asleep only to be awakened by the words "Boat people! Boat people" which someone is shouting on the shore. Thus the search for self-fulfillment and self-gratification is both presented and ironized as Gray questions what it means to pursue pleasure in the context of suffering.

Lasch's book is especially helpful, for it allows us to see contemporary narcissism not as an idle, meaningless self-absorption but as an understandable and justifiable survival or coping mechanism in the face of historical barbarism. The narcissistic age is beset by fears that develop not only from its historical awareness but also from the realization that the holocausts of the past may prefigure even more radical atrocities, including the annihilation of humanity itself.

Thus Gray's character, Jack Daniels, who is chained in a waterproof chamber, high on coffee and blue-flake cocaine anxiously awaiting the moment when he can finally fire his nuclear missile at the Russians, allows Gray to voice his own anxiety about nuclear war. Gray is directing his satire not at the U.S. Navy, or patriotism, or the military, but at a casual, irresponsible desire to use atomic weapons. "I can tell you I thought I was looking my death in the face," he says. The threat of nuclear war, the memory of holocausts in Germany and Cambodia, the fear of ecological disasters create a climate of crises in which narcissism itself, according to Lasch, becomes a form of survivalism. Gray's perfect moment is not a romantic transcendence but a brief instant freed from "phobias," anxieties, and fears; when it is over, he is back in "fearful time" again.

Swimming to Cambodia negotiates the relation of the political and the personal, the historical and the biographical. The double-layered backdrop of the performance captures this tension between personal, even narcissistic, experience (in the blue sky) and historical/political awareness (in the maps).

The central activity of *Swimming to Cambodia* is memory—both personal and collective. Our way of coming to know and understand history is entirely problematic ("We don't know what went on," he says). "I titled this work *Swimming to Cambodia*," he explains, "when I realized that to try to imagine what went on in that country during the gruesome period from 1966 to the present would be a task equal to swimming there from New York." The truth is beyond our imagination. Hence history is portrayed in a curiously mediated way. Facts are presented as reported discourse, information is gleaned from eyewitness reports, and even American history is conveyed by an outsider. *Swimming to Cambodia* does not deny the existence of the past; it does question whether we can ever know that past in any other than a mediated way—like the forms of mediation (books, videos, films) through which Gray's own performance may very well come to us.

How does one comprehend the history of the twentieth century, with its holocausts in Germany and Cambodia? As Lasch observes, the only art appropriate to such atrocity is a minimal art, an art stripped bare and reduced to its simplest counters. A desk. A map. A glass of water. A single man talking:

> And they were laughing. There was a lot of laughter, a *lot* of laughter. And eyewitnesses said that if you pleaded for your life, they laughed harder. If it

was a woman pleading for her life, they would laugh even harder. And they would take the half-dead bodies and throw them into American bomb craters, which acted as perfect graves. It was a kind of visitation of hell on earth. Who needs metaphors for hell, or poetry about hell? This actually happened. Here on this earth. Pregnant mothers disembowelled, eyes gouged out, kids (children) torn apart like fresh bread in front of their mothers. And this went on for years until two million people were either systematically killed or starved to death by the same people. And nobody can really figure out how such a thing could have happened.

(*Swimming,* film version)

Viewed in this way, history is difficult if not impossible for the psyche to assimilate. It seems both real and fantastic, so Gray must repeat, "This actually happened. Here on this earth." According to Kristeva's analysis, the abject—the horrible—borders the fantastic, fuses the imaginary and the real: "The corpse, seen without God and outside of science, is the utmost of abjection. It is death infecting life. Abject. It is something rejected from which one does not part. . . . Imaginary uncanniness and real threat, it beckons to us and ends up engulfing us." The abject is experienced both inside and outside the self: "Excrement and its equivalents (decay, infection, disease, corpse, etc.) stand for the danger to identity that comes from without: the ego threatened by the non-ego, society threatened by its outside, life by death." Rather than repressing the abject and the horrible, Gray exposes them—both within himself and outside. *Swimming to Cambodia* begins with a story about a bad drug trip:

> Up it came, and each time the vomit hit the ground
> I covered it over with sand, and the sand I covered
> it with turned into a black gauze death mask that
> flew up and covered my face . . . until I looked
> down to see that I had built an entire corpse in the
> sand and it was my corpse.

(*Swimming,* film version)

The abject thus operates at a variety of levels within the monologue: physical (nausea), personal (death), and political (autohomeogenocide). Gray's laughter is not empty laughter, but a "way of placing or displacing abjection." His humor confronts and contains the abject of history and of the self. Spalding Gray is a comedian of crises who is not trivializing the tragic but bodying it forth. "After all, what is this film about? Survival! Whose survival? My survival" (*Swimming,* film version). And ours.

David Montrose (review date 8 January 1993)

SOURCE: "This Is Real Serious Talk," in *Times Literary Supplement*, January 8, 1993, p. 17.

[*In the following review, Montrose offers an unfavorable assessment of* Impossible Vacation.]

Introducing his autobiographical monologue, **Monster in a Box** (1991), Spalding Gray mentions how, at the age of eighteen, inspired by Thomas Wolfe, he vowed to become a writer. More than thirty years later, he came up with a truly Wolfean manuscript: 1,900 handwritten pages, the aforesaid "monster". Assuming the Max Perkins role, Gray's American editors have helped to cut and adjust "that sprawling mess" into the relative dwarf now published. Although primarily an account of the interruptions which beset **Impossible Vacation, Monster in a Box** does provide a synopsis of the original text. From this, it is apparent that the ending has been substantially truncated; a sudden jump earlier in the narrative—from 1968 to 1976—is also presumably the result of editing.

Although commissioned to write a novel, Gray was careful, in the monologue, always to call **Impossible Vacation** a book: "I don't know how to make anything up." (Wolfe, similarly, refused to call *Look Homeward, Angel* a novel.) It began as a "simple travelogue" about Gray's inability "to take pleasure when in very pleasurable places". But, partway through, he realized that his first foreign vacation, in Mexico during 1967, coincided with his mother's suicide. This illumination made him realize that he was "working with very classical themes": how every boy, to achieve manhood, "must first . . . kill his mother off." To emphasize this big subject, Gray dedicates the book "To my Mother, *Creator and Destroyer*" and appends a portentous epigraph. What subsequently meets the eye, however, primarily bears the marks of travelogue.

The book's opening sections are the most effective, dealing with the New England childhood and youth of Gray's narrating *alter ego,* Brewster North, with particular regard to beach summers and Mom, a progressively deranged Christian Scientist, to whom he was so attached that, at twenty-two, while yearning to "hang out" in Provincetown, he found himself unable to leave her: every day, he would drive a few miles down the road and then turn back. Despite oedipal hints, the attachment appears to spring from emotional affinity: she was his best friend; they would watch Bergman films together and, afterwards, "stay up late talking all of this real serious talk about loss of faith. . . ." Sensing that their relationship is "too sticky and warm to be right," Brewster blames Mom: his failure to "fly the nest" proves she is not "a good mother." Later, after he has flown—to New York, Texas, Mexico—she is held responsible for his fear of intimacy with others: "Because Mom . . . couldn't get enough intimacy from her family," she ensured, albeit un-

consciously, that they could never find it elsewhere. Brewster's attachment—which survives Mom's suicide—is largely asserted, rarely exhibited, and proves correspondingly unpersuasive. The same applies to Mom's culpability, although the point here may be that it exists mainly in Brewster's imagination; certainly his two brothers seem unaffected.

From childhood, too, date Brewster's fantasies about visiting Bali. The adult Brewster promises himself a "perfect vacation" there; first, however, he must find a life—free of the past, of Mom—from which to take that vacation. The remainder of the book follows his spiritual and geographical wanderings in pursuit of meaningful existence: Theatre, drugs, Zen, sex (especially), pornography, the Bhagwan, psychotherapy, Amsterdam, India, the Himalayas, California, and Grand Canyon (finally), where, in a moment of satori, he determines to write his "true story": "I would dare to remember my ghosts. Then maybe, after I captured them, I could take that vacation. . . ."

Gray's reminiscing style, in which telling prevails over showing, narrative over dialogue, has worked admirably in his published monologues (snippets of which reappear here). **Impossible Vacation** has little of their artistry, however, being carelessly and dully written, a series—the early episodes aside—of inconsequential tales without Gray's usual humour and charm: a section dealing with America's Bicentennial, for example, is both querulous and snooty. Gray's ostensible themes, meanwhile, are generally submerged; references to Mom provide the only evidence that Brewster is not a mixed-up Way-seeking butterfly, but the victim of a more profound wound. The consolation is that Gray should be able, if he wishes, to rescue some fine monologues from this still raw material.

Elizabeth Young (review date 29 January 1993)

SOURCE: A review of *Impossible Vacation*, in *New Statesman & Society,* January 29, 1993, p. 47.

[*In the following review, Young offers a favorable assessment of* Impossible Vacation.]

Spalding Gray and Scott Bradfield are both writers who are extremely sophisticated about fiction. They know exactly what it is and what it should do, how it should be constructed, written and read. They also seem to have a faint, sad sense that most of it will soon be forgotten, that it is all perhaps a doomed endeavour, yet both continue to believe that people need stories. "We tell ourselves stories in order to live," wrote Joan Didion, and Gray's first novel turns on this realisation.

It is difficult not to see Gray's novel as autobiographical. Like the author, the narrator, Brewster North, is a New England Wasp, an actor by profession, whose mother commits suicide and who starts a career in dramatic monologues by talking about her death. Gray, of course, went on to incorporate other material into his act and eventually to publish *Swimming to Cambodia.*

Although it presumably contains fantastical elements, *Impossible Vacation* is probably best read as an additional emotional subtext to the author's public revelations. It is the story of a tormented young intellectual who seeks escape from his "Boston Brahmin" family by maniacally chasing enlightenment down all the well-worn 1960s culs-de-sac. He studies Zen and yoga, drops acid and vitamins. He travels to India and joins Bhagwan Shree Rajneesh's tasteless free-love Poona commune. He listens seriously to people who live in tepees. All the while he is haunted by memories of his almost parodically John Cheever-type family, with their antic high-jinks, insanity and tight-lipped alcoholism.

Gray brings an unusual degree of insight to familiar themes. Brewster North is a very perceptive narrator who understands that at the heart of his quest is a desire to achieve the fashionable 1960s state of "just being". He yearns to attain what seems to be a hassle-free state of harmony. This move away from the old world of clocks and rules and delayed gratification into what Fredric Jameson has termed the "endless present" has come to be seen as one of the fundamental definitions of postmodernist consciousness.

Gradually, North comes to realise that his whole self, his talent, his purpose in the world, lies in his ability to tell stories and that in stories one is always connected to the past and to "the great and always present sadness behind words." The "endless present" eschews language. Consequently, what appears to be a light and amusing Bildungsroman is not only less oppressive than Gray's dramatic monologues but also actually more revealing of the author's life and times than his autobiographical work.

Gay Brewer (essay date Summer 1996)

SOURCE: "Talking His Way Back to Life: Spalding Gray and the Embodied Voice," in *Contemporary Literature,* Vol. 37, No. 2, Summer, 1996, pp. 237-58.

[*In the following essay, Brewer examines Gray's attempt to integrate the mind and body in his autobiographic monologues. According to Brewer, "The reciprocity between life and stage, audience perception and validation of the 'real,' is crucial to Gray's art and its complexity."*]

Spalding Gray's art is the autobiographic monologue, a composite of reality and artifice. His works, most prominently *Swimming to Cambodia* and *Monster in a Box,* share adventures achieved in the pursuit of artistic expression and colored by an obsession with the unattainable—life as art, encapsulated and preserved. The vanity of the unceasing voice—neurotic, amusing, revelatory, self-indicting—conflates with the artist's purpose, the eventual formulation, with practice, of perfect autobiographical "moments." In interviews, Gray realizes the illusoriness of such a goal, "the search for paradise and perfect moments and the mistaken idea of paradise as being a place outside of the mind." The achievement of the perfect moment is to be both sought and avoided, the imperfection of contemporary society being a primary impetus for Gray to be wandering voyeur and raconteur. "Perfection" in this context constitutes a release from the restrictions of Gray's hyperactive mind. The integration of mental and physical then approaches a rare spiritual gratification. Gray's artistic process of organizing his life into public performance parallels a movement that his monologic stories generally demonstrate in content, from isolated experimentation to reunion with audience, and finally, in *Gray's Anatomy,* to the central importance of the body. Despite being a performer ostensibly empowered by "talk," Gray in his latest work reveals the body to be as crucial as the voice to his artistic quest. The body centers the performer and offers itself to be witnessed and adored. Without a foundation in the physical, "perfect moments" sought by the mind/voice cannot be sustained.

In *Swimming to Cambodia,* the author reacts with paradoxical relief to a barely failed "moment" that would have ended his adventure by fulfilling it. "Oh My God!—almost. About a number nine on my scale of ten for Perfect Moments." If this ambivalently sought "perfection" had been achieved, he "would have had to go home that afternoon." Nevertheless, a coalescence of persistent themes shortly follows; water, baptism, and male initiation all manifest Gray's attraction-repulsion to immersing himself uninhibitedly in the waters:

> Suddenly, there was no time and there was no fear and there was no body to bite. There were no longer any outlines. It was just one big ocean. My body had blended with the ocean. And there was just this round, smiling-ear-to-ear pumpkin-head perceiver on top, bobbing up and down. And up the perceiver would go with the waves, then down it would go, and the waves would come up around the perceiver, and it could have been in the middle of the Indian Ocean, because it could see no land.

This passage offers insight into Gray's central preoccupation—the loss of self and submersion of the "I." Here nature is the catalyst, and escape from narcissism, albeit momentarily, marks the event's special quality. Richard

McKim notes that the "unstated . . . irony" of the scene "is that he, like so many of us, finds it easier—and more pleasurable—to experience oneness with the universe than with other people." What is particularly interesting in Gray's case is that he continually defines and grounds himself in the context of others, in being "perceived" more than in "perceiving." The two are integral for him, and inescapable. As soon as the "perfect moment" is achieved, Gray rushes to an audience to validate his experience.

For Gray, this dependence upon audience is crucial to the crafted persona of his monologues. The author makes no distinction between the necessity of audience to his performing stage self and to his living, "real" self: "I tend to disappear when I'm alone. It's hard to explain. It feels like I'm not there, like I'm psychically disappearing, that I don't exist. . . . I think the eyes actually inflate you, make you larger than you are through their energy. When you lose that, it's almost like withdrawal. No one's seeing you, so you're not seeing the things around you." Gray traces his discovery of the importance of the audience's "eyes" to his long run as Hoss in Sam Shepard's *Tooth of Crime*. He realized that rather than work with and off of fellow actors, he preferred the relationship between himself and the audience, the bathing glow of uninterrupted attention on his physical body in the theatrical space: "I even found I was more intensely alive during the performance than I was when I wasn't performing. . . . Everything disappeared in the room and the audience and I were one. . . . That was the most exciting point for me because it allowed a confrontation with the audience's eyes that I would never forget." Such a response clearly led to the blooming of Gray's monologic style, a theatrical device by which he is "interested in working my way back to life through theatre. . . . Now I'm trying to use theatre as a tool to come back to reexamine my everyday life as Spalding Gray."

In his seminal essay "Spalding Gray's *Swimming to Cambodia* and the Evolution of an Ironic Presence," William W. Demastes establishes that Gray indeed "creates a sophisticated theatrical persona, who himself reenacts an awakening onstage designed to sensitize the audience to its own awareness." Demastes usefully divides the "several Spalding Grays" at work into the private citizen "observer-of-events," working in a "nearly reportorial fashion," who turns his results over to Gray the artist; the piece is then "presented by Gray the *naive* performer, who appears fully incorporated into the system and is unaware of the ironies introduced into his presentation by the artist Gray, who shaped the material reported by the observer Gray." The result of what Demastes sees as this "espionage" is that "while Gray's work may *appear* supportive of the status quo, it presents a persona who ironically utilizes an empowered naivety to undermine itself and the authority it seems to uphold." For the purposes of discussing Gray's monologues, the "Spalding Gray" referred to is the "naive" raconteur, the "character" Spalding Gray relating his picaresque episodes. The more complex intentions of Spalding Gray the self-conscious artist are behind and implied by the actions of the stage persona, with the audience left to infer the subversions. Demastes offers the distinction that "Gray the performer is immersed; it is the behind-the-scenes artist Gray who is ironically detached and subtly confrontational." This style "charms as it undermines," mesmerizing both self and audience by the development of a community feeling. "Gray observes that we've all been consumed; in fact, he *demonstrates* it by 'leading' with his own presence." Recently, Gray applied a dance analogy to his stage work: "it's like dancing with a partner. You're reciprocal, you're going back and forth, you're leading sometimes, sometimes they're leading you. It's interactive."

The reciprocity between life and stage, audience perception and validation of the "real," is crucial to Gray's art and its complexity. Gray denies being a writer in any traditional sense, and he has also shied from the term "artist": "First of all, I don't think of myself as a performance artist. Artist I am not. I am a humorist. I don't think many artists have a good sense of humor. I do first person narratives. . . . The other thing to remember is that I was trained as an actor. Bob Dylan used to say, 'I may look like Robert Frost, but I feel like Jesse James.'" In the tradition of his self-claimed profession, Gray bears the sadness of the clown. The audience may laugh, but he is not allowed to: "I can't tell the difference between the world's sadness and my own." Gray equates the elusive dichotomy between humor and sadness, between his responsibility to his audience and a talent divisive to his own personality, with an essential division in his psyche: "I have an enormous sense of humor in a public space and I can make people laugh. I help people laugh. But I don't laugh a lot myself. I'm rather morbid and have a somewhat depressive nature. . . . I'm a Gemini. Split. The name Spalding in Old English means a meadow cleft by a spring." Gray acknowledges that the psychological causes of such a split are elusive, perhaps rooted in his severe upbringing and in a discomfort with the physical body often present in his work: "Growing up a Christian Scientist, it took so long for me to realize I had a body. I had to use a mirror to prove I had a body. . . . the mirror is a witness. You become a lover of yourself."

The analogy is obvious: the audience as mirror, the self-reflection seen in hundreds of eyes the amplified reflection of a child in his mother's bedroom. The term "witnessing," moreover, lends a religious implication to theatrical appearance and to the revelation of personal experience: "For whatever reasons, it seems to me that nothing is real until it's witnessed. That's part of why I work in front of audiences. . . . A terrific need for witness, and when it's not there, I have the witness within me, which is the writer, the writer's eye that watches." This internal eye, for Gray, is the constant monitor and recorder that he knows will transform what it witnesses into monologue and then performance. An elaborate paradox emerges, essential to this continuing voice—the dependence upon an audience to test and validate experience, which in turn heightens the dangers of experience turned directly into product: "I turn things into a story so quickly that I don't feel them. . . . Often, if someone asks me how I feel I tell them an anecdote rather than the feeling, because I'm so fast, I'm so good at it. . . . When I'm not in front of an audience, I tend to need one so badly that I get in situations where I just begin to perform." Ironically, Gray turns himself into pure perceiver, a filtering, theatrical machine that produces story from experience, leaving individual human feeling and reaction stranded. Performance is integral to a manic attempt at definiteness, at an impossible wholeness approachable only through public witness, the witnessing itself the very culprit of the experience's susceptibility to disintegration. David Denby senses much of this in his apprehension of the fleeting, frantic quality of Gray's delivery:

> In *Swimming to Cambodia,* the actor and monologuist Spalding Gray talks fast—faster than an evangelist working a country fair, faster than a stand-up comic in Las Vegas, or a late-night-TV appliance salesman, or a patient on an analyst's couch trying to make himself interesting. Gray, who bears a fleeting resemblance to all those American types, gives the impression of someone trying to express everything he's ever felt or thought—at *once,* before it flies away. . . . Although he always comes back to himself, he cannot be accused of narcissism and monomania. Before our eyes, his ego shreds.

This sympathetic, inescapable cycle of neurosis renders Gray's talking head—and its preoccupation with self—tolerable, troubling, and endearing. Live audiences are bound up and incriminated in this process, if only unconsciously. The act of artistic expression is, for Gray, inseparable from the notion of composition and revision: "My monologues are not prewritten. They are developed with audiences. . . . You play phrases like a jazz musician might. It would never be there the first night. There would just be the struggle of telling a story. . . . The audience doesn't know that. It knows what it sees, and what it sees is not a rewrite, it's what the monologue is at that point." Performance is both validation and purgation, with the audience cast as therapeutic testers, "perceivers" of the artist's ongoing "life" art. Gray is his own most accomplished creation, a tiring commitment that partially explains his attempt to create a more distanced fictional voice in the novel *Impossible Vacation.* The impulses to be "perceived" and to be the released "perceiver" are equally necessary to artistic assimilation. Throughout Gray's work he surrenders to the voices of others, often with no more

judgment than a flat recollection of events that supplies its own irony. Always Gray is a willing audience, and his willingness suggests, again, the reciprocal attention the audience receives from any speaker. Indeed it is difficult to maintain, in Gray's world, a meaningful distinction between perceiver and perceived. In *Swimming to Cambodia,* a large portion of the material is derived from reenactments of conversations in which Gray is a passive, secondary participant: with the director Roland Joffe, Jim the coked-up Marine, the U.S. ambassador, Ivan the "devil," the actors and technicians on the set, his girlfriend Renée, and so on, a stream of characters already recorded, placed, selected, and returned to Gray's audience as offered experience. In other words, what Gray often witnesses is his own not-quite passivity, an acute ear and mind enlivened by the circle of its apprehension-performance-response.

The idea and nature of film and its technology constitute another important issue framing Gray and his relationship to his audience. Both *Swimming to Cambodia* and *Monster in a Box* were filmed live, although with the oddness that Gray performed chiefly to the lens. "The idea of having a live audience was essential for me." With *Monster,* he "went out and thanked them for coming and told them that they would be looking at me looking at a camera and I hoped that would be interesting for them. I like working with cameras but I prefer having an audience present." For the audience watching the films, the peripheral "live" audience lends an added dimension of theatrically to the viewing, but as several critics pointed out, film viewers can't get over the experience that the performances *aren't quite live to them,* that the technology of the camera causes a separation from the performer. For Gray, this gives the film audience a requirement "to make their own film. . . . You have seen so many movies before that offer a kind of literal representation of reality. When it's not there, there is the motivation for the audience to make self-cinema." In *Swimming to Cambodia,* the actor relates a similar revelation about his own performance in *The Killing Fields.* On camera "[i]t didn't matter what I was thinking, so long as I was thinking something. Because everyone looking at the film would be thinking their own thoughts and projecting them on me." As an actor, Gray eschews a psychological approach. Performance is about surrendering to the rhythms of spoken language; audience reaction is imagination and projection. This self-revelation, too, can be pinpointed to the *Tooth of Crime* production: "The fact that the language was so well constructed allowed me a sort of private self within which to daydream, to have my own associations." The primary triangle of performance—and indeed of energized, sustainable existence—is "the audience movement, my movement, and the rhythms of the language."

Fluidity of speech is paramount for Spalding Gray, and J. Hoberman is correct in the assessment that Gray's frantic delivery is symptomatic of a voice barely controlled, a verbal release valve for a tumultuous psyche: "Like America itself, he's at once affably self-absorbed and eerily detached—he gives the sense of watching his life unreel like a movie"; the monologues' "natural subject is an anxiety seemingly held in check through a combination of pithy detail and cascading language." The stage version of *Swimming to Cambodia* is severely edited for the eighty-seven-minute Jonathan Demme film. Roughly, the film is focused on the actual filming of *The Killing Fields* and Gray's performance in the eroticized camera space. In the published monologue, the entire second section takes place after filming is completed, detailing difficulties Gray has both leaving Thailand and reintegrating into America. Within this section the actor says farewell to "Joy . . . my Pat Pong girlfriend." Neither speaks the other's language, and what Gray has perceived as an easy enjoyment of the body, beyond language, erodes into self-incrimination:

> but there were times when I was able to steal a secret glance and then I would see another side of Joy. I would catch her in a slightly drained and more reflective melancholy state, and I realized . . . how little I knew or wanted to know. Most of all realized that I could never get to it without language. . . .
>
> . . . And when the stage lights went out and the house lights came up at quarter to one, I could see everyone scatter like cockroaches under fluorescent light. And I could see the bruises like rotten fruit on the girls' legs.

Stranded by silence, the Gray persona can detect only the glossy sheen of the Asian pleasure houses, staged performances of which he is a willing, guilty audience. This scene culminates, on the personal level, the themes of American culpability persistent throughout the monologue, with Gray himself representing the emotional and geographic isolationism for which he indicts his country.

"I am a fan of the spoken word," asserts Gray, and "spoken word" should be interpreted as referring to both his own words and those of others. This issue of language, however, is problematic. On the one hand, the spoken word suggests dialogue, openness, avenues of communication and, perhaps, understanding between peoples. On the other, it leads back to Gray's primary dilemma, the separation from a direct experience with life. The inability to distinguish between play and real and the difficulty of living in the present are bound up with the predominance of a torrential, omnipresent language which cannot be quieted. Near the end of the stage version of *Swimming to Cambodia,* Gray, summering in the Hamptons, is overcome with regret about his failed "mission" in Thailand. Always he desires the other place, the lost

perfection approachable only in memory and language. "And I looked up from the hammock to see Tom Bird, this mighty Vietnam veteran, standing over me saying in a deep strong voice, *'SPALDING! BE HERE NOW!'* . . . And Tom bellowed again, *'SPALDING! BE HERE NOW!* Do you think I want to be here?' And suddenly I realized that this strong, silent man was also suffering. He just knew how to shut up about it." Torn between self and other, between experience and recollection, between media and history, between the practical and the exotically spiritual, Spalding Gray's dichotomous, conflicted, neurotic voice cannot be silent. This is both his affliction and his salvation. In the monologue *Terrors of Pleasure,* Gray recounts auditioning for a television movie, a love story in which he plays an artist. Trying to find his character through his sketching, Gray is chastised for overreliance on a simple prop. Isn't what he truly desires the flesh-and-blood woman in front of him by the fire? His response epitomizes the paradox of his monologic persona and perhaps the "real" man as well: "'Oh, you mean I'm not really an artist?' Because any real artist would rather sketch than make love."

Gray followed *Swimming to Cambodia* with *Monster in a Box* (1991), a monologue that deals extensively with the author's anxiety in trying to complete his novel *Impossible Vacation.* Much of Gray's difficulty with his nineteen-hundred-page "monster" is rooted in the central concern of all his work: the relationship of performer with audience, the blurring of perceiver and perceived. The monologues, "written" with audiences, represent a very different process from the isolated activity of novel writing: "It felt too much as if I were losing my body; why would I want to turn a well-choreographed eyebrow into a word? I was also losing silence: a theatrical pause always gives space for the ineffable, and there's no place for that in print." Gray's point is a cogent one, stressing not only the importance of audience but also the crucial significance of the actor's physical body during performance. Although Gray's "talking head" on-stage offers an ocean of pure language, the importance of the present living body cannot be overstressed. Critic Stanley Kauffmann sees the lack of Gray's physical presence as the primary deficiency of the filmed monologues. Anyone who has witnessed a live Spalding Gray performance would be unlikely to argue with such an assessment. The live shows are funnier and more vivid and moving than the films, and the films more than the printed texts, as if the words are vitiated as they move farther from the performer's body.

Gray anticipates this problem of distance, romantically attempting to incorporate the physical into the creative process: "I write in longhand, because it's the closest to speaking; it feels like an extension of my body, coming from the muscles, like painting." In *Monster in a Box,* Gray explains beginning the novel as a kind of experiment in regression, an inward-seeking attempt at private therapy: "I thought the monologues were making me too extroverted. I wanted to pull back into my more introverted self and go back in and explore the private self, the shadow self." The result is a novel notably darker in tone than the Spalding Gray of stage, but a text only truly effective to the extent that the well-known monologic voice nevertheless informs one's reading. The title *Monster in a Box* itself suggests the antagonism between Gray and his venture into fiction. Painful physical limitations imply the experiment's failure: "Then I got down to the writing, and it was awful. I don't know why anyone would want to do it. It stinks. It's like a disease. It's an illness, writing. It steals your body from you. There's no audience. You're alone. My knuckle was swelling up. I had an arthritic knuckle from the pen pressing against it so hard while writing longhand." Even in this situation, the author transferred the written word into the spoken: "I really had no idea what I was writing until I read it aloud for the tape. I saw how I had split myself—I'd become my own audience."

Gray accepts the offer of a Nicaragua fact-finding expedition as a happy interruption: "I would much rather be actually going to Nicaragua than staying in L.A. not being able to write about not being able to go to Provincetown." However, the performer's anxiety is far from ended. Although *Monster in a Box* assumes the comic picaresque structure that has become Gray's trademark, its particular recurring theme is the actor's separation from audience and the neurosis that ensues from this estrangement. While *Swimming to Cambodia* finds Gray continually in the company of other actors and artists, *Monster in a Box* deals more with a persona increasingly isolated by its growing celebrity. The subplots of writing the novel and of life in Hollywood—the movie capital where much of the monologue is set—suggest that these other arts intrude on a life in the theater. As he stares at a blank page or into a lens, where is the audience that Gray has always depended upon as "my receptor, my editor, my therapist"? One reviewer noted that "much of *Monster in a Box* shows Gray confronting a culture that's just as self-absorbed as he is: Hollywood." A recurring joke in the work is Gray's despairing attempts to locate anyone to interview on-stage who isn't involved in the movie industry. Even an earthquake only momentarily interrupts the universal topic of one's "project." The moment in *Swimming to Cambodia* when Gray feels invincible in the eroticized space of the camera is recalled by a similar experience in a movie theater: "And what's amazing is that every time I notice a celebrity looking at me, and I'm in their gaze, I'm not afraid of death or dying." If recognition within the gaze is crucial to the author's integrated existence, then this power is heightened within the gaze of the celebrity elite in Hollywood, the world capital of celebrity worship. The image on the film is immortal, and if Gray feels inexplicably safe in the camera's lens, then by extension why not in the refracted gaze of its stars? One reviewer commented, "Gray appears

to have identified a 20th Century strain of *hubris*—the arrogance of pride that, in Greek drama, was a provocation to the gods—peculiar to moviemakers: They feel immortal and infallible on a shoot." For Gray, who finds health and solidity before an audience, what safer haven than the eyes of the movie gods?

"I speak rather than write. My words on a page are like everyone else's, but when you give it voice, it's different. The Spalding Gray of the monologues is a combination of Huckleberry Finn and Candide." As critics have occasionally pointed out, Gray's monologues are essentially novelistic in their narrative emphasis and languid, circular structure, making Gray's venture into proper fiction, while perhaps inevitable, nevertheless unnecessary. The Spalding Gray of the monologues—a creation identified by its author as part fiction and part real, a synthesis of innocence, wit, and adventurousness—suffers through the first half of *Monster in a Box* without the audience that relieves and defines him. With no pressure released through performance, Gray is overcome with too much raw experience:

> By now I'm hysterical and desperate. I come back to the house saying, "Renée, they told me I should find a therapist. I don't know what to do. They're probably right, but I have to interview the L.A. people. I don't have time to find a good therapist. I'd have to look at so many—and the Monster and—K.O.'s outside—and the mothers of the heroes and the martyrs want me to go tell President Reagan—!"

Gray the author is fully aware of his dependence on performance, and the fractured, suffering Gray depicted in *Monster in a Box* can only be cured by one method. Busy with the "L.A. Other," in which he is forced to move outside of his own neuroses and question others in front of an audience, Gray escapes for the interviews' duration his own introverted fragmentation: "I didn't find a therapist, but I completed the project. And I went and collapsed in front of my dressing room mirror and I thought, now that's interesting. I haven't thought about death or dying for two weeks. Isn't it therapeutic to surround yourself with people weirder than yourself!" Both his mental and physical states are improved, clarifying the notion that it is not merely monologic performance that restores Gray but also the ameliorative effect of dialogue, interaction, and discovery in a theatrical space. Shortly after the interviews, perhaps enabled by them, Gray finds his therapist, a Freudian psychoanalyst comically anachronistic in Los Angeles. Gray recognizes the rightness of "the old slow talking cure" for his hypochondria. The doctor dismisses Gray's physical symptoms—sweating feet, dry mouth—as psychosomatic and suggests to his patient that "your problems have to do with what's in that book. Would you tell me the story of that?" As Gray has already demonstrated to us, writing the novel is a failed therapeutic exercise. In an interview, he has added that "[a]t one point I thought that in order to write my book I'd have to have my therapist in Los Angeles come over and sit in a corner of the room, so he could witness me, as a writer." Telling the novel to an audience is in essence the purpose of *Monster in a Box.* The monologue addresses Gray's need, if not to "talk" his novel as he does to the doctor, at least to "talk about" the work and thereby complete and validate it with an audience. Apparently, the method works. Dr. Peter announces that Gray is "much better" and "able to relate to me now in a non-performance mode." He clears his patient for the next episodic adventure, a Russian film festival. Gray is ready to assimilate and take notes on more experience.

In Russia, Gray quickly locates an audience, as is always his concern, but this section of the monologue continues to discredit the notion that Gray is primarily dependent upon language. While one might assume that the performer would be at a disadvantage in front of a volatile foreign crowd, an opposite truth emerges. Only the film of *Swimming to Cambodia,* which loses its Russian translation, is sabotaged by faulty language. "I said, 'Stop! Stop the film, please!' People were walking out in droves, the place was a shambles, everyone was talking. 'Stop! Misha, please tell them to stop. I want to get up and apologize.'" Once Gray locates his audience and is able to initiate a spontaneous live performance, he is seductive and confident within his body: "I thought, maybe I should stand up and show the Russians my body. So I stand up. It's cabaret situation. . . . I myself would like to just get up and moonwalk, if I could, for the Russian audience—but, I don't know how to moonwalk—or do a body roll from the sixties with a little B. B. King music, you know." The story he finally communicates through his translator Misha is archetypal Gray—"flocking" through the Hermitage in the safety of movie stars and being recognized by a group of American high school students. It is a slapstick treatment of familiar themes: the self-defining empowerment of celebrity, the American worship of flash—literally, with the children's cameras—over art and history, and finally, Gray's compulsion for recognition to validate his presence. "I've been recognized—thank God I've been recognized—for being on the David Letterman show. They are over there asking me, 'What is David Letterman really like?'"

Throughout *Monster in a Box,* the Gray persona finds, through his need to be physically seen, a hyperreality on the stage, a heightened sense of the "now." Paradoxically, this discovery conflates the present with a realized past, artifice with reality. For Gray, insight happens only in the context of performance. He explains the attraction to his novel's fictional protagonist Brewster North of playing Konstantin, the young writer in Chekhov's *The Sea Gull:* "he likes the fact that Konstantin gets to shoot himself in the head at the end

of every performance and then come back the following night to play himself again." Play, therapy, repetition, rebirth—these are the salve for a dislocated psyche. In the film *Clara's Heart,* Gray plays a grief counselor signing books. "They want me to sign his name on camera? I won't do it—I won't sell my soul for that price. I'm keeping the book off camera and signing *my* name across the picture and then handing it out to all the extras, pretending it's my book, finished at last." The problems of "real" life are solved in the camera's eye, and for the duration of performance the actor is cured. He knows who he is.

Gray realizes the therapeutic repetition of performance in his role as the Stage Manager in the Broadway revival of *Our Town:* "And now here I was going to a funeral—Emily's funeral—eight shows a week and this was giving me a sense of closure around the issue of having missed my mother's funeral." It is appropriate, perhaps inevitable, that a monologue about the necessity of audience and the preferred "reality" of stage ends with a lengthy retelling of Gray's involvement with the Wilder production. Through the play's language, Gray is "swept back to New England where I used to believe in God and eternity and all the things the play is about." This "softening up" that the play causes allows him to purge himself of the novel and to transcend the failure of isolated writing. Gray has been "on-stage" continuously during the last episode, and the self recalled is by far the most peaceful, calm, and integrated to be found in *Monster in a Box.* Performance is existence: "And as I pull the curtain closed at the end of the play—I'm not acting—I'm crying." Not coincidentally, the closing of the Wilder play marks the conclusion of Gray's monologue, and in turn the "monster" is also quieted. Its protagonist wonders whether he should write his own story or "skip the story and try to take a vacation instead." The peace found on-stage has passed into the fictional world, implying that the best vacation is an escape into the reality of theater.

The importance of the body in Gray's theatrical performances emerges as the primary theme of his most recent monologue, *Gray's Anatomy* (1993). In this work, the human body, with its imperfections and frailties, literally and thematically takes center stage. Through Gray's discovery of a debilitating eye condition, his mortality is rendered immediate to him. As the author searches for alternative healing, he meditates on his own existential doubts and fears, on his desire for magic over the "real," and on the relationship of his self-consciousness and his language to the failing ability of clear sight. Gray has noted that he wavers "from a very practical, cynical, hard-core view of life and then am drawn towards flighty, more spiritual things. . . . I am a doubter, and I haven't doubted my doubt yet. But I am curious about ways of thinking, ways of coping. I'm most interested in how someone deals with the fact that at any moment they could disappear forever." These are the conflicting pulls, and the fearful curiosity, that inform *Gray's Anatomy.*

Gray's attitudes toward neurosis and the unsatisfiable longing for the "other" place isolate the separation between mind and body central to his predicament: "I'm a Freudian to that extent, that I believe culture breeds neurosis. . . . The way that I would define neurosis—I think really it has to do with not being present. If I think of anything that's neurotic in me it's the inability to be in the place that I'm in when I'm in it, with my body and mind, and that I'm longing for someplace else." Such a separation happens not only in daily life but in the nightly life of theater, where the body is present but the actor's mind casts back to the other place: "That's the shadow side of my work, because my work is recollection. . . . What I quite simply mean is I mine my neurosis, that's the thing that I'm chipping away at." While the mind is engaged in the mazelike recalling of the previous night's memory, the body remains present and central: "So when I sit down at a table now, all I'm doing is centering myself at the base of my spine to that chair. And I'm moving out of that all the time. I'm coming up. I'm three inches off the chair. My feet are moving, my arms are moving. I'm sweating. It's a physical event for me to tell these stories. They're very animated." In the newest monologue, the author admits he can see only the "internal film of the place I've just left." Such is the "disease" of which he wants to be cured. The prescription he receives from a bemused healer is a drawing of a Balinese icon, a headless man: "His eyes are twinkling in his chest and his nose is in the center of his body. He had no mouth, which I could relate to." The little man is an appropriate companion for Gray—a being without spoken language whose centrality and intelligence originate from the chest. Gray finds himself "embarrassed" and "self-conscious" talking aloud to the drawing. Their relationship is founded on faith, magic, and the body.

Spalding Gray has increasingly focused his work on the physical. *Gray's Anatomy,* as its title suggests, moves slightly away from Gray's motifs of performance and language except as they contextualize his failing sight and an exploration of doubt realized in the body. In his recollections of Christian Science healing, Gray delineates an upbringing that equated health with the power of language: "Look, when you're dealing with a Christian Science practitioner and you're talking about the disease, you really have to be quite careful not to name it. . . . because to name it gives it power. You're supposed to refer to it as 'an error.'" Gray contacts a healer, who insists on ambiguous references to the eye problem and to fidelity—no other treatments are allowed. Gray rejects him. "I hung up, realizing why it was I had left Christian Science in the first place." For Gray, despite his superstition and doubts, the "not naming" is impossible. The predominance of language in his self-absorption—and his livelihood—makes "naming" unavoid-

able and amplifies its danger: "I listen enormously to the spoken word and have a more vivid image from the spoken." Later in the text, a Filipino psychic surgeon again warns of the danger of fixating—a form of internal naming?—on an illness: "Also, if you are thinking of the AIDS all the time, and I'm sure you do, you will get it. You will manifest it through your thought, you see." Gray responds with the story of "the man who was told that if he stirred a pot of water long enough without once thinking of elephants, it would turn into gold." Hypochondria is therefore made real. Sickness originates in the body through the mind. If Gray cannot escape the self-consciousness that may induce his illness, he can nevertheless seek a similarly mystical cure. He considers possible first causes of the eye's injury. Tellingly, all suggestions of cause are mental or psychological rather than physiological. An explosive "tear" of mourning over his mother's suicide? Too much "I" in his novel's first-person? Or as his "New Age friends" suggest, "Well, what is it you *don't want to see* . . . ?"

Gray realizes that his livelihood is dependent upon his sight and ability to discern the physical specifics of the world: "This is what I totally depend on in order to tell stories. I tell stories about the details of things. If I lost the detail in my right eye, what could I possibly do?" In *Monster in a Box,* the performer needs an audience; in *Gray's Anatomy,* the failing body needs an outlet of physical labor. In a bizarre anecdote that culminates in Gray cleaning up debris at a Jewish synagogue, the author is liberated by work that draws him out of the mind's self-concerns. He is "pretending" to be a Bowery bum, "Peter with perfect eyes," and is energized by the character's new identity and strong body: "I'm feeling great. I'm raking up the leaves, I am sweeping up the broken white plastic knives and forks, and paper cups and plates left over from parties, and I'm whipping it up!" He refuses a ride back from Williamsburg and walks "over the Brooklyn Bridge back to the city feeling triumphant! I think, there is something I can do if I lose my sight in my right eye. I can do something other than tell stories!" Repeatedly in the monologue the emphasis is on the present human body, usually Gray's own. When Azaria Thornbird recounts her astral projections, Gray's response is one of physical self-adoration: "Didn't you ever consider making love to yourself? Because, I mean, that's the first thing I would want to do if I found myself leaving my body." Instead of being able to move outside of the body, however, Gray feels trapped within its condition, isolated by the peculiarity of his affliction and his entrance into the "Bermuda Triangle of Health" between fifty and fifty-three years old: "I was coming into it, and I was feeling lonely, because I was the only one I knew with a macula pucker."

The theme of vision in *Gray's Anatomy* is an effective metaphor for the author's delving into notions of doubt, darkness, uncertainty, and a pervasive chaos. One critic notes Gray's talent for making "grand, inductive leaps to social and moral philosophy from isolated, personal experience. . . . [his] seamless transitions between the ridiculous and the tragic." The comic revelations perpetuated by increasingly arcane healing treatments symbolize the refusal to age gracefully, to adapt to decay, and to acknowledge the whole notion of chaos and fuzziness—that is, uncertainty—that the subject of failing eyesight inevitably produces. Gray is informed by his therapist that "[a]ll things are contingent, and there is also chaos. . . . In other words . . . shit happens. Give up on this magical thinking and this airy-fairy Disneyland kind of let's pretend and your Hollywood la-la fantasy, please. Do the right thing. Get the operation." A "joke" throughout the piece is that not only are Gray's psychological explanations for his illness misguided, but that his "condition is idiopathic. Meaning, no known cause."

Gray's Anatomy is one of the author's most universal and timeless pieces. The monologue's themes are two: aging rendered graceless by the fear of meaningless death, and the acceptance of "reality." These may signal the beginnings, at middle age, of maturation beyond the child's world of hope and magic. Gray grasps at every slim chance of faith and ritual—an Indian sweat lodge, palming, a Brazilian healer, a Filipino psychic surgeon—to ward off aging, entropy, and death. These treatments are highly theatrical, with comic yet compelling "performances" by the participants. Nevertheless, they supply no cure to Gray as actor or audience. The palming treatment, which leaves its patient in a self-created and self-imposed darkness, exemplifies his anxiety: "I also realize that the more I look inside, the more I don't see a self to heal. I can't get any sense of such a thing. There's no core, no me. All I see is darkness, which is more and more frightening for me. It feels just like death." Gray acknowledges, employing the appropriated term, "I don't know who my Creator was. I always thought I was idiopathic. You know. No known cause." Shortly afterwards, in the doctor's waiting room, he admits that he has grown "used to this by now, waiting in the fuzz." Even after Gray has exhausted every alternative and undergoes traditional surgery, no miraculous recovery occurs. "After fourteen days, I go into the hospital to have the patch removed. I know this is supposed to be the dramatic part of the film: *Will the man see again or not?* It's nothing as dramatic as a movie." He sees as if "driving in a rainstorm" or looking through "the bottom of an empty Coke bottle." He has chosen a solution free of magic, but the results are "not great. Things are less distorted, but they are really blurry." That is as good as he can expect "it"— the eye, the life, the doubt—to get; the operation brings neither crippling disaster nor clarity and true resolution.

The complementary subplot to the play's subject of physical isolation is the engagement of Gray and his long-time companion Renée. Her practical reason for wanting commitment is to assure access to Gray as he grows older: "you're going to get sicker a lot more and you'll be in the hospital again. I think it's time we got married." The impending marriage centers the monologue and its concerns of mortality, adult responsibility, and self-doubt. The movement from boyfriend and girlfriend to husband and wife—"It sounds so serious. It sounds so biblical, so Old Testament"—is a difficult semantic leap for the fifty-year-old man, one which epitomizes the journey from magic to reality and from childhood to maturity, a journey not fully desired. When the topic of marriage is initially broached, Gray gets "fuzzy" trying to think about it, linking the subject with vision. Not until he has had the eye surgery is he able to agree to the reasonableness of the union. The two acts represent a necessary movement toward acceptance of mortality and the limitations of human life: "I begin to realize that there are tricks in the world, and there's magic in the world. But there's also reality. And I have to begin to cope with the fact that I'm a little cockeyed. . . . But I don't have a whole lot of time to dwell on it. Because Renée—who is over to my right—wants to get married." His fiancée is aligned with the right, the right eye, the blurry, cockeyed quality that Gray begins to recognize as life.

As the wedding day approaches and Gray's anxiety predictably escalates, he turns a final time to the body to alleviate the tension of his overactive mind: "The one thing that kept me sane during that time was bodysurfing. I love to bodysurf, particularly when the water's cold; it really grounds me and wakes me up at the same time. I was in the water bodysurfing every day." This activity culminates in the play's hilarious and poignant climax, in which Gray, caught in a "sea puss" that threatens to drown him, turns his cry for physical survival into a wail of human angst: "HELLLLLLLLLLLLLP! I'M DROWNING! HELP, I'M GETTING MARRIED! HELP, I'M GROWING OLD! HELP, I'M GOING BALD! HELP, I'M GOING BLIND! HELP, I'M GOING TO DIE! HELP, I'M GOING TO LEAVE THIS EARTH FOREVER ONE DAY! HELLLLLLLLLLLLP!" Gray is the hyped-up Everyman, a Prufrock drowning in a sea of his own hysteria, fear, and regret. The scene parodies the "perfect moment" from *Swimming to Cambodia.* The men who rescue Gray recognize his bobbing head from the earlier movie poster and turn the near-tragedy into a photo opportunity. One senses that what Gray identifies as the center of his neurosis, the inability of mind and body to be integrated in the present, has somehow been addressed. He has been "rescued" from the danger of a disintegration that he has pursued and cultivated in earlier works. The body, preeminent throughout *Gray's Anatomy,* here returns as a symbol of the entire person's inadequacy and uncertainty, suggesting a moment of terrified unity with the mind.

Gray goes through with the marriage, indulging in pleasures which may have contributed to his eye problems: "We run down to the sea together to look out, and then we went back to the house to celebrate. I drank vodka and I drank white wine and I ate big fish. I ate steamed vegetables and I ate wedding cake. I drank coffee and I smoked a cigar." Despite the context in which the marriage takes places—the irreparable blurring of Gray's vision, the hurricane damage that nearly postpones the wedding—one can't help but notice that *Gray's Anatomy* concludes on a note of union and qualified optimism. It is perhaps Gray's funniest work, despite its theme, and ultimately may be his most life-embracing. Despite the limitations of body and language, despite the continual disappointments of the ideal versus the real, life is livable and can be enjoyed. "And I ate and I drank and I smoked . . . *everything* that could make me blind." The pleasures which destroy us also sustain us; death is part of living. Gray implies that in moving over the threshold, to traditional medicine and traditional union, he has faced and accepted this central paradox. He brings the drawing of the Balinese man down to the beach wedding "to be a witness"; there is after all magic in the world to offset reality, and finally the body and mind will not be separated.

Laurie Stone (review date 23 December 1996)

SOURCE: "It's a Slippery Slope," in *The Nation,* December 23, 1996, pp. 33-4.

[*In the following review, Stone offers a generally unfavorable review of* It's a Slippery Slope.]

Spalding Gray is our bard of self-absorption. He's learned to see it with detachment, turning it into a subject, a hot tub big enough for a group soak. In *Monster in a Box,* he found the measure of his talent: his eye for irony and incongruity; his capacity to show himself as vulnerable without undercutting the effect with aggression; his ability to weave story elements into charged arrangements, so that even details that at first seem random eventually gain significance. He presented his prurient, blabbermouth personality as the deviant spawn of his tight-lipped, undemonstrative, alcoholic WASP nest; the leakage that diminished him in childhood was transformed into comic strength.

The serious trouble chronicled in his next monologue, *Gray's Anatomy,* made him funnier. A retinal malady that threatened blindness to his left eye was like a discipline or calling. The blur was focusing. Training on a real infirmity rather than hypochondria, Gray entered a space cleared of self-importance and whining. He was naked and intimate, no membrane protecting him, so we were transported to his side of the eyeball. The sufferer was aware that his ordeal was enormous and ordinary, and he juggled these irreconcilables without dropping either.

His new piece, *It's a Slippery Slope,* . . . is a scrapbook of his narcissism, and damned if he doesn't deepen the gaze—at least for the first sixty minutes. Spalding is nearing 52, the age at which his mother committed suicide, and he's tempted to meet her in Valhalla. Instead he takes up skiing, exchanging his anxious, New York boho head trip for an in-the-moment flight from consciousness. On the mountain he's home, embracing his New England heritage, clambering up and slithering down the big mom-tit in the sky he has longed to join ever since mooning out the window of his high school geometry class.

The monologue is bravura stand-up unreeled with grand minimalism-his acting honed to a Beckettian simplicity that ripples out levels of meaning from a sip of water or the slight rearrangement of his feet beneath the desk at which he's stationed. His plaid shirt is as much clown garb as Bozo's red nose; his circumflex eyebrows shoot asides to the audience, like bubbles of thought above a cartoon character's head. His writing is spare as a haiku and galumphing as a shaggy dog, as he embellishes his themes: the laws of triangles, emotional depression and geological elevation, acting instead of living, the evasion of consequences.

Between monologues he wonders if he creates crises for material. He feels his life is becoming one big memory and that he's lost touch with sensation. He questions why each day he forgets that you only live once, while white-knuckling through existence dreading mortality. There are hilarious set pieces, among them a ski lesson in which he unprotestingly permits himself to be called Sterling. Cast as a suicide in a Soderbergh film, he strolls through his hotel with bloody makeup on his wrists and fails to get a ·rise out of anyone until, seized by a "diabolical 11-year-old Halloween energy," he waves them before an astonished old woman and cries, "Have you got anything for my wounds?" Classically stalled, conversations with his father are sporadic, but he reports one as the old man nears his end, a follow-up to their last chat, conducted on a golf course, when 14-year-old Spuddy was told the facts of life. Loosened by a couple of beers, Gray gropes for a Hallmark moment. "You had three sons, and I'm the middle. Why am I the only one who isn't circumcised?" Father: "You're not?" There is more dick-waving here than in previous works, and this is where the piece goes slack (or, if you prefer, plows into a snowdrift). We've been on the road with Spuddy for years, but those were the days when he was with his "girlfriend" (and later wife) Renee Shafransky, who was not only a character in his pieces but the director of several of them. He didn't confide, as he does now, that he used to have wild affairs on his tours. Unlike the "impingencies" of *Monster in a Box,* about a man who can't write a novel, and of *Gray's Anatomy,* about a man who may be going blind—both struggles with the self—the crisis at the core of *Slippery*

Slope is Gray's affair with a woman who bears him a son and the subsequent dashing of his bond with Renee.

Faced with the consequences of his impact on others, Gray loses his thread. He stops spinning tales of fear and loathing—and psychobabbles: "Renee and I fused, she became very involved with my work. . . . I had to propose to Renee in front of my therapist, who knew I was having an affair with Kathy. . . . Kathy was simple, she liked the outdoors. . . . Kathy had no leftover mothering energy." The unrealness of Renee to Spalding has fogged other narratives. Apart from being devoted to him and resourceful, she is always shadowy, instrumental to Spalding rather than palpable in her own right. At the end of *Anatomy,* when Renee presses to solidify their union with marriage, the gallant self-observer becomes a kvetch. Fear of aloneness and illness have made him passive, and in that state he has agreed to the wedding. Once he's through the operation, however, he wants to escape. This, too, could have been a subject: the way we make regrettable promises while feeling helpless. Instead he portrays himself as the reluctant bridegroom and casts Renee as the old ball and chain. In *Slope,* we can see why the marriage in *Anatomy* comes off false—he was still fucking Kathy!

But spilling the beans doesn't turn him honest. Renee's suffering is mentioned but not taken in by the narrator or presented to the audience. Gray has no impulse to protect the women. He admits that, over both of them, he chooses the mirror of himself he sees in his offspring—"There is always another woman, but never another son." Instead of satirizing this peak act of narcissism, Gray squanders the best chance thus far of his career and waxes reverential, declaring his boy a "little Archimedes [who] had the geometry to split up me and Renee." It's not a crime to love your kid, even to prefer him above others, but Gray speaks as if reproduction in itself is ennobling—redeems all that filthy stuff

he was doing when it was just his dick and pleasure. Talk about returning to your Puritan roots.

FURTHER READING

Criticism

Hornby, Nick. Review of *Impossible Vacation,* by Spalding Gray. *Times Literary Supplement* (14 January 1994): 20.
  An unfavorable review of *Impossible Vacation.*

Johnson, Brian D. "The Talking Cure: A Performer Bases His Career on Confession." *Maclean's* (13 July 1992): 44.
  Offers a brief overview of Gray's career and favorable assessment of *Impossible Vacation* and *Monster in a Box.*

King, W. D. "Dramaturgical Text and the Historical Record in the New Theatre: The Case of *Rumstick Road.*" *Journal of Dramatic Theory and Criticism* 7, No. 1 (Fall 1992): 71-87.
  Examines the composition, structure, and performance strategies of *Rumstick Road.*

Queenan, Joe. Review of *Monster in a Box,* by Spalding Gray. *National Review* (20 July 1992): 43-4.
  A tempered review of *Monster in a Box.*

Interview

Panjabi, Gita. "Spalding Gray: Writing the Spoken, Speaking the Written." In *In the Vernacular: Interviews at Yale with Sculptors of Culture,* edited by Melissa E. Biggs, pp. 151-88. Jefferson, NC: McFarland, 1991.
  Gray discusses his early influences, creative processes, and the artistic concerns of his monologues.

Additional coverage of Gray's life and career is contained in the following sources published by Gale: *Contemporary Authors,* Vol. 128, and *DISCovering Authors Modules: Popular Fiction and Genre Authors.*

John Irving
1942-

American novelist, short story writer, essayist, and memoirist.

The following entry presents an overview of Irving's career
through 1996. For further information on his life and works,
see *CLC,* Volumes 13, 23, and 38.

INTRODUCTION

Upon the publication of his bestseller *The World According
to Garp* (1978), also adapted into a Hollywood film, Irving
emerged as a major literary figure. The enormous success
of *The Hotel New Hampshire* (1980) fortified his reputation
as a writer whose novels bridge the gap between literature
and mainstream fiction. Influenced by the sprawling, plot-
driven novels of Victorian authors such as Charles Dickens,
Irving's intricately developed, multilevel stories are permeated by dark comedy, perverse irony, and bizarre violence
that underscore the dangerous uncertainty of human life and
the erosion of conventional values in modern society. The
popularity of subsequent novels—*The Cider House Rules*
(1985), *A Prayer for Owen Meany* (1989), and *A Son of the
Circus* (1994)—brought further praise for what critics describe as memorable characters, absorbing plots, and sardonic social satire.

Biographical Information

Born John Winslow Irving in Exeter, New Hampshire, Irving was the oldest of four children. Irving attended Phillips
Exeter Academy, a boys' prep school where his father taught
Russian history and where, as a member of the team, Irving
developed a lifelong passion for wrestling. A mediocre student and undiagnosed dyslexic, Irving soon realized his desire to become a writer. After graduating from Exeter in
1961, he studied briefly at the University of Pittsburgh and
the University of Vienna before settling at the University of
New Hampshire, from which he received a bachelor's degree in 1965. He married his first wife, Shyla Leary, in 1964,
with whom he shares two sons. His first publication, the short
story "A Winter Branch," appeared in *Redbook* magazine in
1965. Irving attended the famed University of Iowa Writers
Workshop, where he studied with novelists Vance Bourjaily
and Kurt Vonnegut, earning a Masters in Fine Arts in 1967.
Over the next two years, Irving worked as an assistant professor of English at Windham College in Putney, Vermont,
while completing his first novel, *Setting Free the Bears*
(1969). He then returned to Vienna for several years to work
on a film version of the novel which was never released.

With the aid of a Rockefeller Foundation grant in 1971-72,
Irving completed his second novel, *The Water-Method Man*
(1972). From 1972 to 1975 he was a writer-in-residence and
visiting lecturer at the University of Iowa while working on
his third novel, *The 158-Pound Marriage* (1974). He was
awarded a National Endowment for the Arts fellowship in
1974-75 and named a Guggenheim fellow in 1976-77. In
1975, Irving worked as an assistant professor of English at
Mount Holyoke College while writing *The World According to Garp.* With the overwhelming success of *Garp,* including an American Book Award and nomination for the
National Book Award, Irving earned enough to abandon
teaching for full-time writing. His first three novels were
soon republished together as *Three by Irving* (1980) and his
next novel, *The Hotel New Hampshire,* was a Book-of-the-
Month selection and instant bestseller. *The World According to Garp* and *The Hotel New Hampshire* were also
adapted into major motion pictures in 1982 and 1984 respectively. Irving's subsequent novels, *The Cider House Rules,
A Prayer for Owen Meany,* and *A Son of the Circus* were
similarly greeted by critical approval and an eager popular
audience. Irving has also published a volume of short sto-

ries and essays, *Trying to Save Piggy Sneed* (1996), and a memoir, *An Imaginary Girlfriend* (1996). Divorced from his first wife in 1981, Irving married Janet Turnball in 1987.

Major Works

Irving's structurally complex fiction revolves around the misadventures of eccentric characters involved in tragicomic searches for self-identity and meaning. Their stories are often punctuated by inexplicable violence, maiming, and death, suggesting the absurdity of good intentions in the face of fate and bad luck. Through the misfortunes and comic reversals of his characters, Irving addresses serious social concerns surrounding the family, sexuality, gender relations, and the relationship between life and art. Several recurring motifs and narrative techniques characterize his work, notably the presence of bears, prep schools, wrestlers, Vienna, rape, illegitimate children, and the incorporation of family histories, journal entries, letters, flashbacks, and multiple perspectives to present the story. *Setting Free the Bears* begins with the picaresque travels of two bohemian students—narrator Hannes Graff and Siegfried Javotnick, or Siggy—as they traverse Austria on motorcycle. The second half of the novel, completed by Hannes after Siggy's accidental death, consists of excerpts from Siggy's journal that detail his family's suffering under Nazi and Russian oppression and Siggy's plot to free the animals at the Vienna Zoo, a gesture intended to avenge his European ancestors. *The Water-Method Man* follows the disappointments of Fred "Bogus" Trumper, an endearing, though equivocal, husband, boyfriend, and doctoral candidate who struggles against boredom to translate an Old Low Norse epic poem. Trumper relates his despair through reflection on his failed marriage, fear of commitment to his pregnant girlfriend, and a friend's production of a film about himself with a less-than-optimistic title. The title of the novel refers to Trumper's treatment for a painful urinary tract ailment which becomes a metaphor for his ceaseless discomfort and dread. *The 158-Pound Marriage* reveals the disastrous effect of an ill-conceived mate-swapping scheme involving two married couples. Though initiated with the promise of honesty and guiltless pleasure, the adulterous relationships among the four participants soon degenerate into a source of acrimonious sexual jealousy and emotional pain. *The World According to Garp* recounts the life of T. S. Garp from his illegitimate conception to his untimely death. Raised by Jenny Fields, a nurse and renowned feminist whose autobiography attracts a devoted following, Garp becomes a high school wrestling champion, marries a local sweetheart with whom he has two children, and writes several modestly successful novels. After mutual infidelities, including one that inadvertently leads to the death of their youngest son and the sexual mutilation of his wife's lover, Garp befriends a transsexual ex-football player, adopts a young rape victim, and is finally assassinated by a feminist extremist. *The Hotel New Hampshire*, a family saga beginning in 1939, follows three decades of the troubled Berry family, headed by Win Berry and his wife, Mary, proprietors of three hotels in New Hampshire, Vienna, and Maine. The narrator, John Berry, is the middle child of five, including Frank, Franny, Lilly, and Egg. Violence and the grotesque dominate the novel: Franny is raped by prep school football players, then engages in a brief incestuous affair with brother John; Lilly, a dwarf and blocked author, commits suicide; their grandfather, Iowa Bob, is literally scared to death when their taxidermically preserved dog, Sorrow, falls out of a closet; Mary and Egg die in a plane crash en route to Vienna. Despite successive tragedies and personal crises, the family remains a positive source of collective strength and resiliency. *The Cider House Rules* recounts the work of Dr. Wilbur Larch, an ether-addicted obstetrician, between the 1890s and mid-twentieth century. His Maine orphanage, St. Cloud, doubles as a clinic for safe, illegal abortions. Though Dr. Larch does not encourage abortion among his patients, he recognizes the dismal plight of his parentless charges and grooms one orphan, Homer Wells, to succeed his medical practice at St. Cloud. Homer later abandons the orphanage for work at Ocean View Orchard, where he becomes involved in a love triangle and fathers a daughter. The title of the novel refers to a list of regulations intended to guide the behavior of the orchard workers, symbolizing the coercive, hypocritical rules of society that are better defied or ignored. *A Prayer for Owen Meany*, steeped in Protestant theology and New Testament allusions and set in a quaint New England town, relates the unusual friendship between John Wheelwright, an illegitimate child who seeks the identity of his biological father, and Owen Meany, an undersized Christ-figure distinguished by his belief in predestination and irritating high-pitched voice—his dialogue in the novel is rendered in all capital letters. Owen accidentally kills John's mother with a foul baseball, discovers his death date in a vision during a school production of *A Christmas Carol*, and converts John to Christianity through the example of his extraordinary sacrifice. The film *Simon Birch*, released in 1998, was "suggested" by *A Prayer for Owen Meany* and was created with Irving's blessing, although many important elements of the story were changed. As in much of Irving's previous fiction, *A Son of the Circus* involves a large cast of quirky characters and unusual circumstances. The novel features Dr. Farrokh Daruwalla, an Indian-born orthopedic surgeon who lives in Toronto, anonymously writes screenplays for popular crime films, and periodically returns to Bombay to work in a children's hospital and to study the genetics of dwarfism among Indian circus clowns. Rife with subplots and tangential excursions, the story essentially revolves around the long-unsolved murder of an Indian golfer.

Critical Reception

Irving is considered among the most imaginative and entertaining contemporary American novelists since Kurt Vonnegut and Joseph Heller. An exceptional storyteller whose intelligent novels appeal to both academic and mainstream readers alike, Irving dismisses any demarcation between high literature and popular fiction and asserts the primacy of plot and content over style. An admirer of Dickens and Thomas Hardy, both of whom wrote for mass audiences, Irving is praised for his remarkable ability to immerse large casts of engaging characters in unpredictable plots imbued with provocative contemporary issues such as feminism, sexuality, and religion. As many critics note, his work effectively merges the realism and morality of the conventional novel with the sophisticated metafictional techniques of postmodern writers, especially through the frequent use of texts within texts and flashbacks. Though most critics applaud Irving's unsettling juxtaposition of life-affirming compassion and macabre brutality, others find fault in elements of melodrama and his sensational depiction of explicit sex and excessive violence. While *The World According to Garp* is generally considered his finest work, Irving has received considerable critical approval for his earlier novels, particularly *The Water-Method Man,* as well as *The Hotel New Hampshire* and *The Cider House Rules.*

PRINCIPAL WORKS

Setting Free the Bears (novel) 1969
The Water-Method Man (novel) 1972
The 158-Pound Marriage (novel) 1974
The World According to Garp (novel) 1978
The Hotel New Hampshire (novel) 1981
The Cider House Rules (novel) 1985
A Prayer for Owen Meany (novel) 1989
A Son of the Circus (novel) 1994
Trying to Save Piggy Sneed (short stories and essays) 1996
The Imaginary Girlfriend (memoir) 1996
A Widow for One Year (novel) 1998

CRITICISM

Jack Beatty (review date 23 September 1981)

SOURCE: "A Family Fable," in *The New Republic,* September 23, 1981, pp. 37-8.

[*In the following review, Beatty contrasts* The Hotel New Hampshire *with* The World According to Garp.]

It's extraordinary what a little feeling can do for a novel. To prepare for *The Hotel New Hampshire,* I read *The World According to Garp,* and disliked it intensely, not for its slap-stick sex or for its "comic and ugly and bizarre" preoccupation with mutilation and death, but for its shallowness, its quality of energy without feeling. The novel conveyed only one emotion—self-love. Garp, Irving's writer-hero, was so taken with himself that the title of the last chapter jarred: how could there possibly be "Life After Garp"? Who would want to go on living without that paragon? I frankly hated *Garp,* and picked up the new novel expecting to hate it too. Instead I liked it. Feeling made the difference. In *Garp,* it all flows back on Irving's alter ego; in *The Hotel New Hampshire,* it flows out, bringing a whole family to life on a wide current of care.

John Irving is a talented but facile writer. His prose never encounters those resistances—emotional, moral, epistemological—that energize memorable statement. It never strains at meaning; it just sweeps you along, its easy momentum lulling your critical faculty and rocking you back to a childlike state of wonder. In this 400-page book, for example, I can find only one moment of verbal felicity: "Harold Swallow, darting through the trees, guiding us like a hush up the path. . . ." One pauses over that "like a hush up a path," to admire it. But that is just what Irving doesn't want, for if we stop we might start asking questions that would undermine our pleasure in a novel so willfully unrealistic. So Irving keeps us moving, sacrificing rhetoric to pace, as in the most primitive narrative forms, the fable and the fairy tale. In fiction like this, meaning lies near the surface of the story and in the voice of the storyteller.

The Hotel New Hampshire is a family saga; the storyteller is John Berry, the middle child, a brother and sister fore and aft. Not a novelist like Garp, he is the family annalist, the compiler of its collective story. It begins at a hotel on the Maine coast in 1939, and ends there many years and many adventures later. Along the way, two members of the family die in a plane crash; John's older sister is raped by the backfield of a prep school football team; his older brother grows into a homosexual; his little sister stops growing ("'You're no dwarf, dear,' Mother whispered to Lilly, but Lilly just shrugged. 'So what if I am?' she said, bravely. 'I'm a good kid.'"); and, in a moment of extreme if improbable peril for the whole Berry tribe, his father makes a heroic gesture that costs him his eyes. The two props of the plot are the father's attempts to make his dream of running a successful hotel come true, first in New Hampshire, then in Vienna. The Vienna hotel is occupied by whores, with whom young John investigates the holy mysteries, and by a cell of terrorists who plan to blow up the Vienna State Opera and then take the Berrys hostage. A subplot has John falling in love with his sister, Franny; and oh, there is so much more; for sheer quantity of astonishing happenings and eccentric characters, *Hotel* beats *Raiders of the Lost Ark* cold.

The novel has the manic rhythm of a cartoon; crisis follows

crisis in a spiral of woe; and, at each crisis, the Berry family comes together in a moving tableau of solidarity. Family is one of the novel's values; imagination is the other. That faculty is seen in a double light. On the one hand, it is a defense, a way of coping with troubles. The lack of it can be disabling, and one character commits suicide when her imagination fails. On the other hand, the attempt to realize everything you imagine can be dangerous. Father Berry's lavish efforts to live out his dreams result in several deaths; and the price he ultimately pays himself, being blinded, is a fitting emblem of his benighted condition all along. Moreover, throughout the novel imaginative pranks backfire, leading to tragic unintended consequences. Irving's double view of the imagination, I suspect, is even behind his preoccupation with the Nazis. They, after all, tried to do *everything* they imagined, with what terrible results we know.

John Berry's voice, however, returns us to a warmer idea of the imagination: its power of sympathy. "You've got to get obsessed and stay obsessed," John's grandfather, a football coach, urges him. Coach Bob's advice is about weight-lifting, and John follows it fanatically. But his deeper obsession is with his family. How can I make father happy? How will grim Frank turn out? How I miss Mother and Egg! How I long for Franny! This anxious love is the pulse of his mind.

Someone calls John "a weight lifting maiden aunt"; in another vocabulary, he would be a *mensch*. His moments of caring, together with the larger set-pieces of family solidarity, make the human element in a novel otherwise unbearably farcical. John Berry and John Irving remind us that the imagination is not simply a Rube Golberg faculty of invention; it is also a moral force, a way of sharing others' lives, others' burdens. We all want to check in to the Hotel New Hampshire. It is "the sympathy space" where we can be fully known and yet fully loved, and where a powerful imagination holds us fast and won't let us die.

Caryn Fuoroli (review date January 1982)

SOURCE: "In the Family," in *The Progressive,* Vol. 46, January, 1982, pp. 51-2.

[*In the following review, Fuoroli offers praise for* The Hotel New Hampshire.]

Weak writers may repeat themselves in book after book, while great writers, often obsessed, reexamine their subjects persistently; F. Scott Fitzgerald returned to the very rich again and again, and William Faulkner to the psychological blood sports and themes of Mississippi, novel after novel. A world which constantly threatens to inflict violence and

sudden death is set against the saving virtues and emotional risks of the family and of art.

After *The World According to Garp,* John Irving's tragicomic treatment of New England schoolmasters, Viennese prostitutes, and performing bears will prompt nods of recognition rather than gasps of wonder. He has retained and refined his greatest strength—a narrative control so powerful that readers seem to surrender their will. In his new book, he has become more articulate. *The Hotel New Hampshire* is a compelling novel; Irving's old obsessions become disturbing, while illuminating new experience.

Irving follows the Berry family through three decades and their serial ownership of three hotels. Each is called "The Hotel New Hampshire," although the second is in Vienna and the third in Maine. The narrator, John Berry, describes himself as "the middle child, and the least opinionated." He is the even-handed reflector of his family—of Father's aspirations and Mother's gentle acceptance, and of his four siblings. Frank, the oldest, is fussy in mind and body. Franny is vehement and outwardly sure of every move. John, next in line, is Franny's adoring ally. Lilly and Egg, the smallest sister and brother, in their different ways remain childlike forever.

As a family, the Berrys form a virtually self-enclosed world. Franny explains, "We *aren't* eccentric, we're *not* bizarre. To each other . . . we're as common as rain." And John agrees, "We were just a family. In a family even exaggerations make perfect sense; they are always logical exaggerations, nothing more." As readers we are absorbed into this insular family circle. We understand their logical eccentricities—why Frank preserves and stuffs the corpse of their old dog, Sorrow; how Egg got his name; why they encourage each other to "keep passing the open window."

The family's closeness is a defense against the terrifying and tragic non-Berry world. On one Halloween, Franny is gang raped in the woods near the first Hotel New Hampshire. That Thanksgiving, a visiting doctor announces that Lilly is a dwarf. On Christmas the children's grandfather, Iowa Bob, is scared to death when the dog Sorrow, taxidermied in an attack posture, tumbles out of a closet. While other families celebrate their holidays, the Berrys face new horrors.

Violence is one of those inexplicable horrors which strikes from without. Usually viewed from the perspective of the victim, it is embodied in the icy arrogance of Franny's football hero rapist. And death, like violence, is always an imminent possibility. The plane carrying Mother and seven-year-old Egg to Vienna drops into the Atlantic as suddenly and senselessly as Sorrow fell out of Bob's overstuffed closet.

In the face of this constantly threatening world, the family finds what internal stability it can and explores its internal tensions. Like the Berrys and their mentor, an Austrian nicknamed Freud, Irving brings to the surface our deepest dreams and fears. Incest is not a subterranean theme or a repressed desire, but a fact in John's and Franny's lives. Lilly writes a bestseller called *Trying to Grow*, but she is tormented by her own limitations as an artist. Similarly, the sudden deaths and physical disabilities which haunt Irving's world are our most frightening, half-conscious thoughts brought to life in his fiction.

With its explicit fears, its atmosphere of inevitable, unpredictable doom, *The Hotel New Hampshire* is a dark novel, despite its humor. The comedy is not a relief from tragedy but an increasingly desperate means by which the family endures and bounces back.

The novel is at times awkward. The family's heroic response to a terrorist attack in Vienna seems a clumsy plot device which gets the Berrys home and makes them famous. The novel's several tag lines, especially "sorrow floats," are overused, and quickly become aphorisms. Irving has a dangerous tendency to preach. The third Hotel New Hampshire becomes a platform from which his narrator tells us about the value of rape crisis centers, when Irving might have dramatized their importance to much greater effect.

But Irving rarely loses his footing. He has written an uncompromising novel, for he refuses to sentimentalize or evade the most wrenching emotions, and he insists we must cry and laugh at a world we cannot control.

Evan Carton (essay date Fall 1986)

SOURCE: "The Politics of Selfhood: Bob Slocum, T. S. Garp and Auto-American-Biography," in *Novel,* Vol. 20, No. 1, Fall, 1986, pp. 41-61.

[*In the following excerpt, Carton examines "the issue of the individual's uncertain identity and political complicity" in* The World According to Garp.]

As an idea and a commodity, the personalized life in America numbers among our most popular notions. This curious cultural circumstance reflects the disparity that various critics have observed between our governing model of selfhood and its consequences: that of a privileged, personally empowered and singularly expressive identity whose realization, in Fredric Jameson's words, ironically "maims our existence as individual subjects and paralyzes our thinking about time and change just as surely as it alienates us from our speech itself." Such an irony is hardly new in American

literature. Indeed, Sacvan Bercovitch takes it to originate our literary history—a theory that helps explain the strange typological affinity between the seventeenth century Americans whose quest to empty or annihilate the self rendered it an obsession, and their twentieth century countrymen whose obsession to fill and preserve the self renders it a void.

The connection between the Puritan and the modern self is, to a significant degree, a national one, for it is America, or an image of America, that invests the former and divests the latter. The representative "superindividual" of Cotton Mather's *Magnalia Christi Americana* "is America itself," Bercovitch observes, and he argues that this powerful conflation "obviates history by inverting it into a still higher form of personal narrative." Ultimately, Bercovitch writes, "the concept of 'Americanus' designates a comprehensive social-divine selfhood that surmounts the anxieties of secular time, since the very notion of 'social' has been transformed (by association with the idea of the new continent) into the realm of rhetoric—of sacred past and sacred future unified in the self-celebrating imagination." These remarks lose none of their suggestiveness when they are read (as no doubt they were written) with modern America in mind—a culture that understands history as selective biography, that labors prodigiously to image a "social-divine selfhood" capable of surmounting "the anxieties of secular time," and that still tends to sacrifice the facts, and the notion, of the social to the rhetoric of the national. More important than any thematic application of Bercovitch's thesis, though, is the structure of exchange that its insistence on inversion, sublimation and transference identifies. For, if the realms of personality and imagination consume politics and society, they must themselves become loci of political significance and subjects of social analysis.

Bercovitch calls his representative rhetorical mode "auto-American-biography," and it is the disrupted and confusing form of this description that makes it a useful one. America itself, the term implies, may be the author and/or the subject of such a biography; at the very least, nationality comes between the self and his life and perhaps even automates his history. The "unique power" that auto-American-biography "confers upon the solitary 'true perceiver'" thus begets a lonely impotence, the union with America that produces the representative self consumes it. Such is the ironic legacy of Bercovitch's seventeenth century hermeneutics, the same legacy whose nineteenth century renewals and reversals Quentin Anderson examines. Writing a few years before Bercovitch, Anderson is concerned not with the sublimation of the Puritan self by a myth of America but with the subversion of modern America by a myth of the self. Here again, however, a structure of exchange inheres, and while Anderson tends to see his theme as the individual's imaginative usurpation of (hence, his actual alienation from) social reality, his title points toward a more complexly interactive relation between The Imperial Self and the burgeoning imperialist democracy.

This historical relation suggests that, in a significant way, Tony Tanner and others are wrong when they remark "how singularly a-political the American hero tends to be." More often, the hero of American fiction is *singularly* political, a figure who personally incorporates the national politics and who, therefore, is not "reluctant" (as Tanner claims) but *unable* "to offer any ideas about the kinds of structure which he thinks should replace the structurings in the existing society against which he is rebelling." Such a hero is unideological only to the extent that he carries America's own willful unconsciousness of the ideological bases and implications of its values and desires, as if politics were simply what election year rhetoric takes it for: the art of being true to the individual/national self. This art, in any event, becomes increasingly difficult to sustain as the reciprocal empires of the self and the nation break down in modern America and as the neat dichotomous construction of their relationship (a matter either of identity or of opposition) gives way to a more unsettling sense of complicity—a term that I mean to designate an uncertain, associative relationship in which identity is more fluid than fixed, and power can neither be monopolized nor relinquished.

The two novels I will consider, Joseph Heller's *Something Happened* and John Irving's *The World According to Garp,* both confront the issue of the individual's uncertain identity and political complicity. Each conjoins a claim to represent contemporary social reality in America with an exploration of the power, the boundaries and the nature of the self. Each, by means of a central character who is partially and problematically authorial, makes self-conscious use of language's double role as a vehicle of personal power and a medium of social control. Sharing numerous details, the two seem to comprise a pair of expansive and formally ambitious male works in which (ostensibly) solitary voices seek to exercise and extend dominion over their listeners and their worlds in the manner of America's classic poetic imperialist, Walt Whitman. But, for all their material similarities, *Something Happened* and *The World According to Garp* respond in radically different ways to the world they hold in common. Despite its apparent formal openness, its existentialist rhetoric and its playful juxtapositions of the factual and the fictive, Irving's novel is reactionary in its model of the self and in the politics that that model supports and requires; however oppressive its environment and defensive its bureaucratic narrator, Heller's novel points toward a revisionary possibility for both personal and political identity. Each text, then, and especially their relationship, may help illuminate for us the strategies and stakes of the politics of selfhood. . . .

The World According to Garp would appear to be a richly

polytextual novel. Not only does Irving's bestseller interpolate dreams, short stories, chapters, synopses and reviews of imaginary novels, jokes, journal entries and fragmentary polemical writings into the fictional life it recounts, but it extends the privileges of authorship and commentary to other characters besides its dominant cultural critic and individual talent, T. S. Garp. Two chapter titles—"The World According to Marcus Aurelius" and "The World According to Bensenhaver"—explicitly assert the novel's multivalence. Within the text, moreover, the titular formula attaches to still other and ostensibly different representations of reality, such as "the world according to Jenny Fields," a world whose requirement that every woman be "either somebody's wife or somebody's whore" Jenny defies both in the immaculate conception of her child and in the publication of her autobiography, *A Sexual Suspect.* In contrast to *Something Happened,* *The World According to Garp* is, as its reviews duly note, "a sumptuous novel" that presents "a marvelous assortment of characters," almost all of whom write. Yet, however variegated its cast and its narrative surface, this is a book "wherein the world falls under one embracing tone of voice," a tone that accommodates, legitimates and ultimately embraces the world whose stranglehold Heller exposes and seeks to break.

> **Not only does Irving's bestseller [*The World According to Garp*] interpolate dreams, short stories, chapters, synopses and reviews of imaginary novels, jokes, journal entries and fragmentary polemical writings into the fictional life it recounts, but it extends the privileges of authorship and commentary to other characters besides its dominant cultural critic and individual talent, T. S. Garp.**
>
> **—*Evan Carton***

Garp's world is ours. This is the proposition that Irving's epilogue flatly states and that the entire novel, despite its baroque form and self-mocking air, consistently advances. It is a proposition to which huge numbers of readers have assented, and its truth lies in the enthusiasm of their assent. For *The World According to Garp* constitutes a peculiarly convenient and comforting model of our world, one that, like an uninterpreted dream, offers both immersion in life and immunity from it, both the company of others and solipsism, both the fantasy of omnipotence and the luxury of uncontrol. This, I want to argue, is the source of the book's appeal (and also of its demagoguery); this, too, is why it is so easy to read uncritically and why its pervasive brutality may elicit so little moral or even emotional response. Garp's model of the world is not an interpretation but a dream—albeit a public and topical one, like the evening news—designed precisely to moot the issue of interpretation, to thwart inquiry into its own motives and effects and, hence, to alleviate the reader's interpretive responsibility in the novel and, implicitly, in life. It is a world whose precepts are so truistic that their articulation and acceptance seem to entail no obligation. ("Later he wrote that 'human sexuality makes farcical our most serious intentions'"; "But in the world according to Garp, we are all terminal cases.") And, by virtue of the self-exemption that their very conventionality confers, the author of these precepts manages to appear as an "original": "Even at fifteen, one [sic] could sense his instinct for a personal aesthetic," the narrator remarks. Indeed, Garp's "personal aesthetic" might be described as the ideology of exemption.

From his mythic origin to his martyrdom at age thirty-three, and on into the days of his disciples (chronicled in the novel's last chapter, "Life After Garp"), Garp is curiously exempt from the world that, as writer and protagonist, he represents. While he fully enjoys the pleasures of that world, shares its shortcomings and violently suffers the fate that it holds for all, Garp nonetheless remains apart, constant, his character as uninfluenced by the events that assail it as, he insists, his art is unimplicated in the realities it plays upon. In these respects, Garp's life imitates by inverting the example of Christ, the willing representative of a world from whose sins he was exempt. To recognize this inversion is to reject the readiest explanation of Garp's Christic associations: that they are meant ironically to indicate the mad, but noble, ambition of a writer whose fiction seeks "to keep everyone alive, forever," a citizen whose "one vast and naive wish [is to] make the world *safe*," yet a man whose messianic energies, both imaginative and practical, only hasten his own and others' doom. The novel allows, and at moments even seems to invite, such a critical assessment of its hero, but this is not the relation to Garp that its pace, plot, characterizations and narrator ultimately encourage the reader to establish. Instead, *The World According to Garp* casts the reader in a more passive, in fact a voyeuristic, role and elicits his secret identification with Garp, his vicarious satisfaction through him and even something approaching (but never acknowledged to be) the "blind loyalty" that the epilogue reminds us "Garp had been the type, after all, to compel." To his believers, moreover, Garp, like Christ, provides recompense—not escape from and triumph over, but escape and triumph in human isolation, aggression and helplessness. For, if Christ's mystery is the redemption of a fallen world by his engagement, Garp's is the ratification of an irremediable world by his detachment (and a justification of his detachment by the world's irremediability), a feat that Irving's shrewd mixture of fictional modes facilitates.

To draw on Northrop Frye's taxonomic definition: Garp is a hero of romance who, paradoxically, moves through a realm of irony, "a scene of bondage, frustration [and] ab-

surdity," and it is this deterministic environment, rather than "the postulates of romance," whose establishment insures his transcendent status. In *The World According to Garp*, "the ordinary laws of nature" and failings of human nature are heightened, rather than suspended, and enforced so relentlessly that the hero's exploits, whatever their character or consequences, seem a creative necessity; here, Garp's power is validated and his exemption guaranteed not by the abrogation of the "rule of probability" but by the attenuation of any standard of accountability. "I don't blame you. . . . I don't blame me, either. . . . Only in this way can we be whole again," read the notes that Garp gives to his wife after the apocalyptic convergence of bad weather, driveway fellatio, raging husbandly vigilance, a missing stick shift knob and a lightless, speeding car-parking trick has killed one of their sons, blinded the other, and unmanned Helen's graduate student. Both the accident and the novel are contrived to win the reader's approval of this judgment and to promote Garp's vision not of human interdependence in a world of incomplete personal autonomy but of an insular and fantastic wholeness in a world of amputees.

> **To draw on Northrop Frye's taxonomic definition: Garp is a hero of romance who, paradoxically, moves through a realm of irony, "a scene of bondage, frustration [and] absurdity," and it is this deterministic environment, rather than "the postulates of romance," whose establishment insures his transcendent status.**
> *—Evan Carton*

This vision of wholeness is first authored and embodied, however, not by Garp but by his mother Jenny Fields, whose insouciant self-direction instantly renders it attractive. But the liberation that the novel grants its "famous feminist" is private, defensive, even self-contemptuous; when Jenny tries to convert her personal experiences and resources into political ones, she accomplishes little, prompts mainly scorn and precipitates her destruction. In fact, neither a feminist sensibility nor a conviction of her independent worth underlies the four demands that make Jenny a sexual suspect ("I wanted a job and I wanted to live alone. . . . Then I wanted a baby, but I didn't want to have to share my body or my life to have one"). What motivates her from the outset is a desperate instinct to protect herself against a world in which sexual intercourse is more murderous than generative and denotes not relationship, nor even supplementation of the self, but bodily affliction perpetrated or received. This world is established in the accounts of Jenny's only two sexual encounters that open and close chapter one. In 1942, Jenny uses a scalpel to dissuade (and almost de-nose) an insistent soldier in a movie theatre; in 1943, she nurses a ball turret gunner who has been messily lobotomized by flak shards and who is regressing rapidly toward a foetal degeneration except for his persistent and "impressive erection" from which she draws one "last shot" to produce T. S. Garp. Jenny claims "the rights of an individual" in defense of her self-engineered pregnancy, but her act—like the nurse's uniform she wears throughout her life to hide her despised breasts and to prevent her being viewed as "somebody's wife or somebody's whore"—does not express so much as it insulates and, in its way, effaces her. Jenny's function as a character is similarly deceptive, as Garp himself suggests in a remark that describes not only his mother's relation to her patients and followers but also the service she performs for Irving's reader: "I sometimes think that's what Mom is *for*. . . . She makes people happy by letting them think she is something that she isn't." The individuality of Jenny Fields—like every expression of what passes for feminism in *The World According to Garp*—finally accommodates rather than challenges a masculinist ideology and model of the self and reinforces the association of sex with violence on which it is based. Accordingly, thirty-three years after Nurse Fields inseminates herself astraddle the voiceless, dying gunner, Technical Sergeant Garp, in order to save herself from sexual relationship and him from complete extinction, a young woman with an amputated tongue, who shares some of Jenny's physical features and is disguised in a popular mock nurse's uniform sold under the trade name "Jenny Fields Original," shoots Garp the son, whom she has accused—in a phrase whose variations comprise a virtual refrain in the novel—of having "fucked [her] sister to death."

Garp's originality, like his mother's, is prompted by a demand for total self-determination. Like Jenny's, too, it is ironic, not only in its ultimate personal consequences but in its pervasive and disguised complicity with the social order that it presumes to disdain. Garp is set apart from the beginning by his extraordinary conception and by his name, which, thanks to a dead and unknown father to whom his mother was never related, is (as Jenny insists) "all his own." Aloof and preternaturally calm as a child, Garp becomes convinced "of [his] own uniqueness" in his adolescence and decides to extend and redeem his originality by becoming a writer. The occupation allows him a controlled engagement with the world which more properly comprises, as nursing does for Jenny, a form of detachment. The sheer privacy of creation also appeals to Garp, who "love[s] the idea of never having to go out," and the act of authorship at least fosters the illusion of godly power in a man who feels "an urgent need to protect the few people he loved from what he imagined 'everyone else' was like." But, despite his distinctiveness, his aesthetic insulation and his paternalistic caution, Garp is repeatedly mistaken for and aligned with a rapist whom he encounters in the park, his art reflects or exploits the world's most typical and tawdry aspects, and his actions

maim and kill the ones he seeks most to shelter. As his renegade mother fulfills conventional female roles ("Jenny always said that she was, first and foremost, a nurse") and effectively complies with an ideology from which she disassociates herself, so Garp embodies in his "always personal" life and reproduces in his "original" work the world from which he claims independence. For, the "one embracing tone of voice" that emerges from the "writer's long-sought trance" is nothing other than the voice of the dominant culture, a voice that rationalizes, temporizes, burlesques and finally vindicates what we're told some "serious women" suspect: "a kind of killer instinct in him—basically male and basically intolerant."

As this description suggests, a radical opposition between men and women and a radical identification of sex and violence sustain one another and together inform *The World According to Garp*. So intrinsic are these two structures, in fact, that both assume inevitability and resultant legitimacy; and, despite the narrator's illustrations and lamentations of their consequences, both support the imperial selfhood that the novel celebrates in Garp. The most extreme expression of the text's sexual politics is the forty-page opening chapter of Garp's third novel, *The World According to Bensenhaver*. That chapter, by far the longest excerpt from Garp's work, depicts the abduction and rape of a young housewife, Hope Standish, by an atavistic farm boy, mad for a human orifice. Hope manages to eviscerate her attacker with his own fishing knife, and Oren Rath, who had meant to dispose of her when he was finished, comes and dies simultaneously in an uncontrollable confluence of bodily fluids which "[empty] by quartfuls—by gallons." Hope's defensive butchery of Oren Rath is carefully crafted by Irving, and proudly hailed by the police inspector Arden Bensenhaver, as an apt requital of his dehumanization of her. But Rath is more than simply repaid; he is repaid in kind with an animal frenzy that reiterates his world as it obliterates him. Indeed, for the reader, Hope's revenge serves the same purpose as the fact, revealed at the story's conclusion, that Garp's editor could only place this excerpt in *Crotch Shots*, "a porno magazine of . . . loathsome crudity": both afford the reader *ex post facto* critical detachment and easy moral exemption from Bensenhaver's world without requiring that he challenge its premises or consider his own vicarious implication in it. Irving typically disguises or disowns his ratification of *The World According to Bensenhaver*, but he consistently ratifies it, right down to the tribute to the long suffering Hope with which the synopsis of Garp's novel concludes: "Somehow implicit in the novel is the sense that women are better equipped than men at enduring fear and brutality, and at containing the anxiousness of feeling how vulnerable we are to the people we love. Hope is seen as a strong survivor of a weak man's world." Such an endorsement, of course, grants Hope no redemptive power and acknowledges no revisionary social possibility; what the passage really endorses is the world that it describes, a "weak man's world" that is its own apology and that is almost justified in its cruelty by the "implicit" fortitude of its victims.

That Garp stands not for communal endurance and vulnerability but for solitary power and refuge, and that he takes this antithesis to represent the relation between female and male modes of identity, is evidenced by the contrasting associations that his actual mother and his imaginary father hold for him. In response to Jenny's charge that Garp doesn't bother "to keep up with what's going on," the narrator observes: "What was 'going on,' in Garp's opinion, was never as important as what he was making up—what he was working on. One of the things that upset him about his mother (since she'd been adopted by women's politics) was that she was always discussing the *news*." Later in the same scene, when Jenny defends a radical feminist response to a highly publicized rape by insisting that "Rape is every woman's problem," the narrator adds: "Garp hated his mother's 'everyone' language most of all. A case, he thought, of carrying democracy to an idiotic extreme." The constitutive ·dichotomy of *The World According to Garp* appears here in several of its most characteristic forms. News is opposed to art, as politics is to selfhood, as contingency and capitulation are to control and dominance. Significantly, these same oppositions inform a late passage that is the reciprocal of this encounter between mother and son. Just before his death, Garp is "working on what he called his 'father book,' or 'the book of fathers,'" an enterprise that begins to restore him to himself and to the "writer's long-sought trance."

> Because he was inventing a father, Garp felt more in touch with the spirit of pure imagination that he felt had kindled [his first story] "The Pension Grillparzer." A long way from which he had been falsely led. He had been too impressed by what he now called the "mere accidents and casualties of daily life, and the understandable trauma resulting therefrom." He felt cocky again, as if he could make up anything.

The working title of Garp's unfinished novel, *My Father's Illusions,* is another of Irving's self-defensive satires, an acknowledgment of the realm of irony in which the hero's romantic ideal is thwarted. But the patriarchal vision is not dispelled by its identification as a fiction; on the contrary, it is rendered all the more supreme. Even the mother's disillusionment helps sanction the father's illusion as the supreme fiction of Garp's world, the one ideology in the novel that can sustain life. Jenny's early labors as a nurse of wrecked soldiers establish a world of threatened, disfigured and partial individuals. Her later experiences as an advocate and caretaker of wounded women pointedly suggest that the self is not fulfilled, compensated or reconceived by social or po-

litical union but only subjected—indeed, self-subjected—to more violence and mutilation. This is the proposition emblematized by the Ellen James Society, the novel's representative political organization, a group of women who have had their own tongues amputated as a gesture of solidarity with a raped eleven-year-old whose attackers cut off hers in order to protect themselves from her testimony. Against the silence of the Ellen Jamesians, Garp defines and defends his voice, his privacy and his art. The absolute centrality of this antithesis is confirmed by the two Ellen Jamesian attempts on Garp's life, the first of which proves suicidal for the assailant and the second fatal for Garp. Long before these events, however, the battle line is drawn in a way that is calculated to win more than the reader's (and not only the male reader's) allegiance to Garp but his acceptance of the terms of the battle. "Although he felt deeply disturbed by what had happened to Ellen James," the narrator explains, "[Garp] felt only disgust at her grown-up, sour imitators." Here, the issue is construed as a comparison between the innocence of a child and the manipulativeness of adults, between a genuine personal tragedy and its public imitation. As such, it is hardly a contest, and it becomes even less of one when Ellen James herself, having read *The World According to Bensenhaver* eight times, appears and seeks asylum in the home of T. S. Garp. Ellen, who wants to be a writer and who later publishes a book of poems, poignantly and asocially entitled *Speeches Delivered to Plants and Animals*, reports that "the Ellen Jamesians had only prolonged her anguish" and "made her into a very public casualty," an assertion that ratifies Garp's view of the group's action as "a shallow, wholly political imitation of a very private trauma." Again, the language is revealing in its insistence on a stark opposition between the political and the private, on the priority of the private and on the profane and superficial imitativeness of the political. Political 'wholeness,' the Ellen James Society seems to indicate, is achieved by the partialization of the self. This is clearly Garp's judgment, and the narrator's modification of Garp's attitude toward Ellen Jamesians does not so much contest as reinforce it. While it "was generally true that they were an inflammatory political group of 'feminist extremists,'" the narrator states (in a phrase whose curiously gratuitous 'political' bears an almost hysterical stress), there were "occasional individuals among the Ellen Jamesians" who were prompted not by "wholly political concerns" but by "a most personal identification."

Personal identification is the only acceptable social motive in *The World According to Garp.* Ironically, though, such a motive precludes the community and ultimately attenuates the individuality that it is meant to foster, instead reproducing (and helping to produce) a violative and alienating world. The character Roberta Muldoon, who personally identifies both with Garp and with the Ellen Jamesians, literally embodies this irony. An ex-Philadelphia Eagle tight end who becomes Jenny Fields' devotee and bodyguard after his sex change, the humane Roberta (born Robert) is easily regarded as the novel's true moral standard, the figure who reconciles politics and privacy, the female and the male. But Roberta augurs no social reconciliation; however appealing her character, she remains an oddity, "a tight end with tits," an inevitably parodic impersonation of the idea of harmony between the sexes. In fact, Roberta herself is neither freed from sexual confusion nor able, as a result of her complex experience, to accommodate sexual ambiguity. Instead, her operation double-locks her inside two fixed natures and dooms her alternately "to think like a woman *and* like a Philadelphia Eagle." Accordingly, she vacillates between tears and curses, between passive romantic victimization and crippling cross-body blocks. And it is this vacillation, this double status as victim and larger-than-life hero (she is six-four), that at last renders Roberta the strange figure of Garp's world—a world in which the self is at once trapped and unconditionally licensed, molested and paradoxically authorized by its inescapable molestation.

In *The World According to Garp,* the individual's cosmic helplessness and personal complexity converge to produce a self enjoined to indulgence and exempt from accountability. It is a situation that comprises a Puritanism without God, a world of apocalypse, characterological determinism and self-absorption with no measure of judgment and no prospect of redemption. Hence, the blamelessness of Garp and Helen for the driveway carnage or of anyone in Garp's world, including reader and narrator, for its excessive and indiscriminate brutality. Confronted with the sheer gratuitousness of the novel's central incident, for example, the reader can scarcely contest the logic of Helen's retrospective view: "in her later life, the whole business with Michael Milton would more often make her angry than it would make her sad—because she was strong enough to believe that she was a good woman, which she was, who'd been made to suffer disproportionately for a trivial indiscretion." But Helen's view, on examination, is disturbingly detached and constitutes a voyeuristic attitude toward her own life. It is this voyeurism and not her disproportionate suffering, moreover, that engenders the guiltless, solipsistic Helen of the preceding passage, an agent—like everyone else in the novel—of the authorial sensibility for which she has suffered.

That sensibility represents itself as quintessentially artistic. Throughout the novel, art is conceived as the haven of the personal and the original, a luxurious shelter from the "mere accidents and casualties of daily life." In defense of this conception, Helen repeatedly argues that "politics" and "crusades" are "the kind of thing people do who *can't* write," while Garp deplores the "destruction of art by sociology and psychoanalysis" and insists that "art and social responsibility [are] two distinct acts." These terms are by now familiar: the enemies of art are precisely the enemies of the personal, original, insular self. But, if the novel's images of

art and the self are analogous, its celebrations of the two share the same irony. Just as the individual's unequivocal authorization is a function of his general powerlessness, so art's use lies in what Garp calls its "basic uselessness." Since neither can escape or significantly affect the world (the world, that is, according to Garp), both art and the self find definition in the assumption of an attitude, a tone, of detachment. This is the tone of Garp's fiction and of Irving's, the writer's tone that Garp opposes to the one in which his mother discusses politics and the news. Yet this tone—in the voyeurism it manifests and elicits, and in its professional indiscriminateness, its cynical good nature, its comfortable fatalism and its disavowal of self-implication—bears a strong resemblance to that of a television newscast. Before and after *The World According to Bensenhaver,* a novel that is "largely looked upon as *news,*" Garp's texts and *The World According to Garp* itself offer a full line of news items: the rape story; the incompetent terrorist; the rescue story; the successful deviant; the natural disaster story; the sexual revolution; the animal story; the politician's public tears and lost election. And, although Garp continues to trumpet art's opposition to news, his response to the objection that his work is "X-rated soap opera" echoes the popular journalist's inevitable answer to charges of sensationalism and distortion: "Life is an X-rated soap opera."

The common denominator of Garp's seemingly contradictory claims that art provides an insular refuge from life and an accurate reflection of it is their antagonism toward interpretation. In both cases, art is unequivocal—it is purely what it is or simply what the world is. Garp's representations of his fiction always take one or the other of these forms. When "an associate professor of women's studies somewhere" examines *The World According to Bensenhaver,* for instance, Garp objects that "it's a *story,* and I made it up"; the fact that the review is favorable does not placate him: "'It's not *it* she liked,' Garp said. 'She liked something else.'" Garp's idea that interpretation violates a work's intrinsic identity, turns it into "something else," is more subtly advanced by the narrator, who offers the reader a sampling of the critical response to each of Garp's novels. Invariably, that response is contradictory, jargonistic and self-serving. Hence, *Second Wind of the Cuckold* is pronounced "alternately, 'brilliant' and 'dumb,'" hailed as bitterly truthful" and chided for not having "refined away" enough bitterness to allow "a purer truth" to emerge. "More nonsense was compiled concerning the novel's 'thesis,'" we are apprised, and the message is clear: interpretation is nonsense. The proliferation of meanings renders all meanings equal (or meaningless) and, as a narrative strategy, anticipates and neutralizes any criticism of Garp (or Irving). The reader, then, is freed to make any frivolous meaning he wants and freed of having to make a meaning at all (or of having to admit that he does). He, too, is a model of the self as the novel's conceives it—creatively (personally) authoritative or critically (politically) helpless or, alternately, both. He may replace the text or be replaced by it but he cannot be held responsible for it or hold it responsible to himself.

Thus Garp, Irving, and the reader surmount "the anxieties of secular time" by substituting "a comprehensive social-divine selfhood" for the experience of relationship on which interpretation, history and community depend. In ***The World According to Garp,*** we might say, character, reader and text are identical but effectively unrelated. Each is informed by what Walter Benn Michaels has described as a "nineteenth century scientist model" of autonomous identity, and Irving's feat lies in the ease with which he adapts that model to, and even bolsters it by, a chaotic and coercive contemporary world. The trick is performed by a radical polarization of Cartesian alternatives that can no longer stand independently in the modern world but may appear to hold each other up antithetically, alternatives that Michaels—citing Pierce's critique of Descartes—contests in an essay called "The Interpreter's Self":

> In rejecting the Cartesian goal of neutrality, [Pierce] rejects on the one hand a notion of the self free to assert its subjectivity without constraint and on the other hand a notion of the self wiped clean of prejudice and ready to accept determinate meaning. These two positions are simply the flip sides of the context-free self, active and passive; one generates any interpretation it pleases, the other denies that it interprets at all.

Irving's novel exemplifies the possible (perhaps the actual) consequences of "the Cartesian goal of neutrality" when the interpreter's text is the world. In it, the self is "free to assert its subjectivity without constraint" *because* it is objectively "wiped clean" of social power and obligation and "ready to accept [the world's] determinate meaning." By the generalization and multiple reproduction of this antithesis, the novel protects it against collapse, naturalizes it and renders it a seeming inevitability. The antithesis informs Irving's treatment of sex and violence, underlies his polarization of men and women and of "one" and "everyone," and explains, as it requires, his shrewd vacillation between ironic detachment from and "personal identification" with Garp. Detachment and identification, however, are "simply the flip sides" of the self's denial or failure of relation, just as they are versions of the interpreter's refusal or failure to engage in interpretation.

Irving's title deems his novel's world an interpretation and implies an interpretive role for the reader. ***The World According to Garp,*** however, is ideologically committed to a context-free self (or the dream of one), a self that is paradoxically both unconstrained and determined. This commitment necessitates, even comprises, an antipathy toward interpretation, for, as Julia Kristeva has noted, interpretation means mutual indebtedness. Heller's novel not only illustrates this etymological meaning, by its powerful implication of the reader in Slocum's antiphonal voice, but conveys its social as well as its hermeneutic force. What happens in *Something Happened* is that the false opposition that informs Garp's world and ours, the polarity of procreative authority (the novelist's, the self's, the reader's) and pre-scriptive fate (the world's, society's, the text's), is collapsed. The desperate opposition that appears to preserve an "original" and "always personal" identity in ***The World According to Garp*** is shown, in *Something Happened,* merely to conceal its loss; the picture of freedom painted by and in Garp is seen as a disguised portrait of bondage. . . .

Interpretation, selfhood and politics are bound by the fact that each offers an opportunity to assume, and a mode of assuming, responsibility without complete control. Michaels approaches this position when he rejects the alternatives of the unconstrained subject and the determinate object in "The Interpreter's Self," but he undermines it in a later essay, "Is There a Politics of Interpretation?" Michaels answers his title's question in the negative. Political action presumes "the primacy of choice," he writes; since we do not freely choose our interpretations (since we cannot choose, that is, to believe or disbelieve the interpretations of which we are convinced), they cannot properly be called political and "we are not morally responsible for [them]." The trouble with this argument is that it silently reconstructs the very model of the context-free self that "The Interpreter's Self" had dismantled and bases its notions of personal and political responsibility on that false model. In fact, as my readings of *Something Happened* and ***The World According to Garp*** have illustrated, a quite significant politics shapes and is shaped by our interpretation of selfhood. A very real politics, too. Indeed, one might describe Ronald Reagan's electoral rhetoric as that of "auto-American-biography." Fusing the nation and the individual in the first speech of his re-election campaign, the President announced that the 1984 election offered to both "the deepest, sharpest, most important choice in modern times—greater freedom or coercion. This sharp, clear antithesis of freedom and coercion, this "choice," depends upon the dream, the myth of the desocialized self. A more problematic, and more promising, synthesis of responsibility and interdependence still awaits that myth's repudiation.

Janice Doane and Devon Hodges (essay date 1986)

SOURCE: "Women and the World According to *Garp*," in *Gender Studies: New Directions in Feminist Criticism,* edited by Judith Spector, Bowling Green University Popular Press, 1986, pp. 60-9.

[In the following essay, Doane and Hodges examine the portrayal of strong female characters and feminist issues in The World According to Garp. *Providing a feminist analysis of the novel, Doane and Hodges assert that "*Garp *protects narrative conventions and with them reinforces patriarchal power."]*

Until recently, many feminist critics have defined the feminist novel on the basis of theme and character. One such critic, for example, writes that a novel "can serve the cause of liberation" and "earn feminist approval" if it performs "one or more of the following functions: 1) serves as a forum for women, 2) helps achieve cultural androgyny, 3) provides role models, 4) promotes sisterhood, 5) augments consciousness raising." The importance of focusing on the relation between gender and narrative structure, rather than on character, can be shown through an examination of a novel that seems to make feminism a central concern, John Irving's *The World According to Garp.*

The hero of that novel receives this rave review for one of his books: "The women's movement has at last exhibited a significant influence on a significant male writer." Irving's *Garp* begs for a similar review. It sympathetically discusses feminist issues such as rape, single motherhood, the aspirations of women for political power, domestic role reversal. In a gesture toward androgyny, it provides characters who prove the viability of transsexuality. Its major women characters are strong and capable. One of them, Garp's mother Jenny Fields, is a champion of feminists, who authors her life and insists upon directing her own destiny. The other, Garp's wife Helen, is an exemplar of intelligence and cool professionalism. She supports the family while Garp minds the children, cooks and cleans—an arrangement that satisfies them both.

Yet surely even a cursory feminist analysis of this novel would reveal a strong ambivalence about feminism. All of the strong female characters are uncomfortable with the label "feminist," although, in their words, they are "not anti-feminist!" The narrator tells the reader that Jenny "felt discomfort at the word *feminist.* She was not sure what it meant but the *word* reminded her of feminine hygiene and the Valentine treatment" (the torturous treatment for syphilis in males). In the text, *feminism* always designates a simplistic ideology and those who embrace the term are extremists. But the deeper evidence of ambivalence about feminism is built, as we shall show, into the novel's form. Despite *Garp*'s thematic performance of feminist criteria, the book ignores the fact that feminists formulate such criteria to challenge the male hegemony over writing and to end the silence of women. But though American feminists know that the male control of writing must be challenged, they rarely explicitly consider what *The World According to Garp* so self-consciously plays upon: the conventions of narrative and

writing. We propose to open a feminist discussion of male control over writing by revealing how *Garp* protects narrative conventions and with them reinforces patriarchal power.

At first it seems that *The World According to Garp* defends women's right to claim traditionally male prerogatives. The book begins with a description of Garp's mother, Jenny. Jenny competently defends herself against "male lust" and staunchly commits herself to single motherhood, thus undercutting the male's traditional rights over her body and his place as head of the family. She is neither a dutiful daughter nor anyone's wife and we are encouraged to admire her because of this. Furthermore, she recounts her rebellion against traditional sex roles in an autobiography that "bridges the usual gap between literary merit and popularity." The book, entitled *A Sexual Suspect,* is popular because it speaks for a multitude of women who soon become Jenny's followers. All this seems to suggest that women can have control over themselves and writing—but what is the status of Jenny's writing?

Although she is an influential writer, Jenny's book is "no literary jewel." Garp puts it more bluntly when he says that the book has "the literary merit of the *Sears Roebuck* catalog." His metaphor points out what he considers to be the book's main flaws: a mundane prose style and simple-minded organizational scheme. The only way that Jenny can bind her story together ("the way fog shrouds an uneven landscape," the narrator tells us) is with this opening sentence: "In this dirty-minded world, you are either somebody's wife or somebody's whore, or fast on the way of becoming one or the other." This sentence provides the book with a unity of tone—strident assertiveness—presumably appropriate to her thesis: the right of individual women to refuse their two traditional options. Garp's literary assessment of Jenny's style thus becomes an unspoken commentary on her thesis. We are led to believe that Jenny's literary prose style is evidence of a dogmatic and somewhat simple-minded view of the world. "Disharmonious," "rambling," "messy," Jenny's book is a testament to her failure to produce a truly coherent work that could capture the "complexity" of "human behavior." Unlike "art," *A Sexual Suspect* can only catalogue experience—it is "about me"—and render it in a literal-minded way.

Jenny is the central woman character in the novel, and *A Sexual Suspect* is the most powerful instance of women's writing. In order to limit the authority of this writing, the novel retains, in order to denounce, the idea of "literal writing." The notion that literal writing even exists rests upon the assumption that language is transparent so that words are able to represent accurately their referents—the world or the self. This assumption informs much literary criticism, including feminist literary criticism which valorizes women's writing that is somehow particularly close to life. Elizabeth

Janeway, for example, writes in the *Harvard Guide to Contemporary American Writing* that "If there is a woman's literature, it will derive from an area of experience, worthy of exploration which is known pretty exclusively to women and largely overlooked by men." She goes on to say that "authentic literature reflects actual life." Her second statement, less cautious than her first, binds her to a view of literature that Irving easily denounces in the name of "art," although, as we will show, his "art" also claims to represent the world. But it is in his interest to set up this false opposition to give his own writing a special value. Literature based solely on experience is proved to be shapeless and timebound through Jenny's book. Her messy story is timely but ephemeral: after Jenny's death, *The Sexual Suspect* is never printed again. Irving further critiques "literature that reflects actual life" by suggesting that the writer devoted to actual life cannot sustain the act of writing: having captured and depleted her subject matter—"me"—Jenny has no more to write.

In *The World According to Garp,* autobiographical writing is called the "worst" kind of writing. With this judgment, the most powerful form of women's writing in the novel is discredited. But to be fair, *Garp* does provide alternative forms of writing by "better" women writers, though these alternatives are withdrawn as soon as they are offered. One character, Alice, writes beautifully. She cares about language as a thing in itself, rather than as a mere tool for reflecting life, but she is unable to finish a single novel. Another, Ellen James, is a good poet. But her collection of poems, *Speeches Delivered to Animals and Flowers,* and her genre, the lyric poem, are made to seem peripheral in a novel whose very subject matter privileges the narrative rendering of complex human behavior.

The writing of the major male character, Garp, is set in opposition to the writing of all these women. It is imaginative rather than literal, beautifully written, complete and complex—in short, it makes Garp into what the narrator calls a "real writer." The opposition between male and female writing is set in sharpest relief at the beginning of the novel through the contrast of Jenny's writing with Garp's. Irving juxtaposes the ease with which Jenny steadily produces her 1,158 page life story with the difficulty with which T. S. Garp writes a short story that has very little to do with his own experience. While Jenny's story comes from memory, Garp's story, "The Pension Grillparzer," is drawn from an interior source that is privileged in the novel—imagination. "Imagination, Garp realized, came harder than memory."

Though serious reviewers "chide" Jenny for "her actual writing," her book becomes a "household product." Garp's story, on the other hand, "would first appear in a serious journal where nobody would read it." But even though he initially lacks an audience, Garp's is the more fecund mode of writing. "The Pension Grillparzer" is the first of several "serious stories" published in "a serious way" that culminate in a book, *The World According to Bensenhaver,* which wins him everything: it is both serious and popular. Still (because it is so "imaginative"), "The Pension Grillparzer" is considered his best work by everyone in the novel whose judgment seriously counts. This high evaluation of Garp's work, placed next to derogatory remarks about Jenny's book, is Irving's way of teaching us the importance of "imagination" in writing. And this lesson is repeated over and over in the novel.

All that is said about imaginative fiction in Garp invites the reader to admire rather than understand it. As in literal writing, language is transparent in the fictional world but its referent is different: literal writing reveals the "real world" whereas good fiction reveals "imagination." Claiming that a work that is "imaginative" is an important maneuver because distancing writing from the world elevates its status. The "imaginative" work is freed from the exigencies of history and thus enters the realm of eternal objects. Furthermore, the apparent autonomy of the imaginative work insures its "wholeness"—imaginative work is true to itself. This "inner truth" must be worshipped rather than articulated. Reviewers who use redemptive strategies of interpretation are the objects of Garp's scorn: he mutters about "The destruction of art by sociology and psychoanalysis." Immutable, whole, true, the work of art is "better" than the known and knowable world.

Yet for all of Garp's insistence on the separateness of the imaginative work, he also claims that it is "better" than literal-minded fiction because it is closer to the world. A leap of faith is required if we are to accept this paradox. Apparently the creation of an autonomous work requires such mastery and artistry that the work is assured of being mysteriously complex. And since life itself is mysterious and complex, the work is true to life. This logic bestows a godlike power on the author and helps us accept the *thesis* that art is a sacred ideal. For all his efforts to differentiate fictional and literal writing, the two forms converge: Garp insistently promotes a theory of writing that depends on his notion of "reality"—his writing, so we are encouraged to believe, is the "real" thing.

What is women's relationship to this valorized realm of writing? In the novel, women are destined to consume rather than produce "art." Garp, the incarnation of the active male imagination, is a "natural storyteller," while his audience consists of women, who like his wife Helen seem to be "natural" spectators for this writing. Jenny, a prolific "bad" writer, is simply awed by "real writing." Upon reading her son's first story, "Jenny marvelled at her son's imagination." She is not only awed, but silenced: she reads many books, but "she had nothing to say about them." Helen, too, is a voracious reader, but acknowledges she cannot write. Nevertheless, her fine critical intelligence allows her to appreciate fully works of imagination. In fact, all of the women readers—including Alice, the babysitter Cindy, and Mrs. Ralph—are cast into the role of born consumers and spectators, awed and seduced by the display of male authority.

Men, on the other hand, are active, productive readers and writers. Garp reads only to produce fiction and writes fiction to seduce women. When Garp's writing does not seduce women—be it Helen, Alice or Cindy—it still functions in a procreative way to increase his family. At the end of the novel, he attracts Ellen James by *The World According to Bensenhaver* and eventually adopts her. *The World According to Garp* clearly advocates, then, a familiar dichotomy between an active male principle and a passive female principle. This familiar sexual dichotomy, assumed by the novel to be a fact of nature, determines who will write and who will read. "Real" writing, in this novel, is intimately connected with the "active" male and his sexuality.

It is not only this particular novel, of course, that makes the claim that only men can produce "art." Men have long appropriated the power of writing by maintaining as natural and inevitable the metaphorical link between pen and penis, author and patriarch. In *Garp,* the thematic opposition between male and female writers serves this end. But finally it is the very structure of the novel itself, its narrative conventions, that most strongly defends the equation of author and patriarch. Several modern theorists have pointed out the ways in which the conventions of narrative, and particularly of the novel, give expression to and serve the interests of patriarchy. "The purpose of narrative," writes Dianne Sadoff, "including the narrative about purpose or vocation, is to seek the figure of the father, to write the paternal metaphor and to acquire paternal authority." This paternal authority is inscribed in narrative form through the structuring of a significant sequence of events that moves toward a conclusion which bestows both finality and integrity on the text. The conventions of the novel—sequence, finality, integrity—are therefore not neutral. "The novel," as Edward Said points out, "most explicitly realizes these conventions, gives them coherence and imaginative life by grounding them in a text whose beginning premise is paternal."

The story of Oedipus, which has become the patriarchal myth par excellence, is the paradigm for narrative structure. Without Oedipus, Roland Barthes tells us, story-telling is impossible:

> The death of the Father would deprive literature of many of its pleasures. If there is no longer a Father, why tell stories? Doesn't every narrative lead back to Oedipus? Isn't storytelling always a way of searching for one's origins, speaking one's conflicts with the Law, entering into the dialectic of tenderness and hatred? . . . As fiction, Oedipus was at least

good for something: to make good novels, to tell good stories.

The passage from ignorance to knowledge, the familiar trajectory of the realistic novel, re-enacts the Oedipal drama. But this passage of discovery, it is important to note, is specifically dependent upon the discovery of sexual difference. In the Oedipal drama, the son moves from the naive assumption that everyone has a penis to the discovery of women's lack. This discovery of castration and the anxiety it provokes propel him towards reconciliation with the Law of the Father, the Symbolic Order.

The plot of *The World According to Garp* perfectly re-enacts the classical trajectory of the traditional novel.
—Janice Doane and Devon Hodges

The plot of *The World According to Garp* perfectly re-enacts the classical trajectory of the traditional novel. It is the story of the life and development of a male writer, who, by learning his craft, which entails writing stories that become more and more obviously the Oedipal story (*My Father's Illusions* is his last novel), finally acquires patriarchal authority. But Garp also literally represents what the structure of this dream depends upon: the fear of castration and the corresponding insistence upon sexual differences defined by "castration" (or lack). This fear is represented when Helen bites off Michael Milton's penis; but more threatening to Garp is the graphic equation of castration and silence in the figures of the Ellen Jamesians—women who cut off their own tongues. Here women seem to choose what the Oedipal drama makes necessary: women are defined by silence and by a lack that is perceived as mutilation. The familiar trajectory of the novel, then, depends as much upon the drama of silencing and castrating (mutilating) the female as it does upon reconciling the son to the father. It is the demands of the novelistic structure itself which inscribe, not only male authority and female silence, but the violence done to women as well.

Irving not only relies on this structure but defends it in a way that Roland Barthes does not. Roland Barthes poses his questions about the death of the father and its consequences for narrative as part of a meditation on modern writing that both performs and subverts the conventions of traditional narrative. In some sense, *The World According to Garp* is also a meditation on the death of the father and its consequences for narrative and the male writer. Certainly because it is about the development of a writer, the book has occasion to perform and comment upon the conventions of narrative writing. *Garp* opens with the death of the father (Garp's), like nineteenth-century novels which often begin by presenting the reader with fatherless orphans. But unlike the nine-teenth-century novel, *Garp* connects the death of the father to the rise of woman, particularly the rise of the mother to power. In response to his shift of power, Garp, the hero-writer, becomes more and more adamant about protecting patriarchy, not only, as we have seen, by equating "real writing" with male writing, but also by protecting traditional narrative conventions.

One of Garp's early experiences demonstrates Irving's defensive response to challenges to traditional conventions. When the young Garp submits his first story for publication, it is rejected by one journal because the story "does nothing new with language or with form." Puzzled, Garp consults his teacher, Mr. Tinch, who taught him how to write by teaching him respect for "good old-fashioned grammar." But Mr. Tinch, who reeks of death and decay, is simply as puzzled as Garp. The rotting Mr. Tinch seems to embody Irving's awareness of the decay of "old-fashioned" standards and conventions; nonetheless, Irving valorizes Garp's adherence to them. When Garp's writing becomes more "successful," i.e., popular, the same journal requests one of his stories. Garp triumphantly shoots back a nasty rejection on the rejection slip he had received so many years ago: "I am still doing nothing new with language or with form. Thanks for asking me though." Success has vindicated Garp's inflexibility with form. Experimenting with narrative convention, we are meant to understand, is simply a fad. What really counts—to everybody—is success, which becomes a validation for the truth of traditional narrative form.

By adhering to conventions which meet expectations and insure our pleasure, a writer is likely to be successful. Unconventional writing sacrifices the pleasure of structuring meaning in familiar ways and by doing so, challenges the status of any particular meaning as absolute. Irving cannot acknowledge that conventions of writing create the impression of truth because that acknowledgement would threaten his belief in his truthfulness and his seriousness. For Irving, narrative structure is a natural way to achieve and reflect the truth. But narrative is not natural; Irving simply naturalizes an important narrative convention—the convention of narrative sequence, of the significant accumulation of events toward an inevitable "truth." Thus Irving's conventionalism, which parallels Garp's, becomes a way of defending his own seriousness and a success that accompanies his adherence to the familiar.

Garp achieves his success with a book entitled *The World According to Bensenhaver.* Both the book's title and its major concerns, of course, are meant to parallel **The World According to Garp.** The sequence of events in both books is generated by sexual violence: both depend upon erotic polarization and the violence that ensues from it to make things happen. In the beginning of *The World According to*

Bensenhaver Hope Standish is raped. **The World According to Garp** is powered by a first sentence that sets men and women in opposition: "Garp's mother, Jenny Fields, was arrested in Boston in 1942, for wounding a man in a movie theater." A simple plot summary demonstrates that the rest of the novel continues to rely on the war between the sexes: Jenny does not want to have anything to do with men. She writes a book in defense of this position. Her book attracts a group of feminist extremists, the Ellen Jamesians, to Jenny and Garp. These women have banded together to make the raped and mutilated eleven-year-old Ellen James a political cause, and in the end kill Garp. The battle of the sexes is reproduced within Garp's family where sexual tensions between Garp and Helen lead to a catastrophe in which Helen sexually mutilates a man and Garp kills one of his own children. In sum, sexual violence is what happens in the novel.

In each book, the sequence of events seems contrived to fulfill the popular demand for violence, but Irving works to extol the "seriousness" of his violent narrative by defending the seriousness of Garp's novel. Jillsey Sloper, in her defense of *The World According to Bensenhaver,* acts as Irving's mouthpiece. Jillsey Sloper is a reader who has an intuitive access to what makes a work popular as well as a feeling for the deeper truths of literature. She finds "sick" (i.e., violent) books compelling: "This book is so *sick.* You *know* somethin's gonna happen, but you can't imagine *what.*" But she dignifies this perversity by saying that "it feels so true"—the narrator comments later that Jillsey uses "true" in the "good way," not as in "real life." Here we have it again: Garp's writing is not like life and yet it is a perfect representation of it; as Jillsey explains, with "true" books one can say, "Yeah! That's just how damned people *behave* all the time!"

There are several "truths" being defended here. One is that Garp is a serious writer, who can capture the "truth" of human behavior. Another is that narrative sequence, what happens, is natural—there is a compelling human "instinct" to want to know what happens—and this narrative sequence is fully adequate to expressing human behavior. Finally, male power is necessary and inevitable, so sexual violence is as well. For their "truth," Irving and Garp depend upon the "naturalness" of an active male principle and a passive female principle, a polarization that is erotic, violent, hierarchical, and gives rise to women's victimization. Irving's narrator is clearly unhappy about this victimization and insists on decrying male violence in the form of rape. But it doesn't matter. Irving's explanation for rape, finally, is male lust, an extreme form of the active male principle. Rape, then, is another consequence of the facts of nature. And in the figure of the Ellen Jamesians, who cut off their own tongues in sympathy with Ellen James, Irving entertains the notion that the extreme of female "nature"—masochism—is also a cause of the victimization of women. This victimization in turn generates a "natural" sequence of events—a true narrative. Narrative is naturalized, is itself the truth.

Because in classical narrative it is so important to know "what happens," and to know the meaning of what happens, the conclusion is always privileged. "Truth, these (traditional) narratives tell us, is *at the end* of expectation." This truth is conventionally embodied in the hero's death—the moment when meaning is conferred upon his entire life, giving the narrative—normally the story of his life—coherence as well. "A novelist is a doctor who sees only terminal cases" is the way Garp chooses to formulate this convention. Having naturalized narrative sequence by naturalizing violence between the sexes, Irving makes seemingly inevitable the novel's conventional momentum toward death. Our hero, Garp, must die as a result of sexual violence, and his death confers meaning upon the novel.

If we were to pay attention only to the subject matter, it would seem as though Irving were proposing something like the following: feminism is exacerbating the battle between the sexes, and bringing more violence into society. The best-intentioned men are becoming weaker, are less emotionally capable of dealing with this violence. They are mutilated or killed—they cannot endure. The best of women are stronger. They deal with violence wisely and they will survive, just as Helen and Hope do. But when we see the importance of the form of narrative, that death is what confers meaning on the whole of the narrative, we can see how, in fact, Irving is saying that the survival of women is insignificant since men will endure in more important ways. Garp's death serves only to make his life more important. In death, Garp becomes the all-powerful father that he could never quite be in life.

The last chapter, "Life After Garp," tells how the surviving characters of the novel devote the rest of their lives to making Garp's life more important and meaningful by remembering it. Helen, Roberta, Duncan, Jenny, various biographers and critics, all join in a chorus dedicated to singing Garp's praises. Having apparently conceded the loss of the father in the beginning of his novel, Irving reminds us here that the father, in his death, simply becomes more important.

An analysis of traditional narrative conventions teaches us how the death of the father can make him larger than life. Paradoxically, patriarchy can be served by assaults on it, and this means that feminism can be made the obstacle of its own ends. In *Garp,* not only does the death of the father at the hands of a feminist extremist dignify the hero at the expense of feminist ideology, but Irving can also use the feminist issue of rape to entrench patriarchal power by making sexual violence seem "natural" and by using it to generate and naturalize narrative sequence. Irving easily writes a book that

meets thematic criteria for the "feminist" novel—he includes strong female characters who are attractive survivors—without ever jeopardizing the patriarchal power inscribed in traditional narrative conventions. So rather than concentrating on whether or not a work of fiction truthfully represents women—a critical focus which assumes that a transparent writing is possible—feminist critics should examine how writing creates the illusion of truth. In the novel, and in *The World According to Garp,* truth is structured in such a way as to guarantee paternal authority and to silence women no matter how much they seem to speak.

Wendy Steiner (review date 19 May 1989)

SOURCE: "The American Wholegrain," in *Times Literary Supplement,* May 19, 1989, p. 535.

[*In the following review, Steiner offers a generally unfavorable assessment of* A Prayer for Owen Meany.]

Suppose that your best friend accidentally killed your mother with a Little League baseball. Suppose he was a near-midget whose voice never changed and whose parents believed he was the product of a virgin birth. Suppose he saw himself as God's instrument, knew the date of his death from a vision of his gravestone that appeared during a production of *A Christmas Carol,* and died a hero exactly as a dream of his foretold. Would this be enough to cement your faith in Christianity? John Irving's latest blockbuster, *A Prayer for Owen Meany,* poses this question. Needless to say, the book puts more than a little strain on the reader's ability to keep a straight face.

A Prayer for Owen Meany is the story of John, the outcome of his mother's "little fling" on a trip to Boston. She dies before divulging his father's identity, and only the intrusion of Owen Meany's ghost reveals the truth, Owen, John's best friend, is an undersized genius too good for this world, John's family are New England gentry with Mayflower connections; Owen's are social and psychological cripples. With all his advantages, John turns out a cranky old bachelor; despite all his limitations, Owen emerges a spiritual Horatio Alger. He is the moral voice of his school and ultimately a Christ-figure—he once played baby Jesus in a Christmas pageant. John spends his mature years griping about Reagan from the safe distance of Canada; Owen sacrifices all to rescue some deracinated Vietnamese orphans.

One of Owen's other achievements is to have taught John how to write. He transforms John from an incompetent schoolboy into a successful English major, and it is Owen, presumably, whom we must thank for *A Prayer for Owen Meany.* But perhaps Owen died before he completed his instruction, for we still have to contend with writing seminar sentences such as "The ungainly boy lived for reaching the legal age for legal slaughter." With more training, John might have been confident that the reader would connect the various armless symbols in the book—a statue, a totem, a dressmaker's dummy, a stuffed armadillo, and finally Owen himself—and so might have spared us his well-meant summaries. Owen might also have done more to protect John's high-school students from the literary advice of their teacher. John recommends Timothy Findley's *Famous Last Words* as an example of a bold novelistic opening: a father shows his son a panoramic view of Boston and then leaps to his death; "imagine that. That ranks right up there with the opening chapter to *The Mayor of Casterbridge,* wherein Michael Henchard gets so drunk that he loses his wife and daughter in a *bet;* imagine that!"

Irving diagnoses America's ills as a matter of gender. He subtly names Owen's murderer "Dick", and enlists half the American literary canon in his support. Like William Carlos Williams in *Paterson* and *In the American Grain,* he equates women, the land and the Indians as the spontaneous, passionate victims of male aggression and insensitivity. As a womanly man, Owen is a version of the transsexual football player in **The World According to Garp;** an armless Indian totem and a statue of Mary Magdalene are his symbols. Irving echoes *The Great Gatsby* when he reads Marilyn Monroe's death as the desecration of the American land: "It's a beautiful, sexy, breathless country, and powerful men use it to treat themselves to a thrill." He even pilfers *The Scarlet Letter* to condemn puritanism and hypocrisy: John's mother's secret identity is "The Lady in Red," his unknown father turns out to be a doubting clergyman, and his cousin becomes a rock star called Hester the Molester.

Like all of Irving's novels, *A Prayer for Owen Meany* seems both more and less than one book. It cannot decide whether to be a folksy *Bildungsroman* set in New Hampshire, a full-scale Christian/Freudian allegory, or a commentary on American politics. The reminiscences of Owen and John's childhood are so long and so lacking in comic or psychological punch that one would be hard-pressed to tolerate them from a friend. From the unappealing first-person narrator they are unspeakably tedious. And since that narrator is quite obviously Irving's shadow, we might lay a certain self-indulgence at the author's door. But, most irritatingly, the tone of *A Prayer for Owen Meany* oscillates between 1960s ranting and a sentimentalized Proust; its 543 pages have all the subtlety of a wholegrain madeleine.

Robert Towers (review date 20 July 1989)

SOURCE: "The Raw and the Cooked," in *The New York Review of Books,* July 20, 1989, pp. 30-1.

[*In the following excerpt, Towers offers a tempered assessment of* A Prayer for Owen Meany.]

During the past decade in particular, the line separating fiction from autobiography has frequently seemed on the point of being almost erased. Novel after novel has appeared in which not only the background and chronology but also the major events of the first-person narrator's life closely parallel what is publicly known of the author's. The material is offered up uncooked, so to speak, without the subtlety and depth derived from imaginative transmuting of personal experience into fiction. The gains in journalistic immediacy are generally offset by the absence of the play of novelistic invention (a very different matter from autobiographical fibbing in the manner of Ford Madox Ford or Lillian Hellman).

Conversely, certain novels by writers of whom we know nothing except what is revealed on the dust jacket can have an autobiographical tone that at once distinguishes them from other realistically grounded stories in the first person that we unhesitatingly accept as fiction. One is not tempted to read *The Catcher in the Rye* as a largely factual account of an episode in J. D. Salinger's adolescence. . . .

By contrast, John Irving's seventh novel is unmistakably a work of the imagination, with a distinct, if cumbersome, shape of its own. *A Prayer for Owen Meany* calls to mind a great galleon slowly ploughing its way, with much tacking and detouring, along an intricately plotted course toward its destined port. Irving, who sees himself as a neo-Dickensian, has, like Tom Wolfe in *The Bonfire of the Vanities,* chosen a sprawling, nineteenth-century model, whose principle is one of incorporation rather than of exclusion, a model designed to appeal to a diversified, nonacademic (but not frivolous) audience—in short, to whatever is left of that once large readership of bourgeois fiction. To induce its readers to undertake a voyage lasting more than five hundred pages, such a work needs what the narrator of *A Prayer for Owen Meany* calls a "bold beginning"—a subject on which he "harangues" his students in a course in Canadian literature. The bold (not to say loaded) beginning of this novel goes as follows:

> I am doomed to remember a boy with a wrecked voice—not because of his voice, or because he was the smallest person I ever knew, or even because he was the instrument of my mother's death, but because he is the reason I believe in God: I am a Christian because of Owen Meany.

The narrator is not only doomed to remember but, like the Ancient Mariner, to tell, in often exhaustive detail, the complex story sketched in that opening sentence, and in the course of the telling he attaches a dozen or more subplots to the major events.

The narrator is Johnny Wheelwright, born to a well-to-do New Hampshire family with roots going back to the earliest Puritan settlements. As a child he lives with his warm, attractive mother and his austere grandmother in a fine old Federal house in the town of Gravesend, which, like its prototype Exeter, contains a famous boys' school. The odd thing about Johnny is his birth: he is illegitimate, the result of a "fling" which his otherwise respectable mother had with a man whom she met on the Boston & Maine Railway. Even after she marries, providing the boy with a kind and loving stepfather, she never tells her son who his real father is, and thus that old novelistic quest—the search for the father—becomes one of the more prominent subplots.

Johnny's best friend is a strange, intense child,

> who was *so* small that not only did his feet not touch the floor when he sat in his chair—his knees did not extend to the edge of his seat; therefore, his legs stuck out straight, like the legs of a doll. It was as if Owen Meany had been born without realistic joints.

Worse, the boy has a high-pitched voice that strikes people as both disturbing and uncanny. (Throughout the novel Owen's dialogue, as well as his writing, is set in capital letters—a device that becomes not only distracting but tiresome.) But this Dickensian grotesque has a formidable intelligence, physical adroitness, and an impressive moral authority that is bolstered by his ardent Christian belief. The son of a lower-middle-class granite quarrier, Owen has inexplicably rejected his family's Catholicism and become an Episcopalian. From a remarkably early age, he sees himself as God's instrument and develops a quasi-Calvinist view of his life as predestined.

The manifold action of *A Prayer for Owen Meany* lends itself no more easily to summary than that of *Bleak House,* but two main events convey some of the melodramatic and even gothic aspects of the book. In the last inning of a Little League baseball game, the eleven-year-old Owen is asked to take Johnny's turn at bat. He does so, hits the ball harder than he has ever hit it before, and the ball kills Johnny's mother, who has befriended the boy and whom he dearly loves.

At Christmas that same year Owen plays the part of the Christ Child in a Nativity pageant and the part of the Ghost of Christmas Yet to Come in a production of *A Christmas Carol.* His performance in a rehearsal in the latter role is electrifying, and terrifies the actor playing Scrooge.

> When Owen pointed [at Scrooge's grave], it was all of a sudden, a convulsive, twitchy movement—his small, white hand flashing out of the folds of the cloak, which he flapped. He could glide slowly, like a skater running out of momentum; but he could also *skitter* with a bat's repellent quickness.

On the night of the play's opening, Owen, guiding Scrooge, approaches closer than before to the papier-mâché gravestone, bends over it—and faints. He has had a vision of his own name on the gravestone, together with the date of his death some sixteen years in the future. The possible fulfillment of this vision, augmented later by a detailed dream of the circumstances of Owen's death, provides the main element of suspense for several hundred pages to come.

Giving and withholding, hinting and foreshadowing, Irving manipulates the elements of suspense as shamelessly as did his nineteenth-century master. As Dickens did, he flirts with the supernatural, especially in the form of precognition. Having aroused the reader's curiosity concerning the fate of the main characters, Irving can indulge in various sideshows and diversions. We learn a great deal about the history of Gravesend and its illustrious academy, which both Johnny and Owen attend. We are treated at great length to the narrator's opinions on Ronald Reagan and the contra scandal, the Vietnam War, American moral blindness, and contemporary Canadian literature. We are introduced to enough distinctively drawn characters to populate an entire village—among them the Congregational and Episcopalian ministers and their families, two headmasters of the Gravesend Academy, and assorted lesser masters, worthies and eccentrics and teen-agers of the town, Johnny's boisterous male cousins and their angry sister Hester, the entire depraved family of a soldier killed in Vietnam. . . .

But how interesting does John Irving make this material? Nowhere do we find the power, vision, or humor that would merit a comparison with Dickens. The Christian theme is obviously central to the novel, yet one is left in some doubt how it is to be taken. *A Prayer for Owen Meany* is steeped in the ritual and practice of mainline Protestantism, with frequent quotations of the familiar hymns and carols, and extended passages from Isaiah, the Gospels, and *The Book of Common Prayer.* Owen's identification with the life and passion of Jesus Christ is presented, without a hint of irony, as lying at the very core of his behavior. Yet what the novel conveys is a sense of religiosity, rather than religion, of the miraculous rather than the spiritual. It is hard to give imaginative credence to Owen's bizarre conviction without more to go on than the narrator's reporting of his words and actions, especially since the narrator himself does not inspire total confidence. Too often the Christian elements seem merely another aspect of the novel's sensationalism.

Admirers of *The World According to Garp* will, I think, find the new novel a lesser work—though it seems to me far stronger than either *The Hotel New Hampshire* or *The Ci-*

der House Rules. Although it requires what for many will seem an inordinate suspension of disbelief, the story of Owen and his fate has a lurid power, especially in the novel's final pages. Once he surrenders to the headlong rush of events, Irving shows himself a master of narrated action. But he is less successful in bringing his other major character, Johnny Wheelwright, to life in his own right, though nearly as much space is devoted to the narrator and his problems, sexual and otherwise, as to Owen. The fault seems to lie in the quality—at once overexplanatory and diffuse—of Johnny's voice and the consequent blurring of the outlines of his personality. A number of the other characters, including the rather important figure of the grandmother, fail to transcend convenient stereotypes. Although the culmination of the extended set piece centering upon the Christmas pageant and play rises to a scream of (melo)dramatic intensity, the preliminaries are exhaustingly protracted and—to me—boring. Yet, despite this and other too frequent *longueurs,* many readers will probably read on. The power of raw curiosity to keep things moving is not to be underestimated.

Edward C. Reilly (essay date 1991)

SOURCE: "Understanding John Irving," in *Understanding John Irving,* University of South Carolina Press, 1991, pp. 1-13.

[*In the following excerpt, Reilly provides an overview of the settings, characters, themes, and literary techniques employed in Irving's fiction.*]

Except for *Setting Free the Bears,* his only novel with European settings and characters, John Irving's novels take place in twentieth-century United States, especially Maine and New Hampshire. Irving analyzes contemporary problems and issues plaguing his characters' lives. In addition, random violence and sudden death stalk his fictional worlds, a concept that has its inceptions in *Setting Free the Bears.*

Set primarily in Vienna, Austria, *Bears* traces Vienna's history from before the *Anschluss* (Austria's "union" with Nazi Germany in 1938) to after World War II. While admitting that *Bears* contains a "large" researched "historical center"—"the Yugoslavian resistance in World War II, the Russian occupation of Vienna . . . the Nazi *Anschluss* of Austria in '38"—Irving claims that his succeeding novels do not have researched material as a "central part of them. In the novel imagination wins out over research." For Irving, however, the violence, terror, and murders that preceded and followed the *Anschluss* not only established the precedent for World War II's brutal, chaotic fury, but also for the violence and bizarre deaths lurking in the postmodern world.

Vienna also becomes a secondary but important setting in *The Water-Method Man, The 158-Pound Marriage, The World According to Garp,* and *The Hotel New Hampshire,* novels in which his American characters, especially children, travel to Vienna as part of their maturing processes and the novels' bildungsroman motifs. Irving says, for example, "Growing up in a foreign country, you leave home in that sense. . . . And I attempt in writing . . . to use the experience of someone else's history, another country's history even, to make somebody painfully aware of his own meager grip on his or her surroundings." Although Irving lived in Vienna during 1963 and 1964 and he and his family later lived in Vienna from 1969 to 1972, he emphasizes that Vienna is a "fairyland, really, more than a real place . . . a license to dream. And when I get there—when my characters journey there, or when they start there, or when they end up there— it's a place simply where 'something else' can happen." His characters who experience Vienna, however, learn from its history so that they may better understand those forces shaping their lives, or as the narrator says about Garp's return to Vienna with his family, "The streets, the buildings, even the paintings in the museums, were like his old teachers, grown older."

Although alluding to Wally Worthington's experiences in Burma when his plane is shot down during World War II, *The Cider House Rules* is the only novel in which the characters make no trips to a foreign country. In *A Prayer for Owen Meany,* Irving introduces another secondary but significant setting, Toronto, Canada, where Johnny Wheelwright reflects on the forces, especially the Vietnam War, that changed his and his friends' lives. While Vienna plays a violent role in twentieth-century history, Toronto is a tranquil no-man's-land; however, just as Vienna is the catalyst by which Irving assesses World War II's effects on his characters and their world, Toronto provides the basis for analyzing the Vietnam War's effects on the characters and the United States.

Whether in Vienna, Toronto, or the United States, Irving's settings underscore the violence and death that he sees at the core of life. Yet, in refuting critics who fault his plots for excessive violence, Irving asserts: "How could anyone who reads the newspaper think it excessive? I think events in American social and political life have borne me out. There have been more assassinations than exist in the novel, certainly more radical and terrorist groups. Perhaps I can be accused of having too sweet a disposition or being too optimistic, but not too violent or excessive." Although the violence and death within his plots may emphasize "how perilous and fragile our lives can be," Irving maintains that his literary vision is affirmative, a point emphasized in his wry comment about *Garp:* "I've written a life-affirming novel in which everybody dies." "There are no happy endings," Irving says, but "that's no cause for some blanket cynicism or sophomoric despair. That's just a strong incentive to live purposefully, to be determined about living well." This maxim often governs his characters' lives, especially the Berry family in *Hotel New Hampshire.*

Irving praises Charles Dickens, John Cheever, and Kurt Vonnegut, who all write about their characters with "grace and affection." Grace and affection certainly apply to the way Irving writes about his characters. Critics label Irving's characters zany, wacky, or eccentric, yet in their determination to live well and purposefully, their fears, follies, vanities, and virtues are recognizably human. While admitting that he did not especially admire Siggy or Hannes in *Bears,* Bogus Trumper in *Water-Method Man,* or the narrator in *158-Pound Marriage,* Irving "admired and cared for" the *Garp* characters, an admiration certainly extending to his succeeding characters.

In developing his characters, Irving subjects them to extreme situations—"sexual situations or violent ones or whatever"—to bring out the "best and the worst aspects of ourselves . . . the things we admire or despise about people":

> Basically I always try to place my characters under the most and least favorable circumstances to see how they will react, to test them. In *Garp* this strategy was very self-conscious: I wanted to create characters whom I greatly admired and then bless them with incredibly good fortune in the first half of the novel. . . . But in the second half of the novel, I visit all the worst kinds of extreme things on these people to see how they would deal with extremes of adversity, just as earlier they had to cope with success.

This emotional-extremes technique is most effective in Irving's bildungsroman motifs as children like T. S. Garp, the Berrys, Homer Wells, Johnny Wheelwright, and Owen Meany learn and mature from their experiences with life's extremes. For example, his child characters usually lose either one or both parents. Siggy Javotnik's father, Utch's parents, and Garp's father are World War II victims; the Berrys' mother dies in a plane crash; Homer Wells never knew his father or mother; and a foul ball kills Wheelwright's mother. The bildungsroman motif not only develops these characters' rites-of-passage but also complements the novels' actions, settings, and themes—for example, Garp and the Berrys travel to Vienna to learn more about life, death, love, and happiness.

How his characters live happy, meaningful lives varies from novel to novel, but the bases for their happiness remain constant: accepting responsibility; appreciating life's beauties and gifts; refusing to be intimidated by life's nebulous forces; and especially loving friends and family. The family unit,

in fact, becomes the "defense against the abyss" of the contemporary world, and Irving says he "could not state a better or broader opinion of family life" than in *Garp.* Moreover, in refuting critics who fault him for the bizarre forces plaguing his fictional families, Irving retorts:

> But let's take a simple family of four. Those two children will have, say, two children, making eight people. Is it claiming too much that out of the eight, someone is going to hit the wall? In a car crash, a plane crash, a wipeout, a premature tragedy, of course, it will happen! Someone is going off the deep end. They may not jump out a window, they may take drugs until they are useless, but certainly one of those eight isn't going to make it.

To complement the plot twists that carry his characters from fortune to misfortune, Irving juxtaposes the tragic with the comic. The tragic-comic extremes also drive his characters to the edge and determine their worth or worthlessness. Regarding life, Irving declares: "When people are happy—when we're in love, when we have orgasms of one kind or another, when we're proud of our children or high on ourselves—it strikes me that we are happy indeed. And who can say the world isn't comic, especially at those times? But we have pain too. Quite simply, the pain wins." As the narrator in *Garp* says, "an evening could be hilarious and the next morning murderous."

> **To complement the plot twists that carry his characters from fortune to misfortune, Irving juxtaposes the tragic with the comic. The tragic-comic extremes also drive his characters to the edge and determine their worth or worthlessness.**
> **—Edward C. Reilly**

Despite the pain and tragedy, Irving's novels end affirmatively because his characters have meaningful, happy lives. Indeed, Irving's affirmative vision is evident in some of his concluding chapter titles: "Congratulations to All You Survivors" (*Bears*); "The Old Friends Assemble For Throgsgafen Day" (*Water-Method Man*); "Life After Garp" (*Garp*). His other novels conclude with affirmative images and sentences: "You've got to get obsessed and stay obsessed. You have to keep passing the open windows" (*Hotel New Hampshire*); "there was no fault to be found in the hearts of either Dr. Stone or Dr. Larch who were—if there ever were—Princes of Maine, Kings of New England" (*Cider House*); "they were the forces we didn't have the faith to feel, they were the forces we failed to believe in. . . . Oh God, please give him back" (*Owen Meany*).

Among Irving's other literary techniques are refrains that Irving defines as those "little litanies . . . that serve to mark how far you've come, and also forewarn you about where you're going. . . . In *The Hotel New Hampshire* there are several refrains: Sorrow floats, keep passing the open windows, everything as a fairy tale." Other such verbal refrains would include the "gale of the world" (*Bears*); the "whole thing" (*158-Pound Marriage*); the "rules" and "wait and see" (*Cider House*); the "voice" and the "dream" (*Owen Meany*). Refrains also comprise actions—riding motorcycles (*Bears*); writing a dissertation (*Water-Method Man*); weight lifting (*Hotel New Hampshire*); reading from *David Copperfield, Great Expectations,* and *Jane Eyre* (*Cider House*); or slam-dunking basketballs (*Owen Meany*). Although critics often interpret these refrains as needless repetition, they form the plot threads that augment settings, characterizations, conflicts, and themes; they also illuminate Irving's intricate plotting techniques.

In addition to refrains, Irving's metaphors highlight the novels' themes. While World War II, a clogged urinary tract, writing, and cities may be metaphors, Irving's sport metaphors typify their functions: "To use one of my wrestling metaphors," says Irving, "if you're going to prepare yourself mentally and physically for a tough match on the weekend, the best way to do it is to get the shit kicked out of you by one of your teammates on Tuesday or Wednesday. If you work with something that is brutal and demanding, day-by-day, you'll be better equipped to deal with the real traumas later on." In this sense, wrestling prepares Garp for his writing career; weight lifting gives John Berry the strength to protect his family by squeezing the life out of Arbeiter, a German terrorist; and slam-dunking basketballs enables Meany to consummate his life's quest. Moreover, because of the grueling discipline required for both sports, Garp and John Berry can deal with the personal traumas haunting their lives, and Meany can accept his ultimate fate.

Symbols also underscore the novels' meanings, and Irving believes that symbols should always be clear: "There's not much point in symbols if people don't understand them. If you're going to be symbolic, you'd better let people know you are." Irving's symbols range from wrestling rooms, hotels, a foul ball, an armadillo, bears, to the Under Toad and the Berrys' Labrador retriever, Sorrow. The Under Toad and Sorrow symbolize life's overwhelming forces—e.g., terror, violence, and death. In contrast, in *Bears* and *Hotel New Hampshire* bears suggest the characters' bearish tenacity to survive when confronting those forces. As do refrains, Irving's symbols acquire depth and meaning as the plots develop and thus highlight his intricate plotting techniques.

Irving's are action-filled, expansive novels, facts attributable to his appreciation of and love for nineteenth-century fiction. In addition to Turgenev, Tolstoi, and Dostoevsky, he admires Thomas Hardy and especially Charles Dickens, whom he still reads for pleasure. "I was raised," says Irving, "on European novels, particularly British nineteenth century; I like character and storytelling; I like plot." Irving also appreciates Joseph Conrad, Virginia Woolf, and John Hawkes. Irving even refers to his works as "big novels" since they trace "somebody's life in its *entirety* . . . I mean to move characters through time, so we can see how they've changed—in their lives and by their lives. I think the novel that interests me now is a novel that shows us how people *end up*. I feel I am programmed to write big novels, or at least long ones."

Because he admired the nineteenth-century novels, especially Dickens, Irving is fond of epilogues. "I begin with an ending, or an idea of an ending. I begin with a sense of an epilogue, and in that way there is at least an objective ahead of you." While his epilogues recount events and lives after the novel's official close—e.g., the "Life After Garp" section—Irving's epilogues are necessary for his "big novels": "I knew a novel that did not convey the passage and perspective of time did not interest me. I wanted to write about the passing of and perspective of time and the softening of pain. An epilogue inevitably has nostalgia in it—it's a way of saying, 'It's not so bad what happened to that little child.' No one has a 'happy ending.' 'Ending' is by definition not a happy occurrence."

Irving's novels may be about prep school life, writers' lives, wrestling, Vienna, and Toronto, all experiences common to Irving's life, but he adamantly claims that his novels are not solely autobiographical, "I honestly don't think I could have eked out even one novel from the experiences in my own life." He does concede, however, that while he may use autobiography as a "stepping-off point in fiction . . . something to use up and get over," translating these experiences into fiction comprises the art. "I don't even feel obligated in my fiction to tell the truth. The truth of what's happened to me is mostly irrelevant to what I write about."

Because he focuses on contemporary issues that include homosexuality, transvestism, mate-swapping, equal rights, radical extremism, incest, rape, abortion, and violence, some critics label Irving a "trendy" or "popular" writer; because of his probing insights into and analyses of these issues, other critics label him a "serious" writer. Although in conceding that he writes sentences and paragraphs that keep the reader interested, Irving claims that these "openly seductive" elements are not aspects of "commercialism but part of the writer's responsibility":

> Art has an aesthetic responsibility to be entertaining. The writer's responsibility is to take the hard stuff and make it as accessible as the stuff can be made. Art and entertainment aren't contradictions.

It's only been in the last decade, or last twenty years, that there has somehow developed this rubric under which art is expected to be difficult. . . . By creating a taste for literature that needs interpretation, we, of course, create jobs for reviewers, for critics, for the academy. I like books that can be read without those middlemen.

While Irving's subject matter may be the "stuff" of popular fiction, his analyses of and insights into these contemporary problems are the "stuff" of serious fiction. R. Z. Sheppard establishes Irving's place in contemporary American fiction: "In the 50s J. D. Salinger produced *Catcher in the Rye*, the *Huckleberry Finn* of the Silent Generation. Readers in the 60s and early 70s rallied around Kurt Vonnegut's *Cat's Cradle* with its 'karass,' and the casually philosophical 'so it goes' from *Slaughterhouse Five*. The end of the decade belongs to Irving and Garpomania." **The World According to Garp** provided Irving the critical accolades he deserved, and **The Hotel New Hampshire, The Cider House Rules,** and **A Prayer for Owen Meany** have further enhanced John Irving's critical reputation as an "accessible" serious writer.

Kim McKay (essay date Winter 1992)

SOURCE: "Double Discourses in John Irving's *The World According to Garp*," in *Twentieth Century Literature*, Vol. 38, No. 4, Winter, 1992, pp. 457-75.

[*In the following essay, McKay examines the dual narrative voice of Garp as both biographer and fiction writer. According to McKay, "the narrator's struggle with the languages of fiction and biography is the mirror image of Garp's struggle as a writer with the forces of memory and imagination."*]

In **The World According to Garp** John Irving forms a type of dialogue within the narration by creating a narrator who uses a double discourse: that of the biographer and that of the fiction writer. It is not unusual in the *Bildungsroman* genre, to which this novel most certainly belongs, for the narrator to adopt the role of biographer to a certain extent. *Bildungsroman* narrators do not generally, however, adopt that stance as explicitly as Irving's narrator does. As Michael Priestly notes, the narrator "is intended to be Garp's official biographer." Using evidence from secondary sources, paying particular attention to the incidents in Garp's life that appear in his fiction, and evaluating Garp's writing and artistic philosophy, the narrator often adopts an academic language—that of literary biography. The text he creates is one suitable for fictive future students of Garp's work, who also want to be informed about his life. As presented in this language, Garp is not a character created but a historical fig-

ure for study. When he does treat Garp as a character, however, the narrator adopts the language of fiction. Calling attention to his omniscient power over the text, the narrator manipulates the sequence of events, spins metaphors, creates a persona, adopts comic and satiric attitudes, and uses the present tense—the techniques of the fabricator.

Using both the language of biography and that of fiction, the narrator's discourse reflects an important conflict that develops in Garp as artist, that of memory versus imagination. In his youth Garp's imagination seems to be easily accessible to him. But as he develops in this *Kunstlerroman*, he relies more and more on memory, although he fights that reliance. As Gabriel Miller writes, "one problem he [Garp] must contend with during the novel is an inability to separate his own personal life from his fiction." During his stay in Vienna as a young man, Garp creates a wonderful short story from only a few details from his experience. But he knows, even this early in his career, that "Imagination . . . came harder than memory" because he has watched his mother Jenny Fields at the typewriter. In the time that she writes her entire autobiography, Garp manages only one rather lengthy short story. Always conscious of the lesson learned from reading Marcus Aurelius, that the difference between good and bad writers is not subject matter but "intelligence and grace," Garp chooses a subject quite separate from his experience for his first novel. Ironically, he later feels that his novel, *Procrastination,* suffered from being too distant from his life. No amount of intelligence and grace could overcome the lack of first-hand knowledge of Vienna during the Russian occupation. In his next novel, *Second Wind of the Cuckold,* Garp attempts to weld biography and fiction by simply altering the events of his life, but he produces a work of questionable literary value. His short story "Vigilance" is almost literally autobiography, and the result is a comic but "small" story. In his third novel, *The World According to Bensenhaver,* Garp uses autobiographical material, but, by narrating through the consciousness of a character unlike himself, he manages to apply imagination and to create rather than simply record. Finally he rediscovers the balance between memory and art. In the novel he is writing when he dies, *My Father's Illusions,* Garp has the same imaginative control of experience that he achieved in his first piece of fiction. His growth as a writer, then, encompasses his regaining as an adult the aesthetic perspective that he had as a young man.

Just as Garp is drawn toward the language of memory, the narrator is influenced by the language of fiction, the art form of his *Kunstlerroman* hero. When the narrator commences the text he seems sure of his biographical approach, but soon he becomes seduced by the fiction writer's freedom with his material, as well as by Garp's life and art, and his discourse begins to reflect techniques borrowed from the fabricator's craft. Conversely, Garp begins his career determined to use only imagination, but soon he becomes seduced by the ease of recording his life, the narrator's ostensible task. His discourse begins to reflect techniques borrowed from the biographer's craft. In this way the narrator's struggle with the languages of fiction and biography is the mirror image of Garp's struggle as a writer with the forces of memory and imagination. This double tension creates a kind of dialogue in the narration, a trait indicative of Irving's earlier novels as well.

In his first two novels and, to a lesser extent, in his third novel Irving experimented with the kind of layered narrative voices and incorporated genres that provide the complex dialogue in *Garp.* Indeed, in *Setting Free the Bears,* his first novel, Irving relies on three voices, each of which raises a question about the division between biography and fiction. Although Hannes Graf is Irving's central narrator in *Bears,* his voice controls only parts one and three. In part two Hannes transcribes, apparently word for word, Siegfried Javotnik's notebooks, much as the narrator in *Garp* presents Garp's fiction. Once the text is turned over to Siggy in part two, though, it picks up not one but two voices. One voice is Siggy's as he records his watches while planning the zoo break; these records make clear that Graf is Siggy's intended audience. The second is Siggy's as historian and autobiographer; the audience in these segments is the more general, unknown audience of any text whose writer hopes, as Siggy seems to have hoped, that it will be published. Although Siggy credits his source for the biographical events that occur prior to his ability to remember them, "At least Ernst Watzek-Trummer claims so, and I take my history from him," the dialogue he quotes extensively surely comes from his imagination. In other words, he, not unlike Garp in Irving's fourth novel, creates fiction from his life. Siggy is not, however, the only writer in this text who feels free to adapt biography by employing fictional techniques; as we learn in part three, Hannes has altered his sources for part two by choosing and reshaping, as the fiction writer does: "Of course, there's more to the notebook than that. And, of course, the zoo watches and the autobiography don't appear together in the original; it was my idea to interleaf them."

In his second novel, *The Water-Method Man,* Irving continues to weave a novelistic whole from various voices. The pattern of the first five chapters exemplifies the narrative structure: chapter one uses the first-person narration of Fred Bogus, chapter two uses a third-person narration, chapter three uses no narrator per se, for it consists of a letter, chapter four uses Bogus as narrator again, and chapter five returns to the third-person narrator. Irving does, however, break from the neat arrangement of one narrator per chapter and mix the controlling voices within chapters, as he does in chapter ten. Within the third-person narration, in a manner perfected by Irving's narrator in *Garp,* the narrator shows his proximity to the central character when he presents the

character's language as his own, as he does through his use of exclamation marks and his lack of quotation marks in the second sentence that follows: "Trumper listened to Colm's sweet breathing. How fragile children's faces are in sleep!" Parallel to the narrative style of *Garp* in another way, this novel incorporates parts of a film script as well as reviews of the completed film, letters, lines and explication of the Norse poem "Akthelt and Gunnel," and a chapter from the novel *Vital Telegrams.* In addition, Irving explores the effects of the present tense in a text that is predominantly in past tense, as he does in chapter eleven when Bogus shifts from past to present and back to past without a page break or any other cue. In *The Water-Method Man,* then, Irving's multi-layered narrative suggests the fractured mind and spirit of his central character, a method of storytelling Irving returns to with great success in *Garp.*

Irving abandons the plural voices he established in the first two novels in his third one, *The 158-Pound Marriage,* and chooses a single first-person narrator who is a historical-novelist, a choice that seems to refuse the tension Irving has established between the two sides of that hyphen. Speaking of this novel, Harter and Thompson claim that Irving fails to "create a multidimensional narrative persona who can embody an artistically integrated human experience, an experience that should be revealed through its narration." Certainly *The 158-Pound Marriage* is Irving's weakest novel to date, due in large part to its narrative limitations. Yet in its uneasy blend of history and fiction we can see Irving struggling with a theme and a style that remain key to his work. For example, when the anonymous narrator adopts his friend Severin's point of view, complete with extensive dialogue in a scene from which the narrator was most surely absent (chapter 8), he is practicing his trade, coaxing fiction from second-hand information, as both Garp and the narrator in *Garp* do.

In regard to Irving's interest in narrative voices and the conflict between life and art, biography and fiction, the first novels represent crucial experiments in form and theme. Not until *Garp,* however, does Irving shape a text that codifies voice and theme so effectively. In an analysis of the narration of *Garp* the theory of Susan Lanser is most helpful. As Lanser suggests, a study of the phraseological and psychological stances of a narrator reveals the ways in which he or she is affected by the textual world. "Phraseological stance" refers to the "languages" in the text. This stance reflects a range of discourse styles from diegetic to mimetic, in which pure diegetic discourse is the narrator's own language and mimetic discourses are written records he or she provides for the reader. A midway point is a character's indirect tagged discourse. As Lanser notes, the range between diegetic and mimetic indicates "not only phraseological form, but also the degree to which the narrator is involved in a given segment of discourse." Psychological stance is a measure of the narrator's distance from or affinity with a character or event. It refers not only to the quantity of information given about a particular character or event but also to the kind of information given—subjective or objective. Subjective information reveals the perceiver's ideology while objective information does not. Psychological stance further incorporates "how" a character is seen, whether the vision is internal or external. In addition, the depth of the vision, whether the perceiver supplies only what can be seen and heard or also supplies the thoughts of the character, might be considered. Through these indications one can determine the degree to which the narrator approves or disapproves of the character.

The secondary sources Irving's narrator uses in **Garp** correspond to the most mimetic manner of expression in Lanser's description of the phraseological stance—journals and written records. The narrator's adoption of Garp's fiction style also reveals his phraseological stance, for this is a language borrowed from the character; therefore it is a kind of hybridization. But the narrator's reproduction of large parts of Garp's fiction and his interest in the events in Garp's life that influenced his fiction are indications of the narrator's psychological stance. In addition, the depth of the narrator's "subjective information" about Garp reveals his affinity with Garp—a further measure of his psychological stance.

The first sentence of the novel establishes the narrator as researcher and the text as "fictionalized history," in its attention to detail, date, and place: "Garp's mother, Jenny Fields, was arrested in Boston in 1942 for wounding a man in a movie theatre." The speaker assumes that we know the Garp spoken of, and that, indeed, we are reading this book because its title announces Garp as its subject. The first sentence also suggests that the narrator feels no need to write "T. S. Garp," for in the tradition of literary criticism and biography one often refers to well-known writers by their last names. As he proceeds, the narrator continues in the biographical format when he quotes from various written records. Mikhail Bakhtin calls such external documents "incorporated genres": "All these genres, as they enter the novel, bring into it their own languages, and therefore stratify the linguistic unity of the novel and further intensify its speech diversity in fresh ways." These genres are mimetic elements from the phraseological stance, in Lanser's terminology. But the prominence the narrator assigns to them in his text reveals his psychological stance—his admiration and respect for the artist. In the narrator's biography these genres are sources of information about the life he portrays. (In Irving's novel they serve a similar purpose, though a fabricated one: they introduce a voice apart from the narrator's and a language separate from the narration.) One finds quotations from Garp's journals and personal papers, Jenny Fields's published autobiography, Garp's fiction, and his critical reviews, all of which stratify

the novel while for the most part they suggest the narrator's role as biographer.

In the first two chapters the narrator provides twenty-six quotations of Garp's words from an unknown source. One finds such references throughout the novel (except for chapters 6 and 10-15), but not to the extent that one finds them in the beginning, when the narrator initiates his role as biographer by providing evidence of his research. Seemingly taken from Garp's journal, although we never hear of his writing one, the first quotations are autobiographical in content. They provide evidence to support the narrator's recounting of Jenny Fields's early years: "'My mother,' Garp wrote, 'was a lone wolf'"; "'My mother,' Garp wrote, 'was not one for making fine distinctions'"; and "'My mother,' Garp wrote, 'went through her life on the lookout for purse-snatchers and snatch-snatchers.'" At times the narrator uses his storehouse of biographical material to form a larger part of his narration. For example, the narrator quotes Garp's explanation of what a ball turret gunner is after he establishes the fact that "Garp's father was a ball turret gunner." Generally, however, the narrator selects only one or two sentences from the famous writer's papers and marks the quotation with the narrative tag "Garp wrote."

Quotations from Jenny Fields's autobiography work in a similar fashion, but the source for this information is clearly Jenny's autobiography, *A Sexual Suspect*. As biographer, Irving's narrator uses these quotations to provide evidence of the influence Garp's mother had upon him. The narrator records Jenny's famous words: "I wanted a job and I wanted to live alone. That made me a sexual suspect. Then I wanted a baby, but I didn't want to share my body or my life to have one. That made me a sexual suspect, too." Jenny manages to conceive without sharing her body. And Garp's *Bildung* is clearly shaped by the manner of his conception. His ideology is also influenced by this strong woman's very certain ideas about the rights of the individual and those of women in particular. The narrator quotes her on the subject of Garp's father:

> "Of course I *felt* something when he died," Jenny Fields wrote in her famous autobiography. "But the best of him was inside me. That was the best thing for both of us, the only way he could go on living, the only way I wanted to have a child. That the rest of the world finds this an immoral act only shows me that the rest of the world doesn't respect the rights of an individual."

The most important texts for the biographer, however, are T. S. Garp's novels and stories. A particularly generous biographer, this narrator goes beyond the usual reproduction of passages from the writer's work and reprints for us in full Garp's first notable piece of fiction, the short story "The Pension Grillparzer." Like an academic biographer, the narrator does not discuss the work so much as he describes the period of Garp's life from which it comes. For this purpose the narrator tells us that "In his time spent in pensions, Garp discovered that a water closet was a tiny room with nothing but a toilet in it. . . . The W. C., of course, would also feature prominently in Garp's story." In addition, the narrator explores the evolution of the story:

> He saw a four-member circus unload from Hungary, or Yugoslavia, at a railroad station. He tried to imagine *them* in his story. There had been a bear who rode a motorcycle, around and around a parking lot. A small crowd gathered and a man who walked on his hands collected money for the bear's performance in a pot balanced on the soles of his feet; he fell, occasionally, but so did the bear.

Because that description precedes Garp's short story in the text, the narrator has prepared us for the parallels between the events in Garp's life and his first work of fiction. He further explores the story's creation when he describes Garp's visit to the writer's room in the museum that Jenny has directed him to: "The writer . . . was named Franz Grillparzer; Garp had never heard of him." Soon we learn that Garp has made progress with his story and has decided to incorporate a bad circus and a pension named Grillparzer. And, guiding us through the young writer's development, the narrator as biographer divides the story into two parts in his own text: the first part Garp wrote before he understood the meaning of death, but the second part follows the death of Charlotte, the whore Garp came to love.

Conversely, we receive only the narrator's summaries, not excerpts, of Garp's first and second novels. The first, entitled *Procrastination,* is called "'historical.' It is set in the Vienna of the war years, 1938-45, and through the period of the Russian occupation." The narrator summarizes the novel for us, records the various reviews it received, and comments on the book's impact: "It was, of course, never a popular book, and it hardly made T. S. Garp into a brand name; it would not make him 'the household product'—as he called her—that his mother had become." Although Garp avoids the autobiographical in his work because, as the narrator writes (borrowing Garp's adjectives), "He knew about all the shitty autobiographical associations that make those rabid readers of gossip warm to an occasional fiction," Garp's second novel clearly uses events from his life. The narrator-biographer makes that evident when he carefully details the Garps' affairs with Alice and Harrison Fletcher upon which the novel is based. Garp insists that *Second Wind of the Cuckold* is "*not* about *us* . . . It's *not* about any of that. It just *uses* that." But, as the narrator says, the novel "*was* about four people whose finally unequal and sexually striving relationship is a bust." As Gabriel Miller asserts, "Garp's

vision is a limited one, consistently colored by autobiography and his obsession with death; he's unable to get beyond his personal life." The reader has no doubt, nor does the biographer, that Garp's second novel bears a strong resemblance to the Garps' and the Fletchers' experiment in neighborly love and that Garp uses too much memory and not enough imagination in its creation.

The narrator reveals the source for Garp's short story "Vigilance" by relating in the chapter entitled "The Eternal Husband" how Garp, suffering from writer's block, chases cars on his street. As he approaches them, he berates the drivers for speeding where children play. Three chapters later, in "It Happens to Helen," the narrator records Garp's short story "Vigilance" in full. Written to try to win Helen back, just as Garp used "The Pension Grillparzer" to get her to marry him, this story has none of the merit of Garp's earlier story. Helen knows why: "I mean, what *is* it? A self-parody? You're not old enough, and you haven't written enough, to start mocking yourself. It's self-serving, it's self-justifying; and it's not about anything except yourself, really." In other words, it is a record of his life, not art. The story is Garp's attempt to use only the language of memory. But the biographer shows the relation of Garp's life to his art, how the two intertwine, by printing the short story.

The final piece of Garp's fiction reproduced by the narrator is the first chapter of *The World According to Bensenhaver.* By the time the narrator presents this chapter, the reader knows of not one but perhaps three biographical impulses behind the gruesome rape story. First of all, as the son of Jenny Fields, the famous feminist who helps abused women (the Ellen Jamesians, for example), Garp has been exposed to female suffering for most of his life. In addition, Garp has found in the park a young girl who has just been raped. Although he catches the rapist and becomes a hero, Garp feels responsible: "Rape, Garp thought, made men feel guilty by association." Finally, the novel that Garp writes is influenced by the disastrous car crash that kills his son, Walt. Unlike the autobiography of "Vigilance," however, as Harter and Thompson note, in this novel Garp has found "an objective distance." In fact, these critics see the first chapter of *The World According to Bensenhaver* as a measure of "Garp's maturing aesthetic purpose and vision." He is beginning to learn how to control the facts of his life with his imagination.

In the narrator's text as biography, one finds another incorporated genre, the critical reviews of Garp's fiction. The inclusion of these reviews suggests that, as a student of the famous writer Garp, the narrator has done his homework. He records Garp's first rejection: "The story is only mildly interesting, and it does nothing new with language or with form. Thanks for showing it to us, though." And in reference to Garp's *Procrastination* the narrator reproduces these reviews: "It is amazing that the now-famous son of Jenny Fields has actually grown up to be what he said he wanted to be when he grew up." Another reviewer wrote, "Young Mr. Garp is still writing about bears. Perhaps, when he grows up, he'll write something about people." A critic of *Second Wind of the Cuckold* "called the novel 'bitterly truthful,' but he hastened to point out that the bitterness doomed the novel to the status of 'only a minor classic.'" "The novel confused nearly everyone; even its reviews were confusing" the narrator writes. Ironically, *The World According to Bensenhaver*, which Garp's publisher John Wolf thought was so pornographic as to warrant publication in the pornographic *Crotch Shots*, earned Garp this very winning review:

> "The women's movement has at last exhibited a significant influence on a significant male writer" wrote the reviewer, who was an associate professor of women's studies somewhere. She went on to say that *The World According to Bensenhaver* was "the first in-depth study, by a man, of the peculiarly *male* neurotic pressure many women are made to suffer." And so forth.

These mimetic records establish the separation of the narrator's voice from the voices he records. But on a psychological plane his recording of these genres suggests the high value he applies to them.

In addition to quoting his sources, the biographer discusses Garp's thoughts about writing and provides an informed summary of Garp's aesthetic ideas. This subjective approach and the display of Garp's unconscious thoughts further reveal the narrator's psychological stance—his affinity and approval. In such discussions the narrator approaches Garp's essential aesthetic problem, the tension between memory and art. We learn that Garp thought "a writer's job is to imagine everything so personally that the fiction is as vivid as our personal memories." Similarly, the narrator writes, "What was 'going on,' in Garp's opinion, was never as important as what he was making up—what he was working on." That the two impulses, what's going on and what's made up, are implicated is clear from the narrator's claim that "His first novel, *Procrastination*—in his opinion—suffered from the pretentious weight of all the fascist history he had taken no real part in. His second novel suffered from his failure at imagining *enough*—that is, he felt he had not imagined far enough beyond his own fairly ordinary experience." In these passages the narrator explores Garp's struggle to find a subject and a style without succumbing to autobiography or losing vividness by relying too heavily on imagined life. A degree of the difficulty Garp experiences in that struggle is suggested when the narrator quotes Garp's metaphor about writing: "If you are careful, . . . if you use good ingredients, and you don't take any shortcuts, then you can usually cook something very good. . . . With writing, I find, you can have

all the right ingredients, give plenty of time and care, and still get nothing." The narrator also shares Garp's frustration with the insignificance of his life's work. For instance, he quotes Garp's consideration of the lack of social value in art: "Art doesn't help anyone . . . People can't really use it: they can't eat it, it won't shelter or clothe them—and if they're sick, it won't make them well."

Irving's narrator, using the language of the biographer, quotes written records as evidence for his claims about Garp's life and discusses his aesthetic philosophy. Harter and Thompson refer to "the tone and technique of the objective biographer who deftly sketches . . . in matter-of-fact, even journalistic form" the first two pages of the novel. This is the language of memory that Garp strives to keep to a minimum in his fiction. Beneath the surface of this biographical style, however, the narrator tends to manipulate the text with the techniques of a fiction writer. Influenced by Garp's language, the narrator uses figurative language, creates a persona, adopts a comic and satiric approach, and writes in the present tense. These are indications of the influence of Garp's language on the narrator's. This imaginative language is the one that Garp strives to make dominant in his own work.

Rather than simply retelling events as they occurred, a method Garp as fiction writer tries to avoid, but a method the biographer would not normally avoid, the narrator uses the fictional methods of foreshadowing and withholding information. For instance, the narrator foreshadows the car accident when he describes Garp's driveway trick. If Garp knew the children were sleeping upon his return home at night, he would turn off the car's engine and the lights and coast up the driveway, using the momentum from the descent of the road leading to it. Helen called this practice "puerile and dangerous," a comment that stays with the reader. In further preparation for the accident's outcome, the uncovered metal shaft of the Volvo's stick shift has been described at some length and mentioned frequently. As a result, as soon as the reader learns that Garp and the boys will arrive home while Helen and Michael are still parked in the dark driveway, he understands the potential for disaster. The narrator as fiction writer adds to the suspense he establishes when he refuses to chronicle the accident immediately. Although we suspect the collision, the chapter ends with Walt's response to the feeling of climbing up the driveway without lights and engine: "It's like a dream!" A few paragraphs into the next chapter, we learn of the injuries to Duncan, Helen, Michael, and Garp. But we don't learn of Walt's death until twenty pages later.

His role as a fiction writer's biographer also affects the narrator's discourse stylistically. Although he uses few metaphors in the text, compared to many other third-person narrators, he does employ figurative language. The chapter

"Second Love, Second Children," for instance, opens with a comic description of Walt's name that as a writer Garp would surely envy: "He was simply a *t* at the end of a wall. Walt: like a beaver's tail smacking water, like a well-hit squash ball." The narrator has the advantage of distance that allows him to apply figurative language to his depiction of Duncan's lost eye, which he describes as "a kind of tidal irrigation of the hole where Duncan's right eye had been." The narrator also knows how to incorporate anthropomorphic images poetically. For instance, when Helen's student hands Garp the note she has written saying that Helen is having an affair with the student's ex-boyfriend, the narrator writes: "The slow unwrapping of the note—so it wouldn't tear—made sounds as crisp as autumn, though all around Garp it was a cold March, the hurt ground thawing to mud. The little note snapped like bones as he opened it." And the narrator displays the influence of Garp's language on his own when he uses a metaphor taken from Garp's first short story: "like a bear holding a great through of food in his forepaws." The narrator also enjoys Garp's Under Toad story. He uses the image as the source of several metaphoric passages: "His voice against the stolid stone buildings bounced back to him like the froggy belching of the Under Toad, the foul and warty beast whose sticky nearness he felt like breath"; "The room reeked of toad"; "Garp heard the cold hop of the Under Toad thudding across the cold floors of the silent house." After the attack of the woman in the white Saab, "he heard the croak of the vile-tasting Under Toad in his dry throat."

Seeming to forget his role as biographer, the narrator allows his voice to invade the text in a manner befitting the narrator in one of Garp's own novels. He makes personal comments and observations and uses exclamation and question marks. For example, he seems to have transported himself to the scene of Garp's early years when, after mentioning the books that Jenny brings into the infirmary annex, he exclaims, "What a wet dream for lovers of literature, to lie sick at Steering! At last, a hospital with something good to read." Only one of two voices could be responsible for such an exclamation: Garp's or the narrator's. Since there is no suggestion that Garp has taken charge of the narration, one must assume that the narrator has appropriated Garp's language. The same is true when the narrator describes the scene of the cannon: "Hundreds of prophylactics! A display of arrested reproduction. Like dogs urinating around the borders of their territory, the boys of the Steering school had left their messes in the mouth of the mammoth cannon guarding the Steering River." This is a passage that the writer of *The World According to Bensenhaver* might have written with some pride. In addition to these signs of the narrator's other voice, he joins in the narrative as only a homodiegetic narrator could. For instance, he says of Garp's and Alice's lovemaking, "And they made love, of course, and despite what everyone knows about such things, it *was* special." The narrator also suddenly speaks openly to the reader as he has

not before. He writes of Garp's conflict with the Ellen Jamesians, "They let Garp seethe. What else could they do? It was not one of Garp's better points: tolerance of the intolerant. Crazy people made him crazy." Not only can the narrator use the language that Garp struggles to master as fiction writer, but he can also analyze from an objective distance.

Not unlike Garp's voice as we know it from his fiction, the narrator's voice is often comic and satiric. For instance, when Garp realizes that the old man he finds in the park is not the one who raped the young girl, the narrator describes the man as the one "whose mustache had been innocent." In a satiric tone, the narrator discusses the effect of the car accident on Michael: "Helen may have supposed that biting off three quarters of a student's penis was fairly high on the scale of conceivable abuse to students." Similarly, when Garp feels that he is finished as a writer but might be a marriage counselor, the narrator echoes Garp's comic idea by using that image of Garp in the chapter entitled "The Eternal Husband": "Garp the marriage counselor, full of advice"; and "The marriage counselor is the I'm-sorry man, like a doctor with bad luck—the one who gets to diagnose all the terminal cases." But one of the narrator's favorite Garp-like touches is his use of Alice Fletcher's speech impediment: "Garp knew about writers who couldn't *white*"; "The good-byes that Garp imagined conducting with Alice were violent scenarios, fraught with Alice's incoherent speech and always ending in desperate lovemaking—another failed resolution, wet with sweat and sweet with the lush stickum of sex, oh yeth"; "Did Garp love Alice? Oh yeth"; and "She couldn't *thtop*." Ironically, the narrator makes a point of letting us know that Garp's saying "I've *thtopped*" is a "short, cruel imitation of poor Alice Fletcher."

When the narrator shifts into the present tense for the first half of the chapter entitled "Mrs. Ralph," he breaks most profoundly from the biography he began and adopts not only the voice of Garp's fiction but also its tense. Garp's "Vigilance," for instance, uses the present tense. The narrator's present-tense segment follows Garp's narration of Walt's bedtime dog story, in the chapter entitled "The Dog in the Alley, the Child in the Sky." It is as if the tense shift were the narrator's response to his relative silence in that chapter (it takes less involvement to record his character's speech than it does to describe the character's feelings, thoughts, and actions). With the change in tense come a new perspective and voice. The segment opens with these metaphors: "Like a gunman hunting his victim, like the child molester the parent dreads, Garp stalks the sleeping spring suburbs, green and dark; the people snore and wish and dream, their lawn mowers at rest." Clearly the suburban scene and the mock-heroic tone present an image that the writer of "Vigilance" might employ, but this voice is the narrator's. Indeed, in the opening paragraphs of the segment, the narrator makes the fabricator's language his own. For instance, he describes Mrs. Ralph's breath as "a startling mixture of a fresh-cut lawn and cigarettes." The scene in her kitchen receives similar treatment:

> There is a litter of dishes in the sink, a bottle of gin on the kitchen table, the sour smell of slashed limes. The cord to the overhead light . . . had been substantially lengthened by one sheer leg and hip of a woman's pair of panty hose . . . The nylon foot, spotted with translucent stains of grease, dangles in the breeze above the gin.

Secure in this voice, the narrator even invents a word: "In the blackened houses an occasional dog *snorfles*." And, like a good fiction writer, the narrator makes sure he connects images in this segment with previous chapters. So we find that he returns to Garp as "the marriage counselor," the "marriage-counsel man." No longer does the tense separate the narrator from Garp's world, Garp's language.

Once Garp is shot, the narrator as biographer would have to depend on the words of those close to Garp to complete his life story. But the narrator as fiction writer does not have that limitation. In fact, he can apply imagination and phrase Garp's last thoughts, revealing his psychological affinity: "If he could have talked, he would have told Helen not to be frightened of the Under Toad anymore. It surprised him to realize that the Under Toad was very familiar—as if he had always known it, as if he had grown up with it." The narrator pursues fictive techniques to such an extent that he even records Garp's thoughts in interior monologue: "Don't worry—so what if there is no life after death? There is life after Garp, believe me. Even if there is only death after death . . . be grateful for small favors. . . . Oh yeth, as Alice Fletcher would have said." Certainly, the narrator has not used a biographical source for those words.

Yet in the final chapter, "Life After Garp," the narrator again employs a clearly academic language, ending his study in the biographer's language even though he has not always relied solely on biographical techniques. The first sentence of the chapter, sets a tone for the conclusion of the text: "He loved epilogues, as he showed us in 'The Pension Grillparzer.'" The final chapter allows the biographer to discuss openly the conflict in Garp's writing between memory and imagination. Analyzing Garp's conflict, the narrator writes, "He had been too impressed by what he now called the 'mere accidents and casualties of daily life, and the understandable trauma resulting therefrom.'" In other words, he has been unable to leave his life out of his fiction. But his last work of fiction brings a clearer vision. Although Garp does not complete *My Father's Illusions,* the narrator tells us that "Because he was inventing a father, Garp felt more in touch with the spirit of pure imagination that he felt had

kindled 'The Pension Grillparzer.'" Garp dies, then, on the verge of reaching his full growth as a writer.

As Irving's novel moves toward its conclusion, it becomes clear that Garp needs some of the language of memory in his fiction to make it vivid, and the narrator needs some of the language of imagination in his biography to make it whole. At first Garp uses imagination like an artist; at first the narrator uses facts like a biographer. Yet just as Garp progressively relies more on autobiography until it threatens to overwhelm his creative ability, the narrator relies more on fictional techniques until they threaten the factual account of the life he relates. Finally, both writers resolve their aesthetic conflicts. As a result, Garp's *Bildung* becomes a kind of return to where he began with "The Pension Grillparzer," in which he used imagination to control memory. And, conversely, the narrator returns to using memory to control imagination, his initial narrative stance. In this way, Irving shapes a narration that re-creates the hero's struggle between the forces of memory and imagination, a struggle that represents a large part of Garp's *Bildung* as a writer. But *The World According to Garp*'s continual debate about the value of the two languages ends as it begins: in the dialogue between them, art finds its form.

> **Irving shapes a narration that re-creates the hero's struggle between the forces of memory and imagination, a struggle that represents a large part of Garp's *Bildung* as a writer.**
>
> —*Kim McKay*

After *Garp,* Irving continues his interest in the *Bildungsroman* as well as his interest in the relation between the story and its narration. In *The Hotel New Hampshire,* Irving's first-person narrator seems to have learned Garp's lesson about using imagination when rendering the facts of one's life. In fact, when John writes, "But the first of my father illusions was . . . ," recalling the novel Garp is writing when he dies entitled *My Father's Illusions,* Irving seems to suggest a relation between these two fictional creations. Trained in the search for literary patterns and parallels, John extends that training to his life, which he presents as a "story," a fairy tale, to be precise. For instance, while the family's reading of *The Great Gatsby* might be a biographical fact within the realm of the novel, it is John's imagination that seeks out and establishes parallels between Gatsby and his father. And although his father has relatively little direct discourse in the novel, John, desiring to show him as the hero of the family tale, often "reads" him as a third-person omniscient narrator might:

Father looked at Franny. It reminded me of the looks

he occasionally gave mother; he was looking into the future, again, and he was looking for forgiveness—in advance. He wanted to be excused for everything that *would* happen. It was as if the power of his dreaming was so vivid that he felt compelled to simply act out whatever future he imagined—and we were being asked to tolerate his absence . . . from our lives, for a while.

John also analyzes other people in his life as if they were truly characters, rather than real people in the real life he purports to be telling. For example, after establishing the idea that the whores and the radicals in Vienna treated him well, John says that "despite their day-and-night differences, they bore more similarities to each other than *they* might have supposed." But John's vision of his life as a fictional construct prompts him not only to note but also to develop such similarities. With John as narrator, Irving provides, once again, a narrative that represents in its style the major concerns of the text, in this case the creation of a text that resembles a Gatsby-like American dream.

Cider House Rules, Irving's next novel, centers on an entirely different set of motifs from his previous novels, but the tension between imagination and biography remains, along with the attendant narrative approach. Indeed, this text represents a combination of the techniques in *Garp* and *Hotel.* Just as the narrator in *Garp* quotes from Garp's journal and Jenny's novel, this third-person narrator regularly quotes from Dr. Larch's notebooks, thereby layering a second voice into the text: "'Here in St. Clouds,' Dr. Larch wrote in his journal, 'we have only one problem.'" This narrator also involves himself in the telling, showing his proximity by the use of exclamation marks and the adoption of the character's language. Apparently enjoying Irene's fear of her husband, who is unrecognizable either as himself or as a human, dressed as he is in a beekeeper's suit, the narrator writes, "No doubt this was what had been molesting the hives! The ghost of a beekeeper of bygone days!" And suspending time in order to heighten his images, this narrator, like the narrator of *Garp,* calls attention to his power over the textual world. At the end of chapter four we are shown by way of their shadows reaching across a field behind the orphanage that Homer is now taller than Larch. As if the narrator has stretched that image through space and time, several pages into the next chapter the station master sees "the towering shadows of Wilbur Larch and Homer Wells." And just as John in *Hotel* explores the connections between his story and *Gatsby,* this narrator continually weaves in references to *David Copperfield* and *Jane Eyre,* other novels in the *Bildungsroman* tradition, thereby establishing parallels between Homer and David, Wally and Steerforth, Melony and Jane, and Homer and Rochester. Combining the allusiveness to similar novels and the layering of narrative voices, *Cider*

House Rules is evidence of Irving's continuing growth as a storyteller.

The narration of *A Prayer for Owen Meany,* Irving's latest novel, shows the author experimenting still further with the relationship between narrator and text. Owen, the focus of the first-person narrator's, Johnny's, memoir, is said to have an extraordinary memory, but memory is also the narrative method which shapes Johnny's text and adds layers to his discourse. In one example Johnny juxtaposes the town's production of *A Christmas Carol* and his memory of the baseball game that kills his mother. After quoting Christmas Past's warning to Scrooge, the narrator leaps into memory, writing, "With a shudder I realized that it had been *my father* in the bleachers—it had been *my father* she waved to the instant she was killed." The number of pages given to the brief episode of his mother's death is inordinate to actual time, but memory works by selectively expanding and contracting time. Similarly expanded is the Christmas Pageant, in which Owen plays the Christ Child, and the *Christmas Carol,* in which Owen plays the Ghost of the Future, events which establish Owen's "special" quality. Irving's text gains another layer of memory, therefore another voice, when Johnny weaves more than twenty-five of his present-tense diary entries into his past-tense text. The three selves, shown in memories reached through events in the past time of the narrative, in memories reached through the present time of the narration, and in journals representing the present time of the narration, are juxtaposed via this narrative. The coexistence of those selves suggests the influence that the past has on the present and that memory has on the individual, major themes in the novel.

Irving's handling of the narration is clearly essential to his success as a writer. In *A Prayer for Owen Meany* the elongated layers of memory that are punctuated by diary entries provide the perfect narrative vehicle for a text concerned with time and memory. The power of the third-person narrator in *Cider House Rules,* as seen in the manipulation of time, the proximity to the characters, and the weaving in of journal entries, enables Irving to shift from subjective to objective vision, a movement that supports that novel's theme of one's responsibility to others. In *The Hotel New Hampshire* the first-person narrator's presumed task doesn't give him the power of the narrator in *Cider House Rules,* but he claims the freedom of a third-person narrator anyway, a fitting approach for his American fairy tale. As we have seen in some detail, the narration of *Garp* re-creates the character's conflict as a writer through its use of incorporated genres, manipulated tense, and shifting proximity to the characters. On the other hand, Irving's *The 158-Pound Marriage* lacks the techniques displayed in the other novels, resulting in a single-level narrative without the force to give substance to the characters portrayed. Yet in the earlier novel *The Water-Method Man* the mix of voices, in-

corporated genres, and tense shifts provides a suitably fractured surface with which to portray its main character. Even
in his first novel, **Setting Free the Bears,** Irving found that
incorporated genres present other voices that can serve any
number of relationships to the main voice, allowing the novelist to accent theme through narrative style. Irving's power
to create fascinating plots has long been accepted; these plots
depend to a large extent, however, upon a handful of narrative techniques and the layers of discourse they bring to the
text.

Raymond J. Wilson III (essay date Fall 1992)

SOURCE: "The Postmodern Novel: The Example of John
Irving's *The World According to Garp*," in *Critique: Studies in Contemporary Fiction*, Vol. XXXIV, No. 1, Fall, 1992,
pp. 49-62.

[*In the following essay, Wilson examines the postmodern
construction of* The World According to Garp, *particularly
elements of metafiction, irony, and the gothic bizarre in the
novel.*]

As a novel that recapitulates within itself a history of twentieth-century fiction, John Irving's **The World According to
Garp** illustrates a key aspect of postmodernism, that of formal replenishment. The earlier segments of **Garp** exhibit
strong elements of modernism whereas in its final third,
Irving's book is a postmodern novel of bizarre violence and
black humor, flat characters, and metafiction—a mode of
writing one might expect from the pen of John Barth, Robert Coover, or Thomas Pynchon. Specifically, in its first segment, **Garp** is the artist's *bildungsroman* like James Joyce's
A Portrait of the Artist as a Young Man. Then **Garp** becomes
a mid-century novel of manners dealing with the surface
tone, the daily rituals, and the social patterns of American
couples, its chief drama being found in adultery and sexual
interaction—a novel such as one might have expected from
John Updike or John Cheever. However, in John Barth's concept of a literature of exhaustion, imitation of earlier modes
is a basic strategy of the postmodern novel. Thus, despite
Garp's shifts of mode, as a contemporary fiction operating
in three modes, it must be intrinsically postmodern throughout. My analysis proceeds in two stages: first, a theoretical
overview of postmodernism, followed by the specific example of **The World According to Garp.**

Postmodern Fiction

The term *postmodern* requires careful investigation. Since
the 1960s, readers have noticed a difference in some of our
fiction; attempting to discuss this new fiction without long
circumlocutions, critics invented a term: *postmodern fiction.*

Attempts to define this expression followed its use but led
to a problem. As John Barth points out, no agreement has
been reached on a definition; and because widespread agreement has not yet been reached even for a definition of modernism, we cannot expect a rapid agreement on a definition
of postmodernism. In this situation we might find it effective not to attempt a strict logical definition but simply to
list those characteristics that first made us notice a difference. In this essay, I suggest a noninclusive list: (1) a propensity to contain and reuse all previous forms in a literature
of exhaustion and replenishment; (2) a zone of the bizarre,
where fantasy best expresses our sense of reality; (3) a turning away from penetration into the psychological depth of
character as the primary goal of fiction; and (4) a propensity for metafiction, in which writing draws attention to the
techniques and processes of its own creation.

A literature of exhaustion and replenishment

The postmodern novel contains all the earlier modes of the
novel, contains them intrinsically within the process by
which a literature of exhausted possibilities replenishes itself. Such commentators as Albert J. La Valley, Herman
Kahn, and Christopher Lasch may see causes of change in
recent literature in deep cultural contexts. La Valley says that
the new literature reflects a new consciousness that has been
"inspired in part by the breakdown of our culture, its traditions, and its justifications of the American social structure;"
Kahn and Wiener refer to our culture as being in the "Late
Sensate" stage, our art, including literature, reflecting a culture in the state of decline; and Lasch argues that "Bourgeois
society seems everywhere to have used up its store of constructive ideas" and that there is "a pervasive despair of understanding the course of modern history or of subjecting it
to rational direction." However, the originator of the expression "literature of exhaustion," John Barth, referred to it as
"the literature of exhausted possibilities" and says that by
"'exhaustion' I don't mean anything so tired as the subject
of physical, moral or intellectual decadence, only the
usedupness of certain forms or exhaustion of certain possibilities." Despair might be the reaction of a contemporary
writer of fiction when he or she faces the realization that the
limited number of possible variations in the form of fiction
may have already been explored, but Barth has an answer.
While today's author may panic at the idea of being condemned to merely repeat what a Flaubert, a James, a
Fitzgerald, or a Joyce has discovered and what countless others have already repeated, Barth finds the situation "by no
means necessarily a cause for despair."

The escape from panic, Barth finds, comes in a story by
Borges. In the story "Pierre Menard, Author of *Quixote*,"
Borges described his character Menard's astonishing effort
of will in producing—composing, not copying—several
chapters of Cervantes' *Don Quixote.* Borges's narrator points

out that despite being verbally identical the recomposition is a new, fresh work: what for Cervantes was merely an everyday, workmanlike style of prose is for Menard a clever, playful use of quaint, semi-antiquated diction; what for Cervantes were mere commonplaces of conventional rhetoric can be for Menard a series of radical, exciting departures from the accepted wisdom of his day. Barth points out that it would have "been sufficient for Menard to have *attributed* the novel to himself in order to have a new work of art, from the intellectual point of view." However, Barth feels that "the important thing to observe is that Borges *doesn't* attribute the *Quixote* to himself, much less recompose it like Pierre Menard; instead, he writes a remarkable and original work of literature, the implicit theme of which is the difficulty, perhaps the unnecessity, of writing original works of literature. Barth believes that Borges's "artistic victory," emerges from confronting "an intellectual dead end," and employing it "against itself to accomplish new human work."

In its reuse of earlier forms, we can see how *The World According to Garp* is related to postmodern works by John Barth and Robert Coover. In "Menelaiad," a story in *Lost in the Funhouse,* John Barth parodies the Greek epic form; and in *The Sot-Weed Factor,* Barth contorts the genre of the eighteenth-century novel. It would be a mistake to think that Barth is writing an epic or an eighteenth-century novel. Nor is Barth really writing a Richardsonian epistolary novel in *Letters.* Instead, Barth writes a postmodern novel that plays with the form. Similarly, Coover is not writing a mystery in *Gerald's Party:* instead, this novel, as William Gass is quoted as saying on the dust jacket, "sends up the salon mystery so far it will never come down. What comes down is a terrible indictment of our desires." Just so, *The World According to Garp* plays with the modernist forms of the artist's *bildungsroman* and the mid-century American comedy of manners and necessarily makes an implicit comment upon them, as I shall argue later. *Garp,* by its reuse of modernist forms, stands in the same territory as these works by Barth and Coover.

By reusing existing forms this new fiction opens for itself doors to endless opportunities for freshness. Borges's story, for example, is itself a parody of the critical article. The postmodern novel's parody reveals a literary form returning to its point of origin to renew itself. Barth points out that the *Quixote* is itself a parody of an earlier form—the poetic romance. One thinks immediately of Defoe's stories parodying news articles and his novels in the form of personal reminiscences. Richardson is said to have begun *Pamela* as a model set of letters for young ladies and to have thus invented the English epistolary novel almost by accident.

The zone of the bizarre

Because the term *zone* comes from *Gravity's Rainbow,* this category highlights the relationship between *Garp* and Thomas Pynchon's great novel. Speaking of the zone of occupation in defeated Germany, Brian McHale says that as *Gravity's Rainbow* unfolds, "hallucinations and fantasies become real, metaphors become literal, the fictional worlds of the mass media—the movies, comic-books—thrust themselves into the midst of historical reality." As such, "Pynchon's zone is paradigmatic for the heterotopian space of postmodernist writing." *The World According to Garp* has a zone, as I shall argue, that fits *Gravity's Rainbow*'s paradigm. Brian McHale suggests that behind all the postmodernist fictional construction of zones "lies Apollinaire's poem, 'Zone' (from *Alcools,* 1913), whose speaker, strolling through the immigrant and red-light districts of Paris, finds in them an objective correlative for modern Europe and his own marginal, heterogeneous, and outlaw experience." However, an even better explanation might be found in Philip Roth's observation that "the toughest problem for the American writer was that the substance of the American experience itself was so abnormally and fantastically strange, it had become an 'embarrassment to one's own meager imagination.'" "If reality becomes surrealistic," Joe David Bellamy asks, "what must fiction do to be realistic?" It must become bizarre, goes one answer.

The bizarre connects realistic fiction to fantasy and myth. Fantasy is an old form that takes on new implications when used consciously by the contemporary writer, not as an alternative or escape from reality but as the best method available for catching the emotional essence of our era. The distinction between fantasy and myth is not always easy to maintain when one looks at individual stories, although theoretically a mythically structured story may maintain a surface sense of realism the way a fantasy story cannot.

Also connected to the bizarre characteristic of these zones is the postmodern novel's black humor. In *The Fabulators,* Robert Scholes says that black humorists, in a century of historical horror, deal with the absurdity of "the human situation" by seeing it "as a cosmic joke." He suggests that in contrast to the existentialist, the black humorist offers an alternative: "The best response is neither acquiescence nor bitterness"; rather one must play "one's role in the joke in such a way as to turn the humor back on the joker or cause it to diffuse itself harmlessly on the whole group which has participated in the process of the joke."

As the extreme epitome of the atmosphere of much postmodern fiction, the zone of the bizarre compensates for its retreat from the strict tenets of realism by evoking echoes of no-less-real feelings from our personas pasts, feelings that today we can experience only in dreams or in moments of great stress—of terror, perhaps—when our "normal" functioning breaks down. Although we repress these feelings, we react with a mixture of anxiety and secret welcoming when the television news reports events that cannot be grasped without reference to such emotions. Through the bizarre, postmodern fiction taps and reflects this source of emotional power and does so, not despite, but because of its departure from the formal tenets of "realism," which center on an attempt to penetrate into the depths of character.

The turn away from psychological depth in character

Umberto Eco notes the shift in contemporary novels, where an author "renounces all psychology as the motive of narrative and decides to transfer characters and situations to the level of an objective structural strategy." Eco sees this "choice familiar to many contemporary disciplines" as one in which an author passes "from the psychological method to the formalistic one." Eco's words fit with Robert Scholes's prediction that the key element in the coming new fiction would be a new dimension of the "care for form." This noncharacter orientation provides a point of reference between *The World According to Garp* and Robert Coover's *The Universal Baseball Association,* which is organized neither by plot nor by revelation of its intentionally flat characters but by the structural relationship of game and ritual and the progressive transformation of the one into the other.

Metafiction

Metafiction is another instance where fiction turns away from outside reality and seeks a subject intrinsically suited to the written word. In this method, the technique of composition becomes to some extent the subject of fiction itself. If television and movies are vastly better adapted to creating an illusion of reality—the depiction of objects—then fiction must find other subjects for its own survival, just as painting turned to the nonrepresentational when painters recognized the photograph's power to recreate a scene accurately. In the metafictional dimension, we see the connection of *The World According to Garp* to other postmodern fiction, for example to the stories John Barth's *Lost in the Funhouse,* especially the title story, in which the implied author presents himself as trying—and failing—to write a conventional story by the cookbook-recipe method but actually writing a postmodern story. Of another story in the volume, "Autobiography," Barth says in his author's note, that it is "the story, speaking of itself."

The World According to Garp *as Postmodern Fiction*

Reuse of earlier forms

As a novel that shifts from mode to mode, *The World According to Garp* illustrates the postmodern as a literature of replenishment: *Garp* recapitulates within itself a history of the twentieth-century novel, performing a tacit critique of the earlier forms. Irving starts in an early twentieth-century

mode. Reviewing the fiction of this era, Irving Howe says that whereas nineteenth-century realism studied social classes, early twentieth-century fiction studied the rebellion of the Stephen Dedaluses against behavior patterns imposed by social classes in a particular country. In this conception, the modern novel came into being when James Joyce reconstructed the existing form of the *bildungsroman* to create *A Portrait.* More than merely recasting the autobiographical novel into the "individuating rhythm" of *Dubliners,* Joyce helped form the modern consciousness itself. D.H. Lawrence's *Sons and Lovers* shares this feature with Joyce's *A Portrait:* and although Lawrence's novel retains more of the trappings of nineteenth-century realism than Joyce's book, both create characters that do not fit into their own world but who express an aesthetic that is familiar in our intellectual climate. John Irving achieves similar effects in his *bildungsroman.*

The *bildungsroman* form is suited to linearity of narrative flow, reflecting the linear growth of a boy's life. In the McCaffery interview, John Irving claimed that he was "very conscious of attempting to make my narrative as absolutely linear as possible. . . . With my first four novels I was always troubled," says Irving, "particularly with *Garp,* about the convoluted flow of my narrative. . . . *Garp* was, in fact, a kind of minor breakthrough for me just in the sense that it was the first novel I managed to order chronologically." Irving rejects the unreadable masterpieces of high modernist literature and implies that he is returning to the simpler forms of earlier days; however, no nineteenth-century author could have written *The World According to Garp.* John Irving is moving on into postmodernism, as the three-segment analysis of the novel can demonstrate.

As in the early works of Joyce and Lawrence, the opening section of *Garp* fits the genre's depiction of parents and childhood surroundings. In the chapter entitled "Blood and Blue," Garp's near fall from a roof and his being bitten by a dog parallel Stephen Dedalus's being shouldered into a playground puddle and having his hands smacked by his teacher. And similarly, the succeeding chapters fulfill other criteria for the genre, combining Garp's sexual initiation with an encounter with pain and death in the demise of a prostitute named Charlotte.

Garp's involvement with the death of this "whore," whom he had come to know better than Joyce's Stephen knew the prostitutes he visited, precipitates Garp's forming his working aesthetic as a writer. Combined with the play of Garp's imagination on the war damage at the Vienna zoo, the death of Charlotte ties Garp's emergence as an adult to his emergence as a writer: a creator and reflector of modern consciousness like Stephen Dedalus. Garp had been unable to finish the story that would make him a "real writer." "The

Pension Grillparzer," as the story was called, consisted of two major elements that Garp was having trouble reconciling: a continuous line of hilarious, almost farcical action, low comedy, approaching slapstick that coexisted with a somber theme generated by a dream-omen of death. After Charlotte's death, Garp fell under "a writer's long-sought trance, wherein the world falls under one embracing tone of voice." Here, Irving's narrator emphasizes the importance of what Gerard Genette, following Tzvetan Todorov, has called "aspect," or "the way in which the story is perceived by the narrator."

Visiting the zoo that still bore the signs of war damage, "Garp discovered that when you are writing something, everything seems related to everything else." In the evidences of war Garp saw the connection between larger human history and each person's individual history and so was able to finish the story. His notion of modern consciousness is that "the history of a city was like the history of a family—there is a closeness, and even affection, but death eventually separates everyone from each other." It may be that this is an aesthetic as appropriate for the post-Hiroshima era as Stephen Dedalus's aesthetic was for the era he heralded. Finishing the story after having formed his guiding aesthetic, Garp met Helen's standard for a "real" writer and thus "earned" a wife for himself. Thus, Irving completed the segment of the novel with the forecast that "in their stubborn, deliberate ways," Helen and Garp would fall in love with each other "sometime after they had married."

Irving's implicit comment on the Joycean *bildungsroman* is ironic. By writing in the form, Irving is affirming the value of the early modernist mode, despite his rejection of excessively complicated modernist literature in the McCaffery interview. However, even an affirmation is a comment, and a comment on modernism is not modernism; by its nature, a comment on modernism must be something standing outside of modernism, viewing it, and implicitly judging it. The existence of bizarre violence and the associated vein of black humor, even in the first section of the book, contributes to irony. The novel opens to the backdrop of a war, and Jenny Field's brusque categorizing of the wounded into classes of Externals, Vital Organs, Absentees, and Goners certainly contains an element of the blackly humorous. In its vividness, Jenny's slashing of a persistent masher verges on the gothic. Garp's being bitten by a dog is merely an element of *bildungsroman,* but Garp's biting off the ear of the dog verges on the bizarre. With their hint of anti-realist absurdism, these elements provide a counterpoint to the modernist mode, repeatedly rupturing it, threatening to radicalize the novel into the postmodern, and foreshadowing the third section where the transformation does occur. Implicit in these ruptures is the notion that the early modernist mode has difficulty expressing a contemporary reality that itself has become postmodern.

A similar point and counterpoint arises in the second section of the novel. Here, John Irving introduces a mid-century novel of manners, a section of *Garp* that approximates the aura of an Updike novel or a Cheever story. The central characteristic of the cultural attitude found in mid-century can be illuminated by an insight Stanley Kaufmann drew from the words of a contemporary Italian filmmaker: "When Vittorio de Sica was asked why so many of his films deal with adultery, he is said to have replied, 'But if you take adultery out of the lives of the bourgeoisie, what drama is left?'" The middle segment of Irving's novel, which culminates with Garp's discovery of Helen's affair with Michael Milton, contains the tale of a suburban marriage, its fidelities and infidelities: Garp's sexual encounter with a babysitter, his resisting an attempted seduction by "Mrs. Ralph," and a temporary swap of sexual partners between the Garps and a couple named Harry and Alice—a situation like that with which Updike dealt in his novel *Couples.*

The suburban domestic tale fits Howe's belief that mid-century fiction, having abandoned the rebellious stance of a Stephen Dedalus, studied the search for values (looking for them, to some degree, in marriage) by a people who live in a world where social class may still exist but where it no longer dominates every detail of daily existence or predestines one to as limited a range of expectations as did the earlier class system. Fitting with Howe's analysis, the point of reference in the middle of *Garp,* as in the mainstream American novel in the middle of the century, is sociological; the question asked is whether monogamous marriage, as it is found in suburbia, can sustain or bring happiness to people of any sensitivity. What Garp said about his second novel might describe both the midsection of *Garp* and the American novel at mid-century: it was "a serious comedy about marriage," Garp said, "but a sexual farce."

The central section is made ironic by isolated outcroppings of the bizarre, which implicitly undermine our belief in the fruitfulness of this modernist form. The marriage-comedy/sex-farce enclosed an episode in which Garp helps in the capture of a man who habitually rapes little girls, a sequence that takes on ominous implications when Garp happens to meet the rapist who has been released on a legal technicality, collecting tickets at a basketball game. Implicit in the counterpoint created by the intrusion of public and epochal violence into the private and personal is the conclusion that a mode, such as mid-century modernist realism, the Updike/Cheever comedy of manners, which exists to reveal the private and personal, loses its force.

The reader can guess at the historical moment recreated in Irving's implicit irony from a comment Saul Bellow made about novelists of the early 1960s who sought to "examine the private life." Bellow says that some "cannot find the [private] life they are going to examine. The power of public life has become so vast and threatening that private life cannot maintain a pretense of its importance." Unhappy with the situation in which modernist fiction found itself, some authors began turning away, as Irving Howe has noted, from "realistic portraiture" to express their spirit in "fable, picaresque, prophecy, and nostalgia." Novels by these writers, Howe says, "constitute what I would class 'post-modern fiction.'" Howe was identifying a trend that came to be designated, much more inclusively, by the term he used in 1959.

We are deeply involved in the serio-comic complications of Garp's marriage-comedy/sex-farce when an auto accident wrenches us into the post-modern mode—the accident that killed one of Garp's little boys and maimed the other. The transfer between modes comes from a shattering experience—the accident and its physical and emotional consequences. An analogy (with an important difference) can be seen in the work of Saul Bellow. Irving Howe says that when Bellow writes in *Henderson the Rain King,* "that men need a shattering experience to 'wake the spirit's sleep,' we soon realize that his ultimate reference is to America, where many spirits sleep." Bellow, though he keeps his mode in the realistic mainstream, takes his character to Africa for the shattering experience; Irving keeps the scene in America, but this America has become a postmodern "zone" and is no longer the familiar scene of an Updike novel.

The zone of the bizarre

The nearly gothic episodes of the first two sections prepare us for the novel's final section. The salient events in the third section are intrusions of public life into the private: assassinations, mob violence, and highway mayhem, much of it not accidental. The public/private dichotomy presents itself most clearly in Garp's refusal to accept the fact that a strictly women's memorial service for his mother, Jenny Fields, is not a private funeral but a public, political event. It would be unthinkable to bar a son from the one, but unthinkable to welcome a man to the other.

As for the bizarre, not only is the setting moved to Jenny Field's madcap home for "injured women" at Don's Head Harbor; but even more significantly, we suddenly find ourselves in a world as strange as the fictional zones of a Thomas Pynchon or a John Hawkes, if not one reaching the extremes of a William Burroughs. In the final section of Irving's novel, T. S. Garp expresses the dominant feeling: "*Life* is an X-rated soap opera." Akin to both fantasy and myth, this feeling becomes progressively objectified when the horrible "Under Toad" first grows from a family joke, introduced analeptically, into a code word for speaking about a hovering fear. Then, although the reader's mind tries to reject overt supernaturalism, the Under Toad becomes a veritable character, a vengeful beast who at times becomes as

real as Grendel in the Old English poem. The myth-fantasy dimension of Irving's novel would thus partake of what Tzvetan Todorov calls "the fantastic"; in the book of that name, Todorov defines the state as a hovering between "the uncanny," in which apparently supernatural events receive some ultimate natural explanation, and "the marvelous," in which the supernatural becomes the norm. McHale finds such "hesitation" to be characteristic of postmodernist fiction.

Significantly, the Under Toad is mentioned only in the third section of the book, although its origin—in a little boy's misunderstanding of his father's warning about the "undertow" on the beach—occurs in the chronological middle of the book. There may be technical reasons why Irving decided to develop the Under Toad only in retrospect, after the reader knows of little Walt's death. Even so, it is clear that the fantasy and myth aspects of the Under Toad contribute to a mode of postmodernism in the novel's concluding section, reminding us for example of Pynchon's notion that the modern world can only be fathomed through the agency of paranoia. The Under Toad's myth and fantasy elements would have been less appropriate in the more realistic, comic-farce mode of *Garp*'s center section, but they provide an ideal backdrop for black humor.

Garp's death itself typifies black humor "in its random, stupid, and unnecessary qualities—comic and ugly and bizarre" in the words of the novel itself. "In the world according to Garp," the novel says, "an evening could be hilarious and the next morning could be murderous." These elements of the bizarre, myth/fantasy, and black humor distract the reader from a feature that arouses curiosity when first noticed, that the characters have flattened out.

Flatness of character

The third section, more than the first two, bears out the postmodern ethic by which to declare a character psychologically flat need not be to denigrate the author's skill. Irving's mistrust of over psychologizing may have led to his statement that "the phrase 'psychologically deep' is a contradiction of terms." Irving feels that such a view "is a terribly simplistic and unimaginative approach. Ultimately it is destructive of all the breadth and complexity in literature." Complexity in the final third of *Garp* arises from structure, from ironic genre manipulation, from the problematic nature of the text's relationship to the world, and not from any probing of psychological motive that might lead to internal character revelation. The third section of the text is marked by a lack of interest in motive: of assassins, of the Ellen Jamesians, of Garp when he insists on performing actions that he knows draw destruction down upon himself, even though he desires safety. While reflecting the postmodern distrust of "the subject" as a useful category, the flattening of character in the third section of *Garp* may, even more, express a sense of the individual's powerlessness within an absurd situation.

The novel draws its unity, not from continuity of plot, as in the premodernist novel, nor from analysis of character, a feature of modernist fiction, but partially from the operation of motif: a repetition of impaired speech that interacts with a counter-motif of "writing."
—*Raymond J. Wilson III*

The novel draws its unity, not from continuity of plot, as in the premodernist novel, nor from analysis of character, a feature of modernist fiction, but partially from the operation of motif: a repetition of impaired speech that interacts with a counter-motif of "writing." Garp's father had a speech impediment stemming from profound brain damage suffered in war. From then on, the novel contains numerous other instances of impaired speech, depicted either as a temporary or a permanent condition. Apparently permanently afflicted are Alice Hindman, whose speech problem is a psychological outgrowth of her marriage problems; Ellen James, who was raped and left tongueless by men who did not have the sense to realize that she was old enough to implicate them by writing; the Ellen Jamesians, women who have their tongues removed in sympathy with Ellen; and Garp's high school English teacher Tinch and Tinch's eventual replacement, Donald Whitcomb who was to become Garp's biographer. Temporarily "struck dumb" were the young girl whose rapist Garp had helped capture, and Garp himself—for a long while after his auto accident and for the few moments he lived after being shot by Pooh Percy. Pooh's rage, her inarticulate curses from a gaping self-wounded mouth, forms a near-tableau at the end of Garp's life to match the one at its beginning when his future father's decreasing level of articulation from "Garp" to "Arp" to "Ar" led Jenny to realize that he was soon to die and spurred her to get on with the business of Garp's conception. In between, Garp was to wonder "Why is my life so full of people with impaired speech?" He then asks, "Or is it only because I'm a writer that I notice all the damaged voices around me?"

Compensating for the flatness of character, providing coherence within the zone of the bizarre, these repeated elements are the motor oil for the postmodern fictional machine. Their theme of speech brings us to the author's means of speaking to us, his fiction. Having made ironic modernist realism's implicit claim to tell us about the world, the postmodern fictionist has questioned the writer's own instrument, and he or she thus often turns to examine it in the reader's presence. Irving is not exempt from this tendency toward metafiction.

Metafiction

Irving's novel alludes to the phenomenon of metafiction when discussing the rejection note that Garp received for "The Pension Grillparzer": *"The story is only mildly interesting, and it does nothing new with language or with form."* Tinch, Garp's former instructor, said he really did not understand the "newer fiction" except that it was supposed to be "about it-it-itself. . . . It's sort of fiction about fi-fi-*fiction*," Tinch told Garp. Garp did not understand either and, in truth, cared mainly about the fact that Helen liked the story. But although Garp was not interested in metafiction at this stage of his career, we can see that Irving is to some degree practicing this aspect of the new fiction in the third section of *Garp*. While the accounts of Garp's earlier novels may bear a certain resemblance to Irving's own earlier works, these need not be considered metafictional manifestations; one merely suspects Irving of a certain wry humor of self parody, while he remains in the traditional mode of autobiographical fiction or even within the mere technique of an author drawing on his own experience for his fiction. In contrast, when we enter the third section we encounter Garp's novel *The World According to Bensenhaver,* with its obvious similarity in title to **The World According to Garp.** Although there are significant differences between the novel we are reading and the one we are reading about, the parallels and even the comedy of the differences cannot help but act as implicit comments upon the technique and compositional process of **Garp.**

"'Life,' Garp wrote," according to the novel, "'is sadly *not* structured like a good old-fashioned novel. Instead, an ending occurs where those who are meant to peter out have petered out.'" Such a metafictional comment in the third section does not surprise us. Indeed, we see this mode occurring repeatedly. When Garp's publisher, John Wolf, was dying he asked Garp's son Duncan "What would your father say to this? . . . Wouldn't it suit one of *his* death scenes? Isn't it properly grotesque?" To the extent that we could ask this question equally of Irving as of Garp, the question has metafictional implications, as does what Wolf said about Garp's own grotesque mode of dying: "It was a death scene, John Wolf told Jillsy Sloper, that only Garp could have written." When a character in a novel says that a death scene in that novel occurred in a way which "only" the dying character could have written, we are involved with metafiction.

The structure of the final chapter, which opens with a comment on Garp's fictional technique, has further metafictional implications: "He loved epilogues, as he showed us in 'The Pension Grillparzer.' 'An epilogue,' Garp wrote, 'is more than a body count. An epilogue, in the disguise of wrapping up the past, is really a way of warning us about the future.'" And the final chapter—the nineteenth, identical to the number of chapters in *The World According to Bensenhaver*—ends with just such an epilogue. Irving's narrator makes the metafictional element nearly explicit: "He would have liked the idea of an epilogue, too," says the narrator after Garp's death, "—so here it is: an epilogue 'warning us about the future,' as T. S. Garp might have imagined it." Thus the final twenty pages of the novel present us the interesting metafictional element situation of an author writing the epilogue to his character's death as the narrator says the character would himself have imagined it. Metafiction, combined with the zone of the bizarre and the turn away from psychological depth makes the third section of the novel postmodern. While the first two thirds exhibit far less of these characteristics and more of those of earlier modes, these sections exhibit the postmodern reuse of earlier forms; thus, *Garp* is postmodern throughout.

In writing this novel, Irving stays true to his rejecting the spirit of the unreadable masterpieces of high modernism, but he is not returning to the mode of the nineteenth century; he is moving forward into postmodernism. In his desire to avoid the esoteric, Irving might find an ally in John Barth, who in "The Literature of Replenishment: Postmodernist Fiction" offers his "worthy program" in hopes that the postmodern mode may become a fiction "more democratic in its appeal" than the marvels of late modernism, reaching beyond the "professional devotees of high art" but perhaps not hoping to reach the "lobotomized mass-media illiterates." In its best-seller popularity, *The World According to Garp* has at least fulfilled that aspect of Barth's program for postmodern fiction. This success may be described by the proposition that the postmodern novel, besides its special characteristics, also contains all earlier fictional forms, and John Irving's use of two of them opens his novel to a fruitful variety of combination and interaction.

Irving Weinman (review date 9 April 1993)

SOURCE: "Short Shrifts," in *Times Literary Supplement*, April 9, 1993, p. 21.

[*In the following review, Weinman offers tempered criticism of* Trying to Save Piggy Sneed.]

The dust-jacket announces this volume of eight short pieces by John Irving as "a perfect introduction to his work". But the unfamiliar reader would do better to start with any of his seven novels than with these six short stories (all separately published between 1972 and 1982, introduced here by a memoir and closed by an essay). It is not that Irving's fiction-writing virtues aren't displayed in the stories: inventive

incident, deft characterization and vivid language are all here. Despite these admirable qualities, however, the stories, on the whole, don't work. Over the space of a novel, Irving's loosely structured incidents, narrated with appealing garrulousness, accumulate depth and intensity, and character is deepened bit by bit. This technique doesn't work in short stories, where the demand is for focus and intensity, and it is on such novelistic incidents, with their concomitant bitty characterization, that Irving structures most of these tales.

One, **"The Pension Grillparzer,"** comes verbatim from his most famous novel, *The World According to Garp.* In the novel, the episode helps to develop character and the sense of how a writer comes to tell stories (Garp is a novelist); out of context, it is a whirl of characters (nine, not counting the bear) and happenings that don't cohere. Still, it is full of fine sensual detail: "The hall rug was thin, the color of a shadow." "Shadow" means not only the shadow of its former self but the illusions, dreams and memories which fill the pension.

The short-story form also highlights Irving's tendency to overwrite, which is less noticeable in the shifts and sprawl of the novel. Like his model, Dickens, he leaves little room for the reader's inference. He will keep telling even after he's shown. The story **"Interior Space"** opens:

> George Ronkers was a young urologist in a university town—a lucrative situation nowadays; the uninformed liberality of both the young and old college community produced a marvel of venereal variety. A urologist had plenty to do.

After "a lucrative situation" and "a marvel of venereal variety," the last sentence is already understood.

A different kind of overwriting is found in **"The Pension Grillparzer."** Inspecting her bedroom at the pension with an apprehensive eye, the grandmother sees: "The bed had an unsettling ridge at its center, like fur risen on a dog's spine—was almost as if a very slender body lay stretched beneath the bedspread." In this tale of unicycling bears and ghastly dreams, the comparison of the bed's ridge to a dog's risen hackles is cleverly sinister, but Irving adds the dash, and the heavy, plodding qualified second simile which crushes the effect of the first.

The short story's rejection of novelistic implant isn't the only problem. **"Almost in Iowa,"** in which a man's breakdown is told through his relation to his Volvo, aims for effects incompatible with Irving's four-square, realistic strengths. It is as of he had tried to become Donald Barthelme. (Even Barthelme found that difficult.)

There are two good stories in the collection: the very short

"Brennbar's Rant," and **"Weary Kingdom,"** about a matron at a girls' college. The latter is the one in which Irving's novelistic talents are best redefined for short fiction. The middle-aged matron, Minna, must face the play of passion and sexuality between the kitchen-help, Angelo, for whom she's felt some matronly concern, and a new employee, Celeste. Irving's descriptions mediate delicately between Minna's repressed sensuality and her half-unconscious attraction to sexy Celeste. It's a sensitively rendered story of sentiment, in which Celeste may be heavenly, but little Minna is never a mere stereotype of the repressed old maid.

Robert Towers (review date 4 September 1994)

SOURCE: "Dr. Daruwalla and the Dwarfs," in *The New York Times Book Review,* September 4, 1994, pp. 1, 22.

[*In the following review, Towers offers praise for* A Son of the Circus.]

A dozen or so years ago, the newly revived *Vanity Fair* ran a color photograph of John Irving in his wrestler's outfit that seemed to reveal more about his fiction than about the wrestler himself. A bold frontal stance, a (mostly) good-natured aggressiveness, muscularity, an inclination to show off, to take risks—these are qualities we have come to anticipate in Mr. Irving's novels since *The World According to Garp* first hurtled him to fame. Like Dickens, to whom he has often been too facilely compared, he is a "big" novelist, unafraid of extravagant plots, of grotesque or freakish characters, of sensationalism, of sentimentality. He is also, as his 1989 novel, *A Prayer for Owen Meany,* demonstrated, willing to confront religious experience, to indulge in hints of the miraculous. In one respect his new book is his boldest yet: it is set almost entirely in India, where Mr. Irving (as he tells us in an author's note) has spent less than a month, and its principal character is an Indian, albeit a deracinated one.

Though the author is careful to claim that *A Son of the Circus* is not a novel "about" India, a country that "remains obdurately foreign" to him, the sights and sounds and smells of Bombay, its topology and folkways, its slums, clubs and circuses, its beggars and prostitutes, are teemingly present on nearly every page. With the help of Indian friends, Mr. Irving has clearly taken considerable pains to get the details right, and, as a quick journalistic overview, his picture is (judging from my own now-distant experience of the country) sufficiently convincing.

The figure—at once a character and a guide—through whose sensibility the reader experiences most of the novel's multitudinous events is well chosen for the purpose. A Western-

ized, English-speaking Parsi (rather than a Hindu or Muslim), Farrokh Daruwalla is an orthopedic surgeon who is married to an Austrian and spends most of his time in Toronto. Though a Canadian citizen and an Anglican convert, Dr. Daruwalla feels compelled to return to his native Bombay every four or five years to work at the Hospital for Crippled Children, to indulge his passion for circuses and to take blood samples from the dwarfs who make up the majority of circus clowns in India. By the last activity, he hopes to find a genetic marker for achondroplasia, the defect that causes the clowns' dwarfism. Dr. Daruwalla is presented as a kindly and decent man, a little naïve: "Because his medical practice was an exercise of almost pure goodness, he was ill prepared for the real world. Mostly he saw malformations and deformities and injuries to children; he tried to restore their little joints to their intended perfection. The real world had no purpose as clear as that."

Despite the novel's exotic coloration, the author's many admirers will soon enough feel at home in the world according to John Irving—a world populated not only by dwarfs but also by identical twins separated at birth (one a pseudo-Indian film star, the other an American Jesuit), by transvestite eunuchs (*hijras*), simple transvestites (*zenanas*) and "complete" transsexuals. A lascivious child prostitute who may be H.I.V. positive and a beggar boy whose foot has been crushed by an elephant are there to distress us while simultaneously giving our heart-strings a good tug. Complications are piled upon complications. In addition to being a surgeon, a circus fan and a researcher into dwarfism, Dr. Daruwalla is also a secret writer of film scripts that feature a detective known as Inspector Dhar, a sneering, handsome character played by the twin whom the doctor has unofficially adopted. Since Inspector Dhar is hated by Indian men and adored by Indian women, the prospective reader can easily imagine the possibilities for comedy or catastrophe that occur when the other twin—who is unaware of his brother's existence—arrives from America to teach at a Jesuit mission school.

There are, I would guess, perhaps a dozen subplots (some of them embryonic) in *A Son of the Circus.* One, set 20 years before the present action (but subsequently linked to it), involves an American hippie who, after the murder of her drug-dealing German lover, finds herself in possession of an enormous hollow dildo filled with Deutsche marks. There is, however, a main plot, which, though often out of sight, serves as a kind of spine for this novel of multiple concerns. It centers on the attempt to discover and then to trap the murderer of an elderly Indian golfer at the Duckworth Sports Club—a murderer who may also be the serial killer of so-called "cage-girl" prostitutes, who are exhibited in enclosures along the alleyways in Bombay's extensive red-light district. (The bellies of the prostitutes have all been embellished with the ink-drawn cartoon of an elephant's head, one of whose eyes is the victim's navel.)

Dr. Daruwalla is a major participant in this quest, for he had, 20 years earlier, seen such a cartoon on the corpse of a murdered girl and has used the motif in a recent film, "Inspector Dhar and the Cage-Girl Killer," that appears to have provoked a new round of killings. The chief suspect is soon revealed to be a member of the highly respectable Duckworth Club, a married woman of a certain age referred to as "the second Mrs. Dogar." Is it possible that she is none other than a transsexual once known to the doctor as a beautiful but vicious youth called Rahul? The entrapment, in which a real Indian police inspector and his neurotic American wife (formerly the dildo-carrying hippie) play a significant part, entails an elaborate scheme whose intricacies and improbabilities are amusing to follow.

As his readers have come to expect, Mr. Irving in addition to his affinity for freaks and misfits and his penchant for bizarre, violent and farcical incident, has serious themes to explore—or at least to toy with. In *A Son of the Circus,* which is dedicated to Salman Rushdie, the theme of exile— the state of being a perpetual immigrant—is repeatedly sounded in the case of Dr. Daruwalla, who is at home neither in Toronto, where he is subject to racist abuse, nor in India, where he feels overwhelmed by the country's misery and chaos. Questions of gender and homosexuality—is the latter genetically determined or simply a "life style" choice?—also figure prominently in the novel; both of the identical twins are revealed to be gay, as are two of Dr. Daruwalla's medical colleagues in Canada. The distinctions between real and spurious religious experience are brought into play in connection with Dr. Daruwalla and the Jesuit missionary; even the old paradoxes of free will and predestination are once again rehearsed.

The trouble with these thematic excursions is that they tend to be superficial, insufficiently grounded in the characters and inadequately dramatized in the novel's action. I found them a little boring, interruptions rather than enhancements of my pleasure in the lively progression of events. More seriously, the characters themselves, while often striking in their conception, do not really cohere. As we have seen, Farrokh Daruwalla, the protagonist, is presented as an exile not only in Toronto and Bombay but also in the world itself—an interesting idea. The problem is that the doctor, meant to be both the embodiment of goodness and the eternal immigrant, remains little more than a collection of externally presented attributes. Though we are often made party to his thoughts, no real inwardness is achieved. We never learn why he moved to Canada in the first place. Nor does his curious conversion (the result of what he interprets as a miraculously bitten toe!) seem in the least congruent with what else we are told about him. Similarly, Rahul, as the countervailing embodiment of pure evil, remains a symbolic monster, chillingly sinister but never for a moment human.

While Mr. Irving's approach can lead to prose that is annoyingly perfunctory, even glib, it has its advantages too: the narrative pace never bogs down for long. The reader is swept along by a torrent of vigorously dramatized incidents, jostled by a crowd of instantly (if momentarily) vivid characters. Though seldom memorable or particularly quotable, the language has an energy that keeps pace with the fecundity of invention. The exuberance—and sheer nerve—of John Irving's Indian tour de force goes a long way toward compensating for whatever fictional weaknesses the critical reader is likely to perceive. All things considered, I found it his most entertaining novel since *Garp.*

Sven Birkerts (review date 4 February 1996)

SOURCE: "A Son of the 19th Century," in *The New York Times Book Review,* February 4, 1996, p. 9.

[*In the following review, Birkerts offers tempered criticism of* Trying to Save Piggy Sneed.]

Reading *Trying to Save Piggy Sneed,* John Irving's ninth book but only his first compendium of assorted prose, duplicated for this reviewer the sensation of moving in a large airplane over a long stretch of tarmac before suddenly, thankfully, achieving liftoff. Mr. Irving's miscellany—divided into "Memoirs," "Fiction" (six short stories) and "Homage"— shows how one of our most widely read novelists fares in what he might consider a triathlon of lesser events. What we find, in this order, are disappointments, confirmations and surprises.

The author, an avowed Dickens lover, has from the first demonstrated a good bit of the master's ability with passionate impersonation: his fictional characters strike us as autonomous creatures rather than as just so many refractions of one basic creative sensibility. Sadly, though, Mr. Irving cannot quite manage what the successful memoirist must: he is unable to passionately impersonate himself.

The three essays in the "Memoirs" section fail to engage because Mr. Irving cannot, for once, determine what is compelling and what is not. And so a beguilingly entitled work of autobiographical disclosure like *The Imaginary Girlfriend* becomes, finally, a series of dropped names and seemingly endless accounts of wrestling matches, first those of the young Irving, then those of his teen-age sons. "The referee had blown the whistle for the injury without giving me points for my reversal," Mr. Irving writes, "so the score was still 6-6—and I was still on the bottom." There is only so much that the non-aficionado cares to follow. A better reversal would have been a reversal of strategy, with the psychological struggle of making a writer's life taking precedence over the literal sweat and tears.

Fortunately, this first section is followed by a suite of six previously uncollected stories, including the justly celebrated **"Pension Grillparzer,"** which the author originally attributed to T. S. Garp in *The World According to Garp.* In these works we find displayed a generous range of authorial imagination. Mr. Irving conjures up the marital life of a college-town urologist (**"Interior Space"**), the yearning solitude of a matron at a girls' school in Boston (**"Weary Kingdom"**) and, somewhat less convincingly, the relationship between a driver on an existential errand and his Volvo (**"Almost in Iowa"**).

Supple and energetic as a stylist, Mr. Irving also knows just how to create in the reader's mind a vivid impression of an existing world—and just how to populate it. No one who reads, say, **"The Pension Grillparzer"** will forget the story's antic traveling family and its encounter with the peculiar denizens of a broken-down rooming house, in particular Duna, the unicycle-riding circus bear who "had very good balance but . . . was careless."

So much in Mr. Irving's work goes back to Dickens, that one main source. Indeed, two of the three essays in the "Homage" section are about his hero. The first, **"The King of the Novel,"** shows Mr. Irving to be a spirited and persuasive belletristic essayist. Writing mainly about *Great Expectations,* he very deftly uses the novel as a lens through which to see the man's entire life and work. On page after page, he shares insights that not only cut to the core of Dickens's endeavor but incidentally illuminate the novelist's privileged art. Justifying Dickens's often extraordinary plots, Mr. Irving abruptly asserts, "Just accept as a fact that everyone of any emotional importance to you is related to everyone else of any emotional importance to you," and with this simple yet metaphysically insightful premise, he invites us to ponder a kind of realism that verisimilitude cannot address.

One of the delights of this essay is Mr. Irving's frequent citation of G. K. Chesterton, whose observations ("The great fool is a being who is above wisdom and not below it") sit like sugared almonds on what is already a rich concoction. Their aptness provokes an odd notion: that John Irving's work shows us where the 19th century might have got to had it just kept going.

Andrew Rosenheim (review date 4 February 1996)

SOURCE: "Catch-As-Catch-Can," in *Times Literary Supplement,* February 4, 1996, p. 9.

[In the following review, Rosenheim offers a generally favorable assessment of The Imaginary Girlfriend.*]*

Evelyn Waugh's Mr Pinfold maintained that "most men have the germs of one or two books only; all else is professional trickery". One of the appealing things about the popular American novelist John Irving is his unwillingness to use any tricks at all, or to pretend that the same themes do not recur in his work. Bears, motor cycles, Vienna and, most of all, the sport of wrestling figure prominently and repetitively in his novels, and this curious set of preoccupations has spawned the imaginative plots that are this writer's greatest strength.

The Imaginary Girlfriend is a memoir, atypically short for Irving, which details the major (really, with writing co-dominant) role which amateur wrestling has played in his life. He is quick to admit that wrestling holds little popular appeal, although the amateur sport in America bears no relation to its grotesque professional cousin. It is instead a highly disciplined but low-status sport, finding particular favour in the Midwestern states (Iowa, Nebraska), where the sheer harshness of the winters drives all sport inside.

Irving is, in fact, a New Englander of a privileged sort, who, being the son of a teacher at Phillips Exeter, was able to attend that prestigious boarding school. Yet he manages to portray himself consistently as an underdog, less wealthy than his classmates, academically struggling because of an undiagnosed (and then unknown) dyslexia. In wrestling he found a sport in which, though never talented, he could become competent through hard work, much as he suggests that his success as a writer has come from graft and compulsive rewriting rather than any intrinsic gift. In the light of his subsequent success, this modesty could well seem disingenuous, but the patent sincerity of his passion gives an appealing authenticity to this memoir, though his absorption in the technicalities of his wrestling career can be monotonous.

Far more interesting are the vignettes of the paternal figures and colourful colleagues Irving encountered in one of the few sports where money exercises no influence—and discipline and self-denial (making the weight involves the abstemiousness of a jockey) are all. Ted Seabrooke, Irving's coach at Exeter, was quick to spot his pupil's determination, and to explain that a lack of natural talent could be offset by hard work; "I began to take my lack of talent seriously," says Irving endearingly. Later, when Irving studied at the University of New Hampshire but coached at Exeter, he found Seabrooke joined by the more raffish character of Cliff Gallagher, who "was a little dangerous; he showed the Exeter boys a great number of holds that had been illegal for many years."

Alternating with these memories are shorter accounts of

Irving's development as a writer. Spurred first by an encouraging teacher at Exeter, he ended up as a student at UNH, then attended the famed Iowa Writers Workshop. Here the characters encountered are more famous but less interestingly evoked. The late Thomas Williams (author of the wonderful novel *The Hair of Harold Roux*), Kurt Vonnegut and John Cheever all encouraged Irving, but their appearances in *The Imaginary Girlfriend,* along with a cameo by Robertson Davies, hold none of the resonance of his wrestling mentors. Or, indeed, of the taxi-driver who drove Irving and a teammate to West Point from Manhattan for a meet, then stayed to cheer them on and rifle the locker room of the participants' valuables.

The same lack of force accompanies Irving's account of his early struggles as a writer and the sources for his much-repeated themes. His year abroad in Vienna during his college days, for example, occupies only nine pages in the book; they are characterized chiefly by his lingering distaste for an Austrian anti-Semitism he and a Jewish friend found endemic. Bears play no role at all, nor motorcycles, and, except for one black-and-white still of his second wife and fleeting mentions of his first, women are nowhere to be found. Wrestling more than writing seems to be the protagonist's obvious first love, though it is a tribute to Irving's skill as a writer that a sport of such minority interest is made so compelling and alive.

FURTHER READING

Criticism

Harter, Carol C., and James R. Thompson. "The Man and the Writer: 'Novelist as Cultural Hero.'" In *John Irving,* pp. 1-19. New York: Twayne Publishers, 1986.
> Examines Irving's artistic development, narrative concerns, and public perception.

Miller, Gabriel. "Life and Art." In *John Irving,* pp. 1-24. New York: Frederick Ungar Publishing, 1982.
> Provides an overview of Irving's artistic development, narrative concerns, and critical reception.

Page, Philip. "Hero Worship and Hermeneutic Dialectics:

John Irving's *A Prayer for Owen Meany."* *Mosaic* 28, No. 3 (September 1995): 137-56.
> Examines hermeneutical tensions in *A Prayer for Owen Meany* as a source of multiple interpretations of metaphors, events, characters, and gender relations in the novel.

Rockwood, Bruce L. "Abortion Stories: Uncivil Discourse and *Cider House Rules."* In *Law and Literature Perspectives,* edited by Bruce L. Rockwood, pp. 289-340. New York: Peter Lang, 1996.
> Explores issues surrounding the legalization of abortion and Irving's pro-choice position in *The Cider House Rules.*

Sheppard, R. Z. "Life into Art." *Time* (31 August 1981): 46-51.
> Offers an overview of Irving's life and the publishing success of *The World According to Garp.*

Shostak, Debra. "The Family Romances of John Irving." *Essays in Literature* 21, No. 1 (Spring 1994): 129-45.
> Explores the significance of family origins, paternal authority, and Oedipal conflicts in Irving's novels.

———. "Plot as Repetition: John Irving's Narrative Experiments." *Critique: Studies in Contemporary Fiction* 37, No. 1 (Fall 1995): 51-70.
> Examines the function of recurring themes and motifs, such as bears, wrestling, Vienna, and physical deformities, in Irving's fiction.

Interviews

Freeland, Alison. "A Conversation with John Irving." *New England Review* 18, No. 2 (Spring 1997): 135-42.
> Irving discusses his artistic concerns, literary influences, and the publication of *Trying to Save Piggy Sneed* and *An Imaginary Girlfriend.*

McCaffery, Larry. "An Interview with John Irving." *Contemporary Literature* 23, No. 1 (Winter 1982): 1-18.
> Irving discusses his artistic development, thematic preoccupations, and the critical reception of *The World According to Garp.*

Additional coverage of Irving's life and career is contained in the following sources published by Gale: *Authors and Artists for Young Adults,* **Vol. 8;** *Bestsellers,* **89:3;** *Contemporary Authors,* **Vols. 25-28R;** *Contemporary Authors New Revision Series,* **Vol. 28;** *Dictionary of Literary Biography,* **Vol. 6;** *Dictionary of Literary Biography Yearbook,* **Vol. 82;** *DISCovering Authors Modules: Novelists and Popular Fiction* **and** *Genre Authors;* **and** *Major Twentieth-Century Writers.*

Jay McInerney
1955-

American novelist, short story writer, and editor.

The following entry presents an overview of McInerney's career through 1996. For further information on his life and works, see *CLC*, Volume 34.

INTRODUCTION

McInerney achieved literary recognition as a chronicler of yuppie angst and upscale glamour during the 1980s. His enormously popular debut novel, *Bright Lights, Big City* (1984), presents an insider's view of the fast-paced nightlife and cocaine subculture of the young, privileged elite in New York City. In subsequent novels, including *Ransom* (1985), *Story of My Life* (1988), *Brightness Falls* (1992), and *The Last of the Savages* (1996), McInerney offers similar portraits of disaffected affluent professionals harried by isolation, drug and alcohol abuse, and their inability to find meaning or love in contemporary upper-class society. Praised for his satirical wit, McInerney is regarded as a gifted social observer of the hedonistic excesses and psychological torpor personified by the wildly prosperous young, urban professional of the 1980s.

Biographical Information

Born in Hartford, Connecticut, McInerney spent his childhood in several cities in North America and Europe, including London and Vancouver, the result of his father's frequent transfers as an international sales executive. After completing high school in Pittsfield, Massachusetts, where his family eventually settled, McInerney attended Williams College, from which he received a bachelor's degree in philosophy and a minor in English in 1976. An aspiring writer, McInerney briefly worked as a reporter for the *Huntington County Democrat,* a local newspaper in Flemington, New Jersey. In 1977, he departed for Japan on a Princeton-in-Asia fellowship, where he attended classes at the Institute for International Studies near Tokyo, taught English at Kyoto University, and worked as a textbook editor for Time-Life Publications in Osaka, Japan. Returning to the United States in 1979, McInerney took work as a fact checker for the *New Yorker* magazine, then as a reader of unsolicited manuscripts at Random House. Upon the encouragement of Raymond Carver, McInerney left New York City and his failed first marriage to begin graduate writing courses at Syracuse University in 1981. Three years later, McInerney married Merry Reymond, a doctoral student, and published his best-selling first novel, *Bright Lights, Big City,* an expansion of his short story "It's Six A.M. Do You

Know Where You Are?" which appeared in the *Paris Review* in 1982. With the stunning success of *Bright Lights, Big City,* an early installment in Random House's newly launched "Vintage Contemporaries" paperback series, McInerney achieved fame and became a representative of the "Literary Brat Pack"—a media-appointed group of young writers, including Bret Easton Ellis, Tama Janowitz, and David Leavitt—whose demand for large advances and similar novelistic concerns distinguished them as a new generation of high-profile authors. McInerney produced his much anticipated second novel, *Ransom,* in 1985, and a third, *Story of My Life,* in 1988. He also collaborated on the screenplay for *Bright Lights, Big City,* which was adapted into a motion picture in 1988. During the 1990s, McInerney entered into a third marriage (to Helen Bransford, a jewelry designer) and published additional novels, including *Brightness Falls* and *The Last of the Savages.* He also edited *Cowboys, Indians, and Commuters* (1994), an anthology of sixteen short stories by young American writers, and has contributed to numerous popular magazines, including *Esquire, Playboy, Vogue,* and *The New Republic.*

Major Works

McInerney's novels relate the disorientation and fragmentation of modern urban life through the experiences of moneyed, upwardly mobile characters whose failed relationships, drug and alcohol addictions, and effete entertainments reveal their superficial concerns. *Bright Lights, Big City,* largely based on McInerney's own life, follows an aspiring writer in his early twenties who works as a fact checker for a highbrow literary magazine resembling *The New Yorker,* binges on cocaine and alcohol at exclusive Manhattan nightclubs, and laments his recent divorce from Amanda, a fashion model, and the death of his mother. From the uncommon second-person point of view, the unnamed narrator describes the frenetic cycle of work, late-night parties, and casual sex sustained by copious amounts of "Bolivian Marching Powder," a euphemism for cocaine. After a period of uninterrupted drugging to numb the painful loss of his wife and mother, the narrator emerges from a cocaine haze to confront his feelings of alienation and lost self-identity. *Ransom* features a young American expatriate, Christopher Ransom, who flees to Japan to study the ancient art of karate and to escape the expectations of his father, a successful writer of banal television programs who presses his son to embrace capitalism. While in Kyoto, Ransom recalls the deaths of his friends, Ian and Annette, in a debacle along the Pakistan-Afghanistan border involving hashish-dealing kidnappers and a drug overdose. After a confrontation with his father, who attempts to lure his son back to the United States with a seductive woman, Ransom is killed in a sparring match with a vicious martial arts student. *Story of My Life* follows the demise of twenty-year-old Alison Poole, a self-proclaimed "postmodern girl," as she slips further into alcoholism and cocaine dependency. Set in Manhattan, Alison's first-person monologue describes her unhappy upbringing, escalating drug habit, and preoccupations with sex, fashion, and shallow stockbrokers. All but abandoned by her womanizing father who molested her as a child and poisoned her favorite horse to collect the insurance money, Alison briefly finds purpose and naive self-awareness in acting classes before her addiction lands her in a Minnesota drug treatment center. In subsequent novels, McInerney writes about similar characters as they gradually settle down and approach mid-life. In *Brightness Falls,* part business thriller and roman à clef about the publishing world, McInerney chronicles the waning prosperity and amorality of the 1980s through the marital crisis of Russell and Corinne Calloway—both New York professionals in their early thirties—and the mercurial success of Jeff Pierce, a newly famous young author who succumbs to heroin addiction. The title of the novel is taken from Thomas Nashe's fatalistic Elizabethan poem "A Litany in Time of Plague." Seduced by the allure of wealth and power, Russell, an editor at a distinguished publishing firm, unsuccessfully attempts to usurp the company in a hostile takeover. His marriage to Corinne, a highly paid stockbroker and morally conscious soup kitchen volunteer, is also shaken by mutual infidelities—Russell's with an attractive financier and Corinne's with Jeff. Their eventual reconciliation highlights the importance of love and security over the corrupting influence of greed and ruthless ambition. *The Last of the Savages* explores contemporary race issues in the Deep South through the friendship of former prep school roommates Patrick Keane, a New Englander of modest origins, and Will Savage, a wealthy descendant of aristocratic Memphis planters. Narrated by Patrick, a prosperous New York corporate lawyer in his late forties, the story relates Will's extreme guilt over his family heritage of slave ownership, which he compensates for by promoting black blues musicians and radical politics. While Patrick enjoys the fruits of an Ivy League education and a prestigious career, Will resents his bigoted father, marries a black singer, and struggles to overcome a drug addiction that renders him sterile.

Critical Reception

Upon the publication of *Bright Lights, Big City,* McInerney emerged as a leading new voice in contemporary American fiction. His heady depiction of rampant cocaine abuse, sexual encounters, and after-hours parties among the trendy New York elite attracted a large popular audience and much critical discussion, becoming itself a handbook of yuppie debauchery during the mid-1980s. The cynical narrator of *Bright Lights, Big City* has been favorably compared to J. D. Salinger's Holden Caulfield in *The Catcher in the Rye.* While some critics praise McInerney's authentic, streetwise voice and unabashed description of arrogant decompensation during the heyday of Reaganomics, others find fault in McInerney's second-person narrative, ephemeral colloquial style, and apparent glorification of the profligate lifestyle portrayed in the novel. Though *Ransom* failed to live up to the promise of his literary debut, McInerney was praised for wry humor and perceptive analysis of the tragically spoiled and fashionably addicted in *Story of My Life, Brightness Falls,* and *The Last of the Savages.* Both *Brightness Falls,* a satire of New York greed and corruption akin to Tom Wolfe's 1987 novel *The Bonfire of the Vanities,* and *The Last of the Savages* are admired for McInerney's effort to address larger social issues. Frequently compared to F. Scott Fitzgerald, whose evocation of the Lost Generation and gilded age of the 1920s defined an era, McInerney is regarded as a literary spokesperson for the disillusioned young professional of the 1980s.

PRINCIPAL WORKS

Bright Lights, Big City (novel) 1984

Ransom (novel) 1985
Story of My Life (novel) 1988
Brightness Falls (novel) 1992
*Cowboys, Indians, and Commuters: The Penguin Book of
    New American Voices* [editor] (short stories) 1994
The Last of the Savages (novel) 1996

CRITICISM

Ruth Doan MacDougall (review date 5 October 1984)

SOURCE: "Having Fun in New York," in *The Christian Science Monitor,* October 5, 1984, p. B5.

[*In the following review, MacDougall offers a favorable assessment of* Bright Lights, Big City.]

The nameless hero of this very funny first novel narrates the story in second person—a device that runs the risk of becoming gimmicky and tedious but instead triumphs, emphasizing the distance the hero feels from his collapsing life.

A "perennial new kid" in school, he grew up with a feeling "of always standing to one side of yourself, of watching yourself in the world even as you were being in the world, and wondering if this was how everyone felt."

A few months ago, however, the world had seemed his oyster. He was 24 years old. He was married to beautiful Amanda, whom he had met in Kansas City, where he had gone after college to work as a reporter. They'd moved to New York, and he had landed an impressive-sounding job at "the magazine" (could it be *The New Yorker*?).

When he met Amanda, she was working for a florist, unaware that she was a perfect Size 8 and possessed "neo-classical" cheekbones which could earn $150 an hour. But in New York she soon had a contract with a modeling agency, and though at first she hated the work, eventually she was caught up in it, flying to Europe for showings. And one day four months ago she phoned from Paris to say she wasn't coming home. Ever.

Now the hero's career at the magazine is on the skids. Mr. McInerney has a wonderful time with this magazine, especially with the hero's Department of Factual Verification on the 29th floor, where "the layout suggests a condo for high-rise gophers" and the people "speak as if they were weaned on Twining's English Breakfast Tea." The department is ruled by a tyrant who is just waiting for our friend to slip up; if she [the tyrant] "had her way you would have

been expelled long ago, but the magazine has a tradition of never acknowledging its mistakes." The hero, trying to verify the facts and spelling in a sloppy article, is about to make her wish come true.

He seeks escape from his problems in the night life of Manhattan, accompanied by an ad-agency friend "whose mission in life is to have more fun than anyone else in New York City," and who, as they move from night spot to night spot during each evening's spree, "takes pride in his timing, being on time by being the latest." The hero keeps finding himself snorting cocaine in bathrooms while longing to be home in his apartment reading Dickens or at least watching "Family Feud."

Other hapless heroes, such as Kingsley Amis's "Lucky Jim," come to mind. The trick is not to exasperate the reader, and Mr. McInerney has us solidly on his hero's side, aware of the grief that underlies the humor.

At the end, the revelation of a greater grief doesn't fit all that went before. A rereading shows that McInerney tried to hint at it, but the reader hasn't been properly prepared. Even so, the revelation is handled with the same skill that shines throughout the novel. His is a true talent.

Roz Kaveney (review date 24 May 1985)

SOURCE: "Solutions to Dissolution," in *Times Literary Supplement,* May 24, 1985, p. 572.

[*In the following excerpt, Kaveney offers praise for* Bright Lights, Big City.]

The urban unease that these novels depict has in them its artistic equivalent, a sense of less than absolute commitment to technical strategies adopted. The novel has traditionally celebrated community; can its traditional mechanisms be as readily applied to the corruption or disappearance, in the modern American city, of any participation in a common social existence? The narrative perversities of Jay McInerney, Gloria Naylor's frequent descents into the barn-storming of melodrama and soap opera, the insecurity which causes Dyan Sheldon constantly to over-egg her stylistic pudding—these serious flaws in three otherwise admirable books point to a sense that traditional fictions might not be ideally suited to the depiction of contemporary urban life, but just the best solution that comes readily to these authors' hands.

McInerney's ***Bright Lights, Big City*** is in many ways a stunning debut; reservations have to do with tone, with uncertainty as to whether McInerney is manipulating our judgment of the amoral, sentimental, charming hero, describing journalistically and leaving us to draw conclusions, or colluding more deeply than he knows in his protagonist's flaws, telling us more than he intends. The unnamed hero (addressed throughout, for no obvious reason, in the second person) works—on the brink of dismissal for incompetence—in the Department of Factual Verification at a Famous New York Magazine, has been left by Amanda, the successful model he found in a Kansas bar and taught to be trendy, and is busily corroding his septum with "the powder that made Bolivia famous" in more night clubs than anyone could cope with in the course of an early morning. In one week he accepts the loss of his job, his wife and his year-dead mother; the writing he always means to get round to might be his salvation, or perhaps the preppy cousin of a friend might be; in the meantime, "You will have to learn everything all over again."

What saves all this from looming sentimentality is McInerney's very precise eye and ear, and his sense of the comedy that comes from character. His hero is the type who would fail consistently to perceive that the two women he and his friend Tad are escorting are considerably more interested in each other than in them. At the same time, a Chandlersque palette full of urban description convinces us that there is something to this self-wasting voice worthy of our consideration and our regard. If the other people in the novel are either caricatures (his dragon-lady boss, Clara) or play consoling roles (the Tough Younger Brother, the Supportive Older Woman Colleague) and forgive him his derelictions, that is how someone as selfish and stressed as he is would in general characterize the world around him. His first step on the way to reform is his acceptance that he never knew his mother as an individual rather than a role until the hour of her death, that he has never known, nor ever will know, his wife Amanda at all. *Bright Lights, Big City* combines slick but accurate phrase-making, excellently-paced scenes of comic embarrassment and a tone at once languid, rich and economical; over-insistence on the heart of gold the hero wears on his sleeve is no more than a minor irritation.

Ron Loewinsohn (review date 29 September 1985)

SOURCE: "Land of the Also Rising Sun," in *The New York Times Book Review,* September 29, 1985, p. 42.

[*In the following review, Loewinsohn offers unfavorable assessment of* Ransom.]

Jay McInerney is a serious, gifted artist. His first novel, *Bright Lights, Big City,* is a brilliant and moving work—unique, refreshing, imaginatively powerful and authentically

conceived. *Ransom,* on the other hand, while dealing competently with some of the same themes—alienation, self-alienation and the need for context and continuity—rarely rises above the level of mere competence. It feels thoroughly conventional, thoroughly uninspired.

It is concerned with a group of young, rootless American expatriates in an exotic foreign land where one of them attempts to reconstruct his ravaged self in a corrupt and corrupting environment, and it reads like a transistorized version of *The Sun Also Rises*—that is, miniaturized, reduced. Hemingway set his action in Paris and Spain; Mr. McInerney places his characters in Japan.

Where bullfighting provided Hemingway with a central metaphor, karate does the same for Mr. McInerney. Like bullfighting, karate is a national sport-cum-ritual-cum-esthetic and moral proving ground, and like Hemingway, Mr. McInerney uses the purity and intensity of commitment to this violent art as a gauge of his various characters' human worth. Both books focus on male companionship and competitiveness, and in both books the protagonist acts as a pimp—selling or giving the woman he is involved with to another man. (The epigraph to *Bright Lights, Big City* is quoted from *The Sun Also Rises*.)

Ransom tracks the adventures of Christopher Ransom, an American in his mid-20's, during one spring in Kyoto, where he has gone because he had imagined Japan as "a place of austere discipline which would cleanse and change him." In the novel's flat-footed, explanatory style, we are told (rather than shown) that Ransom "had lost his bearings spiritually, and he wanted to reclaim himself." So he takes up karate as a form of penance and purification. He feels guilty about the flabby privilege of his upper-middle-class background, and guilty by association with his father, a playwright who sold out years before, getting fat writing scripts for television sitcoms. But mostly (we are told) he embraces the pain and asceticism of karate as a "partial redemption after what had happened to Ian and Annette."

We are told what happened to Ian and Annette in a series of coy, melodramatic flashbacks. Two years earlier, bumming around the Pakistan-Afghanistan border with the international punks-on-dope set, Ian (a college acquaintance of Ransom's) is supposedly kidnapped while buying hashish, and Ransom tries to buy back his freedom, offering a night with Annette, his heroin-addict French girlfriend, as part of the ransom. Was Ian really kidnapped? Was Annette killed by an overdose? Was Ransom responsible for her death? Do we care?

Meanwhile, back in Japan, Ransom has become involved in attempting to rescue a young woman (she says she is a Vietnamese refugee) from the clutches of an overlord in the

Yakuza, the Japanese equivalent of the Mafia. But there is more: Ransom's father, who wants him to come home, sends an emissary, Rachel, who makes set speeches about business as "the new logos . . . the Tao of Capital." Then the father himself shows up and makes speeches equating the entertainment business with "what we're all in . . . the power business."

Ransom is not without its strengths. Its descriptions of karate drills and matches are well done. At its most competent, it offers unsentimental, insightful observations of contemporary Japan, including its grossnesses and its sometimes lethal attraction for Westerners who see in its rituals and traditions the embodiment of their dreams of order, cohesiveness and belonging. As heavy handed as Mr. McInerney often is with dialogue and explanation, he often handles metaphors and symbols deftly—as he does with the awakenings and scriptwriting.

But the book reads like a terribly uncertain first novel—explaining too much, summarizing when it needs to render, and deaf to its own lame phrases. It has none of the linguistic brio or Raymond Chandler-style humor of *Bright Lights, Big City.* In a sense *Ransom* is a first novel: Mr. McInerney has said that he began writing *Ransom* first, and before completing it was inspired to write *Bright Lights, Big City.*

Ransom is an honest, even dogged attempt to work seriously with important subjects. If this seriousness joins up again with the energetic inventiveness he displayed in *Bright Lights, Big City,* Mr. McInerney is likely to write much better novels than this.

P. J. O'Rourke (review date 16 September 1988)

SOURCE: "Bookshelf: 'Story of My Life,'" in *The Wall Street Journal,* September 16, 1988, p. 23.

[*In the following review, O'Rourke offers a favorable assessment of* Story of My Life.]

Oh no, it's rich kids leading empty lives, taking harmful drugs and having sex too often (then feeling empty, drugged and tired). In *Story of My Life,* Jay McInerney seems to be adding another volume to the dread and burgeoning category of "Self-Helpless Books."

The browser's first instinct is to take the author, the characters, the author's ex-friends upon whom the characters are based (and the producers, directors and studio executives who will turn it all into a movie any minute now) and ship them to Bangladesh so that the impoverished farmers

of that flood-plagued nation will have something to stand on during monsoon season. The more so because Mr. McInerney has shaken this particular coca bush before, in his clever but twerpy *Bright Lights, Big City:* Spoiled, cocaine-addicted, self-described writer hates job and estranged wife, annoys reader in second person singular, remembers that his mom is dead, finds self and promises to be good from now on.

This time a much more spoiled, much more cocaine-addicted, self-described actress hates dad and dumb pals, annoys reader in present tense, remembers that her horse is dead, finds mental hospital and promises to be sad from now on.

> **Mr. McInerney makes Alison Poole likable, which is hard enough, but the thing that should win him a "Snorty" (or whatever award they give in the dope fiction field) is that he makes her interesting.**
> **—P. J. O'Rourke**

There's only one surprise here, but it's a big one. *Story of My Life* is a very good book. Not since Alfred Jarry tackled waste management in "Ubu Roi" has better art been made from less promising materials.

Alison Poole—the novel's combined spokesmodel, Greek chorus, tragic heroine and gofer, who's "twenty going on gray"—begins with a burst of the inchoate, "I'm like, I don't believe this s—-," and continues for 188 pages without pausing to breathe. She and whelps of her ilk spin and dribble from Gomorrah to acting class to Nell's to suicidal despair powered by immense amounts of drugs and silliness. Alison's voice is note-perfect, vacant-cranium, Manhattan brat chatter. And before you can say, "McInerney has a fine ear, but if this girl doesn't shut up I'm going to run his book through the Robot Coupe," Alison has won you over.

She's funny and she has a way with words:

> I mean you could get paper cuts from this guys lips and I don't even want to mention his tongue . . . it reminds me of this diagram I saw once in a magazine about these lamprey eels that glom onto salmon and suck their insides out.

There's something sweetly pathetic about her saying, "I'm like, I insist on honesty," to a postmoral world where turpitude is a fashion statement and crimes are shouted from the rooftops. Yes, she's self-obsessed, but every other available obsession seems to offer worse results. And, sure, she hates herself. Most modern kids hate themselves. It's touching how Alison knows so many good reasons for doing so.

Mr. McInerney makes Alison Poole likable, which is hard enough, but the thing that should win him a "Snorty" (or whatever award they give in the dope fiction field) is that he makes her interesting. This is possible only because *Story of My Life* is not really about what it's about. Mr. McInerney's true subject is barbarism. Without once looking away from his chosen microcosm of snotty children at loose ends, Mr. McInerney is able to describe a larger world in which hordes of wild bourgeoisie descend from god-knows-where in leased BMWs and lay waste to a civilization. They plunder its foreign reserves, carry away its tax loopholes and feast midst the spoil of its cities, leading lives of aristocratic indulgence unhampered by noblesse oblige.

The essence of barbarism isn't actually rapine, however, it's ignorance. And Alison's mind—a fairly good mind—is absolutely empty.

> He says . . . truth isn't always an unalloyed virtue. I go, a what? Unalloyed, he says. That means pure. And I'm like, no wonder I don't know it. And he says, there are times when it's better to spare people's feelings, keep the social fabric intact. And I'm like, the social fabric? What the hell is that? I go, is that like dacron polyester or something? I mean really, he believes this . . . ? Actually, it's more like silk, he says. It's a delicate thing. It's like nonexistent is what I'm saying, I go. We're all just pieces of lint if you ask me.

The elders in Alison's tribe are no better equipped for ratiocination:

> My parents never gave a s—- whether I went to school or not, they were off chasing lovers or bottles, leaving us kids with the cars and the credit cards. . . . Is that my fault? I mean, if someone told you . . . that you could either go to school or not what do you think you would have done? Pass the trigonometry, please. Right.

It's impossible to imagine the characters portrayed—or even mentioned—in this book performing any act of civic virtue. It's not that they're dropouts or anti-establishmentarian. They just don't know civic virtues exist. They don't know anything.

Alison would have us believe she's screwed up because her father poisoned her favorite jumping horse for the insurance money and maybe made a pass at her. This is nonsense. There are thousands of Alisons bouncing around New York City. They can't all have had molesting, equicidal dads.

Alison comes to a tragic end. She's sent to an expensive drug rehab clinic. The tragedy isn't hers, of course. She'll be fine. She'll come out of therapy just as ignorant, irresponsible and useless, but healthy. The tragedy is ours. We'll have to listen to her babble about the virtues of AA and interactive psychoanalysis for the rest of her life.

Democracy, science, commerce and industry have brought to millions the comforts and possibilities once reserved for a few members of a civilized elite. Pleasure and privilege have grown enormously in our society. Duty and culture have not kept pace. *Story of My Life* is about people who were given the toga of citizenship and threw a toga party.

Carolyn Gaiser (review date 25 September 1988)

SOURCE: "Zonked Again," in *The New York Times Book Review,* September 25, 1988, p. 12.

[*In the following review, Gaiser offers an unfavorable assessment of* Story of My Life.]

Nelson Algren once observed in conversation that "no matter how many novels you write, it sure as hell doesn't get any easier. Each new book is a whole new ball game." That familiar metaphor takes on fresh meaning here, aptly conveying the sheer chanciness of an artistic enterprise in which even a writer as gifted as Jay McInerney may produce a disappointing novel. A very disappointing one.

Story of My Life is Mr. McInerney's third work of fiction. In 1985, he won critical acclaim for his first novel, **Bright Lights, Big City,** a fast-paced, witty, yet oddly moving book about an aspiring young writer adrift in Manhattan—deserted by his wife, high on cocaine and headed for a breakdown.

With this funny valentine to New York (which captured the city in many moods and weathers), Mr. McInerney proved himself not only a brilliant stylist but also a master at characterization. In his second novel, **Ransom,** he brought the Japanese city of Kyoto alive with equal ease; he has a keen eye for the incongruities of urban life.

Unfortunately, his distinctive style and humor are missing from the pages of *Story of My Life,* a pallid version of **Bright Lights, Big City,** told from a young woman's point of view. Mr. McInerney has narrowed his scope drastically in this claustrophobic tale of a "former rich girl" and her headlong slide into alcoholism and cocaine addiction.

In hip (hipper-than-thou) slang, the narrator, 20-year-old

Alison Poole, describes two months of high living on the Upper East Side. Overprivileged but undereducated, she is "not a happy unit." Her much-divorced parents (alcoholic mother and womanizing father) make her wish she were "an orphan. With a trust fund." As the novel opens, the man she's "in lust with," the stockbroker-playboy Skip Pendleton, has just dropped her; she finds a profitable way to get revenge after her father fails to send the tuition check for her acting classes.

"Acting is the first thing that's made me get up in the morning," Alison admits. "The first year I was in New York I didn't do anything but guys and blow." (Riding had been her first love until her favorite horse died.) Though a promising actress, she is beset by distractions: sessions at the tanning salon, nights at Nell's, a popular club, and the constant lures of cocaine and casual sex.

In a state of denial about her own life, Alison finds much to criticize in her friends. They offer a whole panorama of addictions. There's Francesca, hooked on food and the thrill of meeting famous people; "incredibly beautiful" Didi, a "coke monster"; and Jeannie (Alison's roommate), a compulsive spender prone to squandering the rent money.

Just as Alison has fallen in lust, again, with Dean Chasen (a bond trader whose mind attracts her), her "maniac" older sister, Rebecca, flies into town: "She's like an entire heavy metal band on tour." Soon Alison starts skipping class for all-night coke binges. She's not sure if "it's a vicious circle [or] cycle," but enough catastrophes strike to convince her she needs help.

Though the plot teems with activity, the effect is episodic. Mr. McInerney fails to develop his theme—of an abused child's revenge on herself and others—beyond a superficial level.

Then there's the weather problem; we don't know for certain what season it is until page 139, when Alison attends a Kentucky Derby party. Such crucial externals, including the landscape of Manhattan, simply don't exist for her. The monomania of drug dependency takes a heavy toll on the narrator—and on the novel.

Mr. McInerney has created in Alison Poole a thoroughly convincing female voice, but not a very winning character. Her constant flippancy undermines any potential for pathos, and her near inarticulateness cripples the prose. The unrelieved use of slang, coupled with a general lack of structure, causes the novel to read, at times, like the random jottings of a diary kept by a zonked-out teen-ager.

One can only hope that in his next novel Mr. McInerney moves on to a new theme and a new setting—where the weather in the streets and the weather of the heart fire his imagination as they did in *Bright Lights, Big City.*

James Wolcott (review date 10 October 1988)

SOURCE: "Yada Yada Yada," in *New Republic,* October 10, 1988, pp. 38-41.

[*Below, Wolcott offers unfavorable review of* Story of My Life.]

Beware of a novel built upon a catch-phrase. A flip curl eventually loses its hold. Story of my life, toss-away phrase for a toss-away life, is the signature curl of Alison Poole, postmodern boy-toy by night, aspiring actress by day. "Acting is the first thing that's made me get up in the morning. The first year I was in New York I didn't do anything but guys and blow. Staying out all night at the Surf Club and Zulu, waking up at five in the afternoon with plugged sinuses and sticky hair. Some kind of white stuff in every opening. Story of my life." So it, like, fries Alison's bacon that her much-divorced Daddy would rather encourage his latest squeeze than fork over money for her drama school tuition. "He actually believes her when she says she's writing a novel but when I want to spend eight hours a day busting ass at Lee Strasberg's it's like, *another one of Alison's crazy ideas.* Story of my life."

Acting class is about Alison's speed because it showcases her exhibitionism (she boasts in one class about a blowjob she gave that morning) and doesn't bother the Do Not Disturb sign tacked to her brow. It allows her to be her: a hysterical airhead. Alison can only handle a soft curriculum. "[W]hat were the two things that you were never supposed to mix in chemistry class or you'd like blow up the whole school? Not oil and water—something else. So much for my education. Blanks that never got filled in. None of the above. Story of my life." Her friends are blank capsules who hiphop like jumping beans. "Story of Skip's life, trading commodities." "She said she's totally in lust, she'd met a great new guy. Story of her life."

Story of my life. Totally in lust. Can't rape the willing. Shivering wreck. Legend in his own mind. Give me a break. Yada yada yada. Unhappy unit. ***Story of My Life*** becomes a daisy chain of catchphrases. "Story of my life, right? . . . But then I remember my little problem, which makes me a mondo unhappy unit." All talk, no texture, Jay McInerney's third novel speaks in Valley Girl lingo spread with a thick crudola of New York chutzpah. Nerviness and spaciness cross voltage behind spiked eyeballs.

Stylistically McInerney is walking a swinging tightrope.

Novels written entirely in pop idiom seldom succeed, not only because idiom changes (today's trendy expression is tomorrow's corny antique: "pour me a cup of java," said the beatnik to the bearded lady), but because non-stop hipness is too narrow a mode for the full spectrum of human feeling. All-talk novels, from Andy Warhol's *a* to Bret Easton Ellis's *The Rules of Attraction,* are narrow bands of static, nigh on unreadable. Even Norman Mailer, one of McInerney's heroes, couldn't sustain the pop braggadocio with his Texas stud narrator swinging his dong in *Why Are We in Vietnam?* The novel became a no-exit language machine, an orgone box of pun and hyperbole.

McInerney does make a game try. The early pages of *Story of My Life* have a snazzy rhythm and snotty attack. Take Alison's friend Didi, for example. "If Didi made a list of her favorite things I guess cocaine would be at the top and sunlight wouldn't even make the cut." Or take Skip in commodities, still mooning after his college sweetheart. "And I'm like, give me a break, Skip. Give yourself a break. This is ten years after. This is nineteen eighty-whatever." In a daze of drugs and shrinking daylight, Alison grazes at in-spots that already seem passé (Nell's, for instance) and grills herself brown at the tanning salon. But mostly she talks trash. Alison's telephone line is her intravenous tube. Much of the novel consists of telephone calls—

> So of course the phone rings. A guy's voice, Barry something, says, may I speak to Alison Poole?
>
> And I'm like, you're doing it.
>
> I'm a friend of Skip's, he says.
>
> I go, if this is some kind of joke I'm like really not amused.
>
> Hey, no joke, he goes. I'm just, you know, Skip told me you guys weren't going out anymore and I saw you once at Indochine and I thought maybe we could dinner sometime.
>
> I'm like, I don't believe this. What am I?—the York Avenue Escort Service?
>
> I go, did Skip also tell you about the disease he gave me? That shrinks this Barry's equipment pretty quick. Suddenly he's got a call on his other line. Sure you do.

—and answering messages. "I call Dean again and get his machine. Story of my life." Alison herself seems to have a brain equipped with call-waiting. Every new thought makes an interruptive [click].

McInerney has a flair for flash intros. He illuminates Alison's circle of coke-whore friends with a strobe light, its pulsations catching the ghostly ruin beneath their glamour. He also has an ear for how cunty-mouthed a coke whore like Alison sounds: "Alex was really pissed when I read in *Vogue* or somewhere that there's like twelve hundred calories or something like that in an average load of come. Because at the time I was kind of anorexic and the last thing I was looking for was a way to swallow an extra thousand-plus calories." Sex for Alison's circle is a competitive ranking; one of her gal pals records all of their bedmates on a computer file, compiling data on length, width, position, duration.

Since this band of narcissists thinks the world pivots on their pelvises, every setback is shrilly inflated to global status. Pregnant, Alison throws herself a pity party. "And I don't have a nickel to my name, I owe everybody in the western hemisphere, I'm like a fucking Third World country— empty treasury, exploding birth rate. Jesus." (Earlier in the novel she had lied about an abortion to pry money out of a former beau for her portion of the rent.) Ironic that McInerney recently told *New York* magazine, "I'm too young to be a one-note kind of guy when I have a more symphonic mind." *Story of My Life* is only alive when its sticks to its bitchy note of petulance. Beyond that, it's a writing exercise.

Symphonic mind or not, so far McInerney hasn't demonstrated the dramatic amplitude or organizational skills to be a novelist. His specialty is the smart-ass monologue. Brief as it is, *Story of My Life* feels force-fed, crammed with familiar junk. "Jeannie's in a real pissy mood and gets right on the phone to her fiancé, so I watch 'Wheel of Fortune' in the bedroom. When she's finally finished . . . she hangs up and calls the deli to order some Diet Coke and a large bag of barbecue potato chips and a pack of Merit Ultra Lights." For variety from all this zoning out and pigging out in front of the TV, we're taken on a needless tour of midtown Manhattan, where Alison pukes at the observation deck of the Empire State Building and purchases a four-pack of vibrators at a porn shop. McInerney even pads the book with oft-told jokes, including the one about Pia Zadora starring in a production of *The Diary of Anne Frank.* (Punchline: "She's in the attic!") He resorts to these stale tricks with the desperation of a host whose dinner party is dying. Losing his cool to flopsweat, he really begins to reach. "I remember I read somewhere that outlaw guy John Dillinger had one that was about a foot and a half long and it's preserved in the Smithsonian or someplace. Now that's what I call the Washington Monument." Waiter—check, please!

Undoing the novel even more than its patchy construction are its banal psychologizing and sappy sense of woe. As *Bright Lights, Big City* and *Ransom* showed, beneath

McInerney's roomy Armani suits beats the heart-shaped pillow of a blatant sentimentalist. His humor is a cover for heartbreak. It's bad enough in small doses, as when Alison heads uptown to a crackhouse and the vials pop under her feet, "breaking like little promises." And when a crack dealer named Mannie, an exploited ethnic literally outclassed by his white customers, leaps suicidally from a sixth-story window, the message is even heavier: the fall of man, no less. (Mannie, geddit?)

Alison later makes a totally out-of-character visit to Mannie in the hospital only so **Story of My Life** can survey man's fallen state. It's state of grace, as Mannie stares like a Moonie into space, emancipated from his chain of pain. "The thing is, he looks happy, which is more than you can say for the rest of us." Mannie is sacrificed to illustrate the posh vacuum of Alison's privileged upbringing. Early in the novel Alison's friends mockingly allude to Elvis Costello's song "Alison," and McInerney seems to have keyed his characterization from the lyric, "Alison, I know this world is killing you." For unlike Mannie, his Alison's a-hurting inside. She's sorrowful empty.

Stripped of its sequins and sticky residue, **Story of My Life** is basically another money-can't-buy-love tale of a poor little rich girl who's been given anything but parental affection. Mommy is a lush, Daddy is a lech. But her heart belongs to Daddy. ". . . I sort of fantasize that he'll pick up the phone some day and say, is that you, Alison?" Shameless, McInerney even plants a "Rosebud" clue to Alison's disaffection, a horse she adored as a child named Dangerous Dan, which her father had killed for the insurance. Denied Daddy's care, she's doomed to hagdom. So young, so used-up: "Ten days from now I'll be twenty-one. It seems like I've been on the planet a lot longer than that." To keep this cornball crying jag going, McInerney strings the reader along by having Alison ask acquaintances what the three biggest lies are. One is, the check's in the mail, two is, I won't come in your mouth, but what's the third? She can't recall. I'm usually hopeless at guessing games, but even I was able to figure out what the third lie was, and sure enough, in the book's final pages, the payoff: "The third lie is, I love you."

No, the third biggest lie is, "Jay, those critics are just jealous!" In retrospect, lucky timing landed a windfall for **Bright Lights, Big City**. It caught the last tailwind of the downtown club scene before tired trendies began settling in as sofa spuds in front of their VCRs. (By the time the movie version starring Michael J. Fox was released, it had no electric scene to plug into.) And McInerney's sarcastic exposure of the workings of the *New Yorker*'s fact-checking department in **Bright Lights** came at a time when the *New Yorker* was still envisioned as a bloodless Henry James arena of sacred hush and elaborate fuss, where enormous qualms were suspended like raindrops from church

cobwebs. Now that William Shawn no longer mystically ministers the magazine's business with his special dematerializing touch, it's a more pedestrian place.

In E. J. Kahn's chatty diary of 1987 at the *New Yorker* (*Year of Change*), there's a revealing swipe at McInerney: "From London, a copy of a Jay McInerney piece in the Sunday *Times* about the *New Yorker*. Its title is 'Goodbye, Mr. Shawn.' McInerney was fired from Shawn's magazine for being a lousy checker, and his article presents evidence of why that was a good idea: 'And somewhere in the mind of every young man or woman who has ever sent a short story or résumé to the shabby offices on West 43rd Street was the knowledge that J. D. Salinger's *Catcher in the Rye* had first appeared in these pages.' 'Twould have been nice if it had, but it hadn't."

Revealing, because **Story of My Life** is also a misplaced homage to Salinger. **Bright Lights, Big City** was so often compared to *Catcher in the Rye* that McInerney seems to have thought it incumbent to end **Story of My Life** in a way that acknowledges the Salingeresque debt. (*Catcher in the Rye* is also one of the few vernacular novels that *has* lasted.) Where Holden Caulfield ends up in some sort of hospital under a shrink's supervision, Alison crashes in some clinic in Minnesota where she has white dreams while under sedation. Horses appear in both of their memories as emblems of childhood reverie. Like Holden, Alison is suspended on the cusp of adulthood, mentally bandaged from trauma. But Salingeresque innocence can't be faked, even by Salinger himself (as his polishing of the coy precocities of the Glass family proved). Where Holden seemed genuinely lost, Alison seems artificially adrift. For McInerney not only sentimentalizes, he moralizes. He's the one who signs her in for treatment. Alison Must Pay for Her Partying. That's why she's in the clinic: she's the symbol of misspent youth. Miss Selfish Cokehead nineteen eighty-whatever.

But the influence of Salinger goes deeper than McInerney's manhandling of his heroine. **Story of My Life** finds McInerney seeking a literary role model to keep him righteous, a great white father in whose moccasins he can walk. In interviews he broods about the fate of being a burnout, a literary lush like Fitzgerald or Capote, and in his new novel he douses one of these hollow men with pissy scorn. On Kentucky Derby day, Alison's boyfriend Dean wagers on a horse named . . . Capote. But Capote can't handle the far turn. After the race, "Dean comes over and goes, I guess it was pretty stupid to think a horse named Capote could go the distance. He says, it's a case of sport imitating life—brilliant start, pathetic finish." *Brilliant start, pathetic finish* is the epitaph that McInerney fears after the fast start of **Bright Lights, Big City**. Careermanship is the true anxiety bedeviling **Story of My Life**. So to woo the gods who safekeep literary health and longevity, McInerney sticks a pin into Capote's puffy effigy (black magic) and lights a stick of incense at the shrine of Salinger (white magic).

But one could argue that the biggest hex on McInerney is his own bad judgment. Case in point: littering the streets and supermarkets of Manhattan this fall are stacks of catalogs for the Learning Annex, a singles mingles "meet market" that offers phony-baloney adult education courses in wine tasting, white collar boxing, the healing power of crystals, etc. On the back cover of the latest catalog is a full-page notice trumpeting a one-night seminar titled "How to Write and Get Anything Published—With Jay McInerney." The course description is priceless. "Heralded as the 'Salinger of the 80's,' applauded by critics as the new wry and passionate spokesman for the upwardly-mobile generation, McInerney stepped out from his lonely 1-typewriter world onto the golden alter [sic] of publishing success." Step right up to the tent, ladies and gentleman. "Spend an evening with this literary phenomenon and find out how he made it to the top, how he continues to stay there, and how you can too."

Even in his cups Truman Capote never sank this low. For all his authorial airs, McInerney has cheesy instincts. He can't be doing the Learning Annex gig because he needs the money; it's instant feedback he's after, quickie acclaim. He's slumming after fame. No wonder *Story of My Life* reads as if it were written for and about groupies. That's his constituency. In *Story of My Life,* Jaybird is giving his fans their fill. But such slim pickings! Mere crumbs scattered along the golden "alter." Like totally not enough.

Josephine Hendin (essay date 1990)

SOURCE: "Fictions of Acquisition," in *Culture in an Age of Money,* edited by Nicolaus Mills, Ivan R. Dee, 1990, pp. 216-33.

[*In the following excerpt, Hendin explores the integration of emotions, individuality, materialism, and commercial culture in* Bright Lights, Big City. *According to Hendin, the novel represents "the compression of the novel of manners into an equivalent of upscale ads."*]

The rich diversity of American fiction has always made newness difficult to characterize. But the 1980s have seen not only the arrival of fresh work by writers who have long established that diversity, but also the fracturing of literary culture along quasipolitical lines: the rise of a multi-ethnic literature encompassing the work of Chinese Ameri-

cans, Indians, African Americans, and European ethnics, a growing gay literature, and new additions to feminist fiction. Powerful novels of Vietnam and its aftermath, many by combat veterans, have added to the cultural ferment. Yet all these often "radical" voices do not so much signal what has changed as serve the traditional end of extending our fiction's longstanding concern with the drama of marginal man beating at the doors of society. The literary revolution of the 1980s has erupted in a fiction of those who have already gained entry.

Perhaps nothing reveals what has changed more than the transformation of those heroes and antiheroes propelled toward mythic stature by an avid college market. The youthcult heroes of one period are made obsolete by those of another. Reflecting the aspirations and anxieties of coming-of-age, cult heroes dramatize the ethos of the day. The sweet brotherliness of Holden Caulfield in recoil from adulthood reflected the 1950s belief in authenticity, innocence, and family as bulwarks against the crassness of the social world. The sexual freedom of Robert A. Heinlein's *Stranger in a Strange Land,* whose Martian hero teaches the benefits of nonverbal communication, communal life, and abandoning possessive jealousy, reflected a 1960s rejection of competitive, acquisitive America. An attack on authority and authoritarianism figured in the feminist assault on the double standard, fueling mass-market bestsellers of the 1970s, from *Fear of Flying* by Erica Jong to the ambitiously belletristic novel of Francine Duplessix Gray, *Lovers and Tyrants.* But the comparable fiction of the 1980s seems to be giving up the counterculture attack on adulthood, authority, and repression. There is in progress a quiet but sharp recoil from the concepts of self and society, from the quest for authentic emotion, from the visions of individualism and possibility that have been animating forces in our literature. In the 1980s we encounter the new Self in its most extreme form: the Hero as Nostril.

In Jay McInerney's *Bright Lights, Big City,* he lives, or rather, inhales in a spiritual confusion in which day and night are confounded:

> The night has already turned on that imperceptible pivot where two A.M. changes to six A.M. You know this moment has come and gone, but you are not yet willing to concede that you have crossed the line beyond which all is gratuitous damage and the palsy of unravelled nerve endings. Somewhere back there you could have cut your losses, but you rode past that moment on a comet trial of white powder and now you are trying to hang on to the rush. Your brain at this moment is composed of brigades of tiny Bolivian soldiers. They are tired and muddy from their long march through the night. There are holes in their boots and they are

hungry. They need to be fed. They need the Bolivian Marching Powder.

The Hero as Nostril is nose without sense, an inhaling mechanism without the power of smell. His habitat is the toilet stall of an expensive restaurant or an *in* disco, for, together with cocaine, he inhales status sites and brand names. His distraught and destroyed senses, mirrored in McInerney's often impressive surreal style and speed-blurred descriptions, are incredibly precise at conveying name-brand identification. The Nostril is determined to inhale only the best.

McInerney has produced a distinctive literary effort: the compression of the novel of manners into an equivalent of upscale ads. In language there is a comparable constriction: the linguistic quest for T. S. Eliot's "objective correlative" is flattened into an exploitation of objects. There is no correlating link of attendant emotion or depth. His hero, who works as a fact-checker at a thinly disguised version of the *New Yorker,* considers himself vastly superior to the girl at the bar who believes the words "decadence and Dexedrine are the high points of the language of Kings James and Lear." He himself is a man who knows the titles of the best works: "*As I Lay Dying, Under the Volcano, Anna Karenina, Being and Time, The Brothers Karamazov,*" even if he has kept himself innocent of their contents. The title is sign supreme, the label whose possession is meant to convey class.

In style and modes of characterization, the youthcult fiction of the 1980s is a fiction not of insurgency but of cultural collaboration. What stands out is an assimilation, to the point of wholesale adoption, of advertising culture. Labels, name brands, surface signs have become the sole social referents and methods of character definition. McInerney's characterization of a man of literary sensibility is effected not through a representation of consciousness but by the ownership of unread books, contempt for the underyuppie class, and the ability to give such imaginative names to cocaine as "Bolivian Marching Powder." What motivates the Nostril-hero is obscure; he has too little feeling for the gradual and now final withdrawal of his wife, a fashion model and perfect label-wearer. In a belated effort at explaining what drives his hero, when the book is nearly over, McInerney introduces his mother who, near death, wishes she could have lived the way he does. Not even a dying mother runs deep.

Bright Lights, Big City was not simply a successful novel. It was a publishing phenomenon. Produced as a paperback original in Random House's Vintage Contemporaries line, it was widely and enthusiastically reviewed, a first novel that rapidly sold out its first printing and justified the "NATIONAL BEST-SELLER" emblazoned on its cover along with that other label of distinction, "MAJOR MOTION PICTURE." Starring Michael J. Fox as the nose who knows, the film had the dazzling surfaces of the novel but not its ability to reflect a stream of consciousness that is itself filled with objects. Hailed by the *Playboy* reviewer as a "*Catcher in the Rye* for the MBA set," the novel's success underscored how aptly its talented twenty-nine-year-old author, in capturing a contemporary hero, had understood the culture's changing values and equation of materialism with the substance of being.

In this literature, character is entirely the product of acts of appropriation indistinguishable from buying. Serial purchases, episodic peaks and lows before scoring, make shopping the ultimate human act. Buying coke is the model for all experience: the purchase of self, the acquisition of other people.

The youthcult fiction of the 1980s differs from any we have encountered before. Most of the fiction that has appealed to college students has involved a sense of social or generational conflict or advocacy of a hedonistic, experiential ethic at variance with the competitive work ethic of American culture. The youthcult novels of the 1980s reflect an enormous shift. . . .

Is the Hero-as-Nostril only the aberrant creation of under-thirty writers who have come of age in the era of cocaine? The condition described in extreme ways in these novels cannot be dismissed so easily, partly because it differs in degree but not in kind from the worldview of many young writers who do not deal with cocaine but instead have tried to write about personal life. According to author David Leavitt, writing as the voice of the under-thirty literary generation in "New Voices and Old Values" in the *New York Times Book Review* of May 12, 1985, they have all "in general limited themselves to the short story, a form they seem to find appropriate to the age of shortened attention spans, fractured marriages and splintering families in which they grew up."

This youth fiction of personal life has been criticized for being insufficiently true to individual differences and for accepting commercially viable, collectivized notions of self. Bruce Bawer, in a pejoratively titled essay, "The Literary Brat Pack," accuses Leavitt, Elizabeth Tallent, Meg Wolitzer, Marian Thurm, Peter Cameron, and others of writing "exactly alike," of having forsaken an original voice to buy the modish sound purveyed to them by writing programs. Their collective, contrived voice is "especially big on the details surrounding 'relationships' . . . the set decorations—the bags of groceries, the copies of *GQ* and *People* . . . [that] tend, time and again, to overwhelm the frail narratives." At fault, Bawer believes, are "professors in university creative writing programs [who] tell their students that this is the way to write: load up on concrete details, relevant or not. The more particulars, the better." But what is at stake may be more than commercially oriented teaching or the vagaries of youth: these talented young writers are mirroring a striking change.

A new definition of the self, a new vision of subjectivity is being reflected in 1980s fictions. Cocaine-based novels are only the most extreme example of cultural change in which the traditional American faith in individualism, in insurgent selves transcending, withstanding, or at least withholding assent from unpalatable environments, is dying.
—*Josephine Hendin*

A new definition of the self, a new vision of subjectivity is being reflected in 1980s fictions. Cocaine-based novels are only the most extreme example of cultural change in which the traditional American faith in individualism, in insurgent selves transcending, withstanding, or at least withholding assent from unpalatable environments, is dying. This recoil from Emersonianism is not simply a crisis of youth. The world, constituted as a relationship and its artifacts, has slowly grown toward being treated as the only known territory; brand names have only now flowered into use as major social referents, whether what is being mentioned is the cookie bought in a supermarket or a luxurious fur. The self so circumscribed is not a youthcult invention but rather a postmodernist construction, a particular emptiness waiting to become a receptacle for the cultural artifacts that surround it. Like Paola, the young woman in Thomas Pynchon's *V.,* who can speak only in nouns, the characters find meaning only in objects. Just as McInerney's ***Bright Lights, Big City*** compresses the novel of manners to an upscale ad and Ellis's *Less Than Zero* reduces the novel of initiation to the equivalent of snuff-porn stills, so new fiction of "sensibility" operates to treat feelings through surfaces, breaking down the distinctions between people and things. In this phenomenological orgy, to borrow from Wittgenstein, the world is all that is the (Gucci) case.

The postmodern sense of fragmentation is now revealing itself in a vision of *emotions* as artifacts, of people as objects in a society whose common culture is increasingly standardized. What is being standardized is the self in fiction and perhaps in theory. This standardization is effected in several ways. Characters in search of a defining place or connection are seen against the linguistic and visual constructs mass culture provides. They seem almost to conform to a Lacanian theory of personality formation as the

effort to discover oneself in "otherness," a differentiation of self as a "signifier" seeking to be assimilated into a purely symbolic order. Being is not intrinsic, not the existential *sine qua non;* individuals are only carriers looking for a sign, a billboard-self. Thus these characters seem doomed to equate personality with external objects, to discover self as and in objectified form. . . .

Material Differences

Something new has been created from the union of materialism and emotion. In the past, object-laden fiction or a literature of objectified emotion was characteristic of such European experimentalist works as Robert Musil's *The Man Without Qualities* or the fictions of Alain Robbe-Grillet and Nathalie Sarraute. In this country, it has been most associated with the experimentalism of such intellectual artists as Thomas Pynchon. Its appearance in 1980s fiction with a broad, even mass-market appeal suggests both its new importance and its changed emphasis.

This 1980s fiction discloses a fascination for advertising culture most simply in the use of brand names in character definition, but more profoundly in utilizing and adapting its processes: compression, packaging, and quantifying. In embracing commercial culture, 1980s fiction focuses on both the illusions it sustains and the manipulative power of its techniques. On the dark side, it seems to embrace the illusion that the unknown can be ruled out and the self defined by packaging glitzy or strong enough to contain and label it. On the brighter side, 1980s fiction finds, in the operative processes for sustaining such illusions, coping devices.

In the movement toward surfaces there may be a search for ways of relieving what is perceived as unalterable in the inner life. Characters seem actively to seek freedom from uncertainty, self-hatred, and pain. The vision of people as victims rather than masters of their own lives may involve a rejection of the power of individual will but also relieves the burden of rage or guilt. Hoping for release into the pictorial surface, the impersonal course of troubled love (quantifiable too as midlife crisis), or the powdered high, cocaine, are ways of pain-killing through different forms of depersonalization. The spectacle, the object, the impersonal texture, and, as Munro puts it, "the pattern," have become synonymous with experience itself. Each of these writers seems to disclose, in visions of standardization, qualified relief from solitariness.

Knowingly or unwittingly, 1980s writers are our pollsters of the contemporary soul. Delving into its ambivalences, they report that collisions between emotion and materialism, individualism and commercial culture, youth and middle age, have forged a new consensus about our shared limitations and vulnerability, a consensus in the shape of a birth: a shelter-seeking self.

Frank de Caro (essay date 1991)

SOURCE: "The Three Great Lies: Riddles of Love and Death in a Postmodern Novel," in *Southern Folklore,* Vol. 48, No. 3, 1991, pp. 235-54.

[*In the following essay, de Caro examines the cultural context and significance of contemporary urban folklore in* Story of My Life, *particularly as revealed in formal and informal communication among the novel's characters.*]

At the Indiana University Folklore Institute in the 1960s two bits of lore circulated relevant to the current essay. One was the title of an imaginary, mock study such as waggish graduate students concoct: "Frontier Humor in the Writings of Henry James." The other was the supposedly true story of a colleague who had undertaken to do a seminar paper on folklore in Ernest Hemingway's writings only to discover too late that he could discover none and that failure loomed. Both pieces of lore make the same assumption about two different writers, namely that neither has much relevance to folk tradition. Indeed, this assumption is a more general one—there are certain writers who are associated with folklore and others—including James and Hemingway—who are not.

Such may be the case for the simple reason that not all writers incorporate folklore into their texts (although Mary Ellen Brown Lewis 1976 suggests that folklore pervades virtually all literature; see her comment quoted below.) On the other hand, the assumptions may stem from yet other assumptions about the nature of folklore and about what kinds of writers are apt to use folklore: "regional" writers, or those who come from an ethnic group with a well-attested oral tradition, or those who describe certain kinds of environments. Such assumptions may not be without base, yet they may also stem from stereotypes which are questionable and limiting. The use of folklore may come to be overlooked in a literary work whose author does not fit one of the standard assumptions or in which the use of folklore is not obvious or profuse.

Indeed, folklorists have come to look at the folklore/literature connection in new ways—for example, setting folklore and literature in the context of performance studies, or considering the mystery novel structurally in terms of the block elements developed by riddle scholars. Nor have they limited themselves to the works of regional or ethnic writers; Thomas Pynchon and Robert Coover, for example,

have both received attention from folklorists. Some years ago now, Lewis had gone so far as to speak of the "current renaissance of the study of folklore and literature." Nonetheless, even in the scholarship of the last twenty-odd years, there has been a preponderance of concentration upon those whom Robert Hemenway, himself writing about Charles Chesnutt, refers to sarcastically as "such giants of American literature as Rowland Robinson and George S. Wasson." To Hemenway's short list could be added (and the publications cited should be seen as examples only) the names Will N. Harben, Ovid Pierce, Doris Betts, Jesse Stuart, Henry Wheeler Shaw, C. F. M. Noland and Ole E. Rolvaag, mostly known as regionalists. In addition, there has been considerable attention accorded African American writers—some of them certainly major figures—including Ralph Ellison, Arna Bontemps, Zora Neale Hurston, and John Oliver Killens, and of course certain nineteenth-century writers, such as Hawthorne, Cooper, Washington Irving and George Washington Harris, whose folklore interests and connections have been long noticed.

Certainly studies of such writers are legitimate and may be even of considerable significance. The recognition of a connection to an oral tradition has been an important factor in the appreciation of African American literature. Other folk traditions lie behind the works of writers from a number of other ethnic backgrounds—Maxine Hong Kingston and Leslie Marmon Silko, for example—and a recognition of those traditions may be a key part of establishing the diversity of American literatures. However, despite significant attempts to put the study of the relationship between folklore and literature on a new footing, "there has been an emphasis on antiquarian and agrarian folklore as it appears in the pastoral literary tradition," as Kenneth Thigpen put it over ten years ago. Perhaps because folklore studies historically have emphasized rural, peasant environments and only recently looked to other milieux, there has been an emphasis upon literature that reflects or depicts some traditional, almost invariably rural folk society or culture. Mary Ellen B. Lewis has written that "Folklore is everywhere; it is a cultural universal. Since all authors come from a culture, they inevitably reflect folkloric elements in any work of literature, because folklore is a pervasive aspect of life. . . . An author may consciously depict the world around him/her and folklore becomes a major way of doing so; or an author may actively seek folklore from written documents or by conscious collecting. And a creative writer may simply use folklore . . . because it is part of the known; it is what is." Thus she implies that folklore, as a cultural universal, might be expected to permeate much literature, perhaps most literature, not merely that which depicts an older, "traditional," agrarian world, though to follow up on such possibilities perhaps requires us to view folklore in ways more in keeping with redefinitions of folklore than with older conceptualizations, to view folklore as a process of direct, interactive communication in cultural contexts, which will, of course, include other media of communication as well.

The present essay deals with a novel which presents folklore "in context" in the sense that the folklore is used by characters in the course of their everyday interactions and as very much a part of their taken-for-granted cultural backgrounds. The folklore appears as one medium of communication in the midst of others. The novel does not depict a traditional, agrarian society but, indeed, an environment far removed from anything that might be called traditional culture. The novel is Jay McInerney's *Story of My Life,* which is set in the urban world of upper-class New York youth culture, a world of hip clubs and cocaine-sniffing securities dealers, acting classes and Russian emigré taxi drivers, of "the cursed and gilded youth of Eighties Manhattan," "the privileged spawn of the most privileged society in history" (as McInerney has described the characters of another novelist). McInerney's use of folklore is hardly all-pervasive, being limited to a joke, a children's rhyme, and a game. However, his use of folklore is insistent—joke, rhyme, game are all repeated—and I will suggest that, despite its sparing use, it is central to an understanding of the novel, being used in fictional performance contexts to delineate character and to express characters' needs and values. It is through seeing the main character's relationship to folklore that the reader most fully appreciates her underlying problems and her attempts to move beyond them.

I have, through my title, taken the liberty of calling McInerney's book a postmodern novel. I hope I may be allowed this usage at least as a convenience, to reemphasize that here is a work of literature from a context quite different from those most often considered for their relationship to folklore in the past; and therefore, that if a work such as this is relevant to folklore studies, perhaps folklore is indeed far more pervasive in contemporary literature and folkloristic approaches indeed more useful in contemporary literary studies than might otherwise be assumed, as Lewis seems to imply.

The parameters of postmodern literature have hardly been clearly established. "Postmodernism is not a monolithic phenomenon," as Hans Bertens says, and, as Bruce Handy writes, "figuring out why any given pundit considers any given work postmodern can be as exasperating and elusive as conceptualizing six-dimensional spheres." I do not intend to construct any detailed explanation of why the work under consideration should be called postmodern. One could note that the novel displays certain characteristics that have been associated with the postmodern: a self-reflexiveness and, indeed, a "self-regarding irony"; its being written in the present tense, "television's only tense," as

Todd Gitlin puts it; a "blasé tone [and] self-conscious bemusement with surfaces"; a "concern about the extension of relationships of alienation within a consumer society."

However, more germane to my current subject is the postmodern tendency toward crossover between the fine and popular arts, one aspect of what John Barth terms the "synthesis" of postmodernism in his discussion of Calvino and Garcia Marquez, "the blurring or juxtaposition of . . . cultural levels," "meshing and mixing" of diverse cultural forms in the same environment—all, of course, a reflection of a postmodern culture which is global, eclectic, mixed, a result of a "shrinking" world, instantaneous communication, and a presumed breakdown of local traditions. Indeed, one finds in *Story of My Life* a smooth blending of expressive cultural forms. Characters attend a performance of *Liaisons Dangereuses,* act out scenes from *Crimes of the Heart* and own framed posters for *Zoo Story,* make references to "Wheel of Fortune," burst into reggae songs, sing lines by Elvis Costello, and, of course, transmit folklore.

This is to say, then, that the folklore in the novel exists in a complex, "living" (if fictional) cultural matrix in which it is one part of a larger whole, one medium among many, with few if any lines of distinction being drawn between them by the characters. This might be seen as a realistic depiction of folklore in contemporary Western society where the structured, oral channels of folk communication are not so central as in pre-industrial, preliterate societies, yet where they may still be significant ways of expressing and communicating in conjunction with other channels.

In writing about folklore and literature, Lewis has also commented that in the past folklorists and literary scholars concentrated only upon one aspect of the folkloric process, the "item" of folklore or what she calls the "product," for example the tale plot or the proverb itself (which might merely be identified, though some commentators also might attempt an explanation of the role of the folk text in the larger work). She says that this ignores other, equally important aspects of the process, the "situation" and the "medium," that is, the social context in which the lore is communicated and the language and style of its communication. Probably such has been the case because it is much simpler to isolate a folklore product than to "corroborate" (Lewis's term) a social context—if there is a context for folkloric performance in a novel or short story, for example, it is necessarily a fictional re-creation and one may judge only with difficulty how accurately it reflects real-life contexts, especially given the comparative paucity of folkloristic data on social contexts. It may be even more difficult to determine how closely an author's literary text might reproduce folk language, especially given the even much field-collected data in print may not reproduce in all effects the spoken original.

However, Lewis also notes that a literary work "may provide typical *situations* and examples of *medium* which clarify and enlarge the understanding of the *product* or text at hand." McInerney does place all of the folklore in the context of the "actual," in the context of human interchange, as his characters interact with each other, thus giving it to us not as text alone but as verbal art of sorts. Furthermore, he seems sensitive to the nuances of spoken language. His use of the present tense may stem not so much from the supposed influence of television on postmodern literature as from being one part of his attempt to "reproduce" the language patterns of his narrator who lives in a world of intense verbal exchange and whose narrative style is certainly colloquial. Though the novel depicts a subculture of which the present writer is certainly not a member, this is a subculture not so decentered from "mainstream" contemporary American culture as to seem foreign, so that one may judge McInerney's folklore inclusions to be reasonably reflective of real usage. Hence the novel may be seen as providing a realistic if not a real social context, so far as the folklore is concerned. In thus providing a fictional model of the transmission of folklore, it may indeed clarify understanding of how folk texts function to provide meaning for people (characters in the fictional context but also author and reader). In presenting the folklore amidst other channels of communication, it clarifies understanding of how folklore texts "operate" in contemporary—or, if you will, postmodern—culture.

The narrator and chief protagonist of **Story of My Life** is Alison Poole, an aspiring actress who reaches her twenty-first birthday in the course of the novel. She and her friends are habitués of the in clubs, consume great quantities of alcohol and cocaine, keep necessarily odd hours, and leave multitudes of messages on each others' answering machines. They may or may not be employed, may or may not take what jobs they have seriously. They are rich but often in need of money, as allowances run out or other sources of funds dry up. They lead lives that are frantically hedonistic with little thought to future consequences (perhaps another reason for the novel's present tense).

Though she is not consciously aware of it, Alison is moving to extricate herself from this high- and hard-living, purposeless existence. In her acting classes she has found something she loves doing, something which is structured, creative, and purposeful. She is willing to "spend eight hours a day busting ass at Lee Strasberg" and, early in the narrative, refuses cocaine, despite the pressure of friends to partake, in order to get to acting class. Unfortunately, at the outset of the novel she is thwarted by the fact that her father, probably off in the Caribbean somewhere with a new

girl friend, has not sent her tuition check. She is forced to obtain tuition money by telling an ex-boyfriend, commodities trader Skip Pendleton, she is pregnant by him and needs funds for an abortion.

Meanwhile she enters into an affair with bond dealer Dean Chasen. Her relationship with him forms the central thread of the rest of the novel, as they sleep with each other and with others, though the plot has many twists and turns. Throughout we get bits and pieces of Alison's troubled relations with her divorced parents, her alcoholic, TV evangelist-watching mother, and her father, who, Alison has come to believe, poisoned her beloved horse, Dangerous Dan, for the insurance money years before.

Finally, Alison discovers she really is pregnant and, ironically, has to use the tuition money finally sent by her father for an abortion. She visits a drug dealer, hospitalized after he jumped out a sixth-story window, love-sick for Alison's cold, scheming sister Rebecca, and lies to him, telling him that Rebecca really cares for him. Soon she attends her twenty-first birthday party, a wild event which goes on for several days. Alienated from Dean because she has slept once again with old flame Skip in order to spite Dean, who had slept with one Cassie Hane, she becomes hysterical after a sudden realization of the quality of love in her life, and tries to jump out a window of the Stanhope Hotel. She manages to call HELP, a counselling agency whose business card has been passed around as a joke throughout the novel, passes into virtual unconsciousness and awakes, sedated, in an institution in Minnesota. After some days of therapy she phones her father and tells him it would have been cheaper to have let her keep the horse, but he professes to not know what she is talking about. She begins to wonder what really happened, wanting to think that ninety percent of the story of her life has been "just dreaming."

The fact of Alison's turning twenty-one—the age of legal adulthood, of majority—suggests that McInerney is concerned with the time-honored American literary theme of coming of age, of maturing, though usually it has been male characters attempting the passage. Indeed much is made of her own day of passage, not only through the party itself but also through the speech one character—ironically, a "prep," a designation that marks not only his style of dress but also his juvenile manner—makes to declare that Alison is now an adult and a woman. Her transition to adult is, of course, hardly a triumphant one—she does wind up in a detox unit—yet from the outset of the novel, maturity has been on her mind. "Men," she says, "I've never met any. They're all boys." Her father is "fifty-two going on twelve," she herself "twenty going on gray." She tells her father to grow up when he whines over the phone about having been left by "his new bimbo Tanya who's a year younger than me."

It is easy to see the fragmented, youth-centered environment in which Alison lives as an immature world of people who really care little for others, who live with a present-centered worldview and little concern for future consequences, and who flout many of the norms of the more sober society of which they are a tenuous part. Alison herself rejects the rules, the "care of the social fabric," which would interfere with her spontaneity and "honesty," with an unbridled, childish self.

Despite this, however, Alison has been taking steps toward order and toward centering herself, though they are perhaps small and tentative steps by some standards. Acting has given her a purpose; it is "the first thing that's made me get up in the morning. The first year I was in New York I didn't do anything but guys and blow. Staying out all night at the Surf Club and Zulu, waking up at five in the afternoon with plugged sinuses and sticky hair. Some kind of white stuff in every opening. Story of my life." When her friends try to take her away from doing a scene for class she asserts: "this is my life, I'm trying to do something constructive with it." Unlike her roommate, she pays her share of the rent. She fantasizes at least about a stable relationship with Dean. She wonders about leaving New York and realizes she is involved only in "all this hysterical noise which is supposedly my life but it doesn't add up to anything." She realizes she will have to find a job.

However, Alison's maturing is linked to something else, to her obsessive concern for honesty, and, indeed, honesty is a central theme of the novel itself. Early in the narrative Alison declares that "real life seems to be about being a liar and a hypocrite," though "if there's one thing I hate it's the usual bullshit." Part of the novel hinges on her father's apparent lying about having sent her tuition check, and her relationship with Dean becomes rocky over questions of honesty, after he has lied about a recent encounter with Cassie Hane:

> You shouldn't have lied about it, I go. I told you that's the one thing I can't stand. I'll be out the door so fast your head will spin. If you want to go out with other girls, fine. If you want to screw them, fine. But don't ever lie to me. Okay?
>
> Okay, he says.
>
> And wear a goddamn rubber, I say. I don't want to die from anything that comes via Cassie Hane.

He denies actually having slept with Cassie and, the following morning, waking up in his bed, Alison confronts him again:

> Back in the bedroom I climb up and sit on Dean's chest. I take a big drink of OJ, then lean over and dribble a little on his face. His eyes flutter open. This boy looks scared. Guilty conscience, I'd say.
>
> Did you fuck Cassie Hane? I go.
>
> He's freaked. He turns his head both ways, then tries to sit up, but I've got him pinned.
>
> I want the truth, I say. Did you fuck Cassie Hane?
>
> Alison, he pleads. I guess he finally recognizes me. Was it the face or the tits, I wonder.
>
> Did you? I go.
>
> Yes, he says, I did. He looks away.
>
> Thank you, I say, climbing down off him. Thank you for finally telling the truth.

"Acting's about honesty," her teacher tells her and that is obviously one of its appeals. She is appalled when Jeannie lies to her father, telling him that Alison spent the rent money. "I'm completely surrounded by liars," she exclaims. Her desire for honesty is a pure and fierce one, yet of course it is—like Holden Caulfield's obsession with phonies—a too simple, an immature complex of reactions to some of the things which bedevil her life. Her own honesty is hardly as pure as she would have it, and part of her maturing must involve approaching the complexity of honesty, dishonesty and truth itself.

The three pieces of folklore McInerney introduces to his narrative, though their meanings are multivalent, can be seen as being connected to these central, interconnected themes of maturity and honesty.

Not quite halfway through the novel Alison is called by her sister Rebecca, who has been trying to remember the words to a childhood nursery rhyme, "the one about Miss Mary Mack." Alison is able to supply some of it: "Oh, right, I go. Miss Mary Mack Mack Mack all dressed in black black black with silver buttons buttons buttons down her back back back. . . ." but can't remember any more despite Rebecca's prodding for additional words. Alison is momentarily "bugged" by her inability to recall more, but Alison does not dwell for long on very much and her mind moves elsewhere.

It is impossible to say exactly what Alison has forgotten,

for the rhyme, collected as a jump rope rhyme and as part of hand-clapping, skipping and marching games, of course, is found in a number of variants in tradition and the lines she remembers are associated with a variety of other rhymes, including "I love coffee, I love tea. / I love the boys, and the boys love me," which certainly could apply to Alison; "One flew East, one flew West, / One flew over the cuckoo's nest," in itself a counting-out rhyme appropriated by Ken Kesey for the title of his first novel; and "Milk in the pitcher, butter in the bowl, / Can't get a sweetheart to save my soul," which could also perhaps relate to Alison, who runs through guys, unable to stick with any one for very long, and whose inability to hold Dean precipitates her breakdown.

Of course it does not matter what lines she cannot recall. What is important is that she cannot recall whatever variant she happened to know as a child, for in the forgetting itself we see the working out of her current position in her life passage. On the one hand her failure to remember suggests a dangerous fragmentation, an inability to connect, to put things together in a meaningful way and mirrors the disconnected and immature world of which she is very much a part. Folklore is a social connective, supportive of society, and the forgetting suggests a distancing from social cohesion, from "care of the social fabric." ("Care of the Social Fabric" is a chapter title and refers to a remark made by Dean.) Then too, insofar as a "nursery" rhyme reflects childhood, the partial forgetting suggests a repression of a painful childhood of murdered horses and grooms who attempt rape without parental interference, a childhood which the reader gets glimpses of throughout but which Alison seems unready to actually confront before the very end of the novel.

On the other hand, in a more positive vein, a moving away from the rhymes of childhood suggests a maturing process, an idea which is reinforced by the second use of "Miss Mary Mack" in the novel, as Alison undergoes her abortion. On the verge of the procedure, she asks for Demerol, but outpatients, she is told, are given only local anesthesia. In pain, she tries to do a "sense-memory" exercise of Dean "talking about Shakespeare or the stock market or something," but, unable to retain the concentration "I try to remember that rhyme we used to say in school—Miss Mary Mack Mack Mack all dressed in black black black, but I draw a blank on the rest. . . ." Her acting teacher has told the class how important it is to "get in touch with your child," though Alison has interpreted this message in line with her own desire for a childlike spontaneity and an ignoring of conventions: "In my experience this is one big problem with older guys, they start to lose their spontaneity in their thirties, start saying what they think they're supposed to say instead of what they feel, sort of like hardening of the arteries. Like, we're all pretty much raving maniacs

as kids, but then some of us get conventional. Not me . . . I'm totally in touch with my child." Now, undergoing an abortion which can be a difficult rite of passage, childhood horseback riding exchanged for gynecological stirrups, she is able to remember even less of the rhyme than she could earlier. It does seem as though her immaturity is slowly slipping away here in drugless pain and confusion with the childhood lore itself. The rhyme, then, looks both ways, back toward her immature self of repression and self-centeredness, and ahead toward a more mature self, which will perhaps forget entirely the rhymes of childhood (or perhaps remember them whole and entire once again).

Alison's transition, however, is in part facilitated by the game called Truth or Dare, which occupies two chapters. The first time the game is played, the rules are explained to Dean, who is unfamiliar with it: "Didi explains the rules. You've got to be into it, she says. Everybody has to swear at the beginning to tell the truth, because otherwise there's no point. When it's your turn you say either truth or dare. If you say truth, you have to answer whatever question you're asked. And if you say dare, then you have to do whatever somebody dares you to do." Truth or Dare thus has rules and a definite structure and seems a traditional form of play for Alison's folk group, though this children's game has become, more or less, an adult one. Indeed, the actual working out of the game follows an even more restricted pattern than the rules allow for. The dares are invariably selected by the women when asked by the men and involve removing clothes. The questions posed when truth is selected invariably have to do with sex and romantic attachments. The first game starts, for example, with Didi asking Alison whether she was physically attracted to Dean when she first saw him, moves on to her asking Alison to rate Skip Pendleton in bed, and asking Dean to rate Alison's body and her own.

The game provides a fixed institution for people whose lives are otherwise chaotic; it provides rules, which lead to the uncovering of reasonably certain truth. Yet they use it not for self-discovery but rather to find out intimate things for gossip and to embarrass (in a sense greatly magnifying potentials inherent in the children's game). If it provides a fixity, they use it to play with dissension, perverting an activity which does promote a level of social cohesion but which falls off into the potential for ill will. The game works, at least in theory, on the honesty Alison so prizes, yet here honesty leads only to the trivial, the shallow, the hateful, so it is not surprising that the disastrous second session of the game leads Alison to challenge herself and her beliefs.

Alison repeatedly makes statements like, "If there's one thing I hate it's dishonesty. Drives me crazy. I hate liars and hypocrites." Yet her own relationship to honesty is hardly so simple. She indulges in the same small dishonesties as most people when she gives males trying to pick her up a false name or the phone number of an escort service as her own. She phones Cassie Hane and Cassie's boyfriend to, anonymously, lie to them to create bad feelings. Her lie about needing an abortion (which comes back to haunt her as truth) is an important element in the plot. Acting, in which she is absorbed, might be seen as a creative use of "lying" in that an actress dissembles to promote an illusion upon the stage. And, in a sense, she lies to the reader, hiding the fact that she has sex with Skip to spite Dean in a vague remark followed in the text by three asterisks. It is only at the second Truth or Dare session that the truth of the asterisks—standing in for an episode, a hardly praiseworthy action, which has been left out of the narrative—emerges. It is forced out by Dean's asking whether she slept with Skip lately—Skip's presence at the session making a lie, which she does contemplate, impossible. The session has already been horrid: Rebecca's feeling up Dean under the table precipitates a flashback to Rebecca's seducing away Alex, Alison's "last real boyfriend," at an East Hampton beach house, and now Alison sees Dean, for whom she has obviously developed strong feelings despite her stated nonchalance about men, slipping further away from her. She begins to think:

> Some impulses you should stifle, right? I never used to think so, I've always done whatever I felt like, I figured anything else and you're a hypocrite like I told Dean, but I don't know, here in the middle of this really ugly Truth or Dare session watching my sister grab my boyfriend's dick, thinking about her and Alex back then, thinking about some of the shit I've done recently, I'm beginning to wonder if a little stifling is such a bad thing. Right now I'd give my grandmother's pearls for a little white lie. The way this game is going, I'd give all my possessions for a dose of amnesia.

The session is interrupted finally by the arrival of Mannie, the Puerto Rican drug dealer, who is searching for Rebecca to express his love to but who winds up throwing himself from the sixth floor window, an event which produces another element in Alison's transition. Just before the abortion, for reasons she cannot explain, she goes to visit Mannie in the hospital. She explains that Rebecca asked her to look in—"which is totally a lie, I don't know why I say it, except maybe to make him feel better." But when he tells her to tell Rebecca that he loves her, it is too much for Alison:

> And I'm like, what are you, nuts? You're crazy, you're really out of your mind. Listen, I go, I hate to be the one to tell you but she's actually a total bitch, she doesn't give a shit about you, she doesn't give a shit

about anybody but herself, she hasn't even asked about you. That's the kind of person Rebecca is.

> He's not really looking at me, he's looking through me, still smiling. . . .

> All he does is say it again—tell her I love her.

> I say, I'm sorry, Mannie, I didn't mean that, it was just jealousy. Becca had to go out of town but she asked me to look in on you and everything. I'm sure you'll hear from her soon, I go.

> I don't know know if he hears me or not. I leave him grinning into outer space like some kind of Moonie, somebody way beyond your basic logic and facts. The thing is, he looks happy, which is more than you can say for the rest of us.

Alison, who has scorned Dean because "he'd rather be pleasant than honest," who has asked whether the social fabric is "like dacron polyester or something," suggesting its artificiality when Dean says "there are times when it's better to spare people's feelings, keep the social fabric intact," has lied to be kind, to make someone happy, to ease pain. Clearly she has learned something, if she's not sure what, about human relations and the complexity of honesty. She has reached for maturity by doing something selfless to help someone else, though it has meant violating her own supposed values.

The Truth or Dare game sessions, in addition to stressing the theme of honesty, also further suggest the immaturity of Alison's world; the children's game has been upgraded to an adult form, yet this merely amplifies its potential for playing with disruptive actions, retaining in essence the childish fascination for daring others and coercing others to say what they would otherwise not. The sessions also serve to advance plot and Alison's development. In promising honesty but delivering something else, the game, especially the second session, forces Alison to move forward, and she does not play the game again in the novel. The third folklore element, the joke, also ties in with questions of honesty and trust but relates to Alison's vision of love as well. The joke appears four times.

In a chapter called "Two Lies" Alison seeks to punish Dean for having sex with Cassie. She climbs into his bed with her clothes on and turns the TV to an evangelist and remembers the revivals "one of my mother's redneck boyfriends took us to," a memory which causes her to think of lying: "This preacher was an amateur, I mean, give me a break, starting with my father I'd grown up around a better class of liar and cheater and con artist than this cracker. I've been lied to by the best. Which reminds me, I suddenly go to Dean, he's kind of whimpering on his side of the bed, hey, I go, what are the three greatest lies in the world?" When Dean waffles, she goes on: "You know. You're an expert on this subject. (This goes right past him.) One, the check's in the mail. Two, I promise I won't come in your mouth, and what's the third?" But the third cannot be recalled, nor can it be later when she asks Alex the same thing, although his second lie differs—"I promise I'll pull it out before I come." Nor can the third lie be recalled still later when she asks her friend Francesca. It is not until the verge of Alison's breakdown that Everett, the "prep," recalls the third lie during the birthday party and his answer plays a role in pushing Alison over the edge.

Alison is, of course, playing with a well-known joking tradition (carried over from oral joke to posters, Ann Landers columns, and cartoons; see, for example, *Funny Times* 5, no. 2 [1990]: 18). Like much obscene folklore, the joke itself seems to have avoided print in scholarly sources. In oral tradition it has a relatively stable structure, with, of course, the usual variations to be expected. *The check is in the mail* seems to be invariably the first lie. The *third* lie acts as punch-line and may be Alison's *I promise not to come in your mouth,* Alex's *I promise I'll pull it out before I come,* or *I promise I'll respect you in the morning,* or *I promise I'll only put it in a little way,* which have also been reported. The *second* lie seems to be the most variable and some tellers of the joke have reported that virtually anything can be put in the second slot, such as *Your car will be ready by noon.* The joke proceeds from an economic lie, to a lie about virtually anything, to a lie which involves male betrayal during sexual intercourse.

Alison has confused and mistold the joke, shifting what should be the punch-line into the second slot, forgetting what is normally the second, "floating" lie. Forgetting part of a joke can be, of course, part of the normal process of joke telling, and forgetting one of the lies, usually the second, has been reported to me by actual tellers of the joke. In the context of the novel, however, this indicates several things. It suggests, again, her disorientation in a fragmented world. As with "Miss Mary Mack" she cannot remember wholes, only bits and pieces; she has difficulty in putting things together. On one level she has difficulty recognizing the lies as a joke at all. Oral sex is so much a part of her life—she mentions it repeatedly, discusses the etiquette of it, muses on the caloric content of semen, uses a memory of fellating Dean in a psychological exercise in acting class—that it is too commonplace to provide much punch for a punch-line. *The check is in the mail* lie also closely mirrors the reality of her existence, for the novel opens with her father's lie that a check is in the mail for her tuition, and this is evidently a recurring motif in her life. Beyond this, however, the joke reflects her vision of

the world as a place of painful dishonesty. Humor, of course, can be a reaction to what is most painful to us, and Alison does to some extent appreciate the humor inherent in the great lies. However, she is more interested in them as a statement of her personal worldview and thus loses sight of them as joke. Indeed, when Dean, upon hearing her ask what are the three greatest lies, asks if this is a joke, she replies, "no, not really. It's just kind of an old proverb or something." To confuse a joke with a proverb perhaps indicates further Alison's difficulty in structuring her life, but more important is the fact that proverbs are popularly supposed to be wise statements of truth. Thus she sees the joke as a statement of the truth of male betrayal and dishonesty, of her father's lies about money, of Dean's lies about other women, of a world in which lying has given her a dark vision of love itself. "Did I say love?" Alison exclaims. "Wash my mouth out with soap." She scrupulously refers to her own feelings as being "in lust" and ponders: "I wonder sometimes if it would have lasted with Alex if he hadn't fucked me over. Then I say—what are you, soft in the head? It never lasts. I haven't seen one example yet." When asked by her doctor why she doesn't make the men in her sex life wear condoms, she replies, "I'm like, for the same reason I don't fuck with my clothes on, you can't beat flesh on flesh. I want contact, right? Just give me direct contact and you can keep true love."

Everett's birthday speech in which he announces Alison's majority also includes assertions of his love for her, though mixed in with similar assertions about Rebecca. As the party continues at Everett's hotel suite, Alison asks him if he knows the third great lie: "That's easy, he says. The third lie is, I love you. And I'm thinking, wow! of course. That's it." This sudden realization of the quality of love in her life, of the fact that she is not loved, of a need for love, of the failure of the possibility of love with Dean hurries her to the breakdown, though also to the realization of her need for help.

There is, however, another important dimension to the folklore in the novel, a relation to riddling, a complexity which may not be immediately apparent until we realize that "Miss Mary Mack" is also found in tradition as a riddle, the answer for which is "coffin." The joke is in question and answer form, that is, of the genre folklorists sometimes term a riddle-joke. And Truth or Dare, though it is not literally a riddling session, approximates the form of such traditional sessions, people gathered together, posing questions and expecting answers.

To see the novel's lore against the background context of riddling suggests several things. First there is the relationship between riddling and transitional states. Several of the contexts in which traditional riddling is encountered involve transitional activities, such as courtship and initiation and death rituals, probably because riddles themselves seem to join disparate, even opposite, entities through metaphor, just as a wake, for example, joins the world of life and that of death, or courtship male and female. Alison is also on a borderline, a frontier between selves, trying to pass into the world of adulthood and leave that of the child. Beyond that, however, riddling involves posing questions which have certain answers. Alison is looking for answers, though not always consciously or directly, and it is interesting that she repeatedly seeks answers to folkloric questions. She asks others what the three great lies are, hoping to find finally a completing answer to fill in her fragmentary one. When the answer does come, it is a dramatic revelation which pushes her toward a new life state. If that state is immediately a seemingly negative one, it can also be seen as another traumatic ritual of initiation which can lead to a more positive, more healthy, more mature life. She also asks herself what the rest of "Miss Mary Mack" is. Though probably she is literally seeking only other, complementary verses, the answer to the "Miss Mary Mack" riddle, "coffin," is in another sense the "rest" of the rhyme. She can be seen here too, if not literally, as seeking an answer to a riddle. If this search does not literally yield an answer, the answer does, in a sense, make itself plain. Her present way of life leads only to the coffin, to death, perhaps physical, more likely moral. Her name itself comes from the Elvis Costello song "Alison," and early in the novel her friends sing to her the line, "Alison, I know this world is killing you." Perhaps her inability to come up with the rest of the rhyme really indicates her desire to avoid death and to affirm its opposite.

Noah Richler has suggested that underneath McInerney's first novel, **Bright Lights, Big City,** "was a rather old-fashioned moral tale about a young man's fall from grace," and another English review notes that **Story of My Life** itself "has the contours of a moral tract." Such a view contrasts with those of most American reviewers, who saw in Alison only "a 20-year old airhead," or "a dumb little New York rich girl" and in the novel only "the whine of the eternal adolescent." A closer reading of the novel than most American reviewers seem to have accorded it reveals something more akin to a moral tale and a tale of progress toward if not exactly to redemption. Winding up in drug abuse therapy may be a prosaic redemption, but it suggests that finally Alison is mature enough to reach out for help and it marks the potential for initiation into a new life beyond. Rather like the protagonist of **Bright Lights, Big City,** Alison undergoes a series of "jarring event[s]" which move her, if very tentatively, toward the realization that she will "have to learn everything all over again." One wonders whether the mostly male reviewers failed to perceive Alison's moral progress because they were unprepared to recognize it as a possibility for a young female protagonist.

It has been suggested that postmodern literature engages in a decentering of moral authority and rejects the possibility for agreed-upon standards of human behavior. McInerney, however, would have Alison look beyond such uncertainty and rise from the moral fall of her world. Three times Dean refers to her as a postmodern girl, and each time her feelings about the label might be seen as ambivalent. When the term is used a fourth time, it is to make the point that Dean has had "enough of the postmodern girls, [and] now . . . wants the good old-fashioned kind." Alison has certainly not become a good, old-fashioned girl (nor would the reader want her to), but she has seen the need for a more constructive life and for love and selflessness and, particularly in her visit to Mannie, demonstrates that she is capable of both and that she can grow out of strongly-held but immature values and into a kinder accommodation with the world. At the end, in finally accusing her father of Dangerous Dan's death, she not only confronts the central issue of a painful childhood but also opens herself to the possibility at least of an alternate truth, that he is not engaging in further dishonesty now but that she herself may have dreamed his partial confession at the time. She has become more compromising in her childish inflexibility about honesty, a little more mellow and perhaps even loving in her attitude toward her father, a little more aware of the complexity of truth itself.

McInerney's use of folklore is only one element of his subtly and gracefully complex novel, but it is an integral part of it. It is used to emphasize Alison's liminality, through its connection to riddling, though also her fragmentation, while it emphasizes too her need for something more than she has possession of—answers, in a chaotic world. Her inability to remember all the lore suggests her failure to achieve personal wholeness or to become part of the social cohesion that folklore promotes. But her persistent asking for the missing pieces suggests a constancy in searching for a whole, for a more positive relationship with the larger world and, indeed, for her own role in caring for the social fabric (which is, after all, the principal function of folklore). While her parents remain "divided, self-absorbed, remote," while Dean remains "a foreigner to himself," Alison has begun to find a few answers to the riddles of love and death.

McInerney's novel presents a realistic depiction of folklore in the contemporary, urban world, indeed in a part of that world far removed from roots in traditional culture. Folklore exists here as one communicative, expressive channel among many, formal and informal, popular and elite. Though it is hardly the central mode of communication in this subculture, it has considerable vitality. It stems from the needs of the subculture (Truth or Dare surely matches the need to probe into those areas, sex and romance, which fixate Alison's crowd) or of individual characters. It communicates attitudes and values (Alison seeks the great lies to make manifest, to encapsulate in fixed form her view of male dishonesty). It is forgotten or remembered according to circumstances (the childhood rhyme being recalled in moments of extreme stress). It pops up in normal encounters of everyday life, as characters reach back into their stores of memory to find fixed forms which are relevant to the shifting moment. It provides connections, however tenuous, to tradition in a world of novelty and of unfixed values.

The novel does "provide typical *situations* and examples of *medium,*" as well as of folklore "product" and, in doing so, does enlarge understanding of texts. We see something of how texts have social and personal uses and meanings, as well as how an author can manipulate texts for literary meaning (and McInerney is a skilled manipulator of various kinds of "texts"). Alison's search to discover missing pieces of folklore and to thereby reconstruct a fragmented former whole is part of a search for her own role in the social fabric, suggestive of folklore's universal function of keeping the social fabric intact. The literary meaning here obviously goes beyond the folklore but it is also inextricably bound up with folklore use, the context—though a fictional one—amplifying text and vice versa, the novel using the folklore to render meaning but also working to give the folklore a certain life within the fictional frame.

Cathleen Schine (review date 31 May 1992)

SOURCE: A review of *Brightness Falls,* in *The New York Times Book Review,* May 31, 1992, p. 7.

[*In the following review, Schine offers qualified praise for* Brightness Falls.]

A trash novel tells you everything you already know about a way of life you will, in fact, never know. A serious novel tells you, in one way or another, what you don't know about the familiar, the personal, the dailiness of life—and so about life itself. *Brightness Falls,* Jay McInerney's fourth novel, is an easy, entertaining trash novel with welcome glimpses of authentic writing—moments of honest pleasure stashed here and there, unobtrusively, almost apologetically.

With the publication of his celebrated first novel, *Bright Lights, Big City,* in 1984, Mr. McInerney became the first, and certainly the best, of the fashionably fallen literary young men of the 1980's. Now he has written a novel about the fall of such fashionable young men, about the fall of the 80's themselves. An ambitious satire addressing almost as many talk-show topics as Oprah herself (bulimia, heroin,

celebrity drug rehabilitation, AIDS, adultery, a miscarriage and more), *Brightness Falls* hits all its targets with great accuracy. But its chichi New York targets are so large, so easy, so pocked already with the arrows of a thousand journalists (and of that *echt* journalist himself, Tom Wolfe), that one wishes Mr. McInerney had aimed at more exotic game. Or that he had forsaken the satirical hunt altogether. For, surprisingly, his real strength lies in small, personal moments.

Mr. Wolfe reveled in the comedy of social incoherence in "The Bonfire of the Vanities," a cold, inhumanly brilliant book. Mr. McInerney, try as he might, cannot be cold. He lacks the rigor and cruelty of a true satirist. A *roman à clef,* *Brightness Falls* is peopled by editors and writers one may or may not recognize from gossip columns and the regular flow of press describing Mr. McInerney's own life. In this story of a young, ambitious couple in New York City in the late 1980's, there are socialites, models, debs and twisted heiresses. In contrast to Mr. Wolfe's, Mr. McInerney's vision of New York is romantic and tragic, which makes all this familiar, knowing social satire oddly naïve. The tragedy culminates in the 1987 crash of the stock market and the threatened breakup of a marriage.

Russell Calloway is a prodigy editor who published a collection of stories by his college friend Jeff Pierce to overwhelming success and has himself been basking in the reflected glory of Jeff's fame and fortune. Russell's wife, Corinne, is a stockbroker who rushes downtown each week to dish out food at a soup kitchen—an ambivalent stockbroker and the conscience of the book, a quiet, hesitant reality principle. In their early 30's, Russell and Corinne have been married for five years and have been together since college. Insulated by their commitment to each other, they seem almost smug to their less settled friends. "Like Scandinavians, they inhabited a hygienic welfare state the laws of which didn't necessarily apply outside the realm."

Just as well, for outside the realm lies a sparkling, tempting City of Greed. "Sloth, gluttony, recreational drugs were out. Narcissism, blind ambition and greed by contrast were free of side- or aftereffects, at least in this life, and who was counting on the other anymore?" The millennial foreshadowing gets heavier and heavier, though only Corinne is able to recognize it. "For lately it seemed to her that the horsemen of the apocalypse were saddling up, that something was coming to rip huge holes in the gaudy stage sets of Ronald McDonald Reaganland." The weather gets hot and stifling. The homeless riot. A whale washes up and dies on the beach during a Hamptons power party. *La dolce vita,* indeed.

Russell is too caught up in his own ambition to notice those pounding hoofbeats (and Mr. McInerney's prose does pound crudely away in the doomy passages about "the city" or "the decade"). He has lost favor with his mentor, the editor in chief of the prestigious publishing house of Corbin, Dern & Company. So he plans a hostile takeover, enlisting the aid of a savage leveraged buyout expert, a young woman he knew at Brown. She in turn goes to Bernie Melman, ruthless takeover artist, for backing, and Mr. McInerney revs up the journalistic satire machine. We learn that hostile takeovers are morally corrupt. That the financial prosperity of the 80's was all a dream. That married men are tempted by Other Women. That rich people are shallow. That brightness falls.

In the prologue to the novel, Jeff, Russell's friend and author, says, "Begin with an individual and you'll find you've got nothing but ambiguity and compassion; if you intend violence, stick with the type." Mr. McInerney, to his credit, attempts both, but he lacks the vicious disgust for the latter, and he lacks the temperament to stick with the former.
—Cathleen Schine

In the prologue to the novel, Jeff, Russell's friend and author, says, "Begin with an individual and you'll find you've got nothing but ambiguity and compassion; if you intend violence, stick with the type." Mr. McInerney, to his credit, attempts both, but he lacks the vicious disgust for the latter, and he lacks the temperament to stick with the former. He is a sincere, earnest cynic. He creates types, certainly—all the rich people here are nothing if not types, emblematic of whatever particular vice the author requires them to represent.

But Mr. McInerney is not heartless enough to dismiss them as a true satirist must. He sympathizes with them. He admires them. He eats lunch with them. Describing a pilgrimage Russell makes to the "21" Club with Melman, in which the financier proudly displays his table clout, Mr. McInerney betrays his own breathless excitement, his fascination with the intricacies of social status:

> If this concern with the pecking order might have seemed obsessive and parvenu to the clinical gaze, Bernie's boyish enthusiasm was disarming, and Russell's critical faculties were somewhat dulled in this shrine to the masculine romance of old New York, where sacramental cocktails with names like Manhattan and Sidecar were still served by uniformed old men who had never attended an acting class, and cigar smoke rose like incense on the altar of power and money.

This boyish belief in the glamour (and danger) of New York can be rather charming, and sometimes is (Mr. McInerney has a wonderful, compassionate sense of how arrogance can be a kind of innocence); but then those apocalyptic hooves come pounding again. The absurdities of the rich and powerful are viewed with such reverence, such extravagant horror, that one realizes that at some level Mr. McInerney himself really believes this stuff, really believes that your character can be judged by your relationship to a table in a restaurant.

This part of *Brightness Falls*—the self-aggrandizement and the acceptance of status as ethics—makes the novel occasionally ludicrous. Most of its moral and emotional energy is invested in contemplating a character's image, as if his image were his soul. Mr. McInerney's genuine insights into fame, power and status come through only when image recedes, when he leaves behind the journalistically circumscribed vision of the 80's and looks instead at Corinne and Russell's marriage and the ways the values of the era can corrupt it. The strains are observed in small details like the choice of a tie or a new style of shirt cuffs, or when one chooses to wake up in the morning. There are wonderful passages about the robust joy of shopping, about minks and tuxedos—the pleasure Russell and Corinne take in acquiring good things. The tyranny of their success is also felt through these acquisitions, the longed-for material possessions that, once they arrive, are somehow demanding and intrusive, an alien presence unbalancing the Calloways' intimate, habitual understanding of each other.

The glancing delicacy of this writing is in sharp contrast to the obvious blows of the more rhetorical sections of the book, but even at his worst Mr. McInerney is disarmingly openhanded. In *Brightness Falls,* the paste and the gems are offered with the same generosity. Jay McInerney's delight in telling a story, even a story you've heard before, is contagious.

Sven Birkerts (review date 7 June 1992)

SOURCE: "McInerney's Redemption," in *Chicago Tribune Books,* June 7, 1992, p. 3.

[*In the following review, Birkerts offers a favorable assessment of* Brightness Falls.]

"Whom the gods would destroy," Cyril Connolly once wrote, "they first call promising." Jay McInerney, the most visible of the much-maligned "brat-packers" of the 1980s, might have done well to have the words stenciled on the front of his favorite T-shirt, for in recent years the track of his astonishing ascendancy has been playing in slow-motion reverse.

Every book after McInerney's **Bright Lights, Big City,** every late-night grimace snapped by the papparazzi of the fashion tabloids, seemed to further erode the magic. It was the writer become object lesson, the F. Scott Fitzgerald story minus only the literary contribution.

But like Rocky Balboa and Freddy Kruger, McInerney is back. And all of those who were licking their chops in expectation of further comeuppance will be disappointed. While it is not *The Great Gatsby,* or even *Tender Is the Night,* McInerney's new novel, **Brightness Falls,** is a solid and durably plotted book. Indeed, fueled by its images of excess and rendered biographically interesting by its undercurrents of felt remorse, it makes for a quick and compelling reading experience.

Brightness Falls is not the name of a Catskills resort town, but a phrase culled from Thomas Nashe's Elizabethan poem, "A Litany in Time of Plague": "Beauty is but a flower / Which wrinkles will devour, / Brightness falls from the air, / Queens have died young and fair, / Dust hath closed Helen's eye. / I am sick, I must die. / Lord, have mercy on us!"

The lines, read at the memorial service of Jeff Pierce, one of the fast-lane characters, express the age-old recognition that finally comes to haunt not only the book's protagonists, Russell Calloway and his wife, Corinne, but also much of the greed-glutted culture around them.

Set mainly in the months preceding the 1987 stock market crash, **Brightness Falls** opens on a heady, even hubristic note. Russell, a rising young editor at the trade house of Corbin, Dern and Company, is throwing a party for Corinne's 30th birthday. Life looks flush: "The electronic buzz of fast money hummed beneath the wired streets, affecting all the inhabitants . . ." And during the course of the increasingly boozy evening we are introduced to a vivid cross-section of hip New York, including Russell's best friend Jeff, who sneaks off to the bathroom to shoot up some drugs, various publishing cronies and an array of models, club groupies and night crawlers.

These are not the kind of people we want to know—their self-congratulatory wryness assures that—but we turn the pages hoping to see some of them writhe. And this they will do.

The novel's main action starts when Harold Stone, Russell's boss at Corbin, Dern, all but quashes one of Russell's pet projects, a behind-the-scenes account of the secret war in Central America. Russell takes it as a blow aimed at his career and retaliates—in spades. With the help of well-con-nected friends (Corinne works as a stockbroker), he figures out the concept of the leveraged buy-out and is soon scheming to take over the firm.

Money always has a nose for opportunity. Quite suddenly—almost improbably—Russell finds himself in cahoots with an attractive deal-maker named Trina and a smarmy and self-important raider named Bernie Melman. Overnight, it seems, he has lifted himself into a new echelon.

We read about conspiracy sessions in the Oak Bar and opulent dinners at the Melman's. As Russell's crony, a young black editor named Washington, observes of the later: "They had tall, thin women with cleavage and short, pudgy men with leverage."

McInerney has planted a two-pronged hook. First, he plays to the reader's fascination with the runaway corruption of Russell's soul. The prospects of wealth and power, not to mention the anticipation of revenge, lure him slowly away from the cautioning Corinne into the arms—albeit briefly—of the seductive Trina.

Then there is the delerium of the deal itself—the calculations and double-crosses, the rising adrenalin as the players move into position. McInerney orchestrates the drama convincingly, registering both the anxiety flashes and the pulse-rushing highs.

The author is also quite adept at rendering the feel of the publishing milieu. We get bright, satirically edged shots of everything from the lunch-hour confabs over advances and reputations to the rituals of male bonhomie at the urinals. Word on the street is that **Brightness Falls** is, in fact, a roman a clef. Alas, lacking the clef, I can only identify the portrait of Victor Propp, the self-important novelist-schemer who keeps drawing astronomical advances on a work no one has ever seen. (If you don't know that one, you can forget about playing Trivial Pursuit, Literary Boomer Edition.)

If the strongest part of **Brightness Falls** is the building tension around Russell's raid, the weakest is its cautionary tale element. Engrossing as Russell's corruption may be, the dynamics of the situation are too simplistic. Corinne, who just wants a baby and some normalcy, is too pat, while the alluring Trina vamps too predictably around the power and sex chords. The marker flags go up: Story with a Moral. And when the big collapse arrives—I'll save the details—a certain disappointment must follow. We know it's time to take our medicine.

Maybe we've all read and watched one too many chronicles from our last gilded age. I'm not thinking of the movie *Wall Street,* though that would fit. No, the true prototype for

Brightness Falls is Tom Wolfe's *The Bonfire of the Vanities.*

The similarities are quite striking. Like Wolfe's Sherman McCoy, Russell plays at being a Master of the Universe (though, to be fair, Russell packs more human dimension, has softer edges). He, too, falls mightily, filling the reader with the same sense of *schadenfreude.*

And like Wolfe, McInerney evokes a rich, if less sumptuously detailed, panorama of New York City life. We get the boardrooms and the vial-strewn corridors and much that lies in between. The pace is Wolfean, with quick jump-cuts from one charged encounter to the next. It's hard not to try to squeeze in one more chapter before hitting the lights at bed-time. *Brightness Falls* may not be a great literary work—it hangs too much on types and simple moral equations for that—but it will be, for its author, a redemption of sorts.

Richard Eder (review date 7 June 1992)

SOURCE: "Campfire of the Vanities," in *Los Angeles Times Book Review,* June 7, 1992, p. 3.

[*Below, Eder offers a negative review of* Brightness Falls.]

Thomas Nashe's "A Litany in Time of Plague" is one of the most celebrated and haunting of Elizabethan poems, with its bony caution to mortality:

> Beauty is but a flower
> Which wrinkles will devour;
> Brightness falls from the air,
> Queens have died young and fair,
> Dust hath closed Helen's eye.
> I am sick, I must die . . . .

Using it for his title, then for a reference, and finally quoting two stanzas at the climactic funeral in his novel about the flourish and decline of glittery New York lives, Jay McInerney manages to turn it into kitsch.

In *Bright Lights, Big City,* published a decade ago, McInerney wrote of privileged post-college kids drifting aimlessly through sex and drugs. It was brittle, hip and sometimes witty; the qualities were sharpened by the vacuum McInerney placed around them.

One thing about a vacuum is that when you fall through it, you go very quickly. Clutching shards of wit and the spirit of the times—and now, 10 years older, having achieved glamorous jobs or other markers of success—McInerney

and his characters plunge without transition into sentimentality. Together, McInerney has talents but not the novelist's necessary talent of delivering his characters. They remain stillborn inside him. They do not speak; he speaks for them.

The figures in *Brightness Falls* have been everywhere. At least, they have been everywhere that such magazines as Vanity Fair and New York have written about. Unlike Tom Wolfe, who works very hard and who, in "Bonfire of the Vanities," delved deeply into a shallow world, McInerney's own fine focus reflects reflections. He is easier on himself, both when he is being smart and when he is being serious. As a result, the seriousness is mushy and the smartness seems prepackaged; it confirms our responses instead of arousing them. *Brightness* is no bonfire; it is a campfire. . . .

Take the funeral. The three principal characters attend, one of them as the corpse. There are Russell and Corinne Callaway, an erstwhile golden couple who have declined into brass. He was a hotshot young book editor who tried to engineer a leveraged buyout of his company, failed and lost his job. She, once beautiful and envied, grows older and plainer and suffers from bulimia *and* anorexia. The marriage is badly shaken by mutual infidelities. Hers was with Jeff, the corpse. He was a glamorously successful young writer who blocked, and went lethally into drugs and a recovery program that came too late.

Now comes Nashe, recited by a poet. He is "an old poet, bearded and calm." The spirit of decor—autumn shades at this point—that governs *Brightness* precludes his being jowly and twitchy. And Corinne, who went to Brown, finally understands the line that Russell, who also went there, had occasionally tried to explain to her.

"And now, suddenly, she could picture it clearly: brightness and beauty and youth falling like snow out of the sky all around them, gold dust falling to the streets and washing away in the rain outside the church, down the gutters into the sea." Nashe falls from the air, becoming Rod McKuen. So much for Brown.

The story of how Russell, Corinne and Jeff, after enjoying the heights, come down sadder, wiser or dead gets started about a third of the way through. Before that, the author takes us on a tour of his New York vanities. Some of his brighter writing is found here.

There is a nice line, for instance, about the Callaways' ability to be carefully successful, fashionable and beautiful—they live "on the very edge of the credit limits on their charge cards"—and a seemingly happy couple. None of their trendy friends can manage the combination. They were, the author writes, like Scandinavia: "a hygienic welfare state, the laws of which didn't necessarily apply outside the realm."

The "seemingly" is a problem. McInerney describes the Callaways' fashionable dinner party—brittle talk, tasteful food and wine, witty but unsound guests—with a signaling that is all too apparent. If you hang your characters up to dry at the start of a book, it's hard to keep them fresh all the way through. The three principals become increasingly inert and dull as we read on.

McInerney does parties, infidelities, a poetry reading, art talk, a fashion-photography session and other stops on the New York walking tour. He does Russell's publishing house with its playboy proprietor, a cynically ambitious black editor and an editorial director who flaunts his literary integrity and conceals his passion for profits and secretaries. He does the leveraged-buyout scheme, and the ball-of-fire young financial wizard who uses Russell for it and then discards him. It is *roman à clef* all the way. The keys are very large, and the doors they open are very small.

McInerney can be witty with his New York set scenes, the boom times of the 1980s and their collapse after the '87 stock-market crash. But his wit is essentially commentary—"Remarks aren't literature," Gertrude Stein said—and there is little wit, reality or tension in the scenes themselves. We miss the sheer gusto—Wolfe again—of discovering how things work and being told about them.

As a Savonarola, McInerney fails to create the world he denounces. Even if they were stronger and pithier, the denunciations would require something to work on. As it is, they are lethargic, forced—a dying whale, symbolizing our world's decay, beaches at a fashionable seaside lawn party—and trite. They dress in black for mourning, but it is black tinsel.

Joseph Olshan (review date 12 June 1992)

SOURCE: "A Golden Couple of the Age of Accretion," in *The Wall Street Journal*, June 12, 1992, p. A12.

[*In the following review, Olshan offers tempered praise for* Brightness Falls.]

Nearly everyone and everything in Jay McInerney's ambitious fourth novel, **Brightness Falls,** is leveraged. Companies falsify their assets with elaborate facades; authors who are paid egregious advances cannot honor their commitments; undesirable body parts are pumped with silicone that might explode should the unlucky patron ride the Concorde.

In his novels and stories of the 1920s, F. Scott Fitzgerald also explored an era's unmet desires and inflated expectations, but with a nostalgia that Mr. McInerney wisely avoids when he writes about the '80s. **Brightness Falls** adopts a Fitzgeraldian tone in the names of its main characters, Russell and Corinne Calloway, a glamorous couple who recall Dick and Nicole Diver in "Tender Is the Night" (Mr. McInerney's penultimate title for this book was "Tender Offers," which may have also included a nod to Gertrude Stein's "Tender Buttons"). A golden couple of the Age of Accretion, the Calloways nonetheless take great pains to preserve their coveted monogamous relationship and their lofty ideals.

Though Corinne really wants to teach and raise a family, she has accepted a high-paying job as a stock analyst to help fund a flamboyant life style. Once a poet Russell, an editor at the venerated publishing firm of Corbin, Dern, can hardly pride himself on his choice of vocation. He is something of a flunky for his authors, the self-destructive Jeff Pierce, whose overnight fame and sybaritic life-style parody Mr. McInerney's own well-publicized downtown era, as well as the cantankerous, manipulative Victor Propp, who bears a resemblance to Harold Brodkey. The young Pierce trades off the success of his first book, squandering royalties and the enormous advance paid for his second work, which never materializes. The aging Propp, even better at this scam, has been threatening to publish a *magnum opus* for more than two decades, and uses his hermetically sealed isolation as well as the nondelivery of a rumored manuscript, to squeeze out ever larger advances from his publisher.

Pierce and Propp, brilliantly delineated by Mr. McInerney, are true creative casualties of '80s life, of the cultural burnout that occurs when the corporate world that supports the artist overheats. "The trouble with art," Jeff Pierce at one point tells Russell, "is the kind of company it attracts. Art tending to be sluttish, inevitably inviting Money up to see its etchings."

Mr. McInerney's writing is ironic, penetrating and at times even lyrical. For all that the author has been criticized for leading a fast life in New York, at least he has observed his night clubs' habitues with the eye of an ornithologist watching an endangered species of bird: ". . . kids in suspenders who believed that they were entitled to make millions, as scary in their way as the remorseless child murderers who inhabited the ghettos to the north, who'd pull the trigger on anyone who stood between them and their momentary desires."

Beyond the dazzle of language, however, is a business thriller plot: Russell's attempted hostile takeover of Corbin, Dern. His partner is a brilliant, savvy black editor named Washington Lee. Backing these literary buccaneers is Bernard Melman, a hilarious stereotype of a New York financier.

Pages turn quickly in the beginning of the novel, but interest flags toward the middle when Mr. McInerney lets his material sprawl. All those parties, modeling shoots and power dinners, though wonderful set pieces in themselves, hang heavily on the monofilament of a takeover plot. There are simply too many entertaining yet ultimately two dimensional news bulletins of life in Manhattan during the '80s.

Worse still, Mr. McInerney suffers from a compulsion to wink and comment as his narrative proceeds. He sets the tone by writing an acknowledgment that is actually a first-name-only homage to a list of people thanked for moral and "oral" support. It's as though the author is daring the knowing reader to match some of these names with the fictional creations that follow. Then, throughout the book, many important moments are diminished by offstage remarks. Consider, for example, when a whale beaches itself in the midst of one of Bernie Melman's Southampton parties, "dwarfing the humans submerged to their waists in the surf. Churning the foam and sand, it was trying to swim onto the shore, as if it had given up on its watery life and hoped to emulate the remote ancestor it shared with these puny, agitated terrestrials."

Here Mr. McInerney has found an image to convey a decade that will soon succumb to its own excess, even as it symbolizes the foundering of the Calloway's marriage. Yet he undermines this important scene by crowding his canvas with description—radio reports, party-guest histrionics, collections to save the whale. In short, his great moment is almost trivialized with cleverness. Almost. Mr. McInerney has all the true instincts of a major novelist, something he may yet become.

Evelyn Toynton (review date September 1992)

SOURCE: "High Life," in *Commentary,* Vol. 94, No. 3, September, 1992, pp. 56-7.

[*In the following review, Toynton gives a negative evaluation of* Brightness Falls.]

"You will have to learn everything all over again." So goes the last line of Jay McInerney's first, most entertaining novel, *Bright Lights, Big City* (1984). The sentence could almost be taken as McInerney's own authorial program, since both he and his characters seem, in book after book, to be learning not exactly everything but the same thing all over again. And what do they learn? That the glittering al-

lure of hip parties, fashionable clubs, naughty drugs—and, in *Brightness Falls,* his latest offering, big money—is really only superficial. That happiness is to be found in the simpler, human things of life—in love, kindness, honest work, fresh bread.

One might find McInerney's seeming amnesia baffling—why is he unable to recall, from one book to the next, that he has already helped us see through the hollowness of the flashy milieu he depicts in such loving detail? But of course the forgetfulness serves a useful purpose, offering his readers a double set of thrills: they can lap up his savvy descriptions of the lifestyles of the hip and fashionable and still be left with a warm sentimental glow when the hero or heroine renounces all that jazz and on the final page affirms the primacy of the heart.

McInerney has been praised as a satirist, but he lacks the satirist's penchant for exposing uncomfortable truths, for striking painfully close to the bone; our complacency is never threatened for a minute. "You are not the kind of guy who would be at a place like this at this time of the morning": that is how *Bright Lights, Big City* begins, and even as its narrator keeps snorting coke, dancing the night away, and treating people badly, he assures us in his ruefully charming way that he is not the kind of guy who does any of those things. No, he is deeper than that:

> You keep thinking that with practice you will eventually get the knack of enjoying superficial encounters, that you will stop looking for the universal solvent, stop grieving. . . . You ask yourself: How did I get here?

The answer, in this particular case, is that he got there because his wife left him and his mother died. Similarly, the narrator in *Story of My Life* (1988) got there—i.e., spends her life ingesting controlled substances and sleeping around and figuring out ways to cadge money out of people—because her parents never gave her any love and her father poisoned her favorite horse for the insurance money. But she too is a superior soul: she keeps telling us in between snorts how much she hates dishonesty in all its forms.

The same strategy is at work in *Brightness Falls,* which attempts to satirize the lives led by three successful New Yorkers in the 80's while making the major characters themselves wholly sympathetic. The novel consists of one desperately manufactured disaster after another: a failed takeover attempt of an important New York publishing firm, a bout with anorexia, financial collapse, incarceration in a drug-rehabilitation clinic, a beached whale, infidelity, betrayal, separation, a street riot, a death from AIDS. All these events, which never manage to seem inevitable, are intended to have a larger significance as part of the impending collapse of our corrupt civilization: "For lately it seemed . . .

that the horsemen of the apocalypse were saddling up, that something was coming to rip huge holes in the gaudy stage sets of Ronald McDonald Reaganland." They are also meant to serve as backdrop for the moral struggle, such as it is, of the main characters.

Unfortunately none of these characters, good, bad, or in-between, is in the least compelling. If this novel is less charming than its predecessors—in fact it is strangely life-less much of the time—that may be partly because it is nar-rated in the third person. The distinctive voices McInerney was able to create for the narrators in his other two New York novels at least made them vividly present to us, whereas all the main characters in *Brightness Falls* remain fatally indistinct. Tired and glib as is McInerney's satire of ambitious young mergers-and-acquisitions specialists, Eurotrash party-hoppers, fashion models, and self-made billionaires on their second wives, his characterizations of them are positively sprightly next to his renderings of sup-posedly three-dimensional persons.

The strongest, deepest relationship in the novel is meant to be that between Russell, an up-and-coming book editor, and his stock-broker wife Corinne, whose moral virtues McInerney insists on with particular heavy-handedness: not only does she brood at regular intervals about the plight of the unfortunate, and volunteer once a week at a mission for the homeless, but she also has deep feelings of ambivalence about her work—"Maybe there was something wrong with her, that she hadn't been able to turn into an actual stock-broker with a stockbroker's haircut and wardrobe and way of looking at the world"—and ends up befriending a pathetic widow whom she has prospected for business. Yet here she is, newly pregnant, talking with her husband:

> "God [he says], I've been such a jerk lately, haven't I?"
>
> "Maybe just a tiny bit of a jerk."
>
> "I've been a pig."
>
> "But now you're cured." She giggled. "A cured pig. A ham, I guess that makes you."
>
> "You're going to be an extremely silly mother."

And so forth.

McInerney's stated aim in *Brightness Falls* was to write "Tom Wolfe's *Bonfire of the Vanities* with real people in it." But there are neither real people nor real satire here. Tom Wolfe may not be enough of a savage moralist, *à la* Evelyn Waugh, to be a great satirist, but he is savage enough to skewer his characters' pretensions with real glee.

McInerney may simply be too happily at home in his world to summon up much gusto for skewering, and he seems to have no opposing vision of what ought to be, apart from a pious, half-hearted belief—maybe it is something some-one told him once—that greed is a very bad thing and people should not care about status, riches, and success, but rather about the homeless, and being nice to their friends and spouses. If he expects to continue being a novelist, he will have to learn everything all over again.

Jefferson Faye (essay date 1992)

SOURCE: "Cultural/Familial Estrangement: Self-Exile and Self-Destruction in Jay McInerney's Novels," in *The Lit-erature of Emigration and Exile,* edited by James Whitlark and Wendell Aycock, Texas Tech University Press, 1992, pp. 115-30.

[*In the following essay, Faye examines the themes of "cul-tural disaffection," alienation, and expatriation in* Bright Lights, Big City, Ransom, *and* Story of My Life. *Accord-ing to Faye, "Each novel may be considered a* bildungsroman *whose action revolves around a familial betrayal as it drives the main character to reject not only relatives, but self."*]

According to Malcolm Bradbury's *The Expatriate Tradi-tion in American Literature,* fictional expatriation is a re-sponse to "a familiar American complaint about cultural barrenness, 'absence of forms,' the need for another cul-ture. . . ." He describes expatriation not as the act of leav-ing but as "the desire to take the path of separatism, condemn the nation for culturelessness, materialism, or innocence, the gesture of protest." In the 1980s we find this cultural disaffection is as strong as ever; in fact, it is the foundation of Jay McInerney's three novels: *Bright Lights, Big City; Ransom;* and *Story of My Life,* which use expatriation as an underlying metaphor for alienation. These novels contain the social awarenesses Terry Eagleton as-cribes to upper-class and lower-middle class novels, both of which he said were "to some extent self-consciously hostile to what they see as the dominant cultural ortho-doxy." This cultural awareness is juxtaposed with what McInerney calls a heightened sense of the importance of familial influence on his protagonists' lives:

> I do think there's a kind of novel that starts with a char-acter *without* a background—an existential novel, I suppose. My own feeling is that one's family history is hugely determinate, and I find that a very rich mine of character determination.

Ransom literally treats an expatriate, largely American

community in Japan. *Bright Lights, Big City* begins with an epigraph from that paradigmatic novel of expatriation, *The Sun Also Rises,* then McInerney introduces a protagonist whose cocaine-driven "brain at this moment is composed of brigades of tiny Bolivian soldiers" while his feet remain in Manhattan. The character's mind is not merely in South America, but also in France with his expatriate wife. He even equates being fired from his job with receiving an "exit visa" as if he were once again changing locales after the wanderings that brought him to New York. The protagonist of *Story of My Life* also exists in a state of spiritual exile, the result of identifying the link between family and culture, one which closely resembles Bradbury's and Eagleton's definitions. I will discuss this connection first in the context of Ransom's father-son conflict, which presents a clear representation of the running themes it shares with *Story of My Life* and *Bright Lights, Big City. Ransom*'s consideration of the outsider beset with family problems creates a perspective through which their cultural disaffiliations can be read; it has a more concrete sense of exile and clearly exemplifies characteristics of McInerney's work as a whole.

McInerney writes about dissatisfaction as it affects his characters, their families, and, in the process, their cultural perspective. Each novel may be considered a *bildungsroman* whose action revolves around a familial betrayal as it drives the main character to reject not only relatives, but self. What I intend to discuss is the means by which McInerney explains the rejection of family as a representation of culture: in alienating himself from his father, Christopher Ransom is reacting to the foundations upon which he was raised and questioning his own—as well as his father's and even society's—cultural priorities. He falls into self-destructive behavior because he has no beneficial support structure from which to operate; Ransom's inability to recover from his father's adverse influence and immediate social circumstances creates an atmosphere of self-alienation—his experiences make him attempt to escape everything, including himself, and he cannot.

Ransom is a death march in which McInerney connects family to culture straightforwardly. Christopher Ransom is an American living in Japan, a man whose name alone may be sufficient to explain his situation: Christ-for-ransom. The fact that he prefers to be called Ransom suggests the skewed reality in which he lives, a constant reminder not of the sanctity of his impending martyrdom, but of the price that is in the process of being paid. He is treading water, biding time before his death; more importantly, he is using his remaining time to criticize the priorities of predominant American popular culture on one hand and of his father on the other, two influences on his life that he finds difficult to separate and cannot change. He describes, ad infinitum, his father's "selling out," abandoning the honor-

able, or truer, art of playwrighting for the "diseased" world of television-screenplay writing. Ransom's rejection of American popular culture becomes hopelessly intertwined with his rejection of his father, as Chris cannot separate his father's abandonment of playwrighting from Chris's childhood, a time which he associates with neglect and his mother's death. Because of his father's attraction to the power games of Hollywood (and use of them elsewhere), Chris identifies Victor Ransom with its evils. Victor's name, too, is tell-tale: the victor is the ransom demand, economics wielding power over uncorrupted aesthetics.

There is more to Ransom's disaffection with power games and the influence of American culture, however. Through a series of flashbacks, the reader learns of Ransom's experiences during the earlier stages of his expatriation. Periodically, McInerney takes him back two years to the expatriate community in Pakistan, near the Khyber Pass: McInerney relates the disappearance of Ransom's friend Ian during a drug-purchasing trip into Afghanistan, and details Ransom's involvement in the accidental overdose of his lover, Annette. In Ransom's eyes Ian's absence was the result of power games: his desire to make a large amount of money very quickly led him to fall in with greedy drug smugglers, who in all likelihood killed him after his kidnapping. Annette died because she accepted her fate as being under the power of a stronger force. She saw heroin as an entity who had chosen her to be an addict; she had neither the strength nor resolve to try to elude its grasp. This sequence is important because it led Ransom to Japan in an attempt to salve his wounds and rediscover his soul. Unfortunately, in Kyoto's pre-rainy season humidity and distorted reality, his emotional injuries only reinforced the festering and spreading of his afflictions; the atmosphere is noxious, and hauntingly familiar.

The environment surrounding Christopher Ransom seems perverse from our perspective. As base as Ransom finds American television, he reacts more negatively to the complete lack of content standards in Japanese television; he also spends a substantial amount of time describing the Japanese emulation of American culture and its juxtaposition with the traditional, honor-framed Japanese language and customs: the picture he draws suggests that the Japanese have developed a polemical culture that is steeped in honor and tradition on one end of the spectrum and is countered by an entirely tasteless, borrowed and distorted popular culture. In fact, this dichotomy is common throughout McInerney's work; for example, it is similar to the perversion McInerney describes in the New York discotheque and party scenes of *Bright Lights, Big City* and *Story of My Life,* but in this situation McInerney emphasizes an ironic twist: the culture Ransom has rejected in the United States is actually the predominant influence upon which the more perverse Japanese television is based. The dark side of

Japanese culture, then, manifests itself, in Jekyll-and-Hyde fashion, as abject commercialism—and it becomes apparent that for the same reasons Ransom does not like the United States he is not a perverse enough character to adapt to life in Japan. Not only is he unable to reconcile himself with his father's and his own failures, but in doing so he has lost the perspective necessary to survive—he cannot see that he hasn't the sense of humor to understand the dichotomy of popular culture: he cannot separate the self-serious from the satirical and merely entertaining.

Ransom's intolerance is obvious and very easy to understand, but equally clear is his inability to escape "trash" television's presence. It can be seen on the television sets of almost every bar he enters, apparently a necessary cog in the decadent American-influenced undercurrent of Japanese culture. And yet there appears to be a difference. American television has always had "tabloid" programs equivalent to those in the latest rage; "America's Most Wanted," "Cops," and even "A Current Affair" are recent examples, but in previous decades there was, among others, "You Asked for It." McInerney offers Japanese television's sardonic "equivalent" in tastelessness: "Sex Crimes."

> *What do we have tonight,* the host asked. He was wearing a pink tuxedo, a blue boutonnière and several pounds of hair spray.
>
> *One gang rape,* the woman responded brightly, *one double suicide, and a love-triangle murder. We'll be right back.*
>
> An ad for instant noodles came on, followed by back to back detergents. . . . The sensei . . . returned and asked what the lineup was.

This television show is a "dramatic re-enactment" of crimes taken directly from police files, and to Ransom it is little more than a blatant appeal to the same voyeuristic tendencies that make people stare at automobile accidents. With the possible exception of Ransom, it seems that no one is immune to its attraction and humor: even his karate sensei, the man with whom Ransom most closely connects the honor and tradition of Japanese culture, participates in this seduction through violence. This is the side of popular culture that Ransom cannot separate from his disappointment with Victor; while more flagrantly appalling than American versions of the same sort of programming, Japanese television's presentation of sex crimes is equal parts Monty Pythonian and cold-blooded appeal to base titillation as a means of selling laundry detergent and ramen noodles. But more than that, McInerney presents this brand of popular culture as both imitation of and influence on life—not only

is it unclear which affects which, but which is more realistic.

To reinforce this point, motivated by concerns for his son's mental and physical condition, Victor has borrowed ideas from television and movies to coerce Ransom into returning to the United States. (He even subscribes to the great American myth that all problems are attributable to drug abuse.) Once Victor tried fooling him into flying to Los Angeles with a ridiculous story about a friend's "free companion ticket" received from her employers. When that didn't work, he sent an actress from Hollywood to pretend she was a Vietnamese refugee in trouble with the Yakuza (the Japanese Mafia). McInerney seems to be suggesting that it is dangerous for even a screenwriter to borrow ideas from old movies for use in the real world—it creates an artificiality which skews perceptions of reality. Sadly, for Ransom, when his father is the agent behind this mixing of unrealistic fantasy and reality, it creates more distance between them. His father's attempt to manipulate Ransom by appealing to his "sense of duty and honor" only reinforces Ransom's perception of him, and makes Ransom realize that he has not been living so much as merely existing: he is in training for what he thinks is a battle of great importance between good and evil. Victor's ability to realize that purpose devalues, even cheapens it. Ransom is no longer living a quest, but instead his life has been reduced to a hackneyed good guys-bad guys movie plot; he now embodies this aspect of popular culture, and yet he cannot escape the fact that at one time he felt he had nothing in common with it.

For Ransom the world has become one of black and white, of hunger for power and humanity. There may have been degrees of grey, but they are still a part of the black; whether it is Victor, Japanese television and businessmen, or Ransom's enemy Frank DeVito, Ransom condemns them all in varying degrees for seeking power. Years before, Victor went to Hollywood for power, and he is unable to understand why his son thinks it tainted. Victor sees himself as strong because he is kinetic—his activity makes things happen—and he sees Chris as passively idealistic in a world Victor perceives as unresponsive to anything but power. Chris accuses Victor of being unresponsive to his needs, and of treating him as a vessel for Victor's own desires. He even calls Victor a lunatic, not realizing that he, too, is a lunatic for the opposite reason—they are equally distant from the "proper" cultural equilibrium. Each tilts at windmills, but neither understands what the other's windmills represent.

By reducing Ransom's life to preparation for a battle between good and evil, McInerney emphasizes the comparison between Ransom and DeVito, an ex-Marine with a colossal yearning for power. DeVito was drummed out of the Marines because he had neither a sense of duty nor honor (the qualities that drive Ransom's life), but instead an overdeveloped sense of self-importance and ruthlessness. DeVito is in Japan because he feels there are opportunities for him that exist nowhere else in the world. He sees Japan as a truly promising capitalistic domain: to DeVito money means power, because everything—with the possible exception of honor—can be obtained for a price. This is the lesson Victor learned, the lesson DeVito learns, and the lesson Ransom refuses to learn. DeVito hates Ransom because he believes Ransom represents everything holding him back: his rural Oklahoman roots, the morality that cost him his career in the Marine Corps, the social consciousness that reduces his influence and power. To DeVito, Ransom's honor represents his greatest shortcoming, so as Japanese tradition dictates, they must fight a duel for the purpose of saving face.

It is fitting, then, that DeVito kills Ransom. For just as Ransom represents DeVito's lackings, so DeVito represents everything Ransom has resisted (and run from) since before he left the United States. DeVito is the personification of the greed and desire for power that drove Victor to Hollywood, that brought about Ian's disappearance and Annette's death, that caused Victor to try to manipulate Ransom rather than reason with him. The final confrontation is fitting because Ransom has decided not to run any more, not to resist any more, and not to give in. He resigns in the face of incomprehensible odds; he knows that he cannot change the world, and he isn't about to continue "moping." It is fitting, too, that he dies as a result of DeVito's win-at-all-costs attitude. In effect he already has a moral victory when he undermines DeVito's assumed authority (he chooses the location of the duel against DeVito's wishes), then when he arrives at the duel's designated place without being observed, and finally when he draws first blood. In that world, however, moral victories are ephemeral; DeVito has the resolve to live and the savvy to fit perfectly in this world—Ransom does not. And Ransom dies unceremoniously, but with honor. That is all he has.

If Ransom is a misled or failed martyr as I have suggested, the protagonists in McInerney's other novels are survivors of their rites of passage, pilgrimage, failure, and self-sacrifice. In *Bright Lights, Big City,* the nameless protagonist begins the novel spiralling in a cocaine- and alcohol-driven whirlpool amid the Manhattan nightlife, but not just for the sake of "pure" hedonism. He is in exile from his "productive" cultural and familial ties: he is unable to cope with the emotional pain resulting from his mother's death after a battle with cancer; his job at an unnamed New York magazine promised a literary career in which "You wanted to be Dylan Thomas without the paunch, F. Scott Fitzgerald without the crack-up," but delivered only dissatisfaction, drudgery, and failure; and his fairytale romance-turned-mar-

riage with his fashion-model wife, Amanda, became a separation auspiciously categorized by her lawyer as "sexual abandonment." These changes are manifested in his responses to popular culture, as he revolts against his instincts, rejecting the positive, and embraces the negative elements of his surroundings.

Bright Lights, Big City's narration reinforces the protagonist's self-division, exposing a process which Michael Ugarte considers an exile's characteristic self-discovery, a process which

> leads the writer, perhaps unwittingly, into a dialogue with him or herself on the very nature of writing and on the problems that arise from an attempt to record reality.

McInerney uses a second-person narrative in which the nameless protagonist refers conversationally to himself as "You," establishing a sense of an everyman—or perhaps an absence of being—through which the protagonist distances himself from his problems by talking to his reflection in the mirror, or to everyone else because he cannot face his own problems. The use of "You" creates an immediate discomfort for the reader. It shows a schism in which the protagonist is exiled from himself, an ethereal voyeur helplessly watching his own self-destruction from the outside. Unused to this language, the reader is seemingly incorporated in the text as still another powerless bystander, which further illustrates the divisive effects of the problem. McInerney literally draws a picture of this process in the description of the protagonist's

> dream about the Coma Baby. . . . The Coma Mom is stretched out on your desk in a white gown. . . . The gown is open around her midsection. You approach and discover that her belly is a transparent bubble. Inside you can see the Coma Baby. He opens his eyes and looks at you.
>
> "What do you want?" he says.
>
> "Are you going to come out," you ask.
>
> "No way, José. I like it in here. Everything I need is pumped in."
>
> "But Mom's on her way out."
>
> "If the old lady goes, I'm going with her. . . . They'll never take me alive," the Baby says.

As the Coma Baby incubates inside a near-dead mother, it awaits a court decision allowing it to be born by caesarian section at the cost of its mother's life. The protagonist faced a similar problem in attempting to fill his mother's expectations and desires before she died, rather than living his own life:

> marriage wasn't high on your list of priorities, although on Amanda's it was. . . . Then your mother was diagnosed and everything looked different. Your first love had given notice of departure and Amanda's application was on file. . . . And, in the end you may have confused what she wanted with what Amanda wanted.

The only way the Coma Baby or the protagonist can survive is if he accepts his mother's death and faces the conditions which have spawned his exile. Rather than allowing others to make his decisions, or set expectations for him, he must take his fate in his own hands. The protagonist does this by arriving at the realization that he must let his mother die. "'I tried to block her out of my mind. But I think I owe it to her to remember. . . . And I was just thinking that we have a responsibility to the dead,'" which is, for him, to go on living.

This is, of course, a decision which takes the protagonist the entire book to reach. Until then he is engaged in systematically dismantling his life. McInerney illuminates the protagonist's situation by explicating the formula for his self-destructive tendencies. In comparing the magazine and the Manhattan club scene, the yuppie equivalent to high culture, with the mass-cultural New York *Post*, McInerney focuses the narrative on the dichotomy of popular culture much the same way he did in **Ransom,** but more significantly. Aside from the actual *Post* headlines he reads, the protagonist periodically considers the embarrassing headlines that could result from his own bizarre experiences; although emotionally incapable of writing autobiographical fiction, he finds ironic comfort in considering the humorous possibilities his life presents as *Post* articles. In what has become a devastatingly pressure-filled existence, only the *Post* is a source of uncompromising pleasure.

> You get a seat and hoist a copy of the New York *Post.* The *Post* is the most shameful of your several addictions. You hate to support this kind of trash with your thirty cents, but you are a secret fan of Killer Bees, Hero Cops, Sex Fiends, Lottery Winners, Teenage Terrorists, Liz Taylor, Tough Tots, Sicko Creeps, Living Nightmares, Life on Other Planets, Spontaneous Human Combustion, Miracle Diets and Coma Babies.

McInerney's use of this tabloid as a means of providing and maintaining hope is much like Don DeLillo's in *White Noise.* The *Post* occupies a similar position to the protagonist's; its perspective is from the outside looking in, and relies upon a less self-indulgent, more facetious view of our culture and of life in general as its saving grace.

It uses the conscientiously ridiculous to maintain a sense of perspective, extolling the idea that all is possible, but recognizes that most important is the style used to present its material: it is not obligated to limit itself to strictly documented events; the *Post* privileges truth over fact. These characteristics are spelled out in direct contrast with the obsessive directive of the protagonist's job at the Department of Factual Verification: the pursuit of correct accentuation, privileging fact over truth. It is depicted as absurdly anal-retentive and counter to his nature: in the protagonist's eyes, he "never stopped thinking of yourself as a writer biding his time in the Department of Factual Verification," as opposed to some of the characters who actually *belonged* there. As a member of its staff, he is at best a misfit, more accurately an outsider, definitely an exiled prisoner.

The protagonist, like the *Post,* experiences a fundamental exile—just as the *Post* is not of the same ilk as the more mainstream newspapers or the magazine, he consistently finds himself on the perimeter of overzealous, tunnel-visioned groups, never quite meshing with their membership, yet unable to escape their influence. From the novel's first lines, McInerney is informing the reader that the protagonist does not fit in.

> You are not the kind of guy who would be at a place like this at this time of the morning. But here you are, and you cannot say that the terrain is entirely unfamiliar, although the details are fuzzy.

As the narrative continues, McInerney continually reiterates this idea; the protagonist feels incapable of escaping his failures, such as Amanda and the magazine. He is pressured by his inability to conform to the "normal" yearnings for a storybook existence; in essence, he fails to separate real life from idealized societal expectations, and the resulting sense of exile is consuming him. His perception of rejection, of unrealized dreams, as examples of our culture's (or life's) cruelty leads him into a world of decadence, but only as a fringe participant. His own idealism does not permit him to truly take part in the club scene: it is intellectually bereft and entirely unwholesome; he is looking for something more.

> The problem is, for some reason you think you are going to meet the kind of girl who is not the kind of girl who would be at a place like this at this time of the morning. When you meet her you are going to tell her that what you really want is a house in the country with a garden.

And yet he is unable to ignore the call of the hedonist Tad Allegash, who leads him to consume large quantities of cocaine and vodka—exiled drugs themselves—and spends each night tramping about Manhattan. He is a stranger, self-exiled from his rightful domain, thrust into the inescapable sub-culture that has enveloped his life, unable to whole-heartedly participate; he does not see a means of escape from what has become a failure-driven, self-destructive impulse. This is due to his only gradually developing awareness that he was used by Amanda.

Amanda, like the magazine, is a reminder of his failure to reach his surrogate dreams. The protagonist cannot help feeling humiliated; in Amanda he thought he was getting the perfect woman: eager to learn, beautiful, ingenuous, "she came right up and started talking to you. As you talked you thought: *She looks like a goddamned model and she doesn't even know it.*" He was mistaken. Early in their relationship she regarded modeling much the same way he thought of his job at the magazine: it was a means to an end, not a self-contained career. They shared the recognition that their jobs were ridiculous until modeling became Amanda's *career,* only a short time preceding his abandonment, and then he could not escape her/its presence. Walking along the street he saw mannequins molded after her, her face in advertisements, and people asked about her. He attempted to escape the images through his work at the magazine, but he was self-destructing there as well: "They want you to relax, go home. You don't want to go home. Your apartment is a chamber of horrors. There are instruments of tortured." For the protagonist it was not a home so much as a reminder of what was lost to him: he had no wife, no true friends, no mother. Even the dust in his apartment prevents his escape from Amanda's expatriation and his own exile.

Unlike the other novels, *Bright Lights, Big City* presents the only possible outcome for the protagonist if he continues on his present path. McInerney introduces Alex Hardy, who, as a dreamer shaped by society's mores, is a longtime editor at the magazine and a dark, alcoholic, exilic vision of the protagonist's future. Hardy is what the protagonist will become if he continues his self-destructive path; aside from some early success, and having shared an office with William Faulkner, Hardy's writing career has produced little despite initial promise—he spends his days stuporously reminiscing about the past rather than acting in the present, and "No one can say whether his drinking is a function of his decline or whether it is the other way around." Hardy is unwilling to recognize the changing times and cannot extricate himself from his long-lost dreams of greatness, much like the protagonist; the difference is that the protagonist is unwilling to stand still. He, like the Coma Baby, is slowly coming to life, slowly rescinding his exile.

In what amounts to a rejection of his accustomed lifestyle's decadence, the protagonist eventually abandons everything that has been destroying him: he forces a release from his

job, sees the end of his relationship with cocaine, recognizes Amanda's shallowness as she introduces a high-class male prostitute as her fiance. He recognizes Amanda and her kindred spirit, Allegash, as two who, knowingly or not, have been reinforcing his situation, blockading him from participation in the cultural mainstream, maintaining his exile. He has come to an important self-understanding about his goals and his past failures. He entered his present lifestyle by following the easy path, as Amanda approached him for her own gain, not his; the wrong job at the wrong kind of magazine was never a way to reach his literary goals; cocaine merely delayed and refocused the pain he was experiencing. He recognizes that "You will have to go slowly. You will have to learn everything all over again," considering not what expectations are superimposed on him from without, but what comes from within.

Story of My Life is concerned with the more dangerous aspects of patriarchal American culture while maintaining much of *Bright Lights, Big City*'s flavor. It, too, describes a train of cocaine-fueled parties, this time colored with frequent, frank sexual interludes. Like *Bright Lights, Big City, Story of My Life* is a novel of self-abuse leading to an awakening, chronicling Alison Poole's struggle with the increasingly inescapable memories of being sexually abused by her father during her childhood; her constant effort to repress the pain he caused has driven her away from her family, the horse stables and suburban lifestyle that were her birthright, and into a numbing decadence. Alison is an emblematic representation of the position held by all women in a society run by men. This is not to say that all women are like Alison, but *Story of My Life* does present a lurid picture of the ease with which women can become disenfranchised—creating a class of exiles—in this society. Rather than chasing the concept of an ideal life (a la *Bright Lights, Big City*'s protagonist), or martyring herself for the salvation of integrity (as did the title character of *Ransom*), Alison's exile is a result of her attempts to avoid reminders of the past. Unlike McInerney's other protagonists, she has been physically exiled from what would normally be considered "home"—her father's psychological sickness has fostered her detachment from her accustomed family situation, leaving her adrift yet financially dependent on him. Alison is attempting to find a stolen innocence, (including reason, purpose and comfort); essentially, she is on a quest for a safe haven. The entire story creates an atmosphere in which Alison is so unable to separate her different self-abuses that she rambles through a stream-of-consciousness narration: she refers constantly to the men in her life who think of her as nothing more than a sexual playtoy (consequently contributing to her rootlessness), and she jumbles references to cocaine-filled parties with angry and disapproving allusions to her father. She can acknowledge vestiges of his pedophilia in his relationships with other women— "always gone for the young ones, haven't we, Dad?"—but suppresses her memories of his sexually abusing her. She repeatedly hints that this molestation is the source of her self-destructiveness, but it is only at the end of the novel, when she is in treatment for cocaine addiction, that Alison's attitudes and behavior are directly explained.

Story of My Life, then, is a novel built around what Ugarte would call Alison's

> existential need to recover something lost (a land, an identity, a place of origin) results from the absence of an integral part of one's being—a fact that causes the exile to perceive of him or herself as less than human. . . . In many ways exile also creates a new self; it creates the distance one needs to objectify the self, to look back at it from a different situation, a different land.

Alison's memories are the key to her behavior: periodically she hints at her father's sexual obsession with her during her time as an adolescent equestrian, and the combination of two passages, one at the beginning of the novel and the other at the end, creates a coherent narrative which explains her relationship with her father and her perceived need to escape him:

> "When I was a kid I spent most of my time on horseback. I went around the country, showing my horses and jumping."

> "Back then my father bought anything for me. I was his sweet thing."

Unfortunately for her father, the time spent on the road kept her away from him, and the majority of her time was spent on a particular horse:

> "Dangerous Dan was the best. . . . I loved that horse. No one else could get near him, he'd try to kill them, but I used to sleep in his stall, spend hours with him every day."

At this point the story could be the fantasy of any pre-teen or adolescent girl, taken directly from *National Velvet* or any other storybook.

> "until Dangerous Dan dropped dead. I loved Dan more than just about any living thing since."

> "When he was poisoned I went into shock. They kept me on tranquilizers for a week."

This teaches young Alison a lesson about how to escape pain, one which contributed to her future efforts to escape her memories.

I quit riding. A few months later, Dad came into my room one night. I was like, uh-oh, not this again. He buried his face in my shoulder. His cheek was wet and he smelled of booze. I'm sorry about Dangerous Dan, he said. Tell me you forgive me. He muttered something about the business and passed out on top of me and I had to go and get Mom.

McInerney does not suggest that any action was taken against Alison's father, and does not say anything about what happened between Alison and her mother. Clearly the issue was not resolved, because it lingered on until Alison's drug treatment helped her to understand what had happened to her.

> After a week in the hatch they let me use the phone. . . . So just for the hell of it I go, Dad, sometimes I wish you'd let me keep that horse.

> He goes, I don't know what you're talking about.

> I go, Dangerous Dan. You remember what you told me that night. After he died.

> He goes, I didn't tell you anything.

> So, okay, maybe I dreamed it. I was in bed after all, and he woke me up. Not for the first time. . . . I'd love to think that ninety percent of it was just dreaming.

Through the events surrounding Dangerous Dan's death, Alison learned that drugs and travelling were apparently efficient escapes from her feelings of betrayal, and subsequently she spent a significant amount of time doing both. Despite the fact that she feels economically bound to New York—"I owe everyone in the western hemisphere, I'm like a fucking Third World country"—the novel is full of references to falsely foreign places she has been to escape her memories. She frequents clubs named Zulu, Indochine, and China Club, and travels by taxi cab on her nights out, so that from her

> apartment to Trader Vic's you get Cuban music, and then from Trader Vic's to Canal Bar you've got Zorba the Greek music and then Indian ragas from Canal Bar to Nell's, Scandinavian heavy metal on the way from Nell's up to Emile's apartment. After that you start singing the Colombian national anthem.

Through the haze of her cocaine addiction Alison sees leaving as the most promising opportunity for the future. She has concerns for her younger sister, Carol, who may be jaded, but has not lost her innocence yet. In her fantasies, Alison would "have Carol kidnapped by Australian bushmen or something and raised by them before she turned out like the rest of us." Mostly, however, she dreams of her own escape.

> I suddenly wonder how long it would take them to notice I was gone if I went out the fire escape or something. What if I just kept going, left New York entirely? I'm getting this really weird feeling like, I'm so involved in all this hysterical noise which is supposedly my life but it doesn't add up to anything, if you step back far enough it's just a dumb buzz like a swarm of mosquitoes. . . . From the planet Jupiter, none of it counts for shit.

While Alison does not act on this impulse, this is a breakthrough for her, one in which she recognizes the pettiness that is surrounding her, and becomes the keystone upon which she builds up enough courage and desperation to actually seek help. She eventually escapes to a Minnesota hospital's detox program. As the above section indicates, until Alison reaches her breaking point, every event in the novel becomes interrelated in a network of nightmarish self-reflexivity, pushing her farther and farther—spiritually if not geographically—from an emotional reconciliation with herself; she has all the subconscious pieces to assemble a complete picture of her life, but lacks the fundamental self-awareness necessary to understand why she cannot function with any success in society, why she remains an exile. That is why her acting career is so important.

If her social life is an attempt to anesthetize herself, acting is a means of understanding and venting her pent-up emotions. She sees acting as a healing experience, rather than an exercise in denial:

> I just love it, getting up there and turning myself inside out. . . . It's like being a child again . . . ever since I can remember people have been trying to get me to stifle my emotions but. . . . Acting is about being true to your feelings, which is great since real life seems to be about being a liar and a hypocrite.

Alison has established a polemical approach to her past, and therefore her state of exile. She nearly admits by default that she is actively denying herself the benefits of being truthful with herself, and her acting is beginning to wear away the ropes which bind her reactions to her memories and feelings. The maintenance of this duality is contributing to Alison's stream-of-consciousness self-examination, a split which Ugarte says occurs naturally in exile:

> The gap between the reality and the description of what happened seems to grow wider as the exile writes. . . . Similarly, the rendition of the experience turns into the object of another description, as in the

typically exilic apology for not recalling an event exactly as it took place.

Her needs are being manifested in her acting lessons. She has already been separated from herself by her father's sexual abuse; it has forced her to subdivide her memories, repressing the times "he came into my room," and effectively exile part of her being into a cerebral limbo. Drama school provides Alison with the opportunity to begin to heal; it is the means by which she can release the pent-up emotions and feelings of betrayal she experiences, and allow her to do so from an outside perspective. By learning about acting, she is enabling herself to create and escape the myths upon which our culture thrives: she is facilitating not only the expression of her own feelings, but those of anyone who observes her at work, conceiving of alternate realities in which they (and she) can find themselves. The acting allows her to vent her frustrations stemming from her treatment by her father and all the men with whom she associates, rather than lashing out at him/them. They are also a window into her pain:

> Anyway, I don't know—I'm just letting myself go limp in the head, then I'm laughing hysterically and next thing I'm bawling like a baby, really out of control, falling out of the chair and thrashing all over the floor . . . a real basket case . . . epileptic apocalypse, sobbing and flailing around, trying to take a bite out of the linoleum . . . they're used to some pretty radical emoting in here, but this is way over the top, apparently. I kind of lose it, and the nurse says I'm overtired and tells me to go home and rest.

Acting lessons represent Alison's positive interaction with the cultural mainstream; through it, she engages in a sort of self-analysis which allows her to continue living from day to day. Acting creates an alternative to, and provides an excuse for abstaining from, the destructive lifestyle in which she finds herself. Rather than taking in foreign substances and losing control over her mind, body and actions, acting makes her establish control over herself by channeling beneficial and detrimental emotions and memories into the creation of a physical state. This necessitates the exclusion of external stimuli and manifests a sense of self-reliance, even self-healing, which she must apply to her non-acting life if she is to survive.

Alison is in an awkward position. Her father's sexual abuse so entirely consumes her that she looks for a way to exorcise it by repeatedly associating with men and women like her father. Every one of her relationships is a power struggle in which she sees herself as the subject of aggressive behavior: she thinks her friend "Didi would make a really good Dictator of a Third World country"; her sister Rebecca is "the Tasmanian Devil, that character in Bugs

Bunny cartoons that moves around in a tornado and demolishes everything in its path"; and her long-time friend Francesca as "like a force of nature, Niagara Falls or something." Although each poses different threats, she feels that with each she must attempt to protect herself from conflict:

> "I could give a shit about the lifestyles of the rich and famous. I'm a lot more worried about survival of the fittest, and like whether I'm going to make the cut or join the club for dinosaurs and dodo birds."

This hostile environment is the result of her attempts to live by a personal code which does not comply with the surrounding rules of order; but just as Ransom is a vessel for Victor's desires, Alison is an actual and metaphorical vessel for her father and those around her. Her resistance is an attempt to stifle the patriarchal tendencies of the culture in which she has inculcated herself. Because she is unable to succeed within the larger scope of her milieu, she is forced to seek outside help and is finally rescued.

McInerney's main characters' inability to respond positively or even in an openly constructive manner when faced with failure creates their need to abandon the mainstream/traditional family and cultural relationships. According to Michael Seidel, "An exile is someone who inhabits one place and remembers or projects the reality of another." In McInerney's novels, the protagonists share a (nearly) fatal mind set, rather than a spatial location, that makes them stumble and fall into an environment that will eventually destroy them if they cannot escape. Their flaw is a life-threatening inability to actualize their idealism. His protagonists are struggling against familial and societal pressures for an artistic freedom of sorts; decadence attacks them in the guise of abuses: cocaine, power, peer pressure. Alison Poole and the protagonist from *Bright Lights, Big City* rectify their problems by changing environments, making the adjustments necessary for survival; the keystones in their survival are recognitions of the corrupting forces' limitations and the subsequent abandonment of the destructive situation created by an artificial world. Christopher Ransom, however, cannot change the way he is and has exhausted his possible safe havens; he is unable to reconcile the differences he has with the world around him (perhaps because he cannot partially attribute the problem to drugs), and therefore experiences a sort of spiritual resignation. In choosing his death at the hands of DeVito, he perversely satisfies all parties by either ensuring their safety from DeVito or making reality fit their expectations. Interestingly, McInerney spends very few lines describing Ransom's death; the important description has unfolded during the course of the novel, and the scraps are left to the tabloid television programs that represent the cultural affiliation of power, money, and tastelessness.

Thomas R. Edwards (review date 23 May 1996)

SOURCE: "Babylon Re-Revisited," in *The New York Review of Books,* May 23, 1996, pp. 28-9.

[*In the following review, Edwards discusses* Bright Lights, Big City, Ransom, *and* Story of My Life, *and finds fault with McInerney's "bad writing" and lack of social and historical understanding in* The Last of the Savages.]

The 1980s in America were not unlike the 1920s, as almost everyone noticed. Costly foreign military adventures had wound down, postwar slumps had turned to booms, friends of business in both parties had power in Washington, the demand for illegal substances was enriching the criminal classes even as the rewards of high finance were making criminals of certain of the rich. And the young, it seemed, were running wild to the corrupting beat of music their elders couldn't see the point of. In both decades the age demanded a new literature commensurate with its power to excite and offend, and as usual the literature business stood ready to oblige.

It is very hard to think of a novelist like Jay McInerney without also thinking of Scott Fitzgerald (about whom McInerney wrote admiringly in these pages). McInerney's latest book, *The Last of the Savages,* is told by a young Irish American of middle-class provincial antecedents, with (for a time) literary aspirations, who pursues his dream of moving on up in ivied eastern schools and colleges and plush settings of the rich at play, though he eventually finds his vocation not in letters but the law.

Yet the Eighties also were different from the Twenties, not least in the narrowing of the audience for serious fiction. My copies of *This Side of Paradise, Tales of the Jazz Age,* and *The Beautiful and Damned* were bought by my parents in (the fly-leaves say) the year of their marriage, 1923. They were young, intelligent, good-looking, college-educated outlanders like Fitzgerald himself; but their college was small, midwestern, and denominational; they came from sober, middle-class, Methodist families, and they were then living in a tiny Ohio hamlet without easy access to bookstores, bootleggers, or other urban amenities. It seems hard to imagine people of their circumstances in the 1980s reading or even hearing about the books that made young writers like McInerney such good copy for the glossy magazines in the Reagan years.

But if McInerney was at first more a cultural phenomenon, or symptom, than a literary one, his books are worth attention. The earlier ones provide sensational, dire impressions of what it was like, for some, to be young, privileged, and American in their time. The unnamed hero of *Bright Lights, Big City* (1984) is a twenty-four-year-old fact-checker for a magazine modeled after *The New Yorker* who idly dreams of being a writer but can't make himself actually write anything; his life centers on celebrity saloons and downtown clubs, where he nearly kills himself on cocaine, drink, sex, and general depression. In *Ransom* (1985, though perhaps written earlier), another young man, after college and a stay among the smugglers and junkies of northwest Pakistan, comes to Japan to seek moral clarity and discipline through karate but finds only violent death. In *Story of My Life* (1988) Alison Poole, an acting student in New York, is at twenty-one beset by drugs, parental neglect, faithless lovers, and lying friends; she ends up in a detox clinic in wintry Minnesota.

Good novels can of course be written about minority cultures like McInerney's white, expensively educated, fairly affluent young people in their twenties in midtown Manhattan or on the new-style Grand Tour. That most of their contemporaries were poorer, and many of them more serious about such matters as careers, social justice, politics, the environment, music and TV shows, the welfare of their friends and even relations, doesn't invalidate these portraits of the deracinated, drugged-out, self-destructive remainder. But McInerney's characters seem generic, and older readers possibly startled by their Babylonian excesses are left free to hope that the author is exaggerating or that he, too, disapproves. At the same time, younger readers can assume that he understands and sympathizes with, if not their worst practices, then at least their fantasies of liberation from work, family, responsibility. These are bring-your-own-irony books, and no offense intended.

McInerney's characters seem generic, and older readers possibly startled by their Babylonian excesses are left free to hope that the author is exaggerating or that he, too, disapproves. At the same time, younger readers can assume that he understands and sympathizes with, if not their worst practices, then at least their fantasies of liberation from work, family, responsibility. These are bring-your-own-irony books, and no offense intended.
—Thomas R. Edwards

Whether they are celebration, satire, or sermon is hard to say. But McInerney's early books convey certain tones and moods of their period with some force. The demise of "family values" we hear so much about every four years certainly figures in the books, whose characters take scant comfort in their parents, most of them divorced, widowed, manipulative, or indifferent to parental duty. No voice speaks out to question the children's conviction that their elders are to blame for their personal ills, including their failure to take charge of their lives.

In such circles parents often determine how money is or is not deployed, and money also points the books toward part of the truth about the 1980s. That was indeed a prosperous time for those blessed with a head start, but as usual some were more prosperous than others. McInerney's young bond salesmen, commodity traders, and ad men, and the outright drones they go to parties with, can afford drugs, club-hopping, and the right clothes: but the author seems to know that they're dining on the crumbs from their masters' tables, that the subordination they so resent is not finally created by their parents but by the economic system they are caught up in. The point is clearest in *Ransom,* where the hero's father, a pedestrian playwright grown rich and powerful as a maker of TV movies, is anxious to redeem his dropout son from dubious foreign distractions. He sends various emissaries to Japan, and finally comes himself, to trick or persuade Christopher Ransom (McInerney is partial to allegorical names) into going home to his heritage. The ambivalent connection between financial and generational sub-ordination also figures, if less boldly, in *Bright Lights* and *Story of My Life,* as in Alison Poole's anger that the rich father she so despises doesn't pay her tuition bills on time.

In these earlier books the main characters, if not fully representative, are at least strongly represented. McInerney seems better at mimicry than at imagining himself into roles as a good actor can, but he "does" people's voices with skill. The *Bright Lights* boy speaks in a present-tense, second-person-as-first-person mode—"I sat down" becomes "you sit down" and so on—that nicely suggests the suspicious way in which he keeps watching himself be narcissistic. Alison Poole, a mix of Holly Golightly, Holden Caulfield, and basic Valley Girl, is vocally less original, but she, too, is consistent, funny, and often touching. And *Ransom,* though told in the third person, keeps close to the damaged, affectless consciousness of Christopher himself.

These books are short and narrow in range, and McInerney has lately been expanding his picture of an America in moral crisis. *Brightness Falls* (1992) is a too-long, old-fashioned novel, with a larger, less freakish, and almost multicultural cast of characters. The leading couple, Corinne and Russell Calloway, are actually married; though they have little money, she is old-line WASP and a stockbroker, he lace-curtain Irish and in publishing. Their friends include a hip literary black man, a young Jewish movie producer, some environmentalists up in Vermont, and a writer, Jeff Pierce, who has published a successful book of stories, is secretly on heroin, and may be gay. The year is 1987, the homeless are in the streets, and some big-time corporate raiders show up, at Russell's instigation, to try for a leveraged buyout of the publishers he works for.

This new inclusiveness is potentially interesting, but what gets done with it lies uncomfortably close to soap opera or a Michael Douglas big-business movie. Russell and Corinne are loving, but the ups and downs of their life together are banal. She wants a baby, he resists, she gets pregnant, he finds he's glad; he has an affair, his first, with a (female) investment banker; Corinne miscarries, becomes bulimic, learns of his infidelity, kicks him out. Their closest friend, Jeff the writer, has to be put in detox; the LBO blows up and Russell, who has borrowed heavily to do some insider trading in his firm's stock, is ruined and must take a (higher-paying) job in Hollywood, which he for some reason finds a gentler place than Manhattan. Corinne quits the investment business to be a paralegal in the DA's office: Russell learns that she and Jeff had an affair before she married Russell; Jeff dies, perhaps of AIDS, though not before finishing a novel about them all—"Jeff's *Ivan Illyich*," Russell calls it at the memorial service. Russell and Corinne gingerly reunite, the Crash of '87 wipes out the high-leverage guys he had aspired to play with, and the story ends with a rather lame variation on the conclusion of Joyce's "The Dead," in which Russell nods off with Corinne asleep beside him, while he muses about death, memory, the empty nest possibly in their future, and the threat of Alzheimer's before the end.

In short, the effort to give the book historical scope and portent fails. The title's allusion to Nashe's great "Litany in Time of Plague," which Russell carefully explains to Corinne, seems overdone, since its most prominent contemporary reference is not medical or moral but financial. And 1987, unlike 1929, was not, after all, the Apocalypse but just a great buying opportunity. The freedom of the third-person narration may have been too tempting—there's room in *Brightness Falls* to say too much too loosely, as in, "He was fleetingly sensitized to the peculiarities of urban life, briefly conscious of the fantastic web of mundane conventions composing this outlandishly complex organism" (i.e., New York City), which no one in the earlier books could have uttered without laughing.

In *The Last of the Savages* McInerney returns to the first person, but bad writing here becomes unexpectedly endemic. After an opening sentence—"The capacity for friendship is God's way of apologizing for our families"—that might have pleased Austen or Tolstoy, we soon read that a major character, the free-spirited Will Savage, "seemed like an avatar of the orgy of the eternal present," which apparently means, if anything, that he loved a good time and showed it. (He puts on some weight as the story advances.) The narrator, Patrick Keane, describes his reaction to a graceless FBI man with a flattop haircut: "Even as

I equivocated, trying to divulge as little information about Will as possible, I was plagued with the notion of picking that rotten pea [a large purple mole] from his face, and strafed with images of tiny airplanes taking off and landing on the special agent's head." "Equivocated" and "divulge" are ponderous, and "information" is redundant (what else can one have to divulge?). "Plagued" and "strafed" are unfortunate choices, but if they must be there, they surely demand "by" and not "with." The whimsical riff on the word "flattop" is simply lame.

Some of the ineptitudes of the novel's prose are just irritating or unintentionally funny, like "flashes of landscape scooped up fleetingly in the cone of the headlights." Others flirt with disaster. Of Will's Southern-bred ease among black people, one reads that he "seemed to belong [among them], but not by virtue of aping the behavior of the local populace, nor of a moist heartiness." At another point we witness a fascinating struggle on the narrator's part not to utter the low word "accordion," for which he substitutes periphrases like "monstrous instrument of torture," "dreadful device," "spawn of some violent coupling of reptile and pipe organ," and "respirating instrument" with, presumably, a facetious intent.

The Last of the Savages is told by someone who is both a snob and a lawyer, and the implication may be that his profession and outlook have spoiled his powers of language. But this man reads good books and once wanted to be a poet, and snobs and lawyers often speak as clearly and effectively as anyone else. If McInerney wants to make Patrick sound stuffy, it remains true that good novelists can make even stuffy people sound interesting.

Patrick Keane is a very successful New York corporation lawyer telling, in the 1990s, of his youth and early manhood. He was Class of '67 at an elite New England boarding school, which he entered as an Irish Catholic "scholarship student from a . . . mill town down the road." His origins are a bit less humble than his terms imply—his large, loud mother with her broad South Boston "a"s may not be a social asset, but she at least has a mink coat, and his quiet father does well for himself as an appliance dealer while Patrick goes on to Yale, Harvard Law, marriage to the daughter of a "patrician" federal judge (the governor of Massachusetts is at the wedding), and a career that might make anyone a little smug.

At prep school Patrick meets and rooms with another of the bold, dominant, male best friends that often appear in McInerney's stories. The aptly named Will Savage is the scion of an old-rich Memphis family prominent in right-wing circles. His disheveled-preppy style is, even in the mid-Sixties, well on the way to hip-psychedelic; he has read Kerouac, Ginsberg, Hesse, D. T. Suzuki; he scorns the

Beatles, preferring the authentic black rhythm-and-blues singers he knows from back home; he's profane of speech and prone to violence, already into alcohol and grass, a rebel who seems charismatic, if not to his parents and teachers, then at least to some of his buttoned-down peers.

After a near-fatal car accident during summer vacation, Will returns to school for his senior year, saying that he "was dead" and "came back," and he soon gathers a little band of "disciples" to whom he imparts his wisdom about music, Eastern religions, and the Beats, along with, possibly, some LSD. ("Look what happened to Jesus," Patrick says to him a little too appropriately during later bad times.) Denied graduation when he takes the rap for Patrick, who brought a girl to their room, and in danger of being drafted for Vietnam, Will slips the faculty some hash brownies and heads for Asia on his own, visiting Japan, Thailand, the Khyber Pass and Ladakh, the Greek Islands, Amsterdam, Rio, and the guerrilla-filled jungles of Ecuador, ingesting local lore and stimulants as he goes.

Patrick, pursuing the main chance in New Haven, wryly calls Will's Grand Tour "a kind of greatest-hits-of-the-hippie-trail," but he's clearly impressed; the reader is supposed to be as well. And Will's later achievement of celebrity and great wealth as a pop impresario with his own music production company has a Gatsby-like grandeur. But he's a *good* Gatsby, even if Patrick can't quite understand (nor can I) exactly how all his benefactions work, especially the "utopian and profitable" project that involves "giving computers to kids from L.A. street gangs, teaching them to program and make music. Sony was throwing money at him, he said, and he'd convinced them to kick in another million to help keep his free clinic in Mississippi up and running."

"I feel like a fucking cliché," Will Savage declares in one of the book's riskier authorial moves. He is indeed a virtual anthology of clichés—hippie hero, Oedipal sufferer, new-age entrepreneur, Lincolnesque emancipator. (He "wanted to liberate us all," says the admiring Patrick, apparently thinking not just of the black performers he sponsored but of what rock and roll seemed to promise a whole generation.) His life is a neo-Faulknerian agon pitting him against his family's history and against his imposing father, Cordell, who knew Richard Nixon, may have killed his own father, does grievous damage to his wife and sons (two of them die), and may even, Will claims, have been complicit in the murder of Martin Luther King. Cordell disinherits Will, his only surviving son, for marrying a black woman, disappears, and later surfaces in London as a rich international arms dealer married to the gorgeous but dumb fiancée of one of his dead sons, with whom Will cuckolds him as a moral gesture.

Will the liberator also presides over Patrick's qualified victory over his own secret self. He gives Patrick his first clear view of the privileged world he so longs to enter, by bringing him home to Tennessee for school vacations. He arranges Patrick's supposed initiation into (hetero) sexual experience, not knowing (nor do we, then) of his drunken submission, while at Yale, to the importunities of his old prep-school English master. Will introduces Patrick to Lollie Baker, a jaunty, sophisticated Memphis girl who for a time is his lover before he marries, and who evidently owes something to her namesake, Jordan Baker from Louisville, the golfer in *Gatsby* who also liked careful men.

Patrick's sex life comes more and more to drive a story that had seemed to have a broader social and historical point. His friendship with Will looked odd from the start to some of their friends, but the enlightened reader at first dismisses this as mere homophobia. For a time he seems just an ambitious, asexual cold fish, or at best a young man who's shy and awkward with women, drawn mostly to ones who seem safely Will's, like Lollie and Taleesha Johnson, the blues singer Will marries. Patrick's own marriage has been less a fulfillment of desire than a career decision. Even accidentally witnessing Will and Taleesha in bed, she on top and he tied up, leads him to reflections that seem too commonplace to say much, least of all about Patrick himself:

> To this day I don't quite know how to interpret this . . . , but I now understand all too well that you can never predict the geometry of appetite, or know for certain what secret passions may roil within the breast of even your best friend.

But the author is playing games with us—the secret passions Patrick here has in mind, we eventually learn, are not Will's but his own, and he won't divulge them even to us until the author is ready. There have been many clues to his homoerotic feelings, but for a long time they seem only theoretical, further demonstrations of his need to feel guilty. When he finally tells us of the encounter with his English teacher, we realize that he had started to describe that evening a hundred pages before; but he stopped the account before it reached the seduction itself, not for his own reasons, I fear, but only so that McInerney can surprise us with it later, as he does with the news that Patrick has had but not mentioned two other homosexual encounters, casual ones at a bookstore and a parkway rest stop. And the concluding revelation, that Patrick has donated the sperm with which Taleesha conceives the child Will is unable to give her, is shamelessly contrived.

Unless they have some believable reason not to do so, first-person narrators really ought to tell us the facts as they come to know them themselves, however they may misunderstand or lie about their meanings. Like the supposition that a pompous character is best shown by making his speech just as pompous as possible, such evidently calculated concealments prevent one from caring much about Patrick Keane or believing in the "freedom" he claims Will Savage has helped him to appreciate. These are not mere technical problems but signs that, for all McInerney's commendable ambition to take on larger subjects in his last two books, he has not fully imagined and understood the people whose social and historical experience he writes about.

Geoff Dyer (review date 26 May 1996)

SOURCE: "Freeing the Slaves," in *The New York Times Book Review*, May 26, 1996, p. 11.

[*In the following review, Dyer cites shortcomings in* The Last of the Savages. *According to Dyer, "We are left with the statement of great purpose rather than its achieved substance and form."*]

As the allusive title suggests, **The Last of the Savages** addresses itself to big themes. Grappling with "the past's implacable claims on the present," it is a novel about—as a character accents it with some incredulity—*history*. It is also, tacitly, a novel about the confrontation with a frontier: a demonstration of a writer coming up against his limitations. In the end it is less the work itself that compels admiration than the author's willingness to extend himself beyond his undoubted strengths.

Jay McInerney has always been most at home within narrow alleys of narrative: a few blitzed-out days in **Bright Lights, Big City,** a few more in **Story of My Life.** We enjoy Nicholson Baker for the way he notices things the rest of us overlook; by providing a narrative inventory—at once definitive and highly contingent—of situations his readers have probably glimpsed for themselves. Mr. McInerney offers the pleasure of recognition (this was explicit in the second-person narration of **Bright Lights**). His previous novel, **Brightness Falls,** was broader, more ambitious, but it relied on that same ability to furnish a catalogue of the life styles that underwrote a particular moment—Black Monday—of historical convergence. In this novel, though, he means not only to offer a cross-sectional view of history but to chronicle it.

The story begins in familiar rites-of-passage territory, with the narrator, Patrick Keane, meeting his prep school roommate, the rebellious Southern aristocrat Will Savage. In galvanic reaction against a family history that has included the brutal suppression of a slave rebellion, Will's self-proclaimed mission in life is "to free the slaves." When he is

an adult this will mean recording blues musicians and becoming a music mogul; in his adolescence it involves inviting Patrick down to the family home in Memphis and getting him stoned at a blues club. While there, Will makes his first advances on Taleesha Johnson, the young black singer he later marries, partly out of love, largely to cause maximum offense to his family, and, symbolically—or so it seems to Patrick—as a way of "healing the jagged rift across the face of our land." While Will becomes a prime mover in 70's counterculture, Patrick works his way to law school and the comforts of corporate life. By middle age the friends' lives exemplify the ways in which a generation defines and is shaped by its era.

As even this résumé makes clear, there is a lot of storytelling, of history—close on three decades—to get through. Conscious of the scale of his allotted task, Mr. McInerney resorts, on occasion, to summary. Dramatically, material is contrived so that it can be dealt with conveniently. How handy for the author, for example, that his narrator is in a taxi when Will and Taleesha's house goes up in flames: by the time he arrives on the scene the fire has only a paragraph left to run. Similarly, a key moment in Patrick's sexual stagnation is dealt with retrospectively, in a paragraph. The reason for this postponement is to maintain suspense about what he calls "the darkest enigma of my being"—but the suspense is proclaimed by lines like that rather than by self-generating increments: if the novel were working well, Mr. McInerney wouldn't need Patrick to persuade us that there was an enigma.

As a way of summarizing some of the problems of authorial summary, let's take a passage from the middle of the book. Patrick and Will are in New York: Will, Patrick says, "was in love and the scent of marijuana was in the air. The slaves were growing their hair out and marching on Washington. The Pentagon would shortly be levitated. Robert Kennedy and Martin Luther King Jr. and Jimi Hendrix were still among us."

That might be O.K. as commentary for a television documentary, where the on-screen images do nine-tenths of the work, but in a novel we need something happening in the foreground. Mr. McInerney duly obliges: "We wandered the downtown streets for hours, pausing in front of various nightclubs which Will considered hallowed." That "various" is a little slack (some pages later, incidentally, we learn that Patrick chose to study history "for a variety of reasons") and so, conscious that he has fallen below the minimum amount of writerly effort needed to fix the scene, Mr. McInerney makes sure that by the end of the sentence his characters wind up somewhere precise, namely the Cedar Tavern. But that's all it is: a name. As soon as we are inside, it melts away entirely, ceases to exist. The characters could be anywhere. A quick establishing shot has been used as a buffer between stock exterior footage and a generic interior.

Throughout the novel this kind of problem is exacerbated by the way that the dialogue has to do more of the narrative load-bearing than in the author's previous novels. Since Will and Patrick drift apart from each other, a given snippet of dialogue often has to provide us with a couple of years' worth of character development. As with a suitcase crammed full of luggage, chunks of dialogue are all the time threatening to burst out of the quotation marks that have been stretched around them.

A lack of concentration is also apparent at a simple linguistic level. During that first night in the blues club Patrick falls into "a kind of hypnotic rapture"; a little later someone shakes his hand "with a kind of fetal languor." Like burglars, writers leave their prints on everything they touch, an invisible but incriminating "kind of" precedes many a turn of phrase in *The Last of the Savages*. The protagonist of *Bright Lights, Big City* dreams of writing perfect prose: "words in the correct and surprising sequence." There are odd felicitous touches here—like the view of "the expensive Pacific"—but what is most surprising about the prose of *The Last of the Savages* is its relative lack of surprises. Will drives Patrick through Memphis at "terrifying speed"; later on, we hear, they "roared out into the night"; later still the car comes "screeching to a halt." These, it might be claimed, are not very significant lapses, but they are indicative of a broader tendency to reach for the nearest phrase to hand, to coast linguistically. It might also be argued that these uninvigorating locutions are those of Jay McInerney's narrator, and there are occasions, certainly, when a low-intensity irony is wrung from Patrick's youthful belief that others "couldn't possibly imagine the sheer vivacity of my being, the poetry of my fierce yearnings and fears." When Patrick writes that he threw himself "into academic life with a vengeance," on the other hand, Mr. McInerney is reclining in his writing chair with a lack of conviction. In a crucial scene, Patrick lets Will take the blame for a serious breach of school rules; we should not let Patrick take the rap for his creator's shortcomings.

These are most significantly exposed in the character of Will Savage himself. For *The Last of the Savages* to succeed, it is not enough that Will imbibe the heady liberationist ferment of his time; he has also to embody it. As a physical presence he is understandably felt most strongly early in the book. Thereafter the book's lack of linguistic attention begins to sap him imaginatively. Drawn to a language that yearns to express the novel's grander ambitions, Mr. McInerney yields to an idiom that radically undermines it. "The benevolent glaze in his eyes had suddenly given way to a menacing intensity." No character can survive this kind of ministration from an author who is busy

applying the glaze to something not yet fully baked. "The gaunt beauty of his youth had dissipated"; that, likewise, is less a response to Will's appearance than a seductive appeal to a vault of sentiment amassed by F. Scott Fitzgerald and coveted by Jay McInerney.

Will Savage believes there is a curse on him and his family, but the eagerness to elide this taint with the curse that "came over to the New World with the first black slave" and has "been here ever since" is accomplished at the level of authorial declaration rather than convincingly manifested in the characters' actions. Will, the last of the Savages, is an engaging, complex character, but we are not persuaded that his story is history. We are left with the statement of great purpose rather than its achieved substance and form.

Carter Coleman (review date 9 June 1996)

SOURCE: "Riding a Ghost Train, Gatsby-Style," in *Los Angeles Times Book Review,* June 9, 1996, p. 10.

[*In the following review, Coleman offers praise for* The Last of the Savages, *but dismisses McInerney's aspiration to match F. Scott Fitzgerald's* The Great Gatsby.]

It is foolhardy for a novelist to go toe to toe with a beloved classic. Whether by accident or design, it's a risk Jay McInerney takes with his fifth novel. *The Last of the Savages* echoes with allusions to *The Great Gatsby,* F. Scott Fitzgerald's tragic tale of a self-invented man whose dreams ultimately destroy him. In doing so, he has written a thoroughly engaging and funny novel that nevertheless suffers by comparison, as almost any novel would.

Both *Savages* and *Gatsby* have narrators who serve as conventional foils to passionate iconoclasts. In *Gatsby,* it is Nick Carraway who tells Jay Gatsby's haunting story. In *Savages,* it is Patrick Keane who recalls his friendship with his wealthy and privileged Gatsby-like friend, Will Savage.

A Southern aristocrat, Savage rooms with Keane, a scholarship student from a New England mill town, at prep school. Savage, in a self-sacrificial gesture vaguely reminiscent of Gatsby, protects his less-privileged friend, taking the blame for having a girl in their room—grounds for automatic expulsion.

Savage never returns to school and goes on to become a legendary record producer. Meanwhile, Keane toils through the Ivy League and eventually ascends into a partnership at a prestigious New York law firm. Through the years, the two friends stay in touch, with Keane coming to the rescue of his still-wealthy but self-destructive friend, who falls into, and finally out of, drug addiction.

At the age of 47, more or less happily married and living in a large Park Avenue apartment, Keane looks back at the course and meaning of his and Savage's lives. It is this reverie that forms the narrative of *Savages.*

After spending part of several years in Tennessee, McInerney, with this book, is taking on an enduring Southern theme: the past in the present. There is a sense throughout *Savages* of the past being, as Savage says, "always with us. Right alongside us, like a ghost train."

The presence of the past in the present is manifested in Savage's inability to forgive himself for being indirectly involved in an accident that killed his younger brother and in his hatred of his family, which owned a plantation in Mississippi before the Civil War.

In particular, he rebels against his father, who is bent on maintaining white racial dominance in the South. Keane is drawn into this hatred when he uses Savage's family history in a Yale thesis about a slave uprising on the Savage plantation in which an antebellum Savage son who sympathizes with the slaves rebels against his father.

With much humor, a keen ear for authentic dialogue and vivid characters, *Savages* evokes the atmosphere of the contemporary South, from black juke joints to white plantations. In one fine paragraph, it captures the essence of Savage's home town: "Memphis possesses a jagged vitality that seems more Western than Southern, as if its inhabitants have never been told that the frontier has moved on and, finally, disappeared. Although physically situated in Tennessee, it is the spiritual capital of Mississippi, the metropolis to which planters sent their wives for finery and their sons for dissipation; and to which the sons and daughters of their slaves migrated to escape the brutal drudgery of the cotton fields. The city was once abandoned to fever, and a riverine funk still hangs over the housing projects of the South Side as well as the mansions to the east."

Besides the rich-man, poor-man theme to *Savages* and *Gatsby,* there is another similarity between the two books. In each, the narrators are Yale graduates. Moreover, Fitzgerald's Carraway and McInerney's Keane seem to have been shaped in part by what Keane calls "the darkest enigma of my being"—a sexual ambiguity that results in Keane having a fleeting sexual encounter with a man. Fitzgerald seems to suggest a similar ambivalence on the part of Carraway, who dates a tomboy professional golfer, never succeeds in a relationship with a woman, complains of a thinning list of single men as he grows older and evasively describes a

drunken encounter with a "pale feminine" art photographer "clad in his underwear."

Ever since **Bright Lights, Big City** established McInerney as a contender for a great American novelist, his trademark punch has been clever similes. *Savages* is peppered with these literary one-liners.

In one, Keane and Savage, still in prep school, sit at opposite ends of a long table in Savage's cavernous dining room, giving a New Year's Eve toast to the portraits of Savage's ancestors on the walls, who are "glowering as if they had anticipated this long afterlife of staring at the living."

McInerney is best at such small moments, some of which are tender as well as wryly humorous. In his first years at the law firm in New York, Keane realizes just how much the city has hardened him when meeting his mother's bus. He rudely dismisses a street person and is made suddenly to see the beggar through his mother's eyes: "a wizened little man with the face of a bewildered child, clearly retarded and now scared, clutching to his chest a shopping bag overflowing with rags and scraps of paper. . . . I saw that she was ashamed of me. She was wondering how she could have raised a son who could respond so heartlessly and brutally to one of God's needy creatures."

But in the end, as the Gatsby of this novel, Will Savage is a disappointing hero. He sets out to free the slaves—both the oppressed blacks of the South and all Americans bonded to the status quo—by the promotion of blues and rock music and by his patronage of radical causes.

But he ends up midlife in Malibu, bloated and unable to father a child from years of high-octane substance abuse. He is left espousing a dubious Timothy Leary-like message of how computers are "going to free us all from the web of corporate power."

Fitzgerald closes *Gatsby* with this famous existential image: "So we beat on, boats against the current, borne back ceaselessly into the past." Some 70 years later, McInerney gives his characters his own cosmic epiphany. It's not a bad moment, but few could match Fitzgerald's for its simplicity, sadness and beauty.

James Campbell (review date 14 June 1996)

SOURCE: "A Slave to Success," in *Times Literary Supplement,* June 14, 1996, p. 24.

[In the following review, Campbell offers tempered praise

for McInerney's effort to address contemporary race relations in The Last of the Savages.]

In 1962, at the height of the Civil Rights movement, James Baldwin published *Another Country,* a novel based on the premise that love conquers all, and involving every racial and sexual permutation then imaginable (in many minds, unimaginable). Three-and-a-half decades later, the contents of the pot having failed to melt, the best of the present crop of white writers seem to feel as uncomfortable with black characters as the worst of their parents' generation did with black neighbours. Race is regarded as Afro turf, and whites who stray on to it are seldom thanked for doing so.

Jay McInerney's attempt to raise the subject in ***The Last of the Savages*** displays this talented writer's characteristic wit and perception, together with an even larger helping than usual of sophomoric sex and class consciousness. Far from shying clear of the comparisons with F. Scott Fitzgerald which his previous four novels have brought him, McInerney here appropriates the narrative device of *The Great Gatsby,* telling the story of a man of ambition, appetite and, eventually, wealth and influence, in the voice of his more modest friend.

Thrown together as room-mates at a New England prep school in 1967, Patrick Keane and Will Savage, like Nick Carraway and Jay Gatsby, are opposites in every sense. Patrick's father sells washers and dryers for General Electric, a fact of which his son is deeply ashamed. Will is the scion of a former slave-owning Memphis dynasty—a fact of which *he* is deeply ashamed. His father is inclined to seek parallels between "our city . . . and the ancient capital of Egypt" for which it was named. At which his son sneers, "The institution of slavery, for instance". To Will, blues and soul music and the expression of a culture which, like everything else good in America, have been exploited and debased by white prospectors. Fuelled by a desire to pay back some of the booty (and by a lot of drugs), he aims to become a mover and shaker in the music business, promoting black musicians to their rightful level. Will's first words to Patrick are "You like the blues?", to which Patrick replies "Sure", confiding to the reader that he is "not entirely certain who or what the blues might be".

Telling a hip story in the voice of a square gives McInerney the opportunity to raise separate but related concerns: the tension between all-out liberalization and self-restraint, the gulf between the 1960s and the 90s. The cost of this is that the focus of McInerney's story—less the conflict of races in American society, than the place where they might meet—remains in the shadows. Anyone wishing to know what has happened in race relations over the past thirty years would hardly ask boring old Patrick, any more than that notorious cokehead Will.

As the story progresses along its historical grid—taking in, scrapbook-fashion, the assassination of Martin Luther King, Vietnam, Kent State, the death of Jimi Hendrix—it becomes difficult for characters to open their mouths without sounding as if they're taking part in a docudrama:

"There was actually a moment, right before I married Will, when I thought everything was getting better."

I thought I knew what she meant. "Then King was shot."

"Yeah, that and a whole lot of other stuff."

By the end of the novel, Will is in pieces, having seen his two brothers die and his father move to London with the fiancée of one of them. He is married to the black singer Taleesha, but is unable to have children. Patrick, on the other hand, has taken "a first-class ticket to the world I so fervently desired" and is working at a New York law firm.

Not just any law firm, mind. Snobbery has the same hold on McInerney as drugs do on some of his protagonists. After the brilliant first half of his 1992 novel, ***Brightness Falls,*** in which the Manhattan cast and setting were established with a sureness of touch and perception worthy of the Fitzgerald comparison, McInerney let the book slide into a Wall Street soap opera, whose principals were careful who they were seen with: "On weekends, there were two ways to determine someone's tax bracket: watch and shoes." Patrick tells his own story, but worries about such things even more—a concern which is both in character and, one feels, close to his creator's heart. Our first meeting with Patrick finds him anxious about whether his clothes, his hair, even his walk, would "pass muster"; later, he keeps an equally sharp eye on others: "If she intended a glamorous Hollywood entrance, she didn't pull it off"; "As if nervous of making some faux pas, she spoke little"; 200 pages on from his first muster-test, still "reading the signs" before risking anything underbred, Patrick is shaking his head over someone's double-breasted suit.

Like anything by McInerney, ***The Last of the Savages*** is reader-friendly. As with ***Story of My Life*** and ***Brightness Falls,*** the story proceeds vividly and in short takes, like a well-paced movie. Will seems tailored for Hollywood; some scenes seem to belong in a rock-and-roll version of *Apocalypse Now*—especially one in which the two friends get wasted in Elvis's Cadillac, which has been installed in Will's Gothic mansion—and there is a subplot involving

Will's runaway father and some heavy underground forces.

A novel about the debt white culture owes to black needs to draw us into places a pair of prep-school room-mates cannot go, and requires more solid black characters than Taleesha and some token soul musicians seen lurking in the gloom of Southern jukejoints. McInerney produces a clever melting-pot twist along the lines of Baldwin's snappy rebuke to anti-integrationists—"We were integrated in the womb"—but there isn't much bad luck and trouble in *The Last of the Savages,* just a white boy's blues.

FURTHER READING

Criticism

Caveney, Graham. "Psychodrama: Qu'est-ce que c'est? Jay McInerney and the Family Saga." In *Shopping in Space: Essays on America's Blank Generation Fiction,* edited by Elizabeth Young and Graham Caveney, pp. 43-74. New York: Atlantic Monthly Press, 1992.

> Examines the fictional presentation and psychological motivations of characters in *Bright Lights, Big City, Ransom, Story of My Life,* and *Brightness Falls.*

Girard, Stephanie. "'Standing at the Corner of Walk and Don't Walk': Vintage Contemporaries, *Bright Lights, Big City,* and the Problem of Betweenness." *American Litera-ture* 68, No. 1 (March 1996): 161-85.

> Explores the publishing history and sociocultural significance of *Bright Lights, Big City* as a reflection of its readers and target audience.

Kaiser, Charles. "A First Novelist on the Fast Track." *The Wall Street Journal* (2 November 1984): 26.

> A favorable review of *Bright Lights, Big City* with brief comment on McInerney and the publication of his first book.

Pinckney, Darryl. "The New Romantics." *The New York Review of Books* (29 May 1986): 30-2.

> An unfavorable review of *Ransom.*

Powers, John. "The MTV Novel Arrives." *Film Comment* 21 (November-December, 1985): 44-6.

> A favorable review of *Bright Lights, Big City.*

Seligman, Craig. "Bright Lights, Big Deal." *Mother Jones* 10 (May 1985): 57-8.

> An unfavorable review of *Bright Lights, Big City.*

Interviews

Pinsker, Sanford. "Soft Lights, Academic Talk: A Conversation with Jay McInerney." *The Literary Review* 30, No. 1 (Fall 1986): 107-14.

> McInerney discusses his literary influences and both the critical and popular reception of *Bright Lights, Big City.*

Terry McMillan
1951-

American novelist, short story writer, and editor.

The following entry presents an overview of McMillan's career through 1997. For further information on her life and works, see *CLC,* Volumes 50 and 61.

INTRODUCTION

McMillan's best-selling novels *Mama* (1987), *Disappearing Acts* (1989), *Waiting to Exhale* (1992), and *How Stella Got Her Groove Back* (1996) describe the frustrations and hard-won pleasures associated with middle-class security and female autonomy—both financial and sexual—among African-American women in modern American society. While focusing on the everyday experiences of energetic, black female protagonists who overcome oppressive men and socioeconomic obstacles to achieve self-actualization, McMillan avoids aligning herself with any specific political or racial agenda. Through zesty, conversational prose and realistic dialogue, McMillan challenges stereotypical views of African-American women and speaks to a large, transracial audience.

Biographical Information

Born in Port Huron, Michigan, McMillan, the oldest of four children, was raised by her mother, a maid and auto factory worker; her parents were divorced when she was thirteen. McMillan became an avid reader while shelving books in a local library as a teenager, but was not exposed to African-American authors until several years later as a student at a Los Angeles community college. After dabbling in poetry, she published her first short story in 1976 at age twenty-five. McMillan earned a bachelor's degree in journalism at the University of California, Berkeley, and a master's in Fine Arts at Columbia University, both in 1979. At age thirty, McMillan experienced an epiphany that prompted her to overcome a drug and alcohol addiction. In 1984, she gave birth to her son, Solomon. She published her first novel, *Mama,* in 1987, which she single-handedly promoted by writing several thousand letters to booksellers and arranging her own publicity tour. McMillan received a National Endowment for the Arts fellowship the next year. She taught creative writing at the University of Wyoming in Laramie from 1987 to 1990, then at the University of Arizona in Tucson until 1992, where she was an associate professor. Her second novel, *Disappearing Acts,* was published in 1989, and *Breaking Ice,* an anthology of African-American fiction that she edited and introduced, was published in 1990. *Wait-*

ing to Exhale, published two years later, was adapted into a popular Hollywood film in 1995. McMillan's fourth novel, *How Stella Got Her Groove Back,* became an instant bestseller upon its appearance in 1996 and was adapted for film in 1998.

Major Works

McMillan's fiction typically revolves around strong, intelligent African-American female characters whose personal crises and romantic entanglements mirror the conflicted aspirations of working-class and upwardly mobile black women. *Mama* relates the difficulties of a poor black family in Michigan and Los Angeles during the 1960s and 1970s. The protagonist, Mildred Peacock, is a twenty-seven-year-old mother of five who struggles against mounting bills and alcoholism to raise her children. When her abusive husband, Crook, leaves the family, Mildred takes on the full financial burden of the household by working odd jobs, hosting rent parties, and briefly working as a prostitute. Mildred is unable to find a suitable male counterpart and sinks further into depression, drink, and debt. In the end, a reconciliation with her daughter, Freda, a recovering alcoholic, and plans to attend community college offer her new hope. *Disappearing Acts* examines the strained love affair between Zora Banks, a college-educated music teacher and aspiring singer, and Franklin Swift, a high school dropout and perennially unemployed construction worker victimized by racial discrimination. Set in New York City, the narrative is presented through the alternating first-person monologues of Zora and Franklin, who disclose their respective expectations and disappointments. Though financially independent and despite Franklin's alcoholism and physical abuse, Zora bears Franklin's child and assumes the role of mother and provider. The novel ends as Zora plans to return to her family with their child, leaving Franklin and their relationship on uncertain terms. *Waiting to Exhale* explores the supportive friendship and romantic frustrations of four self-reliant, professional African-American women in their late thirties. Savannah Jackson is a successful television producer with material security but without a meaningful, long-term relationship. Bernadine Harris, a mother of two children, is divorcing her husband of eleven years after learning that he is having an affair with a younger white woman. Robin Stokes, an insurance underwriter, is single and unhappily dating a succession of deficient men. Gloria Matthews is a self-employed beauty shop owner in search of love, though resigned to the solace she finds in work, food, and caring for her teenage son. In the Phoenix, Arizona, setting, the four women discuss their careers, contemporary social ills, and single parenthood, and declaim the shortcomings of prospective black men, revealing their shared loneliness and deep longing for monogamous heterosexual relationships and conventional domestic arrangements. *How Stella Got Her Groove Back* recounts the fantasy vacation of Stella Payne, a forty-two-year-old affluent black security analyst and single mother who escapes to a luxury Jamaican resort for some much-needed rest. There she meets and falls in love with Winston Shakespeare, a handsome twenty-year-old chef-in-training. A passionate affair ensues on the island and at Stella's palatial California home, where she brings Winston to live with her and her son, Quincy. When Stella loses her lucrative job, she lives comfortably on savings while weighing the risks and benefits of a relationship with a man half her age. McMillan also served as editor of *Breaking Ice*, a collection of fifty-eight short stories and excerpts from novels by African-American writers including Trey Ellis, William Demby, Charles Johnson, Colleen McElroy, Darryl Pinckney, and Gloria Naylor. The anthology includes an introduction and short story, "Ma' Dear," by McMillan.

Critical Reception

McMillan is recognized as a prominent force in contemporary African-American women's fiction. Her first two novels, *Mama* and *Disappearing Acts,* received favorable critical attention and established her reputation as an inno-

vative new voice of middle-class black America. She is also highly regarded for her work as editor of the anthology *Breaking Ice*. While some critics praise McMillan's direct, unpretentious style and authentic portrayal of African-American relationships and social concerns, others fault her for uneven prose, excessive use of profanity, and thinly veiled sociological commentary. *Waiting to Exhale* and *How Stella Got Her Groove Back* won enormous popularity and launched McMillan into celebrity status. Though some critics laud the humor and acerbic honesty of both, others disapprove of McMillan's interest in material wealth and conspicuous consumption over unresolved issues of racial discrimination and women's rights. *Waiting to Exhale* also elicited controversy for its unflattering portrayal of African-American men. Despite the intensity and wide appeal of McMillan's novels, her detractors assert that her work does not stand up to the literary fiction of acclaimed African-American authors Toni Morrison and Alice Walker. *How Stella Got Her Groove Back,* another huge commercial success, was dismissed by many critics as a superficial romance novel. Nevertheless, McMillan's engaging stories, appealing characters, and insightful commentary on recent American-American experience are considered a vital contribution to contemporary popular literature.

PRINCIPAL WORKS

Mama (novel) 1987
Disappearing Acts (novel) 1989
Breaking Ice: An Anthology of Contemporary African-American Fiction [editor] (short stories and excerpts) 1990
Waiting to Exhale (novel) 1992
How Stella Got Her Groove Back (novel) 1996

CRITICISM

Thulani Davis (review date May 1990)

SOURCE: "Don't Worry, Be Buppie," in *Voice Literary Supplement,* May, 1990, pp. 26-8.

[*In the following excerpt, Davis criticizes the assimilation of mainstream white cultural values in* Disappearing Acts *and contemporary African-American literature.*]

Now that the '90s are at hand, it's inevitable that someone will announce a new generation of writers, folks who'll be the bridge to the next century. (WOW!) The "new generation" of African-American writers, novelist Terry McMillan said not too long ago, are "different from a generation before" because "they are not as race oriented, and they are not as protest oriented." I wondered at first who she was talking about. The novelists being published right now are, for the most part, around 40. Most of them began getting published 20 years ago, but those who were the talk of the '70s seem wildly different—and I mean wildly—from the crew McMillan is describing. The young writers back then were full of the anger, rhythms, sexuality, and wicked humor of jazz, r&b, and the '60s. I doubt if anyone would have guessed that the next generation was going to be less "race oriented."

In the poets' cafes Ntozake Shange, Wesley Brown, Charlotte Carter, Pedro Pietri, Gylan Kain, Pat Parker, Victor Hernandez-Cruz, David Henderson, and Lorenzo Thomas were ripping the lid off our neat and tidy preconceptions. Floating from hand to hand were out-of-print copies of J. J. Phillips's *Mojo Hand* and Carlene Hatcher Polite's *Sister X and the Victims of Foul Play.* Ishmael Reed's early books introduced us to the trickster, and Gayl Jones's novels spared us nothing. The energy was outside the mainstream, as it usually is for young writers, and that energy became a credo: let it be raw and raggedy, intense, black, and yes, self-righteous. It was fun.

All of us who're now somewhere around 40—whether we were in the marches, or in the Panthers, or the lonely Negroes at Hendrix concerts, or none of the above—were in the first generation to go en masse into white institutions when the Civil Rights Act and affirmative action took force. Before that time, we knew white America, north or south, largely by way of television (which we watched with some restriction because it was new, and our parents were understandably frightened of it). Like our parents and grandparents, we were, and are still, different. We started out life in a truly separate culture inside America, and therefore first learned to think, like it or not, with Race Mind, the black half of what W. E. B. Du Bois called double-consciousness. African-American literature of the '60s and '70s made the self-conscious choice to give voice to that black language *without* the explanatory context of earlier work. In today's self-censoring atmosphere, Race Mind is carefully muted. The white half of that double-consciousness is more often used for public presentations: Jesse Jackson uses it in speeches, and yet his Race Mind is coded within what he says.

If four novels published in the past few months, including one by McMillan, are any indication, there is a crop of African-American fiction coming in the '90s, written by 40ish folk, that's less interested in race and protest. It speaks in the practiced tongue of white mainstream literature. Melvin Dixon, Marita Golden, Tina McElroy Ansa, and McMillan show in their work a silent—in some cases maybe unconscious—struggle with assimilation. Each of their books describes some part of the lonely, self-involved journey of the middle-class African American who has access to some little piece of the Dream and is as deeply ensconced in American mass culture as in our boisterous yet closely held black world.

More Bup Art than Black Art, these African-American writers' current work shares bourgeois mores and values with lots of other work by the 40-something generation. Buppism moves literature toward the middle of the road: conservative stylistic choices in form and language taken from mainstream American models; a personal focus, as opposed to the ever-enlarging world view that shifted from Mississippi to internationalism in the late '60s, '70s, and early '80s (and, in the case of Alice Walker, included several millennia); the death of the heroic figure, so prominent in black literature as recent as *Beloved* (Morrison raised questions about the nature of heroism in the African-American context); and an absence of protest, which has been replaced by homilies to survival.

Following Baldwin's edict to "take the language apart," African-American writers have been for some time revising or destroying forms to make them more expressionistic. The '90s writers return to story-telling as a private act, the exorcism of existential demons that could be viewed as nonracial. The old Race Mind, once a necessity for survival, is being lost to a naïve pragmatism: we can imitate and join. Despite many efforts to salvage them, the old sayings of the village have one by one been consigned to the place where America put the dog-tags, ankle-cuffs, and bills of sale for the village folk.

Twenty years after the introduction of Africana studies in American universities, African-American scholars have institutionalized the study of black life; they now argue that their black students need the courses to know who they are. As the culture continues to evolve, the language of black experience is disseminated and assimilated by the mass white audience almost as soon as it appears. Race Mind is marketed as late-night style with Arsenio Hall. The larger, more profound wisdom and practice is being lost to a culture that erases everything but success, and does not replenish the spirit.

As we turn the corner of the century, the shared yearnings based on race, gender, generation, or family so common to black fiction could become inscrutable relics of the past, like the Motown records a Bup executive retrieves from the garbage in George Wolfe's play *The Colored Museum,* or those mama-on-the-couch shows he parodies, which actually did once say something about how we folks felt behind the veil in America. . . .

Disappearing Acts, like Terry McMillan's first novel,

Mama, is an energetic and earthy book that takes place wholly within the confines of an intense relationship. While the narrator of *Mama* sounded like a character in the story, in this book McMillan uses two alternating voices that speak directly to the reader. The whole world is filtered through the self-naming, self-mythologizing first-person monologue—from racism to masturbation, parental conflicts to staying on a diet. And because there's no one obvious for Zora Banks or Franklin Swift to tell it to—they are loners in every way—the question is whether these folks are for real. In many ways they are quite ordinary, in other ways they are hardly tangible.

Zora is a young black woman on the lookout for the right man while she pursues singing ambitions; Franklin is a construction worker frustrated by his inability to get steady work in a closed industry. Zora sounds a lot like the narrator of *Mama,* in spite of her *Essence*-style self-improvement rap: "When I started visualizing myself less abundant, and desirable again, that's how I think I was able to get here—to 139 pounds." She likes to tell you straight up how it is: "I've got two major weaknesses: tall black men and food." Though reviewers have said that Franklin dominates the book, he has the same brassy, up-front, I'm-gon'-tell-you-exactly style as Zora. "Don't ask me why I did some stupid shit like that. Ringing that woman's doorbell at that time of morning. And with a lame-ass line like, 'You drink coffee?' . . . She was still pretty, though, even with no makeup. Her skin looked like Lipton tea. I saw them thick nipples sticking out through that pink bathrobe, and I felt Tarzan rising." Yes, a tall black man whose swinging thing was made in Hollywood.

Even though Zora and Franklin are last-week contemporary, they are also like classic folklore characters come to life in Brooklyn. She's the wily black woman of yore, smart-talking Eve who's always got a little something on the rail for the lizard, as we used to say. She's also a sophisticated shopper who likes fancy cheeses and bottled water, and she says shit all the time. Zora has all the pulls and tugs of feminism versus the feminine that a modern black woman who's read Walker and Shange is supposed to have. She's not unlike Zora Neale Hurston's sassy folk women—characters *Cosmo* would never dare to pop-psychoanalyze.

Complicated as Franklin is supposed to be, he is a savvy urban John Henry—he don't take no tea fo' the fever. An intellectual Tina Turner meets a hardhat Ike. They are both bricks and though they may chip each other, they ain't never gonna blend. They live and work in New York City, but are in a very insulated world: their problems are completely personal. Their relationship is doomed by mutual expectations and ended by an outburst of gratuitous male violence. Let's just say it wasn't needed for the love affair to fall apart.

These two are as they are; like other folk heroes, they don't

change much, or drag skeletons out of the closet, and they learn their lessons the hard way. They've been created by years of past mythologizing, drawn their images from popular culture, black and white. They are black, sho'nuff—the last thing I would say about McMillan's people is that they ain't black—but they're black in big, bold strokes. And that means her work will continue to raise questions among African Americans about the fuzzy line between realism and popular misconception. And at the same time, McMillan is, as she said, less race-conscious. She confines herself to the day-to-day life struggle, as told from behind the mask Claude McKay so poignantly described. McMillan uses, almost exclusively, the performance side of black character, emphasizing the most public, most familiar aspects of us. If you smell a little song and dance in the self-sufficient ribaldry, it's there.

> **I suppose the time had to come when race would cease to be the obsession of African-American writers, and in its place would be some form of ordinary life—stripped in varying degrees of "context," depoliticized.**
> —*Thulani Davis*

Still, hard as it may be to imagine, for me at least, I suppose the time had to come when race would cease to be the obsession of African-American writers, and in its place would be some form of ordinary life—stripped in varying degrees of "context," depoliticized. If I can feel it in the street—the dislocation that can no longer be healed by inspiring leaders—I shouldn't be surprised to find it in our literature. I hope for some understanding from novels about African-American life, but perhaps it isn't there to be had. Welcome to the '90s.

The work of Marita Golden, Melvin Dixon, Tina McElroy Ansa, and Terry McMillan seems ambivalent and narrowly focused after nearly two decades of uninterrupted literary conjuring from those fabulous wild women of the '70s and '80s black-lit boom. Morrison, Walker, and company continue to write books that are ambitious, intensely lyrical, and profoundly disturbing; yet clearly their work is only one end of the spectrum. These new novels show that African-American fiction is miscegenating. Though the white world does not intrude in the form of characters, it is very much alive—recognized or not—in the minds of the blacks. The African Americans in these four works have become garden-variety Americans. They seem confined by the African-American culture that has defined and nurtured writers before them.

In the '70s, cultural nationalists ranted about black women writers, vilifying them/us as purveyors of "mulatto consciousness." I was amused by the clumsiness of the term, and, as intended, insulted. Was black culture so circumscribed that we could not merengue, or talk about men, or whatever it was that upset this crew of fuddy-duddies? Or were they just talking about the lightness of certain writers' skin? That happened too. A few weeks ago I heard Trey Ellis, self-appointed propagandist for the New Black Aesthetic invented by my colleague Greg Tate, proudly defining HIS (30ish) generation as "cultural mulattoes." While I think Tate observed that cultural appropriation is a common denominator among a certain cadre of artists, Ellis seems to be defining his generation by the conditions of their upbringing: We are therefore we are, something like that. It sure ain't like announcing you're the New Negro.

The writers of the '90s are sitting in the middle of a big mess—among critics and other artists screaming "Who are we?" while the newspapers holler that black music and white performers equal popular magic. American culture has not been a blending pot so much as a river Lethe for all its peoples, their languages and arts. Have we baptized our children there only to wonder later to whom they pray? I think George Wolfe is right—this cultural nervous breakdown is likely to land us in the Colored Museum. Collard greens and bean pie will be served at the snack bar.

Charles R. Larson (review date 23 September 1990)

SOURCE: "No Time for Any Barriers," in *Chicago Tribune Books,* September 23, 1990, pp. 1, 4.

[*In the following review, Larson offers praise for* Breaking Ice, *which he finds "brilliantly (and almost single-handedly) dispels a number of myths about contemporary African-American literature and the culture that has nourished it."*]

The wonder of Terry McMillan's anthology of recent black fiction, **Breaking Ice,** is that it brilliantly (and almost single-handedly) dispels a number of myths about contemporary African-American literature and the culture that has nourished it. The scope of the stories repeatedly demonstrates the variety and the richness of African-American life—its tragedy and pathos, which we are accustomed to encountering in such literature, but also its humor and absurdity. In the tradition of Zora Neale Hurston's "Their Eyes Were Watching God," many of the stories in this volume inform us that African-American life is not solely a response to racism. More importantly, they illustrate that "protest" in black writing is on the wane and that black writers are no longer taking potshots at members of the opposite sex, as was commonly believed to be the case during much of the past decade.

Those are quite a few myths for one volume to destroy, but McMillan has done her editorial work superbly. As she informs us in her introduction, the 58 stories in the collection were selected from 300 submissions. Clearly there is a renaissance in black fiction.

As far as gender goes, the writers are almost equally divided between males and females, and older established writers with household names appear alongside those whose first publication is in this anthology. The result is glorious variety: everything from traditional well-made stories to experimental stories to science fiction to stories that deal with minority sexual preferences within the minority itself.

As for humor, while the selections by Toni Cade Bambara, J. California Cooper, William Melvin Kelley (whose opening line reads, "Sweaty H. L. Mencken is climbing a steep rocky hill on an island in the Caribbean"), Percival L. Everett and Trey Ellis immediately stand out, those by William Demby and Charles Johnson are in a class by themselves.

In Demby's rollicking "Love Story Black," the narrator undertakes an interview of an aged Afro-American chanteuse for a new up-scale black woman's magazine and ends up being seduced by the crone. The unfolding of the action is delicious.

Johnson's "China" explores with John Cheever-like perfection the shifting relationship between a middle-aged husband and wife whose marriage has slipped into boredom and complacency, largely because the wife has made her husband into a sap. Then the husband becomes interested in kung fu. Within months, their roles are reversed, prompting the wife to conclude, "I want you back the way you were: *sick.*" Perhaps it should be noted that "China" could be the story of any middle-aged couple, black or white, a further indication that African-American writing is becoming increasingly difficult to pigeonhole.

If Johnson's "China" is miles away from any racial context, a number of other works in this collection have taken earlier black themes and issues and imaginatively woven them into new patterns. "Wild Seed," by Octavia Butler (a winner of a Nebula Award for science fiction), is particularly striking. In this richly evocative story about African slavery, a character remarks, "I search the land for people who are a little different—or very different. I search them out, I bring them together in groups, I begin to build them into a strong new people." That remark might have been made 200 years ago, yet the story is set in the future.

John Edgar Wideman's "Fever" is equally impressive, though slavery in this story is placed in a very different context. Using blackness as an ironic metaphor for racism as a whole, Wideman writes, "We were proclaimed carriers of the fever and treated as pariahs, but when it became expedient to command our services to nurse the sick and bury the dead, the previous allegations were no longer mentioned."

Wideman is one of today's best-known and most compelling African-American writers, and "Fever" is one of the highlights of **Breaking Ice.** But several stories by newcomers are every bit as memorable.

"Spilled Salt," by Barbara Neely (who insists that her name be printed without a space), may be the most powerful work in the volume. From the story's simple beginning ("I'm home, Ma."), when a son returns to his mother's apartment after spending four years in prison for rape, to its crashing end ("I'm sorry. I just can't be your mother right now. I will be back in one week. Please be gone."), the story is a holocaust of filial emotions that conveys the anger and rage of every parent who has had to endure the transformation of his or her child into an adult that the parent does not want to know. To be sure, the horror here is viewed from the vantage point of motherhood: "She would have to live with the unblanketed reality that whatever anger and meanness her son held toward the world, he had chosen a woman to take it out on."

Yet another outstanding story, among the many fine ones gathered here, is John McCluskey's "Lush Life," an evocative account of the rush that music provides to those who are truly addicted to the making of it. As two musicians drive in the middle of the night to their next gig, one of them says: "It's this music we play, Billy. It opens people up, makes them give up secrets. Better than whiskey or dope for that. It don't kill you, and you . . . can whistle it the next day in new places. You can loan it to strangers, and they thank you for it.'"

I have two minor quibbles about **Breaking Ice:** the selections excerpted from novels are less satisfying than the self-contained stories, and some of the older writers are represented by material that is inferior to that of their juniors.

Still, what haunts the reader of this anthology is the possibility that black and white writers are beginning to explore a more common territory instead of emphasizing the uncommon barriers that have separated their work in the past. As an African-American university student says in Cliff Thompson's "Judgment," "After a while I stopped thinking of the two of them as my white roommates and thought of them as just my roommates, and then, gradually, as my friends." Or as McMillan herself states at the end of her introduction: "I wish there hadn't been the need to separate our work from others."

C. J. Walker (review date September-October 1990)

SOURCE: "Intriguing Effort Misses Mark," in *New Directions for Women,* Vol. 19, No. 5, September-October, 1990, p. 19.

[*In the following review, Walker finds shortcomings in* Disappearing Acts.]

The book was a smooth read; it had an easy flow. But, I think more likely, expectation kept me reading because Terry McMillan's new book promised great things. **Disappearing Acts** alternates between first-person reflections, reactions and responses of Franklin and Zora.

Franklin introduces himself, "I'm tired of women. Black women in particular, cause that's about all I ever deal with." He continued to fill us in on his way in the world: "Basically, I guess I'm a loner. Ain't got too many friends, ain't too many people worth trusting. Jimmy, a dude I grew up with, stops by every now and then to borrow a few dollars."

Okay, I have a sense of his honesty and the scope of his relationships as he perceives them. He offers his view and his experiences within the male-female sexual dynamic. I learn about his two children and estranged wife. He offers introspection, "I do know I can be a pain in the ass, but that's my nature. I just like to test people, see what they're made of . . . I got discharged from the Navy because of my temper, lack of cooperation." He continues, "But how can taking orders from the white man, killing people that ain't never done nothing to me personally do me some fuckin' good?"

Okay, I'm involved. What is the author going to do with this man, self-described as big and Black? What is his relationship to Zora, who introduces herself with "I've got two weaknesses: tall Black men and food. But not necessarily in that order," going to look like? I accept these two people for who they say they are; I expect Terry McMillan to provide the depth, to go beyond what I can see watching people on the street or catching bits and pieces of lives in my hallway. I want a view of the internal process and transitions if I'm to believe them. I already have my thinking on why they act as they do; I want to know Franklin, know Zora.

Unfortunately, **Disappearing Acts** doesn't deliver. McMillan creates a relationship between a Black man and a Black woman that she wants to be honest and successful, as in possibly happily-ever-after. Her desire is so strong that it interferes with the life of the characters, because she does not provide them with dimension. Bright, brash, clever language; fiery, loud, loving interactions, nakedness, good cliche, sparks of truth glowing. But their lives read like exchange on the Oprah Winfrey show—condensed, directed, framed, the ultimate dictator being the commercial.

Racism affects Franklin at his jobs, in his ability to get/maintain consistent employment, in the fact that he can't hail a taxi. Racial oppression in *Disappearing Acts* is real, but not developed beyond background cliche. Gender oppression while loudly present is not acknowledged at a level that would allow for a straight-on look. I understand that Franklin feels bad and is treated badly, but what does this really have to do with him not picking up his son from the sitter and why can't he and Zora have this discussion? It has to occur between Franklin and himself, Zora and herself, or between them if the changes are to be accepted as genuine.

Zora is waiting, in part, for Franklin to change. For all her dynamic Black woman rap she is quite passive, which makes believable her acceptance of what appears to me to be more of the same from Franklin. But I don't know for sure.

What are Franklin and Zora's nuances? What is their content as well as their context? In the end I know facts about them, but I still don't know them.

Publishers Weekly (review date 23 March 1992)

SOURCE: A review of *Waiting to Exhale,* in *Publishers Weekly,* Vol. 239, No. 15, March 23, 1992, p. 58.

[*In the following review, the critic offers praise for* Waiting to Exhale.]

A racy, zesty, irreverent and absorbing book with broad mainstream appeal, McMillan's third novel (after *Mama* and *Disappearing Acts*) tells the stories of four 30ish black women bound together in warm, supportive friendship and in their dwindling hopes of finding Mr. Right. Savannah, Bernadine, Robin and Gloria are successful professional or self-employed women living in Phoenix. All are independent, upwardly mobile and "waiting to exhale"—to stop holding their breaths waiting for the proper mate to come along. Bernadine is married, but her husband walks out on her for a white woman as the novel opens. They also share speech patterns that some readers may find disconcerting: they utter profanities with panache, unceasingly. Indeed, the novel's major drawback may be the number of times such words as shit, fuck and ass are repeated on every page. These women have a healthy interest in sex, while deploring the fact that most of the men they meet are arrogant, irresponsible and chronically unfaithful. Each character is drawn with authenticity and empathy, and McMillan pulls no punches about their collective bad judgment in choosing partners for romance. After many vicissitudes, two of the heroines find

love, but until then McMillan keeps us constantly guessing about which members of her lively quartet will be thus rewarded. There's nothing stereotyped in her work here: it is fresh and engaging.

Terry McMillan with Wendy Smith (interview date 11 May 1992)

SOURCE: "Terry McMillan: The Novelist Explores African American Life From the Point of View of a New Generation," in *Publishers Weekly,* Vol. 239, No. 22, May 11, 1992, pp. 50-1.

[*In the following interview, McMillan comments on the publication of her early fiction and her critical reception as an African-American writer.*]

Terry McMillan blows into the Viking offices like a cool breeze off the bay in San Francisco, where she lives. She's toting two overstuffed carryalls, while her cab driver staggers under a garment bag crammed to bursting. She directs him to a nearby closet, warmly greets the Viking receptionist, then flings her arms around her editor, Dawn Seferian, and publicity director Paul Slovak. Introduced to her interviewer, she says, "Oh, God—can you give me a few minutes?" and disappears into a maze of cubicles.

When she rejoins *PW,* she's shed the carryalls and her coat, acquired some coffee, but not yet found an ashtray—a scarce commodity in Viking's smoke-free environment, but an essential accessory for someone who finds it easier to talk with a Kool in her hand. One is finally provided by a helpful staffer, and she flings herself with a sigh of relief into the nearest chair.

It's a hectic time for McMillan. Her third novel, *Waiting to Exhale,* will soon be published with an 85,000-copy first printing and a $700,000 floor for the paperback rights. Viking is sending her on a 20-city, six-week tour that begins with a breakfast speech at the ABA in Anaheim and includes nearly 30 bookstore appearances, closing with a July reading at Central Park's Summer Stage festival.

"I don't even believe the stuff that's happened so far," she says. "It's wonderful, it's a writer's dream, but it doesn't really feel like it's happening to me. 'There's this chick I know named Terry McMillan and, gee, I can't wait to read this *Waiting to Exhale*—it sounds like a good book!'"

But McMillan has never been one to hang around waiting for things to happen. Growing up in Port Huron, Mich., the daughter of working-class parents who didn't read to their children, she discovered the magic of books as a teenager shelving books at the local public library for $1.25 an hour. (A biography of Louisa May Alcott excited her because the writer, like McMillan, "had to help support her family at a young age." She started reading furiously, soaking up most of the classics of African American literature while studying at a community college in California, and began writing poetry after a romance went sour. Pretty soon, the lines of verse turned into sentences; she published her first short story in 1976, when she was 25. She wrote her first full-length work, *Mama,* while working as a word processor and raising her infant son alone.

When *Mama* was released by Houghton Mifflin in 1987, she refused to let it meet the usual fate of the first novel: scattered reviews, zero publicity and minimal sales. "I had seen it happen before to friends of mine, really fine writers, whose publishers did nothing except send out a little press release and the galleys. My publisher had come right out and told me what they couldn't do, and I said, 'Fuck this! I'm not just going to sit back; I've never been passive, and I'm not going to start now.'"

Indeed, it's hard to think of a less passive figure than McMillan, dressed dramatically in black stretch pants, a bright purple sweater and a boldly patterned jacket with a matching black-and-purple design, sporting fuschia lipstick and nail polish. With her vibrant brown eyes, wide smile and dimples, she fills the room with personality even before she begins to speak, leaning forward and stabbing the air with her finger when she wants to emphasize a point.

"I wrote about 3000 letters," she continues, on the subject of her promotional efforts for *Mama.* "When I was at some writers' conference I read this book, *How to Get Happily Published* [co-authored by *PW*'s former managing editor, Judith Appelbaum], and I was so grateful; I wrote the author a letter. [Appelbaum] talked about how to promote your own book, and I went to the library, copied these different pages, then I wrote to the chains and the independent booksellers, universities, colleges. I did it all summer long: my friends were hanging out at the beach, and I was licking envelopes. Luckily I worked as a word processor, and the guys in the mail room were so sweet; they mailed my stuff for me.

"I got a shitload of readings, so I set up my own tour, because the publisher wasn't going to send me anywhere. Every week I sent my itinerary to my publicist—and it should have been the other way around. *Mama* sold out its first printing before pub date; my editors called and said, 'Terry, we don't think this would have happened if you had not done all this.'"

"It wasn't that I was stroking myself and thought I had written this incredibly strong, powerful, wonderful book, but if somebody thinks something is good enough to publish, then show your support! I know every book can't get a $100,000 publicity tour, but if you spent $5000 on all of us, it might sell a few more books."

McMillan continued to display a strongminded attitude during debates with Houghton Mifflin over her second novel, *Disappearing Acts,* which was structured as a series of alternating first-person monologues by the book's lovers, Franklin and Zora.

"They were so impressed with Franklin's voice and the fact that I was pulling it off that they wanted me to write the whole book from his point of view. It was going to be this coup: black woman writes story from black man's point of view, it's never been done, blah, blah, blah, blah, blah. Well, I didn't write *Disappearing Acts* to prove anything; that was the way the story had to be told. When my editor told me Zora sounded kind of preppy, I said, 'Look, she's not barefoot and pregnant, living in the projects and getting her ass kicked. I cannot apologize because some of us have been to college, okay?'"

Her already strained relations with the publisher reached a breaking point when Houghton Mifflin indicated it would like to see a completed manuscript of *Disappearing Acts* before making an offer. McMillan's agent, Molly Friedrich, promptly sent the existing chapters to Viking's Dawn Seferian, who bought the project two days later. Published in 1989, the novel received generally excellent reviews and went on to sell more than 100,000 copies in paperback for Washington Square Press.

It also provoked a lawsuit from Leonard Welch, with whom McMillan had a child in 1984, who claimed the portrait of Franklin libeled him. The case was decided in the author's favor last April, and Welch's subsequent appeal was denied.

"I was more embarrassed than anything else," McMillan says, "because I was concerned that people would think I really didn't write fiction, which *Disappearing Acts* was. I relied on some of my experiences with him, but Franklin Swift and this man are two different people. I worried about the effect on other writers, because everybody relies on their own experiences—even the ones that say they make it all up: they're lying! It's not; it's still fiction."

The ongoing lawsuit was only one of the factors that slowed the writing of *Waiting to Exhale,* which wasn't finished until December 1991, a scant five months before scheduled publication. "I had not been under this kind of pressure before," says McMillan. "I get tons of mail about *Disappearing Acts;* I'm so sick of that book I don't know what to do. After about 90 pages [of *Waiting to Exhale*], I'm saying to myself, 'Are they going to think this is as good as *Disappearing Acts*?

Are they going to be disappointed?' Eventually, I just had to say, 'I cannot think about my audience; I can't guess what people are going to like.'"

Once she got into the thick of the novel, not even a move from Tucson to San Francisco could stop her. "I had the movers take my computer last; they were putting books in boxes, and I was sitting there writing. I get to California, I'm sitting in my sister's fiance's office going blind writing on my little laptop that's not backlit, I'm looking for a place to live while my furniture's on a truck somewhere, it's the end of August and I'm supposed to be finishing the book by September 1st! I finished the first draft November 20." There was still a lot of work to be done. "I'm not one of those writers who just edits, especially when I'm working on a first draft. Sometimes I actually delete an entire chapter from the memory so I have to type it all over, because that's the only way I can relive it. I have to stay close to these people, I have to have their experiences, too, and the only way to do that is to start all over—that stuff is cumulative. It can be very exciting, and it can be very painful, but I have to make the emotional investment."

Staying close to her characters means reproducing their salty, often profane language, which later dismayed *PW*'s reviewer. "I was criticized for this with *Disappearing Acts* too," the author responds, "but basically, the language that I use is accurate.

"I said to Dawn when I read that review, 'You know, it's not on every fucking page!' Then I picked up the galley when I was on the airplane coming to New York, and when I got here I called Dawn and said, 'You know, I think they're right: it is on every fucking page!' But so what? That's the way we talk. And I want to know why I've never read a review where they complain about the language that male writers use!"

I appreciate and value all the protest literature of the '60s, but I am tired of carrying this plantation on my shoulders. I know that if it wasn't for Martin Luther King and Malcolm X we wouldn't be able to do some of the things we do now, but I don't need to constantly remind you of that. I'm not trying to prove anything to white folks, and I'm not trying to make them feel guilty—my editor didn't enslave my ancestors. So why do I have to keep belaboring the point?
—*Terry McMillan*

She braced for criticism about *Waiting to Exhale*'s depic-

tion of black men, who are seen only through the often exasperated eyes of her four central female characters. "The men are on the periphery, they're not the focus of this story, therefore they don't get the three-dimensionality that the women do. Periodically, I would stop and say, 'Oh, they're going to be pissed off at me now!' But I said exactly what I meant, and I'm not apologizing for any of it. This book is not meant to represent or portray any gender or group of people. Nobody thinks that a Czech writer is representing all Czechs, or a Russian writer is writing for all Russians."

In her introduction to *Breaking Ice,* the anthology she edited of contemporary African American writing, McMillan argued that her generation of black writers "are a new breed, free to write as we please . . . because of the way life has changed." Her own fiction, which often portrays successful middle-class professionals, is a case in point.

"This is 1992. I appreciate and value all the protest literature of the '60s, but I am tired of carrying this plantation on my shoulders. I know that if it wasn't for Martin Luther King and Malcolm X we wouldn't be able to do some of the things we do now, but I don't need to constantly remind you of that. I'm not trying to prove anything to white folks, and I'm not trying to make them feel guilty—my editor didn't enslave my ancestors. So why do I have to keep belaboring the point?

"Unfortunately, the black people who are the most militant are the ones who seem to be more hung up than anybody on what white people think. 'We're airing our dirty laundry, why can't we portray ourselves more positively?'—to me, that's stuck in the '60s stuff. They make the assumption that we are anthropologists, sociologists, psychologists, when all we are is storytellers. They try to put this weight on our shoulders, which I totally dismiss. I'm prepared for them with this book: 'Why you make the brothers out to look like they ain't shit?' I say, it's only two of 'em in here, not two million. I want to tell my stories on a much more personal level, more intimate. It's not just the black man pitted against white society; it's deeper than that."

Characters drive a novel for McMillan, and right now, despite her commitment to publicize *Waiting to Exhale* and to write a screenplay for *Disappearing Acts,* she's eager to get back to the group of people waiting to be given voice in her new novel. "I'm stacking up stuff about the story and thinking about these people—I've known who they are for a while, I see them and I sort of know the story, but they haven't started talking to me yet. It's like a picture that's out of focus. I don't force things on my characters; I wait and watch then grow. While I'm writing the screenplay, these people keep intruding—and I'm so glad! I can't wait for this summer to be over so we can play some more."

Charles R. Larson (review date 31 May 1992)

SOURCE: "The Comic Unlikelihood of Finding Mr. Right," in *Chicago Tribune Books,* May 31, 1992, p. 6.

[*In the following review, Larson offers favorable assessment of* Waiting to Exhale.]

In the climactic scene of Terry McMillan's wickedly acerbic third novel, **Waiting to Exhale,** four African-American women—Gloria, Savannah, Bernadine and Robin, all between the ages of 34 and 38—celebrate the birthday of the youngest by drinking five bottles of champagne and talking about their on-going problems with men. All of them are single and/or recently divorced and "waiting to exhale"—yearning for the ideal mate who takes your breath away, although he never seems to materialize.

Furthermore, these women are all economically independent, horny and explicit in their feelings. Among other things, they conclude that the problem with black men is that they are "with white women," "gay," "ugly," "stupid," "in prison," "unemployed," "crackheads," "short," "liars," "unreliable," "irresponsible," "too possessive," "dogs," "shallow," "stuck in the sixties," "arrogant," "childish," "wimps" and too "old and set in their ways."

McMillan's dialogue is raunchy and wild, half black street speech and half one-liners. It's as if we're listening to four foul-mouth stand-up comediennes—all of them lashing out blindly at MEN.

Savannah, a TV producer, tells us that she may be hard up, but not to the point where she'll take any man. "There's a big difference between being thirsty and dehydrated." Later she ponders, "How do you tell a man—in a nice way—that he makes you sick?"

Her friend, Bernadine, whose husband of a dozen years has just left her for a white woman, muses, "When you finally come to understand the man you love, that's when you don't love him anymore." Robin, who works as an insurance underwriter, comments on the problem in another way: "In order for a woman to get a Ph.D., she's gotta pass Men 101." When Savannah reveals that she finally met Mr. Right at a convention in Las Vegas, Bernadine responds, "'Ask him if he can get here by fax or Federal Express.'"

While the dialogue sparkles throughout, the F-word appears so frequently that one has the feeling that McMillan is trying to one-up Spike Lee (whose films are alluded to a number of times). Indeed, McMillan seems to have written her novel with one eye on Hollywood and the other on the sisterhood of educated, articulate, independent black women who are very successful in their professions but frustrated and neurotic about the fact that there are so few black men they consider their equals.

This problem of mating is, however, about the only true lament of this otherwise very funny novel. Because of her biting comic tone, McMillan's work is distanced from that of a number of her contemporaries (Toni Morrison, Alice Walker, Marita Golden, for example). Although **Waiting to Exhale** is rooted in ethnicity, that ethnicity is never angry, bitter or bleak. One of McMillan's characters says, "I don't have anything against most white folks." The issue is gender, not race, and, above all, the question of sisterhood.

The setting—Phoenix, Arizona—also makes one rethink stereotypes of African American writing, although the story is only marginally related to its place. At the beginning, McMillan wants us to believe (and perhaps even expect) that her characters will get their men and, as Savannah tells us, still "be able to exhale." As their stories get told, the title gets jerked around a number of times.

The men (a rather grungy lot at best) initially leave the women breathless but finally teach them to inhale and exhale just fine by themselves. It isn't so much a matter of waiting to exhale, then, as it is of facing the reality that there simply aren't enough good men to go around.

To the richness of her four main characters' bonding, McMillan adds a number of revealing variations. Gloria, for example, struggles with the problems of raising her 16-year-old son without the support of a husband. Robin's identity is strongly bound up with her mother's attempts to deal with her husband's steadily debilitating Alzheimer's disease. Both Bernadine (with her own young children) and Savannah wrestle with their mothers' difficult adjustments to widowhood. The scope of these situations expands the domain of McMillan's novel to three generations, implying a sense of growth and continuity.

If what's been said makes **Waiting to Exhale** seem plotless, that is not the case. Rather, McMillan is such a clever storyteller that while the ending seems too predictable about two-thirds of the way through her narrative, everything shifts around once again as a series of final surprises unfold. It's not a pat ending, but something more bittersweet—all good bawdy fun.

When Lorraine Hansbury wrote *A Raisin in the Sun* back in 1959, one critic accused her of writing a Jewish play about people who happened to be black. I can hear readers on the beach this summer laughing away and saying something like that about **Waiting to Exhale.**

These aren't black women; they're most women at a certain

point of no return. And that may make you think about race—if not gender—in a totally different light.

Paula C. Barnes (review date Fall 1992)

SOURCE: A review of *Waiting to Exhale,* in *Belles Lettres,* Vol. 8, No. 1, Fall, 1992, pp. 56-7.

[*In the following review, Barnes offers praise for* Waiting to Exhale, *which she describes as "an important book" that "traces the problems of 'real' women in a real world."*]

Within weeks of its publication, Terry McMillan's **Waiting to Exhale** appeared on *The New York Times* best-seller list exceeding the success of her first two novels, **Mama** and **Disappearing Acts.** Although specifically it tells the story of four African-American women, **Waiting to Exhale** addresses the dilemma of career women who want it all.

Savannah Jackson, Bernadine Harris, Robin Stokes, and Gloria Matthews, all in their late thirties, are reflecting on their lives, and although they seek to move beyond their pasts, they face uncertain futures. Savannah, having lived in four cities in 15 years, is getting ready to make another career move—from Denver to Phoenix. With a decent job, money in the bank, a nice condo, and respectable car, she has everything she needs but a man. Bernadine, the one with it all—husband, two children, home *and* condo, BMW *and* Cherokee—is told by her husband of 11 years that he is leaving her for a younger, white woman. Having placed her own dreams on hold, Bernadine is forced to rediscover them and herself. Robin knows exactly what she wants—love, marriage, and children. With five serious relationships during the past seven years, however, Robin seems to attract the wrong kind of man. Gloria, mother of a 16-year-old son and owner of a beauty shop, substitutes mothering, work, and food for love.

Career advancement, relocation, divorce, aging parents, illness, single parenthood, and the never ending search for love are the problems these women face and the issues McMillan explores. Yet her real purpose soon becomes clear—to sensitize readers to the real-life problems of Alzheimers', AIDS, breast cancer, hypertension, and the need for individual, communal and governmental action. McMillan's work does not match the caliber of Toni Morrison's, Alice Walker's, Gloria Naylor's, or Zora Neale Hurston's (to whom she has been compared), but *Waiting to Exhale* is an important book as it traces the problems of "real" women in a real world. McMillan has created a series of portraits that reveal the resiliency of the black career woman.

Although McMillan tends to over-explain, a flaw seen in her

earlier works, her style is easy, her language bawdy; McMillan herself acknowledges that the novel is X-rated. *Waiting to Exhale* is refreshingly funny, but its message is hard-hitting—in the end, one must learn to depend on one's self for love and happiness.

Frances Stead Sellers (review date 6 November 1992)

SOURCE: A review of *Waiting to Exhale,* in *Times Literary Supplement,* November 6, 1992, p. 20.

[*In the following review, Sellers finds only "modest" literary merit in* Waiting to Exhale, *but notes its appeal among "glitzy, commercial women's novels."*]

Terry McMillan's novel, **Waiting to Exhale,** raced up the *New York Times* bestseller lists immediately after its publication in the United States early last summer, and has lingered near the top for twenty-three weeks. There are already more than 700,000 copies in print. Paperback rights for the book startled the recession-conscious publishing industry by selling for $2.64 million, and McMillan's drop dead stare and Nefertiti hair-style have become familiar features on daytime television talk shows and in glossy magazines across America.

Most black women writers are associated with a recognizable tradition of serious, ideologically inspired black literature, written primarily for "concerned" whites and black intellectuals. McMillan, however, has little truck with ideology of any kind. She writes to entertain, by providing the type of sexy, popular novel that has been making Jilly Cooper and Danielle Steele rich for years.

Written for and about educated black women, **Waiting to Exhale** reflects the growing numbers of successful African-Americans who have fled the drugs and violence of the ghettoes for fashionable neighbourhoods, while trying to preserve a uniquely black cultural heritage. McMillan's characters believe in black solidarity. To act like a white is an act of betrayal. "White folks" hover disconcertingly on the novel's margins.

Waiting to Exhale's four protagonists live in Phoenix, Arizona. Apart from being black, female and thirtysomething, they have one thing in common: "None of us have a man." And they're holding their breath until they get one. Savannah wants to feel "important to somebody," though she's not yet desperate: she's just "thirsty," not "dehydrated." Bernadine has been betrayed by her acquisitive husband, who traded her in for a new trophy-wife, his twenty-four-year-old (blonde) book-keeper. Gloria has given up waiting for a man who can make her toes curl and takes comfort in God, her hair salon, a promiscuous adolescent son and much too much food. Robin's toes curl for "pretty men with big dicks," but she's hung up on an unscrupulous cad and doesn't know a good man when she sleeps with one. *Waiting to Exhale* chronicles these women's bedroom capers in their exhaustive—and exhausting—searches for Mr Right.

He's hard to come by. Black men prove to be "'Stupid.' 'In prison.' 'Unemployed.' 'Crack-heads.' 'Short.' 'Liars.' 'Unreliable.'" And worse. McMillan's generalized male-bashing has understandably alienated some black men. Her portrayal of women may be more sympathetic, but it is equally shallow. Her characters' preoccupation with deodorants, douches and dates soon grows wearisome. And the attention McMillan draws to male-female rifts within the African-American community seems at odds with the black solidarity she otherwise implicitly approves.

But whether her views are politically correct or not, McMillan has bit a nerve. Many African-American women identify with her heroines. Using the vibrant street-talk McMillan grew up speaking, her protagonists tackle sexual issues that most women can relate to.

It may in part be concern to avoid accusations of racism that has prevented some critics putting this book firmly where it belongs—among the glitzy, commercial women's novels. Its one true importance is that it appeals to a market that American publishers have previously overlooked—the new black middle class. But its literary merits are modest.

Darryl Pinckney (review date 4 November 1993)

SOURCE: "The Best of Everything," in *New York Review of Books,* November 4, 1993, pp. 33-7.

[*In the following excerpt, Pinckney praises the sincerity, force, and humor of* Waiting to Exhale *and discusses the novel's place within contemporary African-American literature and culture.*]

Fannie Lou Hamer once said that *she* didn't want to be liberated from men. Her husband was, after all, six foot-two. There was a time, only two decades ago, when many black women looked at the women's movement as a middle-class white concern, a passing political fashion, or argued that black women and white women wanted very different things. No one, they pointed out, expected white women to express solidarity with white men. For black women as black people the real struggle was elsewhere, and it might prove endless. Though Toni Cade Bambara's anthology, *The Black Woman* (1970), discussed the "double jeopardy" of being both black

and female, the historical moment belonged more to the mood of Elaine Brown's album for the Panthers, which included a song with the refrain, "We'll just have to get guns and be men." The year of *Sisterhood is Powerful,* 1971, was also the year George Jackson was assassinated in Soledad Prison.

But in the post-Watergate haze, some black women began to reason that everyone had had a movement except black women: white guys smoked dope and ran the antiwar movement; black dudes had dark glasses and Black Power; white women burned bras and had feminism. A new feature entered the landscape of consciousness-raising groups, theater collectives, and women's journals: politics and literature for black women. From the campus dorm room, this writing had the appearance of an avant-garde, and things avant-garde tended to come to students in the form of anthologies. On the shelf, next to Donald Allen's *New York Poets* and Clarence Major's *The New Black Poetry,* someone in 1975 might have found room for *Black-Eyed Susans,* edited by Mary Helen Washington, a slim paperback containing only ten stories by contemporary black women writers.

The spectacular successes of Alice Walker, Toni Morrison, and now Terry McMillan give the impression that their triumphs were immediate. Surveys of contemporary fiction by black women remind us that before *Song of Solomon,* the previous books of this year's Nobel laureate, *The Bluest Eye* (1971) and *Sula* (1975), got very mixed receptions. Walker's first novel, *The Third Life of Copeland Grange,* appeared over twenty years ago. Her articles in *Ms,* in which she took on the obtuseness of white feminist studies that didn't include the black woman's condition, and the corrective essays Angela Davis wrote on black women and slavery for *The Black Scholar* had, back then in the late 1970s, a feeling of being out there all on their own. This period also saw renewed interest in the New Negro Movement of the 1920s, with the rediscovery of black women writers such as Jessie Fauset, Nella Larsen, and, most importantly, Zora Neale Hurston, who was swiftly elevated to the rank of "foremother."

There used to be a saying down South that the most free people in the United States were the white man and the black woman. Perhaps the saying referred to unholy alliances; but most likely it meant that the black woman could move about unchallenged in a way the black man could not. A story such as Richard Wright's "Bright and Morning Star" gives a sense of her galling mobility: it doesn't occur to anyone in the lynch mob that the grieving mother who has come among them is hiding a gun under her clothes: she can't be a threat. We now know so much about black women in US history that it is almost impossible to retrieve the reality that folk saying could have been describing. If anything, the absence of consideration for the black woman's point of view in this specimen of folk wisdom would support what all the tone-setting essays by black feminists were criticizing when they talked about the black woman's "invisibility." Not surprisingly, during the late 1970s and throughout the 1980s, we were dealing with a privileged consciousness, one that resorted to strategies of exclusion, much like the argument black writers, including militant black women writers, used to make against white critics: How can you know what it feels like, how can you dare to judge this? A similar force field of intimidation surrounded writing by African-American women: you hegemonic male so and so.

To a large extent the "seized word"—taking control of the interpretation and the expression of your own experience—that black feminist criticism called for was the newest link in the chain of "positive images" that cultural nationalism had been advocating since Marcus Garvey. Furthermore, as Gayl Jones has recently suggested in her study of the oral tradition, *Liberating Voices,* making the black woman heard in literature looks, in retrospect, very much like the resolve of the separatist Black Aesthetic movement of the 1960s to free itself from Western cultural domination. The same tendency, Jones points out, is found in many other subordinate cultures: Estonian, Chicano. Even realism in the US since Dreiser can be viewed as a history of "decolonized sensibilities." What these tendencies have in common is their belief in a transformed society.

Some of the many black feminist studies since the 1970s seem less "alternative" histories than positions criticizing an already existing history. Sweeping claims for a distinct black woman's voice and for "female values" impose recent critical ideas on a past that would not have recognized them. Some of the rhetoric amounts to little more than epistemological fantasy or assumes that black men were more unaware of or indifferent to this history than they in fact were. Nevertheless that the "historical face" of the Black is no longer only male marks, at least in print, a generational change as profound as the experience that separates those who knew Jim Crow from those who didn't.

Imaginative writing by African American women is controversial largely as a result of what it has to say about relations between black women and black men. This is too bad. Gayl Jones's *Corregidora* (1975) and *Eva's Man* (1976) were criticized by both black men and black women for portraying unmitigated domestic violence, even though what was truly extraordinary about these fictions as departures was Jones's ear for the vernacular and the spare structure that nevertheless managed to evoke a complicated social setting. In fact, Jones had left out all scenery and social detail. There wasn't even a white side of town.

When Ntozake Shange's "choreopoem" *For Colored Girls Who Have Considered Suicide/When the Rainbow Is Enuf*

hit Broadway in 1976 relations between black men and black women moved as a ruthless topic into mainstream US culture. Someone once described the message of the piece as, "If you think *you*'ve had it bad with black men listen to this." That sensation was followed by Michele Wallace's polemic, *Black Macho and the Myth of the Superwoman* (1979). Wallace let both the machismo of Black Power and the blame-the-female-headed-household of the Moynihan Report have it. Then came *The Color Purple.* By the time its very vocal critics, such as Ishmael Reed, Stanley Crouch, and Trey Ellis, argued that Alice Walker was making black men the villains and letting white society sit back to enjoy the show, black men writers were dismissed as having a bad case of Issue Envy.

The image of the oversexed black woman was a part of the racism that justified rape. This image kept the light-skinned, refined heroine of uplift at the center of many of the novels by black women well into the twentieth century. But now the argument against patriarchy, that the female body should be taken away from men as an object of use, and returned to women to dispose of as they choose, has brought about, in fiction, the comeback of the uninhibited conjure woman on her own terms. It is okay for her to have her nights out, like any man. The defeated or redefined images of loose women and big strong mamas—these brambles have been cleared, the dirt turned over, and Terry McMillan stands on very cultivated ground. Not a weed in sight.

2.

Popular novels ask complicity from the reader in the name of genre: we all know reality isn't like this. But *Waiting to Exhale* never winks at the reader. It comes at you with a completely straight face, with such intensity about its own convictions that the sincerity is irresistible. If the women characters are sentimental about love, then they are fierce about being sentimental; if they are conventional in their expectations, then they are defiantly prepared to be identified as such. The novel is at the same time hilarious, to the verge of camp, but the thoughts and feelings it captures are too much like life for it not to make a striking impression. There's nothing self-aggrandizing or moralizing about it.

It's a book that knows to whom it is addressed. For sheer topicality, McMillan doesn't miss a base on the wide playing field of issues, and her characters touch them in the most self-aware manner. Caring for one's elderly parents, condoms for teen-agers, day care, feeding the homeless on Thanksgiving, diet, high blood pressure, nail care, AIDS, anti-drugs, including Xanax dependence—anything that could be on the professional black women's list of concerns is there, woven into the conversations of supermoms, much like the false braids in the hairstyles McMillan's women disdain at the beauty salon that functions as their club away from the net-working parties haunted by black men.

Waiting to Exhale never winks at the reader. It comes at you with a completely straight face, with such intensity about its own convictions that the sincerity is irresistible.
—Darryl Pinckney

Very with-it and dialogue-driven, *Waiting to Exhale* is the story of four friends in their mid-thirties, each at a critical point in her life. Savannah and Robin are unmarried, childless, and speak in the first person. The two who do have children, Gloria, a single parent, and Bernadine, on the eve of a nasty divorce, are written about in a very internal third person. Though each chapter is from the viewpoint of one of them, laying out her case history, taking up threads of developing situations, the women share a common voice and are moving toward the same pole-position in the self-realization sweepstakes: dreaming of opening a catering service, doing something creative in production work at that cable channel, becoming a mother, or busting the estranged husband who is trying to hide his considerable financial assets. They recognize that black men have treated them the way they have because they, black women, have let them get away with it all these years. The love of a black woman isn't a black man's right, one character tells herself, it's a privilege. In her overdue anger, another character "bams" the phone down a lot.

McMillan's black women read *Essence.* They know that glossies targeted for their white middle-class sisters are just as full of hints, tips, and desperately cheerful features about sex and finding Mr. Right. They know it's a cynical, self-perpetuating market that goes after those gullible, hopeful bucks, which perhaps makes it all right that they continue to flip through it to check out the latest fashions. They may be fools for love, and fools for "bad" dresses they can wear the hell out of, but they are not victims. They make choices. In fact, out there in Phoenix, Arizona, these women act out, act up, and talk about big dick in a way that makes their white female thirtysomething (by now) counterparts in recent fiction of downtown scenes seem tame by comparison.

It used to be said, maybe still is, that blacks talk differently among themselves from the way they do among whites, and *Waiting to Exhale* is an extension of that, showing how differently black women talk among themselves from the way they do in the company of black men. When they are down, they pop their hymns, Paula Abdul or Anita Baker tapes, into the car tape deck. They say "Fuck you" to one another with affection, get drunk, and tell a friend some home truths for her own good. They call each other up and give advice: that they ought to use black men the way black men have been using them. "Get some," they say. Or "get some for me" and "get some to tide you over." And yet for all their rueful independence, cruising, salaries, and responsibilities, the musketeer-like code of "getting some" is apt to be forgotten the morning after. The man is never a trick. He's the one who "got some" and didn't call back.

Savannah, Bernadine, Robin, and Gloria belong to an organization called Black Women on the Move, which is as safe as NOW. McMillan's women have the same relation to affirmative action and the "glass ceiling" as any middle-class white woman. There is nothing overtly feminist in *Waiting to Exhale,* but if the men can make the women doubt their own worth, the women have the last laugh. McMillan makes full, vivacious use of the tactic that makes Kate Millett's attack on Henry Miller in *Sexual Politics* so devastating: ridicule of masculine fantasies of sexual prowess.

> He rolled over on top of me, and since I could no longer breathe, let alone move, I couldn't show him how to get me in the mood. He started that slurpy kissing again, and I felt something slide inside me. At first I thought it was his finger, but no . . . I was getting pissed off about now, but I tried to keep up with his little short movements, and just when I was getting used to his rhythm he started moving faster and faster and he squeezed me tight against his breasts and yelled, *"God this is good!"* and then all of his weight dropped on me. Was he for real?

Terry McMillan's women wouldn't date a white man, though they have nothing against black women who do. But when Bernadine's husband leaves her for his young, blonde bookkeeper, she recovers, burns his clothes and BMW, cuts her hair, drops by the software company she sweated to help him build, and slaps the shit out of the red-faced girl. Sometimes they don't know or don't want to believe that the black men they go out with who are afraid of commitment are already married, but sometimes they do know.

Their lives are full of topics that are covered every week on the *Oprah Winfrey Show,* but these black women never have to ask themselves the very Oprah-like question of why they're attracted in the first place to Scuzzes Who Lie, because, conveniently, for most of the novel's four hundred pages the black men are all No Good or Losers. But they keep the faith in the one black man who won't be like that, who is "sensitive," not threatened, and yet has a dick hard enough to make them quit smoking—it's either that or acupuncture—and when two Mr. Rights do come along, one is an inspired retired handyman, happy to fix everything around the house, and the other vows to use his law practice to get the state of Arizona to stop putting liquor stores in black neighborhoods.

The anxiety of these women about Mr. Right's whereabouts is far from the sensibility of, say, Andrea Lee's Harvard-educated heroine in *Sarah Phillips* (1984), whose notion of the romantic is the inappropriate, unsuitable man. Daughter of old Negro Philadelphia, she suspects that marriage to someone from a background similar to hers would be boring. The difference is one of class, of milieu: McMillan's women work with what they can find, not with what they have been born into. Indeed, what McMillan's women have been born into is what they have gotten away from.

Part of the appeal of McMillan's work lies in the forceful way it reflects the history of black women as also that of a labor force. *Mama* (1987), *Disappearing Acts* (1989), and now *Waiting to Exhale*—each successive novel takes place on a higher level of prosperity as McMillan charts the fortunes of black women rescued or created by higher education. In Ann Petry's grim novel *The Street* (1946), the heroine's job as a maid causes her to lose her marriage and home. She longs to get her son away from the bad influences of the tenement and becomes a bookkeeper. White men look upon her as a whore and she kills the black man who assaults her, an illustration, perhaps, of James Baldwin's contention that in black fiction the place where sex ought to have been was filled by violence. The most convincing way black writers of his day could make something happen to make their point was to have a catastrophe. The times and taboos have changed for McMillan's determined women. You can have a catastrophe and move on. Mobility is opportunity.

In *Mama,* the girl raped at age fourteen in a depressed Michigan town of the 1960s can throw away her hot comb and find sexual fulfillment, Malcolm X, and a community-college education in Los Angeles. She can get away from her mother's life of welfare checks, scrubbing floors, the husband with the brown leather belt, the casual prostitution when there are no jobs or substitute husbands. Even Mama can try to get away from her platinum wig to make a life like her daughter's.

In *Disappearing Acts,* Zora—her daddy liked to read—is a school teacher who wants to make a career as a singer. She gets an apartment in a Brooklyn brownstone with enough space for a practice room and, fortunately or unfortunately, the builder taking a break on the steps looks like "a black Marlboro man." This novel is largely a dress rehearsal for *Waiting to Exhale,* with a similar circle of catty but supportive, slightly differentiated black women friends, except in this case the alternating voices are unequal, male and female. The edge is in the female voice and McMillan struggles to keep up the man's side of the story, to fill out his inner life with sports, beer, bitterness, shame, horniness.

In *Waiting to Exhale,* the black women are professionals whose children are not likely to fall out of the middle class. They are the grandchildren of the insecure migrants that Dorothy West wrote about in *The Living Is Easy* (1947), a novel of black middle-class life in pre-World War I Boston. McMillan's women repay student loans, send cash back home by Federal Express so widowed mothers can keep the gas on, and tolerate for as long as they can the strain of love for sexy but insolvent black men. They are far from the black neighborhoods of fiction that depended on messages of social consciousness. In Phoenix, they choose white suburbs and schools. The extended black family is contained in long-distance phone calls, and political consciousness consists of being annoyed that Arizona has no Martin Luther King Day.

> McMillan's women repay student loans, send cash back home by Federal Express so widowed mothers can keep the gas on, and tolerate for as long as they can the strain of love for sexy but insolvent black men. They are far from the black neighborhoods of fiction that depended on messages of social consciousness.
> —*Darryl Pinckney*

These women have arrived, are just as Keynesian as any white in recent fiction, and tend to spend their way out of crises. They do not question material reward, because it's all been earned. Doubts about having sold out when they get promotions belong to a pre-Anita Hill era. A condo or a Cherokee is no obstacle to having soul—unless it belongs to a black man. Bernadine despises her husband's Porsche and investments because he's competing with the whites he reads about in *Money* magazine. She never wanted a Rolex. When an absent but well-off father turns up to explain that he doesn't want to get back together with the family because he's gay, the wife senses immediately that something is wrong, closes her eyes, and discovers the problem: "He sounds white."

There is a similar equating of the black man's success with loss of his essential blackness in Gloria Naylor's schematic novel of black middle-class life, *Linden Hills* (1985). A black executive who has made it to the oak panels level of General Motors is terrified that he may be falling in love with a black woman. The black colleague from whom he seeks advice is so self-controlled that no toilet paper is visible in his bathroom of French tiles, because he scarcely needs any.

There is nothing satirical about Naylor's tone; so earnest is her fable about black people who drive Stingrays. One black man goes through with a wedding in which his lover acts as best man rather than risk exposure at his law firm or lose prestige among his neighbors. On the other hand, Naylor gives the lesbians in *The Women of Brewster Place* (1982) the courtesy of being ostracized as sexual outlaws, even though they function in the story as agents of gentrification.

This conceit, the hint of sterility and isolation as the price the black man pays for success, is somewhat retrograde, reminiscent of black nationalist days when Whitey, like God, was always a He, and part of attacking Whitey was to cast aspersions on his manhood. "All white men are trained to be fags," Amiri Baraka said in *Home* (1960). He meant that materialism was emasculating, that being a part of the system was a form of cowardice. Baraka's swagger was a re-formulation of a persistent contradiction in black cultural life: free v. bourgeois, earthy v. assimilated, soul brother v. Uncle Tom. It clearly still has its uses as a denunciation, even though black culture is now big business. Hip and main-stream are no longer mutually exclusive, being successful no longer means compromising blackness. The new genera-tion of "post-soul black culture," very savvy about music, film, television, and books as industries, has dissolved the contradiction in a way that black capitalism, affirmative ac-tion, and Buy Black boycotts failed to do.

McMillan allows her women to thrive in this slick new world, where consumption is a form of cultural politics, whereas black men in these books by black women are por-trayed as allowing materialism to betray their spiritual heri-tage. They risk being cut off from their roots until summoned down home to the naturalness of Sweet Beulah Land, much like the tragic mulattoes who used to "pass" in earlier black literature. . . .

These recent novels by McMillan and [Trey] Ellis are not about the black man or the black woman either as alienated or as secure members of a community. They are not even about love. They are concerned with "relationships"—that tired word—and what people put themselves through to find one they wouldn't be ashamed to show off to their best friends. A partner is an acquisition, a form of self-valida-tion. If there has to be a response from black men, then it was written long ago, in, for example, George Wylie Henderson's novel *Ollie Miss,* published in 1935.

Henderson was a contemporary of Zora Neale Hurston's, and *Ollie Miss* bears a remarkable similarity to *Their Eyes Were Watching God* (1937), in content if not in style. Like Hurston's novel, *Ollie Miss* depicts a self-contained complex rural black community. Interestingly enough, there is noth-ing a feminist could fault in Henderson's heroine. Ollie Miss unnerves men because she can plow as steadily as any of them. She is a child of nature, migratory, but not wild. She is ethical, and so far above petty emotion that she is a mys-tery to the men on the farm where she appears one day look-ing for work and is resented by women whose husbands have long ago deserted them. Ollie is not monogamous, though she is in love. Her passion for the wayward man, Jule, back in another town, gives her a protective single-mindedness and a disinclination to explain herself to her new neighbors that is almost Bartleby-like. When she is severely wounded outside a revival meeting in a razor attack by one of the jeal-ous women Jule has taken up with, Ollie, though pregnant, decides that a piece of land, having something to work for, is more important than the strong feelings she and Jule had for each other, feelings that had made neither of them happy.

Throughout the novel, the field-workers who fail to win her affection, the women who can't gain her confidence, and the black proprietor of the farm where she is employed all be-have toward Ollie as people whose daily lives are made up of the observance of powerful, civilizing customs. A woman who can't leave a man who beats her is pitied as not having "the sense she ought to have been born with." Henderson published a sequel about Ollie's son, and then, like so many other writers who had been a part of the Harlem Renaissance, he faded away.

The Harlem Renaissance faded, and so did the declared pur-pose of its young writers to celebrate the richness of black vernacular culture. The Depression wiped out the optimism of the 1920s and by the time Richard Wright was at the pin-nacle of his career in the 1940s the burdens and hopeless-ness of life in the ghetto had become the most representative and the most riveting themes of African American literature. The city, the world made by migration, was the setting for this protest literature, and the problem of the ghetto domi-nated African American fiction as its most valid, meaning-ful subject until very recently.

The ghetto had become synonymous with black culture to such an extent that even works of sheer entertainment car-ried a political message merely through the scenery. Louise Meriwether's *Daddy Was A Numbers Runner* (1969) or Alice Childress's *A Hero Ain't Nothin' But A Sandwich* (1973) may be reinterpreted to extract something "womanist," but previously these novels by women were fictions about the urban condition, along with everything else, mostly written by men. The urban story was largely the black man's story—the bars, the wounds, the desperate improvisations—and per-haps the black woman's story should be seen as part of a more general reaction against this writing that identified black culture as a problem, and the ghetto as a symbol of the pathological. Celebrating the richness of life in the black community has made a comeback, and especially, ironically, because of *Roots,* this revival emphasizes survival, continu-ity, family feeling—the woman's story. The "folk utterance" has become female.

But just as the ghetto as the primary subject became the victim of the complacence of formula, so too "the necessary bread" of the black woman's point of view is being made to do the job of the five loaves and two fishes. Naomi King's *O.P.P.,* a story of deceit among B girls, and Barbara McNeely's *Blanche on the Lam,* which introduces a black maid as a detective, have nothing in common with Jamaica Kincaid's novels of sensibility apart from the intrinsic interest of being about black women. If anything, Terry McMillan's women flying off to conferences in Las Vegas are closer in temperament to the narcissistic young moguls jetting off to the Frankfurt Book Fair in Jay McInerney's *Brightness Falls.* Only McMillan's novel is more accomplished.

Twenty years ago, when June Jordan never failed to rock the house, these black women writers would have been poets. Twenty years ago, the white women who are a large part of the black woman's audience were preoccupied with the bad sport in *The Bell Jar* and the good sport in *Fear of Flying.* It has been suggested that the sales figures for books by black women expose them as commodities, "the flavor of the month," but people have a way of turning against the best seller in the way that everyone everywhere hates the nouveau riche. Yet the immense popularity of a very few black women writers obscures the fact that most novels by black women have a very short shelf life—just like most other books in the US. Then, too, black writing has been so widely accepted as serving a political or moral purpose that it is hard to see as real books that do not make an immediate display of having instrumentality.

It also says something about the cultural moment that you can quickly name over a dozen black male film directors, but have to pause to come up with four black women directors. Rap is very much the young black man's province, and Angela Davis has noted that hip hop's narrow interpretation of the legacy of Malcolm X once again posits black macho as the only response to white supremacy. Maybe there is some frustration among black male writers that they seem unable to muster an equal impact at the moment; maybe some discuss the limelight around black women writers as if it were a continuation of the alleged conspiracy between the master and his concubine, but it makes me think of what Otis Redding is supposed to have said when "Respect" became such a hit for Aretha Franklin: "That girl stole my song." As everyone knows, it was a different song when Aretha sang it.

Donnella Canty (review date April 1996)

SOURCE: "McMillan Arrives," in *English Journal,* Vol. 85, No. 4, April, 1996, pp. 86-7.

[*In the following review, Canty offers high praise for* Waiting to Exhale.]

Move over Alice Walker and Toni Morrison, make room for Terry McMillan. McMillan will need a lot of room on the bench of elite, female African American writers if her latest novel, **Waiting to Exhale,** is any indication of her true talent. In addition to **Waiting to Exhale,** McMillan has two other novels to her credit; **Mama** (1987) and **Disappearing Acts** (1980) were McMillan's first two fictional endeavors. She also edited **Breaking Ice: An Anthology of Contemporary African-American Fiction** (1990), a very popular collection of short stories.

Waiting to Exhale quickly established McMillan as a major force among contemporary female fiction writers. The novel lived up to the praises of my colleagues and turned out to be one of the most well written, true-to-life books I had ever read. McMillan's story-telling strategies and precise command of narrative voice were exceptional.

The plot centers around four thirtysomething friends (Savannah Jackson, Bernadine Harris, Robin Stokes, and Gloria Matthews) who are rediscovering themselves, their lives, and their mates. As if those three major issues are not enough, the four friends also face and deal with political, cultural, social, and economic challenges facing black women. Through their struggle, McMillan depicts the bonds of friendship and relationship in a humorous light by telling each of the twenty-eight chapters from the viewpoints of each friend. The black dialect and voices McMillan uses to tell all of the women's stories draw readers into black culture.

Savannah and Robin are childless and have never been married. Both are attractive professionals climbing the success ladder and in search of the man who can make their imperfect lives complete. Savannah is plagued with a mother who is aging, an apathetic family that has become dependent on her financial support, and a job which does not allow her to express her creative talents. At the same time, Robin is trying to overcome a long-term love affair that ended, leaving her distraught and lonely. After several mistakes with men, Robin decides that she will have a child with or without a husband.

McMillan tells Savannah and Robin's stories in first person which enables the reader to fully comprehend her protagonists' complex, eventful lives. Although the road to happiness is long, curved, and dangerous, these two women ride it smoothly, taking the many bumps as they come.

Bernadine and Gloria are the more experienced and mature of the four women. Gloria is a single parent of a teenage son and owns Oasis, a hair salon/gossip network for black women. She is coping with being alone, deciding whether to tell her son that his father is gay, and relating to her son's interest in white girls. Bernadine, the mother of two girls, wages a divorce battle with a husband who is an executive, as well as a cheat and a liar. When Bernadine finds out about his long-term affair with his young, white bookkeeper, her husband tries to hide his considerable financial assets. Bernadine is forced to consider being alone and working outside the home to maintain the plush lifestyle to which she and the children are accustomed.

The way these two women deal with their situation is simultaneously funny, sad, and realistic. McMillan tells the stories of Bernadine and Gloria in a very revealing third person.

Although McMillan's four main characters are black women, her story is not black or feminist. *Waiting to Exhale* speaks to most women and to the issues surrounding most women, regardless of race. She portrays women as complete, complex, undiminished human beings.

Waiting to Exhale provides a brief glimpse into the talent and capabilities of Terry McMillan. I am making room on my bookshelf and waiting to inhale her next masterpiece.

Publishers Weekly (review date 1 April 1996)

SOURCE: A review of *How Stella Got Her Groove Back,* in *Publishers Weekly,* Vol. 243, No. 14, April 1, 1996, p. 52.

[*In the following review, the critic offers a tempered assessment of* How Stella Got Her Groove Back.]

Her readers may be surprised that, after the gritty, tell-it-as-it-is *Mama* and *Waiting to Exhale,* McMillan has now written a fairy tale. Her "forty-fucking-two-year-old" heroine, divorcee Stella Payne, possesses a luxurious house and pool in northern California, a lucrative job as a security analyst, a BMW and a truck, a personal trainer and an adorable 11-year-old son—but no steady guy. On a whim, Stella decides to vacation in Jamaica, and she narrates the ensuing events in a revved-up voice, naked of punctuation, that alternates between high-voltage energy and erotic languor. Romance comes to Stella under tropical skies—but there's a problem. Gorgeous, seductive Winston, the chef-trainee with whom she enjoys passionate sex (explicitly detailed), is shockingly young: he's not quite 21. Naturally, Stella wonders if he really loves her; endless soul-searching and a few tepid complications occupy the remainder of the narrative. When Stella loses her job, it's no sweat; she has enough savings to maintain her lifestyle. When fate throws two other gorgeous men her way, she immediately decides they are boring and isn't

tempted for a minute. Meanwhile, her intense preoccupation with feminine deodorant sprays and the smell of women's public bathrooms is rather strange, to say the least. McMillan's expletive-strewn narrative accommodates such musings, however, and readers who have been yearning for a Judith Krantz of the black bourgeoisie—albeit one with a dirty mouth and a more ebullient spirit—will be pleased with this fantasy of sexual fulfillment.

Malcolm Jones Jr. (essay date 29 April 1996)

SOURCE: "Successful Sisters: Faux Terry Is Better than No Terry," in *Newsweek,* Vol. 127, No. 18, April 29, 1996, p. 79.

[*In the following essay, Jones discusses the popularity and influence of McMillan's fiction on the publishing industry and other African-American writers.*]

Like James Michener and his generational epics and Tom Clancy and his techno-thrillers, Terry McMillan created a new literary genre with her upbeat novels about contemporary black women. Then she went those other writers one better: she created an entirely new audience to go with her genre. Vanesse Lloyd-Sgambati, a Philadelphia literary promoter, claims that for African-American women desperate for something to read, McMillan's "books have replaced dates in the '90s."

Waiting for McMillan to publish another book, readers pleaded with booksellers for anything similar. "I'd say, 'Read Bebe Moore Campbell'," says Clara Villrosa, owner of Denver's Hue-Man Experience bookstore. "They'd come back wanting more. I'd say, 'Read Tina McElroy Ansa, read Connie Briscoe.'" All these writers began publishing after McMillan, and like her they steer clear of writing about racial problems, concentrating instead on the problems of contemporary African-American women. They also send the same messages: "Girlfriend, you are all right," and "Men, hmmmph!" Briscoe's *Sisters and Lovers* (1994) sold more than 100,000 copies in hardcover and 325,000 in paperback. Her new novel, *Big Girls Don't Cry,* has 100,000 copies in print. Ansa's *Ugly Ways* (1993) sold 92,000 hardcover copies. Excited by these figures, the overwhelmingly white American publishing industry is going to ever-greater lengths to tap the black audience. In June, for example, Knopf will publish 150,000 copies of *Push,* a gritty first novel by black poet Sapphire for which Knopf paid a half-million dollars. Even E. Lynn Harris has more than 152,500 copies of his current best seller, *And This Too Shall Pass,* in print. Commenting on the unlikely success of a black male who writes about bisexual love affairs, Villarosa says, "When you're a female reader and you want love and a contemporary voice, you don't quibble so much about the other."

In the wake of *Waiting to Exhale,* publishers began to realize that black readers and white readers are reached in entirely different ways. "That review in *The New York Times* is not going to sell books," says Lloyd-Sgambati. And forget booking your author on the morning TV talk shows. "At 8 in the morning, most African-Americans aren't watching TV," she says. They're on their way to work. "So radio's a better way of getting the message across." Villarosa works with black sororities and has booked readings in churches. "So much depends on the connection to the community," she says. "The biggest thing with us is word of mouth."

Noting the black community's tradition of "looking to books for wisdom and solace," Will Schwalbe, editorial director at Morrow, argues that anyone who mistakes the sort of books McMillan writes as just beach reading for blacks has undervalued their importance. For these readers, a book "is not a throwaway form of entertainment. It's a vessel of culture," he says. Or as Lloyd-Sgambati observes, a generation ago, "most African-Americans who were reading were probably reading a Bible." Their grandchildren are reading the likes of Terry McMillan. To them, it's gospel.

John Leland (essay date 29 April 1996)

SOURCE: "How Terry Got Her Groove," in *Newsweek,* Vol. 127, No. 18, April 29, 1996, pp. 76-9.

[*In the following essay, Leland discusses McMillan's literary success, critical reception, and wide popularity.*]

It is midmorning. In Terry Mcmillan's home, and the lovebirds are squawking. This is McMillan's modest-size house—the builders are putting the finishing touches on a grand Spanish-style manor around the corner—and the caged birds are able to rock it: four or five of them, brilliant green and red and yellow, splaying shocks of sound and color amid the fierce teal and chartreuse finishings. The lovebird, you might imagine, has a gentle, soothing coo. But you'd be wrong. These things can blow. And beneath their clamor, cutting through it, is the gruff gale force that is Terry McMillan, one of the most robustly embraced authors in America. Into an innocent telephone she growls: "Why do you keep calling?" This would be her son, Solomon, 11, the love of her life.

These have been tumultuous years for McMillan. After the blockbuster success of her 1992 book, *Waiting to Exhale,* she complained openly of the demands made on her by fans and black groups. At one point, she said she wished she'd

never written it. The novel's unflattering portrayals of black men also drew charges of airing dirty laundry in public. At the same time, in the course of a year, she suffered the death of her mother and her best friend. Distraught, she had to shelve a partially completed novel, "A Day Late and a Dollar Short," modeled partly on her mother. Today, though, she is on her game. She is wearing bright turquoise and white and royal blue, with a turquoise bandanna setting off her strong cheekbones and stronger brown eyes. These are colors loud enough to keep up their end of the conversation.

It has been a full moment or two since she has uttered a swear word, a dry spell in which she has discussed men, women—well, maybe an earthy participle slipped in there—and, ultimately, duty. "Do you believe I have to sign all these," she says, hunkering down to a stack of 4,000 photographs from the cover of her new book, *How Stella Got Her Groove Back,* which is due April 29. The book, about a 42-year-old woman who goes to Jamaica and falls in steamy, sweaty love with a man half her age, is autobiographical. McMillan's twentysomething boyfriend, Jonathan, whom she met in Jamaica, quietly introduces himself and smiles; we should all have such a book written with us in mind.

Since *Waiting to Exhale,* her book signings—legendary occasions for soapy catharsis among the mostly African-American women who read McMillan's books—have gotten too big for her actually to sign books. So this time around, fans will get these photos. "But knowing black folks, they'll be like, [dropping into homegirl mode] 'Could I have a stack of these for my other books,' or 'this for my mama,' or 'this is for my sister, girl you know my aunt is in the hospital.'" She could go on, really she could. Because here in this tony bedroom development east of San Francisco, this funky music—this mix of self-satisfaction and an affectionately mocking voice—this is love, Terry McMillan style.

And McMillan is working it. *Waiting to Exhale* has sold nearly 4 million copies. For last winter's film version, which grossed $66 million, women turned out in large groups for the privilege of yelling "go girl" at the screen while four beautiful, successful black women searched for Mr. Wrong. *How Stella Got Her Groove Back* has a first printing of 800,000 copies in hardcover, unheard of for an African-American novelist. The film rights are already sold. She told a conference of black writers that she now commands $6 million a book. Her racy, frothy novels of middleclass black life have overthrown the unattractive publishing-industry wisdom that African-Americans don't read. And she has spawned a cottage industry of black pop fiction writers.

She has not always been embraced. Some other successful black women writers have refused to acknowledge her, which she has admitted hurts. In a recent interview in *The New Yorker,* the critic Albert Murray dismissed her books as "just

Jackie Collins stuff." McMillan is characteristically unapologetic. "I can imitate Alice [Walker] and Toni [Morrison]. I can imitate f——-ing Virginia Woolf, Katherine Anne Porter, Jane Austen. Anybody can." She laughs. McMillan enjoys a hearty, spirited battle with her critics. In the new novel, Stella takes *Waiting to Exhale* to Jamaica. She finds it pale. "I don't know what all the hoopla is about and why everybody thinks she's such a hot writer because her s——- is kind of weak when you get right down to it and . . ." well, she could go on. But McMillan asserts, "This is my voice. I didn't know if I would be taken seriously because of the tone of my work. All I knew is that I wasn't going to change it."

Her colloquial narratives have the casually cathartic flavor of pop songs, allowing them to reach audiences her more literary peers never will. Clara Villarosa, who owns the largely black Hue-Man Experience bookstore in Denver, describes the McMillan revolution this way: "When you look at the literature of Toni Morrison or Alice Walker, a lot of it reported on experiences in rural areas, or back when. Contemporary black fiction, in a black woman's voice, was a total void. These women weren't reading the Toni Morrisons. They'd say, 'Honey, I want it to sound like me.' And when it did, they loved it."

Terry McMillan was born in 1951, in Port Huron, Mich., the first of five children. Her mother raised the children largely by herself; her father, she says, was a bad drunk. "My mother didn't just get beat up," she says. "She fought back. A lot of times she kicked my father's ass." But she says her mother never regretted marrying her father (they divorced when Terry was 13; her father died three years later). "She was of that mind-set of, I have five beautiful kids, that's one thing he did right. I don't share that attitude."

Like a lot of her neighbors, the McMillans struggled; most went through spells without a phone or heat or electricity. "There were a couple winter nights I remember my teeth chattering," she says. "But I don't remember ever feeling poor. I hate that word. We never went hungry." Her mother worked various jobs and lavished her attentions on the kids. "When we got good grades, it was a reflection on her. Even though she only got up to 11th grade, that was her way of saying, 'I'm doing something right.' We didn't have time to fail. She didn't give us that space."

As a child Terry had little interest in literature. The only book in the house was the Bible. But at 16 she got a job for $1.25 an hour, shelving books in the library. There she discovered the Brontes, the biography of Louisa May Alcott—and James Baldwin, an inspiring surprise: she didn't know African-Americans published books. She'd sit on the floor of the travel section, reading and fantasizing. It was her way of escaping Port Huron. When she finally did get out, first to junior college in Los Angeles and later to Berkeley, where

she got pivotal encouragement from Ishmael Reed, it was again reading that helped her escape a bind. "As soon as I read Ring Lardner, his voice jumped off the page. What he was writing about was tragic, and I was cracking up. I realized that it was the same sort of thing I was trying to do in my stuff. Ring Lardner said, 'It's OK Terry, to write the way that you talk.' Ring Lardner was the one who freed me up. Langston Hughes didn't hurt."

In the early '80s, unsure of herself, McMillan battled with cocaine and alcohol abuse (she says she hasn't touched either substance since). By the time she wrote *Mama* (1987), she was a single mother. She remembers editing galleys by night, working as a typist and trying to raise a young baby on her own (she has never married). She promoted the book herself, sending off thousands of letters and reading in every black bookstore that would have her. Through her incendiary readings, she found her audience, many of whom were really discovering fiction for the first time.

> **McMillan writes intimately, sometimes mockingly, about a middleclass black experience in which white America is largely irrelevant. Her best work captures the foibles and rhythms around her in lusty vernacular.**
>
> **—*John Leland***

Hers is a fresh voice, one belonging to what writer Trey Ellis calls the New Black Aesthetic. Writers before her, she says, "dealt with everything from the perspective of race. A lot of them were appealing to a white audience, hoping they would say, 'OK now we understand you people more. Thanks for sharing.'"

Instead, McMillan writes intimately, sometimes mockingly, about a middleclass black experience in which white America is largely irrelevant. Her best work captures the foibles and rhythms around her in lusty vernacular. Check out, for instance, this resolution from Zora, one of the alternating narrators of *Disappearing Acts* (1989), McMillan's most probing work: "I've got a history of jumping right into the fire, mistaking desire for love, lust for love, and, the records show, on occasion, a good lay for love . . . I made up my mind that the next time I'm 'out here'—which just so happens to be right now—it'll have to start with dinner (which won't be me) and at least one or two movies and quite a few hand-holding walks before I slide under the covers and scream out his name like I've known him all my life. Some flowers wouldn't hurt either."

Her lack of racial polemic has earned her a crossover audience, but also heat from some black critics. Elizabeth Nunez, who heads the National Black Writers Conference, worries that McMillan's success signals a cautionary note to black writers: "Hey, if you want to get popular, then stop writing literature that is race-centered. But the truth is that race is central to a black person's experience." At the same time, McMillan has fought with white editors over what constitutes black experience. Houghton Mifflin, which had an option on *Disappearing Acts,* wanted McMillan to drop the middle-class Zora's narrative voice because, she says, she sounded too much like a white girl. "They weren't acknowledging that we had other experiences. Everything was supposed to be racially motivated. We don't just fall in love and get our hearts broken just like everybody else. No, there's got to be something about being exploited. I'm sorry I did not make Zora barefoot, pregnant, getting her ass locked in the projects. But that's not the story I wanted to tell." She ultimately published with Viking.

But enough about critics. For the Sisterfriends, a reading group in Los Angeles, it doesn't matter what academics say. What matters is that McMillan has a new book coming out. *How Stella Got Her Groove Back,* written—like her others—in a little less than a month, is McMillan's most breathless book, and her least fully developed. The heroine, a $200,000-a-year systems analyst, is her least accessible. But this prospect does not seem to bother the Sisterfriends. They already have plans to meet at the largest black bookstore in L.A. on the day it's released to buy copies.

The Sisterfriends is one of dozens of "sista circles" formed around books like McMillan's. They are working women: hairdressers, teachers, secretaries, paralegals. "I love Toni Morrison and Alice Walker," said Candence Walker last week, "but they can be difficult to understand. I read [Morrison's] *The Bluest Eye* twice before it made sense, and then I still think I missed some of it. I never had that problem with Terry." Gladys Johns, holding a finger sandwich, had to laugh. "I admire those [writers], but damn, they depress me. I know we've been victims as black women, but Alice and Toni really stick it to you and I don't want to be reminded of it all the time. Terry talks about problems, but with humor and fun. I laugh through the tears. That's what I need."

These are the women Terry McMillan wants to speak to, and for. She admits that at a screening of *Waiting to Exhale,* she was yelling at the characters as much as the audience. "I don't write about victims," she says. "They just bore me to death. I prefer to write about somebody who can pick themselves back up and get on with their lives. Because all of us are victims to some extent." The stories she tells are, in the end, her own. Critics may never give her the acceptance she wants. But Terry McMillan is not one to hold her breath.

James Wolcott (review date 29 April 1996)

SOURCE: "Terry McMillan," in *The New Yorker,* Vol. 72, No. 10, April 29, 1996, p. 102.

[*In the following review, Wolcott comments briefly on* How Stella Got Her Groove Back *and McMillan's literary success.*]

Waiting to Exhale was for Terry McMillan what *Dinner at the Homesick Restaurant* was for Anne Tyler—a popular breakthrough after years of paying dues. McMillan's previous novels, *Mama* and *Disappearing Acts,* had found a niche with readers, but had done nothing to separate her from the pack of other praiseworthies. Then came *Waiting to Exhale,* a huge best-seller, its liftoff supplied by the jubilant, snappy talk of its female characters—especially when they ragged on men. History and the burden of race didn't give weight to its pages, as they do in much black fiction. Set in Phoenix, *Waiting to Exhale* exulted in light, open, possibility-filled space.

McMillan's new novel, *How Stella Got Her Groove Back,* which is coming from Viking this month, is also set in the airbrushed present. There are a lot of long sentences without commas, to convey the anxious rush of its heroine's acceleration through life. Lots of "You go, girl!" backslap, too. McMillan, who took flak for portraying black men as sneaks and sheiks in *Waiting to Exhale* (a controversy that was re-ignited when the book became a hit movie), tries to make amends here in the form of Winston, whom Stella meets on a vacation in Jamaica. He is so fine: only twenty-one—half Stella's age—he is responsible, polite, and attentive to a woman's needs, and when he and Stella kiss, those long sentences without commas ascend like goldfish bubbles.

The first printing for the book is a monster one million copies, which makes McMillan the Oprah of black fiction, selling and exemplifying the holy trinity of wish fulfillment: money, fame, and romance. McMillan doesn't write for worrywarts. *How Stella Got Her Groove Back,* like *Waiting to Exhale,* is a sexy handbook of self-realization.

Liesl Schillinger (review date 5 May 1996)

SOURCE: "Beneath a Jamaican Moon," in *Washington Post Book World,* May 5, 1996, pp. 1, 8.

[*In the following review, Schillinger commends McMillan's strong female protagonist and portrayal of desublimated female desire in* How Stella Got Her Groove Back. *Schillinger concludes, "women are ready to read about themselves not only as schemers or sufferers, but as the adventurous heroes of their own lives."*]

Is a happy woman in charge of her own fate de facto an unsympathetic character—someone people don't want to read about and cannot empathize with? If so, the defenders of serious literature will no doubt join in unison to eject Terry McMillan's rip-roaring new book, *How Stella Got Her Groove Back,* from the Eden of politically and academically correct approval. Because, in *How Stella Got Her Groove Back,* no women weep; and Stella, in fact, revels. She revels and even gloats at being a woman, revels in being in solitary possession of her mind, her body, her child, her house, her finances, her beauty, her creativity and finally, of her sexy, strapping young dream lover, whom she finds and triumphantly lashes to her side. If this is unserious literature, it is unserious literature of the most serious kind, perhaps even, in its own way, revolutionary.

Terry McMillan is the only novelist I have ever read, apart from writers of children's books, who makes me glad to be a woman. Children's fiction overflows with examples of authoritative girls who control their worlds, fictional and real; from Laura Ingalls Wilder's own Laura, to C. S. Lewis's Lucy, to E. E. Nesbit's Anthea, Lloyd Alexander's Eilonwy, and of course L. Frank Baum's Dorothy—or, perhaps more remarkable, Baum's Ozma of Oz, who actually chose to be transformed from a boy to a girl to claim the Emerald City throne. But the moment the cloak of girlhood is thrown off, and writers choose to write about grown-up girls, any sense of empowerment, opportunity or strength in the female characters is bestowed only to be smashed sooner or later, as the women run through such hurdles as pleasing men, struggling to find a mate, supporting children and, more often than not, coping with emotional, physical or intellectual bullying of some kind, or paying the wages of their own sentimentalized sin.

I was afraid at first that this impression might have been an absurd exaggeration; but then I looked at my bookshelf of favorite books—books I have read and reread, and care about deeply—and was astonished to find my theory amply confirmed. In the A's to F's alone—Amis (both), Austen, Bronte, Cervantes, Dickens, Dostoevsky, Dos Passos, Duras, Eliot, Faulkner, Fitzgerald and Forster—I remembered female characters who, however interesting their tales might have been, principally sought male sanction or suffered, one way or another. Further down the alphabet, in Shakespeare and Wharton, Graham Greene, Hemingway, Virgil, and Maugham, I recalled doomed Lady Macbeth and Lily Bart, prostitutes and spurned wives, the weeping women of the Trojan wars, weeping women, in fact everywhere. (In fairness, I submit, Trollope also makes me glad to be a woman; the exception proves the rule. But then, in his time, and even now, he was often dismissed as an unserious writer.) This

seems to beg the question: Does serious literature want women to be subject or else abject? McMillan abundantly proves that if it does, it shouldn't.

Fans of McMillan's previous novels, the hugely popular *Waiting to Exhale* and the more critically esteemed *Disappearing Acts* and *Mama,* will recognize McMillan's authentic, unpretentious voice in every page of *How Stella Got Her Groove Back.* It is the voice of the kind of woman all of us know and all of us need: the warm, strong, bossy mother/sister/best friend. Fans and enemies alike will also get their share of the brand names that McMillan uses to signify arrival into this country's upper-middle class: BMW and Calvin Klein, Nordstrom's and Macy's. Having just spent an evening with a friend who crowed ecstatically all night over a new pair of Gucci loafers, which did in fact seem to lend her some special glow, I don't find the product emphasis fatuous or crass. Even Emerson recognized that for a woman, which McMillan indubitably is, "the sense of being perfectly well-dressed gives a feeling of inward tranquillity which religion is powerless to bestow." But readers of this book will find more than wise words and icons of wealth; they will find the rare and perhaps unique example of a courtship in which the woman hunts down her own love object herself—and finds the man willing to be wooed.

At the outset of the book, we learn that Stella, 42, an affluent single mom in San Francisco, has gone a little stale, like champagne that's been uncorked and not tasted for too long. She's content, but she spends more time taking care of business and conducting lengthy Molly Bloom-like internal harangues with herself and external harangues with her sisters than trying to find happiness for herself. So, defying her stagnation, she packs herself off to a luxury resort in Jamaica, where from get-go, every young stud's eyes swing appreciatively in her direction. Sure enough, Stella soon finds the "real thing" in the form of a noble, gentle, fine 20-year-old man, Winston Shakespeare. When McMillan describes Stella's first vision of the boy wonder, you want to howl with laughter at her audacity, and shout, "Go, girl!":

> When I look at him I almost have a stroke. He is wearing baggy brown shorts and has to be at least six three or four and he is lean but his shoulders are wide broad and as he walks toward my table all I can think is Lord Lord Lord some young girl is gonna get lucky as I don't know what if she can snag you. . . . when he smiles he shows off a beautiful set of straight white teeth that've been hiding behind and under those succulent young lips.

Name another time you've read a man objectified by a woman in this way, if you can. Stella, of course, turns out to be the lucky girl, and soon finds that she's hooked. Back in California, her sister Vanessa encourages her, while her sister Angela moans in despair at the folly of a May-December romance in which her sister is not May. Vanessa boldly comes to Stella's defense: "Men have been dating younger women for [expletive] centuries and does anybody say anything to them?" she sputters. Women may talk like this to each other, but few of us write like this.

To those who say this could never happen in real life, I offer the evidence of the young dive-master I met last summer in Belize under an apricot moon, whose gallantry and openhearted effusiveness restored my own faith in romance, even if he was no Winston Shakespeare. McMillan's book may be the stuff of fantasies, not reality; but if fantasies could be bought whole, every woman in the country would be lining up to buy them from Terry McMillan. And maybe then other writers would dare to write them, too. And, maybe this is happening right now—and fiction at last is about to understand that women are ready to read about themselves not only as schemers or sufferers, but as the adventurous heroes of their own lives.

John Skow (review date 6 May 1996)

SOURCE: "Some Groove," in *Time,* Vol. 147, No. 19, May 6, 1996, pp. 77-8.

[*In the following review, Skow discusses McMillan's literary success and the wide popularity of her fiction.*]

News flash: Terry McMillan's big-bucks new novel *How Stella Got Her Groove Back* is a silly wish-fulfillment fantasy that barely qualifies as beach literature. Heroine Stella Payne is a beautiful, single, "forty-bleeping-two-year-old" black investment analyst who, though sexy and rich, hasn't had a date in months. Tired of waiting for a black prince to materialize in a paid-for Lexus, she flies to Jamaica on vacation, meets Winston Shakespeare, a tall, golden-brown, bashful 20-year-old assistant cook at a resort hotel, falls in love, and brings him back home as a live-in souvenir.

Correction to news flash: Stella isn't fantasy after all. Author McMillan, 44, single, renowned for griping raucously about no-account African-American men in her bestselling 1992 novel *Waiting to Exhale,* flew to Jamaica on vacation last June and fell in love with tall, golden-brown, bashful, 20-ish resort hotel employee Jonathan Plummer. They now live together, happily ever after, in McMillan's big house in Danville, California. "I don't anticipate us being together for the rest of my life," says the reflexively blunt author, "but right now it works and it's good for him and it works for me and I don't care what anybody thinks . . . Men have done this bleep for years. Nobody ever says anything about them and they marry chicks young enough to be their daughters."

McMillan may be—in fact, no question, she is—a better story than her latest book. As the first wildly successful black pop novelist, she is, as they say, looking good, an attractive woman of about 5 ft. 7 in., taking her ease in an oversize white sweatshirt, jeans and sneakers after a morning photo shoot. For the moment, turbulence is below the surface, but as McMillan's longtime agent Molly Friedrich says, "You don't meet Terry, you experience Terry. She's truly a force of nature."

> The fact that an African-American author was writing about vivid characters with whom many black women could identify had the added effect of proving to booksellers that there is a sizable, previously ignored market for semisoapy black fiction . . .
>
> —*John Skow*

The former writing teacher (Stanford, University of Wyoming) is also a force of corporate profit. Her first two novels were modest successes; her third was *Waiting to Exhale,* which swept the nation's bedrooms, beaches, hair salons, reading groups and rush-hour subway trains, selling almost 700,000 hard copies in the process and 3 million more in paperback. Numbers like these would have drawn any publisher's attention, of course. The fact that an African-American author was writing about vivid characters with whom many black women could identify had the added effect of proving to booksellers that there is a sizable, previously ignored market for semisoapy black fiction—just as the $67 million gross for last year's film version of *Exhale* proved there is a sizable market for semisoapy black movies.

All of which has set the table for McMillan's staggering $6 million boodle from *Stella* (that's the figure she divulged at a black writers' conference in Brooklyn, New York, in March). Viking is printing 800,000 hard copies of the book. Book-of-the-Month Club bought the novel two years ago, as one of its main selections, sight unseen, before it was even written. The movie rights for *Stella* have also been sold, for an undisclosed seven-figure bundle.

Given all that, her toys are not particularly gaudy. She owns a black BMW, a silver Mercedes and a navy blue Toyota Land Cruiser. A pool, of course. And she just moved into a larger and fancier house with, among other refinements, eggplant-colored leather tiles on the office floor. All perfectly normal for a medium-to-big shot in the entertainment industry, and she grumbles when reporters mention that she, or her characters, live high. "What's their point?" she asks. "All these white people write about people in their books having money. What is the problem with us having a little bit? Why are they so bleeping surprised? What is the big bleeping deal?"

Considering the edge of anger that cuts through her conversation—she can get steamed in several directions within the same five minutes—it may be surprising that McMillan writes only glancingly about racial and feminist issues. Stella, in the new novel, is shocked at the bitter poverty in remote parts of Jamaica. And she does advise her sister that the way to stop black kids from gang-banging is to make them listen to *The Autobiography of Malcolm X* in the third grade. But it's the roiling currents among family, friends and lovers that McMillan is most comfortable writing about.

For the moment, however, the temporarily semiserene author has put aside her caricatures of black men, who in *Exhale* were lampooned as triflers who were generally around at bedtime, ooh Baby, but not a good bet for breakfast and a bleeping certainty to be bleeping gone when there were bills to be paid and kids to be reared. She gets along well, she says, though at a distance, with her 11-year-old son Solomon's father, whom she never married (and who sued her unsuccessfully for an unflattering characterization in her second novel, *Disappearing Acts*). She grew up as the eldest of five children in a troubled, hardscrabble household in Port Huron, Michigan. Her father was alcoholic and abusive, and her mother Madeline, working as a maid and in an auto factory, raised the kids mostly on her own. Madeline is the recognizable main character in McMillan's first novel, *Mama;* it's not hard to guess that she was an important source of her daughter's grit and directness.

There is no denying that McMillan's success has changed the industry by proving that there are eager buyers—lots of blacks, lots of whites—for African-American pop fiction, and not just high-end literary novels like the work of Toni Morrison or Alice Walker, who have had best sellers, but also glossy page turners that owe a thing or two to Jacqueline Susann. Ken Smikle, publisher of *Target Market News,* a Chicago-based trade magazine that focuses on black consumers, credits McMillan with "dragging the industry kicking and screaming into what has become a very lucrative situation." The numbers: between 1990 and 1993 the amount of money African Americans spent on books increased 48% (while book buying by whites increased only 10%). Among the beneficiaries are a number of successful, recently published writers, including Connie Briscoe, whose *Big Girls Don't Cry* (HarperCollins) is a somewhat earnest black-businesswoman-makes-good fable, and E. Lynn Harris, author of *And This Too Shall Pass* (Doubleday), the story of a gorgeously muscled N.F.L. quarterback coming to terms with his homosexuality.

As for McMillan, the most self-revelatory writer in the

world—this week, anyway—she grouses that "nobody would dream of asking Toni Morrison who she is sleeping with." Later, her Jamaican friend Plummer, a slim, amiable fellow who studies hotel management at Diablo Valley College, pokes his head into her cluttered office. He admits that he is "flattered" to be the model for Stella's Winston Shakespeare, though "I don't really read books." "But he will," says McMillan, "or else he's moving." Laughter all around.

It's a dubious sort of good luck that the publication of her slightest and fluffiest novel has brought McMillan her greatest reward. The new book starring "Winston" burbles along cheerfully but lacks the satirical bite of *Waiting to Exhale.* There isn't much to the story, which amounts to woman meets boy, gets boy, with no second act, so the author will have to crank up some misery if she carries out her plans to write the screenplay. You can't have a movie without conflict.

How critics will ultimately judge McMillan is a good question. Will she turn out to be, like Danielle Steele and Judith Krantz, just one more queen of the steamy, scented stuff that the publishing industry calls "commercial"? It's possible. But so far McMillan has not written formula glop. And most of the time her chapters, though they can rank nearly as high as Steele's and Krantz's in breathy descriptions of dressing, undressing and furniture, have a brassy realism that saves them from the trash bin. And even though peace has broken out in the author's life, with the usual corrosive effects on a satirical viewpoint, the reader suspects that there are more battle communiques to be written in the ancient and always up-to-date war between the women and the men.

Stella, in *Stella,* picks up a copy of *Exhale,* reads 50 or 60 pages and drops it with the offhand comment that "I don't know what all the hoopla is about and why everybody thinks she's such a hot writer. Hell, I could write the same stuff she writes." Sure, Stella; in your dreams. Which are what pop novels, even largely autobiographical ones, are all about.

Richard Bernstein (review date 15 May 1996)

SOURCE: "Black, Affluent and Looking for More," in *The New York Times,* May 15, 1996, p. C17.

[*In the following review, Bernstein offers a generally positive assessment of* How Stella Got Her Groove Back, *but states that "the issues for Stella are luxuriously banal."*]

Terry McMillan's new novel is like one of those television sitcoms in which a somewhat unconventional family faces the somewhat unconventional plight of one of its members. In this episode, the family member is Stella Payne, an affluent, divorced 42-year-old investment analyst who, trying to put a little excitement back into her life, goes on vacation to Jamaica. There she meets a handsome, gentle, very charming Jamaican and falls in love with him. The problem, which Stella wrestles with for the rest of the novel, is that the man, named Winston Shakespeare, is half Stella's age.

The television people have names for some of the main sitcom genres. There is the dead-mother comedy, for example, in which a father raises the children in the absence of his deceased wife. *How Stella Got Her Groove Back* is a single-mother comedy. Like the better sitcoms, it has a cast of likable, truculent characters, funny lines, smart repartee and a warm and fuzzy ending. It is a good deal more raunchy than anything that would be allowed on television. It is not deeper or more searching than the average sitcom, no more dramatically powerful than a backyard barbecue, but it is an irreverent, mischievous, diverting novel that at times will make you laugh out loud.

Ms. McMillan's previous book, the wildly successful *Waiting to Exhale,* made into a movie, was warmly welcomed as an expression of middle-class black female identity. The 'hood—the world depicted by *Clockers, Menace 2 Society* or Tupac Shakur—was only part of the larger black pageant, Ms. McMillan was reminding us. The larger picture also included middle-class black women with educations, careers and sensibilities who wage a special kind of struggle over the missing ingredients of the affluent life.

How Stella Got Her Groove Back extends Ms. McMillan's excavation of this literary vein. Stella is the owner of a BMW and an expensive house in the San Francisco suburbs; she is a soft touch for her son's requests for money to buy the latest rap CD's; her younger sister is married to a litigator and among her suitors is a judge. But Stella is a rare member of her extended family to experience life at the level of bourgeois anomie. Many others remain in the 'hood. From time to time a relative calls her collect from prison.

Stella's concerns and her consciousness are standard American-suburban, overlaid by the cultural and psychological cues emanating from the experience of being black in America. Her racial awareness is keen and casual at the same time, her reflections often cursory and soon forgotten. When she gets to Jamaica she refuses to go to the nude beach because "I wouldn't want to give white men the pleasure of seeing my black body, considering they used to rape us when we were slaves." She notices, too, when she gets out of the minivan that has taken her from Montego Bay airport to her hotel in Negril, that none of the white people give the driver a tip. She does—$20. "This is like a black thang: You take care of me, I'll take care of you," she explains.

"I basically like most white people as long as they don't act like Nazis or come across like they're superior or richer or classier or smarter," Stella declares, giving expression not to some element in her personal experience but to her awareness of historical oppression. But Stella's main concerns are the stuff of what the movie people call crossover, the transracial interest Ms. McMillan's books inspire. They stem not from being black but from being a woman and from dealing with and needing men.

The issues for Stella are luxuriously banal. Even though she makes more than $200,000 a year, works with a personal trainer who "makes Cindy Crawford look like a zero," and has a man she can call on for "purely maintenance-oriented sex," she is bored and vaguely discontented. "Right now I'm tired of thinking about how uneventful my life has been lately, and I wish I knew what I could do to put the fizz back into it," she declares. Her 11-year-old son, Quincy, has gone off on vacation with his father, which is what enables Stella to take off for Jamaica and to puzzle out her uncommon romantic dilemma.

"What I do know deep down although I keep it secretly secret," she says, "is that I am terrified at the thought of losing myself again whole-heartedly to any man because it is so scary peeling off that protective sealant that's been guarding my heart and letting somebody go inside and walk around lie down look around and see all those red flags especially when right next to your heart is your soul." Stella is far too self-absorbed to be entirely admirable, but she is sassy and bright and her spasms of surliness stem from the vulnerability she tries hard to hide rather than any streak of real meanness.

Her spiky interior thoughts and the spirited, affectionately caustic dialogue she maintains with the rest of the world save her story from triteness, though not always. ("I mean how can we grow if we think we've already arrived at the end?" Stella asks herself near the end of her journey.) Fortunately, Ms. McMillan's ear is generally rather finely tuned. The secondary characters—especially Stella's two sisters and her precocious, empathetic son—are sharply realized.

Ms. McMillan's book, in short, is pretty smooth sailing, rather like Stella's life. Nothing catches very deeply. Quincy is untroubled by his mother's love affair with a near adolescent. Stella's $200,000-a-year job causes her no difficulty (not even when she loses it). Nobody in this book is much interested in anything except sex, love and new acquisitions. It's the American dream realized, Ms. McMillan demonstrating that the black realization of it can be just as slick and anemic as the white.

Terry McMillan with Evette Porter (interview date 21 May 1996)

SOURCE: "My Novel, Myself," in *Village Voice*, May 21, 1996, pp. 41-2.

[*In the following interview, McMillan discusses her critical reception and autobiographical aspects of her fiction, particularly in* How Stella Got Her Groove Back.]

The thing to remember about Terry McMillan is that she's very much a diva, and not just by reputation. With her high cheekbones and almond-shaped eyes, she actually looks the part, even if she seems somewhat younger than her 44 years and is smaller than I'd expected. Her voice is deep, mature, and sounds slightly edgy as she explains she's just finished doing 19 interviews. She became a phenomenon after the success of **Waiting To Exhale,** *both as a book and a movie, and earned a $6 million advance for her latest novel,* **How Stella Got Her Groove Back.** *It's a breathless tale of a middle-aged woman who falls for a 20-year-old while vacationing in Jamaica, and much has been written about the similarities between the novel and McMillan's real life—which includes a young Jamaican boyfriend she met on the island last summer.*

"How long is this gonna take?" she says, after giving me the once-over. I'd heard about her abrasiveness, but when I say an hour, she says okay, and politely ushers me into her hotel suite.

Not long after we sit down, Jonathan Plummer, the "souvenir" Time magazine says McMillan brought back from her trip last year, pokes his head out from the adjoining room. For all the speculation about Plummer being the love interest in McMillan's latest novel, he bears little resemblance to **Stella'***s tropical boy toy. Lanky, slightly stooped, and self-effacing, he's dressed more like a B-boy than a sexy rent-a-dread from Negril. He seems a little uncomfortable with all the attention, but McMillan assures me he's getting used to it. After the brief introduction, he retreats to the other room.*

This seems like as good an opening as any to start talking about the personal issues in McMillan's work.

[Porter:] *People assume your work is autobiographical, that Terry McMillan is Stella, I say, Is she?*

[McMillan:] "Stella isn't a reinvention of myself. She's only part of my persona. I can't believe people actually think my life is like that. What I give [my characters] are my concerns, which for the most part are grounded in reality."

Are you the person that you see written about?

"Pretty much, with the exception of *Time* magazine. [The writer] had a chip on his shoulder from the first line."

More has been written about you than about your work.

"Thank you. That was my point."

Why?

"I think the film may have had something to do with it, and I understand that. But especially with **Stella,** everybody wants to know how much of it is real. How much of it is true. If I said, 'all of it,' what does that mean? People spend a lot of time trying to draw similarities between my life and my work. I've gotten it with every book. 'Which character is you in **Waiting To Exhale,** girl?' Do you think if I was Robin [the sexually promiscuous character], that I would *admit* it? I mean come on—dingbat that she was. I don't think so!"

Sure, but some of the characters in your novels bear a strong resemblance to you, so maybe that has something to do with it?

"Probably. But in **Waiting To Exhale,** out of all the things those women went through, only two of those experiences came close to what I've been through. And even those were lies. But the bottom line is, as a writer I understand or I'm trying to understand what makes people tick. I try to make the characters believable, realistic. I think when people meet me, they're more comfortable assuming that I'm one of these characters because then it makes me not this icon, this larger-than-life figure. I think that's one of the reasons fans do it. On the other hand, I think this guy from *Time* was trying to show that I hadn't written a novel at all—you know what I'm saying. That it was simply a reenactment of my life, which I really resent. Because he wasn't there. You know."

For all the media's winking about excessive self-disclosure, McMillan has yet to write about some of the more difficult things in her life—the deaths in recent years of one of her closest friends and her mother. Even as **Exhale** *was rising to the top of the charts, she was abandoning A Day Late and a Dollar Short, a tale about a mother and daughter. McMillan's new novel, written in just a month, marked an end to her writer's block.*

Was writing **Stella** *therapeutic?*

"Of course. Definitely. Cathartic."

In a way that A Day Late and a Dollar Short *was not?*

"No, no. You can't compare the two. I don't do that."

Because it was about your mother, right?

"No! No! Nope. Not about my mother. It's about a woman

who's in her fifties who in some ways has a part of my mother's persona, but she's not my mother. I had my mother in mind. I just wanted to explore that and I thought about some of the things my mother had said to me and my sisters over the years and that's how it started. But once I lost my mother, it was too close—the idea of writing about a mother who is a little bit too intrusive and invasive in her adult children's lives, I couldn't go there emotionally. I didn't want to.

"*Stella* was different. I embraced that. I hadn't intended to write it. It dictated to me that it wanted to be written and I just sort of paid attention. I hadn't written in almost two years. So when it started coming out, I just gave in to it. I just sort of succumbed, surrendered. And I was not going to stop. I didn't really think it was a novel I was writing. At first it was a poem. Then a little short story. Jonathan was the one who encouraged me. Didn't you, Jonathan?" *she yells in the direction of the other room.*

[Plummer:] "Yeah, I guess so," *he mutters back.*

[McMillan:]"What do you mean you guess so?" *she says, in a way that seems to demand a stronger reply.*

"You did!"

Jonathan emerges from the other room, briefly interrupting the interview.

"I said to Jonathan, you'll see some things in here that you can kind of recognize, but it's not going to be everything that happened between you and me, is it now?" *she says, glancing in his direction.*

Were you apprehensive about getting involved with someone much younger than you?

"Yeah! Yeah! Wait, let me say goodbye to Jonathan. . . ."

She trails off to walk him to the door. There's a brief exchange between the two—a shared joke—and the kind of physical intimacy one usually sees in young couples. Surprisingly, the somewhat brash McMillan seems uncharacteristically girlish, almost giggly and coy, with Plummer. After he leaves, she settles back into the chair.

So what about being involved with a much younger man?

"I think as women we almost inherently question anything that makes us happy. I don't think I thought about it very long. But if you had told me a year ago that I'd be going out with someone in their twenties, I would have laughed in your face. I would've said, 'I don't go out with children.' Really. I'd never even thought about it."

Part of the attraction, she admits, is that Plummer didn't know who she was. "He'd never even heard of my book, which was great," *she chuckles.* "Plus I didn't really give a shit at the time, to be honest. Because I wasn't really thinking that way. All I was thinking was what a good-looking young man he was and one day somebody was going to be *verrry* happy. I don't think it's so much robbing the cradle, it's more like the way interracial couples were years ago."

So far, she's got no regrets. "Life is really short, too short. My girlfriend wasn't even 50 and my mother was 59 when she died. I was thinking, shit, if I blink, I'll be 59. And I don't want to be one of these 'wish I coulda, woulda, shoulda.' Right now it's been almost a year with Jonathan. And it's been a good year. And if it's over next month, I'll be heartbroken. But the bottom line is it's been a good year, a *damn* good year. That's why I wrote the book, so I wouldn't forget it."

In interviews and even in your novels, you've become somewhat notorious for—

"Being so profane?" *McMillan asks, slightly bemused.* "Oh, I can be when you piss me off. When I was being interviewed by the reporter from *Time*, she was being really probing. I said to her, 'If I were Toni Morrison, would you be asking me these fucking questions? Do you ask Anne Tyler who she was sleeping with before she wrote her last book?' I don't think so. 'Do you ask Danielle Steele?' No!

"I was upset because when they interview white writers, they don't ask them what kind of car they drive, or what kind of house they live in. What has that got to do with my work? If I were white they wouldn't ask me these fuckin' questions. And sure enough that's what that muthafucker put in the article. See, now I'm swearing, because they made me mad.

"There are going to be people out there that are going to review the book for what it is. And of course, there are people who are going to review me. There's a backlash to success, especially if you're black and female—black and/or female.

"You know my mama used to say, 'Always have a thick skin, because people are gonna talk about you if you do, and talk about you if you don't. So fuck 'em.'

"If I'd stopped and thought about the fact that I am writing this novel and people are going to find out that I have this young boyfriend and they're going to think that all this stuff is real, I wouldn't have been able to write anything. But I didn't stop long enough to worry about it. All I thought about was my story, and telling it, and feeling it. And that's how I write. And that's why I write."

Sarah Ferguson (review date 2 June 1996)

SOURCE: A review of *How Stella Got Her Groove Back,* in *New York Times Book Review,* June 2, 1996, p. 21.

[*In the following review, Ferguson summarizes the "uncomplicated" message of* How Stella Got Her Groove Back.]

Divorced at 42, with an 11-year-old son and a lucrative job in investment banking, Stella Payne splits her time between a "funky little California castle" outside San Francisco and a cabin at Lake Tahoe. She's got four computers in her office, a personal trainer, a pool and two steam rooms—but make no mistake, it's lonely at the top. "Once you get past the 200,000-a-year mark you are constantly being appraised and as a result always trying to prove your worth," the buppie heroine complains in her infectiously intimate you-go!-girl run-on style. "It's too hectic up here and the race is always on. It's always rush hour but I haven't figured out when to put on my blinker because it's safe to change lanes and I'm also not sure which exit I should take to get off this track altogether." What Stella needs is a little loving. And so, after the inevitable shopping spree (nightgowns, sexy bras and panties, six or seven bathing suits for a nine-day trip), our new best girlfriend heads to an adults-only resort in Jamaica and straight into the arms of a sweet-smelling "maple-syrup-colored" local hunk—who happens to be all of 20 years old. Terry McMillan's first novel since her 1992 best seller, **Waiting to Exhale,** is a guilty-pleasure sex-and-shopping fantasy of the first order, sprinkled with asides on rap music and feminine hygiene and featuring a message as uncomplicated as a glass of fresh-squeezed papaya juice: If aging men can rev their engines with pretty young trophy wives, why can't middle-aged women treat themselves to dreamy, dishy boy toys?

Janet Mason Ellerby (essay date Summer 1997)

SOURCE: "Deposing the Man of the House: Terry McMillan Rewrites the Family," in *MELUS,* Vol. 22, No. 2, Summer, 1997, pp. 105-17.

[*In the following essay, Ellerby examines McMillan's depiction of the African-American family in* Mama, Disappearing Acts, *and* Waiting to Exhale. *In contrast to other mainstream white, middle-class models, Ellerby asserts that "McMillan's polemical novels reject the dominant patriarchal family values reinforced by the Waltons and the Cosbys and propounded by the Christian right."*]

In Terry McMillan's first novel, **Mama,** Mildred's husband is holding fiercely to his notion of being the "man of the house" within the nuclear family:

Crook . . . found his thick brown leather belt. . . . Then he made her drop her coat next to it, then her cream knit dress, and then her girdle. When all she had on was her brassiere and panties, he shoved her into the bedroom where she crawled to a corner of the bed. Crook kicked the door shut and the kids cracked theirs. Then they heard their mama screaming and their daddy hollering and the whap of the belt as he struck her.

"Didn't I tell you you was getting too grown?" Whap. "Don't you know your place yet girl?" Whap.

I juxtapose this disturbing scenario with the following from Jean Bethke Elshtain's *Power Trips and Other Journeys* in which she writes of society's need for the re-instatement of conventional nuclear family values:

Familial authority . . . is . . . part of the constitutive background required for the survival and flourishing of democracy. Family relations could not exist without family authority, and these relations remain the best way we know anything about to create human beings with a developed capacity to give ethical allegiance to the background presumptions and principles of democratic society.

This is not from a Pat Roberson supporter. Elshtain, who explicitly identifies herself as a feminist, makes a case for "the family"—a specific household arrangement of mother, father, and children. She is talking about traditional, mainstream family values—firm, unchanging entities—as the means to secure democracy. Ironically, her stance puts her in the camp of the socially conservative right, those who cheered George Bush when he maintained that we need a nation closer to *The Waltons,* who applauded Dan Quayle's condemnation of Murphy Brown as a single parent, and who want the Legal Defense Fund abolished because it helps poor women get divorces.

McMillan, however, resists following the script written by mainstream American discourse that imposes the cultural ideals of White patriarchal domesticity across the borders of race, class, ethnicity, and sexual preference. In her first three novels, **Mama** (1987), **Disappearing Acts** (1989), and **Waiting to Exhale** (1992), this hegemonic discourse is reconfigured, and her families look nothing like the Waltons. Despite Bush's endorsement, the Waltons represent a damaging American myth, one that idealizes the patriarchal family as the necessary configuration for emotional security and psychological health, the *sine qua non* for a smoothly functioning, moral democracy. As this myth denies racial, ethnic, and class diversity, it encourages debilitating feelings of guilt, betrayal, and rage, since both minority and mainstream American families often cannot or refuse to conform to the myth's prescriptive ideological values.

The monolithic family values the Waltons represented in the 1970s were reinscribed in the 1980s by the Cosbys, another idealized, intact family with professional parents whose first priority was always their well-dressed, Waltonized children. McMillan's polemical novels reject the dominant patriarchal family values reinforced by the Waltons and the Cosbys and propounded by the Christian right. However, such values are an historical arrangement, a construct that is neither "natural, biological, or 'functional' in a timeless way," nor, indeed, descriptive of the majority of families in this country. McMillan's fiction promotes alternatives to the dominant by reconfiguring family arrangements—what they are and what they might become. Her work is important because it depicts Black family life outside the norms idealized by the White middle class. Furthermore, she refuses to define the Black family as a pathological unit that can do nothing more than sustain the conditions of its oppression. Her novels inscribe a counter-narrative to the popular oversimplification of Black family life.

In a clear feminist gesture, McMillan's contemporary African American families allocate to men a different space than the patriarchal center. In fact, her fiction appears to be affirming African American patterns of kinship groups based on mutual aid and community participation.
—*Janet Mason Ellerby*

In a clear feminist gesture, McMillan's contemporary African American families allocate to men a different space than the patriarchal center. In fact, her fiction appears to be affirming African American patterns of kinship groups based on mutual aid and community participation. The women in her novels rediscover their own sustaining power in kinship bonds which have historically served African Americans well in surviving the physical and psychic atrocities of slavery, as well as the hardships of Reconstruction. In *Mama,* for example, a woman must rely on centuries old, "jack-of-all-trades" survival strategies as she struggles to raise five children. Then, in *Disappearing Acts,* a young woman with the apparent necessary ingredients for a happy family learns how these desiderata can be eroded by racism and sexism. Finally, in *Waiting to Exhale,* McMillan depicts four single women struggling to create a sense of kinship for themselves without husbands. Each novel demonstrates the incapacity of patriarchy to meet the needs of contemporary African American women and the power and security of the kinship groups they form. Taken in sequence, the novels move from portraying isolated, disempowered women to depicting a supportive, empowering community that uses the most dynamic part of the African American tradition of kinship to flourish.

In the sociological literature on the African American family, the diminution of the male as patriarch as a result of slavery's systematic demasculinization was widely accepted. Consequently, the slave woman became the center of the family; hence the hypothesis of the Black matriarchy. However, in *Black Families at the Crossroads* (1993), Robert Staples and Leanor Boulin Johnson refute this assumption. A matriarchy is a system of government ruled by women, but the authors argue that African American women under slavery had no privileges or power, only the dual challenge of labor and motherhood. Staples and Boulin Johnson argue that what has been mislabeled a "matriarchy" was, in fact, a "two-pronged burden."

Through a detailed study of families freed before the Civil War, E. Franklin Frazier concludes that these families "have been the chief bearers of the first economic and cultural gains of the race," and it is their descendants that are "still found today in conspicuous places in the Negro world." However, the restrictions placed upon the growth and development of those pronounced free by Emancipation were amplified by the stifling conditions of poverty and illiteracy. That slavery and Jim Crow left its mark on African American families is unquestionable. Recently, however, the classic assumption that slavery created the basis for the instability of marriage and an inversion of traditional gender roles within the African American family has been impressively challenged.

Indeed, it was only after Emancipation that strong roles for African American women began to emerge. During the late nineteenth century, freed Black men found it very difficult, sometimes impossible, to obtain jobs, but this was not so for Black women. By 1880, approximately three times as many Black women as White women were in the labor force. And before 1925, 75% of African American families were intact. However, with the migration from the rural South to the Northern cities came the rise of female headed households. Again, this position as head of household is not synonymous with empowerment for African American women. As their families became vulnerable to the traumatizing experiences of urbanization, Black women lost the support of the extended family and the small community. In addition, their roles continued to be molded by racial bias, which forced most into domestic work for White families. According to Bureau of Census reports from 1992, African American women were the poorest of all gender/race groups, increasingly forced to fend for themselves. As of 1991, only 30 percent of adult African American females were married and living with a spouse.

Furthermore, although White feminists have had some success challenging male domination, Black women have often found themselves the victims of male powerlessness that causes "black men [to] . . . vent their own frustrations on their women." This projection has been vividly represented in fiction by African American writers: in Ann Petry's *The Street,* in Toni Morrison's *The Bluest Eye,* in Alice Walker's *The Third Life of Grange Copeland,* and now in McMillan's fiction. Although many African American feminists have promoted the goals of racial equality, the care and nurturing of children, and the strengthening of the African American family, McMillan's project seems to be somewhat different: she not only calls for a strengthening of the African American family but also urges a reconfiguration of that system.

Even in seemingly healthy family arrangements, most women inhabit conflicting subject positions. One desires autonomy, "defining [herself] and the values by which [she] live[s], . . . moving into a world in which [she] acts and chooses, . . . free to shape [her] future." Another is erotic, desiring the affection, companionship, and emotional commitment embodied in the romantic tradition. McMillan's novels allow us to see these subject positions in conflict. Her readers find her depiction of the ways women struggle with these conflicts entertaining and redeeming. In an interview, McMillan explains that women are reading *Waiting to Exhale* "because they identify—because they want to say, 'I was there, I'm not there anymore,' or 'I'm still there.'. . . They thank me because they are finally reading about what's happening to them now." McMillan is enacting what Louis Montrose describes as "narrating culture in action, culture as lived in the performances and narratives of individual and collective human actors." Her characters are unique women situated in specific histories, cultures, and classes who are partially dominated by and liberated from the domestic ideology of their time and place. And, as "collective human actors," her characters allow readers to identify with the serious complexity of the patriarchal model that continues to influence gender identity and to limit women's autonomy. As part of the African American literary canon, McMillan's novels situate the African American family as a site of struggle, and as Stephanie Coontz maintains, African Americans "are on the cutting edge of a number of changes in our society."

While many African American women are faced with poverty, others are making great professional strides. McMillan's fiction captures this evolving dynamic by looking at both very poor and upwardly mobile, ambitious Black women. She delineates new options for family arrangements to accommodate both women who divorce and women who choose to create families without husbands. She wants to unmask the consistently reified belief that "the most glorious destiny of a woman is reciprocal love with a man" and interrogate "the longing for a unique, synthesizing, romantic connection (with a man) which should result in monogamous bonding and the institution of marriage." In addition, her narratives refute what Patricia Hill Collins calls the "image of 'happy slave,' whether the white-male-created 'matriarch' or the Black-male-perpetuated 'superstrong Black mother.'"

Many women no longer find themselves completely vulnerable to traditional family values. Yet, in much fiction by and about women, the family remains dominant, and plots still move to resolve or efface domestic conflict and impose harmony. McMillan's narratives disrupt such ideological plots by creating narrative spaces where Black families are in crisis, where conflict is not always resolved, where the fissures of contemporary existence are not denied, and, finally, where self-reliance abides with nurturing interdependence.

These themes surface clearly in **Mama.** The protagonist, Mildred, can only realize her eroticism by way of reckless impetuosity. Although her lack of discretion allows her temporary sexual gratification, it also brings with it the loss of power and autonomy. Mildred learns and relearns that sexual intimacy consistently leaves her vulnerable to emotional and physical abuse.

In the opening quote, Mildred is being beaten because she has challenged her husband's masculine subject position. After, she musters the courage to live without him and lays claim to all that is truly hers, saying to herself:

> This is *my* house . . . I've worked too damn hard for you to be hurting me all these years. . . . Like I'm your property. . . . I pay all the bills around here, even this house note. I'm the one who scrubbed white folks' floors . . . to buy it. . . . These ain't your damn kids. They mine. Maybe they got your blood, but they mine.

For Mildred, motherhood is a given; she has no regrets about having had five children. However, part of McMillan's project is to dismantle the stereotype of the resilient African American single mother who can cope with whatever troubles and sorrows life serves her. In fact, Mildred's endurance often sinks "below sea level." Life on her own is so difficult that she continues to put her faith in the mythical family paradigm that includes a steadfast, loving husband who will support his wife and children. She tells her oldest daughter Freda, "A good husband. Some healthy babies. Peace of mind. Them is the thangs you try to get out of life"; however, Mildred's illusions do not have McMillan's endorsement.

Instead, McMillan complicates matters by adding Mildred's erotic desires to the domestic mix. Mildred is not promiscuous, but she wants to have "some fun," and she does attract men. Although her children object, she becomes so erotically aroused by the new men in her life that for awhile "she [can't] remember her children, by name or by face, and in her heart, she [doesn't] have any." But her affairs end as abruptly as they begin, and not without emotional costs to herself and her children. At one point, she pledges to never again "open up her heart so eagerly and generously," but, driven by impossible bills, she turns tricks, hosts poker parties, remarries, divorces, and moves from house to house, from state to state. The constant is her efforts to maintain some form of family stability and financial security by replacing the "man of the house," but each new partnership ends in a disappointing betrayal. Through Mildred, McMillan shows just how tenaciously women will hold on to the ideological promise of rescue by the "right" man; Mildred is a disturbing example of the enduring power of the hegemonic.

Inevitably disappointed, Mildred alone must make a family for her children. However, her ability to do so is conflicted and limited; she can neither give nor receive affection from her children. Ironically, she becomes a patriarch herself, handing out orders and making hostile threats. McMillan does nothing to glamorize single motherhood or to explore the opportunity that a matriarchy might offer; in fact, she undermines the lingering master narrative that the absent father can be effectively replaced by the strong, enduring, loving Black matriarch.

On her forty-eighth birthday, Mildred, struggling with alcoholism, starts drinking in the morning. Her sister-in-law, Curly, brings her a gift—an old picture of Crook, now dead, Curly and Mildred, pregnant with Freda. On the back Curly has written "We always was family. Remember us that way." But Curly's attempt to recreate the family fails. In fact, the picture depresses Mildred so much that she drinks until she passes out. Still, McMillan wants to end on a positive note. Freda, also battling alcoholism, returns home; she has stopped drinking completely; Mildred decides to attend community college. The novel concludes as Mildred does something she has never been able to do before—she tells her daughter she loves her, and they embrace "as if they hugged each other for the past and for the future." A healthy relationship between mother and daughter is a stronger base from which Mildred and Freda can move in positive directions. Given the social constraints of their culture, this image of family is the best McMillan can realistically provide. The embrace is a start, one in which the patriarchal center has been erased, but the authoritarian matriarch is not inscribed as an ironic mirror. Instead Mildred and Freda represent one reconfiguration of family: one parent and one child finding emotional surcease and connection in one another.

In her next attempt to reconfigure family, McMillan gives

us Zora Banks of *Disappearing Acts.* Unlike Mildred, Zora has financial autonomy. She is a teacher and talented singer who describes herself as "a strong, smart, sexy, good-hearted black woman." However, like Mildred, she has had experience with the destabilizing effects of heterosexual desire: "I've got a history of jumping right into the fire, mistaking desire for love, lust for love, and, the records show, on occasion, a good lay for love. But those days are over." However, Zora still locates her opportunities for happiness within a monogamous heterosexual relationship. She admits, "As corny as it may sound—considering this is the eighties and everything—there's nothing better than feeling loved and needed." She is cautious but still under hegemony's sway.

Gayle Rubin argues that to attain a female identity that will conform to the patriarchal family paradigm requires a process of repression and restraint, "based largely on pain and humiliation." The culmination of this process is the "domestication of women"; women learn to live with their oppression. Jane Flax maintains, "The family is the source of women's oppression because under patriarchal domination it is the agency in and through which women and men are engendered—replicating men who dominate, women who submit." That Rubin's and Flax's observations are applicable to Black women is made manifest by Zora's story, which also serves to realistically represent Staples's and Boulin Johnson's argument that many Black men believe, as do many White men, that women who can provide parity in the family threaten masculinity.

When Zora meets Franklin, we witness the impossibility of equality within the traditional family, because authority is automatically given to the male. Franklin, a handsome, intelligent Black man, works sporadically as a construction worker and drinks heavily. Zora's resolution to maintain her equanimity when faced again with sexual desire is quickly overturned, and her subservience is quickly established: Franklin automatically assumes the position of power in the relationship. Zora allows herself to adopt again an emotionally risky subject position within the discourse of domesticity. In spite of her steady job, her artistic talent, her education, and her middle class family ties, she has less capacity to determine the outcome of their relationship than Franklin, who possesses none of these advantages. When she says to him, "This is dangerous, you know," it is Zora who is in danger.

McMillan is unwilling to glamorize their day to day romance; instead, she pinpoints all the outside elements that bring conflict into their home. Franklin is often unemployed because of racism and his own drinking. He should be in the less dominant position, because he can contribute very little to their economic livelihood; however, it becomes Zora's responsibility not only to unobtrusively support him financially, but also to prop up his brittle ego. Her autonomy is threatened further by pregnancy. Franklin insists she have the baby, perhaps to bolster his faltering male ego. Because he knows that Zora wants to maintain rather than transgress conventional family values, he promises to get a divorce so they can marry. Again McMillan demonstrates the tenacious pull of the dominant ideology that delineates a sequence beginning with love and followed by marriage and children.

Their son's birth does nothing to bring the couple under the protective umbrella of the nuclear family. Franklin, in fact, is jealous of the infant. Deprived of most socially acceptable ways to feel "in charge" of himself and his family, Franklin resorts to the only kind of strength he still has—physical force. He rapes Zora. When she begs him to stop because he is hurting her, he shouts at her, "I want it to hurt." When he is finished, he orders her to stay in the bed, saying, "I want you to sleep in it, so you'll know you slept with a real man all night."

Alone again, Zora comes to realize the damaging subject position she has consistently inhabited when in love. She asks herself:

> How many times have I let myself deflate and crumble inside their hearts, dived into their dreams and made them my own? How many times have I disappeared into the seams of their worlds . . . ? And what am I going to do with this ton of love in my heart? . . . And what about the passion that's freezing in my bones right now? What am I supposed to do with it?

Through Zora, McMillan demonstrates how female erotic desire and desire for family lead strong women to vulnerable dependency. Because McMillan has a vision, she cannot conclude the novel by conforming to a generic plot formula of re-united bliss and forgiveness. Franklin does eventually return; he is faring better, but states bluntly that he is not back to stay. Zora tells him that she is leaving New York with the baby. When she suggests that he come and get them when he is divorced, he refrains from telling her that, in fact, he is now divorced. We must assume that Franklin is withholding this information in order to block any immediate attempt to re-establish the relationship; his ambivalence about a long term commitment to Zora and their child is significant. As the novel ends, they are settling down to a game of Scrabble and a night of sex, but McMillan lets us see no further into the future. What is clear is that both are better able to cope with the vexing problems of their lives not as a family unit, but on their own. Rather than conferring sustenance and security, the attempt to create a conventional domestic arrangement diminished Franklin and disempowered Zora. Zora and her child are returning to her hometown and family life with her father. There is potential for a new familial configuration here, one in which Franklin, as husband and father, is not integral or necessary.

In *Waiting to Exhale,* McMillan continues her reconfiguration project, again tackling the problems of families in crisis and the frustrations of single women striving for autonomy concurrent with meaningful heterosexual relationships. The title comes from one character's remarks about what it feels like to wait for all that she has been taught to desire and expect—marriage, security, intimacy, children. She has been holding her breath for years, waiting; her life has been a preparation for her real destination—creating a family. In this novel, McMillan's raunchy and bitter language strikes a resonant chord that echoes the sentiment of thousands of women today. Here she meshes fiction with "culture in action" in order to make specific the point suggested in the two preceding novels; a husband is not an obligatory ingredient when constructing a family.

Rather than call for a strengthening of the African American family based on the patriarchal, mainstream model, or on a matriarchal model, McMillan makes a bold move, reconfiguring the family on a model that hearkens back to early African American kinship patterns, where obligations extended beyond the nuclear family. Many of today's African American leaders see not only self-reliance but also kinship obligation as the critical components for the social organization of Black people. *Waiting to Exhale* revolves around four women all of whom are struggling emotionally, though not financially, as single women who find their lives frustratingly lonely and incomplete. One character, Robin, had been unwilling to revise her image of the family she believed she deserved:

> We would have a houseful of kids. . . . I would be a model mother. We would have an occasional fight, but we would always make up. And instead of drying up, our love would grow. We would be one hundred percent faithful to each other. People would envy us, wish they had what we had, and they'd ask us forty years later how we managed to beat the odds and still be so happy.

But she has had to relinquish this ideal; bluntly she admits, "I was this stupid for a long time."

The women embark on various ventures to find a "real life" with a loving man. For example, they go out dancing together, but only one of them, Bernadine, has a good time and only because she meets a man. The others, Savannah, Robin, and Gloria, feeling dejected and unattractive, go home alone. As Gloria turns out her light, she wonders, "Why are we all out there by ourselves? Are we just going to have to learn how to live the rest of our lives alone?" In the context of the personal lives of single, heterosexual women in contemporary culture, Gloria asks the most compelling question in the novel. McMillan does not appear to want to answer with a resounding "Yes." "Alone" for her does not appear to be a completely satisfying option; but "together" clearly needs redefinition.

After two unredeeming affairs, Savannah answers the question for herself; she is, in fact, going to learn how to live alone in her own home with a sense of contentment because, she insists, "I can't afford to do this shit anymore. It costs too much. And besides, being lonely has never made me feel this damn bad." Her relationships with her extended family and her friends provide her with the emotional sustenance continually denied her in relationships with men.

Bernadine begins an affair with a married man, James, that does seem to hold a promise of some kind of future for the two of them—partly because James's wife dies after a long illness and partly because he can say to her, "I'm not interested in . . . starting something I can't finish. I play for keeps." This kind of informal verbal commitment is rare for a male character in McMillan's novels, but it is also quite clear that Bernadine will not be defined again, as she was in her first marriage, as dependent and inferior.

Gloria, struggling with being overweight and overworked, suffers a heart attack. She almost has to die before Marvin, the widower across the street, decides he will become a part of her life and blurts out to her doctor a false, unasked for claim that he is her husband. Marvin and James, the only two men who want to establish long-term connections, do so after they have watched someone either die or almost die. McMillan seems to be suggesting that it takes the most dire circumstances for men to make genuine commitments.

At the novel's close, Robin, pregnant by a married man, decides to keep the baby who will, she believes, give her something that no man has yet been able to provide—family. She says: "I'll finally have somebody I can love as hard as I want to. Somebody who needs me." And she remarks that it will be to her girlfriends that she will turn for support and advice. McMillan is creating four different possibilities for what it is to be family in the present social configuration. The Cosby family is nowhere to be found, nor is the long-suffering but enduring African American mother. Although two of the women have found romance, these men are not husbands. Gloria and Bernadine are excited about the prospect of erotic intimacy, without sacrificing of their autonomy. Hillary Radner observes that while the novel works against the romantic paradigm, it "*does not* exclude heterosexual exchange as a moment of feminine pleasure. . . . The hero is no longer all powerful, but in his place; he generates only one relationship among many in a community in which the feminine dominates." McMillan draws vivid portraits of women who are successful at liberating themselves from the desire for the patriarchal family, replacing that delusional construct with African American patterns of communal interdependence.

Politicians tell us that in families without fathers, children are at a greater risk of dropping out of school or joining a gang, being physically ill and mentally fragile. McMillan gives us narratives that can help us counter the bleak univocality of such predictions. Unlike Petry's *The Street,* written in 1946, in which Lutie must desert her son Bub because their poverty, loneliness, and desperation have led her to commit murder, in McMillan's fiction, children are offered the possibility of moving in positive directions. In **Mama,** Freda has pulled through the despair of alcoholism; in **Disappearing Acts,** Zora is seeking a better, more stable home in which to raise her son; in **Waiting to Exhale,** Gloria's adolescent son has joined the "Up With People" brigade, and Bernadine and Robin are better able to care for their children within the kinship system they have established. McMillan is suggesting that there are ways to create supportive, secure and intimate families even though men do leave. In **Waiting to Exhale,** it is clear that these women are going to be one another's family, a family based on loyalty, trust, and enduring concern, that is more resilient than their heterosexual relationships.

In order to create a collective resistance to the hegemony of dominant family values, women need to maintain a vigilant awareness of the seductiveness of this norm as it speaks to their own desires and fears. In her fiction, McMillan jettisons conventional domestic ideology. In so doing, she clears ground for reconfigured African American families that allow for the complexity of female desire. She also challenges the ideological centrality of heterosexual romance, while still celebrating loving trust, respect, commitment and connection. Her narratives affirm; her characters offer possibility.

McMillan has been disconcertingly diminished by those who should know better. Prize-winning African American women writers and others have dismissed McMillan's novels as pulp fiction. Radner remarks, "Too self-conscious to be considered 'trash,' [**Waiting to Exhale**] nonetheless constitutes a 'good read' that cannot be dismissed as the symptom of masculine domination, since the novel constitutes a strident diatribe against traditional gender norms." Perhaps McMillan does not write with the same polished facility as Walker, Morrison, and Naylor, nor does she have the historical range of some of her contemporaries, but it is only critical blindness that prevents readers from seeing that McMillan's work is squarely within the African American canon. It is time for a serious critical re-assessment of McMillan's work within African American scholarship. Alone neither of the three novels considered here can stand as a literary master work; taken together, however, the novels are a significant contribution to understanding the evolving African American family.

FURTHER READING

Criticism

Johnston, Tracy. Review of *Waiting to Exhale,* by Terry McMillan. *Whole Earth Review,* No. 78 (Spring 1993): 84.
  A favorable review of *Waiting to Exhale.*

Kaganoff, Penny. Review of *Breaking Ice,* by Terry McMillan. *Publishers Weekly* (21 September 1990): 68-9.
  A favorable review of *Breaking Ice.*

Nichols, Charles H. "Exploring the Frozen Sea Within Us." *American Visions* 6, No. 1 (February 1991): 34.
  A favorable review of *Breaking Ice.*

Payne, James Robert. Review of *Breaking Ice,* by Terry McMillan. *World Literature Today* 66, No. 1 (Winter 1992): 136-7.
  A favorable review of *Breaking Ice.*

Interviews

Randolph, Laura B. "Black America's Hottest Novelist: Terry McMillan Exhales and Inhales in a Revealing Interview." *Ebony* 48, No. 7 (May 1993): 23-4, 26, 28.
  McMillan discusses her early life, artistic development, and career.

"'Stella' in South Africa: Still Looking for Her Groove: Best-Selling Author Terry McMillan Reveals New Details of Art-Imitating-Life Love Affair." *Ebony* 52, No. 2 (December 1996): 116-18.
  McMillan comments on *How Stella Got Her Groove Back* and the autobiographical parallels behind the novel's creation.

Additional coverage of McMillan's life and career is contained in the following sources published by Gale: *Black Literature Criticism Supplement; Black Writers,* **Vol. 2;** *Contemporary Authors,* **Vol. 140; and** *DISCovering Authors Modules: Multicultural, Novelists,* **and** *Popular Fiction and Genre Authors.*

Chaim Potok

1929-

American novelist, nonfiction writer, children's writer, and essayist.

The following entry presents an overview of Potok's career through 1996. For further information on his life and works, see *CLC,* Volumes 2, 7, 14, and 26.

INTRODUCTION

Potok is a Judaic scholar and ordained rabbi whose fiction consistently addresses important issues concerning Jewish religion and culture in contemporary American society. His best-selling novel, *The Chosen* (1967), and its sequel, *The Promise* (1969), won critical praise and a large popular audience. While most of his novels are steeped in Jewish theology, philosophy, and politics, his perceptive treatment of adolescent initiation, community dynamics, and intergenerational conflict transcend their settings to offer striking insight into the modern individual's search for spiritual meaning. Along with *My Name Is Asher Lev* (1972), the sequel *The Gift of Asher Lev* (1990), and *In the Beginning* (1975), Potok explores profound moral and social issues stemming from the Holocaust and the encroachment of secular influences upon traditional Jewish customs and values. A compassionate moralist and faithful observer of human nature, Potok is viewed as a foremost commentator on the postwar Jewish-American experience.

Biographical Information

Born Herman Harold Potok, the eldest of four children, Potok was raised in the Bronx, New York, by Polish-Jewish immigrant parents. His traditional Jewish upbringing included an orthodox religious education at a yeshiva, a parochial school for boys, and a rigorous daily schedule of prayer and study. At age fourteen he read Evelyn Waugh's *Brideshead Revisited,* an important early experience that inspired him to write. Against the wishes of his parents and teachers, Potok took up painting and, in his limited spare time, studied the fiction of Ernest Hemingway, Charles Dickens, Mark Twain, and William Faulkner. Potok attended Yeshiva University, where he earned a bachelor's degree in English with summa cum laude honors in 1950. He then studied at the Jewish Theological Seminary of America, where he was awarded the Hebrew Literature Prize, Homiletics Prize, Bible Prize, the M.H.L. degree, and rabbinic ordination in 1954. After serving as a U.S. Army chaplain during the Korean War, Potok married Adena Sarah Mosevitzky in 1958 and taught at the University of Juda-

ism in Los Angeles and the Jewish Theological Seminary Teachers' Institute. Potok resumed his studies at the University of Pennsylvania, where he earned a doctoral degree in philosophy in 1965. He also worked as managing editor of *Conservative Judaism* and, in 1965, began a nine-year term as editor-in-chief for the Jewish Publications Society in Philadelphia. Potok was also a visiting professor at Bryn Mawr College and the University of Pennsylvania during the 1980s. In 1967, Potok published *The Chosen,* his first and most popular novel, which received the Edward Lewis Wallant Award and was nominated for a National Book Award. The sequel, *The Promise,* won the Athenaem Award. Potok produced additional best-selling novels with *My Name Is Asher Lev, The Gift of Asher Lev, In the Beginning, The Book of Lights* (1981), *Davita's Harp* (1985), *I Am the Clay* (1992), and *The Gates of November* (1996). Combining his narrative skill and scholarly erudition, Potok also published *Wanderings* (1978), a substantial but highly readable historical account of Jewish cultural encounters with other civilizations over many centuries.

Major Works

Potok's central thematic concerns and narrative style are established in *The Chosen,* a novel featuring two scholarly males who grapple with questions of religious commitment, cultural heritage, and the crisis of postwar Jewish identity. Set in the Williamsburg section of Brooklyn against the backdrop of the Second World War and the Holocaust, the story focuses on the rivalry between Hasidic and Orthodox Jews through the relationship of two boys from opposing sects— Danny Saunders, the brilliant son of Hasidic spiritual leader Reb Saunders, and Reuven Malter, the son of progressive Orthodox scholar David Malter. While Danny is raised in strict silence and groomed to succeed his father as head of the insular Hasidic community, Reuven is encouraged to supplement his Talmudic studies with readings in secular philosophy and the humanities. Though both parents learn mutual respect for each other, they remain at odds over their views on the formation of the Israeli state. Much of the narrative revolves around serious theological debate among the yeshiva students and their fathers. After years of painful inner conflict, Danny eventually forsakes his father's expectations by studying to become a Freudian psychologist. *The Promise* follows the development of the two friends as Danny completes his studies in psychology at Columbia University and Reuven prepares for rabbinical ordination at an Orthodox seminary. The conflict in this novel centers largely around Reuven's controversial application of modern textual criticism to Talmudic exegesis. Bearing resemblance to a medieval morality play, Reuven's dispute with his fundamentalist instructors invokes charges of sacrilege and reveals the enduring influence of the unorthodox critical methods learned from his father. *My Name Is Asher Lev* is an adolescent initiation novel that follows the psychological struggle of a young Hasidic boy who takes up painting against the wishes of his parents and conservative community. Told as a first-person retrospective narrative, the story relates Asher's artistic and spiritual maturation under the tutelage of the rebbe and a sympathetic mentor who encourages his talent and introduces him to Western secular and Christian art. However, when Asher outrages the Hasidic community with his painting "Brooklyn Crucifixion," which depicts his mother as a symbolic martyr, he is finally ostracized. Reminiscent of James Joyce's *Portrait of the Artist as a Young Man,* Potok explores the alienation and exile necessary for the aspiring artist to achieve self-actualization. In the sequel, *The Gift of Asher Lev,* Asher reappears in midlife as an internationally acclaimed painter in France. Returning to Brooklyn for his uncle's funeral, Asher is reimmersed in the politics of the Hasidic community and, in atonement for his defection and in recognizing the importance of continuity, agrees to offer his own son to the rebbe as a successor to the dynastic line. *In the Beginning* is an autobiographical novel that relates the historical continuation of Jewish persecution in twentieth-century America. A departure from earlier novels that depict events within the Jewish community, here Potok explores strained relations between Jews and Gentiles in the Bronx during the 1930s and 1940s. The story is told through the perspective of David Lurie, the young son of European Jewish immigrants who is harassed by a violently anti-Semitic neighborhood bully. Potok underscores the seriousness of this local conflict by drawing parallels between David's escalating torment and the international atrocities of the Russian pogroms and Nazi genocide. *The Book of Lights* traces the spiritual quest of two rabbis, Gershon Loran and Arthur Leiden, through their seminary studies and separate paths in the secular world. Potok juxtaposes the creative power of Jewish mysticism with the role of Jewish physicists in the development of atomic weapons through Loran's mystical interest in Cabala and Leiden's extreme guilt over his father's occupation as an atomic researcher. Unlike previous novels that feature male intellectuals, *Davita's Harp* examines the diminutive status of women within Orthodox Jewish custom and education. The female protagonist, Ilana Davita Chandal, is a brilliant student who challenges liturgical prohibitions against Jewish women and, after she is denied an academic award because of her gender, leaves the yeshiva for a secular high school. Potok further expanded his narrative vision in *I Am the Clay,* a novel set in Korea during the Korean War. Evincing Potok's characteristic moral and humanitarian convictions, the story relates the travails of an elderly Korean couple who endure dislocation and chaos by adopting a badly wounded orphan with whom they traverse the countryside and dodge the ravages of war. In *The Gates of November,* Potok follows the family history of Russian Jews who suffer privation and oppression under totalitarian rule in the Soviet Union.

Critical Reception

Potok is highly esteemed for his vivid portrayal of Jewish family life and yeshiva education. His impressive knowledge of Jewish theology and history is also evident in the engaging intellectual debates that often serve as the locus of dramatic tension in his novels. However, some critics view Potok's preoccupation with esoteric religious scholarship as a liability. Though praised for breathing life into such academic matters in *The Chosen* and *The Promise,* Potok has been criticized for relying on stilted dialogue, flat characterizations, predictable plots, and didacticism to expound his philosophical and ethical musings in subsequent novels. His grim depiction of Hasidic life in *The Chosen* also drew condemnation from fundamentalist Jews. Nevertheless, *The Chosen, The Promise, My Name Is Asher Lev, In the Beginning,* and *The Book of Lights* are generally considered his most successful books. The wide appeal of Potok's fiction may be traced to the author's direct narrative style, uncompromising reverence for human life, and ability to paint poignant descriptions of Jewish tradition, communal existence, and parent-child relationships. Potok is also credited for his willingness to tackle serious social and religious issues, particularly those surrounding the dilemma of personal spirituality and Jewish consciousness in the post-Holocaust world.

PRINCIPAL WORKS

The Chosen (novel) 1967
The Promise (novel) 1969
My Name Is Asher Lev (novel) 1972
In the Beginning (novel) 1975
The Jew Confronts Himself in American Literature (criticism) 1975
Wanderings: Chaim Potok's History of the Jews (history) 1978
The Book of Lights (novel) 1981
Davita's Harp (novel) 1985
Ethical Living for a Modern World: Jewish Insights (essays) 1985
The Gift of Asher Lev (novel) 1990
I Am the Clay (novel) 1992
The Tree of Here (for children) 1993
The Sky of Now (for children) 1995
The Gates of November (novel) 1996

CRITICISM

Granville Hicks (review date 29 April 1967)

SOURCE: "Good Fathers and Good Sons," in *Saturday Review,* April 29, 1967, pp. 25-6.

[*In the following review, Hicks offers praise for* The Chosen, *which he describes as "a fine, moving, gratifying book."*]

The impression one gets from most contemporary fiction is that youth today is both disturbed and disturbing. Everyone knows about J. D. Salinger's Holden Caulfield, who, with the best of intentions, gets into one mess after another. But Holden's troubles are nothing compared to the difficulties of other young people we read about. Wright Morris's Jubal Gainer whirls away on his (stolen) motorcycle from crime to crime. John Updike's Rabbit Angstrom runs and runs. The college students in John Nichols's *The Sterile Cuckoo* major in alcohol and sex, but they are tame in comparison with the undergraduates in the late Richard Farina's *Been Down So Long It Looks Like Up to Me.* John Hersey, in *Too Far to Walk,* presents the newest lost generation, complete with LSD. And we are reminded of the hoodlums in the lower depths by such books as Hubert Selby's *Last Exit to Brooklyn.*

We are likely to be startled, therefore, when we are introduced to two brilliant, studious, serious boys, as we are in Chaim Potok's *The Chosen.* Danny Saunders and Reuven Malter are fifteen when we encounter them and they encounter one another, and we leave them after they have been graduated from college, both *summa cum laude.* They have their problems, of course, but these are not the problems that we are used to reading about.

It is a critical commonplace that good boys, like good men and good women, are likely to seem pretty dull in fiction, but Potok succeeds in making his boys interesting as well as credible right from the start. He begins with a softball game, which is essential to the plot and at the same time seizes the reader by his lapel. The scene is Williamsburg, and the time is June of 1944. As a result of the war-time spirit, some of the teachers in the Jewish parochial schools have organized a kind of little league "to show the gentile world that yeshiva students were as physically fit, despite their long hours of study, as any other American student." Reuven Malter, who tells the story, sometimes plays second base and sometimes pitches for the yeshiva he attends. He describes the outlandish appearance of the rival team:

> There were fifteen of them, and they were dressed alike in white shirts, dark pants, white sweaters, and small black skullcaps. In the fashion of the very Orthodox, their hair was closely cropped, except for the area near their ears from which mushroomed the untouched hair that tumbled down into the long sidecurls. Some of them had the beginnings of beards, straggly tufts of hair that stood in isolated clumps on their chins, jawbones, and upper lips. They all wore the traditional undergarment beneath their shirts, and the tzitzis, the long fringes appended to the four corners of the garment, came out above their belts and swung against their pants as they walked. These were the very Orthodox. . . .

The almost demoniacally belligerent leader of the very Orthodox is Danny Saunders, son of the rabbi of a Hasidic synagogue. After a dramatic accident he and Reuven become close friends, and the novel focuses on this friendship and on the relationship between the two sons and their fathers. Reuven's father, a teacher at his yeshiva, is Orthodox but no fanatic, a man of wide knowledge and true tolerance. Reb Saunders, on the other hand, is a zealot, consecrated to the purity of the small sect to which he belongs and held in the utmost reverence by his followers. Both fathers believe in the most rigorous sort of intellectual discipline, and it is no wonder that their sons, one led on by love and the other driven by unsparing severity, excel in school and college.

Because of Reb Saunders's fanaticism his relationship with Danny becomes more and more difficult, and it complicates

Danny's relationship with Reuven. It takes time for the situation to develop to a satisfying conclusion, and Potok handles the passage of the years with marked skill. After the revelation of Hitler's slaughter of the Jews—one million, three million, six million—Reuven's father becomes a staunch and eloquent supporter of Jewish nationalism, and almost wears himself out for the cause. Reb Saunders, however, is an anti-Zionist, arguing that there can be no true Jewish state until the coming of the Messiah. Reuven grows bitter at this, but his father tells him: "The fanaticism of men like Reb Saunders kept us alive for two thousand years of exile. If the Jews of Palestine have an ounce of that same fanaticism and use it wisely, we will soon have a Jewish state." There are times, he has himself learned, when it is not enough to be broad-minded.

Whatever happens, the center of the novel is always the conflict between Danny and his father. It has been taken for granted from his birth that Danny will become a *tzaddik,* a great leader of his people, like his father and grandfather. But, though Danny is a brilliant Talmudist when he is fifteen, he becomes interested in psychology, and before he is graduated from college he has resolved to become a psychologist. The climax towards which the novel builds is the decisive confrontation between Reb Saunders and Danny, which is as surprising as it is moving.

One of the important literary phenomena of the past twenty years is the number of novels written by and about Jews, some of them in the highest rank of contemporary fiction. As has often been pointed out, the persecution and near-extermination of the Jews of Germany and its neighbors had the effect of making Jews in this country acutely aware of themselves as Jews. It has also been said, and I think accurately, that the Jewish writers, in exploring their own predicament, have expressed the sense of alienation that is felt by many men of our times.

The Chosen points to an even more significant conclusion, for it suggests that almost any situation, no matter how unfamiliar to the population in general, may have meaning for the multitude if the author goes deep enough. Who cares about the Hasidim? Not many people, I suppose. But we all know about fanaticism and can recognize that it may have power for good as well as evil. And many of us are either fathers or sons or both. As I began by saying, it is hard to make good boys credible and interesting; it must have been even harder for Chaim Potok to bring to life a pair of good fathers, good in such different ways. But he succeeded, and the result is a fine, moving, gratifying book.

Edmund Fuller (review date 15 May 1967)

SOURCE: "*The Chosen,* Rare, Reverent Novel," in *The Wall Street Journal,* May 15, 1967, p. 18.

[*In the following review, Fuller offers high praise for* The Chosen.]

We are happy to report on a novel of exceptional beauty and freshness. For many readers its combination of theme place and time will be astonishing; elements that seem old, remote, exotic, are shown to be contemporary, close to familiar scenes and rich in meaning for other sorts of lives.

The book is **The Chosen,** by Chaim Potok. At a time when hedonism, vulgarity, brutality, cynicism and corruption are commonplace themes, those of this book are reverence, responsibility, holiness, learning, tradition and the pain of defending these things against the world.

The place is the Williamsburg section of Brooklyn. The time runs from the closing years of the second World War to about 1950. The action is altogether inside a Jewish community that has distinct divisions within itself.

The story begins amusingly on a baseball field with a group of boys about 15 years old. One team is from a school of Orthodox Jews, the other from a school of Hasidic Jews, whose beliefs are so intense and whose ways so rigorous that they regard the merely Orthodox with scorn.

Reuven Malter, who is the narrator, is the son of a respected Orthodox scholar and teacher of the Talmud, the body of Jewish religious law and tradition. Danny Saunders is the son of Reb Saunders, a tzaddik, a holy man, austere and learned, who is the chief rabbi of the local Hasids. Their teams compete with unusual ferocity, like a holy war. Danny hits a ball so hard that it strikes Reuven, the pitcher, in the eye. He is taken to the hospital for eye surgery. From this hostile first encounter, a devoted friendship evolves between Reuven and Danny.

These boys are still part of a closed community—almost closed. Its divisions are from within more than without. They are not yet touched by modes of rebellion so conspicuous today (of course neither were youth in general so affected until some years later). But change, and in a sense, rebellion, are present.

The rule of Reb Saunders, the tzaddik, over the Hasids is virtually absolute, though benevolent. His person is so venerated that the faithful try to touch him as he passes. By tradition, the role of tzaddik is dynastic. Already Danny is the recognized young tzaddik whose whole training is for the succession to this shepherdhood.

Danny, a brilliant scholar, does not simply read books; with his photographic mind he memorizes them. Inevitably in the public library he explores beyond the range of the approved studies of his training. In this, Reuven's father observes that Danny is like the great Spanish Jew of the 12th century, Maimonides, rabbi and physician, who burst the bounds of the pietism of his early training and enlarged the application of Jewish philosophy and theology in his time.

Danny does not want to succeed his father. Reuven, son of the Orthodox teacher, whose father would like him to be a mathematician, wishes to become a rabbi. The development of these extraordinary boys, the relationships that each has with the father of the other, are drawn with tenderness and tension, humor and reverence. Reuven finds disconcertingly that he is a mediator through whom the austere rabbi can communicate with Danny, otherwise sealed from his father by a puzzling silence on the elder's part.

Do not mistake this for a book of interest to Jews only. Its themes are profound and universal, its appeal is to any thoughtful reader, as the musical folk play, *Fiddler on the Roof,* utterly Jewish, has charmed the world. Christendom knows such enclosed groups, clinging to traditions of dress and appearance (the Amish, for instance).

Bitter sectarianism among the devout is also a Christian experience. The struggle to hold fast that which is good is known everywhere. The book touches other universals, too, as a drama of fathers and sons, with the sons' necessary assertion of independence, even in bonds of love.

Chaim Potok (the jacket reveals a strong, fine face) handles superbly the delicate balance of elements, keeping this enclave related to the outer world, from the baseball game to international events, including the establishment of Israel, which occasions some surprising and fascinating reactions. He writes with wisdom, compassion, humor and again, reverence.

Hear Reuven's father, after two heart attacks: "A span of life is nothing. But the man who lives that span, *he* is something. He can fill that tiny span with meaning, so its quality is immeasurable though its quantity may be insignificant. Do you understand what I am saying? A man must fill his life with meaning, meaning is not automatically given to life. It is hard work to fill one's life with meaning. *That* I do not think you understand yet. A life filled with meaning is worthy of rest. I want to be worthy of rest when I am no longer here."

The portrayal of Reb Saunders is a triumph. In Talmudic exposition before the congregation he deliberately introduces mistakes to test Danny—and Reuven on one occasion. We feel the weight of his personality and his quality of holiness, but also a chilling remoteness, as in the seemingly cruel silence he has always maintained with his son except in Tal-

mudic study. We are led to understand the reason even for this, at last, by the wise interpretation of Reuven's father.

When the Hasid realizes that Danny will go from the religious seminary into the world to study psychology at Columbia, he weeps, but blesses him: "All his life he will be a tzaddik. He will be a tzaddik for the world. And the world needs a tzaddik." His ultimate question: "You will remain an observer of the Commandments?" receives Danny's solemn assurance. This is not a change of faith, but of vocation.

This is a rare book of a sort all too easily buried from sight under slam-bang promotions of books in the hour's vogue. Anyone who finds it is finding a jewel. We are much moved by *The Chosen.* It will stay on our bookshelves and be read again.

Sandra Schmidt (review date 20 July 1967)

SOURCE: "Sight Becomes Insight," in *The Christian Science Monitor,* July 20, 1967, p. 5.

[*In the following review, Schmidt offers high praise for* The Chosen.]

The Chosen is a very special book. It deals with a special era—the middle 1940's when war and the end of war was changing the shade of the world—in a special place, the quiet, vivid streets of Williamsburg in Brooklyn, where the heavily Jewish population created an enclave and an atmosphere of special religious and intellectual urgency. The book is a chronicle of intense adolescent friendship between two rather extraordinary boys, and of the unusual relationship in which each stood with his father.

Inner development

The book is also about a certain kind of passage to manhood. The rites are obscure, not the clear Bar Mitzvah that admits the Jewish boy to the community of responsible adults at age 13, but the far more difficult ceremonies that celebrate integrity, compassion, and humanity in the development of the mature man. Danny Saunders is the Hasid, son of the rabbi, the hereditary leader and ruler of a tight ultra-traditional Hasidic community. Destined to follow his father, his phenomenal mind honed by the relentless, precise, and driving study of the Torah which his father demands, he is haunted by a desire for wider, forbidden knowledge—Darwin, Kant, and Freud, and for vistas of life beyond Williamsburg. Reuven Malter, his friend, the "I" of the book, is the son of an Orthodox scholar, raised in a tradition almost as strict but with a mind, merely brilliant, trained to question and explore.

Images of sight and silence frame the episodes of the boys' friendship. A baseball hurled by Danny in a demonically competitive game shatters Reuven's glasses and nearly costs him the sight of one eye—and in the hospital, newly aware of the possibility of darkness, Reuven puts the light of his childhood behind him. Sight becomes insight and as he begins for the first time to see, Reuven begins also to perceive.

Sounding in silence

Reuven was raised in dialogue with his father. Danny's image is silence. His father has not spoken to him, except over interpretations of the Torah, since he was a little boy. It is in listening to this concentrated silence that Danny comes to hear humanity, a sound to which he must respond.

In reviewing **The Chosen** it is impossible not to attempt to explain it. Yet one of the most special qualities of the book is Potok's creation of an intense life that strongly resists explanation. He writes cleanly, with a minimum of detail, and his characters have a spare, introspective honesty that carries conviction. He is also a fine storyteller. Of the many books about Jewish life written in recent years, this is one of the few that does not rely on the automatic connotations, the schmaltz, the Yiddish slang, the Jewish gestalt, to convey its flavor—yet it makes much American Jewish life far more real than, say, *Herzog.* It is a simple, almost meager story about people who are far from typical—yet the warmth and pathos of the dealings between fathers and sons, the understated odyssey from boyhood to manhood, give the book a range that makes it worth anybody's reading.

Times Literary Supplement **(review date 31 August 1967)**

SOURCE: "Trying to Be Jewish," in *Times Literary Supplement,* August 31, 1967, p. 777.

[*In the following excerpt, the critic gives a favorable assessment of* The Chosen.]

Three more novels [Potok's **The Chosen,** Martin Yoseloff's *A Time to be Young,* and Charles Elliott's *The Minority Man*] to add in one way or another to the growing literature of Jewish self-exploration and self-definition, personal and national. . . .

By far the most distinguished of the three, and that in a totally unexpected and unfashionable way, is **The Chosen.** We are back in New York, this time during and just after the last

war. But instead of the search for a new identity amid the slipping faith and lax observance of Murray Ziegler's suburbia there is the fanaticism of the far-out Hasidic sect, which has survived almost unchanged since its establishment in eighteenth-century Poland. It is the story of a friendship between two boys: Reuven, the son of a kindly Orthodox Zionist teacher, and the brilliant Danny, whose father is a fiercely fanatical Hasidic rabbi, whose only verbal contact with his son (according to a traditional Hasidic method of upbringing) is during their Talmudic discussions. The differing claims of their backgrounds upon the boys, the difficulties of a friendship between two orthodoxies, and Danny's fight for release from his inherited role as his father's successor is told within the tight context of total religious belief; the author is himself a rabbi.

Both boys are serious scholars, brilliant and devout, devoted to their basic faith and to their families in a way which makes any rebellion hideously painful. Nothing could be farther from the freedom of Greenwich Village than Danny's anguished struggle to escape from choking orthodoxy without breaking his father's heart. The immediate concerns of the book are totally unfashionable: but the boys' intellectual voracity for symbolic logic, Freud and Talmud are made to seem far more relevant and exciting than anything in Charles Elliott's Libya. The climax of the book, Rabbi Saunders's emotional agony for his son's soul, has a tragic poignancy and exhilaration.

Richard Freedman (review date 14 September 1969)

SOURCE: "A Warm Glow in a Cruel, Cold World," in *Washington Post Book World,* September 14, 1969, p. 3.

[*In the following review, Freedman commends Potok's "vivid" characterizations and narrative presentation of* The Promise, *but finds shortcomings in his excessive exposition of Jewish theology.*]

One of the few remaining pleasures we get from reading popular contemporary novels is that they are filled with well-researched information about a particular place, occupation or way of life. This helps salve the consciences of the swelling horde of readers who feel that fiction is a waste of time.

Thus, from *Hawaii* we learn the detailed history of that exotic state, and *Airport* tells us why we are right to prefer trains. This massive accumulation of facts, with a banal story line and styrofoam characters, is not the loftiest goal of fiction, but it is a time-honored one. As Mary McCarthy once observed, you can get some really workable recipes out of *Anna Karenina,* and you learn a lot about whaling from

Moby Dick. From the novels of Dr. Chaim Potok, a graduate of Yeshiva University and the Jewish Theological Seminary, you learn all about Judaism.

His first novel, **The Chosen,** contained a long expository chapter about the history and traditions of the Hasidic sect in the Williamsburg section of Brooklyn during World War II.

It was deservedly successful, however, not because it made clear the doctrinal differences between the Hasidim and other Orthodox Jews, but because its wealth of arcane lore was successfully dramatized in the story of two friends growing up amid the conflicts created by warring religious denominations. Its heroes, Reuven Malter and Danny Saunders, were believable boys, not too distantly removed, really, from Tom Sawyer and Huckleberry Finn.

Potok's new novel, **The Promise,** suffers from a slight case of sequelitis. The boys are older now. Reuven is studying for the rabbinate; Danny has managed to break away from his Old Testament patriarch of a father to do graduate work in psychology at Columbia.

Reuven struggles against the fanatical fundamentalism of one of his teachers; Danny struggles to wrest the mind and soul of his fiancée's cousin from the grip of schizophrenia, ingeniously using equal parts of Freud and the Talmud. As in **The Chosen,** the characterizations are vivid, the incidents dramatic, the narrative fluid.

Both novels are leagues above the facile, *haimish* Yiddishkeit of a *Fiddler on the Roof* or a *Wednesday Afternoon the Rabbi Ate Blintzes.* There isn't even an overbearing, chicken-soup-wielding mother in the cast.

Yet it is the very intellectual dignity, the gift for austere but fascinating exposition of problems in Jewish scholarship which so distinguish Potok, which also tend to clog **The Promise** and make it a bit disappointing.

What we get, essentially, is layers of Talmudic lore of the highest interest (but irrelevant to fiction) sandwiched between rather ordinary insights into human situations. Shy boys hate their successful fathers, and Potok serves this up as his denouement. Rabbis who escaped Hitler's ovens can be nasty and vindictive, and Potok seems surprised that outrageous suffering doesn't always make us mellow.

In both novels, for instance, he is concerned with bigotry: not between Jew and Gentile, but between Jew and Jew. Reuven has been brought up by his father to be a modern historical critic of the Talmud, employing the kind of scientific exegesis of ancient texts which stunned the Christian world a century ago when it was applied to the Gospels.

The wrath this arouses among the diehard Hasidim nearly costs him his ordination. Potok understands that modern scholarship is necessary, but he also understands the motives underlying old-guard resistance to it. What he doesn't seem to comprehend is that religion by its very nature is a fecund producer of bigotry—with or without reason—and anyone who gets involved in it should be prepared for the consequences.

Over all there is a glow of humane erudition and compassion which suggests that Potok would be an ideal rabbi. But the world of art is a cruel, capricious one, and sometimes an out-and-out monster like Dostoyevsky can render more of the real quality of religious experience than an obviously nice, reasonable man like Chaim Potok.

Dorothy Rabinowitz (review date May 1970)

SOURCE: "Sequels," in *Commentary,* Vol. 49, May, 1970, pp. 104, 106, 108.

[*In the following excerpt, Rabinowitz offers a mixed assessment of* The Promise, *faulting it for intrusive or overly academic psychologizing among the characters.*]

. . . [Chaim Potok's] **The Promise** is no disappointment as its fore-runner, **The Chosen,** is no masterpiece. **The Chosen** stayed at the top of the best-seller list for reasons which are easy enough to imagine. The story of Danny and Reuven and the Brooklyn Hasidic world begins, in **The Chosen,** with a now-famous baseball game in which Reuven's eye is fairly torn out of his head by Danny, batting fiercely for the Yeshiva team out to beat the *apikorsim.* Indeed, the first sixty pages of that novel gave fair promise of an interesting storyteller at work. Very soon thereafter in **The Chosen,** one sees that nothing of that promise will be sustained. After a first fine start, Mr. Potok declines into tract-like psychology with, I suppose, endearing spiritual qualities.

Mr. Potok's problem in **The Promise,** which is exactly worthy of its predecessor, is not with his subject matter. Indeed, the world he apostrophizes in both novels is a rich one. **The Promise** continues with Reuven—his father's son—struggling to stand somewhere between zealots and mere lovers of the Torah, and with Danny, Hasid turned psychologist, doing graduate work at Columbia. Mr. Potok's problem is not lack of a story. He is a yarn spinner, and he knows what a plot is. Mr. Potok's problem is his sensibility—a fatal deficiency, considering his craft. In Mr. Potok's case, the sensibility which is father to language is Jewish-American genteel, and academic to the bone. A standard Potok rendering flows effortless:

Danny went into a lengthy psychological analysis of Willy Loman's delusions and talked about how crucial it was to be able to distinguish between reality and fantasy.

Danny and Reuven talk. This is a novel of many conversations. Typically:

"Yes," he said, "I can understand violence if a person makes a rational decision that his world is utterly evil. . . ."

"Not many people can make a decision like that rationally."

"They ought to read some good books."

"Marx read a lot of good books."

"Marx was full of rage. Books don't do much good when you're that full of rage."

"We're all full of rage. That's something I've begun to think about these days. Who isn't full of rage?"

"Yes. But most people manage one way or another to handle it."

"Why are people so full of rage? How would your friend Freud answer that?"

Such dialogue, sustained as it is with Mr. Potok throughout—for that is the language the sensibility *naturally* assumes—can only be anti-affect in its proprieties. Perhaps Mr. Potok is one of those novelists who will profit by translation into another language. Many are the moving scenes Mr. Potok is about to have, many he conceives. All are muffled in speeches. In addition, a special form of genteel educational psychologizing intrudes, along with a heavily explicit rendering of every thought of every character who has one. (Danny tugs at nonexistent side-locks all through, in an endless motif of allegiance.) It ought to be noted for fans of Mr. Potok and fans of parallelism in general, that there is a spirited volleyball game in the sequel.

Washington Post Book World (review date 3 December 1978)

SOURCE: "Diaspora," in *Washington Post Book World*, December 3, 1978, p. E5.

[*In the following review, the critic finds shortcomings in*

Wanderings but marks the presence of "occasionally brilliant" passages.]

Babylonian chroniclers wrote, in two columns, the histories of Assyria and Babylonia side by side; during their captivity in Babylonia, Jewish scribes adopted the practice as they synchronized the histories of Judah and Israel. In a way, Chaim Potok now has done the same thing, matching the reigns of Abraham and Saul and David to the advancing civilizations of Mesopotamia, Egypt, Greece, Rome, and tracing the movements of the Hebrew peoples eventually through the development of Islam and Christianity. It is an intriguing concept, and one which lends a more solid basis to the ambiguous history related in the Bible. Unfortunately, Potok, who has formerly stuck to fiction for his explorations of Judaic culture, cannot prevent these massive civilizations from overshadowing the Hebrew tribes. As a matter of organization, he has left the Hebrews for last in each section, so that they seem tacked on. Potok has little control over his style, which staggers from prose to parchment to homily. And, he slips into pseudo-Biblical language ("Now these are the achievements of Solomon son of David, king of Judah and Israel"). With its clumsy and sometimes even ungrammatical style, and its excessive punctuation, reading this book is like traversing the Rocky Mountains one hill at a time. And just to make it more difficult, the publishers have chosen a stark and exhausting typeface. However, the saving graces are the occasionally brilliant interpretations of prophetic passages from the Bible, and the beautifully chosen illustrations.

J. D. Reed (review date 19 October 1981)

SOURCE: "Illuminations," in *Time*, October 19, 1981, p. 102.

[*In the following review, Reed offers a favorable assessment of* The Book of Lights.]

Albert Einstein ponders the young rabbi's last name: "Loran. That is, I believe, also the name of a navigational instrument, is it not?" As usual, the physicist is correct: the acronym for long-range navigation also describes the hero of Chaim Potok's fifth and most ambitious novel. Although the author has retained a strong narrative drive, he has abandoned the matzo-barrel homilies that marked such early works as *The Chosen* and *The Promise*. Once again his themes are ethnic, but his concerns are universal.

Orphaned in the late '30s, when his parents were killed in a now forgotten Arab-Israeli battle, Gershon Loran is raised by an uncle in a Brooklyn ghetto. Surrounded by squalor, the teen-ager refuses to succumb to despair. One summer night, he watches a mongrel bitch give birth to a litter of puppies. In a sudden rush of insight, resting on the roof of a tenement, he is seized by the miraculous: "He felt all caught up in the life of Heaven and earth, in the mystery of creation, in the pain and inexhaustible glory of this single moment." *The Book of Lights* charts Loran's search to re-create that epiphany.

In college and later the seminary, Loran retreats from humanity, abandoning the generous philosophy of the Talmud for the magical pronouncements of the Kabbalah. A fellow student wonders: "Do you transform yourself in the night? Do you become a Rabbi Hyde?" No; Loran remains Rabbi Jekyll, a self-described *Zwischenmensch*, a between-man, traversing the border between reality and self-delusion. His girlfriend acutely observes, "Your eyes go somewhere else."

Certainly they are not focused on her, or on his roommate Arthur Leiden, one of Potok's most complex and compelling characters. Leiden's father was a parent of the atomic bomb. The son's heritage is a lifelong nightmare of incinerated birds in his Los Alamos backyard. But if Leiden Jr. is damned at night, he distributes blessings by day: he induces his family to aid Gershon with a scholarship; later Leiden prevails upon "Uncle Albert" Einstein to make the journey from Princeton to the graduation. The favors are not returned; Loran is too busy probing his own psyche. He has plenty of company. In '50s America, the Holocaust is not yet an obsession. Instead, Topic A in synagogues and cafeterias is the sins committed *by* Jews. The elder Leiden reflects, "We tinker with light and atomic bombs . . . No one is on more familiar terms with the heart of the insanity in the universe than is the Jew, and no one is more frenetic and untidy in the search for an answer . . . We offer apocalypses in a pushcart."

And in starched khaki. Still searching for transcendence, Loran enlists in the Army to become the only rabbi in post-truce Korea. As the young chaplain ministers to occupation troops, he wrestles less with the Kabbalah than with morale reports and charts of the VD rate for enlisted men. On leave, he wanders around Japan ill at ease in the crowded cities and out of place in the temples of Kyoto. In Hiroshima, where "all the darkness and light of the species" lurks in the ruins, he is joined by Leiden, now a fellow chaplain. Before the monument to the dead, Leiden recites Kaddish, the prayer for mourners. As a polite but stunned Japanese couple watch in the cold wind of the peace park, Loran sounds an amen that is wrenched from his soul. At last he has found a moral location, an identity outside of selfhood.

The novelist's prose may be excessively plain, but neither his text nor his cast is simple. Potok knows that personal illuminations, like those of physics, are transitory: the glow of a Brooklyn coal furnace, the sunshine on Mount Fuji, the ambiguous light of the atom and the consolations of philoso-

phy do not stay. They must be discovered again and again, generation after generation. Ironically, it is that sense of impermanence that grants the novel its sense of durability and makes it, literally, a book of lights.

John H. Timmerman (essay date 16 May 1984)

SOURCE: "A Way of Seeing: Chaim Potok and Tradition," in *The Christian Century,* May 16, 1984, pp. 515-18.

[*In the following essay, Timmerman examines the tension among individuality, personal growth, and the force of tradition in Potok's fiction.*]

During the past decade Chaim Potok has emerged not only as a pre-eminent American author, but also as one whose books are avidly and widely read. Why has this Jewish author whose books are openly religious in theme and tenor achieved such uncommon public success? Why does he appeal to this age, saturated as it is with the expressive realism that oozes from books, films and television? In a sense Potok addresses those very questions, for the central theme of all of his books has been the enduring and changing religious tradition of a people, and how that tradition shapes the present moment and is shaped by it. As a result, Potok's books leap beyond narrow categories and become universally appealing. His protagonists, always young men of pronounced individual convictions, carry on a warfare with their tradition and, to varying degrees, find their own place and nature in relation to it. Thus, these are the stories of all humankind living in the ongoing matrix of religious, ethnic and cultural beliefs.

In public lectures Potok has often directly addressed people's conflicts with their traditions. These conflicts, the central issue of his fiction, are formulated by the author as providing three possibilities for interaction. A person can totally reject his or her tradition, but this, in Potok's estimation, is reprehensible. Second, he or she may wholly capitulate to tradition and be subsumed by it, an alternative perhaps worse than the first, since it both locks the rest of life out and locks the life of the tradition in. Untouched by any fresh idea, unruffled by any change, such a life constitutes a prison of unmitigated spiritual and artistic sterility. The third alternative, and the healthiest one in Potok's estimation, is the presence of some tension between the individual and tradition, a willingness to question and be questioned. Such spiritual flexibility allows both to grow. At the conclusion of his history of the Jewish people, *Wanderings,* Potok states:

> In some future time, eyes will gaze upon us as we have gazed in his book upon worlds of the past. They will say of us either that we used our new free-

dom . . . to vanish as a people, or that we took advantage of the secret opportunity concealed within the persistent but hidden trauma we are now experiencing—a Jewry and Judaism decisively changed by its confrontation with modern paganism—to re-educate ourselves, rebuild our core from the treasure of our past, fuse it with the best in secularism, and create a new philosophy, a new literature, a new world of Jewish art, a new community, and take seriously the meaning of the word emancipation—a release from the authority of the father in order to become adults in our own right.

The question that the young protagonists of his novels begin to ask of their fathers is, "Can we trust our tradition sufficiently to grow with it, or must we only guard it jealously as a precious memory?"

This issue, which David Stern suggests is "the dilemma of modern Judaism itself" ("Two Worlds," *Commentary* [October 1972]), focuses squarely on how the law for living is conceived within the tradition. If the law is an end in itself, as Reb Saunders of *The Chosen* believes, then clearly there is no room for individual vision. It also then necessarily follows that the law is a static codification of rules, perhaps empty of spiritual vigor. Locked in place at one time, it makes all future time conform to itself. Individual actions must bend backward to achieve this conformity. But the law does not have to be conceived in this manner—and should not be.

Torah is an untranslatable word; as such, it means many things. Isaac C. Rottenberg points out that

> Torah means 'teaching,' 'instruction,' and 'guidance,' but none of these words alone nor all of them together exhaust its meaning, because in the last analysis 'Torah' refers to God's own gracious and righteous presence. Laws, statutes, and precepts are part of Torah, but they are not its essence. Torah must be primarily understood in dynamic terms, not as a set of legal rules ["Law and Sin in Judaism and Christianity," the *Reformed Journal* (November 1979)].

The last sentence particularly is of striking importance. Torah is a means for ordering life, not for dictating life. *Halacha,* precepts leading to the way of a sanctified life, is not a set of rules, but a dynamic, living guide for life. The precepts are not carved in stone, but etched on the spirit—which may respond to, be stimulated by, and receive guidance from them. Because the law is not an end in itself, but a teleological guide to right action, people must be allowed considerable freedom in their exercise of it. The temptation is to use the law to circumscribe life. Rottenberg points out

that "Judaism is deeply aware of the *vetzer hara,* the evil urge which operates within the human heart and makes our lives the scene of a continual moral struggle." Precisely because they clearly recognize the problem of evil, people may try to use the law as a means to avoid moral struggle, rather than to engage in that struggle, with its attendant risks. In *My Name Is Asher Lev,* Potok depicts such a situation in the parents' fear that Asher Lev's artistic vision may come from the *sitra achra*—the Other Side.

We might put the situation a bit differently. People who are aware of the very real presence of the *sitra achra,* which threatens to destroy the tradition, might believe that they must shut their eyes to such a threat. They might feel compelled to shun even the conception of such a threat, lest a chink be found in tradition's armor that, once admitting a corrosive freedom, would eat away at its very supports, eventually bringing about the collapse of the entire structure. A person may try to save a house that seems in danger of falling by shielding it in an armor of steel. But one may also feel the strength of the tradition so powerfully that one opens wide one's vision to life. By freely engaging life, this alternative suggests, tradition grows stronger, gaining muscle through hard experience.

Such is the clear option in two of Potok's best-known novels, *The Chosen* and *My Name Is Asher Lev,* both stories about young Jews coming to a point of decision about their tradition and their individual lives.

Potok has structured both books around the central metaphor of the human eye, or human seeing. Those who use tradition as a means of seclusion from the world are repeatedly described as having narrowing eyes, blank eyes or shut eyes. But those who use it as a base from which to engage the world hold their eyes wide open.

In *The Chosen,* the metaphor rises out of the initial action of the book, a lively and competitive baseball game in which Danny Saunders raps a line drive that strikes Reuven Malter in the eye. Temporarily blinded by the blow—and waking up for the first time to a recognition of himself and his tradition—Reuven recovers in a hospital ward peopled with tragic representatives of life: the nearly blind ex-boxer who has been pummeled brutally and chatters incessantly, and the small boy who stares ceaselessly with blind eyes. This ward of readjusted vision is also the threshold for Reuven's refocusing vision of life: "I lay there a long time, thinking about my eyes." The image of the eye is developed steadily throughout the book, and eventually becomes clearly associated with the conflict between the individual and the tradition. "What's inside us is the greatest mystery of all," says Danny at one point. That exploration of oneself is perhaps life's ultimate adventure. The novel suggests two ways to go about it, one quick and superficial, the other hard and deep.

Reuven's reflection on the two ways to study Torah strikes a forceful analogy:

> Rabbinic literature can be studied in two different ways, in two directions, one might say. It can be studied quantitatively or qualitatively—or, as my father once put it, horizontally or vertically. The former involves covering as much material as possible, without attempting to wrest from it all its implications and intricacies; the latter involves confining oneself to one single area until it is exhaustively covered, and then going on to new material. . . . The ideal, of course, was to be able to do both.

For Potok, a person needs to be deeply rooted in tradition, while also attempting the broad view of life. Always the individual person is the vital link between the bedrock of tradition and the flow of life. "'I learned a long time ago, Reuven,'" says Mr. Malter, "'that a blink of an eye in itself is nothing. But the eye that blinks, *that* is something. A span of life is nothing. But the man who lives that span, *he* is something.'"

Finally, it is people who fulfill the law, not the law that fulfills people. People forge and effect a tradition as much as they are forged by it. The argument of Potok's fiction is for that freedom within the tradition that allows people to hold their eyes open.

For Potok, a person needs to be deeply rooted in tradition, while also attempting the broad view of life. Always the individual person is the vital link between the bedrock of tradition and the flow of life.
—*John H. Timmerman*

In *Asher Lev,* this tension becomes more stark in the compelling drama of a young artist exploring both his gift and his relation to his tradition. The book is even more deliberately structured by the eye metaphor than is *The Chosen.* Many of the novel's characters almost seem to be acting on a stage, in full dramatic posture, with the author providing calculated stage directions. As on the stage, much of what is left unsaid is conveyed by mannerism—here particularly, eye mannerisms. Asher Lev's mother fears her son's gift, recognizing its potential for endangering their tradition. Her eyes are consequently detailed in alternating images of great fear and abject resignation. Early in the book Asher notes that "I saw a flicker of light in her eyes," but when the subject of painting is brought up "the dead look returned to her eyes." When she becomes ill and Asher promises to draw a pretty picture for her, "Her eyes fluttered faintly but remained closed."

The father, whose occupation and preoccupation are to bring others *into* the tradition, to cement the body of believers, reacts with vitriolic anger to Asher's flirting with the *sitra achra* (he readily identifies Asher's painting as such). Repeatedly his eyes are described as "dark," "tired," "narrowing" and "squinting."

In contrast, as an artist Asher Lev discovers his vision always opening. It is important to note that he considers himself "an orthodox Jew." He stands *not* in open rebellion against, but as a troubled seeker of, his place within a tradition. He manifests most clearly and dramatically what we also find in Potok's other young heroes, Reuven Malter and David Lurie.

In the novel's early scenes, Asher Lev frequently stands by the window of his parents' apartment, looking toward the street below. This prison symbolism is embellished in Lev's controversial painting "Brooklyn Crucifixion." In the picture, Lev's mother is tied to the venetian blinds of the apartment window, her arms outstretched in an anguished crucifix. The window functions metaphorically as the threshold between tradition and the larger world. While Asher persists in looking outward, his mother and father are careful to keep the venetian blinds drawn. These blinds are frequently askew, often awkwardly knotted up so that the outside world and inner tradition persist in tortured meeting. Finally, the mother is a slave to the blinds, tied there by the father's austere legalism. In the painting the father looks at the crucified mother, but he does not release her. The three, mother, father and son, portray varying degrees of dealing with tradition as it is metaphorically represented by the window: the father solidly within, the mother caught by the mesh of blinds and the son persistently peering outward.

Lev's outward-looking vision is not simply an impudent rebellion. He cannot help the way he sees. His artistic drive and vision persist in breaking through, as he comes, with terror, to understand:

> That was the night I began to realize something was happening to my eyes. I looked at my father and saw lines and planes I had never seen before. I could feel with my eyes. . . . I felt myself flooded with the shapes and textures of the world around me. I closed my eyes. But I could still see that way inside my head. I was seeing with another pair of eyes that had suddenly come awake.

To try to kill that vision, he realizes, would be to kill himself. In an anguished scene of self-analysis he takes his stand within, but against, a tradition of static law. Compelled finally to complete the crucifixion painting, Lev recognizes that

> it would have made me a whore to leave it incomplete. It would have made it easier to leave a future work incomplete. It would have made it more and more difficult to draw upon that additional aching surge of effort that is always the difference between integrity and deceit in a created work. I would not be the whore to my own existence. Can you understand that? I would not be the whore to my own existence.

But even in so saying, he remains within the tradition. He is "an observant Jew." Thus, while standing *against* the static, legalistic elements of his tradition, he seeks to find his place *within* its dynamic impulses.

Figuring significantly in that process is the crusty old painter, Jacob Kahn, who tutors Lev in the realities of the larger world. At once tender and harsh, arrogant and loving, of keen vision and tormented spirit, Kahn is a strange guide to the spiritually wandering youth. It is important to note, however, that Kahn has been appointed to his heuristic task by the rabbi and has, therefore, received the blessing of the spiritual leader of the faith. The sum of Kahn's teaching may be encapsulated in a quotation from a book, *The Art of the Spirit*, which, ironically, is given to Lev by his mother after she hears that he is being tutored by Kahn:

> Every great artist is a man who has freed himself from his family, his nation, his race. Every man who has shown the world the way to beauty, to true culture, has been a rebel, a "universal" without patriotism, without home, who has found his people everywhere.

Jacob Kahn succeeds where other characters fail: he points out clearly the risks involved in this other world that lies beyond the window of Lev's tradition—and the risks are genuine. The strength of tradition resides in the security it provides. Indeed, to refocus for a moment on the concept of *halacha,* the reason for any codification of law is to attempt a structured certitude within that law. To live *halacha* properly in the dynamic flux of existence is an act of risk and of considerable daring. As Asher Lev discovers, and as Jacob Kahn well knows, it can be a life of anguish. So it is that he immediately counsels Lev to return to his tradition

> "Jacob," the woman said softly. "You are frightening the boy."

> "It is my intention to frighten him out of his wits. I want him to go back to Brooklyn and remain a nice

Jewish boy. What does he need this for, Anna?"

"What did you need it for, Jacob?"

"I know what I went through," he said.

Kahn would spare the boy the pain of the exposed life, of the questioning spirit assaulted by the world's answers. If one persists in asking the right questions, however, and if one possesses the steely courage to sort through the world's answers, this crucible of tension refines and strengthens. Moreover, as a pilgrim in the outside world, the seeker may learn better the place that is his last refuge, his art.

Not all the torment arises from the world outside tradition. In fact, this world is so large that it offers a different kind of security: anonymity, a kind of rootlessness in the face less crowd. It offers security, moreover, from those within the tradition who would gladly reject the troubled seeker. A note is slipped into Asher Lev's Gemara one day:

> Asher Lev
> Won't go to Heav;
> To hell he'll go
> Far down below.

This is perhaps the greater pain: not rejecting one's tradition, but being rejected by it. Where does the seeker go then? If tradition is sometimes a bed of misunderstanding and hatred, and the world a maze of ready but insufficient answers, is he or she left to walk a precarious tightrope buffeted by forces beyond his or her control?

In a sense, Potok's answer is Yes. But one can learn, through experience and effort, to walk that tightrope with confidence. The tormented young protagonists of Potok's novels will never be at ease. The discovery of their individuality is their important task, however—their life-consuming task. After Lev's first summer in Provincetown with Jacob Kahn, he tells his father: "That's what art is, Papa. It's a person's private vision expressed in aesthetic forms." It is a language that few understand, and its vocabulary is ill suited to neat answers which will still the ire of tradition or lay straight the world's maze. It is a private vision that rises from and through the individual, to be expressed in forms constituting the only real language a person can know. For Potok, the solution to the problem of our relationship to tradition seems to lie in precisely this kind of willful person who does not attempt to destroy his or her tradition or to embrace the world wholly, but who builds some bridge, however flimsy, between the two. If this reconciler's language is imperfect and imprecise at first, perhaps we can grow to understand it as we study its vocabulary. Lev discovers his place in the dynamic flux of his heritage, and learns that he is called to work his own unique *mitzvot*—deeds that fulfill God's will. The tension with tradition is not thereby erased, but it is, perhaps, resolved.

People, Lev learns, must by themselves resolve the tension between tradition and the outside world. Compelled, after the exhibit of the crucifixion paintings, to live outside his tradition by his rabbi's orders, Lev seeks solace in the realization that "we must give a balance to the universe." As he leaves home, his parents watch from the living room window. One imagines the hand raised to the cord of the venetian blinds.

Time (review date 25 March 1985)

SOURCE: A review of *Davita's Harp*, in *Time*, March 25, 1985, pp. 80-1.

[*In the following review, the critic gives a mixed evaluation of* Davita's Harp.]

The earnest radicalism of the 1930s has become familiar terrain for fiction. Chaim Potok, a chronicler of the factions within American Jewish culture (*The Chosen, My Name Is Asher Lev*), assiduously attempts to freshen the milieu: his title character and narrator is a thoughtful, believable preadolescent girl; her father is a celebrated radical journalist from an old-line, plutocratic Wasp family, her mother a Jewish émigré.

The narrative deftly captures Davita's particular sense of placelessness and evokes a child's view of events. But in explaining the parents' political fervor and in analyzing their times, *Davita's Harp* too often limits itself to predictable externalities. Potok relies heavily on the imagination of other artists: the explanation for Davita's father's alienation from his timber-tycoon forebears, for example, is that he witnessed a real-life scene of antiunion violence that is vividly evoked in John Dos Passos' *1919,* and Davita comes to understand him by reading the book. He also introduces a surrogate uncle to Davita, a refugee writer whose fables are full of images that heavy-handedly foreshadow Picasso's *Guernica.* Then Davita's father dies as a hero during the bombing at Guernica. Soon after, the child intuitively envisions the battle in Picasso-like terms. Later she sees the work of art and recoils in recognition and insight beyond her years. As the story evolves, the focus shifts from Davita's dogmatic, unhappy parents to her own quiet revolution: yearning for a sense of identity and excluded from the adult world of politics, she becomes a fervent Jew and eventually challenges the patriarchal presumptions of her religion. During the conflict between Davita's reverence for Hebraic tradition and her determination to make a place for herself, the narrative

becomes far livelier and suggests possibilities for a worthier sequel.

Paul Cowan (review date 31 March 1985)

SOURCE: "The Faiths of Her Childhood," in *The New York Times Book Review,* March 31, 1985, pp. 12-13.

[*In the following review, Cowan offers a favorable assessment of* Davita's Harp, *which he describes as "Mr. Potok's bravest book, though it is not his best."*]

Chaim Potok is a writer who defies easy categorization. Though he does not have the instinct for the fast-paced plots and sleek characters that usually make novels popular and though he has not attracted the intellectual following of a Saul Bellow, still, four of his five novels and his one nonfiction book have been best sellers. By exploring the themes that fascinate him, Mr. Potok has opened a new clearing in the forest of American literature.

Davita's Harp is Mr. Potok's bravest book, though it is not his best. It will almost certainly be one of his most popular. Set in New York during the 1930's, it portrays the lives of Communist Party members and religious Jews. Until Mr. Potok's novel *The Chosen,* almost all popular American Jewish fiction—like most ethnic American fiction—focused on protagonists intent on escaping their childhood environments. The characters who were born in Saul Bellow's Chicago and Philip Roth's Newark may remember the neighborhoods they grew up in with affection or rage; their adult speech may retain traces of immigrant English; they may feel tangled emotions toward a parent they have left behind. But they set out to create themselves anew.

Most of Mr. Potok's characters leave their childhood environments too, at considerable pain to the people who love them. In *The Chosen,* Danny Saunders, who was expected to inherit his father's role as a Hasidic rabbi in Brooklyn, decided to study psychiatry. Conversely, in *The Book of Lights,* Arthur Leiden, primed to follow in his father's footsteps and become one of the great physicists of his age, left the genteel scientific community his parents inhabited—paradoxically, the community that created the atomic bomb—to become a rabbi. But the worlds in which Mr. Potok's characters grew up retain a tight hold on their loyalties. Danny Saunders, Arthur Leiden and now Davita Chandal in *Davita's Harp* are all haunted by memories of the past that echo in their present.

Davita is the daughter of Michael Chandal, a gentile from Maine, a left-wing journalist whose father, a lumber magnate, has disinherited him, and Channah Chandal, a Jewish woman from Poland, a Marxist intellectual whose dreadful memories of her stern Hasidic father have left her disillusioned with religion. For the first quarter of the novel, the Chandals' political work sustains them emotionally as they live like urban gypsies, evicted by one landlord after another. They are protected materially by Ezra Dinn, an Orthodox Jew and Channah's friend since childhood.

These are some of Mr. Potok's most disappointing pages. Though Michael is a robust, loving father, Channah—like so many mothers in Mr. Potok's novels—is a somewhat sickly, withdrawn woman. The Chandals talk about the political horrors of the 30's—the Spanish Civil War, Italy's invasion of Ethiopia, lynchings in the South—without ever explaining them to their baffled, terrified daughter. Since Davita, a child when the novel begins, is the novel's sole voice—and since she is so often bewildered—she (and Mr. Potok) fails to furnish much insight into her troubled parents. But Mr. Potok's prose style is so rich that even these pages have an enchanting quality. Soon Channah Chandal's Orthodox *landsmen* find the family an apartment in the Crown Heights section of Brooklyn. That is the urban soil Mr. Potok always describes with a master's certainty. While living in Crown Heights and in the summertime community of Sea Gate, Davita meets a young girl who is a refugee from the Spanish Civil War. She also comes to love a surrogate uncle, a left-wing writer her mother knew as a young woman. Presently the United States Government sends her uncle back to Hitler's Europe. History begins to shape the child's consciousness.

At the same time, Davita ricochets between the religions her parents have rejected. Michael's sister Sarah, a Christian missionary, often stays with the family. One summer she invites Davita to spend time with her in Maine. She teaches the child to pray on her knees and encourages her to believe in Jesus. Davita loves Aunt Sarah but not her creed. Though Davita's parents don't observe any religious ceremonies, the girl is delighted by the way her Orthodox neighbors greet the Sabbath. Their Judaism appeals to her more than Aunt Sarah's Christianity.

As Davita comes to life, so does the book. She can't bear her beloved father's compulsive need to cover the civil war in Spain. He seems to be choosing politics over her. The Sabbaths she experiences intrigue her so much she begins to attend the neighborhood synagogue despite the fact that her mother rejects religion, despite the fact that almost all the yeshiva boys make derisive remarks to the ignorant girl whose father is a gentile. When her father is killed in Spain, Davita insists on saying the mourner's kaddish in the woman's section of the synagogue. In the 1930's this was so rare as to seem almost heretical. But as Davita becomes an increasingly observant Jew—and soon a brilliant student

in a Brooklyn yeshiva—she continues to insist on her rights as a woman within the limits of Orthodox law.

At the very end of the novel, after Davita, now in her early teens, has been denied a prize in the study of the Talmud because she is a girl, she imagines the speech she would have delivered if she had won the award. It reflects the faiths of her childhood—Judaism and radicalism: "I wanted to say that my mother was once badly hurt in Poland because she was a Jewish woman, and my father was killed while trying to save a nun in Guernica, and my uncle died in part because of his politics and in part because he wrote strange stories. I wanted to say that I'm very frightened to be living in this world and I don't understand most of the things I see and hear and I don't know what will happen to me and to the family I love. I wanted to say that I would try to find and join with the side of America that wouldn't hurt people who [fight for justice], and that I would also try not to let this century defeat me."

As the imagined speech suggests, *Davita's Harp* is full of the horrors of the 20th century. As in all of Chaim Potok's novels, those horrors don't simply exist in the minds of intellectuals. They are not symbols. Hitler's death camps, Franco's troops, the atomic bomb kill people the reader has come to love and alter the survivors' lives completely.

Yet they don't defeat Mr. Potok's characters. For there is a sweet, loving bond that links their lives, a bond symbolized by the gentle tones of the small harp that has been fixed to a door wherever Davita has lived. A frail glory infuses the world these people see when they open their doors and windows each morning. Those qualities are unusual in modern fiction. They draw the reader into Chaim Potok's world. The people he depicts live in a community held together by ancient laws. Those people nourish each other in the worst of times. In doing so, they nourish Mr. Potok's readers too.

Cynthia Grenier (review date 29 April 1985)

SOURCE: "In Search of a Spiritual Pacifier," in *The Wall Street Journal*, April 29, 1985, p. 22.

[*In the following review, Grenier praises the "genuine seriousness and moral complexity" of* Davita's Harp, *but finds shortcomings in Potok's "stiff dialogue and stilted characters."*]

Chaim Potok owes much of his popularity as a writer to his handling of Judaic scenes in contemporary American life (***The Chosen, The Promise,*** etc.).

This time, in ***Davita's Harp,*** Mr. Potok heads into new, highly topical territory—woman's role in the Jewish faith—set in the context of American communism in the 1930s. In what may have been a rash venture, he has chosen as his narrative voice that of his pre-pubescent heroine, who recounts her life from birth to menstruation.

Davita is the daughter of two deeply committed Communist Party members—he's the radical son of an old New England family, she's a Russian-Jewish victim of a pogrom. Party meetings are held in their New York apartment, where the harp of the book's title hangs on the door, symbolizing a security that neither religion nor politics can give our heroine. "Again and again I heard the names Roosevelt, Hitler, Stalin, Mussolini, Franco," says Davita. "I heard strange words. Republic, militia, rebellion, coup d'etat, garrison. . . . And names with menacing sounds. Anarchist, Falangist, Fascist."

Soon Davita is piping up in the first grade to tell her classmates that "Stalin is a Communist. He is not afraid to use his power for good purposes." Caution is rapidly instilled when a fellow first grader from an Italian family takes threatening exception to her description of Mussolini as a fascist.

During these early years the family is poor but happy. They know they are working toward the building of what they confidently expect to be a better world.

But then Davita's father, off in Spain for an unidentified "progressive" newspaper, is blown up while trying to rescue a nun in Guernica. Her anguished mother bravely soldiers on for the party and is about to enter into a second marriage with a fellow Communist when Hitler and Stalin sign their 1939 nonaggression pact. Davita remembers the news announcement:

> "My mother turned off the radio. 'Capitalist lies,' she said. 'What they go through to slander us!'
>
> 'What does it mean?' I asked.
>
> 'Never mind.'
>
> 'What does nonagression pact mean?'
>
> 'Finish your supper, Davita.'"

Utterly destroyed morally and psychologically after she is expelled from the party for questioning Stalin's wisdom, Davita's mother is eventually saved by the love of her widowed cousin, an Orthodox Jew and successful lawyer. Remarried, she returns quite easily to the observant Judaism of her Odessa girlhood, although she still reads the New Masses—"for the fine writers it published." As for those years of Stalinist communism, she speaks with a voice that "shook with anger and bitterness, with her sense of having been used and duped and betrayed."

As Davita tells us, "during her years with my father she had thought often about her religious past; now she reflected upon her Communist past. She seemed unable to bring together those two parts of herself. And that haunted her."

All this seems rich material for a novelist. Alas, Mr. Potok is telling Davita's story, not her mother's. And Davita's story is not so much a quest for a moral absolute as for a spiritual pacifier.

Although her parents are both resolute atheists, as befits good party members, Davita at a young age finds comfort in attending synagogue with a neighbor. At her father's death, finding no release in the impersonal party funeral service, Davita says kaddish—the prayer for the dead—at her synagogue, only to discover women don't say kaddish; only men do. The balance of the novel borders on a feminist approach to Judaism, with the heroine discovering that Orthodox Judaism is not an equal-opportunity religion.

As a novelist Mr. Potok seems drawn to ideas of genuine seriousness and moral complexity, ideas that one would like to see contemporary writers handle. One regrets all the more, therefore, the stiff dialogue and stilted characters. Mr. Potok appears most at ease when he sets his scenes in the synagogue or the yeshiva. In fact, a tiny flame of life flickers valiantly in all the Jewish characters. But the *goyim* come off as very strange creations indeed. For example, Aunt Sarah, the New England spinster who goes as a nurse to Ethiopia and the Spanish Civil War talking about "sweet Jesus," sounds more like a Southern Baptist than a Maine Yankee.

There are hints in this book that we have not seen the last of Davita. She imagines herself addressing not just the departed spirits of her father, aunt and family friend, but "the world and . . . this century. . . . I wanted to say that I would try to find and join with the side of America that wouldn't hurt people like Wesley Everest [the Wobbly lynched in Centralia, Wash.], and I would also try not to let this century defeat me." In this passage, she seems not to have learned anything from her mother's experience. But knowing Mr. Potok's passionate concern with things religious, one suspects that Davita, like her mother, will ultimately come back full circle to the faith. Even if it takes two sequels to do it.

Susan Reed (review date 6 May 1985)

SOURCE: "The Melody of *Davita's Harp* May Be New, but

Author Chaim Potok's Judaic Themes Are Familiar," in *People Weekly,* May 6, 1985, pp. 81-3.

[*In the following review, Reed discusses* Davita's Harp, *Potok's early literary career, and reception of his fiction in the Jewish community.*]

Chaim Potok and his wife, Adena, chanced upon the pear-shaped butternut wood instrument during the summer of 1983, while browsing in a Vermont country store. The proprietor explained that it was a door harp, commonly found in the entryways of local houses. Captivated by the sounds the four maplewood balls made as they struck the piano strings, the Potoks bought it and hung in their kitchen.

Two years later the harp has emerged as the prominent and resonant symbol in Potok's sixth and latest novel, *Davita's Harp.* This time the bearded, best-selling chronicler of life among the Hasidim (*The Chosen, The Promise, My Name Is Asher Lev*) turns to the political turbulence of New York in the 1930s. Ilana Davita Chandal is the daughter of Michael Chandal, a WASP newspaperman, and his Polish-Jewish wife, Channah. Both are fervent communists and atheists. A baffled observer of the meetings her parents hold at home, Davita, as she grows older, searches out security in the rituals of Judaism. In spite of her parents' disapproval, Davita becomes interested in religion and later enrolls in the local yeshiva. There she wins top marks, entitling her to the Akiva Award, given to the best student. Instead, the prize is given to a boy. "What would all the other yeshivas think of us?" a Hebrew teacher asks the devastated youngster. "What would the world think about our boys?"

> **In fact, though Potok's novels are set in the narrow world of Orthodox Jews, more than half of his readers are non-Jews. "I write about Jews because it's what I know best," he says. "The human problems that affect them affect any particular group—Lutherans, Seventh-day Adventists, Mormons.**
>
> **—Susan Reed**

"That actually happened to my wife when she was a young girl in Brooklyn," Potok, 56, says, seated in the library of the Tudor house outside Philadelphia, where he lives with his wife and three children. "I've known about it since we were married. Those things sit like a seed in the core of your being. Finally I decided it was time to haul it out and take another look at it. The harp got mixed in along the way and became the central metaphor."

Potok's surroundings mirror the many sides of a writer who has by turns dazzled, disappointed and baffled critics. In the bookcase are the religious texts of Potok the ordained rabbi. Alongside are the numerous bound novels of Potok the best-selling author. There are also copies of *Wanderings: Chaim Potok's History of the Jews,* on which he spent four years of painstaking research in Jerusalem. Above the bookcases are some Munch-like Expressionist paintings. Potok is also an accomplished painter.

In fact, though Potok's novels are set in the narrow world of Orthodox Jews, more than half of his readers are non-Jews. "I write about Jews because it's what I know best," he says. "The human problems that affect them affect any particular group—Lutherans, Seventh-day Adventists, Mormons. My characters are comfortable inside the framework of their tradition but they keep bumping into and up against ideas from the civilization around them. Davita follows the pattern. She doesn't break away in terms of deeds. She breaks away in her mind."

Much the same could be said of Potok, whose father, Benjamin, emigrated to the U.S. from Poland in 1921. As a boy in the East Bronx, Chaim wanted to be a painter. His father, a jeweler, wanted him to be a teacher, at a Talmud academy. At 16, after reading Evelyn Waugh's *Brideshead Revisited,* he turned to writing. "I'll never forget thinking what power there was in words," he says. Though his father considered both painting and writing to be worthless, gentile enterprises, writing seemed more acceptable. "At 17 I sent a story to the *Atlantic Monthly,* and an editor wrote back an encouraging letter," he recalls. "My father was furious, but it carried me a long way." Majoring in English literature, he graduated from Yeshiva University in 1950 summa cum laude and promptly enrolled in the Jewish Theological Seminary, where he was ordained as a Conservative rabbi in 1954. "I never wanted to be a pulpit rabbi," he says. "But I went to the seminary in order to study what it was I wanted to write about."

Suddenly Potok was ordered to Korea as an Army chaplain, like his character Gershon Loran in *The Book of Lights.* The experience transformed him. "I saw suffering the likes of which I never envisaged in my wildest nightmares. And I saw exquisite, forbidden, pagan beauty. And a culture perfectly at ease without Jews or Judaism."

Potok returned home and enrolled in a doctoral program in philosophy at the University of Pennsylvania. Adena, now 52, supported the family as a psychiatric social worker. "We lived dollar to dollar in those days," he says. "We didn't have a penny in the bank. One day I got an offer of three separate pulpits. Each one paid $20,000, which in 1963 was a lot of money. I was working on *The Chosen,* and I remember telling my wife, 'I've been offered this but I don't want to do it. I want to write.' She said, 'Go ahead.'" When the book was published to critical success four years later, financial pressure eased. Potok worked as editor of the Jewish Publication society in Philadelphia and began to turn out a novel about every three years.

Ironically, for a novelist in the mainstream of Jewish writing, Potok has proved most provocative to Jews themselves. Shortly after its publication, *The Chosen* was banned from Orthodox yeshivas. Potok himself was declared persona non grata at several synagogues. "My book upset the Orthodox for a couple of reasons," he explains. "First, the characters end up just a little more secular than they started out. Second, the Orthodox just don't like being written about. The important thing is the study of sacred texts. Writing is a horrible waste of precious Jewish time." Potok smiles knowingly. "Still, they read me."

Edward A. Abramson (essay date 1986)

SOURCE: "*The Chosen*," in *Chaim Potok*, Twayne Publishers, 1986, pp. 7-36.

[*In the following excerpt, Abramson provides an overview of the major themes, characters, and narrative presentation in* The Chosen.]

Jewish and Non-Jewish Worlds

The Chosen is set largely within a Jewish world, the characters approaching and having to cope with their problems within almost self-contained Jewish communities. The novel opens with a dramatic baseball game between a fanatical Hasidic sect of Ultra-Orthodox Jews and a group of Orthodox Jews who follow the commandments but not the particular idiosyncrasies of the Hasids. It is here that we meet Danny Saunders, the son of the leader of the Hasidic sect and heir apparent to his father's post. Because of what we later learn to be pressure from his father not to engage in secular pursuits at all, Danny feels that his team must win, thus proving that they can beat "lesser" Jews at their own game, as it were. He turns the game into a holy war and, in batting a line drive at Reuven, almost blinds him in one eye.

Reuven is the son of the more liberal David Malter, who has been helping choose library books for Danny unbeknown to his father. Danny is a genius and is chafing at the highly restricted Hasidic world that prevents him from expanding his mind with secular reading, particularly psychology. Danny's father, Reb Saunders, has been raising him in silence in order to try to develop his soul since he will be inheriting his father's role as leader of the community. Reb Saunders wants to speak to Danny through Reuven, a process that David Malter understands and encourages. Unfortunately, a hiatus occurs between the two fathers on account of differing views

toward the rebuilding of the State of Israel by secular Jews, and Reb Saunders refuses to allow Danny to speak to Reuven.

When Israel is proclaimed a Jewish state and Jewish boys begin dying to defend it, Reb Saunder's resistance begins to break down; he allows his son to speak to Reuven again, and the central plot concern of whether Danny will leave the community to become a psychologist reemerges. Danny does leave the community to study psychology and does not take on his inherited role; this passes to his younger brother. Reuven, perhaps ironically, becomes a rabbi. The story is a highly Jewish one but, as we shall see, the non-Jewish world and Jewish elements from outside the tightly knit communities within which the novel is set impinge upon the central characters with increasing force.

The only non-Jewish characters who appear in the novel are patients or relatives in the Jewish hospital to which Reuven goes for treatment of his injured eye. The most thoroughly presented is Tony Savo, who occupies the bed next to Reuven. Potok presents him as a decent man who has no anti-Jewish prejudice and who illustrates in a minor way the importance of faith. He has been a boxer, and will lose his eye because of punches received in the ring. He sees Reuven eating while wearing a skullcap and comments on the importance of religion. Then he says, "Could've been on top if that guy hadn't clopped me with that right the way he did. Flattened me for a month. Manager lost faith. Lousy manager." A page later he repeats the point about his manager losing faith. While this remark may be interpreted as the manager "losing faith" in Tony Savo, we learn that Tony wanted to be a priest once but chose the ring instead, a "Lousy choice," he now feels. As these points are made against the background of the radio's reports of the fighting toward the end of World War II, one feels the contrast between the violence in Europe and simple faith. It is a somewhat simplistic comparison but does highlight Potok's feeling that violence implies a lack of faith both in mankind and in something greater than man.

Danny arrives and tries to apologize to Reuven, who will not listen to him. Mr. Savo comments:

> "He one of these real religious Jews?" Mr. Savo asked.
>
> "Yes."
>
> "I've seen them around. My manager has an uncle like that. Real religious guy. Fanatic. Never had anything to do with my manager though. Small loss. Some lousy manager."

There is a dual implication here in that his manager's loss

of faith is seen as being in some way responsible for Tony Savo's plight and the fact that his manager's religious uncle would have nothing to do with him is yet another sign of the manager's faithlessness. However, Danny and the uncle, religious though they are, are "cloppers": "You're a good kid. So I'm telling you, watch out for those fanatics. They're the worst cloppers around." Religion is a good thing, but not the fanatical type of religion followed by the Hasidim; that is destructive. Thus, Potok uses a non-Jew to present the argument at the center of the religious confrontation which pervades the novel. Indeed, much later on when Reuven decides to become a rabbi, he remembers Tony Savo:

"America needs rabbis," my father said.

"Well, it's better than being a boxer," I told him.

My father looked puzzled.

"A bad joke," I said.

The only other non-Jews who appear in the novel are Billy Merrit and, very briefly, his father. Billy's eye operation is unsuccessful, and he remains blind; Mr. Savo has to have one eye removed. Only Reuven completely heals. Indeed, good fortune will follow him throughout the novel, everything he puts his hand to reaching a satisfactory conclusion. It is one of the criticisms which has been leveled at the novel: everything works out well for the protagonists, Potok being at base highly optimistic, at least as far as his main characters are concerned. This issue will be pursued further later in this chapter.

The world outside the Hasidic community has a crucial effect upon Danny Saunders, the central figure in the plot. He tells Reuven that he feels "trapped" by the assumption that he will carry on the generations-old tradition that his family provides the rebbe for the community. He finds study of the Talmud extremely limiting and must sneak off to the public library and seclude himself behind the shelves in order to read books from the secular world. It is noteworthy that "misbehavior" in **The Chosen** consists of a genius reading the writings of some of the best minds of the last two centuries; one is not dealing here with Danny's reading pornography or popular culture. The nature of his reading highlights the repressiveness of the Hasidic world that his father rules.

Danny points out that once he is rebbe he can read whatever he likes since so far as his people are concerned he can do no wrong. Interestingly, he would then also become a type of psychologist, albeit with an all-pervading religiosity. His people would come to him with their personal problems as well as with those relating directly to religious law. It would, however, be fatuous to see the role of rebbe as simply one of religious psychologist. He would have to be seen to be

taking their suffering upon himself; hence Reb Saunder's attempts to develop in him a soul as well as a mind.

In Europe, in another century, the possibilities open to Danny in the secular world would have been far more limited than they are in America. He might have done what Solomon Maimon did in the eighteenth century in Poland; that is, go to Germany and immerse himself in studying the great philosophers and in writing philosophical texts. It is noteworthy here that the subject of Potok's doctoral dissertation was "The Rationalism and Skepticism of Solomon Maimon." Indeed, David Malter cites Maimon as a parallel to Danny. He says: "Reuven, Reb Saunder's son has a mind like Solomon Maimon's, perhaps even a greater mind. And Reb Saunders' son does not live in Poland. America is free. There are no walls here to hold back Jews. Is it so strange, then, that he is breaking his father's rules and reading forbidden books? he cannot help himself."

Danny's attraction to psychology is an attraction to what has become almost a secular religion, with people like Sigmund Freud constituting members of a priestly caste. Not only does Danny discover that he can use the methods of Talmudic study in deciphering Freud's writings, but Reb Saunders finds that he can partially justify his son's choice of vocation in that Danny "will be a *tzaddik* for the world. And the world needs a *tzaddik*." This explains Hugh Nissenson's remark that "Danny's conflict between the secular and the spiritual life has been daringly, and brilliantly resolved." One might also add, given Reb Saunders's perhaps somewhat too easy acceptance of his son's choice, that the conflict has been a bit too comfortably resolved.

Part of the reason for Danny's being drawn to the secular world lies in the comparative weakness of his Hasidic beliefs. Louis Jacobs states that while it is difficult to find a set of Hasidic doctrines that are acceptable to all Hasidic sects, there are "certain basic themes and a certain mood, founded on the pantheistic beliefs that are fairly constant. Among the ideas stressed in every variety of Hasidic thought are: the love and fear of God; *devekut,* 'cleaving' to God at all times; *simhah,* 'joy' in God's presence; *hitlabavut,* 'burning enthusiasm' in God's worship; and *shiflut,* 'lowliness,' 'humility,' construed as a complete lack of awareness of the self." It is noteworthy that Danny does not illustrate in his life any of these beliefs or actions. Indeed, his concerns are almost entirely with how he can achieve self-fulfillment and pursue the secular studies for which he has a growing passion. One critic has stated that "Danny, for want of a better word—the word has been overly used and abused, though it applies here—has been alienated—from his father, from Hasidism, and finally from the Hasidic community itself."

Historical events thrust themselves with great force upon the characters. I have already discussed the reactions of Reb

Saunders and David Malter to the Holocaust and the rebirth of Israel, events that Potok uses to show basic theological differences between the two men and the two religious groups. Potok also mentions the death of President Roosevelt and devotes most space to the Malters' reaction, with Reuven weeping and his father deeply grieved. They are placed within the context of the typical American reaction to the tragic event, as seen by descriptions of people stunned or crying in the street. Danny feels that the death is a "terrible thing," but we are not given Reb Saunder's reaction. This lack of information heightens the reader's sense of the Hasidic leader's apartness from secular, non-Jewish events. It may show some of Potok's bias in favor of David Malter, who has earlier told Reuven that he "should not forget there is a world outside."

The "world outside" includes those American myths that surround the Jewish communities in the novel, in particular that of the American Dream. Although the Hasidic community tries to insulate itself from American influences, this proves impossible. Danny Saunder's interest in secular subjects and his eventual decision to become a psychologist implies something about the openness of American society to new possibilities; however, the fact that Danny must relinquish his Hasidic identity in order to take advantage of these possibilities also tells us something of the demands that America makes on those who would achieve their dreams there. Sheldon Grebstein observes that despite its strong Jewish content, *The Chosen* is a highly American novel:

> Accordingly, the American cultural myth or fable at the heart of *The Chosen* is essentially that of both the Horatio Alger stories and *The Great Gatsby*—the dream of success. In this version the story is played out by an improbable but possible "only in America" cast of Hasidic and orthodox Jews, who demonstrate that people can still make good through hard work, and that severe difficulties can be overcome by pluck, integrity, and dedication. At the story's end the novel's two young heroes are about to realize the reward they have earned: a limitless future. In sum, *The Chosen* can be interpreted from this standpoint as an assertion of peculiarly American optimism and social idealism. Very simply, it says Yes.

Indeed, *The Chosen* does say "Yes" for the two adolescent Jewish boys. Reuven is elected president of his class, receives virtually all *A* grades, and graduates summa cum laude. He also has the choice of becoming either a mathematician or a rabbi. Danny also graduates summa cum laude; is accepted to do graduate work at Harvard, Berkeley, and Columbia; will become a psychologist; and finds that his father accepts his decision not to inherit the *tzaddikate* but pass it on to his sickly brother instead. This

optimism underlies the novel, even at those points where negative elements enter into it. One always has an ultimate belief that the two boys are so basically decent, and are perceived by the author as being so worthy, that in the end their actions will lead to success, and problems which seem very thorny indeed, like Danny's inevitable confrontation with his father over the leadership of the community, will be resolved.

Potok manages to permit the boys to remain strongly Jewish while taking advantage of the opportunities offered by American society.
—Edward A. Abramson

Potok manages to permit the boys to remain strongly Jewish while taking advantage of the opportunities offered by American society. In this he differs from most other Jewish-American authors whose Jewish characters frequently must sacrifice important aspects of their Jewishness in order to take advantage of American opportunity. Indeed, the majority of the characters in twentieth-century Jewish-American writing do not view the relinquishment of their Jewishness as a major sacrifice. Describing a symposium held by the *Contemporary Jewish Record* (*Commentary*'s predecessor) in 1944 entitled "American Literature and the Younger Generation of American Jews," David Daiches observes that "Many of the contributors to the symposium seemed to think that their Americanism had subsumed their Judaism. One writer went so far as to equate the 'Declaration of Independence' with certain Jewish prayers, and Lincoln with Hillel."

The enormous effect of the American Dream or, in Danny's case in particular, American opportunity as an inherent aspect of the Dream, is stated in part by Loren Baritz when he writes that the Jew had almost always "managed to resist the particular physical locale of his Galut by remembering his participation both in history and in the Jewish community. But because when we moved to America we responded to a psychological reversal promised by the American Dream—a promise of the end of Galut—we became more susceptible to the incursions of American utopianism, of America's rejection of the past, of age, and of continuity with Europe." While Danny does not take his attraction to American opportunity so far as to reject the past, to reject Judaism, one can see in his rejection of his father's Hasidism an awareness that American society will permit both a secular profession and a Jewish life. However, even America makes demands of those who wish to use its gifts: Danny Saunders cannot retain his Hasidic way of life and his Hasidic appearance and still become a successful psychologist in America. As Baritz also writes: "Because of America's rejection of the past, of the fierce commitment to the notion that this land will start anew, the American Jew is pulled apart. To be a Jew is to remember. An American must forget." Danny must "forget" some of his Hasidic ways.

Reuven Malter has less intense choices to make than Danny since his type of Judaism does not prevent him from entering the secular world while retaining his Jewish identification. Ironically, he decides to become a rabbi and remain totally in a Jewish environment. Reuven, however, is aware of the necessity that some Jews feel to prove their Americanism. As narrator he points out that some of the teachers of non-Jewish subjects ("English teachers") in the Jewish parochial schools felt it necessary to organize competitive baseball leagues "to show the gentile world that yeshiva students were as physically fit, despite their long hours of study, as any other American student." This feeling arises as a result of America's entry into World War II and the desire on the part of most Jews that they should be seen as able to do their part in the war effort. Indeed, because baseball is the quintessential American game, "to the students of most of the parochial schools, an inter-league baseball victory had come to take on only a shade less significance than a top grade in Talmud, for it was an unquestioned mark of one's Americanism, and to be counted a loyal American had become increasingly important to us during these last years of the war." Thus optimism about America does not totally remove the Jews' awareness of their differences from the majority culture or the need to temper the more extreme external manifestations of their faith on the part of those who wish to become more a part of mainstream American society.

Potok has reservations concerning the importance of the American Dream and American optimism in *The Chosen.* He asserts that "A covering hypothesis regarding the popularity of my work should take into account the many Jewish and non-Jewish readers of Potok . . . in France, Germany, England, Holland, Japan, Australia, the Philippines, and elsewhere, including the Soviet Union. What do all those people know about Horatio Alger, . . . American optimism and social idealism, and the American reverence for the pioneer?" This comment appears in an essay in which Potok addresses himself to remarks made by Sheldon Grebstein a year earlier. While one can sympathize with Potok's point to a degree, it remains true that with its American setting, the nature of Danny Saunders's belief in what is possible, Reuven Malter's basic faith that his future lies in his own hands, and the ultimate success of these characters and, indeed, of David Malter in achieving his goals, the novel exudes a type of optimism that is strongly associated with America. That this optimism and level of success can exist elsewhere is not in doubt; that it underlies, indeed pervades, *The Chosen* is what gives the book its American ethos. Non-Americans can appreciate and understand this ethos because of general cultural dissemination of American ideals and, not incon-

siderably, because of the attitudes that Potok describes in the novel.

The Value of Education

The Chosen could be viewed as a paean to education. All the central characters are intensely and joyfully engaged in learning, and Potok imbues the quest for knowledge with great excitement. Jews have long placed great value upon learning, with communities in Europe supporting, if at a meager level, Talmud students so that they could pursue their studies. It was felt that a valuable and holy gift for a wealthy man to present to a son-in-law was an extended period of financial support after the marriage so that the young man could engage in study. Supporting a religious scholar was a *mitzvah* (good deed), as his study of the holy books reflected upon the religiosity of the family.

The positive attitude toward education can be seen in the verve with which the protagonists engage in complex discussions of difficult texts. Reuven describes a discussion between Reb Saunders, Danny, and himself thus: "It was a pitched battle. With no congregants around, and with me an accepted member of the family, Danny and his father fought through their points with loud voices and wild gestures of their hands almost to where I thought they might come to blows." They do not come to blows, however, as Reuven realizes that "Reb Saunders was far happier when he lost to Danny than when he won. His face glowed with fierce pride. . . . The battle went on for a long time, and I slowly became aware of the fact that both Danny and his father, during a point they might be making or listening to, would cast inquisitive glances at me, as if to ask what I was doing just sitting there while all this excitement was going on: Why in the world wasn't I joining in the battle?" Reuven does join in and finds that he is "enjoying it all immensely. . . ."

One rarely comes across an author who can convincingly present learning as the most exciting aspect of the lives of adolescents. One does wonder at times whether Potok does not overdo this total commitment to books. Where, for instance, is the boys' awareness of sports, popular music, girls. Have they no hobbies? Neither Reuven nor Danny is particularly interested in baseball despite the opening of the novel, and after Danny tells Reuven that his sister had been "promised" at the age of two to the son of one of his father's followers any interest in girls disappears from the story. Reuven attends her wedding, finds her beautiful, but his concern in this novel for female companionship is over. As one might expect, in the film version of the novel a good deal more is made of Reuven's feelings for Danny's sister. She even seems somewhat attracted to him. As in the novel, however, nothing comes of this attraction.

Although Reuven is not Hasidic, Potok seems to have burdened him with many "Hasidic" restrictions: "'Youth' does not have high status in the Hasidic community, since it is regarded as only a preliminary to adulthood. . . . Boys and girls do not meet ambiguities and uncertainties concerning their expected behavior, since the role of youth is to obey their elders and behave in a way that is appropriate for Hasidic people." Reuven is certainly freer than Danny in his opportunities to interact with the secular world and in the fact that he does not feel "trapped" as does Danny. However, because Potok makes Danny a genius and Reuven a near-genius neither boy can be viewed as a representative adolescent.

Both fathers are committed to intellectual pursuits, and the home life of both boys at times resembles a classroom. Indeed, Potok uses the different methods of teaching employed by the fathers to illustrate different approaches to Judaism that are of great importance in the novel. He writes of "the lecture on Hasidism by David Malter to his fifteen year old son (the scientific Western-oriented method of teaching) and the synagogue-set exhortations of Reb Saunders (the traditional Eastern-European method of teaching)." Reb Saunders also engages in Talmudic discussions with his son which, as we have seen, permit disagreement over possible interpretations. These discussions, however, are carried on in private, but, even privately, Reb Saunders would never permit David Malter's method of textual emendation to be used in his presence. In an interview in which Potok was asked what kind of teacher should "teach truths," he replied: "I would say that the teacher should be somebody like Reuven Malter's father. In many ways he exemplifies the Jewish adventure." Education is an inherent part of that adventure in Potok's work.

David Malter is Potok's ideal teacher because despite his Orthodoxy he does not eschew the twentieth century and what it can offer to his understanding of Judaism. This attitude extends to his method of teaching his son and to his expectations of the breadth of his son's interests. Reuven can discuss any topic with his father, although all those discussed are important and worthy ones. David Malter has a respect for secular knowledge that is lacking in Reb Saunders, and a regard for analysis of all issues. Reb Saunders's narrowness, on the other hand, reflects Hasidic views: "If one is educated in Jewish matters, he will rank high only if his education is used to intensify his Hasidic behavior. Education in itself, without Hasidic observances, has little status value. Occupation, income, and residence, too, carry status value only if they supplement Hasidic behavior."

The result of these differing attitudes toward education is that Danny's attempt to pursue secular studies becomes a source for conflict in the novel whereas Reuven's father is proud of his son's ability in mathematics. Indeed, although David Malter is proud that Reuven has decided to become a rabbi,

he tells him that he would have been very pleased if he had decided to become a university professor of mathematics. He knows that Reuven will not give up his Judaism, and he considers a profession in the secular world to be honorable and worthwhile.

Reb Saunders's way of educating his son has apparently failed to give him the "heart" necessary to find the role of *tzaddik* attractive despite his desire to study psychology and his seeming interest in the more "human" Freudian approach as opposed to the clinical orientation of Dr. Applemen, his psychology professor. One critic observes:

> The Saunderses seem to have an excess of head in their (paradoxical streak of zealousness and emotional) makeup; but the Malters have heart *and* head: they are in balance. . . .

> Reuven's studies are "brain" disciplines—logic, mathematics, philosophy—yet it is he who finally turns out to have more "heart" than the brilliant son of a Hasid. Danny, on the other hand, having been raised in the tradition of the Ba'al Shem, should have been a "heart-and-joy specialist." Yet it is he who is all brain. And this produces a keen irony, since Hasidism, a movement that was originally a revolt against arid scholasticism became (as portrayed in *The Chosen*) transformed into its opposite. Piety, joy, even learning, (a late-comer to Hasidism) becomes pietism, rote learning, memorization.

The results of their educations may have produced quite different people, but Reuven and Danny do share an important set of ideals. Like their fathers they are committed to learning and to its best attributes: thoughtfulness, a desire for self-improvement, and a respect for those whose knowledge is greater than their own. In addition, the sort of learning upon which they devote most of their time is religious in nature. This has given both of them a belief in the importance of morality and of the spiritual aspect of man. In short, their belief in the importance of learning has made both of them decent, caring people who are oriented toward higher things.

It is interesting to note that *The Chosen* appears to appeal to adolescent boys and girls when, as has been pointed out, it is not concerned with what might be thought to be the "normal" interests of this age group. An English teacher in a high school in Midland, Texas (not noted for its high Jewish population), has written that "Although there are some difficult aspects in studying this book in high school, after some preliminary research into the practices of the Jewish religion the students on the junior level read the book and rated it highest in interest of all the major works that we studied this year." The other books studied included *The Red Badge of Courage, Huckleberry Finn,* and *The Old Man and the Sea.*

One can speculate that the appeal of the novel lies in its tapping of the honorable and more "spiritual" side of the adolescent personality. Both Reuven and Danny exhibit a wide range of very admirable traits, and the issues they confront are clearly of importance and have a moral dimension.
—Edward A. Abramson

One can speculate that the appeal of the novel lies in its tapping of the honorable and more "spiritual" side of the adolescent personality. Both Reuven and Danny exhibit a wide range of very admirable traits, and the issues they confront are clearly of importance and have a moral dimension. Also, there is the appeal of the exotic, the sense that information about a secret world is being imparted. Indeed, education of non-Jews and of Jews who are not Hasids provides one of the important appeals of the novel. There are long historical passages, virtually lectures, which David Malter delivers to his son concerning the history of Hasidism and of the Jews. There are exciting Talmudic discussions that culminate in six pages describing a class recitation in which Reuven tackles a very difficult passage in the Talmud using different critical methods. Potok manages to make this recitation gripping in its presentation (it continues over four days of class time) on account of both the subject matter and the understanding that the teacher, Rav Gershenson, is believed not to like the method of textual emendation that Reuven's father uses in his articles and which, finally, Reuven is forced to use himself. Since this teacher will be instrumental in deciding whether or not Reuven is permitted to enter the rabbinate, there is an added tension.

Danny lectures Reuven on the intricacies of Freudian psychology and finds that it is necessary to learn German in order to read Freud in the original. While it might be very difficult for even bright high school pupils to identify with either boy on an academic level because of his brilliance, it is not unreasonable to think that admiration of them would be a common feeling. In regard to Danny's reading of Freud, Potok does create difficulties for him in that even with a knowledge of German he cannot grasp the nuances of the case descriptions. A neat relationship between the Talmud and Freud seems to point the way forward: "He had been going at it all wrong, he said, his eyes bright with excitement. He had wanted to *read* Freud. That had been his mistake. Freud had to be *studied,* not read. He had to be studied like a page of Talmud. And he had to be studied with a commentary."

One critic states that even using this method it is unlikely that Danny could fully understand Freud since "such a boy at his age could not confront the works of Freud in any meaningful way. The problem is not one of intelligence—he might grasp the dictionary meaning of the words—but lack of life experience. . . ." The pupils in Midland, Texas might well have more experience of "life" than does Danny with his cloistered upbringing.

The Chosen is an "education" novel, a bildungsroman. The teenage characters develop in mind and character as time passes, their experiences heightening their understanding of themselves and of their place in the world. This form is a very common one in Jewish-American literature:

> The education novel exactly reproduces the central experience of American Jewry: the movement from the enclosed *shtetl* (Eastern European village) environment, with its highly ordered and pervasive moral system (diffused by peasant lore and a necessarily realistic view of humanity), to the exacting demands of an industrial society. . . . America, coming with such suddenness to so many, intensified the cleavage between the domestic religious culture of the Jews and their external lives in a country which regarded them as an anomaly. The novel repeats the pattern of this process by describing a youth outgrowing the protection of the home and encountering the beckoning life without.

The world of the Hasids described in *The Chosen* is very similar to that of "the enclosed shtetl" in its imposition upon its members of a rigid moral and behavior code that attempts to ignore that of the majority culture. As we have seen, both Danny and Reuven are greatly influenced by American society, this causing in Danny's case the cleavage of which Sherman writes. The Jewish writer's version of the education or "initiation" novel tends to place more stress upon family relations than does that produced by his non-Jewish counterpart. This, also, can be clearly seen in *The Chosen* as the relations between the Saunderses and the Malters, and between the respective fathers and sons, occupy the center stage.

Fathers and Sons

Book 1 of *The Chosen* begins with the following quotation from "Proverbs": "I was a son to my father . . . / And he taught me and said to me, / 'Let your heart hold fast my words. . . .'" This epigraph sets the tone not only for the first section of the novel but for the novel as a whole in that father-son relationships are central to the development of the plot and to an understanding of the various conflicts that occur. The virtual absence of women heightens the centrality of the male relations but, of course, it eliminates any consideration of the complexities of family life, a theme that is very common and important in Jewish-American writing. This somewhat artificial situation (unlike Reuven, Danny has a mother and a sister, but they are almost invisible) parallels the somewhat artificial adolescences of the two boys. A feminine element in the plot would have provided a more balanced family life to offset the male-dominated, religious and educational intensity of the novel.

The stress upon fathers parallels a similar stress in Judaism, where God is King, Judge, and Father. When "authority is involved, God the King or Judge; when He offers love and mercy, even to the wicked, He is Father. Symbolic Hebrew religion deceives some into thinking Deity is really fatherhood." Thus, the father can be viewed as a fount of wisdom, one who takes upon himself some of the aura of the Godhead. This can be clearly seen in Danny's reaction to Reb Saunders and, in terms of respecting his knowledge, ethics, and religiosity, in Reuven's reaction to his father.

One of the saying of the Baal Shem Tov illustrates the close links between learning, the Godhead, and fatherhood which exists both in Hasidic and non-Hasidic Judaism: "'The Lord does not object even if one misunderstands what a man learns, provided he only strives to understand out of love of learning. It is like a father whose beloved child petitions him in stumbling words, yet he takes delight in hearing him.' There is honor between father and son. The father is the benevolent teacher; the son is the obedient student." As Malin observes here, the father-son relationship is one of honor and respect, in the words of the Baal Shem Tov. Despite any differences that occur between the fathers and sons in *The Chosen,* a high level of respect remains in force between the father-teacher and his son.

The strength of the two father-son relationships provides a central focus of the novel in that even when rebellion against the father takes place, as it does in Danny's case, the father is not presented in a totally negative light. Potok shows that Reb Saunders's reasons for acting the way he does are not selfish ones but are in the service of higher things: he is seen as a *tzaddik* who suffers for his flock and for the Jewish people and not merely as a tyrannical father. Danny may resent the pressures put upon him by his father, but he still respects and loves him; Reuven has no reason not to love and respect his father, as he is presented as the most admirable character in the novel.

The ways in which the two boys are raised can be seen as reflecting the fanaticism or tolerance of their fathers. Reb Saunders's raises Danny in silence in order to try to give him a suffering soul that will enable him to feel the pain of his people. Danny's brilliant mind is not sufficient in itself for a *tzaddik,* and his father is appalled that as a child Danny seems to lack the human compassion to match his intellec-

tual brilliance. While Reb Saunders is undoubtedly a fanatic, he does suffer greatly because of this method of raising his son. As we have seen he is willing to make the sacrifice in order that a higher cause be served: that of creating the right sort of leader for his people. *A Time for Silence* was the tentative manuscript title of the novel. This shows the importance Potok placed upon silence and its implications for all of the characters, although it has its greatest effect upon Danny and his father.

Reb Saunder's method largely fails in that its primary effect is to drive Danny out of the community and into the secular world. We must wait for **The Promise** to see the positive effects of this method. While a fascination with secular literature explains much of Danny's lack of interest in Hasidism, it seems probable that the harshness of his father's method of raising him contributes to his distaste for both Hasidism and the role of *tzaddik.* One critic feels that Reb Saunders manages virtually to nullify Danny's personality in that "Danny becomes an object, manipulated by his father, rather than a person one relates to." Danny's personality is somewhat flat rather than round, his conflict with his father and Hasidism being more interesting than he is. His ultimate choice of Freudian as opposed to clinical psychology is presented more in scientific than in humanistic terms, in spite of his comments concerning the more "human" appeal to him of the Freudian approach. In his rebellion, Danny reacts to the intolerance of his father.

By contrast, Reuven Malter is raised in an atmosphere of tolerance and love that is exhibited daily rather than assumed to exist without outward signs. However, David Malter is not a *tzaddik* and does not have the responsibilities toward a group of people and the preservation of a dynasty which Reb Saunders does. Because he is not a Hasid, David Malter is not enclosed in a world which makes the sort of extreme demands that Reb Saunders must face daily. Nonetheless, Malter is committed to the preservation of the Jewish people and fights tirelessly for the creation of a Jewish state. His illness and recovery reflect the condition of the Jews as they move from Auschwitz to Israel. He is also an observer of the commandments, which requires a great deal of discipline in his life. His outgoing love for his son and his respect and tolerance for his needs must be seen in relation to his attitude toward Judaism and toward the secular world, attitudes which we have seen to be far different from those of Reb Saunders.

David Malter teaches his son respect for tolerance. He tells him that "Honest differences of opinion should never be permitted to destroy a friendship. . . ." He illustrates this attitude in his reaction to Reb Saunders, who has bitterly attacked him because of his stance concerning the creation of the State of Israel. Reb Saunders is a fanatic, he feels, in his anti-Zionist stance and the extent to which he is willing to heap scorn upon those who disagree with him. Yet, when Reuven finds that his hatred of Danny's father is growing daily, David Malter defends Reb Saunders on account of his faith and the way in which faith such as his has preserved the Jewish people through two thousand years of persecution. He prefers a rational approach: "He disagreed with Reb Saunders, yes, but he would countenance no slander against his name or his position. Ideas should be fought with ideas, my father said, not with blind passion. If Reb Saunders was fighting him with passion, that did not mean that my father had to fight Reb Saunders with passion." The difference between the two fathers cannot be more clearly seen than in this disparate approach toward the treatment of those with whom one disagrees.

One critic views the two approaches in terms of rationality and mysticism: "In the crisis of generations and cultures, the son of the rationalist, who has come to love the tradition because he has been reared in love, chooses to sustain it; the son of the mystic, reared in silence and seeming hatred, turns toward secular science." While the observation is basically sound, one must question whether Reb Saunders is a mystic, since he places so much stress upon intellectual analysis of the Talmud and does not exhibit a particularly Kabbalistic (Jewish mystical) leaning toward religious texts or experience. As noted earlier, Israel Baal Shem Tov, the founder of Hasidism, was much concerned with nonintellectual, mystical experiences as a means of understanding God. Reb Saunders, as indeed Hasidism in general, has deviated from this total stress upon "simple," mystical experience and has established practices that the Baal Shem would not have wholeheartedly supported. While most Hasidic groups still place some emphasis upon religious ecstasy achieved through dance and certain repetitive tunes (the Hasidic *nign*), particularly for the mass of Hasidim, they would nor differ very much in their regard for the types of intellectual analysis of Talmudic texts for the more able among them, as illustrated in the religious discussions between Danny and his father.

In their concern to pass on the Jewish heritage to their sons, both fathers use what could be described as "rational" methods. At the end of the day it is not so much the method used (silence is used by Reb Saunders as a "rational" method to produce a particular result) as the underlying feeling of love each boy either sees or does not in his father which produces the results of which Hochman writes. The son's awareness of his father's love becomes related to the son's feeling for the type of Judaism for which the father stands. To Reuven, Judaism is as much what his father is as it is a tradition and a body of laws and commandments. In choosing to become a rabbi, Reuven reflects both his love of Judaism and the love which his father, as the primary symbol of Judaism in his life, gave to him; in rejecting the *tzaddikate,* Danny reflects both his distaste of the narrow Hasidic world and the

lack of love that his father, as the primary symbol of Hasidism in his life, forced him to endure.

Form and Content

Potok's style in **The Chosen** has been criticized for the flatness of the dialogue, the subservience of characterization to thematic considerations, and a degree of contrivance to create a symmetrical plot structure in which various plot developments end in a neat balance. Sheldon Grebstein writes: "Its style ranges from undistinguished to banal. Its tone is subdued and utterly humorless. Its pace is moderate. Its overall color is gray. With all these handicaps that **The Chosen**— this really Jewish book—should have attained best-sellerdom seems more than a phenomenon; it is truly a miracle. But miracle or not, its 38 weeks on the list is an obdurate fact demanding explanation." Before exploring the possible explanations for the novel's popularity, some analysis of these adverse criticisms is necessary.

The dialogue in the novel is uninspiring and very slow-paced; however, the subjects being discussed are often highly intellectual in content. They are historical, religious, moral, or related to the intricacies of personality as exhibited by high-minded and complex individuals. In short, the dialogue is suitable for the subjects and themes that are central to the novel. Where it does fall short is in its lack of differentiation between different characters, there being little subtlety of nuance in the speech patterns of one character as compared to another. Because the tone of the conversations is almost always highly serious, there is a marked lack of the lighter side of the characters' personalities.

This one-sidedness can also be seen in character descriptions. There is a mechanical quality about most of them. To show suppressed emotion, certain characters' eyes frequently become "misty"; others gesticulate wildly when they talk, or "nod vaguely" to show their preoccupation with other matters than the ones being discussed. Moreover, these physical traits are repeated throughout the novel to the point of becoming too predictable.

As Potok himself points out in an article I will discuss shortly, the characters speak Yiddish almost all of the time. Yet, there is no attempt in the novel at mimesis through setting apart the non-English phraseology by syntactical methods or through presenting it in, say, perfect English as does Henry Roth in *Call It Sleep,* another novel in which many of the characters (the Shearl family and most of their neighbors) speak Yiddish almost all of the time.

One aspect of **The Chosen** which could have created difficulties through interference with the narrative line is the educative aspect. There are a number of "lecturettes" concerning Hasidic and Jewish history which, like the cetology chapters of *Moby-Dick,* intrude into the plot. Indeed, one critic has referred to the novel as "documentary fictionalized." She goes on to write that "Claustrophobic reading, and really, description of 'customs and traditions' however well done, are not basically what a novel should concern itself with." Perhaps, but the depiction of "customs and traditions" is both relevant and suitable for *The Chosen.* Indeed, the intrusions into the novel of this material can be regarded as essential to an appreciation of the plot. Not only is reference made to it during other portions of the text, but Potok uses this educative material in part to explain the various actions and beliefs of the characters. It therefore takes on more importance than mere extraneous material would normally have. While it is not dramatized, neither is it just "dead" exposition.

> **Because the tone of the conversations is almost always highly serious, there is a marked lack of the lighter side of the characters' personalities.**
> —*S. Lillian Kremer*

By no means have all critics found *The Chosen* wanting in all respects; many have had positive reactions and at least one discovered that having liked the novel "somewhat" in April, liked it "quite a lot" in June. He goes on to say that "*The Chosen* has stayed in memory and, staying, has grown." Most reviewers have praised the sincerity, warmth, and humanity of the novel and have responded to the decency and believability of characters presented in such a sympathetic manner. As Granville Hicks observes: "it is hard to make good boys interesting; it must have been even harder for Chaim Potok to bring to life a pair of good fathers, good in different ways. But he succeeded, and the result is a fine, moving, gratifying book." Indeed, one of the strongest aspects of the novel is the characters, despite the weakness of the dialogue. They remain interesting as people because of what they represent and the skillful manner in which Potok shows their struggles to reach admirable but difficult goals while remaining ethical individuals. There was a danger that these characters would become allegorical, mere symbols or types, thus losing their individuality and humanness. Potok has avoided this pitfall through the creation of a story so interesting in the moral issues raised, in the conflicts presented, and in the exoticism of its setting and themes that we are caught up in the flow from the narrative which, in turn, lends the characters weight and depth.

Daphne Merkin states that Potok has consciously eschewed the "attempt to write about situations or characters that might stand in for humanity in general, and has concentrated instead on the particular, writing from an insularly Jewish perspective that denies broader implications." Unquestionably,

Potok's world in *The Chosen* is firmly rooted in a particular place and culture, the characters illustrating the beliefs and practices of a distinct minority. One can think of many novels about which the same observations could be made. This does not mean that "broader implications" are denied. Isaac Bashevis Singer speaks of the importance of literature having an "address": "I would say that literature must have an address, that it just cannot be in a vacuum. This is very important. Many modern writers would like to get rid of this and write about humanity—general humanity, just abstract human beings. This cannot be done. . . . In other words, literature cannot operate in a void above humanity. It is strongly connected with a group, with a clan. . . ."

If within their particular situations the emotions and reactions of the characters are "true to life," they can be said to exhibit realistic human traits, and Potok is certainly writing within a realistic convention. Indeed, as Sheldon Grebstein points out, "Perhaps its greatest achievement stylistically is its verisimilitude, the solidly detailed portrayal of place, time, weather, scene, object, gesture."

The novel is related through the first-person point of view of Reuven Malter, a reliable narrator who, despite his central position in the tale, does not exude infallibility but takes the audience with him in his difficulties in coping with a Hasidic world that is as strange to him as it is to the reader. Reuven mirrors the reader's emotions as he tries to figure out how to cope with Reb Saunders and remain the ethical person whom his father has tried to create. Reuven and David Malter illustrate the plight of any tolerant individual come face to face with intolerance, the doubts and hesitations of the narrator and the advice of his father providing paradigms of a struggle for decency which has universal implications. Reb Saunders illustrates the plight of a man intimately concerned with ethics whose goals, honorable though they may be, cause him to feel justified in using highly dubious means in their attainment. Not an evil man, he exemplifies the complexities involved in moral decisions. His ghettolike world and sense of absolute sureness render him almost impervious to the force of contrary argument. This is his tragedy and that of his son who must attempt self-fulfillment within the narrow world of absolutes that his father hands down or who must leave that world for another.

In an essay entitled "A Reply to a Semi-Sympathetic Critic," Potok attempted to answer the criticisms of his work stated by a number of critics but, in particular, those of Sheldon Grebstein. He states that in a novel he prefers "simplicity to complexity" and compares his problem with dialogue to that faced by Ernest Hemingway. Just as he had to decide how to present the Yiddish which his characters speak almost all of the time, Hemingway had to decide how to communicate in English the Italian and Spanish of, respectively, *A Farewell to Arms* and *For Whom the Bell Tolls,* as well as these languages in various short stories. Potok writes that "He solved it in his way (and it has been said of him too that all his characters sound alike), and I solved it in mine. Style is the right word in the right place, as Jonathan Swift pointed out."

While Potok's dialogue is not as evocative as Hemingway's spare, stripped syntax, Hemingway's influence is clear and frequently results in our being aware of wider implications in the understated phraseology that fills *The Chosen*. Unfortunately, this awareness often fails to occur. When Potok has a character say nothing in response to a statement about which we know he has strong feelings, the effect can be that we fill in the gaps, as Potok probably intends, or that we feel something important has been omitted, the author having taken the easy way out. The problem arises when we do not feel that there is enough information for the gaps to be filled or that the technique is too transparent. Indeed, this problem occurs, at times, in Hemingway's writing as well; however, he manages to make the style work far more frequently than does Potok in this novel.

Potok points out how painstakingly his novels are written, with numerous revisions and rewritings. He says that he uses "a kind of talked style . . . and one would do well to remember who the 'talkers' are in each of the novels and the extent to which their style of talking varies within the limitations of simplicity I have set for them." He is correct when he says that one must remember who the "talkers" are. One tends to change the word stresses in one's own mind according to how one understands the personality of the character who is speaking. While he does provide verbal clues to some speech patterns (Reb Saunders and Rav Gershenson, in *The Promise* both use "Nu," meaning "Well?" or "What?" when they speak), Potok does not make syntactical changes to imitate Yiddish speech patterns as does Bernard Malamud or, as I have mentioned, use flawless English as does Henry Roth. It may well be that reliance upon characterization, without appropriate changes in the diction and syntax of the various speakers, in order to distinguish speech differences is inadequate—too much reliance being placed upon the subjectivity of the reader. Although Potok's style does work to an extent, "simplicity" can be taken too far.

The popularity of *The Chosen* is due to a number of factors, not least of which is the exoticism of its setting. Both Jews and non-Jews found the descriptions of the Hasidic world in particular to be fascinating. This closed world had not been presented before in such an accessible manner or with such interesting characters as Reb Saunders and Danny. The educative aspect of the novel aided its popularity in that readers were not only being told a story with an interesting plot but were learning something at the same time. I have already discussed the optimism and American social ideal-ism that fills the book and supports the American predelection for believing that hard work and decency are rewarded in the end. One must not forget, either, the quality of the presentation of the conflicts in the novel or the appeal of the moral tone with which these conflicts are presented. *The Chosen* achieved best-sellerdom through a stress upon morality, learning, and sincerity presented by unusual characters who inhabit a strange world and in whom the author obviously believes. Far from being a shortcoming, the lack of violence, sexuality, and deceit in the novel proved to be a strong recommendation.

It is interesting to note what changes to the novel the filmmakers thought necessary in order to widen its appeal even further. In addition to the increased romantic interest between Reuven and Danny's sister referred to earlier, the Hasidim are made less objectionable. The notion of Danny's trying to kill Reuven in a baseball game that the Hasidim have turned into a Holy War is absent from the film. Religiosity is toned down. Although Reuven attends a seminary and says that he wants to become a rabbi, we never see either he or his father praying. Reuven occasionally wears a skullcap; his father never does. The stress is upon the contrast between the Americanized Malters and utterly un-Americanized Saunders and Hasidim.

Reb Saunders is portrayed somewhat harsh, particularly in relation to Zionism, but his sympathetic aspects are stressed in Rod Steiger's performance. As a result of omission of the information that Danny's brother is permitted to take on the *tzaddikate,* the crisis created by Danny's refusal is not satisfactorily resolved.

The strongest aspect of the film is its atmosphere and verisimilitude. The setting and characters inspire believability (Potok himself appears briefly as a Talmud teacher). It is not as effective as the novel in the creation of the religious conflict but does nonetheless remain remarkably close to the book in its depiction of intra-Jewish and Jewish-American tensions.

S. Lillian Kremer (essay date 1989)

SOURCE: "Eternal Light: The Holocaust and the Revival of Judaism and Jewish Civilization in the Fiction of Chaim Potok," in *Witness through Imagination: Jewish American Holocaust Literature,* Wayne State University Press, 1989, pp. 300-23.

[*In the following essay, Kremer explores themes and issues surrounding anti-Semitism and the Holocaust in Potok's fiction. According to Kremer, rather than "focus on the atrocities of the Holocaust period and burden of Holocaust survival, Potok generally concentrates on the possibilities of Holocaust restoration."*]

Chaim Potok is a rabbi, scholar, and novelist whose philosophic and ethical views are derived from Torah and Talmud and whose aesthetic theory is derived from Western philosophy, literature, and art. With Saul Bellow, Bernard Malamud, Cynthia Ozick, Arthur Cohen, and I. B. Singer, Potok rejects alienation in favor of the affirmative position of Jewish idealism in the face of evil and suffering. Jewish history, including repeated outbreaks of anti-Semitism and its 1939-1945 genocidal manifestation, resonates throughout Potok's fiction. Because the author believes that "the Jew sees all his contemporary history refracted through the ocean of blood that is the Holocaust," the *Shoah* is always in the background of his fictional universe. Rather than treating the Holocaust directly, Potok generally introduces the topic indirectly and focuses instead on Holocaust restoration through renewal of Judaism and Jewry in America and Israel. Potok's characters are generally devout Jews, conversant in Jewish theology, liturgy, Talmudic studies, and rabbinic commentary and frequently presented in the context of synagogue, yeshiva, and observant Jewish homes. Their pre-Holocaust mission—dedication to the religious life and adoption from and contribution to secular civilization—is enhanced by their post-Holocaust mission—renewal of Judaism and Jewry in the Diaspora and creation and sustenance of a Jewish homeland in Israel. Potok's fictional heroes thus aspire, as the novelist does in *Wanderings,* "to rebuild . . . [Judaism's] core from the treasures of our past, fuse it with the best in secularism, and create a new philosophy, a new literature, a new world of Jewish art, a new community, and take seriously the meaning of the word emancipation."

Because Levi regards the sudden appearance of the watch as an extraordinary burden, he dismisses the possibility of its potential to make the present meaningful by evoking the past. Now he hates God, hates Him with a cold passionless contempt. He expresses the utter despair of the believer, "I believe in perfect faith that You are unworthy of my perfect faith. You no longer merit consideration." No bleaker moment exists in Potok's fiction.
                                        —*S. Lillian Kremer*

The year Potok's popular first novel, *The Chosen* (1967), was published, his short story, **"The Dark Place Inside,"** appeared. **"The Dark Place Inside"** portrays an Israeli Holocaust survivor suffering the trauma of his losses sixteen years after their occurrence. On the joyous occasion of the birth of his fifth son, he mourns the loss of four sons who "had walked the narrow corridor and tasted the smoky waters of poison gas in the shower house, together with their mother." We learn that Levi Abramovich escaped death in a mass shooting when he fell into heavy brush a moment before the bullets met their mark; he survived as a fugitive in the barn of a Polish peasant. He had been hunted like an animal by the Nazis: "They had smashed his face in the hunting and bayoneted him in the killing so that his blood had run in dark pools. . . . But the killing had been poorly accomplished; the peasant's herbs had sealed the wounds." Holocaust memories become a dark force in Levi's being, generally suppressed, but occasionally emerging and overpowering his capacity for regeneration. Unlike the survivors in Potok's novels, who appear in brief cameos and largely in the restorative mode of commitment to Judaism and the Jewish community, Levi has not made peace with the God of the Holocaust. Like I. B. Singer's protestors, he voices his anger against the impotent or uncaring God: "I believe in God. I believe He is the paradigm for all the fools in the universe." Receipt of his murdered wife's watch is the catalyst for Levi's transformation from a matter-of-fact dismisser of the ineffectual divine—"God is stupidity. God is comic. God is a fool"—to the despairing protester. He is alienated from God and man: "There is no one to talk to now. . . . There is not even God to talk to he thought, trying to make it a calm thinking and failing miserably." Tormented by the memory of four dead sons, he thinks the appearance of his dead wife's watch is an absurd cruelty and charges God accordingly: "Master of the Universe, . . . if You are truly real, then You are powerless and cruel. If You are able to prevent evil but are unwilling, You are cruel. If You are willing to prevent evil but are not able, then You are without power. And if You are able and willing, why then is there evil?" Because Levi regards the sudden appearance of the watch as an extraordinary burden, he dismisses the possibility of its potential to make the present meaningful by evoking the past. Now he hates God, hates Him with a cold passionless contempt. He expresses the utter despair of the believer, "I believe in perfect faith that You are unworthy of my perfect faith. You no longer merit consideration." No bleaker moment exists in Potok's fiction.

Much more typical of Potok's treatment of the Holocaust is *The Chosen.* The novel, set in the Williamsburg section of Brooklyn, is the story of two sets of fathers and sons and their practice and study of Judaism, set against the backdrop of the Holocaust and the establishment of the State of Israel. These historic forces remain in the novel's background while the religious issues dividing Jewish orthodoxy claim the novelist's central interest. Nevertheless, the *Shoah* remains a leitmotif and an important influence on the lives of the characters. David Malter, a yeshiva teacher, and his son Reuven are Orthodox Jews open to the influences of Western philosophy and scholarship. Reb Saunders, the dynastic

Hasidic *tzaddik,* resists non-Hasidic thought and expects his son Danny to follow the prescriptions of the Hasidim and assume the religious leadership of his father's congregation. The novel's dramatic tension results from opposing interpretations of Jewish religious writing, worship, and practices by the groups. A measure of difference between the Orthodox and Hasidic fathers is the manner of their response to the Holocaust and the establishment of a Jewish homeland in Israel. Similarly, antithetical reactions to these two dimensions of twentieth-century Jewish history divide the sons.

In a rare instance of American fictional treatment of the Allies' abandonment of the Jews, David Malter addresses Anthony Eden's 1942 House of Commons speech detailing the Nazi genocide plan and Eden's failure to move beyond rhetorical denunciation of the Final Solution. Malter is outraged by British moral failure:

> the whole machinery of democratic expression had been set in motion to impress upon the British Government the need for action—and not a thing was done. Everyone was sympathetic, but no one was sympathetic enough. The British let some few Jews in, and then closed their doors. America hadn't cared enough, either. No one had cared enough. The world closed its doors and six million Jews were slaughtered.

Although the Holocaust is not in the forefront of Potok's young protagonists' discussions, they are deeply concerned about Jewish losses and refer to Hitler's war against Jewry in the context of general war news. With the end of war and release of news of the concentration camps, Reuven expresses bewilderment at the immensity of the Nazi crimes against Jewry:

> The numbers of the Jews slaughtered had gone from one million to three million to four million, and almost every article we read said that the last count was still incomplete, the final number would probably reach six million. I couldn't . . . imagine six million of my people murdered. . . . It didn't make any sense at all. My mind couldn't hold on to it, to the death of six million people.

Reb Saunders spoke "of the Jewish world in Europe, of the people he had known who were now probably dead, of the brutality of the world," interpreting this catastrophe historically, "the world drinks our blood." He laments the slaughter of the six million in the context of an extraordinary history of persecution. Although Saunders reluctantly accepts the Holocaust as "the will of God," a Divine mystery of inaction, he expresses his bewilderment and petitions the Almighty, "Master of the Universe, how do You permit such a thing to happen?" Departing from his characteristic tendency

to explain Jewish beliefs and attitudes, Potok allows the statement to stand without pursuing its theological implications.

In contrast to many writers' focus on the atrocities of the Holocaust period and burdens of Holocaust survival, Potok generally concentrates on the possibilities of Holocaust restoration. David Malter rejects Reb Saunders' acceptance of the Holocaust as God's will, arguing instead "We cannot wait for God. If there is an answer, we must make it ourselves." Instead, he works for "the education of American Jewry and a Jewish state in Palestine." Reb Saunders, bound by the belief in a religious and holy state ushered in by the Messiah, rejects Zionism because it is a secular movement. For some Hasidim, the establishment of a secular state in Israel was regarded as a Torahic violation. For Malter, the way to derive meaning from the slaughter of six million Jews is for American Jews to replace the lost treasures of Judaism, to train teachers and rabbis to lead the people and to generate a religious renaissance among American Jews. He is heartened by a return to the synagogues, even by the Jewishly uneducated, believing that the mission of the religious is to educate the assimilated and return them to Judaism and to the Jewish people. In the immediate aftermath of the Holocaust and before the establishment of the State of Israel, Malter is convinced that Judaism must be rebuilt in America or perish. When Zionism is resuscitated, David Malter responds enthusiastically and works assiduously to realize Zionist goals. At a massive rally in Madison Square Garden, Malter argues the need to arouse the world to the desperate requirement for a Jewish homeland in Palestine, particularly as a haven for those "that had escaped Hitler's ovens." Furthermore, he counters that

> the slaughter of six million Jews would have meaning only on the day a Jewish state was established. Only then would their sacrifice begin to make some sense; only then would the songs of faith they had sung on their way to the gas chambers take on meaning; only then would Jewry again become a light to the world.

When the United Nations voted for the Partition Plan, Malter reacts with an exuberance common in the American Jewish community:

> The death of the six million Jews had finally been given meaning. . . . After two thousand years, it had finally happened. We were a people again, with our own land. We were a blessed generation. We had been given the opportunity to see the creation of the Jewish state.

Sharing his father's dreams, Reuven endangers his own safety to load smuggled arms for the Jewish Army, which must meet the Arab threat to destroy the new nation as soon as it is established.

In deference to his father, Danny refrains from supporting the Zionist movement. As Arab anti-Jewish violence mounts and the toll of Jewish dead increases daily, Reb Saunders' league becomes silent in its opposition to the secular state. Moved by the similarity of Nazi and Arab anti-Semitism, Hasidic opponents lament Jewish blood being spilled again: "Hitler wasn't enough. Now more Jewish blood, more slaughter. What does the world want from us? Six million isn't enough? More Jews have to die?" Their pain over the new outbreak of violence against the Jews of Israel outweighs Hasidic opposition to the secular state, and they end their vocal campaign against the establishment and recognition of Israel.

The sequel to *The Chosen, The Promise,* continues to trace the lives of Reuven Malter preparing for rabbinic ordination and Danny Saunders pursuing a career in clinical psychology. Reuven is at the center of a theological conflict between fundamentalist-traditionalists and religious scholars who bring the tools of scientific textual criticism to the analysis of religious sources. The religious dichotomy dramatized between Hasidic and *Mitnagdic* orthodoxies in *The Chosen* is extended in *The Promise* to a philosophic conflict between Orthodox and Conservative approaches to Talmud study. The Conservative faction is represented by a new character, Abraham Gordon, and the traditionalist faction by several Holocaust survivors who teach at David Malter's yeshiva, and by Rav Kalman who teaches at Reuven's seminary. Gordon is an American scholar who suffered none of the European hardships that Kalman experienced. Yet the Holocaust changed the direction of his life. After experiencing a crisis of faith, Gordon went to Europe for two years of postdoctoral work in logic with the Vienna Circle positivists. He had been in Germany and reported that he "could smell the smoke of the crematoria even before anyone knew what a crematorium was." Realizing that not many Jews would survive Hitler's Europe, Gordon rejected an invitation from Harvard University to teach logic and entered a seminary to aid in rebuilding American Judaism, a Judaism free of fundamentalist dogma that would appeal to progressive thinkers. Although David Malter remains in the Orthodox community, his scholarly techniques of comparative textual analysis and emendation, like Abraham Gordon's, are often discredited by fundamentalists and associated with progressive thinkers. Malter's major antagonist is his son's teacher, a rigorous European Talmudist who has dedicated his life to traditional Talmudic explication.

Unlike Bellow, Wallant, and Elman who focus on physical and psychological traumas of survivorship, Potok, like Singer, examines the religious and theological implications of the concentrationary experience. The reader perceives the survivors through Reuven's impressions of their responses to the unorthodox scholarship of Abraham Gordon and David Malter. Reuven attributes religious zeal of the neighborhood to the influence of the concentration camp traditionalists: "everything traditional was being drawn toward . . . zealousness. They had changed everything merely by surviving and crossing an ocean. They had brought that spark to the broken streets of Williamsburg, and men like Rav Kalman who were not Hasidim felt swayed by their presence and believed themselves to be equally zealous guardians of the spark."

The survivors of the "sulfurous chaos of the concentration camps . . . eyes brooding, like balls of black flame turned inward upon private visions of the demonic," remain steadfast traditionalists, staunchly opposed to modern tampering with orthodox worship, practice, and scholarship. Undefeated by the physical enemy in Europe, they are prepared to do battle with those they perceive to be Judaism's spiritual enemies in America. Representative of the survivors' intolerance for other expressions of Jewish learning and worship are the "newcomers" at David Malter's yeshiva, who denounce his publications as a threat to scripture and support Abraham Gordon's excommunication. Reuven's teacher, Rav Kalman, also rejects other methods in fealty to his teachers and students who died martyrs' deaths. The survivor-purists perceive American Jewish schools, where students do not wear skullcaps and teachers do not believe that the Torah was given to Moses by God, as being ritually "unclean." Such a school in their opinion is "a desecration of the name of God." Potok's survivors bear witness to the Holocaust through their determination to live religiously pure lives, to live according to the commandments, to defend the Torah, and to revitalize the *Yiddishkeit* (Jewishness) that the Nazis sought to destroy. Against the Nazi program of death and destruction, these Jews defiantly stand for the sanctity of life. Potok's survivors are engaged in the restorative process, regenerating Judaism and the Jewish people.

> Here, [in] Williamsburg, they set about rebuilding their burned-out world. Families had been destroyed; they remarried and created new families. Dynasties had been shattered; elders met and formed new dynasties. Children had been killed; their women now seemed forever pregnant.

Unlike the survivors in Singer's fiction who rant against an unjust God, the characters in Potok's novels neither protest God's Holocaust silence nor question their faith in God and dedication to Torah Judaism. As zealous "guardians of the spark," they may be disruptive to progressive American Jewry but even those Americans who have the most to lose from their irresoluteness, understand the zealots' determination to guard the Torah their comrades died for. Despite Hitler's racial ideology, Potok's characters never speak of

Jews dying in Hitler's racial war. Their perception is religious, and the victims died *kiddish ha-Shem*, religious martyrs sanctifying God's holy name.

The characters in Potok's novels neither protest God's Holocaust silence nor question their faith in God and dedication to Torah Judaism.
—*S. Lillian Kremer*

Rav Kalman, the only survivor individually developed by Potok, fiercely protects his scholarly approach to the sacred texts in order to honor God's word and the memory of those Jews who lived their lives and lost their lives in devotion to Torah and God. Through student speculation about his past, we learn that he had been a teacher in a highly reputed yeshiva in Vilna, a city famed for the superiority of its Jewish institutions of learning. It is known that he spent two years in a German concentration camp in northern Poland, the rest is rumor. Some think storm troopers shot his wife and three daughters before his eyes in the woods outside Warsaw. Other speculations focus on his escape and capture:

> he had escaped from a concentration camp, been caught, and escaped again; he had crossed the Polish frontier into Russia and fought with Russian partisans for a year. One rumor had it that he had organized a group of Orthodox Jewish partisans that specialized in blowing up the tracks of German trains carrying Jews to the concentration camps. Another rumor had it that he had been concealed in a bunker for more than a year by a Polish farm family, had been discovered, had been forced to watch the execution of the family, and had somehow escaped again. He was said to have made his way across northern Russia into Siberia and from there to Shanghai, where he had waited out the war under the eyes of the Japanese, who were not possessed of Hitler's feelings toward Jews and who left the few Jews under their rule alone. According to this version of the life of Rav Kalman, he was brought to America by the administration of Hirsch University and was promptly invited to teach in the rabbinical department.

In marked contrast to the fictional characters of Wallant, Malamud, and Singer who either speak directly of their Holocaust experiences or think about them, in Potok's fiction nonsurvivors speculate about the Holocaust suffering of survivors. It is unclear why Potok includes these student speculations rather than incorporating direct survivor commentary. Perhaps they offer the writer a means of briefly referring to multiple holocaustal experiences and avoiding the need to

create other characters with full biographies and dramatic roles in the manner of Singer, Bellow, and Cohen. Rather than dwell on past atrocities, Potok's survivors concentrate on living. Reuven's father verifies the Shanghai episode. The elder Malter comments on the excellence of Rav Kalman's Talmudic reputation and cites Kalman's establishment of a yeshiva in Shanghai as the cause of delay in bringing him to America where his services were coveted as "a great Talmud scholar" and "one of the great men in Orthodoxy."

David Malter, who served as Potok's voice of reason in *The Chosen*, continues in that fashion in the sequel, and it is his observation that Kalman is to be respected as a champion of the Torah. Malter draws an analogy between Kalman's resistance to Nazism and his resistance to weakened religious observance: "He was not of those who believed in going willingly to the crematoria. He was with the partisans and killed German soldiers for Torah. Now he defends it with words."

Just as we discover Kalman's heroism, first in student speculation and later confirmed by David Malter, so we also first learn of Kalman's suffering under Nazi medical experimentation through an exchange he has with Reuven's friend Danny Saunders regarding his treatment of a withdrawn patient. Kalman becomes rigid at Danny's mere mention of the word *experiment* to explain Michael Gordon's psychological therapy. Later we learn that because of the experiments he endured Kalman has not remarried and started a new family. This indirect means of suggesting holocaustal atrocity is typical of Potok's reluctance to use graphic description of torture or direct or dramatic references to the concentrationary universe. The reader can assume from ample historic reference the types of medical experiments Kalman may have witnessed and endured. In addition to Kalman's response to the word *experiment* and speculation about that which he experienced, one of the novel's most sympathetic characters, the modern scholar and victim of Rav Kalman's fierce orthodoxy, Abraham Gordon, addresses the philosophic implications of Kalman's Holocaust suffering:

> The concentration camps destroyed a lot more than European Jewry. They destroyed man's faith in himself. I cannot blame Rav Kalman for being suspicious of man and believing only in God. Why should anyone believe in man? There are going to be decades of chaos until we learn to believe again in man.

The progressives of Potok's fiction, like their Orthodox and fundamentalist brothers, consistently respond to the Holocaust with determination to rebuild Jewry through a revitalized and strengthened Judaism. Unlike the debilitated survivors of Wallant's, Bellow's, and Singer's novels, Potok's survivors are developed not in terms of their physical and psychological disabilities but as Jews strengthened in their commitment to Judaism. They are ever vigilant, ever dedicated, whether as rabbis, scholars, or Zionists, to the survival and flourishing of Judaism and the Jewish people. Beyond Holocaust horror looms a Jewish renaissance.

Potok's fourth novel, *In the Beginning,* continues to evidence his interests in Judaism and Jewish history. The subject is the Jewish encounter with anti-Semitism, including European, Arab, and American variations. Like Bellow, Epstein, Wallant, and Singer, Potok makes a strong case for a causal relationship between the Holocaust and historic Christian anti-Semitism. He departs from some of the others in the extent to which he develops the American and Arab varieties. Although the Holocaust was of import in the earlier fiction, Potok had presented it as a haunted presence in the lives of American Jews and survivors and as further motivation for their commitment to Judaism and Zionism. *In the Beginning* brings historic anti-Semitism, "the dark underbelly of Western civilization," and its holocaustal manifestation to the thematic core and dramatic center of the novel. Addressing the importance of anti-Semitism and the Holocaust on the American-Jewish consciousness, Potok said:

> Probably the American Jew feels . . . quite guilt-ridden . . . For whatever reason, he never did enough at a crucial point in time by way of an effort to get the thing stopped, or to protest it. . . . I don't see how it is possible to think the world through Jewish eyes without having the blood-screen of the Holocaust in front of your eyes as part of the filtering. I'll go even further and say that for thinking people, Jew or non-Jew, I don't think it is possible to think the world anymore in this century without thinking Holocaust.

Readers of Potok's earlier novels will find much that is familiar in the fourth work: narrative that is presented from the point of view of an intelligent, sensitive young boy; a positive and supportive relationship between two males; and vital father-son and teacher-student character constructs. Departure from the previously established patterns is seen in a sustained antagonism between two boys and the significant intrusion of the secular world in terms of economic depression and social conflict.

David Lurie, the first-person narrator, tells his story chronologically from childhood through early adulthood revealing his initiation to anti-Semitism through his father's European memories and his own victimization at the hands of anti-Semitic neighborhood bullies. The narrative is set in an immigrant Bronx neighborhood where transplanted Europeans have retained their Old World fears and prejudices and passed them on to their American-born children. Here

Potok offers an unusual double exposure to anti-Semitism, superimposing a child's American experience on the adult European manifestations. The bustling multiethnic neighborhoods of the Bronx, where Potok spent his childhood, provide the realistic backdrop for antagonistic encounters between Jew and gentile. Urban experience impinges more forcefully on David Lurie than it had on Reuven Malter, Danny Saunders, and Asher Lev. In addition to a yeshiva classroom, a synagogue, and an observant home, the novel's settings include streets, schoolyards, business districts, and a local zoo. Eddie Kulanski, son of Polish immigrants, is described by his Jewish victim as hating Jews with "a kind of mindless demonic rage." Although still a child, this hooligan acts like an adult, expressing prejudice that "bore the breeding of a thousand years." The novel's Jewish protagonist, named for an uncle who died in a pogrom, has been educated in the history of European anti-Semitism and knows of his family's persecution, but is nevertheless surprised to find it prevalent in America. Eddie learns that David's family is from Poland and he spews the Old World venom in his mother tongue, using the Polish epithet *Anonymowe Panstwo,* ("Anonymous Empire") reiterating the slander outlined in *The Protocols of the Elders of Zion*—namely, that Jews secretly conspire first to destroy Christian countries and then to dominate the world. Exemplifying Potok's method of using the novel to inform the reader of Jewish history is the expository speech on the Jewish conspiracy by David's older cousin, Saul:

> This group is supposed to be able to make all kinds of problems for the goyim because it owns most of the banks and newspapers in the world. These old Jews can do almost anything because they have so much money and control the news and what people say and think. They have plans for all the goyishe governments to get into such bad trouble that they'll fail—and then these Jews can take over the world. My teacher said that in Poland they call this secret organization *Anonymowe Panstwo.* It's even in the Polish dictionary, he said. Almost everyone in Poland believes it.

Variations of anti-Semitic attitudes expressed in all historic periods reappear in the microcosm of David's childhood world. In a scene that would be comic were it not for its sinister implications, David is watching his sleeping infant brother when Eddie and an older cousin, who shares his anti-Jewish prejudices, insist on inspecting the baby's horns. Disappointed to find the child hornless, they question David about the age at which he lost his horns. Eddie parrots the oft-repeated Christian charge of Jewish influence and affluence, albeit in childish overtones: "You own all the money, but you don't own this here sidewalk." Paralleling the European model, but on a smaller scale, violent words lead to violent action. After David accidentally rides his tricycle over Eddie's hand, which was poised on the sidewalk in a street game, Eddie seeks revenge. Nothing short of David's Jewish life will suit him. He tries repeatedly to push the tricycle and rider into oncoming traffic. Unable to inflict his murderous desire on David because an adult intervenes, Eddie arranges for his cousin to slash the tire of David's tricycle. On another occasion Eddie and his cousin conduct a surrealistic chase and assault on David, in an environment suggestive of primitive brutality. The cousins ambush the unsuspecting David in the Bronx Zoo. With the rallying cry "for Christ's sake," they molest David, satisfying their lurid curiosity about the appearance of a circumcised penis. During the attack, David suspects the young anti-Semite's pleasure in Jewish pain and asks rhetorically: "Eddie. Have you seen a concentration camp? Did they look good, all those corpses of dead Jews?"

Emphasizing the Christian source and sustenance of anti-Semitism that is dramatically manifested in the conflict between the boys, a Christian neighbor cites the deicide libel as the fuel for nearly 2000 years of murderous Christian anti-Semitism and informs the Jewish innocent of church doctrine and books that perpetuate the infamy. David is persistently puzzled by the motivation for Christian anti-Semitism. As he looks out the window of his small synagogue at a large local church, he wonders "how a statue whose face was so full of love could be worshipped by someone whose heart was so full of hate." To understand why Christians hate Jews so vehemently, David goes to the library to read the New Testament, the ur-text for anti-Semitism. In Matthew, he finds "rage and scorn directed at the scribes and Pharisees. The rabbis of the Talmud . . . called hypocrites! . . . the word *Jews* in the account of the crucifixion. In Mark he finds further expression of hatred for the Pharisees and similar invectives on the crucifixion in Luke and John. Further, David finds corroboration for early Christian anti-Semitism in current Catholic textbooks that he finds in the playground of a nearby parochial school. In *Religion: Doctrine and Practice* by Francis B. Cassilly, S.J., he reads "The widespread popularity enjoyed by this text since its appearance in 1926 is evidence that our Catholic schools consider the fundamental truths of Faith essential to the high-school course in religion." He turns to the index to search for references to Jews and finds the following: "The Jews as a nation refused to accept Christ and since His time they have been wanderers on the earth without a temple or a sacrifice, and without the Messias." Next he finds a Catholic distortion of the Jewish rejection of Jesus: "The Jews rejected Christ mainly because they expected Him to found a never-ending kingdom, as was foretold in the prophecies. This He really did, but the kingdom He founded—the Church—was a spiritual one, not a temporal one such as the carnal Jews were hoping for." The causal link between Catholic anti-Semitism and the success of the Holocaust is manifested in Potok's documentary incorporation of propaganda dissemi-

nated by Father Charles Coughlin and his supporters during the Holocaust.

Potok skillfully juxtaposes David's American anti-Semitic experiences with his father's European encounters, demonstrating how each generation is shaped by this social pathology. Although Max Lurie's animosity for Christians has been regularly and amply refurbished through repetitions of anti-Jewish actions, the Tulchin massacre looms largest in his consciousness as a touchstone of Christian betrayal of Jewry and Jewry's misplaced trust in Christian decency. Max begins his account of the attack on the city objectively and concludes in a passionate denunciation:

> There were in it Jews and Poles. Cossacks attacked it. The Jews fought well. The Poles wanted to surrender. The Jews could have taken over the city from the Poles and continued fighting. But their rabbi would not let them do it. He was afraid that Poles all over Poland would take revenge on all the Jews in Poland. So the Jews of Tulchin gave all their possessions to the Poles to give to the Cossacks. They hoped the Cossacks would take the money and jewels and gold and not destroy the city. The Cossacks took it all from the Poles and then asked the Poles to hand over the Jews. They handed over the Jews, the same Jews who had fought with them to defend the city. The bastard Poles . . . A nice story, yes? The courageous Jews! What Martyrdom! They could have lived if they had converted to Christianity. Not one of them accepted the offer. What was there in Christianity? It is the idolatry of butchers and murders.

It is from this experience that Max knows it is naive for Jews to expect help from gentiles in the Nazi era. As a descendant of a Tulchin massacre survivor, Max rages against the passive Jewish mentality, which tries to negotiate peace when armed resistance is needed to counter enemies bent on slaughtering Jews. Max Lurie shares the contempt for Poles that is common among many of Singer's Jews, because of their extensive experience with Polish anti-Semitism. Certainly the bitterness of Lurie's tone is unprecedented in the fiction created by American-born novelists, but it is authentic in light of Polish-Jewish history. Lurie rages equally against Catholic murderers and Tulchin's rabbi, who trusted Christians to be true to their Jewish neighbors and prevented the Jews from defending themselves.

The ex-machine-gunner spares no details when telling his son of the wholesale butchery of Polish Jews by Russians, Ukrainians, and fellow Poles during World War I. He teaches David about Jewish suffering under Marshall Pilsudski, a national hero, who refused to discomfort Polish peasants by interfering with their violence against Jews. Like Potok's father, Max Lurie returned from serving his country in World War I to the native enemy eager to exercise its anti-Semitic prejudices. Emblematic of traditional Polish anti-Semitism is the scar Max bears from a wound he sustained on a post-war troop train. The train was detained by bandits who stole only from Jewish soldiers. Max refused to surrender his prayer shawl, and a bandit slashed his face. Not one comrade with whom Max served came to his assistance. It is this kind of pervasive Polish anti-Semitism that leads Max to unite the surviving Jews of his unit into the *Am Kedoshim* Society, a Jewish self-defense group. For Max Lurie, two thousand years of Christian betrayal and indiscriminate slaughter of Jews make the formation of aggressive Jewish self-defense units the only viable response to anti-Semitism.

Photography and the visual imagination offer means through which David Lurie engages in his people's suffering. The *Am Kedoshim* photograph and the history it represents serve for Potok as connective tissue for David's comprehension of historic anti-Semitism and as a structural link connecting the microcosm of Lurie family history to collective Jewish experience. Lurie founded the society in the aftermath of World War I to combat Polish anti-Semitism. Opposing passive acceptance of persecution, the men of *Am Kedoshim*

> learned never to forget the harm our enemies inflict upon us. We have learned that when we work together we can defeat our enemies. We will not stand by with our arms folded when our enemies attack us; nor will we do as some of our families did almost three hundred years ago in Tulchin when they decided not to attack the Poles in that city because they feared what Poles in other cities might do to Jews. We leave such righteousness to other Jews, . . . to Jews whose pure souls make them unable to shed goyishe blood.

Growing Depression-era anti-Jewish violence and the rise of Nazism lead the *Am Kedoshim* to send a representative to get Jews out of Europe and to assist those facing the mounting terror.

David's education in anti-Semitism takes a particularly sinister turn with the news of the Hebron Massacre. He expects outbursts of persecution against Jews in Europe, but he is astonished by the slaughter of Jews in Palestine. Although he learns of violence against Jews in Jerusalem, Safed, Tel Aviv, and Haifa, it is the Arab massacre of yeshiva students in Hebron that troubles David most intensely. Max makes the historical analogy between the Tulchin rabbi and the Hebron Jewish leadership. He voices ire against the Hebron leaders who had anticipated Arab violence, yet refused the protection of the Jewish self-defense organization in order to avoid antagonizing the British commander who guaranteed community safety on the condition that the Jews do

nothing to provoke the Arabs. As Lurie's response to Hebron becomes a free association with Tulchin, the novelist superimposes a forward glance at the Holocaust in the Hebron Massacre:

> On the fifteenth of August, Tisha B'av, there had been Arab disturbances in Jerusalem. The British said these had been in reaction to the demonstration staged by the followers of Jabotinsky at the Western Wall protesting new British regulations that interfered with Jewish religious services at the Wall. But we knew all about the British, he said. Our dear friends, the British. They announced that they washed their hands of the Jews as a result of this demonstration, and the Arabs took the hint. The day after the demonstration, on Tish B'av, a group of Arabs beat up Jews gathered at the Wall for prayers, and then burned copies of the Book of Psalms. . . . Then the Mufti of Jerusalem spread the rumor that the Jews were ready to capture and desecrate the holy mosques on the Temple Mount in Jerusalem. The Arabs began coming into Jerusalem from all over the country. In Hebron, Arabs who were friends of the Jews reported that messengers of the Mufti had been in the city and had preached in the mosque . . . that the Jews had attacked Arabs in Jerusalem and desecrated their mosques.

> The leaders of the Jewish community of Hebron met secretly. They were informed that the Jewish self-defense organization had sent a message from its headquarters in Jerusalem that it was prepared to dispatch a group of armed young men to defend the Jews at Hebron. At the same time, the leaders were informed that the British district commander had guaranteed the safety of the Jews of Hebron on condition that the Jews do nothing to provoke the Arabs and that no one who was not a resident of the city should enter it. . . . The Jews decided to reject the offer of the self-defense organization. They believed the goyim. They were possessed by the mentality of Tulchin. . . . A band of Arabs returned to Hebron from a mass meeting led by the Mufti and his followers in Jerusalem. They ran through the city attacking Jews. They killed a student they found in the yeshiva. . . . On Shabbos morning, . . . Arabs began coming into the city from all over. They carried rifles and revolvers and knives and swords. The Jews locked themselves in their houses. The police warned the Jews to remain inside. Like sheep, they remained inside. And like sheep, they were slaughtered. They were shot and stabbed and chopped to pieces. They had their eyes pierced and their hands cut off. They were burned to death inside their homes and inside the Hadassah Hospital in Hebron.

Bernard Malamud's treatment of the Russian persecution and incarceration in the Beiliss case is an analogue for the Holocaust. So, too, Potok's description of the Hebron Massacre includes elements in common with the Holocaust. Lurie's description of the Hebron Massacre incorporates all the elements of European Holocaust betrayal. False claims of Jewish intent to destroy Islamic holy places parallels Nazi lies about undue Jewish political and economic influence in Europe. Staging the attack on *Tisha B'au,* a day of fasting, mirrors Nazi "special actions" on Jewish holy days—like the Passover offensive against the Warsaw Ghetto. Britain's betrayal of Jews in Hebron foreshadows Britain's betrayal of the Jews in the concentration camps and Britain's sabotage of the Joel Brand mission to save a small portion of Hungarian Jewry in 1944. Potok's lengthy history lesson, like I. B. Singer's use of the Chmielnicki Massacre in *The Satan of Goray,* corresponds to the holocaustal violence and the methods of deceit used to stir up violence against the Jews— the attacks with armed units, which are then protected and inspired to further atrocities by the government in power.

The recitation of anti-Semitic history and David's experience of anti-Jewish street violence converge in the recesses of his imagination as he juxtaposes his father's militant response with his impotent fear. Introduction of the Holocaust in this novel is an organic outgrowth of Potok's focus on Polish and Arab anti-Semitism. Representative of the novelist's increasing skill and sensitivity for integrating liturgy and theme is his invocation of the Holocaust theme in relation to a Yom Kippur memorial service. As David chants a lament for Torah sages martyred during Roman dominion, he grieves for an anonymous Jew, whose murder in Berlin by uniformed Nazis was witnessed from a passing cab by an *Am Kedoshim* member. The witness later read that "the man, a Jew, was found dead the next morning in an alley near a bookstore." During a subsequent trip to Germany to help Jews, the Nazis inform the witness that they will look kindly neither upon his presence in Germany nor his efforts to rescue Jews. American Jewish efforts to aid European Jews is given scant attention in American Holocaust fiction, but Chaim Potok, like Arthur Cohen, acknowledges the central role of immigrant Jews in this endeavor.

Complementing the theme of the continuum of anti-Semitic persecution through reference to the lamentation liturgy is the introduction of biblical and folkloric material. *Am Kedoshim's* foiled efforts to save Jews, culminating in Max Lurie's rage, find parallel in David's withdrawal into biblical and mythological constructs. He conceives of a flood that would cleanse Lemberg, Warsaw, Lodz, the cities of ancestral persecution, and then the site of his own victimization. Rather than a destructive flood, however, it would be a purging flood in whose aftermath "everything outside would be clean and white and the Angel of Death would have less of a job to do because goyim would not kill Jews and the en-

tire world would be free of accidents. Perhaps the Angel of Death himself would die in the flood; the only one to die." On the occasion of the Hebron Massacre, David retreats into a stream of consciousness revery in which he assumes his father's militant personality, raging as his father has against Jewish passivity in the face of gentile violence. Recalling Russian and Polish anti-Jewish atrocities, the boy soldier rants against the Cossacks, for having "Jewish blood on their sabers. And the Jewish flesh on their whips." He also rebukes the Jews: "You are going to sit there reciting Psalms? When did a Psalm prevent a throat from being torn open?" David imagines taking his father's role: the Jew who fights the oppressor, the machine-gunner and cavalryman, the founder and organizer of the *Am Kedoshim* Society, a holy order for the defense of the Jewish people.

In *The Last of the Just,* Andre Schwarz-Bart incorporates the legend of the thirty-six righteous men as a means of relating the history of anti-Semitic persecution from the eleventh to the twentieth century, culminating in the Holocaust. Potok takes a similar approach in his incorporation of the Golem of Prague myth. Jewish folklore created a mythic *golem,* fashioned from lifeless, shapeless matter by a person who knew God's ineffable name and who could, by its mystic means, breath life into the homunculus. The sixteenth-century *golem* was characterized as a huge and very strong figure with a propensity for exercising its physical power, even in indiscriminate destruction. Although the oral tradition inevitably generates variations, most share commonalities including the *golem's* supernatural capacity to discover and foil anti-Jewish violence and the *golem's* enormous strength, used most often to protect powerless Jews from potent enemies. Viewed within the historic frame of European anti-Semitic terror, it is the *golem's* protective role that appealed to the collective imagination of an oppressed people. For his *Legend of the Golem of Prague,* Rabbi Loew endowed the figure with communal responsibility and moral conscience and thus fashioned "a national protector of persecuted Jews, a God-sent Avenger of the wrongs done to a helpless people."

David's *golem* fantasies coincide with the Third Reich's heightened anti-Jewish violence. Gazing into the dark rectangle of his window shade David imagines a Nazi demonstration, flags and banners waving, torches smoking, and twenty-thousand brown-shirted men shouting and saluting. As the news from abroad becomes more violent, ever more menacing visions appear in David's window shade. He consults with the *golem* and envisions himself performing heroically, shouting down the Nazis, quelling demonstrations, and spying on Nazi strategy sessions. The shadow glows red and the boy imagines a German building ablaze. Another time, he imagines a holocaustal conflagration, a synagogue a flame, and himself plunging swiftly through smoke and fire toward the ark to save the endangered Torah scrolls:

Golem, look what they've done, the brown-shirted servants of the Angel of Death. We must save the Torah scrolls! He came then out of the invisibility in which I had left him and stood beside my bed in the darkness. He bowed in mute acknowledgment of my words, bringing his face close to mine, the face I had molded, my face; then he straightened his massive seven-foot frame and in a leap my eyes could barely discern was suddenly inside the window shade. . . . Through the flames! Into the smoke and through the flames! The flames tore at me but I felt nothing and I moved swiftly through smoke-filled corridors and burst into the heart of the synagogue where the pews were burning and the flames licked at the curtain of the Ark. . . . I tore at the flames with my fingers, beating them away from the sacred words. I gathered the scrolls into my arms and left them with startled sleepy-eyed men on the street. The flames roared in my ears. I slipped from the rectangle and lay in my bed listening to the long clattering of an elevated train. You did well, I murmured. Slowly, the Golem bowed.

Dreams commonly used in European Holocaust literature here, too, reflect anxieties of the impotent while adding mythic elements to link historic brutality and contemporary travail. As Nazi harassment of German Jews escalates, the *golem* recedes. During the Passover season—the celebration of the deliverance of the Israelites from Egyptian bondage—David retreats into silence. The *golem* having failed, David now longs for another Moses to deliver the Jews from the German Angel of Death. Potok closes this section of the novel by juxtaposing the end of the *golem* reveries with the German invasion of Poland and cessation of the delivery of mail to or from the family in Poland. "The silences deepened and grew lengthier as the Nazi darkness spread itself across Europe."

The final segment of the novel, set in the Holocaust era and its immediate aftermath, deals with heightened American anti-Semitism as exemplified by the followers of Father Charles E. Coughlin and his Social Justice Movement. Coughlin spewed anti-Semitic propaganda on his regularly scheduled radio broadcasts and in his tabloid, *Social Justice.* As with the Third Reich, rhetoric inspired action. Roaming gangs of American hooligans ambushed yeshiva boys and old Jews: "platoons of goyim numbering about twenty-five each walking the streets of New York looking for Jews. They would try to sell a copy of *Social Justice* to someone who looked Jewish and if he refused to buy it they would start taunting him and pushing him and then they would beat him and run off." Max Lurie had assured his son that the great difference between European and American anti-Semitism was that anti-Semitism was supported and sponsored by the government in Europe, but the American government re-

jected such behavior. Yet David is a witness to the collaboration of police officers' anti-Semitism, when they passively stand by as a Jew is assaulted in a blatant anti-Semitic attack. Incorporation of the Father Coughlin episode suggests both the Christian foundation upon which Nazi racial anti-Semitism thrived and the support given the Nazis' program of genocide by the churches in Europe.

While hooligans attacked Jews in American streets, genteel anti-Semites in Congress blocked Jewish immigration despite their knowledge of the mass murders occurring in Europe. Although Potok fails to develop this matter at length, he alludes to it in the *Am Kedoshim* rescue worker's assessment of Jewish emigration from Nazi-occupied Europe: "Europe and England will take in a few. So will America. But no country will want many of them." As Germany's Final Solution becomes ever clearer, Max's despair gives way to fatalism. In response to his son's inquiry about assistance for the Jews, Lurie explains: "It is not officially known as yet. When it becomes officially known, then governments will meet and decide that nothing can be done." Since the Jews of America can do little during the war to save European Jewry, the members of the *Am Kedoshim,* like Arthur Cohen's Jews of the Society for the Rescue and Resurrection of Jewry, begin to plan their strategy for helping the surviving remnant. Max advocates the need for a Jewish army in Palestine to counter the anticipated British resistance to Jewish immigration.

Through David's mother, Potok registers the impact of the Holocaust on American-Jewish immigrants whose families were being destroyed in Europe. Ruth Lurie continues to care for her American family's physical needs, but withdraws from them emotionally. Having failed to convince her parents to come to America from Poland when they actually had visas and when exodus was possible, she fears they will not survive the war. Eventually Ruth stops reading the old letters from her parents and, for periods lasting several days, avoids speech. The Luries knew during the second year of the war of the massive death toll of Eastern European Jewry, but it is at war's end that they learn the full impact of the concentration camp atrocities and mass murders. Confirmation is received that the families were transferred from Auschwitz to Bergen-Belsen and no one survived. Over 150 family members perished, a fate similar to that which the Potoks suffered. The novelist, who was David's age at war's end, draws on his own history for David's reaction to "newspaper photographs, the memorial assemblies, the disbelief in the faces of friends, the shock as news came of death and more death." Potok writes, "I remember my father's rage, my mother's soft endless weeping." Predictably, Max rages and Ruth weeps.

Only when he writes of the Bergen-Belsen photographs does Potok treat Holocaust atrocities graphically. "Grotesque forms with skeletal arms and legs and rib cages and heads lay stacked like macabre cordwood on a stone ramp." The enormity of the crime is suggested by "hills of corpses, pits of bones, the naked rubble of the dead and the staring eyes and hollow faces of the survivors." David is overwhelmed by a photograph of dead children, "eyes and mouths open, bodies twisted and frozen with death." From the photographs, David understands the truth of his teacher's assessment of the German contribution to the technology of death and the full implications of the Nazi crime against Jewry: "They destroyed an entire civilization. The Nazis have taught Western civilization that not only making cars but also committing murder can become a mass production industry." In addition to realistic rendering, Potok composes an imagistic revery in which David imagines the Bergen-Belsen newsphotos while walking along a parapet overlooking the Hudson River. As he looks at the railroad tracks and a shanty town across the river, he falls down a rocky bluff and cuts his finger, which bleeds profusely. The river begins to flow red—all the world is red. As a freight train passes, he imagines the central holocaustal vision of the trains that crisscrossed German-occupied Europe, behind whose sealed doors he envisions "a multitude of writhing human beings packed together riding in filth and terror." The photographs of Bergen-Belsen atrocities catapult David from traditional to secular biblical scholarship and to a determination to dedicate his life

> to fighting what these accident-makers are doing with . . . the most beautiful photograph of all; that is to say, the picture of my people in the Bible. As a result of the fusion of these two metaphors, he leaves his Orthodoxy, enters one of the metaphors: the secular world, in order to understand better the other metaphor: the photograph, the Bible, which is the picture of his people at a certain period of time.

The final confrontation with anti-Semitism comes to this boy from modern Bible criticism. David follows the path of Potok's colleagues who entered the field of Bible scholarship "to change the attitude of that discipline toward Jews." He loves the Torah and decides to join the ranks of its detractors to prove them wrong, to discredit their insertion of anti-Semitic innuendo in their writing, to use textual criticism—the scholarly method abhorrent to traditionalists—to save the Torah from its detractors. The child who sought to save the Torah from the flames of the anti-Semites in his *golem* fantasies has matured and found a substantive way to contribute to Torahic preservation. However, his method distresses his father who objects to textual criticism because of its association not only with all that he hates about modern Germany but with nineteenth-century German Jewish scholar's creation of Reform Judaism, which he regards as the destruction of Torah Judaism.

The novel's final Holocaust reference appears in the postwar era. David, a biblical scholar, travels to Germany to inspect a manuscript. There he sets out on his quest "into the final beginnings" of his family. In the land of annihilation, standing at the entrance to Bergen-Belsen, David is seized by paralytic terror. Inclined to flee, he is urged forward by his Uncle David's voice and by a vision of his teacher commanding him to view the remains of a family devoted to Torah. Out of the wind, his Uncle David, the victim of the Lemberg pogrom, urges him to a new beginning, implying that out of the ashes Judaism will arise again. For David the revitalization takes the form of biblical scholarship. He reads the numbers of the dead, the dead in the hundreds of thousands in Bergen-Belsen, and laments his family losses: "Who lies beneath my feet? I am walking on the dead of my family's beginnings." In this place of barbarism, Potok celebrates Jewish dignity in a superimposed dialogue between Max and his brother, David. They celebrate the living David, who, carrying his uncle's name, will bring new life to old roots. In an allegoric juxtaposition, Potok contrasts the poison of one civilization with the fruit of its victims. Germany's use of modern technology to exterminate millions of Jews and the millions they would have begotten is contrasted with the ancient Jewish Leverite marriage, which symbolizes Judaism's will to survive despite the world's effort to destroy it. Young David is living testimony to the Torahic encouragement that a childless widow may marry her husband's brother and name the first son of the union for the dead husband, thereby perpetuating his name in Israel. David follows his uncle's scholarly path and is perceived by the family as "the resurrection of the dead." Unlike the ghost of the murdered in Renaissance and Jacobean drama who returns to demand vengeance, Uncle David's ghost demands devotion to Judaism and Jewry. At Bergen-Belsen Uncle David strengthens his nephew's commitment to Jewish scholarship. The novel concludes with David's recitation of the Mourner's Kaddish, a prayer for the dead, but a prayer filled with hope for Jewish survival on the site that witnessed the murder of so many Jews.

The continuity suggested by David's incantation of the Kaddish is given dramatic realization in this novel, as in all Potok's fiction, through the renewed vigor of Jewish-American education, manifested in David Lurie's scholarship, and through building and sustaining a vibrant Israel, the mission Max Lurie adopts as his own. Recalling David Malter's turn from Holocaust defeat to Zionist promise in *The Chosen,* Max Lurie rejects passivity in the wake of the European debacle. Like Potok's father, Max is also a fervent Irgunist and supporter of Vladimir Jabotinsky's militant approach to Jewish immigration and survival in Israel. "With grim and silent satisfaction" that Benjamin Max Potok possessed, Lurie supports Irgun raids for Jewish rights in Palestine.

Illustrative of Potok's growing craft as a novelist is his successful integration of biblical and sacred textual matter with the historic themes of the novel, particularly the incorporation of Genesis subjects, language, and imagery. The Genesis parallels operate structurally, thematically, and allusively. The title is derived from the first word of the Hebrew Bible, *Bereshith.* As Genesis traces the history of the Israelites and their relations with other peoples, so too does Potok now abandon the closed societies of his early fiction, the parochial enclaves of Williamsburg and Crown-Heights, for a multiethnic Bronx neighborhood; this neighborhood serves as a microcosm for twentieth-century Jewish interaction with the gentile world. Toward the end of Genesis, Joseph recapitulates the lesson of his career: that God brings good out of evil, and that He will bring the Jewish people out of Egypt and to the land He promised the patriarchs. Potok invokes this redemptive voice to celebrate the remnant's emergence from European Holocaust bondage and its going forth to rebuild and to restore the land and people of Israel. Similarly, during the worst period of Holocaust suffering, the nineteen-year-old David recalls his *Bar Mitzvah* Torah reading: the entry of the Jews into Egypt and its accompanying prophetic reading from Amos regarding restoration of the fortunes of the Jewish homeland and those who would rebuild the ruined cities and inhabit them. Potok's Jews, survivors and American Jews, are determined to make a new beginning after the Holocaust, a beginning that rejuvenates Judaism and Jewry. Whether the new beginning is in Israel or in the Diaspora is unimportant to them; however, that it support Israel as the Jewish homeland and maintain Judaism in Israel and in the Diaspora is of paramount significance. Chaim Potok's dedication to the State of Israel, Jewish scholarship, and the creation of fiction addressing the dynamics of Jewish civilization testify to his celebration of Judaism and Jewry. Potok adds his voice to Emil Fackenheim's affirmation for Holocaust restoration through commitment to Judaism and Jewry, since, like Fackenheim, Potok believes that "the alternative [to Jewish commitment] is to say Hitler succeeded, that everybody really died for nothing."

Andy Solomon (review date 6 May 1990)

SOURCE: "Potok's Exiled Asher Lev Revisits His Hasidic Roots," in *Chicago Tribune Books,* May 6, 1990, p. 7.

[*In the following review, Solomon finds weaknesses in* The Gift of Asher Lev, *but notes Potok's "knowledgeable insights to share about art."*]

It is sometimes difficult, says a critic in response to artist Asher Lev's latest Paris show, to find the distinction between establishing an individual style and repeating oneself. He

might be speaking to Chaim Potok about this sequel to the superb 1972 novel, *My Name Is Asher Lev.*

Potok has marginal success with sequels. The power of his debut novel, *The Chosen* (1967), stemmed largely from its artlessness, the author's refusal to obtrude on his characters' deep-rooted decency and passion for ideas. Its sequel, *The Promise,* also a trenchant book, seemed marred by Potok's new self-consciousness, his effort not only to tell his tale but also to sound like a writer. His third novel, *My Name Is Asher Lev,* was even better than *The Chosen.* But *The Gift of Asher Lev* is a weaker sequel than *The Promise.*

Asher's plight in the earlier book, which covered his boyhood and adolescence, was an enhanced version of Conservative rabbi Potok's own. Asher could not solve the conflict between his artistic calling and the values of Hebraic tradition. An artist born into a community of Ladover Hasidim, Asher lives in a world that considers art a worthless vanity at best and a blasphemy at worst. Unlike Roth's or Malamud's protagonists, Potok's feel passionately bound to their orthodox identities and have no wish to join the mainstream culture. Asher's was an insoluble conflict. Ultimately, the Ladover's rebbe, its spiritual and political leader, exiled Asher to France.

When *The Gift of Asher Lev* opens, 20 years have passed, Asher, now a world-renowned painter, has married Devorah, whose parents were killed by the Nazis. They live in Southern France with their daughter, Rocheleh, and son, Avrumel. Then a call comes from Brooklyn. Asher's beloved Uncle Yitzchok has died.

Back for the funeral among his parents and former neighbors, Asher almost immediately longs to return to France. "We came for my uncle's funeral, not mine," he tells Devorah. But events conspire against him.

Devorah begins making Asher's parents her own. And Uncle Yitzchok, whose chain of thriving jewelry stores helps finance Ladover schools, oddly had become an art collector. Having bought one of Asher's paintings only to see its value more than double in a year, Yitzchok decided "there's more to art than meets the eye." His will makes Asher trustee of his enormously valuable collection. Asher can do with it what he wishes, provided the profits go to the Ladovers.

The rebbe and Asher's father urge him to keep his family in Brooklyn. Gradually, Asher comes to believe he knows the real reason. The aging rebbe needs a successor for his worldwide movement. Asher's father seems likeliest, but his own advanced years dictate the need for a clear successor to him as well. They must want Avrumel, his son, Asher suspects.

The material for a gripping story is all there, and there is much about the book to admire. As usual, Potok excels at capturing the concrete details of his settings. He tries more earnestly than before to portray not only the severity but also the joy and song of the Hasidic environment. Most importantly, Potok's is a world of intense meanings; ideas and behavior matter deeply to his characters, and even a mild rudeness can be portentous.

Unfortunately, Potok's early strengths are absent. Never a masterly stylist, here he often narrates what should be shown and describes many things too inconsequential to relate. At times he recreates perfectly the syntax of Hasidic English: "'They're repaving this whole section of the parkway,' the driver said. 'Months they're working on it. New trees also they'll put in.'" But often his dialogue, like his narration, falls flat.

Worse still, Potok never mines the conflicts Asher faces. Despite international acclaim, Asher fears he may have lost his creative vision. Artists slash ears off and stick shotguns in their mouths over such things, but Asher says and does little that reflects artistic agony. Surrounded by neighbors who consider him an embarrassment, who taunt him as an impious sinner, Asher remains torpid. Even expected to give up his son, Asher merely utters a line about how he had hoped to see the boy grow up in his own home.

As Asher sleepwalks through these pages, so too does the plot wander, despite some resolutions that form toward the end. The world of the Hasidim is intriguing, and Potok has knowledgeable insights to share about art. But Asher Lev casts far less spell in this revisit than he did two decades ago.

Nikki Stiller (review date 13 May 1990)

SOURCE: "Art Is an Affliction," in *The New York Times Book Review,* May 13, 1990, p. 29.

[*In the following review, Stiller finds shortcomings in* The Gift of Asher Lev, *particularly the novel's "sanitized" characters who lack development.*]

Jewish artists have long felt a conflict between Jewish tradition and the individual talent. Susskind von Trimberg, the medieval Jewish troubadour, thought of going back to the ghetto if his gentile patron went bankrupt. Heinrich Heine, a heretic if ever there was one, wished to die facing Jerusalem. Marc Chagall, best known of Jewish painters, borrowed much of his imagery from Christian peasants.

Chaim Potok has concentrated in his novels on the pull between secular self-fulfillment and communal Jewish values.

In *The Chosen,* for example, a teenager destined to replace his father as the head of a Hasidic dynasty finds himself impelled to study psychology instead of Torah. In *My Name Is Asher Lev,* and now in *The Gift of Asher Lev,* Mr. Potok has sought to make the conflict more dramatic. His main character is a painter, that is, one who speaks through the graven images that the very Orthodox consider prohibited by the Second Commandment.

In the earlier work, a child in a Hasidic household is overpowered by the desire to paint. Some indulge him, but his father, a narrow man devoted to the welfare of the Ladover, a group closely resembling the Lubavitcher, attempts to staunch the boy's genius. The Rebbe, as the community's spiritual leader, wisely recognizes Asher's calling and rescues him. When Asher begins to exhibit nudes and crucifixions, however, the Rebbe exiles him to Paris for the good of the Brooklyn community. Art for most of these Hasidic Jews is "foolishness" or worse—a gift from the other Side. Moreover, it is just after World War II: Hasidism is endangered in Russia, and the Holocaust's shadow is everywhere. The most pressing issue is collective survival.

In the sequel, taking place in the 1980's, conditions are more relaxed. The Rebbe employs television for reaching larger audiences, his followers prosper internationally. In the meantime, Asher Lev has become famous, but his passion for painting has worn thin. He's living with his family on the Côte d'Azur, and he's run out of inspiration. As the novel opens, he is recalled to Brooklyn for his beloved uncle's funeral. From the outset, the questions are: How can the artist and the community be reconciled, and what can each give the other?

Unfortunately, *The Gift of Asher Lev* offers simplistic answers. Asher, feeling trapped, wants to escape immediately after the week of mourning. But his wife, Devorah, and their children prefer Ladover *heimischkeit*—warmth and bustle—to artistic isolation in the south of France. The Rebbe intercedes, and the condolence call lengthens. What's more, wealthy Uncle Yitzchok, a secret art lover, has willed his nephew a world-class art collection. Asher remains in Brooklyn to claim it.

Asher is revitalized by his renewed contact with his people. To regain his artistic freedom, however, he must leave his family, including his little boy, with the Ladover as a sacrificial gift demanded by the Rebbe. Asher's father, successor to the aged leader, wants little Avrumel to succeed him in turn as Rebbe. Asher's father will teach the child pious Ladover ways. The child will teach the philistine grandfather, and thus the community, something about art. How neatly it all works out.

For Mr. Potok is conducting a guided tour of reality—something that perhaps accounts for his widespread popularity. The Hasidim are colorful in their long coats and kerchiefs. Anyone who has read Arthur Frommer's travel books can recognize St-Paul-de-Vence, the Rue des Rosiers, the allusions to Cézanne, Picasso. The predictable prevails in the obvious motif of Abraham and Isaac, and in the prose: a presentiment is "precise, stark, lucid"; the synagogue air is "stale, warm, faintly malodorous." Despite the synagogue air, the characters have been sanitized. Most are Good. A few merely lack understanding, though Cousin Yonkel is the devil incarnate. No Alexander Portnoys here! Asher Lev is relentlessly solemn, Devorah, a survivor, relentlessly benign. Asher has depicted his mother somehow crucified on a Venetian blind, she suffers from angst. His brave little daughter suffers from asthma.

No one suffers from serious doubt, and this allows the reader a complacent superiority to the novel's poor benighted folk. Unlike the protagonist of Chaim Grade's masterpiece, "The Yeshiva," Asher never considers abandoning orthodoxy. He wonders why there's no *brucha,* or blessing, for pagan beauty, but not whether to adhere to a sect that perceives beauty as pagan. He complains about the Jewish edict that forbids him to pray at Chagall's grave in a Christian cemetery, but does not consider defying it. While Asher decides to vote his own choice in a Presidential election, rather than obeying the Rebbe, and has cut off his earlocks, too, his only real deviance is his painting. Even this is perceived not as a choice but an affliction. Mr. Potok does not wrestle with the angel of autonomy. Though the novel begins with a trip back home, for all the distance Asher Lev has come, he might as well have stayed on Brooklyn's Eastern Parkway.

Brian Morton (review date 2 November 1990)

SOURCE: "Banished and Banished Again," in *Times Literary Supplement,* November 2, 1990, p. 1182.

[*In the following review, Morton presents a favorable assessment of* The Gift of Asher Lev *which, according to the critic, "heralds a new sophistication in Potok's art."*]

With the possible exception of Bernard Malamud, the postwar Jewish-American novelists have given out a version of Judaism that is secular and social, and largely passive. "Jewishness," a ready shorthand for qualities such as seriousness, humaneness, anguished historical awareness, rather than a system of beliefs, has provided a backdrop against which to play out dramas of self-discovery, rebellion and accommodation. In sharp contrast to these, Chaim Potok has shown a marked awareness of the internal tensions of modern Judaism, which are prior to its conflicts and accommodations with the Gentile world. His Judaism has content, not

just form; beliefs, not just abstract "pieties"; an exact mentality that participates in a wider society at the same time as it belongs to a distinct enclave.

Potok's new novel is about representation and self-representation. Even though he never describes himself, it is clear from the fascinated stares he records that Asher Lev is a distinctive figure, an exotic in his native America if not in his adopted St-Paul-de-Vence. The closest he comes to self-description is to trace his outline in the opaque steam of a bathroom mirror, an image that remains even when a degree of clarity is restored. It is an ironic gesture, and a very significant one. It occurs at a moment when he has, almost literally, lost sight of himself; it is the first sign of his return to artistic activity; and it takes place in Brooklyn, to which he has returned for the funeral of his uncle, a wealthy Jew with a secret art collection.

The Gift of Asher Lev is a sequel to *My Name Is Asher Lev* (1972) and begins, quite properly, *in medias res*—"Afterward I lived in Paris . . ."—with memories of Picasso's death and Lev's exile. The irony of Lev's distance from Yisroel is that it is entirely physical; in sharp contrast to the lukewarm alienations of the Jewish-American novelists, he has been banished from the Ladover Hasidic community in which his father holds high office as secretary to the Rebbe. His crime is to have turned to the Gentile world for images of suffering. *My Name Is Asher Lev* recounts the painting and reception of the "Brooklyn Crucifixion," in which the faces of the crucified are those of Lev's mother and father. That personal treason is compounded by still greater betrayals: the "inauthenticity" of going outside "the tradition" for his imagery; and the enormous risk, less than a generation after Auschwitz, of reminding the Gentiles that Jews were, in the favourite antisemitic slur, "Christ-killers." Now, "banished" again by the savagery of the Paris critics, who consider he is "repeating himself," Lev stops painting. At his uncle's graveside, he wakens to the complexity of his inheritance, not just the secret Cézannes and Matisses in the old man's attic, but also the world of politics and everyday perception that somehow isn't allowed to intervene under the unchanging sky of Saint-Paul (the very name suggests that his exile is a further betrayal). If the clear Provençal air saves his daughter Rocheleh from asthma, it ultimately prevents Lev from breathing at all.

Unlike Malamud's *Pictures of Fidelman* (to which it bears a certain thematic resemblance) and Philip Roth's obsessive fictional investigations of life after *Portnoy's Complaint,* Potok's new novel is more than a portrait of a sensitive individual in conflict with a repressive and philistine heritage, for Lev has been banished from a community whose values he embraces wholeheartedly; he is neither Ishmael nor Cain. His exile "afterward" represents a further humanization of a man almost pharisaically obsessed with his own moral and artistic mission. The novel also heralds a new sophistication in Potok's art, which in the past was short on humour and reticent about whole areas of experience, notably the erotic. *The Gift of Asher Lev* is far less schematic than its predecessor, *Davita's Harp,* though its female protagonist seems to have freed in Potok some of the awareness that surfaces in Lev's passionate relationship with his wife Devorah (a writer of children's books who lost her own childhood in a sealed apartment in Occupied Paris, much like Anne Frank). It is less profound than his first novel, *The Chosen,* written in 1967, but paired with the original Asher Lev novel (which, in retrospect, was disturbingly incomplete) it covers much the same ground with considerable subtlety.

There is a further dimension, which the Rebbe buries in a riddle. The price of Lev's restoration to his people is his physical and personal exclusion. Much as Christ was a sacrificed "missing generation" between God and mankind, Lev's self-sacrificing art is a personal crucifixion, but also, as the old Rebbe recognized, a guarantee that the tradition will pass on from the new Rebbe, Lev's father, to Avrumel, his young son. While Lev sweats in Saint-Paul, the boy is growing up in New York, with an absent father and without the beloved doll that stood for all the book's simulacra of absent people. "Devorah writes me. Avrumel has lately taken to ignoring Shimson and insists on walking to school by himself." Father and son. Of the making of images, and of learning, there is no end.

Irving Abrahamson (review date 17 May 1992)

SOURCE: "Chaim Potok Traces a Korean War Orphan's Existentialist Journey," in *Chicago Tribune Books,* May 17, 1992, p. 6.

[*In the following review, Abrahamson finds shortcomings in* I Am the Clay, *citing Potok's "unsuccessful foray into the realm of existentialist thought" and his simplistic appeal for Christian love.*]

In *The Book of Lights* (1981) Chaim Potok drew upon his experience as a U.S. Army chaplain in South Korea from 1955 to 1957. In *I Am the Clay,* his eighth novel, he draws upon it once again, this time taking the 1950-53 Korean War for his canvas. Potok is not interested in the 38th parallel, in the North Korean invaders and their Red Chinese allies, nor in the clash of armies. What interests him is the impact of the war upon the countryside and its peasant farmers. He renders this impact through the eyes and experiences of an old peasant couple and Kim Sin Gyu, the orphaned young boy they save from death.

Shifting the point of view from one character to another,

Potok pictures a dangerous world: troops in retreat; long processions of refugees; jeeps, trucks and tanks on the go; helicopters whirling overhead; jets streaking by. Thieves, roving gangs of orphans and suspicious South Korean soldiers menace the innocent. Refugees huddle in the night around wood-burning oil drums. Black smoke rises from huge mounds of corpses set afire by flame throwers.

Potok focuses in on the struggle for survival as the farmer, his wife and the boy battle hunger, sickness, cold, exhaustion and the land itself. He traces their emotions, calls up their memories, delves into their spiritual world—their ancestor worship, their acceptance of a world governed by unseen demons, spirits and ghosts.

But Potok draws his title from a hymn that Christian missionaries taught the old woman's mother. The farmer's wife still remembers the song her mother taught her: "Have thine own way Lord have thine own way thou art the potter I am the clay," even as she recalls how to make the sign of the cross—one stroke with the hand horizontally, another vertically.

Though she is totally ignorant of the meaning of the words of the song and the sign of the cross, Potok portrays her as living the life of a Christian, and just hours before her death he formally turns her into one, having her undergo a symbolic baptism. Just as the words "Have thine own way Lord" cross her mind, she suffers a stroke and slips gently into the stream where she has been washing clothes.

Potok chooses as the motto for his story a line from Albert Camus' "The Myth of Sisyphus," and, at first glance, Kim Sin Gyu does have existential possibilities. A survivor of the massacre of his entire family, in the last few pages of the novel—now all of 14 and at a critical point in his life—he invokes the spirits of his dead to protect him and guide him toward his future. But when they do not respond, he faces the stark existential meaning of their absence and asks himself, "Are the spirits as helpless as men? Perhaps there are no spirits anymore . . . and only emptiness is left for us to fill." And his decision to leave the old farmer behind and pursue in Seoul the studies that will lead him into the world of the scholar or the poet comes across as an existential choice, a break with the Korean fatalistic order of things. Determined to go his own way, Kim Sin Gyu—the only character Potok ever names—might well be a Korean youngest brother to Asher Lev.

But Kim Sin Gyu makes his decision before his confrontation with nothingness, not as a result of it. Indeed, his decision is no real choice at all: He is simply consciously fulfilling a destiny predetermined by the centuries-old intellectual tradition to which his family belongs.

Camus' Sisyphus, recognizing that he lives in a universe "without a master," realizes that he alone is "the master of his days." Surely Potok knows that for Camus there is no potter other than man, who must mold his own clay. For all Potok's sleight of hand, his Kim Sin Gyu is a world away from Western individualism and existentialist thought.

If Potok makes a case for anything at all, it is for Christian love. The old farmer's attitude toward Kim Sin Gyu changes from anger and hatred to love. Likewise, his wife's attitude toward the boy shifts to love from kindness. Kim Sin Gyu himself even leaves the old farmer because of his love for him.

Except for its unsuccessful foray into the realm of existentialist thought, *I Am the Clay,* offers no challenge. But it seems likely that the novel will satisfy Chaim Potok's audience.

Bryan Cheyette (review date 27 November 1992)

SOURCE: "The Sacred East," in *Times Literary Supplement,* November 27, 1992, p. 26.

[*In the following review, Cheyette finds fault with Potok's limited knowledge of Korea and "didacticism" in* I Am the Clay.]

As a young Rabbi, Chaim Potok was a United States Army Chaplain during the Korean War. He served on the front line for sixteen months and this experience later provided the material for his first, unpublished, novel. *I Am the Clay* is evidently a rewriting of this embryonic early work. On one level, Potok could not have moved further from the rather sentimental depictions of New York's Hasidic Jewish community which he has made his own. And yet, the traumatic clash of conflicting cultures within an adolescent hero—which is Potok's perennial theme—is at the centre of this novel no less than his preceding work. Kim Sin Gyu, who takes up this boyish role, remembers his grandfather telling him that "only the wisest and stupidest of men never change. Which are you?" It is the combination of spiritual wisdom coupled with the necessity of modernization which has always preoccupied Potok. As with Reuven Malter in *The Chosen* (1967), Kim Sin Gyu stands on the cusp of the ancient and the modern worlds.

Kim Sin Gyu is discovered lying in a ditch with a shrapnel wound, "a piece of the scale from the dragon of death." He is saved by an unnamed old woman and her husband, who come across him during the retreat from the Chinese and the North Korean army. Most of the novel is taken up with the painful struggle for survival of these three refugees as they move towards an American-made shanty-town and back to their villages in the North. Potok, to his credit, wishes to recount their story from the viewpoint of the victim. But, in attempting laudably to get under the skin of the Korean peasantry, he has adopted a faux-naive style, which often has an oddly condescending tone: "The old man watched in wonder and terror. The machines of the foreigners. How can they be defeated, these giants of pale skin, these devils on our sacred soil?"

Potok's aim is to convey a "sacred" Far Eastern world in which the spiritual realm struggles to overcome an oppressive reality. His clipped, repetitive sentences endeavour to portray the trance-like state of the refugees as they continue to pay homage to their gods and the ever-present spirits which surround them. At the same time, he is happy to cite Shakespeare, T. S. Eliot and Elie Wiesel (among others) in showing the horrors of the Korean War from the perspective of European history. The problem for Potok is that it is impossible for him to let the old man and woman—as they are known throughout—simply speak for themselves. In becoming a surrogate son whom the woman nurtures and the old man jealously rejects, Kim Sin Gyu evokes primeval emotions.

The boy eventually embodies the "magical" dimension which is meant to characterize the Korean peasantry. But, instead of speaking with the authentic voice of the victim, Potok's refugees seem to be mere counterpoints to a brutal Western modernity. The "upside down" world of America is clay-like, filled with machines and "empty" when compared with the primitive, child-like, and spiritually fulfilled East.

By the last and most successful chapter of *I Am the Clay,* a Potok-like chaplain appears and arranges for Kim Sin Gyu to move away from the rural village which he has made his home. His adopted mother's grave, which is the site for the spirits of his deceased family, has to be removed to make way for an American encampment. Once the limits of his "magical" powers are realized, Kim Sin Gyu, not unlike his Kiplingesque counterpart, travels to the Westernized city of Seoul. The synthesis of opposites is the basic pattern to which all of Potok's fiction conforms. But when applied to a world with which he has only a passing acquaintance, his didacticism is exposed as limited and anaemic.

Felicity Barringer (review date 1 December 1996)

SOURCE: "Generation Gap," in *The New York Times Book Review,* December 1, 1996, p. 33.

[*In the following review, Barringer praises* The Gates of

November *as a "fascinating" tale, though finds shortcomings in Potok's overreaching history of Soviet Jewry.*]

Acts of dissent in a totalitarian state can seem incongruously mundane. In some places, it is an act of courage to observe an anniversary, or to hang a sheet with a few words scrawled on it above a busy downtown street.

The last was what Vladimir and Maria Slepak did in June 1978, when they found themselves locked in their Moscow apartment by K.G.B. agents. "Let us go to our son in Israel," read their makeshift placard. K.G.B. agents rushed to break down their apartment door, and Vladimir Slepak—called Volodya by all—spent five years in exile in Siberia. It was the logical culmination of nine years as an "enemy of the people" who showcased the Soviet Union's refusal to permit free Jewish emigration.

Weeks afterward, when Solomon Slepak heard that his estranged son had been sentenced to exile, he had a heart attack and died. A dogmatic Old Bolshevik, he himself had narrowly avoided the net of Stalin's purges more than once, but always justified them to his son by citing the Russian proverb: "Whenever you cut down trees, the chips will fly in all directions." When his only son, and his two grandsons in their turn, renounced the society he had helped to build, he renounced them.

The men and women of Solomon Slepak's generation were young when they created a Communist state on the ruins of the Russian autocracy. Many didn't have time to grow gray before they were devoured by their own creation. And their children were only in their 50's and 60's when the edifice their parents built finally crumbled. A few of them, like Volodya and Masha Slepak, were as committed in their rejection of the state as their parents had been in creating it.

Chaim Potok has won well-deserved praise for his ability to describe the rifts between fathers and sons in novels like *The Chosen* and *My Name Is Asher Lev*. In *Wanderings*, he showed a facility for capturing and conveying accessibly the intricate panorama of Jewish history. In *The Gates of November,* Mr. Potok tries to do it all. Using the taped reminiscences of Volodya and Masha Slepak and their sons, he sets about telling a family tale, a tale that is enmeshed in Soviet history and that is part of Jewish history.

However, it is a tricky thing to write intimate portraits of individuals and also to make them actors in historical dramas. In this case, the result is an often ungainly mixture of the personal and the political, short on insight into the minds and hearts of the father and son whose histories and relationship are the core of the narrative.

Mr. Potok is on more familiar and comfortable turf when describing the Slepaks' struggle to leave Russia. But he overplays his hand: the Slepaks' chronicles are a part of the story of Soviet Jewry, yet the details of distant pogroms are not always a part of the Slepaks' story. Nor are Mr. Potok's all too frequent excursions into Soviet history. The book jolts backward and forward in time, as Mr. Potok tries to weave a larger history into the family narrative. More disconcerting, however, is the multiplicity of voices: now Volodya's, now Masha's, now the voices of their sons, most often Mr. Potok's. Sometimes this produces a cohesive narrative. More often, the result is cacophony.

But the tale remains fascinating. Solomon Slepak defied his mother's wish that he become a rabbi, fled from home at the age of 13, emigrated to New York, converted to Marxism, returned home, commanded Red Army troops in the civil war, murdered comrades and rose to the Communist Party's inner circles.

Volodya Slepak accepted his father's blind faith in Communism until a fierce quarrel in 1952, when Jewish doctors were being arrested on charges of poisoning the country's leadership and an anti-Semitic purge was apparently averted only by Stalin's death. Seventeen years later, he and Masha surrendered their comfortable lives for the dissident's lot: the slow choking off of employment, friendships and, eventually, freedom. Too often in *The Gates of November* they seem less three-dimensional people than simulacra, the literary equivalent of wax figures in Madame Tussaud's museum. Even so, their heroism as people and as Jews cannot help being moving.

David M. Shribman (review date 12 December 1996)

SOURCE: "Fathers and Sons," in *The Wall Street Journal*, December 12, 1996, p. A10.

[*In the following review, Shribman offers high praise for* The Gates of November, *which the critic describes as a "gripping" story.*]

Let me tell you a story: Twenty years ago, as the last remnants of snow lingered on the edges of Moscow's sidewalks, I took a decrepit elevator to the eighth floor of an apartment building on Gorky Street. Loaded down with jeans, sweaters and books, I stepped into an extraordinary world; the redoubt of a refusenik family that, through grit and guile, had battled the Soviet authorities to a standstill.

This was the home of Vladimir Slepak, his wife and sons. In times of tension and detente alike, it had become a gathering place: for Russian Jews who were fighting to leave their native land; for visitors who wanted to offer a bit of solidarity along with their sweaters; and for KGB agents who wanted to keep an eye on the intrigue and intelligence that swirled around the supper table.

There you spoke by writing messages on magic slates, and the idiom was that of struggle: tales of hunger strikes, knocks in the night, forced entries by the KGB (you could see the splinters they had left behind on the very doorway you had just passed through), arrests, secret trials, Siberian prisons. Two years later, Vladimir himself was sentenced to five years of exile in Siberia.

Now the Soviet Union is gone and so are the Slepaks, along with the sad suspicion (you couldn't repress it in that cold apartment so long ago) that the privations and prejudices of communism might well outlive us all. The Soviet Union is a pile of rubble in history's trash heap and the Slepaks, now in Israel, are free to think whatever they like and worship the way their forefathers did.

But that is only the half of it, as I discovered in racing through Chaim Potok's **The Gates of November.** Yes, this was the struggle of a stubborn family against a stubborn system, and the story would be enduring and ennobling for that alone. But the rest of the story is gripping as well, the struggle of father and son, revolutionary and refusenik: Solomon Slepak, one of the Bolsheviks who built the Soviet Union, vs. Vladimir Slepak, one of the dissenters who helped tear it down.

To this tragic struggle Chaim Potok, rabbi and novelist, brings a sharp ear, a sharp eye and a soft heart. This is a family chronicle, the tale of two men, each in his way an incurable idealist. Each, in his way, wanted to remake the world, to better it. Each, in his way, was a fighter. Each, in his way, was a hardened survivor.

Born a Jew in Russia, made a revolutionary in early 20th-century America, Solomon Slepak was one of the few (Trotsky and Bukharin were among the others) who reversed their journey of immigration. He returned to Russia on a cargo ship to take part in the great romantic dramas of the period, the Russian Civil War (where he eventually commanded 10,000 men against Cossack bands) and the building of Soviet Russia (a process that cost many of its supporters dearly).

"The Russian Jews who gave themselves heart and mind to the Bolshevik cause were, like Soloman Slepak, men and women who embraced a cruel between world," writes Mr. Potok. They were "no longer part of the world of their Jewish beginnings, which they had long since abandoned, and not yet fully a part of the world of Russia, which loathed and feared Jews."

But few between-worlds have been so fascinating, so intoxicating: Solomon traveled on Comintern missions to China on money likely raised by the sale of the czar's jewels, and family legend has it that it was he who persuaded Sun Yat-sen, the early Chinese revolutionary leader, to allow Communists into the Kuomintang in 1922. Master of 11 languages, Solomon somehow avoided the spasms of arrests that caught so many of his fellow travelers in the Stalin years.

Solomon named his son for Lenin, but the clarity of the red dream was lost on the younger Slepak. He took his lessons in Marxist Ideology, Principles of Marxism-Leninism and Marxist Political Economy, but there were so many mysteries in his early life: books thrown out after their authors were arrested, photographs inked out after their subjects fell from favor, relatives and friends suddenly regarded as imperialist spies.

And so the break came as the son discovered that the ideal society the father was building had no room for Jews. It was a simple plastic radio, black and yellow and measuring 12 by 8 by 4 inches, that opened the son's eyes with news from the West—and opened the rift with his father. Vladimir Slepak worked on the air-defense system of the Soviet Union but could no longer defend the Soviet system.

It took protests, imprisonment, petty harassment and a chilly desert exile before the exit visas to Israel finally came. By then the Soviet Union was on its last legs and Vladimir's father had died. A year ago there arrived information from the KGB files: Vladimir Slepak's five years of internal exile had been illegal after all; he was guilty of no crime. But Mr. Slepak's struggle was not for nothing, because now the modern KGB recognizes that it is no crime to want to live in freedom.

FURTHER READING

Criticism

Dembo, L. S. "Asher Lev: The Mariolatry of a Hasid." In *The Monological Jew: A Literary Study,* pp. 112-6. Madison, WI: University of Wisconsin Press, 1988.
    Examines Asher Lev's sacrilegious interest in Christian and pagan art in *My Name Is Asher Lev.*

Interviews

Kauvar, Elaine M. "An Interview with Chaim Potok." *Contemporary Literature* XXVII, No. 3 (Fall 1986): 291-317.
    Potok discusses his literary influences, artistic concerns, Judaism, and major themes in his novels.

Additional coverage of Potok's life and career is contained in the following sources published by Gale: *Authors and Artists for Young Adults,* Vol. 15; *Authors in the News,* Vols. 1 and 2; *Contemporary Authors,* Vols. 17-20R; *Contemporary Authors New Revision Series,* Vols. 19 and 35; *Dictionary of Literary Biography,* Vols. 28 and 152; *DISCovering Authors Modules: Novelists; Major Twentieth-Century Writers;* and *Something about the Author,* Vol. 33.

Ezra Pound
1885-1972

(Also wrote under the pseudonyms B. H. Dias, Abel Saunders, and William Atheling) American poet, critic, translator, prose writer, essayist, and editor.

The following entry presents an overview of Pound's career. For further information on his life and works, see *CLC*, Volumes 1, 2, 3, 4, 5, 7, 10, 13, 18, 34, 48, and 50.

INTRODUCTION

An erudite and highly controversial poet and critic, Ezra Pound is considered one of the preeminent literary figures of the twentieth century. Renowned for his *Cantos,* an ambitious series of historiographic meditations that excavate the cultural legacy of modern civilization, Pound developed experimental verse forms distinguished for their technical virtuosity, linguistic invention, and broad assimilation of European and Asian literature. Widely praised for their prodigious learning and epic scope, *The Cantos* document Pound's heroic effort to reconstruct two thousand years of Western history in a montage of ancient myth, literary arcana, and historical fragment. An influential theorist, translator, and prominent intellectual mentor during the early decades of the century, Pound also formulated many of the enduring aesthetic principles of High Modernism, particularly as delineated in his Imagist and Vorticist movements and in numerous critical works. Though castigated for endorsing fascist regimes during the Second World War, Pound is regarded as a brilliant radical thinker who revitalized contemporary literature with his challenging poetry and innovative artistic ideals.

Biographical Information

Born Ezra Loomis Pound in Hailey, Idaho, a frontier mining town, Pound was the only child of Isabel Weston Pound, a descendent of Henry Wadsworth Longfellow, and Homer Loomis Pound, a government bureaucrat. His grandfather, Thaddeus Coleman Pound, was a successful entrepreneur and outspoken Republican congressman who impressed the young Pound as a model of the selfless public figure and independent thinker. In 1889, Pound moved with his family to Philadelphia, where his father was employed as an assayer for the United States Mint. He made his first visits to Europe with his family in 1898 and 1902. At age fifteen Pound enrolled at the University of Pennsylvania, where he befriended poets William Carlos Williams and Hilda Doolittle ("H.D."). Pound transferred to Hamilton College in upstate New York, earning a degree in philosophy in 1905, then re-

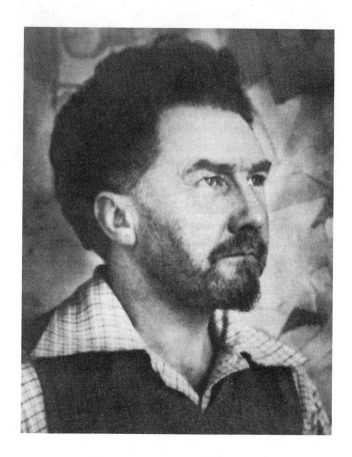

turned to the University of Pennsylvania to complete a master's degree in Romance languages in 1907. Upon graduation he took a teaching appointment at Wabash College in Indiana. Dismissed after only one term, he sailed for Europe in 1908. After a stop in Venice, where he published his first volume of poetry, *A Lume Spento* (1908), Pound settled in London and entered the literary circles of William Butler Yeats, Ford Madox Ford, and T. E. Hulme. He soon won acclaim as a poet with *Personae* (1909) and as a literary critic with *The Spirit of Romance* (1910). Pound founded the Imagist movement in 1913, which he abandoned the next year for Vorticism, another avant-garde school invented by Pound, Wyndham Lewis, and sculptor Henri Gaudier-Brzeska. Pound also played an important role as an advocate for emerging writers such as T. S. Eliot and James Joyce and as a contributor to numerous literary magazines, notably *Poetry, The Egoist, The Little Review,* and *The New Age.* Pound married Dorothy Shakespear in 1914, though maintained a life-long extramarital relationship with Olga Rudge beginning in the early 1920s. He began work on *The Cantos* in 1915; the first installments appeared in *Poetry* in 1917, then in *The Fourth Canto* (1919) and *Quia Pauper Amavi*

(1919), which contains Cantos 1-3. Disillusioned with England and the carnage of the First World War, Pound produced *Hugh Selwyn Mauberley* (1920) and relocated to Paris, where he encountered Dadaist artists and fellow expatriates Ernest Hemingway and Gertrude Stein while working as a foreign correspondent for *The Dial*. In 1924 Pound moved to Rapallo, Italy, and devoted himself to *The Cantos* and the study of Chinese culture. Amid the international depression of the 1930s, Pound became increasingly interested in monetary reforms elucidated in *ABC of Economics* (1933). He also established his allegiance to Italian dictator Benito Mussolini, whose fascist political and economic programs he defended in *Jefferson And/Or Mussolini* (1935). During the Second World War, Pound denounced the American government and an alleged Jewish conspiracy in regular Rome Radio broadcasts. Upon the Allied occupation of Italy in 1945, he was arrested for treason and incarcerated at a military prison in Pisa, inspiring *The Pisan Cantos* (1948), the controversial winner of the Bollingen Prize for Poetry in 1949. After a nervous breakdown in 1945, Pound was declared mentally unfit for trial and detained in a psychiatric institute near Washington, DC, for the next twelve years. Upon his release in 1958, Pound returned to Italy, where he continued to work on his *Cantos* in virtual silence until his death at age eighty-six. He was awarded a fellowship from the Academy of American Poets in 1963.

Major Works

A prolific poet, literary critic, and author of diverse treatises, Pound's artistic development reflects his abiding effort to revive modern art and society in a new unity of past and present. Drawing heavily upon forgotten or neglected classics of European, American, and Asian letters, Pound's mature poetry represents a synthesis of archaic forms, sophisticated allusion, and avant-garde tropes informed by his artistic, political, and economic beliefs. His first volume of poetry, *A Lume Spento,* displays his early lyrical style, affinity for classical and medieval subjects, and the influence of Robert Browning, Charles Algernon Swinburne, and François Villon. The poem "The Tree" from this volume is regarded as one of Pound's best short compositions. Subsequent collections—*A Quinzaine for this Yule* (1908), *Personae, Exultations* (1909), *Provença* (1910), and *Riposte* (1912)—reveal Pound's technical mastery and assimilation of Anglo-Saxon, Asian, Pre-Raphaelite, and French and Italian troubadour verse, evident in oft anthologized poems such as "Sestina: Altaforte" and "Ballad of the Goodly Free." As the leader of the Imagist movement, a descendent of French Symbolism, Pound fortified his commitment to the tenets of clarity, concrete language, and *le mot juste,* or "the right word." His interest in Chinese writing exerted a profound influence on his poetry and precipitated the invention of his ideogrammatic method, an extension of Imagist principles inspired by the condensed precision and immediacy of Chinese characters. This approach justified the incorporation of foreign phrases, Chinese pictographs, and even musical scores in his writing to express a specific mood or concept. Pound's translations in *Cathay,* a collection of verse by eighth century Chinese poet Rihaku, also known as Li Po, are noted for their elegiac tone and austere beauty. These early translations, along with *The Sonnets and Ballate of Guido Cavalcanti* (1912), anticipate Pound's adoption of dramatic masks, or speaker personae, through which to interpret past events in terms of modern analogues and subjective states. In "Homage to Sextus Propertius," contained in *Qui Pauper Amavi,* Pound interpolates the work of Roman poet Sextus Propertius with modern references, Latinate puns, and scatological humor aimed at contemporary figures. *Hugh Selwyn Mauberley,* a long poem permeated by the polemical tone of Vorticism, decries the tragedy of the First World War and the ambivalence of postwar English society. Through his caricature of Mauberley, rendered in conventional verse forms, Pound eschews the purely aesthetic concerns of his earlier writing in favor of greater social consciousness, marking a decisive shift in his self-identity as a poet. Pound invested his lifelong creative aspirations in *The Cantos,* the collective title given to 117 cantos produced between 1915 and 1968. Cantos 1-3, known as the "Ur-Cantos," offer a prospectus for his project. Drawing parallels to Odysseus's descent into the underworld in Homer's *Odyssey* and Dante's journey through heaven and hell in *The Divine Comedy,* Pound introduces his own epic story of cultural loss and reclamation. Though Pound's conception of *The Cantos* changed over time, the central motif involves the disinterment of the past to facilitate understanding and order in the modern world. Presented in alternately rhetorical, dramatic, and narrative modes, *The Cantos* are in large part an eclectic, multilingual palimpsest of Greek myth, Confucian philosophy, European history, economic theory, and contemporary affairs. Despite his expatriation and harsh criticism of American culture and capitalism, Pound maintained a distinctly American sensibility, evident in his admiration for Thomas Jefferson and John Quincy Adams, who appear as champions of political will in *The Cantos. The Pisan Cantos,* among the best known, reflect Pound's fragile emotional state during his imprisonment after the Second World War. In this moving sequence, Pound expresses his despair in an introspective, elegiac tone characteristic of his later cantos. In addition to *The Cantos,* Pound also produced significant works of criticism, including: *The Spirit of Romance,* a collection of critical essays on medieval literature based on his lectures at Regent Street Polytechnic in 1909; *How to Read* (1931), in which he delineates the concepts "melopoeia," "phanopoeia," and "logopoeia"—referring, respectively, to the musical, visual, and intellectual quality of poetic language; *Guide to Kulchur* (1938), Pound's writings on art, literature, politics, and economics; and *Patria Mia* (1950), in which he discusses artist patronage.

Critical Reception

Though widely recognized as one of the most important poets of the century, Pound is the subject of contentious critical debate. Acclaimed for his originality and intellectual gifts, Pound's complex allusive verse, his association with numerous literary movements, and his idiosyncratic political ideals—particularly his fascist loyalty—complicate interpretation of his work. Many critics hail *The Cantos* as his magnum opus and a highspot of twentieth century literature, calling attention to the extraordinary range and depth of Pound's expansive, though ultimately unrealized, literary and philosophical vision. Measured against the masterpieces of Homer and Dante, which Pound aspired to equal, most critics view *The Cantos* as a formidable achievement undermined by its lack of unity and difficult linguistic experiments. Pound's detractors question the efficacy of his ideogrammatic method and its implementation in *The Cantos*, especially where the use of cryptic language and obscure scholarly references render passages inaccessible. *The Pisan Cantos*, which polarized the literary community as the winner of the Bollingen Prize for Poetry in 1949, is now regarded as one of the best sequences of *The Cantos*. Most of Pound's early poetry, including that of the once celebrated *Hugh Selwyn Mauberley*, is overshadowed by the accomplishment of *The Cantos*. Recent critical attention is directed at Pound's preoccupation with the past, his ethical concerns, his relationship with American literary tradition in commonalities with Ralph Waldo Emerson, and textual analysis of *The Cantos*. A foremost poet, critic, translator, and literary impresario who cultivated many of the century's greatest writers, notably Eliot and Joyce, Pound is regarded as one of the dominant intellectual forces of modern literature.

PRINCIPAL WORKS

A Lume Spento (poetry) 1908
A Quinzaine for this Yule (poetry) 1908
Personae (poetry) 1909
Exultations (poetry) 1909
The Spirit of Romance (criticism) 1910
Provença (poetry) 1910
Canzoni (poetry) 1911
The Sonnets and Ballate of Guido Cavalcanti [translator] (poetry) 1912
Ripostes (poetry) 1912
Cathay: Translations by Ezra Pound for the Most Part from the Chinese of Rihaku, From the Notes of the Late Ernest Fenollosa, and the Decipherings of the Professors Mori and Ariga [translator] (poetry) 1915
Gaudier-Brzeska: A Memoir Including the Published Writings of the Sculptor and a Selection from his Letters (prose) 1916

Lustra (poetry) 1916
Noh; or, Accomplishment: A Study of the Classical Stage of Japan [with Ernest Fenollosa] (criticism) 1916
Pavannes and Divisions (criticism) 1918
The Fourth Canto (poetry) 1919
Quia Pauper Amavi (poetry) 1919
Instigations of Ezra Pound, Together with an Essay on the Chinese Written Character by Ernest Fenollosa (criticism) 1920
Hugh Selwyn Mauberley (poetry) 1920
Umbra (poetry) 1920
Poems 1918-21 (poetry) 1921
The Natural Philosophy of Love [translator; original by Rémy de Gourmont] (essays) 1922
Indiscretions (autobiography) 1923
Antheil and the Treatise on Harmony [under pseudonym William Atheling] (criticism) 1924
A Draft of XVI Cantos (poetry) 1925
Personae: The Collected Poems (poetry) 1926
A Draft of the Cantos 17-27 (poetry) 1928
Selected Poems (poetry) 1928
A Draft of XXX Cantos (poetry) 1930
Imaginary Letters (prose) 1930
How to Read (criticism) 1931
ABC of Economics (criticism) 1933
ABC of Reading (criticism) 1934
Make It New (criticism) 1934
Eleven New Cantos: XXXI-XLI (poetry) 1934
Homage to Sextus Propertius (poetry) 1934
Alfred Venison's Poems: Social Credit Themes [under pseudonym The Poet of Titchfield Street] (criticism) 1935
Social Credit: An Impact (prose) 1935
Jefferson And/Or Mussolini (prose) 1935
Polite Essays (criticism) 1937
The Fifth Decad of Cantos (poetry) 1937
Confucius: Digest of the Analects [translator] (prose) 1937
Guide to Kulchur (prose) 1938
What Is Money For (prose) 1939
Cantos LII-LXXI (poetry) 1940
A Selection of Poems (poetry) 1940
Carta da Visita [*A Visiting Card*] (prose) 1942
L'America, Roosevelt e le Cause della Guerra Presente [*America, Roosevelt and the Causes of the Present War*] (prose) 1944
Oro e Lavoro [*Gold and Work*] (prose) 1944
Introduzione alla Natura Economica degli S.U.A. [*An Introduction to the Economic Nature of the United States*] (prose) 1944
Orientamenti (essays) 1944
Confucius: The Unwobbling Pivot and the Great Digest [translator] (prose) 1947
If This Be Treason . . . (broadcasts) 1948
The Pisan Cantos (poetry) 1948
The Cantos (poetry) 1948

CRITICISM

Philip E. Bishop (essay date Winter 1989)

SOURCE: "'And Will the World Take Up Its Course Again?': Paranoia and Experience in the *Pisan Cantos*," in *Texas Studies in Literature and Language,* Vol. 31, No. 4, Winter, 1989, pp. 536-53.

[*In the following essay, Bishop discusses Pound's effort to continue his epic historical vision in* The Cantos *after his traumatic imprisonment in Pisa and the demise of Mussolini. According to Bishop, "the jarring tonalities and circuitous associations" of his verse beginning with "Canto 74" "is the drama of Pound's recovery."*]

The relation between Ezra Pound's *Pisan Cantos* and his alleged mental illness has not been satisfactorily explained. Some scholars ignore this complication entirely and explicate the *Pisan Cantos* without reference to Pound's certified mental incompetence. Others question the psychiatric verdict reached at Pound's trial, a verdict that might taint the literary value of those much-admired later cantos. This skepticism has been buttressed by claims that trial psychiatrists exaggerated Pound's symptoms to protect him from prosecution. But if Pound was not a psychotic (E. Fuller Torrey calls him a sociopath), then he deserved to stand trial for treason and might well have been executed. This can

hardly be a great solace to Pound's critical defenders. Among the major Pound critics, only Eva Hesse asserts that Pound's paranoid condition may have affected the style and structure of the poems written at Pisa. But her reading of Pound's paranoid style remains highly theoretical, and the antipsychiatric twist to her argument may be, quite simply, mistaken. Indeed, if Torrey is correct, Pound's psychiatrists may have saved his life.

Or, it may be that the *Pisan Cantos* saved his life. Certainly, Pound's mental illness and these cantos shared the same traumatic setting: the wire cage at Pisa. They both arose from the shambles of ideological belief and poetic aspiration left when Pound was arrested for treason. From the cage at Pisa, Pound could see that his political hero was dead; his political enemies, triumphant; and his epic poem, discredited. The poetic project that Pound had pursued with such irascible energy had momentarily reached an end—a dead end. From this end, however, came a different beginning. Both Pound's symptoms and his *Pisan Cantos* were the means of recovering from this trauma, of going on with the **Cantos** and with his life. But both the poem and the life were inalterably changed. A reading of **"Canto 74"** reveals, I believe, that Pound's recovery was based upon false hopes and guilt-ridden despair. With **"Canto 74,"** the course of his epic poem was diverted from history and toward delusion.

As is typical of Pound's life, his captivity in Pisa is a matter of dispute. The poet was arrested in May 1945 by Italian partisans and was eventually taken by jeep, handcuffed to an accused murderer and rapist, to the U.S. Army Detention Training Center at Pisa. This was a sprawling complex where soldiers convicted of violent crimes could work their way back into the regular army. Pound was placed in a cage normally reserved for prisoners under the death sentence. The cage had been reinforced with air-stripping, and the camp had been instructed to take special measures to prevent escape or suicide. In an affidavit Pound's lawyer, Julian Cornell, described the poet's predicament:

> Pound was placed in solitary confinement in a steel cage specially built for him in the prison yard. He knew not whether he would rot away in this cage or be taken out and hanged as a traitor. . . . Not far away were the pens in which long term offenders were confined, but all other prisoners were forbidden to speak to Pound, and could not come near him.
>
> . . . After enduring the tropical sun all day, neither sleep nor rest came with the night—electric lights glared into the poet's cage and burned into his bloodshot eyes. The cage was devoid of all furniture. Pound lay upon the cement floor in his blankets, broiled by the sun and wet by the rain.

After about three weeks of struggle to maintain his sanity, the wretched man fell ill. The heat and the glare, added to the hopelessness of being held incommunicado and the torture of solitary confinement, were more than his aging mind could bear. Pound was stricken with violent and hysterical terror. He lost his memory. He became desperately thin and weak until finally the prison doctor feared for him.

. . . The period of violent insanity apparently began about mid-June, to endure for three months or more.

After twenty-five days in the cage, Pound was moved to more comfortable quarters on the recommendation of camp psychiatrists. The psychiatrists found no evidence of delusion or psychosis. They described the poet's condition as a "transitory anxiety state" characterized by confusion, claustrophobia, and fatigability. Despite this reassuring diagnosis, Pound's mental condition remained at issue during his time at the camp. Fearing a mental breakdown, the doctors ordered Pound removed from solitary confinement and eventually granted some special privileges. A month later, the DTC commander reported that his most important prisoner had adjusted to prison life and was "mentally competent." By officially certifying Pound's mental health, the army was trying to avoid later trouble in trying Pound for treason. Despite their efforts four psychiatrists testified at Pound's trial that the poet suffered from delusion and grandiosity focused on his economic and political ideas. Pound was pronounced incompetent to stand trial and admitted to the government psychiatric hospital at St. Elizabeths.

Pound's mental suffering, whatever its proper psychiatric name, is but one aspect of the calamity at Pisa. Pound's twenty-five-year poetic project, the *Cantos,* was devastated by the events of 1945. Just a few days before Pound's arrest, Mussolini had been executed. Newspapers ran photographs of the Duce and his mistress, hung by their heels "like a bullock," as Pound later wrote in **"Canto 74."** In the 1930s and 1940s, Pound had repeatedly expressed his hope that fascism would rescue Western civilization from decay. Mussolini's death and Germany's impending defeat were the final disappointment of this political hope.

With fascism's demise, there came a crisis of purpose in Pound's masterwork. The *Cantos'* purpose had always been tentative and often obscure. From the beginning the poem's complex fabric of allusion, imagery, and opinion had been stretched upon a fragile narrative frame. This framework consisted of two overlapping stories. One story told the *history* of Western civilization's struggle against evil; the heroes of this story were Malatesta, Jefferson, Mussolini, and other leaders temporarily able to order and direct their subjects' lives. The second story was the *autobiography* of

Pound's efforts to foster sound design and wise authority—Pound's efforts, in other words, to be a minor hero in history. His retelling of Western history in the poem is guided by Pound's eccentric beliefs about money, language, and politics. For example, much of **"Cantos 42-44"** is devoted to the founding of the Sienese Monte dei Paschi Bank, a momentous historical event in light of Pound's Social Credit opinions. (The founding of a public bank promised credit to farmers and freedom from usurious bank rates.) At the same time, the *Cantos* are sprinkled with references to current events that vindicated Pound's telling of history. There is constant interaction between Pound's polyglot beliefs and the emerging plot of his epic poem. Pound looked for (and found) confirmation of his beliefs in historical events, both past and present. As Michael Bernstein aptly describes it, Pound's heterodox beliefs unite in the *Cantos* "as *narrative,* where 'plot' become the realization of theory, and theory the privileged begetter of plot."

> The *Cantos'* purpose had always been
> tentative and often obscure. From the
> beginning the poem's complex fabric of
> allusion, imagery, and opinion had been
> stretched upon a fragile narrative frame.
> —*Philip E. Bishop*

In 1945, however, history had refuted much of Pound's theory. The "plot" of Pound's poem was predicated on a series of moments when wise government and sound money had triumphed in history. Following his anthropologist friend Leo Frobenius, Pound called these "paideuma." Pound's examples of enlightened government included Malatesta's regime at Rimini, Jeffersonian America, and Mussolini's fascist Italy. Mussolini was positioned at the end of this history, where he was supposed to realize the best ideas of Pound's historiography and economics. The *Cantos* were telling and were to tell this story of triumph. With the fall of the Duce, however, the narrative progress of the *Cantos* was disrupted. Not only had they lost their historical plot, but, as Bernstein adds, they also had lost their primary audience, needing "to reach—and guide—a Jefferson (or, in Pound's case, a Mussolini), capable of ordering the nation by the authority of his judgments." In other words, Mussolini was both the *Cantos'* ideal audience and the historical agent who would put their ideas into action. Prior to Pisa the *Cantos* had established themselves as a peculiarly open-ended historical narration. Their completion—indeed, their validity as historical truth—was contingent upon a fascist victory in World War II.

So, in fact, the crisis at Pisa was threefold. Personally, Pound suffered the distress of imprisonment and apprehension about his impending trial. Pound, the ideologue, saw his opinions refuted by fascism's military defeat. Pound, the epic poet, saw the forward progress of his "poem including history" halted. The *Cantos* were blocked by the collapse of that historical "paideuma"—Mussolini's Italy—which might have vindicated Pound's masterpiece. It is this last crisis that interests me most, but the revival of the *Cantos* at Pisa was closely linked to the personal and ideological aspects of this trauma. This threefold crisis was united in the poet's own experience as an intensely personal cataclysm. Pound was to say later of his days at Pisa that the "world fell on me." Hugh Kenner has written that, just as Pound seemed ready to begin his Dantean Paradiso, "everything collapsed." Kenner continues:

> For he seems to have assumed that his Paradiso when he came to write it would correspond to and be validated by a demonstrable public order, most probably in Italy. The Douglas insights seemed so accessible to comprehension, so simple of application, that theory ought to issue in practice as inevitably, and as rapidly, as electromagnet theory had issued in the telegraph. All it required was a statesman (Mussolini, perhaps) with the requisite will. So events and the poem ought to have run in counterpart, toward a *paradise terrestre.*

Before 1945 the *Cantos'* historical and autobiographical narratives had pointed toward a utopian end. In Pisa, Pound could no longer intend to write an epic that would end in reconciliation and the revelation of truth. He could not write a *Commedia:* history had prevented it. Pound's imprisonment and the Allied victory had profoundly disturbed his poem's relation to historical time. The *Cantos* stood at a chasm in time that had to be bridged if the saga was to continue.

"**Canto 74,**" the first of the *Pisan Cantos,* had to cross this gap between Pound's shattered vision and his uncertain future. It had somehow to recover from the trauma of the cage. The poetic tactics of this recovery are revealed in the canto's style. The poem's hallucinatory and dream-like qualities were intensified, as if to compensate for the *Cantos'* suddenly impoverished relation to history. Lacking a political or ideological explanation for his predicament, Pound grasped at the meager "contents" left him: cherished memories of old friends, piecemeal quotations from earlier cantos, disjointed perceptions of the hostile world that surrounded him at Pisa. And instead of historical narration, the poem reverts to a mythic or archaic time as the means for ordering its fragmentary contents. These poetic tactics try to make sense of Pound's traumatic experience at Pisa, to discover some point from which the *Cantos* may begin again. These tactics constitute the paranoid style of the *Pisan Cantos.*

The use of the term "paranoia" in this context does not imply a clinical judgment about Pound's condition in 1945. In psychiatry, paranoia is a mental condition involving deluded ideas of grandiosity and persecution, ideas that cannot be refuted by logic. In pathological cases, paranoia is a symptom of schizophrenia, the profound disordering of thought. But paranoia is also an act of imagination. Deluded ideas explain the paranoid's experience in terms of his own distorted perception and idiosyncratic logic. The paranoid's delusions are a genuine creation, a making or *poiesis.* Existential analyst Ernest Becker calls paranoia "truly a kind of poetics, a weaving of images around the limitations of the human situation, the plight of a peculiarly limited organism." The poetics of paranoia responds to a world that is indifferent to the paranoid's existence. It creates the (deluded) perception of a world that cares about the paranoid, even if only by hating him. This *poiesis* of paranoia helps to explain Pound's writings at Pisa; it was the bridge to Pound's future.

In this light, paranoid thinking has a distinctively constructive or affirmative character. Phenomenological and existential analysts in particular have stressed the affirmative cast of the paranoid delusion. They see the delusion as an original and elaborate explanation of the sufferer's role in the world; although impossible for others to understand, the delusion makes "sense" to the paranoid. Becker describes it as a way of dramatizing or "staging" value: "When the world reflects a lesser image than the patient has worked for, then there is a need for esthetic reordering. Paranoid fantasy is a principal device for righting the imbalance, for warding off the invasion of meaninglessness into a life that feels it has achieved so much that ought to be meaningful." Cut off from ordinary experience by their own distorted thinking, paranoids concoct idiosyncratic ideas about the world's rules of operation. These rules typically exaggerate the sufferer's importance in the world (i.e., they are grandiose), and they often blame the sufferer's predicament on agents of persecution (i.e., they are "paranoid").

A peculiar form of paranoid delusion has special relevance to Pound's case and the *Pisan Cantos.* It is called the "deranged experience of the world's end" (*Weltuntergangserlebnis*). The sufferer believes that he or she is the sole survivor of a world catastrophe, often a catastrophe for which the patient is responsible. The most famous paranoid of Freud's era, jurist Dr. Daniel Paul Schreber, believed that, as lone survivor of an apocalypse, he would soon become mother to a new human race fathered by God. Freud recounted the delusion in his theoretical analysis of Schreber's case: "Voices told him that the work of the past 14,000 years had now come to nothing, and that the earth's allotted span was only 212 years more; and during the last part of his stay in Prof. Flechsig's sanatorium he believed that that period had already elapsed." Moreover,

Freud noted, Schreber came to believe that the global catastrophe was the "inevitable result" of his own illness, the consequence of Schreber's privileged bond with God and of his conflict with analyst Flechsig. Such an apocalyptic delusion offers the paranoid a means of restoring temporality and value to his experience. It allows one to say, "Time begins again, now, and I am at the center of it." In this kind of delusion, an imaginary and idiosyncratic time scheme replaces the historical experience of one's existence. The author of the delusion is often (as with Schreber) responsible for the world's end, or is charged (again as with Schreber) with a divine mission to rescue humanity. In short, the *Weltuntergangserlebnis* provides its author's life with a rationale and power that were missing in real time.

The Rome radio speeches offer ample evidence of Pound's intensifying paranoia and grandiose ideas during the war years. The poet had journeyed to the United States in 1939, expecting to avert world war by speaking personally with President Roosevelt and congressional leaders. This inflated sense of self-importance was matched with a virulently anti-Semitic paranoia. The Rome broadcasts were rife with Pound's own version of a Jewish conspiracy to destroy Western civilization:

> SOMETIME the Anglo Saxon may AWAKE to the fact that the Jewish kahal and secret forces concentrated or brought to focus in the unappetizin' carcass of Franklin D. Roosevelt do NOT shove Aryan or non-yittisch nations in WARS in order that those said nations may WIN wars. The non-Jew nations are shoved into wars in order to destroy themselves, to break up their structure, to destroy their social order, to destroy their populations.

In Pound's peculiar version of this vulgar notion, the poet's own literary research and translation were the key to salvation. One trial psychiatrist testified that Pound's "remarkable grandiosity" focused on his mission to save the U.S. Constitution and on his belief that "he has the key to the peace of the world through the translations of Confucius." Pound told his examiners that he had given himself up in Italy to offer his services to the U.S. government as a diplomat or emissary. Pound viewed his imprisonment as a "double-cross," possibly engineered by agents of the British Secret Service.

These deluded ideas play an important role in **"Canto 74,"** where they enabled Pound to reconstruct his relation to history. **"Canto 74"** dramatizes Pound's tentative efforts to regain contact with a world that now was the scene of his devastated hope. Despite the trauma of the cage, Pound was not silent for long. Even before his move to more hospitable quarters, Pound had evidently started to work on new cantos: parts of **"Canto 74"** were drafted on toilet paper. The camp's commander permitted him to use a few books and the company typewriter, hoping that writing might improve Pound's mental state.

These new poems had to bridge the gap between the first seventy-one cantos and a perilous future. **"Canto 76"** was to ask, "And will the world take up its course again?" **"Canto 74"** contains two answers to that question. One is based on a deluded hope, the other on a deluded fear. The hope was that Pound could mold the shattered pieces of his new world into a mythic substitute for history. The substitute's ingredients consisted of all that Pound could see, hear, and remember in the camp at Pisa. There are recollected moments of happiness; brief glimpses of natural order and beauty; and the residual desire for a redemption that history had now denied Pound. But Pound's hope coexisted with a fear: that he, Ezra Pound, and his epic poem had betrayed the fascist cause and helped to destroy the fascist paideuma. For years Pound had believed that language and writing were decisive tools in sound government. Pound expected that his writing—the *Cantos* above all—would undergird a fascist regime in Italy and the rest of Europe. The events of 1945 forced Pound to consider his own complicity in fascism's catastrophic failure. **"Canto 74"** contains the poignant, furtive admission that the *Cantos* had failed, too, and that their author deserved his punishment.

Pound's hope and fear are visible at different moments in the opening canto of the Pisan sequence. They represent the centrifugal and centripetal forces in the *Pisan Cantos*. Under their alternating influence, the poem's perceptions—grasshoppers "in coito," the crate made into a writing desk, remembered snatches of earlier cantos—either meld into brief, glistening lyrical fragments, or degenerate into babbling and verbal clutter. One moment the reader is in paradise, the next in hell.

The paradise of the *Pisan Cantos* has been altered from the earlier sequences, though. Paradise is not to be found in or at the end of history. Rather, paradise is located in an archaic time, which moves according to the changeless rhythms of Pound's own private myth. The chief token of this archaic time is the story of Wagadu, cited several times in **"Canto 74."** Wagadu is an African goddess who returns four times to rebuild her nation after catastrophes induced by human error.

> 4 times was the city rebuilded   HOOo Fasa
>   Gassir, Hooo Fasa   dell'Italia tradita
> now in the mind indestructible, Gassir, Hoooo
>   Fasa,
> With the four giants at the four corners
> and four gates mid-wall Hooo Fasa
> and a terrace the colour of stars

Pound most likely heard this myth from Leo Frobenius and his researchers during their visit to Rapallo in 1939. Frobenius reports the myth as follows:

> Every time the guilt of man caused Wagadu to disappear she won a new beauty which made the splendor of her next appearance still more glorious. Vanity brought the song of the bard which all peoples imitate and value today. Falsehood brought a rain of gold and pearls. Greed brought writing as the Burdama still practice it today which in Wagadu was the business of the women. Dissension will enable the fifth Wagadu to be as enduring as the rain of the south and as the rocks of the Sahara, for every man will have Wagadu in his heart and every woman a Wagadu in her womb. Hoooh ! Dierra, Agade, Silla ! Hooh ! Fasa !

One can imagine the myth's impact on Pound when he first heard it. It echoes themes long prominent in his own writing: the association of writing with gold and avarice; a series of great civilizations destroyed by human error; and a heroic savior who promises to build a final and lasting paradise.

"Canto 74" suggests that Pound superimposed the reappearances of Wagadu upon his history of paideuma; the fourth city of Wagadu is identified with "Italia tradita," or Italy betrayed. In 1945 this Italy was gone, erased by the Allied victory, by the "error" of Roosevelt, Churchill, and the international conspiracy against fascism. The fifth city of Wagadu is associated with the ancient Median capital, Ecbatan, which was built during the reign of Deioces ("Dioce"). Earlier in the *Cantos,* Ecbatan would have been cited as a historical example of paideuma. In **"Canto 74,"** however, the city of Dioce represents an event beyond history:

> yet say this to the Possum: a bang, not a whimper,
>   with a bang not with a whimper,
> To build the city of Dioce whose terraces are the
>   colour of stars

In this context the city of Dioce is an alternate figure for the last Wagadu, preserved in the heart of the true believer. The sole remaining believer, though, was Pound. Because no Deioces or Mussolini existed to build the city in fact, Pound had to build it in his mind, or rather, in his poem. The *Pisan Cantos* are Pound's attempt to construct this inward paradise, his persistent affirmation that Wagadu is not lost:

> I believe in the resurrection of Italy
>   quia impossibile est
> 4 times to the song of Gassir

> now in the mind indestructible
> . . . .
> I surrender neither the empire nor the temples
>   plural
> nor the constitution nor yet the city of Dioce
> each one in his god's name

The final Wagadu, the last paradise of order and beauty, now could exist only "in the mind indestructible," as a phantasmal paideuma preserved against all hope of realization.

Deprived of its narrative design by this new inwardness, Pound's epic devolves into a composite of lyrical fragments and allusions. These are the building blocks of the phantasmal city of Dioce. The roll call of Pound's literary friends in **"Canto 74"** is a good example:

> Lordly men are to earth o'ergiven
>   these the companions:
> Fordie that wrote of giants
>   and William who dreamed of nobility
>   and Jim the comedian singing:
> "Blarrney castle me darlin'
>   you're nothing now but a StOWne"
> and Plarr talking of mathematics
>   or Jepson lover of jade
> Maurie who wrote historical novels
>   and Newbolt who looked twice bathed
>   are to earth o'ergiven.

This passage is, first of all, a poignant counterpoint to Pound's desolation at Pisa. It recalls Pound's life as literary entrepreneur and go-between in London; in its first line, the passage echoes **"The Seafarer,"** one of Pound's earliest and most controversial translations. As a figment of Pound's earlier literary life, these lines preserve the memory of companionship against the ignominious isolation at Pisa. Similar fragments, to be internalized and protected, are provided by natural beauty:

> Hooo Fasa, and in a dance the renewal
> with two larks in contrappunto
> at sunset
> . . . .
> nor is it for nothing that the chrysalids mate in the
>   air color di
>   luce
> green splendour and as the sun thru pale fingers

But these brief glimpses of natural order and remembered happiness are always broken off, alternating with Pound's rage at his persecutors and his anxious uncertainty. Deprived of any hope for historical redemption and denied the "plot" of history, the *Pisan Cantos* merely suspend these bits of paradise in a web of poetic suggestion. Paradise, says

"Canto 74," "n'est pas artificiel / but spezzato [shattered] apparently."

Massimo Bacigalupo sees these fragments as evidence of a newfound "neo-platonism" in Pound's philosophy. He calls these disconnected images *formae,* that is, ideal aesthetic shapes that resemble the ephemeral "rose in the steel dust," the image that closes **"Canto 74."** Such a reading aptly underscores the idealism of this style: beauty is, indeed, an ephemera endangered by contact with the world of historical experience. Like the "diamond in the avalanche," these fragments of a hard and enduring beauty have been uprooted by history, scattered and buried in the calamity of 1945.

But Pound's was a curiously solipsistic platonism. The *formae* in the **Pisan Cantos** were the constituents of his poetics of delusion. The remains of paradise were themselves disparate: the orderly processes of nature, history's brief moments of sane government, the accomplishments and convictions of Pound's earlier career. Someone had to collect these shards of paradise and protect them from the dispersion of historical time. Of course, the only person qualified for such a project and aware of its necessity was Pound himself. Paradise would be "indestructible" only if Pound could preserve its remnants in new cantos. Thus, the *Cantos* acquired their new mission at Pisa: not to end history but to recover from it.

Out of this impulse emerged a new and precarious mission for the *Cantos* as a whole. Before the war Pound had hoped that Mussolini's Italy would be the earthly paradise. His epic poem was to be a useful prod and commentary for this new age, but not the agent of historical change itself. With Mussolini's demise, however, the very existence of paradise—even as phantasm—depended upon Pound's ability to imagine and record it. Thus, the cantos composed at Pisa were the fragile vehicle of paradise, threatened by history and by Pound's own confusion and dementia.

> **Before the war Pound had hoped that Mussolini's Italy would be the earthly paradise. . . . With Mussolini's demise, however, the very existence of paradise—even as phantasm—depended upon Pound's ability to imagine and record it.**
> —*Philip E. Bishop*

The grandiosity of this new mission for the *Cantos* is evident: the salvation of Western civilization rested upon Pound's poetic prowess. Paradise would be lost if that prowess weakened, if the *Cantos* "failed to cohere" as Pound had feared they might. For years Pound had insisted that muddled writing could undermine the state. Now, in the detention camp at Pisa, these convictions pricked the author with a bitter and self-accusing question: Had the obscurity of the earlier *Cantos* contributed to fascism's defeat? Would a failure in these new cantos—the degeneration of style into babble, the disintegration of form into rubble—mean the end of paradise?

These questions cast a shadow of guilt and complicity upon the **Pisan Cantos**' phantasmal paradise. The Wagadu myth, whose fifth city is the refuge of paideuma, also hints at the poet's responsibility for disaster. In the myth's framing story, the prince Gassire pursues a holy song of the poet's immortality. This song, to be played on a magic lute, would endure long after the battles had been fought and the poet was dead. But Gassire's quest for the immortal song causes incessant war among his people; the magic "lute of Gassir," it turns out, must be hallowed by his own sons' blood. In seeking beauty and immortality through the lute, Gassire finds that he has been banished and Wagadu has been lost. **"Canto 74"** refers repeatedly to the lute of Gassire and his cry, "Hooo Fasa." These references indicate that, in the midst of Pound's own banishment, Frobenius's story reinforced the poet's sense of guilt and betrayal. The story explained how, while reaching for paradise, Pound had reached hell and was caught there in a cage.

There is other such evidence in **"Canto 74."** For example, the canto twice refers to Ugolino, a character in Dante's *Inferno.* Ugolino betrayed his native city Pisa for private gain. As punishment, he was shut up in the Torre della fame with his sons and left to starve. Ugolino was consigned to the depths of hell by Dante, himself the victim of betrayal. By raising his eyes from the ground to the horizon, Pound could see Ugolino's tower to the left of Pisa's more famous landmark:

> dry friable earth going from dust to more dust
>   grass worn from its root-hold
>   is it blacker? was it blacker? Nux animae?
>   is there a blacker or was it merely San Juan with
>   a belly ache
>   writing ad posteros
>   in short shall we look for a deeper or is this the
>   bottom?
>   Ugolino, the tower there on the tree line
> Berlin dysentery phosphorus
>   la vieille de Candide
>   (Hullo Corporal Casey) double X or burocracy?
>   Le Paradis n'est pas artificiel
>   but spezzato apparently
> it exists only in fragments

This passage is typical of the **Pisan Cantos**' laconic and disjointed style, a style that sets off intricate correspondences and identifications. The "friable earth" here is most likely the dirt path worn by Pound's vigorous exercise rounds. In it the poet apparently sees the dispersion, darkness, and threat of death that haunt him. His question to St. John of the Cross, whether this is the darkest "night of the soul," is answered by the allusion to Ugolino, walled up in a Pisan prison and cannibalizing the bodies of his dead sons. Ugolino's awful recourse from starvation suggests Gassire, who sacrificed his sons to hallow the magic lute. Completing the circuit of identification, Ugolino recounts his guilty crime "to posterity," through the voice of the immortal poet Dante, just as Pound speaks to posterity in his own epic. From Ugolino the passage moves on to Berlin, a fascist capital betrayed; to dysentery, Pound's own "belly ache" in captivity; and the phosphorus, a false and deceiving light that contrasts with the "color of light" cited so frequently in this canto as a figure of paradise. The highly condensed and allusive identification with Ugolino suggests that Pound may be perpetrator as well as victim of betrayal. The question about betrayal is addressed to Pound's jailer, Corporal Casey: Is the cause of Pound's suffering a "double-cross," a betrayal of truth for private gain (as with Ugolino)? Or is it "burocracy," the dispersion of administrative power from a single leader? The passage rises from this dark self-examination to affirm that paradise is not artificial, as Baudelaire proclaimed, but it is "spezzato," in pieces. Paradise is friable, worn from its root-hold in history.

This brief passage illustrates how easy it is to explicate the *Pisan Cantos* without explaining them. The poems' labyrinthine associations stimulate multiple and sometimes mutually contradictory readings. No one reading is more authoritative as long as it is referenced just to the poem itself. To explain the Pisan poems, one must connect them to the circumstances of their composition, to a poet suspended between vain hopes for redemption and the self-accusing realization of failure.

Another moment of implicit self-accusation in **"Canto 74"** appears in the "wanjina" passage. Again, Pound recalls a myth told to him by Frobenius. The Australian wondjina were icons whose mouths had been removed; **"Canto 74"** equates them to Ouan Jin, a transliteration of the Confucian term for "literary gent" (*wen jen*).

> but Wanjina is, shall we say, Ouan Jin
> or the man with an education
> and whose mouth was removed by his father
>   because he made too many *things*
> whereby cluttered the bushman's baggage
> vide the expedition of Frobenius' pupils about
> 1938 to Auss'tralia
> Ouan Jin spoke and thereby created the named
> thereby making
>   clutter
> the bane of men moving

> and so his mouth was removed
> as you will find it removed in his pictures in
> principio verbum
>   paraclete or the verbum perfectum:sinceritas

In one of its aspects, this passage accords with the paradisal impulse of **"Canto 74."** Beauty and truth may be contained in the "verbum perfectum," here a synonym for Confucian "sinceritas." Guy Davenport has rightly termed this passage a parable of the poetic act. The writer's sincerity invites God to dwell with humans. But for the blessed paraclete to descend, the "man with an education" must be silent. Davenport writes, "The ellipsis takes its energy from the iconographic paralleling of word, mouth, and logos, the absence of the latter, in accordance with John 16:7, being prerequisite for the appearance among men of the Paraclete, thus equating, seemingly, the mouthless Wanjina with the fertile presence of God in man."

The "wanjina" parable has a darker aspect that Davenport overlooks. He quite admittedly disregards the Australians' belief that if the wondjina had mouths, all humanity would perish in a catastrophic deluge. It is the end of the world again, this time brought on by the "man with an education" who speaks (or writes) excessively and thereby creates clutter. With the "wanjina," once again, the writer is complicit in catastrophe. He has violated Confucius's dictum of "sinceritas": "To communicate, and then stop, that is the / law of discourse . . . simplex munditiis." It was precisely this prescription that the *Cantos* at Pisa could not obey. To be silent would be to admit that paradise *was*, after all," "artificiel." To go on speaking, on the other hand, was to create the poetic clutter of the *Pisan Cantos*. Thus, the mouthless "wanjina" may be equated to Ezra Pound himself: the man with an education, or, shall we say, the erudite poet indicated for treason, the "bane of men moving."

The implicit self-indictments of **"Canto 74"** are the underside of Pound's grandiose conception of the writer in history. Writers who made "clutter" aided the downfall of wise leaders and the decline of civilization. For the first time in the *Pisan Cantos,* Pound turned this accusation against himself, if only briefly and by implication. It was a bitter truth that Pound could only take in small doses and that did not cure his hope for paradise. But by the last cantos, the self-accusation had prevailed:

> But the beauty is not the madness
> Tho' my errors and wrecks lie about me.
> And I am not a demigod,
> I cannot make it cohere.
> . . . .
> That I lost my center
>   fighting the world.
> The dreams clash

and are shattered and—
that I tried to make a paradiso
terrestre.

. . . .

I have tried to write Paradise . . .
Let the Gods forgive what I
have made
Let those I love try to forgive
what I have made.

Traces of this insight appear in the dark moments of **"Canto 74."** In Gassire, Ugolino, and the "wanjina," the canto offers figures of the poet who had betrayed his people and his paradise. These are the sobering antidotes to the delusion that paradise could be preserved "in the mind entire." Eventually, in Pound's old age, a bitter and disillusioned sanity prevailed, and work on the *Cantos* stopped. "I ruin everything I touch. I have been mistaken, always," he told a reporter in 1963. Of the *Cantos* he said, "They are a botch."

There was, as yet, no such recantation at Pisa. The ideological rag-bag of Pound's fanaticism was still intact in the *Pisan Cantos.* Pound's ideas about fascism, Jews, and money had not changed; indeed, he continued to advocate those ideas while at St. Elizabeths. What had changed was those ideas' relation to history and to Pound's epic ambition. **"Canto 74"** had to blaze a new path to paradise, a path that did not lead through history. The *Cantos'* new mission, as I have called it, was to preserve paradise as a purely interior phantasm. This phantasm was encapsuled in the broken fragments, the *formae,* of Pound's Pisan style. The preservation of these fragments gave Pound reason to continue writing at and after Pisa. But the recovery at Pisa was bought at an awful cost to Pound's ambition: the admission, in **"Canto 74,"** that paradise exists only as a figment and can never be redeemed by historical time. The paranoid moment of the *Pisan Cantos* was to continue—as delusion—an epic poem which could no longer be history.

Thus, the unique enterprise of Pound's *Cantos* recovered from its trauma and continued beyond 1945, even though it was to end in acknowledged failure. Pound's was the only epic in the Western tradition to so orient itself toward the future horizon of history. Certainly Dante had taken no such risk; the *Commedia* was ostensibly a recollection of Dante's journey into the afterlife. But by claiming the terrain of historical narration, the *Cantos* were vulnerable to the intrusion of historical events. The eventuality of history had not vindicated Ezra Pound, but rather victimized him. Pound's own history, the catalog of paideuma, had come to a cataclysmic end. **"Canto 74,"** with its jarring tonalities and circuitous associations, is the drama of Pound's recovery from this catastrophe. By turning inward, this and the succeeding cantos sought to rescue Pound's convictions and aspirations from the ash heap of history. As ideas, their failure was de-

served. As poetry, their success continues to animate and to intrigue the readers of this complex work.

Vincent Miller (essay date Winter 1990)

SOURCE: "Mauberley and His Critics," in *ELH: English Literary History,* Vol. 57, No. 4, Winter, 1990, pp. 961-76.

[*In the following essay, Miller offers a reexamination of critical dispute surrounding* Hugh Selwyn Mauberley *from its publication to the present. "Once Pound's greatest success," writes Miller, "it is today perhaps his least respected poem."*]

I

Ezra Pound's **Hugh Selwyn Mauberley** is, one must hasten to say, an overconsidered poem. Disagreed about for half a century, interpreted in contradictory fashions, whoever speaks of it has to begin by explaining how he reads it. Once Pound's greatest success, it is today perhaps his least respected poem. [T. S.] Eliot, one recalls, thought whatever else he was sure of, he was sure of **Mauberley;** Donald Davie, himself very intelligent, tells us that it only appeals to "thin and constricted and rancorously distrustful sensibilities." There's a difference of opinion to think about.

Such disagreements do have a way of working themselves out. Twenty-five years ago, in *Essays in Criticism,* A. L. French published a perceptive and now famous essay, damning **Mauberley** and all the upstart modernist literature it seemed to him to represent. It is obvious enough today that French's intelligence and his dislike of what seemed to him chaos come again were getting in each other's way. That gives one hope. For **Mauberley** criticism had its origin among critics caught up, as French was, in a battle of pro-modernists versus anti-modernists, pro-Poundians versus anti-Poundians, which skewed perceptions and created mindsets still with us. It is time to write the story up, see it clearly, and escape its limitations. For **Mauberley** is not only one of Pound's major poems, essential to his development and to that of modernist literature, it is still, as Hugh Kenner pointed out forty years ago, "at its deepest levels . . . unread."

> For **Mauberley** is not only one of Pound's major poems, essential to his development and to that of modernist literature, it is still, as Hugh Kenner pointed out forty years ago, "at its deepest levels . . . unread."
>
> —*Vincent Miller*

A few basic things everyone is agreed about, and one of them must be mentioned at the outset, however familiar: that Mauberley is one of two kinds of artist Pound had spent several years differentiating—a kind characterized by what he called "Epicurean receptivity, a certain aloofness, an observation of contacts and auditions." Poets of this type are, Pound held, aesthetes withdrawn from action and given to the passive "perception of beauty," which makes them easily distinguished, at least in theory, from those who have what Pound called "the Propertian attitude": poets inspired by passionate love and able to create new worlds out of their "kinship to the vital universe." Pound's critics agree that Mauberley is a beauty-loving aesthete and that he fails as a result to change what he finds a crass and vulgar world.

And that is about all they agree upon. Serious differences surface as soon as any attempt is made to determine what Mauberley's aestheticism and failure, described in the poem's second section, have to do with the scathing attack upon his civilization that makes up the first, or with that section's beautiful concluding love lyric, **"Envoi."** The story begins with F. R. Leavis, who in 1931 responded to the poem's many aestheticisms by concluding that it should be read as Mauberley's poem, Mauberley being a mask through which Pound was not only brilliantly condemning modern commercial vulgarity and writing a lovely lyric, but also confessing his own ineffectual aestheticism. Widely accepted, the view set up a "Pound is (or isn't) Mauberley" argument that has dogged the poem ever since. It remained dominant—with individual critics disagreeing how completely Pound should be identified with Mauberley—until Kenner, in his ground-breaking study of Pound's works in 1950, claimed that Pound was not in *Mauberley* confessing his own weaknesses through a persona, creating a poem readers liked because it sounded like a familiar Eliotic "introspection," but instead writing with Flaubertian objectivity about England and the poetic voice represented by Mauberley. In 1955 in his detailed and still invaluable study of the poem, John Espey agreed, making Pound a virile, passionate, Propertian poet condemning an ineffectual, unvirile aesthete and his crassly commercial world. The stage was now set for all that was to follow, for subsequent critics found attempts to read the entire poem as the creation of a Propertian Pound difficult if not unworkable.

A few examples will suffice. In 1956 Thomas Connolly argued that all of the poem's first section had to be read as Mauberley's. In 1961 Davie agreed that would be best, though he felt individual poems in the first section could just as easily be read as Pound's because Pound and Mauberley had not been "sufficiently differentiated." In 1963 George Dekker agreed they were not, and suggested that this was because Pound was criticizing Mauberley while at the same time trying to purge himself of his own Mauberley-like tendencies. In 1965 William Spanos found Mauberley's voice

so nearly omnipresent that he argued that Mauberley must be thought of as speaking all of the poem except **"Envoi."** Recently Ronald Bush has made another suggestion: that Mauberley speaks the poem's first section in tonalities which Pound deliberately echoes in speaking the second. And to cite but two more conclusions, both recent, Massimo Bacigalupo has now returned to Leavis's original view that the poem is autobiographical throughout, while Jo Brantley Berryman has argued that Pound himself disagreed with almost everything said in its first section and was therefore clearly not writing autobiographically.

This is a brief sample—though only a sample—of the tangle of different readings that have resulted from imposing on the poem the question of Pound's relation to Mauberley. Looking back, one wonders how that particular question ever got as entrenched as it now is, and must conclude that it became the standard way of considering the poem not just because of critics convinced and sometimes anxious to prove that Pound was as much, or nearly as much, an aesthete as Mauberley, but also because of those convinced and anxious to prove that he wasn't. For their main defense was to put Pound into the poem and argue that he was criticizing in his own Propertian voice both modern culture and one of its typical aesthetes. This made it absolutely necessary to distinguish Pound's way of writing from Mauberley's within the poem. And when that, as we have seen, proved impossible to do in any way that could be agreed upon, it left *Mauberley* criticism in its present state, distorting in the process both what Pound thought of Propertius's kind of writing and what he thought of the aesthetic. Pound had run into similar attempts to save him by making him into a virile and passionate Propertian as early as 1913.

> Oh my fellow sufferers, songs of my youth,
> A lot of asses praise you because you are 'virile',
> We, you, I! We are 'Red Bloods'!
> Imagine it, my fellow sufferers—
> Our maleness lifts us out of the ruck
>   Who'd have foreseen it?

"The Condolence"

Pound had—as any careful re-reading of his prose shows—much more respect for the aesthetic kind of writing than his critics have had; and we are, as a result, much better off assuming that he at least initially began *Mauberley,* just as he suggested he had to John Drummond, intending to use the aesthetic voice of a very British Hugh Selwyn Mauberley to communicate his scorn of recent British culture to a "blockheaded epoch," an epoch he had found incapable of understanding the *Homage to Sextus Propertius*'s emphasis on sex and its seemingly flippant, sex-oriented condemnation of bourgeois crassness, imperialism, and war.

He had, as we know, been using a similar voice—"effete and overcivilized," he called it—for somewhat similar purposes, writing a series of "Imaginary Letters" for the *Little Review* under the name of Walter Villerant, knowing it a voice to which English audiences were trained to respond. (*Mauberley* was Pound's first and only marked English success.) It was not a mode he despised in any of its manifestations, of which Mauberley is but one. Instead it was one of two kinds of writing—the first receptive, diagnostic, sensitive, and beauty-loving; the second passion-born and creative—which, starting in 1912 in his **"Psychology and Troubadours,"** he had by the time he began *Mauberley* spent almost a decade differentiating. Both of these at their best he admired, and both can be found in his work from beginning to end.

While he was writing *Mauberley,* he was, in fact, learning at least as much from Henry James, whom he thought an aesthete, as from Remy de Gourmont, whom he found Propertian. For he was finding in James not only hints for the overcivilized Mauberley—as Espey thoroughly proved—but, as Bush has made clear, techniques essential to the advances he was at the time beginning to make in **"Cantos 4-7."** What Bush finds so important here is that it was in these cantos that Pound found the narrative voice that would enable him to write his epic, a voice that, he wrote John Quinn, came from the middle of himself and not from some mask. If the Jamesian aesthetic mode played an integral part in that achievement, it cannot be seen as something he was in 1919 doing anything but learning how to use.

All of which suggests that Pound set out in *Mauberley* neither to condemn aestheticism in general, nor to confess his own aesthetic failures, nor to differentiate himself from an aesthete named Mauberley; rather, he set out to make use of the nineties' version of the aesthetic mode to communicate what he had failed to communicate in the *Homage*—seeing, at the same time, how far he could within its limits develop its possibilities. No reading of *Mauberley* which tries to see in it a Propertian Pound differentiating himself from a minor aesthete (or trying to), or that has less respect for the aesthetic mode than Leavis, who found the poem a significant achievement, can evaluate that attempt—or even see its existence.

II

The place to begin any serious reconsideration of *Mauberley* criticism is with its concluding poem, **"Envoi"**—for even those who think *Mauberley*'s first section is Mauberley's poem see **"Envoi"** as something beyond his reach. **"Envoi"** is, they point out, written in the great English lyric tradition that stretches back to Shakespeare and beyond. It cannot, they are sure, be confused with anything an aesthete might write. Famous as the poem is, let me start by quoting it. It is the pivot point about which *Mauberley* turns and merits being looked at still another time.

> Go, dumb-born book,
> Tell her that sang me once that song of Lawes:
> Hadst thou but song
> As thou hast subjects known,
> Then were the cause in thee that should condone
> Even my faults that heavy on me lie,
> And build her glories their longevity.
>
> Tell her that sheds
> Such treasure in the air,
> Recking naught else but that her graces give
> Life to the moment,
> I would bid them live
> As roses might, in magic amber laid,
> Red overwrought with orange and all made
> One substance and one colour
> Braving time.
>
> Tell her that goes
> With song upon her lips
> But sings not out the song, nor knows
> The maker of it, some other mouth,
> May be as fair as hers,
> Might, in new ages, gain her worshippers,
> When our two dusts with Waller's shall be laid,
> Siftings on siftings in oblivion,
> Till change hath broken down
> All things save Beauty alone.

Rereading this lovely lyric, with its echoes of Edmund Waller's "Go, Lovely Rose," of Shakespeare, and of a hundred Elizabethan songs and sonnets, one can understand why so many critics have felt that Pound was in it writing of passion as the kind of "intellectual instigation" he claimed it to be in Propertius and the troubadours. But he wasn't. It is true that "Go, Lovely Rose," which **"Envoi"** so brilliantly echoes, is a carpe diem poem that urges its hearer to consider youth's brevity and accept physical passion. Thus the song which the girl in **"Envoi"** sings to the poet—and sings specifically to him, so he tells us, "recking naught else but that her graces give / Life to the moment"—does have a Propertian import. But the most significant thing about the poet's reply is not that it echoes Waller's song but that it echoes it only to move in exactly the opposite direction from that song's meaning. For what it seeks is not a passionate acceptance of life and love, but an escape from human mutability into the frozen permanence of an art world where the girl's beauty can be preserved like "roses in magic amber laid, / Red overwrought with orange and all made / One substance and one colour / Braving time." This is a beautifully refurbished Elizabethan poetic cliché, but it is not about love in any Propertian sense. It is about Beauty, its loss in this world, and its preservation in art.

Its relation to the rest of *Mauberley* is, as a result, dramatically different from the relation of Propertius's passion for Cynthia to the poems of Pound's *Homage*. Propertius's passion is central to all he speaks of, present in every poem, conditioning all he thinks and feels. The **"Envoi"** poet's concern for the singing girl is, in contrast, neither passionate nor related to *Mauberley*'s other concerns. It is, of course, only in part two of *Mauberley* that we are told of Mauberley's response to a girl's beauty that "he made no immediate application / Of this to relation of the state." But it is that very lack of relationship that accounts for the placement of **"Envoi"** as an envoi—an afterword, a postscript—to the social criticism of *Mauberley*'s first section. And what is differentiated thereby is the order of passionate love basic to the entire *Homage* from the love of beauty that animates all of *Mauberley,* **"Envoi"** included.

III

It is at this point that Pound's opinion of Waller's poetry takes on significance. Pound thought Waller "a tiresome fellow" whose talent was "fathoms below Rochester's," a poet whose merit was the result of his being fortunate enough to write in the "'style of a period'" whose "musical criteria . . . were of prime order." This is significant because Pound believed, as he put it in his essay on Cavalcanti, that the Elizabethan modes of song and sonnet writing which had established those criteria had done so at a price—that of losing the very qualities he pictures his aesthete Mauberley as also lacking: "masculinity," "fervor," "intensity." This conclusion he reached in deciding that the poetic techniques of the best Elizabethan lyricists would not allow him to translate into contemporary English these three essential qualities of Cavalcanti's sonnets.

"But by taking these Italian sonnets," he finally concluded, "by sacrificing, or losing, or simply not feeling and understanding their cogency, their sobriety, and by seeking simply that far from quickly or so-easily-as-it-looks attainable thing, the perfect melody . . . you find yourself in the English *seicento* song-books." And there you find, "quite often," he said, "a Mozartian perfection of melody" accompanied by a "wisdom, almost perhaps an ultimate wisdom, deplorably lacking in guts." And this because in them, escaping life's sobering realities, "death has become melodious; sorrow is as serious as the nightingale's, tombstones are shelves for the reception of rose leaves." One has at this point only to recall the **"Envoi"** poet's "when our two dusts with Waller's shall be laid, / Siftings on siftings in oblivion," or his lines about roses "in magic amber laid," to see that Pound was not uncritical of the poetic tradition **"Envoi"**'s verbal beauty renews.

Given these facts, we are pushed toward two conclusions. First, Pound intended **"Envoi"** to be read as Mauberley's work; and second, he intended it to be an example of the kind of poem the beauty-loving aesthete, continuing a long tradition, wanted to write—or was able to write—in 1919, the date of **"Envoi."** For Mauberley does change. The dates here are important. Pound stressed them by dating neither the rest of the poem's first section, nor the poem as a whole—only **"Envoi"** and the immediately following second section, dated 1920. In 1919 the **"Envoi"** poet responds to a beautiful girl's song about love by telling her that what that song arouses in him is not a Propertian desire for her love, but a desire to write a death-defying song preserving for future generations the memory of her evanescent loveliness. In 1920 Mauberley comes to realize—"a year late" we are reminded—that his devotion to beauty rather than to passionate living has had a price:

> Mouths biting the empty air
> The still stone dogs,
> Caught in metamorphosis, were
> Left him as epilogues.

IV

In 1957 Pound changed the title of his poem from *Hugh Selwyn Mauberley (Life and Contacts)* to *Hugh Selwyn Mauberley (Contacts and Life)* and wanted the fact noticed: "Note inversion in sub-title of Mauberley, NOT Life and Contacts, but the actual order of the subject matter." This seems to suggest that the actual order of his poem about Mauberley makes its first section an account of Mauberley's contacts—and not, as many critics were concluding, Pound's own—just as it makes the second section what almost everyone was granting and still grants, an account of Mauberley's life.

But what makes this so important? The contacts are obviously Pound's. He did, however, at the time he began *Mauberley,* have a problem. As Bush has made us aware, he had come to believe—influenced by what he saw as Laforgue's advance over Flaubert—that "ideas," in Pound's words, have "little value apart from the modality of the mind which receives them." That is, all a writer actually manages to convey is his *"façon de voir,"* his "modality of apperception." Pound's problem in 1919 was that he had not as yet been able to create a language in which he could express all that made up his own "modality of apperception." And until he solved that problem—which he began to do that year with **"Canto 4"**—he was consciously confined to exploring those partial aspects of his own vision for which, up to that time, he had found the language. Since 1916 he had explored one such aspect in what he called the "archaic language" of his Provençal poems; still another in the contrastingly "realistic" *moeurs contemporaines* poems; and still another in the Propertian and Laforgian *Homage to Sextus Propertius.* These poems he published together in 1921, along with the aesthete-oriented *Mauberley,* and **"Cantos 4-7."** And it was of this volume that he wrote Quinn, telling him that in contrast to the other poems the four new cantos "come out of the middle of me and are not a mask, are what I have to say. . . ." This makes *Mauberley,* all of it, including the first section and its **"Envoi,"** spoken through a mask.

But can't the mask be that of a Pound who, still developing, is not yet fully able to express himself, an "E.P."—as he is referred to in the poem—who embodies an aspect of Pound but not all of him? This would get us out of some of our problems; and it echoes a suggestion K. K. Ruthven made in 1969. But since it gives us Pound using the mask of a partial self to write about what we have to conclude is another Pound mask, the argument becomes more involuted than we would like, and ends up entangled in the same old side-issue, as it tries to differentiate the Pound-Propertian mask from the Mauberley-aesthetic one.

The battle between Poundians and anti-Poundians, modernists and anti-modernists may not be entirely over—may only have assumed another form—but it seems time to conclude that Pound wrote the first section of *Mauberley* in Mauberley's voice, using him, warts and all, as a "surface" that allowed him to "condense the James novel." Nothing in *Mauberley*'s first section, **"Envoi"** included, grows from passion in any Propertian sense. The section echoes Gautier in almost every one of its individual poems, as Espey has shown us, and of Gautier's aestheticism there can be no question. And it has what Pound thought a Jamesian subject, *moeurs contemporaines,* treated from an English aesthete's disdainful, culture-soaked, beauty-loving point of view. To conclude that Pound had deserted his practice of speaking through masks and was writing in his own voice—when it seems clear he had not yet found that voice—and that he was doing so by imitating an aesthete's poems and metrics, is but one more of those strangely involuted conclusions which critics of the poem's first section, seeking to put Pound into the poem, have offered us.

V

If *Mauberley*'s second section must, like the first and for the same reasons, be read as an expression of Mauberley's *"façon de voir,"* it must be read as Leavis read it, as a turn inward toward self-analysis. It is important, then, to place its composition in Mauberley's life.

In the poem's second section, we are told that during a three-year period Mauberley "drank ambrosia" and had some relationship with a girl "among whose phantasmagoria" he "moved." In 1919, toward the end of that relationship, he

wrote **"Envoi."** Shortly after writing it but before 1920, the date of the poem's second section, the relationship collapsed: "came end to that Arcadia." Bewildered, adrift, Mauberley found himself "unable in the supervening blankness / To sift TO AGATHON from the chaff" until he found a new way of registering realities: "until he found his sieve . . . / Ultimately his seismograph."

Having found that seismograph, Mauberley charts his own failure in relation to his world's. And given the precise and beautiful finality of the analysis, it is not enough to say of the section as Bush very perceptively has—leading us in exactly the right direction, toward a single evolving consciousness—that it is written in a less "youthfully vigorous version of the restless, abstracted voice" of the first. What Bush's view does not give enough weight is a perception of aestheticism's viable future, one which, born in the first section under the influence of Gautier, has in both sections, as a result of what Pound found or thought he found in Laforgue, been deepened and put to new uses.

That Pound sought in *Mauberley* to bring into English poetry what Gautier had achieved in French is another thing all the poem's critics agree upon. Evaluating the work of what he called "the men of 'the nineties,'" Pound had decided by the time he wrote *Mauberley* that the nineties poets had accomplished in English what Gautier had accomplished in France by 1830, but had failed to go on to emulate the "hardness" and "clearness" of his later *Émaux et Camées.* What he found in Laforgue that makes Laforgue important to *Mauberley* was another advance to catch up with: "the next phase after Gautier in French poetry."

Laforgue was, as Leo Weinstein has pointed out, a poet different from the aesthetes before him because he didn't react as they did with dissoluteness, rebellion, and hashish. As Weinstein goes on to say, he "understood and admired his predecessors" but—like Mauberley—"was also aware of how puerile certain aspects of . . . [their] revolts were and to what extent they were a pose." Out of that awareness, a part of the tradition he criticized, he developed, Weinstein says, a "less spectacular" attitude which "turning inward . . . produced works of . . . urbane irony (often self-irony, the anti-dote for self-pity) and wit."

What we can find in *Mauberley,* in both its sections, are exactly the ironic Laforgian characteristics of language and attitude that Weinstein defines. And Pound himself singled them out. What Pound saw in Laforgue was, he said, an artist "nine-tenths . . . critic" who took "literary poses and *clichés* . . . as his subject matter" and wrote about them, "not [in] the popular language of any country but [in] an international tongue common to the excessively cultivated". This is, of course, just what Mauberley does, with exactly the attitude Weinstein defines and in exactly the language Pound describes. He writes of the literary poses and clichés of the English aesthetes of the nineties and their late-Victorian world as well as those that typify his own England, and, finally, "turning inward" with "self-irony" and "wit," his own "Olympian *apathein*" and its inevitable consequences.

And when we come to Mauberley's deepest feelings about himself and his world, another aspect of Laforgue's poetry takes on significance. For Pound thought it was perhaps Laforgue's greatest merit that he was able to present his criticisms in such a way as to use them as "a vehicle for the expression of his own personal emotions." Mauberley's "personal emotions" become more than an aesthete's stereotypical dandyism as soon as we realize that Pound's study of Laforgue paid dividends here also. To that we can now turn.

VI

Perceiving that aestheticism and science come to share, at a certain point in their development, a similar stance and a similar strategy, Laforgue had, as Pound pointed out, "dipped his wings in the dye of scientific terminology." Hence, in Laforgue's case, such phrases as the one Pound quotes, which describes the beardless Pierrot as having "un air d'hydrocephale asperge" [an air of a hydrocephalic asparagus stalk]. And hence also one aspect of *Mauberley*'s second section, imbued as it is with a carefully poised analytic objectivity not at all unlike that with which an internist, in the highly technical language of his art, charts the course of some terminal disease; let us, to keep the parallel, even assume it his own. The similarity here is obvious. A language that informs us that "for three years, diabolus in the scale, he drank ambrosia . . . came end to that Arcadia" shares characteristics with the one a doctor would use if he wrote of his own state that his melanoma was resected but had in fact already metastasized. Both the doctor and the aesthete have, that is to say, substituted for what Yeats in "Byzantium" called "the mire of human veins," a world of carefully distanced intellectual precisions that screen and structure and give new emotional weight to a messy reality from which they must remain, as a condition of their art, detached.

What Laforgue was mocking and exploiting with his "scientific terminology" was, then, a methodology and an attitude coming into prominence all about him. At their worst they created the slant of mind for which Flaubert's Homais, without intelligence or character, won his Legion of Honor. At their best they animate the objectively distanced concern and skill Flaubert finds in the heroic Dr. Larivière, and perfects in himself so he can write *Madame Bovary,* ("*Emma Bovary, c'est moi!*") To any understanding of that attitude and its enabling techniques Homais is a key. For what Homais has appropriated, and so delightfully caricatures, is

just what he thought it: a most promising method of dealing in Olympian detachment with the petty, the vulgar, and the painful. He dines with Dr. Larivière hoping to enjoy a learned discussion of Emma's death agony. ("'*Saccharum,* doctor?' said he, offering the sugar.") What is involved in Mauberley's poetic experiments is, then, much more than an aesthete's lack of Propertian drive. It is the evolving nature of dominant western attitudes.

VII

Much of what is accomplished in *Mauberley*'s first section has been clear for decades—however miscredited to Propertian virility. Something of what is accomplished in its second becomes obvious as soon as one stops trying to impose a Pound versus Mauberley question on the poem and compares the two sections' final lyrics, noting how different they are in their similarity.

> Luini in porcelain!
> The grand piano
> Utters a profane
> Protest with her clear soprano.
>
> The sleek head emerges
> From the gold-yellow frock
> As Anodyomene in the opening
> Pages of Reinach.
>
> Honey-red, closing the face-oval,
> A basket-work of braids which seem as if they
>   were
> Spun in King Minos' hall
> From metal, or intractable amber;
>
> The face-oval beneath the glaze,
> Bright in its suave bounding-line, as,
> Beneath half-watt rays,
> The eyes turn topaz.

"Medallion"

The author of this poem, writing a new tribute to the singing girl, does seek, like the author of **"Envoi,"** the comfort of life's aesthetic surfaces to escape its painful depths. He too loves the permanence of amber and the lasting beauty of art. But his love of art and artifice is not, like that in **"Envoi,"** an Elizabethan echo.

And that it is not, and that it arouses as a consequence no favorable reflexes, tells us something important about the conditioning influence Elizabethan lyric poetry has had upon English poetic expectations down even into the twentieth century. For it is not too much to say that Elizabethan lyricists were, like the author of **"Envoi"** more than three hundred years later, obsessed with mutability, that they too yearned for worlds of artificial permanence that would outlast their animal flesh: marble, or the gilded monuments of princes, or this powerful rhyme. What is important here is that the Elizabethan songs and sonnets which satisfied that yearning contained, Pound felt, a wisdom, almost perhaps an ultimate wisdom, lacking, he concluded, in guts.

It is a conclusion that seems at first surprising but isn't. For it is one that had sooner or later to surface in a post-Elizabethan world which had come to think of art as a total and honest expression of—rather than, as the Elizabethan lyricists did, a carefully and beautifully wrought complement to—life's realities. And when the change was finally complete, what was needed was not of necessity what we find in Yeats's Byzantium poems: some passionately intense expression within the poem itself of the agonizing difference between art and life. A different solution—Mauberley's kind of solution, Laforgue's kind—would merely include within the poem quietly and with deflating irony the knowledge Elizabethan poets felt needed no acknowledgment at all: that any work of art is a created counterpoint to, not a substitute for, the breathing human life whose existence it replaces only at a cost.

In some ways the two approaches—Mauberley's and Yeats's—have like results. In their love of beauty and artifice and their awareness that art is not a living thing, both poets create worlds that are critical of and ambivalent about their own points of view. Bodies of hammered gold are as insistently artificial and life-denying as braids spun from metal or intractable amber; and the young in one another's arms are as vivid a definition of a breathing world lost as *Mauberley*'s still stone dogs biting the empty air. But, from the point of view that creates *Mauberley*'s final lyric, to pretend with great intensity that the artificial is better than the living, as Yeats can seem to do, while at the same time complaining passionately that it isn't, as Yeats can also seem to do, is to lack—what Yeats would scorn to have—"sobriety." There is, however, something to be said for sobriety. One can, in some moods, find seas that are mackerel-crowded, dolphin-torn, and gong-tormented a little much. Despite his genius, Yeats remained, as Eliot remarked, "perhaps a little too much the weather-worn Triton among the streams." One cannot conceive of the poet who wrote **"Medallion"** yearning to be an artificial bird.

Putting **"Medallion"** by Yeats's Byzantium poems and at the same time by any of the sonnets Shakespeare mocked in "My mistress' eyes"—sonnets praising, not hair like braids spun from metal or amber, but lips of coral, breasts like snow or ivory—does therefore reveal something about it. We need only assume that the voice of **"Medallion"** is as aware of the nature of the tradition he is working in as Shakespeare was, and as Pound certainly was—and as critic after critic

reading **"Medallion"** has suddenly become without fully realizing it. When we do, **"Medallion"** becomes at once a more significant attempt to explore the continuing possibilities of an English poetic tradition than **"Envoi,"** and as significant an attempt as "Sailing to Byzantium." And what is most important, of course, is that it becomes so at exactly the points most often criticized as effete failures, those points that unfold a world of carefully defined aesthetic surfaces insistently what they are and nothing more: a world where "beneath half-watt rays, / The eyes turn topaz," or a girl's head "emerges" from a "gold-yellow frock / As Anadyomene in the opening / Pages of Reinach." In its insistence upon what art worlds are and aren't, this world differs markedly from the verbally intoxicating, reality-defying one of roses "in magic amber laid" of **"Envoi,"** whose merit, after all, is that it is not a modern poem at all but a beautifully crafted poetic echo.

The resulting emotions, being new and significant, are, as Kenner noted almost forty years ago, complexly fused and not readily definable. ("Beauty? Irony? Geometrical and optical fact?" Kenner asked of **"Medallion"** in 1950.) One might add that they are also, as in event proved, not readily apprehensible—either in **"Medallion"** or in the second section as a whole, where they occur in a variety of ways. But it is their presence that makes *Mauberley*'s entire second half an even more interesting accomplishment than its first, whose achievements are more readily responded to—though they are finally of the same order.

All of which makes the entire poem just what Pound suggested that it was—its author's "farewell" to London and to an indigenous and beloved English poetic tradition that had come down to him through the nineties. This tradition, he believed, had from the start sought to escape from life's mutabilities, and had now before it in a new age—so far as he could see—only the delicately poised, brilliantly diagnostic, and finally ineffectual dead ends his poem defined.

One may note, however, in a final concession to those who condemn Mauberley for lacking what they see as sexual drive and all that Pound thought could grow from passion, that they are in their way right. There are indeed definite limitations to the approach taken in *Mauberley:* those Pound felt limited Laforgue's acceptance. "The red-blood," Pound noted, "has turned away [from Laforgue]. . . . Delicate irony, the citadel of the intelligent, has," he pointed out, "a curious effect on these people." "They wish always to be exhorted, at all times . . . to do those things which almost anyone will and does do whenever suitable opportunity is presented." Despite which, the brilliance of at least some of the poems in *Mauberley*'s first section, the precision and the carefully distanced pathos of its second, and even—as Berryman has pointed out—the severe, clear, metallic beauty of **"Medallion,"** have impressed critic after critic who has read the poem, yearning all the time, as the new century was, as in fact Ezra Pound himself was, for something more red-blooded, something less delicately ironic.

Cary Wolfe (essay date March 1991)

SOURCE: "Ezra Pound and the Politics of Patronage," in *American Literature,* Vol. 63, No. 1, March, 1991, pp. 26-42.

[*In the following essay, Wolfe examines contradictory aspects of Pound's democratic and elitist sentiments, particularly concerning the relationship between art and economics. Wolfe contends that "Pound's literary ideology has at least as much in common with Ralph Waldo Emerson's individualism as it does with Benito Mussolini's fascism."*]

Few writers, modern or otherwise, have inspired more criticism, and more of it theoretically polarized and mutually hostile, than Ezra Pound. The critic who would engage Pound's work finds himself or herself framed from the outset by a kind of critical Cold War, one which forces him into something resembling the role of Marc Antony at the funeral in *Julius Caesar.* Pound critics come time and again *either* to bury *or* to praise this strange and disturbing individual, who is seen by turns either as a fascist and anti-Semite in his very composition and genesis or as a literary genius whose "true" self (the self that produced the stalwart poetry of high modernism) can somehow be separated from the pathological embarrassment who penned and delivered the maniacal Rome Radio speeches.

If I've just glanced synoptically at the theoretical oversimplification of this well-nigh proverbial condition of Pound studies, then let me be a bit clearer about its critically disabling consequences. A politically engaged criticism of Pound would by definition need to move beyond this kind of displacement of broad economic, social, and ideological problems onto Pound the unique (so it goes) and therefore romanticized subject of admiration or revulsion. It is here, at this juncture and against this pressing critical necessity, that the either-orist imperative of Pound studies exerts its institutionally powerful and politically disabling force. If we want to come to terms with the ideological character of Pound's cultural project, we need to explore what is precisely ideological about it: namely, its internally contradictory, fractured, and self-conflicted nature, its capacity to attract subjects even as it repels others. But it is exactly this sort of contradiction—itself the very mark of ideological formations—that the current climate of Pound studies forestalls in advance.

In practical terms, the contradiction that the political critic of Pound needs to engage is that Pound's palpable attractions—his early defense of individual difference in the face of economic Taylorization and imperialism, his recognition that the aesthetic is at once fully social and even economic—are inextricably wedded to his reprehensible obsessions. And we need to be able to do all of this, moreover, without making the one a mere epiphenomenon of the other. Only by doing so can we provide an adequate picture of Pound's literary ideology in its power and complexity, instead of a facile caricature of it. And only by doing so can we dispel the politically naive impression that once we have unmasked Pound's ideological failures, we have once again made the world safe for literary democracy.

For my purposes, we need to recognize that Pound's literary ideology has at least as much in common with Ralph Waldo Emerson's individualism as it does with Benito Mussolini's fascism, and at the same time we need to realize that this isn't necessarily good news. Pound's liberationist Emersonian side cannot be separated from his authoritarian fascist side: that, it seems to me, is the powerful and disturbing political point that the polarization of Pound studies mitigates against.

In an exacting discussion of Pound's early aesthetic, Michael Levenson has recently argued that something like an abrupt change took place in Pound's position between the autumn of 1913 and the early months of 1914. During this period, Pound discovered Allan Upward's philosophy of radical egoism, and that discovery, Levenson argues, transformed what had been Pound's liberal humanism into a virulently anti-democratic and elitist egoism. The artist, Pound now declares in his essay **"The New Sculpture"** of February 1914, "has dabbled in democracy and he is now done with that folly."

Levenson's argument is perfectly correct in pointing up this dimension of Pound's individualism, but it does not go far enough. In Pound's letters of the period, for instance, we find not a break but rather a vacillation between the two positions, and throughout his career he would alternate between pronouncements which were both radically elitist and radically democratic. **"Patria Mia,"** for instance (written in 1910-1911), staged its social critique on behalf of the individual "of whatever age or sex or condition," and in **"Murder By Capital"**—written in the same year as *Jefferson and/or Mussolini*—Pound declared, as if in reaction to his Blastian pronouncements: "If there was a time (and I admit that there was) when I thought this problem [of art's commodification] could be solved without regard to the common man, humanity in general, the man in the street, the average citizen, etc., I retract, I sing palinode, I apologise."

Pound's individualism, like Emerson's, never really abandoned either of its extremes, and as with Emerson's we can trace in it nothing like a clean linear development from one pole to the other. We find not a break, then (as even this brief survey suggests), but rather the uneasy and sometimes violent coexistence of two latent possibilities, two different—and finally irreconcilable—political vectors which the ideology of individualism might follow. In the career of Pound, nowhere are these conflicting and inseparable tendencies clearer than in his early writings on patronage. In these proposals—for they were proposals, motivated not a little by impinging economic desperation—we are able to glimpse the antinomies of Pound's literary ideology, contradictions which would in time enable, if not exactly produce, the disastrous political consequences of Pound's later and infamous career.

In a letter written to Margaret Anderson in 1917, Pound made clear his idea of a proper relation between the artist and his economic context: "My whole position," he wrote, "and the whole backing up of my statement that the artist is 'almost' independent goes with doing the thing as nearly as possible without 'money.'" Throughout the period 1910-1917 Pound had mounted in his critical prose a wide-ranging critique of what intellectual and literary work had become under capitalist modernization. In **"Provincialism: The Enemy"** (1917), for instance, he complained, as Emerson had in many places, that the university was chiefly in the business of "habituating men to consider themselves as bits of mechanism for one use or another." This supposed last bastion of the life of the mind had become, in Pound's estimation, "one with the idea that the man is the slave of the State, the 'unit', the piece of the machine." And things were no better for the writer who sought to make it outside the walls of academe. In **"Patria Mia,"** Pound shrewdly observed that the extreme division of labor of the assembly line had found its way into the large-circulation magazines upon which aspiring writers in America were largely dependent for their sustenance. What Pound identified at the very outset of his career was nothing less than the Taylorization of *literary* production: "As the factory owner wants one man to make screws and one man to make wheels and each man in his employ to do some one mechanical thing that he can do almost without the expenditure of thought, so the magazine producer wants one man to provide one element, let us say one sort of story and another articles on Italian cities and above all, nothing personal."

So it is not so surprising, given his diagnosis of the conditions of literary production which dominated both sides of the Atlantic, that the ideal relation Pound envisions in his letter to Anderson is in essence *no* relation. A supportive economy for the artist was not in the cards, he thought, because his experience told him that the story of this unhappy marriage was mainly one of slavish repetition of formulae being rewarded by a commodity system which found experi-

ment and invention too risky for investment. Doing the thing as nearly as possible without "money" meant taking oneself foremost as an artist, not as a producer of commodities. You cannot, Pound says here in so many words, be a good artist and a good capitalist subject at the same time. The artist can only be half a self so long as "The lute sounds like a cash register, and a cadence is weighed down with a 'job.'" But Pound well knew that if the artist was "almost" independent, a whole nightmare of poverty, repetition, and economic coercion (necessity) was contained in that "almost."

But this didn't mean, at this early juncture in his career, changing the basic structure of the economic system so that this sort of schizophrenia might no longer plague those who want to be artists. Instead, it seemed to indicate that the economic realm *itself* was unredeemable, a burden, at best, to be tolerated: not a job but a "job," and not money but "money." Not work, in other words, but the abstract labor it had become in a system ruled by the commodity.

Artists have to eat, however, and the truth Pound knew about capitalist economy was not, for all its truth, edible. In 1918, Pound would discover Social Credit economics, which would "include creative art and writing in an economic scheme" by issuing a national dividend to all citizens except the wealthy—and to those cultural producers, of course, whose work was not "as vendible as bath-tubs." But well before the turn to Social Credit, Pound had his own ideas about how artists and writers were going to survive in an economy that held out little promise for experiment and invention. At the very outset of his career, Pound provided a glimpse not only of the modernist mover and shaker he would become but also of the limitations of his ideological inheritance when pushed to address problems which were economic in origin.

In surprising detail and with the kind of passion that creeping poverty inspires, Pound in **"Patria Mia"** proposed a system of patronage as the only means by which the artist might be free enough from the law of the commodity long enough to achieve something which might outlast its economic context. Looking back over history and its periods of artistic energy and decline, he concluded that the lesson of that history was quite clear: "Art was lifted into Alexandria by subsidy," he declared, "and by no other means will it be established in the United States." The "free" market of literary enterprise had been given a fair shake, and it had summarily put the genteels and the *Atlantic* in the executive suite of American culture. (It had also returned Pound's work, from *Harper's* and other like-minded magazines, stamped "rejected.") So what now?

"Patria Mia" and **"The Renaissance"** (1914) both attempted to answer that question. Aware of the difficulty of his position—"I write barefacedly," he admitted, "call me an opportunist"—Pound nevertheless felt that somebody had to address the would be patron, and in **"Patria Mia"** he put his considerable rhetorical skills to the task. He reasoned that the current millionaire in early twentieth-century America was not that different, in economic power, from the feudal lord—and "no more a permanent evil" either. Both are on the earth for a short period, amass great wealth and power, and then shuffle off this mortal coil more or less in infamy. "Nevertheless," Pound reckoned, "there seems to be no reason why he should not confer upon society, during his reign, such benefits as he is able." "The centralisation of power in his hands," he continued, "makes it very easy for him to display a virtue if he have one." And just how might that virtue be displayed? How might that extraordinary concentration of economic potency be distributed so as to leave a mark which might testify to the virtue of the millionaire long after he is gone?

Pound shrewdly reasoned—foreshadowing here his later talents of negotiation and general avant-garde salesmanship—that the gifts of the patron might be thought of as really a sort of investment, but in a different kind of economy.
—Cary Wolfe

Pound shrewdly reasoned—foreshadowing here his later talents of negotiation and general avant-garde salesmanship—that the gifts of the patron might be thought of as really a sort of investment, but in a different kind of economy. The patron might be a big stick on Wall Street in 1910, but what about his place on the great balance sheet of the ages? The Medici, Pound reminds us, "retain honour among us not for their very able corruption of the city of Florence, but because they housed Ficino and various artists and in doing so even reaped certain credit due their forerunners, the Orsini." Our advance man of modernism says to the twentieth-century millionaire, in so many words, that you'll never make your mark until you can walk with the Medici, and the only way to do *that* is to find a way to make your capital continue to earn interest across the centuries, where *real* success is measured. And just for good measure he underscores the point with his punning play on the "credit" which has accrued to the name Medici—a kind of friendly takeover of the house of Orsini's posterity made possible by the Medici's zeal in artistic investment.

Having begun, first, by flattering the modern millionaire (by calling him a lord), and having then moved subtly to force him to question his own economic potency in the world-class league of the Medici, Pound then follows up with the rhetorical roundhouse of the *carpe diem* theme: "It is his function as it is the function of any aristocrat to die and to leave

gifts. Die he must, and he may as well leave gifts, lest people spit upon his tomb and remember him solely for his iniquities." And then the final parry from this sometime fencer. There is still hope, Pound tells him, you may yet endure by doing the right thing—the only thing—which can save your otherwise cursed name: "Also his order must pass as all things pass from this earth, save masterwork in thought and in art. It is well, therefore"—the tone pontifical now—"that he leave behind him some record for consideration."

At this point, the would-be patron—if he has a virtuous bone in his body or the least self-doubt about his posterity—is ready for the details. Sold, he now has to face the bill of goods. First, the patron must not think that all he need do now is buy some famous art and wait for the accolades. "An old thing has a fixed sort of value," Pound admonishes; "One acquires property in acquiring it." It is not retention you must be concerned with, Pound tells our millionaire, but invention. If you support the established artist whose work is behind him, you may "bolster up your own self-respect," but "you do nothing to assist awakenings or liberations." What is wanted is not hero-worship or a fetish for masterpieces but an age, a "Risorgimento," which will, as the young Pound put it, "make the Italian Renaissance look like a tempest in a teapot."

Doubling back now to reassure the patron, who's beginning to wonder what he's gotten himself into, Pound brings his business sense to bear: "It is most economical to do this when they are in the energetic state, to wit, at the beginning of their course, in the years when they will work for least money. Any artist who is worth powder to blow him to Sheol wants, at the start, liberty to do his work and little beyond this." The patron, in other words, can get the most bang for his buck by giving a little money to a lot of struggling young artists—by enabling, as it were, the most invention per pound.

As **"Patria Mia"** unfolds, Pound will articulate his plans in greater detail, suggesting, for instance, that we should have a decent college of the arts in New York or San Francisco where the young artist might be housed and fed during "the impossible years." And this is reasonable enough; we can subsidize so-called "research," he reminds us, so why not what the researchers study? But these details can be taken up later—and indeed they are, here, in letters, and in **"The Renaissance."** For now, Pound's bottom line—and almost the last line of this long essay—is that "there should be a class of artist-workers free from necessity." Pound had done his rhetorical job. Would the millionaire now do his?

In 1915 Pound wrote to John Quinn, a New York lawyer whose support (mostly for other artists) he cultivated:

   My whole drive is that if a patron buys from an artist who needs money (needs money to buy tools, time and food), the patron then makes himself equal to the artist: he is building art into the world; he creates.

If he buys even of living artists who are already famous or already making £12,000 per year, he ceases to create. He sinks back to the rank of a consumer.

A great age of painting, a renaissance in the arts, comes when there are a few patrons who back their own flair and who buy from unrecognized men. In every artist's life there is, if he be poor, and they mostly are, a period when £10 is a fortune and when £100 or £200 a year without worry (without spending their time running to dealers, or editors) means a peace of mind that will let them work and not undermine them physically.

Among the many significant issues raised in this passage, one of the most striking has to be Pound's equation of the patron and the artist. Pound could have perhaps put this line to good use in his sales pitch in **"Patria Mia,"** where he had admonished the patron not to think of his involvement as a matter of acquiring property for the sake of personal enrichment, but rather to look at it from the vantage of production and circulation. If money is purely instrumental (as it is here for Pound), then the real trick for the patron is to make money productive, to transform it from a thing frozen in the "fixed value" of the masterpiece hanging on the wall into a constructive agency at work in the world. By helping the struggling artist buy time, food, and tools, the patron creates not art, but what makes art possible. He creates, in other words, the *conditions of invention* which capitalist economy could not provide.

In fact, this hope was nothing new in American literary ideology. As Emerson put it, in almost identical terms, the men of capital "must drive their craft poetically." Their economy must be "inventive, alive" to be distinguished from "parsimony, which is a poor, dead, base thing." For Emerson, making capital poetic meant making it fluid, a circulating power channelled by the active soul toward the cultivation of men, not of more capital. Pound's distinction in the letter to Quinn between the productive and acquisitive patron might well be drawn in Emerson's terms, which are the same terms of **"Patria Mia,"** where Pound had set the pioneering entrepreneur—"a man of dreams, in a time when dreams paid"—against the modern businessman whose fetish is "the nickel-plated cash register": "The first man," Pound wrote in an Emersonian moment, "deals with men, the latter deals with paper."

And just what might this "dealing" look like? Pound pro-

vides a clue in **"Canto 8,"** where his model patron, Sigismundo Malatesta, writes of the *Maestro di pentore:*

> And in order that he may enter my service
> And also because you write me that he needs cash,
> I want to arrange with him to give him so much
>   per year
> And to assure that he will get the sum agreed on.
> You may say that I will deposit security
> For him wherever he likes.
> And let me have a clear answer
> For I mean to give him good treatment
> So that he may come to live the rest
> Of his life in my lands—
> Unless you put him off it—
> And for this I mean to make due provision,
> So that he can work as he likes,
> Or waste his time as he likes. . . .

The master painter, it seems, will have it considerably better than Pound's modern artist under patronage. But Malatesta is really a model, not an out-of-reach anachronism. Pound made this much clear in a less public moment, when he wrote to Harriet Monroe, "A decent system would give [the writer] time to loaf in a library. Which while perhaps less important than loafing in pubs, is still a part of the complete man's loafing." When we cast about for the sort of world implied in these whimsical lines, it is perhaps not so surprising that the utopian world of art which Pound sketched in his early essay **"The Serious Artist"** seems to fit the bill perfectly. In that world, which art both envisions and promotes, "you can admire, you can sit in the shade . . . you can do as you jolly well please."

The pall of Pound's later politics makes it easy to miss the echo here of the almost identical world-after-capital which Marx and Engels imagined in *The German Ideology,* that new world which "makes it possible for me to do one thing today and another tomorrow, to hunt in the morning, fish in the afternoon, rear cattle in the evening, criticise after dinner, just as I have mind, without ever becoming hunter, fisherman, shepherd or critic." Of course, Pound was no Marxist, but in his early career he wasn't sure *what* he was—he had been radicalized, we might say, but not yet, in any coherent sense, politicized. But through the window of the early, "romantic" Marx, we can sharpen our sense of Pound's challenge to the deadening effects of modern capitalist production. Pound too had seen too many "crippled" and "one-sided" people (as Marx called them) in a society which treated them as economic agents only. Like Marx's world after capital, Pound's world of art would promote instead what Marx called "the total life of the individual," and Pound's proposals for patronage register the force of Marx's diagnosis of the fundamental structure of the commodity:

that where abstract exchange value is the rule, repetition is its cultural application.

Emerson, Marx's contemporary, had had a similar idea—with similar critical point—when he observed in his punning way, "'Tis very costly, this thinking for the market in books or lectures"—costly, that is, within exactly the same economy Pound had imagined in his letter to Margaret Anderson. Musing in his journals on the ideal conditions of literary production, Emerson envisioned, with a little guilt and in terms even more radical than Pound's just the right situation in which the unanalyzable, undisciplined self—what "Self-Reliance" called *Whim*—might be nurtured to creation: "If I judge from my own experience I should unsay all my fine things, I fear, concerning the manual labor of literary men. They ought to be released from every species of public or private responsibility. To them the grasshopper is a burden. I guard my moods as anxiously as a miser his money. For company, business, my own household-chores untune and disqualify me for writing." In his more poetic moods, Emerson had to admit that the relation between the writer and economies of all kinds save the whimsical was mostly antagonistic, that the whole man who tills at day and writes at night might not be, after all, the poetic man. And finally—to join the metaphors in these two passages from his journals—he had to admit that it is "costly" to fritter away the capital of "moods" on those quotidian things not worthy of its expenditure. (Apparently, a little parsimony is fine if one is close in the right kind of economy.) This poetic capital of the innermost self Emerson, like a miser, loves not for what it might buy or acquire but rather for its own sake. It is a kind of latent power kept shiny by his refusal to circulate it in any economy other than a lyric one.

Elsewhere in his journals, Emerson provides a passage which may therefore be seen to be pregnant with anticipation of Pound's modernist distinction between what he called, in an early review, the unique "lump gold" of individual expression and the repetitive, featureless "coin" or "paper money" of common knowledge and accepted convention. As Emerson put it: "We all lean on England, scarce a verse, a page, a newspaper but is writ in imitation of English forms . . . & sometimes the life seems dying out of all literature & this enormous paper currency of Words is accepted instead." Instead of dealing in the "paper currency of words," Emerson, like Pound, would have the American literary self pay in that nugget or lump gold which defines itself against all earthly economies. Only then could the work of art realize itself fully, not as a bearer of economic value but as what Emerson's metaphor tells us it is and what Pound thought it should be: a kind of "permanent property . . . given to the race at large."

The radical individualism of Pound and his ideological father Emerson may have led them both to reach many of the same conclusions about those institutions and practices which seemed an all-out assault on the first principle of their American politics, but what, exactly, did both envision as a more beneficent social and economic structure which might take that individual into just account? In his writings on patronage, Pound suggests something of what that world might look like, the kind of social and economic organization which might allow the self to get on with the business of being lyric.

For Pound's own part, nowhere is that picture clearer than in the essay **"The State,"** written in 1927, which shows the aesthetic economy of the early essays very much alive and well in his later career. This essay makes the same sort of distinction between "transient" and "permanent" goods which Pound, in so many words, had been making all along. In the first category, **"The State"** places, more than a little eclectically, "fresh vegetables," "fake art," and "pseudo-books." Though he doesn't really say so, what holds this rather fanciful sampling together is not only the fact that these things for immediate consumption do not survive the momentary needs they fulfill, but mainly that they are produced *for the purpose* of being consumed.

"Permanent goods," however, are not economically determined by-products of the rule of the commodity. "Scientific discoveries," "works of art," and "classics" are produced with an eye toward not transient economic value but permanent aesthetic value and intellectual law. What makes Pound's economy in **"The State"** of signal interest, however, is his criterion for inclusion in this latter category. These sorts of things are, as he puts it, "never consumed; or they are, in jargon, 'consumed' but not destroyed by consumption." What this means, of course, is that the permanent goods of art are not really consumed at all; their value is not dissipated by use. Like gold, they still remain gold no matter what material form they take or the uses to which they are put.

But **"The State"** provides the opportunity to explore as well the sort of social configuration which this overarching economy might determine. In a passage rich in implication, Pound writes: "The capitalist imperialist state must be judged not only in comparison with unrealised utopias, but with past forms of the state; if it will not bear comparison with the feudal order; with the small city states both republican and despotic; either as to its 'social justice' or its permanent products, art, science, literature, the onus of proof goes against it."

It is clear, not only in this passage but in the essay as a whole, that the efficacy of the state is now to be judged largely by the extent to which it makes possible and encourages the permanent products of Pound's economic hierarchy. The state is now seen, in Pound's words, as a "convenience," itself a kind of transient commodity, and when it can no longer provide the conditions of invention for the enduring goods of culture, then it too is used up and can be discarded.

And when we ask, "Who shall judge the convenience of the State?," Pound responds: "The party that follows [the artist] wins; and the speed with which they set about it, is the measure of their practical capacity and intelligence." The aesthetic economy which derives from Pound's earliest work now determines the efficacy of political structures, and the artist—and only the artist—can measure them against the gold standard of art and "permanent property" to determine their value. **"The State,"** then, fleshes out the disturbing contradictions embedded in Pound's early ideas about patronage and the sort of social organization they imply. In the passage which we just examined, Pound's examples (the feudal order, the pre-capitalist city-state) seem offhand, but in fact they are quite symptomatic of his fatal tendency, early and late, to dissociate ethical, economic, and political concerns, the better to assimilate all of these to an essentially ethical—and often strictly aesthetic—framework.

Of course, Pound didn't propose in his writings on patronage a return to a feudal economic order, but that's precisely the point. The dissociation of the ethical, political, and economic dimensions that allowed Pound early in his career to hold up the energetic entrepreneur as a model of democratic self-reliance—while at the same time attacking the conditions and effects of capitalism—is the same kind that could lead him to propose a system of patronage while at the same time arguing, as he did in **"Patria Mia,"** that "There need be little actual change in the existing machinery," that what was needed was "simply a more conscious and more far-calculating application of forces already present." For Pound, it is not a question of the structure of economic relations which entrepreneurship, for example, reproduces and perpetuates. Rather, it is a matter of making an essentially ethical distinction between "good" entrepreneurs and bad, "good" uses of the existing economic structure and those which are more short-sighted.

This same kind of dissociation is at work in Pound's early proposal for patronage, and now, reading by the light of **"The State,"** we are in a better position to judge the politics of that proposal. It is not only that Pound's patronage model depends upon the perpetuation of an aristocracy of the capitalist rich who are as remote from the exploited mass as the feudal lord. Pound's plan is also hopelessly naive; for all its seeming economic detail, it is finally a *purely ethical* matter. It is all *noblesse oblige,* it stands or falls by the good graces of the patron, and it has very little to do with basic structural changes in an economic mode of production whose effects Pound quite sincerely abhorred—effects not only on artists but also, as he wrote in the *Cantos,* on "folk of / ANY

CONDITION." Pound's early social vision may be strong, as negative critique, for individual difference. But what Pound's writings on patronage reveal is that his early politics, when pushed to pragmatic, positive application, are dangerously regressive and undisturbed about the binding logic of political structures and the way in which cultural practices reproduce those structures.

If, as Jean-Paul Sartre (a very different modernist) put it in *Search for a Method,* praxis must always be viewed in terms of the future social organization it implies and suggests, then Pound's patronage model appears to be a kind of cultural practice in reverse. But of course this sort of practice, at least in Sartre's terms, is no practice at all; it is a repetition of the past, not a transformation of it. How true this is of Pound's later career, of his growing attraction to ancient China and to an essentially Populist vision of a pre-capitalist past free of plutocratic machination and Taylorized production. And Pound's model of patronage is an early sign as well of his increasing tendency (again like the Populists) to address economic problems in terms of not production but distribution. For the artist, patronage may indeed be a kind of "solution," through distribution, to problems created by the mode of production which Pound never tired of attacking. But it is a solution, of course, only for those artists who receive the patron's good will and therefore his cash.

Finally, the ultimate irony and central contradiction of Pound's patronage model is that it makes the artist dependent on that very economic structure Pound deplored, only now it is not the artist but those democratic others who must pay the price commanded by the permanent property of art. For the economic fact is that the capital of the patron depends upon that very economic system, and upon the exploitation of those who create its wealth—and so, therefore, does the artist and the art which was supposed to be that system's antithesis. If no abstract labor, then no exchange value; if no exchange value, then no surplus value; if no surplus value, then no capital; if no capital, then no patron; and if no patron, then no "free" artist, no "permanent" aesthetic property. Under patronage, the artist isn't really independent; rather, it is simply *another kind* of dependence—dependence, in this case, upon the continued existence of an aristocracy of capital.

If Pound had read much Emerson he would have found that his ideological ancestor himself had struggled to find the same kind of balance of economy and culture. What does England do with its surplus value, Emerson asked in *English Traits,* what is the "compensation" for the fragmenting and exploitive effects of this mode of production? "A part of the money earned returns to the brain to buy schools, libraries, bishops, astronomers, chemists and artists with," he wrote. "But the antidotes are frightfully inadequate and the evil requires a deeper cure, which time and a simpler social organization must supply." Unlike the later Emerson, whose early agrarian critique had long since lost (even for him) its critical force, Pound would spend a good part of his later career looking back to the times of Confucius and Jefferson for that simpler social organization which might dictate the culturally beneficial commerce of the good state. And he would find its modern avatar in Benito Mussolini who, like "T.J." (or so Pound thought), was set against "machinery or at any rate the idea of cooping up men and making 'em all into UNITS, unit production, denting in the individual man, reducing him to a mere amalgam."

But Emerson, at age fifty, recognized the difficulty of being both democratic and aesthetic, and he saw that the permanent property of art had a price that not the artist but democracy would have to pay if it indulged patronage. As he put it in a letter to Thomas Carlyle: "America is incomplete. Room for us all, since it has not ended, nor given sign of ending, in bard or hero. 'Tis a wild democracy, the riot of mediocrities, & none of your selfish Italies and Englands, where an age sublimates into a genius, and the whole population is made into paddies to feed his porcelain veins, by transfusion from their brick arteries."

Porcelain veins and brick arteries, the body aesthetic and the body economic, Emerson's two types of clay to Pound's two kinds of gold. Emerson never really found a way to put them together in the body politic. And neither, despite the fearful political price, did Pound.

Laszlo K. Géfin (essay date Spring 1992)

SOURCE: "So-Shu and Picasso: Semiotic/Semantic Aspects of the Poundian Ideogram," in *Papers on Language and Literature,* Vol. 28, No. 2, Spring, 1992, pp. 185-205.

[*In the following essay, Géfin examines the aesthetic and ethical concerns behind Pound's ideogrammic method, particularly the use of Chinese pictographs and literary allusion in* The Cantos.]

Ezra Pound's "ideogrammic method" has had an uneven history during the last fifty years, some critics accepting it as the structural mode of composition of *The Cantos,* some accepting it but disparaging its use, others arguing against it in favor of other textual procedures, and still others dismissing it altogether. In the most general terms, the method denotes Pound's nontransitional, or paratactical, juxtaposition of textual fragments of varying length and complexity, such as bits of what appear to be poetry, historical data, quotations from or allusions to other texts, or autobiographical detail—in his own words, "first heaping together the necessary components of thought." Although Pound claimed to

have discovered the method after editing in 1913-14 Ernest Fenollosa's essay, "The Chinese Written Character as a Medium for Poetry," he began to call his poetic method "ideogrammic" only in the 1930s, offering his most complete definition in *Guide to Kulchur:*

> At last a reviewer in a popular paper . . . has had the decency to admit that I occasionally cause the reader "suddenly to see" or that I snap out a remark . . . "that reveals the whole subject from a new angle".
>
> That being the point of the writing. That being the reason for presenting first one facet and then another—I mean to say the purpose of the writing is to reveal the subject. The ideogrammic method consists of presenting one facet and then another until at some point one gets off the dead and desensitized surface of the reader's mind, onto a part that will register.
>
> The "new" angle being new to the reader who cannot always be the same reader. The newness of the angle being relative and the writer's aim, at least this writer's aim being revelation, a just revelation irrespective of newness or oldness.

The passage may appear straightforward, but it invites closer scrutiny and clarification. For one, Pound admits to having a "subject" with "facets," but more importantly, that this subject precedes or preexists its presentation. Then the presentation is said to consist of Pound's serially adducing various "facets" of the subject in no apparent order but from different angles, directed toward "the reader." The latter is not some implied or ideal reader, but represents a variety of "real" readers ("who cannot always be the same reader") conceived as having minds with "surfaces" that have "dead" or "desensitized areas"—presumably areas of ignorance, repressed or forgotten knowledge, "false" notions about a "subject." At the moment when correct facet coincides with non-desensitized area, a "just revelation" supposedly occurs. Like the subject, the "writer's aim" to bring about such a revelation also appears to exist before the process of presentation.

It is this textual practice that Pound came to call ideogrammic. It complicates matters, however, that Pound recommended and used the "ideogrammic method" not only as a mode of composition applicable to poetry alone, but as a critical and pedagogic device. He even went as far as to say that the method is the "method science," and that he had "approached" the method as early as 1913 in **"The Serious Artist."** In that essay he juxtaposed some lines by Cavalcanti, Dante, Villon, Yeats, and from the Anglo-Saxon poem "The Wanderer," in order to demonstrate by example "that passionate simplicity which is beyond the precisions of the intellect." In another essay, entitled **"The Teacher's Mission,"** Pound proposes the method be used in education; in answer to the question, What ought to be done [to improve the quality of teaching], he offers: "Dispassionate examination of the ideogrammic method (the examination and juxtaposition of particular specimens—e.g. particular works, passages of literature) as an implement for acquisition and transmission of knowledge." These "critical ideograms"—or his "musical ideograms" in the concerts he organized at Rappalo (putting together works by Janequin, Corelli, Vivaldi, Debussy, Bartók, and others)—differ from the poetic use of the method because they quite obviously were not created to form lasting or determinate wholes, "thoughts," of which they are the "necessary components." They can be assembled and disassembled at will; the components remain fluid, and not solidified into poetry, which is Pound's main intent in **The Cantos:** "that certain images be formed in the mind / to remain there" (**"Canto 74"**).

My main interest in this paper is twofold. First, I wish to examine Pound's claim for what I call his "narrative of understanding:" that the gradual adducement of textual particles in a finite series or group can lead to a clear and exact apprehension of the right relationship between them, and then proceed to the formulation of a correct idea, concept, or general statement regarding a specific subject, or "thought," of which they were the "necessary components." Second, I would like to establish whether the ideogrammic method, applied expressly to literary composition, can qualify as poetry. I will proceed by looking at a group of text fragments from **The Cantos** comprising an "ideogram" in the light of certain seminal theories of language and signs, particularly those of Benveniste, Peirce, and Jakobson; Compagnon's investigation of citations; and recent text theory. While Pound had no formal interest in linguistics and semiotics, he was intensely involved with the practical aspects of language use, especially in literature. "Language was obviously created, and is, obviously, USED for communication," he wrote; it would appear that the ideogrammic method of writing is "obviously" intended for the communication of images and ideas to different readers, and privileged by Pound because he believed it to be a mode of communication superior to Western narrative discourse.

1

The semiotic aspect of Pound's ideogrammic project is quite sensible: provide a poetic sign system that communicates better than others. On one semiotic level at least, Pound's method is similar to the Chinese written sign, in that the latter combines heterogeneous signs to form a new sign. A small number of Chinese ideograms are actually hieroglyphic—stylized images of objects and events—so that in Peircean terms they may be called iconic. Pound's preference for the

Chinese sign over Western modes of representation derives from Fenollosa who disparaged the phonetic word because it "does not bear its metaphor on its face" in favor of the Chinese sign whose "etymology is constantly visible." True, Chinese readers would no more be aware of this "visible etymology" than would Western readers of the metaphoric roots of a great many words and phrases; but the point here is that Pound (along with Fenollosa) privileges iconic referentiality over abstract (in Peirce's word, symbolic) relations.

Pound makes it clear in his "narrative of understanding," however, that even if the subject precedes the act of presentation, his aim is not representation, i.e., some form of mimesis, but "revelation," the full and just revelation of the (supposedly concealed) subject. While the revelation takes place through the medium of language (it is Pound's "snap[ping] out a remark" that causes the reader "suddenly to see"), at the moment the "subject" is revealed, the medium presumably self-destructs, leaving nothing behind. It is not surprising, therefore, that Pound's narrative of understanding is couched in sculptural terms (facets, angles, surfaces) rather than those of language. Like the Chinese ideogram, a poetic practice of "presenting one facet and then another" of a subject would reconstruct (by reverse repetition) the process whereby concepts and ideas are created from particulars—particulars that are not arbitrary signs but still-fresh traces of their natural antecedents. The symbolic sign, though it is composed in the units of the non-referential western alphabet, would first transpose itself to the level of iconicity, and at the last stage of revelation merge with subject and mind, or more precisely, disappear at the moment when mind and subject are fused.

Pound's "narrative of understanding," then, appears to minimize and even negate the immanence of language affecting all aspects of poetic (and other) communication. The consequences of this (Platonic, hermetic, gnostic) naivete (if it can be characterized as such) would be far-reaching. The anti-language stance of the narrative may, however, lose its impact if Pound's actual practice of ideogrammic writing in **The Cantos** runs counter to the claims he makes. At any rate, it will be important to examine the particular textual components of a poetic ideogram not only semiotically (as signs in a system), but more decisively in terms of semantics (as words in actual use, in sentences as part of discourse). This is Benveniste's distinction of the "double signification" inherent in language: "La langue combine deux modes distincts de signifiance, que nous appelons le mode SEMIOTIQUE d'une part, le mode SEMANTIQUE de l'autre" 'language combines two distinct modes of signification, which we call the semiotic mode on the one hand, and the semantic mode on the other.' The *processing* of a sign/word according to these two modes moves on equally distinct levels; as Benveniste writes, "Le sémiotique (le signe) doit être RECONNU; le sémantique (le discours) doit être

COMPRIS" 'The semiotic (the sign) is to be recognized; the semantic (discourse) is to be understood.'

Benveniste refers only in passing to the poetic use of language, which he sees as restricting language's "double signification" to the semantic level, excluding the semiotic or lexical. But his general distinction of semiotic and semantic helps to see how ideogrammic poetic composition passes back and forth between *signification* of the semiotic level to *meaning* in discourse. Pound's theoretical suppositions about the language of literature appear to correspond roughly to Benveniste's. "Literature is language charged with meaning," Pound writes; on the other hand, when he attempts to give a definition of poetry, he borrows from Dante—"'A canzone is a composition of words set to music'"—adding, "I don't know any better point to start from" because Dante's statement [he notes]

> starts the reader or hearer from what he actually sees or hears, instead of distracting his mind from that actuality to something which can only be approximately deduced or conjectured FROM the actuality, and for which the *evidence* can be nothing save the particular and limited extent of that actuality. (Pound's emphases)

Pound appears to distinguish between a general (semiotic-lexical) significance and particular (semantic) meaning in the definition of literature/poetry, and to favor the semiotic formulation—foreshadowing Benveniste's added recognition and understanding as they apply to semiotics and discourse, respectively. This distinction is particularly important for interpreting poetic ideograms.

Ethics and aesthetics are inseparable: the beautiful is functional, the functional is accurate, and accuracy is the sign of good writing.
—*Lazlo K. Géfin*

Furthermore, consistent with his (elevated) view of the writer's role, Pound insists that the "justness" of ideogrammic presentation implies an ethical imperative, which subsumes the aesthetic. "Your language is in the care of your writers," he wrote, and "writers as such have a definite social function exactly proportioned to their ability AS WRITERS. This is their main use." Ethics and aesthetics are inseparable: the beautiful is functional, the functional is accurate, and accuracy is the sign of good writing. "Bad art," he wrote as early as 1913, "is inaccurate art. It is art that makes false reports," or as he later put it, "Good writers are those who keep the language efficient. That is to say, keep it accurate, keep it clear." Pound's insistence on the ideo-

grammic method, then, is commensurate with his "totalitarian" demand: writers are "good" because they can reveal subjects to readers in their totality, while the natural/textual traces that led to the revelation are capable of repeating the process for any number of new readers. In this movement from particulars to universals, from signification to meaning (and back again), poets, aware *a priori* of the subject *as a whole* before releasing a few select "facets" in writing, turn signs into words in order to reveal the specific thought in its totality and truth. Pound's ethics of writing is thus characteristically ambitious in that it promises to deliver interpretation from the bane of indeterminacy, since ideogrammic writing, in being faithful to nature's processes, cannot but be precise. What he maintained in general, that "a certain limpidity and precision are the ultimate qualities of style," ought all the more to be applicable to his own practice in particular. The entire narrative of understanding, after all, indicates Pound's frustration with contemporary reception of modern poetry, especially his *Cantos,* which he characterized as "an endeavour to communicate with a blockheaded epoch."

2

The Cantos provides nearly limitless examples to test Pound's practice against the theory. One passage, from the early part of **"Canto 2,"** includes a variety of components. It is preceded by the beginning lines of the canto, which is a disputation between Pound's persona and Robert Browning: "Hang it all, Robert Browning, / there can be but the one 'Sordello.' / But Sordello, and my Sordello?" It is a brief scene of what appears to be an "anxiety of influence" about how Pound is to launch his own epic project without trudging over the same ground already mapped out by his precursor. Pound, however, without any real anxiety cuts off the dispute by the introduction of a line from a medieval biography of Sordello in the original Provençal, "Lo Sordels si fo di Mantovana" 'Sordello was from Mantua,' as if to suggest that his own mode of dealing with the past will be more faithfully historical rather than fictive. The citation would thus prefigure the direction of Pound's own epic venture, at once "diagnostic" in its scrupulous historicity and "curative" in its evocation of enduring mysteries—proceeding along lines Browning had presumably failed or neglected to touch.

While a specific citation may thus be called "just," allusions are more diffuse, and resist immediate, uniform understanding. Allusions by their nature call into question the notion of accuracy, authority, and justness, as evident from the passage in **"Canto 2"** that follows the Sordello section:

> So-shu churned in the sea.
> Seal sports in the spray-whited circles of cliff-
>   wash,
> Sleek head, daughter of Lir,

                    eyes of Picasso
        Under black fur-hood, lithe daughter of Ocean;

These five lines I would consider a discursive unit, or ideogram. Following the semicolon after "Ocean," the next line, "And the wave runs in the beach-groove," is a deflection from the composite image of seal and "lithe daughter." Furthermore, this line also provides a transition to a passage concerned with Helen of Troy, and although the seascape is reintroduced in more detail a little later, that scene may itself be seen as an introduction to Pound's transliteration of Ovid's tale of Pentheus and Acoethes, which takes up the bulk of the canto.

How does the reader ("who cannot always be the same reader") attempt to make sense of the passage? This group of lines is indeed a "heaping together," as Pound had said, but in what manner are these lines "components of thought"? What thought? And who can this So-shu be? Looking up various guides and annotated indexes to **The Cantos** makes it clear that So-shu as verbal sign is neither clearly iconic nor indexical, for every entry offers a different interpretation. According to Terrell, So-shu is the name of the Han dynasty poet Ssu-ma Hsiang-ju, "a representative of the rhyme-prose school criticized by Li Po in an allegory from which the line quoted is derived via a translation by Fenollosa in the Fenollosa Notebooks (inedit)," Ssu-ma being criticized for "creating foam instead of waves." So-shu is also the Japanese equivalent of the Taoist philosopher Chuang Tzu, but Pound may also be confusing him with Li Po. In Cookson's *Guide* Pound "told his daughter" that So-shu is a figure from Chinese mythology; but Cookson adds, somewhat incongruously, that "this is possibly a Chinese myth of Pound's invention." Christine Froula quite categorically states that the name *is* of Pound's making. Like the author of the *Companion,* she, too, derives her gloss from unpublished material in the Pound archives: "The name [So-shu] Pound used in this image, which is his own invention, is 'Ka-hu' (Yale MSS). He probably preferred 'So-shu' because of its onomatopoeic sound rather than for the sake of any allusion."

Froula's conclusion, with her "probably" conveying doubt, seems to me to be evasive and inadequate. Since it is not necessary to pretend that I am reading **"Canto 2"** for the first time, it may be revealed at this point that the name So-shu comes up again some one hundred lines later ("And So-shu churned in the sea, So-shu also, / using the long moon for a churn-stick"). In Froula's view, "The So-shu image, an invented Orientalism, personifies the moon and the shaft of light it casts down to the ocean." This is hasty and unconvincing, not the least because in the cluster of lines under discussion "churned" in no way implies the presence of the moon as churn-stick. Nonetheless, what may be clear at this stage is that "So-shu" does resist semantic integration, i.e.,

understanding; it can only work as a verbal sign and must be recognized as such. Even with the above scholia, it may be unsafe to go beyond the statement "So-shu: unidentified Chinese-sounding name." But it is doubtful that we are dealing with an instance of chinoiserie here, some vaguely suggestive (of what?) onomatopoeia. If this were the case, one would have to infer that Pound never wanted the verbal sign "So-shu" to be anything but a lexeme, arresting its potential to be turned from sign into word in discourse and activated as meaningful—an unlikely proposition. In contrast to Froula, I would suggest that Pound would not want to stop here, nor want readers to dismiss the line as nothing more than a (tantalizing) sign without referent. Taking Pound's narrative of understanding seriously, we may conclude that the first "facet" he has presented of his "subject" has met with "desensitized areas" in the minds of most readers, including those of learned exegetes. The inconclusive recognition of So-shu, when seen as churning in the sea (especially since it is not certain at this point whether the verb "churned" is to be read as transitive or intransitive), may produce such reactions as absurd, nonsensical, or at best, "provocative." The reader perceives the line, not as a "thought," but only as its component, and goes on reading, exactly as Pound would wish.

The next line, a "natural image" of a seal moving vigorously in the sea, lets us re-read the line on So-shu in terms of the seal in the water, more than likely compelled by the parallel construction of "So-shu churned" and "Seal sports"; and we may attempt to make them cohere, this time semantically, taking the verb as intransitive and figurative ("So-shu churned," i.e., moved in the sea with great agitation), even noticing the difference in tense, that So-shu churn*ed,* while the seal "sports." We may conflate the two actions, in which the sporting of the seal resembles the churning movements of So-shu. So-shu, however, does not stand for "seal" in Chinese. . . . At any rate, this So-shu performed something in the sea in the past that the seal is performing at the present time, a churning motion. Human and animal activities may thus seem to partake of a common ground, a relationship similarly integrated with larger and wider natural processes. Moreover, the past tense of "So-shu churned" when contrasted with the present tense of "Seal sports" may suggest the unique historicality of human action, while seals sport outside time, or in all times: So-shu's time (in an unknown past time, or, if we provisionally accept the *Companion* as a guide, in the 2nd century B.C.), Pound's time (in 1922 when he was writing the canto), and our own.

However, if "churned" is a transitive verb, denoting that something solid is being produced from a liquid, the apparent resemblance turns into difference. And the difference is ironic: the verb "sports" suggests a pleasurable action, frolicking and playing in the water, something that is natural to the animal, in the light of which So-shu's churning may be seen as mad or futile, or, at least, "unnatural." Furthermore, juxtaposed to the sporting seal, the image of a certain So-shu actually involved in churning the water may give way to a purely figurative rendering, in which case churning in the sea ("futility") is just another (more exotic?) way of saying "beating a dead horse." More importantly, depending on whether "churned" is read as transitive or intransitive verb, two diametrically opposed meanings may be generated of the sentence "So-shu churned in the sea"; and the image of the sporting seal may be coerced to sustain either interpretation with equal force. (And even if the more complete reference to So-shu and the moon as churn-stick are brought forward to dispel the indeterminacy and intransitive reading, it may not succeed completely, for as soon as we "stop thinking" of So-shu with a churn-stick, the verb "churned" reverts back to being undecidable.) The line "Seal sports" may be a new "facet" of the subject, but instead of clarifying what had been stated in the previous line, it has made So-shu and his(?) action indeterminate. It would seem "the reader's mind," though not as "desensitized" as before, is still far from being able to grasp the meaning as distinct from significance.

Is the obstacle of indeterminacy (transitive/intransitive, literal/figurative) insurmountable? Are we faced with a "rhetorical" situation in discourse when, according to de Man, "it is impossible to decide by grammatical or other linguistic devices which of the two meanings (that can be entirely incompatible) prevails"? In de Man's view, the figural, or what to him denotes the same entity, the rhetorical potentiality of language may be equated with literature itself. De Man points to Monroe Beardsley's assertion that "literary language is characterized by being 'distinctly above the norm in ratio of implicit [or, de Man would say, rhetorical] to explicit meaning.'" While the nature of poetic discourse will be discussed below, it may be said at this point that figurality is a potential of language that already exists explicitly on the grammatical level; its presence neither proves nor disproves whether the text in question is literature. While aware of the differences inherent in semiotics and semantics, de Man fails to consider the Benvenistian distinction of "double significance," or what Sándor came to call "diaphoricity," the unstable ("purely differential") nature of the verbal sign when considered semantically. However, Sándor (rightly) goes one crucial step further. In his view, "meaning at the lexical level is diaphoric"; and "[a]t the sentence level . . . literal or figurative or both according to intention, and if the intention is unclear (on either side), meaning will be diaphoric even at the sentence level. The possibility that *language* can be given without clarity about how it is being used, and how it is to be used, renders it fundamentally diaphoric in nature." Indeterminacy, then, is specific to language, not to literary discourse alone. In other words, it is not only the reader's mind that contains "desensitized" areas; language, seen from the level of discourse, is similarly

"desensitized," i.e., resistant to meaning production. The reader's mind remains "desensitized" because a sign is always differential. Although "activation" (transposition of sign to word) may appear to delimit radical polysemy, as Sándor suggests, "it is impossible to know what is being activated without knowing the context in which it is meant to be done." Even syntagmatic contextuality is not sufficient to do away with diaphoricity. Assume the case of a reader who reads **"Canto 2"** for the first time, without fast-forwarding to the second reference to So-shu. The fact that So-shu's churning took place in the sea, coupled with the seal in the next line seen in a similar activity, may tip the balance, however slightly, toward taking "churned" as an intransitive verb, thereby assuming a resemblance between the two acts. But the sea as mutual environment ("context") may not be enough to generate a single meaning: there is no reason why the same verb ("churned") in the sentence "So-shu churned in the yard" may not be read intransitively, especially if reinforced by "Dog sports in clouds of dust" or some clause like it. Similarly, intention, whether clear or not, as deducible from language does not by itself guarantee unambiguous interpretation. On the one hand, Pound may himself assume that the particular "facet" he releases is precise in its referentiality because it corresponds exactly to his "intention," as the latter appears to him; in this case he would be blissfully unaware that words can (and will) disrupt intention. On the other hand, his insistence on the ideogrammic method, especially in his narrative of understanding, attests to his latent suspicion that *le mot juste* is a mirage, and the production of meaning a precarious process.

Both Benveniste and Sándor assert that when verbal signs are turned into words, the syntagmatically generated meaning of a word "depends on the other words in the sentence, and, ultimately, on the total idea of the sentence." So-shu churning and seal sporting may thus depend on additional units of the "total idea" of the ideogram in order to attain meaningfulness in themselves. Readerly interest is sustained, not because a safe and comfortable meaning derives from the juxtaposition of the two lines. Rather, readers experience the excitement/irritation of simultaneous resemblance and difference uniting them, the sole source of comfort being an awareness of the obtuse and desensitized nature of both language and human consciousness, the latter also in part constituted by language. In this awareness we may in fact have made the first tentative move toward a "sensitization" of both.

In the next line, "Sleek head, daughter of Lir," quickly reread together with the first two, the proliferation of sibilants ("So-shu churned," "Seal sports," "Sleek head") reinforces a sense of unity between the lines. "Sleek head" may thus at once be connected to "seal," although "daughter of Lir" is uncomfortably close to permit such convenient allocation. Does "sleek head" belong to the seal, to "daughter of Lir," or to both? Who is "daughter of Lir?" Who is "Lir"? The *Companion* entry asserts an "Old Celtic sea-god. Pound regards seals as being Lir's daughters [cf. chapter 'Branwen the Daughter of Llyr' in *Mabinogion,* where Branwen means 'White Cow']." The entry is of little help, for glossary becomes interpretation (an endemic weakness, incidentally, of the *Companion* as a whole) and substitutes a presumption to know for facts. Even if Pound did "regard" seals as daughters of Lir, could he, with all his insistence on precision and clarity, deliberately conflate and confuse a white cow with a black seal? It seems more "natural" to regard, simply, "daughter of Lir" as sea-nymph, and "sleek head" as something belonging both to the seal and to the nymph. This would, after all, be an instance of how Pound conceived of the poetic image, as a "superposition," i.e., "one image set on top of another"—a definition, incidentally, coming right after his acquisition of the Fenollosa manuscripts.

Thus, So-shu and his/her churning, even with the moon as churn-stick, appears to be neither a meaningless Orientalism nor a deprecatory allusion. Sporting seal and sea goddess are united both for having sleek heads and for being creations of a sea-god, "churning" the sea (like So-shu?) and producing solid beings. Whether So-shu is a Chinese myth of Pound's invention or not, the verbal sign is filled with at least some meaning because of the proximity of Lir, his daughter/seal, and the sea. Pound presents both oriental and western "facets" of mythology, as if to alert the reader by this juxtaposition/conflation that mythic consciousness is our universal heritage, even as he treats the seal itself as real, actual, and un/demythologized. The identity of So-shu as a nature deity or a metonym for the transforming energy of nature is augmented by the context of the name in its second occurrence. To the story of the kidnapped Bacchus's exacting his revenge by metamorphosing the pirates into fishes and other sea creatures (though not expressly into seals), Pound tags another myth of his own, of a sea nymph turned to coral as she was fleeing "a band of tritons." After the sea-nymph's "smooth brows" lie in "ivory stillness" under the water's surface, come the lines:

> And So-shu churned in the sea, So-shu also,
> using the long moon for a churn-stick . . .
> Lithe turning of water,
> sinews of Poseidon,

followed by a return of the seascape. It seems likely that just as So-shu received a semblance of identity by the proximity of Lir's daughter in the first ideogram, in the same way the presence of Poseidon's name performs something similar. Both the descriptive phrase "Lithe turning of water" and the kenning "sinews of Poseidon" signify "waves"; and even if the ". . ." after "churnstick" are inserted to suggest a cut to another scene, the waves may still be seen as the result of So-shu's churning, "also" involved in transformation

alongside other, western deities. Yet diaphoricity is not annulled, as some readers remember So-shu's attempt to ape divine potency as ludicrously pretentious.

3

Nonetheless, the "superposition" of seal and sea-nymph is an important new "fact." The Ovidian fusion-in-distinction would be neatly completed by "Under black fur-hood, lithe daughter of Ocean" ("Ocean" in Liddell and Scott is *Okeanos,* god of small waters, i.e., another Lir), were it not for the insertion of "Eyes of Picasso." Why Picasso? How "just" is the sudden intrusion of this proper name, and his "eyes"? The *Companion* relates that "the reference to Picasso's seal's eyes evokes the artist's faculty for changing the shape of the things he sees," and adds a non sequitur: "In ancient mythology the seal is the animal most closely linked with Proteus, who among other things used to assume the shape of a seal." Among other things, indeed. As for the other guides, Cookson does not even bother with an entry for "Picasso," and in Brooker we learn merely that Picasso was "the painter and famous instigator of Cubism. Pound at one time contemplated a book on Wyndham Lewis, Brancusi, Picasso and Picabia." Thus "illuminated," and as desensitized as ever, we turn to Froula, who writes: "Pablo Picasso (1881-1973), whose eyes Pound thought resembled a seal's." Again, the troubling inference about "Pound thought." No wonder that Froula, too, follows up with a non sequitur: "Pound saw a good deal of his [Picasso's] work while living in Paris, and admired it." But is this sufficient reason to include reference to his eyes, we may ask, even if Pound did think that Picasso had eyes that looked like a seal's? What if "Eyes of Picasso" does not mean "Picasso's eyes," but refers to certain eyes the painter painted (and Pound "admired")? Is it enough to say, as does Peter Makin, that "Eyes of Picasso" and "black furhood" are "specificities of texture"? Or, as Hugh Kenner "explains," the reference is legitimate, for Picasso was a "metamorphoser of vision"? But was not every great modernist painter, or every great painter for that matter, just such a "metamorphoser"? All entries beg the question: if "Eyes of Picasso" is meant to communicate as a signifier, what is its signified? And if activated as a verbal sign, what is its meaning in its semantic context? Is the context provided by Pound a "sufficient phalanx of particulars," as he insists in **"Canto 74,"** that would prevent its dispersal as a "facet," never finding a "sensitized" area in a reader's mind where it could register with a certain "justness"?

Before attempting semantic activation, it might be useful to establish the status of "Eyes of Picasso" as a verbal sign. In his discussion of Peirce's semiotics, Roman Jakobson has suggested that the division of signs into iconic, indexical, and symbolic is based on the dichotomy of contiguity and similarity. An icon is a sign of factual similarity, an index a sign of factual contiguity and symbol of imputed [i.e., artificially designated] contiguity. But, through the interpretant, symbolic signs may acquire a certain measure of iconicity and indexicality; there may arise certain semiotic hierarchies within symbolic signs as well. Thus, the symbolic sign "seal" may be said to be iconic for readers who "know" seals, the sign on the page evoking a "factual similarity" between itself, the interpretant in their mind, and the actual seal somewhere in the sea or zoo. If seal is made to "stand for" "daughter of Lir," it becomes an index and the relationship is that of "factual contiguity." So-shu, on the other hand, is indeterminate by itself; only by relating it to its contextual neighbors "daughter of Lir" and "sinews of Poseidon" is it possible to confer a meaning, however ephemeral, upon it. The sign thus hovers between "factual" and "imputed"; it takes some form of conscious decision on the reader's part whether So-shu, like Lir, will be taken for a sea-god.

"Eyes of Picasso," however, seems to fit none of these categories. Jakobson has said that the intersection of the two dichotomies of factual/imputed and similarity/contiguity "admits a fourth variety" of relations between signifier and signified: *imputed similarity.* Jakobson assigns this fourth relation to music, glossolalic poetry, and abstract art, indicating a "message which signifies itself." Taking this cue from Jakobson, Antoine Compagnon postulates that the Chinese characters (pictographs and ideograms) inserted by Pound in the text of *The Cantos* constitute just such a sign: "un graphisme asignifiant ou un signifiant sans signifié" 'a nonsignifying graphic mark or a signifier without signified.' Inexplicably, Compagnon disregards readers who recognize such signs (because they read Chinese), and would make an effort to activate the sign in an attempt at meaning formation. Compagnon names Jakobson's unnamed fourth term *symptom,* and comes to invest it with much more than an absence of referentiality:

> ce qui manque au symptôme et ce qui fait le propre du signe, c'est la signification, la pensée de la separation ineluctable du langage et de l'être, du mot et de la chose. Ignorant la signification, le symptôme présume de la coincidence rigoureuse de la parole et de ce que'elle designe. [Le symptôme corresponde] à la collusion du langage et de l'être: il est lui-même objet réel, c'est à dire être.

> [what is missing in the symptom, and what is essential to the sign, is signification, the idea of the ineluctable separation of language and being, of words and things. Ignoring signification, the symptom presupposes the rigorous coincidence of language and what it denotes. The symptom corresponds to the collusion of language and being: it is

itself a real object, that is to say, it exists in its own right.]

This conjunction of sign and referent, signifier and signified is close to Pound's own aesthetic and ethical intentions. His adoption of the ideogrammic method for poetic composition indicates a desire to find a mode of poetic expression where sign and referent will eventually coincide. His definition of the poetic image—"that which presents an intellectual and emotional complex in an instant of time," giving a "sense of sudden liberation . . . from time limits and space limits"—is nearly identical to the revelatory qualities he claimed for both Chinese and poetic ideograms. Kenner may be correct in averring that for Pound "Chinese written characters are neither archaic nor modern. Like cave paintings they exist now, with the strange extra-temporal persistence of objects in space."

The problem is, of course, that as soon as such pictograms are copied from a dictionary and are inserted in an alphabetically organized sign system or text, they lose a measure of their extra-temporal persistence and willy-nilly *become part of that text.* Pound did not intend it otherwise: as one may glean even from a cursory look at a page with Chinese characters in *The Cantos,* pictograms invariably repeat, and thus emphasize, the sense provided by the English text. Correctly or even approximately identified, their semiotic status quickly loses that of a "nonsignifying graphic mark;" they become instead thematic reinforcers to western modes of signification whose effectiveness Pound, following Fenollosa, considered inferior to that of Chinese writing.

If, as Compagnon asserts, Chinese signs in an English text are "symptoms," they are still "symptomatic" of something else. For Fenollosa (and Pound) they signify a more "natural" (in Peircian terms, iconic/indexical rather than symbolic) mode of communication. Even though they are not "real objects," "existing in their own right," (neither Fenollosa nor Pound would make such a claim), they are closer to objects than alphabetic signs. As Fenollosa wrote,

> Chinese notation is something much more than arbitrary symbols. It is based upon a vivid shorthand picture of the operations of nature. In the algebraic figure and in the spoken word there is no natural connection between thing and sign: all depends upon sheer convention. But the Chinese method follows natural suggestion.

The juxtaposition of unrelated pictograms results in the formation of ideograms. "In this method of compounding," writes Fenollosa, "two things added together do not produce a third thing but suggest some fundamental relation between them." This is the process of metaphor, "the use of material images to suggest immaterial relation"; and metaphor, "the revealer of nature, is the very substance of poetry." Here lies the root of Pound's ideogrammic method, which he thought proceeds according to the Chinese method of juxtaposition. Its main virtue is that of a "just revelation," analogous to the power of ancient metaphors in Chinese picture writing, because these "primitive metaphors," Fenollosa declared, "do not spring from arbitrary subjective processes. They are possible only because they follow objective lines of relations in nature herself."

Pound, following Fenollosa, refuses to acknowledge that in spite of what he sees as "natural suggestion" in certain pictograms, the compounds (ideograms) are without exception conventional. And just as the Chinese ideograms in *The Cantos* are neither self-signifying "graphic marks" à la Compagnon nor icons/indices as Fenollosa had thought, so Pound's poetic ideograms fall short of revealing nature and her processes without residue. In the ideogram of So-shu, seal, and Lir's daughter, the line "Eyes of Picasso" as a verbal sign is diaphoric rather than metaphoric—even if one were to accept Froula's suggestion that Pound "thought" Picasso's eyes resembled those of a seal. In fact, diaphoricity may have come about precisely because the mode of association has been so subjective and private (perhaps a kind of in-joke). Thus, even if "Eyes of Picasso" is "recognized" on the semiotic level, on the level of discourse it eludes understanding. One can of course speculate and offer various hypotheses. The phrase may be taken to mean the presence of a kind of Emersonian-Fenollosian "transparent eyeball" fusing the vision of oriental and Western gods and goddesses with the world of humans and animals into a complex. Or the phrase may mean the disruptive human presence in the world of creators and creatures. Or it may have a host of other meanings. One thing, however, seems to be certain: instead of mitigating the endemic disseminate effect of diaphoricity, by inserting "Eyes of Picasso" in a barely intelligible semantic context Pound in fact amplifies it. Now, as Sándor argues, "the indeterminacy of diaphors may also result, of course, from intention and decision. . . . It is possible to produce sentences by which nothing is actually said." Clearly, such a notion runs counter to the very nature of Pound's poetic project and his "narrative of understanding" outlining the values of the ideogrammic method. "Eyes of Picasso" fails the litmus test of his own cherished ideals of precision and accuracy in meaning formation, making in the end of the entire ideogram, in Sándor's words, "just a heap or sequence of unconnected (and unconnectable) verbal signs." Such sequences may still be endowed with meaning by readers; Sándor allows for the activation even of a shopping list as a poem. Such sequences, however, cannot properly be called *poetic;* according to Sándor, "poeticity" consists in certain texts' being "processable at large, not as an idiosyncratic chiffre that has a certain effect in a single mind due to unique associations." It is the "nature" of allusions to operate in the manner described by Sándor, even if

they alluringly conjure up a network of interconnected (and interconnectable) loci of meaning. "Eyes of Picasso," in being just such an allusive chiffre, prevents the ideogram in which it is placed to function meaningfully.

4

Although Compagnon's notion of the symptom does not bear close scrutiny, it is significant that his idea of the ideogram as "itself a real object" that "exists in its own right" is close to Pound's own aesthetic ideology. Yet Pound's beliefs in the dissolution of the materiality of "facets" and "aspects" in the moment of revelation, and so in the concomitant disappearance of the abyss between *res* and *verba,* are belied both by his practice and by some of his rhetorical devices. Latent doubts about the ideogrammic method persist. In *Guide to Kulchur,* for example, he cites at length Gaudier-Brzeska's "Vortex," follows with a discussion of his own theory of Great Bass, and then adds sections on Leibniz and Erigena. At this point he interrupts the presentation and writes, *"These disjunct paragraphs belong together, Gaudier, Great Bass, Leibniz, Erigena, are parts of one ideogram, they are not merely separate subjects."* Or, after a similar presentation of unconnected "facts" in the same book, he again explains: "Let the reader be patient. I am not being merely incoherent. I haven't 'lost my thread' in the sense that I haven't just dropped one thread to pick up another of a different shade. I need more than one string for a fabric." Here, as in his "narrative of understanding," Pound again allegorizes his practice. Deliberately or not, but in any case revealingly, he obscures the linguistic nature of his enterprise: he is involved neither in presenting sculptural "facets" nor textural "threads," but in a project of discourse, composed of signs and words, that never coincide with the subject they intend at best to evoke or allude to. The very nature of the image as symptom/ideogram is a desire to erase the *difference* between "facet" and "subject"; in that, Pound's modernist image is not far removed from the Romantic image where, as Kermode put it, "there is no disunity of being," ultimately betraying, in de Man's words, a "nostalgia for the object," which has become "a nostalgia for an entity that could never, by its very nature, become a particularized presence."

Pound's nostalgia for an ideal poetic writing has from the beginning had ethical implications. Hence his insistence on precision, control, and accuracy as indispensable attributes of a mode of discourse the aim of which is a "just revelation." "Good writing," he stated in 1913, "is writing that is perfectly controlled, the writer says just what he means. He says it with complete clarity and simplicity." And there are "various kinds of clarity":

> There is the clarity of the request: Send me four pounds of ten-penny nails. And there is the syntac-

tical simplicity of the request: Buy me the kind of Rembrandt I like. This last is an utter cryptogram. It presupposes a more complex and intimate understanding of the speaker than most of us ever acquire from anyone. It has as many meanings, almost, as there are persons who might speak it. To a stranger it conveys nothing at all.

"Eyes of Picasso," in contradistinction to "So-shu churned in the sea," is too private an allusion ever to make the journey from "the Rembrandt I like" to "ten-penny nail." And since *The Cantos* are studded with a vast number of private and cryptic allusions similar to "Eyes of Picasso," the text as a whole, apart from its historiographic dimension, resists the transposition of its verbal signs to the level of words, which is the level of discourse. An excessive reliance on allusions in poetry as is evident in Pound's (and the early Eliot's) writing may stem from their ostensible exactness and specificity when compared to concepts and abstract statements; it is in fact easy to perceive them as iconic/indexical signs or, as tropes, metaphors rather than diaphors. But allusions do not arrest diaphoricity; on the contrary, allusion is the diaphoric trope par excellence, a device of simultaneous nostalgic substitution *and* dislocation.

The ideogrammic method of juxtaposing disjunct textual fragments may continue to offer possibilities for poetic composition; it will, however, have to do without the ideal of a "natural" precision Pound had envisaged for it, as a way to "write Paradise" in a language that would ultimately transcend its materiality and fuse with its subject in a moment of "just revelation."

Frank Lentricchia (essay date Spring 1993)

SOURCE: "Ezra Pound's American Book of Wonders," in *South Atlantic Quarterly*, Vol. 92, No. 2, Spring, 1993, pp. 387-415.

[*In the following essay, Lentricchia examines the modernist ideals and Emersonian influence behind Pound's ambitious innovation in* The Cantos. *According to Lentricchia, "The form he invented is at once the representation of a culture he thought to be in fragments and an offering of hope for a different kind of future, rooted in the narrative of common lineage and destiny."*]

As a social and literary critic Ezra Pound is a celebrant of the intensely peculiar: the apparently primordial, autonomous force which he believed stood under and propelled all expression: what rescues Homer or Dante, Chaucer or Shakespeare—his chief examples—from what would otherwise have been their certain aesthetic and political fate as

rank imitators, the lackeys of someone else's mind. Pound's word for this substance of substances was *virtu*. In his populist American logic: *individuality*, therefore *virtue*, and therefore (the aesthetic turn on his politics) *virtuosity*, and he saw it threatened at its virile heart by the culture of capitalism and its commodity-based economy. The virtuous artist was Pound's persistent emblem of the free individual, and his representation of a generous ideal of culture that he would see translated into the social sphere at large: "Having discovered his own virtue," Pound wrote, "the artist will be more likely to discern and allow for a peculiar virtu in others." This, Pound's live and let live company of literary worthies, is his measure of actual social decency at any given time and the basis of his political criticism of what he thought American capitalism had done to our fundamental political ideals.

When Pound told his story of *virtu*, a story he obsessively told, he talked the ahistorical psychology of genius; when he talked the dilemma of the artist in modern America he told another story: that of the vulnerability of genius to social pressures, the curious inability of the primordial and the autonomous to stay primordial and autonomous. This second story is the backbone of Pound's career, the backbone, in other words, of high modernism. The necessity of reimagining the social sphere is initially a literary necessity; social change pursued in order to ensure the life of the artist. Later, and more grandly, in Pound's theorizing of the 1930s, in an odd utopian echo of a famous passage in Marx, social change is pursued in order to ensure that every man may fish in the morning for his sustenance and pursue criticism and poetry in the afternoons; social change on behalf of the artist in us all; society totally reimagined from the aesthetic point of view.

But if it is precisely as a celebrant of a linked literary and political *virtu* that Pound achieved his own *virtu* as a critical voice—he became the polemical engine of high modernism—then the oddity of Pound the poet is that he was haunted for his entire career by the suspicion that he was not original, that he was a poet of no *virtu* whatsoever. Out of this haunting by the spirits of literary history's virtuous powers he fashioned a practice from *A Lume Spento* through *The Cantos* more continuous than the usual views of his poetic evolution (including his own) have generally allowed.

If no *virtu*, then no self; if no self, then nothing to express: Pound's life as a poet is in constant, if implicit, dialogue with the archetypal and revolutionary American desire, announced in Emerson's "Nature" essay of 1836, for radical origination in a new land ("new lands, new men, new thoughts"), a desire for self-creation that Emerson thought would be realized only if we could forget history, rid ourselves of the old man of old thoughts from the old land. Emerson says, free yourself from tradition and you'll cease building "the sepulchers of the fathers." In order to kill himself off as an expression of history and simultaneously re-birth himself as the first man living utterly in the present—like a rose, as Emerson put it in "Self-Reliance," with no concern for past or future roses—a man must "go into solitude," not only from society but also from his "chamber"—the place where "I read and write," where though no one is bodily present, "I" am "not solitary," because "I" have the unwanted company of all those represented selves who populate my books. The "I" must therefore be emptied of everything, including its literary company. And the virgin American woods, Emerson thought, is the context which might induce the necessary ascetic action, the place where "I" may escape all mediation and confront nature "face to face"—the place where "I" can say, at last, "I am nothing." With the historically layered self presumably so negated, the "I"—this urgent and almost passive emptiness which is not quite nothing—becomes a capacity for reception ("a transparent eyeball"), a hollowed out space anxious to be filled: desire in its purest form—in Emerson, a no-self gratified, become filled up, and so rescued at the last moment from nothingness by the inflowing currents of the Transcendental Self.

Pound replayed Henry James's criticism of America as a place whose cultural newness made a certain kind of literature improbable.
　　　　　　　　　　　　　　—*Frank Lentricchia*

Pound's effort to rethink lyric practice is inseparable from Emerson's dynamic of American desire, which in its turn is an expression of the quintessence of the immigrant imagination on its never-ending crossing of a real or metaphoric Atlantic, the immigrant who would leave "I" behind in the suffocating ghetto of a real or a metaphoric Europe (say, some small town in the Middle West), leave behind the "I" that is for a magically fulfilling self that we are not but would become—Vito Andolini become Vito Corleone, James Gatz become Jay Gatsby. In Pound the Atlantic crossing is reversed and (in the trajectory of his biography) taken all the way back, from Idaho to Philadelphia to Italy. An American expatriate who left his country because he believed its cultural and economic system denied him literary selfhood, Pound took his American desire to make it new, the "nothing" that "I am," back to European ground, and in a cluster of his earliest poems figured himself precisely as a determinate emptiness of literary longing seeking writerly identity in re-contact with international literary tradition, which is what he had in glamorous substitution for Emerson's Transcendental Self. What Pound learned very early was that the Emersonian promise of selfhood couldn't be delivered; Emerson's American woods, after all, was only natural, there was no literature there, no *selva oscura,* no Yeatsean mytho-

logical mystery. Our so-called virgin land was a nightmare to Pound precisely for its solitude and its purity.

So as a reverse immigrant he fled the literary death whose name was natural immediacy, fled an America where he enjoyed the sorts of freedoms and comforts that classic immigrants coming to America had sought, and went to Italy—his twenty-third birthday still several months off—seeking cultural life in the very period when millions of Italians from the south of Italy fled their homes (such as they were) for America in hopes of improving an economic base that Pound's family had already secured and upon which (thanks to his father's generous understanding) he could—and did—modestly draw in his expatriation. In effect, Pound replayed Henry James's criticism of America as a place whose cultural newness made a certain kind of literature improbable. James's key judgment of American society—he thought it "denuded"—signifies what for him and for Pound had been lost in the new world. James's solution was to drop the innocent American rose down into the context of European experience: "[O]ne might enumerate the items of high civilization," James wrote, "as it exists in other countries, which are absent from the texture of American life until it should become a wonder to know what was left." The effect of such absence on an English or French imagination "would probably," he surmised, "be appalling." On himself and on Pound the impact of such absence provided the energy and often the structure of the writing they would do.

In a brief poem from *A Lume Spento,* his first volume of poetry, Pound stages the predicament of his empty American "I" gazing into the mirror of desire; he sees "I" represented as a series of incompatible images; the denuded "I" who *is* comes before the mirror and presumably "before" what is represented in the mirror as the foundation of representation. But this "I" is represented as somebody else, as the "he," the consciousness Pound would take on: "O strange face there in the glass! / O ribald company, O saintly host!" **"On His Own Face in a Glass"** stages the moment of self-awareness as a moment of some shock and anxiety ("I? I? I?"), a moment of self-awareness in which he comes to know that there is no self anterior to representation to be aware of and that all the self that can ever be exists in the magical medium of representation, in literature now envisioned, as the pilgrims and other immigrants imagined America itself, as a mirror of transforming desire. Pound's primary poetic tone for such knowledge was mainly confident, even grateful, as if in one stroke—the shape his entire career would take bears heavily upon the point—he had discovered a role to play which coordinated all of his impulses as poet, literary historian, critic, anthologist, and translator, with this last activity (the man was a graduate student in philology and what we call comparative literature) providing the cohesion which made the role unified, lent it identity, so that he did become a self of sorts.

In the concluding poem of *A Lume Spento* Pound represents his soul as a "hole full of God" through which the "song of all time blows. . . . As winds thru a knot-holed board." And in his first English volume, *A Quinzaine for this Yule* (1908), he represents the "I" similarly as a "clear space"—

> 'Tis as in midmost us there glows a sphere
> Translucent, molten gold, that is the "I"
> And into this some form projects itself:
> Christus, or John, or eke the Florentine;
> And as the clear space is not if a form's
> Imposed thereon,
> So cease we from all being for the time
> And there, the Masters of the Soul live on.

These early poems about poetry—so stilted, so unmodern in diction—escape mere conventionality by the extremity of their representation of the self seeking inspiration and poetic selfhood. As Pound figures it, his pre-poetic self is much less than that favorite romantic figure of self at home in the world, unanxiously dependent; self as aeolian harp awaiting the winds of nature that will stir it into music. Pound's pre-poetic self is in possession of no resources of its own. In what sense it is a self is hard to say: "Thus am I Dante for a space and am / One François Villon." But when not Dante or Villon, what then? Just who is this "I" who ceases to be when the virtuous and manly masters of his soul fill the hole of self? The self as translator, the self of no virtue, becomes a medium of the *virtu* of others, and Pound's poems, *The Cantos* most especially, become a kind of international gallery, a hall of exhibits of the originality that he lacked and which without his heroic retrieval would be locked away in a cultural dead space, of antiquarian interest only. Pound's famous avant-garde directive, "make it new," really means "make contemporary what is old." Pound is a man without a center in whom the old masters can "live on"; his poetry is the lifeline and medium of their persistent historicity. His poetry's "modernity" would lie in its creation of a usable literary and political past, exemplary in force: a model to live by and a cultural community to live *in*.

If the absence of *virtu* is no condition to be overcome in a search for an original self of his own but the durable basis of everything Pound did as a poet—an absence of identity that he came comfortably to accept as his identity, a trigger of poetic production, early and late—then in one important sense Pound never really "evolved" as a poet. The numerous and dramatic shifts in style we can note from *A Lume Spento* to *The Cantos*—and not only from volume to volume but often within a given volume—are not evidence of the dissatisfied, self-critical young writer groping toward his one and only true voice, but the very sign of his voice and all the maturity he would ever achieve. The word Pound frequently used to describe this persistent mark of change in his poetic writing was *metamorphosis,* from "the tradition

of metamorphoses," as he explained in 1918, "that teaches us that things do not always remain the same. They become other things by swift and unanalysable process." Pound's theory of myth is based on an attempt to explain the moment when a man, after walking "sheer into nonsense," tried to tell someone else about it "who called him a liar." The man was forced to make a myth, "an impersonal or objective story woven out of his own emotion, as the nearest equation that he was capable of putting into words."

Among the manifestations of Pound's obsession with protean energy there is his radically avant-garde idea of literature as "something living, something capable of constant transformation and rebirth"; his doctrine of the image, which asserts that in the presence of the genuine work of art we experience "the sense of sudden liberation; that sense of freedom from time and space limits; that sense of sudden growth"; and his statement in *The Spirit of Romance* that myth takes its origin subjectively, in a moment when we pass through "delightful psychic experience." In the period spanning the many stylistic changes from his earliest poems to his early *Cantos,* Pound changed not at all on the value of metamorphosis for the sort of writer (himself) who explained the process of writing to himself in his earliest poems as an experience of walking sheer into nonsense—becoming Christ, Villon, or Dante, God or a tree—a writer who would project the psychic value of his own aesthetic experience as the real value of *reading* his poems. Pound's reader would also be freed from the self of the moment, liberated into some strange and bracing identity, joining the writer in mythic experience in order to take on with Pound what he, like Pound, does not possess.

The unsaid assumption of Pound's poetics is that his typical reader is not everyman but an American like himself, in need of what he needs—a reader, in other words, not only with no *virtu* of his own but a reader who does not want to be fixed and crystallized with a "self," a reader for whom avant-gardism, though not known as such, is the ruling philosophy of everyday life in the land of opportunity and infinite self-development. From the delightful, because liberating, psychic experience of the poet and the parallel experience of his American reader, this projection: the reformation of literary history in his own (and America's) image via the bold antidefinition of literature as writing without historically prior and persistent identity, writing without a prior "self" to rely on—a nonidentity of sheerest possibility, an absence of essence: "constant transformation," constant rebirth into a newness of (these are equivalents) an American and a modern literary selfhood. Never mind that "constant transformation" also describes the dream of consumer capitalism, avant-garde of capitalist economics.

Metamorphosis is the unprecedented master category in

Pound's literary theory. In spite of the explicit Ovidian allusion, the theory is not Ovidian. Nor does Pound draw upon a notion of biological metamorphosis: the man who comes "before" the glass cannot be traced, not even obscurely, as a surviving form in the new self (hence Pound's shocked "I?"). But if there is to be metamorphosis in any recognizable sense of the word, there must be a prior something which undergoes transformation. If the prior "something" is, as in Pound, a determinate nothing, a hole needing filling and fulfilling, valuable ("golden") precisely because of its amorphic condition, then Pound, like Emerson, has pressed metamorphosis to the edge of its limiting boundary: the classic American dream, self-origination *ex nihilo*. Pound theorizes metamorphosis, a process of self-emergence, as Emerson had theorized it: on a condition of potential-for-self only, not on the transformation of one self into another; a condition without a memory out of which a self might emerge which is nothing but memory, and so—the irony and paradox of Pound's career—no self at all.

Even as he turned out small poem after small poem and a shocking number of pages of prose, Pound was all along—perhaps as early as 1904, while a student at Hamilton College—working himself up to write a long poem of epic size, "long after" (Pound speaking) "mankind has been commanded never again to attempt a poem of any length." He apparently began work in earnest on this poem sometime in 1915, published his first three "cantos," as he called them, in *Poetry* in 1917, only soon thereafter to suppress them and begin anew. After an initial volume appeared in 1925 as *A Draft of XVI Cantos,* gatherings of cantos were published with regularity, to the end of Pound's life, including the infamous *Pisan Cantos* in 1948 and two volumes, in 1955 and 1959, written in the insane asylum. The least taught of the famous modernist texts, the collected volume, *The Cantos of Ezra Pound*—one hundred and seventeen cantos' worth—appeared in 1970, reprinted ten times as of this writing, this latter fact strong testimony on behalf of our continuing fascination with the high modernists, including this one whose major work is widely assumed to be unreasonably difficult, often pure gibberish, and, in its occasional lucid moments, offensive to most standards of decency.

Just what kind of literary thing he was writing Pound had trouble deciding. He was keenly conscious of his epic predecessors and often glossed their intentions as his own: to give voice to the "general heart," to write "the speech of a nation" through the medium of one person's sensibility. Yet for all his classic desire and expressed contempt for romantic poetry, Pound was also marked by its contrary aesthetic: "[T]he man who tries to explain his age instead of expressing himself," he writes, "is doomed to destruction." In Pound the poetics of *The Odyssey* and *The Divine Comedy* are complicated by the poetics of *The Prelude* and *Song of Myself:* refocused by Pound in the lens of Wordsworth, Whitman, and Poe, *The Divine Comedy* becomes Dante's "tremendous lyric."

Classic ambition and romantic impulse would surface constantly through the long publishing history of *The Cantos.* An "epic is a poem including history," Pound wrote in 1935, in the midst of a decade during which he was writing cantos that "included" history and chunks of the historical record with stupefying literality: redactions of Chinese history in **"Cantos 52-61,"** extract after extract from the writings of John Adams in **"Cantos 62-71."** In 1937, in *Guide to Kulchur,* he declared (with a nod to Kipling) that his long poem would tell "the tale of the tribe," but in the same book he also described *The Cantos* with analogy to Bartok's Fifth Quartet as the "record of a personal struggle." Then, in the middle of the journey, in 1939, he struck a new note, this one neither epic nor romantic: "As to the form of *The Cantos:* All I can say or pray is wait till it's there. I mean wait till I get 'em written and then if it don't show, I will start exegesis. I haven't an Aquinas-map; Aquinas *not* valid now." And with that nostalgic glance back at the cultural context of his beloved Dante, Pound approached the clarity he achieved in 1962 in his *Paris Review* dialogue with Donald Hall.

With over a hundred cantos done, he gave Hall a definition—antidefinition, really—of the poem's form that marked it "modernist" in strictest terms. Not Homer or Dante, but Joyce and Eliot stand behind Pound's search for a form "that wouldn't exclude something merely because it didn't fit." With this insouciant gesture Pound declares the classic concern of aesthetics for the decorous relationship of genre to subject matter beside the modernist point. He tells us that the literary form that can include what doesn't fit is the authentic signature of modern writing, the sign that the literature of our time has adequately taken the measure of its exploded culture.

Like Wordsworth, Pound felt himself an outsider in his society, a literary radical who knew that his poetry was unrecognizable as such by mainstream culture. As a consequence, he set himself the task (in Wordsworth's phrasing) "of *creating* the taste by which he is to be enjoyed." His project was to provide epic substance for a culture grounded in none of the assumptions that typically had nourished the epic poet: a culture no longer capable of issuing a valid rhetorical contract between writer and reader. In a culture that cannot read him—here is the motivating contradiction of *The Cantos* and much high modernism—Pound would write a poem that his culture needs to read in order to make itself truly a culture. "The modern mind contains heteroclite elements. The past epos has succeeded when all or a great many of the answers were assumed, at least between author and audience. The attempt in an experimental age"—he means socially as well as aesthetically experimental—"is therefore rash."

Rash or no, Pound persisted in epic intention because, as he told Hall, "there *are* epic subjects. The struggle for individual rights is an epic subject, consecutive from jury trial in Athens to Anselm versus William Rufus, to the murder of Becket and to Coke and through John Adams." So the poem that Pound had mainly written by 1962 found its home not in a specific Western culture and place, as classical epics had done, but in Western culture as a whole, as the grand story of struggle, not yet won, for individual rights; and it found its strange literary form in an age of experiment that demanded he invent his own. The form he invented is at once the representation of a culture he thought to be in fragments and an offering of hope for a different kind of future, rooted in the narrative of common lineage and destiny.

Pound knew that in order to tell the tale of the tribe he needed a tribe to tell it to, knew he didn't have one, and in *The Cantos*—a poem without unifying epic hero, or stability of cultural scene—he gave us the unlikely record of one poet's effort to create through means unclassical a new classical situation for writing. What he ended up achieving was a poem whose experimental character overwhelms all cultural and social goals, except those that bear on the welfare of writers. *The Cantos* would resuscitate a community of letters for modern writers, in order that they might join a tradition of radical experimenters and their noble patrons, all those who waged their struggle for individual (largely aesthetic) rights against the grain; a tradition brought to life for an age (our own) cut off from nourishment and patronage, a home for our contemplative (but only our contemplative) life.

In this light, Pound's title, *The Cantos,* is tellingly odd. It is the nontitle of a writer who apparently never saw the need to make up his mind—who, if he could have lived forever, would probably not have pinned a crystallizing title (like *The Waste Land* or *The Bridge*) onto his experiment. Calling a poem *The Cantos* (and shall we say *The Cantos* "is" or *The Cantos* "are"?, to decide that question is to decide much) is like calling a novel *Work in Progress* while you're writing it and then to publish it under that title, or maybe the title *The Chapters;* like a Renaissance sonneteer deciding to call his sequence *The Sonnets.* To publish sections of this poem, forever in progress, with the words "a draft of" included in the title only underscores the tentativeness of the writer's intention. Unlike all the epics we know, *The Cantos* names as its substance aesthetic form itself, without ever claiming, as Wordsworth and Whitman had in their romantic versions, the substantial coherence of a binding subjectivity.

Not that there isn't a discernible subjectivity afloat in the poem: there is, but it doesn't congeal as a "self" whose autonomous presence is projected in the autobiographical narrative of a poet's mind. For much of the way, "Ezra Pound" appears to us in the shape of a desire: as a generous capacity for reception, a subjectivity virtually transparent, a facilitating vehicle, a literary producer (in the theatrical sense of that word, a gatherer of artistic forces), a man, by his own account, of no *virtu,* an absence of selfhood, a hole, a mirror for others. This tissue of masks, this incessant scholarly quoter—translator, alluder, medium of pastiche, tradition's own ventriloquist; this poet as anthologist, poet of the specimen, patron and exhibitor of styles, heroes, and cultural contexts which are given space in the literary gallery and curriculum called *The Cantos,* is an active and empathetic memory trapped in the dead present of his culture, casting a long lifeline into the past (tradition's own lifeguard) in order to rescue by transmitting tradition, and in so transmitting bring his own culture back to life again.

The Cantos approached as if they were written by a poet-without-a-self unveil themselves as a vast texture (text, textile, interweaving) of discourses lyric, satiric, narrative, dramatic, and nonliterary (historical, epistolary, technical); Pound's influential idea of the heterogeneous image (an "intellectual and emotional complex in an instant of time") writ very large; an immense vortex; or, in the perfect metaphor from the discarded first canto (drafted in 1912), a "rag-bag," best form of all for a poet who didn't want to exclude something merely because it didn't fit; the form of a poetry by and for the culturally homeless.

And so the centrality for *The Cantos* of those storied modernist metaphors drawn from the visual and spatial arts: like *montage,* a stark juxtaposition which yields its significance in some third, unnamed thing to be construed (imagined, created), by an active reader in the process of interpretation, whose own imaginative life will be the force which brings Pound's cultural hope to realization, and who is charged with voicing the poem's otherwise unvoiced vision, with making the diagnosis, distributing Pound's medicine; who appreciates Pound properly and therefore earns his own entry into the community of letters by transforming himself from passive consumer in the culture of capital into resourceful, self-reliant free agent; Pound's critic become the reader as modernist, co-maker of *The Cantos,* and coworker in the enterprise of culture-making. And of course the metaphor of *collage,* surrealist version of the rag-bag, a composition whose diverse and incongruously placed fragments—drawn from all manner of media—ask us (as does montage, but now on the scale of the entire work) to take the thing as a whole, not as a narrative but as a form hung in space, in order to "view" it in its entirety: under the pressure of these metaphors, *The Cantos* become a difficult structure of fragments signifying not the imitation of fragmentation by the means of fragmentation but some missing total vision (or the desire thereof) whose presence in any given canto must be supplied by an engaged reader. So read, *The Cantos* become a vision of social and cultural health sporadically in evidence and constantly threatened by the historical process; a vision of the free individual gathering himself against history's gloom of diseased economics; a vision contemplated and disseminated by those who must read Pound in a thickening contemporary cultural darkness almost complete. *The Cantos* may be the clearest example we have of the doubled character of modernist literary desire: to pursue aesthetic innovation for the purpose of instigating social change; a poem whose unparalleled formal sumptuousness—a cornucopia of literary texture—calls forth those mediators who would join Pound's lifelong experiment in cultural hope to a world of possible readers.

"And then went down to the ship / Set keel to breakers, forth on the godly sea. . . ." That is how *The Cantos* begin, in a strange world modified by gods, with Pound translating from the eleventh book of *The Odyssey,* the descent into the underworld. Assuming the mask of an epic hero already written, Pound voyages, "Heavy with weeping" (the tone is elegiac, the subject is cultural loss), to a place of darkness, dimly lit with torches, for a colloquy with the dead, the prophetic Tiresias in particular. Ezra Pound, Odyssean poet, makes his descent to the West's literary underworld in order to conjure the ghosts of writers past in a poetry of reading. Homer's hero summons the dead with the ritual blood of sacrifice; Pound, with the blood of scholarly poetic labor, would summon Homer via a Latin translation made by Andreas Divas in the Renaissance, period of classical recovery; presses his Latin Homer through the alliterative strong rhythms of Anglo-Saxon poetry and then into modern English—thereby producing the effect of a triple translation for the benefit of the modern English reader, an illusion of three literary traditions simultaneously present in culturally mixed traces of diction and proper names, a palimpsest, writing over writing for a period, his own, which Pound hoped would also be a time of cultural recovery.

The first of *The Cantos* begins the project of a new *risorgimento* as if it were already in progress—the first word of the first canto is "and." We are offered a stylistic exhibit of heroic endeavor, by a poet-patron, toward the end of which the stylistic exhibitor himself comes forward, breaking out of the mask of Odysseus. In an abrupt comic descent from the heroic decorum of his tone and diction Ezra Pound speaks—"Lie quiet Divas"—so revealing himself in that moment as a haunter of libraries and old bookstores—in the dramatic fiction of **"Canto I,"** a man pouring over a rare book—searching for the traces of a usable tradition, and finding them in the text of Divas's translation.

The eleventh book of Homer's epic: Odysseus's youngest companion, Elpenor, asks Odysseus to provide proper burial, lest he restlessly and forever wander the earth's surface; and he requests a memorial so that he may enjoy afterlife in his culture's collective memory: just so does Pound grant Divas, another unhappy ghost, similar (if imagined) requests

in order that Divas may "lie quiet." And Pound's autobiographically aggressive translation of Homer's epitaph for Elpenor ("*A man of no fortune, and a name to come*") links him to Elpenor and Divas both, and to a literary history merging ancient, Renaissance, and modern cultures in an overarching triplet rhyme of tradition-making, the point of literary history being its own transmission; the immortality of writers depending on other writers who remember long.

Pound, a bibliophile and cultural genealogist, gives the citation as a kind of epitaph: "I mean, that is Andreas Divas, / In officina Wecheli, 1538, out of Homer." Divas and Wecheli (the bookmaker), those, too, are names of heroes in the commemorative world of *The Cantos,* heroes as significant as Odysseus. For one more line and a half Pound returns now in his own voice—the spell of recovery is broken—to the Homeric narrative, then (as it were) flips the pages to the back of the book that Wecheli made, this time quoting the Latin of Georgius Dartona of Cyprus, whose translation of the Homeric hymns was bound in with Divas's work: some enamored phrases about Aphrodite ("thou with dark eyelids"), who was assigned the defenses of Crete, phrases whose Latin will be strange to the modern reader, but much less strange than the idea they contain, absurd to the modern mind (Pound knows this), of art active in the world, beauty in defense of the city. At the end of **"Canto I"** Pound comes forward as a voice among old books, trying to breathe life into voices he feared silenced by his culture. In that act, he creates a voice of his own.

> Two mice and a moth my guides—
>   To have heard the farfalla gasping
>   as toward a bridge over worlds.
> That the kings meet in their island,
>   Where no food is after flight from the pole.
> Milkweed the sustenance
>   as to enter arcanum.
>
> To be men not destroyers.

That is how *The Cantos* end, with Pound writing lyric notes: on the forms of his confusion ("M'amour, m'amour / what do I love and / where are you?"); on his regrets ("Let the Gods forgive what I / have made / Let those I love try to forgive / what I have made"); on his econo-aesthetic obsessions ("La faillite de François Bernouard, Paris"— Bernouard, unsung, unknown in poetry until this moment in *The Cantos,* a contemporary version of Wecheli, a hero in the cultural struggle for *risorgimento,* a French bookmaker who went bankrupt printing the classics and who functions here as an incarnation of history's truth, Pound-style: the destruction of the honorable by a dishonourable economic system that will not permit the valuing of beauty and beauty's patrons). Notes on his unceasing hatred for the human costs of war and the cold-blooded calculation of the secure-from-battle ("the young for the old / that is tragedy"); notes on his sustaining confidence in the liberating power of the image as the bedrock of personal redemption, aestheticist life preserver of Pound's youth coming in handy at the end of a life of failed larger design ("For the blue flash and the moments / benedetta"); notes on his grandiose ambition ("I have tried to write Paradise"), his anchoring modesty, his disavowal of ambition ("Do not move / Let the wind speak / that is paradise"); notes on his cultural deprivation, having to go it, as Dante did not, without a Virgil-like teacher for his guide ("Two mice and a moth my guides—"): all his notes the verbal condensation of desire, and desire, the gathering ambience of *The Cantos,* become palpable, the real subject of this last collection, *Drafts and Fragments* (1969).

In this final fragment of the final canto (**"117"**), a collage representative of virtually everything Pound thought about in *The Cantos* as a whole, the striking note sounded is not in some final revelation for poet and reader but in the variegated sounds of the poet's voice—in Pound's tonal agility, his compression of a range of vocal attitudes: the desperate old man, speaking painfully in the dark, sometimes in the curious mixed tones of prayer and imperative; sometimes in gentle self-directive; sometimes in fragments of amazement ("That I lost my center / fighting the world"; "That the kings meet in their island / where no food is after flight from the pole"); sometimes in desire's timeless infinitive ("To have heard the farfalla gasping / as toward a bridge over worlds"). Fragment following fragment, in a poem heavy with sharply etched perceptions and feelings freed (largely) from reason's habitat of correct English syntax: a poem of reason undone, and in its unravelment of reason displaying the constituents of a mind trying to strip itself of the authoritative power of utterance it used to command (half-wanting to fail, still desiring authority); wanting to enter the realm of the unspeakable with the monarch butterflies in need of no food—those king figures of the soul entering the last mystery. The final line is the one Pound (according to his lover, Olga Rudge) wanted to finish *The Cantos* with; a line impossibly poised in tone and form, hung between yearning and self-confident imperative; "To be men not destroyers."

Between the first and the last of *The Cantos* in a cluster which occupies the virtual center of the entire work—approximately fifty lie either side of it—fall the Chinese and American history cantos (**"52-72"**), a section nearly one quarter the length of the complete cantos, and presenting the one continuous stretch of writing to be found in *The Cantos of Ezra Pound;* a chronological span recounting some five thousand years of Chinese history, from 3000 B.C. through the eighteenth century A.D., mediated for America by the French Enlightenment (when Chinese texts began to be translated), an era in European thought which eventually

passed formatively into the social theories of John Adams and the founding fathers.

There's a point to Pound's history, but the point is not easy to grasp because his history is told in a rush of names, dates, references, and events presented largely without explanation or narrative connection. The effect is one of relentless obscurity, which is maybe Pound's intention: to rub our noses in the fact that we've been cut off from the sources of what he imagines as social vitality, that we have no tradition, that we need to make another Odyssean journey back, to another cultural underworld, this one not Western, and that we can do it but it will take scholarly work. Such work would itself, presumably, be salutary, a sign that we are recovering (in both senses of the word), for in doing the work that Pound asks, we begin the process of self-healing. And if enough of us who do this work of recovery will only disseminate its findings, we will be on our way to cultural and not just personal healing as the active readers that Pound needs in the corporate effort to make the bridge between the isolated island of the modern world and the mainland of cultural history. The payoff will be a renovated economics, with justice for all, and a renovated language in which the word will bear the right name. Like an honest currency (in Pound that means an imagist economics), the word will not go the way of abstraction because it will be ligatured to real goods extant. And economics and poetics alike will be underwritten by a benevolent totalitarian (Confucius a more perfect totalitarian than Aristotle, Mussolini the hopeful modern instance), who protects money and words, properly ligatured, from manipulation by usurers, gun manufacturers, the fantastic international Jewish conspiracy, and other corrupters, financial and aesthetic, real and imaginary.

So do the Chinese and Adams cantos work in theory; in practice, and by the measure of Pound's aesthetic, they are a literary disaster. The aesthetic and the great majority of the cantos insist on heterogeneity in texture, voice, and form; the Chinese and Adams cantos present a homogeneous voice of didactic intent. The aesthetic and the great majority of the cantos insists on fragments and the surprising and delightful juxtapositions of montage which invite creative reading; the Chinese and Adams cantos progress by a principle of deadly smooth continuity which puts the reader into the passive position of a student listening to a lecturer with no dramatic talent. The literary project of *The Cantos* is modernist, but **"Cantos 52-71"** fulfill no one's idea of modernist writing, or even, perhaps, of interesting writing.

The Chinese/Adams cantos fail because they lack the anchor of cultural poverty that motivates Pound's project for redemption. The Chinese/Adams cantos give us a portrait of the poet comfortable in his views, speaking without duress from nowhere. But at their most riveting *The Cantos* evoke as their true speaking subject, however minimally, the presence of a writer—*The Cantos* are "about" a writer as much as they are "about" anything—a writer in struggle, working against the grain, under the inspiration of the muses of memory, those muses his only hope in a culture without memory. As in **"Canto 1,"** for example, where, at the end, we finally see Pound, book in hand, meditating on ancient ideals of heroism and beauty from a place where those ideals are not honored. Or in **"Canto 2"** where Pound fictionalizes himself, Whitman-like, a brooder at the seashore, a man for whom all mythologies of the sea are simultaneously present, from Homer to Ovid to Picasso, but with no mythology of his own to be at home in. "And"—the linguistic sign of pound's consciousness, eager to bind together—here in **"Canto 2"** becomes the sign of a mind which says "and" because it cannot say "because"—because it cannot trace a logical path to its leap into Ovid's *Metamorphoses,* the presiding cultural exhibit of **"Canto 2."**

"And by Scios": Pound becomes a first-person participant in the story of the kidnapping of the young Dionysius by sailors who would sell him into slavery (not knowing who he was). The episode retold from Ovid is a story whose chief characters, in many variants, dominate **The Cantos,** a story of money lust and mythic power; poetry turned against and vanquishing greed (usually the story ends badly in **The Cantos,** but not here); Dionysius unleashed, and Pound in attendance, awestruck, retelling the consequences for the ears of worldly power ("Fish scales on the oarsmen," "Arms shrunk into fins"): "And you Pentheus, had as well listen . . . or your luck will go out of you." **"Canto 2"** concludes with a return to the brooding poet in his place on the shore. With his vision lapsed into the desolation of the present, and the Ovidian memory fading fast, now only an afterimage mediating his experience of the sea, Pound presses Homer's epithet of the wine-dark sea through Ovid's Bacchus ("wave, color of grape's pulp"); Pound, a writer whose detailed and life-endowing memory of literary tradition unsettles him for life in his own world.

Can these, or any of Pound's literary exhibits, make our dry cultural bones dance again? Can his specimens of cultures past make any difference? Do Pound's heroes from ancient and Renaissance worlds (forerunners all of *Il Duce?*) translate as our heroes, or do they best remain where they are, exemplars for his imaginative life, beacons in his struggle through cultural darkness? In his last canto Pound says, "I have tried to write Paradise": a line whose force lies not in the vision glimpsed, nor even in the vision glimpsed-and-then-lost, but in the effort of writing a Paradise that can be lived only in the act of writing, sustained in and by a writing that cannot sustain it for very long. The quintessential fact about Pound's paradise is that it cannot be culturally transported outside **The Cantos.** The most moving (if implicit) image of **The Cantos** is of a writer working mightily at the retrieval of the West's great cultural highs, who be-

lieves that if he can only talk eloquently enough, incessantly enough, about what he loves, the subjects of his love will spring to life before him, talked back to life, if only he would not lose heart (as so frequently he does), lose vocal energy and intensity (this, too, part of the image), and in so doing remind himself and us where we all are.

One of the strong, comically pathetic moments to **The Cantos** occurs in the **Pisan** group when Pound admits defeat and in the same breath tries to build out of defeat's humble gifts a new paradise. If *Il Duce* is the summation of the heroic tradition, then what can Pound save of tradition with "Ben and la Clara *a Milano* / by the heels at Milano"? And he answers in **"Canto 74:"**

> Le Paradis n'est pas artificiel
> but spezzato apparently
> it exists only in fragments unexpected excellent
> 　　sausage,
> 　The smell of mint, for example,
> 　Ladro the night cat

And the reader's equivalent, the unexpected excellent literary sausage of a broken paradise, lies in scattered but numerous moments of individual elegance, sudden interventions of Pound's virtuosity in the midst of his historical labor of recuperation. As in **"Canto 13,"** where he presents in doctrinally constrained dialogue the Confucian ethic and social ideal, a canto intended to make a point about order, personal and public, and who underwrites it:

> If a man have not order within him
> He can not spread order about him;
> And if a man have not order within him
> His family will not act with due order;
> 　And if the prince have not order within him
> He can not put order in his dominions.

Pound assigns those lines to Kung himself, the man whose authority stems from the wisdom that cannot be questioned, an oriental voice drawn through Western timbres of biblical propheticism: the constant Poundian conjunctive ("and") now marking unshakable certitude ("And if a man," "And if the prince," and you better believe it). And we will hear that supremely self-possessed voice again, whenever Pound feels his doctrinal oats. But in the midst of this canto about the origin and dissemination of right political authority, we watch the poet in pursuit of something else, like a bloodhound after the irrelevant detail—in a long aside going off the doctrinal tract, seduced by the unfolding, self-pleasuring movement of his own conceit; the familiar Poundian conjunctive now marking lyric momentum:

> And Tian said, with his hands on the strings of his
> 　lute

The low sounds continuing
  after his hands left the strings,
And the sound went up like smoke, under the
  leaves,
And he looked after the sound. . . .

Within the doctrinal program of **"Canto 13"** these lines move with the grace that passes the reach of doctrine; the unexpected and unexpectable gift of cantabile, for no ends beyond the singing itself.

Elsewhere—strikingly so in the Malatesta group (**"Cantos 8-11"**)—Pound's minor beauties engage major preoccupations, not as food for isolated aesthetic indulgence but as medium of historical work. **"Cantos 8-11"** concern the exploits of an obscure fifteenth-century Italian professional soldier of fortune, Sigismundo Malatesta, complete political cynic with a singular passion for art and artists: just the sort of passion for which Pound will forgive anything (and with Malatesta there is apparently much to forgive), a type of the Poundian hero who achieved what he achieved "against the current of power" and found his truest expression of selfhood as patron par excellence, in unswerving devotion to the building of the Tempio Malatestiana in Rimini: Malatesta, in other words, as figure of the poet Pound would be in *The Cantos,* building in the Tempio, as Pound would build, a "little civilization," part pagan, part Christian.

Pound's method in the Malatesta group is cagily documentary: he quotes heavily from chronicles, letters, legal documents, papal denunciations; inserts his own retelling, sometimes as on-site narrator, in recreation of scenes for which no documentation exists. These cantos take the shape of a boiling polylogue, some voices friendly, most not, to Sigismundo's person and desire; they give off an ambience of thickest treachery—of men (including Sigismundo) willing to do anything, he for the love of art, they for the love of power. The arrangement of the documents is dramatic: Pound's purpose is to conjure his obscure hero (**"Canto 8"** opens with incantatory rhetoric), show him in the act of emerging from corruption, his voice freeing itself, sailing above, somehow uncontaminated; a voice elegant, dignified, gracious, lyrical, and promising violence, a man whose passion rescues him even from the evil that he does. The strength of Pound's showing lies not in the narrative of Sigismundo—its confusions overwhelm even Pound—but in the rhetorical effects he manages in honor of his hero. Pound loves the man, and his love creates a verbal habitation that insulates him from the garbage of his circumstances. We know not Malatesta but Pound "writing Malatesta"—not "of" or "about" Malatesta, but writing Malatesta as in "writing poetry"; or "writing Paradise"; or in this translation of one of Malatesta's letters concerning what he would do for Piero della Francesca:

So that he can work as he likes
Or waste time as he likes
(*affatigandose per suo piacere or no
  non gli manchera la provixione mai*)
  Never lacking provision.

The prose meaning of Pound's English captures the prose of Malatesta's Italian, but with its arrangement into a versified parallel, like two lines of poetry with a full caesura at the end of each line, the translation adds an eloquence beyond the touch of its prose sense. Pound's translation becomes a stylistic index, the verbal maneuver that directs us by dint of its phrasing alone to the generous soul of Malatesta. And the sandwiched Italian original proves Pound's translating fidelity, his capacity for living transmission:

    With the church against him,
    With the Medici bank for itself,
    With wattle Sforza against him
    Sforza Francesco, wattle-nose,
    Who married him (Sigismundo) his (Francesco's)
    Daughter in September,
    Who stole Pesaro in October (as Broglio said
      "bestialmente"),
    Who stood with the Venetians in November,
    With the Milanese in December,
    Sold Milan in November, stole Milan in December
    Or something of that sort,
    Commanded the Milanese in the spring,
    The Venetians at midsummer,
    The Milanese in the autumn
    And was Naples' ally in October, . . .

From this swamp of political confusion, this comic litany of the months and seasons of Byzantine betrayal, spoken, no doubt, in some smoke-filled backroom, comes a line from another level, elevated in syntax and tone, with a Latin phrase at the end (like an anchor of final authority) telling us what Malatesta did—the Latin working for Pound (as languages other than English often did) as some talismanic discourse, the facilitator of magical transcendence from politics to the plane of art: "He, Sigismundo, *templum aedificavit.*" "He Sigismundo"—a phrasing repeated often in the Malatesta group—not only clarifies just who it is among these obscure political actors that Pound is talking about, but adds the sound of awe, like an epitaph which registers the shock of the memorialist, that in the midst of all this, he, Sigismundo, did what he did: "In the gloom, the gold gathers the light against it."

In his introduction to the *Active Anthology* Pound says that experiment "aims at writing that will have a relation to the present analogous to the relation which past masterwork had to the life of its time." He insists: "[W]ithout constant experiment literature dates." He means that literary experimentation is the response to the challenge posed by social change that writers come to terms with a new world. The implication is that the true history of literature is the discontinuous non-history of experiment, a series of modernist revolutions (what Pound means by "master work") in evidence across the ages, whose relations to one another lie not in content, form, or value, but in the incomparable fact of radical originality. Radical as in "root"; originality as in deriving from an "origin": a literature rooted in an origin, the origin here being the writer's salient historical situation. The severe discipline of a modernist aesthetic relegates "literature" as such, or "literariness" as such, to the status of empty concepts, because no writer who would be modern (original) in any age (rather than the voice of some other time) has anything to lean on. Original writing (the essence of which is that it has no essence) proceeds, as always, in the dark, driven by difficult questions, the answers to which are never known in advance: What is it like to be alive now? What strange, new forms has human being assumed here, in this place? Would we, if we could, do some social experimentation? New World writing—the project of an "American" literature—is the exemplary moment of modernist literature.

Pound thought Eliot insufficiently moved by the experimental spirit. Of Eliot's modernist benchmark, "Tradition and the Individual Talent," he wrote: "This kind of essay assumes the existence of a culture that no longer subsists and does nothing to prepare a better culture that must or ought to come into being." If Western culture, as Pound told Donald Hall, is the struggle for individual rights, beginning with jury trial in Athens, then ever since the late eighteenth century we have been living in an age of revolution for individual rights in relation to which Eliot's "existing monuments" of literary tradition can have no organic significance. Pound thought "existing monuments" a contradiction, thought we needed "something living" and might have sought (he would have been stunned by this suggestion) support from Emerson for his political reading of the course of the West: the necessity, as Pound put it, to respect the "peripheries" of the individual.

The chief sign of the times, Emerson wrote in "The American Scholar," is the "new importance given to the single person. Everything that tends to insulate the individual—to surround him with barriers of natural respect, so that each man shall feel the world is his, and man shall treat with man as a sovereign state with a sovereign state—tends to true union": he meant, tends to just community. Emerson thought the revolutions of democratic change he was witnessing had implication for revolutions of cultural freedom, the individual and national rights of intellect and imagination. "Our day of dependence, our long apprenticeship to the learning of other lands, draws to a close.... We have listened too long to the courtly muses of Europe." Or, in the equally

clarion call from the opening paragraph of "Nature": "Why should not we have a poetry and philosophy of insight and not of tradition . . . ?"

Emerson, in the optative mood, spoke on behalf of the American cultural achievement he hoped would come to pass, an aesthetic birth which would, in Pound's words, bear relation to its present that past art bore to the life of its time. Pound's criticism of Eliot sounds suspiciously like the criticism of a nativist leveled at an expatriate who in fleeing his country has also fled Emerson's challenge to American writers (whether here or abroad) to resist the seductions of Old World culture, to make the cultural journey over the Atlantic to America, to come home, not in order to embrace the American imagination but in order to create it.

But Pound, like Eliot, was a reverse American immigrant, an unlikely ally of Emerson, who seemed all along to have intended to seek out those courtly muses who inspired no revolutions on behalf of any individual. Emerson probably had Longfellow in mind when he wrote the following, but the stricture implied seems to fit Pound even better: "I ask not for the great, the remote, the romantic; what is doing in Italy or Arabia, what is Greek art, or Provençal minstrelsy; I embrace the common, I explore and sit at the feet of the familiar, the low." Pound's theory of experimentation is in the American grain, but his practice in *The Cantos,* his pamphleteering of the 1930s, his Rome Radio broadcasts during World War II—are they not betrayals? Had not Pound written, in the outrageously entitled *Jefferson And/Or Mussolini:* "The heritage of Jefferson . . . is HERE, NOW *in the Italian peninsula* at the beginning of fascist second decennio, not in Massachusetts or Delaware"?

Perhaps, though, the failure was less Pound's than Emerson's, whose visionary essays of the 1830s and 1840s on the future of the American writer, who would be nourished in experimental freedom by an original culture, do not come close to comprehending what would become the crisis of the modern writer, whose classic situation in the age of revolution is one in which he feels himself irremediably outside, in uncertain relation to the culture of his time. Pound in New York, in 1910, on the eve of decisive expatriation, gathers his data for his first and most sustained critical meditation on American culture (**"Patria Mia"**). He reflects upon life in a democratic culture and concludes (in effect) that there has been no improvement upon the situation of cultural deprivation Emerson had observed in the 1830s. He leaves America, confirmed in his judgment that we are a people committed to the exigencies of the practical life and the cash nexus; with a sense that the cost of a new land was severance from the cultural past of Europe, a loss enhanced by the dry imitations of English verse he read in the organs of the literary marketplace; and with a belief that the marketplace is the instrument of amnesia, the great barrier to the past which would seem to ensure, for those who did not take Pound's expatriate option, the permanent triviality of American writing, and for those like Pound, who would not or could not write to its demands—for all writers in America's post-aristocratic culture, of modest middle-class means (or less)—permanent anxiety about economic survival; the choice of the literary vocation a choice of poverty and the contempt of mainstream society.

The exciting new culture Emerson had prophesied turned out to be mass culture, engineered by a culture industry feeding its commodities to democratic man, not a culture, as Emerson had hoped, organic with the life of the ordinary man. Pound, not alone among American writers, believed that the American common man (in Emerson's exultant phrasing: "new lands, new men, new thoughts") was of no literary interest except as he might serve as the object of the ridiculing satiric gaze.

Far from being the expression of an American who had forsaken his culture, *The Cantos* are the work of an American experimenter standing at cultural ground zero. This experimenter is a man not unlike Henry James's archetype of the American, who works himself curiously up to cultural snuff—the archetypal modern as major autodidact, of no cultural patrimony, who by sheer effort of discipline acquires all there is to know and whose typical vocal posture before the great European cultural treasures is one of stunned awe; who will address Homer, Ovid, and Dante, *talk* to them in worshipful apostrophe, speak their names as only an adoring American could speak them, as the names of gods; an American who will find certain moments in these writers so excellent that he will repeat them over and over in *The Cantos,* as if he were recording them in a notebook of the most important quotations of the great writers I have read. For all its complexity, *The Cantos* is often the book of wonders of a precocious American student.

By the measure of the ambitious desire of culture-making that moved their writing, *The Cantos* are a failure. They do not engender (or recover) a unified vision or a single narrative; rest upon no stable foundation of concepts; offer no odyssey of character; and for these failures we probably should be grateful. *The Cantos* "are," not "is." *The Cantos* narrate, quote, translate, dramatize, sing, and rant—as literary montage and collage they invite readers to supply the missing totality which would make sense of all the fragments, but what is missing, or only subtly present, is not some deep-seated story that binds all the pieces together into a social whole, but the writer in the act of trying to make sense of his circumstances. In Wallace Stevens's words: "[T]he poem of the mind in the act of finding / What will suffice." It may be that there is a sense in which every age is an age of experiment, and that all writing proceeds in the dark in an effort to find the socially companionable form, but the modernist believes (in this believing is being) that he proceeds in darkness apparently total. Dante and Milton had the cultural gift of the Christian map: Joyce, Eliot, Stevens, and Pound believed their cultures had little to give; believed that they were living in a time when all the stage sets (again Stevens's figure) were being struck (*being* struck: they were witnesses to various dissolutions). They found that the privilege of living in an age of revolution was more than matched by the burdens of modernist culture; they found that they could take nothing for granted; that every thing would need to be re-imagined.

The world of *The Cantos* is close to the world of the later Yeats, who saw the destruction of the great country house as the socially symbolic moment of modernism's inauguration: the end of the politically and socially privileged class and all the artistic life (in all senses) that it ensured and supported (in all senses); the end of the writer's security, the underwriting of his vision blotted out in social upheaval. Adrift in a new world, Yeats is left with his memories and Pound, passionate American reader of the classics, is left with the desire for memory within a new social system— secular, democratic, capitalist—which has no use for the past, and offers no structural support for its artists, whom it does not believe can defend its cities. And it is much worse for Pound, because unlike Yeats he never saw the gracious old American estate which is also cultural matrix—there is no American experience of this; we have no exemplary Coole Park for memory to cherish in the lineage of our American cultural blood, no Coole Park which in unforgiving recollection can be the measure of modernist loss. Unlike Yeats, Pound nurses no delicious and bitter nostalgia (no return-pain), unless we choose to credit his longing (as I do) as a paradox of nostalgia—a New World desire to return to the cultural home he never had.

In the notorious *Pisan Cantos* ("74-84") the poet as modernist steps forward, holding back nothing. Written in a military detention camp in Pisa at the end of the war, and awarded the first Bollingen Prize for Poetry in 1949, to the shock and anger of at least half of the English-speaking literary world, these poems as well as any in the modernist tradition figure forth the modernist writer as the quintessential outsider, in prison now, which is just about where the modernist has always thought he was; literally old, which is what modernist poets often feel even when they're young (as if they had never experienced vaulting zest for life: culturally desiccated from the start, Prufrocks all—a figure Eliot invented as an undergraduate); an old man without a country whose open subject now is himself incessantly in conversation with himself, in elegiac remembrance of writers ancient, Renaissance, and contemporary, friends all, the literal ones also now all dead: Ford, Joyce, Yeats "to earth o'ergiven"; talking his favorite opinions: how economic justice can be ensured through just distribution and reform of the money system; how to collar the "buggering banks"; the role of the "yidds" in the world's exploitation; the cattle-like nature of the "goyim"; the death of Mussolini and the failure of fascism; the desire to build the ideal city; Pound, an old man quoting his favorite phrases poetic and political, and then quoting them again and again; remembering his earlier cantos, alluding to the heroic figures therein; quoting his own lines, especially the one in the first canto about losing all companions: all this talk as if (Robert Frost's phrase) "the talk were all," and it is.

> Pound-the-modernist is a writer in extremis because extremity is his norm; a writer who creates in his experiment a poem precisely adequate to the cultural circumstances of a man, unlike Homer, without a story to tell.
> —*Frank Lentricchia*

The *Pisan Cantos* are jail-talk from solitary confinement (who at Pisa could Pound talk to?), jail-talk gone about as far as the modernist can take it. In the saying of his memories, in their linguistic retrieval and preservation of cultures past (especially the cultures made by writers, recalling what they wrote and sometimes what they did) Pound projects an image of the modernist writer working from the shards of tradition and frustrated political obsession but not working them up into a new culture—placing them, instead, side by side, as he counts the losses. Pound-the-modernist is a writer in extremis because extremity is his norm; a writer who creates in his experiment a poem precisely adequate to the cultural circumstances of a man, unlike Homer, without a story to tell.

No one will take Pound, after what he has revealed, as hero, or moral guide. The Pound in the *Pisan Cantos* is the best answer to the Pound who venerated heroes and thought Mussolini would underwrite economic justice and the independence of the individual. *The Cantos* are a poetry full of heterogeneity to the point of chaos, an indescribable mixture whose ingredients of anti-Semitism and fascism are not of the essence because, in this experiment, nothing is of the essence. The most typical moments of *The Cantos* are those which defy the expectations of typicality: like the moment when out of nowhere we hear a black man speak (blacks in *The Cantos* appear as "coons," "niggers," and "negroes") and we learn that Pound has been done (by this black man) a risky act of charity—against regulations he has been spoken to, and, more, has been built a box upon which to set his typewriter: "[D]oan you tell no one / I made you that table," words that will be repeated through the *Pisan Cantos,* in the same way that phrases from the literary giants are repeated, until Mr. Edwards-who-made-the-box assumes the

status of Sigismundo-who-made-the-Tempio. Mr. Edwards takes his commemorative place with Malatesta because, like Malatesta, he achieved what he achieved against the current of power. (What Mr. Edwards calls a "table," Pound calls a "box"; Mr. Edwards is an imaginative writer of another order.) He, Mr. Edwards, *boxum aedificavit.* And the significance of this act of patronage and charity for the whole of *The Cantos?* Only that a poetry which was written with no encouragement from its culture, and with no possibility of gaining cultural centrality, was helped a little along its way by a patron of the arts who couldn't read it, and who could have no intention, surely, of helping this particular poem come to life and to print.

Ming Xie (essay date Spring 1993)

SOURCE: "Elegy and Personae in Ezra Pound's *Cathay*," in *ELH: English Literary History,* Vol. 60, No. 1, Spring, 1993, pp. 261-81.

[*In the following essay, Xie discusses Pound's interpretation of Chinese verse in* Cathay. *According to Xie, Pound differs from "the Victorian masters of the elegiac before him" through "his skillful and extensive reliance upon the speaker-persona as the primary device for rendering subjective emotion and elegiac mood, as amply and successfully demonstrated in* Cathay.*"*]

Pound first published his *Personae* in 1909, including two previous collections of his poems. The title "Personae" was used again for his collected poems of 1926, and for the selection from these of 1928. That Pound attached great importance to the idea of personae is best summed up in his "Vorticism" of September 1914, in which he called his translations as well as his poems but a series of "elaborate masks." By the time he wrote this, Pound had already possessed the literary manuscripts left by Ernest Fenollosa for about a year and had begun working on them, including the poems that were to make up his *Cathay.* Pound no doubt also had his Chinese poems in mind when he spoke of "casting off" complete masks of the self in his translations. In 1920, he again referred to **"The Seafarer,"** *Cathay,* and **"Homage to Sextus Propertius"** as his "major personae." Yet these Chinese poems were significantly different from his previous experiments with personae. His previous personae were, as Hugh Kenner puts it, "deliberate dramatizations which extend the modes of thinking and feeling accessible to the quotidian inhabitant of a given London decade." And the connection with Browningesque dramatic monologue was often superficial, in that Pound was more interested in the idea of the intense lyrical moment. But what sharply distinguishes Pound from the Victorian masters of the elegiac before him, with the partial exception of [Robert] Browning, is his skillful and extensive reliance upon the speaker-persona as the primary device for rendering subjective emotion and elegiac mood, as amply and successfully demonstrated in *Cathay.*

What sharply distinguishes Pound from the Victorian masters of the elegiac before him, with the partial exception of [Robert] Browning, is his skillful and extensive reliance upon the speaker-persona as the primary device for rendering subjective emotion and elegiac mood, as amply and successfully demonstrated in *Cathay.*
                                        —*Ming Xie*

Pound was consciously using his *Cathay* translations as a counterbalance against what he saw to be the droning of a corrupt elegiac lyricism, as is in his view characteristic of much mid- and late-Victorian poetry. The speakers in [Alfre, Lord] Tennyson's dramatic monologues often seem to drown in a certain dramatically deliberate exaggeration of their melancholy mood. Yet this kind of masterly control and modulation of elegiac cadence and dramatic contrast, not at all rare in Tennyson at his best, was also frequently susceptible to the risk of overly dramatized pathetic excessiveness, particularly in the later imitation or parody of this cadence by lesser Tennysonian epigones. Consider the following version of Kêng Wei's "Lonely" as translated by Herbert Giles:

> The evening sun slants o'er the village street;
>   My griefs alas! in solitude are borne;
> Along the road no wayfarers I meet,—
>   Naught but the autumn breeze across the corn.

The diction of this version has the effect of setting poems in an unspecified period of a romanticized past, and also of naturalizing whatever is poetically different and individualized in an alien poem. Giles's debased and streamlined Victorian elegiac cadence and movement weigh so heavily that the original Chinese poem all but disappears.

To put the late Victorian elegiac tradition in perspective, we might go to [Samuel Taylor] Coleridge who provides a succinct formulation in 1833:

> Elegy is the form of poetry natural to the reflective mind. It may treat of any subject, but it must treat of no subject *for itself:* but always and exclusively with reference to the poet himself. As he will feel regret for the past or desire for the future, so sorrow and love become the principal themes of elegy. Elegy presents every thing as lost and gone, or absent and future. The elegy is the exact opposite of

the Homeric, in which all is purely external and objective, and the poet is a mere voice.

[Matthew] Arnold is of course often ambivalent about the elegiac aspects of his poetry, and criticizes this aspect of his work in his "Preface" to the "Poems of 1853," where he contends strongly against poetry as an allegory of the poet's state of mind and strongly for poetry as representation of an action: "What is not interesting, is that which does not add to our knowledge of any kind; that which is vaguely conceived and loosely drawn; a representation which is general, indeterminate, and faint, instead of being particular, precise, and firm. . . . What are the eternal objects of poetry, among all nations and at all times? They are actions; human actions. . . ." But in practice Arnold is often drawn to elegy and the elegiac even though in his best poems he attempts to exorcise this characteristic collusion.

Arnold's "A Summer Night" provides a prominent example of the nineteenth-century displaced elegy, that is, a poem devising the location and occasion for the feeling expressed by elevated fancy rather than speaking from a context that is literally the predicament of such feeling:

> In the deserted, moon-blanched street,
> How lonely rings the echo of my feet!
> Those windows, which I gaze at, frown,
> Silent and white, unopening down,
> Repellent as the world; but see,
> A break between the housetops shows
> The moon! and, lost behind her, fading dim
> Into the dewy dark obscurity
> Down at the far horizon's rim,
> Doth a whole tract of heaven disclose!

This kind of poem for the most part depends for its effect upon associative meanings generated from within the frame set up by the poet, so that the whole subject matter of the poem is thoroughly subordinated to the dominant emotional or psychological mood imposed by the poet himself. Thus the poet's attention is almost solely devoted to his own elegiac states of mind, without any effort to ground such feelings in the immediate, circumscribed actualities that surround the poet or the poetic persona in the first place. Even when actualities are presented, as often they are with great brilliance and precision by the early Tennyson, they are tacit but unmistakable "objective correlative" devices for expression of prevailing mood; as Eliot succinctly puts it in his essay on "In Memoriam," Tennyson characteristically uses dramatic situation as the occasion for "stating an elegiac mood."

Pound's use of the elegiac is quite different. Consider his version of T'ao Ch'ien's **"To-Em-Mei's 'The Unmoving Cloud,'"** for example:

The clouds have gathered, and gathered,
  and the rain falls and falls,
The eight ply of the heavens
  are all folded into one darkness,
And the wide, flat road stretches out.
I stop in my room toward the East, quiet, quiet,
I pat my new cask of wine.
My friends are estranged, or far distant,
I bow my head and stand still.

Here the sensibility and susceptibility of the poet functions as an impersonal agency for the mood of the persona, giving a complete primacy to the narrative situation from which that mood arises and not appropriating or contaminating it with any oblique opportunism on the part of the poet. The poet establishes the persona as the source and primary sanction for feeling and then tunes his own mood into a matching sympathetic resonance. Pound's version has objectified successfully a mood of the persona, and it invites the reader to experience the distinctness of that mood. This mood is not the same as the Tennysonian elegiac mood which depends for its effect on the reader's more or less subjective identification and often exhibits a progressive, tacit conflation between lyrical mood, the ostensibly dramatized occasion for speech, and the reader's emotional response—a notable aspect of Tennyson's "power of embodying himself in ideal characters," in the words of his friend Arthur Hallam, "or rather moods of characters, with such extreme accuracy of adjustment, that the circumstances of the narration seem to have a natural correspondence with the predominant feeling, and, as it were, to be evolved from it by assimilative force." Hugh Kenner has commented at length on Pound's version:

> The objects, the images, clouds, rain, darkness, the wide flat road, exist not as stage-dressing, as atmospheric props for a display of the writer's chagrin, but as a constellation intrinsically and inevitably related to the inherent mood. (This is a manner of speaking; whether these relationships "existed" before the poet made his stanza is irrelevant to our technical inquiry). They are allotropic components into which the mood, the initial poetic "idea," has been fragmented. Nor is the mood threadbare and familiar, existing for the reader as an evoked memory. It is particular and new.

However, the rhythm and implied outlook of the description in T'ao Ch'ien's original poem firmly imply a central and sponsoring *consciousness,* a center of dramatized personal awareness, which at once functions as the focus and reference for a coherence of implicit feeling as it gradually declares itself by what is observed and what is thought. The explicit tense-logic of the grammar in Pound's version positions a meditative self in a present moment, made desolate by nostalgic contrast with past memories, whereas in more condensed imagistic presentations, this implied consciousness would be denied controlling coherence of a unified mood and may be either reduced or excluded altogether, replaced instead by various other *techniques* such as those of brevity, juxtaposition, and so on.

Michael Alexander suggests that "*Cathay* is in many ways a deeply Tennysonian volume in its matter, its colour, its emotion. But its versification, melody, use of image and directness of language are indeed very different. This difference presents itself primarily as a difference in the 'nature', in the actual landscape. . . ." Certainly the use of landscape or natural imagery in classical Chinese poetry most frequently suggests and embodies an inexorable sense of melancholy and elegiac mood. But the crucial point here is that, though there is a thematic and modal correlation of melancholy thoughts and feelings with expanses of rain-washed landscapes, for the Edwardian or Georgian English reader the codes for these Chinese landscapes, linking them to understood conventions of feeling, were so different that the mood seemed to arise directly from the disjunct economies of description. Vast and empty expanse of water or mountain; imminent snow or darkening twilight; falling rain over a lake or river; solitary human figures in mist: these are a few of the most common images used by various Chinese poets and painters, mostly of the T'ang and Sung period, to suggest a kind of metaphysical loneliness and their elegiac consolation through submerging their subjectivity in the natural landscape itself. Quite often in Chinese poetry no immediate occasion is invoked at all and the feeling of solitude and consolation seems universalized, by means of diminished foreground, although the individual viewer is positioned along various points of the landscape.

This phenomenon in Chinese poetry has much in common with the diffuse and dynamic perspective in many Chinese landscape paintings. Parts of the represented field of view are separated from other parts, and are treated as if remote or floating with reference to the human figures "tethering" the mood to its focus; yet the formal articulation and composition of these levels and zones of separation allow the viewer to read the picture-surface, its recessions and elevations, as coherently *viewed:* this is a kind of ordering and ordered perspective usually called a "parallel perspective" or a "multiple station-point." Earlier Chinese landscape views of more panoramic or extended vertical dimension (lofty mountains and great waterfalls, for example) assumed several separate viewpoints, so that the viewer was "imagined as standing point blank in front of that part of the surface on which the object is presented." The effacement of subjective feeling, the presence of cosmic melancholy, the enormous scale of natural landscape, the absence of personal pronouns: all these help to make up a distinctive class of poems of pictorial solitude and plaintive consolation. These qualities have been well captured by Pound, in the opening lines of his **"canto 49"**, which is based on a series of Chinese landscape poems inscribed on paintings:

> Rain; empty river; a voyage,
> Fire from frozen cloud, heavy rain in the twilight
> Under the cabin roof was one lantern.
> The reeds are heavy; bent;
> and the bamboos speak as if weeping.

"And the bamboos speak *as if* weeping": had this piece been an attempt at imagist writing, the younger Pound would surely have struck out this weakly explicit comparative. Yet here it is just, and it works, because the "surface" description of natural objects, while displacing any explicit expression of hidden emotion, also dramatizes the displaced and thus invisible depth of that emotion. Generically, the notable thing about these poems in **"canto 49"** is their extreme brevity, since in nineteenth-century (and also earlier) English poetry the elegy invariably implies and occasions a more developed amplitude of expression. Yet the fragmented appearance of Pound's images is deceptive, for paradoxically there is a strongly implied presence of narrative continuity: the semicolons here function similarly as the colon in that they are quasi-narrative markers which point both forward and backward and thus link the seemingly isolated images into an implied sequence of expressive narration.

Cathay was published in April 1915, with Pound's Anglo-Saxon adaptation **"The Seafarer"** included between **"The Exile's Letter"** and the **"Four Poems of Departure."** The whole collection could be construed as having a topical meaning and significance when it first appeared, as probably the **"Seafarer"** insertion was originally meant to suggest a certain implicit relation between the thematic formula of the First World War. Indeed, Kenner thinks that *Cathay* is "largely a war book, using Fenollosa's notes much as Pope used Horace or Johnson Juvenal, to supply a system of parallels and a structure of discourse" by means of "an oriental obliquity of reference." This is no doubt true. From among the diverse wealth of the Fenollosa notes for Chinese poems at Pound's disposal at the time, he selected only a dozen or so to make up *Cathay,* evidently more interested in the type of poems that embrace themes of war and exile, separation and heroism, and other related themes.

Again, the coupling of **"The Seafarer"** with **"The Exile's Letter"** in particular is significant for Pound, who believes that the *Seafarer* is the only European poem of the period that can be weighed on the same scale as Li Po's "The Exile's Letter." Pound's sense of the equivalence of the two poems is more than a mere comparison in terms of the national literatures they are supposed to represent. Pound's secularization of the Anglo-Saxon *Seafarer* is not motivated by sheer textual considerations: "The groundwork may have

been a longer narrative poem, but the 'lyric', as I have accepted it, divides fairly well into 'The Trials of the Sea,' its Lure and the Lament for Age." Pound's emphasis on the "lyric" suggests that he regarded *The Seafarer* as a dramatic lyric. The unhesitant dramatic quality of feeling and mood and the directness of address in the form of the dramatic lyric link Pound's **"The Seafarer"** with poems like **"The Exile's Letter"** or **"The River-Merchant's Wife: a Letter,"** and the poet of *The Seafarer* with **"Rihaku,"** with Pound presiding over both. It is the elegiac genre and theme of exile that led Pound to translate *The Seafarer* as we have it now. Pound stresses the elements of exile and solitude and nostalgia even more than the original Anglo-Saxon poem. The Anglo-Saxon elegy deals chiefly with the theme of exile, as different from the tradition of the classical pastoral elegy. Though it is strongly conditioned by its generic and rhetorical formulae, *The Seafarer* clearly exhibits a dramatization and projection of subjective mood, the emotional predicament inherent in a mode of life given individual focus in an explicitly personal narrative, as is similarly the case in Pound's **"The Exile's Letter"** with its form of personal statement and individualized narrative. **"The Seafarer"** and **"The Exile's Letter"** share a similarity of attitude and value in their respective personae—a recognizable type of individual predicament (seafarer and exile) and a defiance through indifference to conventional attitudes. It is thus possible for Pound to enact, through his adopted Anglo-Saxon and Chinese masks, his own personal and historical situation. Although never unmistakably explicit, this meaning is nevertheless implied clearly enough. In selecting the group of **"Rihaku"** poems of exile and solitude, Pound follows his own generic considerations, and in translating them, develops his own generic framework and personal style which have been determinants for the later writings in the *Cantos*.

The sense of exile and estrangement is also markedly different from melancholy: this is perhaps why Pound deliberately introduces a strong note of antibourgeois stringency into his version of *The Seafarer.* With the *Cathay* poems, he tries to employ radical structural strategies, for example, a greater reliance on and exploitation of the individual speaker in each poem. In these poems Pound follows the prosaic realism of the original Chinese and accentuates the particular emotional and psychological qualities that reside within the completeness of each individual speaker. **"The River-Merchant's Wife: a Letter"** and **"The River Song"** are examples of this strategy.

Pound's own gradual evolution from his experiments with the "hokku-like" sentences, the epigrams and epitaphs in the earlier poems, to the longer *Cathay* poems in which the elegiac mood prevails, indicates his gradual generic modulation of the epigrammic into the elegiac, paralleled by his developing theory of the Image. As a result Pound extended the repertoire of elegy by modulating it into a mixture of styles and moods: the epigrammic, the rhetorical, the dramatic, the narrative, the epistolary, and so on, all to be unified in a cluster of simple, natural and distinct images.

The connection between Pound's haiku images and his earlier epigrams might be viewed as the logical precedent for what he sets out to do in the *Cathay* poems. Alastair Fowler suggests that "rejection of Victorian poetic diction by the modernists has had the indirect effect of making the survival of elegiac poetry depend on epigram, which now provides its usual external form." David Lindley's distinction between epigram and elegy is also extremely suggestive here: "Where epigram pushes the lyric towards compression, elegy opens it, among other things, to quasi-personal 'passionate meditation.'" It might be said that Pound's apparent ignorance of Chinese and Chinese literary forms has perhaps enabled him to modulate and transpose freely the original Chinese poems in terms adapted to his own generic experiments and expressive considerations. He was perhaps fortunate enough not to be in a position to render literally from the original Chinese; he evidently derived a stimulus to innovate forms of a more immediate expressiveness from this ostensibly unpromising activity, that of translating from a language not fully understood. His Provençal versions, by contrast, do not have this radical directness.

Pound's **"Lament of the Frontier Guard,"** for instance, shows his ability to handle creatively, yet still under constraints, Fenollosa's notes for the poem:

> By the North Gate, the wind blows full of sand,
> Lonely from the beginning of time until now!
> Trees fall, the grass goes yellow with autumn.
> I climb the towers and towers
>   to watch out the barbarous land:
> Desolate castle, the sky, the wide-desert.

It is notable that Pound's new title for the poem makes the poem a monologue spoken by the guard: what in the original is the "barbarian pass" (*hu-kuan*), the whole corridor across which the invaders push southwards, is for Pound "the North Gate": it is but the last outpost of the empire left to be defended by those posted to it. Thus the guard is lonely, hence the whole place is so; the "desolation" of that emptiness is personalized by the voice which speaks of it: the guard's tour of duty seems to last for ever, in its wearisome isolation, and yet it is the briefest interval in a vast expanse of time matching the vastness of space.

Pound here has grasped the latent psychology of this contrast, following the hints from Fenollosa, because he was ready to import a little of Browning's psychology of dramatic mood, entitling the poem as **"The *Lament* of the Frontier Guard"** (Li Po's title is simply "Ancient Style, No. 14"), to bring in a central defining pronoun "I" (Li Po's poem does

not specify the singularly personal speaker) as the locus or pivot for these contrasts: thus trees, formerly standing "naturally," fall to the ground, but towers and castles, built by man, hold out against this wastage of time. Yet by an irony already latent in the mood of the "lament" the wastage of time will eventually destroy all the works of man, the high heaps again covered with natural vegetations:

> Desolate castle, the sky, the wide desert.
> There is no wall left to this village.
> Bones white with a thousand frosts,
> High heaps, covered with trees and grass;

In the Chinese line "desolate-castle-empty-vast-desert," the middle character "empty" is ambiguous enough to serve both as a "verb" reinforcing "vast desert" and as a "verb" (past participial in this case) looking back to "desolate castle": the desolate castle *made more empty* by the vastness of the desert. Pound's version captures this pivotal image in its complexity as well as its simplicity. Partly the complexity is given by the interactive ambiguities of the key terms at the start and finish of the line, with their associations and overtones in English: "desolate" and "desert." The castle is *desolate* because as a far outpost it is solitary and alone, far from human habitation, on the edge of the barren emptiness which is the *desert*. But the dreary sorrow of personal isolation and wretchedness is matched by seeing the barbarous lands as *deserted,* forlorn and abandoned. All these aspects interact and empty their senses into the vast neutral emptiness of *sky* "Desolate castle, the sky, the wide desert."

> And sorrow, sorrow like rain,
> Sorrow to go, and sorrow, sorrow returning.
> Desolate, desolate fields,
> And no children of warfare upon them,
>   No longer the men for offence and defence.

Here omitting the word "tears" supplied by Fenollosa's crib, Pound has grafted "like rain" straight on to "sorrow, sorrow," thus effecting a memorable abstract-concrete simile. Since in Western tradition fighting soldiers are not supposed to weep at their posts but instead often turn their emotion into a kind of half-joke, as in the exotic last line of Pound's version, the overall shape and development of sorrowful feeling is itself "translated": "A gracious spring, turned to blood-ravenous autumn, / A turmoil of wars-men, spread over the middle kingdom." Note the tacit pun on ravening/raven (the carrion bird of ill omen on the battlefield), and the comparably tacit reference to heroic warrior-elegy in the north-European tradition in Pound's line near the end of the poem: "Ah, how shall you know the *dreary* sorrow at the North Gate." "Dreary," from the Anglo-Saxon *dreorig,* means dark with spilled blood. Pound here assembles and draws upon his latent precedents, to diagnose and express the fundamental mood of the poem. The word "dreary," in variant archaic forms, also appears in Pound's **"The Sea-farer"** and in **"canto 1"**.

It must be stressed here, though, that the Anglo-Saxon *Seafarer* represents a kind of proto-elegy in which the primitive oral element predominates, whereas the more modern kind of elegy or elegiac poem is distinctively personal. The generic framework of classical elegy has gradually evolved into the poem of the elegiac mood during the major part of the nineteenth century. Tennyson's *In Memoriam* would be a pivotal example, because it was so complex and so massively influential. In the late eighteenth century, [Thomas] Gray ("Elegy Written in a Country Churchyard"), [Oliver] Goldsmith ("The Deserted Village") and [William] Cowper ("The Poplar-Field") had defined for later Romanticism and the whole nineteenth century "the elegiac tone as a mood rather than as a formal mode." "Farm House on the Wei Stream" by the T'ang poet Wang Wei, as translated by Amy Lowell, reminds one of the elegiac poems by Goldsmith (his "The Deserted Village" for example):

> The slanting sun shines on the cluster of small
>   houses upon the heights.
> Oxen and sheep are coming home along the distant
>   lane.
> An old countryman is thinking of the herd-boy,
> He leans on his staff by the thorn-branch gate,
>   watching.
> Pheasants are calling, the wheat is coming into ear,
> Silk-worms sleep, the mulberry-leaves are thin.
> Labourers, with their hoes over their shoulders,
>   arrive;
> They speak pleasantly together, loth to part.
> It is for this I long—unambitious peace!
> Disappointed in my hopes, dissatisfied, I hum
>   "Dwindled and Shrunken."

Of course, it is the community which has "dwindled" for Goldsmith, as the rural population leave the fields of their forefathers; whereas in the more individualized personal mood-elegy it is the individual speaker who is isolated and unhappy from the separating consciousness and sometimes tacit self-congratulation of his own sorrowfulness. The narrative and thus prospective element diminishes as the retrospective element increases, eventually to produce an overwhelming mood devouring everything: this is what Pound was to see as the corrupt elegiac lyricism most typical in Victorian poetry. However, first-person autobiographical elegy is a much more difficult case, because it is frequently the *ambiguity* of the self or person presented that may cause the reader the greatest difficult. Arthur Waley's version of "The Chrysanthemum in the Eastern Garden" by Po Chü-i is one such example:

> The days of my youth left me long ago;

> And now in their turn dwindle my years of prime.
> With what thoughts of sadness and loneliness
> I walk again in this cold, deserted place!
> In the midst of the garden long I stand alone;
> The sunshine, faint; the wind and dew chill.
> The autumn lettuce is tangled and turned to seed;
> The fair trees are blighted and withered away.
> All that is left are a few chrysanthemum-flowers
> That have newly opened beneath the wattled
>   fence.

Here within the objective setting of the garden the elegiac self tries to establish its own present validity and solidity by way of reflection and *anagnorisis;* yet the very identity of this self is threatened by the multiple functions it tries to embrace: the elegiac self is both the focus and occasion of present feeling, while also serving as the free epitome of its recognition. In addition there is the bound subjectivity of the first-person self. Across the pattern of these shifting relations the reader's position is not at all easily determined.

By contrast, Pound consciously strives for the clear presentation of narrative and emotion and displays a much more effective use of the dramatic lyric medium to render precisely the predicament of the original Chinese protagonists. And here the elegiac poetry of Thomas Hardy can serve as a useful comparison. Pound has said that Hardy "woke one to the extent of his own absorption in *subject* as contrasted with aesthetes' preoccupation with 'treatment.'" "Hardy at his best stems out of Browning, as Ford does, and does so by shedding his encrustation." Pound praises Hardy's elegies of 1912-1913 as the best among Hardy's poems. The *Cathay* poems also display the importance of a certain kind of provincialism of feeling, feeling deeply rooted in details of the actual circumscribed world of the protagonists. In this respect they closely resemble Hardy's "dramatic or personative" poems, especially those from his *Poems of 1912-13:* "The Going," "The Voice," "After a Journey," and "A Wet August," for example, though Hardy is frequently more dramatic and ironic. But the similarities abound: both Pound and Hardy are often concerned with the reality of memory and retrospection, regret and melancholy, time and consolation. One chief characteristic of Hardy's speaking voice in the first-person elegiac poem which differentiates him from Pound is the ghostly, barren, and depersonalized present self as compared to the vitality and personal involvements of the remembered past life: this is a principal irony for Hardy, that the narrating voice is always belated in regard to the events which have meaning for it, isolated in an empty present in which memory can be called upon but no longer shared, except vicariously, with the reader.

The use of natural imagery in the *Cathay* poems is often of primary importance. There is a natural relation of the natural setting to the speaking and observing persona in the poems, as well as a sense of distance that separates the observer or speaker from the natural world that he or she observes. But the resulting tension is precisely what is most important in any good poem. Here Pound differs from Hardy's procedure, partly because of the translator's constraints but more importantly because of Pound's complete trust in the matter of his Chinese poems; there is no arbitrary or dramatic staging of either personae or natural images for certain subjective effects. In Hardy's verse the inevitability of emotion and sadness often combines with the installation of certain particular figures or scenes to produce an elaborate apparatus for capturing and rendering past experiences. Most of the *Cathay* poems do not exhibit this elaborateness with regard to both scene and persona; these poems seem more reticent in their articulation of personal loss and sadness. For example, the image of "flowers falling" at the end of Pound's version of **"The Exile's Letter"** by Li Po functions both as a reminder of the distance between the persona and the natural setting and as the persona's subjective identification with the natural world:

> And if you ask how I regret that parting:
> It is like the flowers falling at Spring's end
>   Confused, whirled in a tangle.

Such images exhibit the sense of control and restraint, so characteristic of much of Chinese poetry, in the expression of strong emotion and feeling, especially passionate love between man and woman. Such reticence and impassivity are very well conveyed in most English translations from the Chinese, including those of Arthur Waley. But it must have suited Waley to maintain a coyly decorous absence of recognizably particular and overtly personal emotion in Chinese poetry, a kind of Edwardian or Georgian reticence and understatement about personal and intimate feelings. Pound himself in part suffers from this coyness of his age, while trying hard to shake it off. As for Hardy, characteristically, all passion lies in the past, so for Pound it was often found most alive in the forms of alien and remote cultures, whereas Waley by contrast has sought to bury passionate expression of feeling or emotion in respectable discretion and understatement.

Pound has complete trust in the subject-matter of the poems he translates; the emotions of the personae in these poems are completely real for him. He is always seeking out specific European cognates whenever he discusses Chinese poetry. The form and subject-matter of **"The River-Merchant's Wife: a Letter,"** for example, has its cognates in European literary traditions too: especially in some of Browning's poems such as "Men and Women" which, Pound believes, belong to the tradition of Ovid's "Heroides" and Theocritus' idyls, while the special feature of Li Po's poem is its grace and simplicity. The "simplicity" and beauty of this poem (both the original Chinese poem and Pound's ver-

sion of it) consist chiefly in the convincing speaking voice of the persona, yet full of emotional maturity and sophistication.

A. R. Orage believed that Pound's **"The Seafarer"** is "a little less perfect; it has not the pure simplicity of its Chinese exemplars. On the other hand, it is as we should expect, a little more manly in its sentiment." Orage also noted the similarity between Browning's "Bishop Bloughram's Apology" and Pound's **"The River-Merchant's Wife: a Letter"** in terms of their "natural" simplicity: "The difference is that Browning was 'perfecting' the expression of a powerful and subtle mind, while Rihaku was perfecting the mind relatively of a child. The extension of the directness and simplicity, the veracity and the actuality aimed at by vers librists, into the subtler regions than the commonplace is advisable if they are not to keep in the nursery of art." Perhaps deliberately, Pound has brought over and constructed the image of a tender, ordinary, yet emotionally sophisticated and mature woman in his rendition of **"The River-Merchant's Wife: a Letter"**:

> While my hair was still cut straight across my
>   forehead
> I played about the front gate, pulling flowers.
> You came by on bamboo stilts, playing horse,
> You walked about my seat, playing with blue
>   plums.
> And we went on living in the village of Chokan:
> Two small people, without dislike or suspicion.
>
> At fourteen I married My Lord you.
> I never laughed, being bashful.
> Lowering my head, I looked at the wall.
> Called to, a thousand times, I never looked back.
>
> At fifteen I stopped scowling,
> I desired my dust to be mingled with yours
> Forever and forever and forever.
> Why should I climb the look out?
>
> At sixteen you departed,
> You went into far Ku-to-yen, by the river of
>   swirling eddies,
> And you have been gone five months.
> The monkeys make sorrowful noise overhead.

In Pound's version the emotion of the woman speaker is presented within her confined perspective through particular stages of emotional development and psychological retrospection, out of which emerge different shades of meaning and significance. It is significant that Pound finds it necessary to divide the original Chinese poem into different stanzas or strophes, in order to delineate more sharply and contrastively the successive stages of retrospection and revelation. In the original Chinese poem, due to lack of speci- fied relations of tense or number, the narrative sequence is not explicitly established by the syntactical markers. It is therefore all the more difficult for the English translator to grasp the intimations of feeling and attitude in the original and to devise an effective inner logic of psychological de- velopment.

Thus the English translator is called upon to utilize what- ever resources in English he or she can muster, in order to present a convincing structure of feeling and sensibility in a new English poem. The word "still" in Pound's first line, for instance, is absent from both the original Chinese poem and Fenollosa's transcriptions. Pound's "still" thus introduces into the narrative a prefigured sense of lost innocence, nos- talgic pleasure, and subsequent frustration from the point of view of the woman speaker before she married her present "Lord." Her girlish confidence in perpetual romance is im- plicit in "Forever and forever and forever" (this is, in fact, Pound's addition), because the ironies inherent in life had by that stage not yet made their first appearance: at the start of the poem the reader is asked to recognize that he, as a reader, knows more of what is to come than she does ("still"). A sense of retrospective ambivalence and nostal- gia is thereby subtly implied.

If in the first part of the **"River-Merchant's Wife: a Let- ter"** he more or less follows Fenollosa's original phrasings, Pound departs significantly from them in the second half in terms of rhythm and speech representation as necessitated by his own adopted strategy of translating the poem into a dramatic lyric, a structure of feeling generated from within the speaking persona.

> You dragged your feet when you went out.
> By the gate now, the moss is grown, the different
>   mosses,
> Too deep to clear them away!
> The leaves fall early this autumn, in wind.
> The paired butterflies are already yellow with
>   August
> Over the grass in the West garden;
> They hurt me. I grow older.

This is a strikingly direct presentation of emotional naked- ness of the woman speaker, dramatizing as it does the subtle- ties of love, sorrow and ambivalence by closely following the inner speech rhythm of the speaker herself. Pound's "The leaves fall early this autumn, in wind," modifying Fenollosa's notes but still retaining the essentials, wonderfully recreates the emotional implication of the Chinese line as a whole. It is comparable to Hardy's closing lines in the "The Voice" (1912). In Pound's **"River-Merchant's Wife: a Letter,"** there is a complex psychological interaction between the tone of playful, childish innocence, carefree and ironically

insouciant ("I never looked back"), and the sorrowful grav- ity of a young wife suddenly made older by the loneliness and anxiety of separation. Because the young wife in Li Po's poem is unpracticed in grief, she feels all the more sharply what are in fact all the traditional signs of her desertion and solitariness: the moss, the paired butterflies, and the autumn leaves falling in wind. Freshly to her, they hurt. To put the full stop after *me,* and then state "I grow older," is a display of great control and objectivity on the part of Pound the translating poet. The young woman *feels* that she is grow- ing older, aging by having to bear this hurt so early in life by an abrupt gap in the onflow of her short-lived happiness. The *ending* (represented by the full stop) of her happiness makes her realize that life's bitterness and wantonness have started and await her in the future: "They hurt me. I grow older." She is too demure to complain openly, and Pound, through his tacit understanding, remains rather too discreet to hint at this, since she seems to have no reason to reproach her husband who as a merchant has to rely on his travel for their survival, so that his is not a tacit abandonment.

In Pound's version, this acute sense of time and change is again captured in the word "already" of the following line: "The paired butterflies are already yellow with August." The woman has begun to notice *for the first time* the change of the seasons and to recognize the painful images of their tran- sience and mutability. And then she reminds herself that what makes leaves fall, early or not, is not grief or anxiety but wind ("The leaves fall early this autumn, *in wind*": "in wind" is poignantly isolated by a comma), so that the source of her present predicament is a natural cause for a natural phenom- enon. Yet there is an even more somber underlying sugges- tion that grief itself may be "natural," part of the "natural" course of things, the autumn season coming earlier or later, inciting "natural" human emotion but beyond human con- trol.

"The River Song" is made up of two poems by Li Po, the title of the second poem being versified and submerged in Pound's version. The dramatic irony in the new context of Pound's version emerges from the persona's unique position and perspective, the ironic contrast between the two parts of the poem being generated from within the poem through the speaker's individualized response to a succession of im- ages underscored by the very sequence of narration and re- flection:

> He returns by way of Sei rock, to hear to hear the
>   new nightingales,
> For the gardens at Jo-run are full of new nightin-
>   gales,
> Their sound is mixed in *this flute,*
> Their voice is in the twelve pipes *here.*

Here, the word "this" in "this flute" echoes the first word in

Pound's version: "This boat is of shato-wood . . . ," thus binding the whole poem together across the diverse parts and aspects of the two Chinese poems thus conflated. The specified reference to the dramatic-lyrical persona clinches the whole poem's meaning with an intensely dramatic disclosure. In Pound's new poem, if we take it that the poem's speaker is a poet, out carousing on a splendid and expensive boat and entertained with flute and pipes, remembering how he had lingered in the Emperor's garden "awaiting an order-to-write" ("And I *have moped* in the Emperor's garden. . . ." and then the memory changed into the past tense), we can indeed take the section starting "the eastern wind" to be the poem that he writes or recalls, leading back into the garden where he awaited his order and the sound of those remembered nightingales "rhyming" with the flute and pipes on the boat *here* ("*This* boat . . . ," "the twelve pipes *here*"). If so, the conflation of the two poems would indeed be deliberate, because in Pound's new poem the first contains as it were the setting for the writing of the second, and also contains its author. In this respect, the poem is more akin to what Pound defines as the "Noh" image rather than being merely Browningesque monologue. But in one respect, the "moping poet" of Pound's version can be seen as a piece of Browningesque irony, in that the court-poet, waiting for the imperial nomination of a theme for composition, heard the nightingales' singing as "aimless" because he was not free to respond to it or even to take notice of it. The exaggerated cacophony of these birds ("five-score") is in sharp contrast with all the potentially sensitive and interesting images that were wasted simply because the poet was unassigned. But now, in the poem's present tense, the poet is in full spate of delicate observation and description: "the fine birds sing to each other" and so on. In this light, Pound's version is not a literal translation, but a rendering and reshaping of the original persona in a new dramatic-lyrical situation.

Thus Pound consciously or unconsciously superimposes Browningesque monologue and Poundian lyrical persona to from one poem. He emphasizes the *virtù* of the persona of the poem being translated. In the "Lament" poem, for example, Pound introduces near the end of his version "Ah, how shall you know the dreary sorrow at the North Gate," where the "Ah" testifies to the extent to which Pound is able to enter into the original Chinese and emerge out of it with a transmuted sense of emotional paradox and irony, unifying the whole apparatus of the rhetorical voice in the traditional planctus cry of the lament poem.

In *Cathay* Pound frequently invokes vocalized speakers, whether the personae themselves or the projected voices of the personae, whereas these voices are mostly absent or only latent in their Chinese originals. Pound ends **"To-Em-Mei's 'The Unmoving Cloud'"** with the birds' speech:

> The birds flutter to rest in my tree,
> and I think I have heard them saying,
> 'It is not that there are no other men
> But we like this fellow the best,
> But however we long to speak
> He can not know of our sorrow.'

I think I have heard them saying this is purely Pound's own addition. Pound's version dramatizes the presence of the birds, not in order to displace the focus of personal elegiac meditation of T'ao Ch'ien's poem and thus to transform it into a different poem about the sorrow of the birds, but to find an analogy of sorrowful feeling in the birds themselves. Thus the emotion of the solitary who cannot speak his feelings directly because he has no human company is mimicked with a peculiar pathos by the birds who have plenty of company and many voices but who also cannot communicate their sorrow. The birds are given a kind of demotic speech ("this fellow") because they are also a common bunch: their fanciful grief thus imagined and imputed must of course be all in the mind and heart of the desolate human onlooker. But the solitary human figure has momentarily become all transparent—a kind of objective vehicle for embodying a mood—so that the reader does not really see him, but rather sees *through* his eyes and *beyond* him to a nature outside his window from which he has been alienated, so that the solitary human can only *think* that he hears the message of the birds.

The individualized perspective in *Cathay* is for the most part retrospective and is almost always tinged with an elegiac coloring. Yet this coloring is not a general, all-pervasive mood or atmosphere enveloping or devouring the individual speakers in the poems. It also often tends to leave the emotional stance of the translating poet (Pound in this case) somewhat uncommitted, in a kind of sympathetic neutrality, not by any implicit collusion expressing his own personal elegiac feeling. Thus the expression of this elegiac mood or feeling exists on three levels: that of the original Chinese poet being translated, that of Pound the translator, following Fenollosa's often neutral and uncommitted cribs, and finally the implied voice or stance of the resulting poem in English. These three levels are often not easily distinguishable; in a given poem they may exist simultaneously as a kind of superimposition of one upon the other.

Tennyson and other Victorian poets often, if not always, invoked a kind of elegiac collusion, whereas, to Pound, Joyce in his *Dubliners* was very close to the pathos and sense of suppressed unhappiness in his characters but remained fastidiously impartial in the matter of his own feelings. For Pound, Flaubert was the master to be set in contrast to the Tennysonian tradition. With the *Cathay* poems Pound comes closer to the Browningesque dramatic monologue, in that they depend very much on the individual speakers and their narratives for dramatic development and psychological truth, rather than solely on generalized moments of subjective lyricism. The speaker of each of the poems in *Cathay* is engaged in a particular dramatic monologue, dramatizing the narrated facts or events or imaginings in his or her individual life. However, the dramatic monologue of the *Cathay* poems differs greatly from the characteristic Browning monologue. Browning's speakers are often there to provide some striking perspective on certain unusual moral or emotional motives. Yet it has to be emphasized that in English the Chinese poems are decidedly unusual, especially so to the English readers of the time when *Cathay* was first published. The unusual for Pound is often replaced by the *culturally* distant, unfamiliar and hard to retrieve as vital rather than merely antiquarian.

The *Cathay* poems as a whole do not provide some extraordinary moral perspective in which the reader would be invited to judge morally; rather, they almost invariably invite the reader to participate and sympathize in an ordinary yet highly individualized emotional or psychological perspective, except that the exotic and unfamiliar context—alien culture, lack of historical background or perspective as well as strange, unknown names—makes this for the Western reader "ordinary" only by an act of consciously maintained vicarious projection, not altogether different from, if not more extreme than, Browning's Renaissance Italy. Pound's narratives in *Cathay* do exert this leverage on the Western reader's imagination by presenting, as if in realistic description, actions and settings which a Western reader can only reconstruct by rather exotic envisagement. So the mood is muted and low-key, as if belonging to a familiar naturalism of emotional coding where hints and intimations are all that is needed. And yet all these narratives are to a significant degree alien and unfamiliar: they represent a remote and strange domesticity and moral ambiance which the Western reader cannot take in knowingly but must rather apprehend by acts of extended and parallel intuition. So that what looks so strange can yet seem so familiar, and it is perhaps the nuances of implied irony that give the rhythm of a poem its tension and laconic artfulness.

Salah el Moncef (essay date Spring 1995)

SOURCE: "Gold, Representation, and the Reversible Dynamic of Symptomatic Return in Ezra Pound," in *Boundary 2,* Vol. 22, No. 1, Spring 1995, pp. 117-42.

[In the following essay, Moncef examines Pound's disdain for gold as a symbol of evil. According to Moncef, "the malevolent aspect of gold exists in its own right throughout Pound's works; however, within this negative imaginary dimension of gold, there also lies its positive *function as a master-signifier of discursive and economic author-ity."]*

Gold and silver have been established by a general agreement as the means of purchasing all goods, and as a pledge of their value, because these metals are rare, and useless for any other purpose: of what consequence was it to us, then, that they should become more common, and that to mark the value of any commodity, we should have two or three signs in place of one? . . . [A]miable simplicity, so dear to our holy Prophet, constantly recalls me to the artlessness of the olden time, and the peace which reigned in the hearts of our first fathers.

—Montesquieu, *The Persian Letters,* Letter 106

So much has been written about Pound's obsessive deprecation of gold that one can hardly avoid approaching the subject without confronting a sort of Manichean division whereby gold is relegated to an almost exclusively "evil" function in his works. Even if we limit ourselves to the vague parameters of "good" and "evil," however, a close inquiry into the symbolic (that is, discursive) implications of gold in Pound's writings reveals its highly ambivalent function of a condensed signifier that points to a complex interplay of both "good" and "malevolent connotations." As Peter Nicholls rightly argues, when viewed against the background of a debilitating overproduction of monetary signifiers, gold undoubtedly emerges in Pound's writing as a malevolent master-signifier, the obsessive index of a "psychological" fear of the *dislocation* of "the genuinely creative signifying system." I shall argue that this anxiety ultimately reflects the poet's fear of symbolic castration through dislocution and his relegation to the status of a dead author. Considering the recurrence of Pound's *explicitly* negative statements about gold and money, it is tempting to take his words at face value and see in his obsession with the destabilization of monetary and discursive referentiality a desire to reject gold as *the* cause of the destabilization—which would be a typically Poundian strategy.

One way to deal with the facile one-sidedness of this temptation is to articulate Pound's fear for the "genuinely creative signifying system" as a motive inseparable from his fear for the monetary signifying system. The analogous relation between a literary medium of representation based on nonreferentiality and the dissemination of meaning in what Pound defines as an "abstract" monetary discourse has been investigated by Jean-Joseph Goux, who posits the principle of nonreferential money as the paradigm of a literary discourse "devoid of . . . evocative capacity":

The token, as a word or a currency devoid of all evocative capacity, is therefore, in turn, the symbol of formalized reason. . . . Thus all exchange [monetary, discursive] is done through a mediating substitute, or a substitute of a substitute, indefinite deferral. . . . Nowhere *presence*. Always *deferral*.

In Pound's works, a similar occurrence of gold as the master-signifier of a morbid overproduction of dead, non-"evocative" monetary signs (the **Hell Cantos**) and its elusive otherness vis-à-vis the poet (**"Canto 1"**) argue for its qualification as the symptomatic signifier of a subject fearing a fundamental loss of symbolic mastery at the hands of an all-powerful agency.

For this reason, one might argue that Pound's conscious pronouncements on the relation between usurious gold and the dislocation of the order of monetary and discursive representation is the simple sum of a binary education in a paranoid construct. From a Manichean perspective, the obsession with "usurocratic" gold in particular and the "toxicology of money" in general is the subjective symptom of a suppressed fear of physical dislocation and discursive dislocution: the literal and the symbolic castration of the authorial self. In **"Canto 74,"** for instance, this symptomatic return of Pound's subjective fear of physical and symbolic castration emerges transformed into the *social* symptom of a usury-sapped, impotent "culture [that] lies shattered in fragments," a culture whose incomprehensible economic structure "has become a closed book to the aesthetes." My adoption of the term *symptom* in relation to Pound's dislocation-dislocution anxiety owes much to the Freudian dynamic of symptomatic return, the "substitutive process" whereby a repressed "instinctual impulse" returns in a "displaced" way: in Pound's case, castration anxiety returns in the form of an obsession with the deconstructive influence of usurocracy on the order of discursive and monetary representation.

Having examined this dimension of gold, however, the same disturbing question remains: all negative aspects of the question considered, does Pound write binarily about gold as an exclusively "good" or "evil" agency; or does the latter emerge throughout his career (and often against his authorial intentions) as an ambiguously "good" *and* "evil" signifier that can invest itself with a baffling form of reversibility, an alternate power of attractiveness and repulsiveness that the poet's conscious comprehension fails to corner? Even if, admitting to a shift in his outlook on the question, we argue that Pound's conception of gold *becomes* predominantly negative at a certain point in his career, we are still likely to miss the extremely ambivalent and far-reaching meaning of this signifier's double function as a telling index of the ideological dynamic at work in his poetic, cultural, economic, and political agendas. As I shall try to demonstrate, the very assumption of gold as the signifier of reversibility answers the first part of the question by ruling it out as simplistic.

If we stop ascribing to gold an exclusively negative capacity of subversiveness, its symptomatic emergence in Pound's imagination starts occupying the double role of an agency that is debilitating not simply through sheer inert malevolence but through a mortifying *power* of subjection. As I have suggested above, the malevolent aspect of gold exists in its own right throughout Pound's works; however, within this negative imaginary dimension of gold, there also lies its *positive* function as the master-signifier of discursive and economic author-ity. This function of gold as a condensed signifier becomes emblematic of the poet's and society's impotence only insofar as its supplementing power is withheld from the "right" poet or the "right" politician who suffers from its demonic otherness—that is, its alienation and its misappropriation by the subverters of concrete monetary and discursive representation: the agents of abstract usurocracy. This reversibility of the function of gold (its protean capacity to shift, according to who possesses it, from the signifier of monetary and discursive power to the demonic emblem of impotence) partly explains Pound's ambivalence toward the monopolizers of wealth in general. Hence the fundamental impossibility of simplistically polarizing the function of gold as "good" or "evil," and the necessity of viewing it as a condensed signifier and a strong motive force behind Pound's economics and poetics: one of his key metaphors for rationalizing the systemic contradictions of the order of monetary and discursive representation.

At this level of conflation between subjective and systemic rationalization, the integration of the marginal usurpers of gold in the Poundian demonological scene becomes a conditional *necessity* in Pound's views on monetary and discursive representation in particular, and in his cultural and political outlook in general. Those usurpers, the aliens of the Western economic and cultural scene, are naturally the usurers who, through a strange effect of displacement, are transferred beyond the purely economic sphere and made to function as the morbid other of the true poet, the "perverters of language," whose presence saps the poet's voice, condemning it to the symbolic castration of dislocution. If we assume, as Pound does, that the hoarding of gold and then the dissemination of its imaginary value along a chain of signifiers without objectal signifieds implies the loss of all meaning, then it seems quite plausible to posit it as the paradigm of an *initially* referential discourse that gets sucked into what is, in Pound's poetics, the equivalent of a spatial black hole. By this black hole I mean, of course, the "muzziness" of nonreferential chaos, the discursive element that absorbs the "soft" poet unable to "cut in hard substance." It is a measure of the complexity of gold as a condensed signifier that it has come to occupy this conflationary point where a seemingly subjective symptom ends up reflecting a broader literary, cultural, and economic symptom. Subsequently, what might be initially discerned as Pound's subjective symptom emerges, in the final analysis, as a manifestation of the foundational symptom of the *social order* and its systems of symbolic representation. Because of this isomorphic conflation of the subjective and the social realms, gold, as an elusive signifier floating in the others' sphere (the usurers), can be viewed as the symptomatic signifier of both a culture's and a poet's subjection to the order of symbolic representation under its various guises.

Having established gold as the signifier of subjection, however, we should not overlook its role as an ideologically overdetermined agency that can stitch the seamy tissue of the monetary discourse that Pound criticizes at the level of its incidental margin rather than at the level of its foundational core. This mutation in the function of gold occurs when the state puts the fragmented economic fabric under the aegis of its normative design and reappropriates gold and the monetary order for their "true" function. Subsequently, from the **Hell Cantos** to the **[Chinese] Dynastic Cantos,** gold shifts from the signifier of "soft" amorphousness and perversion to the politically functional signifier of the state's unifying authority. When he envisions this reappropriation, Pound argues (consciously or unconsciously) in a strictly ideological way: namely, by repressing the fact that it is the system of monetary representation itself that is based on a fundamental slippage impossible to halt even through the supplementation of state mediation; by repressing the fact that *any* order of monetary representation (state-supplemented or "usurocratic") must posit as its *raison d'être* an endless combinatory drift of abstract monetary signifiers with no objectal signifieds. To frame the reappropriation of gold in Poundian terms is simply to state that the sole mediation of the right state suffices to restore the transparency of a referential equivalence between monetary sign and economic thing. The same applies to the appropriation of the order of signification by the concrete word of the author-itative poet who "compose[s] to the feel of the thing"—the poet who can capture the objectal thingness of the world in the *word*. At this level, we clearly recognize the conflation between Pound's artistic agenda and his politico-economic views. In effect, when, in anticipation of his later *economic* views, he announces, as early as 1912, his "scientific answers" to the social justification of literature, he envisions the coining of a "self-sustaining" objectal word in no need of further discursive supplementation as the only instrument of the poet's social credit:

> [L]anguage, the medium of thought's preservation, is constantly wearing out. It has been the function of poets to new-mint the speech, to supply the vigorous terms for prose . . . poets may be "kept on" as conservators of the public speech, or prose, perhaps, becoming more and more an art, may become . . . self-sustaining.

Needless to say, the only way to keep language from "wearing out" into the amorphous muzziness of usurious hell is to cut it in the "hard substance" of concrete referentiality.

Thus, Pound seems to imply, only when *re*considered from the perspective of objectal concreteness will the newly acquired author-ity of the poet, like the renewed signification of the stamped gold coin, be taken at face value.

Later, in a 1919 text, the two functions (monetary and discursive) are more explicitly paired; their dialectical interplay, however, is cast in such a way as to shed a totally different light on Pound's association of the reappropriation of gold with the reappropriation of discursive author-ity:

> *The genius can pay in nugged and in lump gold; it is not necessary that he bring up his knowledge into the mint of consciousness, stamp it into either the coin of conscientiously analyzed form-detail knowledge or into the paper money of words, before he transmit it* [Pound's emphasis] . . . the sudden coagulation of bits of knowledge collected here and there during the years, need not be re-sorted and arranged into coin. This sort of *lump-payment is not mediumistic* [my emphasis]; it is mastery.

Passages such as this one reveal the bedrock of Pound's contradiction, a contradiction that, let me say again, cannot be limited to a phase in his career but represent a motif that recurs throughout his works. On the one hand, his synthetic monetary-discursive metaphor implies that "lump" gold and the word of the true poet can be creditable only when they do not bear the stamp of a system of representation—that is, when they appear in their full embodiment of prediscursive thingness. On the other hand, throughout his career, he asserts ad nauseam that the only way of guaranteeing a stable monetary and discursive order is to trust their "new-minting" to the regulating mediation of the state and the poet—sole preservers of a monetary and a poetic discourse "which represent . . . something alive." If we follow this self-contradictory assertion from its premise to its logical conclusion, the assumptions we can make about it can only be imaginary. For what Pound seems to imply by his non-"mediumistic" gold is no less than the death of *any* medium of monetary and discursive representation, be it state-/poet-endorsed or usurocratic. Thus, as in the passage from **"Art Notes,"** the contradictory split between the presymbolic anarchy of the monetary signified called non-"mediumistic" gold and the normative mediation of the order of signifiers provides a nodal Manichean metaphor for Pound's aporic quest. This aporic quest is embodied in a contradictory war waged against monetary and poetic discourse with its own impotent weapons: as with any monetary signifier that attempts to point to its signified in its premonetary thingness, a sign-thing is a fundamental logical contradiction in that the very presence of the one implies the irredeemable cancellation of the other.

In the more moderate passages where he discusses money

exclusively, Pound is aware of the impossibility of a monetary order based on unmediated thingness. In order to close the gap opened by such an impossibility, he resorts to a process of rationalization whereby usurocratic deconstruction is made to represent the subversive force obscuring the referential relation between money and its specular double: the realm of things. During such moments, his political and cultural thought appears with its fundamental ideological contradictions. That is when he starts arguing simultaneously that gold is a monetary element whose evil lies solely in its misappropriation (its "false representation") *and* in its "inherent" liability to end itself to abstract manipulation:

> The durability of metal gives it certain advantages not possessed by potatoes or tomatoes . . . in addition to this potentiality for unjust manipulation inherent in metallic money . . . man has invented a document provided with coupons to serve as a more visible representation of usury. . . . No! it is not money that is the root of the evil. The root is greed, the lust for monopoly. . . . All that is needed is a kind of money that cannot be kept waiting in the safe.

A similar indicator of Pound's contradictory diagnosis of a monetary order that is inherently speculative *and* potentially redeemable lies in his assertion, shortly before his discussion of inflation and stamp scrip, that silver money can actually serve as "a ticket for the orderly distribution of WHAT IS AVAILABLE. It may even be an incentive to grow or fabricate more grain or goods that is, to attain abundance." Although he deposits money as an inherently speculative economic factor, the emphasis on the fact that *ultimately* the false representation of usurious monopolizers is only a marginal phenomenon whose expansion has reached the core of a culture and an economy "shattered in fragments." In this context, I intend the term *core* as a structural component that Pound sees at work in the fabric of Western society, for, his contradiction aside, what he seems to discern in the false representation of money by the betrayers of language *ultimately* not a phenomenon intrinsic to the structure of monetary representation. Through this emphasis on the ultimate productive function of money, he manages to repress the inherently speculative an disseminatory nature of monetary discourse by ascribing its excessive malfunctions a displaced and incidental phenomenon: the subversive manipulations of usurocaratic cell that has worked its way from the margins of the socioeconomic fabric to its central core. It is against the background of this complex repression of a disseminatory quality inherent in the monetary as well as the discursive order that gold emerges as a reversible signifier. The first dimension of its reversibility is its liability to become a symptomatic signifier pointing to the death of the monetary and discursive thing through a cancellation of referential totality ("fragmentation"). The second dimension of

its reversibility lies in its imaginary figuration as a signifier of potential empowerment through reappropriation of the non-"mediumistic" objectal other of money and language. In both cases, Pound's works emerge as the line of osmosis between the symptom of an individual and the symptom of a society meshed in an involuted ideological process whose obsessive aim is a desperate attempt to rationalize the unreasons of reason.

Which brings me to the oft-discussed question of the historicity of Pound's works—the irreducible relation between his poetics, his economics, and his totalitarian politics. By focusing on the symbolics of Pound's socioeconomic and poetic obsessions, the following discussion primarily attempts to sound the profound discursive irrationality of his totalitarian politics. In this sense, my interpretation of the symptomatics of Pound's work intends to reveal not so much the historical context of his political affiliation as the conceptual and *symbolic limits* of that affiliation, the inescapable bedrock of contradiction and ambivalence upon which his ideologically determined rationalizations repeatedly run aground. This does not mean, however, that we should conceive Pound's political, economic, and poetic re-expression of his anxiety in a static way. Paradoxically enough, Pound's fixation on the need to oppose author-itative order to disintegration, his obsession with the historically determined concept of the "conspiratorial Jew" as a principle of socioeconomic rationalization, and so on are discursive loci that are crucial for revealing both the symbolic condensation of his socio-economic discourse and the baffling openness of his poetics to almost all types of totalitarian theories and practices. Thus, we can argue that the symbolic condensation of Pound's monetary and discursive obsessions is perhaps the key element in explaining his often incoherent synthesis of totalitarian principles as disparate as European feudalism, American populism, and Italian fascism. In the final analysis, the most telling symptom of the symbolic condensation of Pound's discourses—a condensation that the expresses politically through a disorienting capacity for ideological ventriloquism—is perhaps that ultimate Poundian paradox; the unrelenting, and yet constantly wavering, belief in *the* Poem pregnant with the aggregate echoes of an author-itative order to come.

. . . . .

The obsessive nature of Pound's desire to recover the non-"mediumistic" objectal double of language already manifests itself in as early a poem as **"Near Perigord."** In it, the rhetoric of desire that gives birth to Maent as a poetic persona and a historical object reveals Pound's concern with precise discursive representation as a token of the author-ity of the poetic word. It is true that, for Pound as well as for Bertrans, Maent is only a factitious fantasy object that "has no existence, no form outside the tyranny" of the poetic construct.

Stating Maent's existence uniquely in terms of her subjection to the poetic frame, however, is an incomplete assessment of her role in Bertrans's and in Pound's poems as well as a considerable understatement of the "tyranny" of which *she* is capable. For is not her subjection to the tyranny of a factitious construct also, and by the same token, a sign of her rebellion against the possessive desire that she manages to elude even while it claims to capture her in words? In other words, because of Maent's unwillingness to manifest herself physically to the poet, Bertrans's poem stands as the imaginary supplement that, by, hopelessly trying to bridge the gap of her absence through substitutive intercourse, points to its own referential impotence. As is indicated by the conclusion of **"Perigord,"** the construct that tries to synthesize fact and fiction retrospectively in a master-artifact, the poet and the historian eventually have to admit that a "shifting change" is the outcome of *any* discursive attempt (factitious or factual) to rationalize Maent's absence into presence. And if Pound "fails to detect the seam between fact and fiction" in Bertrans's poem, it is precisely because he finds himself unwittingly *occupying* that seam in exactly the same way Bertrans did!

Placed against Pound's concern with the referential authority of poetic discourse, we see, then, how crucial the Bertrans-Maent substitutive relation is for him. For even when we momentarily disregard the quotations from Bertrans's poem, we realize that it is through a similar dialectical interplay of presence and absence that Maent is initially posited as the condensed matrix of historical and discursive truth animating **"Perigord"**'s rhetoric of desire. What we find in the excerpts from Bertrans's poem only serves as further corroboration of Maent's key role. In effect, through Bertrans, we learn that all the supplementary parts he erects against Maent's absence—"'The voice at Montfort, Lady Agnes' hair, / Bel Miral's stature, the viscountess' throat'"—put "'all together, are not worthy of'" the real thing as a whole. Thus, against Bertrans's incremental drift of imaginary substitutes (including his poem), Maent emerges in her double function as the longed-for specular double of discourse, a source of desire that teases the grasp of the poet-lover (Bertrans) and the poet-historian (Pound) who try to capture, respectively, the real thing of amorous fantasy and historical imagination through the poetic word. Through her double existence in Bertrans's and in Pound's poem, Maent can therefore be viewed as the nodal signifier of discursive author-ity—the transcendent sphere where "somewhere, in the Other, it knows" the truth.

Another more significant dimension of Maent's double function concerns her position as a reversible signifier both for Bertrans and for Pound. For although she may be the real thing of Bertrans's writerly desire, and the matrix of historical truth for Pound, she ultimately turns into the matrix of truth as a vacant otherness that sucks, and suckers, the poet's

power of expression through her teasing elusiveness. Pound expresses this totally different dimension of Maent in his final realization that her factitious existence as a steady referential whole in any poem is only an *other* substitutive supplement: a gaping *black hole* that absorbs the poet's energy through its vampishness. This vampishness of Maent, the presumed referent of poetic representation, ultimately degenerates into discursive vampirism, a "disease of proliferation" that can suck the poet's creative vitality unto death.

It is the final metamorphosis of the vampish Maent into an alien vampiric other that qualifies her as a reversible signifier: that which marks the poet's initial belief in the truth of discursive thingness as well as the symptomatic return of his fear of (symbolic) castration. In the latter case, Maent's poetic persona can be viewed as the master-index of the powerless moment when the poet can speak himself to death without being able to capture the living object of his imaginary representation, the moment when "truth stammers" despite all the poetic supplements deployed.

> So to this last estrangement, Tairiran!
> There shut up in his castle, Tairiran's,
> . . . .
> Gone—ah, gone—untouched, unreachable!
> She who could never live save through one person,
> And all the rest of her a shifting change,
> A broken bundle of mirrors . . . !

Given Maent's eventual emergence as the symptomatic signifier that represents fragmentation in poetic as well as in historical discourse, Pound realizes that the only person who can have intercourse with her as an unmediated, living whole is, after all, Tairiran; as to both poets, they can only evoke her as a dead object of fantasy condemned by the very substitutive constructs of their poetry to live as a reflection in fragmented imaginary mirrors. This debilitating otherness of Maent and the incapacity of the poet's imaginary attempt to relate to her as a living whole in his poetic mirror become all the more telling of Pound's concern with the dialectical interplay between discursive author-ity and impotence as we learn that **"Perigord"** is initially set against an intertextual background of (symbolic) castration. In this respect, it is important to know that Dante, the master that Pound uses to supplement his poem, sees in Bertrans's decapitation a vicarious mutilation of his own voice; hence, probably, the opening of Dante's Canto with the ominous six lines indicating the powerlessness of the poetic word in particular and of language in general. The intertextual resonances of **"Perigord,"** then, create a double play of reflection: at one level, we have Dante, the poetic master, who starts his Canto with an acknowledgment of discursive powerlessness, contemplating another mutilated master; at a second level, we have Pound, a young poet aspiring to mastery, contemplating the powerlessness of both predecessors.

The same dialectical interplay between discursive author-ity and the impotent poetic voice informs **"Canto 1,"** the Canto in which Pound the cultural crusader merges indistinctly with the figure of Odysseus, the literary epitome of the drifting adventurer, as the central subject or the *Bildungsgedicht.* Here, the discursive author-ity in which I am most interested concerns the intricate symbolic overtones surrounding Odysseus's/Pound's desired appropriation of the golden wand and its capacity to endow the holder with access to the underworld. Far from being a clearly positive or negative symbolic factor, the function of the golden wand is ambivalent in the sense that it operates as a reversible signifier marking a *division* within the (poetic) subject between a proleptic access to discursive author-ity and a denial thereof. But before proceeding to the analogical relation between the (poetic) subject aspiring to discursive mastery and the reversibility surrounding the precarious appropriation of the golden wand, I would like first to turn to one of Pound's remarks on the relation between literary discourse and life as a biological process. In a plea for the importance of literature, he argues that

> the function of literature as a *generated* prize-worthy *force* is precisely that it does incite humanity to continue living. . . . They ["lovers of *order*"] regard it as dangerous. . . . They try to *tame it down.* They try to make a *bog,* a *marasmus,* a great putridity in place of a sane and active ebullience. (my emphasis)

With the same degree of precariousness (the potential movement of the poetic word between the (pro)creative drive of phallic generation and the "boggy" stillness of anal degeneration), a similar dialectical interplay between access to the life-generating power of the poetic word and the stillness of symbolic castration operates as the central motif of **"Canto 1."** Again, this interplay finds its locus of conscious return in *one* condensed signifier loaded with a reversible function: the phallic golden wand of Tiresias. In this Canto, the persona of Odysseus/Pound in the underworld emerges as that of the vicarious redeemer of the "impotent dead," invoking the authority of "Pluto the strong," god of gold and precious stones, and waiting to hear the pronouncement of Tiresias, holder of the golden wand. For it is Tiresias, seer and representative of the author-itative word, who holds the power of access to the underworld through his possession of the phallic signifier. Thus, from the outset, phallic author-ity is systematically associated with discursive author-ity. And it is to a paternal figure of author-ity that Odysseus/Pound turns, hoping to obtain the golden key to the word and the underworld. Through its function as the signifier of (discursive) potency, the golden wand stands in antithetical relation to the general lethargy of the impotent dead. Subsequently, it appears as a power-endowing source, enabling the holder to occupy the key role of redeemer of the under-

world rough his author-itative function as recorder of the hell dwellers' misfortunes. Those hell dwellers are the people *"with a name to come"*—that is, a name hibernating in the underworld and waiting to be resurrected through the poet's desired function of naming. "I bid remember me," says the impotent Elpenor, asking for a prospective resurrection of his body through an inscription of his name, *"A man of no fortune, and with a name to come. / And set my oar up . . ."* (Pound's emphasis).

Access to the underworld and the resurrection of dead names through the golden wand refer us to the golden bough of Hermes, another prophet of the word and a "begetter" of discursive author-ity. Insofar as he aspires to the prospective moment of (re)generating the dead names through remembrance, inscription, and naming (the author's function), Odysseus/Pound, like Hermes, waits with deference for Tiresias's word. If we consider Hermetic virtues as a whole—that is, in their (pro)creative biological/symbolic function as the "male origin of life"—then the bough of Hermes is the signifier antithetical to the (pro)creative stasis of the dwellers of the uterine underworld who cannot inscribe their names.

For the aims of this essay, I will focus on the symbolic function of the sailor/poet in relation to the (pro)creative Hermetic word, especially insofar as it foreshadows a *proleptic* moment of appropriation. For it is obvious that Odysseus's/Pound's deference to Tiresias's refusal ("I stepped back") is the placatory gesture of an effaced "noman" aspiring to future possession of the signifier of discursive author-ity. Its most significant implication, however, is that it is at the same time a sign of *deferral,* indicating that the sailor/poet is still like the impotent dead: a *"name to come"* condemned through paternal decree to drift "over dark seas" before acceding to the author-ity of the seer with the golden wand.

With its central image of the sailor/poet aspiring to the signifier of discursive and (pro)creative power held by an other, this first Canto lays the foundation of the poet's identity as an initially dispossessed and selfless vacancy in the process of being impregnated with the voices of author-ity—the Odyssean "noman," who defines himself as a receptacle pregnant with other voices. In this sense, the pronouncement "by no man these verses" can be viewed as emblematic of the poem's obsessive strategy of endless supplementation through the presence of other author-itative men. In this qualification of the poetic persona as a mediator delivering other men's voices, we already see an anticipation of the derivative "ego scriptor" of the **Pisan Cantos** emerging "from the wreckage of Europe" and trying to represent, through the agency of retrospective naming, the deeds of great men reduced to figures "with a name to come"—that is, a name awaiting rebirth through the discursive intercession of a Hermetic poet destined to represent all the dead names of the Western scene.

When viewed as a masked *affirmation* of the ego scriptor, however, it is precisely this selfless vacancy of the dispossessed poet that grants him natural *author-ity*. In an earlier text, we already discern an inceptive form of this ambivalent function of the poet as a selfless reflector of "many men's" voices:

> The so-called major poets have most of them given their *own* [Pound's emphasis] gift but the peculiar term "major" is rather a gift to them from Chronos. I mean that they have been born upon the stroke of their hour and that it has been given them to heap together and arrange and harmonize the results of many men's labor. This very faculty for amalgamation is a part of their genius and it is, in a way, a sort of *unselfishness*. (my emphasis)

This view of the poet as a "modest," "unselfish" (shall we read "selfless"?) entity is important only insofar as it acquires a double relevance. First, it qualifies the naturally "gifted" poet as the representative of all significant poetic voices, thus making his poetry the ultimate "amalgamation" of author-itative poetic expression. Second, when applied beyond the poetic sphere, Pound's definition of the poetic voice as an amalgamating matrix empowers the latter to represent, thanks to the poet's natural genius for "harmonization," the various figures of political and cultural author-ity. It is probably in the light of this ambivalent interplay between selfless effacement and the poet's natural "gift" of multiple representation that we should read the pronouncement "There be thy mirror in men."

A strong indicator of Pound's conception of himself as a selfless receptacle filled with other men's author-ity and "labor" appears in his attempt to reaffirm the role of his Poem as the source of rebirth of the poet-son through the word. Needless to say, it is important to remember the political affiliation underlying this ambivalent filiality: more than ever, the poet-son of the **Pisan Cantos** reiterates his role as the specular double of Mussolini, the man in whose mutilation the name of the father (sole guarantor of the stability of the order of monetary and discursive representation) finds its literal dislocation. The (re)generation of the order of discursive representation in, and through, the poet (the specular double of the dead father) is a major motif in **"Cantos 74"** and **"80."** In effect, in both Cantos, the ego scriptor of **"Canto 76,"** the "lone ant," the synecdochical part of the "broken ant-hill" of dead names, looks forward to a rebirth of "the wreckage of Europe" through the word spoken in the name of the dead father(s).

In **"Cantos 74"** and **"80,"** the motif of the rebirth of the

figure(s) of authority in the word of the poet is played out against an intricate amalgamation of pagan myths of the son as specular double of the father and the Christian myth of the incarnation of God the Father in the son's word. This relation to the father(s), symbolized through the filial image of "DIGONOS" (the "twice-born"), allows the ego scriptor to function as a specular double symbolically reborn, through the discursive agency of the poem, out of the dead name(s) of the father(s):

> . . . Odysseus
> > the name of my family.
> . . . .
> but a precise definition
> > transmitted thus Sigismundo
> > > thus Duccio, thus Zuan Bellin, or trastevere
> > > > with La Sposa
> Sponsa Cristi in mosaic till our time / deification
> > of emperors.

Paradoxically, it is only insofar as he accepts the Odyssean image of a noman that the poet can accede to his symbolic role as the ego scriptor destined to incarnate the dead name(s) of the father(s) through the "verbum perfectum." In other words, facing the crippling author-ity of other men's names, the poet can only affirm his symbolic/second birth through his author-ial death; hence the necessity of giving poetic credit to his Poem through the endless drift of other author-itative names and voices integrated in order to supplement the ego scriptor's voice. Because he perceives it as an "amalgamating" necessity, supplementation in Pound becomes a poetic form of rationalization—that is, a justification through poetic method of the specular relation of desire that defines the poet in relation to other authoritative men. Thus, in a way that is strongly illustrative of his amalgamating practice, Pound posits this specular relation as a premise to be applied with the rigor of an aphoristic statement: "There be thy mirror in men."

It is probably from the paradoxical perspective of a self-negating affirmation of the ego scriptor (simultaneously a male specular double and a female receptacle) that we should read Pound's emphatic assertion of his "nomanhood" in relation to Ouan Jin, the "man of letters" and the negative Poundian alter ego who tries to usurp the father's function of creating the world through the word:

> "I am noman, my name is noman"
> but Wanjina is, shall we say, Ouan Jin
> or the man with an education
> and whose mouth was removed by his father
> > because he made too many *things*
> . . . .
> Ouan Jin spoke and thereby created the named

thereby making

clutter.

In stark Manichean opposition to the excessive discursive "clutter" of the son, Pound then introduces immediately the biblical word of the creation. The latter, as we know from the earlier **Hell Cantos** and *A Visiting Card,* was betrayed through a usurious clutter of abstraction whose monetary and discursive "falsification" has caused the power of (pro)creative referential discourse to degenerate into the "satanic transubstantiation" of the word. The latter, with its metaphoric suggestion of a relapse into anal amorphousness, represents the ultimate "falsification" of the natural generation of wealth through a chaotic overproduction of nonreferential signs. (If, at this point, I refer to a process of causality in relation to this Manichean polarity in Pound's vision, it is not so much to delineate a clear-cut opposition as to point out a process of ideological rationalization whereby the systemic failures inherent in monetary and poetic discourse are ascribed to a factor judged external and incidental to the order of monetary and poetic discourse.) The first passages of *A Visiting Card,* in which the nonreferential amorphousness and fragmentation of the order of words is not only justified by but also yoked to the monetary falsification of usury, provide a good instance of Pound's ideological rationalization according to the vague terms of concrete good and abstract evil:

> We find two forces in history: one that *divides, shatters,* and *kills,* and one that contemplates the *unity* of the mystery.

> "The arrow hath not two points."

> There is the force that falsifies, the force that destroys every clearly delineated symbol, dragging man into a maze of abstract arguments, destroying not one but every religion. (my emphasis)

The resurrection of the "arrow" with one point, the seminal word-as-God-incarnate reerected as an antidote against the abstract forces that disseminate, "shatter," and "kill," is the event that Pound seems to celebrate in the Christian intimations of a reincarnation and a regeneration of the name of the Father through the word of the Son. Like those who emerge out of "the gates of death" after having "swum in a sea of air strip / through an aeon of nothingness," the poet turns to Christ's affirmation of His and God's rebirth and proliferation in the seminal word. The imagery of rebirth out of the chaos of death ("nothingness") is further sustained by an apposition of the dark "souterrain" (an agrarian metaphor for the underworld?) and the grain ready to sprout:

> if calm be after tempest
> that the ants seem to wobble

> as the sun catches their shadows
> . . . .
> with a smoky torch through the unending
> labyrinth of the souterrain
> or remembering Carleton let him celebrate Christ
> in the grain
> and if the corn cat be beaten
> Demeter has lain in my furrow.

More than just a homage to a secular figure of agricultural productivity (Carleton), the celebration of "Christ in the grain" has deeper symbolic connotations related to the biblical motif of the (pro)creative seminal word, the specular bind between the name of the Father and the word of the Son. In effect, using a similar agrarian image of proliferation after death, Jesus-as-God-incarnate posits His physical death as the necessary condition of a resurrection of the name of the Father through the filial word (John 12:24, 28).

Through the appropriation of the biblical interplay between the death of God-in-Jesus and His resurrection in the seminal word, Pound's affirmation of other men's rebirth by means of the (pro)creative agency of the Poem comes to stand for the matrix (the "furrow," the line) pregnant with the dead names' life to come. It is probably in this sense that "the [poetic] *forma,* the concept rises from death"—a dictum that refers us back to Pound's early-phrased desire to see the true poet new-mint language. For it is through such a regeneration of the dead order of representation that the perennial word of the hard poet, like the hard gold coin of the true leader, can be made to transcend its death by usurious disincarnation and dissemination: "The bust outlasts the throne / The coin Tiberius." Naturally, by confining it to the bearing of other men's names, Pound qualifies the (pro)creative poetic word as partaking of an exclusively homoerotic process. By virtue of its exclusiveness, this positing of a phallocentric order of representation as the antidote against the uterine stasis of death is not devoid of ambiguity. As we have seen in **"Canto 1,"** the initial positing of the life-giving word of the Hermetic poet as an affirmation of the redemptive virile ego scriptor is always already a reversible function in the sense that, ultimately, it reveals the ambivalent position of the poet as both a potential holder of the seminal phallic word *and* a vacant noman. For even while aspiring to appropriation of the name of the father in **"Canto 80,"** the ego scriptor still has to assert himself defensively—that is, as the matrix of the deferential noman, the furrow pregnant with the seed of names hibernating in the underworld of the Western scene. In a strangely infectious way, this reversible function if the ego scriptor (a specular double of other men and a female matrix) eventually marks the reversibility of the Poem itself: its status as an androgynous signifying body oscillating between its ideal of formalized being and its nightmare of fragmented nothingness, between the chaos of uterine vacancy and the (pro)creative plenitude of semantic presence.

. . . . .

As I have tried to demonstrate, the death stasis of the order of representation and its representatives appears in the *Cantos* as the symptom of a fragmented culture whose dislocation is rendered in the paroxysmal climax of the *Pisan Cantos* but whose liability to a collapse through a dislocution of the voices of author-ity already finds its inception in "Canto 1." With Pound's vision of the "amalgamating" function of the poet's voice in mind, we can see the cultural dimension of his invocation of the names of the impotent dead and the powerless figures of "Cantos 1, 76," and "80." If the poem fails to redeem the broken anthill of the Western scene by reviving its author-itative voices, however, we already know Pound's justification of this failure as well as the outcome of the justification. The outcome is, first, a repression of the inherently dislocutionary nature of discourse and the disseminatory nature of the monetary order; and, second, a symptomatic return of this repression in the deconstructive powers of usurious monetary misrepresentation—the betrayers of language.

In the **Hell Cantos,** usury is represented as a dissembling signifying force that eludes concrete, as well as meaningful, representation—a disseminating agency threatening creative and *pro*creative power:

> with usura
> hath no man a painted paradise on his church wall
> *harpes et luz*
> or where virgin receiveth message
> . . . .
> with usura
> . . . . . .
> no picture is made to endure nor to live with
> but is made to sell and sell quickly
> with usura, sin against nature,
> is thy bread as dry as paper,
> . . . .
> It slayeth the young man's courting
> It hath brought palsy to bed, lyeth
> between the young bride and her bridegroom.

The usurious overproduction of dead monetary signifiers, the false representation of wealth, can turn "natural" (referential) art into an "unnatural," infinitely reproducible and marketable surface—a "picture." Likewise, instead of producing the real thing called bread, usury transforms the latter into a sign falsely represented on, and by, paper. This complete subversion of the natural thingness of the order of monetary and discursive representation, symbolized by the castration (the "palsy") of the male procreative capacity, eventually

culminates in the images that refer to the misappropriation of gold and precious stones by usura and the discursive consequences of such a misappropriation. If, as Rabaté argues, we posit gold as being initially the signifier that "connotes the work of the poet writing with care," then it does not seem unwarranted to argue, against Rabaté's diachronic framing, that even in the later "Canto 45," for instance, the absence of gold from the weaver's work can be taken as a metaphoric expression of the usurpation of natural meaning from the poet's discourse:

> It rusteth the craft and the craftsman
> It gnaweth the thread in the loom
> None learneth to weave gold in her pattern
> Azure hath a canker by usura; cramoisie is
>   unbroidered
> Emerald findeth no Memling.

Pound's metaphoric equation of the misappropriation of gold with the monetary and discursive misrepresentations of the usurocratic "perverters of language" appears more emphatically in the **Hell Cantos'** association of the monetary overproduction of nonreferential signifiers with the "perversion" of anal sterility. It is true that in the **Hell Cantos,** as well as in "Canto 45," the signifiers of wealth (gold, jewels, money) seem the loathsome tokens of unnatural (noncreative) perversion—nameless, amorphous objects sucked in by the "mud" of chaotic anality. As the early and late Cantos how, however, it is this very regression of gold, the "natural" signifier of monetary and discursive referentiality, to the "ooze" and "lost contours" of anal amorphousness that necessitates the reestablishment of its author-iative status as the master-signifier of hard money and the hard word. Ultimately, and despite their attempts to defile jewels in the mud of hell chaos, the dwellers of Pound's hell end up "howling to find them unstained."

It is, then, in view of Pound's desire to restitute the true function of a disappropriated gold that the latter should be regarded as a reversible signifier in his works: it can shift from the usurious sphere of anal amorphousness and death to the (pro)creative sphere of the true political author-ity, which, as announced in *Gold and Work,* concerns itself with the referential dimension of money in concrete economic terms of vital creation of goods. In this sense, the later Cantos—with their scenes of reappropriation of gold by figures of authority—represent Pound's ideological belief that the monetary-discursive hell of the Western world is not a phenomenon inherent in discourse and in capital but an incidental occurrence redeemable through the utopian centralization of the monetary order—a belief already expressed in *A Visiting Card:* "State or imperial money has always been an assertion of sovereignty. Sovereignty carries with it the right to coin or print money." Hence the constant emphasis (in "Canto 87," for instance) on a strict state control of issue rather than the nature of capital itself: "attention to outlet, no attention to source, / That is: the problem of issue. / Who issues it? How?" The master-metaphor for such a state of affairs (which is ultimately an affair of the state) is the libidinal tapping of perverse usurious excess. Hence the "order" and the "norm" of the **Dynastic Cantos**, which rise against the "semitic" fragmentation, the "grades and gradations" of a social body aspiring to "corporate" homo-geneity: "CHI KING ostendit incitatque. Vir autem rectus / et libidinis expers ita domine servat."

It is in view of an "attention to outlet" and the author-ity that issues and controls gold that such figures as William Jennings Bryan and Thomas Hart Benton (other paternal figures) are "Willing to see a currency of hard money," a "currency of intrinsic value" antithetically opposed to the usurocratic overproduction of "unconvertable [sic] paper." From this perspective of the recuperation of gold by the right figures of author-ity, it seems reasonable to suggest that for Bryan, as well as for the hard poet who posits himself against the anal overproduction of the soft poet, the only standard that should be erected as the index of monetary and discursive referentiality is hard gold. It is through a desire to reaffirm what is out of circulation, what needs to be new-minted, that Bryan rebels against the disseminatory power that has dispossessed him of his gold:

> Young Bryan
> . . . . . .
> Wanted gold, coins not then in circulation,
> . . . .
> Asked for the state of his account. The teller
>   took up packages of bills and
>   asked in what size notes he wd/ have it.
> "I want money."
>   said Mr. Randolph.
> The teller, beginning to understand him, said:
>   Silver?

For both the figure of author-ity and the poet lost in the usurocratic ooze of disseminatory overproduction and misrepresentation, value on paper is still not the real thing of monetary and discursive representation. In this respect, perhaps the most important aspect of Pound's works stems from his obsessive belief that the mission of both figures lies in a search for the real thing outside the confines of formalized monetary and discursive representation (the bank, the soft word). It is a measure of the importance of such works that they should survive as the traces of a reversible struggle between a bondage to the chains of monetary and discursive signification and the aporic utopia of their identity as the incarnation of thingness beyond (or rather before) discourse.

FURTHER READING

Criticism

Beach, Christopher. "Ezra Pound and Harold Bloom: Influences, Canons, Traditions, and the Making of Modern Poetry." *ELH: English Literary History* 56, No. 2 (Summer 1989): 463-83.

> Compares Pound's modernist theories of literary innovation and influence with those of contemporary literary critic Harold Bloom.

Casilo, Robert. "The Italian Renaissance: Pound's Problematic Debt to Burckhardt." *Mosaic* 22, No. 4 (Fall 1989): 13-29.

> Discusses the influence of historian Jacob Burckhardt's *The Civilization of the Renaissance in Italy* on Pound's conception of Renaissance scholarship, cultural and aesthetic ideals, and historical view of Italian fascism.

Dasenbrock, Reed Way. "Ezra Pound, the Last Ghibelline." *Journal of Modern Literature* XVI, No. 4 (Spring 1990): 511-32.

> Examines Pound's affinity for Mussolini in terms of his admiration for Italian culture and Dante's political ideals.

Goldensohn, Barry. "Pound and Antisemitism." *Yale Review* 75 (Spring 1986): 399-421.

> Discusses Pound's anti-Semitic views and fascist loyalties.

Hartnett, Stephen. "The Ideologies and Semiotics of Fascism: Analyzing Pound's *Cantos* 12-15." *Boundary 2* 20, No. 1 (1993): 65-93.

> Examines the historical context and semiotic representation of Pound's fascism and anti-Semitism in *The Cantos*.

Kronick, Joseph. "Resembling Pound: Mimesis, Translation, Ideology." *Criticism* XXXV, No. 2 (Spring 1993): 219-36.

> Explores the mimetic function of ideology, economics, and aesthetic representation in Pound's poetry.

Nicholls, Peter. "'A Consciousness Disjunct': Sex and the Writer in Ezra Pound's *Hugh Selwyn Mauberley*." *Journal of American Studies* 28 (1994): 61-75.

> Examines issues of sexuality, romantic desire, and authorial identity in "Medallion" from *Hugh Selwyn Mauberley*.

————. "An Experiment with Time: Ezra Pound and the Example of Japanese Noh." *Modern Language Review* 90, No. 1 (1995): 1-13.

    Explores Pound's assimilation of temporal structures from Noh theater to create dramatic movement in *The Cantos.*

Tryphonopoulos, Demetres P. "Ezra Pound's Occult Education." *Journal of Modern Literature* XVII, No. 1 (Summer 1990): 73-96.

    Examines the significance of Pound's exposure to theosophy and psychic spirituality, gained through association with occult circles including William Butler Yeats and G.R.S. Mead.

Additional coverage of Pound's life and career is contained in the following sources published by Gale: *Concise Dictionary of American Literary Biography, 1917-1929; Contemporary Authors,* **Vols. 5-8R, and 37-40R;** *Contemporary Authors New Revision Series,* **Vol. 40;** *Dictionary of Literary Biography,* **Vols. 4, 45, and 63;** *DISCovering Authors; DISCovering Authors: British; DISCovering Authors: Canadian; DISCovering Authors Modules: Most-Studied and Poets; Major Twentieth Century Writers; Poetry Criticism,* **Vol. 4; and** *World Literature Criticism.*

Kenneth Rexroth
1905-1982

American poet, translator, critic, essayist, editor, dramatist, and autobiographer.

The following entry presents an overview of Rexroth's career through 1995. For further information on his life and works, see *CLC*, Volumes 1, 2, 6, 11, 22, and 49.

INTRODUCTION

Associated with various avant-garde movements throughout his career, notably Cubism and the Beat Generation, Rexroth's highly regarded meditative poetry incorporates eclectic elements of Judeo-Christian, classical, modernist, and Eastern influences. A skilled translator in several languages, noted literary critic, and outspoken political dissenter, Rexroth's radical libertarianism and mystical orientation produced a controversial confluence of ideas in his work. Though marginalized by East Coast literary critics and academics during much of his life, Rexroth's evocative depiction of the natural world and erotic love is now widely praised for its visionary spiritual awareness and universality. Much of his best known verse appears in *The Art of Worldly Wisdom* (1949), *The Signature of All Things* (1950), *In Defense of the Earth* (1956), *The Homestead Called Damascus* (1963), and *The Collected Shorter Poems* (1966). A poet of remarkable range and ability, Rexroth's distinct prophetic voice, iconoclastic appropriation of disparate literary traditions, and devotion to the craft of poetry and translation attracted international critical attention and exerted an important influence on contemporary American literature.

Biographical Information

Born Kenneth Charles Marion Rexroth in South Bend, Indiana, Rexroth was the only son of Charles, a pharmaceuticals salesman, and Delia Rexroth; their travels to New York City and Europe exposed the young Rexroth to modern art and fostered his lifelong interest in painting. After moving to Indiana and then Michigan, the family settled in Chicago where the Rexroths' marriage deteriorated due to Charles' alcoholism and philandering. Delia, a loving mother who encouraged Rexroth's creativity, died of gangrene in 1916, and Charles succumbed to liver disease two years later. Orphaned at age thirteen, Rexroth was taken in by an aunt in Chicago; he eventually dropped out of high school and attended the Chicago Art Institute, where he immersed himself in the bohemian art and intellectual scene of the Chicago Renaissance. During the early 1920s, Rexroth entered into

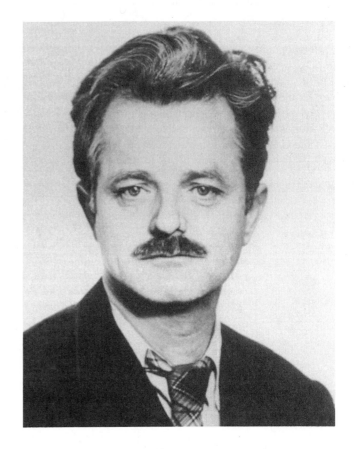

a love affair with his social worker, Lesley Smith, whom he followed to Smith College in New York City. While in New York, Rexroth attended the New York Art Students League and worked for several radical leftist publications. When his relationship with Smith ended, Rexroth began a vagabond existence, hitchhiking to the West Coast, back again to Chicago in 1924, and then traveled to Europe, the American Southwest, and Mexico. In 1927 Rexroth married Andrée Deutcher, an artist, and moved to San Francisco where he became increasingly active in leftist politics during the Depression. Rexroth's first published poems appeared in *Blues,* a small literary magazine, in 1929, but he remained unrecognized until his poem "A Prolegomenon to a Theodicy" appeared in Louis Zukofsky's *Objectivist Anthology* in 1932. He was awarded the California Literature Silver Medal for his first two books of poetry, *In What Hour* (1940) and *The Phoenix and the Tortoise* (1944). After his first wife died in 1940, Rexroth married Marie Kass, a nurse, whom he divorced in 1948. That same year, Rexroth returned to Europe on a Guggenheim Fellowship and, the next year, published a third volume of poetry, *The Art of Worldly Wisdom.* In the 1950s Rexroth emerged as a leading figure of the San Francisco Poetry Renaissance and mentor for Beat writers such as Allen Ginsberg. He produced additional volumes of poetry, notably *The Signature of All Things* and *In Defense of the Earth,* as well as verse drama in *Beyond the Mountains* (1951), and collections of translated French, Spanish, Japanese, and Chinese poetry. Rexroth received the Chapelbrook Award and Eunice Teitjens Award from *Poetry* magazine in 1957, a Shelley Memorial Award and Amy Lowell Fellowship in 1958, and a Longview Award in 1963. During the 1960s and 1970s, Rexroth maintained a prolific output of poetry, including *The Homestead Called Damascus* and *The Morning Star* (1979), more translations of Asian poetry, and essays on society and literature. Rexroth's third marriage to Marthe Larsen produced two daughters and ended in divorce in 1961. He was awarded a grant from the National Academy of Arts and Letters in 1964 and subsequently taught at San Francisco State College, the University of Wisconsin in Milwaukee, and the University of California at Santa Barbara. In 1967 he received a Rockefeller grant on which he travelled to Europe and Japan. Rexroth relocated to Santa Barbara in 1968, and married his fourth wife, poet Carol Tinker, in 1974. He resided in Santa Barbara until suffering a fatal stroke in 1982. He was presented with the Academy of American Poets' Copernicus Award in 1978 in recognition of his lifetime achievement.

Major Works

Rexroth's large and remarkably varied body of work stems from a core of artistic, political, and literary preoccupations centered largely upon communion with the natural world, non-violent protest, and transcendental philosophy. *In What Hour* contains Rexroth's early attempts to unify personal and humanitarian concerns in verse about the execution of Sacco and Venzetti, the Spanish Civil War, and the death of his first wife. In the tradition of Walt Whitman and William Butler Yeats, Rexroth displays the characteristic nature imagery, contemplative lyricism, and pacifistic morality that permeates so much of his work. His despair over the outbreak of the Second World War, especially the split between East and West, foreshadows Rexroth's lifelong effort to reconcile the transcendental legacy of both cultures. Rexroth examines the interrelationship of self-identity and social conscience in *The Phoenix and the Tortoise,* an assemblage of political verse, satire, elegies, and passionate love poems modelled on those of D. H. Lawrence. The more abstract influence of Cubism is prominent in *The Art of Worldly Wisdom,* in which Rexroth evokes elementary forms and intuitive word associations reminiscent of the work of Gertrude Stein, James Joyce, and the Imagist poetry of Ezra Pound. The latter volume contains "A Prolegomenon to a Theodicy," an extended meditative poem that incorporates allusions to Dantean Hell and visionary Christian imagery akin to John Milton's *Paradise Regained. The Signature of All Things,* named after the work of German mystic Jakob Boehme, reveals the strong influ-

ence of the eighth-century Chinese poet Tu Fu on Rexroth's verse, marked by an increasing tendency toward an oriental aesthetic in direct, spare lyrics. Rexroth's affinity for Asian culture is also evident in *Beyond the Mountains,* a tetralogy of verse drama that combines characters from classical Greek tragedy with elements of Noh drama, a stylized ancient Japanese form of theater involving dance, poetry, and mime. *In Defense of the Earth* is a diverse collection of personal statement, Japanese translations, epigrams, and highly charged love poetry. This volume also contains two of Rexroth's best known poems—"A Letter to William Carlos Williams," a touching tribute to one of his greatest influences, and "Thou Shalt Not Kill," an elegy commemorating the death of Dylan Thomas in which he offers a bitter indictment of conformist pressures and conventional morality in contemporary American society. The title poem of *The Homestead Called Damascus* is among Rexroth's most famous long works. Originally composed during the 1920s, this philosophical poem traces Rexroth's introspective quest for spiritual meaning through the dialogue and metaphysical speculation of two brothers and an omniscient narrator who ponder with skepticism the received wisdom of the ages. Written in the Symbolist style, the poem shows the influence of T. S. Eliot's *Wasteland.* In *An Autobiographical Novel* (1966), Rexroth offers additional insight into his intellectual and personal growth through the first six decades of his life. His well-informed interest in Asian literature and Buddhist philosophy is displayed in numerous volumes of Chinese and Japanese verse translations, as well as in *The Heart's Garden, The Garden's Heart* (1967), whose title poem describes a visionary journey into nature and the Tao. In this work, Rexroth sublimates the emotionalism of his earlier verse with serene landscape imagery and sensuous reflection that portray the quiet search for enlightenment and actuality. Along with several collections of essays, particularly *Bird in the Bush* (1959) and *Assays* (1961), literary criticism in *Classics Revisited* (1968) and *With Eye and Ear* (1970), and social commentary in *The Alternative Society* (1970) and *Communalism* (1974), Rexroth displays his wide-ranging interests, provocative insights, and erudition.

Critical Reception

Rexroth is widely recognized as a gifted poet and translator whose indefatigable commitment to the creative life attests to the conviction and seriousness of his work, yet he was excluded from scholarly criticism and anthologies for many years. His detractors typically object to his avid contentiousness and anarchistic contempt for the literary establishment and consumer culture. However, as a model for radical free thinkers and "grandfather of the Beats," Rexroth achieved a rare independent perspective as a genuine autodidact and leading figure of the West Coast literary scene. Though eschewing affiliation with any artistic or political ideology, especially the modernist presumptions of Lawrence, Eliot, and

Pound, Rexroth formulated a heterogenous personal style that freely assimilated elements of their work along with that of Whitman, Yeats, Tu Fu, Williams, Wallace Stevens, and the French Surrealists. Rexroth is consistently praised for his unusual ability to distill deep philosophical musings and multicultural literary allusions in highly accessible verse that captures the immediacy of sensuous experience in lucid language and arresting metaphor. While "The Homestead Called Damascus," "A Prolegomenon to Theodicy," and "The Heart's Garden, the Garden's Heart" are considered among his finest long works, Rexroth's shorter poems, particularly his elegies and erotic love verse, are considered equally accomplished. In addition, Rexroth's renderings of Chinese and Japanese poetry are considered among the best in the English language. He is also credited for his efforts to introduce female Asian poets to Western readers in several volumes devoted to translations of their work.

PRINCIPAL WORKS

In What Hour (poetry) 1940

The Phoenix and the Tortoise (poetry) 1944

The Art of Worldly Wisdom (poetry) 1949

The Signature of All Things: Poems, Songs, Elegies, Translations, and Epigrams (poetry) 1950

Beyond the Mountains (verse drama) 1951

The Dragon and the Unicorn (poetry) 1952

Fourteen Poems by O. V. de L. Milosz [translator] (poetry) 1952

A Bestiary for My Daughters Mary and Katherine (poetry) 1955

One Hundred Poems from the French [translator] (poetry) 1955

One Hundred Poems from the Japanese [translator] (poetry) 1955

Thou Shalt Not Kill (poetry) 1955

In Defense of the Earth (poetry) 1956

One Hundred Poems from the Chinese [translator] (poetry) 1956

Thirty Spanish Poems of Love and Exile [translator] (poetry) 1956

Bird in the Bush: Obvious Essays (essays) 1959

Assays (essays) 1961

Poems from the Greek Anthology [translator] (poetry) 1962

The Homestead Called Damascus (poetry) 1963

Natural Numbers: New and Selected Poetry (poetry) 1963

An Autobiographical Novel (autobiography) 1966

The Collected Shorter Poems (poetry) 1966

The Heart's Garden, the Garden's Heart (poetry) 1967

Classics Revisited (essays) 1968

Collected Longer Poems of Kenneth Rexroth (poetry) 1968

The Spark in the Tinder of Knowing (poetry) 1968

Pierre Reverdy: Selected Poems [translator] (poetry) 1969

The Alternative Society: Essays from the Other World (essays) 1970

Love in the Turning Year: One Hundred More Poems from the Chinese [translator] (poetry) 1970

With Eye and Ear (essays) 1970

American Poetry in the Twentieth Century (essays) 1971

Sky Sea Birds Tree Earth House Beasts Flowers (poetry) 1971

The Orchid Boat: Women Poets of China [translator with Ling Chung] (poetry) 1972

The Elastic Retort: Essays in Literature and Ideas (essays) 1973

Communalism: Its Origins to the Twentieth Century (essays) 1974

New Poems (poetry) 1974

One Hundred More Poems from the Japanese [translator] (poetry) 1974

On Flower Wreath Hill (poetry) 1976

The Silver Swan: Poems Written in Kyoto, 1974-75 (poetry) 1976

The Burning Heart: Women Poets of Japan [translator with Ikuko Atsumi] (poetry) 1977

The Love Poems of Marichiko (poetry) 1978

Li Ch'ing Chao: Complete Poems [translator with Ling Chung] (poetry) 1979

The Morning Star (poetry) 1979

New and Selected Poems (poetry) 1979

Saucy Limericks and Christmas Cheer (poetry) 1980

Excerpts from a Life (poetry) 1981

Between Two Wars (poetry) 1982

Selected Poems (poetry) 1984

Thirty-Six Poems by Tu Fu [translator] (poetry) 1987

World Outside the Window: The Selected Essays of Kenneth Rexroth (essays) 1987

More Classics Revisited (essays) 1989

CRITICISM

Janet Overmyer (review date 9 January 1969)

SOURCE: "Seeing the Classics as New," in *Christian Science Monitor*, January 9, 1969, p. 5.

[*In the following review, Overmyer offers a favorable assessment of* Classics Revisited.]

John Crow, a witty and wise Shakespearian authority, has said that the difficulty with writing on Shakespeare today is that by now all the intelligent things have been said, so that anyone hoping to come up with a new observation is reduced to saying something unintelligent.

Before reading this book, one might have said the same of

the sixty classics on which Kenneth Rexroth, best known as a poet, has written sixty brief, revealing essays which first appeared in the Saturday Review. After all, hasn't all the intelligence about such works as *The Iliad, The Republic, Don Quixote,* and *War and Peace* already been disseminated? Can readers unfamiliar with them be lured to read the poems of Tu Fu, *The Epic of Gilgamesh,* or *Njal's Saga*? The answers to these questions are no and yes, respectively.

> **Although he is sometimes adversely critical, he is plainly excited by each book and, what is more to the point, he can excite others into wanting to read it also.**
> **—*Janet Overmyer***

While Rexroth has obviously read much of the scholarship surrounding each of the works, his special talent lies in being uncorrupted by it, so that he approaches each classic as though it were a brand new book, just arrived for review. He goes immediately to the heart of each, indicating its theme(s), style, and pertinence in a few pithy paragraphs. Although he is sometimes adversely critical, he is plainly excited by each book and, what is more to the point, he can excite others into wanting to read it also. (After reading the original *Saturday Review* articles, I rushed out and bought *The Epic of Gilgamesh* and *The Tale of Genji*; after rereading these reviews, I see I will have to buy several more.)

By making the contents of these classics interesting to and relevant for man today, Rexroth demonstrates plainly why "classic" rightfully means a literary work alive with transcendent insight, not a tiresome tome one must struggle through for a book report in English 10-A. For instance, he comments that *The Odyssey* resembles the ever-recurring dream of the traveling man who wonders what his wife is doing at home. Livy's history, *Early Rome,* is a myth of how the aristocrats of the day supposed themselves to be; it provided models for generations of heroes to come, in many different countries and cultures. Marco Polo had "what we have lost—an ecumenical mind, an international sensibility;" he did not find distant persons and customs strange, no matter how outlandish. Casanova's *History of My Life* possesses a "peculiar naked profundity" by revealing that Casanova, "a man without interiority except for a profound awareness of the vanity of human wishes," knew that the passage of time has no meaning.

Rexroth is at times highly controversial, as when he says that *The Brothers Karamazov* contains "general ideas reduced to foolishness and hysteria," and that tragedy is neither impressive, nor even believable, when it is so garrulously articulate. Still, the opposition probably stirred up by such comments will force the reader back to the book to formulate his rebuttal, which is precisely what Rexroth intends.

Not the least of the virtues of this book is that the reader is told, for the works that must be read in translation, which are the best and most inexpensive editions. If this book were handed to students in Comparative Literature courses, it would do more to arouse interest than any number of dull, learned lectures by dull, learned pedagogues who equate solemnity with profundity.

Times Literary Supplement (review date 30 April 1971)

SOURCE: "The Transcendental Redoubt," in *Times Literary Supplement,* April 30, 1971, p. 499.

[*In the following review, the critic offers a positive assessment of* With Eye and Ear, *drawing comparisons between Rexroth and Ralph Waldo Emerson.*]

The Azimuth Press has found a gnomon in Kenneth Rexroth. Even his style tends towards the gnomic, ranging the heavens of literature from China to Peru: "*Don Quixote, The Tale of Genji, The Dream of the Red Chamber,* the *Satyricon,* these are the world's major works of prose fiction." Or of D. H. Lawrence: "He is certainly one of the major poets of the twentieth century, along with Guillaume Apollinaire and William Carlos Williams." Or: "So the fifty odd stories in *The Farmer's Daughters,* the collected stories of William Carlos Williams, are amongst the most precious possessions of the twentieth century in any language."

The claims sound heady; but this is part of the intoxication of the Pacific West where *The Pillow Book and Prayer Mat of Flesh* loom far closer across the ocean. A spiritual renewal needs its champion and California—that heterogeneous land of *nabis,* Zen Buddhists, Gnostics Tantric or underground Catholics—has launched an erudite prophet to descend on the priesthood of the new Jerusalem. Woe unto that "minor American academic critic of the now-forgotten Reactionary Generation, Professor R. P. Blackmur"! Woe unto "that strange alliance of penitent Marxists and Southern Cavaliers whose organs of literary intimidation were the now-forgotten quarterlies, the *Kenyon* and *Partisan Reviews*"! "Woe unto you, lawyers! for ye have taken away the key of knowledge: ye entered not in yourselves, and them that were entering ye hindered."

The effect of these scattered reviews and articles, gathered from more than a decade, is like some old San Francisco dwelling with its wooden bay-windows, its millwork acanthus leaves and volutes holding up the cornices and plaster cupids on the ceilings, and marble or Italian-tile fireplaces. "Somehow I've always lived in such a place", Kenneth Rexroth explains, "and live in one now." But the Bay Area is not exactly the Mediterranean, nor is the house exactly an Italian villa. There is something too grandiose, too gimcrack, even oddly Anglophile about the whole carpentry. This may not be quite the site for seeing life steadily and seeing it whole (a favourite maxim): but as a Catholic redoubt against the Masada of Mornington Heights (or "Old Left Establishment, one of the numerous clones of Philip Rahv"), it supplies its own strange, fitful illumination.

The pressures of consensus thought, at least, are flouted. Individuals and individual achievements alone are celebrated: Defoe, Frank Norris, Ford Madox Ford, Sei Shonagon, D. H. Lawrence, Kafka, Sir Thomas More, Sir Thomas Browne, Tolstoy. Only one thread binds this encyclopedic journey through past and present: what has kept civilization going all these years? And the answer acknowledged is Maritain's: "The prayers of the contemplatives in the monasteries."

So the contemplative reader moves from a long discursive essay on **"The Spiritual Alchemy of Thomas Vaughan"** to **"Smoky the Bear Bodhisattva"** (celebrating Gary Snyder and Philip Whalen). In many ways Kenneth Rexroth resembles Emerson. Perhaps he is the Pacific reincarnation of that transcendentalist, who made his own passage to California exactly a century ago.

Thomas Parkinson (essay date 1976)

SOURCE: "Kenneth Rexroth, Poet," in *Ohio Review,* Vol. 17, No. 2, 1976, pp. 54-67.

[*In the following essay, Parkinson discusses the poetry and literary accomplishment of Rexroth through examination of* The Phoenix and the Tortoise. *According to Parkinson, "To Rexroth poetry envisions and embodies life on a scale and grandeur that none of his poetic contemporaries has attempted to reach."*]

Many readers have difficulty in disengaging Rexroth as poet from Rexroth as social critic, Rexroth as man of letters, Rexroth as poetic warrior carrying on a vendetta with those who do not see the world of poetry as he does. One distinguished writer remarked scornfully in my presence that he did not consider Rexroth a poet but a politician. In the interests of dinner table decorum I didn't bother to press him to a clearer definition, but the remark was so pejorative in tone that it was hardly necessary. Now the poetic community has before it the **Collected Shorter Poems** and the **Collected Longer Poems** from New Directions, and the matter is there to be explored afresh.

I say "explored" deliberately, because magisterial criticism seems to me impertinent to most current literature, and because the poetry of Rexroth is special in the contemporary canon: because it gives a world to explore, it is not predicated on convention or a break from convention, it is not tuned to the sequence of fads that absorbs so much energy better invested. In an age of fashions without style, this body of work has style. There is integrity of manner because there is integrity of vision that is not clouded by polemics or confined to the merely aesthetic. The poetry articulates, often overtly but more often by example, a devotion to the contemplative life. Insofar as it is a record of events, it records the anguish and reward of pursuing the contemplative life in a world of spiritual, religious environmental, and economic agony. When the world intrudes on the quest it is sometimes met with fury and invective, scorn, sarcasm, contempt, and hatred.

Style is a by-product. Writers of stature do not say, "I must develop a style," and then go about deliberately seeking mannerisms that will set them apart from their contemporaries and past convention. Style is a by-product of an habitual disposition toward experience. The man who devotes his life to an art or to the arts does so because he has a love for the medium of that art and what has been accomplished through that medium, and he has an intuitive and often secretly arrogant belief that he has something to do with or say through that medium, something of importance. He is persuaded (with little objective reason persuaded), with the fatality of birth, that there is something he can do that no one else can do, and that the art is his work. He has a vocation. How many people have felt that persuasion and then, after disappointment and neglect, sometimes justified, have turned to some other mode of being. Henry James said once that a man can be taught the techniques of an art but he cannot be taught the one necessity, courage. To be an artist at any time demands courage; to be an artist in California from 1927, when Rexroth first established himself in San Francisco, through the Reagan regime, when Rexroth resettled in Santa Barbara, demands heroism.

And he will have something to do with or say through that medium. The implied distinction sets Rexroth apart from, say, Ezra Pound. When Rexroth writes of the Revolution of the Word, he is saying something very complex. Certainly he has in mind the *logos,* and there is an underlying religious motive. Certainly too he is thinking of the revolution of the word that began with Baudelaire and Whitman, continued through Pound and Apollinaire, and is the heritage of the modern age, the attempt through changing the medium of verse to change sensibility and hence in effect the structuring of society. But he also means the revolution *through* the word, and his affection for the poetry of D. H. Lawrence is revealing (for Eliot was quite right in saying that in Lawrence's poetry at its most transcendent one is not aware of the poetry but of what one is seeing through the poetry). Like any poet, Rexroth is concerned with what he can do *with* the medium, but his stress is on what can be done *through* words. He uses as epigraph for his **Collected Shorter Poems** a translation from an anonymous Provençal poem:

> When the nightingale cries
> All night and all day,
> I have my sweetheart
> Under the flower
> Till the watch from the tower
> Cries, "Lovers, rise!
> The dawn comes and the bright day."

Poets growing up between 1920 and the present have used Ezra Pound's early poems as the best working out of poetic problems. Rexroth knew this, and his incidental comments in conversation on Pound's prosody set all those young associates, as I then was, wondering. Pound rendered the same poem:

> When the nightingale to his mate
> Sings day-long and night late
> My love and I keep state
> In bower
> In flower
> 'Till the watchman on the tower
> Cry:
> > "Up! Thou rascal, Rise,
> > I see the white
> > > Light
> > > And the night
> > > > Flies."

Here is a difference.

The Pound version is a pedagogue's delight, and that was one of Pound's functions. He instructed an entire generation of American poets. Seldom has the poetic game been so nakedly given away; the leading of vowel tones that Duncan talks about mysteriously is not one bit a mystery here. The diphthong *ai* becomes the long *e*, the long *e* and diphthong *ai* continue until the diphthong *au* takes control, and finally the diphthong *ai* dominates and concludes. The poem is formulated in circular design—it is all there, evident. Who can not like it, teacher, student, or poet? Rexroth knew all that, and deliberately set about determining the motive of his collected shorter poems by denying it.

The Rexroth version does not point to itself but to the experience. Anyone who thinks that this is an accident has very little sense of the recent history of poetry—the Pound version points to itself, to its fine shadings, to its subtleties, to its movement and recoil and ultimate satisfaction of expectations established in the opening line. Irresistible. I admire

it gratefully—any pedagogue would—but there is something lost to the experience in the Pound version. Rexroth appeals to the common experience of the dawn song, Pound to the overt artifice of his special treatment.

The Pound poem makes a convention new: the Rexroth poem attempts to recreate a traditional experience. The difference represents in miniature Rexroth's definition of his poetic function. Conventions irritate him to the point of indifference, so that he is not even interested in destroying them. Traditions, the core experience of the race, as embodied in wisdom whether poetical or philosophical or historical or religious—these are the substance of his concern. He writes poetry to discover and render wisdom. Wisdom is useless knowledge, knowledge after the fact, and the fact never recurs in precisely that form. It is not paradoxing to say that genuine wisdom is unique in the same way that a genuine poem is. It makes a generous accurate statement about the special form that a universal recurring problem, and an insoluble one, takes. The human effort to be good, the hunger for righteousness, is its sad area for contemplation.

This is why, after the first two books, **The Art of Worldly Wisdom** and **In What Hour,** Rexroth settles into a relatively fixed mode of prosody, normally syllabic in structure. Although sympathetic to innovative writing, he publishes few experiments with language because of his basic persuasion that what poetry lets us see is more important than its texture, that verbal process is only incidentally revelatory, that knowledge, experience, understanding are the materials. His admiration for Tu Fu, Catullus, Baudelaire, Lawrence, and Stevens shows his own motivation. That is the lineage of the visionary and moral traditionalist.

But Rexroth has his special particular tone, that of the civilized man in a barbarous world, self-conscious and socially aware, speaking in an urbane ironic voice. Of art and letters, girls and wine, food and politics, children and music, nature and history, the conversation of a club that never existed on land or sea. Perhaps, thinking of the poetry, the hardest thing to comprehend is just that tone—all one can do is listen, for its modulations, its sudden surge to anger, its suave inversion of its own plausibility, its tinge of sadness, its rage against insensitivity. It goes on talking, talking, a reminder of possibility in the darkening years.

This was the ground of his appeal, especially with the poems from **The Phoenix and the Tortoise** on to the present. Nobody else was thinking of writing poetry in just those terms. Nobody else had the boldness to define his poem's subject as so large and inclusive:

> . . . And I,
> Walking by the viscid, menacing
> Water, turn with my heavy heart

In my baffled brain, Plutarch's page—
The falling light of the Spartan
Heroes in the late Hellenic dusk—
Agis, Cleomenes—this poem
Of the Phoenix and the tortoise—
Of what survives and what perishes,
And how, of the fall of history
And waste of fact—on the crumbling
Edge of a ruined polity
That washes away in an ocean
Whose shores are all washing into death.

It could have been written yesterday; it was published in 1944. Rather than talk about the two formidable collected volumes, I should prefer to look closely at the volume that for me still embodies the reasons for my admiration and indebtedness to the poetry of Rexroth.

II.

I have several copies of *The Phoenix and the Tortoise.* One of them is worn from reading. The binding is broken. I don't know how many times I have read it. Except for books used in teaching, very few books in my library show equivalent wear.

The seasons revolve and the years change
With no assistance or supervision.
The moon, without taking thought,
Moves in its cycle, full, crescent, and full.

The white moon enters the heart of the river;
The air is drugged with azalea blossoms;
Deep in the night a pine cone falls;
Our campfire dies out in the empty mountains.

The sharp stars flicker in the tremulous branches;
The lake is black, bottomless in the crystalline
  night;
High in the sky the Northern Crown
Is cut in half by the dim summit of a snow peak.

O heart, heart, so singularly
Intransigent and corruptible,
Here we lie entranced by the starlit water,
And moments that should each last forever

Slide unconsciously by us like water.

I have been reading this poem for twenty-five years with deepening pleasure. It is not a pleasure that comes from recognizing new relations within the poem that had evaded me before but instead a joy that grows as my experience grows, makes the poem more true because I have, at least quantitatively, more opportunity for knowing what the truth is or

might be. The quietness of notation, the directness of that the natural world lives on without assistance or supervision, the rightness of the perceptions. Perhaps the poem has conditioned my experience so that it has become difficult to distinguish between the two, but if so its power is dual, the power to alert the sensibility, the power to vindicate.

There are others of the short poems that show the same kind of imagination at work. The view here shown, of the break between man and nature, the adoration of a natural structure that has an integrity and beauty of design beyond human touch or apprehension, the elegiac realization of human separation from such an order, its failure to be in a way analogous to the biological and astronomical order—there is great poignance in it. The poem immediately following it shows knowledge, the attentiveness that lets us see in what fullness it is the same basic biological design:

Now, on this day of the first hundred flowers,
Fate pauses for us in imagination,
As it shall not ever in reality—
As these swifts that link endless parabolas
Change guard unseen in their secret crevices.
Other anniversaries that we have walked
Along this hillcrest through the black fir forest,
Past the abandoned farm, have been just the
  same—
Even the fog necklaces on the fencewires
Seem to have gained or lost hardly a jewel;
The annual and diurnal patterns hold.
Even the attrition of the cypress grove
Is slow and orderly, each year one more tree
Breaks ranks and lies down, decrepit in the wind.
Each year, on summer's first luminous morning,
The swallows come back, whispering and weaving
Figure eights around the sharp curves of the swifts
Plaiting together the summer air all day,
That the bats and owls unravel in the nights.
And we come back, the signs of time upon us,
In the pause of fate, the threading of the year.

James Broughton once said about the reputations of Bay Area artists, whether poets or film-makers, that they suffered in relation to those of New York artists because they were interested in, believed in, natural and aesthetic beauty, were not at all bashful in reacting to it or trying to make it. The beauty of this poem—and it is beautiful—parallels the beauty of, grows from, the natural order of the world. The poem has faith in that order, even to the weaving and unweaving of flight patterns by swift, swallow, bat, owl. The subject is old. In the Mediterranean spring and summer, whether in Italy or California, I am moved by the changing of the guard when the swallows suddenly seem to diminish and move more clumsily because the bats have taken over—there is a poem dimly in my memory on the subject. It must be one of the genuinely classical human observations.

The poem's faith in the almost military regularity of nature, the breaking of ranks by the cypress trees, the swifts' changing of guard—this is not an aesthetic but an experienced order: "The annual and diurnal patterns hold." The vocabulary of nature is limited but endless; the human entity is more varied but has a definite term, is not irreplaceable, as the fog necklaces on the fencewires are. There is pathos here without self-pity, and the curious thing is that this poet who speaks so frequently of personality as necessary to poetry, as inevitable, and does so sometimes with rancor and vigor that seem excessive to the subject, should himself become in these poems more type than person. Nobody else could have written such poems, but the style, as I have already asserted, is more the way of expressing a complex disposition toward experience than the assertion of personal uniqueness. These poems stand as refractions of general design, parts of the universe rather than expressions of a separate individualism.

The term "classic" keeps forcing itself on my attention as I contemplate this body of work. At times Rexroth exhibits that enviable gift of getting to the ground of experience that one sees in the poetry of Lawrence or Yeats when they are at their least effortful. The theme of these two poems is close to that of "The Wild Swans at Coole," but the poems are much more selfless than Yeats' moving lyric. For in one of its aspects, Rexroth's poetry strikes the same nerve as "I have a gentil cok" or "The Maidens Came," poems that are not often part of critical discussion because there is nothing much to do but admire them. His feeling toward nature has none of the egotism that afflicts Keats or Wordsworth or, to take the really egregious example, Hopkins. Perhaps this is because Rexroth has lived closer to wilderness than to what Europeans call "nature"; it is one thing to listen to a nightingale on Hampstead Heath and something very different to walk in the hills of Marin county or lie by a dwindling camp fire in the Sierra. Wilderness has a way of putting human emotions in their proper place.

At the base of many of the shorter poems, then, is the recognition of an extra-human order, non-social, transcendent. Yet there is no sentimentalizing of nature, no infusion of it with human quality. It is a measure and norm, indifferent.

Among the other shorter poems are numerous erotic poems, sometimes set in wilderness, sometimes urbanely Roman or Mediterranean. Rexroth seemed to fix on several qualities in his life in California that extended to analogies to other cultures and geographies, and his favorites were the Orient and the classic world of the Graeco-Roman tradition. His later work would result in his book of translations from Mediterranean poetry and his two books of poems from the Japanese and the Chinese—beautifully printed, lovingly rendered, these books have achieved the status of ideal Christmas presents. Their tone was already present in the translations that conclude *The Phoenix and the Tortoise,* and it infused the style of the entire book. Somehow he discovered among the dreary stretches of Ausonius the one poem surely by him and genuinely fine. From the medieval *Carmina,* he chose the brilliant "Rumor Laetalis." They are adaptations—the tone is what mattered to him.

The special quality of this poetry, however, is pleasure in the language and in the experience. The pleasure grows from the clear fact that the poet knows what he means, he says what he means, and he means what he says. Sometimes the poetry appears declarative, what is sometimes disparagingly called the poetry of statement, as if cogency and fullness of statement did not in themselves have suggestion and overtone enough:

> . . . I have only the swindling
> Memory of poisoned honey.
>
> Poetry and letters
> Persist in silence and solitude.
>
> . . . In ten years
> The art of communication
> Will be more limited.
> The wheel, the lever, the incline,
> May survive, and perhaps
> The Alphabet. At the moment
> The intellectual
> Advance guard is agitated
> Between the Accumulation
> Of Capital and the
> Systematic Derangement of
> The senses, and the Right
> To Homosexuality.

These several statements, the cheated lover, the neglected poet, the saddened intellectual—all of them have the overtone of their voice, one that is widely diffused. They are characteristic, and compared to other verse of the period they have a quality of sustained judgment, of ultimate good sense, of wry factualness, that is extraordinary. The capacity for making judgments appear factual, to reify the moral imagination, is not so frequent that one can take such poetry lightly. It is not just that this was the way things were, but the way they are, their continuousness, and alas, their permanence.

III.

The long poem. Since 1912 the quality and quantity of poetry in the United States has steadily grown. Looking at the recent output of a small press sent to me for review, I find myself murmuring Yeats' words about the Rhymers' Club, "I don't know whether any of us will become great or famous, but I know one thing—there are too many of us." The very growth of poetic technique and skill, however, had for a long time a deleterious effect. First, the exploration of new methods turned the poet's attention from what he could do through words to what he could do with them—a very salutary thing for the art. The novelist knew no such inhibitions, and from Gertrude Stein and James Joyce on, novelists incorporated the new poetic devices into their work until, finally, the novel had become so Alexandrian as to lead literary historians to declare that *Finnegans Wake* was the novel's funeral.

At the same time there was a determined effort to reclaim from the novel much of the ground lost by the modern poem's tendency toward the compact, the elliptical, the privately symbolic. These efforts are well known, and the line from the *Cantos* of Pound through Williams' *Paterson* to Olson's *Maximus* poems is clear to see. Crane's *Bridge* does not fall entirely outside that line of development, but its use of closed forms seems to shunt it toward another line of development.

The Bridge, The Four Quartets, **The Phoenix and the Tortoise.** The sequence does not seem exactly right, but it seems to me more appropriate than placing Rexroth's poem in the Pound-Williams-Olson lineage. In fact, Rexroth stands outside both lineages, but it might be helpful to see his poem in conjunction with the *Four Quartets,* which were written and published, except for the first of them, during the Second World War. For the *Quartets* are in effect war poems, poems written to celebrate the religious and historical continuity of England when that continuity seemed most menaced, poems also designed to place the poet's religious responsibility for the spiritual state of his world. **The Phoenix and the Tortoise** is also a war poem but written from outside the war, and from outside any state or national loyalty. Its loyalties are placed in another realm. At the same time, it is a religious meditative poem on history, on what abides and what perishes, on the place of man in nature and the cosmic resonance of individual responsibility.

"Meditations in a cold solitude." The cold in this line is physical, night by the sea, and the solitude of the poem comes from the contemplation of tragedy. Remote on the Pacific shore, there is nothing to sustain except what in the cultural imagination gets across the Sierra. His memory broods over, ruminates on, what makes for historical continuity as he stands

> . . . here on the edge of death,
> Seeking the continuity,
> The germ plasm of history,

The epic's lyric absolute.

He can find that absolute in love, in the sacrament of marriage, in sexual abandon, in the imperious remoteness of geology, in courtesans and trivial survivals: the baby, the rose, the pear tree, the coin that outlives Tiberius, vulnerable mere data. Tragedy—

> . . . beyond the reach
> Of my drowsy integrity,
> The race of glory and the race
> Of shame, just or unjust, alike
> Miserable, both come to evil end.

History apart from irreducible values of biology and personality (in a sense not at all conventional) he sees from an Augustinian perspective. History, the public articulation of human energy, is evil and at best tragic, and the state is the organization on massive scale of the evil motives of men. In the midst of the Second World War, this isolated clear look has an austerity and compassion that are unique and, now, all the more accurate:

> Men drop dead in the ancient rubbish
> Of the Acropolis, scholars fall
> Into self-dug graves, Jews are smashed
> Like heroic vermin in the Polish winter.

Christianity, when its communal and metaphysical sanctions give out, places an intolerable and even paralyzing burden on the believer. Eugene O'Neill's life is one bitter monument to that fact. There are many others. Christianity cannot accommodate tragedy; all its habits and drifts are toward ultimate resolutions, and the insoluble it cannot admit. If one maintains the ethic of Christianity without belief in its rituals and dogmas, then all that sacrifice, repentance, and prayer are self-flagellating. The Augustinian doctrine of history without a Day of Judgment leaves one caught in a world of pointless cruelty. After describing some of the horrors of the Second World War, Rexroth shifts the burden to his own shoulders:

> This is my fault, the horrible term
> Of weakness, evasion, indulgence,
> The total of my petty fault—
> No other man's.
>
> And out of this
> Shall I reclaim beauty, peace of soul,
> The perfect gift of self-sacrifice
> Myself as act, as immortal person?

He walks on, through the light of nature, clouds, and sea, as the sun rises:

My wife has been swimming in the breakers,
She comes up the beach to meet me, nude,
Sparkling with water, singing high and clear
Against the surf. The sun crosses
The hills and fills her hair, as it lights
The moon and glorifies the sea
And deep in the empty mountains melts
The snow of winter and the glaciers
Of ten thousand thousand years.

The answer is love, is sacramental marriage. In the terms of Rexroth's preface, "I have tried to embody in verse the belief that the only valid conservation of value lies in the assumption of unlimited liability, the supernatural identification of the self with the tragic unity of creative process." This is to be achieved by the movement from the self to the other, and through that other to universal commitment.

Rexroth claims no individual credit for the idea, citing Lawrence and Schweitzer as predecessors:

> The process as I see it goes something like this: from abandon to erotic mysticism, from erotic mysticism to the ethical mysticism of sacramental marriage, thence to the realization of the ethical mysticism of universal responsibility—from the Dual to the Other. These poems might well be dedicated to D. H. Lawrence, who died in the attempt to refound a spiritual family. One of the poems is a conscious paraphrase of one of his.

> *The Phoenix and the Tortoise* is an attempt to portray the whole process in historical, personal and physical terms. I have tried to embody in verse the belief that the only valid conservation of value lies in the assumption of unlimited liability, the supernatural identification of the self with the tragic unity of creative process. I hope I have made it clear that I do not believe that the Self does this by an act of will, by sheer assertion. He who would save his life must lose it.

Unlimited liability is a product of the imagination. If a president who declared an aggressive war intervening in the lives of remote and innocent people had to conduct it by personally strangling each man, woman, and child of the "enemy," there would be no such wars. But since he has no personal responsibility, he can allow and even threaten and encourage actions that would make slow strangulation a welcome death.

One difficulty is that the people endowed with imagination are the ones most deeply hurt, in the moral sense. To live in the twentieth century with full imaginative sensibility operative at the highest level is to have a molecule painfully cut out of one's body each second of each day, as some peasant dies from fragmentation bombs, as some black chalks up another hopeless second in the concentration camps that are called corrective institutions, as some baby dwindles away from his possibilities in some disease-ridden hut or tenement. And those who are doing the cutting believe in their righteousness. "Why should we pour our money into the rat-hole of some slum? If you've seen one slum you've seen them all."

So the title poem of *The Phoenix and the Tortoise* stands in its integrity as a witness to the love of true righteousness, of mercy, of pity, of love, of knowledge and understanding. How can one be good in an evil world? the classic traditional question that never leaves us, our moral doom.

The poem seems to me the most perfect artistically of the long meditative poems of the twentieth century. It cannot be reduced to a series of barren meditations relieved by occasional bursts of lyric felicity. The texture is even in its interest and appeal. Rexroth can think in verse, and unlike so many of the large established poetic imaginations of the twentieth century, he is not a truncated man, a literary specialist with some cranky notions about economics or language or religion or history. He knows the fashions of his age, and he knows what is faddish and impertinent in them. He is not taken in by the thought of the moment that is there only to feed an empty desire for false novelties. The only comparable poems are Eliot's *Four Quartets,* and to choose them over Rexroth's poem strikes me as a foolish act. *The Phoenix and the Tortoise* is a saddening poem *not* because it doesn't shape a valid artistic form—it does—but because even the world of 1944, the agonies of that terrible war, seems more possibly habitable than the world that has come out of the post-war years. Now it would be hard to say that the annual and diurnal patterns persist, power is so heavily concentrated and so savagely misused.

IV.

I have insisted on talking of Rexroth as poet and concentrated on a single book in so doing because economy requires some selectivity. What I have said of *The Phoenix and the Tortoise* does not "cover" his poetry, which is diverse and rich beyond the limits of any single book. *The Collected Shorter Poems* and *The Collected Longer Poems* provide a massive body of work for exploration. The whole seems to me unique and overwhelmingly useful. Utility, beauty, integrity, fullness of vision, and a knowledge of the world that extends beyond the latest critical book on Mallarmé while including it. To Rexroth poetry envisions and embodies life on a scale and grandeur that none of his poetic contemporaries has attempted to reach. At the same time he has not neglected precision of observation, clarity of articulation, verbal play and prosodic invention.

In a curious way, for his fellow poets, and especially those younger ones who take him with appropriate seriousness, he doesn't tell us much about poetry. His later work, from *The Phoenix and the Tortoise* on, settles into an adaptation of Apollinaire's revivifying of the eight syllable line in French, with variations, and of modern poets in English Rexroth seems to have profited most from the study of Apollinaire. Still, if one wants the experience of Apollinaire's qualities, better to go to him directly. If one wants to learn the rich vocabulary of forms that is the heritage of the modern period, Rexroth has less to offer than Stevens, Neruda, Pound, Williams, Desnos, Eluard, Rilke, Yeats, even Auden. Rexroth offers something else, a model for emulation that one can neither imitate nor loot because it is all of a piece, a fully ordered design of a recognizable universe to which one can give imaginative assent. I don't know what the term major exactly means, but if the body of Rexroth's poetic work is not a major achievement, then we can forget the term.

David Kirby (review date 30 May 1980)

SOURCE: "Quiet Satisfaction," in *Times Literary Supplement,* May 30, 1980, p. 620.

[*In the following review, Kirby gives a favorable assessment of* The Morning Star.]

The first section of *The Morning Star* consists of very short poems, glimpses of the natural world with or without the human presence:

On the forest path
The leaves fall. In the withered
Grass the crickets sing
Their last songs. Through dew and dusk
I walk the paths you once walked,
My sleeves wet with memory.

What is attempted here is the directness and clarity more commonly associated with Japanese than with Western art, a method which the haiku poet Noboru Fujiwara has described as "a weeding out of all that would clutter, muddy, confuse, leading to great incisiveness, clear purpose." Reviewing Rexroth's *One Hundred Poems from the Chinese* (in the June 1957 number of *Poetry*), William Carlos Williams commented on the absence of metaphor in Oriental verse. Metaphor is more at home in cultures where the dualistic nature of things is taken for granted, for metaphor consists of an object and its reference—flint and steel, says Williams, which spark when struck together. Nor does Rexroth put much of himself into these poems of the first section, and this too is understandable from an Oriental perspective. In *A Mediator's Diary,* Jane Hamilton-Merritt recalls her discussions of the creative process with a Thai monk who pointed out that the truly religious do not write at all, much less parade their own egos for the world's admiration.

> In its directness and clarity, *The Morning Star* should appeal greatly to adolescents, because they have read nothing; not at all to university undergraduates, because they have read T. S. Eliot; and greatly again to older readers, because they have read much.
> —*David Kirby*

The second section of *The Morning Star* is a meditation on mortality and eternity, and the third section, a translated sequence called **"The Love Poems of Marichiko,"** forms what Rexroth calls "a sort of little novel". The strongest of the three sections, these poems dwell on the delights of passionate and illicit love. To the Eastern mind, writes Joseph Campbell in *Myths to Live By,* only illicit love is passionate, and it is certainly passionate here:

As I came from the
Hot bath, you took me before
The horizontal mirror
Beside the low bed, while my
Breasts quivered in your hands, my
Buttocks shivered against you.

But as the Buddha says, "The combinations of the world are unstable by nature", and the affair ends badly:

Chilled through, I wake up
With the first light. Outside my window
A red maple leaf floats silently down.
What am I to believe?
Indifference?
Malice?
I hate the sight of coming day
Since that morning when
Your insensitive gaze turned me to ice
Like the pale moon in the dawn.

The tone throughout *The Morning Star* is one of quietism; the passion in **"The Love Poems of Marichiko"** simply throws into relief the solitary, minimal, introspective nature of Rexroth's persona. How different this is from the Rexroth of *The Phoenix and the Tortoise* (1944), who sounds like Lawrence and Pound and Whitman, or the one who wrote this, in *In Defense of the Earth* (1956), about Dylan Thomas:

And all the birds of the deep sea rise up
Over the luxury liners and scream,
"You killed him! You killed him.
In your God damned Brooks Brothers suit,
You son of a bitch."

In those days Rexroth sounded like a *nabi*, a term he applies to Allen Ginsberg in **With Eye and Ear** (1970), one of those bearded, bad-smelling crazies who came down periodically from the hills to Jerusalem and denounced everyone, or simply like an "old-fashioned American sorehead", as Alfred Kazin once called Rexroth. Now he appears to belong, or to want to belong, at least as much as a publishing writer can, to the Buddhist bodhisattvas or the yamabushi of Japan or the zaddiks of Hasidism or the Shiite hidden imam. These are Rexroth's heroes, as one sees from his prose writings and from an interview with him in Volume Two (1979) of an American Buddhist magazine called *Zero;* their goal is to ignore the world, to "live unknown." One might characterize this change with Rexroth's own words (from his essay on Rimbaud in **Bird in the Bush,** 1959): "True illumination always results in a special sweetness of temper, a deep, lyric equanimity and magnanimity. The outstanding characteristic of the mystic's vision is that it is satisfying. He is never frustrated, at least not in our worldly sense."

In its directness and clarity, *The Morning Star* should appeal greatly to adolescents, because they have read nothing; not at all to university undergraduates, because they have read T. S. Eliot; and greatly again to older readers, because they have read much.

Morgan Gibson (essay date 1986)

SOURCE: "'Poetry Is Vision'—'Vision Is Love': Rexroth's Philosophy of Literature," in *Revolutionary Rexroth: Poet of East-West Wisdom*, Archon Books, 1986, pp. 32-48.

[*In the following essay, Gibson examines the evolution of Rexroth's poetic style, literary influences, and conception of personal vision and communal sacrament. According to Gibson, "Rexroth shows that vision is organic consciousness, sympathetic, clear, and steady, communing, communicating, realizing the many in the one, the one in the many, the universality of each being."*]

According to Rexroth's theory and practice, poetry is vision. Poets and critics have often used this term carelessly, but in Rexroth's work "vision" has several definite meanings that cohere in his organic philosophy of literature-in-community.

"Vision," referring to phases of a creative process of con-sciousness, sometimes means contemplation, in which the poet communed with nature and those he loved, and in which he periodically had oceanic, ecstatic experiences of realization, illumination, or enlightenment. At these times, sensation, perception, thinking, and feeling, especially love, were clarified, purified, and radically expanded; so he claimed that "vision is love." As experience became intellectualized, vision came to mean the act of philosophizing and also the worldview projected by philosophizing; so vision is both sensuous and abstract, nonverbal and literary, personal and transpersonal. Rexroth's world vision is both conservative in reviving and uniquely synthesizing Hebraic-Christian, classical, Buddhist, and modern traditions of spiritual realization, and revolutionary in its vigorous opposition to the prevailing impersonality and alienation of modern society, technology, and culture. As Rexroth's personal experiences were expressed in poetry, vision became the act of poetic communication, evolving from interpersonal communion and recreating community. His vision is uniquely his, yet is also universal in scope and validity because it realizes the person in world community. Rexroth's world vision reveals his, and our, "Being in the World," as Heidegger put it.

"Poetry is vision," Rexroth asserts in **"Poetry, Regeneration, and D.H. Lawrence,"** "the pure act of sensual communion and contemplation." Does he mean all poetry, or the best of it? Obviously his idea is normative rather than descriptive, characterizing the poetry of Lawrence, Yeats, Blake, Whitman, poetry that he translated by Tu Fu, Li Ch'ing Chao, Sappho, Dante, and his own. He means by "vision" the essence of poetry, the quality that makes it true poetry, the quality often ignored by critics who emphasize form, structure, construction, or technique at the expense of imagination, or identify artifice as poetry itself. Craftsmanship is important in Rexroth's own poetry and all poetry that he values, but as a means to an end rather than as an end in itself. What, in his opinion, does poetry at its best communicate? Visionary experience: vision itself. And what is that?

He defines poetic vision as an *act,* a dynamic transformation of experience rather than as passive reflection; and it is a *pure* act, unlike impure acts of ordinary experience that lack unifying aesthetic concentration. There may be a suggestion that poetry is a purifying act, as in Aristotle's idea of catharsis; but in Rexroth's view poetry does more than purge impure emotions, for *communion* implies that poetry is an intimate experience of mutuality, a sacramental act of commemoration in which we may be mystically united with others and perhaps with reality as a whole. Such communion is *sensual,* for delightful sounds of language indicated by the artistry of calligraphy or typography evoke the imagined world of the poem. So poetry is a *contemplative* act, arising in deep, clear, open-minded, loving awareness. The text and form of the poem reveal the visionary act which is the essential poetry.

Rexroth shows that vision is organic consciousness, sympathetic, clear, and steady, communing, communicating, realizing the many in the one, the one in the many, the universality of each being. In vision, the observer is united with the observed, the poet communes directly with other beings, and all interact in community which extends through galaxies and transpersonal dimensions of mind that he called Buddha-worlds. Such thinking must be experienced in poetry itself, not abstracted from it as doctrine, just as in understanding music we must experience music musically.

Visionary experience—essentially formless—sometimes takes form; but *a* vision is not vision, as Rexroth carefully points out in *The Heart's Garden, The Garden's Heart:* "visions are / The measure of the defect / Of vision." Because true vision is clarified interpersonal consciousness, not hallucination, dream, or fantasy, Rexroth's poetics is opposed to surrealism and dada, as shown in his cubist poem, **"Fundamental Disagreement with Two Contemporaries,"** which alludes to Tristan Tzara and André Breton. Similarly, Rexroth refused to identify true vision with the drug highs of the Beat generation, for he doubted that Allen Ginsberg's and Jack Kerouac's frantic searches for vision in *Howl* and *On the Road* got them beyond confusion. According to Rexroth, vision is habitual clear-mindedness:

> The illuminated live
> Always in light and so do
> Not know it is there as fishes
> Do not know they live in water.
>
> . . . .
>
> St. John of the Cross said it,
> The desire for vision is
> The sin of gluttony.

"The True Person"

Rexroth insisted that vision is personal, the experience of a "true person" in community. "The universalization of the human soul, the creation of the true person," was evident in the life of Albert Schweitzer, for example. Such a person is neither merely a self-made man, nor someone who simply loses himself in work or meditation. He or she loses ego, but not the whole person, which is realized in creative interaction with others. Rexroth takes himself for granted as an integral person instead of condemning himself as a sinner or striving to change himself into someone else.

Rexroth's personalism is aesthetic as well as ethical and psychological. Because vision is personal, he typically stands undisguised in his poetry and prose instead of concealing himself behind an impersonal literary construction, a mask, like Yeats, or an "objective correlative," like Eliot and the New Critics. Rexroth's poetic theory and most of his practice challenge the impersonality of much modernist literature and criticism, particularly as Eliot dogmatized in "Tradition and the Individual Talent" about the necessity of the poet's losing his personality as he learns to express not himself but his medium. Rexroth's "progress" as poet was radically subversive of Eliot's principles, for Rexroth's work was a continual revelation of personality, his own and the personalities of the many poets from many cultures whose work he translated after imaginatively conversing with them. He might have argued against James Joyce's Stephen Dedalus that the true poet remains in his handiwork like a pantheistic god, instead of invisibly behind it like the god of Roman Catholicism. Rexroth openly participates in much of his poetry, excepting his plays, and even in them the characters' tragic lives dramatize the poet's philosophical personalism, which links each one with the fate of the human race, as the chorus proclaims near the end of *Beyond the Mountains:*

> There are countless
> Iphigenias marching to
> Their deaths at this moment in all
> The dust motes of the rising sun.
>
> There are no things in the real
> World. Only persons have being.
> Things are perspectives on persons—
> A mote of dust is a distant
> Person seen with dusty interest.

Communion: "Communication Raised to the Highest Power"

Rexroth's poetry typically arises out of preverbal, preconceptual, visionary experiences similar to those described in the sutras and tantras, D. T. Suzuki's Zen writings, William James's *Varieties of Religious Experience,* Martin Buber's *I and Thou,* Jacob Boehme's *The Signature of All Things,* George Fox's *Journals,* Vedanta, and other sources referred to throughout his work; but he remained skeptical of dogmatic and theoretical explanations, especially those depending upon an Absolute or a supernatural god. His sense that "The Holy is in the heap of dust—it is the heap of dust" was no different from the Quaker Inner Light, Blake's "Heaven in a wild flower," the emptiness of the Buddha-nature, but such an intuition cannot be forced into a dogmatic system, for such experience can only be intimated artistically, not defined scientifically.

Rexroth's "perfect communion with others" was often erotic, but at the same time it transcended physical attraction. In his many love poems, the women are spiritual beings, sometimes human, sometimes divine, as in the seventeenth poem of *The Silver Swan,* when, before dawn in Japan, he imagines a nude girl taking form from the light of the Morning Star: "her / Body flows into mine, each / Corpuscle of light merges / With a corpuscle of blood or flesh." But the erotic mysticism that permeates his poetry is but one kind of communion and, as we learn from his introduction to *The Phoenix and the Tortoise,* it is but a phase in the development of the person out of despair, through sacramental marriage, to a realization of universal responsibility. With this responsibility, a person acts with compassionate consciousness of world community. So communion of two persons in the "mutual being" of love entails, by implication, responsibility for all beings in universal community; for each is inseparable from all.

In regarding poetry as vision, Rexroth meant that it arises out of contemplation and communion to become communication and so was not complete as merely private experience. So he can also, without contradiction, say that poetry is "interpersonal communication raised to the highest power." "It communicates the most intense experiences of very highly developed sensibilities," he wrote in one of his most important essays on aesthetics, **"Unacknowledged Legislators and Art pour Art,"** in which he emphasized the personal origin of poetry and its communication not predominantly of feeling or thought, but of whole experiences: "A love poem is an act of communication of love, like a kiss." Such communication has a strong ethical value, strangely reminiscent of Matthew Arnold's "criticism of life"; or in Rexroth's words "symbolic criticism of values." So love poems and nature poems become criticisms of a dehumanized culture based on the alienation of people from one another, from their own nature, and from the universe as a whole. But such moral and intellectual functions of poetry are never separated from its emotional, psychological, sensuous, and spiritual aspects, for it "widens and deepens and sharpens the sensibility."

Most poetry in the Western world is more or less corrupted with rhetoric and manipulation . . . with program and exposition, and the actual poetry, the living speech of person to person, has been a by product.
—*Kenneth Rexroth*

Rexroth felt that Chinese and Japanese poetry often communicates experiences of such "highly developed sensibilities" more directly and purely than most European poetry because "Most poetry in the Western world is more or less corrupted with rhetoric and manipulation . . . with program and exposition, and the actual poetry, the living speech of person to person, has been a by product." This extraordinary statement, which might well be debated, may suggest

one reason for Rexroth's turn from cubism, prevalent in his theory and practice of poetry as well as painting between the World Wars, to the poetry of natural speech, which became his predominant mode from *The Phoenix and the Tortoise* (1944) on. Also, terms from European and American philosophy and historical struggles, so prominent in his poetry before *The Heart's Garden, The Garden's Heart* (1967), were used less often as oriental and especially Buddhist themes and imagery filled his poetry, both original work and translations.

In Rexroth's view, communication rests upon some preunderstanding from communion and community. A message is not transmitted mechanically by means of a text, from sender to receiver; rather, meaning evolves from preestablished community, some kind of mutual existence and mutual interest. Out of I-Thou, meaning comes. Unless we share consciousness, we can understand nothing. True communication, through poetry and other arts, helps us realize mutual being.

"The Craft Is the Vision and the Vision Is the Craft"

In emphasizing vision, Rexroth may seem to underplay skill; but in fact he was a meticulous craftsman in both poetry and prose, and his criticism of literature places a high premium on artistic technique, not as an end in itself as in aestheticism, but as a means of communicating experience. He appreciated subtle forms and techniques of many kinds of art such as action painting, progressive jazz, and the Revolution of the Word that were often condemned as obscure; but they moved him because of his sensitivity to craftsmanship and his curiosity about its meaning. "Purposive construction of any kind is a species of communication," he wrote, "just as any kind of communication must be structured." And in successful visionary poetry such as Lawrence's *Birds, Beasts, and Flowers,* "the craft is the vision and the vision is the craft."

Rexroth's own craftsmanship is impressive, and his prosody deserves a long study. He wrote some rhymed quatrains and limericks as well as a few unpublished sonnets, but most of his poetry is in free verse and in syllabic patterns that are intricately melodious; for example, the nine-syllable lines of most of *The Homestead Called Damascus,* the 7 to 8 syllable lines of most of *The Dragon and the Unicorn, The Heart's Garden, The Garden's Heart,* and of parts of *Beyond the Mountains,* and the seven syllable lines of many shorter poems such as **"The Reflecting Trees of Being and Not Being"**:

> In my childhood when I first
> Saw myself unfolded in
> The triple mirrors, in my
> Youth, when I pursued myself

Wandering on wandering
Nightbound roads like a roving
Masterless dog, when I met
myself on sharp peaks of ice.
And tasted myself dissolved
In the lulling heavy sea,
In the talking night, in the
Spiraling stars, what did I
Know?

If this passage is read aloud so that the seven syllables of each line are given equal duration, sound and meaning are fused with great clarity and dignity. Syllabic verse seems eminently suited for Rexroth's poetics of visionary communication in that it focuses attention directly on sound's meaning, the sense of sense, with more control than free verse because of regular line-lengths, whereas rhymed and accentually metered verse divides attention between the abstract sound system and the actual sound and meaning of language. In transmitting experience with maximum directness, Rexroth did not want the playful tension between abstract and actual patterns of sound, which are appropriately enriching in other kinds of poetry. He seems to have been influenced by syllabic verse in Japanese, Chinese, and French, which he translated profusely, more than by contemporary practitioners of syllabics in English such as W. H. Auden, Marianne Moore, and Dylan Thomas. Why he chose to write lines of certain length is not certain, but they feel normal in English, in which we are accustomed to alternating lines in ballad stanzas of eight syllables (not counting truncations and other frequent variations) and in most poems before free verse, pentameter lines of ten syllables: Rexroth seems to have discovered natural line-lengths from seven to nine syllables without regular accentual patterns. The seven-syllable lines (mixed with five-syllable lines) of Japanese haiku and tanka also influenced his practice. The framework of seven syllables, in this poem, allows for full freedom of speech, while at the same time providing emphases at the ends and beginnings of lines—"first," "Saw," "Youth," "myself," "Wandering" (repeated), "Nightbound," "roving," "Masterless," "Myself," "ice," "dissolved," "sea," "Spiraling," "I," and "Know."

There are also profuse echoes from line to line, supporting the unrolling theme, in parallelism indicated in the following diagram:

In my childhood
    when I first /Saw myself
        unfolded in/ The triple mirrors
in my/Youth
    when I pursued myself /
        Wandering on wandering /
        Nightbound roads
            like a roving / Masterless dog,

When I met / Myself
    on sharp peaks of ice, /
And tasted myself
    dissolved /
        In the lulling heavy sea, /
        In the talking night,
        In the / Spiraling stars,
    what did I / Know?

This subtly constructed poem of cosmic vision continues with his questioning what he knows now, as he imagines his blood flowing out to the nebulas and back. Losing himself in the vastness of the universe, he knows only faces of other persons, mostly of his beloved, beyond space and time.

Rexroth explained how he deliberately patterned vowels and consonants to enhance the melody of much of his verse, a method that he seems to have learned in part from Japanese poetry:

> Most of these poems are in syllabic lines. (Sometimes after the poem is cast in syllabic lines it is broken up into cadences.) Against this is counterpointed a rhythm primarily of quantity, secondarily of accent. In addition, close attention is paid to the melodic line of the vowels and to the evolution of consonants (p-b-k, m-r-l-y, *etc.*). In most cases a melody was written at the time of the poem.

What is important here is that the melody is inherent in the poem's language, in the rise and fall of pitch in the spoken poem, rather than being determined by an abstract form imposed upon natural speech.

Indeed, Rexroth's poetry is most often in the direct statement and address of "natural numbers," in the normal grammar of actual speech. Symbolism characterizes *The Homestead Called Damascus,* his first long poem written between 1920 and 1925, but this mode was then abandoned. A third mode, described by Rexroth as cubism or objectivism, was practiced mostly between the World Wars, with such work collected chiefly in the latter half of *In What Hour* (1940) and *The Art of Worldly Wisdom* (1940), though some also appears later.

The Vicarity of Symbolism

In his youth, Rexroth wrote symbolist poetry which evolved into *The Homestead Called Damascus,* his first long philosophical poem. This musical narrative of the traumatic quests of two brothers is full of symbols and myths of decadence, sacrifice, and fertility—a rambling home full of the bric-a-brac of imperialism; dreams of Tammuz and Adonis, castrated; Persephone and a black stripper promising sexual-spiritual revitalization. The brothers have vague, inconclusive, meandering metaphysical and theological conversations and helpless fantasies about a beautiful Renaissance maiden who occasionally rides past on a white horse. The poem echoes Stevens, Yeats, Aiken, Proust, James, French symbolist poets, anthropological scholars such as Frazer, Weston, Harrison, Cornford, Murray; and the strongest influence of all, Eliot, whose *The Waste Land* had enthused Rexroth until he realized that Eliot stood against everything that he was working for. The style of **Homestead** was not compatible with Rexroth's emerging aesthetic theory and practice of cubism and later of direct utterance, so he wrote nothing else like it and did not publish it for thirty years. Moreover, symbolism, suggesting a transcendent reality remote from immediate experience, grew from a metaphysic opposite to his idea of immanence, that the "Holy is the heap of dust" and is not symbolized by it. Nevertheless, the poem is a remarkable achievement that deserves to be honored for its own sake, for the sensuousness of its sound, the complexity of its characters and their interactions, the suggestiveness of its imagery, and its philosophical implications:

> I know this is an ambivalent
> Vicarity—who stands for who?
> And this is the reality then—
> This flesh, the flesh of this arm and I
> Know how this flesh lies on this bone
> Of this arm, this is reality—
> I know. I ask nothing more of it.
> These things are beautiful, these are
> My sacraments and I ask no more.

The Revolution of the Word: Cubism and Objectivism

Rexroth's cubist poetry and painting launched him into the international avant-garde between the two World Wars, when the Revolution of the Word was in full swing. It was a comprehensive revolution, not only of language, but also of the mind and of life itself. Whereas symbolist poetry seemed to be a language of aristocratic decadence, cubism appealed to his ambition to reconstruct language along with everything else. His youthful, elitist commitment to change the world was lifelong, though his modes of writing changed.

Rexroth's earliest cubist poems were written as early as 1920, but were not published in little magazines after 1929 and were not collected until 1949, when they appeared in *The Art of Worldly Wisdom,* including, along with short poems, *A Prolegomenon to a Theodicy.* Such writing was called "objectivist," but he preferred to describe his work as cubist, involving "the analysis of reality into simple units and the synthesis of the work of art as a real parallel to experience," as in Eisenstein's films, some of the poetry of Apollinaire, Cocteau, Cendrars, MacOrlan, Deltier, Soupault,

Aragon, Tzara, Eluard, and especially Reverdy in France, Williams, Pound, Stein, Winters, Arensberg, Lowenfels, and Zukofsky in America, songs of preliterate people such as American Indians, and of course cubist painting.

Rexroth vigorously and originally promoted the cubist aesthetic, theoretically and practically, in his own paintings, poems, essays, and translations from the French.
—Morgan Gibson

Rexroth vigorously and originally promoted the cubist aesthetic, theoretically and practically, in his own paintings, poems, essays, and translations from the French. His analytical mind was attracted to the direct, definite reconstruction of experience as an art object, which he distinguished from the dreamy suggestiveness of symbolism and surrealism. **"In the Memory of Andrée Rexroth,"** the agonizing elegy opening *The Art of Worldly Wisdom,* is Rexroth's cubism at its best, at once personal and objective:

> is a question of mutual being
> a question of congruence or
> proximity a question of
> a sudden passage in air beyond
> a window a long controlled fall
> of music . . .

Rexroth's introduction to Reverdy contains his strongest defense of cubism, which as a young man he was sure would be the future of American poetry: "Its revolution is aimed at the syntax of the mind itself." Such poetry, he claims, induces in the reader

> Vertigo, rapture, transport, crystalline and plangent sounds, shattered and refracted light, indefinite depth, weightlessness, piercing odors and tastes, and synthesizing the sensations and affects, an all-consuming clarity.

This claim cannot be argued, but only tested in the actual experience of reading cubist poetry—such as, for example, the last section of **"Andromeda Chained to Her Rock the Great Nebula in Her Heart"**:

> Eyes in moss
> Salt in mouth
> Stone in heart
> An owl rings the changes of silence
> Torn head
> Crow's wings
> Black eyeballs

Poison seeps through the parabolic sand
The rock on fire
Ice falls towards the sun.

Reading such a passage, I experience vertigo and some of the extreme sense impressions described by Rexroth, but not, I regret to say, an "all-consuming clarity," which more aptly characterizes the poems in "natural numbers" rather than cubist poems. The phenomena that he describes are comparable to those of mystical experiences; but he is careful to make a fundamental distinction between religious experiences, which are "necessitated and ultimate," and visionary poems, which are not. Poetry may communicate vision in the sense of communion, I-Thou, without being itself a vision of transcendent being.

Why did Rexroth turn away from cubism after it had made him internationally famous? In the 1953 preface to *The Art of Worldly Wisdom,* he explains that because even some of his friends in the avant-garde did not comprehend his cubist poems, he decided to reach a wider community of readers by writing very much as he spoke, in normal syntax. Nevertheless, some cubist poems continued to appear even in his late books, in the section called "Gödel's Proof" at the outset of *The Collected Shorter Poems,* for example. He never gave up on cubism, helping to revive it in essays and translations of French poetry.

Though not much in favor today, Rexroth's cubist poetry nevertheless shows his early artistic originality, his immense intellectual power, and his contribution to a worldwide cultural transformation that continues today in "language poetry" and other manifestations. In practicing cubism, he analyzed and controlled the elements of language in innovative ways that carried over to "natural numbers," especially in startling juxtapositions of particulars of experience and the phrasings of direct address. Whenever in later years he returned to cubism in his poetry, translations, and essays, it was a reminder that the Revolution of the Word and of Life had not been extinguished, even during the repressiveness of the cold war.

"Natural Numbers"—"Striving to Write the Way I Talk"

Rexroth's most characteristic, successful, and popular mode of poetic communication might be called "natural numbers," a term used in the title of one of his books, referring to poetry that stylistically approximates, in syntax and diction, actual speech of person to person. From about 1920 on he wrote translations from Greek, Chinese, Japanese, and Latin in this mode, starting with translations of Sappho:

> . . . about the cool water
> the wind sounds through sprays
> of apple, and from the quivering leaves

slumber pours down . . .

The classical directness and clarity of ancient poetry, especially of Japanese tanka, mastered through the art of translations, infused his original poems as well. Among the earliest of these is the sequence for Leslie Smith entitled **"The Thin Edge of Your Pride,"** dated 1922-1926, containing such perfect imagist passages as:

> After an hour the mild
> Confusion of snow
> Amongst the lamplights
> Has softened and subdued
> The nervous lines of bare
> Branches etched against
> The chill twilight:

Rexroth had become famous as a cubist before the poems in "natural numbers" began appearing in periodicals in the mid-1930s. He speaks through the "natural" poems as if a listener is present, so the poems are intense, dramatic speech-acts, typically expressing love or friendship, often grief, sometimes outrage and social protest. Even if a listener does not seem to be present, in poems of meditation and lone reminiscence, for instance, the voice remains so intimate that the reader becomes Rexroth's *confidant.* In autobiographical poems such as **"A Living Pearl"** and contemplative poems in the mountains such as **"Lyell's Hypothesis Again"** and **"Toward an Organic Philosophy,"** the words draw us toward him as if we are sitting beside a campfire under the stars, listening to him talk.

> **[Rexroth] speaks through the "natural" poems as if a listener is present, so the poems are intense, dramatic speech-acts, typically expressing love or friendship, often grief, sometimes outrage and social protest.**
> **—Morgan Gibson**

Direct address is also evident in the revolutionary rhetoric of the poems in the first half of *In What Hour,* the antiwar memorial for Dylan Thomas called **"Thou Shalt Not Kill,"** the ethical speculations of *The Dragon and the Unicorn,* and the dramatic tetralogy *Beyond the Mountains,* stylistically influenced by Japanese No drama. "I have spent my life striving to write the way I talk," Rexroth wrote, and his public readings convincingly demonstrated the relationship between his writing and speaking. Even when technical terms from the sciences, philosophy, politics, and theology enter his prose and poetry, along with literary and historical allusions from the major civilizations, there is a natural flow of living speech, an acceptance of the Tao, the way things naturally are, except in the symbolist and cubist poems, in which language has been willfully, sometimes forcefully, reconstructed. "Natural numbers" became the appropriate mode for the Buddhist worldview that grew in importance in Rexroth's work from World War II on, for in Buddhism, the will and ego turn out to be illusions floating in calm, compassionate contemplation.

"Actual Poetry Is the Living Speech of Person to Person"

The evolution of Rexroth's chief poetic mode, "natural numbers," from lyrical, elegiac, and satirical to dramatic forms, supported and was supported by his idea that "actual poetry is the living speech of person to person." His friend William Carlos Williams, with whom he had many affinities, believed that "you have no other speech than poetry," and Whitman had heard America singing in its common speech. Rexroth thought that poems are derived from the poetic flow of living speech, that poems are realized orally, that texts like scores of music are indications of oral performance, an art which he practiced and promoted extensively long before readings became commonplace. Through this process, poetry unites poet and audience in community. This approach counteracts the pedantic idea that poetry is fundamentally on the page or in the mind as an object of impersonal analytical study, or that poetry is some kind of artificially constructed arrangement of words that no one would ever conceivably say to one another. For Rexroth, true poetry realizes the spiritual union of Martin Buber's I-Thou.

Not all actual speech can be poetry, of course, for much talk is thoroughly debased; but poetry cannot be poetry unless it is vital communication from sensibility to sensibility, actualized in speech from one to another. The idea would have been readily accepted by the ancient Greeks, Chinese, and Japanese, among others who thought of poetry as song that unites performers and audience.

When Rexroth implies that poetic communication depends on sensibility, he seems dependent on Wordsworth, who defined a poet as "a man speaking to men—a man, it is true, endowed with more lively sensibility, more enthusiasm and tenderness, who has greater knowledge of human nature, and a more comprehensive soul, than are supposed to be common among mankind." Despite this fundamental agreement about the poet's nature and function, however, there are differences of emphasis; for whereas sensibility for Wordsworth is innately endowed, for Rexroth it can be developed to the qualitative magnitude necessary for true poetry: so poets may be made as well as born.

Poetry as Communal Sacrament

According to Rexroth, poetry originates in personal vision (communion with others), takes form in the direct communication of living speech, person-to-person, and functions sacramentally in community. In **"American Indian Songs"** he shows how song, and art generally, unite the individual to society and nature. People alienated from nature, from each other, and from themselves, as most people are in modern secular, industrial or postindustrial society, cannot imagine living organically; so poetry has a revolutionary function in reminding us that we *do* live in nature, in some kind of community, invaded and broken though it may be by technological forces that divide us from each other. In *An Autobiographical Novel* Rexroth wrote eloquently about the sacramental activities of organic societies:

> In the rites of passage—the fundamental activities and relationships of life—birth, death, sexual intercourse, eating, drinking, choosing a vocation, adolescence, mortal illness—life at its important moments is ennobled by the ceremonious introduction of transcendence: the universe is focused on the event in a Mass or ceremony that is itself a kind of dance and a work of art.

He centered on his own rites of passage and those of his family: his birth, sexual and intellectual awakenings of adolescence, his parents' illnesses and deaths, hopes for a religious vocation that climaxed during a retreat in an Anglo-Catholic monastery, and his lifelong commitment to the vocations of poet, artist and revolutionary. He wrote to and about his children and their growing awareness of the universe in **"The Lights in the Sky Are Stars," "Mary and the Seasons," "Xmas Coming,"** and many other poems. He heartrendingly commemorated his mother in two elegies and his first wife Andrée in three elegies. Some of his most intensely erotic poems are the Marichiko poems. Eating and drinking are celebrated in several appetizing passages in *The Dragon and the Unicorn* and elsewhere. Countless nature poems center on ritualistic observations of seasonal cycles and the motions of heavenly bodies.

Of all rites of passage, Rexroth seems to have been most preoccupied with marriage, for his spiritual aim was to move

> from abandon to erotic mysticism, from erotic mysticism to the ethical mysticism of sacramental marriage, thence to the realization of the ethical mysticism of universal responsibility . . .

In sacramental marriage as distinct from a merely legal bond, the I-Thou of interpersonal communion (the original vision of poetry) is realized and celebrated as the center of community, uniting each person with humanity as a whole, in universal responsibility. The union of the loving couple is the nexus of the mystical union of all. The theme is prominent in *The Phoenix and the Tortoise,* the Marichiko poems, and many others.

Rexroth's poetry is typically sacramental whether it celebrates erotic and marital union or processes of nature, humanistic revolts for freedom, or visionary creations. His poetry as a whole transmits a boundless reverence for life and love of humanity.

Most comprehensively of all the shorter poems **"A Letter to William Carlos Williams"** reveals Rexroth's visionary poetics, his commitment to poetry as interpersonal communion, communication of vision, and communal sacrament. In intimate direct address, Rexroth compares Williams to St. Francis, Brother Juniper, and Yeats's Fool of wisdom and beauty. He praises Williams's quiet affection for red wheelbarrows, cold plums, Queen Anne's lace; his stillness like that of George Fox and Christ, from which the authentic speech of poetry emerged. Then Rexroth prophesies that a young woman, walking one day in a utopian landscape by "the lucid Williams Rivers," will tell her children that it used to be the polluted Passaic in the Dark Ages; and just as the river flows through nature, Williams's veins, Rexroth's speech, history, the imagined woman and her children, as well as those of us who read the poem—flowing like the Tao, the Way of Lao-tzu—so all participate in the universal community of all beings, revealed in poetry:

> And that is what a poet
> Is, children, one who creates
> Sacramental relationships
> That last always.

Leo Hamalian (essay date Summer 1989)

SOURCE: "Scanning the Self: The Influence of Emerson on Kenneth Rexroth," in *South Dakota Review*, Vol. 27, No. 2, Summer, 1989, pp. 3-14.

[*In the following essay, Hamalian compares Rexroth's tireless self-reflection, scholarship, poetic sensibility, and role as cultural spokesperson with that of Ralph Waldo Emerson.*]

One of the crucial links between the Beat poets and the other avant-garde movements of the 1950s was Kenneth Rexroth. He served more or less as liaison between the younger generation and modernists like William Carlos Williams and Ezra Pound. A political activist for most of his life, he championed curiosity in scholarship and experimentalism in the arts and acted as a kind of *pater familias* for many poets of the '50s. One of his early disciples, Robert Duncan, found in Rexroth a learned poet able to converse as easily about Oriental philosophy or anarchism as about modernist art or jazz, and he admired him for supporting the idea of poetry unconfined to national borders of poetic schools.

Though clearly a citizen of the world, keenly attentive to international trends, Rexroth was primarily a spokesman for a special kind of American sensibility that unites relentless self-scrutiny with observation of forces at work in the immediate reality of the external world. In retrospect his poetry may be viewed along with that of Charles Olsen and Williams as one of the inescapable forces in American poetry written since World War II. From his moment to ours, American poets are either following the trail he blazed or operating as a counter-movement to his practice or implicit poetics. Speaking recently at the Guggenheim Museum in New York, Gary Snyder said as much in an overdue acknowledgement of Rexroth's significant and enduring presence on the American literary scene.

His career is marked by seemingly contradictory currents to which he himself contributed. He wrote nature poetry about the American West, commented on popular culture for the media, and devoted himself to translations from a variety of languages, at the same time eking out a marginal existence by working at odd jobs which afforded him a chance at a literary career (at times he was unemployed: then his second wife, Marie, supported them while he performed domestic duties). The psychic conflicts that must have been aroused by these contradictions might have silenced a lesser spirit or led him to the brink. Rexroth drew on some deep unifying force within himself, gathered these diverse energies together into a coherent entity, and never ceased to praise the primacy of the single self in the act of achieving almost total integration and autonomy, of becoming its own cosmos. He resisted the demands of the rival selves (unlike Eliot and Pound, who submitted their *daemon* to the claims of other cultures). Though he never lost his faith, he remained too sceptical toward the rigidities of religious profession and fought the pull of nature to become a pantheist as Robinson Jeffers had. Once his own psyche was forged to his own satisfaction, he always sought to give his readers back to themselves, rather than them to him. In willing them to be free, he most recalls the urgings of Ralph Waldo Emerson. Indeed, more than any other poet of our age, it was Rexroth who enhanced the Emersonian tradition at a time when allegiance to external authority seemed to be dangerously ascendant. His poetry and criticism embody one of Emerson's central ideals: "In all my lectures," he wrote in his *Journals,* "I have taught one doctrine, namely, the infinitude of the private man." One might say the same of Rexroth. He never shunted responsibility for the world's failure away from individuals. Instead he stood resolutely by his dialectic of love, death, and growth, the strenuous cycle through which a mortal might transcend his own and the world's limitations. That dialectic, unspoken as doctrine but inescapable in the poems, is crucial to understanding Rexroth. Implicit in its operation are the forces that unify his apparently antipodal selves.

Thus, if there is a single overriding truth that emerges from Rexroth's work, it is his conviction that all genuine subjectivity is a high but difficult achievement while supposed objectivity is merely the failure of having become an amalgam of other selves and opinions. Yet he does not deny the stiffening power of the distanced view. There is something peculiarly Emersonian in the way Rexroth, in both his poetry and his prose, continually records the influx of insights that give his work their individualistic flavor, then retreats into an almost studied scepticism. Like Emerson, he is a man armed with a vision of another, perhaps clearer reality which he feels compelled to verify in the pragmatic world.

This feeling for the ideal is in the native tradition. American writers have always claimed knowledge of a "republic of the spirit," a revivified Eden, which permitted them to realize the limitations but also the immanent holiness of the natural world, and to celebrate both simultaneously. Rexroth's poetry would grow out of the tensions and similarities between the world of his visions and the world of reality, and the myth which as a poet he would create out of this conflict. *A Homestead Called Damascus,* which he began writing at the age of fifteen, reveals to the alert reader how these forces were working their way into his poetry. Furthermore, early in his career, he shows a range of interests Emersonian in scope. The 19th century Unitarians, led by Emerson, broke away from puritanism with romantic and revolutionary gusto and explored the world as their predecessors never had. That freedom—which Emerson called "heroic"—was made available to Rexroth and others who embraced Emerson's openness of spirit. It would soon become evident that Rexroth's true subject was a free human response to whatever swam into his ken. Much of his best poetry can be taken as meditations on the broad range of human engagements—reactions observed in himself or others, stories heard or read, and the responses of his imagination, in dream, in fantasy, in vision. Ultimately he learned to embrace them as one, to fuse them and to write about this collective experience—which is to say, the myths of his time and place. Thus Rexroth often will appear to fluctuate between a possible transfiguration, an Edenic assumption, and a watchful worldliness—but will always be sensitive to the danger of believing that either passion or sophistication alone can bring one to the state of wisdom. In a letter to Louis Zukovsky in 1931, Rexroth comments that "Emerson was one of our greatest poets and one of our best philosophers, but he kept the two activities separate." What Rexroth acquired in the following years was the gift of unifying the two, so that his finest poems unfold as lyric meditative journeys of a man confronting the world imaginatively and immediately, unbound by hoops of sterile tradition.

Rexroth's first thirty years suggest an unrelenting struggle to extract the precious ore from the flux of his hard mid-Western experience. He was bent on overcoming its limitations without wholly repudiating it. Like D. H. Lawrence, whom he would later use and discard, Rexroth was forever forging himself in a kind of inner Faustian drama of which he was, naturally, the hero (the wit who remarked that Rexroth's supreme fiction was Rexroth himself, was not far off the mark). Early in childhood he learned a vital lesson from his mother, Delia Rexroth. She made the world of books available to him, with the most American of admonitions: that which you get from another is never truly instructional, but always stimulation. You taught yourself. Having learned this lesson young from a mother who had Amerindian blood and abolitionist views, Rexroth would later on proclaim as a principle the conviction that great poets call us forth to ourselves, rather than to the causes that we may yearn to serve. Rexroth's mother taught him how to interpret the world according to the principle that there is no method for doing so except through oneself, even though her own temperament would eventually restore her (as his would him) to the lap of the authoritarian Catholic Church. Despite her religious bent, Delia Rexroth apparently never encouraged her precocious son to flee from his individuality. On the contrary, she seems to have urged him to value it above all else, even in its eccentric manifestations.

During these early years, his formal education took place in the bleak classrooms of Elkhart, Toledo, and Battle Creek public schools, while his real education was conducted in the special study his mother had built for him as a counterweight to the platitudes that children were forced to endure in the elementary schools of the day. Against the unimaginative conservatism of the American school system, she pitted her own definition of a proper education, which called upon the mind and spirit to judge conventional wisdom with Emerson's "iron string" of the liberated mind (which W. H. Auden calls "the free man's worship") as a guiding principle.

So it would appear that already there were implanted in young Rexroth the seeds of the dialectic quality which perhaps flourishes best on American soil: that gift, the willingness to quarrel with one self rather than to assert dogmatically, would on one hand challenge the young radical poets who mobilized in San Francisco during the 1950s and on the other would be misappropriated by reactionaries who idealized individualism for its own ends. Indeed, it is ironic that Rexroth's vision of humanity, though couched in the call for a small community of the spirit, should have taken shape as an elitist vision, if elite in the best sense of the word. That too was real and came from his mother's constant reminder that the Rexroth clan was special, different from the lumpen proletariat of the small Midwestern cities where Rexroth grew up.

Confronted with the fluctuating fortunes of an alcoholic father forced to become a travelling salesman of drugs, living the life of what George Bernard Shaw called "downstarts," the youthful Rexroth clung to the image of individualism as his most precious heritage, and more importantly, as his only hope for an imaginative life amid impoverished circumstances. Based on what appears to have been his mother's faith in the Emersonian ideal, there developed in him the belief that the only literary and critical method worth embracing was the investigation of the self. Though he continued to work at a variety of odd jobs and enlisted in the ranks of radical organizations that required total fealty, he remained wary of any occupation or cause which might stamp him inwardly with its insignia. He ingested huge chunks of the past in history, philosophy, and the classics, ransacking the public libraries of Elkhart, Toledo, and later Chicago, where the museums also provided him with a self-education in art and painting which the public schools could not equal. He seems to have steeped himself in the scholastics, especially Thomas Aquinas and Duns Scotus, who preached among other things the doctrine of individual conscience, and the mystical idealist Jakob Boehme, who sent him into ecstasies. He delighted in consuming without discretion almost anything that fed his appetite for intellectual stimulation, that exercised the inner Self he had learned to prize as his most precious possession. He was already developing the ability to absorb diverse materials from many cultures, yet not leave his own center. For the youthful Rexroth, already rooted in his immediate reality, the past was neither a prescription nor a burden; it was rather an aesthetic experience. He used the past to enhance the present and to catapult himself into the future, using his sense of himself as his gyroscope. While he welcomed the warming wisdom of the past, he was careful to shear away from its authority. Even his early poetry reflected a mind dominated by a powerful sense of individualism, mellowed by the slanting sun of old European culture but not profoundly modified by it or made discontent with its own landscape. And perhaps reading through Emerson, he concurred with the old sage that engagement with the present moment in a particular place provided the gunpowder of the mind. At the same time, it became increasingly clear to him that a writer could not maintain a literary career like Emerson's without immense commitment to studying and reading (later on, as an unconscious tribute to this obsession of his, one San Francisco writer would complain, "Rexroth wants *us* to read everything"). The apprentice, Rexroth concluded, had to submit to a monastic mode of life, either in or out of a monastery.

After travelling extensively in the West, sometime around 1928 Rexroth came to New York for a second time and rented a basement apartment on Grove Street, in the same building where Allen Tate and Hart Crane, "that tragic enragé," were living. The Jazz Age was then in full swing. Robert Benchley and Dorothy Parker were the toasts of the Algonquin parties. Weekend parties at the Boosevain home in Jamaica Estates were presided over by Edna St. Vincent Millay. Rexroth flirted with the fringes of this scene (alluded to in *Homestead*), but he had neither the means nor the notoriety to participate except as an observer in that fast-paced life. Moreover, he disliked the unavoidable aspects of New York City life—the dirt, the noise, the tension, and he was soon considering alternatives. He started attending church at St. Luke's, a pre-Revolutionary church run by Peter Schlueter, "one of the most remarkable men in the history of Anglo-Catholicism in America." About mid-February of that year, Rexroth was baptized into the church and left Sin City in a snow-storm for the Holy Cross Monastery across the Hudson River from Poughkeepsie, ready to give up the world for a religious vocation—or at least a monastic one. There is no way to be sure how long he actually stayed, since his own accounts vary and the Monastery of the Holy Cross retained no record of his attendance. If we examine the events of his previous years, (described in *An Autobiographical Novel*), we get some understanding of how the vagaries of a difficult and relatively rootless, survival-type of boyhood could have driven him toward the security of that peaceful patch of ground overlooking the Hudson River and its verdant valley. He apparently hoped, in the presence of like-spirited sympathetic souls, to recover the meaning of theodicy in an age of faithlessness and agnosticism, to fire anew the idea of God in his own heart. From Boehme he had learned that God was equal to mind, the vital mind which is a form of imaginative, intellectual, and moral action that Emerson had tried to embody and to recommend as a counter to the ills of his age. Emerson had demanded that we reconsider and re-examine the value and trustworthiness of all received knowledge and of the intellectual habits that load our faith in that knowledge, and now Rexroth was facing a similar dilemma of doubt and belief, described in surrealistic detail in *A Homestead Called Damascus*. The late Robert Fitzgerald puts it very well, as if he were talking about Rexroth: "So hard at best is the lot of man, and so great is the beauty he can apprehend, that only a religious conception of things can take in the extremes and meet the case. But it seems to me there are a few things everyone can humbly try to hold onto: love and mercy (and humor) in everyday living; the quest for the exact truth in language and affairs of the intellect; self-recollection or prayer; and the peace, the composed energy of art."

It worked for a time, apparently, but the straining for freedom of action apparently overwhelmed all other impulses. Furthermore, Rexroth's craving for intellectual experience and literary associations could not be satisfied through the limited resources of the monastery (though he seems to have made good use of a lively library on the premises). After about two months of religious experience, he discovered that he was not a natural-born monk and that his temperament was better suited to a kinetic active life than to a contemplative one. He returned to New York long enough to ship out for Europe as a mess-steward aboard a rusty old freighter.

On his return to Chicago, Rexroth met and married a young painter named Andree Shaefer. Together they headed for California and decided to live there. They spent some time on the Monterrey Peninsula in the area of Carmel and around Big Sur, camping, hiking from site to site, and tramping mountain trails. Soon the dramatic setting began to infiltrate his sensibility and perception. Relatively isolated from European influences, his thinking became American in a very special sense. In somewhat the same way as Robinson Jeffers, Rexroth slipped into the spell of the American West, of the California spaces, the mountains, the forests, the wild terrain, and the Pacific Ocean itself. Especially the area around Carmel had a visual splendor almost dreamlike, a "soft-focus mirage of dunes and crashing white water and guano-washed rock islets and sheer cliffs falling into the surf and forest and meadows and clinging mists and windbent stands of cypresses" (Danny Santiago). The place created a pervading, even comforting conviction that no artistic accomplishment could ever match this landscape, arousing in him once more a sense of a sacramental presence in all things. He filled his poems in progress with the stamp of that discovery. In these poems, there is nowhere a trace, not one blurring image of language or perception rooted in other cultures or geographies (though he never seems to have forgotten Apollinaire). The yet unspoiled California land breathes into and through Rexroth—and it is for this quality that William Everson calls him one of the finest nature poets in American literature. However much Rexroth may have contributed to the ferment of American letters later on in his San Francisco days, his discovery of America, in its specific local manifestations, was to be no less important a contribution. Once young writers like Snyder, Whalen, Levertov, Everson, and McClure experienced these poems, the body of America could no longer be the same to them—or to us. Rexroth had learned the significance of place (his reading of Lawrence helped), but at the same time, he never lost sight of the risk of putting place before person—of allowing place, no matter how alluring, to be the designator of personality, to the point that feelings about love, sex, and inner life are excluded. What John Ashbery said about Frank O'Hara's work applies to Rexroth's: "Even at its most abstract, even when it seems to be speaking about something else, it is poetry emerging out of his life." Yet there is little about it that we can call "confessional" in the same breath that might be appropriate for Robert Lowell, Sylvia Plath, or Allen Ginsberg. Rexroth does not linger over aberrant aspects of himself, nor does he dally much with quirky or bizarre reflections, in the hope that his self-absorption will make them seem exemplary rather than eccentric. He wastes little time analyzing himself or turning his personality inside out. "I have always been too busy being a poet or a painter or a husband or a father or a cook or a mountain climber to worry about my personality," he would boast in his autobiography. If he does talk about himself in his poetry, it is mainly because he cannot avoid himself as the maker of the poem, al-

most exactly as Emerson confronts himself in his "confessional" essays. In the end, the poem materializes as a natural setting for the ruminations of a man seemingly caught up in the big and little phenomena that make up the unknowable substance of our existence. It is an open poetry, American in its openness, and it has a powerful appeal to those people who, in a phrase of Kenneth Koch, are "dying for the truth."

It was during this period that one of the most important developments in his poetics begins to emerge. Emerson had hoped that for his generation the ancient precept, "Know thyself" and the contemporary precept, "Study nature" (espoused by Thoreau and dismissed by James Russell Lowell as mere sentiment and "one more symptom of the general liver complaint"), would become a single precept, a single piece of advice. Self-knowledge, for Emerson, was inextricably linked to the search for a stable center, an authoritative moment, an expression or mode of action in a centrifugal field. He was intent on schooling himself in endless diffusion and indeterminacy as the context for that search, so that certitude and even rigid consistency would be constantly under query. Only in this way could one know oneself. And the search had to be in the world, the world that looked like an abyss but which Emerson sensed was a constant becoming, a complex and ever-changing arena for courageous human action that discourse was incapable of capturing. Rexroth experimented with ways to blend knowledge of self with knowledge of place (Emerson, of course, was stalking the idea of the integration of sensibility). When Rexroth was successful, the physical observed metaphorically was carried into his inner or invisible world and his poetry acquires a new commanding power that grows out of this union. His poetry was never far from nature and never far from himself. He was in the world and the world was in him as the sea is in the fish and the fish is in the sea (St. Catherine in Siena). This quality gave his work a rugged honesty, strength, and fragility not common in the poetry of his day.

> **When Rexroth was successful, the physical observed metaphorically was carried into his inner or invisible world and his poetry acquires a new commanding power that grows out of this union.**
> **—Leo Hamalian**

Aside from the visual splendors it offered, the Carmel area was "an outpost of bohemia, a place of artists, near artists, and would-be artists" (Kevin Starr, in *Americans and the California Dream, 1850-1915*), the perfect setting for anyone bent on merging self-knowledge and nature. But Rexroth may have been drawn to Carmel for other reasons. Carmel had the reputation of being "progressive" (Langston Hughes lived there for years) and Rexroth was no doubt exposed to what Kevin Starr calls Carmel's "loquacious socialism" and "posturing reformism." When he later became politically active in San Francisco, Rexroth shrewdly stripped his own style of socialism of the posturing (whether he succeeded in shedding the loquaciousness as well is a matter of debate). For a while he was a member of the Communist Party, but its demands for conformity with the Party line outraged a conscience that was closer to Emerson's than Stalin's.

The radical movement in politics, originating in the struggle against the power of the railroads and land-owners in the West, swept through the San Francisco area shortly before the Rexroths arrived there. Along with it came the Marxist aesthetic which combined the demand for an American poetry derived from Whitman with the Soviet demand for a revolutionary literature. Fused, these two strains created a body of work that was peculiarly the product of the left-wing poets of the decade, mainly Rexroth and Patchen. It is worth noting that these two poets who were writing from a leftist perspective in the thirties became the beacons for the "beat generation" of the fifties and the sixties. The Rexroth-Patchen heritage was carried forward into the new poetry of social protest associated with Ginsberg and his cohorts. Robert Bly's interest in translating Spanish and South American poets may well come from looking back at the thirties, when Williams and Rexroth were translating Pablo Neruda's political poetry. Baraka, who knew Rexroth, developed his experiments with reading poetry to jazz in night-clubs where the political left gathered for entertainment.

In Rexroth's criticism of the capitalist system, in both his essays and his poetry ("You did, you son-of-a-bitch in your Brooks Brothers suit") often sounds inflexible and even merciless, nevertheless his individualism never alienated him from his nativist roots. In one respect it made him a spokesman for it—he was for a time in San Francisco an extremely popular columnist with unpopular views. The younger poets of the following generation, whose often eccentric individualism did in fact alienate them from their roots, nonetheless tried to take up the Rexroth tradition and at first treasured him for re-introducing the artist in his role as shaman—a mystical, priestly political figure in pre-historic cultures, the figure who stood at the entrance to a spiritually renovated future. It was Rexroth who recognized with incisive clarity the energizing reality of America. For him, America dealt in transformation: it suggested an endless series of possibilities, extending like the reflections of two mirrors set facing one another, stretching on, replica after replica, to the vanishing point. It suggested one adventure after the other, one wondrous day after the other, one improvement after the other. It suggested rejuvenation, the pain of impoverished childhood overcome and transcended, and even endless love once deemed lost. The real promise was immortality. Where other writers of the same intensity had

a darkened vision of our customary existence as though seen through a begrimed window, Rexroth's vision remained optimistic and flickered with the light of paradise not yet rendered a vanishing fantasy by events.

Here we may have the key to Rexroth's magnetism for those writers who sought him out on Scott Street. Rexroth returned them to the human economy that Emerson had in mind when he wrote: "The one thing in the world, in value, is the active soul." It may not be an exaggeration to say that Rexroth altered the course of American poetry through his influence on some of the best minds of the following generation who sought to fashion a poetry that could become an instrument for political and social change, that might create an ambience for nourishing his vision.

Donald Hall (essay date 1991)

SOURCE: "Kenneth Rexroth," in *American Writing Today,* edited by Richard Kostelanetz, Whitston Publishing Company, 1991, pp. 82-92.

[*In the following essay, Hall provides an overview of Rexroth's literary accomplishments. According to Evans, Rexroth's poetry "is a poetry of experience and observation, of knowledge and allusion, and finally a poetry of wisdom."*]

Among Kenneth Rexroth's lesser accomplishments, he appears as a character in two famous novels. James T. Farrell put him in the *Studs Lonigan* trilogy (1932-35), where he is a kid named Kenny working in a drugstore. With more creative denomination, Jack Kerouac called him Rheinhold Cacoethes in *The Dharma Bums,* that 1958 Beat Generation testament, where he is the figure we recognize: anarchist, leader of San Francisco's literary community, and poet.

For decades he has written lines like these, setting human life in a context of stone:

> Our campfire is a single light
> Amongst a hundred peaks and waterfalls.
> The manifold voices of falling water
> Talk all night.
> Wrapped in your down bag
> Starlight on your cheeks and eyelids
> Your breath comes and goes
> In a tiny cloud in the frosty night.
> Ten thousand birds sing in the sunrise.
> Ten thousand years revolve without change.
> All this will never be again.

One thing that is without change is that everything changes. Like many of the greatest poets—Wordsworth, Keats, Frost,

Eliot—Rexroth returns continually to one inescapable perception. Maybe this elegiac vision of permanent stone and vanishing flesh derives from the great private event of his middle years—the death of his first wife Andrée in 1940 after 13 years of marriage. Her name and image return decades after her death.

But Rexroth is not limited to elegy; he is the most erotic of modern American poets, and one of the most political. The great public event of his young life was the execution of Sacco and Vanzetti. Years after the electrocution he wrote **"Climbing Milestone Mountain"**:

> In the morning
> We swam in the cold transparent lake, the blue
> Damsel flies on all the reeds like millions
> Of narrow metallic flowers, and I thought
> Of you behind the grille in Dedham, Vanzetti,
> Saying, "Who would ever have though we would
>   make this history?"
> Crossing the brilliant mile-square meadow
> Illuminated with asters and cyclamen
> The pollen of the lodgepole pines drifting
> With the shifting wind over it and the blue
> And sulphur butterflies drifting with the wind,
> I saw you in the sour prison light, saying,
> "Goodbye comrade."

In Rexroth's poems the natural world, unchanged and changing, remains background to history and love, to enormity and bliss.

As a young man, Rexroth was a Wobbly—an Industrial Worker of the World, or IWW—and he studied Marxism as a member of a John Reed Club. Later he became anarchist and pacifist, ideologies which his mature philosophic poems support with passion and argument. His politics of the individual separates him from the mass of Americans—and obviously from Stalinists—and yet joins him to all human beings; it is a politics of love—and Rexroth is the poet of devoted eroticism. **"When We with Sappho"** begins by translating from a Greek fragment, then continues into a personal present:

> ". . . about the cool water
> the wind sounds through sprays
> of apple, and from the quivering leaves
> slumber pours down . . ."

> We lie here in the bee filled, ruinous
> Orchard of a decayed New England farm,
> Summer in our hair, and the smell
> Of summer in our twined bodies,
> Summer in our mouths, and summer
> In the luminous, fragmentary words

> Of this dead Greek woman.
> Stop reading. Lean back. Give me your mouth.
> Your grace is as beautiful as sleep.
> You move against me like a wave
> That moves in sleep.
> Your body spreads across my brain
> Like a bird filled summer;
> Not like a body, not like a separate thing,
> But like a nimbus that hovers
> Over every other thing in all the world.
> Lean back. You are beautiful,
> As beautiful as the folding
> Of your hands in sleep.

This passionate tenderness has not diminished as Rexroth has aged. His latest book includes the beautiful **"Love Poems of Marichiko,"** which he calls a translation from the Japanese; however, a recent bibliography lists the translation of Rexroth's **"Marichiko"** *into* Japanese: in the middle of his eighth decade, the poet has written his most erotic poem.

His work for 40 years has moved among his passions for the flesh, for human justice, and for the natural world. He integrates these loves in the long poems and sometimes in briefer ones like **"Lyell's Hypothesis Again"**:

Lyell's Hypothesis Again

> *An Attempt to Explain the Former*
> *Changes of the Earth's Surface by*
> *Causes Now in Operation*
> *Subtitle of Lyell: Principles of Geology*

> The mountain road ends here,
> Broken away in the chasm where
> The bridge washed out years ago.
> The first scarlet larkspur glitters
> In the first patch of April
> Morning sunlight. The engorged creek
> Roars and rustles like a military
> Ball. Here by the waterfall,
> Insuperable life, flushed
> With the equinox, sentient
> And sentimental, falls away
> To the sea and death. The tissue
> Of sympathy and agony
> That binds the flesh in its Nessus' shirt;
> The clotted cobweb of unself
> And self; sheds itself and flecks
> The sun's bed with darts of blossom
> Like flagellant blood above
> The water bursting in the vibrant
> Air. This ego, bound by personal
> Tragedy and the vast

Impersonal vindictiveness
Of the ruined and ruining world,
Pauses in this immortality,
As passionate, as apathetic,
As the lava flow that burned here once;
And stopped here; and said, 'This far
And no further.' And spoke thereafter
In the simple diction of stone.

. . . . .

Naked in the warm April air,
We lie under the redwoods,
In the sunny lee of a cliff.
As you kneel above me I see
Tiny red marks on your flanks
Like bites, where the redwood cones
Have pressed into your flesh.
You can find just the same marks
In the lignite in the cliff
Over our heads. *Sequoia
Langsdorfii* before the ice,
And *sempervirens* afterwards,
There is little difference,
Except for all those years.

Here in the sweet, moribund
Fetor of spring flowers, washed,
Flotsam and jetsam together,
Cool and naked together,
Under this tree for a moment,
We have escaped the bitterness
Of love, and love lost, and love
Betrayed. And what might have been,
And what might be, fall equally
Away with what is, and leave
Only these ideograms
Printed on the immortal
Hydrocarbons of flesh and stone.

The poet writes best when his passions coalesce.

It is the strength of Rexroth's language that it proscribes nothing. He uses words from the natural sciences and from mathematics, as well as philosophical abstractions which modern poetic practice is supposed to avoid. If he sometimes aims to speak in "the simple diction of stone," he refuses the temptation to purity: this same brief poem uses classical reference, scientific terminology and Latin taxonomy, earth-history, the "flagellant blood" of Christianity, and intimate common speech: "tiny red marks on your flanks / like bites. . . ."

In **"Lyell's Hypothesis Again"** we hear Rexroth's characteristic rhythm—swift and urgent, slow and meditative, pow-erful; his line hovers around three accents, mostly seven or eight syllables long. (Much of his poetry is strictly syllabic.) It is remarkable how little Rexroth's line has changed over 40 years, in a world of poetic fashions. This steadfastness or stubbornness recalls his patience over publication: he did not publish a book of poems until 1940, when he was 35 years old, although he had been writing since the early 1920s. Later, in **The Art of Worldly Wisdom** (1949), he collected and published work from his Cubist youth. Some had appeared in Louis Zukofsky's *An Objectivists' Anthology* (1932).

When we try to describe a poet's style, it can be useful to name starting points, but that is not easy with Kenneth Rexroth. He has said that Tu Fu was the greatest influence on him; fair enough, but there is no analogy between the Chinese line, end-stopped, with its count of characters, and Rexroth's run-in enjambed syllabics. In temperament and idea Rexroth is close to D. H. Lawrence, about whom he wrote his first major essay in 1947. But Lawrence's best poems take off from Whitman's line—and Rexroth's prosody is as far from Whitman's as it can get. Perhaps there is a bit of William Carlos Williams in his enjambed lines; maybe Louis Zukofsky. We could say, throwing up our hands, that he is a synthesis of Tu Fu, Lawrence, and Mallarmé. To an unusual extent, Rexroth made Rexroth up.

. . . . .

He was born in Indiana in 1905 and spent most of the 1920s in Chicago's Bohemia—poet, painter, and autodidact. Late in the decade he moved to San Francisco where he has lived much of his life, moving down the coast to Santa Barbara only in 1968. He was the poet of San Francisco even before Robert Duncan, Philip Lamantia, Kenneth Patchen, and William Everson (Brother Antoninus). For decades he has advocated the poetry of the West, the elder literary figure of the city where poetry came to happen: Jack Spicer, Philip Whalen, Michael McClure, Lawrence Ferlinghetti, Lew Welch, Joanne Kyger. . . . His influence on the young is obvious, clearest in Gary Snyder, who is worthy of his master. When young writers from the East arrived in the 1950s—Allen Ginsberg, Jack Kerouac, Gregory Corso—they attended gatherings at Rexroth's house, and it was Rexroth who was catalyst for the 1955 Six Gallery reading that was the public birth of the Beat Generation.

Later, alliances altered. . . . Talking about Kenneth Rexroth, it is easy to wander into the history of factionalism, for he has been partisan, and few polemicists have had a sharper tongue. Inventor of *"The Vaticide Review"* (apparently referring to *The Partisan Review,* but it can stand in for all the quarterlies), he wrote in 1957 of poet-professors, "Ninety-nine percent of them don't even exist but are androids manufactured from molds, cast from Randall Jarrell by the lost wax process." On the west coast he has been a constant, grumpy presence. If the West has taken him for granted, the East has chosen to ignore him, perhaps because he has taken potshots at the provincial East forever and ever. The *Harvard Guide to Contemporary American Writing* (1979), which purports to cover the scene since 1945, will do for an example: the poetry critic quotes *none* of Rexroth's poetry but sputters about his "intemperate diatribes." Nor does Rexroth make the *New York Review of Books* shortlist of Approved Contemporaries. Which is a pity, because he is better than anyone on it.

Taste is always a fool—the consensus of any moment; contemporary taste is the agreement of diffident people to quote each other's opinions. It reaffirms with complacency reputations which are perceived as immemorial, but which are actually constructed of rumor, laziness, and fear. As a writer ages and issues new volumes, he or she is reviewed as if the writing had remained the same, because it would require brains and effort to alter not only one's past opinion but the current professional assessment.

Perhaps the consensus of our moment, product largely of the East and the academy, is especially ignorant, especially gullible. Or perhaps it is only—in the matter of Kenneth Rexroth—that the taste-makers are offended by Rexroth's morals. In fact they *ought* to be because the ethical ideas that Rexroth puts forward with such acerbity are old-fashioned and individual—anathema to the suburban, Volvo-driving, conformist liberalism of the academy. He stands firm against technocracy and its bureaus and hierarchies, to which the university is as devoted an institution as General Motors. Rexroth's morals derive in part from Indiana before the First World War, in part from centuries of oriental thought, and in part from the radical non-Marxist thinking of late 19th-century Europe.

He has not been wholly without attention. James Laughlin of *New Directions* has been his loyal publisher who keeps his poetry in print. Morgan Gibson wrote a book about him which lists many reviews and articles about his poetry; a magazine called *The Ark* devoted a 1980 issue to his work; his reading aloud to music, which is superb and innovative, can be heard on several tapes and records.

Still, he should be acclaimed as one of the great poets of our literature because he has written poems like **"The Signature of All Things."**

> My head and shoulders, and my book
> In the cool shade, and my body
> Stretched bathing in the sun, I lie
> Reading beside the waterfall—

Boehme's "Signature of all Things."
Through the deep July day the leaves
Of the laurel, all the colors
Of gold, spin down through the moving
Deep laurel shade all day. They float
On the mirrored sky and forest
For a while, and then, still slowly
Spinning, sink through the crystal deep
Of the pool to its leaf gold floor.
The saint saw the world as streaming
In the electrolysis of love.
I put him by and gaze through shade
Folded into shade of slender
Laurel trunks and leaves filled with sun.
The wren broods in her moss domed nest.
A newt struggles with a white moth
Drowning in the Pool. The hawks scream,
Playing together on the ceiling
Of heaven. The long hours go by.
I think of those who have loved me,
Of all the mountains I have climbed,
Of all the seas I have swum in.
The evil of the world sinks.
My own sin and trouble fall away
Like Christian's bundle, and I watch
My forty summers fall like falling
Leaves and falling water held
Eternally in summer air.

. . . . .

Deer are stamping in the glades,
Under the full July moon.
There is a smell of dry grass
In the air, and more faintly,
The scent of a far off skunk.
As I stand at the wood's edge,
Watching the darkness, listening
To the stillness, a small owl
Comes to the branch above me,
On wings more still than my breath.
When I turn my light on him,
His eyes glow like drops of iron,
And he perks his heard at me,
Like a curious kitten.
The meadow is bright as snow.
My dog prowls the grass, a dark
Blur in the blur of brightness.
I walk to the oak grove where
The Indian village was once.
There, in blotched and cobwebbed light
And dark, dim in the blue haze,
Are twenty Holstein heifers,
Black and white, all lying down,
Quietly together, under

The hugh trees rooted in the graves.

. . . . .

When I dragged the rotten log
From the bottom of the pool,
It seemed heavy as stone.
I let it lie in the sun
For a month; and then chopped it
Into sections, and split them
For kindling, and spread them out
To dry some more. Late that night,
After reading for hours,
While moths rattled at the lamp—
The saints and the philosophers
On the destiny of man—
I went out on my cabin porch,
And looked up through the black forest
At the swaying islands of stars.
Suddenly I saw at my feet,
Spread on the floor of night, ingots
Of quivering phosphorescence,
And all about were scattered chips
Of pale cold light that was alive.

Starting from his reading in a Christian mystic (Jacob Boehme, 1575-1624), he writes vividly of the natural world, he refers to *Pilgrim's Progress,* he ranges out into the universe of stars and focuses back upon the world of heifers and minute phosphorescent organisms. It is a poetry of experience and observation, of knowledge and allusion, and finally a poetry of wisdom.

This poem comes from the ***Collected Shorter Poems*** (1967). There is also a ***Collected Longer Poems*** (1968); they are five in number, including **"The Phoenix and the Tortoise,"** a 30-page meditative philosophic poem from the early 1940s, and **"The Dragon and the Unicorn,"** from the second half of the same decade, which describes European travel and argues on a high level of abstraction. Best of the long poems is the latest, **"The Heart's Garden, the Garden's Heart"** (1967).

There is also a collection of verse plays. There are many volumes of prose: ***An Autobiographical Novel*** (1966), several volumes of essays both literary and political, and a rapid polemical literary history called ***American Poetry in the Twentieth Century*** (1971). In addition, Rexroth has translated from Latin, Greek, French, German, Spanish, Swedish, but it is his work in Chinese and Japanese which is deservedly best known—beginning with ***One Hundred Poems from the Chinese*** (1956). Certainly his verse translations remain among the best work in an age of translation.

But if we look for the best, we look to his own poems. To end with, here is a lyric from his *New Poems* of 1974:

Your Birthday in the California Mountains

A broken moon on the cold water,
And wild geese crying high overhead,
The smoke of the campfire rises
Toward the geometry of heaven—
Points of light in the infinite blackness.
I watch across the narrow inlet
Your dark figure comes and goes before the fire.
A loon cries out on the night bound lake.
Then all the world is silent with the
Silence of autumn waiting for
The coming of winter. I enter
The ring of firelight, bringing to you
A string of trout for our dinner.
As we eat by the whispering lake,
I say, "Many years from now we will
Remember this night and talk of it."
Many years have gone by since then, and
Many years again. I remember
That night as though it was last night,
But you have been dead for thirty years.

Donald Gutierrez (essay date 1992)

SOURCE: "Kenneth Rexroth: Poet, Radical Man of Letter of the West," in *Northwest Review,* Vol. 30, No. 2, 1992, pp. 142-55.

[*In the following essay, Gutierrez discusses Rexroth's literary career and critical reputation. According to Gutierrez, Rexroth "remains probably the most underrated poet in 20th-century American literature."*]

They say I do not realize
The Values of my own time.
What preposterous nonsense!
Ten years of war, mountains of dead,
One hundred million armed men
And billions of paper dollars
Spent to disembowel mankind.
If they go on forever,
They will have realized less
Value than I can in one hour
Sitting at my typewriter.

　　　　　　　Kenneth Rexroth, **"Me Again"**

I

The single most intriguing fact about Kenneth Rexroth is that this significant American literary figure remains probably the most underrated poet in 20th-century American literature.

There are a number of reasons for this unenviable status, and probably more to be discovered. Geographical location has something to do with it. Moving to San Francisco in 1927, Rexroth was a long distance from New York, where reputations are most readily made (and destroyed) in the arts. In his fascinating, iconoclastic *An Autobiographical Novel* (1966), Rexroth claims that he wanted to steer clear of the publicity and careerist "troughs" of the Big Apple. He wanted privacy, his own space, and a place where artists were generally accepted and were not in vicious rivalry with each other. All this he felt he found in San Francisco, traditionally a strong union town with a sophisticated European ambience. He lived in San Francisco until the 1970s, then spent the remainder of this life in Santa Barbara, California, where he taught part-time at the University of California. Besides being a poet much of his life, a fine translator of verse, a political radical and a social critic of formidable perceptiveness and satiric bite, a playwright and journalist, Rexroth was also a painter with one-man shows in three major American cities, the co-founder of the San Francisco Poetry Center, and the organizer in San Francisco of active, well-attended Anarchist educational and political meetings as well as of bi-weekly literary meetings in his own home.

Despite this wealth of West-Coast cultural and social activities and engagement, Rexroth over the decades alienated the centers of power in academe and the East Coast with a battery of polemics against the dominant values found in key intellectual, critical journals like *Partisan Review* and the *Kenyon Review*, the pervasive magisterial influence of T. S. Eliot's literary criticism, and the New Critics (whom, with typical and justifiable derision, Rexroth described as Cornbelt Metaphysicians). His Bohemian posture (*pose*, his foes urged) identifying himself with the world avant-garde and with political radicalism did not endear him to American English Departments with their pronounced orientation towards American and English literature, and at most political liberalism, nor did he win many academic allies when he did give poetry readings at universities in the 1960s and 1970s, accompanied either by considerable arrogance to his academic hosts, or by moves on faculty wives or on attendant attractive women. A Communist in the 1920s, then a philosophic Anarchist at least into the 1950s, Rexroth had deep roots in Midwestern "native" radicalism, the powerful syndicalism of the IWW and the Indiana Populist Socialism of men like Eugene V. Debs. Also, Rexroth's identification as a Beat guru in the mid-1950s for his championing of young poets like Allen Ginsberg, Gregory Corso, Gary Snyder, Robert Duncan, Denise Levertov and others, stigmatized him *then* as a kind of elderly literary barbarian, "Daddy of the Beats" (as East-Coast literary critic Alfred Kazin impudently called him). This misrepresented associa-

tion blinded people to Rexroth's real stature as a complex literary mind, and certainly did not draw attention to his own verse. Yet being stigmatized for championing literary artists of the fame of Duncan, Ginsberg, Levertov, and Snyder should by now have stigmatized the stigmatizers.

This ignorance about him was a shame, for the truth of the matter is that Rexroth was actually enormously erudite—and he was a splendid poet as well. An orphan by 13, self-taught, Rexroth developed a deep hostility towards universities and towards most English Departments in particular, which he regarded as supporting, through the New Critics or more traditional critical orientations, an artistic and political reaction that was anathema to his conception of a vital vanguard art and a "self-actualizing" communalist society. To what extent, then, Rexroth was intentionally victimized by the power centers of literary America is hard to determine. Surely, paranoid interpretations are all too tempting to explain the markedly inadequate acknowledgment of one of the truly exceptional literary artists and men of letters of America.

Consider what he accomplished. As Lee Bartlett (who recently edited Rexroth's letters to James Laughlin for New Directions) has said, "Rexroth.... published over 1,000 pages of poetry, ten volumes of translations from six languages, eight volumes of literary and social criticism and an autobiography" (*American Poetry,* Winter 1984). Indeed, Rexroth's autobiography (edited by Linda Hamalian) which covers his life up to the late 1940s, was published recently. One of his books of criticism, entitled *Classics Revisited,* which first appeared in separate essays in *The Saturday Review,* is highly readable, distilling in a few pages the central wisdom or force of classics from *The Iliad* to *Leaves of Grass* (a second volume of these *Saturday Review* essays, entitled *More Classics Revisited,* is now also in print). He also wrote a tetralogy of verse plays based on ancient Greek models called *Beyond the Mountains.* Published by New Directions, these plays were also performed by The Living Theatre in New York City. Among his books of verse alone, such works as *In What Hour* (1940), *The Phoenix and the Tortoise* (1944), *The Signature of All Things* (1950), *In Defense of the Earth* (1956), *The Heart's Garden, The Garden's Heart* (1975), *The Dragon and the Unicorn* (1952), a book-length verse "travelogue", *The Love Poems of Marichiko* (from *The Silver Swan,* 1978), not to mention numerous fine translations of Chinese and Japanese verse, should have given him eminence among 20th-century American poets, as should his activity as a West-Coast iconoclast and polyhistor in acute, entertaining and provocative weekly book reviews for the Berkeley listener-supported Pacifica station KPFA.

All of this (and it is not an exhaustive list of Rexroth's creative, journalistic, and social-political activities by any means), yet Rexroth has generally received scant attention particularly in—but also beyond—literary academia in America. To this day, he is not represented by a single poem in many of the most frequently used college anthologies of American literature. Significantly enough, some good poets know and respect, and in some cases, revere his verse.

Why have some important poets held either Rexroth or his verse in high regard? For one thing, Rexroth, somewhat like Ezra Pound (whom he detested), was a generous supporter of promising younger literary artists and of vanguard art generally. He was for years a mentor and inspiration to such distinctive poets as Robert Duncan, William Everson, Philip Lamantia, the Beats (Rexroth's promotional journalism had much to do with getting *both* the San Francisco Renaissance, including Duncan, Jack Spicer, and others, and the Beat writers off the ground). As William Everson said in a mid-1980s interview, "Rexroth got the thing [the San Francisco Renaissance] started in San Francisco, then Ginsberg took it back East and sold it to *Time*. Kerouac and his group wrote for ten years before the Beat Generation emerged, and it was Rexroth who made the difference" (*Talking Poetry: Conversations in the Workshop with Contemporary Poets*, Lee Bartlett). He read the work of these and other poets, recommended them to the great publisher of New Directions, James Laughlin, told them what to read, in short, provided the rudiments of a vital, general education as he did for many people through his Pacifica broadcasts and his reviews and essays. He also magnanimously aided all kinds of people in trouble with the authorities, including Japanese-American friends and acquaintances during the Earl-Warren-conceived State of California program for the detention of Japanese Americans during World War II. Further, he counselled young men about being conscientious objectors to war and indeed was in significant contact with "conchees" stationed during World War II in a C.O. detention camp in Waldport, Oregon. Last but not least, many poets admired his verse, particularly for its paradoxical blend of deep passion and masterful tonal and prosodic control.

But there was a downside to all this genuine and kind helpfulness. Rexroth was sometimes not an easy person to get along with. He demanded loyalty from his "followers"; he expected them to remain as he had defined them as being, and when they followed their own inevitable paths of self-development as artists, he seemed to have felt betrayed. Robert Duncan in his last years was so alienated from Rexroth that he would not even talk to Rexroth scholars about him, nor would Marthe Larsen, Rexroth's third wife, to whom Rexroth dedicated the seven splendid **"Marthe"** poems, written during the mid-1950s and designed (unsuccessfully, in the long run) to win back his estranged wife. Even U. C. Berkeley's Thomas Parkinson, long a strong supporter of Rexroth, in an English Department hostile to the poet, described him in a 1983 memoir as a "morally discontinuous"

personality. It appears that Rexroth was capable of startling mood-swings. Also, evidence from Rexroth scholars like John Tritica, now completing a definitive bibliography of Rexroth's work, and from eye-witness reports, indicates that Rexroth estranged a lot of people, including old friends and admirers, by his unpredictable offensiveness. He used to be fond of saying that of the one-hundred worst persons in the world, 90% were poets, and even if in periods of self-dissatisfaction he might have included himself among that select society, such an opinion was not likely to develop new friendships or sustain old ones among poets.

> **[Rexroth] used to be fond of saying that of the one-hundred worst persons in the world, 90% were poets, and even if in periods of self-dissatisfaction he might have included himself among that select society, such an opinion was not likely to develop new friendships or sustain old ones among poets.**
> —*Donald Gutierrez*

No doubt some of Rexroth's cantankerousness and rages had to do with his career frustrations. He was a man whose full and complex worth as a social critic, political radical and polemicist, translator and poet (not to mention gourmet cook and mountain climber) was far from fully acknowledged. Eliot Weinberger, a New York-based poet and verse translator, has asserted that Rexroth deserved the status of a Neruda in Chile, a Paz in Mexico, a McDiarmid in Scotland; he deserved, that is, the national esteem of an artist who could serve as the intellectual conscience of a nation. But few if any poets or literary figures are revered in the United States unless they are distortingly popularized like Robert Frost (a process to which Frost certainly contributed) or self-mythicized like Ernest Hemingway. It was most unlikely that a Bohemian-Anarchist California man of letters would ever receive such accolades in America. After all, he made it very clear throughout his career that he was ideologically disconnected from the "heartbeat" of America, most certainly in its megacorporation aspects. And though he could (and did) expend a lot of energy convincingly implying how at home he was in the American radical tradition, mid-20th-century America was not a comfortable epoch for radicals of any stripe.

Further, as an anti-Stalinist radical, Rexroth was, according to Robert Duncan, subjected to a lot of hostility and pressure from American Stalinists, especially during the 1930s (and possibly, I would add, up into the early 1950s when McCarthyism began putting American Communists and fellow travellers—including many liberals—under severe pressure). As one who listened to Rexroth's brilliant, pompous, idiosyncratic and often hilarious KPFA broadcasts during the 1950s, I was often struck by his bottomless rancor towards Stalinists and Stalinism. This impression, persuasively created by a man who seemed versed in all the complexities and contradictions of 20th-century international radicalism in theory and practice, was counterweighted by Rexroth's sense of the formidable evil also resident in the American State and in the unrelenting rapacity and philistinism of American Capitalism ("spreading inexorably / As bacteria spread in tissue," as he put it in another context in a savagely dark visionary poem ironically titled **"Strength through Joy"**).

If a radical poet feels no affiliation with the two most powerful and threatening societies of his day he might well feel alienated, especially in a culture that would hardly pay attention to political advice or moral denunciation from a *famous* poet like Frost, let along an "eccentric" Bohemian-Anarchist poet like Rexroth. How "alienated" a person really is in contemporary American society can be hard to determine; one need not be a sociologist to realize that mass people in modern urban, industrial societies lack communal bonds or support. Some advertising executives or CEOs, for example, might be more alienated from their family, friends, or themselves, than a poet of disaffiliation. Rexroth, on the other hand, often came on as if he were part of a cultured, "hip" community of individuals who despised *Life Magazine* or *Time,* the academic poets and critics, the diabolical wiles of Madison Avenue and GE, and so on. It was the Hip versus the Square: the latter category emphatically including the half-educated, claimed Rexroth, denizens of most college English Departments. In view of the ongoing academic institutionalizing of American intellectuals and artists that accelerated after World War II, Rexroth's incessant derision of academics (especially English Department ones) actually represented an ideological impulse essential to the sustaining of a vigorous and independent American intelligentsia, the sizeable *lack* of which partly explains the rampant corruption and concentration of power in American public life for the past thirty years or so. At its worst, Rexrothian in-group communalism shrunk to a personal snobbery, and one did have the marked impression listening to Rexroth on KPFA or reading him that he had drunk the best wines, loved the most gorgeous women, read all of the important books in every major field (this he probably came close to doing), participated in the most exciting events and knew the most significant or worthy people in the 20th century. (It is not accidental that Rexroth's first autobiography, *An Autobiographical Novel,* is so titled—his primary publisher James Laughlin, though a great friend of Rexroth's, insisted on adding the word "novel" [*American Poetry,* Spring 1989]).

Rexroth is hard to come to grips with as a biographical subject partly because he was a "confabulator"—that is, he told

imaginative untruths that are themselves so vivid or entertaining or instructive that the element of lying pales. We don't know whether Rexroth's father really ate chicken and drank gin on his Terre Haute home porch with Gene Debs, or Rexroth met D. H. Lawrence in Santa Fe, or was in the same picket line that John Steinbeck describes in a famous novel when one (says Steinbeck) or eight (claims Rexroth) strikers were killed by company goons. But Rexroth telling such stories, and he had hundreds of them, might be like a novelist mediating some valuable experience—and, sometimes, he definitely was telling the (little known or incorrectly perceived) truth.

However, given Rexroth's proclivity for embroidering the truth, it can be difficult discovering his real sense of his position or "location" in American society from the 1950s on considering that he had already achieved sufficient work as a *poet* (and polemicist) to have received substantial critical recognition—and yet did not receive it. Rexroth was given some awards and recognition (including a Guggenheim in 1948, a Shelley Memorial Award, a National Institute Award and two California poetry awards), but nothing that bestowed eminence upon him, at least nothing comparable to, say, the far less gifted Delmore Schwartz's meteoric rise and New York critical encouragement. Nor has Rexroth received the kind of critical attention and deification bestowed by numerous academic critics on Robert Lowell, John Berryman, John Ashbery, Sylvia Plath and the like, over the past few decades. It is surely significant that many of these highly touted poets, as well as their praisers, are Easterners. Rexroth, though originally a Midwesterner, born in South Bend, Indiana (in a house still standing), and associated in his adolescence and early adulthood with Chicago, came West as a young man (following, he says, not Horace Greeley's but the formidable Anarchist Alexander Berkman's advice to Go West: "Go back," Rexroth claims Berkman said to him in Paris, "There is more for you in the Far West than there is here. You can probably become famous here but you'll be just another one" (*An Autobiographical Novel*). If this damaged his career, it also may have helped his verse immeasurably.

II

One way the move West might have enhanced his verse is by endowing it with regional definition and location. The significance of this regionality in Rexroth's work has not yet been sufficiently appreciated, though Gary Synder understood it, nor has the claim made by Robert Duncan that Robinson Jeffers in his coastal California landscapes influenced both Rexroth and Everson. Aside from the value to Rexroth of San Francisco as a liberated, sophisticated city receptive to artists, the West, particularly the wilds of California, with its great mountain ranges, was a source of creative stimulation to Rexroth both as a subject and as a medium of meditation and contemplation. American poets like John Matthias, David Ray and James Wright have regarded Rexroth as a *major* American poet or creative inspirer. Indeed, poets have generally thought more highly of Rexroth than critics, a situation perhaps analogous to pro-ball players who have a more authoritative idea than sports writers about who the good players in the league really are. As James Wright memorably put it in 1980, "I believe [Rexroth] has saved many poets from imaginative death" ("For Kenneth Rexroth," *The Ark,* 1980). If Rexroth is actually a major poet—Harvard's David stows on Rexroth the thin honor of being the finest of the *minor* San Francisco poets (along with whom he cites Philip Whalen, Jack Spicer and Michael McClure)—this is in no small part due to his love and nature verse. The centrality of places like Mt. Tamalpais, the Coast Range, and the Sierra Nevadas in his best nature verse is evident.

In the early three-part poem **"Toward an Organic Philosophy,"** from **In What Hour,** both California mountain ranges provide setting and embody substance in the poem. Professor Perkins has implied that Rexroth's verse lacks intensity and surprise (although he admits—without explaining why—that Rexroth is best quoted in full. Such a stricture, however, overlooks a "Western" aspect of Rexroth's verse which is integral to his poetic achievement—the "Asian" dimension. Consider the last six lines from Part I of **"Towards an Organic Philosophy"** entitled **"Spring, Coast Range":**

> There are tiny hard fruits already in the plum trees.
> The purity of the apple blossoms is incredible.
> As the wind dies down their fragrance
> Clusters around them like thick smoke.
> All the day they roared with bees, in the moonlight
> They are silent and immaculate.

Intense these lines are not, nor are they surprising. Rexroth once described the essential quality of Yeats' Japanese Noh or Dance plays as an utterly unWestern dramatic process, with no modulated character of the sort that leads to the inevitable crisis of a Western tragedy (**Bird in the Bush; Obvious Essays**). Rather a dance must incorporate and release all the energy of accumulating frustrations or longings or obsessions.

Now many of Rexroth's nature poems don't even have that sort of dramatic (let alone terpsichorean) character, and thus eschew intensity. But influenced as they are by the character of Chinese verse to depict with acute accuracy the sheer appearance of nature as also representing its deepest reality, of seeing, that is, appearance and reality as one, Rexroth achieves a purity of expression and authenticity of representation that are truly remarkable. In the six lines above, the plum tree fruits, the tree's fragrance, the roaring of the bees, the moonlit silence of the trees, are so clearly described and thus apprehended that a kind of serenity is achieved that one

would call natural mysticism were not such an intellectual formulation almost a violation of the essential spirit of the poem. In the poem, Spring in the Coast Range has been sharply imagized, and when Rexroth moves on to **"Fall, Sierra Nevada,"** we should realize that his operative poetics in this poem (and in many of his best nature poems) is in effect "Asian"—the representation of nature phenomena and being so clearly and sharply and fully There, so irrefragably existent, as almost to embody *presentation:*

> —At noon a flock of hummingbirds passed south,
>   Whirling in the wind up over the saddle between
>   Ritter and Banner [Sierra Nevada mountain
>   peaks]
>
> —   The ventriloquial belling
> Of an owl mingles with the bells of the waterfall,
>
> —Just before moonset a small dense cumulus
>   cloud,
>   Gleaming like a grape cluster of metal,
>   Moves over the Sierra crest and grows down
>   the westward slope.

How intense, how surprising is a Sung-Dynasty vase? A Sung vase Rexroth's verse may not be, but its excellence resides in part within that constellation of aesthetic values.

However, there is a kind of "Western" purposefulness in this three-fold poem after all. The verse ends as follows:

> 'Thus,' says Tyndall, 'the concerns of this little
>   place
> Are changed and fashioned by the obliquity of the
>   earth's axis,
> The chain of dependence which runs through
>   creation,
> And links the roll of a planet alike with the
>   interests
> of marmots and of men.'

If there is a "philosophy" behind this verse, it is implied in the Tyndall quote—the "chain of dependence" which "runs through creation" and which identifies the common interests of humans and all other animals. This is not so much an ecological ethic or aesthetic, though it certainly is pre-environmentalist in its acute awareness of the sensitive ecosystemic interrelation of all living creatures on the earth. Rather, Rexroth's poem records natural phenomena so sensitively, accurately and authentically as to make us remember or realize that human culture, with all of its distractions, horrors and self-importance, is not the only or even the primary plane of earthly existence.

Indeed, the West in Rexroth's work (as in that of Witter

Bynner, rather like Rexroth a very underrated poet but a well regarded translator of Asian verse, Gary Snyder and Morris Graves) has often meant serious interest in Oriental culture. Asia has been highly influential for some West Coast artists, as of course it has been more and more for the entirety of West-Coast society. Rexroth has long been interested in Asian philosophy and art, and he had many American-Asian friendships and connections going back to the early 1940s and probably before then. One leading Japanese literary scholar, Sanahide Kodama, has even claimed that Rexroth's Asian verse translations are easily superior to Ezra Pound's. According to Kodama, "There is no doubt that among major American poets, Kenneth Rexroth best understood Japanese culture" (*American Poetry and Japanese Culture*). Kodama goes on to say something equally impressive about Rexroth:

> After World War II, the new generation of American poets tried to search for something deeper than exoticism, poetical forms or device; they tried to explore the values of Japanese spiritual life. The most influential of them was Kenneth Rexroth, who maintained an interest in Japanese culture when nearly all Americans had rejected it just before and during the war, and who re-interpreted it as a new source of values for the post-war generation. In the values underlying the world of Classical Japanese poetry and Shingon Buddhism, he sensed the possibility that there might be a means to save modern civilization from destruction. In place of Western rationalism and individualism, he could find in Japanese works a new world view in which man and nature are in coexistent, harmonious relationship."

This compounding in Rexroth's work of humanity and nature reached a deeply poignant climax in Rexroth's three elegies to his first wife, Andrée Dutcher:

> Now once more gray mottled buckeye branches
> Explode their emerald stars,
> And alders smoulder in a rosy smoke
> Of innumerable buds.
> I know that spring again is splendid
> As ever, the hidden thrush
> As sweetly tongued, the sun as vital—
> But these are the forest trails we walked together,
> These paths, ten years together.
> We thought the years would last forever,
> They are all gone now, the days
> We thought would not come for us are here.
> Bright trout poised in the current—
> The raccoon's track at the water's edge—
> A bittern booming in the distance—
> Your ashes scattered on this mountain—
> Moving seaward on this stream.

Perkins, who quotes this first elegy, can't find anything to say about it. I can. What is remarkable about it is the absence of overt lament or sorrow. The grief is only implied, very quietly in the 8th line "But these are the forest trails we walked together," which introduces the dead beloved. The main expression of the loss occurs in three lines in the center of the poem:

> We thought the years would last forever,
> They are all gone now, the days
> We thought would not come for us are here.

These lines and much of Rexroth's best verses, are impressive in the utter bareness, lucidity, and "classical" restraint of their language. Rexroth believes, rather Miltonically, that language in verse should be as simple, direct and sensuous as possible. Yet, as in those three lines, the simplicity and directness of the language, by its very lack of "literary" ornamentation or pose, but also by careful choice, generate considerable force. Showing "Rexroth," like most of us, victimized by the illusion of love as something beyond time or contingency, the poem elicits our identification at the deepest emotional level, and in Rexroth's adroit use of "we" and "us" in the twelfth line, his condition of being "dead" along with his dead wife is movingly (if quietly) conveyed.

But the entire poem and its core of deep, silent lament are underscored by a nature description which exhibits Rexroth's skill in presenting the exact nuance or nature of things—the "*buckeye* branches" and their "emerald stars," the "*smoldering* alders", the "hidden *thrush*." All this carefully weighted exactness comprises one dimension towards Rexroth's complex ideal of communicating the "holiness of the real" which is "accessible in total immanence." But these quoted bits from Rexroth's *great* poem, **"Time Is the Mercy of Eternity,"** are ironic in the context of the **"Andrée Rexroth"** elegy because what for Rexroth, what for any husband or lover, made the real most *holy* is now missing—it, she, Andrée, is now dead, and thus, though nature is as vital and beautiful as it was before, it is also crucially, poignantly different.

III

Rexroth was a unique figure in American literary culture. There are people in our society who are Bohemians or poets or social radicals but few who combine these roles with his enormous general knowledge and highly distilled wisdom. Not all of Rexroth's essays are fine, but many of them, in their combination of trenchant insight, broad knowledge, and iconoclastic vigor and wit, are fine indeed, and, if one can put up with Rexroth's man-of-the-world tone and occasional arrogance and pretentiousness, enriching and memorable. Both volumes of his autobiography are vivid and eye-opening reading from a quite different perspective on art and thought, and on modern life and society than one would generally encounter even among iconoclasts, apolitical radicals and other members of the ideological minority. More than a few people who heard Rexroth's KPFA book talks or read his prose felt that this man, over and beyond his affectations and posturing, possessed from the late 1920s into the 1970s a visionary sense of the radical ways in which 20th-century societies were willfully destroying civilization and the earth itself and thus ultimately the human race. People in the late 1950s scoffed at his jeremiads, exposures, revelations; today, their truth is common knowledge to most children over six.

Kenneth Rexroth almost single-handedly urged that there was a West-Coast, Western-American culture that, if not as publicized and powerful as that of the East Coast, was nevertheless worthy and self-sufficient. Polemicist, verse translator, enduring radical, lecher, transvalutationist and wit, Rexroth himself embodied no little portion of the West that he inhabited most of his life and whose culture he did so much to enhance in merit, esteem and durability—no mean achievement for David Perkins' "minor" San Francisco poet:

> See, The sun has fallen away,
> Now there are amber
> Long lights on the shattered
> Boles of the ancient apple trees.
> Our bodies move to each other
> As bodies move in sleep;
> At once filled and exhausted,
> As the summer moves to autumn,
> As we, with Sappho, move towards death.
> My eyelids sink toward sleep in the hot
> Autumn of your uncoiled hair.
> Your body moves in my arms
> On the verge of sleep;
> And it is as though I held
> In my arms the bird filled
> Evening sky of summer.

(from **"When We with Sappho,"** in
The Phoenix and the Tortoise)

David Barber (essay date Fall 1993)

SOURCE: "The Threading of the Year," in *Parnassus*, Vol. 18, No. 2, Fall, 1993, pp. 267-90.

[*In the following essay, Barber provides analysis of Rexroth's poetry and literary development. According to Barber, "however boldly his personal history carries the impress of beatnik San Francisco and beatific Kyoto, his*

reckonings with the wilderness bear the telltale marks of Jeffersonian and Emersonian bloodlines."]

In his later years Kenneth Rexroth came to assume the very appearance of a weathered Chinese sage. That drooping mustache and the incalculable crinkles round the eyes, the high forehead and the set of the square chin, something about the mixed air of gruffness and whimsy in that battered physiognomy—one feels certain, gazing at the snapshots of this doughty septuagenarian, that we have seen him countless times in the corner of an inkbrushed screen, a venerable figure dwarfed by cliffs and all but lost in swirling mists, ever watchful, scroll in hand.

And so in a way we have. Rexroth looked toward Asia every bit as purposefully as another Midwestern kid by the name of Eliot took to Britannia, and his transformation into an Oriental poet-scholar was no less convincing or complete than Eliot's reincarnation as an English don. Translations and imitations from the Chinese began appearing in Rexroth's collections of poetry during the 1940's, and his initial pair of New Directions anthologies, *One Hundred Poems from the Japanese* (1955) and *One Hundred Poems from the Chinese* (1956), became touchstone volumes as they passed through their many editions. From the start there was a refreshing candor and undisguised ardor about it all. "I have chosen only those poems whose appeal is simple and direct . . . poems that speak to me of situations in life like my own," Rexroth stated in his notes to the Chinese volume. "I have thought of my translations as, finally, expressions of myself."

That candor and ardor never slackened. As he grew older Rexroth read widely in Buddhism, and lived for a time in Kyoto, courtesy of a Fulbright. In the last decade of his life he produced or coauthored six collections of Far Eastern poetry, assemblages spanning a panoramic range of periods, styles, and sensibilities. Thanks in large part to the accessibility of the texts and the sturdiness of Rexroth's renderings, this portfolio of translated verse not only found an ample following but to a sensible degree can be said to have formed and cultivated that wider readership. Self-schooled in this enterprise as in everything else, splendidly undaunted by his lack of fluency and scholarly bona fides, he became his day's foremost popularizer of Chinese and Japanese verse, the translator most likely to have introduced the common reader to the women court poets of Japan or the gnomic utterances of Tu Fu.

Rexroth also published two collections of original verse during his last rush of industry in the 1970's. You can now read them side by side in the single trim edition recently published by Rexroth's old camping chum James Laughlin under the title *Flower Wreath Hill: Later Poems.* And with that book in hand and a few biographical facts at your disposal you might tell an absorbing story about a stormy iconoclast from the American Heartland who reinvented himself as a contemplative imagistic poet in the Golden State, a story of how an avant garde firebrand turned his back on the dialectics of the West and the precepts of modernism to embrace the distilled quietism of the East. You would observe that a full half of *New Poems* (1974) is given over to Chinese translations or adaptations, and that most of *The Morning Star* (1979) was written in the gardens and temples of Kyoto. You would point out that in the poems from Rexroth's own hand, the line between poet and translator has blurred almost beyond recognition: One sees the same highly concentrated structures, the same containment, the same cultivation of open line and frozen image, a kindred predilection towards sequence and diary notation.

Finally, you would unfold the tantalizing dance of veils behind **"The Love Poems of Marichiko,"** the sequence of fifty erotic lyrics that close out the book. Five of these poems first appeared in Rexroth's *One Hundred More Poems from the Japanese* (1974), and the poet was glossed in the end-notes as "the pen-name of a contemporary young woman who lives near the temple of Marishi-ben, in Tokyo." In the notes to the **"Love Poems,"** however, one comes across a wink and a nudge. "Notice," Rexroth writes, "that the sex of the lover is ambiguous." This Marichiko, it emerges, is a fabrication, cross-cultural identification turned inside out, translation in drag. What better climax to a virtually lifelong intimacy with Far Eastern verse? Rexroth, on the final pages of his last book, speaks to us as a Japanese woman.

It is an almost irresistible story, resonant with psychobiographical reverberations and socioliterary overtones. There is no disputing or diminishing the importance of the Orient to the contrarian temperament and tempestuous career of Kenneth Rexroth. There's also no denying that the cultural tradewinds blowing out of California in the 1950's and 1960's helped sweep Rexroth along: The aura hovering over those New Directions paperbacks glimmered all the brighter as an amalgamation of Eastern mysticisms and wisdoms took on a faddishness in youth culture and as hybrid variations on open forms began to attract a growing faction of metrically disaffected poets. As a longtime resident of the state and the tribal elder of the San Francisco literary caravansary, as an evolutionary link between the California of Jeffers and the California of Snyder and Hass, as a driving force in both the countercultural and crosscultural permutations of the regional imagination, Rexroth is a natural when cast as the framing spirit of what contemporary punditry insists we call the "Pacific Rim." If he hadn't reinvented himself, it may have been necessary for us to invent him.

An arresting story, then, but one that's rather too available. A story, finally, that remains more colorful than sufficiently insightful, and one that helps explain why Rexroth, to quote poet (and former Rexroth student) Sam Hamill, is "among

our best-known and least-read poets." It not only encourages us to lazily stylize an irrepressibly eclectic personality, but deprives us of much incentive to grapple with a body of poetry distinctive for its robust unorthodoxy and bracing restlessness. It condescends too quickly to the presumption that Rexroth's diehard Bohemian leanings and fire-breathing disdain for Eastern Seaboard snobbery bred an animus toward his own Americanness. It perpetuates the impression, this narrative line does, that Rexroth lacked the requisite quotient of modernist irony and ambiguity to himself become a fully realized poet in an age of anxiety, that he was forced to compensate for the unevenness and coarseness of his own verse by co-opting the Orient's polished refinements of sense and sensibility. It justifies his marginality and excuses his neglect. It gives his metamorphosis the cynical spin of a good career move.

> **Rexroth is a natural when cast as the framing spirit of what contemporary punditry insists we call the "Pacific Rim." If he hadn't reinvented himself, it may have been necessary for us to invent him.**
> —*David Barber*

Like so many others, I suspect, my first brush with Rexroth was as the name on the spine of those compact and handsomely packaged New Directions "100 Poems" paperbacks, which I regarded as standing invitations to steal a march on Milton-loving prep-school teachers everywhere. The name was not the spur. Rexroth was, as far as this Southern California schoolboy was concerned, merely the humble translator, and as such, properly shadowy. I don't think it would have much mattered to me if I'd been told at that time that Rexroth was living some 90 minutes north in Santa Barbara, ever the cantankerous polymath and for many the dean of California poets. What mattered to me was the mystique of all that white space on the pages, the allure of those calligraphic brushstrokes, the attar of erotica that seemed to promise a hidden garden of significance. What mattered was the sensation of being spoken to directly and intimately by an alien tongue across the ages:

> Tumult, weeping, many new ghosts.
> Heartbroken, aging, alone, I sing
> To myself. Ragged mist settles
> In the spreading dusk. Snow skurries
> In the coiling wind. The wineglass
> Is spilled. The bottle is empty.
> The fire has gone out in the stove.
> Everywhere men speak in whispers.
> I brood on the uselessness of letters.
>
>   ("Snow Storm" [Tu Fu])

So it was jarring, some years later and the Milton-lovers safely behind me, to discover that shadowy humility was not exactly Rexroth's forte. Threading my way through the largely embalmed Bohemian quarter of San Francisco in the dawn of the Reagan *risorgimento,* I would spin squealing postcard racks and come across the same photo time and again. It was a blurry, noirish shot of Rexroth declaiming his verse to the accompaniment of a jazz ensemble sometime in the throes of Eisenhower America, bulldog jaw jutting into the nicotine haze, all pugnacity and bardic torque. Who was the nightclubbing Homer, this leather-lunged hipster doyen? Could he possibly be the same canny soul who had made the T'ang master Tu Fu seem my contemporary?

I indulge in this scrap of personal reminiscence because I am convinced that the Rexroth of initial impressions and general acquaintance is more often than not a caricature, a "figure" whose singularity is most conveniently filed away as the headstrong sum of his polarized selves. Depending on which way we want the compass needle to quiver, he can be emblematic of a certain kind of aggrieved excess, a certain brand of generational dissonance and provincial dissent, a certain mixed breed of cosmopolitan primitivism that could call itself neither redskin nor paleface, a certain fearless vigor which is also a certain endless quandary. And depending on one's own cherished notions of artistic essence, an appraisal of Rexroth's powers can lend itself instinctively to either salutary ideals or cautionary tales. As a constellation of contradictions, enthusiasms, and antagonisms, he is perhaps surpassed only by that other notable maverick from the American interior—Little Dipper to Pound's Big. In Yeatsian terms, alas, he made the fatal error of seeking perfectibility in both the life and the art, eternally falling short of reconciling a life of action and a poetry of inwardness.

"He is no writer in the sense of the word-man," wrote Williams of Rexroth. "For him words are sticks and stones to build a house—but it's good house." And true enough, the mature Rexroth did not write poems that anyone would be tempted to call, with a nod to Williams, "little word machines." Much of his writing seems to be one species or another of pedagogy—lectures and lessons, sermons and tracts. As anyone who's read across Rexroth's bully-pulpit prose knows well, his was an incorrigibly discursive and dialectical mind, a polemical intellect of nearly inexhaustible capacity, wheels within wheels. The verse, too, often seems to have been composed in the spirit of instruction and exhortation. Rexroth's pair of long poems from the 1940's, **"The Phoenix and the Tortoise"** and the European travelogue **"The Dragon and the Unicorn,"** are sprawling monuments to his mania for association and assimilation, running commentaries crammed with arcana and opinion, diatribe and panegyric, cerebral pontification and encyclopedic information:

> Bath a stageset for Terence,
> One of the world's unlikely
> Cities, as freakish as Venice.
> In the midst of its colonnades
> And the swarming well-fed people,
> Bath Abbey, immense and absurd,
> Like the skeleton of a
> Whale or a dirigible,
> Built by Walpole Gothicizing,
> The most eighteenth-century
> Product of the Middle Ages.
>   (from **"The Dragon and the Unicorn"**)

But we do wrong by Rexroth if we overstate his didacticism and only have ears for his windier topicality. This was also a poet who all his life wrote quietly wrought and intensely intimate homages and elegies, love lyrics and pacts. It's fetching irony, in light of the above remark by the good doctor of Paterson, that one of the most moving and telling of these is Rexroth's 1946 poem, **"A Letter to William Carlos Williams,"** in which Rexroth lionizes Williams as "the first / Great Franciscan poet since / The Middle Ages" and praises the "wonderful quiet / You have, a way of keeping / Still about the world. . . ."

> Nowadays, when the press reels
> With chatterboxes, you keep still,
> Each year a sheaf of stillness,
> Poems that have nothing to say,
> Like the stillness of George Fox,
> Sitting still under the cloud
> Of all the world's temptation . . .

Let others celebrate William's earthiness; in Rexroth's eyes he shall be known for his saintliness, his Quaker-like gravity, a containment that verges on mysticism. The poem closes with an affectionate prophecy, the Passaic having become "the lucid Williams River" and a young woman imparting the essence of the poet to her young ones as they stroll alongside.

> '. . . And the
> Beautiful river he saw
> Still flows in his veins, as it
> Does in ours, and flows in our eyes,
> And flows in time, and makes us
> Part of it, and part of him.
> That, children, is what is called
> A sacramental relationship.
> And that is what a poet
> Is, children, one who creates
> Sacramental relationships
> That last always.'

One might well expect that Rexroth would hold keen admiration for Williams. His own sense of measure and cadence owed something to Williams' perceptually alert line, as did his colloquial worldliness and moral allegiance to the local. His is arguably the most moving and incisive tribute we have for a poet who inspired a great many. But this Williams of stillness and sacrament, of "wonderful quiet," seems also a selective embodiment of the kind of poet Rexroth himself wished to become, a personification of the knowing reserve and meditative concentration his early verse only fitfully sustained.

Our leading story, of course, would have it that Rexroth learned to keep still about the world, at long last, by donning the robes of the Buddhists and assuming the manner of the classical poets of the East. "Sitting still under the cloud / Of all the world's temptation"—aren't we already closer here to the Yangtze than to the Passaic? But Rexroth is one of those poets who only grow more distorted the more we squint at him through the lens of artistic development; we must take care not to twist him into the lotus position quite so briskly and willfully. He is never quite the poet we expect him to be, or rather, we are obliged to revise our sense of his reach and his grasp the further we read on. To traverse the nearly 800 pages of his poetry amassed in the *Collected Shorter,* the *Collected Longer,* and *Flower Wreath Hill* is only to confirm that there are no shortcuts around the manysided soul that was Kenneth Rexroth. It's chiefly for this reason that I want for the rest of this essay neither to take the high road of eulogy nor the low road of apology but rather to locate Rexroth in a very particular clearing, a place apart form the forking paths where poets are hustled into their rightful anthologies or obscurities, a buffer zone somewhere between that squealing postcard rack and that hanging inkbrushed screen:

> All day I walk over ridges
> And beside cascades and pools
> Deep into the Spring hills.
> Mushrooms come up in the same spot
> In the abandoned clearing.
> Trillium and adder's tongue
> Are in place by the waterfall.

This is from a poem called **"Hapax,"** and it too appears among the autumnal offerings of *Flower Wreath Hill,* early in the book under the section title **"Love Is an Art of Time."** Contrary to the collection's Oriental cast, the poem opens with a bow to the Christian calendar ("Holy Week. Once more the full moon / Blooms in deep heaven / Like a crystal flower of ice.") and bears the curiously exculpatory epigraph, **"The Same Poem Over and Over."** It's a nocturne set in an unspecified patch of Rexroth's beloved California ranges—a valedictory piece of meditation spoken at the end of a daylong ramble through the upcountry so familiar to the poet that "A heron lifts from a pool / As I come near, as it

has done / For forty years, and flies off / Through the same gap in the trees." The tone is reverent; the language direct and unadorned. A general atmosphere of monkish solitude prevails throughout, the poem by gradual degrees convincing us that it was intended all along as a rough-hewn prayer: "Back at my cabin / In the twilight an owl on the same / Limb moans in his ancient language. / Billions and billions of worlds / Full of beings larger than dinosaurs / And smaller than viruses, each / In its place, the ecology of infinity. / I look at the rising Easter moon. / The flowering madrone gleams in the moonlight."

"Hapax" is not by any stretch one of Rexroth's most accomplished works. In fact, it's a poem that can seem to confirm one's worst suspicions about his relative indifference to linguistic tension or prosodic rigor, his disdain for psychological intricacy and dramatic irony, the mulish matter-of-factness of his compositional method, his weakness for the scenic and susceptibility to fuzzy mysticism. A commentator disposed to unkindness could well claim that not only is the scenery distinctively California but so too is the poem's cosmic bathos and its over-eagerness to be "at one" with the universe. Rexroth's religiosity appears for the most part to be a matter of vibes rather than spirit, the end-product of the poem's predetermined rhetoric of transcendence. The operative phrase, "ecology of infinity," sounds as if it should be the slogan of a Silicon Valley software firm.

But it is in this vein, I would argue, that Rexroth did write some of his most transparent and transfigured poems throughout his life—poems that shuttle more surely than this one between natural pieties and elective affinities, poems at once grounded in the immediate and bent toward the beyond, poems of *en plein aire* mindfulness and loamy ongoingness that ask to be read as authentic spiritual exercises, devotional verse. **"Hapax,"** for all its seeming offhandedness, is an Easter poem set down in good faith—which is not to say that it enunciates a Christian creed, but that it seeks an emptying of self as a condition of spiritual consolation. It is here, in abandoned clearings, in alpine retreats, in periodic monastic solitudes, that we come upon Rexroth's variants on "poems that have nothing to say," to borrow his encomium for Williams. It is here, in poems where a stripped-down declarative idiom corresponds to a greater stripping-away of pretense and ingenuity, that we find a self-made contemplative poet for whom significance has become a test of artlessness.

I daresay one can find in Rexroth's writings a précis or an ars poetica for each and every paradox his temperament was heir to. It's curious nonetheless to observe him glossing this particular reconstitution of his poetic humors as the most effortless of conversion experiences, in a little wartime poem called **"Precession of the Equinoxes":**

Time was, I walked in February rain,
My head full of its own rhythms like a shell,
And came home at night to write of love and
   death,
High philosophy, and brotherhood of man.

After intimate acquaintance with these things,
I contemplate the changes of the weather,
Flowers, birds, rabbits, mice and other small deer
Fulfilling the year's periodicity.

And the reassurances of my own pulse.

This rather sounds like the poem one would write in the autumn of one's days, disabused of youthful illusions and disencumbered of overblown ambitions. In fact, Rexroth was not yet forty, and not nearly the master of his nervous system that these lines would have us believe. As such, one can't help thinking that the poem is wise to its own wishful thinking, set down more as a prospectus than a fait accompli. Rexroth, in any event, certainly didn't become a contemplative overnight, and breaking with his past was no simple matter of losing himself in the birds and the stars. That "time was" takes us back only a year or so to the hot-blooded auguries and maledictions that fill the pages of his first book, *In What Hour* (1941), and a disposition given to spasms of rampant self-doubt. "Time was," he seems to have been teetering on the brink of jettisoning the fairest hopes of art and language and learning altogether: "What is it all for, this poetry, / This bundle of accomplishment / Put together with so much pain? / . . . What words can it spell, / This alphabet of one sensibility?"

Born a round generation behind Pound and Williams in 1905, Rexroth came of age while the Lost Generation was sowing its oats and the dashing Europe of the charter modernists was counting its dead in the trenches. We might therefore exonerate him for what might appear like grandstanding pessimism in the above passage, which can be found at the beginning of a set piece titled **"August 22, 1939."** Like the canonic poem of Auden's that's dated ten days later, Rexroth's is an epochal lamentation written in the throes of one of the modern era's darkest hours. And like Auden, just two years his junior, Rexroth was attempting to raise his voice against the march of armies and the sleep of reason—a "world in stupor," to borrow one of the many majestically disabused phrases from **"September 1, 1939."**

I daresay one can find in Rexroth's writings a précis or an ars poetica for each and every paradox his temperament was heir to.
—*David Barber*

Poetry makes nothing happen, Auden had testified in his elegy to Yeats earlier that year, but of the two poems written at the close of that grim summer, Rexroth's is the bleaker as well as the cruder deposition on the futility of the poet. The role reversal, if you will, is perhaps more noteworthy than the synchronicity. Central casting surely would have called for the rough-and-ready Midwestern autodidact, not the urbane Oxonian, to have been "one of the faces along the bar" that "clings to their average day," and keeps alive "an affirming flame." Yet it is Rexroth rather than Auden who seems to have been rendered abject by a "low, dishonest decade," coarsely cursing the darkness where his emigré contemporary nurses sparks of luminous humanism. **"August 22, 1939"** ends not with a gesture of affirmation but a bray of exasperation: "What are we doing at the turn of our years / Writers and readers of the liberal weeklies?"

Certainly, this poem of clenched fists catches Rexroth at the turn of *his* years, still more the fiery lefty than the full-blown man of letters. It is not, like Auden's, a poem for the ages but a broadside on the times. Liberals or no, the initial readers of *In What Hour* were no doubt more apt than we to recognize that the date of the poem salutes the anarchists Sacco and Vanzetti (executed August 23, 1927) and to place its unattributed quote from Marx's *Kapital* ("From each according to his ability, / Unto each according to his needs"). **"August 22, 1939"** is one of a number of poems in the collection that rage and grieve over the bitter harvest of partisan struggle or rail at the various avatars of the Big Lie. At times this pitch of righteous declamation and unrepentant disenchantment turns Rexroth into a cross between a soapbox Marxist and an Old Testament prophet:

It is later than you think, fires have gone over
Our forests, the grasshopper screamed in our corn.
Fires have gone over the brains of our young girls,
Hunger over young men and fear everywhere.
The smell of gas has ascended from the streets,
Bloomed from the cartridges, spread from wall to
   wall,
Bloomed on the highways, and seeped into the
   corn.
It is later than you think, there is a voice
Preparing to speak, there are whisperings now
And murmurings and noises made with the teeth.
   (from **"The Motto on the Sundial"**)

But *In What Hour* ran against the grain of cultural orthodoxy in calmer and more collected ways too. There is a clear-eyed as well as a wild-eyed poet at work in this Depression album of poems. As Robert Hass has suggested, we find in its pages a sensibility taking root: a Midwestern outcast remaking himself into a California citizen-poet, a fierce moral intelligence fighting the good fight at the far margins of the nation. Although it's evident that Rexroth's radical disaffection from the centers of official culture made the Bay Area an appealing base of operations, it's also plain that his embrace of the California hinterlands stemmed from impulses at least as elemental as ideological. An avid and delicate alertness to his adopted region's natural history, a charged responsiveness to its open sprawl and utter scale, ground the more durable passages in *In What Hour,* revealing backcountry affinities and reflective leanings one doesn't usually associate with hardboiled anarchists:

> Autumn in California is a mild
> And anonymous season, hills and valleys
> Are colorless then, only the sooty green
> Eucalyptus, the conifers and oaks sink deep
> Into the haze; the fields are plowed, bare, waiting;
> The steep pastures are tracked deep by cattle;
> There are no flowers, the herbage is brittle.
> All night along the coast and the mountain crests
> Birds go by, murmurous, high in the warm air.
>
> (from **"Autumn in California"**)

Readers whose acquaintance with California isn't limited to glossy postcards of the Golden Gate or celluloid montages of Hollywood palms can attest to the rightness of that "sooty green" and that oak-devouring haze, but one needn't be a native to be impressed by the fine-spun attention Rexroth musters for a "mild / And anonymous season" that few writers in his day (and no great number in our own) would deem worthy of more than passing notice. A Currier and Ives calendar of stock seasonal footage is next to useless in coming to terms with the muted annual cycle of the Californian countryside, and Rexroth's precedence in paying homage to this terra incognita is a credit to both his sense of nuance and his sensible knack for "making it new." The ear must shake off the echoes of intoxicating Keatsian stanzas before it can pick up the unprepossessing stateliness of *this* ode to autumn, and that's arguably all to the good: The ruminative texture of the above passage, the chariness toward fully ripened rhyme ("Mild"—"valleys"; "green"—"deep") and verbal dazzle ("Birds go by"), seem altogether more fitting to the hazy, colorless, and anonymous character of the landscape under scrutiny than the chiming couplets, lush pentameters, and rapturous sprung rhythms that a verdant, dramatically transitory clime wrings from its laureates.

Rexroth had been a resident of San Francisco for more than a decade when *In What Hour* came off the presses. He also had some twenty years of literary industry already behind him, much of it hyperactive philosophical collage and programmatic dabblings in Objectivist serialism. These experimental proclivities apparently withered as the breadlines formed and his political activism intensified, but what really seems to have brought Rexroth back from the brink of linguistic cubism was his growing intimacy with Northern California's coastal wilds and Sierra ranges. It is surely not

a trifling biographical detail that Rexroth was periodically under the employ of the Federal Writers Project during these years, contributing unsigned descriptive sketches and touring squibs to such publications as the *WPA Guide to California* and a *Field Handbook of the Sierra Nevada.* These commissions had to be a happy circumstance for an enthusiast of the trail like Rexroth, and it's safe to say that the grit and dirt he picked up along the way was a decided blessing for his poetry. Amid such abstruse set pieces as **"Dative Haruspices"** ("Film and filament, no / Donor, gift without / Reciprocity, transparent / Tactile act, an imaginary / Web of structure sweeps / The periphery of being . . .") and **"New Objectives, New Cadres"** ("By what order must the will walk impugned, / Through spangles of landscapes, / Through umbers of sea bottom, By the casein gleam of any moon / Of postulates and wishes?") that take up considerable breathing room in his first collection, one welcomes the tempered measure that marks Rexroth's epistles from the mountains:

> Frost, the color and quality of the cloud,
> Lies over all the marsh below my campsite.
> The wiry clumps of dwarfed white bark pines
> Are smoky and indistinct in the moonlight,
> Only their shadows are really visible.
> The lake is immobile and holds the stars
> And the peaks deep in itself without a quiver.
> In the shallows the geometrical tendrils of ice
> Spread their wonderful mathematics in silence.
>
> (from **"Toward an Organic Philosophy"**)

> In the long day in the hour of small shadow
> I walk on the continent's last western hill
> And lie prone among the iris in the grass
> My eyes fixed on the durable stone
> That speaks and hears as though it were myself.
>
> (from **"A Lesson in Geography"**)

Lines like these assure us that Rexroth from early on was wholly conscious of casting himself as a poet in honorable regional exile, and they also affirm the elements of style that were coalescing into trustworthy habits of composition. The "outdoors" poetry of *In What Hour*—lean and economical in its syntax and its diction, coolly observant and solemnly meditative in its essential register, its balance of trust placed in the testimony of the senses rather than the force of rhetorical address—assumes the concentrated plainspoken form that Rexroth would avail himself of increasingly in the years to come. Implicit in this streamlined prosody is a finetuned moral sensibility. Steeped in the organic rhythms and seasonal variations of the California landscape, this is verse that divines in ecology a higher ethical order that might expunge the taint of a corrupt and corrosive social ethos. More simply, the mountaintop had become for Rexroth the most reliable place to steel the conscience and clear one's head. Here is the opening of **"Hiking in the Coast Range,"** a poem commemorating the death of two dockworking unionists:

> The skirl of the kingfisher was never
> More clear than now, nor the scream of the jay
> As the deer shifts her covert at a footfall;
> Nor the butterfly tulip ever brighter
> In the white spent wheat; nor the pain
> Of a wasp stab ever an omen more sure;
> The blood alternately dark and brilliant
> On the blue and white bandanna pattern.

What bears out the intensity and urgency of these clean-hammered lines are their scrupulous attentiveness and inherent clarity: the balance of cadences and concentration of stresses ("white spent wheat," "omen more sure"), the taut quasi-scriptural deployment of successive negations and accumulating pivots, the deft interlocking of naturalistic and emblematic detail as the passage moves from "skirl" to "scream" to "wasp stab." This is not the voluble and splenetic poet who elsewhere confounds oracular power with oratorical volume; this is not the poet whose moral imperatives are largely indistinguishable from his imperious moods. It is the difference between grandiloquence and gravity; between a short fuse and a drawn bowstring.

What's striking as one thumbs toward the midpoint of the *Collected Shorter* is the hush that falls over Rexroth's later backcountry poetry of the 1940's and 1950's, the hue and cry of causes and the outbursts of anathema fading out like crackling radio signals.
—*David Barber*

Even so, **"Hiking the Coast Range"** is still in its own way a public poem written on the barricades. The hiker has hied to the hills to galvanize his resistance to injustice in the polis and to gird his lions for renewed class warfare. What's striking as one thumbs toward the midpoint of the *Collected Shorter* is the hush that falls over Rexroth's later backcountry poetry of the 1940's and 1950's, the hue and cry of causes and the outbursts of anathema fading out like crackling radio signals. In their place one hears a virtual liturgy of earthly delights and soulful gleanings, poems claiming sovereignty in what a later, blither generation of Californians would champion as the here and now. A handful are examples of the forthright and singularly unaffected love poetry that is justly accorded a place of honor among Rexroth's more devoted readers. Initially most distinctive for an unblinkered erotic candor rarely encountered in mid-century American poetry (Rexroth was an acolyte of Sappho long before **"Marichiko"** was so much as a rustle

in a kimono), these amatory poems retain their boldness on the far side of the sexual revolution because they are unmuddied by either sentimentality or lubricity and unblemished by Puritan and Freudian galls alike. Up where the air is clear, Eros routs Thanatos from the field, if only for the most fleeting of interludes. As demonstrated in the exemplary **"Lyell's Hypothesis Again"** (Charles Lyell was the preeminent geologist of the early nineteenth century and one of the forefathers of modern geological time), Rexroth's sylvan settings are vivid environments, not allegorized Gardens, and his grasp of the material world vastly exceeds that of your average passionate shepherd:

> Naked in the warm April air,
> We lie under the redwoods,
> In the sunny lee of a cliff.
> As you kneel above me I see
> Tiny red marks on your flanks
> Like bites, where the redwood cones
> Have pressed into your flesh.
> You can find just the same marks
> In the lignite in the cliff
> Over our heads. *Sequoia*
> *Langsdorfii* before the ice,
> And *sempervirens* afterwards,
> There is little difference,
> Except for all these years.

Encountering other such poems (**"Floating," "Still on Water," "When We with Sappho"**) that twine in a double helix around the force of nature and power of desire, we are reminded of Rexroth's admiration for the eroticized, mystical pulse of D. H. Lawrence's poetry, which he praised in his rousing 1947 introduction to the first American edition of Lawrence's *Selected Poems,* for achieving its visionary authority in "the pure act of sensual communion and contemplation" and reaching its highest mastery in Lawrence's explicit love poems to Frieda composed during the couple's travels along the Rhine. This cluster of lyrics, declared Rexroth in his best Poundian manner, comprise "the greatest imagistic poems ever written," capturing the romantic union of a man and woman in so primal and natural a state that "everything stands out lit by a light not of this earth and at the same time completely of this earth. . . ." That line could serve as the epigraph for Rexroth's own intermittent poetry of spiritualized Eros and conjugal grace, his Lawrentian tendency—revealed nowhere more indelibly than in these closing lines of **"Floating"**—to spot the fingerprints of the divine in the couplings of humankind:

> Move softly, do not move at all, but hold me,
> Deep, still, deep within you, while time slides
>   away,
> As this river slides beyond this lily bed,
> And the thieving moments fuse and disappear

In our mortal, timeless flesh.

Memorable though they are, Rexroth's present-tense lyrics celebrating a flesh-and-blood Other under an open sky are outnumbered by wilderness poems conceived in the absence of companionship or the aftermath of passion. Most of them take the form of soliloquies rather than direct addresses to the beloved, and they chronicle more hours spent in soulmaking than lovemaking. Much as Rexroth cherished having a mate by his side as he scaled peaks and forded brooks, the evidence of these poems lays bare an even deeper need to wrestle with body and spirit in perfect solitude. The impulse is ancient, and at this late date often wearily formulaic, yet the verse Rexroth mined on a "high plateau where / No one ever comes, beside / This lake filled with mirrored mountains" (**"Time Is the Mercy of Eternity"**) or "On the ground beside lonely fires / Under the summer stars, and in / Cabins where the snow drifted through / The pines and over the roof" (**"A Living Pearl"**) stands out as some of the most measured and least derivative he would ever compose. While these meditations always assume a monastic distance from the madding crowd, they seldom indulge in the presumptions of holy loneliness; while they commonly incline toward mysticism, they rarely court the thin air of worldly detachment. The rituals of purification Rexroth invokes are better described as escapes *into* the world, revolving as they do around the pleasures of the flesh and the manifestations of place, sharply specific as they are about the passage of the seasons, the changes in the weather, the fluctuation of waters and the cycles of flowerings, the comings and goings of creatures. "Nature poetry" is almost always an enfeebling appellation, but especially so for these benedictions and baptisms written at the intersection of natural history and preternatural mystery:

> Forever the thought of you,
> And the splendor of the iris,
> The crinkled iris petal,
> The gold hairs powdered with pollen,
> And the obscure cantata
> Of the tangled water, and the
> Burning, impassive snow peaks,
> Are knotted here together.
> This moment of fact and vision
> Seizes immortality,
> Becomes the person of this place.
> The responsibility
> Of love realized and beauty
> Seen burns in a burning angel
> Real beyond flower or stone.
>
>   (from **"Incarnation"**)

"This moment of fact and vision"—here, in a phrase, is Rexroth's plumbline, the unit of measure by which he set about divining the limits of knowing and the depths of be-

ing as he lit out for the timberline. Yet the poems Rexroth consecrates to such moments have precious little in them of Romantic self-exaltation and sublimity: The visionary awakenings that grip this poet on his lonely summits or beside his rushing streams are specimen reaffirmations of recurrence, of continuity, of pattern, of the habitual and the diurnal, of responsibility. The "burning angel / Real beyond flower or stone" that appears in the closing lines of **"Incarnation"** gains all the greater purchase on reality by virtue of the fact that we are in the hands of a poet who is inordinately attentive to flowers and stones and by virtue of the fact that we have been paced through a poem that begins not in inspiration but perspiration: "Climbing alone all day long / In the blazing waste of spring snow, I came down with the sunset's edge / To the highest meadow. . . ." The elevation of the soul and the attainment of serenity pivots not on "either/ors" but hangs in the balance between infinitely renewable "ands" and "thens."

The alpine wilderness, to be sure, was where Rexroth sought a peace surpassing all understanding, and in certain poems he enshrines his waterfalls and meadows and glades as the way stations of a pilgrim. Occasionally, they verge on ecstatic experience, glimpses behind the veil. In **"The Signature of All Things"** (the title poem of Rexroth's 1949 collection, named after the seminal work of the 16th-century German mystic Jacob Boehme) he lays the text aside and "gaze[s] through shade / Folded into shade of slender / Laurel trunks and leaves filled with sun" until "My own sin and trouble fall away? Like Christian's bundle." In **"Time Is the Mercy of Eternity"** he stares into a high-country pool upon an August evening and discerns "that the color / Of the water itself is / Due to millions of active / Green flecks of life . . . / The deep reverberation / Of my identity with / All this plentitude of life / Leaves me shaken and giddy." But for the most part, in transcribing his communions with nature, Rexroth succumbs neither to grandiosity nor to giddiness. The devotional integrity of his compactly built verse paragraphs derives from their implicit insistence that looking closely, speaking directly, and feeling deeply can (and perhaps must) merge into a steadfast and continuous sacramental habit of mind.

There is a rugged humility in Rexroth's readiness to be steadied by the cyclical and his willingness to be schooled by the commonplace. Observation, these poems intimate, incubates perception; description, revelation. "Although / I expect them, I walk by the / Stream and hear them splashing and / Discover them each year with / A start," he writes of a salmon migration in **"Time Spirals."** And again, in **"Doubled Mirrors,"** tramping down a familiar road at night and descrying a "glinting / Everywhere from the dusty gravel," Rexroth hunkers down for a remedial seminar in wonder: "I suspect what it is / And kneel to see. Under each / Pebble and oak leaf is a / Spider, her eyes shining at / Me with my reflected light / Across immeasurable distance." The salmon spawn every year, it is an old story; the spiders proliferate under the leaf-fall at summer's end, there's nothing remarkable in it; and there is Rexroth, expecting and suspecting, lingering over his yoked moments of fact and vision as if they were a rosary.

Rexroth is never more firmly in possession of his tone and touch as when he seems to be simply marking time, nothing the hour, fixing the night sky, taking stock of what stirs around him. His finest poems of this ilk, with their delicacy and accuracy of perception, their owlishness and gravitas, their fastidious rhythms and spare syntax literally portray a man coming to his senses. What commends them—the poems and the senses—is their exemplary composure. Time and again in this poetry of the interior Rexroth cultivates keen regard where others might have lapsed into wild rapture—dedicating himself not to leaps of faith but rather, as he articulated in one of his most lovely poems, to "pauses of fate." The poem is **"We Come Back,"** from the 1944 collection *The Phoenix and the Tortoise,* and it follows in its entirety:

> Now, on this day of the first hundred flowers,
> Fate pauses for us in imagination,
> As it shall not ever in reality—
> As these swifts that link endless parabolas
> Change guard unseen in their secret crevices.
> Other anniversaries that we have walked
> Along this hillcrest through the black fir forest,
> Past the abandoned farm, have been just the
>   same—
> Even the fog necklaces on the fencewires
> Seem to have gained or lost hardly a jewel;
> The annual and diurnal patterns hold.
> Even the attrition of the cypress grove
> Is slow and orderly, each year one more tree
> Breaks rank and lies down, decrepit in the wind.
> Each year, on summer's first luminous morning,
> The swallows come back, whispering and weaving
> Figure eights around the sharp curves of the
>   swifts,
> Plaiting together the summer air all day,
> That the bats and owls unravel in the nights.
> And we come back, the signs of time upon us,
> In the pause of fate, the threading of the year.

Here, I submit, is the most telling and limpid draft of "the same poem over and over" that the elder Rexroth makes reference to at the head of **"Hapax."** For all its classical elegance of bearing and the formal mastery of its syllabics, it is a supplicant's poem and a sacramental incantation. For all its worldliness, it seeks meaning in provisionality and in the shedding of metaphysical conceits and moral precepts. If any poem was ever a "sheaf of stillness" it is this one: In that

pause of fate an orgy of motion becomes a tapestry of eternal forces and the vernal turns autumnal as our eye works down the page. Stated baldly in **"Hapax,"** the "ecology of infinity" is a shibboleth, a buzzline. Inscribed in the "endless parabolas" of swifts and the "fog necklaces on fencewires" that "seem to have gained or lost hardly a jewel," it's a spiritual condition made manifest and a phrase redeemed.

I don't want to give the impression that this pietistic poet of the woods and rockfaces is the "true" Rexroth or a Rexroth to be extolled at the expense of all the rest there are to go around. Nor would I venture to say that this medley of work constitutes anything so commanding as a "period" or anything as coherent as a system of thought. Notwithstanding the auspiciously titled "Toward an Organic Philosophy," one of the contemplative respites among the fiery polemics of *In What Hour,* this is not a poet to whom we turn for grandly mounted summas. In the years roughly spanning Pearl Harbor and the McCarthy hearings (one instinctively reaches for political watermarks when considering a muckraker of Rexroth's caliber), Rexroth's poems cover a teeming variety of subjects in a variety of forms and registers: urbane epigrams (**"Me Again"**), erotic homages (**"A Dialogue of Watching"**), memoirs bittersweet and unrepentant (**"The Bad Old Days," "A Living Pearl"**), playful verse for his daughters (**"A Bestiary," "Mother Goose"**), outright screeds (most notoriously, **"Thou Shalt Not Kill,"** an ostensible elegy for Dylan Thomas that some adherents of incendiary anaphora hail as an ur-"Howl"), and of course, the earliest of his floodtide of Chinese and Japanese translations. But I believe these intermittent Hapaxes hold up so well precisely because they occupy an honestly arrived-at middle ground between Rexroth's more vexed compulsions and volcanic convictions, sinning neither on the side of preachiness or aloofness. For that reason they are also some of the most humane poems from Rexroth's hand, urgent without straining after effects, serious without resorting to homiletics, thoughtful without thirsting for themes. Theirs is a versification and idiom of proportion, which in turn bears out the rectitude and the scrupulousness of the speaker's self-reflection.

What they are surely not, this group of contemplative verses occasioned by travels upcountry and downriver, are California eclogues or Sierra idylls, numbers written in honor of some idealized, half-mythical territory of honeyed light and stirring vistas. Proportion presupposes equilibrium, and the landscapes that loom so large in Rexroth's field of vision are as empirical and historical as they are archetypal and sanctified. As fleshed out in poems like **"We Come Back," "Time Is the Mercy of Eternity," "Time Spirals,"** or **"Lyell's Hypothesis Again,"** Rexroth's California has fewer links to the legendary island that the first European mapmakers drew or the promised land that the nineteenth-century popular imagination painted than it has ancestral ties to an innately Protestant branch of debate over the conception of nature as scripture and geography as destiny. Call him Ishmael: The deeper Rexroth penetrates into the region's lonely isolation, the more inescapably he becomes entangled in uniquely American contours of imagination and realms of spirit. However much his work asks to be understood with reference to Marx or in light of Tu Fu, however boldly his personal history carries the impress of beatnik San Francisco and beatific Kyoto, his reckonings with the wilderness bear the telltale marks of Jeffersonian and Emersonian bloodlines.

Seeking expression through nature, argued Emerson in "The Poet," "is a very high sort of seeing, which does not come by study, but by the intellect being where and what it sees; by sharing the path or circuit of things through forms, and so making them translucid to others." In Rexroth's backcountry poetry, California—and the so-called American Century that he waged such a holy war against—finds a glowing ember of Transcendentalism, no longer a creed or a mission but a latent aptitude for, in Emerson's words again, "the condition of true naming . . . resigning himself to the divine aura which breathes through forms. . . ." Wherever else Rexroth's long and winding paper trail leads us, it also runs through the vicinity of Concord, and that is where, just now, this reader would like to leave him:

> Deer are stamping in the glades,
> Under the full July moon.
> There is a smell of dry grass
> In the air, and more faintly,
> The scent of a far off skunk.
> As I stand at the wood's edge,
> Watching the darkness, listening
> To the stillness, a small owl
> Comes to the branch above me,
> On wings more still than my breath.

Thomas Evans (essay date 1995)

SOURCE: "Kenneth Rexroth," in *American Poetry: The Modernist Ideal,* edited by Clive Bloom and Brian Docherty, St. Martin's Press, 1995, pp. 93-104.

[In the following essay, Evans examines the significance of Eastern philosophy, particularly the fusion of "Buddhism and anarcho-pacifist attitudes," in Rexroth's contemplative poetry.]

Kenneth Rexroth should be remembered, primarily, for his contemplative verse; but this was by no means the extent of his best work. By the end of the Second World War he was already well known on the West Coast as a discerning critic,

an essayist who covered an encyclopedic range of subjects, an accomplished painter, and a long-time political activist; and, throughout the later part of his life, for his translations from French, Swedish, Greek, Latin, Spanish, Chinese and Japanese, which drew attention to previously unacknowledged European and Oriental poets.

He was born in Indiana in 1905, and raised by parents who held liberal views. From the beginning, his mother encouraged him to develop his artistic abilities and to allow no-one to compel him to choose a career other than that of writer and artist. In *An Autobiographical Novel* he mentions that, from earliest memory, he had experienced an 'awareness, not a feeling, of timeless, spaceless, total bliss.' Such experiences gave him the determinative philosophy to achieve his ambitions. When he was orphaned, at the age of thirteen, he set out resolutely to fulfil his aspirations. Often finding himself well in advance of his classmates, he took to educating himself with dedication, and was soon influenced by the works of H. G. Wells, the French 'literary Cubists,' various Christian mystics, and classical Chinese poetry; he also met D. H. Lawrence, G. K. Chesterton, the Loeb family, Louis Aragon, Tristan Tzara and many other luminaries of the 1920s. And it was throughout the Twenties and Thirties that he developed his profound love of the countryside, mainly by exploring the mountains of the North West. At the same time he became actively involved with such movements as the John Reed Club and the International Workers of the World (IWW). He visited Sacco and Vanzetti in their prison cells, and the memory of this encounter—and their subsequent executions—was instrumental in directing his political tendencies. His early activities shaped a lifelong belief in anarcho-pacifism.

Rexroth had a turbulent personal life. He had an adoring mother, and the psychological damage of being orphaned at an early age may have affected his marriages. His wives had to compete with the idealised memory of Delia Rexroth. He was married four times, and, whenever a marriage ran into trouble, seemed unable to accept that his misdemeanours were a cause of friction. Yet, in contrast to this domestic instability, his verse reflects a poetic identity of one searching with contemplative detachment for a means of coming to terms with his existence.

In the last twenty or so years of his life, Rexroth became increasingly attracted to Chinese and Japanese culture—the subject of numerous essays, poems and translations. His knowledge was extraordinarily wide (his favourite reading was the seven volumes of Joseph Needham's *Science and Civilisation in China,*) but he was selective in what he chose to introduce into his own verse. He identified strongly with the basic principles of Mahayana Buddhism, which imbued his later poetry with an enhanced spirituality. Indeed, it is curious that Rexroth did not come earlier to Buddhism, since it advocates a lifestyle similar to the one he had aspired to. Although there are allusions to Buddhist beliefs in, for example, **"The Dragon and the Unicorn"** (1944-50), it is not until we come to a poem like **"On Flower Wreath Hill"** (1974) that we can observe him embracing Buddhist principles, after time spent in intense study to acquire an integrated understanding of the faith. It is this understanding which illuminates the contemplative aspect of such poems.

Analysed from a Buddhist point of view, much of Kenneth Rexroth's poetry can be seen as a meditation on the impermanence of all substance—the Mahayana concept of Sunyata. His love for the natural world does not present a contradiction since it is by intense contemplation on its wonders and beauty that one arrives at a realisation of this concept. In a sense, many of his poems become gateways to an understanding of that which lies beyond all changing substance, Sunyata, or Voidness (Sunya is Void, Sunyata Voidness), through their visionary evocation of this impermanence in nature, and the doctrine of Sunyata is manifest in their transcendental imagery. In later works it is also addressed directly as an explicit theme.

There are further Buddhist perspectives when Rexroth's poetry incorporates his political convictions. His anarcho-pacifism merged naturally with an actively compassionate form of Buddhism; it engendered a poet-narrator as a Bodhisattva figure. The Bodhisattva postpones Nirvana in order to serve mankind; Rexroth, the contemplative, retains his belief in political activism and participation in self-governing community.

I

It was in *An Autobiographical Novel* that Kenneth Rexroth affirmed his faith in the Noble Eightfold Path of Buddha which culminates in Nirvana. The Noble Eightfold Path is a highly disciplined way of life for those who would conquer desire, since the second of the Four Noble Truths teaches that the cause of suffering in the world is desire.

To some, it is a way of life which rejects responsibility for social problems; this is, of course, not so. Those who transcend suffering and desire do not transcend compassion, and for a Buddhist the issue of social responsibility and participation is one of major importance; for a Mahayana Buddhist it is an ideal embodied in the Bodhisattva, who dedicates his life to it. The ideal influences and informs Rexroth's work at least from 1944, when he began writing the long didactic poem, **"The Dragon and the Unicorn,"** and later in **"The Heart's Garden, the Garden's Heart"**: 'I will not enter Nirvana / Until all sentient creatures are saved'; and it is a belief which fuses with his anarcho-pacifist assertion that patriarchal, hierarchical society represses man's natural forms of communication (concurring on this point with the Marxist concept of 'human self-alienation'), and that the individual has the capability to take on more responsibility for the sustenance of his existence than he is given by a capitalist society; in this he endorses George Woodcock's theory of 'individual capability' and introduces it into **"The Dragon and the Unicorn"** where he states that love can only exist as a kind of Gnostic cult 'Until men learn / To administer things. . . .'

It follows, he maintains, that society functions more effectively without government when it is replaced by hitherto repressed, natural co-operation and voluntary organisation within the community. Rexroth has explored the implications of this with great faith in its practicability, and in the possibility of a 'community of contemplatives', motivated by Agape (brotherly love), which a Bodhisattva would practice on principle. Sir Herbert Read, whose political writings influenced Rexroth from his youth, claims, in his essay **"Anarchism and the Religious Impulse"** that 'a religion is a necessary element in any organic society' since it represents a natural authority which effectively counters the artificial authority of government. Therefore, a religion that is itself hierarchical cannot accommodate the needs of an anarchist society; but the Bodhisattva principle encourages the individual to take an active part in the 'religion' of the community and excludes a hierarchical structure. 'Buddhist Agape,' so to speak, becomes the religion, and compassion becomes instinctive instead of a tiresome necessity.

There is a further, more spiritual level on which this 'symbiosis' of Buddhism and anarcho-pacifism exists in Rexroth's poetry. In the Avatamsaka Sutra (Avatamsaka means 'flower wreath,' the inspiration for Rexroth's poem **"On Flower Wreath Hill"**) occurs the image of the 'Jewel Net of Indra,' in which reality is likened to a net, each knot of which can be compared to a 'jewel' or the perspective of an individual human being, which is reflected in all the other 'jewels' or perspectives. Our separate perspectives are thus bound together by a single infinite law. By contemplation on the interdependence of all the other 'jewels,' rather than by selfish introspection, one becomes bound to them on an intuitive level; in Rexroth's words, everything is 'in its place, the ecology / Of infinity.' In the poem **"Hapax,"** from which this line is taken, the Net is a feature of the organic world; the closer a community is to such an organic world, the closer it comes to perpetuating a fully integrated existence in a substantial universe—as far as this is possible in Buddhism, where all substance is impermanent.

Rexroth also uses the image of the Net in **"On Flower Wreath Hill,"** to create the peace that spreads in Nature when the Net is no longer shaken or disturbed by human disharmony; even the 'Spider's net of jewels has ceased / to tremble.' His perception of the Net becomes a sustaining religious experience in this poem. Although it is true that he perceives this net in the architecture of nature rather than in the 'architecture' of community, the Net has a social function, as a subsidiary part of its universal purpose, since it binds together mutually supportive human beings. Significantly, Rexroth told an interviewer, 'A life lived according to the Buddha law will not need much from politics.' In the same interview, Rexroth maintained that 'the religious experience is self-sufficient.' This takes on a broader significance in the context of his desire for an organic community: the impetus provided by the experience is a compelling but intuitive force, and is the ultimate affirmation of man's link with mankind. The community is bound by the experience to work for its own health and Agape becomes instinctive.

The religious experience sustains the health of the Buddhist anarcho-pacifist community, while war preserves the health of the hierarchical capitalist state—a sentiment expressed in **"The Dragon and the Unicorn"**: 'War is the health of the State? / War against its own members.' War is the Health of the State' is the title of an essay by Randolph Bourne, in which he observes that man was always fundamentally and naturally gregarious, and that individualism came later. As he travels through Chicago in **"The Dragon and the Unicorn,"** Rexroth witnesses the products of 'self-alienated man' in the drastically commercialised cityscape, and understands 'What Marvell meant by desarts / Of vast eternitie. Man / Gets daily sicker and his Ugliness knots his bowels.' The industrial panorama is the result of a social system which functions by pitting man against man and by denying the gregarious instinct.

Having absorbed an IWW antipathy towards organisations which prosper through the destruction of workers' solidarity, Rexroth frequently felt morally obliged to introduce a didacticism into his poetry (typically in **"Thou Shalt Not Kill,"** 1956). But in much of his later poetry he excludes an overt political stance, since by its very nature it functions as a catalyst for Mahakaruna, 'great compassion.' It evokes a powerful, unifying religious experience which, as Rexroth has said, transcends politics.

In his lifetime, Rexroth came close to witnessing something approaching his ideal in movements on the post-war West Coast, an area with a strong tradition of oriental awareness and anarcho-pacifism. The dynamism may have been lost, but its spirit remains in his verse.

II

I referred earlier to Rexroth's poetry as being a gateway to a perception of what lies beyond all transient matter: Sunya, the Void. This Mahayana doctrine permeates his later work; most notably in **"On Flower Wreath Hill."** It is worth concentrating on this poem; but before doing so, a fuller explanation of Sunya is necessary.

Sunyata (Voidness) is basic to the Mahayana school of Buddhism, although it has roots in the earlier school of Hinayana. It is the belief that what we know as reality is only comparatively real to us, but what exists as comparative reality is a component part of ultimate reality: 'The One is all things, and is incomplete without the least of them.' All things which exist in our comparative reality are impermanent and possess no real content, i.e. they are Void of content. They are manifestations of the Void, ultimate reality, which lies beyond them. For a Buddhist to fulfil the essence of this Void is enlightenment, the only absolute. This is the doctrine of Mind Only or Void Only: Sunyata.

This is the ultimate theme of **"On Flower Wreath Hill"** but the poem is also laden with references to Japanese and Buddhist mythology, and bears the powerful influence of the Late T'ang poet Tu Fu, particularly in the way Rexroth intersperses descriptive passages with personal meditations. Buddhism was at a peak in China throughout the T'ang dynasty, and the poetry of this period that is not political often contemplates the world of nature. (Ezra Pound and Arthur Waley were dissatisfied with their translations of Tu Fu, whereas Rexroth translated many of Tu Fu's poems with great sensitivity.)

Parts One and Two of the poem introduce the theme of transience by establishing links between the ancient past and the present, demonstrating the cyclical nature of time. As the narrator walks through the forest, he considers the fallen leaves and the burial mound beneath them which contains a long-dead princess; he is concerned not only with the change of tangible matter (Anicca) but with the nature even of abstract concepts such as honour and beauty: 'Who was this princess under / This mound overgrown with trees / Now almost bare of leaves?' The imagery of leaves is extended when Rexroth very probably refers to an episode in the life of the Buddha, when he grasped a handful of leaves from the ground, and asked his disciples which were more numerous, the leaves in his hand or those on the trees of the forest, (the former being the truths he had told them and the latter being the ones he had not revealed).

And now, for Rexroth, on the brink of religious revelation, 'There are more leaves on / The ground than grew on the trees.' In the lines that follow this quotation, Rexroth considers the paradox that nostalgic memory perpetuates delusions of immortality, despite earlier intuition of impermanence. After expanding on the theme of the silence and natural glory of Autumn, in Parts Three and Four, he returns in Part Five to yet another distraction from complete knowledge of Sunyata: memories of suffering, painful memories reverberate through his consciousness like a temple bell. Each part of the poem, in sequence, depicts inner conflict or comparatively serene contemplation; for, in Part Six, he reflects with equanimity on the royal dead beneath their shattered grave-stones, whom no-one remembers.

The penultimate section abandons the influence of Tu Fu upon the structure of the poem (description followed by reflection), in favour of a not entirely satisfactory combination of Buddhist mythology, and ultimately an emphatic affirmation of Annica: 'Change rules the world forever. / And man but a little while.' These lines bid farewell to doubt, and clear the way for the confident tone of the final section.

In the first verse of Part Eight, the narrator generates an anticipatory tension with images of the world being 'alive,' and of his body being penetrated with electric life. He sits in the darkness on a 'Sotoba,' a grave marked by symbolic stones representing earth, water, air, fire and ether. These remind him of impermanence, which for the first time leads him to contemplate directly what lies beyond, in emptiness: 'The heart's mirror hangs in the void.' (In his essay 'Poetry and Mysticism,' Colin Wilson sees man as becoming 'an enormous mirror that reflects reality.' Again we return to the Avatamsaka Sutra and the Jewel Net of Indra. The imagery of the Net is handled with consummate skill; initially it is only referred to obliquely, in terms of silver and pearls that gleam on a young girl's sleeves, an image which is transposed to a mist of silver and pearls (Interestingly, Rexroth has suggested that one should approach illumination 'as though an invisible mist was coming up behind you and enveloping you.' These oblique references reflect the poet's gradual progression towards full realisation of the Net.

The fifth verse of this final section reflects on Annica, change, in the organic world, in the pattern of the seasons, and acts as a precursor to the harmony of the last verse; here the Net of Indra has ceased to tremble. It prepares us for a kind of frozen tableau of a mist whose every drop is lit by moonlight—transcendental architecture in which each part is a component of a harmonious whole.

In the last fifteen lines, Rexroth experiences Absolute Reality, a revelation of Void Only. In the forest, the mist and the moon, he sees the Net of Indra, linking partial reality to Absolute Reality. The sense of perfect harmony between the temporal world and infinity is strengthened by the soundless music of Krishna's flute which summons the Gopis, or milkmaids, to dance and become Real.

"On Flower Wreath Hill" is Rexroth's most significant exposition of Buddhist philosophy. His shorter poem, **"Void Only"** is less artistically impressive, but it is an explicit statement of Sunyata which is at least effective in its concrete language, paring down his view-point to an Absolute: 'Only emptiness / No limits' (there is an erotic version of this poem in **"The Silver Swan"**). What **"On Flower Wreath Hill"**

and **"Void Only"** have in common is their handling of Sunyata, which is direct and explicit. But, in **"On Flower Wreath Hill,"** the reader is prepared gradually for the experience, which occurs in the last verse, whereas in **"Void Only,"** the poet (and by implication, the reader) is almost surprised by it, as he wakens from a dream.

In other poems, such as **"Towards an Organic Philosophy"** and **"A Spark in the Tinder of Knowing,"** Rexroth implies Voidness, rather than addressing it directly, and through this method creates the style of poetry for which he is best known. Richard Eberhart once said of Rexroth's poetry that it achieved a 'calmness and grandeur, as if something eternal in the natural world has been mastered.' In Buddhist terms, the Net of Indra provides that 'something eternal,' a successful image for the inter-relationship of all things. In **"Towards an Organic Philosophy,"** he describes three landscapes which have been subjected to different kinds of change, such as glaciation in the Sierras, and finds a common factor in 'The chain of dependence which runs through creation' (a quotation from Tyndall). As in **"The Dragon and the Unicorn,"** shift of scene leaves an impression of constant change, the gentle motion of Annica.

"The Spark in the Tinder of Knowing" takes a single scene in which man communes with nature and finds in himself the peace which stills the landscape, a suggestion of the Void beyond Annica. But, just as **"Towards an Organic Philosophy"** attempts to create no more than the impression of Sunyata, through an expression of nature's part in Oneness, so this poem stops short of probing the implications of Annica. In this Rexroth is putting into effect Keats's Negative Capability, thus relying on the power of transcendence.

When he came to write **"On Flower Wreath Hill,"** Rexroth did not abandon his transcendental descriptiveness, for it was a technique which had made him original and influential, but he combined it with explicit statements. Later poems such as **"Confusion of the Senses,"** **"Privacy,"** or **"Red Maple Leaves"** show that he retained his ability to sensualise his mystical organic philosophy without needing to define it. But it would be reckless to categorise his poems rigidly, since there is a reflective, contemplative element in so many of them.

It is also important to realise that, despite the depth and breadth of his erudition, Rexroth was unwilling to give unconditional allegiance to any one school of Buddhism, preferring to absorb those teachings which confirmed and broadened his own intuitive and intellectual concepts. He found them in Jakob Boehme, A. N. Whitehead, Tu Fu, Whitman and many others, but it was most demonstrably in the fundamental beliefs of the Mahayana school—above all in the doctrine of Sunyata—that he encountered the consummate vision of reality that he had sought.

III

Rexroth wrote contemplative verse, based on an organic philosophy strongly influenced by Mahayana Buddhism. The two poets he influenced above all, William Everson and Gary Snyder, preserved the essence of his belief in an organic Reality, but other religious influences broadened their vision. William Everson's loosely contemplative poetry was affected by his conversion to Catholicism. Gary Snyder felt an active kinship with nature and propounded a work ethic within that particular environment; and his beliefs were complemented by his formal Zen education in Japan.

Snyder was of a younger generation of poets; it was Rexroth and Everson who planted the seeds of organic philosophy in the San Francisco Renaissance, for it was they who had turned to religion to sustain their pacifist integrity throughout the Second World War. The War ended the era described in *An Autobiographical Novel,* and Michael Davidson writes of a subsequent elegiac mode in much of Rexroth's and Everson's work. In his collection of poems *The Signature of All Things* (1949), Rexroth finds it hard to shake off his sense of utter loss and the futility of human endeavour: 'Finally you say, "I am not / Weeping for our own Troubles / But for the general chaos / Of the world."' In Everson's 'October Tragedy' there is the same sentiment: 'Do not sing those old songs here tonight.'

Rexroth and Everson may share this elegiac mood, but they have different emphases. In the organic world, Rexroth finds equanimity (see for example, **"Hojoki"** or **"Advent"** which is dedicated to Everson), whereas Everson almost succumbs to the pathetic fallacy: 'Bitter is the quiet singing of the cricket, / And the silent pools lie black beneath still reeds.'

Although poets of Snyder's generation maintained the religious impulse, it took a more dynamic, exuberant form under the influence of Zen Buddhism. There was a determination to renew society and banish the stupor of the late Forties and the Fifties. However, only Snyder retained a dedicated organic sensibility from Rexroth's and Everson's lead (although Rexroth was by far the more influential of the two). Much to Rexroth's distaste, Snyder's poetry also showed the influence of Ezra Pound in its form and method. Under these influences, Snyder evolved his own approach to nature, which was as distinct from Rexroth's as his Buddhism.

Although Rexroth was by no means aloof from the natural world, his poetic stance is far more passive than Snyder's. His search is always for what points to the eternal in nature, while Snyder, following the more dynamic Zen philosophy, involves himself with nature viewed as a friend who is generally the stronger, supportive partner, but who is currently subjective to the same abuse as exploited people. In 'Revolution in The Revolution in The Revolution,' the landscape is personified as being 'Among the most ruthlessly exploited classes: / Animals, trees, water, air, grasses.'

Despite their differences, Rexroth and Snyder share the conviction that urban life contains little that is energising and revitalising, an opinion which is encapsulated in Snyder's 'Before the Stuff Comes Down,' in which he leaves the consumerism of suburbia and greets the Californian landscape as if it were a gust of fresh air: 'Suddenly it's California: / Live oak, brown grasses.' As the title implies, it is a vulnerable resource.

In his essay 'Buddhism and the Possibilities of a Planetary Culture,' Snyder refers to the Avatamsaka Sutra and the interdependence of all things, but he sees it as having more value as a reason for practical effort than as a basis for contemplation. Rexroth's emphasis is on the latter as the basis of a supportive community. Different schools of Buddhism affected the work of Rexroth and Snyder, but they were united in their belief in anarcho-pacifism and in Buddhism's contribution to an autonomous American poetry.

What, then, are the influences on the San Francisco Renaissance which are traceable to Rexroth? For Everson, they are the values of solitary contemplation, which he saw in terms of Catholicism and Jungian psychology; for Snyder, Rexroth provided an exemplar, in the preceding generation, as one who had fused Buddhism and anarcho-pacifist attitudes. His view of the landscape in terms of his organic philosophy served as a model for Everson and Snyder, and perhaps even for poets like Richard Eberhart, whose work reflects a similar sense of decay and regeneration (as in Eberhart's 'Rumination').

Oriental literature and mythology, and much else, were all sources for Kenneth Rexroth, but he created a mature American poetry which William Carlos Williams quickly acknowledged. He is ultimately an American contemplative whose vision was given shape by Buddhism. These lines of his were inscribed on his gravestone:

> As the full moon rises . . .
> The swan sings
> In sleep
> On the lake of the mind.

FURTHER READING

Criticism

Gutierrez, Donald. "The Holiness of the Ordinary: The Literary-Social Journalism of Kenneth Rexroth." *Northwest Review* 32, No. 2 (1994): 109-28.
    Examines Rexroth's significant contributions as a literary critic and social commentator.

————. "Introduction: The Crystalline Poetry of Kenneth Rexroth." In his *"The Holiness of the Real": The Short Verse of Kenneth Rexroth,* pp. 19-52. Madison: Fairleigh Dickinson University Press, 1996.
    Provides an overview of Rexroth's poetic style, influences, and major artistic concerns.

————. "The West and Western Mountains in the Poetry of Kenneth Rexroth." *North Dakota Quarterly* 62, No. 3 (Summer 1994-1995): 121-39.
    Examines Rexroth's evocation of the American West Coast and California in his poetry.

Hamalian, Linda. "Early Versions of 'The Homestead Called Damascus,'" in *North Dakota Quarterly* 56, No. 1 (Winter 1988): 131-47.
    Explores the origin, development, and composition of "The Homestead Called Damascus."

Woodcock, George. "Realms beyond the Mountains: Notes on Kenneth Rexroth," in *Ontario Review* 6 (1977): 39-48.
    Provides discussion of Rexroth's poetry, artistic achievement, and political concerns.

Interviews

McKenzie, James J., and Robert W. Lewis. "'That Rexroth—He'll Argue You into Anything': An Interview with Kenneth Rexroth." *North Dakota Quarterly* 44, No. 3 (1976): 7-33.
    Rexroth comments on contemporary American poetry, art, education, culture, and politics.

Carl Sagan
1934-1996

American scientist, nonfiction writer, novelist, and critic.

The following entry presents an overview of Sagan's career through 1997. For further information on his life and works, see *CLC*, Volume 30.

INTRODUCTION

An internationally renowned astronomer, Sagan is among the most influential popular interpreters of science in recent times. Best known for his role as the host of the award-winning television documentary *Cosmos,* Sagan is also recognized for his efforts to win credibility for the scientific search for extraterrestrial life and as a leading advocate for nuclear arms reduction. The best-selling author of *The Cosmic Connection* (1973), *The Dragons of Eden* (1977), *Cosmos* (1980), and the novel *Contact* (1985), Sagan celebrated the joy of scientific discovery and captured the imagination of a mass audience with his compelling speculations on the mechanizations of the universe and evolution of human life.

Biographical Information

Born Carl Edward Sagan in New York, Sagan was raised by his Russian-immigrant father, a garment cutter, and American-born mother in the Bensonhurst section of the city. Fascinated with the night sky as a youth, Sagan became engrossed in science fiction, particularly the novels of Edgar Rice Burroughs, and at age twelve announced to his grandfather his desire to become an astronomer. Four years later he left for the University of Chicago on a scholarship, where he earned an undergraduate degree in 1954 and a Ph.D. in astronomy and astrophysics in 1960. While at Chicago, Sagan earned a reputation as a nonconformist and even organized his own series of campus lectures. In 1957, Sagan married his first wife, scientist Lynn Alexander; a second marriage to Linda Salzman in 1968 also ended in divorce, and was followed by a third marriage to writer Ann Druyan. In 1960, Sagan began his scientific career as a research fellow in astronomy at the University of California at Berkeley. There he developed important hypotheses about the surface temperature of Venus and Martian wind storms. He then took up a teaching position at Harvard University while working at the Smithsonian Astrophysical Observatory in Cambridge, Massachusetts. Denied tenure at Harvard, Sagan left for Cornell University in 1968, where he worked as a teacher and director of the Laboratory for Planetary Studies until his death in 1996. Sagan also contributed to the de-

velopment of NASA space-probe projects over several decades, including the unmanned Mariner 9 and Viking missions to Mars and subsequent Pioneer and Voyager missions to distant planets. His first major publication, *Intelligent Life in the Universe* (1963), was followed by the success of *The Cosmic Connection, The Dragons of Eden,* winner of a Pulitzer Prize in 1978, and *Broca's Brain* (1979). A popular guest on the talk show circuit, Sagan's fame as the unofficial spokesperson for the scientific community grew in 1980 with the PBS television program *Cosmos,* a thirteen-part series in which Sagan traversed a computer-simulated galaxy in search of the origins of the universe and life—both human and extraterrestrial. His book *Cosmos,* based on the television series, won a Hugo Award in 1982. Sagan's only novel, *Contact,* winner of a Locus Award, was adapted as a film in 1996. In his late works, *Shadows of a Forgotten Ancestor* (1992), *Pale Blue Dot* (1994), *The Demon-Haunted World* (1995), and *Billions and Billions* (1997), Sagan continued to take on the central mysteries of human nature and existence. He was also a prolific contributor to both scientific journals and popular magazines. He died in Seattle, Washington, of pneumonia, a complication resulting from myelodysplasia, a bone marrow disease from which he was recovering.

Major Works

Sagan's popular writings on the promise of modern science won wide appeal largely for their unusual ability to translate complex subjects into awe-inspiring commentaries on the possibility of space travel, human evolution, and life on other planets. With the publication of *Intelligent Life in the Universe,* a translation and abridgement of the work by Russian astrophysicist I. S. Shklovskii, Sagan emerged as a leading spokesperson for exobiology, the study of extraterrestrial environments and potential life forms. The book was one of the first of its kind to take the subject seriously. *The Cosmic Connection* provides a comprehensive outline of recent advances in planetary science, including the probable origins of the universe, stars and planets, and life on Earth. Sagan further expanded his ambitious investigations into the design and evolution of the universe in his television program and book *Cosmos,* both of which feature a semi-omniscient Sagan as cosmic guide and instructor aided by stunning intergalactic illustrations and photographs. *Pale Blue Dot* similarly explores the birth of the universe and solar system, space travel, and the future colonization of other planets through "terraforming." The title alludes to an astonishing photograph of Earth taken by the Voyager spaceprobe as it left the solar system, drawing attention to the humbling revelation that our planet is merely one among countless others. In *A Path Where No Man Thought* (1989), a collaboration with atmospheric scientist Richard Turco, Sagan reexamines the threat of nuclear war and the implications of "nuclear winter," a theory developed by Sagan and several other experts in 1983. According to their research, a massive nuclear strike could produce enough smoke to obscure the sun, resulting in a darkened, frigid, and uninhabitable world. Published as the Cold War drew to an end, in the book Sagan and Turco warn against the continuing danger of nuclear holocaust and recommend drastic reductions in U.S. and Soviet nuclear arsenals to a level of "minimum sufficient deterrence." In *The Dragons of Eden,* Sagan discusses contemporary neurophysiology and the genetic origin of human intelligence. His speculation, largely concerned with the history of human behavior, focuses on the interplay among three hypothetical stages of human brain development: the first and lowest is the reptilian R-complex, a vestige of our pre-mammalian progenitors that is responsible for aggression and ritual; the second is the limbic system, similar to that of birds and lower-order mammals, from which emotions and religion derive; the third and highest is the more developed neocortex or primate brain. *Shadows of Forgotten Ancestors,* co-written with his wife Ann Druyan, is a highly readable survey of human evolution, covering the birth of the solar system, formation of DNA, and study of physiological and behavioral similarities among humans and primates. *Broca's Brain,* named after nineteenth-century anatomist Paul Broca, who identified the source of articulate speech in the frontal lobe, contains a diverse collection of essays on the solar system, planetary exploration, robots, extraterrestrial intelligence, famous scientists, pseudoscience and religion, and a call for greater public support for science and technology. In *The Demon-Haunted World,* Sagan holds the verifiable achievements of science and scientific method against dubious, unsubstantiated examples of phenomena and superstition. Seeking to demystify stories of UFO sightings, alien abductions, miracles, astrology, and New Age versions of spirituality, Sagan exalts the superiority of empirical testing and the ability of certain branches of science to predict the future. Revealing his abiding interest in the search for extraterrestrial life, *Contact,* his only work of fiction, explores the possibility of communication with a distant planet. In this science fiction thriller, scientists receive radio transmissions from the star system Vega. From these signals, in the form of rebounded television images of Hitler's 1936 Olympic games, they are able to decrypt mathematical instructions for the construction of a spacecraft. After two failed launches, an international crew is transported to an Earth-like environment where they encounter doppelgangers and apparitions. Discredited upon their return—Earth witnesses note that the vehicle never left the ground and their entire excursion lasted only twenty minutes—an American member of the crew, Eleanor Arroway, seeks to verify their voyage and discovers God's signature in a mathematical extrapolation of pi.

Critical Reception

Sagan is consistently praised for his great ability to communicate the esoteric dilemmas and discoveries of modern science to a general audience. In addition, he is highly regarded for his significant contributions to the study of Mars and Venus, NASA space exploration, and the nuclear disarmament movement. However, criticized and even resented by some members of the scientific community, he has been derided for his controversial interest in extraterrestrial life and accused of oversimplifying complex subjects to the point of inaccuracy for his nonspecialist viewers and readers. Others object to Sagan's materialist view of evolution, tendency toward reductionism, vehement denial of a godlike creator, and glorification of technological progress and the primacy of human reason. Despite his detractors, Sagan's infectious enthusiasm for science and dauntless speculation on the great mysteries of our cosmic origins inspired renewed public interest in the scientific enterprise. Along with Jacob Bronowski and Stephen Jay Gould, Sagan is credited for the popularization of science in the twentieth century.

PRINCIPAL WORKS

The Atmospheres of Mars and Venus [with W. W. Kellogg] (nonfiction) 1961

Intelligent Life in the Universe [with I. S. Shklovskii] (nonfiction) 1963

Planets [with Jonathan Leonard] (nonfiction) 1966

The Cosmic Connection: An Extraterrestrial Perspective (nonfiction) 1973

The Dragons of Eden: Speculations on the Evolution of Human Intelligence (nonfiction) 1977

Broca's Brain: Reflections on the Romance of Science (essays) 1979

*Cosmos (nonfiction) 1980

Comet [with Ann Druyan] (nonfiction) 1985

Contact (novel) 1985, [with Ann Druyan and others] (screenplay) 1997

A Path Where No Man Thought: Nuclear Winter and the End of the Arms Race [with Richard Turco] (nonfiction) 1989

Shadows of Forgotten Ancestors: A Search for Who We Are [with Ann Druyan] 1992

Pale Blue Dot: A Vision of the Human Future in Space (nonfiction) 1994

The Demon-Haunted World: Science as a Candle in the Dark (nonfiction) 1995

Billions and Billions: Thoughts on Life and Death at the Brink of the Millennium (nonfiction) 1997

*Cosmos was originally produced as a thirteen part television series for PBS in 1980.

CRITICISM

Bruce Cook (essay date June 1980)

SOURCE: "Carl Sagan's Guided Tour of the Universe," in *American Film*, Vol. 5, June, 1980, pp. 22-7.

[*In the following essay, Cook examines Sagan's popular presentation of science and astronomy on the television program* Cosmos.]

This fall, when PBS launches *Cosmos,* its most ambitious series to date, the total effect may be a little like a thirteen-week funding appeal. But there will be no ringing telephones or heartfelt solicitations. The new show is far slicker than that. In fact, it may just be the slickest production of its kind ever undertaken on either side of the Atlantic. And why not? The driving force behind *Cosmos,* the man who will smile at you week after week during this guided tour of the universe, is none other than Carl Sagan, television's top pitchman for science.

Sagan, no less than Carroll O'Connor or Mary Tyler Moore, is a television phenomenon. Still boyish, though now in his forties, this professor of Astronomy and Space Sciences at Cornell University (where he heads its Laboratory for Planetary Studies) has made frequent appearances on the "Today" show, "The Dick Cavett Show," and has practically graduated to guest host status on "The Tonight Show." Because of his fluency, articulateness, and ready wit, he has become the unofficial spokesman for the entire scientific community. If the American public elected the top scientist the way it does the president of the United States, then Carl Sagan would win hands down.

Sagan means to use every ounce of his considerable clout in the service of science. He sees the series as a grand opportunity to remind that vast taxpaying public of the importance of science, the grand adventure of it, at a time when the public seems to have lost its enthusiasm for the ambitious programs of space exploration he is advocating. *Cosmos* is so much bread upon the water. Only time will tell if this sort of soft sell-cum-audience education will really pay off. Sagan will only know it has paid off when the appropriations start rolling in.

Cosmos is so much Carl Sagan's baby that it may astonish his fans to learn that the putative father wasn't present at the precise moment of conception. That honor goes to a twenty-nine-year-old producer at KCET, Los Angeles's innovative public television station. Greg Andorfer had done some work on "The Age of Uncertainty," the series on economics with John Kenneth Galbraith, which was essentially a BBC project. He wondered why that sort of series—"the large intellectual landscape thing that television does best"—was always done by the BBC. Why, he asked himself, can't we do it, too?

He thought about the right sort of subject for such a series, recognizing that what he was after would have to be a so-called created documentary. It wasn't simply out there for the shooting a la Robert Flaherty. What, then?

"Astronomy!" Andorfer said, snapping his fingers, as he recalled, during a recent interview, the moment *Cosmos* was created. "It not only has to do with science but with the big questions that people ask in religion, et cetera." Practically in the same instant he thought of the subject, he began to consider who might be the right host for a show with such a broad subject.

At first, a number of science fiction writers came to mind—Ray Bradbury, Arthur C. Clarke, Fred Hoyle (who doubles as an astronomer). "Then," Andorfer said, "I thought of what should have been obvious right from the start—that Carl Sagan was the right one. I got together with him, and a couple of years later, here we are, finishing up the series."

"Well," he added, "it wasn't quite as easy as all that. We had to raise a $180,000 planning grant for the thirteen shows we had in mind. And then we did the serious business of going out and finding the money for the shows themselves. The entire series was budgeted at $8 million."

That makes it the most costly project ever undertaken by public television. It is being underwritten by the Atlantic Richfield Company, the Arthur Vining Davis Foundations, and the Corporation for Public Broadcasting. Coproducing the series and contributing to it modestly are the BBC and West Germany's Polytel International. KCET, however, is shouldering the greatest part of the burden. Its facilities (formerly Monogram Studios in the Silverlake district of Los Angeles) and its staff are now being taxed to the limit by the project.

The show's shooting schedule, stretched out over a year, called for more than forty locations all over the world. For instance, a sequence was shot in the Cavendish Laboratories in Cambridge, England. Scenes were filmed in Italy for a segment on the life of Leonardo da Vinci, and in Czechoslovakia and West Germany for the life of Johannes Kepler. And so on, in Egypt, India, Greece, and in locations all around the United States.

By far the biggest single item on the production budget, however, is the one labeled "special effects." Even a movie like *Star Wars* offered only minutes of special effects. But *Cosmos,* because of its nature and length, will offer two and a half hours of movie magic metered out as needed through the series' thirteen hours. This will include computer animation handled at the Jet Propulsion Laboratory in Pasadena, Magicam miniature work at Paramount, and optics done at Motion Pictures, Inc. There, Jamie Shourt and Robert Blalack, who both worked on special effects for *Star Wars,* were involved in the production of a whole array of special effects for *Cosmos*—among them, and most spectacular of all, the so-called cosmic zoom.

What is it? Greg Andorfer describes it as a "sports car ride from one edge of the universe to the other." A voyage from here to eternity may not be possible in actuality, but its simulation will be at least technologically accurate. Carl Sagan and his staff have taken great pains to see to that. The idea was that the space vessel on which we travel with him through the universe must steer a course that is both feasible and reasonably direct. All told, it took about half a year just to plan. On screen it will occupy only twenty-five minutes of a single show.

Nowhere was this attention to detail and accuracy more evident than in the work I saw when I went with Greg Andorfer to the studios of Motion Pictures, Inc. In front of a wall of storyboards from the cosmic zoom sequence, my guide

traced the course through successive shots. "We live on the upper edge of the third spiral arm of the Milky Way," Andorfer said. "It's four-and-a-half light-years to the nearest star, Alpha Centauri—nearest besides the sun, of course. But just look at all the stars there are!"

His hand swept in an arc at the renderings that surrounded us. Stars shone down from every side. "There are probably ten planets around each star in the universe," he explained. "Consider the number of stars. Why, it's almost impossible that there is not other life in our galaxy."

That would qualify in certain scientific circles as rank Saganism. And, indeed, Carl Sagan's philosophy and speculations have permeated not only the narrative portions of *Cosmos,* but also the thinking and talking of many of those connected with the series. This seems particularly the case with Andorfer, who quotes him often and in detail. Sagan, in fact, will seldom be offscreen during the show's thirteen hours. Even during the cosmic zoom, for example, the astronomer will be on screen most of the time pointing out the sights as they pass by. Galaxies will flash by in animation and by rear projection.

"We're shooting Carl on a huge Chroma-Key stage," Andorfer said. "On another stage we're shooting the background model. We can cut back and forth to Carl in close-up, too. That will work a lot better than just voice-over. As we go along, and he comments, we'll project lights on his face in close-up and get a real sense of drama."

On the way back to KCET, Andorfer talked about the role played by special effects in the *Cosmos* series: "The main point in the effects is not to get stuck on one process. We use one and then another and combine some. We're using a conventional animation stand, a horizontal animation stand, computer animation in multi-axis and multi-plane, and motion-repeating photography with models or artwork. In other words, it's a wide palette of techniques, and we're trying hard to use all the colors available to us."

Once back, we looked in on a sound stage where another, slightly more primitive sort of special effects shooting was under way, involving miniatures, models, and tabletop photography. Earlier Andorfer had shown me a miniature of a Martian canyon—"a tributary of Valles Marineris, the largest canyon on Mars." It had been done by artist Don Davis, who used the latest flyby pictures of the red planet to ensure accuracy. On the sound stage, a crew was filming a much more fanciful sort of model.

"This is a Martian city we're shooting," Andorfer explained, waving his hand over a big horizontal representation of a slightly dilapidated art deco city of the future. It would be used to present the ideas of Percival Lowell and others who were sure the "canals" of Mars confirmed the presence of intelligent life. "They were wrong, of course, but their notions provided a great incentive to explore space," Andorfer said. Why a dilapidated model? To represent, Andorfer explained, "that the ideas are discredited, so the Mars they envisioned is in a state of disrepair."

The crew shooting the sequence was also getting it all down on videotape beforehand, just to make sure it looked right before they shot the film. The playback of the sequence, however, didn't come close to satisfying the large Englishman who was in charge.

His name was Adrian Malone. As a BBC producer, he was responsible, along with Michael Gill, for the many "large intellectual landscape" series produced by the network. Between them they account for (among others) "Civilisation," "America," "The Ascent of Man," and "The Age of Uncertainty." The two are now out on their own developing projects. Malone himself, as executive producer, has been seeing *Cosmos* through from start to finish. As resident catalyst and all-around wizard on *Cosmos,* he was a very busy man, and an interview, it turned out, took weeks to arrange.

When at last I sat across the desk from him, Adrian Malone barely noticed me for the first few minutes, so intent was he on telling a telephone caller just what he thought of the quality of a sequence he had viewed. "It looked like a bloody carpet commercial," he roared. "When we wanted it out of focus, it was sharp as a wink. You knew what we wanted."

After a few more choice comments, he abruptly hung up. Then he smiled and shrugged. "Well," he said, "there you have me in action." Malone joined the *Cosmos* project after he decided to leave the BBC and come to work in this country. Andorfer called him and sent him the plans for the show. "Then," Malone recalled, "I met Carl Sagan and Gentry Lee, who is his partner, in New York, and they said great things. But when I realized that the whole thing was not formed, and they didn't want me to come in and just put their ideas down on film, but wanted me to contribute, *then* I was taken with the idea."

What got him interested in a scientific series was an incident during the shooting of "Civilisation." Malone recalled, "Sir Kenneth Clark was being filmed in the Rotunda room in Greenwich, going from a painting on one side of the room to one on the other. In the exact center of the room was one of the early instruments used in computing Greenwich mean time. He stopped a moment in mid-passage, looked at it rather blankly, and said, 'This seems to be a scientific object of some sort.' Well, I mean, really! This smug ignorance on the part of so many of the most cultured people about the things in this world that affect their lives most directly." How did he collaborate with Carl Sagan? "My practice is

usually to write a lot of stuff in the way of notes, treatments, and suggestions," Malone said, "and then get together with the intellectual mentor—in this case, Sagan. What complicated this was the distance factor. We met again, though, a number of times in Ithaca, New York, and I would go tramping up and down the hills with him, back and forth between his office and the Howard Johnson's where I was staying. What we were doing, actually, was making stories out of the material. It's my contention, you see, that if you can't make something into a story, then you can't properly communicate it."

"In the end," he continued, "Carl wrote the right-hand side, and I did the visuals. Then I dictated the treatment, which went to 350 pages. The budget was done from this, the right people were brought in, everything was storyboarded, and locations were chosen."

The treatment called for millions of dollars' worth of special effects. Malone's BBC projects had required little in the way of movie magic, and this presented some problems at first. "When I first came into it," he said, "I was not up to Hollywood's standards on special effects. But I did know what we wanted and needed, and I was willing to be unpleasant if that was what it took to get it." In one instance, not satisfied with one outfit's work, Malone said, "I rebuilt their machinery and retrained their people. No doubt about it, though. This is where the best work is done, right here in Hollywood."

Adrian Malone is so satisfied with what Hollywood has to offer that he intends to make it his home base as he continues to work with Michael Gill on their many projects. These include two on the drawing board, a series on myth with the anthropologist Joseph Campbell, and another on the future of world energy with economist Daniel Yergin; and two screenplays, one a science fiction piece and the other about Jebe the Arrow, a lieutenant of Genghis Khan's.

At one point, I had asked Adrian Malone to characterize his relationship with Carl Sagan, and he brought up Jacob Bronowski, with whom he had worked on "The Ascent of Man." "Jacob and I were quite close, rather a father and son sort of relationship," he said. "Sometimes I didn't like him, but I always loved him. With Carl, however, it was quite different. We are, for one thing, in the same age bracket. There are rivalries and territories to be defended. The relationship is sometimes an acerbic and tense one, but it is creative tension."

"Carl is intellectually ambitious," he added. "One can see that from his books. What it's been like on *Cosmos* is having two fairly mettlesome horses put together to pull a carriage. We get going at a hell of a speed, but we're often out of step, and there's some danger the carriage may tip over.

We have different styles. When I go at a canter, he may gallop."

Carl Sagan, in the judgment of his scientific colleagues, always seems to be going at a gallop. But they disagree on his direction. One of them, in Henry S. F. Cooper, Jr.'s *New Yorker* profile of Sagan, calls him "the greatest menace since the black plague." Another, in the same profile, offers this defense: "Someone has to propose ideas at the boundaries of the plausible, in order to so annoy the experimentalists or observationalists that they'll be motivated to disprove the idea. Otherwise, there is a powerful temptation for an experimenter to design experiments for just what he knows."

The point is that Sagan's views on the cosmos are controversial. But he is so boyish, so winning, so persuasive that an audience may not always make a distinction between Sagan's speculations and scientific facts.

He is a self-described "carbon chauvinist." That is, he believes profoundly in the existence, somewhere out there, of intelligent life based on a chemical equation not totally unlike our own. With the intention of proving this, he has trained not only in astronomy (his primary field), but also in biology and chemistry. Cooper quotes one of Sagan's colleagues on the 1976 Viking mission as saying, "Sagan desperately wants to find life someplace, anyplace—on Mars, on Titan, in the solar system or outside it. In all the divergent things he does, that is the unifying thread. . . . People say, 'What a varied career he has had,' but everything he has done has had this underlying purpose."

It was during that mission, in which Sagan played such an important part, that he determined to make use of television in order to spread his ideas and advance the cause of science.

"I was working with Gentry Lee of the Jet Propulsion Lab in Pasadena," Sagan recalled recently. "We were both on the imaging team for the Viking lander. Gentry was in charge of engineering. And here it was, an epochal mission, and we were both very disappointed at the way it was presented to the public. We naturally thought about how we would do it ourselves. And this thinking got so serious that we formed a production company, intending to present something, a special or a series, not just on the planets but on the cosmos. And that's how we came here."

Carl Sagan was talking to me in his office at KCET, which he shares with his personal staff and two writers who assisted him on **"Cosmos."** ("Steve Soter and Annie Druyan did some ten percent of it. She did the Alexandria library sequence. It's good.") But Sagan himself was rarely in. He spent most of his time, when in town, on the sound stage.

But as production was winding down, he spent more and more time out of town, shuttling back and forth between Los Angeles and the East Coast, and hiding out wherever he could to write. He was finishing up the book version of *Cosmos,* which he insists will not be just a transcription of his scripts, but rather an amplification of them.

Sagan described the upcoming series as "a *general* view of the universe," moving from the atom to the cosmos. "We'll be treating historical things," he explained with characteristic enthusiasm, "and a great many of the *big* questions."

Such as? "Well, such as the likelihood of making contact with life on other planets," he replied. "What will such contact mean? Will there be a high level of technology? Can they teach us? Keep us from destroying ourselves? Politics becomes quite important in this. In fact, there's hardly a field of human endeavor that's not involved in the implications and ramifications of this single question." But he added, "Some things we're doing just because they're fun—or beautiful, or interesting. Yes, doing something to increase the audience's understanding—now, *that's* fun."

Had he found it a problem tailoring technical material to a general audience? "What my experience has indicated is that people are a whole lot smarter than they are given credit for," Sagan said. "For a scientist to explain what he knows requires a certain mind cast. You have to remember what your mind was like just before you understood what you now know. It's just a matter of getting it across with a little creative effort, with visuals and metaphors and asking questions. It's a particular kind of writing, certainly, but I don't find it much different from the kind of thing that I do off the cuff on the Carson show."

"We're not just presenting conclusions to the audience," he explained. "We're also trying to get across the method by which the conclusions are reached. In my opinion, the fun of understanding is built in to every one of us. Some have it beaten out of them in schools, but everyone is basically a scientist. It's how we understand the world. That's what we're assuming. That's what we're building on. I can't predict how successful we'll be in communicating these concepts to a large audience, but from my previous experience, I'd say we'll be very successful."

Sagan gave one example of the show's methods. "For instance," he said, "we discuss astrology as we lead in to astronomy—in this way, using what people know about to get them to understand what they don't. In the same way a lot of kids are turned on to science by science fiction in books and movies. This future-oriented aspect is vital for young people. They have to live in the future. They have to start thinking, What if?"

Cosmos hopes to get people to consider the possibilities in somewhat the same way that science fiction does. "One theme in the series," Sagan said, "is the playfulness and the sense of fun in science. A lot of science fiction films have this. *Star Wars* did. It was not the least bit pretentious, and it got a lot of science wrong. And every time this happens, they've lost an opportunity to teach, an opportunity to get across the tremendous, real possibilities of science. We're going to get it right. We're also going to keep that sense of fun and enthusiasm and get it across to the audience."

In this way, Sagan hopes to win an audience for science. "Real science," he said. "This is an area where individuals matter. Maybe out of all the millions of people we interest, a few thousand will choose careers in science. Maybe a hundred of those will make real contributions. Out of that hundred—who knows? An Einstein? A Kepler?" Or, at least, a couple of Sagans.

Frederic Golden (essay date 20 October 1980)

SOURCE: "The Cosmic Explainer," in *Time,* October 20, 1980, pp. 62-3, 65-6, 68-9.

[*In the following essay, Golden provides an overview of Sagan's career and his production of the television program* Cosmos.]

> *Scene: A living room in Brooklyn, circa 1946*
>
> *Grandfather:* What do you want to be when you grow up?
>
> *Boy:* An astronomer.
>
> *Grandfather:* Yes, but how will you make a living?

Flashing through the heavens like an extraterrestrial Tinker Bell, the spacecraft looks like something by H. G. Wells out of Walt Disney. At the helm is none other than the boy from Brooklyn, now fully grown and, among several other things, a real astronomer. With a nonchalant gesture over his magical controls, he guides the ship on a voyage made possible only by the imagination, with the help of a Hollywood special-effects crew. Into the arms of giant galaxies he goes, through halos of stars, past a blinking pulsar, skirting the edge of a black hole, even reconnoitering a distant planet that seems to be inhabited.

It is an extraordinary journey, surmounting all barriers of space and time. The pilot-guide does not pause to question such miracles. Nor does he stint on bold speculation. Passing one planet, he muses, "Intelligent beings may have evolved and reworked this planetary surface in some massive engineering enterprise." Finally returning to the vicinity of home, he talks of "a single, ordinary, yellow dwarf star surrounded by a system of nine planets, dozens of moons, thousands of asteroids and billions of comets—the family of our sun." He fantasizes about large, tenuous life forms in the stormy atmosphere of Jupiter and about small, microbial ones in the reddish volcanic soil of Mars. To the space traveler, the earth is the shore of a cosmic ocean: "Recently, we have waded a little way out, maybe ankle-deep, and the water seems inviting."

So it goes when Carl Sagan, creator, chief writer and host-narrator of the new public television series *Cosmos* takes the controls of his fantasy spaceship. Sagan's grandfather can rest easy now. His grandson is not only making a living, thank you, he has also become a star—indeed, a supernova of sorts—in the scientific firmament. Sagan's books, ranging from speculations about life beyond the earth (*The Cosmic Connection*) to ruminations about the reptilian ancestry of the human brain (*The Dragons of Eden*) have sold millions of copies and have been translated into a dozen languages. His lectures, on campus as well as off, attract overflow crowds. He is at home on late-night TV bantering with Johnny Carson about heavenly bodies, both human and astronomical. He has also talked with Jimmy Carter about such esoteric matters as black holes and exobiology (the study of possible extraterrestrial life).

Now, at 45, the Cornell-based scientist is displaying his didactic gifts in his largest classroom yet. The first two of *Cosmos*' 13 weekly episodes may have attracted more viewers (perhaps as many as 10 million each) than any regular series in PBS history. With a budget of $8.5 million, *Cosmos* was three years in the making, involved a production staff of 150 people and was filmed at 40 locations in twelve countries. It features special effects rivaling those in *Star Wars,* computer animation, scale models and painted backdrops as dazzling as anything ever attempted on television.

The series' name comes from the Greek word for the ordered universe, the antithesis of chaos. It is an apt choice. *Cosmos* is nothing less than Sagan's attempt to make sense out of what is for many people the hopelessly baffling world of 20th century science. To unfold his story he roves through two millennia of scientific progress, often shuttling back and forth over the centuries like some Wellsian time traveler. He travels the earth as well. One moment he is seated in a café on the Aegean island of Samos, home of Pythagoras and Aristarchus, explaining the first stirrings of Greek scientific prowess. At another moment, he is strolling through the venerable Cavendish Laboratories of England's Cambridge University, recounting the birth of modern atomic physics. At still another, he is standing in the bleak wastes of Death Valley, discussing the efforts of the Viking landers to find living things on Mars. Alas, concedes Sagan, they have found no sure trace of life—yet.

Sagan sends out an exuberant message: science is not only vital for humanity's future well-being, but it is rousing good fun as well.
—*Frederic Golden*

In the casualness of turtleneck jersey and chino pants, his butcher-boy haircut tousled by the wind, Sagan sends out an exuberant message: science is not only vital for humanity's future well-being, but it is rousing good fun as well. Even the most scientifically untutored person can—indeed, must—grasp its essentials. As Sagan insists, "There is nothing about science that cannot be explained to the layman."

Physicists among his colleagues shudder at such popularization and simplification. After all, science has a long tradition, often violated to be sure, of modesty and understatement, even of calculated obfuscation, so that only an elite priesthood will be privy to its secrets. Other than the irrepressible Sagan, how many scientists would buzz a simulated Martian volcano, as he does in one *Cosmos* sequence; or rummage through a re-creation of the famed library of Alexandria, pretending to read long-lost papyrus scrolls; or attempt to explain the paradoxes of special relativity while bicycling through the hills of Tuscany, where the young Einstein once wandered? Sagan also issues some open challenges. To creationists, who argue for a biblical interpretation of life's beginnings, he states that evolution is not a theory, it is a fact. As for reports that creatures from other worlds have landed on earth, he dismisses them with a shrug. Astrology, Sagan insists, is a fraud.

There are more than a few milligrams of arrogance in all this. The camera lingers too often on the Sagan profile. His lyrical language sometimes lapses into flowery excess, and occasionally *Cosmos'* galloping pace struggles to a crawl. But without a doubt, Sagan makes science as palatable as the apple pie he lovingly cuts up in a Cambridge University dining room in order to make a point about matter. He is the quintessential schoolmaster; he makes such a classical experiment as Christian Huygens' determination of the distance of the stars with only a perforated brass disc seem as vivid today as when it was performed three centuries ago. In the words of one admiring reviewer, he is the prince of popularizers, the nation's scientific mentor to the masses.

Since the beginnings of science, every age has had its tradition of explainers, often scientists themselves, who clarified new and difficult ideas. In the 19th century, T. H. Huxley served as the spokesman of Darwinian evolution. Later such skilled popularizers as Arthur Eddington and Bertrand Russell helped interpret the startling new worlds of relativity and quantum mechanics.

Today more and more scientists seem to be matching their talent for experimentation with a surprising gift for exposition. One of them is a Harvard paleontologist named Stephen Jay Gould, 39, author of two pellucid collections of essays on evolution (*Ever Since Darwin, The Panda's Thumb*). Another is Dr. Lewis Thomas, 66, whose humane writings on biology and medicine in the pages of the *New England Journal of Medicine* became the basis for two bestsellers (*The Lives of a Cell, The Medusa and the Snail*). Others include Physicists Jeremy Bernstein, 50, a regular contributor to *The New Yorker;* Robert Jastrow, 55, head of the Goddard Institute for Space Studies; and Princeton's Gerard O'Neill, 53, the leading apostle of space colonization. There is also the British physician Jonathan Miller, whose medical series *The Body in Question* is running on PBS and is the basis of a current book. Most prolific of all is Isaac Asimov, 60 (with 218 books to his credit at last count), a chemistry Ph.D. and one-time medical-school instructor.

A decade or so ago, much of the public would have turned a deaf ear to these voices of science, eloquent as they are. The subject was unpopular, even in disrepute. Science, or more accurately its offshoot technology, was being blamed for much that was wrong with the world: the growing despoliation of the environment, the chemical devastation of the Vietnamese countryside, the spread of nuclear weaponry. Even the first flush of excitement about landing men on the moon quickly turned into boredom after repeated video exposure of the dusty, lifeless lunar surface. Many people pressed loudly and insistently for more attention to earthly problems. NASA is still suffering budgetary blues from this outcry. Indeed, only last week the space agency's beleaguered boss, Robert Frosch, announced he was quitting, reportedly because of lack of financial support.

But even when science was attracting little popular interest, plenty was going on. Investigators were making enormous strides, especially those involved in basic research—inquiries with no immediate practical payoff. Some researchers were probing the inner secrets of the atomic nucleus, others, like Sagan himself, looked out to the mysteries of the planets and the stars. Still others discovered how the earth's surface, found to be unexpectedly mobile, has been shaped and reshaped over the ages. Perhaps most startling of all were the explorations on the very frontiers of life. For the first time, scientists were beginning to understand and manipulate DNA, the basic stuff of heredity.

Eventually, the awe of science overcame the indifference toward it. As Lewis Thomas explains, "The more that is learned about nature, particularly the puzzling aspects—the queernesses being uncovered by the physicists, for example—the more engrossing it becomes." Adds Asimov: "We feel that if we do not understand science and the changes science makes possible, we may find ourselves overwhelmed."

In a turnabout as sudden as some of the scene shifts in *Cosmos*, ennui has turned into enthusiasm. Public curiosity about science, if not financial support of it, seems to be rocketing upward. Some signs: the New York *Times* has created a special weekly section to report the news of science, and other newspapers have expanded their science staffs and coverage. Some half a dozen new mass-market science magazines have been launched within the past few years, the most recent being Time Inc.'s new monthly *DISCOVER*. There is a growing readership for books on scientific topics, as opposed to those on such pseudoscientific hokum as UFOs, astrology and parapsychology.

Television's interest grew too. In the early 1970s, PBS began importing BBC science specials, like Nigel Calder's programs on astronomy, physics, the new biology. In 1974, one of the PBS stations, WGBH in Boston, took the plunge with its own Nova series. Now, counting *Nova,* Sagan's *Cosmos,* and Miller's *Body,* PBS is running seven separate science series.

The commercial networks long gave science short shrift, except when it came to moon landings or *Mr. Wizard*-like kiddie shows. Now they too are moving into expanded coverage. ABC has a possible science series for next year, an offshoot of *20/20* tentatively titled *Quest.* At CBS, programmers are considering whether to give Walter Cronkite's *Universe,* an occasional half-hour science news show that has got a moderately good reception, a regular evening time slot. One factor that will surely affect the decision: the response of viewers to Sagan's *Cosmos.*

Playing the part of pacesetter is nothing new to Sagan. While growing up in Brooklyn's Bensonhurst section, the son of a U.S.-born mother and a Russian-immigrant father—a garment cutter who rose to factory manager—he was already thinking of the heavens while other children were preoccupied with stickball and marbles. He recalls: "I remember seeing the stars and asking my friends what they were. They told me that they were 'lights in the sky.'"

Unsatisfied, Sagan went off to the library and asked for a book on the stars. The librarian gave him one on the Hollywood variety: Jean Harlow and Clark Gable. When he finally got the right book, he learned that the stars were enormously distant suns. "This just blew my mind. Until then, my universe had been my neighborhood. Now I tried to imagine how far away I'd have to move the sun to make

it as faint as a star. I got my first sense of the immensity of the universe. I was hooked."

The hook worked its way in deeper when Carl also stumbled into science fiction. He was especially taken with the Martian tales of Edgar Rice Burroughs, who wrote of sensuous princesses, six-legged beasts of burden, evil warlords and a Virginia gentleman named John Carter, who miraculously transported himself to the Red Planet simply by gazing at it. The dark-eyed youngster, looking up at the night sky from a Brooklyn lot, tried vainly to follow his hero into space. It was a dream that Sagan has never forgotten. Phobos, the name of one of the moons of Mars, now appears on the license plates of Sagan's bright orange Porsche.

It was not until the Sagan family moved to Rahway, N.J., that Carl realized he actually could become a professional astronomer. All along he had felt he might have to go into the clothing business with his father, perhaps as a salesman. But his high school biology teacher assured him that astronomers, like the famous Harlow Shapley, were really paid for their work. In 1951, at 16, he entered the University of Chicago on a scholarship. Nine years later, he left with a Ph.D. in astronomy and astrophysics.

During his undergraduate years at Chicago, Sagan spent some summers breeding fruit flies in the Indiana University laboratory of the famed geneticist Hermann Muller, who won a Nobel Prize for showing that X rays could cause mutations. It was ideal training for an astronomer who would become the premier spokesman for exobiology. He also showed early gifts as a popularizer. He organized a highly successful campus lecture series on science, characteristically including himself as one of the speakers; some faculty members dismissed it as "Sagan's circus," but it drew S.R.O. crowds.

Even at that stage of Sagan's career, some of his professors detected rebelliousness in him, a penchant for shunning the work at hand in order to explore other interests. Recalls Physicist Peter Meyer, who is now director of Chicago's Enrico Fermi Institute, "He told me he would rather spend time with problems in astronomy than go through the hardships of classical physics." Today Meyer concedes that it is precisely this restlessness of intellect that enables Sagan to see the broader picture, letting him point out, for example, where biology and chemistry converge with astronomy. Says another scientist: "Sagan can separate the momentous from the minute. He can tell the story without cluttering detail."

Still, for all his extracurricular interests, including a young biologist named Lynn Alexander whom he would shortly marry, Sagan was a highly productive researcher. As always, he was iconoclastic. Although most astronomers were studying the more distant realms of the stars and galaxies, Sagan opted for the nearby planets, under the tutelage of the late Gerard Kuiper. He realized that planets were the most likely places for extraterrestrial life to be found in his lifetime. He also anticipated that the U.S. would soon embark on an ambitious program of planetary exploration. At a party just before Sputnik I spurred American space activity, Sagan made a perspicacious wager: he bet a case of chocolate bars that the U.S. would reach the moon by 1970. He won with five months to spare.

Sagan published his first paper at 22. Its title was an echo from his days with Muller and a sign of his growing interest in exobiology: "Radiation and the Origin of the Gene." A key point was that radiation may have been the trigger for the combination of the first DNA molecules. Eventually some 300 more papers would follow, including a particularly brilliant bit of deduction about the planet Venus. At the time, many scientists still regarded Venus as a kind of sister planet of the earth with a benign climate. But radio emissions from the planet were hinting at puzzlingly high temperatures. Sagan pointed out that a Venusian atmosphere of carbon dioxide and water vapor would trap solar heat, create a "greenhouse effect" and raise surface temperatures far above those of the earth. His prediction was soon confirmed by Soviet landers. The planet's surface temperature proved to be about 480° C (900° F), high enough to melt lead.

In 1960, Sagan headed for the University of California at Berkeley, where he spent two years as a research fellow; he insisted on taking a turn at teaching a class, even though the terms of his contract did not require it. At the Stanford University School of Medicine he delved into the origins of life. Then he went off to teach and do research at Harvard and the Smithsonian Astrophysical Observatory in Cambridge, Mass.

Collaborating with his first graduate student, James Pollack, he offered a novel explanation for the periodic lightening and darkening of parts of Mars' surface. Some scientists had suggested that the changes were due to seasonal variations in plant life. Sagan and Pollack argued that the fluctuations were varying dust patterns kicked up by winds of ferocious force. Years later, closeup photos of Mars confirmed their thesis.

At Harvard, Sagan was a highly popular lecturer, talking about such things as UFOs (he debunked them) and the idea of extraterrestrial life (he promoted it). He was divorced from Lynn (after two children, Dorian, now 21, and Jeremy, 19) and married to Linda Salzman, an artist. His career appeared to be taking off. But in spite of his professional flair, Harvard never offered him tenure. So, in 1968, when Cornell University beckoned with an offer to set up a laboratory of planetary studies, he promptly accepted it and moved to rural Ithaca, N.Y.

Even Sagan's scientific friends acknowledge that he does not have the patience or persistence for the slow, painstaking experimentation and data collection that is at the heart of the scientific process. Nor has he come close to the kind of breakthrough work that wins Nobel Prizes. But he more than compensates with other significant talents. He has a penchant for asking provocative questions. Sometimes, as Sagan fully concedes, this can rile others. But such prodding can inspire students and colleagues, lead to brilliant new insights and generally create a mood of intellectual excitement.

> **As a planetary expert, Sagan was called upon by NASA to act as an adviser and scientific investigator on unmanned space missions. He did not always endear himself to the space agency. One irritant was his outspoken opposition to the moon landings. Robots, he argued, could do the job better and cheaper and with no risk to life.**
> —*Frederic Golden*

At Sagan's Cornell laboratory, one of the main objectives was to try to unravel the mystery of how the building blocks of life—amino acids, proteins and DNA—could have evolved on the primordial earth. Although he and the Russian astrophysicist I. S. Shklovskii lived half a world apart, they collaborated in writing *Intelligent Life in the Universe,* still probably the best treatise on the prospects for extraterrestrial life. As a planetary expert, Sagan was called upon by NASA to act as an adviser and scientific investigator on unmanned space missions. He did not always endear himself to the space agency. One irritant was his outspoken opposition to the moon landings. Robots, he argued, could do the job better and cheaper and with no risk to life.

In 1973, during a brief appearance on the *Tonight* show to promote *Cosmic Connection,* his first really popular book, he so impressed Host (and astronomy buff) Johnny Carson that he was soon invited back, for a choicer spot on the show. That second appearance gave Sagan a chance to tell the story of the evolution of the universe and the beginnings of life in his inimitable cadences: "Fifteen billion years ago, the universe was without form. There were no galaxies, stars or planets. There was no life. There was darkness everywhere." When Sagan's soliloquy ended, said a reviewer, 100,000 teen-age listeners must have vowed on the spot to become astronomers. One thing is certain: Sagan captivated Carson, who kept inviting him back for further appearances. Indeed he became such a frequent guest that students would greet his return to the Ithaca lecture halls with a mock *Tonight* show-type introduction: "He-e-e-re's Carl!"

Yet even without Carson's patronage, Sagan's public star

would surely have risen. Just before NASA sent off its twin Pioneers 10 and 11 to Saturn and Jupiter, he had persuaded the space agency to attach plaques identifying the ships' origins on the remote chance that they might be intercepted when they finally passed out of the solar system. The idea was a triumph over bureaucratic caution. The plaques, drawn by Linda, depicted nude male and female earthlings, and provoked worldwide comment.

For Sagan these overtures to anyone out there were equally important as signals to earth. They are part of what he calls cosmic consciousness-raising, his attempt to alert earthlings to the excitement and wonder of the universe. It was just such consciousness-raising that first stirred thoughts in Sagan's mind of doing a television program on space exploration.

Back in 1971, the Mariner 9 spacecraft had just become the first ship from earth to orbit another planet. The target was Sagan's old favorite, Mars. In less than a year of reconnaissance, the robot accumulated more information about the Red Planet than had been gathered in three centuries of earlier observation from earth. Yet to Sagan's chagrin, the feat was virtually ignored by American television. Four years later, the even more spectacular Viking landings on Mars were again all but ignored. Sagan decided something had to be done. Joining up with an equally dismayed colleague at the Jet Propulsion Laboratory, B. Gentry Lee, Sagan sought sponsors for a TV film on space exploration. What they ended up with was an agreement with KCET, the Los Angeles PBS station, for an even bigger project: a full science series somewhat like Jacob Bronowski's acclaimed *The Ascent of Man*, with Sagan as guide and principal author. *Ascent*'s British producer, Adrian Malone, was even recruited to ride herd on the enterprise.

That was no easy job. Inevitably, there were disagreements, some over scientific accuracy, others involving personality. Sagan, a novice at TV production, admits that he ruffled feelings among the TV staff with his constant questioning. There were logistical problems. A severe snowstorm hit Death Valley just before the *Cosmos* team was scheduled to re-enact a Viking landing. A few miles away, the U.S. Air Force was conducting bomb runs. In addition, word came that Sagan's father had developed lung cancer. Over the ten months of illness that led up to his father's death, Carl frequently had to be away from the filming for days at a time.

There were other changes in Sagan's life during this period. He separated from his wife Linda, leaving her and their son Nicholas, 10, behind in Ithaca. He moved to Los Angeles with a New York novelist named Ann Druyan, 31, who had been collaborating with him on a record of terrestrial photographs and sounds (*Murmurs of Earth*) for placement aboard the Voyager spacecraft, as well as helping him with the *Cosmos* script. After Sagan's divorce, they hope to marry.

Having discovered the excitement of show business, Sagan is eager to continue in it. Says he: "Television is one of the greatest teaching tools ever invented, particularly for teaching science." One project on tap is a feature film with a scenario by Sagan (but no acting role for him), about an encounter with extraterrestrial life. The tentative title: *Contact*. It may be a while, however, before that adventure goes before the cameras. After a two-year absence Sagan is due to resume teaching and research at Cornell in January. He must also straighten out his divorce proceeding which now threatens to become a court battle over the division of property (Sagan has retained flamboyant "palimony" Lawyer Marvin Mitchelson). Finally, he professes a desire to go back to research, at least part time, something that he has found virtually impossible to pursue with his multiplying interests.

Watching with wonder—and no doubt a little envy—the whirling star named Sagan, some of his colleagues feel that he has stepped beyond the bounds of science. They complain that he is driven by ego. They also say he tends to overstate his case, often fails to give proper credit to other scientists for their work and blurs the line between fact and speculation. But they probably represent a minority view. Most scientists, increasingly sensitive to the need for public support and understanding of research, appreciate what Sagan has become: Americas most effective salesman of science. His pitch in *Cosmos*—and indeed in all his popularizing—is classic Sagan. Says he: Science is a joy. It is not just something for an isolated, remote elite. It is our birthright." What scientist could disagree?

William J. Harnack (essay date July-August 1981)

SOURCE: "Carl Sagan: Cosmic Evolution vs. the Creationist Myth," in *The Humanist*, Vol. 41, July-August, 1981, pp. 5-6.

[*In the following essay, Harnack discusses the success of the television program* Cosmos *and Sagan's appearance before the American Humanist Association to receive its Humanist of the Year award in 1981.*]

On April 18, 1981, the American Humanist Association, at their Fortieth Annual Conference held in San Diego, named Carl Sagan 1981 Humanist of the Year.

In his address, Sagan simply yet eloquently noted that plants, animals, and humans are all part of a whole. The Greeks, in glimpsing the distribution of the elements of the cosmos, had a vision of surpassing importance. We now know that we can make all the essential building blocks of life. We believe the single-cell organism, the first form of life, was like a free-floating molecular complex—like DNA—or "naked gene." Yet there is more to discover.

Although most people throughout history have chosen to believe that "God did it" when trying to understand the complexities of the universe, Sagan proceeded to take a scientific approach. He began with the elemental composition of the universe and expanded his analysis to make comprehensible the two conflicting views of the direction of the universe—the theory of an expanding and infinite universe as opposed to an oscillating one. He paused, sensing the audience's wish to know which one was true, and added, "You don't have to make up your minds right now. Wait till the data are in. Keep an open mind."

This theme was the thrust of a very interesting and, to humanists constantly under assault by the religious right these days, inspiring speech.

Why choose Carl Sagan as Humanist of the Year?

As one of the most popular figures in the world today, Carl Sagan combines a solid academic background as an astronomer and researcher with the identifiability of a film or rock star. He is a teacher who can communicate such seemingly unfathomable concepts as black holes, via various media, to a roomful of people, such as assembled in the Hotel San Diego, or to millions through his books and television programs.

Cosmos, Sagan's television series about the origin, design, and direction of the universe, was the most widely seen series in the history of public television in America. Aired this past year (with a beautiful follow-up book published by Random House), *Cosmos* was one reason for granting this year's award to Dr. Sagan. This series proved something that needed to be proved—both regarding television programming and, more importantly, about the nature of the American public. To quote Sagan, "People are more intelligent than publishing house executives and television programmers believe. *Cosmos* was popular because it presented a cosmic perspective as opposed to the creationist view," with which, he went on to say, one is bombarded just about anytime one turns on the set.

For this alone, humanists applaud Carl Sagan. The showing of *Cosmos* was coincidental with the formation of the Moral Majority and the largest swing to a religiopolitical right this country has ever experienced. Yet many people, hungry not necessarily for Jerry Falwell's truth but rather for truth based on their own understanding of the data, tuned in in record-

breaking numbers. "We are by nature a scientific species," Sagan reminded us. "We are descended from the guys who 'figured it out.'"

While he centered on the most up-to-date explanations of the origin and nature of the universe—and why these disprove fundamentalists who literally "add up the begats" in the Bible and conclude that the Earth is about six thousand years old—the afternoon debate between Tim LaHaye and Gerald Larue was clearly on his mind. As a scientist and a seeker of all evidence, the New Right's opposition to other views bothers him. "Creationists do not want the other view [evolution]," and then, realizing his audience, "the view that, for some reason I don't understand, they credited you people for. When I first read their stuff, I didn't know who the secular humanists were. Turned out it was just you guys!" The audience laughed.

He explained that every culture has had a "creation myth," and he finds it troubling that the theory of evolution has been dismissed by many as "only a theory"—explaining that the word theory has an unfortunate connotation. "Because it is not written in stone, it is a no less well-developed way of knowing."

During the discussion period, AHA administrator Fred Edwords asked for a response to the creationists' claim that the perfect balance for life on Earth is evidence of their view. Dr. Sagan dismissed their argument as "confusing cause and effect" and explained that differing conditions may produce different life forms. Bette Chambers, coordinator of the Association's *Statement Affirming Evolution as a Principle of Science,* asked about the possibility of more forums for debate between scientists and creationists in scientific organizations including the American Association for the Advancement of Science. Sagan responded that, while many of his colleagues seem to be afraid to air the opposition's views, believing in the Sam Goldwyn theory that "publicity is good, and good publicity is better," he thinks such forums are an excellent idea because "truth will out."

Sagan cautioned that even some humanists proclaim too much before enough data are in. He mentioned as cases in point "those committed atheists who believe there is compelling evidence that no god exists" and the AHA's statement concerning astrology, with which he largely agrees but believes is too "authoritarian."

He concluded by stating that he is very glad that the AHA exists and considers the award a great honor.

"The pursuit of science should be fun," Sagan observed, and the aim of science, quoting Socrates, is "to know a deep thing well." We can thank Carl Sagan for helping millions achieve these objectives.

Cynthia Thomiszer (essay date September 1982)

SOURCE: "Brain Theory and Literary Criticism: Sagan on Art," in *Essays in Arts and Sciences,* Vol. XI, September, 1982, pp. 87-95.

[*In the following essay, Thomiszer considers Sagan's application of scientific discovery to explain the origin and significance of art in* The Dragons of Eden. *According to Thomiszer, "to confuse aesthetics with empiricism, as Sagan does, is to further confuse an already clouded issue."*]

Science and art, so long perceived as mighty opposites, are enjoying a new recognition of kinship. The "two cultures," a model based on the disparate results of science and art, has been discarded. In its place has arisen a unified approach to both activities that focuses on their shared point of departure: both art and science represent man's attempt to know himself and his world. That the pursuit and expression of knowledge is the basis of science and art is hardly a new idea. However, what has changed in the last few years is our understanding of the processes which science and art employ to establish and express their particular truths. According to the traditional argument, science taught through repeatable experiment, art through reconstructed experience. These processes were seen as complementary, but not identical, and their results were said to be equally valuable, though in a technological society, science always seemed to be a little "more equal."

> **A scientific model, such as the Newtonian world machine, shares with the humblest lyric poem a uniquely human exercise in metaphor: our brain translates our knowledge into symbols, ranks and orders it within a recognizable model, or, in the case of genius, creates a new model.**
> **—Cynthia Thomiszer**

In these post-Einsteinian days of relativity and circularity, the old arguments for "separate but equal" are dying out. Though science and art *may* have separate fields to explore, and not necessarily even that, there is a growing recognition that both use the same tool: the brain. Further, there is an increasing awareness that the brain works by making models, both scientific and artistic, by which we comprehend reality. A scientific model, such as the Newtonian world machine, shares with the humblest lyric poem a uniquely human exercise in metaphor: our brain translates our knowledge into symbols, ranks and orders it within a recognizable model, or, in the case of genius, creates a new model. In her probing essay "Is Art All There Is?," Annie Dillard names this process the "creating of contexts"; Thomas Kuhn speaks

of "models," Northrop Frye of "metaphors," but all three are describing the essential activity of the brain, whether that brain is creating physics or the Prince of Elsinore. There is only one culture, and that culture is the one generated by the human brain.

All of this good fellow feeling between science and art grew out of epistemological questions that began with Descartes. Inevitably the problems of knowing would force us to the source of knowledge itself, the brain. And thus, the brain is becoming the central icon in contemporary man's study of himself, replacing the Medieval interest in the soul and the Renaissance attention to the self. We think, therefore we are. But the only way to study how we think is to use the source of our thinking, the brain, and there is nowhere to stand in order to see our brain objectively. Despite this epistemological circularity, scientists are deducing what they can about the way our brain works. Can their research tell us anything about art? And since this research is written almost exclusively by scientists, does it reflect any bias against art, a vestige of the "separate, but not so equal" doctrine of the past? These are the questions I will briefly pursue.

One place to begin our study is to look at the gross physical configuration of the brain and speculate on its mechanisms. Of course, this approach forces a reification between brain and mind and between mind and idea, but it is precisely this blend of fact and fancy that Carl Sagan offers in *The Dragons of Eden.* Though there are many books with a more scholarly focus, Sagan is an enormously successful popularizer of scientific research—*Dragons* was a best seller for many months—and thus, his book has been most influential on the general public's conception of the human brain. More to the point, he tells us much, both directly and indirectly, about the place of art in brain research.

The first thing a humanist would probably note in reading *Dragons of Eden* is the ease with which Sagan moves between science and art. For example, the scientific research he cites in the opening chapters offers a *physical* basis for many familiar and ancient literary truths, including the myths of Cassandra, Phaedrus, and Prometheus. More to the point, the various myths provide a vehicle for expressing scientific fact. Thus, science is used to confirm art and art is used to express science as if Sagan perceives no incompatibility between the methods or products of the two.

If, in Sagan's book, scientific research enjoys "borrowed interest" from literary myth, the book itself plunders freely from the world of art. *The Dragons of Eden* supports Morris Kline's assertion that "science is rationalized fiction." Part of this fictitious effect derives from Sagan's style, which incorporates metaphors, irony, puns, and well-chosen allusions. But the artifice of the book runs deeper. The information about the evolution of the brain is selected and arranged for maximum effect, taking on the configurations of a plot. There is even a flashback "dream sequence." The central character is, of course, the brain, whose random evolutionary fortunes produce a hero at once picaresque and epic. But the brain is not alone. Also peopling its little world is an array of secondary characters, among them scientists and a collection of so-called lesser animals, both mythical and real. Sagan himself acts as a semi-omniscient narrator who contemplates his character but cannot penetrate its ultimate mystery.

W. P. Ker has defined the plot of an epic as "the defense of a small place against odds," in which the "small place" represents some civilized outpost or relatively advanced hero. The history of the brain subscribes to this formula, for it is the story of a small place which grew to control the world against incredible natural odds. Our brain evolved through accretion, new areas simply emerging over the old without replacing them. Therefore, the "deep and ancient parts" of our pre-mammalian heritage continue to function even today. Our first brain, the R-complex, is reptilian; we are, as Sagan's title suggests, the dragons of Eden. The second stage to emerge (the limbic system) parallels the structure of birds and non-primate mammals (a fact that gives new resonance to the insult "birdbrain"). The final area to evolve was the neocortex or primate brain. Thus, it is not "a heavy bear" that goes with us, but a chimp, a lizard, and a sparrow. The "animal within," long noted by artists and observers of human behavior, is more like a zoo.

Our epic hero is the neocortex with its metaphorical geography, the two "hemispheres" and four major lobes. This civilized and civilizing brain alienates us from non-primates, producing those mental activities we suspect are peculiarly "human": language, imagination, rational analysis. As Odysseus placed certain limits on the witch Circe in order to defend himself, the neocortex dominates but does not destroy the other brains within us. They continue their own functions, the R-complex busying itself with matters of "hierarchy, ritual, and aggression" while the gentler limbic system provides strong emotions, altruism, and religion. Physically, man internalizes his own psychomachia, incorporating both the good and bad angels in his own brain.

Although the brain's accommodation of these competing parts is, in many ways, a model of cooperation, Sagan does suggest that the various brains are sometimes uneasy "headfellows." The neocortex consistently wins, as heroes must, through superior resources and intellect. However, the more primitive brains make their own compelling demands, including a demand for art. Art serves, it seems, as a clarifying experience against genuine internal confusion and struggle.

In other words, Sagan's model of and speculations on the brain do not present an alien figure. Rather, our brain subscribes to familiar models created by and perpetuated in literature and art. Previously the interchange between science and literature has been approached as if it were a one-sided exchange: Newton's impact on Pope, Darwin's influence on Dickens, Einstein's effect on the structure of the modern novel. In Sagan's book, the balance is righted somewhat. Now we see the impact of literature on science: Art provides a model to explain scientific findings. One might even note that art and culture seem to predispose a scientist to see phenomena in a certain way—an attack on scientific "objectivity" which, while hardly original, deserves to be remembered periodically. Sagan gracefully weaves together literary myth and scientific research, establishing in the process a hard scientific reason for careful study of myth and art. For Sagan at least, scientific and literary models seem to have merged.

Sagan's ideas about art are not always given so indirectly. In the book he cites two theories about the physical origin of art: art originates in the genetic memory, and art originates in the brain itself, especially the R-complex and the right hemisphere.

Sagan's speculation that some art arises from a biological memory reposited in the genetic code produces a theory of art similar (at least in results) to Jung's concept of the collective unconscious. The only biological memory Sagan discusses at length is the speculation that our DNA holds within it some memory of a time when mammals and reptiles fought a guerilla war for control of the earth, warmblooded mammals waking at night to forage for reptile eggs, coldblooded reptiles rising at day to stalk sleeping mammals. Such a memory may explain the story of the garden of Eden and the nearly universal human antipathy for snakes, as well as the human habit of eating eggs for breakfast. All readers of western literature can cite examples of anti-reptile bias in our written culture. Shakespeare, for example, reserves his reptile imagery for his most treacherous villains, who are variously described as lizards and snakes, and, ironically, for his tragic protagonists. Othello "had rather be a toad" than a cuckold; Lear knows himself well enough to warn Kent "Come not between the dragon and his wrath."

Even whole Shakespearean plays seem constructed around a mammal-reptile battle. *Anthony and Cleopatra* centers on three characters who embody the characteristics Sagan outlines. Octavius, a coldblooded and rigidly hierarchical reptile, is a daytime character, markedly uneasy in his one nighttime scene when he observes the drunken celebration of the spontaneous, warmblooded mammals. Antony leads the mammals; a creature of the night, he is a lover, poet, dreamer, and drinker, comfortable with his peers and subordinates. Cleopatra is the serpent of the Nile, who recognizes her affinity with the reptiles in her dying description of the asp that kills her: "Dost thou not see my baby at my breast That sucks the nurse asleep?" But Cleopatra is ambivalent. Her relationship with Antony shows a capacity for love, and Sagan tells us that mammals invented that particular emotion. When Enobarbus speaks of Antony as a "bellows," he describes quite accurately Antony's warmblooded effect on Cleopatra.

Sagan's theory of a genetically-based origin for art raises other issues as well. If we have a biologically-induced perception of the reptile as "the enemy," and yet have the working vestigial brain of a reptile within us, is all our aggression ultimately self-directed? Are we fighting the beast without or the animal within? Again Shakespeare's tragic heroes come to mind. Inevitably, Shakespeare's heroes recognize some affinity between themselves and the enemy they sought to destroy. Lear sees Goneril as "a disease within my flesh which I must needs call mine." The complex interchange between Othello and Iago provides a more developed example of the same bonding. Even Prospero offers an ambiguous recognition of Caliban: "This thing of darkness I acknowledge mine." Shakespeare's protagonists do follow the circular pattern Sagan's theory would suggest, each pursuing an enemy only to discover that he pursues a darkness within his own soul.

After noting these points of similarity between Sagan's model and Shakespeare's, what conclusions can we draw? Probably not many. Given sufficiently large categories, it takes no special ingenuity to make everything fit or to see what has been left out in the process. Does Shakespeare resort to reptile imagery because it is in his DNA or because it is a traditional image he inherited from Genesis, or both? For that matter, does Sagan's theory on reptiles reflect a bias in his own education which, presumably, included readings in Genesis and Shakespeare? Obviously these questions strike at the foundation of scientific observation and expression. Thus, I note similarities with interest, but not conviction.

Genes, however, are not the only source of art that Sagan postulates. As the Greeks had two gods for art, so too the brain itself has two possible generators of art. The first of these is the R-complex, whose "elementary needs" force us to face our personal dragons in a therapeutic process similar to catharsis. From this source derives our ritualistic and hierarchical art, the art the Greeks called Apollonian.

The second source of art is the right hemisphere of the neocortex, the place of intuition, sexuality, dreams, and creativity itself, a veritable cornucopia of Dionysian delight. Sagan devotes most of his discussion to dreams, which serve, he suggests, as entertainment and problem solvers. There is a marked similarity between the function of dreams, then, and the traditional function of art: to teach and to delight. Certainly the link between art and dreams is a literary commonplace extending from the medieval dream vision to Strindberg's *A Dream Play*. With Sagan's theory in hand, we can offer a scientific theory about why this link exists.

Further, the recognition of the right hemisphere as the source of creativity provides a particular physical point at which we may link science and art. Physics is created in the right hemisphere as surely as *Hamlet*, a point eloquently argued some years ago by Jacob Bronowski and supported by Sagan himself. Not only do art and science share a physical point of origin, but they undergo a similar process of "logical editing" in the left hemisphere to achieve the form, language, and line of reasoning that make them comprehensible. No longer separate but equal, science and art are now united by the confirmation of science itself.

Or are they? Though Sagan himself argues for this material unity, he suffers from *a priori* assumptions that reflect a clear bias toward science as a "higher" work of the brain than art. Since brain research is largely written by scientists, and since their writings have a decided impact on the way we view ourselves and our world, I fear we must be alert for such a bias or succumb to a new version, this one "scientifically based," of separate and unequal. For example, though Sagan calls repeatedly for a fruitful merger of both hemispheres, he shares with most of western culture a decided bias towards the work of the left hemisphere—the work of logic and analysis. Since this is such a common bias, Sagan's expression of it becomes a problem only when he begins to associate science almost exclusively with the left hemisphere and art with the right. It is the American way for people to rise above their origins, but one may justly question the practice when engaged in by models of reality. Science and art begin in the same right hemisphere and move through the same left hemisphere "translator and editor." But Sagan appears to underestimate the formal properties of art: its discipline, structure, revision, logical development, and comprehensibility. In other words, the impact of the left hemisphere on art is largely ignored, as if art were truly created in a "fine frenzy rolling" rather than heavily edited in tranquility.

Sagan also charges that art is not susceptible to a test of validity:

> I know of no significant advance in science that did not require major inputs from both cerebral hemispheres. This is not true for art, where apparently there are no experiments by which capable, dedicated, and unbiased observers can determine to their mutual satisfaction which works are great.

Sagan's conclusions not only contradict his earlier statements, but also show a rather selective memory of history.

The history of science is fraught with examples of unrecognized greatness, unrecognized, we should note, by other scientists as well as politicians and priests. The ease with which a scientific theory is accepted or rejected today comes largely from the test applied to it: a scientifically constructed model of truth called empiricism. When the model for truth was constructed by theologians and not scientists, scientific theory did not fare so well. However, now that we have a firmly entrenched scientific test for truth, why does art so stubbornly resist its criteria? Why are there "no experiments by which . . . observers can determine . . . which works are great"?

We demand more of art than we do of science, and our tests for art are both more complex and less precise. Empiricism is a true/false test, easy to pass or fail; aesthetics is an essay exam, harder to complete and harder to grade.
—Cynthia Thomiszer

First, Sagan has shifted his terms on us: "great" is now substituted for "true." If, in fact, all we asked of art was "truth," we could presumably apply the criteria of verisimilitude to any work. But we demand of art not only truth, but beauty and moral "rightness." When such tests have been applied to science, science itself has had trouble receiving a passing grade. Carlyle, for example, found Darwin's theory not false, but ugly, leading him to conclude that, though the theory might well be correct, still "the less said of it, the better." And today's renewed debate on evolution finds Darwin's theories under attack for lacking moral rightness as well as conflicting with Biblical models of truth. When we ask our science to be beautiful or right as well as true, we find few theories that are unanimously considered "great." But we ask only that our science be true within a narrowly defined sense of that word. In other words, we demand more of art than we do of science, and our tests for art are both more complex and less precise. Empiricism is a true/false test, easy to pass or fail; aesthetics is an essay exam, harder to complete and harder to grade. But to confuse aesthetics with empiricism, as Sagan does, is to further confuse an already clouded issue.

Judging from our journals and conferences, humanists have shown great and justified interest in brain research. This is not surprising since, to some degree, we teach applied brain theory every time we discuss a writer who is interested in the way men create and solve their problems. (And what writer is not, finally, dealing with that issue?) However, at the moment, scientific theory about the brain is neither subtle nor complex enough to make the aesthetic discriminations we demand of literary criticism. Brain theory cannot tell us

how Oedipus knew the answer to the Sphinx' riddle and yet failed to know himself, nor why Hamlet can only think in circles. It is as far as we can go for the moment to note, to ourselves and to our students, that science seems to be confirming models of reality established by artists long ago. These points of conjunction between art and science may ultimately prove to be a recognition of identical twinship or, if a persistent anti-art bias continues to infiltrate the argument, brain research may simply provoke a new version of the old sibling rivalry.

Thomas M. Lessl (essay date May 1985)

SOURCE: "Science and the Sacred Cosmos: The Ideological Rhetoric of Carl Sagan," in *Quarterly Journal of Speech*, Vol. 71, No. 2, May, 1985, pp. 175-87.

[*In the following essay, Lessl examines elements of religious discourse and rhetoric in Sagan's television program* Cosmos. *According to Lessl, Sagan's* Cosmos *provides "a mythic understanding of science which serves for television audiences the same needs that religious discourse has traditionally satisfied for churchgoers."*]

> A bomb outrage to have any influence on public opinion now must go beyond the intention of vengeance or terrorism. It must be purely destructive . . . . You anarchists should make it clear that you are perfectly determined to make a clean sweep of the whole social creation. But how to get that appallingly absurd notion into the heads of the middle classes so that there should be no mistake? That's the question . . . . A bomb in the National Gallery would make some noise. But it would not be serious enough. Art has never been their fetish . . . . But there is learning—science. Any imbecile that has got an income believes in that. He does not know why, but he believes it matters somehow. It is the sacrosanct fetish.
>
> —Joseph Conrad, *The Secret Agent*

The sanctity of science in modern society is perhaps greater than that observed by Conrad's fictional anarchist seventy years ago. Like the archetypal Sky Father of primitive religion, who in his union with Earth Mother brought forth the sustenance of life, science as the great modern provider is likely to be deified by the society reaping its benefits. But like other sacred objects, science is a symbol of both hope and despair. American society wavers between regarding modern science as Prometheus and as Pandora.

Although science's privileged status may result from the material benefits it affords, in many situations scientists find it expedient actively to promote their status. In such cases the intermingling of scientific and cultural symbols produces a rhetoric often more characteristic of religious than scientific discourse.

A particularly useful example is the popular television series *Cosmos,* written and narrated by Carl Sagan, professor of Astronomy and Space Sciences at Cornell University. *Cosmos* does not easily fit any of the descriptions previously set forth in the science-as-rhetoric literature. Clearly targeted for nonscientists, it seems to have only minimal concern for maintaining scientific integrity. While it bears marks of science journalism, *Cosmos* also seems not to be bothered by journalistic standards of neutrality; it is at times plainly polemic. While in the genre common to previous expeditions into science education by public television, *Cosmos* is a hybrid generic form; it sets the instructional elements of the series within a larger mythical framework reminiscent of numerous works of science fiction. This presentation of science, I believe, creates a mythic understanding of science which serves for television audiences the same needs that religious discourse has traditionally satisfied for churchgoers.

> **While in the genre common to previous expeditions into science education by public television, *Cosmos* is a hybrid generic form; it sets the instructional elements of the series within a larger mythical framework reminiscent of numerous works of science fiction.**
> —*Thomas M. Lessl*

Science is often carefully distinguished from religion, but this differentiation is much more the consequence of the history of the conflict between scientists and the church than a conflict inherent to science and religion. Indeed, science gained a good deal of momentum in previous centuries because it was regarded as a sub-branch of natural theology which, if properly executed, could reveal God in His creation. Until science was secularized in the late nineteenth century, it was legitimated both for scientists and for the public as an enactment of religious mission. Although modern scientists are less willing to justify their work as empirical support for theological positions, science must be legitimated by the institutional powers that allow its continuation. When scientific rhetoric satisfies religious impulses, as I shall argue is the case with *Cosmos,* it serves two purposes—the practical purposes of maintaining the privileged status of science in society and the religious purpose of grounding faith in an unimpeachable body of knowledge.

Science in the Public Realm

Four characteristics of rhetoric as defined by [Kenneth] Burke are particularly applicable to popular treatments of the brand of science seen in *Cosmos.* First, rhetoric is an attempt to create consubstantiality, a sense of shared substance. For the scientist, the need for identification with a nonscientific audience creates a rhetorical dilemma, because the material of science is intrinsically foreign to the uninitiated layman, and to step outside of science to find common ground is to betray the ethos of the scientific community. In this light, one should not be surprised to find the popularizer of science regarded by his professional peers as an outcast or heretic.

Second, the situation that brings forth rhetoric will always be characterized by divisions which occur at several levels. Scientists fight a continuous political battle over allocations of funds for research programs which are increasingly expensive, while numerous critics, Senator William Proxmire being most prominent, press scientists to make other than scientific justifications for their work. Scientists are also in perennial conflict with other interest groups over control of the educational system. A salient example is the most recent resurgence of arguments over whether the biblical story of creation should be given status in public schools equal to that of the scientific theory of evolution. This confrontation must be regarded as more than just a debate centering on the differences between science and religion. The educational system is the very lifeline of science; it is the means through which the scientific community renews and socializes its membership.

Such divisions are resolved, according to Burke, through a third characteristic of rhetoric—presentation of symbols of identification through which people can mediate reality and organize their actions. The artifacts of science sometimes become the symbols of nonscientific culture (as did the mammoth Saturn rockets of the national space program), but, for the most part, the machines of scientific research are not only revered but also regarded mysteriously by the uninitiated; moreover, they rarely serve as objects of identification. Science seems to be more successful with the general public when it uses its own natural objects of inquiry (stars, planets, galaxies, living organisms) as its symbols. Unlike technological artifacts, the natural objects of scientific inquiry already have a sacred quality for the public at large and can act as common symbols uniting science and society.

Fourth, in acting together, people share a common substance; they share common sensations, concepts, images, and ideas that unite them in attitude and spirit. Rhetoric that successfully mediates between science and society symbolically brings the layman into the scientific frame of mind. The lay person needs to view himself metaphorically, "as if" he were a scientist, just as the religious believer needs to see himself as saint-like, or the political activist as an important part of the electoral process. Since the nonscientist can only participate in a limited portion of the scientific enterprise, mediational rhetoric like *Cosmos* is likely to focus on the underlying values and premises guiding scientific research and to identify those values and premises with public needs. The particular attention paid by Sagan to instructing the audience in the ethos of science, attention which can be construed as a rhetorical attempt to establish a common ground, sets the series apart as an explicitly persuasive venture.

The particular attention paid by Sagan to instructing the audience in the ethos of science, attention which can be construed as a rhetorical attempt to establish a common ground, sets the series apart as an explicitly persuasive venture.
—*Thomas M. Lessl*

Cosmos, which as a television series is comparable only to Jacob Bronowski's *The Ascent of Man* after which it was modeled, is an ambitious attempt to bridge the division between the scientific community and the general public. With a budget of eight million dollars, it is the most expensive program in the history of public television. Sagan estimates that the series has been viewed by 140 million people worldwide since its first appearance in the fall of 1980, approximately three percent of the world's population. The series, which is the joint product of Sagan's own company (Carl Sagan Productions) and KCET-TV of Los Angeles, consists of thirteen one-hour episodes. While each of the episodes is self-contained and can be viewed meaningfully in isolation, there are numerous symbols and themes which acquire special meaning when the programs are viewed consecutively. As Carl Sagan has said, *Cosmos* is about science in the "broadest sense." Most fundamentally, it is an exploration of the methods and premises of science through a historical overview of science, through biographical vignettes of great scientists, and through speculations into the future of science. The thesis advanced by Sagan is that the scientific perspective, as a manner of perceiving the cosmos, is in fundamental harmony with nature itself. Sagan's concept of science as the "cosmic perspective," or natural way to knowledge, is developed as the series progresses through Sagan's various metaphoric elaborations of the concept of evolution.

Evolutionary Myth

Evolution, as the term is applied in *Cosmos,* might be best understood as an example of a world hypothesis or root metaphor. Just as in countless religions where human activities and experiences have divine archetypes in the eternal realm, so also in scientific messages such as *Cosmos* we find

that the activities and experiences of the scientist have an eternal paradigm, in this instance, cosmic evolution. Conformity to evolution is the defining quality of the scientific temperament, as demonstrated in Sagan's various biographical portrayals of notable scientists in the series. Conversely, Sagan attempts to show that the failure of various individuals and societies to surrender to the progressive movement of cosmic evolution accounts for human evils and, ultimately, for the potential extinction of the species. With evolution as the empirical basis for all values in *Cosmos,* scientists, as the individuals best equipped to understand and interpret evolution, become by implication both seers and saints. As seers, scientists hold the keys to all cosmic secrets, making the ways of evolutionary progress known to the human species. As saints, they are in closest touch with the evolutionary essence of the cosmos; they purify the human species by their redeeming presence among us, and as teachers they bring us closer to what will pass as ultimate.

The groundwork for Sagan's evolutionary mythology is laid in the second episode of the series, "One Voice in the Cosmic Fugue." Because so much is at stake (rhetorically and philosophically) with the evolutionary metaphor, Sagan spends a good deal of time reaffirming the soundness of evolutionary theory and refuting theistic notions of creation. While the validity of evolutionary theory is well established among most scientists, Sagan asserts flatly that "evolution is a fact, not a theory." Many scientists would privately agree with Sagan's statement, but within the world of scientific talk, such an assertion may be regarded as an heretical violation of the principle of falsification, and is therefore a patently unscientific statement. A factual treatment of evolutionary theory is, however, rhetorically important to the cosmic myth. By calling evolution fact, the process of evolution is removed from dispute; it is no longer merely a scientific construct, but now stands apart from humankind and its perceptual frailties. Sagan apparently wishes to accomplish what Peter Berger calls "objectification," the attribution of objective reality to a humanly produced concept. If Sagan's audience can accept the factuality of evolution, all the meanings that can thereafter be derived from evolutionary doctrine are likely to be taken as truths about the universe. The theory of evolution and the universe appear to be co-extensive.

With evolution no longer regarded as a mere human construct, but now as part of the natural order of the cosmos, evolution becomes a sacred archetype against which human actions can be weighed. Evolution is a sacred object or process in that it becomes endowed with mysterious and awesome power, a power distinct from, but yet related to, humankind. In Biblical and tribal religions, the co-extension of the human social world and the sacred cosmos was demonstrated through geneological tracings of the lineage of present members of the faith back through time to some ultimate beginning in sacred time. In this way the integrity and authority of the present social order is reaffirmed and legitimated as part of the natural order. Mircea Eliade would want to place evolution (as Sagan uses the term) outside the temporal cycles of time as a divine model within which the events or experiences of history are conceptualized. By placing history within cosmic evolution, Sagan in effect reidentifies it with nature, and thus stabilizes the transient and disordered events of the present within an eternal spectrum of evolution. The events of human history take on a new reality to the extent that they retrace natural evolutionary time.

Sagan makes his most explicit identification of scientific history and the eternal cosmic order in the second episode of **Cosmos.** Cosmic evolution, beginning with the "Big Bang," begets chemical evolution, which begets biological evolution, which begets human evolution, which begets scientific evolution. In such a progressive time spectrum, science is clearly made to stand at the pinnacle of history. Science is the crowning feature of evolution and is endowed with natural authority as the descendent of the cosmos. Just as the Church is regarded as the "body of Christ," and thus given its authority as the consubstantial representative of God on Earth, Sagan refers to science as the "way for the Cosmos to know itself." Scientists are the "eyes, and ears, thoughts and feelings of the Cosmos."

Neurological Hierarchy

Implicit in the "cosmization" of science is an epistemological chain-of-being rooted in the spectrum of evolution. Given its assumptions, some modes of consciousness are likely to be deemed superior to other ways of knowing because they are further along the evolutionary spectrum. The criterion for superior development is natural selection, the mechanism of evolution. Through natural selection the trait of the individual or group that is likely to allow that individual or group to survive is going to be passed on to future generations. With time, certain traits that were once serviceable for survival no longer contribute to evolutionary success. In a chain-of-being that places science at its forefront, scientific modes of thought are consequently valued and prescientific ways of thinking are regarded as deleterious to survival, if not merely obsolete. In human terms, then, conformity to scientific modes of thought becomes the standard against which good and evil are defined.

The moral superiority of science is illustrated in "The Persistence of Memory," the eleventh episode of **Cosmos,** where Sagan outlines an evolutionary model of the brain borrowed from biologist Paul MacLean. According to this model, the brain is divided into three parts which are hierarchically ordered on the basis of evolutionary age. The oldest portion, the R-complex or "reptilian brain," is the part responsible for what Sagan suggests are our more sinister propensities:

"Aggression, ritual, territoriality, and social hierarchy." The R-complex is, for Sagan, a scientific version of original sin. The second part of the brain, the limbic system, inherited from our mammal ancestors, brings both good and bad. Sagan attributes to this part of the brain "our concern and care for the young," but also "moods and emotions" that obscure our rationality. The newest part of the brain, the cerebral cortex, is the seat of art and science, "the point of embarkation for all our cosmic journeys." The cerebral cortex is the biological counterpart to science, which Sagan depicts as a great library filled with loose leaf notebooks to which humans can add and subtract knowledge.

In telling his tale, Sagan is teaching more than a science lesson. His moral becomes quickly apparent. In contrast to the unlimited logicality and flexibility of the cerebrum, Sagan depicts the lower portions of the brain, "the brain's basement," as dangerously rigid, an unfortunate inheritance of outdated evolutionary "baggage":

> Emotions and ritual behavior patterns are built very deeply into us. They're part of our humanity, but they're not characteristic of the human. Many other animals have feelings. What distinguishes our species is thought. The cerebral cortex is a way of liberation. We need no longer be trapped in the genetically inherited behavior patterns of lizards and baboons, territoriality and aggression and dominance hierarchies. We are, each of us, largely responsible for what gets put into our brain, for what we as adults want to end up caring for and knowing about. No longer at the mercy of the reptile brain, we can change ourselves. Think of the possibilities.

The inherent rectitude of the scientific mindset seems to be implied by this hierarchical view of the brain, as well as a corresponding sinfulness in what is less than scientific. Sagan depicts science as standing at the apex of evolutionary history; anything that is unscientific is anachronistic. Since the cerebral cortex is capable of liberating the individual from the bondages of the lower parts of the brain, science, as the outward expression of the cerebrum, is the way of salvation from the various human propensities for self-destruction that arise from the primitive brain and its corresponding political, religious, and social manifestations. The failure of humans to order their behavior according to this evolutionary hierarchy is the fundamental Saganian version of the fall of man.

The condition of the human species, as portrayed by Sagan, is one of evolutionary crisis brought about by the failure of the cerebral portion of the triune brain completely to subjugate the lower portions of the brain. This understanding of the human condition is implicit in Sagan's analogous comparison of these three brain systems to the evolution of modern systems of urban transportation. In the technological evolution of transportation systems, an older, outdated transit system will continue to operate during the construction (evolution) of a new system meant to replace the old, because the city (organism) cannot shut down during construction. Similarly, Sagan imagines, during the evolution of the cerebral cortex, it was necessary that the lower portions of the brain continue to function in order that the species would survive. Because of this, the lower brain portions survive, by Sagan's suggestion, as vestigial organs which must now be brought into submission to the completed cerebral cortex. If left in operation the old parts of the brain will conflict with the smooth operation of the new parts, just as an old transit system might compete with a new system.

The fact that this mandated neurological order is incomplete, finds expression throughout *Cosmos* in Sagan's dramatic depictions of scientific history as an epic of ongoing conflict between science and its subcortical competitors—"territoriality, and aggression, and dominance hierarchies." This depiction of the human dilemma is nowhere more clear than in Sagan's discussion of ancient Greco-Roman society, a civilization which Sagan compares to our own as having great scientific potential, but which may fail because of the reptilian influence. The villains of this drama are not the demonic emperors of Rome, nor its citizens, but the scientists, Plato, Pythagoras, and Aristotle, who in their contempt for the public, for experiment, and for applications of science that would serve the masses, showed the residual reptilian influences in themselves. These scientists were unable to raise the public consciousness above mysticism and superstition. Consequently, Sagan reminds us, it was the unenlightened masses who came to burn the great Alexandrian library which, for Sagan, is the key symbol of all ancient and modern learning.

Sagan's lesson is clear. Science is a redemptive enterprise, which, if turned rhetorically upon the public, can elevate society above the neurological conflict that led to the stagnation of Ionian science, and ultimately ancient civilization. Two thousand years later, the costs of this stagnation are magnified for Sagan, who believes that if the more empirically and experimentally-oriented scientists of Ionia had won out over Plato, Pythagoras, and Aristotle, our civilization might now be "going to the stars."

Scientific Teleology

Thus far, I have attempted to show how evolutionary thinking serves as Sagan's justification for the privileged hierarchical position of science in the cosmic scheme, and how it provides a basis for understanding the problem of evil and the related goodness of the scientific way. Evolution also operates as the scientific grounding for Sagan's teleological vision in which humankind comes to know itself through a full knowledge of the cosmos.

Throughout *Cosmos,* when Sagan speaks about his most fundamental premises, we find a man who fits very well into the scientific traditions of rationality and skepticism. When the subject matter is orthodox scientific theory, Sagan is hesitant to accept any argument on faith, or to ascribe other than natural causes to any phenomenon. Here Sagan seldom diverges in his description from the dominant mechanistic model of nature. But this is Sagan the scientist. When Sagan the cosmologist speaks, a different set of epistemic principles seems to be in force. Suddenly, through the subtle suggestiveness of metaphor, Sagan breathes life into the formerly dead machine universe, transforming it into a self-determining, purposive cosmos. The fact that this vitalism is given to nature through deliberate metaphor is important. The ambiguity of figurative speech allows Sagan the capacity to transgress the more rigid norms of scientific description. When Sagan refers to the early existence of a star as its "adolescence," he evokes a sense of being, and consequently purpose and meaning; but also, to the extent that he can be perceived as being "only figurative," he provides himself with a disclaimer against charges of being unscientific.

Two metaphors are of particular importance in Sagan's rhetoric. For ordinary scientific terms such as universe and evolution, Sagan substitutes the metaphors *ocean* and *voyage.* Sagan's use of the oceanic metaphor to stand, archetypally, for the scientific cosmos epitomizes the gradual reversal of the older meaning of the sea as chaos to its present more benevolent meanings. The sea is a useful scientific metaphor because of its essential connectedness to evolutionary theory, and because of the sense it has more recently achieved of being something conquerable. Translated into Sagan's cosmology, the universe becomes a familiar place, the evolutionary sea from which the human species comes. Perhaps more important, it is a sea which the human species can journey upon and thus control through science. Sagan's first episode, which is titled "The Shores of the Cosmic Ocean," reveals Sagan's representation of science as a journey occurring within the almost mystical scene of macrocosmic/microcosmic interplay:

> The surface of the earth is the shore of the cosmic ocean. From it we have learned most of what we know. Recently, we have waded a little way out, maybe ankle deep, and the water seems inviting. Some part of our being knows this is where we came from. We long to return, and we can, because the cosmos is also within us. We are made of star stuff. We are a way for the cosmos to know itself.

In certain respects Sagan's image of the human as the microcosmic reflection of the cosmos is a naturalistic version of the Judeo-Christian idea of man created in the image of God. In both cases the belief in a fundamental identity with some absolute entity obliges the individual to behave in accordance with the character of that entity. Since the character of Sagan's cosmos is evolutionary, the appropriate business of the human species is science which actively carries on the evolutionary work of the cosmos. Sagan's journey is thus a sacred voyage, a pilgrimage to the place of our origins and beyond.

Sagan's metaphor of scientific journey would also have us draw literal parallels between science, especially space exploration, and historic seafaring. Perhaps desiring to lend support to the scientific crusade of space exploration, Sagan depicts space travel as a continuation of the oceanic exploration of past centuries, which he regards as a scientific enterprise. Sagan depicts the seventeenth century Dutch Republic, which combined a vigorous program of marine exploration with its pluralistic capitalism, as the ideal model of a scientific society. Sagan asserts that it cost the Dutch more to finance explorations in the Far East then it presently costs to send robot explorers to nearby planets. But because this society respected knowledge more than material gain, Sagan would have us believe, the Dutch Republic flourished economically. Sagan's lesson is clear: science is productive of economic and social health. By implicit contrast, current politicians who see money spent on scientific research as wasteful are a threat not only to science, but also to modern civilization as well. Again, science is depicted by Sagan as the redemptive means of humankind.

The decision to follow a vigorous program of scientific research is more than a matter of economic prosperity; for Sagan it is a question of survival. In "Who Speaks for Earth," the final episode of *Cosmos,* he envisions the human race standing at an intersection of choice similar to, but more severe than, that faced by the ancient Greeks, of whether to pursue science in its purity or to regress as the ancients did into subservience to the reptilian brain. The choice is not between alternative policies, but between right and wrong, knowledge and ignorance, progress or retrogression.

Like much of biblical prophecy, Sagan's prophetic vision in the final segment offers two perspectives: one of optimism and human redemption through a new scientific consciousness of cosmic citizenship, and one of apocalyptic doom through nuclear self-destruction. In presenting this message, Sagan adopts two of the rhetorical conventions of the traditional seer. First, Sagan identifies his message literally as a nightmare he once experienced. As such the message takes on a meaning of its own, as if it did not come from Carl Sagan but was passed on to him through inspiration from without. Second, Sagan adopts the perspective of extraterrestrial beings he imagines inhabiting the universe, and

whom he also imagines to be morally superior to ourselves. In taking this perspective, Sagan is doing something rhetorically similar to the biblical prophet who, after uttering a moral rebuke to the people of Israel pronounces, "Thus says the Lord." Sagan gives divine authority to his analysis of the human situation by confidently attributing his own opinions to extraterrestrials who act as the scientific equivalent of deity.

In the dramatization of his vision, Sagan takes his audience, via cinematic illusion, to the outskirts of a distant planet inhabited by an advanced civilization much like our own. Though the inhabitants of this planet have the qualifications to move up the evolutionary ladder into "cosmic citizenship," they instead destroy themselves before Sagan's eyes with their own technology. Horrified, Sagan decides to return to his own planet Earth, only to find that it has also self-destructed. Sagan goes on to ponder the causes and consequences of this human tragedy from his vantage point in space as a failure to follow the scientific way:

> There would be no more big questions, no more answers, never again a love for a child, no descendants to remember us and be proud, no more voyages to the stars, no more songs from the Earth. I saw East Africa, and thought: a few million years ago we humans took our first steps there. Our brains grew and changed; the old parts began to be guided by the new parts, and this made us human, with compassion, foresight, and reason. But instead we listened to that reptilian voice within us, counseling fear, territoriality, and aggression. We accepted the products of science; we rejected its methods.

Taking the judgmental mantle of the extraterrestrial, Sagan elevates himself into the prophetic office, and makes his own view of the human situation appear to be transcendent of localized considerations. As I noted previously, Sagan makes his own beliefs seem to come from some authoritative consciousness outside himself:

> How would we explain all this to a dispassionate extraterrestrial observer? What account would we give of our stewardship of the planet Earth? We have heard the rationales offered by the super powers. We know who speaks for the nations, but who speaks for the human species? Who speaks for Earth? From an extraterrestrial perspective our global civilization is clearly on the edge of failure in the most important task it faces, preserving the lives and well-being of its citizens and the future inhabitability of the planet.

For Sagan, the tragedy of potential human extinction is magnified beyond its already unfathomable scope because it is not only the destruction of the human species but also the "waste of four billion years of cosmic evolution." Thus, to allow our species to die would be a great disservices to the cosmos that formed us, since we, as cosmic matter raised to consciousness through science, are the only way for the cosmos to come to know itself. The moral imperative of *Cosmos* is to think and act scientifically. This ethic is most clearly expressed in the final utterance of the series: "Our obligation to survive and flourish is owed, not just to ourselves, but to that Cosmos, ancient and vast, from which we spring."

Implications

The inherent religiosity of *Cosmos* can best be accounted for if we view it within the context of a larger, more complex rhetorical situation. In the broadest historical spectrum, *Cosmos* represents an attempt to restore or to replace a culturally based scientific ethos that was originally rooted in Western religion, but gradually eroded as science became increasingly secularized in the last two hundred years.

In its history, science cannot be thought of as an expression of individual cognition or personal expertise carried out in remote isolation from social or political concerns. Science is best conceived in history as a social achievement built upon cooperative effort and sustained by the coordination of scientific and unscientific concerns. While science had its earliest inception on the mainland of Europe through Galileo and Descartes, it was in Protestant England that science seems to have taken a permanent hold, not because of some special quality of mind possessed by the British, but because of a visionary rhetoric linking scientific enterprise to the Christian mission. From the pulpits of several upper class London churches of the seventeenth century, science was preached as a weapon against the growing threat of atheism and deism, as means of positive proof of God's existence, and as the means to carry out the millennial programs of Christendom. In England, a firm foundation was constructed for modern science. Instead of being the esoteric concern of a handful of academics, science became the champion of a larger body of socially and politically powerful individuals.

At our end of the spectrum of modern scientific history stands *Cosmos,* a contemporary attempt to fill a vacuum left by the gradual erosion of the previous religious understandings of science's place in the unfolding human destiny. Like the formerly predominant theistic justifications for science, *Cosmos* is an attempt to ground science in a higher order, to place science within the realm of the sacred, and consequently to remove it from the banalities of profane existence. By speaking the words of science in a sacral mode, Sagan is responding to an enduring human need that spans not only the history of science but also human history: the need to make what is human more than human, to make the deeds of humans the deeds of the gods, to make the order of human society the order of the universe, and the hopes of the species the purposes of nature. Sagan's rhetoric is representative of what Stephen Toulmin has identified as the new cosmology, which, modifying the tradition of intellectual detachment science inherited from Cartesian dualism, reunites natural science with natural religion, giving science a voice in how humans define themselves in the greater order of things.

Unlike the previous theistic rationale for science, *Cosmos* is grounded in a naturalistic understanding of reality, making Sagan's religious thinking more akin to the Eastern tradition and the pre-Christian roots of Western culture than to that of the Protestant forbearers of modern science. And, in fact, when Sagan chooses to make explicit connections between his vision of science and religion, it is with Eastern religious thought that Sagan identifies. But while *Cosmos* is rhetoric stemming primarily from a naturalistic model, the values that dominated the older theistic vision of science still persist, albeit in different form. *Cosmos* might be best seen as lying in the intersection of two worldviews, one the theistic perspective that shaped early modern science but that has since gradually declined, and the other a kind of naturalism which was previously implicit in the scientific perspective, but now repeatedly comes to the surface. From the millennialism of the old theistic vision *Cosmos* inherits its preoccupation with progress as a value, and inherits the underlying sense of purpose it projects into the cosmos. From the naturalistic vision *Cosmos* brings to the viewer a sense of the relatedness between the human species and the universe, a relatedness which manifests itself in ecological values of self-preservation and respect for nature. These two fundamental visions of purpose and interrelatedness are the interpretations of a sacred text composed chiefly of evolutionary materials from within science rather than from an external text, as was the case with previous attempts to align science with popular beliefs. In the light of *Cosmos,* Richard Weaver's claim of pre-eminence for the god-term of "progress" is somewhat antiquated. If *Cosmos* is reflective of the current scientism of our society, we must recognize the equal status of a set of terms encircling a god-term of "adaptiveness."

After a lapse of about eighty years or more in which popular justifications for science were political and practical rather than religious, *Cosmos* represents a return to a religious rhetoric of science. This singular, but widely popular rhetoric, may represent a fundamental difficulty the scientific community faces in its interface with the nonscientific public. The increasing sophistication of scientific research places greater pressure on scientists to justify their demands for the funding of work that, while enormously expensive, is also increasingly difficult for the nonscientific public to understand and therefore appreciate. Simultaneous with the increasing financial demands that science makes on the American public is a growing moral distrust of science. A recent study by the National Science Foundation shows a rising uneasiness with science since 1957 when public support of science was boosted by the political ramifications of Sputnik. Among individuals attentive to science in the period between 1957 and 1979, the belief that the benefits of scientific research outweigh the harmful results declined from 96 to 90 percent. Among the nonattentive public the decline was from 87 to 66 percent. More significant perhaps is the rising belief that scientific discoveries tend to break down people's ideas of right and wrong. Among those who are attentive to science this belief increased during that twenty-two year period from 11 percent to 27 percent. Among the general public the increase is more alarming, from 24 percent in 1957 to 42 percent in 1979.

The popular distrust of science reflected in these figures is not a new development. Every generation has its own versions of the Faustian legend, but the contemporary versions are fueled by a new sense of mortality increasingly making its way into the human consciousness in the aftermath of Hiroshima and Nagasaki. The scientist of popular drama is more often than not a tragic figure, a sorcerer's apprentice who freely invents, but who cannot control, the magic of his inventions. It is not scientists and science so much that people fear, but that scientists and everyone along with them will become the victims of scientific inventions. Science in the midst of a world it has technologized faces a great moral quandary. As the edifice of scientific achievements rises to the heavens, so also does the length of its shadow stretch across the earth. Science not only taught us how to systematize production, but also how to systematize the extermination of a whole people. Science not only gave the world medicine to prolong life, but also the possibility for greater numbers to starve. Science not only brought the mysteries of the atom to light, but also the atomic technology that darkens our future. Science not only empowers all that is good in the human character, but also brutality, self-indulgence, and arrogance.

The moral neutrality that scientists wish to claim for their work does not obtain in the public world where the artificial distinction between scientific work and its consequences becomes invisible. But as these consequences become more apparent, a rhetoric of science that is successfully to maintain a working relationship with the larger public that supports science must respond to the moral meanings of science in the world. Such a response moves scientific discourse from its traditional realm of the epistemic into the realm of the ethical, which means in effect into the narrative arena of public dialogue. Carl Sagan's *Cosmos* is one instance of this transformation. As an attempt to portray science as a righteous force, as a holy movement culminating in the cos-

mic drama, Sagan projects a moralistic vision of science, a theodicy vindicating the ethical integrity of the scientific way. As such, as communication not just about what is and is not but also about what is good and bad, *Cosmos* has its rhetorical roots in the traditions of religious discourse as much as in the scientific.

Len Ackland (review date 6 January 1991)

SOURCE: "Chilly Scenes of Nuclear Winter," in *The New York Times Book Review,* January 6, 1991, p. 7.

[*In the following review, Ackland offers praise for* A Path Where No Man Thought.]

At their summit meeting in February, Presidents George Bush and Mikhail Gorbachev are scheduled to sign the Strategic Arms Reduction Treaty (START). That will be a good step toward disarmament and many people are bound to reckon that the threat of a global nuclear catastrophe has died with the cold war. But, in fact, the risk is far from gone.

In *A Path Where No Man Thought* Carl Sagan and Richard Turco, who were on the scientific team that devised the concept of nuclear winter, remind us that the risks of nuclear war, even of a relatively "small" one, are unacceptably high. Given the possibility of nuclear winter—the "darkening, cooling, enhanced radioactivity, toxic pollution, and ozone depletion" that would follow a nuclear holocaust—the authors note that the reliable prevention of nuclear war still "deserves by far the highest priority of all the entries on the policymaker's agenda" despite the lessened tension between the superpowers.

This book, regardless of its awkward title, is a valuable updating of the scientific and policy controversies that have surrounded the concept of nuclear winter since Mr. Sagan, Mr. Turco and three of their colleagues, Brian Toon, Tom Ackerman and Jim Pollack, introduced it in the journal *Science* in December 1983.

The original analysis of nuclear winter followed a 1982 study by Paul Crutzen and John Birks, published in the Swedish journal *Ambio,* in which they analyzed the atmospheric effects of the enormous quantities of smoke that would be generated by nuclear war. To this analysis the Turco and Sagan team added the idea that the smoke would lead to a severe temperature drop on the earth's surface. And they used dozens of different war scenarios to calculate the magnitude and duration of the cooling. Their most startling conclusion, which has been fundamentally upheld in subsequent studies by many other scholars, is that a nuclear war involving hundreds of warheads (in a world where more than 50,000 now exist) could bring on a nuclear winter, under certain conditions.

Here Mr. Sagan, a professor of astronomy at Cornell University and the creator of the television series **Cosmos,** and Mr. Turco, a professor of atmospheric sciences at the University of California, Los Angeles, repeatedly delineate where scientific facts end and considered speculation begins. "In this book, we do not claim that a given sort of nuclear war will inevitably produce a given severity of nuclear winter; the irreducible uncertainties are too large for that," they write. "What we do claim is that the most likely consequences of many kinds of nuclear war constitute climatic and environmental catastrophes much worse than the worst our species has ever encountered—and that prudent national policy should treat nuclear winters as a probable outcome of nuclear war."

The obvious, and unfortunately unrealistic, way to avert nuclear winter is to completely abolish nuclear weapons. But even though nuclear war can't be made impossible, Mr. Sagan and Mr. Turco argue that nuclear winter can be. This can be accomplished by reducing "the nuclear arsenals to levels at which threshold quantities of smoke cannot be generated, no matter how a nuclear war is 'fought' or who is in charge of the nuclear-armed nations."

Members of the progressive arms control community, such as the physicist Frank von Hippel, have long argued that nuclear arsenals should be drastically cut to some small number of invulnerable strategic weapons that would deter nuclear attack by insuring a devastating retaliatory strike. To this idea of a "minimum deterrence," Mr. Sagan and Mr. Turco add the goal of insuring against nuclear winter and thus come up with the term "minimum sufficient deterrence." They figure that the United States and the Soviet Union should have no more than 100 to 300 strategic warheads each, and that other states with nuclear weapons should reduce their arsenals too. The last third of the book focuses on how we might reach these goals.

The authors admit that their plans for minimum sufficient deterrence "are rough sketches only, intended to stimulate and encourage better artists and draftsmen." And their humility is warranted, for as they stray into the morass of weapons and strategies, more and more muck sticks to their arguments. For example, even while they advocate cutting strategic weapons to about 2 percent of their current number, the authors equivocate on calling for an immediate comprehensive nuclear test ban that would curtail new weapon development.

I was disappointed that only one of the book's 22 short chapters (each of which is supplemented by lots of sidebars) was devoted to the problems of proliferation. Given the increasing possibility of regional nuclear wars between rivals such as India and Pakistan or between various countries in the Middle East, there should have been a more complete discussion of the nuclear winter scenarios that would result from such conflicts. Another weakness of the book is the authors' propensity to understate the role that factors other than nuclear winter have played in changing the world's attitudes toward nuclear weapons and policies during the past seven years. Did the nuclear freeze movement have no part? Was the emergence of Mikhail Gorbachev so insignificant?

Such blemishes do not, however, negate this book's value and timeliness. It is an important reminder that much remains to be done before we can scratch the danger of catastrophic nuclear war from the top of the human agenda.

Alan Robock (review date March 1991)

SOURCE: "The Imparsible Dream?," in *Bulletin of the Atomic Scientists,* Vol. 47, No. 2, March, 1991, pp. 43-4.

[*In the following review, Robock offers praise for* A Path Where No Man Thought.]

Soon after the theory of nuclear winter was published, Carl Sagan gave a briefing on the subject on Capitol Hill. Sagan described how, after a nuclear war, the thick smoke from burning cities and industrial plants would block out so much sunlight that the earth's surface would become cold and dark. Agriculture would be impossible for years and most of the world's population would starve to death. After his presentation, one member of the audience called him aside. "Carl," he said, "if you think the mere threat of the end of the world is enough to change the way people in Washington and Moscow think, you clearly haven't spent enough time in either place."

Yet Sagan and coauthor Richard Turco are still determined to change the way people think. The first two-thirds of *A Path Where No Man Thought* is a description of the theory of nuclear winter for the nonscientist. The authors describe the climate system and the nuclear arsenal, and compare the effects of cities burning from non-nuclear causes, such as the 1906 San Francisco earthquake and the fire bombings of World War II, to the nuclear-ignited fires at Hiroshima and Nagasaki. They review climate model calculations and describe the effects of cooling caused by natural events such as forest fires and volcanic dust clouds, a memorable example of which occurred in 1816, the "year without a summer" following the eruption of Tambora in Indonesia.

Sagan and Turco, both prominent scientists, urge that for reasons of strategic stability, economic progress, and the threat of nuclear winter, the global nuclear arsenal should be reduced from its current level—approximately 50,000 warheads—to 300. Three hundred warheads would provide what they call "Minimum Sufficient Deterrence" (MSD). At such a level, they argue, stable deterrence is possible, yet no combination of computer failures, accidents, miscalculations, or insanity in high office could create a nuclear winter that would kill billions of people. The authors see MSD as only a step toward the goal of a world completely free of nuclear weapons.

Their continuing crusade also raises the issue of scientists' responsibility to society when, in the course of their investigations, they discover great dangers. In 1984, at one of the first conferences on nuclear winter, at the National Academy of Sciences, a scientist from Lawrence Livermore National Laboratory told me he thought that responsibility ended with the publication of results in scientific journals, and that it was up to the experts in politics to deal with the implications of those results. My response to such statements is that nuclear arsenals exist precisely because experts have been running things.

Sagan and Turco point out that scientists have been rewarded for creating weapons of mass destruction, but when they warn of the weapons' dangers, as Leo Szilard did in 1945, they have been ignored or considered unpatriotic. Still, the authors hope to enlist others in the effort. "It's hard to think of more worthy work. We hope that many established scholars, but particularly large numbers of young people, will consider devoting a part of their lives to finding the path" to an MSD regime, they write.

The theory of nuclear winter has provided a new context in which to examine existing assumptions about nuclear war. And that reexamination happened only because scientists tried to warn the world of the current policies' dangers. The world seems to be a much safer place than it was in 1982 and 1983 when the first nuclear winter papers were published. It is difficult to know how much of this change was induced by the theory of nuclear winter, although some future historian may be able to tell us. Certainly, the inclusion of the concept of nuclear winter in the speeches of Mikhail Gorbachev, the prime architect of improved East-West relations, suggests that it has played a part. The Cold War is over, but the arms race continues. Perhaps the ideas in this book will inspire continued progress toward a safer, more peaceful world.

Rudy Abramson (review date 15 January 1995)

SOURCE: "Light-Years from Home," in *New York Times Book Review,* January 15, 1995, pp. 12-13.

[*In the following excerpt, Abramson gives a favorable assessment of* Pale Blue Dot.]

Carl Sagan became a consultant to the National Aeronautics and Space Administration when it was still in its formative stage. During the more than three decades since, he has briefed astronauts for journeys to the moon, helped resolve some of the most intriguing mysteries about Mars and Venus and reigned as one of the principal gurus of planetary exploration.

Though honored for both public service and scientific achievement, Mr. Sagan is more renowned as a popularizer of space exploration. In 1978 he was awarded a Pulitzer Prize for his book *The Dragons of Eden.* In *Pale Blue Dot* he returns to familiar topics: the origin of the universe, the birth of the solar system, the development of life on Earth, the evolution and demise of stars and the prospect of life elsewhere among the galaxies. But this time he struggles to define a future for the human species after Earth, our "pale blue dot," and the rest of the solar system have met destruction in the dying throes of the sun.

Mr. Sagan's book offers lavish illustrations—telescopic images, pictures from robot space vehicles and paintings executed so perfectly as to be mistakable for the stunning photographs. With them, he marshals revelations by numerous planetary probes, especially two Voyager spacecraft now plunging through the Milky Way. Launched in 1977, the Voyager robots brushed past Jupiter and Saturn, and Voyager 2 went on to the neighborhood of Uranus and Neptune before heading out of the solar system. Together, they have sent back the equivalent of a 100,000-volume encyclopedia, Mr. Sagan says, including photographs of the two distant planets that previously had been nothing more than fuzzy dots taunting astronomers.

Unfortunately, the awe-inspiring work of the repaired Hubble Space Telescope is not included in *Pale Blue Dot.* More than Voyager, Mariner, Galileo or any of the planetary explorers, Hubble's recent discoveries have advanced what Mr. Sagan persuasively presents as the fundamental achievement of space science and exploration: humanity's changing perception of the universe and, consequently, of itself. The perception is still changing slowly, despite three decades of planetary probes and the tentative beginnings of human flight into space. But, after looking back to the humbling discovery that Earth is not the center of the universe and tracing the revelation of the cosmos as we know it today, Mr. Sagan soars to an inspirational, and evidently serious, conclusion that "a central element of the human future lies far beyond the Earth" and even beyond the solar system and our corner of the Milky Way.

People alive today may someday walk on Mars and on the

asteroids near Earth. Extrapolating recent advances in technology, Mr. Sagan concludes that within a few centuries space vehicles may be able to travel near the speed of light. And, hundreds of generations into the future, he believes, their passengers will have evolved into a species significantly different from 20th-century earthlings.

"But unless we destroy ourselves first," he predicts, "we will be inventing new technologies as strange to us as *Voyager* might be to our hunter-gatherer ancestors. . . . In time, the designs will become more elegant, more affordable, more efficient. The day will come when we overcome the necessity of jumping from comet to comet. We will begin to soar through the light-years and, as St. Augustine said of the gods of the ancient Greeks and Romans, colonize the sky."

Mr. Sagan confesses that he argued with himself on the way to his remarkably optimistic prediction that humanity will one day travel beyond the solar system, colonize other worlds and perhaps even make contact with civilizations from other planetary systems. And well he might. Human space flight has enjoyed an uncertain beginning.

Although the Apollo moon landing project generated the enthusiasm and Federal appropriations that made robot missions to the planets possible, the project was the result of cold war competition, not a love of science or exploration. The space shuttle program has never been altogether certain of its objectives, nor has the much-debated and redesigned international space station.

When the Bush Administration offered a human mission to Mars as the next great American space objective, the idea was greeted with little enthusiasm from Capitol Hill or the public. Such an expedition, Mr. Sagan concludes, "is now probably too expensive for any one nation to pull off by itself," even if that were an appropriate national undertaking.

Not only is human flight expensive, but space accidents in the United States and the former Soviet Union have proved the enterprise to be dangerous by its very nature. And in the United States, there has been little political tolerance for accidents. . . .

Mr. Sagan nominates the scientists and engineers who designed, built and operated the Voyager spacecraft as "role models for an America seeking excellence and international competitiveness," recommending that they be honored on postage stamps. Many of those involved in the Apollo program would echo that recommendation for Mr. Lovell's crew and the Mission Control team that got them back. Nearly 25 years later, the aborted moon landing mission is still widely remembered as NASA's finest moment.

Phillip Morrison (review date May 1995)

SOURCE: "Candid Camera," in *Scientific American,* Vol. 272, No. 5, May, 1995, pp. 106-7.

[*In the following review, Morrison offers praise for* Pale Blue Dot, *concluding that "no recent book has done better at making plain the subtle nature and fascination of scientific investigation."*]

This book opens with a generous gift to us all. It was made early in 1990, when the space probe *Voyager* completed its scripted dozen-year tour of duty. Well beyond Neptune and far north of the plane of the solar system, the craft received a final set of new commands, no part of the original mission. Look back, *Voyager,* to the now distant inner planets! Carl Sagan and a few others had argued and waited years for the Jet Propulsion Laboratory and NASA to schedule a shoestring effort to snap just one candid portrait of the earth among the planets. They succeeded brilliantly.

The spacecraft recorded a mosaic of 60 frames, planets against the sky. It sent the bits to far-off earth; that slow video transmission from past its design range took three months. The four planets in clear view would at best be mere dots of light. (The glare of the sun only six light-hours away from the camera masked nearby Mercury. Pluto and Mars happened to be poorly placed. Uranus and Neptune were so faint that they required long exposure; they could not help themselves from moving, so their images are streaked.) Our earth entire is seen as one bright bluish dot in the image that faces the title page.

The cloud-and-sea-marked blue marble we know well from closer space views dwindled to a featureless dot once the telescopic camera was carried a few thousand times farther away. The earth was for the first time put into the same perspective as the other planets in the sky. In 1957 a metal ball from a human workshop had been set into the heavens; mere speed transformed it into something celestial, "shining, circular, and perpetual" in orbit. Aristotle was denied and Newton confirmed. One after another the planets became close-up scenes, real places, a red Mars landscape looking not unlike the Arizona desert. Here they are at last as wandering stars: the earth, too.

Anyone can now *see* at once that Copernicus was right. The earth is only one planet among planets; blue, yes, but then icy Neptune is blue as well. Sagan eloquently draws an inference about this our home. "On it everyone you love . . . every human being who ever was, lived out their lives . . . Every hunter and forager, every hero and coward, every creator and destroyer of civilization. . . . Every saint and sinner in the history of our species lived there—on a mote of dust suspended in a sunbeam."

Around us stretches a vast cosmic darkness, studded with countless pools of myriads of suns. Only the abstract laws of physics seem to bring any order; no Designer is visible, no Parent seen to care for us. Yet the universe of science is no petty place; it is dauntingly large, old, diverse, even humbling. A religion to match our awesome data, Sagan thinks, may someday emerge. We are not center stage. "We have not been given the lead in the cosmic drama. Perhaps someone else has. Perhaps no one else has . . . a good reason for humility." The self-serving conclusion is what the author mistrusts above all.

After this high thinking, Sagan catches his readers up in a dozen exciting, personal, even audacious reviews of what we have found and may yet seek in space. Colorful and fresh space images are plentiful in these pages, along with paintings, diagrams, maps and some graphs, but no equations at all. Many of these treat issues Sagan has been close to. Here he is more than an author; he is an original researcher, articulate and engaged.

A sample of three out of many rich topics will have to suffice. One is a witty little essay. The French use a mild expletive, *sacre-bleu*. Translate it: Good heavens! Like our "geez," it is a euphemism for invoking Deity. The earth's distant signature is that sacred blue. Yet just outside the air, astronauts see a black sky with stars, even in sunlight. All airless moons and asteroids share black skies.

Molecular light scattering from the density fluctuations of any molecule is preferentially blue; what scatters is removed from the direct path, so that the long low light of any sunset is rendered in red hues. Venus has an atmosphere so thick that down at ground level it is always sunset, as the sky color reported by the *Venera* landers confirms. The meager sky above the rusty deserts of Mars looks pale salmon, colored by the long-lasting residues of finest dust, stirred up into the high air by windstorms. The two giant planets are certainly dark at the prodigious depths of their atmospheres. All we see there from without is the cloud layers that lie highest. The unearthly blue skies of Neptune and Uranus are puzzling; easy answers do not appear quite to work. Does some unknown blue stuff lie there inside? *Sacre-jeune, sacre-rouge, sacre-noir!* For this reader, awe of plenitude arises from this game of words.

Are we alone in the Milky Way? The most ambitious of searches for radio signals from putative distant sharers of our own scientific curiosity has been pressed for seven years by Paul Horowitz of Harvard University; it was financed by private gift, largely from Steven Spielberg of *E.T.* The modest radio dish in use is surplus, but the student-built multichannel receiver is world class, automatically monitoring eight million simultaneous narrow-frequency channels.

Signals that rise far above the noise are the candidates for our attention and are tested for origin from interference or for electronic fault. A few are culled from 60 trillion observations over the entire sky. Not one of the finds repeats. One fact, says Sagan, co-author of the analysis, "sends a chill down my spine." Of the 11 best candidates, eight lie within or close to the band of the Milky Way, where most stars collect. A fair bet against that happening by chance should pay off at better than 100 to 1. Probably these are rare, nonrepeating chip errors; without repeats or other structure we remain ignorant and very properly withhold belief. We will keep on listening, now without federal support. "Science offers little in the way of cheap thrills. The standards of evidence are strict. But . . . they allow us to see far, illuminating even a great darkness."

This book glowingly communicates current wonders and large issues still ahead, like future "interplanetary violence" against the earth by collisions both random and intentional. It displays openly the hopes and judgments of one gifted, adept and devoted human being, surely sometimes right and sometimes wrong. No recent book has done better at making plain the subtle nature and the fascination of scientific investigation.

Arthur C. Clarke (review date June 1995)

SOURCE: A review of *Pale Blue Dot*, in *Sky & Telescope*, Vol. 89, No. 6, June, 1995, pp. 54-5.

[*In the following review, Clarke offers praise for* Pale Blue Dot, *but objects to Sagan's reference to Wernher von Braun as a "Nazi-American."*]

An honest reviewer must disclose any special interest, and in the case of this book I have several, starting with David Hardy's magnificent Marsscape on the dust jacket. A slightly different version appears on page 328, which was used for the jacket of my own book *The Snows of Olympus: A Garden on Mars*. Frankly, I'm not sure which I prefer: they're both beautiful, but there's a subtle distinction between the two paintings. Not only has the planet on the front of **Pale Blue Dot** been terra-formed, it's been mirror-imaged, presumably by rotation through the fourth dimension!

My friendship with Carl, who in Japan would be regarded as a national treasure, began more than 30 years ago. My account of our adventures at the 1964 New York World's Fair appears in Roddy McDowall's *Double Exposure: Take Three*. The book and TV series **Cosmos** still remain paragons of that difficult art, popular science presentation, and **Pale Blue Dot** is a worthy successor.

How I wish that the opening chapters—especially "The Great Demotions" and "A Universe Not Made for Us"—were required reading in all high schools! Despite the biblical promise: "Ye shall know the truth, and the truth shall set you free" (1 John 8:32), many people cannot face the truths of science that Carl so eloquently sets forth. Worse still, they may not even be able to hear them above the current babble of "new age" imbecilities and the megawatts of pious flimflam emitted by cynical—or ignorant—televangelists. Carl suggests, "A religion that stressed the magnificence of the Universe as revealed by modern science might be able to draw forth reserves of reverence and awe hardly touched by the conventional faiths. Sooner or later, such a religion will emerge." Perhaps. But would it be, like Buddhism, a religion without God?

Pale Blue Dot gives a fine survey of the great discoveries made during the (first) golden era of the space age and will help to keep up the spirits of those who are waiting impatiently for the second to begin. The numerous illustrations—who would have imagined, a generation ago, that such wonders would ever be revealed to us?—are so well reproduced that many, such as the Landsat or SPOT images of Earth, invite and even withstand examination with a magnifying glass. It will certainly be a surprise to most people to see that the U.S.-Mexican border is as prominent from space as it is in an atlas, owing to different agricultural practices.

By fortunate timing *Pale Blue Dot* has been able to take advantage of the most dramatic astronomical event in recorded history. The impact of Comet Shoemaker-Levy 9 on Jupiter is not only of great scientific interest, but it has also at last given an indisputable reason for developing advanced space technologies to protect our home from future cosmic bombardments. As Carl points out, hazards from comets and asteroids must apply to all planets, so no galactic civilization can be both long-lived and non-technical. "Their eventual choice, as ours, is spaceflight or extinction," he explains. I am glad that, despite more urgent and obvious problems, Congress has gotten the message—and I am flattered that NASA has adopted the name Spaceguard, which I proposed more than 20 years ago, for its planned survey of near-Earth threats.

Two other themes that this book discusses in considerable depth are terra-forming other planets (to make them more habitable) and the continuing search for extraterrestrial intelligence (SETI). Despite the ignorant hostility of some critics, it is difficult to imagine a more important quest. If SETI succeeds, it will give us some assurance that—despite the daily disasters on the evening TV news—intelligence does have survival value and is not an evolutionary aberration that dooms its possessors.

Unfortunately, I must end this review with a very serious

criticism. Although I can understand (and even share—I was in the V-2 rocket target area) the feelings of those who condemn anyone who ever helped the Third Reich, Carl does my late friend Wernher von Braun a grave injustice by referring to him as a "Nazi-American." Wernher's scarcely disguised contempt for the Nazis often put him in serious danger. He was probably lucky to have escaped execution after being arrested and jailed by Heinrich Himmler (who had earlier failed to win his support by conferring SS rank on him—this most unwelcome "honor" would have been suicidal to reject). As is recorded in fascinating detail in Ernst Stuhlinger and Frederick Ordway's definitive biography *Wernher von Braun: Crusader for Space,* Wernher agonized over the moral issues involved for the rest of his life. However, his position was no different from that of all patriotic scientists and engineers in time of war.

As Carl rightly says, von Braun "more than anyone else, actually took us into space." He was also a warm and delightful human being, sincerely admired by all those who knew and worked for him—whatever their national origins. I hope, therefore, that the next edition of *Pale Blue Dot* will rectify this posthumous insult to one of the greatest men of our age.

Francisco J. Ayala (review date 26 July 1996)

SOURCE: A review of *The Demon-Haunted World,* in *Science,* Vol. 273, No. 5274, July 26, 1996, pp. 442-43.

[*Below, Ayala presents a favorable review of* The Demon-Haunted World, *but disagrees with Sagan's reductionist view of scientific truth.*]

In 1961 while driving at night in the White Mountains, Betty and Barney Hill sighted a bright object in the sky that seemed to follow them. Fearing for their safety, they left the main highway and took narrow roads, arriving home two hours later than they had expected. The experience prompted Betty to read a book that described UFOs as spaceships navigated by little men from other worlds, who sometimes abducted humans. Soon thereafter, she began experiencing a repetitive nightmare in which she and Barney were abducted and taken aboard a UFO. In a few days they were describing a pancake-like UFO with uniformed figures visible through the craft's windows. This and other motifs of the Hills' account are similar to those found in the 1953 motion picture *Invaders from Mars.* Later, Barney described the enormous eyes of the aliens, just 12 days after aliens were so portrayed in an episode of the television series *The Outer Limits.* The Hills' story was made into a 1975 movie purporting that short, grey alien abductors are among us in the psyches of millions of people.

Carl Sagan tells that he met with the Hills for several hours, and writes: "There was no mistaking the earnestness and sincerity of Betsy and Barney, and their mixed feelings about becoming public figures." Nevertheless, there are many reasons to doubt that the events described by the Hills happened in the world outside their mental experience. Sagan pursues this and other case histories of a demon-haunted world with the sure-footedness of a well-informed observer, the narrative skills of an engaging raconteur, and the subtle destructiveness of an experienced educator.

We encounter the Man in the Moon, the Face of Mars, the Dragon in the Garage, and countless stories of UFO sightings, abductions by aliens, and miraculous apparitions. Sagan meticulously debunks each story by noting absence of verifiable information, uncovering suspicious coincidence of conditioning circumstances, and pursuing other lines of reasoning that would persuade an impartial reader that the claimed experiences resulted from dreams and hallucinations, rather than from events in the outside world. We are provided a long list of typical offerings at the table of pseudoscience and superstition: astrology, the Bermuda Triangle, Big Foot, the Loch Ness monster, extrasensory perception, bleeding statues, divining rods, pyramidology, palmistry, numerology, faith-healers, Ouija boards, and much more.

Sagan tackles antiscience, in addition to pseudoscience. Science has been under attack for centuries, he proclaims. The nemeses of our time are postmodernists and deconstructionists (he does not use the latter term) who deny the objectivity of science. "Some even allege," he laments, "it's entirely subjective, as is, they say, history." Sagan sees that historical accounts are often self-promotional; what really happened is colored by subjective biases. Scientists also have biases and breathe the prevailing prejudices of their environment. But science is a collective enterprise endowed with the error-correcting process of empirical testing. In science, "you can rerun the event as many times as you like, examine it in new ways, test a wide range of alternative hypotheses." Scientists are biased and commit mistakes, but "Science thrives on errors, cutting them away one by one. False conclusions are drawn all the time, but they are drawn tentatively. Hypotheses are framed so they are capable of being disproved."

Science is the candle in the dark of the book's title, and Sagan seeks to characterize its distinctive attributes. One, according to him, is that science can predict the future. "Not every branch of science can foretell the future—paleontology can't—but many can and with stunning accuracy. If you want to know when the next eclipse of the Sun will be, you might try magicians or mystics, but you'll do much better with scientists." Here Sagan and I part company. In the matter of foretelling the future I don't think that astronomy is

the rule and paleontology the exception, but the other way around.

Scientists predict the course of rockets and the statistical distribution of populational events, but that is in my book a long way from foretelling the future. Yet I think it correct to assert that "science is predictive," as the slogan goes. Indeed, being predictive of unknown facts is essential to the process of empirical testing of hypotheses, the most distinctive feature of the scientific enterprise. A hypothesis is tested empirically by ascertaining whether or not predictions about the world of experience derived as logical consequences from the hypothesis agree with what actually becomes observed. What is being predicted in this process is an unknown state of affairs, not necessarily a future event. And the prediction is made by logical deduction from the hypothesis.

The hypothesis that chimps are more closely related to humans than to gorillas is tested by examining DNA segments from each species, which the hypothesis predicts will be more similar between human and chimp than between chimp and gorilla. The evolutionary divergence of humans, chimps, and gorillas happened in the distant past, and their DNA is already there. When I now examine it, I test my hypothesis. Sagan has gone astray by failing to distinguish prediction in the logical sense (by deduction) from prediction in the temporal sense (foretelling the future), which is not an essential feature of science.

Sagan has much to say about reductionism as a distinctive feature of science that accounts for much of its success. Science seeks understanding of an event or process by investigating its component elements and underlying processes. The success of this analytical mode is unquestionable (although the antithetical mode is also successful; in matters of research strategy, what counts is success, not how we get there). We might call this kind of research strategy "methodological" or "strategical" reductionism.

But Sagan claims much more. He writes: "Until the middle twentieth century, there had been a strong belief . . . that life was not 'reducible' to the laws of physics and chemistry, that there was a 'vital force,' an 'entelechy,' a tao, a mane that made living things go." He tells the story of the 18th-century chemist Joseph Priestley, who found no difference in the weight of a mouse just before and after its death. Nothing had departed with death, at least nothing that could be weighed. Most scientists would agree, I suppose, with this kind of reductionism (let's call it "ontological" or "physical"). Living things are exhaustively composed of atoms, if we remove all the atoms that make up a mouse body, nothing is left. But accepting this kind of reductionism does not in any way entail the claim that biology is reducible to the laws of physics and chemistry. This is an epistemological claim, which can be shown to be mistaken by simply pointing out that the origin of species or symbolic language (or the majority of the subjects worth of investigating in biology and other disciplines) cannot be explained by the laws of physics or chemistry.

Sagan might state a conviction that such reductionism (of, say, the laws of biology to the laws of physics) will be accomplished in the future. But this is a statement of faith. The late philosopher Karl Popper argued that complete epistemological reduction of a discipline to another is impossible in principle. Sagan asks rhetorically: "Why should some religious people oppose the reductionist program in science, except out of some misplaced love of mysticism?" Popper's opposition to the (epistemological) reductionist program in science was certainly not religiously motivated, nor was he particularly appreciative of mysticism.

Richard Lewontin (review date 9 January 1997)

SOURCE: "Billions and Billions of Demons," in *New York Review of Books,* January 9, 1997, pp. 28-32.

[*In the following review, Lewontin challenges Sagan's defense of science and scientific method in* The Demon-Haunted World.]

"But the Solar System!" I protested.

"What the deuce is it to me?" he interrupted impatiently: "you say that we go round the sun. If we went round the moon it would not make a pennyworth of difference to me or my work."

—Colloquy between Dr. Watson and
Sherlock Holmes in *A Study in Scarlet*

I first met Carl Sagan in 1964, when he and I found ourselves in Arkansas on the platform of the Little Rock Auditorium, where we had been dispatched by command of the leading geneticist of the day, Herman Muller. Our task was to take the affirmative side in a debate: "*Resolved,* That the Theory of Evolution is proved as is the fact that the Earth goes around the Sun." One of our opponents in the debate was a professor of biology from a fundamentalist college in Texas (his father was the president of the college) who had quite deliberately chosen the notoriously evolutionist Department of Zoology of the University of Texas as the source of his Ph.D. He could then assure his students that he had unassailable expert knowledge with which to refute Darwinism.

I had serious misgivings about facing an immense audience of creationist fundamentalist Christians in a city made fa-

mous by an Arkansas governor who having detected a resentment of his constituents against federal usurpation, defied the power of Big Government by interposing his own body between the door of the local high school and some black kids who wanted to matriculate.

Young scientists, however, do not easily withstand the urgings of Nobel Prize winners, so after several transparently devious attempts to avoid the job, I appeared. We were, in fact, well treated, but despite our absolutely compelling arguments, the audience unaccountably voted for the opposition. Carl and I then sneaked out the back door of the auditorium and beat it out of town, quite certain that at any moment hooded riders with ropes and flaming crosses would snatch up two atheistic New York Jews who had the chutzpah to engage in public blasphemy.

Sagan and I drew different conclusions from our experience. For me the confrontation between creationism and the science of evolution was an example of historical, regional, and class differences in culture that could only be understood in the context of American social history. For Carl it was a struggle between ignorance and knowledge, although it is not clear to me what he made of the unimpeachable scientific credentials of our opponent, except perhaps to see him as an example of the Devil quoting scripture. The struggle to bring scientific knowledge to the masses has been a preoccupation of Carl Sagan's ever since, and he has become the most widely known, widely read, and widely seen popularizer of science since the invention of the video tube. His only rival in the *haute vulgarisation* of science is Stephen Jay Gould, whose *vulgarisations* are often very *haute* indeed, and whose intellectual concerns are quite different.

While Gould has occasionally been enlisted in the fight to protect the teaching and dissemination of the knowledge of evolution against creationist political forces, he is primarily concerned with what the nature of organisms, living and dead, can reveal about the social construction of scientific knowledge. His repeated demonstrations that organisms can only be understood as historically contingent, underdetermined Rube Goldberg devices are meant to tell us more about the evolution of human knowledge than of human anatomy. From his early *Mismeasure of Man,* which examined how the political and social prejudices of prominent scientists have molded what those scientists claimed to be the facts of human anatomy and intelligence, to his recent collection of essays, *Eight Little Piggies,* which despite its subtitle, *Reflections on Natural History,* is a set of reflections on the intellectual history of Natural History, Gould's deep preoccupation is with how knowledge, rather than the organism, is constructed.

Carl Sagan's program is more elementary. It is to bring a knowledge of the facts of the physical world to the scientifically uneducated public, for he is convinced that only through a broadly disseminated knowledge of the objective truth about nature will we be able to cope with the difficulties of the world and increase the sum of human happiness. It is this program that inspired his famous book and television series, *Cosmos,* which dazzled us with billions and billions of stars. But Sagan realizes that the project of merely spreading knowledge of objective facts about the universe is insufficient. First, no one can know and understand everything. Even individual scientists are ignorant about most of the body of scientific knowledge, and it is not simply that biologists do not understand quantum mechanics. If I were to ask my colleagues in the Museum of Comparative Zoology at Harvard to explain the evolutionary importance of RNA editing in trypanosomes, they would be just as mystified by the question as the typical well-educated reader of this review.

> **The reason that people do not have a correct view of nature is not that they are ignorant of this or that fact about the material world, but that they look to the wrong sources in their attempt to understand.**
> —*Richard Lewontin*

Second, to put a correct view of the universe into people's heads we must first get an incorrect view out. People believe a lot of nonsense about the world of phenomena, nonsense that is a consequence of a wrong way of thinking. The primary problem is not to provide the public with the knowledge of how far it is to the nearest star and what genes are made of, for that vast project is, in its entirety, hopeless. Rather, the problem is to get them to reject irrational and supernatural explanations of the world, the demons that exist only in their imaginations, and to accept a social and intellectual apparatus, Science, as the only begetter of truth. The reason that people do not have a correct view of nature is not that they are ignorant of this or that fact about the material world, but that they look to the wrong sources in their attempt to understand. It is not simply, as Sherlock Holmes thought, that the brain is like an empty attic with limited storage capacity, so that the accumulated clutter of false or useless bits of knowledge must be cleared out in a grand intellectual tag sale to make space for more useful objects. It is that most people's mental houses have been furnished according to an appallingly bad model of taste and they need to start consulting the home furnishing supplement of the Sunday *New York Times* in place of the stage set of *The Honeymooners.* The message of *The Demon-Haunted World* is in its subtitle, *Science as a Candle in the Dark.*

Sagan's argument is straightforward. We exist as material beings in a material world, all of whose phenomena are the consequences of physical relations among material entities. The vast majority of us do not have control of the intellectual apparatus needed to explain manifest reality in material terms, so in place of scientific (i.e., correct material) explanations, we substitute demons. As one bit of evidence for the bad state of public consciousness, Sagan cites opinion polls showing that the majority of Americans believe that extraterrestrials have landed from UFOs. The demonic, for Sagan, includes, in addition to UFOs and their crews of little green men who take unwilling passengers for a midnight spin and some wild sex, astrological influences, extrasensory perception, prayers, spoon-bending, repressed memories, spiritualism, and channeling, as well as demons *sensu strictu,* devils, fairies, witches, spirits, Satan and his devotees, and, after some discreet backing and filling, the supposed prime mover Himself. God gives Sagan a lot of trouble. It is easy enough for him to snort derisively at men from Mars, but when it comes to the Supreme Extraterrestrial he is rather circumspect, asking only that sermons "even-handedly examine the God hypothesis."

> The fact that so little of the findings of modern science is prefigured in Scripture to my mind casts further doubt on its divine inspiration.

> But of course, I might be wrong.

I doubt that an all-seeing God would fall for Pascal's Wager, but the sensibilities of modern believers may indeed be spared by this Clintonesque moderation.

Most of the chapters of *The Demon-Haunted World* are taken up with exhortations to the reader to cease whoring after false gods and to accept the scientific method as the unique pathway to a correct understanding of the natural world. To Sagan, as to all but a few other scientists, it is self-evident that the practices of science provide the surest method of putting us in contact with physical reality, and that, in contrast, the demon-haunted world rests on a set of beliefs and behaviors that fail every reasonable test. So why do so many people believe in demons? Sagan seems baffled, and nowhere does he offer a coherent explanation of the popularity at the supermarket checkout counter of the *Weekly World News,* with its faked photographs of Martians. Indeed, he believes that "a proclivity for science is embedded deeply within us in all times, places and cultures." The only explanation that he offers for the dogged resistance of the masses to the obvious virtues of the scientific way of knowing is that "through indifference, inattention, incompetence, or fear of skepticism, we discourage children from science." He does not tell us how he used the scientific method to discover the "embedded" human proclivity for science, or the cause of its frustration. Perhaps we ought to add to the menu of Saganic demonology, just after spoon-bending, ten-second seat-of-the-pants explanations of social realities.

Nearly every present-day scientist would agree with Carl Sagan that our explanations of material phenomena exclude any role for supernatural demons, witches, and spirits of every kind, including any of the various gods from Adonai to Zeus. (I say "nearly" every scientist because our creationist opponent in the Little Rock debate, and other supporters of "Creation Science," would insist on being recognized.) We also exclude from our explanations little green men from Mars riding in space ships, although they are supposed to be quite as corporeal as you and I, because the evidence is overwhelming that Mars hasn't got any. On the other hand, if one supposed that they came from the planet of a distant star, the negative evidence would not be so compelling, although the fact that it would have taken them such a long time to get here speaks against the likelihood that they exist. Even Sagan says that "it would be astonishing to me if there weren't extraterrestrial life," a position he can hardly avoid, given that his first published book was **Intelligent Life in the Universe** and he has spent a great deal of the taxpayer's money over the ensuing thirty years listening for the signs.

Sagan believes that scientists reject sprites, fairies, and the influence of Sagittarius because we follow a set of procedures, the Scientific Method, which has consistently produced explanations that put us in contact with reality and in which mystic forces play no part. For Sagan, the method is the message, but I think he has opened the wrong envelope.

There is no attempt in **The Demon-Haunted World** to provide a systematic account of just what Science and the Scientific Method consist in, nor was that the author's intention. The book is not meant to be a discourse on method, but it is in large part a collection of articles taken from *Parade* magazine and other popular publications. Sagan's intent is not analytic, but hortatory. Nevertheless, if the exhortation is to succeed, then the argument for the superiority of science and its method must be convincing, and not merely convincing, but must accord with its own demands. The case for the scientific method should itself be "scientific" and not merely rhetorical. Unfortunately, the argument may not look as good to the unconvinced as it does to the believer.

First, we are told that science "delivers the goods." It certainly has, sometimes, but it has often failed when we need it most. Scientists and their professional institutions, partly intoxicated with examples of past successes, partly in order to assure public financial support, make grandiose promises that cannot be kept. Sagan writes with justified scorn that

We're regularly bombarded with extravagant UFO

claims vended in bite-sized packages, but only rarely do we hear of their comeuppance.

He cannot have forgotten the well-publicized War on Cancer, which is as yet without a victorious battle despite the successful taking of a salient or two. At first an immense amount of money and consciousness was devoted to the supposed oncogenic viruses which, being infectious bugs, could be exterminated or at least resisted. But these particular Unidentified Flying Objects turned out for the most part to be as elusive as the Martians, and so, without publicly calling attention to their "comeuppance," the General Staff turned from outside invaders to the enemy within, the genes. It is almost certain that cancers do, indeed, arise because genes concerned with the regulation of cell division are mutated, partly as a consequence of environmental insults, partly because of unavoidable molecular instability, and even sometimes as the consequence of a viral attack on the genome. Yet the realization of the role played by DNA has had absolutely no consequence for either therapy or prevention, although it has resulted in many optimistic press conferences and a considerable budget for the National Cancer Institute. Treatments for cancer remain today what they were before molecular biology was ever thought of: cut it out, burn it out, or poison it.

The concentration on the genes implicated in cancer is only a special case of a general genomania that surfaces in the form of weekly announcements in *The New York Times* of the location of yet another gene for another disease. The revealing rhetoric of this publicity is always the same; only the blanks need to be filled in: "It was announced today by scientists at [Harvard, Vanderbilt, Stanford] Medical School that a gene responsible for [some, many, a common form of] [schizophrenia, Alzheimer's, arteriosclerosis, prostate cancer] has been located and its DNA sequence determined. This exciting research, say scientists, is the first step in what may eventually turn out to be a possible cure for this disease."

The entire public justification for the Human Genome Project is the promise that some day, in the admittedly distant future, diseases will be cured or prevented. Skeptics who point out that we do not yet have a single case of a prevention or cure arising from a knowledge of DNA sequences are answered by the observations that "these things take time," or that "no one knows the value of a newborn baby." But such vague waves of the hand miss the central scientific issue. The prevention or cure of metabolic and developmental disorders depends on a detailed knowledge of the mechanisms operating in cells and tissues above the level of genes, and there is no relevant information about those mechanisms in DNA sequences. In fact, if I know the DNA sequence of a gene I have no hint about the function of a protein specified by that gene, or how it enters into an organism's biology.

What is involved here is the difference between explanation and intervention. Many disorders can be *explained* by the failure of the organism to make a normal protein, a failure that is the consequence of a gene mutation. But *intervention* requires that the normal protein be provided at the right place in the right cells, at the right time and in the right amount, or else that an alternative way be found to provide normal cellular function. What is worse, it might even be necessary to keep the abnormal protein away from the cells at critical moments. None of these objectives is served by knowing the DNA sequence of the defective gene. Explanations of phenomena can be given at many levels, some of which can lead to successful manipulation of the world and some not. Death certificates all state a cause of death, but even if there were no errors in these ascriptions, they are too general to be useful. An easy conflation of explanations in general with explanations at the correct causal level may serve a propagandistic purpose in the struggle for public support, but it is not the way to concrete progress.

Scientists apparently do not realize that the repeated promises of benefits yet to come, with no likelihood that those promises will be fulfilled, can only produce a widespread cynicism about the claims for the scientific method. Sagan, trying to explain the success of Carlos, a telepathic charlatan, muses on

> how little it takes to tamper with our beliefs, how readily we are led how easy it is to fool the public when people are lonely and starved for something to believe in.

Not to mention when they are sick and dying.

Biologists are not the only scientists who, having made extravagant claims about their merchandise, deliver the goods in bite-sized packages. Nor are they the only manufacturers of knowledge who cannot be bothered to pick up a return package when the product turns out to be faulty. Sagan's own branch of science is in the same business. Anxious to revive a failing public interest in spending large amounts on space research, NASA scientists, followed by the President of the United States, made an immense fuss about the discovery of some organic molecules on a Mars rock. There is (was) life (of some rudimentary kind) on Mars (maybe)! Can little green men in space machines be far behind? If it turns out, as already suggested by some scientists, that these molecules are earthly contaminants, or were produced in non-living chemical systems, this fact surely will not be announced at a White House press conference, or even above the fold in *The New York Times*.

Second, it is repeatedly said that science is intolerant of theories without data and assertions without adequate evidence. But no serious student of epistemology any longer takes the naive view of science as a process of Baconian induction from theoretically unorganized observations. There can be no observations without an immense apparatus of preexisting theory. Before sense experiences become "observations" we need a theoretical question, and what counts as a relevant observation depends upon a theoretical frame into which it is to be placed. Repeatable observations that do not fit into an existing frame have a way of disappearing from view, and the experiments that produced them are not revisited. In the 1930s well-established and respectable geneticists described "dauer-modifications," environmentally induced changes in organisms that were passed on to offspring and only slowly disappeared in succeeding generations. As the science of genetics hardened, with its definitive rejection of any possibility of the inheritance of acquired characteristics, observations of dauer-modifications were sent to the scrap heap where they still lie, jumbled together with other decommissioned facts.

The standard form of a scientific paper begins with a theoretical question, which is then followed by the description of an experimental technique designed to gather observations pertinent to the question. Only then are the observations themselves described. Finally there is a discussion section in which a great deal of energy is often expended rationalizing the failure of the observations to accord entirely with a theory we really like, and in which proposals are made for other experiments that might give more satisfactory results. Sagan's suggestion that only demonologists engage in "special pleading, often to rescue a proposition in deep rhetorical trouble," is certainly not one that accords with my reading of the scientific literature. Nor is this a problem unique to biology. The attempts of physicists to explain why their measurements of the effects of relativity did not agree with Einstein's quantitative prediction is a case no doubt well known to Sagan.

As to assertions without adequate evidence, the literature of science is filled with them, especially the literature of popular science writing. Carl Sagan's list of the "best contemporary science-popularizers" includes E. O. Wilson, Lewis Thomas, and Richard Dawkins, each of whom has put unsubstantiated assertions or counter-factual claims at the very center of the stories they have retailed in the market. Wilson's *Sociobiology* and *On Human Nature* rest on the surface of a quaking marsh of unsupported claims about the genetic determination of everything from altruism to xenophobia. Dawkins's vulgarizations of Darwinism speak of nothing in evolution but an inexorable ascendancy of genes that are selectively superior, while the entire body of technical advance in experimental and theoretical evolutionary genetics of the last fifty years has moved in the direction of emphasizing non-selective forces in evolution. Thomas, in various essays, propagandized for the success of modern scientific medicine in eliminating death from disease, while the unchallenged statistical compilations on mortality show that in Europe and North America infectious diseases, including tuberculosis and diphtheria, had ceased to be major causes of mortality by the first decades of the twentieth century, and that at age seventy the expected further lifetime for a white male has gone up only two years since 1950. Even *The Demon-Haunted World* itself sometimes takes suspect claims as true when they serve a rhetorical purpose as, for example, statistics on child abuse, or a story about the evolution of a child's fear of the dark.

Third, it is said that there is no place for an argument from authority in science. The community of science is constantly self-critical, as evidenced by the experience of university colloquia "in which the speaker has hardly gotten 30 seconds into the talk before there are devastating questions and comments from the audience." If Sagan really wants to hear serious disputation about the nature of the universe, he should leave the academic precincts in Ithaca and spend a few minutes in an Orthodox study house in Brooklyn. It is certainly true that within each narrowly defined scientific field there is a constant challenge to new technical claims and to old wisdom. In what my wife calls the Gunfight at the O.K. Corral Syndrome, young scientists on the make will challenge a graybeard, and this adversarial atmosphere for the most part serves the truth. But when scientists transgress the bounds of their own specialty they have no choice but to accept the claims of authority, even though they do not know how solid the grounds of those claims may be. Who am I to believe about quantum physics if not Steven Weinberg, or about the solar system if not Carl Sagan? What worries me is that they may believe what Dawkins and Wilson tell them about evolution.

With great perception, Sagan sees that there is an impediment to the popular credibility of scientific claims about the world, an impediment that is almost invisible to most scientists. Many of the most fundamental claims of science are against common sense and seem absurd on their face. Do physicists really expect me to accept without serious qualms that the pungent cheese that I had for lunch is really made up of tiny, tasteless, odorless, colorless packets of energy with nothing but empty space between them? Astronomers tell us without apparent embarrassment that they can see stellar events that occurred millions of years ago, whereas we all know that we see things as they happen. When, at the time of the moon landing, a woman in rural Texas was interviewed about the event, she very sensibly refused to believe that the television pictures she had seen had come all the way from the moon, on the grounds that with her antenna she couldn't even get Dallas. What seems absurd depends on one's prejudice. Carl Sagan accepts, as I do, the duality of light, which is at the same time wave and particle, but he thinks that the consubstantiality of Father, Son, and Holy Ghost puts the mystery of the Holy Trinity "in deep trouble." Two's company, but three's a crowd.

Our willingness to accept scientific claims that are against common sense is the key to an understanding of the real struggle between science and the supernatural. We take the side of science *in spite* of the patent absurdity of some of its constructs *in spite* of its failure to fulfill many of its extravagant promises of health and life, *in spite* of the tolerance of the scientific community for unsubstantiated just-so stories, because we have a prior commitment, a commitment to materialism. It is not that the methods and institutions of science somehow compel us to accept a material explanation of the phenomenal world, but, on the contrary, that we are forced by our *a priori* adherence to material causes to create an apparatus of investigation and a set of concepts that produce material explanations, no matter how counterintuitive, no matter how mystifying to the uninitiated. Moreover, that materialism is absolute, for we cannot allow a Divine Foot in the door. The eminent Kant scholar Lewis Beck used to say that anyone who could believe in God could believe in anything. To appeal to an omnipotent deity is to allow that at any moment the regularities of nature may be ruptured, that miracles may happen.

The mutual exclusion of the material and the demonic has not been true of all cultures and all times. In the great Chinese epic *Journey to the West,* demons are an alternative form of life, responsible to certain deities, devoted to making trouble for ordinary people, but severely limited. They can be captured, imprisoned, and even killed by someone with superior magic. In our own intellectual history, the definitive displacement of divine powers by purely material causes has been a relatively recent changeover, and that icon of modern science, Newton, was at the cusp. It is a cliché of intellectual history that Newton attempted to accommodate God by postulating Him as the Prime Mover Who, having established the mechanical laws and set the whole universe in motion, withdrew from further intervention, leaving it to people like Newton to reveal His plan. But what we might call "Newton's Ploy" did not really get him off the hook. He understood that a defect of his system of mechanics was the lack of any equilibrating force that would return the solar system to its regular set of orbits if there were any slight perturbation. He was therefore forced, although reluctantly, to assume that God intervened from time to time to set things right again. It remained for Laplace, a century later, to produce a mechanics that predicted the stability of the planetary orbits, allowing him the hauteur of his famous reply to Napoleon. When the Emperor observed that there was, in the whole of the *Mécanique Céleste,* no mention of the author of the universe, he replied, "Sire, I have no need of that hypothesis." One can almost hear a stress on the "I."

The struggle for possession of public consciousness between

material and mystical explanations of the world is one aspect of the history of the confrontation between elite culture and popular culture. Without that history we cannot understand what was going on in the Little Rock Auditorium in 1964. The debate in Arkansas between a teacher from a Texas fundamentalist college and a Harvard astronomer and University of Chicago biologist was a stage play recapitulating the history of American rural populism. In the first decades of this century there was an immensely active populism among poor southwestern dirt farmers and miners. The most widely circulated American socialist journal of the time (*The Appeal to Reason!*) was published not in New York, but in Girard, Kansas, and in the presidential election of 1912 Eugene Debs got more votes in the poorest rural counties of Texas and Oklahoma than he did in the industrial wards of northern cities. Sentiment was extremely strong against the banks and corporations that held the mortgages and sweated the labor of the rural poor, who felt their lives to be in the power of a distant eastern elite. The only spheres of control that seemed to remain to them were family life, a fundamentalist religion, and local education.

This sense of an embattled culture was carried from the southwest to California by the migrations of the Okies and Arkies dispossessed from their ruined farms in the 1930s. There was no serious public threat to their religious and family values until well after the Second World War. Evolution, for example, was not part of the regular biology curriculum when I was a student in 1946 in the New York City high schools, nor was it discussed in school textbooks. In consequence there was no organized creationist movement. Then, in the late 1950s, a national project was begun to bring school science curricula up to date. A group of biologists from elite universities together with science teachers from urban schools produced a new uniform set of biology textbooks, whose publication and dissemination were underwritten by the National Science Foundation. An extensive and successful public relations campaign was undertaken to have these books adopted, and suddenly Darwinian evolution was being taught to children everywhere. The elite culture was now extending its domination by attacking the control that families had maintained over the ideological formation of their children.

The result was a fundamentalist revolt, the invention of "Creation Science," and successful popular pressure on local school boards and state textbook purchasing agencies to revise subversive curricula and boycott blasphemous textbooks. In their parochial hubris, intellectuals call the struggle between cultural relativists and traditionalists in the universities and small circulation journals "The Culture Wars." The real war is between the traditional culture of those who think of themselves as powerless and the rationalizing materialism of the modern Leviathan. There are indeed Two Cultures at Cambridge. One is in the Senior Common Room, and the other is in the Porter's Lodge.

Carl Sagan, like his Canadian counterpart David Suzuki, has devoted extraordinary energy to bringing science to a mass public. In doing so, he is faced with a contradiction for which there is no clear resolution. On the one hand science is urged on us as a model of rational deduction from publicly verifiable facts, freed from the tyranny of unreasoning authority. On the other hand, given the immense extent, inherent complexity, and counterintuitive nature of scientific knowledge, it is impossible for anyone, including non-specialist scientists, to retrace the intellectual paths that lead to scientific conclusions about nature. In the end we must trust the experts and they, in turn, exploit their authority as experts and their rhetorical skills to secure our attention and our belief in things that we do not really understand. Anyone who has ever served as an expert witness in a judicial proceeding knows that the court may spend an inordinate time "qualifying" the expert, who, once qualified, gives testimony that is not meant to be a persuasive argument, but an assertion unchallengeable by anyone except another expert. And, indeed, what else are the courts to do? If the judge, attorneys, and jury could reason out the technical issues from fundamentals, there would be no need of experts.

What is at stake here is a deep problem in democratic self-governance. In Plato's most modern of Dialogues, the *Gorgias,* there is a struggle between Socrates, with whom we are meant to sympathize, and his opponents, Gorgias and Callicles, over the relative virtues of rhetoric and technical expertise. What Socrates and Gorgias agree on is that the mass of citizens are incompetent to make reasoned decisions on justice and public policy, but that they must be swayed by the rhetorical argument or guided by the authority of experts.

> Gorgias: "I mean [by the art of rhetoric] the ability to convince by means of speech a jury in a court of justice, members of the Council in their Chamber, voters at a meeting of the Assembly, and any other gathering of citizens, whatever it may be."

> Socrates: "When the citizens hold a meeting to appoint medical officers or shipbuilders or any other professional class of person, surely it won't be the orator who advises them then. Obviously in every such election the choice ought to fall on the most expert."

Conscientious and wholly admirable popularizers of science like Carl Sagan use both rhetoric and expertise to form the mind of masses because they believe, like the Evangelist John, that the truth shall make you free. But they are wrong. It is not the truth that makes you free. It is your possession of the power to discover the truth. Our dilemma is that we do not know how to provide that power.

Stephen Jay Gould (essay date 31 January 1997)

SOURCE: "Bright Star among Billions," in *Science,* Vol. 275, No. 5300, January 31, 1997, p. 599.

[In the following essay, Gould praises Sagan's contribution to the popular presentation of science.]

Saul despised David for receiving ten thousand cheers to his own mere thousand. We scientists often stigmatize, for the same reason of simple jealousy, the good work done by colleagues for our common benefit. Because we live in a Philistine nation filled with Goliaths, and because science feeds at a public trough, we all give lip service to the need for clear and supportive popular presentation of our work. Why then do we downgrade the professional reputation of colleagues who can convey the power and beauty of science to the hearts and minds of a fascinated, if generally uninformed, public?

This narrow-minded error—our own Philistinism—arises in part from our general ignorance of the long and honorable tradition of popular presentation of science, and our consequent mistake in equating popularization with trivialization, cheapening, or inaccuracy. Great scientists have always produced the greatest popularizations, without compromising the integrity of subject or author. In the 10th century, Galileo wrote both his major books as dialogues in Italian for generally literate readers, not as formal Latin treatises designed only for scholars. In the 18th century, the Swiss savant J. J. Scheuchzer produced the beautifully elaborate eight-volume *Physica sacra,* with 750 full-page copperplate engravings showing the natural history behind all Biblical events. In the 19th century, Charles Darwin wrote the *Origin of Species,* the most important and revolutionary of all scientific works, as a book for general readers. (My students often ask me where they can find the technical monograph that served as the basis for Darwin's popular work; I tell them that the *Origin of Species* fulfills both allied, not opposing, functions.)

With the death of Carl Sagan we have lost both a fine scientist and the greatest popularizer of the 20th century, if not of all time.
—*Stephen Jay Gould*

With the death of Carl Sagan we have lost both a fine scientist and the greatest popularizer of the 20th century, if not of all time. In his many books, and especially in his monumental television series *Cosmos*—our century's equivalent of Scheuchzer's *Physica sacra* and the most widely viewed presentation in the entire history of science—Carl explained the method and content of our discipline to the general pub-

lic. He also conveyed the excitement of discovery with an uncanny mix of personal enthusiasm and clear presentation unequaled by any predecessor. I mourn his passing primarily because I have lost a dear friend, but I am also sad that many of us never appreciated his excellence or his importance to all of us, while a few of the best of us (in a shameful incident at the National Academy of Sciences) actively rejected him. (Carl was a remarkably sanguine man, but I know that this incident hurt him deeply.) Too many of us never grasped his legendary service to science.

I would epitomize his excellence and integrity in three points. First, in an age characterized by the fusion of high and pop culture, Carl moved comfortably across the entire spectrum while never compromising scientific content. He could joke with Johnny Carson, compose a weekly column for *Parade,* and write a science fiction novel while maintaining an active laboratory and publishing technical papers. He had foibles aplenty; don't we all? We joked about his emphatic pronunciation of "billions," and my young son (much to Carl's amusement) called *Cosmos* the "stick-head-up show" because Carl always looked up dreamily into the heavens. But the public watched, loved, and learned. Second, for all his pizzazz and charisma, Carl always spoke for true science against the plethora of irrationalisms that surround us. He conveyed one consistent message: Real science is so damned exciting, transforming, and provable, why would anyone prefer the undocumentable nonsense of astrology, alien abductions, and so forth? Third, he bridged the gaps between our various cultures by showing the personal, humanistic, and artistic side of scientific activity. I will never, for example, forget his excellent treatment of Hypatia, a great woman, philosopher, and mathematician, who was martyred in Alexandria in 415 A.D.

You had a wonderful life Carl, although too short. You will, however, always be with us, especially if we as a profession can learn from you that the common touch enriches science and extends an ancient tradition that lies at the heart of Western humanism, and does not represent (when properly done) a journalistic perversion of the "sound bite" age. In the words that John Dryden wrote about another great artist, the musician Henry Purcell, who died even younger, "He long ere this had tuned the jarring spheres and left no hell below."

Jerry Adler (essay date 31 March 1997)

SOURCE: "Unbeliever's Quest," in *Newsweek,* March 31, 1997, pp. 64-7.

[In the following essay, Adler discusses Sagan's unshakable

faith in science over religion even in the face of fatal illness.]

A man of science, Carl Sagan didn't want prayers; he wanted proof. He died still waiting for evidence.

Carl Sagan, the famous scientist and author, never asked for anyone to pray for him, although in his final illness many people did anyway. For two years prayers for his health filled the great Cathedral of St. John the Divine in New York. They rose (if prayers do rise) to the heaven Sagan had never seen in all his years of searching the sky, and were heard (if prayers are heard) by the God Sagan never called on. And God (if he exists) let Sagan die anyway, late last year, at the untimely age of 62, leaving behind a wife, five children and much unfinished work on the earth he loved so well. But he died in what amounted, for him, to a state of grace: resisting the one temptation to which almost everyone submits in the end, the temptation to believe.

Not that the Kingdom of Heaven held no interest for Sagan, an astronomer who found the solar system too confining for his speculations on cosmic origins, human consciousness and evolution. For most of the last decade of his life he engaged in a wide-ranging dialogue with religious leaders on the question whose answer held the potential to put either preachers or cosmologists out of business: does God exist? He argued the negative, although his formal position was agnostic, awaiting proof. On the other side were primarily mainstream, liberal Protestant clerics, such as the Rev. James Parks Morton, then dean of St. John the Divine, and the Rev. Joan Brown Campbell, general secretary of the National Council of Churches, whom Sagan met in the environmental movement. But he also exchanged views with believers of a more conservative bent, such as Robert Seiple, head of the Christian relief organization World Vision. Sagan was fascinated by the phenomenon that educated adults, with the wonders of science manifest all around them, could cling to beliefs based on the unverifiable testimony of observers dead for 2,000 years. "You're so smart, why do you believe in God?" he once exclaimed to Campbell. She found this a surprising question from someone who had no trouble accepting the existence of black holes, which no one has ever observed. "You're so smart, why don't you believe in God?" she answered.

Sagan never set out to finish the work of the Enlightenment singlehandedly. "I started out very much enjoying the idea of an omnipotent, omniscient, benevolent God who like a benign parent was watching out for me," he wrote to one of his correspondents. "I was brought to skepticism by the slow realization that the 'evidence' [for religion] is anecdotal . . . But if there is evidence of such a God, or any other God, I feel it is my responsibility to try and know about it."

For that matter, Sagan's early career suggested he had the potential to become as big a public nuisance as Shirley MacLaine. Twenty years ago, as a scientist on the Viking Mars probe project, he was known as a particularly visionary believer in the possibility of life on other planets, to the point where some of his colleagues at NASA considered him a flake. But it was only the possibility he believed in. When Mars landers found nothing but rocks, he accepted the evidence—as, years earlier, he had himself published a seminal paper showing that Venus was too hot to support life. Thus "Carl's major contributions to science each flew in the face of his own most cherished expectations," remarks his wife and sometime collaborator, Ann Druyan. He thought believers should be just as willing to jettison their beliefs in response to evidence. A religion whose highest sacrament is heresy might have won Sagan's allegiance, but he never found one.

Sagan developed many of these ideas in his 1995 book, ***The Demon-Haunted World,*** a defense of science against the superstitious nonsense that he saw in American culture, from alien abductions to "recovered memories" of satanic ritual abuse. He managed to suggest, with considerable circumspection, that the evidence for most religion is not very much stronger. Sagan's insistence on dealing only with "evidence" put his correspondents at a seeming disadvantage, at least until the time Campbell asked him, "Carl, do you believe in love?"

"And he said, 'Of course I do.' He was very much in love with his wife. And I said, 'Can you prove love exists?' And at first he said, 'Well, certainly,' but eventually he agreed that love, like faith, has something unprovable at its core, but that doesn't mean it doesn't exist."

But that was still a long way from accepting the claims of organized religion. Sagan reserved particular scorn for petitionary prayer, which by its very utterance renders God's qualities of omnipotence, omniscience and benevolence mutually contradictory. Does God need to be reminded that someone is sick, Sagan asked. Or does he know, but he won't do anything about it unless someone else asks him to?

Of course, many believers have wrestled with these same questions. Morton began praying for Sagan after he was diagnosed with myelodysplasia, a disease related to leukemia, in the winter of 1995. "That prayer works is very clear," Morton says, "although how, I don't have a clue." If God had actually cured Sagan with a visible miracle, as in the Bible, Morton would have been only a little less astonished than the patient himself. "Look at it psychologically," he says. "It helped keep his spirits going. If your spirits are up, your body works better. Any kind of mechanistic notion of changing the molecules, that's nonsense."

But Seiple, from a very different religious tradition, had a more direct appreciation of the power of prayer. In a letter shortly before Sagan was to undergo a marrow transplant, he asked about his condition so he could "pray more intelligently" for a cure. "I have already begun to pray," he reassured Sagan, "and, as I have tried to persuade you, prayer has been the most necessary part of bridging the gap between the divine and our humanity."

Sagan was eventually to have three bone-marrow transplants, and by last summer seemed to be recovering. Campbell had dinner with him in the fall and said, "I think you're going to make it," to which he replied, smiling, "I'm praying I'm going to make it." Then he contracted pneumonia, a side effect of his radiation treatment. His friends prayed harder, but Sagan never wavered in his agnosticism.

"There was no deathbed conversion," Druyan says. "No appeals to God, no hope for an afterlife, no pretending that he and I, who had been inseparable for 20 years, were not saying goodbye forever."

Didn't he want to believe? she was asked.

"Carl never wanted to believe," she replies fiercely. "He wanted to know."

FURTHER READING

Criticism

Chapman, Clark R. "Carl Sagan: An Appreciation." *Sky & Telescope* 93, No. 3 (March 1997): 6-7.
A brief overview of Sagan's career and scientific contributions.

Eicher, Dave. "Carl Sagan: 1934-1996." *Astronomy* 25, No. 3 (March 1997): 28.
A brief summary of Sagan's professional accomplishments and public role.

Randi, James. Review of *The Demon-Haunted World,* by Carl Sagan. *Skeptical Inquirer* 20, No. 4 (July-August 1996): 46-7.
A favorable review of *The Demon-Haunted World.*

Interviews

"Carl Sagan: A Slayer of Demons." *Psychology Today* 29, No. 1 (January-February 1996): 30, 32-3, 62, 65, 67.
Sagan comments on *The Demon-Haunted World* and the importance of scientific knowledge.

Sanoff, Alvin P. "Science and Religion: 'Similar Objective, Different Methods': A Conversation With Carl Sagan." *U.S. News and World Report* (1 December 1980): 62-3.
Sagan discusses the possibility of extraterrestrial life, space travel, and differences between scientific and religious explanation.

Additional coverage of Sagan's life and career is contained in the following sources published by Gale: *Authors and Artists for Young Adults,* **Vol. 2;** *Contemporary Authors,* **Vols. 25-28R;** *Contemporary Authors New Revision Series,* **Vols. 11 and 36;** *Major Twentieth-Century Writers;* **and** *Something about the Author,* **Vol. 58.**

☐ Contemporary Literary Criticism

Indexes

Literary Criticism Series
Cumulative Author Index
Cumulative Topic Index
Cumulative Nationality Index
Title Index, Volume 112

How to Use This Index

The main references

Camus, Albert
1913-1960 ...... CLC 1, 2, 4, 9, 11, 14,
32, 69; DA; DAB; DAC; DAM DRAM,
MST, NOV; DC2; SSC 9; WLC

list all author entries in the following Gale Literary Criticism series:

BLC = *Black Literature Criticism*
BLCS = *Black Literature Criticism Supplement*
CLC = *Contemporary Literary Criticism*
CLR = *Children's Literature Review*
CMLC = *Classical and Medieval Literature Criticism*
DA = *DISCovering Authors*
DAB = *DISCovering Authors: British*
DAC = *DISCovering Authors: Canadian*
DAM = *DISCovering Authors Modules*
  DRAM = *dramatists;* *MST* = *most-studied*
  authors; *MULT* = *multicultural authors;* *NOV* =
  novelists; *POET* = *poets;* *POP* = *popular/genre*
  writers; *DC* = *Drama Criticism*
HLC = *Hispanic Literature Criticism*
LC = *Literature Criticism from 1400 to 1800*
NCLC = *Nineteenth-Century Literature Criticism*
PC = *Poetry Criticism*
SSC = *Short Story Criticism*
TCLC = *Twentieth-Century Literary Criticism*
WLC = *World Literature Criticism, 1500 to the Present*
WLCS = *World Literature Criticism Supplement*

The cross-references

See also CA 89-92; DLB 72; MTCW

list all author entries in the following Gale biographical and literary sources:

AAYA = *Authors & Artists for Young Adults*
AITN = *Authors in the News*
BEST = *Bestsellers*
BW = *Black Writers*
CA = *Contemporary Authors*
CAAS = *Contemporary Authors Autobiography Series*
CABS = *Contemporary Authors Bibliographical Series*
CANR = *Contemporary Authors New Revision Series*
CAP = *Contemporary Authors Permanent Series*
CDALB = *Concise Dictionary of American Literary Biography*
CDBLB = *Concise Dictionary of British Literary Biography*

DLB = *Dictionary of Literary Biography*
DLBD = *Dictionary of Literary Biography Documentary Series*
DLBY = *Dictionary of Literary Biography Yearbook*
HW = *Hispanic Writers*
JRDA = *Junior DISCovering Authors*
MAICYA = *Major Authors and Illustrators for Children and Young Adults*
MTCW = *Major 20th-Century Writers*
NNAL = *Native North American Literature*
SAAS = *Something about the Author Autobiography Series*
SATA = *Something about the Author*
YABC = *Yesterday's Authors of Books for Children*

Annensky, Innokenty (Fyodorovich) 1856-1909 **TCLC 14**
See also CA 110; 155

Annunzio, Gabriele d'
See D'Annunzio, Gabriele

Anodos
See Coleridge, Mary E(lizabeth)

Anon, Charles Robert
See Pessoa, Fernando (Antonio Nogueira)

Anouilh, Jean (Marie Lucien Pierre) 1910-1987 **CLC 1, 3, 8, 13, 40, 50; DAM DRAM; DC 8**
See also CA 17-20R; 123; CANR 32; MTCW

Anthony, Florence
See Ai

Anthony, John
See Ciardi, John (Anthony)

Anthony, Peter
See Shaffer, Anthony (Joshua); Shaffer, Peter (Levin)

Anthony, Piers 1934- .... **CLC 35; DAM POP**
See also AAYA 11; CA 21-24R; CANR 28, 56; DLB 8; MTCW; SAAS 22; SATA 84

Antoine, Marc
See Proust, (Valentin-Louis-George-Eugene-) Marcel

Antoninus, Brother
See Everson, William (Oliver)

Antonioni, Michelangelo 1912- .... **CLC 20**
See also CA 73-76; CANR 45

Antschel, Paul 1920-1970
See Celan, Paul
See also CA 85-88; CANR 33, 61; MTCW

Anwar, Chairil 1922-1949 .... **TCLC 22**
See also CA 121

Apollinaire, Guillaume 1880-1918 **TCLC 3, 8, 51; DAM POET; PC 7**
See also Kostrowitzki, Wilhelm Apollinaris de
See also CA 152

Appelfeld, Aharon 1932- .... **CLC 23, 47**
See also CA 112; 133

Apple, Max (Isaac) 1941- .... **CLC 9, 33**
See also CA 81-84; CANR 19, 54; DLB 130

Appleman, Philip (Dean) 1926- .... **CLC 51**
See also CA 13-16R; CAAS 18; CANR 6, 29, 56

Appleton, Lawrence
See Lovecraft, H(oward) P(hillips)

Apteryx
See Eliot, T(homas) S(tearns)

Apuleius, (Lucius Madaurensis) 125(?)-175(?) **CMLC 1**

Aquin, Hubert 1929-1977 .... **CLC 15**
See also CA 105; DLB 53

Aragon, Louis 1897-1982 .. **CLC 3, 22; DAM NOV, POET**
See also CA 69-72; 108; CANR 28; DLB 72; MTCW

Arany, Janos 1817-1882 .... **NCLC 34**

Arbuthnot, John 1667-1735 .... **LC 1**
See also DLB 101

Archer, Herbert Winslow
See Mencken, H(enry) L(ouis)

Archer, Jeffrey (Howard) 1940- ..... **CLC 28; DAM POP**
See also AAYA 16; BEST 89:3; CA 77-80; CANR 22, 52; INT CANR-22

Archer, Jules 1915- .... **CLC 12**
See also CA 9-12R; CANR 6, 69; SAAS 5; SATA 4, 85

Archer, Lee
See Ellison, Harlan (Jay)

Arden, John 1930-**CLC 6, 13, 15; DAM DRAM**
See also CA 13-16R; CAAS 4; CANR 31, 65, 67; DLB 13; MTCW

Arenas, Reinaldo 1943-1990 . **CLC 41; DAM MULT; HLC**
See also CA 124; 128; 133; DLB 145; HW

Arendt, Hannah 1906-1975 .... **CLC 66, 98**
See also CA 17-20R; 61-64; CANR 26, 60; MTCW

Aretino, Pietro 1492-1556 .... **LC 12**

Arghezi, Tudor .... **CLC 80**
See also Theodorescu, Ion N.

Arguedas, Jose Maria 1911-1969 **CLC 10, 18**
See also CA 89-92; DLB 113; HW

Argueta, Manlio 1936- .... **CLC 31**
See also CA 131; DLB 145; HW

Ariosto, Ludovico 1474-1533 .... **LC 6**

Aristides
See Epstein, Joseph

Aristophanes 450B.C.-385B.C.**CMLC 4; DA; DAB; DAC; DAM DRAM, MST; DC 2; WLCS**
See also DLB 176

Arlt, Roberto (Godofredo Christophersen) 1900-1942**TCLC 29; DAM MULT; HLC**
See also CA 123; 131; CANR 67; HW

Armah, Ayi Kwei 1939-... **CLC 5, 33; BLC 1; DAM MULT, POET**
See also BW 1; CA 61-64; CANR 21, 64; DLB 117; MTCW

Armatrading, Joan 1950- .... **CLC 17**
See also CA 114

Arnette, Robert
See Silverberg, Robert

Arnim, Achim von (Ludwig Joachim von Arnim) 1781-1831 ...... **NCLC 5; SSC 29**
See also DLB 90

Arnim, Bettina von 1785-1859 .... **NCLC 38**
See also DLB 90

Arnold, Matthew 1822-1888**NCLC 6, 29; DA; DAB; DAC; DAM MST, POET; PC 5; WLC**
See also CDBLB 1832-1890; DLB 32, 57

Arnold, Thomas 1795-1842 .... **NCLC 18**
See also DLB 55

Arnow, Harriette (Louisa) Simpson 1908-1986 **CLC 2, 7, 18**
See also CA 9-12R; 118; CANR 14; DLB 6; MTCW; SATA 42; SATA-Obit 47

Arp, Hans
See Arp, Jean

Arp, Jean 1887-1966 .... **CLC 5**
See also CA 81-84; 25-28R; CANR 42

Arrabal
See Arrabal, Fernando

Arrabal, Fernando 1932-.... **CLC 2, 9, 18, 58**
See also CA 9-12R; CANR 15

Arrick, Fran .... **CLC 30**
See also Gaberman, Judie Angell

Artaud, Antonin (Marie Joseph) 1896-1948 **TCLC 3, 36; DAM DRAM**
See also CA 104; 149

Arthur, Ruth M(abel) 1905-1979 ...... **CLC 12**
See also CA 9-12R; 85-88; CANR 4; SATA 7, 26

Artsybashev, Mikhail (Petrovich) 1878-1927 **TCLC 31**

Arundel, Honor (Morfydd) 1919-1973**CLC 17**
See also CA 21-22; 41-44R; CAP 2; CLR 35; SATA 4; SATA-Obit 24

Arzner, Dorothy 1897-1979 .... **CLC 98**

Asch, Sholem 1880-1957 .... **TCLC 3**
See also CA 105

Ash, Shalom
See Asch, Sholem

Ashbery, John (Lawrence) 1927-**CLC 2, 3, 4, 6, 9, 13, 15, 25, 41, 77; DAM POET**
See also CA 5-8R; CANR 9, 37, 66; DLB 5, 165; DLBY 81; INT CANR-9; MTCW

Ashdown, Clifford
See Freeman, R(ichard) Austin

Ashe, Gordon
See Creasey, John

Ashton-Warner, Sylvia (Constance) 1908-1984 **CLC 19**
See also CA 69-72; 112; CANR 29; MTCW

Asimov, Isaac 1920-1992 **CLC 1, 3, 9, 19, 26, 76, 92; DAM POP**
See also AAYA 13; BEST 90:2; CA 1-4R; 137; CANR 2, 19, 36, 60; CLR 12; DLB 8; DLBY 92; INT CANR-19; JRDA; MAICYA; MTCW; SATA 1, 26, 74

Assis, Joaquim Maria Machado de
See Machado de Assis, Joaquim Maria

Astley, Thea (Beatrice May) 1925- ... **CLC 41**
See also CA 65-68; CANR 11, 43

Aston, James
See White, T(erence) H(anbury)

Asturias, Miguel Angel 1899-1974 **CLC 3, 8, 13; DAM MULT, NOV; HLC**
See also CA 25-28; 49-52; CANR 32; CAP 2; DLB 113; HW; MTCW

Atares, Carlos Saura
See Saura (Atares), Carlos

Atheling, William
See Pound, Ezra (Weston Loomis)

Atheling, William, Jr.
See Blish, James (Benjamin)

Atherton, Gertrude (Franklin Horn) 1857-1948 **TCLC 2**
See also CA 104; 155; DLB 9, 78, 186

Atherton, Lucius
See Masters, Edgar Lee

Atkins, Jack
See Harris, Mark

Atkinson, Kate .... **CLC 99**
See also CA 166

Attaway, William (Alexander) 1911-1986 **CLC 92; BLC 1; DAM MULT**
See also BW 2; CA 143; DLB 76

Atticus
See Fleming, Ian (Lancaster); Wilson, (Thomas) Woodrow

Atwood, Margaret (Eleanor) 1939-**CLC 2, 3, 4, 8, 13, 15, 25, 44, 84; DA; DAB; DAC; DAM MST, NOV, POET; PC 8; SSC 2; WLC**
See also AAYA 12; BEST 89:2; CA 49-52; CANR 3, 24, 33, 59; DLB 53; INT CANR-24; MTCW; SATA 50

Aubigny, Pierre d'
See Mencken, H(enry) L(ouis)

Aubin, Penelope 1685-1731(?) .... **LC 9**
See also DLB 39

Auchincloss, Louis (Stanton) 1917-**CLC 4, 6, 9, 18, 45; DAM NOV; SSC 22**
See also CA 1-4R; CANR 6, 29, 55; DLB 2; DLBY 80; INT CANR-29; MTCW

Auden, W(ystan) H(ugh) 1907-1973**CLC 1, 2, 3, 4, 6, 9, 11, 14, 43; DA; DAB; DAC; DAM DRAM, MST, POET; PC 1; WLC**
See also AAYA 18; CA 9-12R; 45-48; CANR 5, 61; CDBLB 1914-1945; DLB 10, 20; MTCW

Audiberti, Jacques 1900-1965**CLC 38; DAM DRAM**
See also CA 25-28R

43; DAB; DAM MST, POET
See also CA 9-12R; 112; CANR 33, 56; CDBLB 1945-1960; DLB 20; DLBY 84; MTCW
Bettelheim, Bruno 1903-1990 .... **CLC 79**
See also CA 81-84; 131; CANR 23, 61; MTCW
Betti, Ugo 1892-1953 .... **TCLC 5**
See also CA 104; 155
Betts, Doris (Waugh) 1932- ...... **CLC 3, 6, 28**
See also CA 13-16R; CANR 9, 66; DLBY 82; INT CANR-9
Bevan, Alistair
See Roberts, Keith (John Kingston)
Bey, Pilaff
See Douglas, (George) Norman
Bialik, Chaim Nachman 1873-1934 **TCLC 25**
Bickerstaff, Isaac
See Swift, Jonathan
Bidart, Frank 1939- .... **CLC 33**
See also CA 140
Bienek, Horst 1930- .... **CLC 7, 11**
See also CA 73-76; DLB 75
Bierce, Ambrose (Gwinett) 1842-1914(?)
TCLC 1, 7, 44; DA; DAC; DAM MST; SSC 9; WLC
See also CA 104; 139; CDALB 1865-1917; DLB 11, 12, 23, 71, 74, 186
Biggers, Earl Derr 1884-1933 .... **TCLC 65**
See also CA 108; 153
Billings, Josh
See Shaw, Henry Wheeler
Billington, (Lady) Rachel (Mary) 1942- **C L C 43**
See also AITN 2; CA 33-36R; CANR 44
Binyon, T(imothy) J(ohn) 1936- .... **CLC 34**
See also CA 111; CANR 28
Bioy Casares, Adolfo 1914-1984 **CLC 4, 8, 13, 88; DAM MULT; HLC; SSC 17**
See also CA 29-32R; CANR 19, 43, 66; DLB 113; HW; MTCW
Bird, Cordwainer
See Ellison, Harlan (Jay)
Bird, Robert Montgomery 1806-1854 **NCLC 1**
Birney, (Alfred) Earle 1904-1995 **CLC 1, 4, 6, 11; DAC; DAM MST, POET**
See also CA 1-4R; CANR 5, 20; DLB 88; MTCW
Bishop, Elizabeth 1911-1979 **CLC 1, 4, 9, 13, 15, 32; DA; DAC; DAM MST, POET; PC 3**
See also CA 5-8R; 89-92; CABS 2; CANR 26, 61; CDALB 1968-1988; DLB 5, 169; MTCW; SATA-Obit 24
Bishop, John 1935- .... **CLC 10**
See also CA 105
Bissett, Bill 1939- .... **CLC 18; PC 14**
See also CA 69-72; CAAS 19; CANR 15; DLB 53; MTCW
Bitov, Andrei (Georgievich) 1937- ... **CLC 57**
See also CA 142
Biyidi, Alexandre 1932-
See Beti, Mongo
See also BW 1; CA 114; 124; MTCW
Bjarme, Brynjolf
See Ibsen, Henrik (Johan)
Bjoernson, Bjoernstjerne (Martinius) 1832-1910 .... **TCLC 7, 37**
See also CA 104
Black, Robert
See Holdstock, Robert P.
Blackburn, Paul 1926-1971 .... **CLC 9, 43**
See also CA 81-84; 33-36R; CANR 34; DLB 16; DLBY 81
Black Elk 1863-1950 **TCLC 33; DAM MULT**

See also CA 144; NNAL
Black Hobart
See Sanders, (James) Ed(ward)
Blacklin, Malcolm
See Chambers, Aidan
Blackmore, R(ichard) D(oddridge) 1825-1900 **TCLC 27**
See also CA 120; DLB 18
Blackmur, R(ichard) P(almer) 1904-1965 **CLC 2, 24**
See also CA 11-12; 25-28R; CAP 1; DLB 63
Black Tarantula
See Acker, Kathy
Blackwood, Algernon (Henry) 1869-1951 **TCLC 5**
See also CA 105; 150; DLB 153, 156, 178
Blackwood, Caroline 1931-1996 **CLC 6, 9, 100**
See also CA 85-88; 151; CANR 32, 61, 65; DLB 14; MTCW
Blade, Alexander
See Hamilton, Edmond; Silverberg, Robert
Blaga, Lucian 1895-1961 .... **CLC 75**
See also CA 157
Blair, Eric (Arthur) 1903-1950
See Orwell, George
See also CA 104; 132; DA; DAB; DAC; DAM MST, NOV; MTCW; SATA 29
Blais, Marie-Claire 1939- **CLC 2, 4, 6, 13, 22; DAC; DAM MST**
See also CA 21-24R; CAAS 4; CANR 38; DLB 53; MTCW
Blaise, Clark 1940- .... **CLC 29**
See also AITN 2; CA 53-56; CAAS 3; CANR 5, 66; DLB 53
Blake, Fairley
See De Voto, Bernard (Augustine)
Blake, Nicholas
See Day Lewis, C(ecil)
See also DLB 77
Blake, William 1757-1827 . **NCLC 13, 37, 57; DA; DAB; DAC; DAM MST, POET; PC 12; WLC**
See also CDBLB 1789-1832; CLR 52; DLB 93, 163; MAICYA; SATA 30
Blasco Ibanez, Vicente 1867-1928 **TCLC 12; DAM NOV**
See also CA 110; 131; HW; MTCW
Blatty, William Peter 1928- **CLC 2; DAM POP**
See also CA 5-8R; CANR 9
Bleeck, Oliver
See Thomas, Ross (Elmore)
Blessing, Lee 1949- .... **CLC 54**
Blish, James (Benjamin) 1921-1975 . **CLC 14**
See also CA 1-4R; 57-60; CANR 3; DLB 8; MTCW; SATA 66
Bliss, Reginald
See Wells, H(erbert) G(eorge)
Blixen, Karen (Christentze Dinesen) 1885-1962
See Dinesen, Isak
See also CA 25-28; CANR 22, 50; CAP 2; MTCW; SATA 44
Bloch, Robert (Albert) 1917-1994 .... **CLC 33**
See also CA 5-8R; 146; CAAS 20; CANR 5; DLB 44; INT CANR-5; SATA 12; SATA-Obit 82
Blok, Alexander (Alexandrovich) 1880-1921 **TCLC 5; PC 21**
See also CA 104
Blom, Jan
See Breytenbach, Breyten
Bloom, Harold 1930- .... **CLC 24, 103**
See also CA 13-16R; CANR 39; DLB 67
Bloomfield, Aurelius

See Bourne, Randolph S(illiman)
Blount, Roy (Alton), Jr. 1941- .... **CLC 38**
See also CA 53-56; CANR 10, 28, 61; INT CANR-28; MTCW
Bloy, Leon 1846-1917 .... **TCLC 22**
See also CA 121; DLB 123
Blume, Judy (Sussman) 1938- ... **CLC 12, 30; DAM NOV, POP**
See also AAYA 3; CA 29-32R; CANR 13, 37, 66; CLR 2, 15; DLB 52; JRDA; MAICYA; MTCW; SATA 2, 31, 79
Blunden, Edmund (Charles) 1896-1974 **C L C 2, 56**
See also CA 17-18; 45-48; CANR 54; CAP 2; DLB 20, 100, 155; MTCW
Bly, Robert (Elwood) 1926- **CLC 1, 2, 5, 10, 15, 38; DAM POET**
See also CA 5-8R; CANR 41; DLB 5; MTCW
Boas, Franz 1858-1942 .... **TCLC 56**
See also CA 115
Bobette
See Simenon, Georges (Jacques Christian)
Boccaccio, Giovanni 1313-1375 ... **CMLC 13; SSC 10**
Bochco, Steven 1943- .... **CLC 35**
See also AAYA 11; CA 124; 138
Bodel, Jean 1167(?)-1210 .... **CMLC 28**
Bodenheim, Maxwell 1892-1954 .... **TCLC 44**
See also CA 110; DLB 9, 45
Bodker, Cecil 1927- .... **CLC 21**
See also CA 73-76; CANR 13, 44; CLR 23; MAICYA; SATA 14
Boell, Heinrich (Theodor) 1917-1985 **CLC 2, 3, 6, 9, 11, 15, 27, 32, 72; DA; DAB; DAC; DAM MST, NOV; SSC 23; WLC**
See also CA 21-24R; 116; CANR 24; DLB 69; DLBY 85; MTCW
Boerne, Alfred
See Doeblin, Alfred
Boethius 480(?)-524(?) .... **CMLC 15**
See also DLB 115
Bogan, Louise 1897-1970 . **CLC 4, 39, 46, 93; DAM POET; PC 12**
See also CA 73-76; 25-28R; CANR 33; DLB 45, 169; MTCW
Bogarde, Dirk .... **CLC 19**
See also Van Den Bogarde, Derek Jules Gaspard Ulric Niven
See also DLB 14
Bogosian, Eric 1953- .... **CLC 45**
See also CA 138
Bograd, Larry 1953- .... **CLC 35**
See also CA 93-96; CANR 57; SAAS 21; SATA 33, 89
Boiardo, Matteo Maria 1441-1494 .... **LC 6**
Boileau-Despreaux, Nicolas 1636-1711 . **LC 3**
Bojer, Johan 1872-1959 .... **TCLC 64**
Boland, Eavan (Aisling) 1944- .. **CLC 40, 67; DAM POET**
See also CA 143; CANR 61; DLB 40
Boll, Heinrich
See Boell, Heinrich (Theodor)
Bolt, Lee
See Faust, Frederick (Schiller)
Bolt, Robert (Oxton) 1924-1995 ..... **CLC 14; DAM DRAM**
See also CA 17-20R; 147; CANR 35, 67; DLB 13; MTCW
Bombet, Louis-Alexandre-Cesar
See Stendhal
Bomkauf
See Kaufman, Bob (Garnell)
Bonaventura .... **NCLC 35**

See also DLB 90

Bond, Edward 1934- **CLC 4, 6, 13, 23; DAM DRAM**

See also CA 25-28R; CANR 38, 67; DLB 13; MTCW

Bonham, Frank 1914-1989 .... **CLC 12**

See also AAYA 1; CA 9-12R; CANR 4, 36; JRDA; MAICYA; SAAS 3; SATA 1, 49; SATA-Obit 62

Bonnefoy, Yves 1923-... **CLC 9, 15, 58; DAM MST, POET**

See also CA 85-88; CANR 33; MTCW

Bontemps, Arna(ud Wendell) 1902-1973 **C L C 1, 18; BLC 1; DAM MULT, NOV, POET**

See also BW 1; CA 1-4R; 41-44R; CANR 4, 35; CLR 6; DLB 48, 51; JRDA; MAICYA; MTCW; SATA 2, 44; SATA-Obit 24

Booth, Martin 1944- .... **CLC 13**

See also CA 93-96; CAAS 2

Booth, Philip 1925- .... **CLC 23**

See also CA 5-8R; CANR 5; DLBY 82

Booth, Wayne C(layson) 1921- .... **CLC 24**

See also CA 1-4R; CAAS 5; CANR 3, 43; DLB 67

Borchert, Wolfgang 1921-1947 .... **TCLC 5**

See also CA 104; DLB 69, 124

Borel, Petrus 1809-1859 .... **NCLC 41**

Borges, Jorge Luis 1899-1986 **CLC 1, 2, 3, 4, 6, 8, 9, 10, 13, 19, 44, 48, 83; DA; DAB; DAC; DAM MST, MULT; HLC; PC 22; SSC 4; WLC**

See also AAYA 19; CA 21-24R; CANR 19, 33; DLB 113; DLBY 86; HW; MTCW

Borowski, Tadeusz 1922-1951 .... **TCLC 9**

See also CA 106; 154

Borrow, George (Henry) 1803-1881 **NCLC 9**

See also DLB 21, 55, 166

Bosman, Herman Charles 1905-1951 **T C L C 49**

See also Malan, Herman

See also CA 160

Bosschere, Jean de 1878(?)-1953 ... **TCLC 19**

See also CA 115

Boswell, James 1740-1795 . **LC 4; DA; DAB; DAC; DAM MST; WLC**

See also CDBLB 1660-1789; DLB 104, 142

Bottoms, David 1949- .... **CLC 53**

See also CA 105; CANR 22; DLB 120; DLBY 83

Boucicault, Dion 1820-1890 .... **NCLC 41**

Boucolon, Maryse 1937(?)-

See Conde, Maryse

See also CA 110; CANR 30, 53

Bourget, Paul (Charles Joseph) 1852-1935 **TCLC 12**

See also CA 107; DLB 123

Bourjaily, Vance (Nye) 1922- ....**CLC 8, 62**

See also CA 1-4R; CAAS 1; CANR 2; DLB 2, 143

Bourne, Randolph S(illiman) 1886-1918 **TCLC 16**

See also CA 117; 155; DLB 63

Bova, Ben(jamin William) 1932- ...... **CLC 45**

See also AAYA 16; CA 5-8R; CAAS 18; CANR 11, 56; CLR 3; DLBY 81; INT CANR-11; MAICYA; MTCW; SATA 6, 68

Bowen, Elizabeth (Dorothea Cole) 1899-1973 **CLC 1, 3, 6, 11, 15, 22; DAM NOV; SSC 3, 28**

See also CA 17-18; 41-44R; CANR 35; CAP 2; CDBLB 1945-1960; DLB 15, 162; MTCW

Bowering, George 1935- .... **CLC 15, 47**

See also CA 21-24R; CAAS 16; CANR 10; DLB 53

Bowering, Marilyn R(uthe) 1949- .... **CLC 32**

See also CA 101; CANR 49

Bowers, Edgar 1924- .... **CLC 9**

See also CA 5-8R; CANR 24; DLB 5

Bowie, David .... **CLC 17**

See also Jones, David Robert

Bowles, Jane (Sydney) 1917-1973 **CLC 3, 68**

See also CA 19-20; 41-44R; CAP 2

Bowles, Paul (Frederick) 1910-1986 **CLC 1, 2, 19, 53; SSC 3**

See also CA 1-4R; CAAS 1; CANR 1, 19, 50; DLB 5, 6; MTCW

Box, Edgar

See Vidal, Gore

Boyd, Nancy

See Millay, Edna St. Vincent

Boyd, William 1952- .... **CLC 28, 53, 70**

See also CA 114; 120; CANR 51

Boyle, Kay 1902-1992 **CLC 1, 5, 19, 58; SSC 5**

See also CA 13-16R; 140; CAAS 1; CANR 29, 61; DLB 4, 9, 48, 86; DLBY 93; MTCW

Boyle, Mark

See Kienzle, William X(avier)

Boyle, Patrick 1905-1982 .... **CLC 19**

See also CA 127

Boyle, T. C. 1948-

See Boyle, T(homas) Coraghessan

Boyle, T(homas) Coraghessan 1948- **CLC 36, 55, 90; DAM POP; SSC 16**

See also BEST 90:4; CA 120; CANR 44; DLBY 86

Boz

See Dickens, Charles (John Huffam)

Brackenridge, Hugh Henry 1748-1816 **N C L C 7**

See also DLB 11, 37

Bradbury, Edward P.

See Moorcock, Michael (John)

Bradbury, Malcolm (Stanley) 1932- **CLC 32, 61; DAM NOV**

See also CA 1-4R; CANR 1, 33; DLB 14; MTCW

Bradbury, Ray (Douglas) 1920- **CLC 1, 3, 10, 15, 42, 98; DA; DAB; DAC; DAM MST, NOV, POP; SSC 29; WLC**

See also AAYA 15; AITN 1, 2; CA 1-4R; CANR 2, 30; CDALB 1968-1988; DLB 2, 8; MTCW; SATA 11, 64

Bradford, Gamaliel 1863-1932 ...... **TCLC 36**

See also CA 160; DLB 17

Bradley, David (Henry, Jr.) 1950- .. **CLC 23; BLC 1; DAM MULT**

See also BW 1; CA 104; CANR 26; DLB 33

Bradley, John Ed(mund, Jr.) 1958- .. **CLC 55**

See also CA 139

Bradley, Marion Zimmer 1930- **CLC 30; DAM POP**

See also AAYA 9; CA 57-60; CAAS 10; CANR 7, 31, 51; DLB 8; MTCW; SATA 90

Bradstreet, Anne 1612(?)-1672 **LC 4, 30; DA; DAC; DAM MST, POET; PC 10**

See also CDALB 1640-1865; DLB 24

Brady, Joan 1939- .... **CLC 86**

See also CA 141

Bragg, Melvyn 1939- .... **CLC 10**

See also BEST 89:3; CA 57-60; CANR 10, 48; DLB 14

Brahe, Tycho 1546-1601 .... **LC 45**

Braine, John (Gerard) 1922-1986 **CLC 1, 3, 41**

See also CA 1-4R; 120; CANR 1, 33; CDBLB 1945-1960; DLB 15; DLBY 86; MTCW

Bramah, Ernest 1868-1942 .... **TCLC 72**

See also CA 156; DLB 70

Brammer, William 1930(?)-1978 .... **CLC 31**

See also CA 77-80

Brancati, Vitaliano 1907-1954 .... **TCLC 12**

See also CA 109

Brancato, Robin F(idler) 1936- ....**CLC 35**

See also AAYA 9; CA 69-72; CANR 11, 45; CLR 32; JRDA; SAAS 9; SATA 97

Brand, Max

See Faust, Frederick (Schiller)

Brand, Millen 1906-1980 .... **CLC 7**

See also CA 21-24R; 97-100

Branden, Barbara .... **CLC 44**

See also CA 148

Brandes, Georg (Morris Cohen) 1842-1927 **TCLC 10**

See also CA 105

Brandys, Kazimierz 1916- .... **CLC 62**

Branley, Franklyn M(ansfield) 1915- **CLC 21**

See also CA 33-36R; CANR 14, 39; CLR 13; MAICYA; SAAS 16; SATA 4, 68

Brathwaite, Edward Kamau 1930- . **CLC 11; BLCS; DAM POET**

See also BW 2; CA 25-28R; CANR 11, 26, 47; DLB 125

Brautigan, Richard (Gary) 1935-1984 **CLC 1, 3, 5, 9, 12, 34, 42; DAM NOV**

See also CA 53-56; 113; CANR 34; DLB 2, 5; DLBY 80, 84; MTCW; SATA 56

Brave Bird, Mary 1953-

See Crow Dog, Mary (Ellen)

See also NNAL

Braverman, Kate 1950- .... **CLC 67**

See also CA 89-92

Brecht, (Eugen) Bertolt (Friedrich) 1898-1956 **TCLC 1, 6, 13, 35; DA; DAB; DAC; DAM DRAM, MST; DC 3; WLC**

See also CA 104; 133; CANR 62; DLB 56, 124; MTCW

Brecht, Eugen Berthold Friedrich

See Brecht, (Eugen) Bertolt (Friedrich)

Bremer, Fredrika 1801-1865 .... **NCLC 11**

Brennan, Christopher John 1870-1932 **T C L C 17**

See also CA 117

Brennan, Maeve 1917- .... **CLC 5**

See also CA 81-84

Brent, Linda

See Jacobs, Harriet A(nn)

Brentano, Clemens (Maria) 1778-1842 **N C L C 1**

See also DLB 90

Brent of Bin Bin

See Franklin, (Stella Maria Sarah) Miles (Lampe)

Brenton, Howard 1942- .... **CLC 31**

See also CA 69-72; CANR 33, 67; DLB 13; MTCW

Breslin, James 1930-1996

See Breslin, Jimmy

See also CA 73-76; CANR 31; DAM NOV; MTCW

Breslin, Jimmy .... **CLC 4, 43**

See also Breslin, James

See also AITN 1; DLB 185

Bresson, Robert 1901- .... **CLC 16**

See also CA 110; CANR 49

Breton, Andre 1896-1966 **CLC 2, 9, 15, 54; PC 15**

See also CA 19-20; 25-28R; CANR 40, 60; CAP 2; DLB 65; MTCW

Breytenbach, Breyten 1939(?)- . **CLC 23, 37; DAM POET**

See also CA 113; 129; CANR 61

Bridgers, Sue Ellen 1942- .... **CLC 26**
See also AAYA 8; CA 65-68; CANR 11, 36; CLR 18; DLB 52; JRDA; MAICYA; SAAS 1; SATA 22, 90

Bridges, Robert (Seymour) 1844-1930 **T C L C 1; DAM POET**
See also CA 104; 152; CDBLB 1890-1914; DLB 19, 98

Bridie, James .... **TCLC 3**
See also Mavor, Osborne Henry
See also DLB 10

Brin, David 1950- .... **CLC 34**
See also AAYA 21; CA 102; CANR 24; INT CANR-24; SATA 65

Brink, Andre (Philippus) 1935- **CLC 18, 36, 106**
See also CA 104; CANR 39, 62; INT 103; MTCW

Brinsmead, H(esba) F(ay) 1922- .... **CLC 21**
See also CA 21-24R; CANR 10; CLR 47; MAICYA; SAAS 5; SATA 18, 78

Brittain, Vera (Mary) 1893(?)-1970 . **CLC 23**
See also CA 13-16; 25-28R; CANR 58; CAP 1; DLB 191; MTCW

Broch, Hermann 1886-1951 .... **TCLC 20**
See also CA 117; DLB 85, 124

Brock, Rose
See Hansen, Joseph

Brodkey, Harold (Roy) 1930-1996.... **CLC 56**
See also CA 111; 151; DLB 130

Brodsky, Iosif Alexandrovich 1940-1996
See Brodsky, Joseph
See also AITN 1; CA 41-44R; 151; CANR 37; DAM POET; MTCW

Brodsky, Joseph 1940-1996 **CLC 4, 6, 13, 36, 100; PC 9**
See also Brodsky, Iosif Alexandrovich

Brodsky, Michael (Mark) 1948-........ **CLC 19**
See also CA 102; CANR 18, 41, 58

Bromell, Henry 1947- .... **CLC 5**
See also CA 53-56; CANR 9

Bromfield, Louis (Brucker) 1896-1956 **T C L C 11**
See also CA 107; 155; DLB 4, 9, 86

Broner, E(sther) M(asserman) 1930- **CLC 19**
See also CA 17-20R; CANR 8, 25; DLB 28

Bronk, William 1918- .... **CLC 10**
See also CA 89-92; CANR 23; DLB 165

Bronstein, Lev Davidovich
See Trotsky, Leon

Bronte, Anne 1820-1849 .... **NCLC 71**
See also DLB 21, 199

Bronte, Charlotte 1816-1855 **NCLC 3, 8, 33, 58; DA; DAB; DAC; DAM MST, NOV; WLC**
See also AAYA 17; CDBLB 1832-1890; DLB 21, 159, 199

Bronte, Emily (Jane) 1818-1848 **NCLC 16, 35; DA; DAB; DAC; DAM MST, NOV, POET; PC 8; WLC**
See also AAYA 17; CDBLB 1832-1890; DLB 21, 32, 199

Brooke, Frances 1724-1789 .... **LC 6**
See also DLB 39, 99

Brooke, Henry 1703(?)-1783 .... **LC 1**
See also DLB 39

Brooke, Rupert (Chawner) 1887-1915 **T C L C 2, 7; DA; DAB; DAC; DAM MST, POET; WLC**
See also CA 104; 132; CANR 61; CDBLB 1914-1945; DLB 19; MTCW

Brooke-Haven, P.

See Wodehouse, P(elham) G(renville)

Brooke-Rose, Christine 1926(?)- .... **CLC 40**
See also CA 13-16R; CANR 58; DLB 14

Brookner, Anita 1928- **CLC 32, 34, 51; DAB; DAM POP**
See also CA 114; 120; CANR 37, 56; DLB 194; DLBY 87; MTCW

Brooks, Cleanth 1906-1994 **CLC 24, 86, 110**
See also CA 17-20R; 145; CANR 33, 35; DLB 63; DLBY 94; INT CANR-35; MTCW

Brooks, George
See Baum, L(yman) Frank

Brooks, Gwendolyn 1917- **CLC 1, 2, 4, 5, 15, 49; BLC 1; DA; DAC; DAM MST, MULT, POET; PC 7; WLC**
See also AAYA 20; AITN 1; BW 2; CA 1-4R; CANR 1, 27, 52; CDALB 1941-1968; CLR 27; DLB 5, 76, 165; MTCW; SATA 6

Brooks, Mel .... **CLC 12**
See also Kaminsky, Melvin
See also AAYA 13; DLB 26

Brooks, Peter 1938- .... **CLC 34**
See also CA 45-48; CANR 1

Brooks, Van Wyck 1886-1963 .... **CLC 29**
See also CA 1-4R; CANR 6; DLB 45, 63, 103

Brophy, Brigid (Antonia) 1929-1995 **CLC 6, 11, 29, 105**
See also CA 5-8R; 149; CAAS 4; CANR 25, 53; DLB 14; MTCW

Brosman, Catharine Savage 1934- ..... **CLC 9**
See also CA 61-64; CANR 21, 46

Brother Antoninus
See Everson, William (Oliver)

The Brothers Quay
See Quay, Stephen; Quay, Timothy

Broughton, T(homas) Alan 1936- ..... **CLC 19**
See also CA 45-48; CANR 2, 23, 48

Broumas, Olga 1949- .... **CLC 10, 73**
See also CA 85-88; CANR 20, 69

Brown, Alan 1950- .... **CLC 99**
See also CA 156

Brown, Charles Brockden 1771-1810 **N C L C 22**
See also CDALB 1640-1865; DLB 37, 59, 73

Brown, Christy 1932-1981 .... **CLC 63**
See also CA 105; 104; DLB 14

Brown, Claude 1937- **CLC 30; BLC 1; DAM MULT**
See also AAYA 7; BW 1; CA 73-76

Brown, Dee (Alexander) 1908-.. **CLC 18, 47; DAM POP**
See also CA 13-16R; CAAS 6; CANR 11, 45, 60; DLBY 80; MTCW; SATA 5

Brown, George
See Wertmueller, Lina

Brown, George Douglas 1869-1902 **TCLC 28**
See also CA 162

Brown, George Mackay 1921-1996 **CLC 5, 48, 100**
See also CA 21-24R; 151; CAAS 6; CANR 12, 37, 67; DLB 14, 27, 139; MTCW; SATA 35

Brown, (William) Larry 1951- .... **CLC 73**
See also CA 130; 134; INT 133

Brown, Moses
See Barrett, William (Christopher)

Brown, Rita Mae 1944- **CLC 18, 43, 79; DAM NOV, POP**
See also CA 45-48; CANR 2, 11, 35, 62; INT CANR-11; MTCW

Brown, Roderick (Langmere) Haig-
See Haig-Brown, Roderick (Langmere)

Brown, Rosellen 1939- .... **CLC 32**
See also CA 77-80; CAAS 10; CANR 14, 44

Brown, Sterling Allen 1901-1989 **CLC 1, 23, 59; BLC 1; DAM MULT, POET**
See also BW 1; CA 85-88; 127; CANR 26; DLB 48, 51, 63; MTCW

Brown, Will
See Ainsworth, William Harrison

Brown, William Wells 1813-1884 ...**NCLC 2; BLC 1; DAM MULT; DC 1**
See also DLB 3, 50

Browne, (Clyde) Jackson 1948(?)- .... **CLC 21**
See also CA 120

Browning, Elizabeth Barrett 1806-1861 **NCLC 1, 16, 61, 66; DA; DAB; DAC; DAM MST, POET; PC 6; WLC**
See also CDBLB 1832-1890; DLB 32, 199

Browning, Robert 1812-1889 **NCLC 19; DA; DAB; DAC; DAM MST, POET; PC 2; WLCS**
See also CDBLB 1832-1890; DLB 32, 163; YABC 1

Browning, Tod 1882-1962 .... **CLC 16**
See also CA 141; 117

Brownson, Orestes (Augustus) 1803-1876 **NCLC 50**

Brownson, Orestes Augustus 1803-1876 **NCLC 50**
See also DLB 1, 59, 73

Bruccoli, Matthew J(oseph) 1931- ... **CLC 34**
See also CA 9-12R; CANR 7; DLB 103

Bruce, Lenny .... **CLC 21**
See also Schneider, Leonard Alfred

Bruin, John
See Brutus, Dennis

Brulard, Henri
See Stendhal

Brulls, Christian
See Simenon, Georges (Jacques Christian)

Brunner, John (Kilian Houston) 1934-1995 **CLC 8, 10; DAM POP**
See also CA 1-4R; 149; CAAS 8; CANR 2, 37; MTCW

Bruno, Giordano 1548-1600 .... **LC 27**

Brutus, Dennis 1924- **CLC 43; BLC 1; DAM MULT, POET**
See also BW 2; CA 49-52; CAAS 14; CANR 2, 27, 42; DLB 117

Bryan, C(ourtlandt) D(ixon) B(arnes) 1936- **CLC 29**
See also CA 73-76; CANR 13, 68; DLB 185; INT CANR-13

Bryan, Michael
See Moore, Brian

Bryant, William Cullen 1794-1878. **NCLC 6, 46; DA; DAB; DAC; DAM MST, POET; PC 20**
See also CDALB 1640-1865; DLB 3, 43, 59, 189

Bryusov, Valery Yakovlevich 1873-1924 **TCLC 10**
See also CA 107; 155

Buchan, John 1875-1940 ..... **TCLC 41; DAB; DAM POP**
See also CA 108; 145; DLB 34, 70, 156; YABC 2

Buchanan, George 1506-1582 .... **LC 4**
See also DLB 152

Buchheim, Lothar-Guenther 1918- .... **CLC 6**
See also CA 85-88

Buchner, (Karl) Georg 1813-1837 . **NCLC 26**

Buchwald, Art(hur) 1925- .... **CLC 33**
See also AITN 1; CA 5-8R; CANR 21, 67; MTCW; SATA 10

Buck, Pearl S(ydenstricker) 1892-1973 **CLC 7,**

See also BW 1; CA 125; CANR 56

Dacey, Philip 1939- .... **CLC 51**
　　See also CA 37-40R; CAAS 17; CANR 14, 32,
　　64; DLB 105

Dagerman, Stig (Halvard) 1923-1954 **T C L C 17**
　　See also CA 117; 155

Dahl, Roald 1916-1990 CLC 1, 6, 18, 79; DAB;
　　DAC; DAM MST, NOV, POP
　　See also AAYA 15; CA 1-4R; 133; CANR 6,
　　32, 37, 62; CLR 1, 7, 41; DLB 139; JRDA;
　　MAICYA; MTCW; SATA 1, 26, 73; SATA-
　　Obit 65

Dahlberg, Edward 1900-1977 .. **CLC 1, 7, 14**
　　See also CA 9-12R; 69-72; CANR 31, 62; DLB
　　48; MTCW

Daitch, Susan 1954- .... **CLC 103**
　　See also CA 161

Dale, Colin .... **TCLC 18**
　　See also Lawrence, T(homas) E(dward)

Dale, George E.
　　See Asimov, Isaac

Daly, Elizabeth 1878-1967 .... **CLC 52**
　　See also CA 23-24; 25-28R; CANR 60; CAP 2

Daly, Maureen 1921- .... **CLC 17**
　　See also AAYA 5; CANR 37; JRDA; MAICYA;
　　SAAS 1; SATA 2

Damas, Leon-Gontran 1912-1978 .... **CLC 84**
　　See also BW 1; CA 125; 73-76

Dana, Richard Henry Sr. 1787-1879 NCLC 53

Daniel, Samuel 1562(?)-1619 .... **LC 24**
　　See also DLB 62

Daniels, Brett
　　See Adler, Renata

Dannay, Frederic 1905-1982 . **CLC 11; DAM
　　POP**
　　See also Queen, Ellery
　　See also CA 1-4R; 107; CANR 1, 39; DLB 137;
　　MTCW

D'Annunzio, Gabriele 1863-1938 TCLC 6, 40
　　See also CA 104; 155

Danois, N. le
　　See Gourmont, Remy (-Marie-Charles) de

Dante 1265-1321 .... **CMLC 3, 18; DA; DAB;
　　DAC; DAM MST, POET; PC 21; WLCS**

d'Antibes, Germain
　　See Simenon, Georges (Jacques Christian)

Danticat, Edwidge 1969- .... **CLC 94**
　　See also CA 152

Danvers, Dennis 1947- .... **CLC 70**

Danziger, Paula 1944- .... **CLC 21**
　　See also AAYA 4; CA 112; 115; CANR 37; CLR
　　20; JRDA; MAICYA; SATA 36, 63; SATA-
　　Brief 30

Dario, Ruben 1867-1916 .... **TCLC 4; DAM
　　MULT; HLC; PC 15**
　　See also CA 131; HW; MTCW

Darley, George 1795-1846 .... **NCLC 2**
　　See also DLB 96

Darrow, Clarence (Seward) 1857-1938 T C L C
　　81
　　See also CA 164

Darwin, Charles 1809-1882 .... **NCLC 57**
　　See also DLB 57, 166

Daryush, Elizabeth 1887-1977 ...... **CLC 6, 19**
　　See also CA 49-52; CANR 3; DLB 20

Dasgupta, Surendranath 1887-1952 TCLC 81
　　See also CA 157

**Dashwood, Edmee Elizabeth Monica de la Pas-
　　ture** 1890-1943
　　See Delafield, E. M.
　　See also CA 119; 154

Daudet, (Louis Marie) Alphonse 1840-1897

NCLC 1
　　See also DLB 123

Daumal, Rene 1908-1944 .... **TCLC 14**
　　See also CA 114

Davenport, Guy (Mattison, Jr.) 1927- **CLC 6,
　　14, 38; SSC 16**
　　See also CA 33-36R; CANR 23; DLB 130

Davidson, Avram 1923-
　　See Queen, Ellery
　　See also CA 101; CANR 26; DLB 8

Davidson, Donald (Grady) 1893-1968 CLC 2,
　　13, 19
　　See also CA 5-8R; 25-28R; CANR 4; DLB 45

Davidson, Hugh
　　See Hamilton, Edmond

Davidson, John 1857-1909 .... **TCLC 24**
　　See also CA 118; DLB 19

Davidson, Sara 1943- .... **CLC 9**
　　See also CA 81-84; CANR 44, 68; DLB 185

Davie, Donald (Alfred) 1922-1995 . CLC 5, 8,
　　10, 31
　　See also CA 1-4R; 149; CAAS 3; CANR 1, 44;
　　DLB 27; MTCW

Davies, Ray(mond Douglas) 1944- ... **CLC 21**
　　See also CA 116; 146

Davies, Rhys 1901-1978 .... **CLC 23**
　　See also CA 9-12R; 81-84; CANR 4; DLB 139,
　　191

Davies, (William) Robertson 1913-1995 C L C
　　2, 7, 13, 25, 42, 75, 91; DA; DAB; DAC;
　　DAM MST, NOV, POP; WLC
　　See also BEST 89:2; CA 33-36R; 150; CANR
　　17, 42; DLB 68; INT CANR-17; MTCW

Davies, W(illiam) H(enry) 1871-1940 TCLC 5
　　See also CA 104; DLB 19, 174

Davies, Walter C.
　　See Kornbluth, C(yril) M.

Davis, Angela (Yvonne) 1944- **CLC 77; DAM
　　MULT**
　　See also BW 2; CA 57-60; CANR 10

Davis, B. Lynch
　　See Bioy Casares, Adolfo; Borges, Jorge Luis

Davis, Harold Lenoir 1896-1960 ...... **CLC 49**
　　See also CA 89-92; DLB 9

Davis, Rebecca (Blaine) Harding 1831-1910
　　TCLC 6
　　See also CA 104; DLB 74

Davis, Richard Harding 1864-1916 TCLC 24
　　See also CA 114; DLB 12, 23, 78, 79, 189;
　　DLBD 13

Davison, Frank Dalby 1893-1970 ..... **CLC 15**
　　See also CA 116

Davison, Lawrence H.
　　See Lawrence, D(avid) H(erbert Richards)

Davison, Peter (Hubert) 1928- .... **CLC 28**
　　See also CA 9-12R; CAAS 4; CANR 3, 43; DLB
　　5

Davys, Mary 1674-1732 .... **LC 1**
　　See also DLB 39

Dawson, Fielding 1930- .... **CLC 6**
　　See also CA 85-88; DLB 130

Dawson, Peter
　　See Faust, Frederick (Schiller)

Day, Clarence (Shepard, Jr.) 1874-1935
　　TCLC 25
　　See also CA 108; DLB 11

Day, Thomas 1748-1789 .... **LC 1**
　　See also DLB 39; YABC 1

Day Lewis, C(ecil) 1904-1972 . **CLC 1, 6, 10;
　　DAM POET; PC 11**
　　See also Blake, Nicholas
　　See also CA 13-16; 33-36R; CANR 34; CAP 1;
　　DLB 15, 20; MTCW

Dazai Osamu 1909-1948 .... **TCLC 11**
　　See also Tsushima, Shuji
　　See also CA 164; DLB 182

de Andrade, Carlos Drummond
　　See Drummond de Andrade, Carlos

Deane, Norman
　　See Creasey, John

**de Beauvoir, Simone (Lucie Ernestine Marie
　　Bertrand)**
　　See Beauvoir, Simone (Lucie Ernestine Marie
　　Bertrand) de

de Beer, P.
　　See Bosman, Herman Charles

de Brissac, Malcolm
　　See Dickinson, Peter (Malcolm)

de Chardin, Pierre Teilhard
　　See Teilhard de Chardin, (Marie Joseph) Pierre

Dee, John 1527-1608 .... **LC 20**

Deer, Sandra 1940- .... **CLC 45**

De Ferrari, Gabriella 1941- .... **CLC 65**
　　See also CA 146

Defoe, Daniel 1660(?)-1731 LC 1; DA; DAB;
　　DAC; DAM MST, NOV; WLC
　　See also CDBLB 1660-1789; DLB 39, 95, 101;
　　JRDA; MAICYA; SATA 22

de Gourmont, Remy(-Marie-Charles)
　　See Gourmont, Remy (-Marie-Charles) de

de Hartog, Jan 1914- .... **CLC 19**
　　See also CA 1-4R; CANR 1

de Hostos, E. M.
　　See Hostos (y Bonilla), Eugenio Maria de

de Hostos, Eugenio M.
　　See Hostos (y Bonilla), Eugenio Maria de

Deighton, Len .... **CLC 4, 7, 22, 46**
　　See also Deighton, Leonard Cyril
　　See also AAYA 6; BEST 89:2; CDBLB 1960 to
　　Present; DLB 87

Deighton, Leonard Cyril 1929-
　　See Deighton, Len
　　See also CA 9-12R; CANR 19, 33, 68; DAM
　　NOV, POP; MTCW

Dekker, Thomas 1572(?)-1632 .. **LC 22; DAM
　　DRAM**
　　See also CDBLB Before 1660; DLB 62, 172

Delafield, E. M. 1890-1943 .... **TCLC 61**
　　See also Dashwood, Edmee Elizabeth Monica
　　de la Pasture
　　See also DLB 34

de la Mare, Walter (John) 1873-1956 TCLC 4,
　　53; DAB; DAC; DAM MST, POET; SSC
　　14; WLC
　　See also CA 163; CDBLB 1914-1945; CLR 23;
　　DLB 162; SATA 16

Delaney, Franey
　　See O'Hara, John (Henry)

Delaney, Shelagh 1939- CLC 29; DAM DRAM
　　See also CA 17-20R; CANR 30, 67; CDBLB
　　1960 to Present; DLB 13; MTCW

Delany, Mary (Granville Pendarves) 1700-1788
　　LC 12

Delany, Samuel R(ay, Jr.) 1942- CLC 8, 14, 38;
　　BLC 1; DAM MULT
　　See also AAYA 24; BW 2; CA 81-84; CANR
　　27, 43; DLB 8, 33; MTCW

De La Ramee, (Marie) Louise 1839-1908
　　See Ouida
　　See also SATA 20

de la Roche, Mazo 1879-1961 .... **CLC 14**
　　See also CA 85-88; CANR 30; DLB 68; SATA
　　64

De La Salle, Innocent
　　See Hartmann, Sadakichi

Delbanco, Nicholas (Franklin) 1942- **CLC 6,**

13
See also CA 17-20R; CAAS 2; CANR 29, 55; DLB 6

del Castillo, Michel 1933- .... **CLC 38**
See also CA 109

Deledda, Grazia (Cosima) 1875(?)-1936
TCLC 23
See also CA 123

Delibes, Miguel ....**CLC 8, 18**
See also Delibes Setien, Miguel

Delibes Setien, Miguel 1920-
See Delibes, Miguel
See also CA 45-48; CANR 1, 32; HW; MTCW

DeLillo, Don 1936- **CLC 8, 10, 13, 27, 39, 54, 76; DAM NOV, POP**
See also BEST 89:1; CA 81-84; CANR 21; DLB 6, 173; MTCW

de Lisser, H. G.
See De Lisser, H(erbert) G(eorge)
See also DLB 117

De Lisser, H(erbert) G(eorge) 1878-1944
TCLC 12
See also de Lisser, H. G.
See also BW 2; CA 109; 152

Deloney, Thomas (?)-1600 .... **LC 41**
See also DLB 167

Deloria, Vine (Victor), Jr. 1933- ..... **CLC 21; DAM MULT**
See also CA 53-56; CANR 5, 20, 48; DLB 175; MTCW; NNAL; SATA 21

Del Vecchio, John M(ichael) 1947- ... **CLC 29**
See also CA 110; DLBD 9

de Man, Paul (Adolph Michel) 1919-1983
CLC 55
See also CA 128; 111; CANR 61; DLB 67; MTCW

De Marinis, Rick 1934- .... **CLC 54**
See also CA 57-60; CAAS 24; CANR 9, 25, 50

Dembry, R. Emmet
See Murfree, Mary Noailles

Demby, William 1922- **CLC 53; BLC 1; DAM MULT**
See also BW 1; CA 81-84; DLB 33

de Menton, Francisco
See Chin, Frank (Chew, Jr.)

Demijohn, Thom
See Disch, Thomas M(ichael)

de Montherlant, Henry (Milon)
See Montherlant, Henry (Milon) de

Demosthenes 384B.C.-322B.C. ...... **CMLC 13**
See also DLB 176

de Natale, Francine
See Malzberg, Barry N(athaniel)

Denby, Edwin (Orr) 1903-1983 .... **CLC 48**
See also CA 138; 110

Denis, Julio
See Cortazar, Julio

Denmark, Harrison
See Zelazny, Roger (Joseph)

Dennis, John 1658-1734 .... **LC 11**
See also DLB 101

Dennis, Nigel (Forbes) 1912-1989 .... **CLC 8**
See also CA 25-28R; 129; DLB 13, 15; MTCW

Dent, Lester 1904(?)-1959 .... **TCLC 72**
See also CA 112; 161

De Palma, Brian (Russell) 1940- .... **CLC 20**
See also CA 109

De Quincey, Thomas 1785-1859 ...... **NCLC 4**
See also CDBLB 1789-1832; DLB 110; 144

Deren, Eleanora 1908(?)-1961
See Deren, Maya
See also CA 111

Deren, Maya 1917-1961 .... **CLC 16, 102**

See also Deren, Eleanora

Derleth, August (William) 1909-1971**CLC 31**
See also CA 1-4R; 29-32R; CANR 4; DLB 9; SATA 5

Der Nister 1884-1950 .... **TCLC 56**

de Routisie, Albert
See Aragon, Louis

Derrida, Jacques 1930- .... **CLC 24, 87**
See also CA 124; 127

Derry Down Derry
See Lear, Edward

Dersonnes, Jacques
See Simenon, Georges (Jacques Christian)

Desai, Anita 1937-**CLC 19, 37, 97; DAB; DAM NOV**
See also CA 81-84; CANR 33, 53; MTCW; SATA 63

de Saint-Luc, Jean
See Glassco, John

de Saint Roman, Arnaud
See Aragon, Louis

Descartes, Rene 1596-1650 .... **LC 20, 35**

De Sica, Vittorio 1901(?)-1974 .... **CLC 20**
See also CA 117

Desnos, Robert 1900-1945 .... **TCLC 22**
See also CA 121; 151

Destouches, Louis-Ferdinand 1894-1961**CLC 9, 15**
See also Celine, Louis-Ferdinand
See also CA 85-88; CANR 28; MTCW

de Tolignac, Gaston
See Griffith, D(avid Lewelyn) W(ark)

Deutsch, Babette 1895-1982 .... **CLC 18**
See also CA 1-4R; 108; CANR 4; DLB 45; SATA 1; SATA-Obit 33

Devenant, William 1606-1649 .... **LC 13**

Devkota, Laxmiprasad 1909-1959 . **TCLC 23**
See also CA 123

De Voto, Bernard (Augustine) 1897-1955
TCLC 29
See also CA 113; 160; DLB 9

De Vries, Peter 1910-1993 **CLC 1, 2, 3, 7, 10, 28, 46; DAM NOV**
See also CA 17-20R; 142; CANR 41; DLB 6; DLBY 82; MTCW

Dexter, John
See Bradley, Marion Zimmer

Dexter, Martin
See Faust, Frederick (Schiller)

Dexter, Pete 1943- ... **CLC 34, 55; DAM POP**
See also BEST 89:2; CA 127; 131; INT 131; MTCW

Diamano, Silmang
See Senghor, Leopold Sedar

Diamond, Neil 1941- .... **CLC 30**
See also CA 108

Diaz del Castillo, Bernal 1496-1584 .... **LC 31**

di Bassetto, Corno
See Shaw, George Bernard

Dick, Philip K(indred) 1928-1982**CLC 10, 30, 72; DAM NOV, POP**
See also AAYA 24; CA 49-52; 106; CANR 2, 16; DLB 8; MTCW

Dickens, Charles (John Huffam) 1812-1870
NCLC 3, 8, 18, 26, 37, 50; DA; DAB; DAC; DAM MST, NOV; SSC 17; WLC
See also AAYA 23; CDBLB 1832-1890; DLB 21, 55, 70, 159, 166; JRDA; MAICYA; SATA 15

Dickey, James (Lafayette) 1923-1997 **CLC 1, 2, 4, 7, 10, 15, 47, 109; DAM NOV, POET, POP**
See also AITN 1, 2; CA 9-12R; 156; CABS 2;

CANR 10, 48, 61; CDALB 1968-1988; DLB 5, 193; DLBD 7; DLBY 82, 93, 96, 97; INT CANR-10; MTCW

Dickey, William 1928-1994 .... **CLC 3, 28**
See also CA 9-12R; 145; CANR 24; DLB 5

Dickinson, Charles 1951- .... **CLC 49**
See also CA 128

Dickinson, Emily (Elizabeth) 1830-1886
NCLC 21; DA; DAB; DAC; DAM MST, POET; PC 1; WLC
See also AAYA 22; CDALB 1865-1917; DLB 1; SATA 29

Dickinson, Peter (Malcolm) 1927-**CLC 12, 35**
See also AAYA 9; CA 41-44R; CANR 31, 58; CLR 29; DLB 87, 161; JRDA; MAICYA; SATA 5, 62, 95

Dickson, Carr
See Carr, John Dickson

Dickson, Carter
See Carr, John Dickson

Diderot, Denis 1713-1784 .... **LC 26**

Didion, Joan 1934-**CLC 1, 3, 8, 14, 32; DAM NOV**
See also AITN 1; CA 5-8R; CANR 14, 52; CDALB 1968-1988; DLB 2, 173, 185; DLBY 81, 86; MTCW

Dietrich, Robert
See Hunt, E(verette) Howard, (Jr.)

Dillard, Annie 1945- **CLC 9, 60; DAM NOV**
See also AAYA 6; CA 49-52; CANR 3, 43, 62; DLBY 80; MTCW; SATA 10

Dillard, R(ichard) H(enry) W(ilde) 1937-
CLC 5
See also CA 21-24R; CAAS 7; CANR 10; DLB 5

Dillon, Eilis 1920-1994 .... **CLC 17**
See also CA 9-12R; 147; CAAS 3; CANR 4, 38; CLR 26; MAICYA; SATA 2, 74; SATA-Obit 83

Dimont, Penelope
See Mortimer, Penelope (Ruth)

Dinesen, Isak .... **CLC 10, 29, 95; SSC 7**
See also Blixen, Karen (Christentze Dinesen)

Ding Ling .... **CLC 68**
See also Chiang, Pin-chin

Disch, Thomas M(ichael) 1940- .... **CLC 7, 36**
See also AAYA 17; CA 21-24R; CAAS 4; CANR 17, 36, 54; CLR 18; DLB 8; MAICYA; MTCW; SAAS 15; SATA 92

Disch, Tom
See Disch, Thomas M(ichael)

d'Isly, Georges
See Simenon, Georges (Jacques Christian)

Disraeli, Benjamin 1804-1881 .... **NCLC 2, 39**
See also DLB 21, 55

Ditcum, Steve
See Crumb, R(obert)

Dixon, Paige
See Corcoran, Barbara

Dixon, Stephen 1936- .... **CLC 52; SSC 16**
See also CA 89-92; CANR 17, 40, 54; DLB 130

Doak, Annie
See Dillard, Annie

Dobell, Sydney Thompson 1824-1874 **NCLC 43**
See also DLB 32

Doblin, Alfred .... **TCLC 13**
See also Doeblin, Alfred

Dobrolyubov, Nikolai Alexandrovich 1836-1861
NCLC 5

Dobson, Austin 1840-1921 .... **TCLC 79**
See also DLB 35; 144

Dobyns, Stephen 1941- .... **CLC 37**

Evarts, Esther
See Benson, Sally
Everett, Percival L. 1956- .... **CLC 57**
See also BW 2; CA 129
Everson, R(onald) G(ilmour) 1903- . **CLC 27**
See also CA 17-20R; DLB 88
Everson, William (Oliver) 1912-1994 **CLC 1, 5, 14**
See also CA 9-12R; 145; CANR 20; DLB 5, 16; MTCW
Evtushenko, Evgenii Aleksandrovich
See Yevtushenko, Yevgeny (Alexandrovich)
Ewart, Gavin (Buchanan) 1916-1995 **CLC 13, 46**
See also CA 89-92; 150; CANR 17, 46; DLB 40; MTCW
Ewers, Hanns Heinz 1871-1943 ..... **TCLC 12**
See also CA 109; 149
Ewing, Frederick R.
See Sturgeon, Theodore (Hamilton)
Exley, Frederick (Earl) 1929-1992 **CLC 6, 11**
See also AITN 2; CA 81-84; 138; DLB 143; DLBY 81
Eynhardt, Guillermo
See Quiroga, Horacio (Sylvestre)
Ezekiel, Nissim 1924- .... **CLC 61**
See also CA 61-64
Ezekiel, Tish O'Dowd 1943- .... **CLC 34**
See also CA 129
Fadeyev, A.
See Bulgya, Alexander Alexandrovich
Fadeyev, Alexander .... **TCLC 53**
See also Bulgya, Alexander Alexandrovich
Fagen, Donald 1948- .... **CLC 26**
Fainzilberg, Ilya Arnoldovich 1897-1937
See Ilf, Ilya
See also CA 120; 165
Fair, Ronald L. 1932- .... **CLC 18**
See also BW 1; CA 69-72; CANR 25; DLB 33
Fairbairn, Roger
See Carr, John Dickson
Fairbairns, Zoe (Ann) 1948- .... **CLC 32**
See also CA 103; CANR 21
Falco, Gian
See Papini, Giovanni
Falconer, James
See Kirkup, James
Falconer, Kenneth
See Kornbluth, C(yril) M.
Falkland, Samuel
See Heijermans, Herman
Fallaci, Oriana 1930- .... **CLC 11, 110**
See also CA 77-80; CANR 15, 58; MTCW
Faludy, George 1913- .... **CLC 42**
See also CA 21-24R
Faludy, Gyoergy
See Faludy, George
Fanon, Frantz 1925-1961 ... **CLC 74; BLC 2; DAM MULT**
See also BW 1; CA 116; 89-92
Fanshawe, Ann 1625-1680 .... **LC 11**
Fante, John (Thomas) 1911-1983 ..... **CLC 60**
See also CA 69-72; 109; CANR 23; DLB 130; DLBY 83
Farah, Nuruddin 1945- **CLC 53; BLC 2; DAM MULT**
See also BW 2; CA 106; DLB 125
Fargue, Leon-Paul 1876(?)-1947 ... **TCLC 11**
See also CA 109
Farigoule, Louis
See Romains, Jules
Farina, Richard 1936(?)-1966 .... **CLC 9**
See also CA 81-84; 25-28R

Farley, Walter (Lorimer) 1915-1989 **CLC 17**
See also CA 17-20R; CANR 8, 29; DLB 22; JRDA; MAICYA; SATA 2, 43
Farmer, Philip Jose 1918- ....**CLC 1, 19**
See also CA 1-4R; CANR 4, 35; DLB 8; MTCW; SATA 93
Farquhar, George 1677-1707 ... **LC 21; DAM DRAM**
See also DLB 84
Farrell, J(ames) G(ordon) 1935-1979 **CLC 6**
See also CA 73-76; 89-92; CANR 36; DLB 14; MTCW
Farrell, James T(homas) 1904-1979 **CLC 1, 4, 8, 11, 66; SSC 28**
See also CA 5-8R; 89-92; CANR 9, 61; DLB 4, 9, 86; DLBD 2; MTCW
Farren, Richard J.
See Betjeman, John
Farren, Richard M.
See Betjeman, John
Fassbinder, Rainer Werner 1946-1982 **CLC 20**
See also CA 93-96; 106; CANR 31
Fast, Howard (Melvin) 1914- **CLC 23; DAM NOV**
See also AAYA 16; CA 1-4R; CAAS 18; CANR 1, 33, 54; DLB 9; INT CANR-33; SATA 7
Faulcon, Robert
See Holdstock, Robert P.
Faulkner, William (Cuthbert) 1897-1962 **CLC 1, 3, 6, 8, 9, 11, 14, 18, 28, 52, 68; DA; DAB; DAC; DAM MST, NOV; SSC 1; WLC**
See also AAYA 7; CA 81-84; CANR 33; CDALB 1929-1941; DLB 9, 11, 44, 102; DLBD 2; DLBY 86, 97; MTCW
Fauset, Jessie Redmon 1884(?)-1961 **CLC 19, 54; BLC 2; DAM MULT**
See also BW 1; CA 109; DLB 51
Faust, Frederick (Schiller) 1892-1944(?) **TCLC 49; DAM POP**
See also CA 108; 152
Faust, Irvin 1924- .... **CLC 8**
See also CA 33-36R; CANR 28, 67; DLB 2, 28; DLBY 80
Fawkes, Guy
See Benchley, Robert (Charles)
Fearing, Kenneth (Flexner) 1902-1961 . **C L C 51**
See also CA 93-96; CANR 59; DLB 9
Fecamps, Elise
See Creasey, John
Federman, Raymond 1928- ....**CLC 6, 47**
See also CA 17-20R; CAAS 8; CANR 10, 43; DLBY 80
Federspiel, J(uerg) F. 1931- .... **CLC 42**
See also CA 146
Feiffer, Jules (Ralph) 1929- ..... **CLC 2, 8, 64; DAM DRAM**
See also AAYA 3; CA 17-20R; CANR 30, 59; DLB 7, 44; INT CANR-30; MTCW; SATA 8, 61
Feige, Hermann Albert Otto Maximilian
See Traven, B.
Feinberg, David B. 1956-1994 .... **CLC 59**
See also CA 135; 147
Feinstein, Elaine 1930- .... **CLC 36**
See also CA 69-72; CAAS 1; CANR 31, 68; DLB 14, 40; MTCW
Feldman, Irving (Mordecai) 1928- ..... **CLC 7**
See also CA 1-4R; CANR 1; DLB 169
Felix-Tchicaya, Gerald
See Tchicaya, Gerald Felix
Fellini, Federico 1920-1993 .... **CLC 16, 85**
See also CA 65-68; 143; CANR 33

Felsen, Henry Gregor 1916- .... **CLC 17**
See also CA 1-4R; CANR 1; SAAS 2; SATA 1
Fenno, Jack
See Calisher, Hortense
Fenton, James Martin 1949- .... **CLC 32**
See also CA 102; DLB 40
Ferber, Edna 1887-1968 .... **CLC 18, 93**
See also AITN 1; CA 5-8R; 25-28R; CANR 68; DLB 9, 28, 86; MTCW; SATA 7
Ferguson, Helen
See Kavan, Anna
Ferguson, Samuel 1810-1886 .... **NCLC 33**
See also DLB 32
Fergusson, Robert 1750-1774 .... **LC 29**
See also DLB 109
Ferling, Lawrence
See Ferlinghetti, Lawrence (Monsanto)
Ferlinghetti, Lawrence (Monsanto) 1919(?)- **CLC 2, 6, 10, 27, 111; DAM POET; PC 1**
See also CA 5-8R; CANR 3, 41; CDALB 1941-1968; DLB 5, 16; MTCW
Fernandez, Vicente Garcia Huidobro
See Huidobro Fernandez, Vicente Garcia
Ferrer, Gabriel (Francisco Victor) Miro
See Miro (Ferrer), Gabriel (Francisco Victor)
Ferrier, Susan (Edmonstone) 1782-1854 **NCLC 8**
See also DLB 116
Ferrigno, Robert 1948(?)- .... **CLC 65**
See also CA 140
Ferron, Jacques 1921-1985 .... **CLC 94; DAC**
See also CA 117; 129; DLB 60
Feuchtwanger, Lion 1884-1958 .... **TCLC 3**
See also CA 104; DLB 66
Feuillet, Octave 1821-1890 .... **NCLC 45**
See also DLB 192
Feydeau, Georges (Leon Jules Marie) 1862-1921 .... **TCLC 22; DAM DRAM**
See also CA 113; 152; DLB 192
Fichte, Johann Gottlieb 1762-1814 **NCLC 62**
See also DLB 90
Ficino, Marsilio 1433-1499 .... **LC 12**
Fiedeler, Hans
See Doeblin, Alfred
Fiedler, Leslie A(aron) 1917- . **CLC 4, 13, 24**
See also CA 9-12R; CANR 7, 63; DLB 28, 67; MTCW
Field, Andrew 1938- .... **CLC 44**
See also CA 97-100; CANR 25
Field, Eugene 1850-1895 .... **NCLC 3**
See also DLB 23, 42, 140; DLBD 13; MAICYA; SATA 16
Field, Gans T.
See Wellman, Manly Wade
Field, Michael 1915-1971 .... **TCLC 43**
See also CA 29-32R
Field, Peter
See Hobson, Laura Z(ametkin)
Fielding, Henry 1707-1754 **LC 1; DA; DAB; DAC; DAM DRAM, MST, NOV; WLC**
See also CDBLB 1660-1789; DLB 39, 84, 101
Fielding, Sarah 1710-1768 .... **LC 1, 44**
See also DLB 39
Fields, W. C. 1880-1946 .... **TCLC 80**
See also DLB 44
Fierstein, Harvey (Forbes) 1954- ... **CLC 33; DAM DRAM, POP**
See also CA 123; 129
Figes, Eva 1932- .... **CLC 31**
See also CA 53-56; CANR 4, 44; DLB 14
Finch, Anne 1661-1720 .... **LC 3; PC 21**
See also DLB 95
Finch, Robert (Duer Claydon) 1900- **CLC 18**

See also AAYA 22; AITN 1; BW 2; CA 29-32R; CAAS 6; CANR 18, 41, 60; CLR 6; DLB 5, 41; INT CANR-18; MAICYA; MTCW; SATA 24

Giovene, Andrea 1904- .... **CLC 7**
See also CA 85-88

Gippius, Zinaida (Nikolayevna) 1869-1945
See Hippius, Zinaida
See also CA 106

Giraudoux, (Hippolyte) Jean 1882-1944 **TCLC 2, 7; DAM DRAM**
See also CA 104; DLB 65

Gironella, Jose Maria 1917- .... **CLC 11**
See also CA 101

Gissing, George (Robert) 1857-1903**TCLC 3, 24, 47**
See also CA 105; DLB 18, 135, 184

Giurlani, Aldo
See Palazzeschi, Aldo

Gladkov, Fyodor (Vasilyevich) 1883-1958 **TCLC 27**

Glanville, Brian (Lester) 1931- .... **CLC 6**
See also CA 5-8R; CAAS 9; CANR 3; DLB 15, 139; SATA 42

Glasgow, Ellen (Anderson Gholson) 1873-1945 **TCLC 2, 7**
See also CA 104; 164; DLB 9, 12

Glaspell, Susan 1882(?)-1948 .... **TCLC 55**
See also CA 110; 154; DLB 7, 9, 78; YABC 2

Glassco, John 1909-1981 .... **CLC 9**
See also CA 13-16R; 102; CANR 15; DLB 68

Glasscock, Amnesia
See Steinbeck, John (Ernst)

Glasser, Ronald J. 1940(?)- .... **CLC 37**

Glassman, Joyce
See Johnson, Joyce

Glendinning, Victoria 1937- .... **CLC 50**
See also CA 120; 127; CANR 59; DLB 155

Glissant, Edouard 1928- . **CLC 10, 68; DAM MULT**
See also CA 153

Gloag, Julian 1930- .... **CLC 40**
See also AITN 1; CA 65-68; CANR 10

Glowacki, Aleksander
See Prus, Boleslaw

Gluck, Louise (Elisabeth) 1943-**CLC 7, 22, 44, 81; DAM POET; PC 16**
See also CA 33-36R; CANR 40, 69; DLB 5

Glyn, Elinor 1864-1943 .... **TCLC 72**
See also DLB 153

Gobineau, Joseph Arthur (Comte) de 1816-1882 .... **NCLC 17**
See also DLB 123

Godard, Jean-Luc 1930- .... **CLC 20**
See also CA 93-96

Godden, (Margaret) Rumer 1907- ... **CLC 53**
See also AAYA 6; CA 5-8R; CANR 4, 27, 36, 55; DLB 161; MAICYA; SAAS 12; SATA 3, 36

Godoy Alcayaga, Lucila 1889-1957
See Mistral, Gabriela
See also BW 2; CA 104; 131; DAM MULT; HW; MTCW

Godwin, Gail (Kathleen) 1937- **CLC 5, 8, 22, 31, 69; DAM POP**
See also CA 29-32R; CANR 15, 43, 69; DLB 6; INT CANR-15; MTCW

Godwin, William 1756-1836 .... **NCLC 14**
See also CDBLB 1789-1832; DLB 39, 104, 142, 158, 163

Goebbels, Josef
See Goebbels, (Paul) Joseph

Goebbels, (Paul) Joseph 1897-1945**TCLC 68**

See also CA 115; 148

Goebbels, Joseph Paul
See Goebbels, (Paul) Joseph

Goethe, Johann Wolfgang von 1749-1832 **NCLC 4, 22, 34; DA; DAB; DAC; DAM DRAM, MST, POET; PC 5; WLC 3**
See also DLB 94

Gogarty, Oliver St. John 1878-1957**TCLC 15**
See also CA 109; 150; DLB 15, 19

Gogol, Nikolai (Vasilyevich) 1809-1852**NCLC 5, 15, 31; DA; DAB; DAC; DAM DRAM, MST; DC 1; SSC 4, 29; WLC**
See also DLB 198

Goines, Donald 1937(?)-1974**CLC 80; BLC 2; DAM MULT, POP**
See also AITN 1; BW 1; CA 124; 114; DLB 33

Gold, Herbert 1924- .... **CLC 4, 7, 14, 42**
See also CA 9-12R; CANR 17, 45; DLB 2; DLBY 81

Goldbarth, Albert 1948- .... **CLC 5, 38**
See also CA 53-56; CANR 6, 40; DLB 120

Goldberg, Anatol 1910-1982 .... **CLC 34**
See also CA 131; 117

Goldemberg, Isaac 1945- .... **CLC 52**
See also CA 69-72; CAAS 12; CANR 11, 32; HW

Golding, William (Gerald) 1911-1993**CLC 1, 2, 3, 8, 10, 17, 27, 58, 81; DA; DAB; DAC; DAM MST, NOV; WLC**
See also AAYA 5; CA 5-8R; 141; CANR 13, 33, 54; CDBLB 1945-1960; DLB 15, 100; MTCW

Goldman, Emma 1869-1940 .... **TCLC 13**
See also CA 110; 150

Goldman, Francisco 1954- .... **CLC 76**
See also CA 162

Goldman, William (W.) 1931- ....**CLC 1, 48**
See also CA 9-12R; CANR 29, 69; DLB 44

Goldmann, Lucien 1913-1970 .... **CLC 24**
See also CA 25-28; CAP 2

Goldoni, Carlo 1707-1793**LC 4; DAM DRAM**

Goldsberry, Steven 1949- .... **CLC 34**
See also CA 131

Goldsmith, Oliver 1728-1774**LC 2; DA; DAB; DAC; DAM DRAM, MST, NOV, POET; DC 8; WLC**
See also CDBLB 1660-1789; DLB 39, 89, 104, 109, 142; SATA 26

Goldsmith, Peter
See Priestley, J(ohn) B(oynton)

Gombrowicz, Witold 1904-1969**CLC 4, 7, 11, 49; DAM DRAM**
See also CA 19-20; 25-28R; CAP 2

Gomez de la Serna, Ramon 1888-1963**CLC 9**
See also CA 153; 116; HW

Goncharov, Ivan Alexandrovich 1812-1891 **NCLC 1, 63**

Goncourt, Edmond (Louis Antoine Huot) de 1822-1896 .... **NCLC 7**
See also DLB 123

Goncourt, Jules (Alfred Huot) de 1830-1870 **NCLC 7**
See also DLB 123

Gontier, Fernande 19(?)- .... **CLC 50**

Gonzalez Martinez, Enrique 1871-1952 **TCLC 72**
See also CA 166; HW

Goodman, Paul 1911-1972 ...... **CLC 1, 2, 4, 7**
See also CA 19-20; 37-40R; CANR 34; CAP 2; DLB 130; MTCW

Gordimer, Nadine 1923-**CLC 3, 5, 7, 10, 18, 33, 51, 70; DA; DAB; DAC; DAM MST, NOV; SSC 17; WLCS**

See also CA 5-8R; CANR 3, 28, 56; INT CANR-28; MTCW

Gordon, Adam Lindsay 1833-1870 **NCLC 21**

Gordon, Caroline 1895-1981**CLC 6, 13, 29, 83; SSC 15**
See also CA 11-12; 103; CANR 36; CAP 1; DLB 4, 9, 102; DLBY 81; MTCW

Gordon, Charles William 1860-1937
See Connor, Ralph
See also CA 109

Gordon, Mary (Catherine) 1949-**CLC 13, 22**
See also CA 102; CANR 44; DLB 6; DLBY 81; INT 102; MTCW

Gordon, N. J.
See Bosman, Herman Charles

Gordon, Sol 1923- .... **CLC 26**
See also CA 53-56; CANR 4; SATA 11

Gordone, Charles 1925-1995**CLC 1, 4; DAM DRAM; DC 8**
See also BW 1; CA 93-96; 150; CANR 55; DLB 7; INT 93-96; MTCW

Gore, Catherine 1800-1861 .... **NCLC 65**
See also DLB 116

Gorenko, Anna Andreevna
See Akhmatova, Anna

Gorky, Maxim 1868-1936**TCLC 8; DAB; SSC 28; WLC**
See also Peshkov, Alexei Maximovich

Goryan, Sirak
See Saroyan, William

Gosse, Edmund (William) 1849-1928**TCLC 28**
See also CA 117; DLB 57, 144, 184

Gotlieb, Phyllis Fay (Bloom) 1926- ..**CLC 18**
See also CA 13-16R; CANR 7; DLB 88

Gottesman, S. D.
See Kornbluth, C(yril) M.; Pohl, Frederik

Gottfried von Strassburg fl. c. 1210- **CMLC 10**
See also DLB 138

Gould, Lois .... **CLC 4, 10**
See also CA 77-80; CANR 29; MTCW

Gourmont, Remy (-Marie-Charles) de 1858-1915 .... **TCLC 17**
See also CA 109; 150

Govier, Katherine 1948- .... **CLC 51**
See also CA 101; CANR 18, 40

Goyen, (Charles) William 1915-1983**CLC 5, 8, 14, 40**
See also AITN 2; CA 5-8R; 110; CANR 6; DLB 2; DLBY 83; INT CANR-6

Goytisolo, Juan 1931- . **CLC 5, 10, 23; DAM MULT; HLC**
See also CA 85-88; CANR 32, 61; HW; MTCW

Gozzano, Guido 1883-1916 .... **PC 10**
See also CA 154; DLB 114

Gozzi, (Conte) Carlo 1720-1806 .... **NCLC 23**

Grabbe, Christian Dietrich 1801-1836**NCLC 2**
See also DLB 133

Grace, Patricia 1937- .... **CLC 56**

Gracian y Morales, Baltasar 1601-1658**LC 15**

Gracq, Julien .... **CLC 11, 48**
See also Poirier, Louis
See also DLB 83

Grade, Chaim 1910-1982 .... **CLC 10**
See also CA 93-96; 107

Graduate of Oxford, A
See Ruskin, John

Grafton, Garth
See Duncan, Sara Jeannette

Graham, John
See Phillips, David Graham

Graham, Jorie 1951- .... **CLC 48**

See also CA 111; CANR 63; DLB 120
Graham, R(obert) B(ontine) Cunninghame
See Cunninghame Graham, R(obert) B(ontine)
See also DLB 98, 135, 174
Graham, Robert
See Haldeman, Joe (William)
Graham, Tom
See Lewis, (Harry) Sinclair
Graham, W(illiam) S(ydney) 1918-1986 **CLC 29**
See also CA 73-76; 118; DLB 20
Graham, Winston (Mawdsley) 1910- **CLC 23**
See also CA 49-52; CANR 2, 22, 45, 66; DLB 77
Grahame, Kenneth 1859-1932 **TCLC 64; DAB**
See also CA 108; 136; CLR 5; DLB 34, 141, 178; MAICYA; YABC 1
Grant, Skeeter
See Spiegelman, Art
Granville-Barker, Harley 1877-1946 **TCLC 2; DAM DRAM**
See Barker, Harley Granville
See also CA 104
Grass, Guenter (Wilhelm) 1927- **CLC 1, 2, 4, 6, 11, 15, 22, 32, 49, 88; DA; DAB; DAC; DAM MST, NOV; WLC**
See also CA 13-16R; CANR 20; DLB 75, 124; MTCW
Gratton, Thomas
See Hulme, T(homas) E(rnest)
Grau, Shirley Ann 1929- .. **CLC 4, 9; SSC 15**
See also CA 89-92; CANR 22, 69; DLB 2; INT CANR-22; MTCW
Gravel, Fern
See Hall, James Norman
Graver, Elizabeth 1964- ..... **CLC 70**
See also CA 135
Graves, Richard Perceval 1945- .... **CLC 44**
See also CA 65-68; CANR 9, 26, 51
Graves, Robert (von Ranke) 1895-1985 **CLC 1, 2, 6, 11, 39, 44, 45; DAB; DAC; DAM MST, POET; PC 6**
See also CA 5-8R; 117; CANR 5, 36; CDBLB 1914-1945; DLB 20, 100, 191; DLBY 85; MTCW; SATA 45
Graves, Valerie
See Bradley, Marion Zimmer
Gray, Alasdair (James) 1934- .... **CLC 41**
See also CA 126; CANR 47, 69; DLB 194; INT 126; MTCW
Gray, Amlin 1946- .... **CLC 29**
See also CA 138
Gray, Francine du Plessix 1930- ..... **CLC 22; DAM NOV**
See also BEST 90:3; CA 61-64; CAAS 2; CANR 11, 33; INT CANR-11; MTCW
Gray, John (Henry) 1866-1934 ...... **TCLC 19**
See also CA 119; 162
Gray, Simon (James Holliday) 1936- **CLC 9, 14, 36**
See also AITN 1; CA 21-24R; CAAS 3; CANR 32, 69; DLB 13; MTCW
Gray, Spalding 1941- **CLC 49, 112; DAM POP; DC 7**
See also CA 128
Gray, Thomas 1716-1771 **LC 4, 40; DA; DAB; DAC; DAM MST; PC 2; WLC**
See also CDBLB 1660-1789; DLB 109
Grayson, David
See Baker, Ray Stannard
Grayson, Richard (A.) 1951- .... **CLC 38**
See also CA 85-88; CANR 14, 31, 57
Greeley, Andrew M(oran) 1928- ..... **CLC 28;**

DAM POP
See also CA 5-8R; CAAS 7; CANR 7, 43, 69; MTCW
Green, Anna Katharine 1846-1935 **TCLC 63**
See also CA 112; 159
Green, Brian
See Card, Orson Scott
Green, Hannah
See Greenberg, Joanne (Goldenberg)
Green, Hannah 1927(?)-1996 .... **CLC 3**
See also CA 73-76; CANR 59
Green, Henry 1905-1973 .... **CLC 2, 13, 97**
See also Yorke, Henry Vincent
See also DLB 15
Green, Julian (Hartridge) 1900-
See Green, Julien
See also CA 21-24R; CANR 33; DLB 4, 72; MTCW
Green, Julien .... **CLC 3, 11, 77**
See also Green, Julian (Hartridge)
Green, Paul (Eliot) 1894-1981 **CLC 25; DAM DRAM**
See also AITN 1; CA 5-8R; 103; CANR 3; DLB 7, 9; DLBY 81
Greenberg, Ivan 1908-1973
See Rahv, Philip
See also CA 85-88
Greenberg, Joanne (Goldenberg) 1932- **CLC 7, 30**
See also AAYA 12; CA 5-8R; CANR 14, 32, 69; SATA 25
Greenberg, Richard 1959(?)- .... **CLC 57**
See also CA 138
Greene, Bette 1934- .... **CLC 30**
See also AAYA 7; CA 53-56; CANR 4; CLR 2; JRDA; MAICYA; SAAS 16; SATA 8
Greene, Gael .... **CLC 8**
See also CA 13-16R; CANR 10
Greene, Graham (Henry) 1904-1991 **CLC 1, 3, 6, 9, 14, 18, 27, 37, 70, 72; DA; DAB; DAC; DAM MST, NOV; SSC 29; WLC**
See also AITN 2; CA 13-16R; 133; CANR 35, 61; CDBLB 1945-1960; DLB 13, 15, 77, 100, 162; DLBY 91; MTCW; SATA 20
Greene, Robert 1558-1592 .... **LC 41**
See also DLB 62, 167
Greer, Richard
See Silverberg, Robert
Gregor, Arthur 1923- .... **CLC 9**
See also CA 25-28R; CAAS 10; CANR 11; SATA 36
Gregor, Lee
See Pohl, Frederik
Gregory, Isabella Augusta (Persse) 1852-1932 **TCLC 1**
See also CA 104; DLB 10
Gregory, J. Dennis
See Williams, John A(lfred)
Grendon, Stephen
See Derleth, August (William)
Grenville, Kate 1950- .... **CLC 61**
See also CA 118; CANR 53
Grenville, Pelham
See Wodehouse, P(elham) G(renville)
Greve, Felix Paul (Berthold Friedrich) 1879-1948
See Grove, Frederick Philip
See also CA 104; 141; DAC; DAM MST
Grey, Zane 1872-1939 .. **TCLC 6; DAM POP**
See also CA 104; 132; DLB 9; MTCW
Grieg, (Johan) Nordahl (Brun) 1902-1943 **TCLC 10**
See also CA 107

Grieve, C(hristopher) M(urray) 1892-1978 **CLC 11, 19; DAM POET**
See also MacDiarmid, Hugh; Pteleon
See also CA 5-8R; 85-88; CANR 33; MTCW
Griffin, Gerald 1803-1840 .... **NCLC 7**
See also DLB 159
Griffin, John Howard 1920-1980 ..... **CLC 68**
See also AITN 1; CA 1-4R; 101; CANR 2
Griffin, Peter 1942- .... **CLC 39**
See also CA 136
Griffith, D(avid Lewelyn) W(ark) 1875(?)-1948 **TCLC 68**
See also CA 119; 150
Griffith, Lawrence
See Griffith, D(avid Lewelyn) W(ark)
Griffiths, Trevor 1935- .... **CLC 13, 52**
See also CA 97-100; CANR 45; DLB 13
Griggs, Sutton Elbert 1872-1930(?) **TCLC 77**
See also CA 123; DLB 50
Grigson, Geoffrey (Edward Harvey) 1905-1985 **CLC 7, 39**
See also CA 25-28R; 118; CANR 20, 33; DLB 27; MTCW
Grillparzer, Franz 1791-1872 .... **NCLC 1**
See also DLB 133
Grimble, Reverend Charles James
See Eliot, T(homas) S(tearns)
Grimke, Charlotte L(ottie) Forten 1837(?)-1914
See Forten, Charlotte L.
See also BW 1; CA 117; 124; DAM MULT, POET
Grimm, Jacob Ludwig Karl 1785-1863 **NCLC 3**
See also DLB 90; MAICYA; SATA 22
Grimm, Wilhelm Karl 1786-1859 .... **NCLC 3**
See also DLB 90; MAICYA; SATA 22
Grimmelshausen, Johann Jakob Christoffel von 1621-1676 .... **LC 6**
See also DLB 168
Grindel, Eugene 1895-1952
See Eluard, Paul
See also CA 104
Grisham, John 1955- .... **CLC 84; DAM POP**
See also AAYA 14; CA 138; CANR 47, 69
Grossman, David 1954- .... **CLC 67**
See also CA 138
Grossman, Vasily (Semenovich) 1905-1964 **CLC 41**
See also CA 124; 130; MTCW
Grove, Frederick Philip .... **TCLC 4**
See also Greve, Felix Paul (Berthold Friedrich)
See also DLB 92
Grubb
See Crumb, R(obert)
Grumbach, Doris (Isaac) 1918- **CLC 13, 22, 64**
See also CA 5-8R; CAAS 2; CANR 9, 42; INT CANR-9
Grundtvig, Nicolai Frederik Severin 1783-1872 **NCLC 1**
Grunge
See Crumb, R(obert)
Grunwald, Lisa 1959- .... **CLC 44**
See also CA 120
Guare, John 1938- . **CLC 8, 14, 29, 67; DAM DRAM**
See also CA 73-76; CANR 21, 69; DLB 7; MTCW
Gudjonsson, Halldor Kiljan 1902-1998
See Laxness, Halldor
See also CA 103; 164
Guenter, Erich
See Eich, Guenter
Guest, Barbara 1920- .... **CLC 34**

See also CA 25-28R; CANR 11, 44; DLB 5, 193

Guest, Judith (Ann) 1936- **CLC 8, 30; DAM NOV, POP**
See also AAYA 7; CA 77-80; CANR 15; INT CANR-15; MTCW

Guevara, Che .... **CLC 87; HLC**
See also Guevara (Serna), Ernesto

Guevara (Serna), Ernesto 1928-1967
See Guevara, Che
See also CA 127; 111; CANR 56; DAM MULT; HW

Guild, Nicholas M. 1944- .... **CLC 33**
See also CA 93-96

Guillemin, Jacques
See Sartre, Jean-Paul

Guillen, Jorge 1893-1984 .... **CLC 11; DAM MULT, POET**
See also CA 89-92; 112; DLB 108; HW

Guillen, Nicolas (Cristobal) 1902-1989 **C L C 48, 79; BLC 2; DAM MST, MULT, POET; HLC; PC 23**
See also BW 2; CA 116; 125; 129; HW

Guillevic, (Eugene) 1907- .... **CLC 33**
See also CA 93-96

Guillois
See Desnos, Robert

Guillois, Valentin
See Desnos, Robert

Guiney, Louise Imogen 1861-1920 **TCLC 41**
See also CA 160; DLB 54

Guiraldes, Ricardo (Guillermo) 1886-1927 **TCLC 39**
See also CA 131; HW; MTCW

Gumilev, Nikolai (Stepanovich) 1886-1921 **TCLC 60**
See also CA 165

Gunesekera, Romesh 1954- .... **CLC 91**
See also CA 159

Gunn, Bill .... **CLC 5**
See also Gunn, William Harrison
See also DLB 38

Gunn, Thom(son William) 1929-**CLC 3, 6, 18, 32, 81; DAM POET**
See also CA 17-20R; CANR 9, 33; CDBLB 1960 to Present; DLB 27; INT CANR-33; MTCW

Gunn, William Harrison 1934(?)-1989
See Gunn, Bill
See also AITN 1; BW 1; CA 13-16R; 128; CANR 12, 25

Gunnars, Kristjana 1948- .... **CLC 69**
See also CA 113; DLB 60

Gurdjieff, G(eorgei) I(vanovich) 1877(?)-1949 **TCLC 71**
See also CA 157

Gurganus, Allan 1947-. **CLC 70; DAM POP**
See also BEST 90:1; CA 135

Gurney, A(lbert) R(amsdell), Jr. 1930-. **C L C 32, 50, 54; DAM DRAM**
See also CA 77-80; CANR 32, 64

Gurney, Ivor (Bertie) 1890-1937 ... **TCLC 33**

Gurney, Peter
See Gurney, A(lbert) R(amsdell), Jr.

Guro, Elena 1877-1913 .... **TCLC 56**

Gustafson, James M(oody) 1925- ... **CLC 100**
See also CA 25-28R; CANR 37

Gustafson, Ralph (Barker) 1909- ..... **CLC 36**
See also CA 21-24R; CANR 8, 45; DLB 88

Gut, Gom
See Simenon, Georges (Jacques Christian)

Guterson, David 1956- .... **CLC 91**
See also CA 132

Guthrie, A(lfred) B(ertram), Jr. 1901-1991 **CLC 23**
See also CA 57-60; 134; CANR 24; DLB 6; SATA 62; SATA-Obit 67

Guthrie, Isobel
See Grieve, C(hristopher) M(urray)

Guthrie, Woodrow Wilson 1912-1967
See Guthrie, Woody
See also CA 113; 93-96

Guthrie, Woody .... **CLC 35**
See also Guthrie, Woodrow Wilson

Guy, Rosa (Cuthbert) 1928- .... **CLC 26**
See also AAYA 4; BW 2; CA 17-20R; CANR 14, 34; CLR 13; DLB 33; JRDA; MAICYA; SATA 14, 62

Gwendolyn
See Bennett, (Enoch) Arnold

H. D. .... **CLC 3, 8, 14, 31, 34, 73; PC 5**
See also Doolittle, Hilda

H. de V.
See Buchan, John

Haavikko, Paavo Juhani 1931- .. **CLC 18, 34**
See also CA 106

Habbema, Koos
See Heijermans, Herman

Habermas, Juergen 1929- .... **CLC 104**
See also CA 109

Habermas, Jurgen
See Habermas, Juergen

Hacker, Marilyn 1942- **CLC 5, 9, 23, 72, 91; DAM POET**
See also CA 77-80; CANR 68; DLB 120

Haeckel, Ernst Heinrich (Philipp August) 1834-1919 .... **TCLC 83**
See also CA 157

Haggard, H(enry) Rider 1856-1925**TCLC 11**
See also CA 108; 148; DLB 70, 156, 174, 178; SATA 16

Hagiosy, L.
See Larbaud, Valery (Nicolas)

Hagiwara Sakutaro 1886-1942**TCLC 60; PC 18**

Haig, Fenil
See Ford, Ford Madox

Haig-Brown, Roderick (Langmere) 1908-1976 **CLC 21**
See also CA 5-8R; 69-72; CANR 4, 38; CLR 31; DLB 88; MAICYA; SATA 12

Hailey, Arthur 1920-**CLC 5; DAM NOV, POP**
See also AITN 2; BEST 90:3; CA 1-4R; CANR 2, 36; DLB 88; DLBY 82; MTCW

Hailey, Elizabeth Forsythe 1938- ..... **CLC 40**
See also CA 93-96; CAAS 1; CANR 15, 48; INT CANR-15

Haines, John (Meade) 1924- .... **CLC 58**
See also CA 17-20R; CANR 13, 34; DLB 5

Hakluyt, Richard 1552-1616 .... **LC 31**

Haldeman, Joe (William) 1943- .... **CLC 61**
See also CA 53-56; CAAS 25; CANR 6; DLB 8; INT CANR-6

Haley, Alex(ander Murray Palmer) 1921-1992 **CLC 8, 12, 76; BLC 2; DA; DAB; DAC; DAM MST, MULT, POP**
See also BW 2; CA 77-80; 136; CANR 61; DLB 38; MTCW

Haliburton, Thomas Chandler 1796-1865 **NCLC 15**
See also DLB 11, 99

Hall, Donald (Andrew, Jr.) 1928- **CLC 1, 13, 37, 59; DAM POET**
See also CA 5-8R; CAAS 7; CANR 2, 44, 64; DLB 5; SATA 23, 97

Hall, Frederic Sauser
See Sauser-Hall, Frederic

Hall, James
See Kuttner, Henry

Hall, James Norman 1887-1951 ..... **TCLC 23**
See also CA 123; SATA 21

Hall, (Marguerite) Radclyffe 1886-1943 **TCLC 12**
See also CA 110; 150

Hall, Rodney 1935- .... **CLC 51**
See also CA 109; CANR 69

Halleck, Fitz-Greene 1790-1867 .... **NCLC 47**
See also DLB 3

Halliday, Michael
See Creasey, John

Halpern, Daniel 1945- .... **CLC 14**
See also CA 33-36R

Hamburger, Michael (Peter Leopold) 1924- **CLC 5, 14**
See also CA 5-8R; CAAS 4; CANR 2, 47; DLB 27

Hamill, Pete 1935- .... **CLC 10**
See also CA 25-28R; CANR 18

Hamilton, Alexander 1755(?)-1804 **NCLC 49**
See also DLB 37

Hamilton, Clive
See Lewis, C(live) S(taples)

Hamilton, Edmond 1904-1977 .... **CLC 1**
See also CA 1-4R; CANR 3; DLB 8

Hamilton, Eugene (Jacob) Lee
See Lee-Hamilton, Eugene (Jacob)

Hamilton, Franklin
See Silverberg, Robert

Hamilton, Gail
See Corcoran, Barbara

Hamilton, Mollie
See Kaye, M(ary) M(argaret)

Hamilton, (Anthony Walter) Patrick 1904-1962 **CLC 51**
See also CA 113; DLB 10

Hamilton, Virginia 1936- .... **CLC 26; DAM MULT**
See also AAYA 2, 21; BW 2; CA 25-28R; CANR 20, 37; CLR 1, 11, 40; DLB 33, 52; INT CANR-20; JRDA; MAICYA; MTCW; SATA 4, 56, 79

Hammett, (Samuel) Dashiell 1894-1961 **C L C 3, 5, 10, 19, 47; SSC 17**
See also AITN 1; CA 81-84; CANR 42; CDALB 1929-1941; DLBD 6; DLBY 96; MTCW

Hammon, Jupiter 1711(?)-1800(?) ..**NCLC 5; BLC 2; DAM MULT, POET; PC 16**
See also DLB 31, 50

Hammond, Keith
See Kuttner, Henry

Hamner, Earl (Henry), Jr. 1923- ...... **CLC 12**
See also AITN 2; CA 73-76; DLB 6

Hampton, Christopher (James) 1946- **CLC 4**
See also CA 25-28R; DLB 13; MTCW

Hamsun, Knut .... **TCLC 2, 14, 49**
See also Pedersen, Knut

Handke, Peter 1942-**CLC 5, 8, 10, 15, 38; DAM DRAM, NOV**
See also CA 77-80; CANR 33; DLB 85, 124; MTCW

Hanley, James 1901-1985 ..... **CLC 3, 5, 8, 13**
See also CA 73-76; 117; CANR 36; DLB 191; MTCW

Hannah, Barry 1942- .... **CLC 23, 38, 90**
See also CA 108; 110; CANR 43, 68; DLB 6; INT 110; MTCW

Hannon, Ezra
See Hunter, Evan

Hansberry, Lorraine (Vivian) 1930-1965**CLC**

See also AAYA 9

Hebbel, Friedrich 1813-1863**NCLC 43; DAM DRAM**
See also DLB 129

Hebert, Anne 1916-**CLC 4, 13, 29; DAC; DAM MST, POET**
See also CA 85-88; CANR 69; DLB 68; MTCW

Hecht, Anthony (Evan) 1923- **CLC 8, 13, 19; DAM POET**
See also CA 9-12R; CANR 6; DLB 5, 169

Hecht, Ben 1894-1964 .... **CLC 8**
See also CA 85-88; DLB 7, 9, 25, 26, 28, 86

Hedayat, Sadeq 1903-1951 .... **TCLC 21**
See also CA 120

Hegel, Georg Wilhelm Friedrich 1770-1831 **NCLC 46**
See also DLB 90

Heidegger, Martin 1889-1976 .... **CLC 24**
See also CA 81-84; 65-68; CANR 34; MTCW

Heidenstam, (Carl Gustaf) Verner von 1859-1940 .... **TCLC 5**
See also CA 104

Heifner, Jack 1946- .... **CLC 11**
See also CA 105; CANR 47

Heijermans, Herman 1864-1924 .... **TCLC 24**
See also CA 123

Heilbrun, Carolyn G(old) 1926- .... **CLC 25**
See also CA 45-48; CANR 1, 28, 58

Heine, Heinrich 1797-1856 .... **NCLC 4, 54**
See also DLB 90

Heinemann, Larry (Curtiss) 1944- ... **CLC 50**
See also CA 110; CAAS 21; CANR 31; DLBD 9; INT CANR-31

Heiney, Donald (William) 1921-1993
See Harris, MacDonald
See also CA 1-4R; 142; CANR 3, 58

Heinlein, Robert A(nson) 1907-1988**CLC 1, 3, 8, 14, 26, 55; DAM POP**
See also AAYA 17; CA 1-4R; 125; CANR 1, 20, 53; DLB 8; JRDA; MAICYA; MTCW; SATA 9, 69; SATA-Obit 56

Helforth, John
See Doolittle, Hilda

Hellenhofferu, Vojtech Kapristian z
See Hasek, Jaroslav (Matej Frantisek)

Heller, Joseph 1923-**CLC 1, 3, 5, 8, 11, 36, 63; DA; DAB; DAC; DAM MST, NOV, POP; WLC**
See also AAYA 24; AITN 1; CA 5-8R; CABS 1; CANR 8, 42, 66; DLB 2, 28; DLBY 80; INT CANR-8; MTCW

Hellman, Lillian (Florence) 1906-1984**CLC 2, 4, 8, 14, 18, 34, 44, 52; DAM DRAM; DC 1**
See also AITN 1, 2; CA 13-16R; 112; CANR 33; DLB 7; DLBY 84; MTCW

Helprin, Mark 1947-**CLC 7, 10, 22, 32; DAM NOV, POP**
See also CA 81-84; CANR 47, 64; DLBY 85; MTCW

Helvetius, Claude-Adrien 1715-1771 ..**LC 26**

Helyar, Jane Penelope Josephine 1933-
See Poole, Josephine
See also CA 21-24R; CANR 10, 26; SATA 82

Hemans, Felicia 1793-1835 .... **NCLC 71**
See also DLB 96

Hemingway, Ernest (Miller) 1899-1961 **C L C 1, 3, 6, 8, 10, 13, 19, 30, 34, 39, 41, 44, 50, 61, 80; DA; DAB; DAC; DAM MST, NOV; SSC 25; WLC**
See also AAYA 19; CA 77-80; CANR 34; CDALB 1917-1929; DLB 4, 9, 102; DLBD 1, 15, 16; DLBY 81, 87, 96; MTCW

Hempel, Amy 1951- .... **CLC 39**

See also CA 118; 137

Henderson, F. C.
See Mencken, H(enry) L(ouis)

Henderson, Sylvia
See Ashton-Warner, Sylvia (Constance)

Henderson, Zenna (Chlarson) 1917-1983**S S C 29**
See also CA 1-4R; 133; CANR 1; DLB 8; SATA 5

Henley, Beth .... **CLC 23; DC 6**
See also Henley, Elizabeth Becker
See also CABS 3; DLBY 86

Henley, Elizabeth Becker 1952-
See Henley, Beth
See also CA 107; CANR 32; DAM DRAM, MST; MTCW

Henley, William Ernest 1849-1903 .. **TCLC 8**
See also CA 105; DLB 19

Hennissart, Martha
See Lathen, Emma
See also CA 85-88; CANR 64

Henry, O. .... **TCLC 1, 19; SSC 5; WLC**
See also Porter, William Sydney

Henry, Patrick 1736-1799 .... **LC 25**

Henryson, Robert 1430(?)-1506(?) ...... **LC 20**
See also DLB 146

Henry VIII 1491-1547 .... **LC 10**

Henschke, Alfred
See Klabund

Hentoff, Nat(han Irving) 1925- .... **CLC 26**
See also AAYA 4; CA 1-4R; CAAS 6; CANR 5, 25; CLR 1, 52; INT CANR-25; JRDA; MAICYA; SATA 42, 69; SATA-Brief 27

Heppenstall, (John) Rayner 1911-1981 **C L C 10**
See also CA 1-4R; 103; CANR 29

Heraclitus c. 540B.C.-c. 450B.C. .. **CMLC 22**
See also DLB 176

Herbert, Frank (Patrick) 1920-1986**CLC 12, 23, 35, 44, 85; DAM POP**
See also AAYA 21; CA 53-56; 118; CANR 5, 43; DLB 8; INT CANR-5; MTCW; SATA 9, 37; SATA-Obit 47

Herbert, George 1593-1633 ..... **LC 24; DAB; DAM POET; PC 4**
See also CDBLB Before 1660; DLB 126

Herbert, Zbigniew 1924- .. **CLC 9, 43; DAM POET**
See also CA 89-92; CANR 36; MTCW

Herbst, Josephine (Frey) 1897-1969 **CLC 34**
See also CA 5-8R; 25-28R; DLB 9

Hergesheimer, Joseph 1880-1954 .. **TCLC 11**
See also CA 109; DLB 102, 9

Herlihy, James Leo 1927-1993 .... **CLC 6**
See also CA 1-4R; 143; CANR 2

Hermogenes fl. c. 175- .... **CMLC 6**

Hernandez, Jose 1834-1886 .... **NCLC 17**

Herodotus c. 484B.C.-429B.C. ...... **CMLC 17**
See also DLB 176

Herrick, Robert 1591-1674**LC 13; DA; DAB; DAC; DAM MST, POP; PC 9**
See also DLB 126

Herring, Guilles
See Somerville, Edith

Herriot, James 1916-1995**CLC 12; DAM POP**
See also Wight, James Alfred
See also AAYA 1; CA 148; CANR 40; SATA 86

Herrmann, Dorothy 1941- .... **CLC 44**
See also CA 107

Herrmann, Taffy
See Herrmann, Dorothy

Hersey, John (Richard) 1914-1993**CLC 1, 2, 7,**

9, 40, 81, 97; DAM POP
See also CA 17-20R; 140; CANR 33; DLB 6, 185; MTCW; SATA 25; SATA-Obit 76

Herzen, Aleksandr Ivanovich 1812-1870 **NCLC 10, 61**

Herzl, Theodor 1860-1904 .... **TCLC 36**

Herzog, Werner 1942- .... **CLC 16**
See also CA 89-92

Hesiod c. 8th cent. B.C.- .... **CMLC 5**
See also DLB 176

Hesse, Hermann 1877-1962**CLC 1, 2, 3, 6, 11, 17, 25, 69; DA; DAB; DAC; DAM MST, NOV; SSC 9; WLC**
See also CA 17-18; CAP 2; DLB 66; MTCW; SATA 50

Hewes, Cady
See De Voto, Bernard (Augustine)

Heyen, William 1940- .... **CLC 13, 18**
See also CA 33-36R; CAAS 9; DLB 5

Heyerdahl, Thor 1914- .... **CLC 26**
See also CA 5-8R; CANR 5, 22, 66; MTCW; SATA 2, 52

Heym, Georg (Theodor Franz Arthur) 1887-1912 .... **TCLC 9**
See also CA 106

Heym, Stefan 1913- .... **CLC 41**
See also CA 9-12R; CANR 4; DLB 69

Heyse, Paul (Johann Ludwig von) 1830-1914 **TCLC 8**
See also CA 104; DLB 129

Heyward, (Edwin) DuBose 1885-1940 **T C L C 59**
See also CA 108; 157; DLB 7, 9, 45; SATA 21

Hibbert, Eleanor Alice Burford 1906-1993 **CLC 7; DAM POP**
See also BEST 90:4; CA 17-20R; 140; CANR 9, 28, 59; SATA 2; SATA-Obit 74

Hichens, Robert (Smythe) 1864-1950 **T C L C 64**
See also CA 162; DLB 153

Higgins, George V(incent) 1939-**CLC 4, 7, 10, 18**
See also CA 77-80; CAAS 5; CANR 17, 51; DLB 2; DLBY 81; INT CANR-17; MTCW

Higginson, Thomas Wentworth 1823-1911 **TCLC 36**
See also CA 162; DLB 1, 64

Highet, Helen
See MacInnes, Helen (Clark)

Highsmith, (Mary) Patricia 1921-1995**CLC 2, 4, 14, 42, 102; DAM NOV, POP**
See also CA 1-4R; 147; CANR 1, 20, 48, 62; MTCW

Highwater, Jamake (Mamake) 1942(?)- **C L C 12**
See also AAYA 7; CA 65-68; CAAS 7; CANR 10, 34; CLR 17; DLB 52; DLBY 85; JRDA; MAICYA; SATA 32, 69; SATA-Brief 30

Highway, Tomson 1951-**CLC 92; DAC; DAM MULT**
See also CA 151; NNAL

Higuchi, Ichiyo 1872-1896 .... **NCLC 49**

Hijuelos, Oscar 1951- **CLC 65; DAM MULT, POP; HLC**
See also AAYA 25; BEST 90:1; CA 123; CANR 50; DLB 145; HW

Hikmet, Nazim 1902(?)-1963 .... **CLC 40**
See also CA 141; 93-96

Hildegard von Bingen 1098-1179 . **CMLC 20**
See also DLB 148

Hildesheimer, Wolfgang 1916-1991 .. **CLC 49**
See also CA 101; 135; DLB 69, 124

Hill, Geoffrey (William) 1932- **CLC 5, 8, 18,**

Ibuse, Masuji 1898-1993 .... **CLC 22**
 See also CA 127; 141; DLB 180
Ichikawa, Kon 1915- .... **CLC 20**
 See also CA 121
Idle, Eric 1943- .... **CLC 21**
 See also Monty Python
 See also CA 116; CANR 35
Ignatow, David 1914-1997 .. **CLC 4, 7, 14, 40**
 See also CA 9-12R; 162; CAAS 3; CANR 31,
 57; DLB 5
Ihimaera, Witi 1944- .... **CLC 46**
 See also CA 77-80
Ilf, Ilya .... **TCLC 21**
 See also Fainzilberg, Ilya Arnoldovich
Illyes, Gyula 1902-1983 .... **PC 16**
 See also CA 114; 109
Immermann, Karl (Lebrecht) 1796-1840
 NCLC 4, 49
 See also DLB 133
Inchbald, Elizabeth 1753-1821 ...... **NCLC 62**
 See also DLB 39, 89
Inclan, Ramon (Maria) del Valle
 See Valle-Inclan, Ramon (Maria) del
Infante, G(uillermo) Cabrera
 See Cabrera Infante, G(uillermo)
Ingalls, Rachel (Holmes) 1940- .... **CLC 42**
 See also CA 123; 127
Ingamells, Rex 1913-1955 .... **TCLC 35**
Inge, William (Motter) 1913-1973 . **CLC 1, 8,**
 19; DAM DRAM
 See also CA 9-12R; CDALB 1941-1968; DLB
 7; MTCW
Ingelow, Jean 1820-1897 .... **NCLC 39**
 See also DLB 35, 163; SATA 33
Ingram, Willis J.
 See Harris, Mark
Innaurato, Albert (F.) 1948(?)- .. **CLC 21, 60**
 See also CA 115; 122; INT 122
Innes, Michael
 See Stewart, J(ohn) I(nnes) M(ackintosh)
Innis, Harold Adams 1894-1952 .... **TCLC 77**
 See also DLB 88
Ionesco, Eugene 1909-1994 **CLC 1, 4, 6, 9, 11,**
 15, 41, 86; DA; DAB; DAC; DAM DRAM,
 MST; WLC
 See also CA 9-12R; 144; CANR 55; MTCW;
 SATA 7; SATA-Obit 79
Iqbal, Muhammad 1873-1938 .... **TCLC 28**
Ireland, Patrick
 See O'Doherty, Brian
Iron, Ralph
 See Schreiner, Olive (Emilie Albertina)
Irving, John (Winslow) 1942- **CLC 13, 23, 38,**
 112; DAM NOV, POP
 See also AAYA 8; BEST 89:3; CA 25-28R;
 CANR 28; DLB 6; DLBY 82; MTCW
Irving, Washington 1783-1859 . **NCLC 2, 19;**
 DA; DAB; DAM MST; SSC 2; WLC
 See also CDALB 1640-1865; DLB 3, 11, 30,
 59, 73, 74, 186; YABC 2
Irwin, P. K.
 See Page, P(atricia) K(athleen)
Isaacs, Jorge Ricardo 1837-1895 ... **NCLC 70**
Isaacs, Susan 1943- .... **CLC 32; DAM POP**
 See also BEST 89:1; CA 89-92; CANR 20, 41,
 65; INT CANR-20; MTCW
Isherwood, Christopher (William Bradshaw)
 1904-1986 .... **CLC 1, 9, 11, 14, 44; DAM**
 DRAM, NOV
 See also CA 13-16R; 117; CANR 35; DLB 15,
 195; DLBY 86; MTCW
Ishiguro, Kazuo 1954- .. **CLC 27, 56, 59, 110;**
 DAM NOV

 See also BEST 90:2; CA 120; CANR 49; DLB
 194; MTCW
Ishikawa, Hakuhin
 See Ishikawa, Takuboku
Ishikawa, Takuboku 1886(?)-1912 **TCLC 15;**
 DAM POET; PC 10
 See also CA 113; 153
Iskander, Fazil 1929- .... **CLC 47**
 See also CA 102
Isler, Alan (David) 1934- .... **CLC 91**
 See also CA 156
Ivan IV 1530-1584 .... **LC 17**
Ivanov, Vyacheslav Ivanovich 1866-1949
 TCLC 33
 See also CA 122
Ivask, Ivar Vidrik 1927-1992 .... **CLC 14**
 See also CA 37-40R; 139; CANR 24
Ives, Morgan
 See Bradley, Marion Zimmer
J. R. S.
 See Gogarty, Oliver St. John
Jabran, Kahlil
 See Gibran, Kahlil
Jabran, Khalil
 See Gibran, Kahlil
Jackson, Daniel
 See Wingrove, David (John)
Jackson, Jesse 1908-1983 .... **CLC 12**
 See also BW 1; CA 25-28R; 109; CANR 27;
 CLR 28; MAICYA; SATA 2, 29; SATA-Obit
 48
Jackson, Laura (Riding) 1901-1991
 See Riding, Laura
 See also CA 65-68; 135; CANR 28; DLB 48
Jackson, Sam
 See Trumbo, Dalton
Jackson, Sara
 See Wingrove, David (John)
Jackson, Shirley 1919-1965 . **CLC 11, 60, 87;**
 DA; DAC; DAM MST; SSC 9; WLC
 See also AAYA 9; CA 1-4R; 25-28R; CANR 4,
 52; CDALB 1941-1968; DLB 6; SATA 2
Jacob, (Cyprien-)Max 1876-1944 .... **TCLC 6**
 See also CA 104
Jacobs, Harriet A(nn) 1813(?)-1897 **NCLC 67**
Jacobs, Jim 1942- .... **CLC 12**
 See also CA 97-100; INT 97-100
Jacobs, W(illiam) W(ymark) 1863-1943
 TCLC 22
 See also CA 121; DLB 135
Jacobsen, Jens Peter 1847-1885 .... **NCLC 34**
Jacobsen, Josephine 1908- .... **CLC 48, 102**
 See also CA 33-36R; CAAS 18; CANR 23, 48
Jacobson, Dan 1929- .... **CLC 4, 14**
 See also CA 1-4R; CANR 2, 25, 66; DLB 14;
 MTCW
Jacqueline
 See Carpentier (y Valmont), Alejo
Jagger, Mick 1944- .... **CLC 17**
Jahiz, Al- c. 776-869 .... **CMLC 25**
Jahiz, al- c. 780-c. 869 .... **CMLC 25**
Jakes, John (William) 1932- .. **CLC 29; DAM**
 NOV, POP
 See also BEST 89:4; CA 57-60; CANR 10, 43,
 66; DLBY 83; INT CANR-10; MTCW;
 SATA 62
James, Andrew
 See Kirkup, James
James, C(yril) L(ionel) R(obert) 1901-1989
 CLC 33; BLCS
 See also BW 2; CA 117; 125; 128; CANR 62;
 DLB 125; MTCW
James, Daniel (Lewis) 1911-1988

 See Santiago, Danny
 See also CA 125
James, Dynely
 See Mayne, William (James Carter)
James, Henry Sr. 1811-1882 .... **NCLC 53**
James, Henry 1843-1916 **TCLC 2, 11, 24, 40,**
 47, 64; DA; DAB; DAC; DAM MST, NOV;
 SSC 8; WLC
 See also CA 104; 132; CDALB 1865-1917;
 DLB 12, 71, 74, 189; DLBD 13; MTCW
James, M. R.
 See James, Montague (Rhodes)
 See also DLB 156
James, Montague (Rhodes) 1862-1936 **TCLC**
 6; SSC 16
 See also CA 104
James, P. D. .... **CLC 18, 46**
 See also White, Phyllis Dorothy James
 See also BEST 90:2; CDBLB 1960 to Present;
 DLB 87
James, Philip
 See Moorcock, Michael (John)
James, William 1842-1910 .... **TCLC 15, 32**
 See also CA 109
James I 1394-1437 .... **LC 20**
Jameson, Anna 1794-1860 .... **NCLC 43**
 See also DLB 99, 166
Jami, Nur al-Din 'Abd al-Rahman 1414-1492
 LC 9
Jammes, Francis 1868-1938 .... **TCLC 75**
Jandl, Ernst 1925- .... **CLC 34**
Janowitz, Tama 1957- .. **CLC 43; DAM POP**
 See also CA 106; CANR 52
Japrisot, Sebastien 1931- .... **CLC 90**
Jarrell, Randall 1914-1965 **CLC 1, 2, 6, 9, 13,**
 49; DAM POET
 See also CA 5-8R; 25-28R; CABS 2; CANR 6,
 34; CDALB 1941-1968; CLR 6; DLB 48, 52;
 MAICYA; MTCW; SATA 7
Jarry, Alfred 1873-1907 .. **TCLC 2, 14; DAM**
 DRAM; SSC 20
 See also CA 104; 153; DLB 192
Jarvis, E. K.
 See Bloch, Robert (Albert); Ellison, Harlan
 (Jay); Silverberg, Robert
Jeake, Samuel, Jr.
 See Aiken, Conrad (Potter)
Jean Paul 1763-1825 .... **NCLC 7**
Jefferies, (John) Richard 1848-1887 **NCLC 47**
 See also DLB 98, 141; SATA 16
Jeffers, (John) Robinson 1887-1962 **CLC 2, 3,**
 11, 15, 54; DA; DAC; DAM MST, POET;
 PC 17; WLC
 See also CA 85-88; CANR 35; CDALB 1917-
 1929; DLB 45; MTCW
Jefferson, Janet
 See Mencken, H(enry) L(ouis)
Jefferson, Thomas 1743-1826 .... **NCLC 11**
 See also CDALB 1640-1865; DLB 31
Jeffrey, Francis 1773-1850 .... **NCLC 33**
 See also DLB 107
Jelakowitch, Ivan
 See Heijermans, Herman
Jellicoe, (Patricia) Ann 1927- .... **CLC 27**
 See also CA 85-88; DLB 13
Jen, Gish .... **CLC 70**
 See also Jen, Lillian
Jen, Lillian 1956(?)-
 See Jen, Gish
 See also CA 135
Jenkins, (John) Robin 1912- .... **CLC 52**
 See also CA 1-4R; CANR 1; DLB 14
Jennings, Elizabeth (Joan) 1926- . **CLC 5, 14**

Author Index

See Irving, Washington

Lanier, Sidney 1842-1881 ..... **NCLC 6; DAM POET**
See also DLB 64; DLBD 13; MAICYA; SATA 18

Lanyer, Aemilia 1569-1645 .... **LC 10, 30**
See also DLB 121

Lao Tzu .... **CMLC 7**

Lapine, James (Elliot) 1949- .... **CLC 39**
See also CA 123; 130; CANR 54; INT 130

Larbaud, Valery (Nicolas) 1881-1957**TCLC 9**
See also CA 106; 152

Lardner, Ring
See Lardner, Ring(gold) W(ilmer)

Lardner, Ring W., Jr.
See Lardner, Ring(gold) W(ilmer)

Lardner, Ring(gold) W(ilmer) 1885-1933
TCLC 2, 14
See also CA 104; 131; CDALB 1917-1929; DLB 11, 25, 86; DLBD 16; MTCW

Laredo, Betty
See Codrescu, Andrei

Larkin, Maia
See Wojciechowska, Maia (Teresa)

Larkin, Philip (Arthur) 1922-1985**CLC 3, 5, 8, 9, 13, 18, 33, 39, 64; DAB; DAM MST, POET; PC 21**
See also CA 5-8R; 117; CANR 24, 62; CDBLB 1960 to Present; DLB 27; MTCW

Larra (y Sanchez de Castro), Mariano Jose de 1809-1837 .... **NCLC 17**

Larsen, Eric 1941- .... **CLC 55**
See also CA 132

Larsen, Nella 1891-1964 .... **CLC 37; BLC 2; DAM MULT**
See also BW 1; CA 125; DLB 51

Larson, Charles R(aymond) 1938- ... **CLC 31**
See also CA 53-56; CANR 4

Larson, Jonathan 1961-1996 .... **CLC 99**
See also CA 156

Las Casas, Bartolome de 1474-1566 ... **LC 31**

Lasch, Christopher 1932-1994 .... **CLC 102**
See also CA 73-76; 144; CANR 25; MTCW

Lasker-Schueler, Else 1869-1945 ... **TCLC 57**
See also DLB 66, 124

Laski, Harold 1893-1950 .... **TCLC 79**

Latham, Jean Lee 1902-1995 .... **CLC 12**
See also AITN 1; CA 5-8R; CANR 7; CLR 50; MAICYA; SATA 2, 68

Latham, Mavis
See Clark, Mavis Thorpe

Lathen, Emma .... **CLC 2**
See also Hennissart, Martha; Latsis, Mary J(ane)

Lathrop, Francis
See Leiber, Fritz (Reuter, Jr.)

Latsis, Mary J(ane) 1927(?)-1997
See Lathen, Emma
See also CA 85-88; 162

Lattimore, Richmond (Alexander) 1906-1984
CLC 3
See also CA 1-4R; 112; CANR 1

Laughlin, James 1914-1997 .... **CLC 49**
See also CA 21-24R; 162; CAAS 22; CANR 9, 47; DLB 48; DLBY 96, 97

Laurence, (Jean) Margaret (Wemyss) 1926-1987 .. **CLC 3, 6, 13, 50, 62; DAC; DAM MST; SSC 7**
See also CA 5-8R; 121; CANR 33; DLB 53; MTCW; SATA-Obit 50

Laurent, Antoine 1952- .... **CLC 50**

Lauscher, Hermann
See Hesse, Hermann

Lautreamont, Comte de 1846-1870**NCLC 12;**

SSC 14

Laverty, Donald
See Blish, James (Benjamin)

Lavin, Mary 1912-1996**CLC 4, 18, 99; SSC 4**
See also CA 9-12R; 151; CANR 33; DLB 15; MTCW

Lavond, Paul Dennis
See Kornbluth, C(yril) M.; Pohl, Frederik

Lawler, Raymond Evenor 1922- .... **CLC 58**
See also CA 103

Lawrence, D(avid) H(erbert Richards) 1885-1930**TCLC 2, 9, 16, 33, 48, 61; DA; DAB; DAC; DAM MST, NOV, POET; SSC 4, 19; WLC**
See also CA 104; 121; CDBLB 1914-1945; DLB 10, 19, 36, 98, 162, 195; MTCW

Lawrence, T(homas) E(dward) 1888-1935
TCLC 18
See also Dale, Colin
See also CA 115; DLB 195

Lawrence of Arabia
See Lawrence, T(homas) E(dward)

Lawson, Henry (Archibald Hertzberg) 1867-1922 .... **TCLC 27; SSC 18**
See also CA 120

Lawton, Dennis
See Faust, Frederick (Schiller)

Laxness, Halldor .... **CLC 25**
See also Gudjonsson, Halldor Kiljan

Layamon fl. c. 1200- .... **CMLC 10**
See also DLB 146

Laye, Camara 1928-1980 **CLC 4, 38; BLC 2; DAM MULT**
See also BW 1; CA 85-88; 97-100; CANR 25; MTCW

Layton, Irving (Peter) 1912-**CLC 2, 15; DAC; DAM MST, POET**
See also CA 1-4R; CANR 2, 33, 43, 66; DLB 88; MTCW

Lazarus, Emma 1849-1887 .... **NCLC 8**

Lazarus, Felix
See Cable, George Washington

Lazarus, Henry
See Slavitt, David R(ytman)

Lea, Joan
See Neufeld, John (Arthur)

Leacock, Stephen (Butler) 1869-1944**TCLC 2; DAC; DAM MST**
See also CA 104; 141; DLB 92

Lear, Edward 1812-1888 .... **NCLC 3**
See also CLR 1; DLB 32, 163, 166; MAICYA; SATA 18

Lear, Norman (Milton) 1922- .... **CLC 12**
See also CA 73-76

Leautaud, Paul 1872-1956 .... **TCLC 83**
See also DLB 65

Leavis, F(rank) R(aymond) 1895-1978**CLC 24**
See also CA 21-24R; 77-80; CANR 44; MTCW

Leavitt, David 1961- ..... **CLC 34; DAM POP**
See also CA 116; 122; CANR 50, 62; DLB 130; INT 122

Leblanc, Maurice (Marie Emile) 1864-1941
TCLC 49
See also CA 110

Lebowitz, Fran(ces Ann) 1951(?)-**CLC 11, 36**
See also CA 81-84; CANR 14, 60; INT CANR-14; MTCW

Lebrecht, Peter
See Tieck, (Johann) Ludwig

le Carre, John .... **CLC 3, 5, 9, 15, 28**
See also Cornwell, David (John Moore)
See also BEST 89:4; CDBLB 1960 to Present; DLB 87

Le Clezio, J(ean) M(arie) G(ustave) 1940-
CLC 31
See also CA 116; 128; DLB 83

Leconte de Lisle, Charles-Marie-Rene 1818-1894 .... **NCLC 29**

Le Coq, Monsieur
See Simenon, Georges (Jacques Christian)

Leduc, Violette 1907-1972 .... **CLC 22**
See also CA 13-14; 33-36R; CANR 69; CAP 1

Ledwidge, Francis 1887(?)-1917 .... **TCLC 23**
See also CA 123; DLB 20

Lee, Andrea 1953- .... **CLC 36; BLC 2; DAM MULT**
See also BW 1; CA 125

Lee, Andrew
See Auchincloss, Louis (Stanton)

Lee, Chang-rae 1965- .... **CLC 91**
See also CA 148

Lee, Don L. .... **CLC 2**
See also Madhubuti, Haki R.

Lee, George W(ashington) 1894-1976**CLC 52; BLC 2; DAM MULT**
See also BW 1; CA 125; DLB 51

Lee, (Nelle) Harper 1926- .. **CLC 12, 60; DA; DAB; DAC; DAM MST, NOV; WLC**
See also AAYA 13; CA 13-16R; CANR 51; CDALB 1941-1968; DLB 6; MTCW; SATA 11

Lee, Helen Elaine 1959(?)- .... **CLC 86**
See also CA 148

Lee, Julian
See Latham, Jean Lee

Lee, Larry
See Lee, Lawrence

Lee, Laurie 1914-1997 **CLC 90; DAB; DAM POP**
See also CA 77-80; 158; CANR 33; DLB 27; MTCW

Lee, Lawrence 1941-1990 .... **CLC 34**
See also CA 131; CANR 43

Lee, Manfred B(ennington) 1905-1971**CLC 11**
See also Queen, Ellery
See also CA 1-4R; 29-32R; CANR 2; DLB 137

Lee, Shelton Jackson 1957(?)- .... **CLC 105; BLCS; DAM MULT**
See also Lee, Spike
See also BW 2; CA 125; CANR 42

Lee, Spike
See Lee, Shelton Jackson
See also AAYA 4

Lee, Stan 1922- .... **CLC 17**
See also AAYA 5; CA 108; 111; INT 111

Lee, Tanith 1947- .... **CLC 46**
See also AAYA 15; CA 37-40R; CANR 53; SATA 8, 88

Lee, Vernon .... **TCLC 5**
See also Paget, Violet
See also DLB 57, 153, 156, 174, 178

Lee, William
See Burroughs, William S(eward)

Lee, Willy
See Burroughs, William S(eward)

Lee-Hamilton, Eugene (Jacob) 1845-1907
TCLC 22
See also CA 117

Leet, Judith 1935- .... **CLC 11**

Le Fanu, Joseph Sheridan 1814-1873**NCLC 9, 58; DAM POP; SSC 14**
See also DLB 21, 70, 159, 178

Leffland, Ella 1931- .... **CLC 19**
See also CA 29-32R; CANR 35; DLBY 84; INT CANR-35; SATA 65

Leger, Alexis

See also BW 2; CA 21-24R; CAAS 6; CANR 13, 25, 53; DLB 33

Major, Kevin (Gerald) 1949-.. **CLC 26; DAC**
See also AAYA 16; CA 97-100; CANR 21, 38; CLR 11; DLB 60; INT CANR-21; JRDA; MAICYA; SATA 32, 82

Maki, James
See Ozu, Yasujiro

Malabaila, Damiano
See Levi, Primo

Malamud, Bernard 1914-1986**CLC 1, 2, 3, 5, 8, 9, 11, 18, 27, 44, 78, 85; DA; DAB; DAC; DAM MST, NOV, POP; SSC 15; WLC**
See also AAYA 16; CA 5-8R; 118; CABS 1; CANR 28, 62; CDALB 1941-1968; DLB 2, 28, 152; DLBY 80, 86; MTCW

Malan, Herman
See Bosman, Herman Charles; Bosman, Herman Charles

Malaparte, Curzio 1898-1957 .... **TCLC 52**

Malcolm, Dan
See Silverberg, Robert

Malcolm X .... **CLC 82; BLC 2; WLCS**
See also Little, Malcolm

Malherbe, Francois de 1555-1628 .... **LC 5**

Mallarme, Stephane 1842-1898 **NCLC 4, 41; DAM POET; PC 4**

Mallet-Joris, Francoise 1930- .... **CLC 11**
See also CA 65-68; CANR 17; DLB 83

Malley, Ern
See McAuley, James Phillip

Mallowan, Agatha Christie
See Christie, Agatha (Mary Clarissa)

Maloff, Saul 1922- .... **CLC 5**
See also CA 33-36R

Malone, Louis
See MacNeice, (Frederick) Louis

Malone, Michael (Christopher) 1942-**CLC 43**
See also CA 77-80; CANR 14, 32, 57

Malory, (Sir) Thomas 1410(?)-1471(?)**LC 11; DA; DAB; DAC; DAM MST; WLCS**
See also CDBLB Before 1660; DLB 146; SATA 59; SATA-Brief 33

Malouf, (George Joseph) David 1934-**CLC 28, 86**
See also CA 124; CANR 50

Malraux, (Georges-)Andre 1901-1976**CLC 1, 4, 9, 13, 15, 57; DAM NOV**
See also CA 21-22; 69-72; CANR 34, 58; CAP 2; DLB 72; MTCW

Malzberg, Barry N(athaniel) 1939- ... **CLC 7**
See also CA 61-64; CAAS 4; CANR 16; DLB 8

Mamet, David (Alan) 1947-**CLC 9, 15, 34, 46, 91; DAM DRAM; DC 4**
See also AAYA 3; CA 81-84; CABS 3; CANR 15, 41, 67; DLB 7; MTCW

Mamoulian, Rouben (Zachary) 1897-1987 **CLC 16**
See also CA 25-28R; 124

Mandelstam, Osip (Emilievich) 1891(?)-1938(?) **TCLC 2, 6; PC 14**
See also CA 104; 150

Mander, (Mary) Jane 1877-1949 ... **TCLC 31**
See also CA 162

Mandeville, John fl. 1350- .... **CMLC 19**
See also DLB 146

Mandiargues, Andre Pieyre de .... **CLC 41**
See also Pieyre de Mandiargues, Andre
See also DLB 83

Mandrake, Ethel Belle
See Thurman, Wallace (Henry)

Mangan, James Clarence 1803-1849**NCLC 27**

Maniere, J.-E.
See Giraudoux, (Hippolyte) Jean

Manley, (Mary) Delariviere 1672(?)-1724**L C 1**
See also DLB 39, 80

Mann, Abel
See Creasey, John

Mann, Emily 1952- .... **DC 7**
See also CA 130; CANR 55

Mann, (Luiz) Heinrich 1871-1950 ... **TCLC 9**
See also CA 106; 164; DLB 66

Mann, (Paul) Thomas 1875-1955 **TCLC 2, 8, 14, 21, 35, 44, 60; DA; DAB; DAC; DAM MST, NOV; SSC 5; WLC**
See also CA 104; 128; DLB 66; MTCW

Mannheim, Karl 1893-1947 .... **TCLC 65**

Manning, David
See Faust, Frederick (Schiller)

Manning, Frederic 1887(?)-1935 ... **TCLC 25**
See also CA 124

Manning, Olivia 1915-1980 .... **CLC 5, 19**
See also CA 5-8R; 101; CANR 29; MTCW

Mano, D. Keith 1942- .... **CLC 2, 10**
See also CA 25-28R; CAAS 6; CANR 26, 57; DLB 6

Mansfield, Katherine**TCLC 2, 8, 39; DAB; SSC 9, 23; WLC**
See also Beauchamp, Kathleen Mansfield
See also DLB 162

Manso, Peter 1940- .... **CLC 39**
See also CA 29-32R; CANR 44

Mantecon, Juan Jimenez
See Jimenez (Mantecon), Juan Ramon

Manton, Peter
See Creasey, John

Man Without a Spleen, A
See Chekhov, Anton (Pavlovich)

Manzoni, Alessandro 1785-1873 .... **NCLC 29**

Mapu, Abraham (ben Jekutiel) 1808-1867 **NCLC 18**

Mara, Sally
See Queneau, Raymond

Marat, Jean Paul 1743-1793 .... **LC 10**

Marcel, Gabriel Honore 1889-1973 . **CLC 15**
See also CA 102; 45-48; MTCW

Marchbanks, Samuel
See Davies, (William) Robertson

Marchi, Giacomo
See Bassani, Giorgio

Margulies, Donald .... **CLC 76**

Marie de France c. 12th cent. - **CMLC 8; PC 22**

Marie de l'Incarnation 1599-1672 ...... **LC 10**

Marier, Captain Victor
See Griffith, D(avid Lewelyn) W(ark)

Mariner, Scott
See Pohl, Frederik

Marinetti, Filippo Tommaso 1876-1944**TCLC 10**
See also CA 107; DLB 114

Marivaux, Pierre Carlet de Chamblain de 1688-1763 .... **LC 4; DC 7**

Markandaya, Kamala .... **CLC 8, 38**
See also Taylor, Kamala (Purnaiya)

Markfield, Wallace 1926- .... **CLC 8**
See also CA 69-72; CAAS 3; DLB 2, 28

Markham, Edwin 1852-1940 .... **TCLC 47**
See also CA 160; DLB 54, 186

Markham, Robert
See Amis, Kingsley (William)

Marks, J
See Highwater, Jamake (Mamake)

Marks-Highwater, J

See Highwater, Jamake (Mamake)

Markson, David M(errill) 1927- .... **CLC 67**
See also CA 49-52; CANR 1

Marley, Bob .... **CLC 17**
See also Marley, Robert Nesta

Marley, Robert Nesta 1945-1981
See Marley, Bob
See also CA 107; 103

Marlowe, Christopher 1564-1593**LC 22; DA; DAB; DAC; DAM DRAM, MST; DC 1; WLC**
See also CDBLB Before 1660; DLB 62

Marlowe, Stephen 1928-
See Queen, Ellery
See also CA 13-16R; CANR 6, 55

Marmontel, Jean-Francois 1723-1799 .. **LC 2**

Marquand, John P(hillips) 1893-1960**CLC 2, 10**
See also CA 85-88; DLB 9, 102

Marques, Rene 1919-1979 ..... **CLC 96; DAM MULT; HLC**
See also CA 97-100; 85-88; DLB 113; HW

Marquez, Gabriel (Jose) Garcia
See Garcia Marquez, Gabriel (Jose)

Marquis, Don(ald Robert Perry) 1878-1937 **TCLC 7**
See also CA 104; 166; DLB 11, 25

Marric, J. J.
See Creasey, John

Marryat, Frederick 1792-1848 .... **NCLC 3**
See also DLB 21, 163

Marsden, James
See Creasey, John

Marsh, (Edith) Ngaio 1899-1982 **CLC 7, 53; DAM POP**
See also CA 9-12R; CANR 6, 58; DLB 77; MTCW

Marshall, Garry 1934- .... **CLC 17**
See also AAYA 3; CA 111; SATA 60

Marshall, Paule 1929- .. **CLC 27, 72; BLC 3; DAM MULT; SSC 3**
See also BW 2; CA 77-80; CANR 25; DLB 157; MTCW

Marsten, Richard
See Hunter, Evan

Marston, John 1576-1634**LC 33; DAM DRAM**
See also DLB 58, 172

Martha, Henry
See Harris, Mark

Marti, Jose 1853-1895**NCLC 63; DAM MULT; HLC**

Martial c. 40-c. 104 .... **PC 10**

Martin, Ken
See Hubbard, L(afayette) Ron(ald)

Martin, Richard
See Creasey, John

Martin, Steve 1945- .... **CLC 30**
See also CA 97-100; CANR 30; MTCW

Martin, Valerie 1948- .... **CLC 89**
See also BEST 90:2; CA 85-88; CANR 49

Martin, Violet Florence 1862-1915 **TCLC 51**

Martin, Webber
See Silverberg, Robert

Martindale, Patrick Victor
See White, Patrick (Victor Martindale)

Martin du Gard, Roger 1881-1958 **TCLC 24**
See also CA 118; DLB 65

Martineau, Harriet 1802-1876 .... **NCLC 26**
See also DLB 21, 55, 159, 163, 166, 190; YABC 2

Martines, Julia
See O'Faolain, Julia

Martinez, Enrique Gonzalez

See Gonzalez Martinez, Enrique
Martinez, Jacinto Benavente y
See Benavente (y Martinez), Jacinto
Martinez Ruiz, Jose 1873-1967
See Azorin; Ruiz, Jose Martinez
See also CA 93-96; HW
Martinez Sierra, Gregorio 1881-1947TCLC 6
See also CA 115
Martinez Sierra, Maria (de la O'LeJarraga)
1874-1974 .... TCLC 6
See also CA 115
Martinsen, Martin
See Follett, Ken(neth Martin)
Martinson, Harry (Edmund) 1904-1978C L C
14
See also CA 77-80; CANR 34
Marut, Ret
See Traven, B.
Marut, Robert
See Traven, B.
Marvell, Andrew 1621-1678 ... LC 4, 43; DA;
DAB; DAC; DAM MST, POET; PC 10;
WLC
See also CDBLB 1660-1789; DLB 131
Marx, Karl (Heinrich) 1818-1883 . NCLC 17
See also DLB 129
Masaoka Shiki .... TCLC 18
See also Masaoka Tsunenori
Masaoka Tsunenori 1867-1902
See Masaoka Shiki
See also CA 117
Masefield, John (Edward) 1878-1967CLC 11,
47; DAM POET
See also CA 19-20; 25-28R; CANR 33; CAP 2;
CDBLB 1890-1914; DLB 10, 19, 153, 160;
MTCW; SATA 19
Maso, Carole 19(?)- .... CLC 44
Mason, Bobbie Ann 1940-CLC 28, 43, 82; SSC
4
See also AAYA 5; CA 53-56; CANR 11, 31,
58; DLB 173; DLBY 87; INT CANR-31;
MTCW
Mason, Ernst
See Pohl, Frederik
Mason, Lee W.
See Malzberg, Barry N(athaniel)
Mason, Nick 1945- .... CLC 35
Mason, Tally
See Derleth, August (William)
Mass, William
See Gibson, William
Masters, Edgar Lee 1868-1950 TCLC 2, 25;
DA; DAC; DAM MST, POET; PC 1;
WLCS
See also CA 104; 133; CDALB 1865-1917;
DLB 54; MTCW
Masters, Hilary 1928- .... CLC 48
See also CA 25-28R; CANR 13, 47
Mastrosimone, William 19(?)- .... CLC 36
Mathe, Albert
See Camus, Albert
Mather, Cotton 1663-1728 .... LC 38
See also CDALB 1640-1865; DLB 24, 30, 140
Mather, Increase 1639-1723 .... LC 38
See also DLB 24
Matheson, Richard Burton 1926- ..... CLC 37
See also CA 97-100; DLB 8, 44; INT 97-100
Mathews, Harry 1930- .... CLC 6, 52
See also CA 21-24R; CAAS 6; CANR 18, 40
Mathews, John Joseph 1894-1979 .. CLC 84;
DAM MULT
See also CA 19-20; 142; CANR 45; CAP 2;
DLB 175; NNAL

Mathias, Roland (Glyn) 1915- .... CLC 45
See also CA 97-100; CANR 19, 41; DLB 27
Matsuo Basho 1644-1694 .... PC 3
See also DAM POET
Mattheson, Rodney
See Creasey, John
Matthews, Greg 1949- .... CLC 45
See also CA 135
Matthews, William (Procter, III) 1942-1997
CLC 40
See also CA 29-32R; 162; CAAS 18; CANR
12, 57; DLB 5
Matthias, John (Edward) 1941- .... CLC 9
See also CA 33-36R; CANR 56
Matthiessen, Peter 1927-CLC 5, 7, 11, 32, 64;
DAM NOV
See also AAYA 6; BEST 90:4; CA 9-12R;
CANR 21, 50; DLB 6, 173; MTCW; SATA
27
Maturin, Charles Robert 1780(?)-1824NCLC
6
See also DLB 178
Matute (Ausejo), Ana Maria 1925- .. CLC 11
See also CA 89-92; MTCW
Maugham, W. S.
See Maugham, W(illiam) Somerset
Maugham, W(illiam) Somerset 1874-1965
CLC 1, 11, 15, 67, 93; DA; DAB; DAC;
DAM DRAM, MST, NOV; SSC 8; WLC
See also CA 5-8R; 25-28R; CANR 40; CDBLB
1914-1945; DLB 10, 36, 77, 100, 162, 195;
MTCW; SATA 54
Maugham, William Somerset
See Maugham, W(illiam) Somerset
Maupassant, (Henri Rene Albert) Guy de 1850-
1893NCLC 1, 42; DA; DAB; DAC; DAM
MST; SSC 1; WLC
See also DLB 123
Maupin, Armistead 1944-CLC 95; DAM POP
See also CA 125; 130; CANR 58; INT 130
Maurhut, Richard
See Traven, B.
Mauriac, Claude 1914-1996 .... CLC 9
See also CA 89-92; 152; DLB 83
Mauriac, Francois (Charles) 1885-1970C L C
4, 9, 56; SSC 24
See also CA 25-28; CAP 2; DLB 65; MTCW
Mavor, Osborne Henry 1888-1951
See Bridie, James
See also CA 104
Maxwell, William (Keepers, Jr.) 1908-CLC 19
See also CA 93-96; CANR 54; DLBY 80; INT
93-96
May, Elaine 1932- .... CLC 16
See also CA 124; 142; DLB 44
Mayakovski, Vladimir (Vladimirovich) 1893-
1930 .... TCLC 4, 18
See also CA 104; 158
Mayhew, Henry 1812-1887 .... NCLC 31
See also DLB 18, 55, 190
Mayle, Peter 1939(?)- .... CLC 89
See also CA 139; CANR 64
Maynard, Joyce 1953- .... CLC 23
See also CA 111; 129; CANR 64
Mayne, William (James Carter) 1928-CLC 12
See also AAYA 20; CA 9-12R; CANR 37; CLR
25; JRDA; MAICYA; SAAS 11; SATA 6, 68
Mayo, Jim
See L'Amour, Louis (Dearborn)
Maysles, Albert 1926- .... CLC 16
See also CA 29-32R
Maysles, David 1932- .... CLC 16
Mazer, Norma Fox 1931- .... CLC 26

See also AAYA 5; CA 69-72; CANR 12, 32,
66; CLR 23; JRDA; MAICYA; SAAS 1;
SATA 24, 67
Mazzini, Guiseppe 1805-1872 .... NCLC 34
McAuley, James Phillip 1917-1976 ..CLC 45
See also CA 97-100
McBain, Ed
See Hunter, Evan
McBrien, William Augustine 1930- ..CLC 44
See also CA 107
McCaffrey, Anne (Inez) 1926-CLC 17; DAM
NOV, POP
See also AAYA 6; AITN 2; BEST 89:2; CA 25-
28R; CANR 15, 35, 55; CLR 49; DLB 8;
JRDA; MAICYA; MTCW; SAAS 11; SATA
8, 70
McCall, Nathan 1955(?)- .... CLC 86
See also CA 146
McCann, Arthur
See Campbell, John W(ood, Jr.)
McCann, Edson
See Pohl, Frederik
McCarthy, Charles, Jr. 1933-
See McCarthy, Cormac
See also CANR 42, 69; DAM POP
McCarthy, Cormac 1933- CLC 4, 57, 59, 101
See also McCarthy, Charles, Jr.
See also DLB 6, 143
McCarthy, Mary (Therese) 1912-1989CLC 1,
3, 5, 14, 24, 39, 59; SSC 24
See also CA 5-8R; 129; CANR 16, 50, 64; DLB
2; DLBY 81; INT CANR-16; MTCW
McCartney, (James) Paul 1942- CLC 12, 35
See also CA 146
McCauley, Stephen (D.) 1955- .... CLC 50
See also CA 141
McClure, Michael (Thomas) 1932-CLC 6, 10
See also CA 21-24R; CANR 17, 46; DLB 16
McCorkle, Jill (Collins) 1958-.......... CLC 51
See also CA 121; DLBY 87
McCourt, Frank 1930- .... CLC 109
See also CA 157
McCourt, James 1941- .... CLC 5
See also CA 57-60
McCoy, Horace (Stanley) 1897-1955TCLC 28
See also CA 108; 155; DLB 9
McCrae, John 1872-1918 .... TCLC 12
See also CA 109; DLB 92
McCreigh, James
See Pohl, Frederik
McCullers, (Lula) Carson (Smith) 1917-1967
CLC 1, 4, 10, 12, 48, 100; DA; DAB; DAC;
DAM MST, NOV; SSC 9, 24; WLC
See also AAYA 21; CA 5-8R; 25-28R; CABS
1, 3; CANR 18; CDALB 1941-1968; DLB
2, 7, 173; MTCW; SATA 27
McCulloch, John Tyler
See Burroughs, Edgar Rice
McCullough, Colleen 1938(?)- CLC 27, 107;
DAM NOV, POP
See also CA 81-84; CANR 17, 46, 67; MTCW
McDermott, Alice 1953- .... CLC 90
See also CA 109; CANR 40
McElroy, Joseph 1930- .... CLC 5, 47
See also CA 17-20R
McEwan, Ian (Russell) 1948- .... CLC 13, 66;
DAM NOV
See also BEST 90:4; CA 61-64; CANR 14, 41,
69; DLB 14, 194; MTCW
McFadden, David 1940- .... CLC 48
See also CA 104; DLB 60; INT 104
McFarland, Dennis 1950- .... CLC 65
See also CA 165

McGahern, John 1934- **CLC 5, 9, 48; SSC 17**
See also CA 17-20R; CANR 29, 68; DLB 14; MTCW

McGinley, Patrick (Anthony) 1937- . **CLC 41**
See also CA 120; 127; CANR 56; INT 127

McGinley, Phyllis 1905-1978 .... **CLC 14**
See also CA 9-12R; 77-80; CANR 19; DLB 11, 48; SATA 2, 44; SATA-Obit 24

McGinniss, Joe 1942- .... **CLC 32**
See also AITN 2; BEST 89:2; CA 25-28R; CANR 26; DLB 185; INT CANR-26

McGivern, Maureen Daly
See Daly, Maureen

McGrath, Patrick 1950- .... **CLC 55**
See also CA 136; CANR 65

McGrath, Thomas (Matthew) 1916-1990**CLC 28, 59; DAM POET**
See also CA 9-12R; 132; CANR 6, 33; MTCW; SATA 41; SATA-Obit 66

McGuane, Thomas (Francis III) 1939-**CLC 3, 7, 18, 45**
See also AITN 2; CA 49-52; CANR 5, 24, 49; DLB 2; DLBY 80; INT CANR-24; MTCW

McGuckian, Medbh 1950- ..... **CLC 48; DAM POET**
See also CA 143; DLB 40

McHale, Tom 1942(?)-1982 .... **CLC 3, 5**
See also AITN 1; CA 77-80; 106

McIlvanney, William 1936- .... **CLC 42**
See also CA 25-28R; CANR 61; DLB 14

McIlwraith, Maureen Mollie Hunter
See Hunter, Mollie
See also SATA 2

McInerney, Jay 1955-**CLC 34, 112; DAM POP**
See also AAYA 18; CA 116; 123; CANR 45, 68; INT 123

McIntyre, Vonda N(eel) 1948- .... **CLC 18**
See also CA 81-84; CANR 17, 34, 69; MTCW

McKay, Claude**TCLC 7, 41; BLC 3; DAB; PC 2**
See also McKay, Festus Claudius
See also DLB 4, 45, 51, 117

McKay, Festus Claudius 1889-1948
See McKay, Claude
See also BW 1; CA 104; 124; DA; DAC; DAM MST, MULT, NOV, POET; MTCW; WLC

McKuen, Rod 1933-......................... **CLC 1, 3**
See also AITN 1; CA 41-44R; CANR 40

McLoughlin, R. B.
See Mencken, H(enry) L(ouis)

McLuhan, (Herbert) Marshall 1911-1980 **CLC 37, 83**
See also CA 9-12R; 102; CANR 12, 34, 61; DLB 88; INT CANR-12; MTCW

McMillan, Terry (L.) 1951- **CLC 50, 61, 112; BLCS; DAM MULT, NOV, POP**
See also AAYA 21; BW 2; CA 140; CANR 60

McMurtry, Larry (Jeff) 1936-**CLC 2, 3, 7, 11, 27, 44; DAM NOV, POP**
See also AAYA 15; AITN 2; BEST 89:2; CA 5-8R; CANR 19, 43, 64; CDALB 1968-1988; DLB 2, 143; DLBY 80, 87; MTCW

McNally, T. M. 1961-......................... **CLC 82**

McNally, Terrence 1939-.... **CLC 4, 7, 41, 91; DAM DRAM**
See also CA 45-48; CANR 2, 56; DLB 7

McNamer, Deirdre 1950- .... **CLC 70**

McNeile, Herman Cyril 1888-1937
See Sapper
See also DLB 77

McNickle, (William) D'Arcy 1904-1977 **C L C 89; DAM MULT**
See also CA 9-12R; 85-88; CANR 5, 45; DLB 175; NNAL; SATA-Obit 22

McPhee, John (Angus) 1931- .... **CLC 36**
See also BEST 90:1; CA 65-68; CANR 20, 46, 64, 69; DLB 185; MTCW

McPherson, James Alan 1943-.. **CLC 19, 77; BLCS**
See also BW 1; CA 25-28R; CAAS 17; CANR 24; DLB 38; MTCW

McPherson, William (Alexander) 1933- **C L C 34**
See also CA 69-72; CANR 28; INT CANR-28

Mead, Margaret 1901-1978 .... **CLC 37**
See also AITN 1; CA 1-4R; 81-84; CANR 4; MTCW; SATA-Obit 20

Meaker, Marijane (Agnes) 1927-
See Kerr, M. E.
See also CA 107; CANR 37, 63; INT 107; JRDA; MAICYA; MTCW; SATA 20, 61

Medoff, Mark (Howard) 1940- ... **CLC 6, 23; DAM DRAM**
See also AITN 1; CA 53-56; CANR 5; DLB 7; INT CANR-5

Medvedev, P. N.
See Bakhtin, Mikhail Mikhailovich

Meged, Aharon
See Megged, Aharon

Meged, Aron
See Megged, Aharon

Megged, Aharon 1920-......................... **CLC 9**
See also CA 49-52; CAAS 13; CANR 1

Mehta, Ved (Parkash) 1934-............... **CLC 37**
See also CA 1-4R; CANR 2, 23, 69; MTCW

Melanter
See Blackmore, R(ichard) D(oddridge)

Melies, Georges 1861-1938 .... **TCLC 81**

Melikow, Loris
See Hofmannsthal, Hugo von

Melmoth, Sebastian
See Wilde, Oscar (Fingal O'Flahertie Wills)

Meltzer, Milton 1915- .... **CLC 26**
See also AAYA 8; CA 13-16R; CANR 38; CLR 13; DLB 61; JRDA; MAICYA; SAAS 1; SATA 1, 50, 80

Melville, Herman 1819-1891**NCLC 3, 12, 29, 45, 49; DA; DAB; DAC; DAM MST, NOV; SSC 1, 17; WLC**
See also AAYA 25; CDALB 1640-1865; DLB 3, 74; SATA 59

Menander c. 342B.C.-c. 292B.C. ..... **CMLC 9; DAM DRAM; DC 3**
See also DLB 176

Mencken, H(enry) L(ouis) 1880-1956 **T C L C 13**
See also CA 105; 125; CDALB 1917-1929; DLB 11, 29, 63, 137; MTCW

Mendelsohn, Jane 1965(?)- .... **CLC 99**
See also CA 154

Mercer, David 1928-1980**CLC 5; DAM DRAM**
See also CA 9-12R; 102; CANR 23; DLB 13; MTCW

Merchant, Paul
See Ellison, Harlan (Jay)

Meredith, George 1828-1909 . **TCLC 17, 43; DAM POET**
See also CA 117; 153; CDBLB 1832-1890; DLB 18, 35, 57, 159

Meredith, William (Morris) 1919-**CLC 4, 13, 22, 55; DAM POET**
See also CA 9-12R; CAAS 14; CANR 6, 40; DLB 5

Merezhkovsky, Dmitry Sergeyevich 1865-1941 **TCLC 29**

Merimee, Prosper 1803-1870**NCLC 6, 65; SSC 7**
See also DLB 119, 192

Merkin, Daphne 1954- .... **CLC 44**
See also CA 123

Merlin, Arthur
See Blish, James (Benjamin)

Merrill, James (Ingram) 1926-1995**CLC 2, 3, 6, 8, 13, 18, 34, 91; DAM POET**
See also CA 13-16R; 147; CANR 10, 49, 63; DLB 5, 165; DLBY 85; INT CANR-10; MTCW

Merriman, Alex
See Silverberg, Robert

Merriman, Brian 1747-1805 .... **NCLC 70**

Merritt, E. B.
See Waddington, Miriam

Merton, Thomas 1915-1968**CLC 1, 3, 11, 34, 83; PC 10**
See also CA 5-8R; 25-28R; CANR 22, 53; DLB 48; DLBY 81; MTCW

Merwin, W(illiam) S(tanley) 1927- **CLC 1, 2, 3, 5, 8, 13, 18, 45, 88; DAM POET**
See also CA 13-16R; CANR 15, 51; DLB 5, 169; INT CANR-15; MTCW

Metcalf, John 1938-......................... **CLC 37**
See also CA 113; DLB 60

Metcalf, Suzanne
See Baum, L(yman) Frank

Mew, Charlotte (Mary) 1870-1928 .. **TCLC 8**
See also CA 105; DLB 19, 135

Mewshaw, Michael 1943- .... **CLC 9**
See also CA 53-56; CANR 7, 47; DLBY 80

Meyer, June
See Jordan, June

Meyer, Lynn
See Slavitt, David R(ytman)

Meyer-Meyrink, Gustav 1868-1932
See Meyrink, Gustav
See also CA 117

Meyers, Jeffrey 1939-......................... **CLC 39**
See also CA 73-76; CANR 54; DLB 111

Meynell, Alice (Christina Gertrude Thompson) 1847-1922 .... **TCLC 6**
See also CA 104; DLB 19, 98

Meyrink, Gustav .... **TCLC 21**
See also Meyer-Meyrink, Gustav
See also DLB 81

Michaels, Leonard 1933- **CLC 6, 25; SSC 16**
See also CA 61-64; CANR 21, 62; DLB 130; MTCW

Michaux, Henri 1899-1984............**CLC 8, 19**
See also CA 85-88; 114

Micheaux, Oscar 1884-1951 .... **TCLC 76**
See also DLB 50

Michelangelo 1475-1564 .... **LC 12**

Michelet, Jules 1798-1874 .... **NCLC 31**

Michener, James A(lbert) 1907(?)-1997 **C L C 1, 5, 11, 29, 60, 109; DAM NOV, POP**
See also AITN 1; BEST 90:1; CA 5-8R; 161; CANR 21, 45, 68; DLB 6; MTCW

Mickiewicz, Adam 1798-1855 .... **NCLC 3**

Middleton, Christopher 1926- .... **CLC 13**
See also CA 13-16R; CANR 29, 54; DLB 40

Middleton, Richard (Barham) 1882-1911 **TCLC 56**
See also DLB 156

Middleton, Stanley 1919-............... **CLC 7, 38**
See also CA 25-28R; CAAS 23; CANR 21, 46; DLB 14

Middleton, Thomas 1580-1627 **LC 33; DAM DRAM, MST; DC 5**
See also DLB 58

Migueis, Jose Rodrigues 1901- .... **CLC 10**

Moore, George Augustus 1852-1933**TCLC 7; SSC 19**
See also CA 104; DLB 10, 18, 57, 135
Moore, Lorrie .... **CLC 39, 45, 68**
See also Moore, Marie Lorena
Moore, Marianne (Craig) 1887-1972**CLC 1, 2, 4, 8, 10, 13, 19, 47; DA; DAB; DAC; DAM MST, POET; PC 4; WLCS**
See also CA 1-4R; 33-36R; CANR 3, 61; CDALB 1929-1941; DLB 45; DLBD 7; MTCW; SATA 20
Moore, Marie Lorena 1957-
See Moore, Lorrie
See also CA 116; CANR 39
Moore, Thomas 1779-1852 .... **NCLC 6**
See also DLB 96, 144
Morand, Paul 1888-1976 .... **CLC 41; SSC 22**
See also CA 69-72; DLB 65
Morante, Elsa 1918-1985 ....**CLC 8, 47**
See also CA 85-88; 117; CANR 35; DLB 177; MTCW
Moravia, Alberto 1907-1990**CLC 2, 7, 11, 27, 46; SSC 26**
See also Pincherle, Alberto
See also DLB 177
More, Hannah 1745-1833 .... **NCLC 27**
See also DLB 107, 109, 116, 158
More, Henry 1614-1687 ....**LC 9**
See also DLB 126
More, Sir Thomas 1478-1535 .... **LC 10, 32**
Moreas, Jean .... **TCLC 18**
See also Papadiamantopoulos, Johannes
Morgan, Berry 1919- .... **CLC 6**
See also CA 49-52; DLB 6
Morgan, Claire
See Highsmith, (Mary) Patricia
Morgan, Edwin (George) 1920- .... **CLC 31**
See also CA 5-8R; CANR 3, 43; DLB 27
Morgan, (George) Frederick 1922- .. **CLC 23**
See also CA 17-20R; CANR 21
Morgan, Harriet
See Mencken, H(enry) L(ouis)
Morgan, Jane
See Cooper, James Fenimore
Morgan, Janet 1945- .... **CLC 39**
See also CA 65-68
Morgan, Lady 1776(?)-1859 .... **NCLC 29**
See also DLB 116, 158
Morgan, Robin (Evonne) 1941- .... **CLC 2**
See also CA 69-72; CANR 29, 68; MTCW; SATA 80
Morgan, Scott
See Kuttner, Henry
Morgan, Seth 1949(?)-1990 .... **CLC 65**
See also CA 132
Morgenstern, Christian 1871-1914 . **TCLC 8**
See also CA 105
Morgenstern, S.
See Goldman, William (W.)
Moricz, Zsigmond 1879-1942 .... **TCLC 33**
See also CA 165
Morike, Eduard (Friedrich) 1804-1875**NCLC 10**
See also DLB 133
Moritz, Karl Philipp 1756-1793 .... **LC 2**
See also DLB 94
Morland, Peter Henry
See Faust, Frederick (Schiller)
Morren, Theophil
See Hofmannsthal, Hugo von
Morris, Bill 1952- .... **CLC 76**
Morris, Julian
See West, Morris L(anglo)

Morris, Steveland Judkins 1950(?)-
See Wonder, Stevie
See also CA 111
Morris, William 1834-1896 .... **NCLC 4**
See also CDBLB 1832-1890; DLB 18, 35, 57, 156, 178, 184
Morris, Wright 1910- ...... **CLC 1, 3, 7, 18, 37**
See also CA 9-12R; CANR 21; DLB 2; DLBY 81; MTCW
Morrison, Arthur 1863-1945 .... **TCLC 72**
See also CA 120; 157; DLB 70, 135, 197
Morrison, Chloe Anthony Wofford
See Morrison, Toni
Morrison, James Douglas 1943-1971
See Morrison, Jim
See also CA 73-76; CANR 40
Morrison, Jim .... **CLC 17**
See also Morrison, James Douglas
Morrison, Toni 1931-**CLC 4, 10, 22, 55, 81, 87; BLC 3; DA; DAB; DAC; DAM MST, MULT, NOV, POP**
See also AAYA 1, 22; BW 2; CA 29-32R; CANR 27, 42, 67; CDALB 1968-1988; DLB 6, 33, 143; DLBY 81; MTCW; SATA 57
Morrison, Van 1945- .... **CLC 21**
See also CA 116
Morrissy, Mary 1958- .... **CLC 99**
Mortimer, John (Clifford) 1923-**CLC 28, 43; DAM DRAM, POP**
See also CA 13-16R; CANR 21, 69; CDBLB 1960 to Present; DLB 13; INT CANR-21; MTCW
Mortimer, Penelope (Ruth) 1918- .... **CLC 5**
See also CA 57-60; CANR 45
Morton, Anthony
See Creasey, John
Mosca, Gaetano 1858-1941 .... **TCLC 75**
Mosher, Howard Frank 1943- .... **CLC 62**
See also CA 139; CANR 65
Mosley, Nicholas 1923- .... **CLC 43, 70**
See also CA 69-72; CANR 41, 60; DLB 14
Mosley, Walter 1952- . **CLC 97; BLCS; DAM MULT, POP**
See also AAYA 17; BW 2; CA 142; CANR 57
Moss, Howard 1922-1987 **CLC 7, 14, 45, 50; DAM POET**
See also CA 1-4R; 123; CANR 1, 44; DLB 5
Mossgiel, Rab
See Burns, Robert
Motion, Andrew (Peter) 1952- .... **CLC 47**
See also CA 146; DLB 40
Motley, Willard (Francis) 1909-1965**CLC 18**
See also BW 1; CA 117; 106; DLB 76, 143
Motoori, Norinaga 1730-1801 .... **NCLC 45**
Mott, Michael (Charles Alston) 1930-**CLC 15, 34**
See also CA 5-8R; CAAS 7; CANR 7, 29
Mountain Wolf Woman 1884-1960 .. **CLC 92**
See also CA 144; NNAL
Moure, Erin 1955- .... **CLC 88**
See also CA 113; DLB 60
Mowat, Farley (McGill) 1921-**CLC 26; DAC; DAM MST**
See also AAYA 1; CA 1-4R; CANR 4, 24, 42, 68; CLR 20; DLB 68; INT CANAR-24; JRDA; MAICYA; MTCW; SATA 3, 55
Moyers, Bill 1934- .... **CLC 74**
See also AITN 2; CA 61-64; CANR 31, 52
Mphahlele, Es'kia
See Mphahlele, Ezekiel
See also DLB 125
Mphahlele, Ezekiel 1919-1983 **CLC 25; BLC 3; DAM MULT**

See also Mphahlele, Es'kia
See also BW 2; CA 81-84; CANR 26
Mqhayi, S(amuel) E(dward) K(rune Loliwe) 1875-1945**TCLC 25; BLC 3; DAM MULT**
See also CA 153
Mrozek, Slawomir 1930-................**CLC 3, 13**
See also CA 13-16R; CAAS 10; CANR 29; MTCW
Mrs. Belloc-Lowndes
See Lowndes, Marie Adelaide (Belloc)
Mtwa, Percy (?)-................................. **CLC 47**
Mueller, Lisel 1924- .... **CLC 13, 51**
See also CA 93-96; DLB 105
Muir, Edwin 1887-1959 .... **TCLC 2**
See also CA 104; DLB 20, 100, 191
Muir, John 1838-1914 .... **TCLC 28**
See also CA 165; DLB 186
Mujica Lainez, Manuel 1910-1984 ... **CLC 31**
See also Lainez, Manuel Mujica
See also CA 81-84; 112; CANR 32; HW
Mukherjee, Bharati 1940-**CLC 53; DAM NOV**
See also BEST 89:2; CA 107; CANR 45; DLB 60; MTCW
Muldoon, Paul 1951-**CLC 32, 72; DAM POET**
See also CA 113; 129; CANR 52; DLB 40; INT 129
Mulisch, Harry 1927- .... **CLC 42**
See also CA 9-12R; CANR 6, 26, 56
Mull, Martin 1943- .... **CLC 17**
See also CA 105
Mulock, Dinah Maria
See Craik, Dinah Maria (Mulock)
Munford, Robert 1737(?)-1783 .... **LC 5**
See also DLB 31
Mungo, Raymond 1946- .... **CLC 72**
See also CA 49-52; CANR 2
Munro, Alice 1931- .... **CLC 6, 10, 19, 50, 95; DAC; DAM MST, NOV; SSC 3; WLCS**
See also AITN 2; CA 33-36R; CANR 33, 53; DLB 53; MTCW; SATA 29
Munro, H(ector) H(ugh) 1870-1916
See Saki
See also CA 104; 130; CDBLB 1890-1914; DA; DAB; DAC; DAM MST, NOV; DLB 34, 162; MTCW; WLC
Murasaki, Lady .... **CMLC 1**
Murdoch, (Jean) Iris 1919-**CLC 1, 2, 3, 4, 6, 8, 11, 15, 22, 31, 51; DAB; DAC; DAM MST, NOV**
See also CA 13-16R; CANR 8, 43, 68; CDBLB 1960 to Present; DLB 14, 194; INT CANR-8; MTCW
Murfree, Mary Noailles 1850-1922 ... **SSC 22**
See also CA 122; DLB 12, 74
Murnau, Friedrich Wilhelm
See Plumpe, Friedrich Wilhelm
Murphy, Richard 1927- .... **CLC 41**
See also CA 29-32R; DLB 40
Murphy, Sylvia 1937- .... **CLC 34**
See also CA 121
Murphy, Thomas (Bernard) 1935- ... **CLC 51**
See also CA 101
Murray, Albert L. 1916- .... **CLC 73**
See also BW 2; CA 49-52; CANR 26, 52; DLB 38
Murray, Judith Sargent 1751-1820**NCLC 63**
See also DLB 37, 200
Murray, Les(lie) A(llan) 1938-**CLC 40; DAM POET**
See also CA 21-24R; CANR 11, 27, 56
Murry, J. Middleton
See Murry, John Middleton
Murry, John Middleton 1889-1957 **TCLC 16**

See also CA 105; CABS 3; CANR 41; DLBY 84

Normyx
See Douglas, (George) Norman

Norris, Frank 1870-1902 .... **SSC 28**
See also Norris, (Benjamin) Frank(lin, Jr.)
See also CDALB 1865-1917; DLB 12, 71, 186

Norris, (Benjamin) Frank(lin, Jr.) 1870-1902 **TCLC 24**
See also Norris, Frank
See also CA 110; 160

Norris, Leslie 1921- .... **CLC 14**
See also CA 11-12; CANR 14; CAP 1; DLB 27

North, Andrew
See Norton, Andre

North, Anthony
See Koontz, Dean R(ay)

North, Captain George
See Stevenson, Robert Louis (Balfour)

North, Milou
See Erdrich, Louise

Northrup, B. A.
See Hubbard, L(afayette) Ron(ald)

North Staffs
See Hulme, T(homas) E(rnest)

Norton, Alice Mary
See Norton, Andre
See also MAICYA; SATA 1, 43

Norton, Andre 1912- .... **CLC 12**
See also Norton, Alice Mary
See also AAYA 14; CA 1-4R; CANR 68; CLR 50; DLB 8, 52; JRDA; MTCW; SATA 91

Norton, Caroline 1808-1877 .... **NCLC 47**
See also DLB 21, 159, 199

Norway, Nevil Shute 1899-1960
See Shute, Nevil
See also CA 102; 93-96

Norwid, Cyprian Kamil 1821-1883 **NCLC 17**

Nosille, Nabrah
See Ellison, Harlan (Jay)

Nossack, Hans Erich 1901-1978 .... **CLC 6**
See also CA 93-96; 85-88; DLB 69

Nostradamus 1503-1566 .... **LC 27**

Nosu, Chuji
See Ozu, Yasujiro

Notenburg, Eleanora (Genrikhovna) von
See Guro, Elena

Nova, Craig 1945- .... **CLC 7, 31**
See also CA 45-48; CANR 2, 53

Novak, Joseph
See Kosinski, Jerzy (Nikodem)

Novalis 1772-1801 .... **NCLC 13**
See also DLB 90

Novis, Emile
See Weil, Simone (Adolphine)

Nowlan, Alden (Albert) 1933-1983 **CLC 15; DAC; DAM MST**
See also CA 9-12R; CANR 5; DLB 53

Noyes, Alfred 1880-1958 .... **TCLC 7**
See also CA 104; DLB 20

Nunn, Kem .... **CLC 34**
See also CA 159

Nye, Robert 1939- .. **CLC 13, 42; DAM NOV**
See also CA 33-36R; CANR 29, 67; DLB 14; MTCW; SATA 6

Nyro, Laura 1947- .... **CLC 17**

Oates, Joyce Carol 1938-**CLC 1, 2, 3, 6, 9, 11, 15, 19, 33, 52, 108; DA; DAB; DAC; DAM MST, NOV, POP; SSC 6; WLC**
See also AAYA 15; AITN 1; BEST 89:2; CA 5-8R; CANR 25, 45; CDALB 1968-1988; DLB 2, 5, 130; DLBY 81; INT CANR-25; MTCW

O'Brien, Darcy 1939- .... **CLC 11**

See also CA 21-24R; CANR 8, 59

O'Brien, E. G.
See Clarke, Arthur C(harles)

O'Brien, Edna 1936- **CLC 3, 5, 8, 13, 36, 65; DAM NOV; SSC 10**
See also CA 1-4R; CANR 6, 41, 65; CDBLB 1960 to Present; DLB 14; MTCW

O'Brien, Fitz-James 1828-1862 ..... **NCLC 21**
See also DLB 74

O'Brien, Flann ....**CLC 1, 4, 5, 7, 10, 47**
See also O Nuallain, Brian

O'Brien, Richard 1942- .... **CLC 17**
See also CA 124

O'Brien, (William) Tim(othy) 1946- . **CLC 7, 19, 40, 103; DAM POP**
See also AAYA 16; CA 85-88; CANR 40, 58; DLB 152; DLBD 9; DLBY 80

Obstfelder, Sigbjoern 1866-1900 ... **TCLC 23**
See also CA 123

O'Casey, Sean 1880-1964**CLC 1, 5, 9, 11, 15, 88; DAB; DAC; DAM DRAM, MST; WLCS**
See also CA 89-92; CANR 62; CDBLB 1914-1945; DLB 10; MTCW

O'Cathasaigh, Sean
See O'Casey, Sean

Ochs, Phil 1940-1976 .... **CLC 17**
See also CA 65-68

O'Connor, Edwin (Greene) 1918-1968**CLC 14**
See also CA 93-96; 25-28R

O'Connor, (Mary) Flannery 1925-1964 **C L C 1, 2, 3, 6, 10, 13, 15, 21, 66, 104; DA; DAB; DAC; DAM MST, NOV; SSC 1, 23; WLC**
See also AAYA 7; CA 1-4R; CANR 3, 41; CDALB 1941-1968; DLB 2, 152; DLBD 12; DLBY 80; MTCW

O'Connor, Frank .... **CLC 23; SSC 5**
See also O'Donovan, Michael John
See also DLB 162

O'Dell, Scott 1898-1989 .... **CLC 30**
See also AAYA 3; CA 61-64; 129; CANR 12, 30; CLR 1, 16; DLB 52; JRDA; MAICYA; SATA 12, 60

Odets, Clifford 1906-1963**CLC 2, 28, 98; DAM DRAM; DC 6**
See also CA 85-88; CANR 62; DLB 7, 26; MTCW

O'Doherty, Brian 1934- .... **CLC 76**
See also CA 105

O'Donnell, K. M.
See Malzberg, Barry N(athaniel)

O'Donnell, Lawrence
See Kuttner, Henry

O'Donovan, Michael John 1903-1966**CLC 14**
See also O'Connor, Frank
See also CA 93-96

Oe, Kenzaburo 1935- **CLC 10, 36, 86; DAM NOV; SSC 20**
See also CA 97-100; CANR 36, 50; DLB 182; DLBY 94; MTCW

O'Faolain, Julia 1932- .... **CLC 6, 19, 47, 108**
See also CA 81-84; CAAS 2; CANR 12, 61; DLB 14; MTCW

O'Faolain, Sean 1900-1991 **CLC 1, 7, 14, 32, 70; SSC 13**
See also CA 61-64; 134; CANR 12, 66; DLB 15, 162; MTCW

O'Flaherty, Liam 1896-1984**CLC 5, 34; SSC 6**
See also CA 101; 113; CANR 35; DLB 36, 162; DLBY 84; MTCW

Ogilvy, Gavin
See Barrie, J(ames) M(atthew)

O'Grady, Standish (James) 1846-1928**T C L C 5**
See also CA 104; 157

O'Grady, Timothy 1951- .... **CLC 59**
See also CA 138

O'Hara, Frank 1926-1966 .**CLC 2, 5, 13, 78; DAM POET**
See also CA 9-12R; 25-28R; CANR 33; DLB 5, 16, 193; MTCW

O'Hara, John (Henry) 1905-1970**CLC 1, 2, 3, 6, 11, 42; DAM NOV; SSC 15**
See also CA 5-8R; 25-28R; CANR 31, 60; CDALB 1929-1941; DLB 9, 86; DLBD 2; MTCW

O Hehir, Diana 1922- .... **CLC 41**
See also CA 93-96

Okigbo, Christopher (Ifenayichukwu) 1932-1967 . **CLC 25, 84; BLC 3; DAM MULT, POET; PC 7**
See also BW 1; CA 77-80; DLB 125; MTCW

Okri, Ben 1959- .... **CLC 87**
See also BW 2; CA 130; 138; CANR 65; DLB 157; INT 138

Olds, Sharon 1942- .... **CLC 32, 39, 85; DAM POET; PC 22**
See also CA 101; CANR 18, 41, 66; DLB 120

Oldstyle, Jonathan
See Irving, Washington

Olesha, Yuri (Karlovich) 1899-1960 .. **CLC 8**
See also CA 85-88

Oliphant, Laurence 1829(?)-1888 .. **NCLC 47**
See also DLB 18, 166

Oliphant, Margaret (Oliphant Wilson) 1828-1897 .... **NCLC 11, 61; SSC 25**
See also DLB 18, 159, 190

Oliver, Mary 1935- .... **CLC 19, 34, 98**
See also CA 21-24R; CANR 9, 43; DLB 5, 193

Olivier, Laurence (Kerr) 1907-1989 . **CLC 20**
See also CA 111; 150; 129

Olsen, Tillie 1913-**CLC 4, 13; DA; DAB; DAC; DAM MST; SSC 11**
See also CA 1-4R; CANR 1, 43; DLB 28; DLBY 80; MTCW

Olson, Charles (John) 1910-1970**CLC 1, 2, 5, 6, 9, 11, 29; DAM POET; PC 19**
See also CA 13-16; 25-28R; CABS 2; CANR 35, 61; CAP 1; DLB 5, 16, 193; MTCW

Olson, Toby 1937- .... **CLC 28**
See also CA 65-68; CANR 9, 31

Olyesha, Yuri
See Olesha, Yuri (Karlovich)

Ondaatje, (Philip) Michael 1943-**CLC 14, 29, 51, 76; DAB; DAC; DAM MST**
See also CA 77-80; CANR 42; DLB 60

Oneal, Elizabeth 1934-
See Oneal, Zibby
See also CA 106; CANR 28; MAICYA; SATA 30, 82

Oneal, Zibby .... **CLC 30**
See also Oneal, Elizabeth
See also AAYA 5; CLR 13; JRDA

O'Neill, Eugene (Gladstone) 1888-1953**TCLC 1, 6, 27, 49; DA; DAB; DAC; DAM DRAM, MST; WLC**
See also AITN 1; CA 110; 132; CDALB 1929-1941; DLB 7; MTCW

Onetti, Juan Carlos 1909-1994 ... **CLC 7, 10; DAM MULT, NOV; SSC 23**
See also CA 85-88; 145; CANR 32, 63; DLB 113; HW; MTCW

O Nuallain, Brian 1911-1966
See O'Brien, Flann
See also CA 21-22; 25-28R; CAP 2

Ophuls, Max 1902-1957 .... **TCLC 79**

See also CA 113
Opie, Amelia 1769-1853 .... **NCLC 65**
  See also DLB 116, 159
Oppen, George 1908-1984 ...... **CLC 7, 13, 34**
  See also CA 13-16R; 113; CANR 8; DLB 5,
  165
Oppenheim, E(dward) Phillips 1866-1946
  TCLC 45
  See also CA 111; DLB 70
Opuls, Max
  See Ophuls, Max
Origen c. 185-c. 254 .... **CMLC 19**
Orlovitz, Gil 1918-1973 .... **CLC 22**
  See also CA 77-80; 45-48; DLB 2, 5
Orris
  See Ingelow, Jean
Ortega y Gasset, Jose 1883-1955 .... **TCLC 9;**
  DAM MULT; HLC
  See also CA 106; 130; HW; MTCW
Ortese, Anna Maria 1914- .... **CLC 89**
  See also DLB 177
Ortiz, Simon J(oseph) 1941-.. **CLC 45; DAM**
  MULT, POET; PC 17
  See also CA 134; CANR 69; DLB 120, 175;
  NNAL
Orton, Joe .... **CLC 4, 13, 43; DC 3**
  See also Orton, John Kingsley
  See also CDBLB 1960 to Present; DLB 13
Orton, John Kingsley 1933-1967
  See Orton, Joe
  See also CA 85-88; CANR 35, 66; DAM
  DRAM; MTCW
Orwell, George . **TCLC 2, 6, 15, 31, 51; DAB;**
  WLC
  See also Blair, Eric (Arthur)
  See also CDBLB 1945-1960; DLB 15, 98, 195
Osborne, David
  See Silverberg, Robert
Osborne, George
  See Silverberg, Robert
Osborne, John (James) 1929-1994**CLC 1, 2, 5,**
  11, 45; DA; DAB; DAC; DAM DRAM,
  MST; WLC
  See also CA 13-16R; 147; CANR 21, 56;
  CDBLB 1945-1960; DLB 13; MTCW
Osborne, Lawrence 1958- .... **CLC 50**
Oshima, Nagisa 1932- .... **CLC 20**
  See also CA 116; 121
Oskison, John Milton 1874-1947 .. **TCLC 35;**
  DAM MULT
  See also CA 144; DLB 175; NNAL
Ossian c. 3rd cent. - .... **CMLC 28**
  See also Macpherson, James
Ossoli, Sarah Margaret (Fuller marchesa d')
  1810-1850
  See Fuller, Margaret
  See also SATA 25
Ostrovsky, Alexander 1823-1886**NCLC 30, 57**
Otero, Blas de 1916-1979 .... **CLC 11**
  See also CA 89-92; DLB 134
Otto, Whitney 1955- .... **CLC 70**
  See also CA 140
Ouida .... **TCLC 43**
  See also De La Ramee, (Marie) Louise
  See also DLB 18, 156
Ousmane, Sembene 1923- .... **CLC 66; BLC 3**
  See also BW 1; CA 117; 125; MTCW
Ovid 43B.C.-18(?)**CMLC 7; DAM POET; PC**
  2
Owen, Hugh
  See Faust, Frederick (Schiller)
Owen, Wilfred (Edward Salter) 1893-1918
  TCLC 5, 27; DA; DAB; DAC; DAM MST,

POET; PC 19; WLC
  See also CA 104; 141; CDBLB 1914-1945;
  DLB 20
Owens, Rochelle 1936- .... **CLC 8**
  See also CA 17-20R; CAAS 2; CANR 39
Oz, Amos 1939-**CLC 5, 8, 11, 27, 33, 54; DAM**
  NOV
  See also CA 53-56; CANR 27, 47, 65; MTCW
Ozick, Cynthia 1928- **CLC 3, 7, 28, 62; DAM**
  NOV, POP; SSC 15
  See also BEST 90:1; CA 17-20R; CANR 23,
  58; DLB 28, 152; DLBY 82; INT CANR-
  23; MTCW
Ozu, Yasujiro 1903-1963 .... **CLC 16**
  See also CA 112
Pacheco, C.
  See Pessoa, Fernando (Antonio Nogueira)
Pa Chin .... **CLC 18**
  See also Li Fei-kan
Pack, Robert 1929- .... **CLC 13**
  See also CA 1-4R; CANR 3, 44; DLB 5
Padgett, Lewis
  See Kuttner, Henry
Padilla (Lorenzo), Heberto 1932- ..... **CLC 38**
  See also AITN 1; CA 123; 131; HW
Page, Jimmy 1944- .... **CLC 12**
Page, Louise 1955- .... **CLC 40**
  See also CA 140
Page, P(atricia) K(athleen) 1916- **CLC 7, 18;**
  DAC; DAM MST; PC 12
  See also CA 53-56; CANR 4, 22, 65; DLB 68;
  MTCW
Page, Thomas Nelson 1853-1922 .... **SSC 23**
  See also CA 118; DLB 12, 78; DLBD 13
Pagels, Elaine Hiesey 1943- .... **CLC 104**
  See also CA 45-48; CANR 2, 24, 51
Paget, Violet 1856-1935
  See Lee, Vernon
  See also CA 104; 166
Paget-Lowe, Henry
  See Lovecraft, H(oward) P(hillips)
Paglia, Camille (Anna) 1947- .... **CLC 68**
  See also CA 140
Paige, Richard
  See Koontz, Dean R(ay)
Paine, Thomas 1737-1809 .... **NCLC 62**
  See also CDALB 1640-1865; DLB 31, 43, 73,
  158
Pakenham, Antonia
  See Fraser, (Lady) Antonia (Pakenham)
Palamas, Kostes 1859-1943 .... **TCLC 5**
  See also CA 105
Palazzeschi, Aldo 1885-1974 .... **CLC 11**
  See also CA 89-92; 53-56; DLB 114
Paley, Grace 1922-**CLC 4, 6, 37; DAM POP;**
  SSC 8
  See also CA 25-28R; CANR 13, 46; DLB 28;
  INT CANR-13; MTCW
Palin, Michael (Edward) 1943- .... **CLC 21**
  See also Monty Python
  See also CA 107; CANR 35; SATA 67
Palliser, Charles 1947- .... **CLC 65**
  See also CA 136
Palma, Ricardo 1833-1919 .... **TCLC 29**
Pancake, Breece Dexter 1952-1979
  See Pancake, Breece D'J
  See also CA 123; 109
Pancake, Breece D'J .... **CLC 29**
  See also Pancake, Breece Dexter
  See also DLB 130
Panko, Rudy
  See Gogol, Nikolai (Vasilyevich)
Papadiamantis, Alexandros 1851-1911**T C L C**

29
Papadiamantopoulos, Johannes 1856-1910
  See Moreas, Jean
  See also CA 117
Papini, Giovanni 1881-1956 .... **TCLC 22**
  See also CA 121
Paracelsus 1493-1541 .... **LC 14**
  See also DLB 179
Parasol, Peter
  See Stevens, Wallace
Pardo Baz<aacute>n, Emilia 1851-1921 **S S C**
  30
Pareto, Vilfredo 1848-1923 .... **TCLC 69**
Parfenie, Maria
  See Codrescu, Andrei
Parini, Jay (Lee) 1948- .... **CLC 54**
  See also CA 97-100; CAAS 16; CANR 32
Park, Jordan
  See Kornbluth, C(yril) M.; Pohl, Frederik
Park, Robert E(zra) 1864-1944 ...... **TCLC 73**
  See also CA 122; 165
Parker, Bert
  See Ellison, Harlan (Jay)
Parker, Dorothy (Rothschild) 1893-1967**C L C**
  15, 68; DAM POET; SSC 2
  See also CA 19-20; 25-28R; CAP 2; DLB 11,
  45, 86; MTCW
Parker, Robert B(rown) 1932-**CLC 27; DAM**
  NOV, POP
  See also BEST 89:4; CA 49-52; CANR 1, 26,
  52; INT CANR-26; MTCW
Parkin, Frank 1940- .... **CLC 43**
  See also CA 147
Parkman, Francis, Jr. 1823-1893 ..**NCLC 12**
  See also DLB 1, 30, 186
Parks, Gordon (Alexander Buchanan) 1912-
  CLC 1, 16; BLC 3; DAM MULT
  See also AITN 2; BW 2; CA 41-44R; CANR
  26, 66; DLB 33; SATA 8
Parmenides c. 515B.C.-c. 450B.C. **CMLC 22**
  See also DLB 176
Parnell, Thomas 1679-1718 .... **LC 3**
  See also DLB 94
Parra, Nicanor 1914- ...... **CLC 2, 102; DAM**
  MULT; HLC
  See also CA 85-88; CANR 32; HW; MTCW
Parrish, Mary Frances
  See Fisher, M(ary) F(rances) K(ennedy)
Parson
  See Coleridge, Samuel Taylor
Parson Lot
  See Kingsley, Charles
Partridge, Anthony
  See Oppenheim, E(dward) Phillips
Pascal, Blaise 1623-1662 .... **LC 35**
Pascoli, Giovanni 1855-1912 .... **TCLC 45**
Pasolini, Pier Paolo 1922-1975 . **CLC 20, 37,**
  106; PC 17
  See also CA 93-96; 61-64; CANR 63; DLB 128,
  177; MTCW
Pasquini
  See Silone, Ignazio
Pastan, Linda (Olenik) 1932- **CLC 27; DAM**
  POET
  See also CA 61-64; CANR 18, 40, 61; DLB 5
Pasternak, Boris (Leonidovich) 1890-1960
  CLC 7, 10, 18, 63; DA; DAB; DAC; DAM
  MST, NOV, POET; PC 6; SSC 31; WLC
  See also CA 127; 116; MTCW
Patchen, Kenneth 1911-1972 ... **CLC 1, 2, 18;**
  DAM POET
  See also CA 1-4R; 33-36R; CANR 3, 35; DLB
  16, 48; MTCW

Pater, Walter (Horatio) 1839-1894 .. **NCLC 7**
See also CDBLB 1832-1890; DLB 57, 156
Paterson, A(ndrew) B(arton) 1864-1941
TCLC 32
See also CA 155; SATA 97
Paterson, Katherine (Womeldorf) 1932-**C L C 12, 30**
See also AAYA 1; CA 21-24R; CANR 28, 59; CLR 7, 50; DLB 52; JRDA; MAICYA; MTCW; SATA 13, 53, 92
Patmore, Coventry Kersey Dighton 1823-1896 **NCLC 9**
See also DLB 35, 98
Paton, Alan (Stewart) 1903-1988 **CLC 4, 10, 25, 55, 106; DA; DAB; DAC; DAM MST, NOV; WLC**
See also CA 13-16; 125; CANR 22; CAP 1; MTCW; SATA 11; SATA-Obit 56
Paton Walsh, Gillian 1937-
See Walsh, Jill Paton
See also CANR 38; JRDA; MAICYA; SAAS 3; SATA 4, 72
Patton, George S. 1885-1945 .... **TCLC 79**
Paulding, James Kirke 1778-1860 ... **NCLC 2**
See also DLB 3, 59, 74
Paulin, Thomas Neilson 1949-
See Paulin, Tom
See also CA 123; 128
Paulin, Tom .... **CLC 37**
See also Paulin, Thomas Neilson
See also DLB 40
Paustovsky, Konstantin (Georgievich) 1892-1968 .... **CLC 40**
See also CA 93-96; 25-28R
Pavese, Cesare 1908-1950 ... **TCLC 3; PC 13; SSC 19**
See also CA 104; DLB 128, 177
Pavic, Milorad 1929- .... **CLC 60**
See also CA 136; DLB 181
Payne, Alan
See Jakes, John (William)
Paz, Gil
See Lugones, Leopoldo
Paz, Octavio 1914-1998**CLC 3, 4, 6, 10, 19, 51, 65; DA; DAB; DAC; DAM MST, MULT, POET; HLC; PC 1; WLC**
See also CA 73-76; 165; CANR 32, 65; DLBY 90; HW; MTCW
p'Bitek, Okot 1931-1982 .... **CLC 96; BLC 3; DAM MULT**
See also BW 2; CA 124; 107; DLB 125; MTCW
Peacock, Molly 1947- .... **CLC 60**
See also CA 103; CAAS 21; CANR 52; DLB 120
Peacock, Thomas Love 1785-1866. **NCLC 22**
See also DLB 96, 116
Peake, Mervyn 1911-1968 .... **CLC 7, 54**
See also CA 5-8R; 25-28R; CANR 3; DLB 15, 160; MTCW; SATA 23
Pearce, Philippa .... **CLC 21**
See also Christie, (Ann) Philippa
See also CLR 9; DLB 161; MAICYA; SATA 1, 67
Pearl, Eric
See Elman, Richard (Martin)
Pearson, T(homas) R(eid) 1956- .... **CLC 39**
See also CA 120; 130; INT 130
Peck, Dale 1967- .... **CLC 81**
See also CA 146
Peck, John 1941- .... **CLC 3**
See also CA 49-52; CANR 3
Peck, Richard (Wayne) 1934- .... **CLC 21**
See also AAYA 1, 24; CA 85-88; CANR 19,

38; CLR 15; INT CANR-19; JRDA; MAICYA; SAAS 2; SATA 18, 55, 97
Peck, Robert Newton 1928- ..... **CLC 17; DA; DAC; DAM MST**
See also AAYA 3; CA 81-84; CANR 31, 63; CLR 45; JRDA; MAICYA; SAAS 1; SATA 21, 62
Peckinpah, (David) Sam(uel) 1925-1984**C L C 20**
See also CA 109; 114
Pedersen, Knut 1859-1952
See Hamsun, Knut
See also CA 104; 119; CANR 63; MTCW
Peeslake, Gaffer
See Durrell, Lawrence (George)
Peguy, Charles Pierre 1873-1914 .. **TCLC 10**
See also CA 107
Peirce, Charles Sanders 1839-1914**TCLC 81**
Pena, Ramon del Valle y
See Valle-Inclan, Ramon (Maria) del
Pendennis, Arthur Esquir
See Thackeray, William Makepeace
Penn, William 1644-1718 .... **LC 25**
See also DLB 24
PEPECE
See Prado (Calvo), Pedro
Pepys, Samuel 1633-1703 **LC 11; DA; DAB; DAC; DAM MST; WLC**
See also CDBLB 1660-1789; DLB 101
Percy, Walker 1916-1990**CLC 2, 3, 6, 8, 14, 18, 47, 65; DAM NOV, POP**
See also CA 1-4R; 131; CANR 1, 23, 64; DLB 2; DLBY 80, 90; MTCW
Perec, Georges 1936-1982 .... **CLC 56**
See also CA 141; DLB 83
Pereda (y Sanchez de Porrua), Jose Maria de 1833-1906 .... **TCLC 16**
See also CA 117
Pereda y Porrua, Jose Maria de
See Pereda (y Sanchez de Porrua), Jose Maria de
Peregoy, George Weems
See Mencken, H(enry) L(ouis)
Perelman, S(idney) J(oseph) 1904-1979 **C L C 3, 5, 9, 15, 23, 44, 49; DAM DRAM**
See also AITN 1, 2; CA 73-76; 89-92; CANR 18; DLB 11, 44; MTCW
Peret, Benjamin 1899-1959 .... **TCLC 20**
See also CA 117
Peretz, Isaac Loeb 1851(?)-1915 ... **TCLC 16; SSC 26**
See also CA 109
Peretz, Yitzhok Leibush
See Peretz, Isaac Loeb
Perez Galdos, Benito 1843-1920 .... **TCLC 27**
See also CA 125; 153; HW
Perrault, Charles 1628-1703 .... **LC 2**
See also MAICYA; SATA 25
Perry, Brighton
See Sherwood, Robert E(mmet)
Perse, St.-John
See Leger, (Marie-Rene Auguste) Alexis Saint-Leger
Perutz, Leo 1882-1957 .... **TCLC 60**
See also DLB 81
Peseenz, Tulio F.
See Lopez y Fuentes, Gregorio
Pesetsky, Bette 1932- .... **CLC 28**
See also CA 133; DLB 130
Peshkov, Alexei Maximovich 1868-1936
See Gorky, Maxim
See also CA 105; 141; DA; DAC; DAM DRAM, MST, NOV

Pessoa, Fernando (Antonio Nogueira) 1898-1935 .... **TCLC 27; HLC; PC 20**
See also CA 125
Peterkin, Julia Mood 1880-1961 .... **CLC 31**
See also CA 102; DLB 9
Peters, Joan K(aren) 1945- .... **CLC 39**
See also CA 158
Peters, Robert L(ouis) 1924- .... **CLC 7**
See also CA 13-16R; CAAS 8; DLB 105
Petofi, Sandor 1823-1849 .... **NCLC 21**
Petrakis, Harry Mark 1923- .... **CLC 3**
See also CA 9-12R; CANR 4, 30
Petrarch 1304-1374 **CMLC 20; DAM POET; PC 8**
Petrov, Evgeny .... **TCLC 21**
See also Kataev, Evgeny Petrovich
Petry, Ann (Lane) 1908-1997 ... **CLC 1, 7, 18**
See also BW 1; CA 5-8R; 157; CAAS 6; CANR 4, 46; CLR 12; DLB 76; JRDA; MAICYA; MTCW; SATA 5; SATA-Obit 94
Petursson, Halligrimur 1614-1674 .... **LC 8**
Phaedrus 18(?)B.C.-55(?) .... **CMLC 25**
Philips, Katherine 1632-1664 .... **LC 30**
See also DLB 131
Philipson, Morris H. 1926- .... **CLC 53**
See also CA 1-4R; CANR 4
Phillips, Caryl 1958-..**CLC 96; BLCS; DAM MULT**
See also BW 2; CA 141; CANR 63; DLB 157
Phillips, David Graham 1867-1911 **TCLC 44**
See also CA 108; DLB 9, 12
Phillips, Jack
See Sandburg, Carl (August)
Phillips, Jayne Anne 1952-**CLC 15, 33; SSC 16**
See also CA 101; CANR 24, 50; DLBY 80; INT CANR-24; MTCW
Phillips, Richard
See Dick, Philip K(indred)
Phillips, Robert (Schaeffer) 1938-.... **CLC 28**
See also CA 17-20R; CAAS 13; CANR 8; DLB 105
Phillips, Ward
See Lovecraft, H(oward) P(hillips)
Piccolo, Lucio 1901-1969 .... **CLC 13**
See also CA 97-100; DLB 114
Pickthall, Marjorie L(owry) C(hristie) 1883-1922 .... **TCLC 21**
See also CA 107; DLB 92
Pico della Mirandola, Giovanni 1463-1494**LC 15**
Piercy, Marge 1936- **CLC 3, 6, 14, 18, 27, 62**
See also CA 21-24R; CAAS 1; CANR 13, 43, 66; DLB 120; MTCW
Piers, Robert
See Anthony, Piers
Pieyre de Mandiargues, Andre 1909-1991
See Mandiargues, Andre Pieyre de
See also CA 103; 136; CANR 22
Pilnyak, Boris .... **TCLC 23**
See also Vogau, Boris Andreyevich
Pincherle, Alberto 1907-1990 ... **CLC 11, 18; DAM NOV**
See also Moravia, Alberto
See also CA 25-28R; 132; CANR 33, 63; MTCW
Pinckney, Darryl 1953- .... **CLC 76**
See also BW 2; CA 143
Pindar 518B.C.-446B.C. ..... **CMLC 12; PC 19**
See also DLB 176
Pineda, Cecile 1942- .... **CLC 39**
See also CA 118
Pinero, Arthur Wing 1855-1934 ... **TCLC 32; DAM DRAM**

See also CA 110; 153; DLB 10
Pinero, Miguel (Antonio Gomez) 1946-1988 **CLC 4, 55**
See also CA 61-64; 125; CANR 29; HW
Pinget, Robert 1919-1997 .... **CLC 7, 13, 37**
See also CA 85-88; 160; DLB 83
Pink Floyd
See Barrett, (Roger) Syd; Gilmour, David; Mason, Nick; Waters, Roger; Wright, Rick
Pinkney, Edward 1802-1828 .... **NCLC 31**
Pinkwater, Daniel Manus 1941- .... **CLC 35**
See also Pinkwater, Manus
See also AAYA 1; CA 29-32R; CANR 12, 38; CLR 4; JRDA; MAICYA; SAAS 3; SATA 46, 76
Pinkwater, Manus
See Pinkwater, Daniel Manus
See also SATA 8
Pinsky, Robert 1940-**CLC 9, 19, 38, 94; DAM POET**
See also CA 29-32R; CAAS 4; CANR 58; DLBY 82
Pinta, Harold
See Pinter, Harold
Pinter, Harold 1930-**CLC 1, 3, 6, 9, 11, 15, 27, 58, 73; DA; DAB; DAC; DAM DRAM, MST; WLC**
See also CA 5-8R; CANR 33, 65; CDBLB 1960 to Present; DLB 13; MTCW
Piozzi, Hester Lynch (Thrale) 1741-1821 **NCLC 57**
See also DLB 104, 142
Pirandello, Luigi 1867-1936**TCLC 4, 29; DA; DAB; DAC; DAM DRAM, MST; DC 5; SSC 22; WLC**
See also CA 104; 153
Pirsig, Robert M(aynard) 1928-**CLC 4, 6, 73; DAM POP**
See also CA 53-56; CANR 42; MTCW; SATA 39
Pisarev, Dmitry Ivanovich 1840-1868 **NCLC 25**
Pix, Mary (Griffith) 1666-1709 .... **LC 8**
See also DLB 80
Pixerecourt, (Rene Charles) Guilbert de 1773-1844 .... **NCLC 39**
See also DLB 192
Plaatje, Sol(omon) T(shekisho) 1876-1932 **TCLC 73; BLCS**
See also BW 2; CA 141
Plaidy, Jean
See Hibbert, Eleanor Alice Burford
Planche, James Robinson 1796-1880**NCLC 42**
Plant, Robert 1948- .... **CLC 12**
Plante, David (Robert) 1940- **CLC 7, 23, 38; DAM NOV**
See also CA 37-40R; CANR 12, 36, 58; DLBY 83; INT CANR-12; MTCW
Plath, Sylvia 1932-1963 **CLC 1, 2, 3, 5, 9, 11, 14, 17, 50, 51, 62, 111; DA; DAB; DAC; DAM MST, POET; PC 1; WLC**
See also AAYA 13; CA 19-20; CANR 34; CAP 2; CDALB 1941-1968; DLB 5, 6, 152; MTCW; SATA 96
Plato 428(?)B.C.-348(?)B.C. .... **CMLC 8; DA; DAB; DAC; DAM MST; WLCS**
See also DLB 176
Platonov, Andrei .... **TCLC 14**
See also Klimentov, Andrei Platonovich
Platt, Kin 1911- .... **CLC 26**
See also AAYA 11; CA 17-20R; CANR 11; JRDA; SAAS 17; SATA 21, 86
Plautus c. 251B.C.-184B.C.. **CMLC 24; DC 6**

Plick et Plock
See Simenon, Georges (Jacques Christian)
Plimpton, George (Ames) 1927- .... **CLC 36**
See also AITN 1; CA 21-24R; CANR 32; DLB 185; MTCW; SATA 10
Pliny the Elder c. 23-79 .... **CMLC 23**
Plomer, William Charles Franklin 1903-1973 **CLC 4, 8**
See also CA 21-22; CANR 34; CAP 2; DLB 20, 162, 191; MTCW; SATA 24
Plowman, Piers
See Kavanagh, Patrick (Joseph)
Plum, J.
See Wodehouse, P(elham) G(renville)
Plumly, Stanley (Ross) 1939- .... **CLC 33**
See also CA 108; 110; DLB 5, 193; INT 110
Plumpe, Friedrich Wilhelm 1888-1931**TCLC 53**
See also CA 112
Po Chu-i 772-846 .... **CMLC 24**
Poe, Edgar Allan 1809-1849**NCLC 1, 16, 55; DA; DAB; DAC; DAM MST, POET; PC 1; SSC 1, 22; WLC**
See also AAYA 14; CDALB 1640-1865; DLB 3, 59, 73, 74; SATA 23
Poet of Titchfield Street, The
See Pound, Ezra (Weston Loomis)
Pohl, Frederik 1919- .... **CLC 18; SSC 25**
See also AAYA 24; CA 61-64; CAAS 1; CANR 11, 37; DLB 8; INT CANR-11; MTCW; SATA 24
Poirier, Louis 1910-
See Gracq, Julien
See also CA 122; 126
Poitier, Sidney 1927-........................... **CLC 26**
See also BW 1; CA 117
Polanski, Roman 1933- .... **CLC 16**
See also CA 77-80
Poliakoff, Stephen 1952- .... **CLC 38**
See also CA 106; DLB 13
Police, The
See Copeland, Stewart (Armstrong); Summers, Andrew James; Sumner, Gordon Matthew
Polidori, John William 1795-1821 . **NCLC 51**
See also DLB 116
Pollitt, Katha 1949- .... **CLC 28**
See also CA 120; 122; CANR 66; MTCW
Pollock, (Mary) Sharon 1936-**CLC 50; DAC; DAM DRAM, MST**
See also CA 141; DLB 60
Polo, Marco 1254-1324 .... **CMLC 15**
Polonsky, Abraham (Lincoln) 1910- **CLC 92**
See also CA 104; DLB 26; INT 104
Polybius c. 200B.C.-c. 118B.C. ...... **CMLC 17**
See also DLB 176
Pomerance, Bernard 1940-.... **CLC 13; DAM DRAM**
See also CA 101; CANR 49
Ponge, Francis (Jean Gaston Alfred) 1899-1988 **CLC 6, 18; DAM POET**
See also CA 85-88; 126; CANR 40
Pontoppidan, Henrik 1857-1943 .... **TCLC 29**
Poole, Josephine .... **CLC 17**
See also Helyar, Jane Penelope Josephine
See also SAAS 2; SATA 5
Popa, Vasko 1922-1991 .... **CLC 19**
See also CA 112; 148; DLB 181
Pope, Alexander 1688-1744 **LC 3; DA; DAB; DAC; DAM MST, POET; WLC**
See also CDBLB 1660-1789; DLB 95, 101
Porter, Connie (Rose) 1959(?)- .... **CLC 70**
See also BW 2; CA 142; SATA 81
Porter, Gene(va Grace) Stratton 1863(?)-1924

TCLC 21
See also CA 112
Porter, Katherine Anne 1890-1980**CLC 1, 3, 7, 10, 13, 15, 27, 101; DA; DAB; DAC; DAM MST, NOV; SSC 4, 31**
See also AITN 2; CA 1-4R; 101; CANR 1, 65; DLB 4, 9, 102; DLBD 12; DLBY 80; MTCW; SATA 39; SATA-Obit 23
Porter, Peter (Neville Frederick) 1929-**CLC 5, 13, 33**
See also CA 85-88; DLB 40
Porter, William Sydney 1862-1910
See Henry, O.
See also CA 104; 131; CDALB 1865-1917; DA; DAB; DAC; DAM MST; DLB 12, 78, 79; MTCW; YABC 2
Portillo (y Pacheco), Jose Lopez
See Lopez Portillo (y Pacheco), Jose
Post, Melville Davisson 1869-1930 **TCLC 39**
See also CA 110
Potok, Chaim 1929- ... **CLC 2, 7, 14, 26, 112; DAM NOV**
See also AAYA 15; AITN 1, 2; CA 17-20R; CANR 19, 35, 64; DLB 28, 152; INT CANR-19; MTCW; SATA 33
Potter, (Helen) Beatrix 1866-1943
See Webb, (Martha) Beatrice (Potter)
See also MAICYA
Potter, Dennis (Christopher George) 1935-1994 **CLC 58, 86**
See also CA 107; 145; CANR 33, 61; MTCW
Pound, Ezra (Weston Loomis) 1885-1972 **CLC 1, 2, 3, 4, 5, 7, 10, 13, 18, 34, 48, 50, 112; DA; DAB; DAC; DAM MST, POET; PC 4; WLC**
See also CA 5-8R; 37-40R; CANR 40; CDALB 1917-1929; DLB 4, 45, 63; DLBD 15; MTCW
Povod, Reinaldo 1959-1994 .... **CLC 44**
See also CA 136; 146
Powell, Adam Clayton, Jr. 1908-1972**CLC 89; BLC 3; DAM MULT**
See also BW 1; CA 102; 33-36R
Powell, Anthony (Dymoke) 1905-**CLC 1, 3, 7, 9, 10, 31**
See also CA 1-4R; CANR 1, 32, 62; CDBLB 1945-1960; DLB 15; MTCW
Powell, Dawn 1897-1965 .... **CLC 66**
See also CA 5-8R; DLBY 97
Powell, Padgett 1952-........................ **CLC 34**
See also CA 126; CANR 63
Power, Susan 1961-............................ **CLC 91**
Powers, J(ames) F(arl) 1917-**CLC 1, 4, 8, 57; SSC 4**
See also CA 1-4R; CANR 2, 61; DLB 130; MTCW
Powers, John J(ames) 1945-
See Powers, John R.
See also CA 69-72
Powers, John R. ....**CLC 66**
See also Powers, John J(ames)
Powers, Richard (S.) 1957- .... **CLC 93**
See also CA 148
Pownall, David 1938- .... **CLC 10**
See also CA 89-92; CAAS 18; CANR 49; DLB 14
Powys, John Cowper 1872-1963**CLC 7, 9, 15, 46**
See also CA 85-88; DLB 15; MTCW
Powys, T(heodore) F(rancis) 1875-1953 **TCLC 9**
See also CA 106; DLB 36, 162
Prado (Calvo), Pedro 1886-1952 ... **TCLC 75**

See also CA 131; HW

Prager, Emily 1952- .... **CLC 56**

Pratt, E(dwin) J(ohn) 1883(?)-1964 **CLC 19;
DAC; DAM POET**
See also CA 141; 93-96; DLB 92

Premchand .... **TCLC 21**
See also Srivastava, Dhanpat Rai

Preussler, Otfried 1923- .... **CLC 17**
See also CA 77-80; SATA 24

Prevert, Jacques (Henri Marie) 1900-1977
CLC 15
See also CA 77-80; 69-72; CANR 29, 61;
MTCW; SATA-Obit 30

Prevost, Abbe (Antoine Francois) 1697-1763
LC 1

Price, (Edward) Reynolds 1933-**CLC 3, 6, 13,
43, 50, 63; DAM NOV; SSC 22**
See also CA 1-4R; CANR 1, 37, 57; DLB 2;
INT CANR-37

Price, Richard 1949- .... **CLC 6, 12**
See also CA 49-52; CANR 3; DLBY 81

Prichard, Katharine Susannah 1883-1969
CLC 46
See also CA 11-12; CANR 33; CAP 1; MTCW;
SATA 66

Priestley, J(ohn) B(oynton) 1894-1984**CLC 2,
5, 9, 34; DAM DRAM, NOV**
See also CA 9-12R; 113; CANR 33; CDBLB
1914-1945; DLB 10, 34, 77, 100, 139; DLBY
84; MTCW

Prince 1958(?)- .... **CLC 35**

Prince, F(rank) T(empleton) 1912- .. **CLC 22**
See also CA 101; CANR 43; DLB 20

Prince Kropotkin
See Kropotkin, Peter (Alekseevich)

Prior, Matthew 1664-1721 .... **LC 4**
See also DLB 95

Prishvin, Mikhail 1873-1954 .... **TCLC 75**

Pritchard, William H(arrison) 1932-**CLC 34**
See also CA 65-68; CANR 23; DLB 111

Pritchett, V(ictor) S(awdon) 1900-1997 **C L C
5, 13, 15, 41; DAM NOV; SSC 14**
See also CA 61-64; 157; CANR 31, 63; DLB
15, 139; MTCW

Private 19022
See Manning, Frederic

Probst, Mark 1925- .... **CLC 59**
See also CA 130

Prokosch, Frederic 1908-1989 ...... **CLC 4, 48**
See also CA 73-76; 128; DLB 48

Prophet, The
See Dreiser, Theodore (Herman Albert)

Prose, Francine 1947- .... **CLC 45**
See also CA 109; 112; CANR 46

Proudhon
See Cunha, Euclides (Rodrigues Pimenta) da

Proulx, Annie
See Proulx, E(dna) Annie

Proulx, E(dna) Annie 1935- ... **CLC 81; DAM
POP**
See also CA 145; CANR 65

**Proust, (Valentin-Louis-George-Eugene-)
Marcel** 1871-1922 **TCLC 7, 13, 33; DA;
DAB; DAC; DAM MST, NOV; WLC**
See also CA 104; 120; DLB 65; MTCW

Prowler, Harley
See Masters, Edgar Lee

Prus, Boleslaw 1845-1912 .... **TCLC 48**

Pryor, Richard (Franklin Lenox Thomas) 1940-
CLC 26
See also CA 122

Przybyszewski, Stanislaw 1868-1927**TCLC 36**
See also CA 160; DLB 66

Pteleon
See Grieve, C(hristopher) M(urray)
See also DAM POET

Puckett, Lute
See Masters, Edgar Lee

Puig, Manuel 1932-1990**CLC 3, 5, 10, 28, 65;
DAM MULT; HLC**
See also CA 45-48; CANR 2, 32, 63; DLB 113;
HW; MTCW

Pulitzer, Joseph 1847-1911 .... **TCLC 76**
See also CA 114; DLB 23

Purdy, A(lfred) W(ellington) 1918-**CLC 3, 6,
14, 50; DAC; DAM MST, POET**
See also CA 81-84; CAAS 17; CANR 42, 66;
DLB 88

Purdy, James (Amos) 1923-**CLC 2, 4, 10, 28,
52**
See also CA 33-36R; CAAS 1; CANR 19, 51;
DLB 2; INT CANR-19; MTCW

Pure, Simon
See Swinnerton, Frank Arthur

Pushkin, Alexander (Sergeyevich) 1799-1837
**NCLC 3, 27; DA; DAB; DAC; DAM
DRAM, MST, POET; PC 10; SSC 27;
WLC**
See also SATA 61

P'u Sung-ling 1640-1715 .... **LC 3; SSC 31**

Putnam, Arthur Lee
See Alger, Horatio, Jr.

Puzo, Mario 1920-**CLC 1, 2, 6, 36, 107; DAM
NOV, POP**
See also CA 65-68; CANR 4, 42, 65; DLB 6;
MTCW

Pygge, Edward
See Barnes, Julian (Patrick)

Pyle, Ernest Taylor 1900-1945
See Pyle, Ernie
See also CA 115; 160

Pyle, Ernie 1900-1945 .... **TCLC 75**
See also Pyle, Ernest Taylor
See also DLB 29

Pyle, Howard 1853-1911 .... **TCLC 81**
See also CA 109; 137; CLR 22; DLB 42, 188;
DLBD 13; MAICYA; SATA 16

Pym, Barbara (Mary Crampton) 1913-1980
CLC 13, 19, 37, 111
See also CA 13-14; 97-100; CANR 13, 34; CAP
1; DLB 14; DLBY 87; MTCW

Pynchon, Thomas (Ruggles, Jr.) 1937-**CLC 2,
3, 6, 9, 11, 18, 33, 62, 72; DA; DAB; DAC;
DAM MST, NOV, POP; SSC 14; WLC**
See also BEST 90:2; CA 17-20R; CANR 22,
46; DLB 2, 173; MTCW

Pythagoras c. 570B.C.-c. 500B.C. . **CMLC 22**
See also DLB 176

Q
See Quiller-Couch, SirArthur (Thomas)

Qian Zhongshu
See Ch'ien Chung-shu

Qroll
See Dagerman, Stig (Halvard)

Quarrington, Paul (Lewis) 1953- ..... **CLC 65**
See also CA 129; CANR 62

Quasimodo, Salvatore 1901-1968 ..... **CLC 10**
See also CA 13-16; 25-28R; CAP 1; DLB 114;
MTCW

Quay, Stephen 1947- .... **CLC 95**

Quay, Timothy 1947- .... **CLC 95**

Queen, Ellery .... **CLC 3, 11**
See also Dannay, Frederic; Davidson, Avram;
Lee, Manfred B(ennington); Marlowe,
Stephen; Sturgeon, Theodore (Hamilton);
Vance, John Holbrook

Queen, Ellery, Jr.
See Dannay, Frederic; Lee, Manfred
B(ennington)

Queneau, Raymond 1903-1976 **CLC 2, 5, 10,
42**
See also CA 77-80; 69-72; CANR 32; DLB 72;
MTCW

Quevedo, Francisco de 1580-1645 .... **LC 23**

Quiller-Couch, SirArthur (Thomas) 1863-1944
TCLC 53
See also CA 118; 166; DLB 135, 153, 190

Quin, Ann (Marie) 1936-1973 .... **CLC 6**
See also CA 9-12R; 45-48; DLB 14

Quinn, Martin
See Smith, Martin Cruz

Quinn, Peter 1947- .... **CLC 91**

Quinn, Simon
See Smith, Martin Cruz

Quiroga, Horacio (Sylvestre) 1878-1937
TCLC 20; DAM MULT; HLC
See also CA 117; 131; HW; MTCW

Quoirez, Francoise 1935- .... **CLC 9**
See also Sagan, Francoise
See also CA 49-52; CANR 6, 39; MTCW

Raabe, Wilhelm 1831-1910 .... **TCLC 45**
See also DLB 129

Rabe, David (William) 1940-... **CLC 4, 8, 33;
DAM DRAM**
See also CA 85-88; CABS 3; CANR 59; DLB 7

Rabelais, Francois 1483-1553**LC 5; DA; DAB;
DAC; DAM MST; WLC**

Rabinovitch, Sholem 1859-1916
See Aleichem, Sholom
See also CA 104

Rachilde 1860-1953 .... **TCLC 67**
See also DLB 123, 192

Racine, Jean 1639-1699 . **LC 28; DAB; DAM
MST**

Radcliffe, Ann (Ward) 1764-1823**NCLC 6, 55**
See also DLB 39, 178

Radiguet, Raymond 1903-1923 ...... **TCLC 29**
See also CA 162; DLB 65

Radnoti, Miklos 1909-1944 .... **TCLC 16**
See also CA 118

Rado, James 1939- .... **CLC 17**
See also CA 105

Radvanyi, Netty 1900-1983
See Seghers, Anna
See also CA 85-88; 110

Rae, Ben
See Griffiths, Trevor

Raeburn, John (Hay) 1941- .... **CLC 34**
See also CA 57-60

Ragni, Gerome 1942-1991 .... **CLC 17**
See also CA 105; 134

Rahv, Philip 1908-1973 .... **CLC 24**
See also Greenberg, Ivan
See also DLB 137

Raimund, Ferdinand Jakob 1790-1836**NCLC
69**
See also DLB 90

Raine, Craig 1944- .... **CLC 32, 103**
See also CA 108; CANR 29, 51; DLB 40

Raine, Kathleen (Jessie) 1908- ...... **CLC 7, 45**
See also CA 85-88; CANR 46; DLB 20; MTCW

Rainis, Janis 1865-1929 .... **TCLC 29**

Rakosi, Carl 1903- .... **CLC 47**
See also Rawley, Callman
See also CAAS 5; DLB 193

Raleigh, Richard
See Lovecraft, H(oward) P(hillips)

Raleigh, Sir Walter 1554(?)-1618 . **LC 31, 39**
See also CDBLB Before 1660; DLB 172

Richardson, Ethel Florence (Lindesay) 1870-
    1946
    See Richardson, Henry Handel
    See also CA 105
Richardson, Henry Handel .... **TCLC 4**
    See also Richardson, Ethel Florence (Lindesay)
    See also DLB 197
Richardson, John 1796-1852**NCLC 55; DAC**
    See also DLB 99
Richardson, Samuel 1689-1761**LC 1, 44; DA;
    DAB; DAC; DAM MST, NOV; WLC**
    See also CDBLB 1660-1789; DLB 39
Richler, Mordecai 1931-**CLC 3, 5, 9, 13, 18, 46,
    70; DAC; DAM MST, NOV**
    See also AITN 1; CA 65-68; CANR 31, 62; CLR
    17; DLB 53; MAICYA; MTCW; SATA 44,
    98; SATA-Brief 27
Richter, Conrad (Michael) 1890-1968**CLC 30**
    See also AAYA 21; CA 5-8R; 25-28R; CANR
    23; DLB 9; MTCW; SATA 3
Ricostranza, Tom
    See Ellis, Trey
Riddell, Charlotte 1832-1906 .... **TCLC 40**
    See also CA 165; DLB 156
Riding, Laura .... **CLC 3, 7**
    See also Jackson, Laura (Riding)
Riefenstahl, Berta Helene Amalia 1902-
    See Riefenstahl, Leni
    See also CA 108
Riefenstahl, Leni .... **CLC 16**
    See also Riefenstahl, Berta Helene Amalia
Riffe, Ernest
    See Bergman, (Ernst) Ingmar
Riggs, (Rolla) Lynn 1899-1954 ..... **TCLC 56;
    DAM MULT**
    See also CA 144; DLB 175; NNAL
Riis, Jacob A(ugust) 1849-1914 ..... **TCLC 80**
    See also CA 113; DLB 23
Riley, James Whitcomb 1849-1916**TCLC 51;
    DAM POET**
    See also CA 118; 137; MAICYA; SATA 17
Riley, Tex
    See Creasey, John
Rilke, Rainer Maria 1875-1926**TCLC 1, 6, 19;
    DAM POET; PC 2**
    See also CA 104; 132; CANR 62; DLB 81;
    MTCW
Rimbaud, (Jean Nicolas) Arthur 1854-1891
    **NCLC 4, 35; DA; DAB; DAC; DAM MST,
    POET; PC 3; WLC**
Rinehart, Mary Roberts 1876-1958**TCLC 52**
    See also CA 108; 166
Ringmaster, The
    See Mencken, H(enry) L(ouis)
Ringwood, Gwen(dolyn Margaret) Pharis
    1910-1984 .... **CLC 48**
    See also CA 148; 112; DLB 88
Rio, Michel 19(?)- .... **CLC 43**
Ritsos, Giannes
    See Ritsos, Yannis
Ritsos, Yannis 1909-1990 .... **CLC 6, 13, 31**
    See also CA 77-80; 133; CANR 39, 61; MTCW
Ritter, Erika 1948(?)- .... **CLC 52**
Rivera, Jose Eustasio 1889-1928 ... **TCLC 35**
    See also CA 162; HW
Rivers, Conrad Kent 1933-1968 .... **CLC 1**
    See also BW 1; CA 85-88; DLB 41
Rivers, Elfrida
    See Bradley, Marion Zimmer
Riverside, John
    See Heinlein, Robert A(nson)
Rizal, Jose 1861-1896 .... **NCLC 27**
Roa Bastos, Augusto (Antonio) 1917-**CLC 45;**

DAM MULT; HLC
    See also CA 131; DLB 113; HW
Robbe-Grillet, Alain 1922-**CLC 1, 2, 4, 6, 8, 10,
    14, 43**
    See also CA 9-12R; CANR 33, 65; DLB 83;
    MTCW
Robbins, Harold 1916-1997 ..... **CLC 5; DAM
    NOV**
    See also CA 73-76; 162; CANR 26, 54; MTCW
Robbins, Thomas Eugene 1936-
    See Robbins, Tom
    See also CA 81-84; CANR 29, 59; DAM NOV,
    POP; MTCW
Robbins, Tom .... **CLC 9, 32, 64**
    See also Robbins, Thomas Eugene
    See also BEST 90:3; DLBY 80
Robbins, Trina 1938- .... **CLC 21**
    See also CA 128
Roberts, Charles G(eorge) D(ouglas) 1860-1943
    TCLC 8
    See also CA 105; CLR 33; DLB 92; SATA 88;
    SATA-Brief 29
Roberts, Elizabeth Madox 1886-1941 **T C L C
    68**
    See also CA 111; 166; DLB 9, 54, 102; SATA
    33; SATA-Brief 27
Roberts, Kate 1891-1985 .... **CLC 15**
    See also CA 107; 116
Roberts, Keith (John Kingston) 1935-**CLC 14**
    See also CA 25-28R; CANR 46
Roberts, Kenneth (Lewis) 1885-1957**TCLC 23**
    See also CA 109; DLB 9
Roberts, Michele (B.) 1949- .... **CLC 48**
    See also CA 115; CANR 58
Robertson, Ellis
    See Ellison, Harlan (Jay); Silverberg, Robert
Robertson, Thomas William 1829-1871**NCLC
    35; DAM DRAM**
Robeson, Kenneth
    See Dent, Lester
Robinson, Edwin Arlington 1869-1935**T C L C
    5; DA; DAC; DAM MST, POET; PC 1**
    See also CA 104; 133; CDALB 1865-1917;
    DLB 54; MTCW
Robinson, Henry Crabb 1775-1867**NCLC 15**
    See also DLB 107
Robinson, Jill 1936- .... **CLC 10**
    See also CA 102; INT 102
Robinson, Kim Stanley 1952- .... **CLC 34**
    See also CA 126
Robinson, Lloyd
    See Silverberg, Robert
Robinson, Marilynne 1944- .... **CLC 25**
    See also CA 116
Robinson, Smokey .... **CLC 21**
    See also Robinson, William, Jr.
Robinson, William, Jr. 1940-
    See Robinson, Smokey
    See also CA 116
Robison, Mary 1949- .... **CLC 42, 98**
    See also CA 113; 116; DLB 130; INT 116
Rod, Edouard 1857-1910 .... **TCLC 52**
Roddenberry, Eugene Wesley 1921-1991
    See Roddenberry, Gene
    See also CA 110; 135; CANR 37; SATA 45;
    SATA-Obit 69
Roddenberry, Gene .... **CLC 17**
    See also Roddenberry, Eugene Wesley
    See also AAYA 5; SATA-Obit 69
Rodgers, Mary 1931- .... **CLC 12**
    See also CA 49-52; CANR 8, 55; CLR 20; INT
    CANR-8; JRDA; MAICYA; SATA 8
Rodgers, W(illiam) R(obert) 1909-1969**CLC 7**

    See also CA 85-88; DLB 20
Rodman, Eric
    See Silverberg, Robert
Rodman, Howard 1920(?)-1985 .... **CLC 65**
    See also CA 118
Rodman, Maia
    See Wojciechowska, Maia (Teresa)
Rodriguez, Claudio 1934- .... **CLC 10**
    See also DLB 134
Roelvaag, O(le) E(dvart) 1876-1931**TCLC 17**
    See also CA 117; DLB 9
Roethke, Theodore (Huebner) 1908-1963**CLC
    1, 3, 8, 11, 19, 46, 101; DAM POET; PC 15**
    See also CA 81-84; CABS 2; CDALB 1941-
    1968; DLB 5; MTCW
Rogers, Samuel 1763-1855 .... **NCLC 69**
    See also DLB 93
Rogers, Thomas Hunton 1927- .... **CLC 57**
    See also CA 89-92; INT 89-92
Rogers, Will(iam Penn Adair) 1879-1935
    TCLC 8, 71; DAM MULT
    See also CA 105; 144; DLB 11; NNAL
Rogin, Gilbert 1929- .... **CLC 18**
    See also CA 65-68; CANR 15
Rohan, Koda .... **TCLC 22**
    See also Koda Shigeyuki
Rohlfs, Anna Katharine Green
    See Green, Anna Katharine
Rohmer, Eric .... **CLC 16**
    See also Scherer, Jean-Marie Maurice
Rohmer, Sax .... **TCLC 28**
    See also Ward, Arthur Henry Sarsfield
    See also DLB 70
Roiphe, Anne (Richardson) 1935- .. **CLC 3, 9**
    See also CA 89-92; CANR 45; DLBY 80; INT
    89-92
Rojas, Fernando de 1465-1541 .... **LC 23**
Rolfe, Frederick (William Serafino Austin
    Lewis Mary) 1860-1913 .... **TCLC 12**
    See also CA 107; DLB 34, 156
Rolland, Romain 1866-1944 .... **TCLC 23**
    See also CA 118; DLB 65
Rolle, Richard c. 1300-c. 1349 ...... **CMLC 21**
    See also DLB 146
Rolvaag, O(le) E(dvart)
    See Roelvaag, O(le) E(dvart)
Romain Arnaud, Saint
    See Aragon, Louis
Romains, Jules 1885-1972 .... **CLC 7**
    See also CA 85-88; CANR 34; DLB 65; MTCW
Romero, Jose Ruben 1890-1952 .... **TCLC 14**
    See also CA 114; 131; HW
Ronsard, Pierre de 1524-1585... **LC 6; PC 11**
Rooke, Leon 1934- .. **CLC 25, 34; DAM POP**
    See also CA 25-28R; CANR 23, 53
Roosevelt, Theodore 1858-1919 ..... **TCLC 69**
    See also CA 115; DLB 47, 186
Roper, William 1498-1578 .... **LC 10**
Roquelaure, A. N.
    See Rice, Anne
Rosa, Joao Guimaraes 1908-1967 .... **CLC 23**
    See also CA 89-92; DLB 113
Rose, Wendy 1948-**CLC 85; DAM MULT; PC
    13**
    See also CA 53-56; CANR 5, 51; DLB 175;
    NNAL; SATA 12
Rosen, R. D.
    See Rosen, Richard (Dean)
Rosen, Richard (Dean) 1949- .... **CLC 39**
    See also CA 77-80; CANR 62; INT CANR-30
Rosenberg, Isaac 1890-1918 .... **TCLC 12**
    See also CA 107; DLB 20
Rosenblatt, Joe .... **CLC 15**

See also Rosenblatt, Joseph

Rosenblatt, Joseph 1933-
See Rosenblatt, Joe
See also CA 89-92; INT 89-92

Rosenfeld, Samuel
See Tzara, Tristan

Rosenstock, Sami
See Tzara, Tristan

Rosenstock, Samuel
See Tzara, Tristan

Rosenthal, M(acha) L(ouis) 1917-1996 . **C L C 28**
See also CA 1-4R; 152; CAAS 6; CANR 4, 51; DLB 5; SATA 59

Ross, Barnaby
See Dannay, Frederic

Ross, Bernard L.
See Follett, Ken(neth Martin)

Ross, J. H.
See Lawrence, T(homas) E(dward)

Ross, Martin
See Martin, Violet Florence
See also DLB 135

Ross, (James) Sinclair 1908- **CLC 13; DAC; DAM MST; SSC 24**
See also CA 73-76; DLB 88

Rossetti, Christina (Georgina) 1830-1894 **NCLC 2, 50, 66; DA; DAB; DAC; DAM MST, POET; PC 7; WLC**
See also DLB 35, 163; MAICYA; SATA 20

Rossetti, Dante Gabriel 1828-1882 . **NCLC 4; DA; DAB; DAC; DAM MST, POET; WLC**
See also CDBLB 1832-1890; DLB 35

Rossner, Judith (Perelman) 1935- **CLC 6, 9, 29**
See also AITN 2; BEST 90:3; CA 17-20R; CANR 18, 51; DLB 6; INT CANR-18; MTCW

Rostand, Edmond (Eugene Alexis) 1868-1918 **TCLC 6, 37; DA; DAB; DAC; DAM DRAM, MST**
See also CA 104; 126; DLB 192; MTCW

Roth, Henry 1906-1995 ..... **CLC 2, 6, 11, 104**
See also CA 11-12; 149; CANR 38, 63; CAP 1; DLB 28; MTCW

Roth, Philip (Milton) 1933- **CLC 1, 2, 3, 4, 6, 9, 15, 22, 31, 47, 66, 86; DA; DAB; DAC; DAM MST, NOV, POP; SSC 26; WLC**
See also BEST 90:3; CA 1-4R; CANR 1, 22, 36, 55; CDALB 1968-1988; DLB 2, 28, 173; DLBY 82; MTCW

Rothenberg, Jerome 1931- .... **CLC 6, 57**
See also CA 45-48; CANR 1; DLB 5, 193

Roumain, Jacques (Jean Baptiste) 1907-1944 **TCLC 19; BLC 3; DAM MULT**
See also BW 1; CA 117; 125

Rourke, Constance (Mayfield) 1885-1941 **TCLC 12**
See also CA 107; YABC 1

Rousseau, Jean-Baptiste 1671-1741 ...... **LC 9**

Rousseau, Jean-Jacques 1712-1778 **LC 14, 36; DA; DAB; DAC; DAM MST; WLC**

Roussel, Raymond 1877-1933 .... **TCLC 20**
See also CA 117

Rovit, Earl (Herbert) 1927- .... **CLC 7**
See also CA 5-8R; CANR 12

Rowe, Elizabeth Singer 1674-1737 ...... **LC 44**
See also DLB 39, 95

Rowe, Nicholas 1674-1718 .... **LC 8**
See also DLB 84

Rowley, Ames Dorrance
See Lovecraft, H(oward) P(hillips)

Rowson, Susanna Haswell 1762(?)-1824 **NCLC 5, 69**

See also DLB 37, 200

Roy, Arundhati 1960(?)- .... **CLC 109**
See also CA 163; DLBY 97

Roy, Gabrielle 1909-1983 **CLC 10, 14; DAB; DAC; DAM MST**
See also CA 53-56; 110; CANR 5, 61; DLB 68; MTCW

Royko, Mike 1932-1997 .... **CLC 109**
See also CA 89-92; 157; CANR 26

Rozewicz, Tadeusz 1921- .. **CLC 9, 23; DAM POET**
See also CA 108; CANR 36, 66; MTCW

Ruark, Gibbons 1941- .... **CLC 3**
See also CA 33-36R; CAAS 23; CANR 14, 31, 57; DLB 120

Rubens, Bernice (Ruth) 1923- .... **CLC 19, 31**
See also CA 25-28R; CANR 33, 65; DLB 14; MTCW

Rubin, Harold
See Robbins, Harold

Rudkin, (James) David 1936- .... **CLC 14**
See also CA 89-92; DLB 13

Rudnik, Raphael 1933- .... **CLC 7**
See also CA 29-32R

Ruffian, M.
See Hasek, Jaroslav (Matej Frantisek)

Ruiz, Jose Martinez ....: **CLC 11**
See also Martinez Ruiz, Jose

Rukeyser, Muriel 1913-1980 **CLC 6, 10, 15, 27; DAM POET; PC 12**
See also CA 5-8R; 93-96; CANR 26, 60; DLB 48; MTCW; SATA-Obit 22

Rule, Jane (Vance) 1931- .... **CLC 27**
See also CA 25-28R; CAAS 18; CANR 12; DLB 60

Rulfo, Juan 1918-1986 ...... **CLC 8, 80; DAM MULT; HLC; SSC 25**
See also CA 85-88; 118; CANR 26; DLB 113; HW; MTCW

Rumi, Jalal al-Din 1297-1373 .... **CMLC 20**

Runeberg, Johan 1804-1877 .... **NCLC 41**

Runyon, (Alfred) Damon 1884(?)-1946 **T C L C 10**
See also CA 107; 165; DLB 11, 86, 171

Rush, Norman 1933- .... **CLC 44**
See also CA 121; 126; INT 126

Rushdie, (Ahmed) Salman 1947- **CLC 23, 31, 55, 100; DAB; DAC; DAM MST, NOV, POP; WLCS**
See also BEST 89:3; CA 108; 111; CANR 33, 56; DLB 194; INT 111; MTCW

Rushforth, Peter (Scott) 1945- .... **CLC 19**
See also CA 101

Ruskin, John 1819-1900 .... **TCLC 63**
See also CA 114; 129; CDBLB 1832-1890; DLB 55, 163, 190; SATA 24

Russ, Joanna 1937- .... **CLC 15**
See also CANR 11, 31, 65; DLB 8; MTCW

Russell, George William 1867-1935
See Baker, Jean H.
See also CA 104; 153; CDBLB 1890-1914; DAM POET

Russell, (Henry) Ken(neth Alfred) 1927- **C L C 16**
See also CA 105

Russell, William Martin 1947- .... **CLC 60**
See also CA 164

Rutherford, Mark .... **TCLC 25**
See also White, William Hale
See also DLB 18

Ruyslinck, Ward 1929- .... **CLC 14**
See also Belser, Reimond Karel Maria de

Ryan, Cornelius (John) 1920-1974 ..... **CLC 7**

See also CA 69-72; 53-56; CANR 38

Ryan, Michael 1946- .... **CLC 65**
See also CA 49-52; DLBY 82

Ryan, Tim
See Dent, Lester

Rybakov, Anatoli (Naumovich) 1911- **CLC 23, 53**
See also CA 126; 135; SATA 79

Ryder, Jonathan
See Ludlum, Robert

Ryga, George 1932-1987 **CLC 14; DAC; DAM MST**
See also CA 101; 124; CANR 43; DLB 60

S. H.
See Hartmann, Sadakichi

S. S.
See Sassoon, Siegfried (Lorraine)

Saba, Umberto 1883-1957 .... **TCLC 33**
See also CA 144; DLB 114

Sabatini, Rafael 1875-1950 .... **TCLC 47**
See also CA 162

Sabato, Ernesto (R.) 1911- **CLC 10, 23; DAM MULT; HLC**
See also CA 97-100; CANR 32, 65; DLB 145; HW; MTCW

Sa-Carniero, Mario de 1890-1916 . **TCLC 83**

Sacastru, Martin
See Bioy Casares, Adolfo

Sacher-Masoch, Leopold von 1836(?)-1895 **NCLC 31**

Sachs, Marilyn (Stickle) 1927- .... **CLC 35**
See also AAYA 2; CA 17-20R; CANR 13, 47; CLR 2; JRDA; MAICYA; SAAS 2; SATA 3, 68

Sachs, Nelly 1891-1970 .... **CLC 14, 98**
See also CA 17-18; 25-28R; CAP 2

Sackler, Howard (Oliver) 1929-1982 **CLC 14**
See also CA 61-64; 108; CANR 30; DLB 7

Sacks, Oliver (Wolf) 1933- .... **CLC 67**
See also CA 53-56; CANR 28, 50; INT CANR-28; MTCW

Sadakichi
See Hartmann, Sadakichi

Sade, Donatien Alphonse Francois, Comte de 1740-1814 .... **NCLC 47**

Sadoff, Ira 1945- .... **CLC 9**
See also CA 53-56; CANR 5, 21; DLB 120

Saetone
See Camus, Albert

Safire, William 1929- .... **CLC 10**
See also CA 17-20R; CANR 31, 54

Sagan, Carl (Edward) 1934-1996 **CLC 30, 112**
See also AAYA 2; CA 25-28R; 155; CANR 11, 36; MTCW; SATA 58; SATA-Obit 94

Sagan, Francoise .... **CLC 3, 6, 9, 17, 36**
See also Quoirez, Francoise
See also DLB 83

Sahgal, Nayantara (Pandit) 1927- .... **CLC 41**
See also CA 9-12R; CANR 11

Saint, H(arry) F. 1941- .... **CLC 50**
See also CA 127

St. Aubin de Teran, Lisa 1953-
See Teran, Lisa St. Aubin de
See also CA 118; 126; INT 126

Saint Birgitta of Sweden c. 1303-1373 **C M L C 24**

Sainte-Beuve, Charles Augustin 1804-1869 **NCLC 5**

Saint-Exupery, Antoine (Jean Baptiste Marie Roger) de 1900-1944 **TCLC 2, 56; DAM NOV; WLC**
See also CA 108; 132; CLR 10; DLB 72; MAICYA; MTCW; SATA 20

Schopenhauer, Arthur 1788-1860 . **NCLC 51**
See also DLB 90

Schor, Sandra (M.) 1932(?)-1990 ...... **CLC 65**
See also CA 132

Schorer, Mark 1908-1977 .... **CLC 9**
See also CA 5-8R; 73-76; CANR 7; DLB 103

Schrader, Paul (Joseph) 1946- .... **CLC 26**
See also CA 37-40R; CANR 41; DLB 44

Schreiner, Olive (Emilie Albertina) 1855-1920
TCLC 9
See also CA 105; 154; DLB 18, 156, 190

Schulberg, Budd (Wilson) 1914-... **CLC 7, 48**
See also CA 25-28R; CANR 19; DLB 6, 26, 28; DLBY 81

Schulz, Bruno 1892-1942 **TCLC 5, 51; SSC 13**
See also CA 115; 123

Schulz, Charles M(onroe) 1922- .... **CLC 12**
See also CA 9-12R; CANR 6; INT CANR-6; SATA 10

Schumacher, E(rnst) F(riedrich) 1911-1977
CLC 80
See also CA 81-84; 73-76; CANR 34

Schuyler, James Marcus 1923-1991 **CLC 5, 23; DAM POET**
See also CA 101; 134; DLB 5, 169; INT 101

Schwartz, Delmore (David) 1913-1966 **CLC 2, 4, 10, 45, 87; PC 8**
See also CA 17-18; 25-28R; CANR 35; CAP 2; DLB 28, 48; MTCW

Schwartz, Ernst
See Ozu, Yasujiro

Schwartz, John Burnham 1965- .... **CLC 59**
See also CA 132

Schwartz, Lynne Sharon 1939- .... **CLC 31**
See also CA 103; CANR 44

Schwartz, Muriel A.
See Eliot, T(homas) S(tearns)

Schwarz-Bart, Andre 1928- .... **CLC 2, 4**
See also CA 89-92

Schwarz-Bart, Simone 1938-.. **CLC 7; BLCS**
See also BW 2; CA 97-100

Schwob, (Mayer Andre) Marcel 1867-1905
TCLC 20
See also CA 117; DLB 123

Sciascia, Leonardo 1921-1989 . **CLC 8, 9, 41**
See also CA 85-88; 130; CANR 35; DLB 177; MTCW

Scoppettone, Sandra 1936- .... **CLC 26**
See also AAYA 11; CA 5-8R; CANR 41; SATA 9, 92

Scorsese, Martin 1942- .... **CLC 20, 89**
See also CA 110; 114; CANR 46

Scotland, Jay
See Jakes, John (William)

Scott, Duncan Campbell 1862-1947 **TCLC 6; DAC**
See also CA 104; 153; DLB 92

Scott, Evelyn 1893-1963 .... **CLC 43**
See also CA 104; 112; CANR 64; DLB 9, 48

Scott, F(rancis) R(eginald) 1899-1985 **CLC 22**
See also CA 101; 114; DLB 88; INT 101

Scott, Frank
See Scott, F(rancis) R(eginald)

Scott, Joanna 1960- .... **CLC 50**
See also CA 126; CANR 53

Scott, Paul (Mark) 1920-1978 .... **CLC 9, 60**
See also CA 81-84; 77-80; CANR 33; DLB 14; MTCW

Scott, Sarah 1723-1795 .... **LC 44**
See also DLB 39

Scott, Walter 1771-1832 .. **NCLC 15, 69; DA; DAB; DAC; DAM MST, NOV, POET; PC 13; WLC**

See also AAYA 22; CDBLB 1789-1832; DLB 93, 107, 116, 144, 159; YABC 2

Scribe, (Augustin) Eugene 1791-1861 **N C L C 16; DAM DRAM; DC 5**
See also DLB 192

Scrum, R.
See Crumb, R(obert)

Scudery, Madeleine de 1607-1701 .... **LC 2**

Scum
See Crumb, R(obert)

Scumbag, Little Bobby
See Crumb, R(obert)

Seabrook, John
See Hubbard, L(afayette) Ron(ald)

Sealy, I. Allan 1951- .... **CLC 55**

Search, Alexander
See Pessoa, Fernando (Antonio Nogueira)

Sebastian, Lee
See Silverberg, Robert

Sebastian Owl
See Thompson, Hunter S(tockton)

Sebestyen, Ouida 1924- .... **CLC 30**
See also AAYA 8; CA 107; CANR 40; CLR 17; JRDA; MAICYA; SAAS 10; SATA 39

Secundus, H. Scriblerus
See Fielding, Henry

Sedges, John
See Buck, Pearl S(ydenstricker)

Sedgwick, Catharine Maria 1789-1867 **N C L C 19**
See also DLB 1, 74

Seelye, John 1931- .... **CLC 7**

Seferiades, Giorgos Stylianou 1900-1971
See Seferis, George
See also CA 5-8R; 33-36R; CANR 5, 36; MTCW

Seferis, George .... **CLC 5, 11**
See also Seferiades, Giorgos Stylianou

Segal, Erich (Wolf) 1937- . **CLC 3, 10; DAM POP**
See also BEST 89:1; CA 25-28R; CANR 20, 36, 65; DLBY 86; INT CANR-20; MTCW

Seger, Bob 1945- .... **CLC 35**

Seghers, Anna .... **CLC 7**
See also Radvanyi, Netty
See also DLB 69

Seidel, Frederick (Lewis) 1936- .... **CLC 18**
See also CA 13-16R; CANR 8; DLBY 84

Seifert, Jaroslav 1901-1986 .. **CLC 34, 44, 93**
See also CA 127; MTCW

Sei Shonagon c. 966-1017(?) .... **CMLC 6**

Selby, Hubert, Jr. 1928- **CLC 1, 2, 4, 8; SSC 20**
See also CA 13-16R; CANR 33; DLB 2

Selzer, Richard 1928- .... **CLC 74**
See also CA 65-68; CANR 14

Sembene, Ousmane
See Ousmane, Sembene

Senancour, Etienne Pivert de 1770-1846
NCLC 16
See also DLB 119

Sender, Ramon (Jose) 1902-1982 **CLC 8; DAM MULT; HLC**
See also CA 5-8R; 105; CANR 8; HW; MTCW

Seneca, Lucius Annaeus 4B.C.-65 . **CMLC 6; DAM DRAM; DC 5**

Senghor, Leopold Sedar 1906- **CLC 54; BLC 3; DAM MULT, POET**
See also BW 2; CA 116; 125; CANR 47; MTCW

Serling, (Edward) Rod(man) 1924-1975 **C L C 30**
See also AAYA 14; AITN 1; CA 162; 57-60; DLB 26

Serna, Ramon Gomez de la

See Gomez de la Serna, Ramon

Serpieres
See Guillevic, (Eugene)

Service, Robert
See Service, Robert W(illiam)
See also DAB; DLB 92

Service, Robert W(illiam) 1874(?)-1958 **TCLC 15; DA; DAC; DAM MST, POET; WLC**
See also Service, Robert
See also CA 115; 140; SATA 20

Seth, Vikram 1952- **CLC 43, 90; DAM MULT**
See also CA 121; 127; CANR 50; DLB 120; INT 127

Seton, Cynthia Propper 1926-1982 .. **CLC 27**
See also CA 5-8R; 108; CANR 7

Seton, Ernest (Evan) Thompson 1860-1946
TCLC 31
See also CA 109; DLB 92; DLBD 13; JRDA; SATA 18

Seton-Thompson, Ernest
See Seton, Ernest (Evan) Thompson

Settle, Mary Lee 1918- .... **CLC 19, 61**
See also CA 89-92; CAAS 1; CANR 44; DLB 6; INT 89-92

Seuphor, Michel
See Arp, Jean

Sevigne, Marie (de Rabutin-Chantal) Marquise de 1626-1696 .... **LC 11**

Sewall, Samuel 1652-1730 .... **LC 38**
See also DLB 24

Sexton, Anne (Harvey) 1928-1974 **CLC 2, 4, 6, 8, 10, 15, 53; DA; DAB; DAC; DAM MST, POET; PC 2; WLC**
See also CA 1-4R; 53-56; CABS 2; CANR 3, 36; CDALB 1941-1968; DLB 5, 169; MTCW; SATA 10

Shaara, Michael (Joseph, Jr.) 1929-1988 **C L C 15; DAM POP**
See also AITN 1; CA 102; 125; CANR 52; DLBY 83

Shackleton, C. C.
See Aldiss, Brian W(ilson)

Shacochis, Bob .... **CLC 39**
See also Shacochis, Robert G.

Shacochis, Robert G. 1951-
See Shacochis, Bob
See also CA 119; 124; INT 124

Shaffer, Anthony (Joshua) 1926- .... **CLC 19; DAM DRAM**
See also CA 110; 116; DLB 13

Shaffer, Peter (Levin) 1926- **CLC 5, 14, 18, 37, 60; DAB; DAM DRAM, MST; DC 7**
See also CA 25-28R; CANR 25, 47; CDBLB 1960 to Present; DLB 13; MTCW

Shakey, Bernard
See Young, Neil

Shalamov, Varlam (Tikhonovich) 1907(?)-1982
CLC 18
See also CA 129; 105

Shamlu, Ahmad 1925- .... **CLC 10**

Shammas, Anton 1951- .... **CLC 55**

Shange, Ntozake 1948- **CLC 8, 25, 38, 74; BLC 3; DAM DRAM, MULT; DC 3**
See also AAYA 9; BW 2; CA 85-88; CABS 3; CANR 27, 48; DLB 38; MTCW

Shanley, John Patrick 1950- .... **CLC 75**
See also CA 128; 133

Shapcott, Thomas W(illiam) 1935-... **CLC 38**
See also CA 69-72; CANR 49

Shapiro, Jane .... **CLC 76**

Shapiro, Karl (Jay) 1913-... **CLC 4, 8, 15, 53**
See also CA 1-4R; CAAS 6; CANR 1, 36, 66; DLB 48; MTCW

Sharp, William 1855-1905 .... **TCLC 39**
See also CA 160; DLB 156

Sharpe, Thomas Ridley 1928-
See Sharpe, Tom
See also CA 114; 122; INT 122

Sharpe, Tom .... **CLC 36**
See also Sharpe, Thomas Ridley
See also DLB 14

Shaw, Bernard .... **TCLC 45**
See also Shaw, George Bernard
See also BW 1

Shaw, G. Bernard
See Shaw, George Bernard

Shaw, George Bernard 1856-1950**TCLC 3, 9,
21; DA; DAB; DAC; DAM DRAM, MST;
WLC**
See also Shaw, Bernard
See also CA 104; 128; CDBLB 1914-1945;
DLB 10, 57, 190; MTCW

Shaw, Henry Wheeler 1818-1885 .. **NCLC 15**
See also DLB 11

Shaw, Irwin 1913-1984 **CLC 7, 23, 34; DAM
DRAM, POP**
See also AITN 1; CA 13-16R; 112; CANR 21;
CDALB 1941-1968; DLB 6, 102; DLBY 84;
MTCW

Shaw, Robert 1927-1978 .... **CLC 5**
See also AITN 1; CA 1-4R; 81-84; CANR 4;
DLB 13, 14

Shaw, T. E.
See Lawrence, T(homas) E(dward)

Shawn, Wallace 1943- .... **CLC 41**
See also CA 112

Shea, Lisa 1953- .... **CLC 86**
See also CA 147

Sheed, Wilfrid (John Joseph) 1930-**CLC 2, 4,
10, 53**
See also CA 65-68; CANR 30, 66; DLB 6;
MTCW

Sheldon, Alice Hastings Bradley 1915(?)-1987
See Tiptree, James, Jr.
See also CA 108; 122; CANR 34; INT 108;
MTCW

Sheldon, John
See Bloch, Robert (Albert)

Shelley, Mary Wollstonecraft (Godwin) 1797-
1851**NCLC 14, 59; DA; DAB; DAC; DAM
MST, NOV; WLC**
See also AAYA 20; CDBLB 1789-1832; DLB
110, 116, 159, 178; SATA 29

Shelley, Percy Bysshe 1792-1822 . **NCLC 18;
DA; DAB; DAC; DAM MST, POET; PC
14; WLC**
See also CDBLB 1789-1832; DLB 96, 110, 158

Shepard, Jim 1956- .... **CLC 36**
See also CA 137; CANR 59; SATA 90

Shepard, Lucius 1947- .... **CLC 34**
See also CA 128; 141

Shepard, Sam 1943-**CLC 4, 6, 17, 34, 41, 44;
DAM DRAM; DC 5**
See also AAYA 1; CA 69-72; CABS 3; CANR
22; DLB 7; MTCW

Shepherd, Michael
See Ludlum, Robert

Sherburne, Zoa (Morin) 1912- .... **CLC 30**
See also AAYA 13; CA 1-4R; CANR 3, 37;
MAICYA; SAAS 18; SATA 3

Sheridan, Frances 1724-1766 .... **LC 7**
See also DLB 39, 84

Sheridan, Richard Brinsley 1751-1816**NCLC
5; DA; DAB; DAC; DAM DRAM, MST;
DC 1; WLC**
See also CDBLB 1660-1789; DLB 89

Sherman, Jonathan Marc .... **CLC 55**

Sherman, Martin 1941(?)- .... **CLC 19**
See also CA 116; 123

Sherwin, Judith Johnson 1936- .... **CLC 7, 15**
See also CA 25-28R; CANR 34

Sherwood, Frances 1940- .... **CLC 81**
See also CA 146

Sherwood, Robert E(mmet) 1896-1955**T C L C
3; DAM DRAM**
See also CA 104; 153; DLB 7, 26

Shestov, Lev 1866-1938 .... **TCLC 56**

Shevchenko, Taras 1814-1861 .... **NCLC 54**

Shiel, M(atthew) P(hipps) 1865-1947**TCLC 8**
See also Holmes, Gordon
See also CA 106; 160; DLB 153

Shields, Carol 1935- .... **CLC 91; DAC**
See also CA 81-84; CANR 51

Shields, David 1956- .... **CLC 97**
See also CA 124; CANR 48

Shiga, Naoya 1883-1971 ...... **CLC 33; SSC 23**
See also CA 101; 33-36R; DLB 180

Shilts, Randy 1951-1994 .... **CLC 85**
See also AAYA 19; CA 115; 127; 144; CANR
45; INT 127

Shimazaki, Haruki 1872-1943
See Shimazaki Toson
See also CA 105; 134

Shimazaki Toson 1872-1943 .... **TCLC 5**
See also Shimazaki, Haruki
See also DLB 180

Sholokhov, Mikhail (Aleksandrovich) 1905-
1984 .... **CLC 7, 15**
See also CA 101; 112; MTCW; SATA-Obit 36

Shone, Patric
See Hanley, James

Shreve, Susan Richards 1939- .... **CLC 23**
See also CA 49-52; CAAS 5; CANR 5, 38, 69;
MAICYA; SATA 46, 95; SATA-Brief 41

Shue, Larry 1946-1985**CLC 52; DAM DRAM**
See also CA 145; 117

Shu-Jen, Chou 1881-1936
See Lu Hsun
See also CA 104

Shulman, Alix Kates 1932- .... **CLC 2, 10**
See also CA 29-32R; CANR 43; SATA 7

Shuster, Joe 1914- .... **CLC 21**

Shute, Nevil .... **CLC 30**
See also Norway, Nevil Shute

Shuttle, Penelope (Diane) 1947- .... **CLC 7**
See also CA 93-96; CANR 39; DLB 14, 40

Sidney, Mary 1561-1621 .... **LC 19, 39**

Sidney, Sir Philip 1554-1586 **LC 19, 39; DA;
DAB; DAC; DAM MST, POET**
See also CDBLB Before 1660; DLB 167

Siegel, Jerome 1914-1996 .... **CLC 21**
See also CA 116; 151

Siegel, Jerry
See Siegel, Jerome

Sienkiewicz, Henryk (Adam Alexander Pius)
1846-1916 .... **TCLC 3**
See also CA 104; 134

Sierra, Gregorio Martinez
See Martinez Sierra, Gregorio

Sierra, Maria (de la O'LeJarraga) Martinez
See Martinez Sierra, Maria (de la O'LeJarraga)

Sigal, Clancy 1926- .... **CLC 7**
See also CA 1-4R

Sigourney, Lydia Howard (Huntley) 1791-1865
NCLC 21
See also DLB 1, 42, 73

Siguenza y Gongora, Carlos de 1645-1700**L C
8**

Sigurjonsson, Johann 1880-1919 ... **TCLC 27**

Sikelianos, Angelos 1884-1951 .... **TCLC 39**

Silkin, Jon 1930- .... **CLC 2, 6, 43**
See also CA 5-8R; CAAS 5; DLB 27

Silko, Leslie (Marmon) 1948-**CLC 23, 74; DA;
DAC; DAM MST, MULT, POP; WLCS**
See also AAYA 14; CA 115; 122; CANR 45,
65; DLB 143, 175; NNAL

Sillanpaa, Frans Eemil 1888-1964 ... **CLC 19**
See also CA 129; 93-96; MTCW

Sillitoe, Alan 1928- ... **CLC 1, 3, 6, 10, 19, 57**
See also AITN 1; CA 9-12R; CAAS 2; CANR
8, 26, 55; CDBLB 1960 to Present; DLB 14,
139; MTCW; SATA 61

Silone, Ignazio 1900-1978 .... **CLC 4**
See also CA 25-28; 81-84; CANR 34; CAP 2;
MTCW

Silver, Joan Micklin 1935- .... **CLC 20**
See also CA 114; 121; INT 121

Silver, Nicholas
See Faust, Frederick (Schiller)

Silverberg, Robert 1935- **CLC 7; DAM POP**
See also AAYA 24; CA 1-4R; CAAS 3; CANR
1, 20, 36; DLB 8; INT CANR-20; MAICYA;
MTCW; SATA 13, 91

Silverstein, Alvin 1933- .... **CLC 17**
See also CA 49-52; CANR 2; CLR 25; JRDA;
MAICYA; SATA 8, 69

Silverstein, Virginia B(arbara Opshelor) 1937-
CLC 17
See also CA 49-52; CANR 2; CLR 25; JRDA;
MAICYA; SATA 8, 69

Sim, Georges
See Simenon, Georges (Jacques Christian)

Simak, Clifford D(onald) 1904-1988**CLC 1, 55**
See also CA 1-4R; 125; CANR 1, 35; DLB 8;
MTCW; SATA-Obit 56

Simenon, Georges (Jacques Christian) 1903-
1989 .. **CLC 1, 2, 3, 8, 18, 47; DAM POP**
See also CA 85-88; 129; CANR 35; DLB 72;
DLBY 89; MTCW

Simic, Charles 1938- .... **CLC 6, 9, 22, 49, 68;
DAM POET**
See also CA 29-32R; CAAS 4; CANR 12, 33,
52, 61; DLB 105

Simmel, Georg 1858-1918 .... **TCLC 64**
See also CA 157

Simmons, Charles (Paul) 1924- .... **CLC 57**
See also CA 89-92; INT 89-92

Simmons, Dan 1948- ..... **CLC 44; DAM POP**
See also AAYA 16; CA 138; CANR 53

Simmons, James (Stewart Alexander) 1933-
CLC 43
See also CA 105; CAAS 21; DLB 40

Simms, William Gilmore 1806-1870 **NCLC 3**
See also DLB 3, 30, 59, 73

Simon, Carly 1945- .... **CLC 26**
See also CA 105

Simon, Claude 1913-1984 ..**CLC 4, 9, 15, 39;
DAM NOV**
See also CA 89-92; CANR 33; DLB 83; MTCW

Simon, (Marvin) Neil 1927-**CLC 6, 11, 31, 39,
70; DAM DRAM**
See also AITN 1; CA 21-24R; CANR 26, 54;
DLB 7; MTCW

Simon, Paul (Frederick) 1941(?)- ..... **CLC 17**
See also CA 116; 153

Simonon, Paul 1956(?)- .... **CLC 30**

Simpson, Harriette
See Arnow, Harriette (Louisa) Simpson

Simpson, Louis (Aston Marantz) 1923-**CLC 4,
7, 9, 32; DAM POET**
See also CA 1-4R; CAAS 4; CANR 1, 61; DLB
5; MTCW

Theroux, Alexander (Louis) 1939- **CLC 2, 25**
   See also CA 85-88; CANR 20, 63
Theroux, Paul (Edward) 1941- **CLC 5, 8, 11, 15, 28, 46; DAM POP**
   See also BEST 89:4; CA 33-36R; CANR 20, 45; DLB 2; MTCW; SATA 44
Thesen, Sharon 1946- .... **CLC 56**
   See also CA 163
Thevenin, Denis
   See Duhamel, Georges
Thibault, Jacques Anatole Francois 1844-1924
   See France, Anatole
   See also CA 106; 127; DAM NOV; MTCW
Thiele, Colin (Milton) 1920- .... **CLC 17**
   See also CA 29-32R; CANR 12, 28, 53; CLR 27; MAICYA; SAAS 2; SATA 14, 72
Thomas, Audrey (Callahan) 1935- **CLC 7, 13, 37, 107; SSC 20**
   See also AITN 2; CA 21-24R; CAAS 19; CANR 36, 58; DLB 60; MTCW
Thomas, D(onald) M(ichael) 1935- . **CLC 13, 22, 31**
   See also CA 61-64; CAAS 11; CANR 17, 45; CDBLB 1960 to Present; DLB 40; INT CANR-17; MTCW
Thomas, Dylan (Marlais) 1914-1953 **TCLC 1, 8, 45; DA; DAB; DAC; DAM DRAM, MST, POET; PC 2; SSC 3; WLC**
   See also CA 104; 120; CANR 65; CDBLB 1945-1960; DLB 13, 20, 139; MTCW; SATA 60
Thomas, (Philip) Edward 1878-1917 . **TCLC 10; DAM POET**
   See also CA 106; 153; DLB 19
Thomas, Joyce Carol 1938- .... **CLC 35**
   See also AAYA 12; BW 2; CA 113; 116; CANR 48; CLR 19; DLB 33; INT 116; JRDA; MAICYA; MTCW; SAAS 7; SATA 40, 78
Thomas, Lewis 1913-1993 .... **CLC 35**
   See also CA 85-88; 143; CANR 38, 60; MTCW
Thomas, Paul
   See Mann, (Paul) Thomas
Thomas, Piri 1928- .... **CLC 17**
   See also CA 73-76; HW
Thomas, R(onald) S(tuart) 1913- **CLC 6, 13, 48; DAB; DAM POET**
   See also CA 89-92; CAAS 4; CANR 30; CDBLB 1960 to Present; DLB 27; MTCW
Thomas, Ross (Elmore) 1926-1995 ... **CLC 39**
   See also CA 33-36R; 150; CANR 22, 63
Thompson, Francis Clegg
   See Mencken, H(enry) L(ouis)
Thompson, Francis Joseph 1859-1907 **TCLC 4**
   See also CA 104; CDBLB 1890-1914; DLB 19
Thompson, Hunter S(tockton) 1939- . **CLC 9, 17, 40, 104; DAM POP**
   See also BEST 89:1; CA 17-20R; CANR 23, 46; DLB 185; MTCW
Thompson, James Myers
   See Thompson, Jim (Myers)
Thompson, Jim (Myers) 1906-1977(?) **CLC 69**
   See also CA 140
Thompson, Judith .... **CLC 39**
Thomson, James 1700-1748 ... **LC 16, 29, 40; DAM POET**
   See also DLB 95
Thomson, James 1834-1882 **NCLC 18; DAM POET**
   See also DLB 35
Thoreau, Henry David 1817-1862 **NCLC 7, 21, 61; DA; DAB; DAC; DAM MST; WLC**
   See also CDALB 1640-1865; DLB 1
Thornton, Hall

   See Silverberg, Robert
Thucydides c. 455B.C.-399B.C. .... **CMLC 17**
   See also DLB 176
Thurber, James (Grover) 1894-1961 . **CLC 5, 11, 25; DA; DAB; DAC; DAM DRAM, MST, NOV; SSC 1**
   See also CA 73-76; CANR 17, 39; CDALB 1929-1941; DLB 4, 11, 22, 102; MAICYA; MTCW; SATA 13
Thurman, Wallace (Henry) 1902-1934 **T C L C 6; BLC 3; DAM MULT**
   See also BW 1; CA 104; 124; DLB 51
Ticheburn, Cheviot
   See Ainsworth, William Harrison
Tieck, (Johann) Ludwig 1773-1853 **NCLC 5, 46; SSC 31**
   See also DLB 90
Tiger, Derry
   See Ellison, Harlan (Jay)
Tilghman, Christopher 1948(?)- .... **CLC 65**
   See also CA 159
Tillinghast, Richard (Williford) 1940- **CLC 29**
   See also CA 29-32R; CAAS 23; CANR 26, 51
Timrod, Henry 1828-1867 .... **NCLC 25**
   See also DLB 3
Tindall, Gillian (Elizabeth) 1938- ...... **CLC 7**
   See also CA 21-24R; CANR 11, 65
Tiptree, James, Jr. .... **CLC 48, 50**
   See also Sheldon, Alice Hastings Bradley
   See also DLB 8
Titmarsh, Michael Angelo
   See Thackeray, William Makepeace
Tocqueville, Alexis (Charles Henri Maurice Clerel Comte) 1805-1859 ... **NCLC 7, 63**
Tolkien, J(ohn) R(onald) R(euel) 1892-1973 **CLC 1, 2, 3, 8, 12, 38; DA; DAB; DAC; DAM MST, NOV, POP; WLC**
   See also AAYA 10; AITN 1; CA 17-18; 45-48; CANR 36; CAP 2; CDBLB 1914-1945; DLB 15, 160; JRDA; MAICYA; MTCW; SATA 2, 32; SATA-Obit 24
Toller, Ernst 1893-1939 .... **TCLC 10**
   See also CA 107; DLB 124
Tolson, M. B.
   See Tolson, Melvin B(eaunorus)
Tolson, Melvin B(eaunorus) 1898(?)-1966 **CLC 36, 105; BLC 3; DAM MULT, POET**
   See also BW 1; CA 124; 89-92; DLB 48, 76
Tolstoi, Aleksei Nikolaevich
   See Tolstoy, Alexey Nikolaevich
Tolstoy, Alexey Nikolaevich 1882-1945 **T C L C 18**
   See also CA 107; 158
Tolstoy, Count Leo
   See Tolstoy, Leo (Nikolaevich)
Tolstoy, Leo (Nikolaevich) 1828-1910 **TCLC 4, 11, 17, 28, 44, 79; DA; DAB; DAC; DAM MST, NOV; SSC 9, 30; WLC**
   See also CA 104; 123; SATA 26
Tomasi di Lampedusa, Giuseppe 1896-1957
   See Lampedusa, Giuseppe (Tomasi) di
   See also CA 111
Tomlin, Lily .... **CLC 17**
   See also Tomlin, Mary Jean
Tomlin, Mary Jean 1939(?)-
   See Tomlin, Lily
   See also CA 117
Tomlinson, (Alfred) Charles 1927- **CLC 2, 4, 6, 13, 45; DAM POET; PC 17**
   See also CA 5-8R; CANR 33; DLB 40
Tomlinson, H(enry) M(ajor) 1873-1958 **TCLC 71**
   See also CA 118; 161; DLB 36, 100, 195

Tonson, Jacob
   See Bennett, (Enoch) Arnold
Toole, John Kennedy 1937-1969 **CLC 19, 64**
   See also CA 104; DLBY 81
Toomer, Jean 1894-1967 **CLC 1, 4, 13, 22; BLC 3; DAM MULT; PC 7; SSC 1; WLCS**
   See also BW 1; CA 85-88; CDALB 1917-1929; DLB 45, 51; MTCW
Torley, Luke
   See Blish, James (Benjamin)
Tornimparte, Alessandra
   See Ginzburg, Natalia
Torre, Raoul della
   See Mencken, H(enry) L(ouis)
Torrey, E(dwin) Fuller 1937- .... **CLC 34**
   See also CA 119
Torsvan, Ben Traven
   See Traven, B.
Torsvan, Benno Traven
   See Traven, B.
Torsvan, Berick Traven
   See Traven, B.
Torsvan, Berwick Traven
   See Traven, B.
Torsvan, Bruno Traven
   See Traven, B.
Torsvan, Traven
   See Traven, B.
Tournier, Michel (Edouard) 1924- **CLC 6, 23, 36, 95**
   See also CA 49-52; CANR 3, 36; DLB 83; MTCW; SATA 23
Tournimparte, Alessandra
   See Ginzburg, Natalia
Towers, Ivar
   See Kornbluth, C(yril) M.
Towne, Robert (Burton) 1936(?)- ..... **CLC 87**
   See also CA 108; DLB 44
Townsend, Sue .... **CLC 61**
   See also Townsend, Susan Elaine
   See also SATA 55, 93; SATA-Brief 48
Townsend, Susan Elaine 1946-
   See Townsend, Sue
   See also CA 119; 127; CANR 65; DAB; DAC; DAM MST
Townshend, Peter (Dennis Blandford) 1945- **CLC 17, 42**
   See also CA 107
Tozzi, Federigo 1883-1920 .... **TCLC 31**
   See also CA 160
Traill, Catharine Parr 1802-1899 .. **NCLC 31**
   See also DLB 99
Trakl, Georg 1887-1914 .... **TCLC 5; PC 20**
   See also CA 104; 165
Transtroemer, Tomas (Goesta) 1931- **CLC 52, 65; DAM POET**
   See also CA 117; 129; CAAS 17
Transtromer, Tomas Gosta
   See Transtroemer, Tomas (Goesta)
Traven, B. (?)-1969 .... **CLC 8, 11**
   See also CA 19-20; 25-28R; CAP 2; DLB 9, 56; MTCW
Treitel, Jonathan 1959- .... **CLC 70**
Tremain, Rose 1943- .... **CLC 42**
   See also CA 97-100; CANR 44; DLB 14
Tremblay, Michel 1942- **CLC 29, 102; DAC; DAM MST**
   See also CA 116; 128; DLB 60; MTCW
Trevanian .... **CLC 29**
   See also Whitaker, Rod(ney)
Trevor, Glen
   See Hilton, James
Trevor, William 1928- . **CLC 7, 9, 14, 25, 71;**

SSC 21
See also Cox, William Trevor
See also DLB 14, 139
Trifonov, Yuri (Valentinovich) 1925-1981
  CLC 45
  See also CA 126; 103; MTCW
Trilling, Lionel 1905-1975 ...... CLC 9, 11, 24
  See also CA 9-12R; 61-64; CANR 10; DLB 28,
  63; INT CANR-10; MTCW
Trimball, W. H.
  See Mencken, H(enry) L(ouis)
Tristan
  See Gomez de la Serna, Ramon
Tristram
  See Housman, A(lfred) E(dward)
Trogdon, William (Lewis) 1939-
  See Heat-Moon, William Least
  See also CA 115; 119; CANR 47; INT 119
Trollope, Anthony 1815-1882NCLC 6, 33; DA;
  DAB; DAC; DAM MST, NOV; SSC 28;
  WLC
  See also CDBLB 1832-1890; DLB 21, 57, 159;
  SATA 22
Trollope, Frances 1779-1863 .... NCLC 30
  See also DLB 21, 166
Trotsky, Leon 1879-1940 .... TCLC 22
  See also CA 118
Trotter (Cockburn), Catharine 1679-1749L C
  8
  See also DLB 84
Trout, Kilgore
  See Farmer, Philip Jose
Trow, George W. S. 1943- .... CLC 52
  See also CA 126
Troyat, Henri 1911- .... CLC 23
  See also CA 45-48; CANR 2, 33, 67; MTCW
Trudeau, G(arretson) B(eekman) 1948-
  See Trudeau, Garry B.
  See also CA 81-84; CANR 31; SATA 35
Trudeau, Garry B. .... CLC 12
  See also Trudeau, G(arretson) B(eekman)
  See also AAYA 10; AITN 2
Truffaut, Francois 1932-1984 .. CLC 20, 101
  See also CA 81-84; 113; CANR 34
Trumbo, Dalton 1905-1976 .... CLC 19
  See also CA 21-24R; 69-72; CANR 10; DLB
  26
Trumbull, John 1750-1831 .... NCLC 30
  See also DLB 31
Trundlett, Helen B.
  See Eliot, T(homas) S(tearns)
Tryon, Thomas 1926-1991 . CLC 3, 11; DAM
  POP
  See also AITN 1; CA 29-32R; 135; CANR 32;
  MTCW
Tryon, Tom
  See Tryon, Thomas
Ts'ao Hsueh-ch'in 1715(?)-1763 .... LC 1
Tsushima, Shuji 1909-1948
  See Dazai Osamu
  See also CA 107
Tsvetaeva (Efron), Marina (Ivanovna) 1892-
  1941 .... TCLC 7, 35; PC 14
  See also CA 104; 128; MTCW
Tuck, Lily 1938- .... CLC 70
  See also CA 139
Tu Fu 712-770 .... PC 9
  See also DAM MULT
Tunis, John R(oberts) 1889-1975 ...... CLC 12
  See also CA 61-64; CANR 62; DLB 22, 171;
  JRDA; MAICYA; SATA 37; SATA-Brief 30
Tuohy, Frank .... CLC 37
  See also Tuohy, John Francis

See also DLB 14, 139
Tuohy, John Francis 1925-
  See Tuohy, Frank
  See also CA 5-8R; CANR 3, 47
Turco, Lewis (Putnam) 1934- ...... CLC 11, 63
  See also CA 13-16R; CAAS 22; CANR 24, 51;
  DLBY 84
Turgenev, Ivan 1818-1883 .... NCLC 21; DA;
  DAB; DAC; DAM MST, NOV; DC 7; SSC
  7; WLC
Turgot, Anne-Robert-Jacques 1727-1781 L C
  26
Turner, Frederick 1943- .... CLC 48
  See also CA 73-76; CAAS 10; CANR 12, 30,
  56; DLB 40
Tutu, Desmond M(pilo) 1931-CLC 80; BLC 3;
  DAM MULT
  See also BW 1; CA 125; CANR 67
Tutuola, Amos 1920-1997CLC 5, 14, 29; BLC
  3; DAM MULT
  See also BW 2; CA 9-12R; 159; CANR 27, 66;
  DLB 125; MTCW
Twain, MarkTCLC 6, 12, 19, 36, 48, 59; SSC 6,
  26; WLC
  See also Clemens, Samuel Langhorne
  See also AAYA 20; DLB 11, 12, 23, 64, 74
Tyler, Anne 1941- . CLC 7, 11, 18, 28, 44, 59,
  103; DAM NOV, POP
  See also AAYA 18; BEST 89:1; CA 9-12R;
  CANR 11, 33, 53; DLB 6, 143; DLBY 82;
  MTCW; SATA 7, 90
Tyler, Royall 1757-1826 .... NCLC 3
  See also DLB 37
Tynan, Katharine 1861-1931 .... TCLC 3
  See also CA 104; DLB 153
Tyutchev, Fyodor 1803-1873 .... NCLC 34
Tzara, Tristan 1896-1963 ...... CLC 47; DAM
  POET
  See also CA 153; 89-92
Uhry, Alfred 1936- ... CLC 55; DAM DRAM,
  POP
  See also CA 127; 133; INT 133
Ulf, Haerved
  See Strindberg, (Johan) August
Ulf, Harved
  See Strindberg, (Johan) August
Ulibarri, Sabine R(eyes) 1919-CLC 83; DAM
  MULT
  See also CA 131; DLB 82; HW
Unamuno (y Jugo), Miguel de 1864-1936
  TCLC 2, 9; DAM MULT, NOV; HLC; SSC
  11
  See also CA 104; 131; DLB 108; HW; MTCW
Undercliffe, Errol
  See Campbell, (John) Ramsey
Underwood, Miles
  See Glassco, John
Undset, Sigrid 1882-1949TCLC 3; DA; DAB;
  DAC; DAM MST, NOV; WLC
  See also CA 104; 129; MTCW
Ungaretti, Giuseppe 1888-1970CLC 7, 11, 15
  See also CA 19-20; 25-28R; CAP 2; DLB 114
Unger, Douglas 1952- .... CLC 34
  See also CA 130
Unsworth, Barry (Forster) 1930- ..... CLC 76
  See also CA 25-28R; CANR 30, 54; DLB 194
Updike, John (Hoyer) 1932-CLC 1, 2, 3, 5, 7,
  9, 13, 15, 23, 34, 43, 70; DA; DAB; DAC;
  DAM MST, NOV, POET, POP; SSC 13, 27;
  WLC
  See also CA 1-4R; CABS 1; CANR 4, 33, 51;
  CDALB 1968-1988; DLB 2, 5, 143; DLBD
  3; DLBY 80, 82, 97; MTCW

Upshaw, Margaret Mitchell
  See Mitchell, Margaret (Munnerlyn)
Upton, Mark
  See Sanders, Lawrence
Urdang, Constance (Henriette) 1922-CLC 47
  See also CA 21-24R; CANR 9, 24
Uriel, Henry
  See Faust, Frederick (Schiller)
Uris, Leon (Marcus) 1924- CLC 7, 32; DAM
  NOV, POP
  See also AITN 1, 2; BEST 89:2; CA 1-4R;
  CANR 1, 40, 65; MTCW; SATA 49
Urmuz
  See Codrescu, Andrei
Urquhart, Jane 1949- .... CLC 90; DAC
  See also CA 113; CANR 32, 68
Ustinov, Peter (Alexander) 1921- .... CLC 1
  See also AITN 1; CA 13-16R; CANR 25, 51;
  DLB 13
U Tam'si, Gerald Felix Tchicaya
  See Tchicaya, Gerald Felix
U Tam'si, Tchicaya
  See Tchicaya, Gerald Felix
Vachss, Andrew (Henry) 1942- .... CLC 106
  See also CA 118; CANR 44
Vachss, Andrew H.
  See Vachss, Andrew (Henry)
Vaculik, Ludvik 1926- .... CLC 7
  See also CA 53-56
Vaihinger, Hans 1852-1933 .... TCLC 71
  See also CA 116; 166
Valdez, Luis (Miguel) 1940- ..CLC 84; DAM
  MULT; HLC
  See also CA 101; CANR 32; DLB 122; HW
Valenzuela, Luisa 1938- CLC 31, 104; DAM
  MULT; SSC 14
  See also CA 101; CANR 32, 65; DLB 113; HW
Valera y Alcala-Galiano, Juan 1824-1905
  TCLC 10
  See also CA 106
Valery, (Ambroise) Paul (Toussaint Jules) 1871-
  1945 ..... TCLC 4, 15; DAM POET; PC 9
  See also CA 104; 122; MTCW
Valle-Inclan, Ramon (Maria) del 1866-1936
  TCLC 5; DAM MULT; HLC
  See also CA 106; 153; DLB 134
Vallejo, Antonio Buero
  See Buero Vallejo, Antonio
Vallejo, Cesar (Abraham) 1892-1938TCLC 3,
  56; DAM MULT; HLC
  See also CA 105; 153; HW
Vallette, Marguerite Eymery
  See Rachilde
Valle Y Pena, Ramon del
  See Valle-Inclan, Ramon (Maria) del
Van Ash, Cay 1918- .... CLC 34
Vanbrugh, Sir John 1664-1726 LC 21; DAM
  DRAM
  See also DLB 80
Van Campen, Karl
  See Campbell, John W(ood, Jr.)
Vance, Gerald
  See Silverberg, Robert
Vance, Jack .... CLC 35
  See also Kuttner, Henry; Vance, John Holbrook
  See also DLB 8
Vance, John Holbrook 1916-
  See Queen, Ellery; Vance, Jack
  See also CA 29-32R; CANR 17, 65; MTCW
Van Den Bogarde, Derek Jules Gaspard Ulric
  Niven 1921-
  See Bogarde, Dirk
  See also CA 77-80

See also CA 85-88; CANR 45; DLB 75; MTCW

Wolfe, Gene (Rodman) 1931- **CLC 25; DAM POP**
See also CA 57-60; CAAS 9; CANR 6, 32, 60; DLB 8

Wolfe, George C. 1954- .... **CLC 49; BLCS**
See also CA 149

Wolfe, Thomas (Clayton) 1900-1938**TCLC 4, 13, 29, 61; DA; DAB; DAC; DAM MST, NOV; WLC**
See also CA 104; 132; CDALB 1929-1941; DLB 9, 102; DLBD 2, 16; DLBY 85, 97; MTCW

Wolfe, Thomas Kennerly, Jr. 1931-
See Wolfe, Tom
See also CA 13-16R; CANR 9, 33; DAM POP; DLB 185; INT CANR-9; MTCW

Wolfe, Tom .... **CLC 1, 2, 9, 15, 35, 51**
See also Wolfe, Thomas Kennerly, Jr.
See also AAYA 8; AITN 2; BEST 89:1; DLB 152

Wolff, Geoffrey (Ansell) 1937- .... **CLC 41**
See also CA 29-32R; CANR 29, 43

Wolff, Sonia
See Levitin, Sonia (Wolff)

Wolff, Tobias (Jonathan Ansell) 1945- . **C L C 39, 64**
See also AAYA 16; BEST 90:2; CA 114; 117; CAAS 22; CANR 54; DLB 130; INT 117

Wolfram von Eschenbach c. 1170-c. 1220 **CMLC 5**
See also DLB 138

Wolitzer, Hilma 1930- .... **CLC 17**
See also CA 65-68; CANR 18, 40; INT CANR-18; SATA 31

Wollstonecraft, Mary 1759-1797 .... **LC 5**
See also CDBLB 1789-1832; DLB 39, 104, 158

Wonder, Stevie .... **CLC 12**
See also Morris, Steveland Judkins

Wong, Jade Snow 1922- .... **CLC 17**
See also CA 109

Woodberry, George Edward 1855-1930 **TCLC 73**
See also CA 165; DLB 71, 103

Woodcott, Keith
See Brunner, John (Kilian Houston)

Woodruff, Robert W.
See Mencken, H(enry) L(ouis)

Woolf, (Adeline) Virginia 1882-1941**TCLC 1, 5, 20, 43, 56; DA; DAB; DAC; DAM MST, NOV; SSC 7; WLC**
See also CA 104; 130; CANR 64; CDBLB 1914-1945; DLB 36, 100, 162; DLBD 10; MTCW

Woolf, Virginia Adeline
See Woolf, (Adeline) Virginia

Woollcott, Alexander (Humphreys) 1887-1943 **TCLC 5**
See also CA 105; 161; DLB 29

Woolrich, Cornell 1903-1968 .... **CLC 77**
See also Hopley-Woolrich, Cornell George

Wordsworth, Dorothy 1771-1855 .. **NCLC 25**
See also DLB 107

Wordsworth, William 1770-1850 .. **NCLC 12, 38; DA; DAB; DAC; DAM MST, POET; PC 4; WLC**
See also CDBLB 1789-1832; DLB 93, 107

Wouk, Herman 1915-**CLC 1, 9, 38; DAM NOV, POP**
See also CA 5-8R; CANR 6, 33, 67; DLBY 82; INT CANR-6; MTCW

Wright, Charles (Penzel, Jr.) 1935-**CLC 6, 13, 28**

See also CA 29-32R; CAAS 7; CANR 23, 36, 62; DLB 165; DLBY 82; MTCW

Wright, Charles Stevenson 1932- ... **CLC 49; BLC 3; DAM MULT, POET**
See also BW 1; CA 9-12R; CANR 26; DLB 33

Wright, Jack R.
See Harris, Mark

Wright, James (Arlington) 1927-1980**CLC 3, 5, 10, 28; DAM POET**
See also AITN 2; CA 49-52; 97-100; CANR 4, 34, 64; DLB 5, 169; MTCW

Wright, Judith (Arandell) 1915- **CLC 11, 53; PC 14**
See also CA 13-16R; CANR 31; MTCW; SATA 14

Wright, L(aurali) R. 1939- .... **CLC 44**
See also CA 138

Wright, Richard (Nathaniel) 1908-1960 **C L C 1, 3, 4, 9, 14, 21, 48, 74; BLC 3; DA; DAB; DAC; DAM MST, MULT, NOV; SSC 2; WLC**
See also AAYA 5; BW 1; CA 108; CANR 64; CDALB 1929-1941; DLB 76, 102; DLBD 2; MTCW

Wright, Richard B(ruce) 1937- .... **CLC 6**
See also CA 85-88; DLB 53

Wright, Rick 1945- .... **CLC 35**

Wright, Rowland
See Wells, Carolyn

Wright, Stephen 1946- .... **CLC 33**

Wright, Willard Huntington 1888-1939
See Van Dine, S. S.
See also CA 115; DLBD 16

Wright, William 1930- .... **CLC 44**
See also CA 53-56; CANR 7, 23

Wroth, LadyMary 1587-1653(?) .... **LC 30**
See also DLB 121

Wu Ch'eng-en 1500(?)-1582(?) .... **LC 7**

Wu Ching-tzu 1701-1754 .... **LC 2**

Wurlitzer, Rudolph 1938(?)- .... **CLC 2, 4, 15**
See also CA 85-88; DLB 173

Wycherley, William 1641-1715**LC 8, 21; DAM DRAM**
See also CDBLB 1660-1789; DLB 80

Wylie, Elinor (Morton Hoyt) 1885-1928 **TCLC 8; PC 23**
See also CA 105; 162; DLB 9, 45

Wylie, Philip (Gordon) 1902-1971 ... **CLC 43**
See also CA 21-22; 33-36R; CAP 2; DLB 9

Wyndham, John .... **CLC 19**
See also Harris, John (Wyndham Parkes Lucas) Beynon

Wyss, Johann David Von 1743-1818**NCLC 10**
See also JRDA; MAICYA; SATA 29; SATA-Brief 27

Xenophon c. 430B.C.-c. 354B.C. ... **CMLC 17**
See also DLB 176

Yakumo Koizumi
See Hearn, (Patricio) Lafcadio (Tessima Carlos)

Yanez, Jose Donoso
See Donoso (Yanez), Jose

Yanovsky, Basile S.
See Yanovsky, V(assily) S(emenovich)

Yanovsky, V(assily) S(emenovich) 1906-1989 **CLC 2, 18**
See also CA 97-100; 129

Yates, Richard 1926-1992 .... **CLC 7, 8, 23**
See also CA 5-8R; 139; CANR 10, 43; DLB 2; DLBY 81, 92; INT CANR-10

Yeats, W. B.
See Yeats, William Butler

Yeats, William Butler 1865-1939**TCLC 1, 11, 18, 31; DA; DAB; DAC; DAM DRAM, MST, POET; PC 20; WLC**
See also CA 104; 127; CANR 45; CDBLB 1890-1914; DLB 10, 19, 98, 156; MTCW

Yehoshua, A(braham) B. 1936- .. **CLC 13, 31**
See also CA 33-36R; CANR 43

Yep, Laurence Michael 1948- .... **CLC 35**
See also AAYA 5; CA 49-52; CANR 1, 46; CLR 3, 17; DLB 52; JRDA; MAICYA; SATA 7, 69

Yerby, Frank G(arvin) 1916-1991 .**CLC 1, 7, 22; BLC 3; DAM MULT**
See also BW 1; CA 9-12R; 136; CANR 16, 52; DLB 76; INT CANR-16; MTCW

Yesenin, Sergei Alexandrovich
See Esenin, Sergei (Alexandrovich)

Yevtushenko, Yevgeny (Alexandrovich) 1933- **CLC 1, 3, 13, 26, 51; DAM POET**
See also CA 81-84; CANR 33, 54; MTCW

Yezierska, Anzia 1885(?)-1970 .... **CLC 46**
See also CA 126; 89-92; DLB 28; MTCW

Yglesias, Helen 1915- .... **CLC 7, 22**
See also CA 37-40R; CAAS 20; CANR 15, 65; INT CANR-15; MTCW

Yokomitsu Riichi 1898-1947 .... **TCLC 47**

Yonge, Charlotte (Mary) 1823-1901**TCLC 48**
See also CA 109; 163; DLB 18, 163; SATA 17

York, Jeremy
See Creasey, John

York, Simon
See Heinlein, Robert A(nson)

Yorke, Henry Vincent 1905-1974 ...... **CLC 13**
See also Green, Henry
See also CA 85-88; 49-52

Yosano Akiko 1878-1942 .... **TCLC 59; PC 11**
See also CA 161

Yoshimoto, Banana .... **CLC 84**
See also Yoshimoto, Mahoko

Yoshimoto, Mahoko 1964-
See Yoshimoto, Banana
See also CA 144

Young, Al(bert James) 1939-**CLC 19; BLC 3; DAM MULT**
See also BW 2; CA 29-32R; CANR 26, 65; DLB 33

Young, Andrew (John) 1885-1971 ...... **CLC 5**
See also CA 5-8R; CANR 7, 29

Young, Collier
See Bloch, Robert (Albert)

Young, Edward 1683-1765 .... **LC 3, 40**
See also DLB 95

Young, Marguerite (Vivian) 1909-1995 **C L C 82**
See also CA 13-16; 150; CAP 1

Young, Neil 1945- .... **CLC 17**
See also CA 110

Young Bear, Ray A. 1950- ...... **CLC 94; DAM MULT**
See also CA 146; DLB 175; NNAL

Yourcenar, Marguerite 1903-1987**CLC 19, 38, 50, 87; DAM NOV**
See also CA 69-72; CANR 23, 60; DLB 72; DLBY 88; MTCW

Yurick, Sol 1925-................................. **CLC 6**
See also CA 13-16R; CANR 25

Zabolotsky, Nikolai Alekseevich 1903-1958 **TCLC 52**
See also CA 116; 164

Zamiatin, Yevgenii
See Zamyatin, Evgeny Ivanovich

Zamora, Bernice (B. Ortiz) 1938- .. **CLC 89; DAM MULT; HLC**
See also CA 151; DLB 82; HW

Zamyatin, Evgeny Ivanovich 1884-1937

Literary Criticism Series
Cumulative Topic Index

This index lists all topic entries in Gale's *Classical and Medieval Literature Criticism, Contemporary Literary Criticism, Literature Criticism from 1400 to 1800, Nineteenth-Century Literature Criticism,* and *Twentieth-Century Literary Criticism.*

Topic Index

Topic Index

Topic Index

Contemporary Literary Criticism
Cumulative Nationality Index

Nationality Index

Nationality Index

Nationality Index

Nationality Index

Nationality Index

CLC-112 Title Index